International Directory of

COMPANY HISTORIES

International Directory of

COMPANY HISTORIES

VOLUME 39

Editor

Tina Grant

ST. JAMES PRESS

AN IMPRINT OF THE GALE GROUP

DETROIT • NEW YORK • SAN FRANCISCO
LONDON • BOSTON • WOODBRIDGE, CT

STAFF

Tina Grant, *Editor*

Miranda H. Ferrara, *Project Manager*

Erin Bealmear, Christa Brelin, Joann Cerrito, Steve Cusack,
Kristin Hart, Melissa Hill, Margaret Mazurkiewicz, Carol Schwartz,
Christine Tomassini, Michael J. Tyrkus, *St. James Press Editorial Staff*

Peter M. Gareffa, *Managing Editor, St. James Press*

Library of Congress Catalog Number: 89-190943

British Library Cataloguing in Publication Data

International directory of company histories. Vol. 39
I. Tina Grant
338.7409

ISBN 1-55862-444-9

Printed in the United States of America
Published simultaneously in the United Kingdom

St. James Press is an imprint of The Gale Group

Cover photograph: Headquarters of the SWX Swiss Exchange in Zurich, Switzerland
(courtesy: SWX Swiss Exchange)

10 9 8 7 6 5 4 3 2 1

CONTENTS

Company Histories

PREFACE

The St. James Press series *The International Directory of Company Histories (IDCH)* is intended for reference use by students, business people, librarians, historians, economists, investors, job candidates, and others who seek to learn more about the historical development of the world's most important companies. To date, *IDCH* has covered over 5,000 companies in 39 volumes.

Inclusion Criteria

Most companies chosen for inclusion in *IDCH* have achieved a minimum of US$25 million in annual sales and are leading influences in their industries or geographical locations. Companies may be publicly held, private, or nonprofit. State-owned companies that are important in their industries and that may operate much like public or private companies also are included. Wholly owned subsidiaries and divisions are profiled if they meet the requirements for inclusion. Entries on companies that have had major changes since they were last profiled may be selected for updating.

The *IDCH* series highlights 10% private and nonprofit companies, and features updated entries on approximately 45 companies per volume.

Entry Format

Each entry begins with the company's legal name, the address of its headquarters, its telephone, toll-free, and fax numbers, and its web site. A statement of public, private, state, or parent ownership follows. A company with a legal name in both English and the language of its headquarters country is listed by the English name, with the native-language name in parentheses.

The company's founding or earliest incorporation date, the number of employees, and the most recent available sales figures follow. Sales figures are given in local currencies with equivalents in U.S. dollars. For some private companies, sales figures are estimates and indicated by the abbreviation *est.* The entry lists the exchanges on which a company's stock is traded and its ticker symbol, as well as the company's NAIC codes.

Entries generally contain a *Company Perspectives* box which provides a short summary of the company's mission, goals, and ideals, a *Key Dates* box highlighting milestones in the company's history, lists of *Principal Subsidiaries, Principal Divisions, Principal Operating Units, Principal Competitors,* and articles for *Further Reading.*

American spelling is used throughout *IDCH,* and the word "billion" is used in its U.S. sense of one thousand million.

Sources

Entries have been compiled from publicly accessible sources both in print and on the Internet such as general and academic periodicals, books, annual reports, and material supplied by the companies themselves.

Cumulative Indexes

IDCH contains three indexes: the **Index to Companies,** which provides an alphabetical index to companies discussed in the text as well as to companies profiled, the **Index to Industries,** which allows researchers to locate companies by their principal industry, and the **Geographic Index,** which lists companies alphabetically by the country of their headquarters. The indexes are cumulative and specific instructions for using them are found immediately preceding each index.

Suggestions Welcome

Comments and suggestions from users of *IDCH* on any aspect of the product as well as suggestions for companies to be included or updated are cordially invited. Please write:

The Editor
International Directory of Company Histories
St. James Press
27500 Drake Rd.
Farmington Hills, Michigan 48331-3535

ABBREVIATIONS FOR FORMS OF COMPANY INCORPORATION

A.B.	Aktiebolaget (Sweden)
A.G.	Aktiengesellschaft (Germany, Switzerland)
A.S.	Aksjeselskap (Denmark, Norway)
A.S.	Atieselskab (Denmark)
A.Ş.	Anomin Şirket (Turkey)
B.V.	Besloten Vennootschap met beperkte, Aansprakelijkheid (The Netherlands)
Co.	Company (United Kingdom, United States)
Corp.	Corporation (United States)
G.I.E.	Groupement d'Intérêt Economique (France)
GmbH	Gesellschaft mit beschränkter Haftung (Germany)
H.B.	Handelsbolaget (Sweden)
Inc.	Incorporated (United States)
KGaA	Kommanditgesellschaft auf Aktien (Germany)
K.K.	Kabushiki Kaisha (Japan)
LLC	Limited Liability Company (Middle East)
Ltd.	Limited (Canada, Japan, United Kingdom, United States)
N.V.	Naamloze Vennootschap (The Netherlands)
OY	Osakeyhtiöt (Finland)
PLC	Public Limited Company (United Kingdom)
PTY.	Proprietary (Australia, Hong Kong, South Africa)
S.A.	Société Anonyme (Belgium, France, Switzerland)
SpA	Società per Azioni (Italy)

ABBREVIATIONS FOR CURRENCY

$	United States dollar	KD	Kuwaiti dinar
£	United Kingdom pound	L	Italian lira
¥	Japanese yen	LuxFr	Luxembourgian franc
A$	Australian dollar	M$	Malaysian ringgit
AED	United Arab Emirates dirham	N	Nigerian naira
		Nfl	Netherlands florin
B	Thai baht	NKr	Norwegian krone
B	Venezuelan bolivar	NT$	Taiwanese dollar
BFr	Belgian franc	NZ$	New Zealand dollar
C$	Canadian dollar	P	Philippine peso
CHF	Switzerland franc	PLN	Polish zloty
COL	Colombian peso	Pta	Spanish peseta
Cr	Brazilian cruzado	R	Brazilian real
CZK	Czech Republic koruny	R	South African rand
DA	Algerian dinar	RMB	Chinese renminbi
Dfl	Netherlands florin	RO	Omani rial
DKr	Danish krone	Rp	Indonesian rupiah
DM	German mark	Rs	Indian rupee
E£	Egyptian pound	Ru	Russian ruble
Esc	Portuguese escudo	S$	Singapore dollar
EUR	Euro dollars	Sch	Austrian schilling
FFr	French franc	SFr	Swiss franc
Fmk	Finnish markka	SKr	Swedish krona
HK$	Hong Kong dollar	SRls	Saudi Arabian riyal
HUF	Hungarian forint	W	Korean won
IR£	Irish pound	W	South Korean won
K	Zambian kwacha		

International Directory of

COMPANY
HISTORIES

The Abbey National Group

Abbey National plc

Abbey House
Baker Street
London NW1 6XL
United Kingdom
Telephone: +44-0870-612-4000
Fax: +44-20-7486-2764
Web site: http://www.abbeynational.plc.uk

Public Company
Incorporated: 1944
Employees: 29,209
Total Assets: £204.4 billion ($291.92 billion) (2000)
Stock Exchanges: London
Ticker Symbol: ANL
NAIC: 52211 Commercial Banking

In the short time that it has been a publicly traded company, Abbey National plc has grown into one of Britain's largest banks. Preferring to emphasize its roots as a building society, Abbey National avoids calling itself a bank as much as possible, despite the fact that retail banking services and wholesale banking operations contribute greatly to its bottom line. Through subsidiaries Abbey National also offers life and general insurance. In addition, it has been very active in taking advantage of the Internet and digital TV to reach new customers.

Origins in the Building Society Movement of the 1800s

Abbey National plc has a long history, growing to become Britain's second largest building society from its 19th-century roots as two separate entities: the National Building Society, established in 1849, and the Abbey Road Building Society, founded in 1874. Later Abbey National became the first such society to convert to a public limited company.

Building societies originated as mutual groups, known as "friendly societies," which proliferated during the urbanization trend of the mid-19th century. As towns and cities swelled, a substitute was needed for the social support traditionally offered by the community in rural areas. The first friendly societies were early forms of insurance—self-help organizations whose members paid regular subscriptions and were entitled to financial help from the group's funds when necessary. From this general concept evolved the "building clubs" of the late 18th century. These were temporary organizations formed to build houses from money collected from subscribers; they were dissolved once that purpose was accomplished. The first known permanent building society was established in 1845, just four years before the National came into being.

The National's founders (among whom were the social reformers and members of Parliament Richard Cobden and Joseph Hume) had a political rather than a commercial agenda. In an age when voting rights were heavily restricted and tied to land ownership, they sought to increase suffrage by increasing the number of those who owned the freehold on their land and were thus entitled to vote. Essentially, then, the National was a land society, not a building society, and was popularly known as The National Freehold Land Society. It was officially named The National Permanent Mutual Benefit Building Society to give the association a legal framework under the Building Societies Act of 1836. The new organization enjoyed tremendous initial success, though not exactly in the way its founders had intended. Relatively few members took electoral advantage of their new status; most were far more interested in the National as a savings and loan institution, and in building on their new land.

Britain in the mid-1800s was economically buoyant and socially progressive. More people were earning more money than ever before, industry was booming, the population was growing, the railroads were revolutionizing travel and communications, and society was becoming ever more urbanized. Yet only a tiny proportion of the population owned their own homes. There was great demand for the National's 30 shares, and within four years the society was the largest of its kind in the country.

Under the 1836 Building Societies Act, societies were not permitted to own land themselves, so the National held its land in the name of trustees until 1856, when it formed the British Land Company for that purpose. With this division of operations, the National moved a step closer to becoming a building—rather than a land—society, a process completed in 1878 when the National and the British Land Company separated.

Unlike the National, the Abbey Road Building Society was formed in recognition of the growing need for home ownership. An outgrowth of a self-help organization, the Abbey Road Baptist Church's benefit society, the association was masterminded by Frank Yerbury, a builder, to purchase houses for its 500 members. Led by conservative directors in its early years, the Abbey Road enjoyed modest but steady success.

Building societies suffered a setback toward the end of the 19th century. In 1892 the Liberator, one of the National's principal competitors, was forced out of business by a combination of unwise speculation and fraud. In the wake of the scandal, tighter government controls were instituted on building societies, and public confidence was severely shaken.

The Abbey Road, and particularly the National, suffered along with the others. But the societies' fortunes improved at the beginning of the 20th century, when an affluent middle class was growing and demanding suburban housing developments. In the cities, much of the older housing had degenerated into slum areas and needed replacement. Another crisis in public confidence occurred in 1911, however, caused by the failure of the Birkbeck. Technically a building society, the Birkbeck operated more as a bank (only ten percent of its assets were in mortgages), but nonetheless its fall caused panic among building society investors and gave pause to building societies (such as the National) that had harbored thoughts of branching out into banking operations. Indeed, a comment made early in 1912 by the National's chairman tried to allay investors' fears: "Now, in the case of the National, we have never done anything, and we never mean to do anything, which remotely or indirectly suggests banking. We never have, and we never will."

World War I curtailed the activities and products of the building societies, and following the war the Liberal government dealt them a further blow by declaring housing for the poor the province of local authorities, giving the building societies their first real taste of how party politics could affect their business. Nonetheless, the interwar years proved, on the whole, prosperous. In 1923, under a Conservative government, a Housing Act was passed to provide a subsidy to private enterprise for house building. Another great building boom was taking place. Whereas in 1919 fewer than ten percent of the population owned their own home, by 1938 that figure had grown to 25 percent.

During this period the Abbey Road prospered. Under the leadership of Harold Bellman, who favored bold initiatives and—heretofore unusual in British business—aggressive marketing, the Abbey Road rocketed from sixteenth to second place in the building society hierarchy. In 1921, the Abbey Road had £1 million in assets; by 1925 assets had risen to £3.6 million and by 1929 to £19 million. For the first time the society ventured out of London; branches were opened in Southend, Watford, Reading, and Blackpool. By 1935, the Abbey Road had 110 branch outlets and employed more than 500 people.

Meanwhile the National, though it had slipped from the high position it had enjoyed in its earliest days, continued on a prosperous course, though it could not compare to the spectacular rise of the Abbey Road at that time. In 1929, Bruce Wycherley took over operations, introducing more modern commercial ideas and machinery, improving profits, and opening new branches. By the late 1930s, the society had a dozen U.K. branches.

Formation of Abbey National in 1944

Business suffered with the outbreak of World War II. Staff shortages were chronic, building materials were lacking, and less building work was being undertaken. As with the Great War, it was a time of stagnation for building societies. Nevertheless, as the end of the war approached, the Abbey Road and the National signaled their intention to continue to expand in the expected postwar boom by announcing, in 1943, their decision to merge. The move became official the following year.

Because the Abbey Road was the second largest building society in the United Kingdom and the National was the sixth, their merger made the new Abbey National a formidable force indeed. But this force was blunted, temporarily, by the postwar Labour government, which embarked on an ambitious program of state-financed building. Almost a million new homes were built and rented by the government.

The building societies still prospered, however, as savings and loan institutions, and by 1951 a Conservative government sympathetic to the building societies' aims had taken power. Party politics continued to ebb and flow, but the 1950s and 1960s were years of expansion for most building societies, and the Abbey National's record was one of steady growth. The demand for privately owned housing was still on the rise (in the 1960s the proportion of owner-occupied houses reached 50 percent), and the Abbey National was firmly ensconced in second place in this favorable market. By the end of 1962, the Abbey National could boast assets of £500 million—as compared with £80 million at the time of the two societies' merger. By 1968, assets had reached £1 billion and the society had nearly 150 branches. Within a few years the Abbey National's assets had doubled and it was opening a new branch office every other week. New products and services were introduced, including Bounty Bonds, which offered life insurance as well as an increased range of savings and property bonds.

The early 1970s were troubled years financially for the country, with house prices, mortgage rates, and inflation all rising dramatically. On two occasions the government offered loans to the building societies in an effort to keep interest rates down. While economic commentators might argue over whether the building societies were partly to blame for these

<table>
<tr><td colspan="2">**Key Dates:**</td></tr>
<tr><td>1849:</td><td>National Freehold Land and Building Society is established.</td></tr>
<tr><td>1874:</td><td>The Abbey Road & St. John's Wood Permanent Benefit Building Society is established.</td></tr>
<tr><td>1944:</td><td>Abbey Road & National Freehold merge to create the Abbey National Building Society.</td></tr>
<tr><td>1989:</td><td>Abbey National converts to a plc.</td></tr>
<tr><td>1996:</td><td>Abbey National merges with National and Provincial Building Society.</td></tr>
<tr><td>2000:</td><td>Cahoot, a separately branded e-bank, is created.</td></tr>
</table>

bleak conditions or whether they were simply victims of the prevailing economic winds, from the societies' point of view their profits and expansion were affected little by adverse conditions. In 1979, the Abbey National had 500 branches across the United Kingdom and assets of £5.8 billion.

Clive Thornton became chief general manager and instituted a number of new initiatives designed to bring Abbey National a higher profile in 1979. An office was opened in Brussels, Belgium (the first overseas office of any building society), the society participated in a loan scheme to renovate housing in inner-city areas, and it introduced various new savings and loans opportunities to attract new customers and offer existing ones more choice. (Thornton even capitalized on the company's address of 221 Baker Street by marketing Sherlock Holmes souvenirs.)

Abbey National's move into areas previously the province of banks was gradual but inexorable. In 1983, it announced its intention to withdraw from its agreement to keep its interest rates in line with those recommended by the Building Societies Association. Under Peter Birch, who succeeded Thornton as chief executive in 1984, the society continued its trend of providing more and varied banking services to its customers. The Abbey National offered improved transaction services, more comprehensive insurance coverage, an increased number of service products—including conveyancing, structural surveys, and financial counseling—and more credit options. In 1988, interest-bearing checking accounts became available to all customers for the first time and the society established a national real estate agency under the name Cornerstone. The result of all this activity was that Abbey National (still firmly in place as the second largest building society in the United Kingdom, with assets of more than £31 billion and more than nine million members) had moved into areas of direct competition with banks.

Although the continually evolving legal definition of building societies allowed such diversification, the Abbey National came to believe that it could operate more efficiently and competitively as a public limited company. As a building society, the Abbey National was prevented by law from diversifying into new businesses, restricted in its capacity to raise capital, and limited in its access to wholesale markets. Especially irksome were the restrictions on the provision of unsecured lending; under the conditions laid down by the 1986 Building

Societies Act, a society could have only 15 percent of its assets in that category, whereas a bank was free to do as it wished.

Abbey National's Conversion to plc in 1989

Intense interest was sparked by the board's proposal to go public, announced in 1988. The conversion of a building society to a public limited company was unprecedented. With no established procedure to follow, the implementation of the plan took a full year. The Bank of England had to carry out a review to grant a banking license. The Building Societies Commission had to be consulted every step of the way. Teams of lawyers ironed out legal questions and potential difficulties. Most important, Abbey National had to inform the public and its members of the ramifications of the proposed change in status. To that end, the society organized a massive media campaign, even including 17 public ''roadshows'' held at various locations around the country where members could ask questions directly of Abbey National's directors.

An opposition group was formed, called Abbey Members Against Flotation, which tried to stop the conversion, accusing Abbey National of underhanded practices in presenting the matter to its customers. There were questions over the fairness of certain proposals; for example, Abbey National had offered to give each member 100 free shares of the new company, but this did not apply to minors, and in the case of joint accounts, only the first-named was to receive shares (invariably, critics pointed out, the husband in married couples' accounts). Opposition and doubts notwithstanding, when it came to the test, of the 65 percent of members who voted, 90 percent voted to go public. On June 6, 1989 the Building Societies Commission officially confirmed Abbey National's conversion to a public limited company.

The controversy did not end with the vote, however, for the flotation was attended by administrative mismanagement and farcical mishaps. Thousands of letters and share certificates were sent to incorrect addresses, refund checks failed to be sent at all, countless people received the wrong number of shares, and in one bizarre and mysterious incident share certificates were discovered burning in a skip outside one of the mailing houses.

Abbey National's success made people forget the debacle of the changeover. It increased its share of the mortgage market by acquiring, in 1994, the U.K. residential mortgage business of the Canadian Imperial Bank of Commerce, retitled Abbey National Mortgage Finance. It was becoming increasingly apparent, however, that the key to future growth for Abbey National was diversification. Home ownership had reached a mature state in the United Kingdom, so that mortgages were becoming stagnant. In 1994 outstanding mortgages grew at only five percent over the previous year.

In 1993, the company acquired a new subsidiary, Abbey National Life, which, together with the previously acquired Scottish Mutual, enabled Abbey National to provide its customers with wide coverage in life insurance, long-term savings, and pension products. The company expanded its business in derivatives, having established in 1993 a joint operation with Baring Brothers & Co., Ltd., called Abbey National Baring

Derivatives. In addition, the bank established operations in several European countries.

But not every attempt to broaden its range of products met with success. In 1990 Abbey National purchased the French bank Fico France, which serviced the commercial property market, the crash of which in the early 1990s brought significant losses. Abbey National also sold its British real estate agency, Cornerstone, in 1993 after four consecutive years of negative returns.

Despite setting a goal of lowering retail lending that accounted for 80 percent of its bottom line in 1994 to just 60 percent by 1997, Abbey National in 1995 made a bid for the National & Provincial, Britain's ninth largest building society. The merger, completed in August 1996 at a cost of £1.35 billion ($2.15 billion), increased Abbey National's share of the home loan market from 12 percent to 15 percent, making it Britain's second largest mortgage lender.

Abbey National, in the meantime, continued its efforts at diversification. It acquired Pegasus Assurance Group for its Scottish Mutual subsidiary in order to add health insurance to the product line. It acquired First National Finance Corporation, which offered home improvement loans, personal loans, and car loans; later, to augment the subsidiary, it purchased three businesses from NatWest Group: Lombard Tricity Finance Ltd, Lombard Motor Finance, and Lombard Business Equipment Leasing Ltd. In 1996 National Abbey acquired Wagon Finance Group, a major U.K. used car finance company; a year later it purchased Cater Allen Holdings Plc, which engaged in the business of wholesale money markets and offshore banking, as well as onshore retail banking.

In 1998 Ian Harley, after 20 years with the firm, became the chief executive officer of Abbey National. He inherited control of a bank that had doubled its profits over the previous five years and, in terms of market capitalization, had grown to become Britain's fifth largest bank. Abbey National's success also made it a rumored acquisition target of larger players, such as National Westminster and Barclays. Harley vowed to increase revenue between two and three times over costs within three years. He lost credibility when 18 months later he had to back down from his numbers. Nevertheless, under Harley's leadership Abbey National had, by 2000, lowered its mortgage and savings business to just 50 percent of profit.

Abbey National also looked to make itself a consumer-friendly brand through innovation and technology. It opened retail outlets in Safeway supermarkets, Britain's third largest chain. It opened Costa Coffee cafes in some smaller branches and teamed with Costa Coffee to open a nontraditional banking superstore. Abbey National created a digital banking service with Sky Digital's interactive television capabilities. After offering e-banking services, Abbey National launched Cahoot, a separately branded e-bank that in addition to financial services teamed with vendors to offer an array of products and lifestyle services, from CDs and computers to travel plans.

By 2000, with the banking industry undergoing a cycle of consolidation, Abbey National appeared that it might become a victim of its own success. Unless it grew too large to be swallowed, the bank was a prime takeover target. It began merger talks with the smaller Bank of Scotland (BoS). The combination of the two would create an entity that could seriously challenge the big four high street banks: HSBC, Barclays, Royal Bank of Scotland, and Lloyds TSB. It was Lloyds that would inject itself in the Abbey National–BoS talks by making an offer to purchase Abbey National, which was quickly rejected. On one hand Lloyds was concerned about the potential of a combined Abbey National–BoS; on the other, the acquisition of Abbey National would make Lloyds the second largest bank in Britain. Once Lloyds made its offer official in early 2001, a prolonged regulatory process and uncertainty was assured. Lloyds promised to retain the Abbey National brand, so that the former building society was destined to continue on. The question of size and control was all that seemed to remain unanswered.

Principal Subsidiaries

Abbey National General Insurance Services, Ltd; Abbey National Leasing Companies; Abbey National Life plc; Abbey National Treasury Services; Cater Allen International Ltd; First National Bank plc; Scottish Mutual plc.

Principal Competitors

HSBC Holdings; Barclays; Lloyds TSB; Citigroup; Halifax.

Further Reading

''Abbey National: Fish and Fowl,'' *Economist,* June 3, 1995, p. 69.

Ashworth, Herbert, *The Building Society Story,* London: Franey, 1980.

Barnes, Paul, ''A Shabbey Habit to Shake Off,'' *Accountancy,* December 1989, pp. 25–26.

Bellman, Sir Harold, *Bricks and Mortals: A Study of the Building Society Movement and the Story of the Abbey National Building Society, 1849–1949,* London: Hutchinson, 1949.

Birch, Peter, ''Abbey National: A Continuous Process,'' *Banking World,* December 1992, pp. 23–24.

Davidson, Andrew, ''Ian Harley,'' June 1998, pp. 52–56.

Fry, John M., ''Abbey National Becomes a Company,'' *Long Range Planning,* Vol. 23, no. 3, 1990, pp. 49–56.

Merrell, Caroline, ''Abbey Rejects 'Inadequate' Lloyds Bid,'' *Times,* February 8, 2001.

Price, Seymour J., *Building Societies: Their Origins and History,* London: Franey, 1958.

Reid, Margaret, ''Sir Christopher Tugendhat—All-Purpose Top Person,'' *Banking World,* January 1992, pp. 16–18.

Ritchie, Berry, *A Key to the Door: The Abbey National Story,* London: Abbey National plc, 1990.

—Robin DuBlanc
—update: Ed Dinger

Acadian Ambulance & Air Med Services, Inc.

300 Hopkins Street
Lafayette, Louisiana 70501
U.S.A.
Telephone: (337) 291-3333
Toll Free: (800) 259-3333
Fax: (337) 291-2211
Web site: http://www.acadian.com

Private Company
Incorporated: 1971 as Acadian Ambulance Service
Employees: 1,400
Sales: $97.9 million (1998 est.)
NAIC: 62191 Ambulance Service

Acadian Ambulance & Air Med Services, Inc. is the nation's largest private, employee-owned ambulance service. Headquartered in Lafayette, Louisiana, the company serves 32 parishes with over half of Louisiana's population, providing both emergency and non-emergency medical transportation. It operates and maintains a fleet of 140 ambulances, five Air Med helicopters, and two fixed-winged aircraft. The company also provides paramedical services to 60 offshore installations in the Gulf of Mexico. Over its history, the company has received many awards and commendations for its community service and various achievements. Notably, it has compiled an excellent record of adapting to new, state-of-the-art technologies, which, in 1999, prompted Microsoft's Chairman Bill Gates to write, in his book *Business @ the Speed of Thought,* that ''Perhaps no emergency services firm in the country has made more use of PC technology than Acadian Ambulance and Air Med Services, in Lafayette, Louisiana.'' Because it has been an innovative company, many of Acadian's programs have served as models for other EMS companies nationwide.

1971–75: Getting Started and Quickly Expanding

In 1971, partners Roland Dugas, Richard Zuschlag, and Rolland Buckner, in their twenties, started up Acadian Ambulance in response to a growing crisis in south-central Louisiana. Up until then, funeral homes had provided ambulance services

for the area, but new federal regulations forced most funeral homes to stop offering the cost-prohibitive service, leaving several small communities at risk of having no ambulance providers at all.

Concerned about the impending difficulty, Acadian Ambulance's three founders teamed up in the late 1960s. At the time, Dugas, just out of the Air Force, was an assistant administrator at Lafayette General Hospital in Lafayette; Zuschlag was a contract employee for Westinghouse; and Buckner was a practical nurse. The three decided to create a private EMS company wholly independent of the area's funeral homes, then took their idea to the Lafayette Police Jury, which was already trying to deal with the crisis.

Although they lacked startup funds, the men proposed hiring and training former Vietnam War medics to staff all the modern ambulances they could arrange to purchase. They wanted to try customer-financing as the means of getting the operation underway, using a telethon to sell subscription memberships, a rather novel idea for south Louisiana. Although skeptical, the Police Jury decided to let the men try and, on July 21, 1971, it authorized Acadian Ambulance Services, Inc. to offer ambulance services throughout Lafayette Parish. Thanks in part to the support offered by important community leaders, the first membership campaign proved successful enough to become the annual means of soliciting memberships.

Initially, Acadian Ambulance's operation was very small. It was headquartered in a World War II vintage quonset hut and consisted of just two ambulances, eight medics, and a managerial staff made up of the three founding partners, with Dugas serving as president. However, after September 1, 1971, when all funeral homes in Lafayette Parish stopped offering the service, Acadian Ambulance had an ambulance-service monopoly throughout the parish, a necessary condition for insuring both the company's survival and its growth.

Grow it did. In 1972, it established an in-house maintenance program, expanded its fleet of ambulances to eight and its membership to almost 26,000 households, up from 8,400 the previous year. It also began providing ambulance services in two adjacent parishes—St. Mary and Vermilion—where offi-

Company Perspectives:

Acadian Ambulance & Air Med Services has been committed to providing the highest level of emergency and non-emergency medical care and transportation since 1971. The most sophisticated technology in the industry, combined with dedicated, caring professionals, has made Acadian a leader in the EMS field, and the largest ambulance company in the country. We are proud that the publisher of the Journal of Emergency Medical Services *editorialized that Acadian 'may be the best ambulance service in the nation.'*

cials had noted Acadian's success in Lafayette Parish and invited the new company to extend services to their parishes. Moreover, Acadian Ambulance quickly developed pre-hospital medical care services far superior to anything previously seen in the region. It also put in place a dispatch system that would became a model for other EMS providers. In` the next year, Acadian also began using a new telemetry radio system that allowed medics to transmit EKGs of heart attack victims from an ambulance to a hospital emergency room, an important step in initiating a new era of on-site cardiac-patient care.

In was also in 1973 that Acadian Ambulance had the largest growth year in its early history, beginning operations in St. Martin, Acadia, Terrebonne, and Jeff Davis Parishes as well as the town of Eunice in St. Landry Parish. Altogether, membership rose to 70,648, up almost 200 percent from 1972. To accommodate its growth, in 1974 Acadian completed a new headquarters building, featuring an advanced Emergency Medical Dispatch Center as its centerpiece. By that time, the company had 100 employees, 75 of whom were registered Emergency Medical Technicians (EMTs). Acadian Ambulance was also expanding into two other parishes: Evangeline and Iberia.

The company continued to develop a very efficient network of stations in the various parishes it served, so that by 1975, with just 33 ambulances, it was able to provide the coverage previously provided by over 100 funeral-home ambulances. At each station, Acadian Ambulance maintained at least one unit, on call around the clock, ready to respond to calls from any of its subscribers, which in 1975 had reached 80,216 households.

1976–80: Advances in Training and National Recognition for Excellence

In 1976, assured that its expansion would continue, Acadian Ambulance began focusing more of its attention on other parts of its mission. Among other things, it was determined to increase the scope and availability of its EMT training. To that end it formalized its courses and achieved a very high level of instruction, fully qualifying student-employees for certification by Louisiana and the National Registry of EMTs. In the same year, the company also began training its employees in I.V. therapy, making an important step forward in trauma care. Moreover, in conjunction with the military, the company began transporting patients by helicopters, a service it would later provide with its own Air Med helicopter fleet.

The following year, Acadian Ambulance received an award from the Robert Wood Johnson Foundation, the first of several national awards that the company has garnered through its history. In 1978, such recognition, plus its proximity to the Gulf of Mexico, earned the company a role in a pioneering project using NASA satellites to communicate from offshore petroleum rigs to hospital emergency rooms.

The company reached a milestone in the next year, 1979, when its membership roll topped 100,000. The company also expanded into sparsely populated Assumption Parish, despite a lack of sufficient revenue generated by membership subscriptions. Its expansion into such lightly populated and sometimes nearly inaccessible regions helped spur Acadian to enhance its technology. Notably, in 1980, it expanded its telemetry system, allowing the transmission of the EKGs of heart attack victims to hospital emergency rooms from virtually any point within the company's service area, no matter how remote.

1981–89: Diversifying and Improving Services

In 1981, when Pointe Coupee Parish and all of St. Landry Parish were added to its service area, Acadian entered into a contract with Petroleum Helicopters, Inc. whereby PHI provided a medically-configured helicopter for Acadian Ambulance. Partly subsidized by two Lafayette hospitals, the helicopter ambulance became the first of what would later become the company's Air Med fleet. Also that year Acadian began providing contract medics to the offshore petroleum industry, working on the same seven-on, seven-off schedule of the other offshore workers.

Part of Acadian's mission from the outset had been to train its employees and, because medical and related technologies kept changing, to retrain them often. In 1983, for example, a new, radio telephone switching system made it possible to transmit EKGs to hospital emergency rooms while EMS personnel used telephones rather than the more intimidating and less comfortable two-way radios. Also that year, the company introduced a model defensive driving system designed to optimize both ambulance service and safety.

In 1985, Acadian commenced extending its service beyond boundaries that until then had kept its service area contained in contiguous parishes. That year it leap-frogged into East and West Baton Rouge Parishes, providing the base for its Capital Area Network. Subsidized in part by two Baton Rouge hospitals, the company also added its second Air Med helicopter stationed in that city, the Capital Area hub. The company soon further increased the size of its Capital service area by expanding into Ascension Parish and established Advanced Life Support service in Livingston Parish.

Over the next three years, despite the general plight of Louisiana's oil-bust economy, Acadian continued to grow, to diversify its services, and to make significant advances in technology and communications. In 1987, for example, it set up a toll-free, statewide telephone number for emergency calls to its newly dedicated Acadian Communication Center. It also added a third air ambulance to its fleet, and, in response to problems ambulances encountered while trying to maneuver at crowded events, the company introduced Med Cart I, a golfcart-like, medically-equipped vehicle.

Key Dates:

1971: Roland Dugas, Richard Zuschlag, and Rolland Buckner start up Acadian Ambulance Service.
1979: Subscription membership tops the 100,000 mark.
1981: Company begins offering airborne EMS in conjunction with Petroleum Helicopters, Inc.
1985: Company expands to the Baton Rouge area and establishes its Air Med Service.
1990: Company logs its millionth patient transport.
1993: Acadian institutes employee stock ownership.
1995: The Commission on Accreditation of Ambulance Services accredits the company.
2000: Acadian introduces its "Millennium Ambulance."

Next, in 1989, Acadian added its first fixed-wing, medically-configured airplane to its Air Med fleet. The twin-engine craft provided the capacity to transport patients much longer distances than were possible with helicopters. In that year, the company also created a new department responsible for vehicle safety, hazardous material programs, and the defensive driving program.

1990 and Beyond

In 1990, Acadian Ambulance reached a major milestone, logging the transport of its millionth patient. The company was also still expanding, extending its services to Avoyelles Parish, where a tax initiative made its service available to all residents. Further, as an addition to the company's marketing and community relations program, it began using a new vehicle, "L'Etoile de Vie" (Star of Life), a hot-air balloon—its only craft to escape medical reconfiguration.

Acadian celebrated its 20th anniversary in 1991. That year it initiated "Acadian on Call," a personal alert system for the disabled and elderly. It also won a major honor when the American Ambulance Association recognized Acadian's community service and marketing program as the best in the nation. Additional awards came soon thereafter, when the company received the United States Senate Innovation Award for its pioneering work in bringing state-of-the-art EMS to sparsely populated rural areas and the development of its widely-imitated communications system. In 1992 Acadian added its second fixed-wing aircraft to its Air Med fleet: a twin-engine, prop jet capable of carrying two patients and up to four medical attendants in addition to its flight crew. The following year, the company introduced "Carpe Diem," a program designed to help its medics best prepare to give aid and comfort to the aged.

The year 1992 also marked the inauguration of Acadian's employee stock ownership program (ESOP). The EMS field's chief spokesperson, Jim Page, asserted at the time that Acadian "may well be the best ambulance service in the nation."

Over the next two years, Acadian continued to initiate programs and to improve existing ones. For example, in 1994 it secured a 311 three-digit phone number (later changed to 511), the first ever granted to an emergency service company. The next year, the Commission on Accreditation of Ambulance

Services accredited Acadian for its compliance with that agency's rigorous standards of excellence. The company also continued to expand, extending its 1995 service range to Rapides, East Feliciana, and St. Tammany parishes, bringing its total coverage to 26 parishes and 44 percent of Louisiana's population, making it the nation's largest privately-owned ambulance service. The expansion prompted Acadian to add a fourth Air Med helicopter to those serving the central Louisiana area. It also purchased a new BK-117 helicopter for service in the Capital Region. Larger than the other helicopters in the company's Air Med service, the BK-117 could carry up to four medics with a single patient or three medics with two patients.

By August 1996, Acadian Ambulance could boast a work force of 1,021 and a fleet of 143 ambulances, four helicopters, and two fixed-wing aircraft. That year the company introduced telemedicine for use offshore. The technology allowed emergency-room physicians at computer terminals to study high-resolution images transmitted by paramedics from offshore sites. Because of Acadian's exemplary record of adopting to such state-of-the-art technology, *Inc. Magazine*/MCI bestowed a National Technology Leadership Award on the company, selecting it from a list of over 800 small-to-mid-size businesses.

Acadian Ambulance's growth continued to the end of the century. In 1998, it expanded its coverage to 33 parishes when it acquired two companies headquartered in Lake Charles: Calcasieu Ambulance Service and LifeCare Ambulance Service. Adding seven parishes to its service area, the acquisitions gave Acadian a service range extending from the Mississippi to the Texas state borders. Changes would give it a different geographic configuration in 2000, when it terminated service in some parishes, started it up in others, and even moved across the state line into Jackson County, Mississippi. At the end of 2000, after entering new parishes and withdrawing from others, it had a 32-parish service area accounting for about 2.3 million people, over half of Louisiana's population. It had always been Acadian's policy to negotiate contracts giving the company term-limited but exclusive rights to providing its services, a major risk-reduction strategy that worked well through its rapid growth cycle. However, its right to be the sole provider of ambulance services has been challenged and has drawn some critical fire. In 2000, the small, Vermilion Parish city of Abbeville permitted another company, Med Express, to offer ambulance services in its jurisdiction. That decision, upheld in court, prompted Acadian to withdraw from Vermilion Parish altogether, giving notice that without the protection of a sole-provider clause in its renewed contracts, Acadian would not do business, a strict but necessary policy, though one that caused Med Express to complain that Acadian had become a "corporate bully." That and the unabashed, unapologetic courting of political figures by Richard Zuschlag, the company's CEO, put the firm on the media's targeting radar in 2000, somewhat tarnishing its image.

Nevertheless, Acadian Ambulance remained a much honored and respected company, noted for its devoted public service and excellent record of adapting to state-of-the art technology. It was clearly positioned for continued growth, both in the quality of its services and its range of coverage. The company's "millennium ambulance," introduced in 2000 and equipped with the most advanced medical and communications technology, seemed almost emblematic of the company itself—a company ever willing to test, evaluate, and adjust to the EMS needs of those for whom it provided its services.

Principal Competitors

Med Express Ambulance Service; American Medical Response Inc.

Further Reading

Blanchard, Kevin, ''Ambulance Service Shuts Offices: Acadian President Says Vermilion Parish Can't Support Two Companies,'' *Advocate* (Baton Rouge), September 1, 2000, p. 10B.

Franics, Bob, ''Pen Tablets Rescue EMTs,'' *PC Week*, August 31, 1998, p. 34.

Jaleshgari, Ramin P., ''VAR PAD Systems Answers the Call,'' *Computer Reseller News*, December 7, 1998, p. 152.

Lear, Calvin, ''Acadian Ambulance Strikes Deal with Mississippi Counterpart,'' *Advocate* (Baton Rouge), July 14, 1995, p. 3B.

Simoneaux, Angela, ''Med Express Can Continue Service: Judge Rules Acadian Ambulance Can't Challenge Permit,'' *Advocate* (Baton Rouge), April 21, 2000, p. 4B.

Walsh, Bill, ''Ambulance Firm Rides on the Favor of Those in Power,'' *Times-Picayune* (New Orleans), June 4, 2000, p. A1.

—John W. Fiero

Alliance Atlantis Communications Inc.

121 Bloor Street East, Suite 1500
Toronto, Ontario M4W 3M5
Canada
Telephone: (416) 967-1174
Fax: (416) 960-0971
Web site: http://www.allianceatlantis.com

Public Company
Incorporated: 1985 as Alliance Communications
    Corporation
Employees: 650
Sales: C$771.6 million (US$498.64 million)(2000)
Stock Exchanges: NASDAQ Toronto
Ticker Symbols: AAC.A; AAC.B; AACB
NAIC: 512130 Cinemas; 513120 Television
    Broadcasting; 513210 Pay and Specialty Television;
    512110 Motion Picture and Video Production; 512120
    Motion Picture and Video Distribution

Alliance Atlantis Communications Inc. is a leading broadcaster, creator, and distributor of filmed entertainment and also has significant ownership interests in eight Canadian specialty television networks. The company's principal business activities are conducted through three operating units: Broadcast, Motion Pictures, and Television. Headquartered in Toronto, Alliance Atlantis operates offices in Los Angeles, Montreal, Edmonton, London, Sydney, and Shannon. The company was created in 1998 by a merger of Canada's two largest film and TV production companies: Atlantis Communications and Alliance Communications.

History of Atlantis Communications

In 1978, Michael MacMillan, a film studies graduate of Queen's University in Ontario, founded Atlantis Communications with three friends and combined financial resources of $300. The fledgling company focused on producing short films for industrial clients as well as for general entertainment purposes. Despite a difficult climate for Canadian entertainment

companies during this time, Atlantis survived. Like many Canadian film and television production companies, it sometimes lived project to project, relying on government grants. In 1983, MacMillan produced a live-action short film, *Boys and Girls,* based on a short story by a Canadian author, and the film received an Academy Award. Thereafter, the company's fortunes increased.

By the beginning of the 1990s, the entertainment industry in Canada had matured, consisting of larger, vertically integrated companies that conducted their own production, distribution, and financing operations. Atlantis had grown and matured at the same time, acquiring considerable financial assets, including studios, real estate, film and television libraries, and rights to other productions. By the 1990s, Atlantis, still headed by MacMillan, had produced for all the major Canadian broadcasters and U.S. networks and had also built an international presence, with offices in Amsterdam, Sydney, and Los Angeles. An estimated 30 percent of Atlantis's business at the time was in foreign markets.

The expanding global market for programming along with advances in technology had made entertainment a truly global industry with much growth potential. Joint productions between foreign entertainment companies were becoming popular, especially for Atlantis, given the concurrent cutbacks in Canadian government funding for such projects. In 1993, the Atlantis television production subsidiary, Atlantis Films Ltd, by then one of Canada's top ranked production houses, sold a minority interest of its shares to American-based E.C. Television, a division of Interpublic Groups of Cos. Inc. Interpublic was one of the world's largest advertising organizations, bringing a broad scope of major advertising clients to the deal. MacMillan told journalists from the *Globe & Mail* in May 1993 that the minority interest was significant in terms of strategic benefits and capitalization. ''It positions us for substantial growth and we're very happy,'' he noted.

In 1995, following a period of steady growth, Atlantis experienced a year of diminished profit. The company restructured in an effort to save millions of dollars in annual overhead. The declining profits were also attributed to delayed production schedules and the cancellation of the company's science fiction

---

TekWar television series on the USA Network. MacMillan predicted that the company would return to normal by year's end and that the outlook for 1996 was good.

History of Alliance Communications

The history of Alliance Communications can be traced to 1972, when two men from Vancouver, Robert Lantos and Victor Loewy, began an enterprise that would eventually become Canada's largest film company. Graduates of McGill University, Lantos and Loewy started Vivafilm, a film distribution company, acquiring the rights to the soft-core porn spoof *Flesh Gordon* among others. With the rights to the John Waters cult film *Pink Flamingos,* Lantos and Loewy next opened an art-house theater, the Rembrandt, in Vancouver, where the Waters film played for months on end, attracting that city's "hippie" culture. Moreover, by the mid-1970s, the pair had moved into the production business as well. In the early years, as Katherine Monk of the *Vancouver Sun* described it in a June 1999 article, these two "swinging entrepreneurs . . . had no idea what they were doing, but it worked."

Eventually, the Rembrandt venture began losing money, and Lantos and Loewy refocused on producing and distributing movies. Lantos's first feature movie was the 1978 *In Praise of Older Women.* In a difficult economic climate for filmmakers, the entrepreneur scraped together the funding for the movie. Following this, he produced several steamy, low-budget movies starring his first wife.

In 1985, Lantos and Loewy combined their production and distribution ventures as Alliance Communications Corporation, which would focus on television and motion picture production. Lantos later recalled the impetus for the move in a 1998 article in the *Ottawa Citizen:* "I wanted to have some real infrastructure, I wanted to have a business. I wanted to hold my head up high when I walked around the Cannes Film Festival or dealt with the Hollywood companies. . . . Something in my nature rebels at being a supplicant. And back when I started, if you were a Canadian in this business you were a supplicant by definition. The plan was that . . . there would be a point in time that I would pass it on to others and I would go back to telling stories."

Throughout the late 1980s and early 1990s, Alliance broadened its scope and geographical reach, adding to its offerings Canadian theatrical distribution, international television and theatrical distribution, financing services for the television and motion pictures industries, broadcasting and animations, and movie publishing, merchandising and licensing. Also during this time, Lantos has produced many significant movies including *The Sweet Hereafter* and *Black Robe*, along with such popular TV fare as *Due South* and *E.N.G.*

By the mid-1990s, Alliance was Canada's largest film and television producer. Influenced by the same financial and global trends as Atlantis had been at that time, Alliance sold a stake to investment dealer Wood Gundy Ltd., and industry analysts speculated that the company would soon go public. Lantos also fueled speculation by saying that consolidation in the Canadian television and film industry was inevitable if Canadian companies hoped to compete internationally.

The 1998 Merger

In July 1998, at a press conference in Toronto, it was announced that Canada's two leading film and television companies, Alliance Communications and Atlantis Communications, would merge. Under terms of the deal, Alliance actually acquired Atlantis, and rechristened the company Alliance Atlantis Communications. Together, the companies were Canada's largest film and television company and ranked sixth worldwide in terms of size and revenues.

Lantos, whom journalists described Lantos as colorful, mercurial, and "a flamboyant mogul," left his executive role (retaining the title of chairman emeritus), to focus on making movies. Lantos's long-time friend and colleague, Loewy, remained with Alliance Atlantis as head of feature film distribution. MacMillan, described as "quiet and methodical," assumed the roles of CEO and chairman of the new company.

Armed with a $12 million severance package, Lantos went on to form a new company, Serendipity Point Films, which struck an exclusive agreement with Alliance Atlantis to produce feature films for at least three years.

When MacMillan took charge of the company, large-budget productions were clearly the way of the future. Alliance had already achieved international renown as the producer of the Oscar-nominated film *The Sweet Hereafter,* while Atlantis's dominance in the Canadian television industry was established, with the company owning and operating several specialty cable tv channels, despite industry predictions that specialty channels could not survive in the Canadian market.

The year following the merger was dedicated to restructuring and reorganization. There were financial challenges connected with bringing the large companies, formerly competitors, together as one. Some 150 jobs were eliminated in the process, while North American offices were consolidated.

In the first quarter of 1998, Atlantic Alliance realized a 48 percent increase in profits, which it attributed to the strong performance of Equicap, their high-margin tax-shelter financing business, as well as high box office receipts from the movie *Austin Powers: The Spy Who Shagged Me,* for which Atlantic Alliance owned distribution rights. By year's end, although the company realized a profit of US$25 million before extraordinary items, the company ultimately reported a loss of $27.3 million, given the $81.4 million charge related to the merger along with Lantos's $12 million severance package.

Key Dates:

1978: Michael MacMillan and friends found Atlantis Communications.
1983: Atlantis film *Boys and Girls,* wins an Academy Award in the short film category.
1985: Robert Lantos and Victor Loewy found Alliance Communications.
1993: Alliance goes public.
1997: Alliance's Television Division receives five Emmy awards and a Golden Globe award.
1998: Alliance Communications and Atlantis Communications merge to form Atlantis Alliance.
2000: Company becomes a board member of the North American Broadcasting Association (NABA); launches online broadcasting with Internet venture, U8TV.
2001: Company receives seven Golden Globe nominations.

Stock prices fluctuated during this time. CanWest Global Communications purchased a 20 percent interest in the company's outstanding stock, triggering speculation as to whether CanWest wanted to take over the company. In response, company executives boosted their holdings of the voting stock. Uncertainties also triggered some investor anxiety, resulting a drop in the value of shares.

Despite financial setbacks, the first year was an active one operationally. The company distributed the widely popular films *Austin Powers: The Spy Who Shagged Me* and *Blair Witch Project.* Its television division created a successful kids' show on U.S. television called *I was a Sixth Grade Alien,* and Peter O'Toole won an Emmy for his work in Alliance's *Joan of Arc* miniseries.

Moreover, the company worked to expand its presence in the cinema business, purchasing Festival Cinemas, a Vancouver-based art-house chain. In a partnership deal with Famous Players, the subsidiary Alliance Atlantic Cinemas, chaired by Victor Loewy, planned to open five new theaters in markets across Canada by the end of 2000. To Alliance Atlantis, the chain represented the potential for higher gross margins for each of Loewy's own films, as well as a guaranteed screen in each major market. Such vertical integration would allow the company to create, control, distribute, and exhibit, ensuring that all profits would go to the company.

In May 1999, Alliance Atlantis launched the New Media Division, the role of which was to cross-promote the various assets—including motion pictures, television production, television distribution, and cable specialty channels—as well as to lead the new media strategy and to develop products for the Internet.

In August of that year, Alliance Atlantis sold 20 percent stake in the company to the German distributor Kimowelt Medien for US$130 million or $21 a share. Under the terms of the agreement, Kimowelt also acquired 50 percent of Alliance Atlantis's U.K. motion picture distribution. Alliance Atlantic

expected the deal would give the company increased access to bigger projects with greater commercial potential, and would lead to a partnership becoming the leader in the United Kingdom. The proceeds from the sale were used to fund future growth and to repay short-term debts.

2000 and Beyond

The year 2000 was one of growth and acquisitions. Karen Palmer observed, in an article for the *Vancouver Sun,* that "Alliance Atlantis is starting to pump up its filmmaking sector, aggressively pursuing international partnerships to produce bigger-budget feature length projects." In July, the company purchased Great North Communications Ltd. of Edmonton, regarded as Canada's leading producer of factual and documentary programming. In September, Alliance Atlantic Communications was accepted as a full member in the North American Broadcasters Association (NABA), giving the company a position on that entity's board of directors.

November 2000 brought the company's entrance to online broadcasting. U8TV, the broadcasting Web site, promised 100 percent Canadian content and plugged the launch of a "reality-based" show called *The Lofters,* which featured live broadcasting of eight people living together in a loft in downtown Toronto. *The Lofters* launched on January 9, 2001.

Motion picture operations remained strong, the largest independent distributor in Canada, with a market share of 15 percent of all films distributed in Canada. Additionally, the unit was the exclusive distributor in Canada of motion pictures from Miramax Films, New Line Cinema, Destination Films, October Films, Artisan Films, and Fine Line Features. Alliance Atlantis Cinemas had 29 screens in seven locations including Toronto, Vancouver, Victoria, and Calgary. By early 2002, the company planned to open an additional 25 screens in five cities. The television department had 12,500 hours of programming in its catalogue, with some 80 percent of its license revenue generated outside of Canada. In fiscal 2000, the unit generated approximately 270 hours of programming on a slate of 14 series sold in over 200 countries. Given the company's history, its alliances, and its strategic partners, it appeared likely that Alliance Atlantis was well positioned for continued growth in scope and profits.

Principal Subsidiaries

Alliance (1991) Distribution Inc.; Alliance Distributing Corp.; Alliance Entertainment Holdings Inc.; Alliance Entertainment U.S.A., Inc.; Alliance Equicap Corp.; Alliance Europe Inc.; Alliance Film Holdings No. 1 Inc.; Alliance Film Holdings No. 2 Inc.; Alliance Hungary Inc.; Alliance International France Ltd.; Alliance International Releasing Corp.; Alliance International Releasing Ireland Ltd.; Alliance Production Services Corp.; Alliance Productions (1993) Ltd.; Alliance Productions Ltd.; Alliance Releasing (1994) Corp.; Amalgamated Moviecorps Inc.; Citadel Entertainment, LLC; Counterstrike Television, Inc.; Johnny Mnemonic Distribution Ltd.; Le Monde Entertainment Sales Corp.; Screenventures International Inc.; True Love Productions I Inc.; True Love Productions II Inc.; Turning April (Canada) Ltd.; U.R. Film Services Ltd.; Western Sky Productions Ltd.; ZigZag Graphics; Atlantis

Alliance Cinemas; Showcase Television (99%); Alliance National Productions Inc. (75%); Partisan Music Productions Inc. (75%); Johnny Mnemonic Productions Inc. (66%); Showcase Television Inc. (55%).

Principal Operating Units

Broadcast; Motion Pictures; Television; New Media.

Principal Competitors

CanWest Global Communications Corporation; Lions Gate Entertainment Corporation.

Further Reading

"Alliance's Profit Soars 48%," *Vancouver Sun,* August 27, 1999.

Atherton, Tony, "Canada's Screen Giants Unite to Become Mega-Company," *Ottawa Citizen,* July 21, 1998.

Enchin, H., "Atlantis Films Sells Stake to Foreign Firms," *Globe & Mail,* May 19, 1993, Bus. Sec.

Kirkland, Bruce, "Alliance Atlantis Gives $1 Million Dollars to Film Center," *Toronto Sun,* September 13, 1999.

Mahood, Casey, "Atlantis Forecasts Lower Profit, Job Cuts," *Globe & Mail,* August 25, 1995.

Monk, Katherine, "Selling Art and Popcorn," *Vancouver Sun,* June 9, 1999.

"NABA Adds Alliance Atlantis to Board of Directors," *Naba News,* September 28, 2000.

Onstad, Katrina, "Alliance Atlantic Join Forces," *Vancouver Sun,* July 24, 1998, pp. D1, D4.

Palmer, Karen, "Films Get a Double Boost," *Vancouver Sun,* September 13, 2000.

Shatkin, Elina, "Alliance Atlantis Forms New Media Division," *Creative Planet Post Industry*, May 28, 1999.

Surrette, Louise, "German Investors Buying 20% of Alliance Atlantis, *Vancouver Sun,* July 31, 1999, p. E4.

—June Campbell

American Medical Association

515 North State Street
Chicago, Illinois 60610
U.S.A.
Telephone: (312) 464-5000
Toll Free: (800) 262-3211
Fax: (312) 464-4184
Web site: http://www.ama-assn.org

Nonprofit Corporation
Incorporated: 1847
Employees: 1,200
Sales: $242.8 million (1999)
NAIC: 81292 Professional Organizations; 92312
   Administration of Public Health Programs

The American Medical Association is the oldest and largest advocacy group representing American physicians. The AMA represents about one-third of the nation's doctors. It publishes the weekly *Journal of the American Medical Association*, one of the most prestigious and influential American medical journals, as well as a host of other journals and books. Members have access to data services and to insurance through its insurance arm. The AMA is one of the nation's leading lobbying forces, and its political action committee, which dispenses money to political campaigns, is also one of the nation's wealthiest. The association runs awareness campaigns on health issues and works to shape governmental policy that affects doctors and patients. The AMA derives about one-quarter of its revenue through its annual membership fees. Other revenue comes from corporate grants and from sale of its publications and data services. Policy for the AMA is set by its 550-member House of Delegates.

Roots in the 19th Century

The American Medical Association was founded by a group of doctors in 1847 who were affiliated with various local and state medical associations. The doctors were concerned that medical education in America was not regulated on a national level. Medical schools had inconsistent standards of what stu-dents had to study and master to graduate as "physicians." A school that termed itself a "medical" school might actually have a curriculum that deviated from what had become "traditional" medicine—healing arts associated with mystic beliefs or unscientific precepts. The AMA opposed healing approaches such as homeopathy, a popular system based on the beliefs of a German physician that prescribed tinctures of herbs and minerals that had been so diluted as to render them biologically inactive. AMA members were traditional medical doctors, and the organization tried to ensure that institutions calling themselves medical schools were not teaching alternative or spiritual healing. It also called for the raising of educational standards. Even the nation's leading medical schools, such as Harvard and Yale, turned out sadly underprepared doctors, and many other medical schools operated neither entry or exit requirements, accepting all who could pay and granting degrees to all who completed the course. The AMA also tried to combat the prevalence of "quack" medicines—potions with secret ingredients of doubtful use or safety, which were widely available before the invention of modern drugs. By 1849 the AMA had established a committee to educate the public about the dangers of quack medicines. The AMA also sought to raise standards of medical journals. Many scientific journals flourished briefly in 19th-century America, and few gave any guarantee that what they published was factual. In 1882 the AMA founded its *Journal of the American Medical Association (JAMA)*. The *Journal* promoted the AMA's views, and set itself high journalistic standards. Nathan Davis, one of the founders of the AMA, was the first editor, and it was published by a firm in Chicago. That city became national headquarters for the association.

The early AMA was a loosely organized group, and it was only one among many American medical associations. By 1901, the AMA had mostly failed in its efforts to influence national medical policy, and the group decided to reorganize. The association adopted a new structure in 1901. Abandoning its early structure of state and local chapters, the group adopted a new constitution in 1901 that gave it a more national character. Decisions were to be carried out by an elected body called the House of Delegates. In 1902 the AMA adopted official permanent headquarters in Chicago. The group was now a nonprofit corporation with the power to conduct business anywhere in the United States. After the reorganization, the group redoubled its efforts to raise standards of medical education. In 1906 the AMA put out its first directory of medical schools. It also put out a directory of licensed physicians that year. After the reorganization, the AMA began to grow quickly, with many states doubling or tripling their membership. By 1906, the AMA had 50,000 members nationwide. The rejuvenated group continued its crusades to promote higher educational standards and to combat medical fraud and quackery. It also put out more journals, following *JAMA* with the *Archives of Neurology and Psychiatry* in 1919 and the *Archives of Surgery* in 1920.

Response to Reform in the 1920s and 1930s

The AMA continued to grow through the 1920s and 1930s. The group spoke authoritatively on a variety of health issues, influencing national policy on such questions as food safety and psychiatric evaluations for people accused of crimes. This was an era of broad social reform, when labor-rights issues were prominent. Reformers and legislators worked to pass laws guaranteeing workers old-age pensions and reimbursement in case of injury. Many reformers were interested in passing legislation that would give workers mandatory health insurance coverage, thus ensuring them of medical treatment. The AMA registered its opinion on compulsory health insurance in 1920, when its House of Delegates passed a resolution condemning any national health insurance policy. The group feared that government would interfere in the relationship between doctor and patient, and that physicians would not be adequately compensated for their services under a compulsory insurance system. Throughout the 1920s, the AMA opposed changes in the way physicians were paid. It disapproved of contract medical practices, in which, for example, a mining company paid a doctor a salary to look after its workers at a mining camp. It also disapproved of group hospital plans, whereby employers or groups would pay a lump fee to hospitals to cover hospitalization costs for its workers or members.

By 1933, the Great Depression had exacerbated already existing problems in the nation's medical care. Huge numbers of unemployed could not afford to pay doctors, and there was no national policy for dealing with this crisis. The AMA worked with the Roosevelt administration in drawing up some legislation that affected health care. For instance the AMA approved the administration's plan to have the government pay for medical care for federal employees under the Civil Works Administration, enacted in 1933. But the AMA continued to oppose any broader form of national health insurance. The AMA had formed a Bureau of Medical Economics in 1931, which spoke out against any insurance plans that might change the way doctors were compensated. The group put out pamphlets, spoke on the radio, and supplied high-school debating teams with material backing the AMA's position against compulsory insurance. The Social Security Act was passed in 1933, giving all

Americans retirement benefits. But largely because of the vociferous opposition of the AMA, the act lacked any national compulsory health insurance. The AMA continued to oppose group health insurance practices in the 1930s, until in 1938 a federal prosecutor pressed charges against the group for threatening to expel doctors who worked for a non-profit cooperative Group Health Association in Washington, D.C. The case was long and complex, and eventually, the AMA paid a fine.

Meanwhile, the AMA continued to crusade against quack medicines. In 1936 the AMA began offering its Seal of Acceptance to food manufacturers who passed standards of safety and hygiene and who did not advertise unproved benefits of their products. The association also spoke out on issues of general nutrition. It recommended enriching milk with vitamin D in 1936, and promoted the use of iodized salt to prevent hypothyroid disease. In 1938 the AMA published a book called *The Normal Diet*. This was the first comprehensive and authoritative listing of what Americans should be eating.

A Strong National Voice in the 1950s and 1960s

The AMA continued to work on familiar issues during World War II and after. The group promoted public health issues such as the fluoridation of drinking water and the curbing of drunk driving. It worked on medical education standards, forming a new committee in the 1940s to accredit programs granting medical degrees in the United States. In 1950, the AMA's Council of Medical Education published for the first time a list of foreign medical schools that met the AMA's standards.

At the same time, the AMA continued to lobby Washington against national health insurance. When President Truman again raised the idea of mandatory national health insurance in 1948, the AMA quickly spoke out against it. The AMA began levying dues from its members for the first time in 1949, which gave the organization ready cash to pay for publicity. Over the 1950s, the association spent millions of dollars on various campaigns to influence opinion against national medical insurance. This fight intensified in the 1960s, when John F. Kennedy came to office pledging to provide medical insurance for the indigent aged, a program that became known as Medicare. The AMA spent heavily to block Medicare. The group claimed 180,000 physician members at that time, and all received posters and pamphlets for their offices to inform patients of their doctor's opposition to Medicare. Its writers produced speeches for members' use, put out radio advertisements and full-page ads in big-city newspapers, and came up with instructions for the AMA's Women's Auxiliary to begin a letter-writing campaign. In 1961 the AMA began contributing money to politicians' election campaigns. As a nonprofit organization, the AMA could not contribute money directly, but it set up an organization called the American Medical Political Action Committee, or AMPAC, to filter money to its candidates. AMPAC apparently had vast resources from the beginning and is still one of the wealthiest political action committees in the nation.

The AMA brought in revenue through annual membership dues and by selling advertising in its publications. Ad revenues rose in the 1960s, peaking in 1967 with $13.6 million, which was more than 40 percent of the organization's total revenue.

After 1967, however, advertising revenue fell sharply following the enactment of new regulations by the Food and Drug Administration that slowed the process of bringing new drugs to market. As a result, pharmaceutical companies cut their advertising budgets, and the AMA found its income shrinking. The AMA raised membership dues to take up the slack, bringing them up from $45 to $70 in 1967. Inflation and the lack of advertising revenue put the association in a perilous financial position at the end of the 1960s, and the AMA began the 1970s in the red.

The 1970s and 1980s

In the early 1970s the AMA began to lose members when several state chapters stopped requiring their members to be AMA members as well. Mostly as a result of this, the AMA lost 11,671 members in 1971. The association was unable to convince board members to raise membership dues enough to make up for lost revenue. At the same time, journal publishing costs were rising quickly. By 1974, the AMA was at the point of having to borrow money to meet its payroll. A new president, James Sammons, took over that year, and he immediately instituted financial reforms. The AMA shut down some of its committees and cut some staff. Members were asked to send in a special $60 assessment to ease the organization's plight. This raised $7 million in 1975. Sammons and a fiscal committee reviewed the dues-collection system and worked actively to recruit members. The AMA began operating under a strict fiscal plan that aimed for increasing membership fees to cover operating costs for a period of five years. Though the number of regular members declined in the late 1970s, growing numbers of residents and students signed up. In 1975 the AMA had just over 179,000 total members. 8,700 were residents, and 8,100 students. By 1982, total membership was 213,400. The number of residents and students had risen sharply, to 27,900 and 26,900, respectively.

Sammons also overhauled the association's publishing ventures. A single group vice-president for publishing became responsible for all publications, and all were reviewed. As a result, some ceased to publish, and others were sold. By 1979, the AMA's publishing division was financially sound. It began bringing in money through new projects with broad consumer appeal, such as the *AMA Family Medical Guide*, published in 1982.

With its finances under better control, the AMA continued to fund national campaigns on public health issues in the 1980s. In 1981 the group recommended more study on the effects of dioxin and Agent Orange, chemical defoliants deployed in the Vietnam War, which could have lingering health effects. The AMA also began a renewed campaign to curb the harmful effects of alcohol in 1982. It called on its state chapters to work for legislation that would raise the legal drinking age to 21. The AMA began educating physicians and healthcare workers in 1984 about the symptoms and treatment of child abuse and neglect, and in 1985 the organization began working toward nationwide curbs on tobacco smoking. The AMA called for a ban on tobacco advertising, and also supported legislation that banned smoking on public transportation. That year the AMA also began an education campaign regarding AIDS that continued through the 1980s.

The 1990s and Beyond

Though total membership in the AMA continued to grow, the percentage of doctors who belonged to the organization declined from the mid-1960s on. At the height of the group's campaign against Medicare, the AMA claimed at least 70 percent of American doctors as members. By the mid-1990s, the AMA represented only about 40 percent of American doctors. The group spent lavishly on its public outreach campaigns, backed by money from its for-profit arms such as its successful publishing division. But revenue from membership did not keep up. The group lost money in 1993 and 1994. A sharp increase in advertising revenues made up the loss in 1995, but by the mid-1990s it was clear that the physicians' group was troubled. Close to 90 percent of doctors over the age of 70 were members, but fewer than 35 percent of those aged 30 to 49. The group had worked hard to sign up students and residents at reduced rates, but the full rate for regular membership was over $400 in the mid-1990s, and apparently many younger doctors felt the price was too high. At the same time, the AMA had taken increasingly conservative political stances, and its political involvement in Washington often displayed mixed motives. For instance, although the group endorsed gun control as a public-health issue, its political action committee also gave generously to the campaigns of politicians who were outspoken supporters of the National Rifle Association. In 1997, the AMA suffered a scandal when it revealed an arrangement it had signed with the Sunbeam Corporation, a small-appliance manufacturer, to give the firm's goods an AMA seal of approval in exchange for royalties. AMA members protested that the arrangement tarnished the group's image. The AMA was forced to break the deal with Sunbeam and eventually had to pay substantial damages to the company. The fracas meant a new loss of members, and that, combined with the payment to Sunbeam, sent the AMA into the red once again. The group also lost money in 1999, ending the year with a loss of $5.4 million. Revenue from dues continued to shrink, and the organization had also had to spend millions to prepare its computers for the year 2000.

The group continued to struggle with ways to attract and retain members in the 2000s. At a meeting in June 2000, the AMA revealed a new plan, to let doctors pay a one-time fee to join for life. At the same time, the AMA entertained proposals to drop dues altogether, and automatically grant membership to all American physicians. By 2000, the AMA claimed only about 30 percent of American doctors as members. The organization had struggled with dwindling membership for decades, and the trend did not seem as if it would reverse easily.

Faced with this probability, the AMA looked for ways to trim its budget and to bring in more money. At its 2000 national meeting, the group announced it would begin to peddle its information technology services. The AMA's executive vice-president, E. Ratcliffe Anderson, claimed in an article in *Modern Healthcare* (June 19, 2000) that the AMA was "probably the most data-rich entity anywhere in the world of medicine." Information technology initiatives, such as a new online health network called "Your Practice Online," would bring the group the financial success it needed in order to continue to fund its work.

Principal Competitors

American Nurses Association; American Academy of Family Physicians.

Further Reading

Booth, Bonnie, "AMA Seeking New Lifetime Membership," *American Medical News,* August 7, 2000, p. 17.

Burrow, James G., *AMA: Voice of American Medicine,* Baltimore: Johns Hopkins Press, 1963.

Campion, Frank D., *The AMA and U.S. Health Policy Since 1940,* Chicago: Chicago Review Press, 1984.

Dreyfuss, Robert, "Which Doctors? The AMA's Identity Crisis," *New Republic,* June 22, 1998, pp. 22–26.

Fishbein, Morris, *History of the AMA 1847–1947,* Philadelphia and London: W.B. Saunders, 1947.

Gibbons, Don L., "Dr. Sammons Weathering Storm," *Medical World News,* December 25, 1989, p. 17.

Gorman, Christine, "Doctors' Dilemma," *Time,* August 25, 1997, p. 64.

Harris, Richard, "Medicare: We Do Not Compromise," *New Yorker,* July 16, 1966, pp. 35–70.

Jaklevic, Mary Chris, "AMA Loses Millions," *Modern Healthcare,* June 14, 1999, p. 3

——, "AMA's Profits Climb 17% in 1996," *Modern Healthcare,* June 23, 1997, p. 20.

McCormick, Brian, "Re-Organized Medicine," *American Medical News,* February 2, 1998, p. 7.

Melcher, Richard A., "The AMA Isn't Feeling So Hot," *Business Week,* September 1, 1997, p. 33.

Thompson, Elizabeth, and Kristen Hallam, "AMA Reminds Members of What It Can Do," *Modern Healthcare,* June 19, 2000, p. 6.

—A. Woodward

American Medical Response, Inc.

2821 South Parker Road
Aurora, Colorado 80014
U.S.A.
Telephone: (303) 614-8500
Fax: (303) 614-8502
Web site: http://www.amr-inc.com

Wholly Owned Subsidiary of Laidlaw Inc.
Incorporated: 1992
Employees: 19,800
Sales: $1.7 billion (1998)
NAIC: 621910 Ambulance Services

American Medical Response, Inc. (AMR) is among the nation's leading providers of ambulance services. Maintaining a fleet of some 4,000 vehicles and 265 site facilities, AMR operates in 35 states, providing basic transport as well as more specialized services, including critical care transport (involving transport, nursing staff, and intensive care equipment) and advanced life support services (involving transport and paramedic staff). Moreover, the company operates a 911 emergency call and response system. AMR was acquired by the Canadian transportation giant Laidlaw, Inc. in 1997; in the late 1990s, Laidlaw began to flounder and in 2000 was struggling to avoid bankruptcy. As a result, Laidlaw put AMR up for sale in October 2000.

Early 1990s Origins

When Paul M. Verrochi, a 42-year-old entrepreneur from Boston, formed American Medical Response in 1992, he knew nothing about the operations of an ambulance service company. He did, however, know something about building large companies through the consolidation of small businesses, and he was familiar with the service industry. Verrochi and his long-time partner and accountant, Dominic Puopolo, had already successfully expanded two service firms (janitorial and asbestos-removal) through acquisition and consolidation. In fact, the two had overseen more than 150 acquisitions over the years. In the early 1990s, Verrochi and Puopolo were looking for a new opportunity when their banker suggested they consider ambulance services.

At that time the ambulance services industry was highly fragmented, consisting of 2,200 small, privately owned, local businesses as well as numerous municipal and county operations at local fire districts, many of whom wanted to privatize. Consolidation in the industry had occurred only regionally, and no publicly owned ambulance service companies existed. Given the growth and aging of the population and an increase in outpatient care, Verrochi viewed both the growth potential for medical transportation services and the benefits of consolidation as great. Verrochi aimed to create and build the leading provider of ambulance services, and his would become the first such to operate nationwide.

Verrochi hired a consultant to assist in targeting companies to purchase in forming American Medical Response. Four regional companies, with potential to expand in their markets, were settled on: Regional Ambulance Services in San Francisco's East Bay area; Professional Ambulance Services in Delaware; New Haven Ambulances Services in Connecticut; and Vanguard Ambulance Services, a 98-vehicle fleet in the San Francisco area. Vanguard was the largest of the acquisitions, having recently consolidated some smaller ambulance service companies under its umbrella. AMR formed with the combined annual revenues of $96 million and headquarters in Boston. The entrepreneurs, who remained with the company, received stock in the new company and cash.

Verrochi took AMR public concurrent with the completion of the acquisitions in August 1992. The initial public offering, at $10.25 per share, raised $23.7 million. Flush with cash, the company purchased Mobile Medic Ambulance Services of Gulfport, Mississippi, in November, Ambulance Service Company of Denver in December, and Buck Medical Services of Portland, Oregon, in January 1993.

Verrochi's strategy for growth involved acquiring "beachhead" companies (the strongest, best-managed providers in a given market) and then expanding to contiguous service areas by purchasing companies in those areas or by placing bids to

---

Company Perspectives:

The American Medical Response team of compassionate professionals will be the leading provider of medical transportation and pathways to health care.

---

supply services in surrounding areas. The new AMR company would then be responsible for identifying potential local targets for acquisition. Because the owner of the local company became a partner in the AMR business, Verrochi valued his personal relationship with each new partner, inviting him to dinner with the Verrochi family.

AMR maintained headquarters in Boston but divided its new businesses by region, retaining local management capabilities while consolidating accounting, payroll, purchasing, and human resources as a means to lower overhead, thus lowering the cost per ambulance trip. By eliminating redundant operations and adding new services, AMR hoped to provide geographically and financially efficient ambulance services.

The use of state-of-the art technology also improved operations and cost efficiency. When AMR acquired the Regional Ambulance Service of Fremont, California, it also gained a Global Positioning Satellite (GPS) system. The GPS allowed dispatchers to call for an ambulance that might be closest to the emergency site based on travel time rather than geographic location. GPS tracked each ambulance every 14 seconds, while computer-aided dispatch determined the travel time to the destination based on traffic patterns. Thus an ambulance further away from the emergency site, but unimpeded by traffic jams or construction, might reach the caller more quickly than another unit. While small companies often did not have the capital to invest in technology, AMR's large regional companies did and thereby provided better service at an ultimately lower cost.

Moreover, GPS proved more cost-efficient to AMR. With the consolidation of two East Bay companies under AMR, 86 vehicles could cover an area that had previously required 100 vehicles. With a fully equipped vehicle costing about $100,000, and annual maintenance on top of that, AMR stood to save millions. The GPS system could coordinate up to 50 911 emergency calls simultaneously in Alameda and Contra Costa counties. AMR hoped to install GPS systems in Denver, Chicago, Connecticut, Mississippi, Philadelphia, and Chicago, when the volume of business allowed for it.

In its first full year in operation, 1993, AMR reported $189 million in revenues and $9.5 million in earnings. Contracts from county and municipal governments comprised approximately two-thirds of AMR's revenues. Such contracts were obtained through bidding and renegotiation and involved the provider's ability to meet standards for response times (usually eight to nine minutes, 90 percent of the time), staffing, vehicle and equipment, quality of service, and insurance. The remaining one-third of AMR's revenues were received primarily from private insurance companies.

AMR's successful foray into consolidating and privatizing ambulance services prompted other companies to go public and follow Verrochi's acquisition strategy. These included Rural/Metro in Scottsdale, Arizona, and CareLine of Irvine, California. Moreover, Laidlaw Inc., a Canadian-based transportation services company, formed MedTrans for the purpose of entering ambulance services industry.

However, the public sector found this new industry trend somewhat disturbing. Local fire districts did not relish the competition, and the public expressed concern about the quality of patient care under a profit-oriented corporation. Northern California was a particularly difficult battleground in bidding on contracts. After a struggle with the public and local fire districts, AMR received a four-year extension contract in Santa Clara County, California, worth $25 million in annual revenues. The contract involved a cooperative alliance with the City of San Jose whose fire department provided first responder paramedic service, Basic Life Support within five minutes of the call, while AMR provided Advanced Life Support within nine minutes.

Focus of Growth

AMR's regional strategy soon proved useful in serving the changing needs of health care insurance providers. Health Maintenance Organizations (HMOs) and Preferred Physician Organizations (PPOs) preferred single source providers to handle local ambulance service needs. AMR's local networks, which covered larger contiguous areas, including multi-county and multi-state areas, fulfilled this need better than a fragmented system. AMR was thus able to secure lucrative contracts with PruCare, US Healthcare, HMO Blue, Cardiology First and FHP Corporation.

In February 1995, AMR signed a contract with Kaiser Permanente of Portland, Oregon, for the handling of non-emergency transport calls as part of Kaiser's managed care plan. Under the pioneer agreement, AMR implemented telephone triage to evaluate the caller's health care needs. Under the controversial program, Kaiser members called a seven-digit telephone, or a toll-free number in outlying areas, instead of 911, to obtain a diagnosis and determine the need for emergency medical care. If emergency care was deemed necessary, the call was transferred to a 911 operator. While AMR and Kaiser viewed this program as more efficient and cost effective, reducing the number of emergency ambulatory services for non-emergency situations, customer concerns centered on the element of risk as the two minutes required to determine need meant the difference between life and death in some circumstances.

Coverage of large, geographic service areas also served AMR well in treating bombing victims at the Alfred R. Murrah Federal building in April 1995. By drawing on resources from Tulsa and communities surrounding Oklahoma City, AMR utilized 127 of 131 of its local personnel to respond to the situation without curtailing services to other emergencies. AMR immediately established an Incident Command Structure in Oklahoma City and performed immediate triage to discern patient needs according to the severity of injuries. Paramedics and technicians treated 517 people within the first 90 minutes and transported 210 people in the first hour. AMR also drew on its Critical Incident Stress Management providers from around the country to assist employees and other public safety responders in coping with the crisis.

Key Dates:

1992: Paul Verrochi enters the ambulance business.
1992: AMR completes four acquisitions and goes public.
1995: AMR reports earnings of $24.5 million on sales of $483.8 million.
1997: AMR is acquired by Laidlaw, Inc. and merges with that company's MedTrans operations.
1999: A restructuring program seeks to streamline AMR's operations.
2000: A struggling Laidlaw puts AMR up for sale.

AMR continued to pursue its acquisition strategy with funds from a secondary stock offering which raised $90 million. AMR had completed a total of 58 acquisitions by the end of 1995, 22 of them in 1995 alone. The largest acquisition in the company's history occurred in October of that year with the purchase of Ambulance Systems of America, of Natich, Massachusetts, whose operations in Massachusetts, New Hampshire, Rhode Island, Maine, and New Jersey was garnering nearly $100 million in annual revenues. That year AMR responded to 1.7 million calls in 26 states with 10,000 employees and a fleet of over 1,700 ambulances. Revenues reached $483.8 million and earnings reached $24.5 million or $1.35 per share.

To meet the needs of its growing company, AMR restructured in late 1995. Paul T. Shirley, originally owner of Vanguard Ambulance Services, was elected CEO and president of AMR in August, and George De Duff, formerly CEO of AMR West, became the company's chief operating officer. Consolidation of operations into six regional units shifted administration into regional offices in the Northeast, Mid-Atlantic, South, Great Lakes, Midwest, and West.

Financial Troubles Mar Late 1990s

In January 1997, AMR was purchased by Laidlaw, Inc., as part of Laidlaw's own aggressive acquisition plan in the transportation industry. Laidlaw paid $40 per share, or an estimated $1.2 billion, for AMR, and then merged it with another of its ambulance service companies, California-based MedTrans. Thus, the two largest ambulance service companies in the United States had combined to create a presence in 34 states, keeping the AMR name. AMR headquarters were moved from Boston to the Denver area and management was restructured into four regions, each with chief financial and operating officers. DeHuff replaced Paul Shirley as CEO upon Shirley's retirement in August 1997.

About a year after Laidlaw purchased AMR, however, some challenges to AMR's system began to emerge. With over 100 companies acquired in a short period of time, AMR had difficulties meeting demands of local communities. Specifically, AMR struggled to adapt to local public safety standards, as it tried to apply its own national standards to local situations. The problems resulted in claims of substandard medical services and delayed response times, with some customers, such as the city of Littleton, CO, documenting response times longer that 12 minutes. Unlike ambulances stationed at local fire districts,

AMR's roving vehicles were often too far away, especially in rural and semi-rural areas. AMR had voluntarily discontinued service to some rural areas, as well in Chicago, but the company also lost key contracts in such cities as Dallas, Houston, Boulder, and Oklahoma City.

Another problem involved the collections for unpaid services. Because local laws required ambulance services to respond regardless of a caller's ability to pay, uncollectible debts remained a hazard of the business. AMR experienced relatively low rates of uncollectible accounts when it first formed, as low as five percent. However, as the company grew and centralized its collections office, it became more difficult to locate customers and collect service bills. Uncollectible bills reached 40 percent of revenues in 1998. While the company recorded revenues of $1.1 billion in 1998, that amount did not include uncollectible bills of $700 million the same year. The discrepancy severely hampered AMR's ability to provide service and to compete with other companies who bid on large contracts. Finally, the company found itself in competition with new companies, some founded by former employees of acquired companies who were not retained by AMR.

While its ambulance service business shrank, AMR focused on program development in partnership with health insurance providers. In May 1998 AMR worked with Sutter Health in San Francisco, implementing a mobile health care unit for on-the-job injuries. The service provided first-aid vans rather than ambulances and charged only for actual care. The fee for an emergency ambulance call was $1,200 while van response was $150 per call. AMR and Sutter designed the service, called SutterHealth@Work, to resolve the problem of non-urgent use of the 911 emergency system, which overloaded the emergency response system. SutterHealth@Work also provided vaccinations, drug screening, and other services.

In late 1998 AMR prepared to open a national call center for American Medical Pathways, a new subsidiary formed to perform triage for health care providers. Located in Kenosha, Wisconsin, the call center served Kaiser Permanente members in 18 states. AMR management had hoped to base the service in Denver, but a tight labor market in Colorado led to the location of the call center in Wisconsin. The location raised concerns about the timeliness of emergency response. While a local system used an enhanced Caller ID system to bring up the name, telephone number, and address of the caller, the Pathways system matched the telephone numbers to addresses in a database of Kaiser members. The system facilitated dispatch of paramedics if the caller was unable to communicate the problem. While the call center was sustained by a $600 million, five-year contract with Kaiser, AMR hoped to attract other health care providers to the system. Anthem Blue Cross Blue Shield in New Haven county, Connecticut, opted for a local Pathways program to serve its Medicare HMO patients.

In early 1999 AMR began to restructure the company. DeHuff resigned as CEO in March, and Laidlaw replaced him with COO John Grainger. Grainger reduced the work force by ten percent, or approximately 2,200 people, and reduced management by 180 positions. AMR scaled back ambulance service operations in Boston and closed operations in Philadelphia as the company was too large to respond to government changes in reimbursement rates. The company lost a contract for Fort Worth, Texas, to Rural/Metro, though it did win bids for a five-year contract in Sonoma County, California, and a four-year contract in Las Cruces, New Mexico. Healthcare provider Humana tested AMR's Pathways program with Medicare HMO patients in Florida during the summer of 1999.

While AMR struggled to manage its holdings, its parent, Laidlaw, succumbed to financial woes of its own, including a tremendous debt burden and irate stockholders. In an abrupt move, in September 1999, Laidlaw announced that it was putting AMR up for sale, with an asking price of $1.6 million. The company had hoped to divest AMR entirely by August 2000, but acceptable offers were not forthcoming. The parent company had already announced that it was "discontinuing" its relationship with AMR, taking AMR off its financial books in order to focus on stabilizing its own balance sheet. As industry analysts speculated on an impending bankruptcy for Laidlaw, a group known as Harlingwood Equity Partners, consisting of former AMR employees and the former CEO of Rural/Metro offered $500 million for AMR. However, Laidlaw did not accept the offer, and by late 2000 AMR was making inroads in its return to profitability. In March 2001, Laidlaw appointed Jack Edwards as AMR's new president and CEO. Edwards was charged with enhancing AMR's value by improving its financial performance.

Principal Divisions

American Medical Pathways.

Principal Competitors

American Medical Alert Corporation; Community Medical Transport, Inc.; Rural/Metro Corporation.

Further Reading

"Ambulance Chasing," *Time*, December 9, 1996, p. 58.

Austin, Marsha, and Aldo Svaldi, "Ambulance Giant Races for Revamp," *Denver Business Journal*, March 5, 1999, p. 1A.

Austin, Marsha, "Critics Attack Emergency System," *Denver Business Journal*, December 25, 1998, p. 3A.

——, "Kaiser's Waiting Game: Sale of AMR Puts Key Partner in Play," *Denver Business Journal*, September 17, 1999, p. 1A.

——, "Laidlaw Dragging Heels on AMR Sale," *Denver Post*, September 5, 2000, p. C1.

——, "Who Will Snatch Up an Ambulance Giant?," *Denver Business Journal*, February 4, 2000, p. 9A.

Bole, Kristen, "Chasing Ambulances," *San Francisco Business Times*, May 22, 1998, p. 3.

Brock, Kathy, "Ambulance Wars Flare Up in Suburbs," *Business Journal-Portland*, October 14, 1994, p1.

——, "AMR Bid Extends Olive Branches to Ambulance Rivals," *Business Journal-Portland*, April 14, 1995, p. 1.

——, "Fire Districts Kill AMR's Sweet Deal for Backup Aid," *Business Journal-Portland*, July 4, 1997, p. 1.

——, "Seeking Stability in a Turbulent World," *Business Journal-Portland*, December 12, 1997, p. 16.

"CEO Spotlight," *Atlanta Business Chronicle*, November 7, 1997, p. 30A.

Darlin, Damon, "Hillary to the Rescue?," *Forbes*, September 12, 1993, p. 76.

Finegan, Jay, "Strength in Numbers," *Inc.*, December 1995, pp. 94+.

Kuzins, Rebecca, "Ambulance Buy: Boston Firm in Driver's Seat," *Business Journal Serving Greater Sacramento*, April 11, 1994, p. 7.

——, "Managed Care Chases Ambulances," *Business Journal Serving Greater Sacramento*, July 18, 1994, p. 1.

Smith, Brad, "Ambulance Firm Top Execs Step Down," *Denver Business Journal*, August 22, 1997, p. 1A.

Svaldi, Aldo, "AMR's Problems Take Their Toll," *Denver Business Journal*, April 16, 1999, p. 3A.

——, "Tale of a Troubled Roll-Up: How AMR Gobbled 250 Rivals to Lead the Pack," *Denver Business Journal*, March 19, 1999, p. 1A.

—Mary Tradii

Arch Wireless, Inc.

1800 West Park Drive, Suite 250
Westborough, Massachusetts 01581
U.S.A.
Telephone: (508) 870-6700
Fax: (508) 366-8966
Web site: http://www.arch.com

Public Company
Incorporated: 1986 as Arch Communications Group Inc.
Employees: 9,000
Sales: $642 million (1999)
Stock Exchanges: NASDAQ
Ticker Symbol: ARCH
NAIC: 513321 Paging; 513322 Cellular and Other
    Wireless Telecommunications

With a new name and a new corporate identity, Arch Wireless, Inc. (formerly Arch Communications Group, Inc.) is positioned to benefit from the growing demand for wireless two-way messaging services and the expansion of the wireless Internet. Founded in 1986 as a local and regional provider of paging products and services in the Boston area and New England, Arch grew by completing more than 30 mergers and acquisitions. For most of the 1990s Arch benefited from strong consumer demand for traditional paging services. In 1998 Arch acquired MobileMedia Corp. to form the second largest paging company in the United States. Around this time consumer demand for advanced messaging services began to take hold. In 2000 Arch acquired PageNet and became the largest paging company with nearly 17 million subscribers. Arch Wireless is now betting that demand from consumers and businesses for its advanced messaging services will more than offset the decline in its traditional paging business.

Growth Through Acquisitions: 1986–97

Arch Communications Group, Inc. was founded in 1986 to provide traditional paging services to the Boston area. In 1992 Arch went public and its stock began trading on the NASDAQ

under the symbol APGR. In 1993 Arch gained a $55 million line of bank credit from a group of financial institutions headed by Bank of New York Co. Arch provided low-cost regional paging services focused on small to medium-sized markets. In New England the company was known as Page New England. It had grown in its first eight years by providing narrow-band wireless communications in underserved paging areas. In five years the paging industry grew more than 20 percent annually to more than 19 million subscribers in 1993. In recent years pagers became more sophisticated, allowing users to receive up to 500-character messages from a personal computer. Subscribers also could receive news headlines, sports scores, and stock quotes on the pagers. The introduction of vibrating pagers made them less intrusive.

In 1993 Arch was one of the fastest growing paging companies. Its subscriber base increased 60 percent to 400,000 users in 13 states, making it the fifth largest public paging company in the United States ranked by number of subscribers. Ranked ahead of Arch were PageNet, the largest paging business with 3.7 million subscribers, and MobileComm, Skytel, and PageMart. By 1994 Arch's larger rivals had launched digital nationwide services that enabled users to receive phone messages anywhere in the United States for a basic service fee ranging from $29.95 to $39 per month. PageNet was planning to spend $1 billion on a nationwide voice-messaging network that would allow subscribers to carry a pocket answering machine.

Arch grew by acquiring smaller paging companies, and the paging industry in general was going through a period of consolidation. From 1986 to 1994 the company made more than 25 acquisitions. In 1994 the company was expanding beyond its base in New England and the mid-Atlantic states to northern Illinois and Wisconsin and further into Florida. The company had yet to turn a profit, and for fiscal 1993 ending August 31 Arch reported a net loss of $5.7 million on revenue of $41.4 million. Nevertheless, the company reported strong operating cash flow, a standard performance measure for paging companies, and was able to increase its bank line of credit to $150 million. Keeping costs low was the key to Arch's strong financial performance.

In mid-1994 Arch launched Arch Nationwide, which relied on a consortium of paging companies to deliver messages. The

Company Perspectives:

Arch Wireless provides two-way messaging and universal access to your preferred information sources, giving you the ability to communicate with everyone, anywhere, anytime and in every direction. Arch Wireless keeps you connected to the wireless web, so you can receive continuous, automatic updates—from stock quotes, to news, to sports, to weather. Our "Arch-smart" service keeps people on the go connected to the right information at the right moment. We are there when you need us most. Arch is your net@hand.

system was slower than that of Arch's competitors and was priced around $19.95 a month. In August 1994 Arch lost out to PageNet in a Federal Communications Commission (FCC) auction of new nationwide frequencies, in which PageNet paid $200 million for three licenses.

By 1997 Arch had grown to more than four million subscribers, and the company relocated its national services division from Dallas to Tempe, Arizona. Its national services division provided turnkey paging services to companies such as US West Communications, which in turn sold paging services to consumers.

Becoming Second Largest
U.S. Paging Company: 1998

In mid-1998 Arch announced that it would acquire MobileMedia Corp., the fifth largest paging company in the United States, for $649 million. Based in Fort Lee, New Jersey, and operating under the name MobileComm, MobileMedia was in bankruptcy. The acquisition gave Arch an additional three million customers for a total of more than seven million customers, making it the second largest paging company in the United States behind PageNet. Also in 1998 Arch sold off its broadcast tower and site management business to OmniAmerica Inc. for $38 million. The sale involved broadcast towers at 134 sites in 22 states.

Arch's growth had come from more than 30 mergers and acquisitions it had made since its inception in 1986. To consolidate its infrastructure, the company created a new customer-care system based on a Java application server and object-relational mapping technology from Novera Software Inc. and Informix databases.

During 1998 the company undertook a major reorganization, reducing the number of its geographically-based divisions from seven to four, which were headquartered in Boston; Charlotte, North Carolina; Columbus, Ohio; and Phoenix. It also split its former national services division into separate national sales and services units. Arch's new organizational structure was expected to be fully implemented by mid-2000.

For 1998 the company reported total revenue of $414 million, up from $397 million in 1997. Net revenue—service and product revenue less the cost of product sales—increased four percent to $384 million from $368 million in 1997. Although the company's net loss increased from $181.9 million in 1997 to $206.1 million

in 1998, its earnings before interest, taxes, depreciation, and amortization (EBITDA) grew from $130.3 million in 1997 to $141.6 million in 1998. Net revenue and EBITDA were two standard measures of performance in the paging industry.

In its annual report for 1998, Arch noted that "the tremendous growth of one-way numeric paging since the early 1990s slowed while consumer demand for today's exciting new advanced messaging services began to take hold." Traditional numeric display paging over conventional networks continued to account for more than 80 percent of the units in service. The coming transition from traditional paging to advanced messaging was marked by the entrance of two paging carriers offering services on NPCS (national personal communications services) networks.

In October 1998 Arch launched an electronic distribution channel called the Arch Paging Online Store. The service gave customers the opportunity to purchase pagers and Arch paging services over the Internet and was available at the company's web site.

Adding Wireless Data Services: 1999–2000

By 1999 Arch and other paging companies, facing a decline in the traditional paging business, were betting on executing their wireless data strategies. Wireless data was at the heart of the two-way messaging revolution. Eventually, consumers would decide whether they preferred to receive wireless data over their pagers, personal digital assistants (PDAs), or cell phones. Mobile phone carriers such as Verizon Wireless and Sprint PCS began to offer wireless data access to e-mail and other information over cell phones. Arch offered wireless data service on a pager-like device made by Motorola Inc. and a snap-on messaging module for the Handspring Visor.

In November 1999 Arch announced that it would acquire its larger rival PageNet, or Paging Network Inc., of Dallas, Texas, for $1.36 billion in stock. The acquisition reflected the declining state of the paging business as more than 70 million Americans now owned wireless phones. At the time PageNet was facing a possible Chapter 11 bankruptcy filing; its latest filing with the Securities and Exchange Commission (SEC) raised questions about the company's ability to service its long-term debt. A key component of the complex deal involved PageNet bondholders, who would become stockholders and own 44.5 percent of the combined company, or more than $500 million worth of stock. PageNet had $1.2 billion of debt outstanding in senior notes and $804 million in bank debt. The combined company's outstanding debt would be reduced to $1.8 billion, 46 percent less than before the merger. In addition, PageNet would spin off its Vast Solutions business unit as a separate company providing wireless services. PageNet stock and bond holders would own about 80 percent of Vast Solutions, with Arch shareholders owning the remaining 20 percent. As of November 1999, Arch had seven million subscribers, and PageNet had 9.7 million. PageNet had not shown a profit since going public in 1991. Its assets included valuable licenses to provide paging services and a comprehensive two-way paging network suitable for carrying e-mail and other types of information.

Key Dates:

1986: Company is founded as Arch Communications Group, Inc. and provides paging products and services in Boston and New England.
1992: Arch Communications goes public.
1998: Arch acquires MobileMedia Corp., the fifth largest paging company in the United States, for $649 million.
2000: Arch completes its acquisition of Paging Network Inc. (PageNet) to form the largest paging company in the United States; Arch changes its name to Arch Wireless, Inc.

Also in November Arch and Juno Online Services, Inc. announced a strategic alliance whereby they would market co-branded pagers and an integrated messaging service to Juno's more than 7.6 million subscribers. The messaging service would provide users with pager notification when they received a message in their Juno mailbox. Arch, in turn, gained direct access to millions of potential wireless messaging customers.

For 1999 Arch reported total revenue of $642 million, net revenue of $607 million, and EBITDA of $209 million. In spite of an overall net loss of $285.6 million, the company was pleased with its financial performance and expected to be able to fund future growth through operations rather than from borrowing. Its operating margins were among the best in the industry.

Arch continued to form strategic alliances during 2000. In January the company announced that it would gain access to thousands of small and mid-sized business through an alliance with BizBuyer.com, a leading on-line business-to-business marketplace. In February Arch and employeesavings.com, a leading provider of Employee Sponsored Value Plans (ESVPs) to Fortune 1000 companies, announced a marketing venture that gave Arch access to more than one million corporate employees and family members. As part of the venture Arch would provide special offers on its services to the employees and their families served by employeesavings.com.

In March 2000 Arch was selected by America Online Inc. (AOL) to provide two-way messaging capabilities for AOL's new Mobile Messenger service. The service offered AOL's e-mail and Instant Messenger service to customers using Arch wireless devices. Under the three-year contract AOL would purchase wholesale access to Arch's paging network. As a result, Arch would be able to offer AOL services to its paging service customers. Arch's network had enough existing capacity that no initial investment was needed to support new sales to AOL. BellSouth Corp. would provide the network for AOL's wireless messaging service, which also would be available through Sprint PCS handsets and handheld devices made by Nokia Inc.

In August Arch reached an agreement with Movil@ccess, Mexico's first personal interactive communications (PIC) provider, that would allow Arch subscribers to roam within major metropolitan areas in Mexico. Under the agreement Movil@ccess customers would be able to roam throughout the United States.

An agreement with OracleMobile, a subsidiary of Oracle Corp., gave Arch users access to Internet content from their devices without requiring a Web browser through a service called Ask@OracleMobile. Among the Ask@OracleMobile services Arch customers could receive were news, eBay, movie guide, package tracking, stock quotes, traffic, flight status, driving directions, horoscope, lottery, dictionary, translations, and weather. Customers also could receive "Instant Alerts" triggered by specific events.

Before Arch was able to close its acquisition of PageNet, a rival bid was submitted by Metrocall Inc., the third largest U.S. paging company, for $1.57 billion. Meanwhile, PageNet was forced to file an involuntary Chapter 11 bankruptcy petition, as the result of actions by creditors holding $3.5 million worth of PageNet bonds that were in default. PageNet responded to Metrocall's offer by filing a voluntary Chapter 11 bankruptcy petition and rejecting Metrocall's bid. Subsequent litigation revived Metrocall's offer, but with PageNet's board of directors favoring Arch, Arch completed its acquisition of Paging Network Inc. in November 2000. With the acquisition Arch gained 5,000 employees and a nationwide two-way network over which it could sell wireless data services. Prior to the acquisition Arch's network covered only 25 percent of the United States, forcing it to lease portions of WebLink Wireless Inc.'s network.

To reflect its transition from a traditional paging company to one that provided two-way Internet messaging and mobile information services, the company changed its name in September 2000 to Arch Wireless, Inc. Its ticker symbol was changed from APGR to ARCH and the corporate tagline became Net@Hand. The company successfully introduced its new two-way messaging services under the Arch Webster brand name in August 2000. The first product was the Arch Webster 100, a two-way interactive messaging service that enabled users to communicate via e-mail using a Motorola T900 interactive messaging device. Other developments included the debut of the Arch Message Center service, which allowed customers to consolidate office and Internet e-mail accounts, address books, schedules, and online files and access them from a Web-connected desktop or through an Arch Wireless messaging device.

With nearly 17 million subscribers, Arch was in a strong position to participate in the growth of interactive messaging and wireless mobile data—an industry projected to grow by 30 percent or more annually over the next five years, from a $6 billion industry to a $25 billion industry. Target markets included corporate accounts, which Arch serviced through its 1,700-member sales force. Two-way messaging was used by corporate field sales personnel, on-site repair workers, and mobile professionals in general, among others. Arch also marketed its services to consumers through numerous retail partners, including home improvement retailer Lowe's, Service Merchandise, and many others. The company also was developing industry-specific services, and in July 2000 Arch reached an agreement with Preferred Healthcare Staffing, Inc. to provide two-way wireless messaging to the company's national staff of healthcare professionals.

Arch claimed that its ReFlex 25 network offered more reliability and was less costly to operate than national PCS networks. ReFlex 25 covered more than 90 percent of the U.S. population and operated nationwide on a standard digital protocol, whereas PCS networks were designed primarily to carry voice signals and operated over a patchwork of digital protocols. Arch also was moving into providing Internet-based wireless information through strategic alliances with companies such as America Online, MyWay.com, OracleMobile, GoAmerica, Inc., and Juno Online Services, Inc.

Principal Competitors

WebLink Wireless Inc.; Skytel; Metrocall Inc.; Verizon Wireless; Sprint PCS; Vodaphone AirTouch plc; BellSouth Mobility.

Further Reading

"Arch Acquires MobileMedia," *HFN: The Weekly Newspaper for the Home Furnishing Network,* August 31, 1998, p. 59.

Collins, Jonathan, "Once You Get 'Em, How Do You Keep 'Em?," *Tele.com,* March 20, 2000, p. 17.

Files, Jennifer, "Addison, Texas-Based Paging Company to Merge with Communications Firm," *Knight-Ridder/Tribune Business News,* November 8, 2000.

——, "Debts Land Addison, Texas-Based Paging Network in Bankruptcy," *Knight-Ridder/Tribune Business News,* July 18, 2000.

——, "Paging Giant Challenges Rival's Bid for Troubled Addison, Texas, Firm," *Knight-Ridder/Tribune Business News,* July 20, 2000.

Freeman, Michael, "Towers as Cash Magnets," *Mediaweek,* April 20, 1998, p. 14.

Howe, Peter J., "America Online Picks Westborough, Mass., Paging Firm for New Service," *Knight-Ridder/Tribune Business News,* February 29, 2000.

——, "Westborough, Mass.-Based Paging Company to Acquire Rival," *Knight-Ridder/Tribune Business News,* November 8, 1999.

Levin, Rich, "Paging Company to Create Java Customer-Care System," *InformationWeek,* August 24, 1998, p. 26.

"Pager, Pager, Who's Got the Pager?," *Business Week,* September 4, 2000, p. 54.

"Paging Company to Provide Tempe with 300 Positions," *Business Journal,* July 4, 1997, p. 4.

Rosenberg, Ronald, "Massachusetts' Arch Communications Defies Predictions for Pager Industry," *Knight-Ridder/Tribune Business News,* September 20, 1994.

—David P. Bianco

Army & Air Force Exchange Service

Army and Air Force Exchange Service

3911 South Walton Walker Boulevard
Dallas, Texas 75236-1598
U.S.A.
Telephone: (214) 312-2011
Toll Free: (800) 527-6790
Fax: (214) 312-3000
Web site: http://www.aafes.com

Government-Owned Company
Incorporated: 1941 as Army Exchange Service
Employees: 54,000
Sales: $6.99 billion (2000)
NAIC: 44512 Convenience Stores; 45211 Department
    Stores; 72211 Full-Service Restaurants; 722211
    Limited-Service Restaurants; 45421 Vending Machine
    Operators; 512131 Motion Picture Theaters (Except
    Drive-Ins)

The Army and Air Force Exchange Service (AAFES) is a government agency within the Department of Defense that operates for-profit stores, restaurants, movie theaters, gas stations, and other businesses on military bases and in the field. Income generated by the service is used to pay for morale, welfare, and recreational programs on bases, which promote cultural events and operate and build such facilities as libraries, gymnasiums, and youth centers for military personnel and their families to use. Only two percent of the agency's funds come from the government; these typically are used to cover transportation costs and wages for a small number of military staffers (the vast majority of AAFES employees are civilians). AAFES stores offer a wide range of products, from food and health-care items to clothing, stereo equipment, and auto parts. Prices are significantly lower than those charged by civilian businesses, and customers pay no sales tax. Through its catalog service, which went on-line in 1996, AAFES customers can order goods from anywhere in the world. AAFES stores are only open to active, reserve, or retired military personnel and their families. With nearly $7 billion in annual revenues, AAFES operates one of the country's largest department store chains.

Late 19th-Century Roots of AAFES

The origins of the AAFES date to the late 19th century, when trading posts were first established on military bases. Until then, itinerant peddlers known as "sutlers" had served the day-to-day needs of soldiers for such items as shaving gear and tobacco. In 1889 the U.S. War Department officially sanctioned the presence of base canteens, and six years later the department issued General Order 46 establishing a system of base exchanges at virtually every military post. Each military organization had its own system for the exchanges, with post commanders typically assigning an officer to run the unit. The commanding officers decided how to spend the profits. Soldiers soon began to refer to these post exchanges simply as "PXs," and they relied on them for basic personal items that the military did not supply.

Shortly before the United States entered World War II, the government was in the process of reorganizing the system. In 1941 the Army Exchange Service was created as a civilian-staffed organization that operated on military bases. A panel of five private-sector businessmen recommended changes to the existing PX system. Ultimately a structure was created whereby a brigadier general headed an executive staff drawn from both military and civilian sectors, with civilians staffing the actual PXs. All independent PX facilities were purchased from their respective owners by the new Army Exchange Service.

With the war, the Army Exchange Service was called upon to support troops in the field, and the War Department created mobile units for this purpose. A catalog service was also started so that troops in remote locales could order items to send home to loved ones. In 1948 the organization was expanded to include the Air Force and was renamed, becoming the Army and Air Force Exchange Service, or AAFES. Air Force Exchanges were called BXs, for base exchanges, while the Army continued to use the acronym PX.

With many U.S. soldiers stationed as peacekeepers around the world following World War II and the Korean conflict, a demand for luxury goods on bases began to develop. In 1960 the government decided to allow foreign PXs to sell such items as electronic equipment and cameras, enabling soldiers to obtain American-made versions of these items overseas.

Company Perspectives:

The Customer is the Business, and the Business is the Customer. This motto describes the way we feel about those we serve—including active duty, retirees, reserve forces, and their families. Around AAFES it is repeated often because we know that the customer is the most important person in the operation of our business. The key to satisfying our customers is our people. Whether an associate is directly serving customers or supporting another associate who is, it is their knowledge and commitment that is at the heart of AAFES' success. As members of the AAFES team, we must each day ask ourselves what we can do to make AAFES a better place to work and a better place to shop. We will never stop our efforts to improve our organization and ourselves. What our customers expect is simple. We must have efficient operations that provide the right merchandise at an excellent price and follow it all up with superior customer service.

During the Vietnam conflict, expensive goods such as televisions and stereo equipment became big sellers at AAFES outlets. AAFES stores were still staffed by civilians in locations where no fighting was expected, but near the front, military personnel operated the exchanges, which were sometimes housed in a tent or the back of a truck.

Competition from the Private Sector

The rise of discount chains in the late 1970s, such as Wal-Mart, hurt business; these chains found it profitable to build stores near military bases. AAFES soon responded by lowering prices and improving customer service. New categories and products such as car care and food concessions were added at larger base facilities. Inventory control was computerized, and stores were redesigned during the 1980s so that they much more closely resembled their civilian counterparts. The military stores also began emphasizing merchandising, paying more attention to displays of goods and store layouts. By 1985 AAFES had 6,000 retail outlets and 2,300 food-service establishments. Worldwide revenues topped $4.8 billion, and the organization employed 70,000 civilian workers. AAFES undertook a further $183 million upgrade during the latter half of the 1980s, when it built a new $58.4 million distribution center in Newport News, Virginia.

AAFES' business was now growing rapidly. Sales reached a peak of $7.4 billion in 1990. Of this, just under $6 billion came from retail sales; nearly $1.5 billion came from concessions, services, and vending, and almost $50 million was from catalog sales. The agency was now operating 130 Burger King franchises and 313 ''Shopette'' convenience stores, with plans to open more of both. AAFES was also arranging to offer H & R Block tax preparation services at some locations. A survey by the A.C. Nielsen Company showed goods cost an average of 23.2 percent less when purchased through AAFES than they did at conventional retail outlets, and this did not take into account the additional savings realized by not paying sales tax. Despite offering such low prices, AAFES was still able to put $229

million into morale, welfare, and recreational development programs during the year. About 70 percent of profits were so used, with the remainder spent to maintain and upgrade AAFES facilities. Starting in 1991, National Guard and Reserve personnel were allowed to buy at the facilities, further increasing AAFES' customer pool.

The end of the Cold War and the subsequent reductions in military forces affected AAFES dramatically, however. With U.S. bases closing all around the world, the agency was forced to shutter some of its facilities. European bases were particularly hard hit, with troops reduced from 500,000 to 100,000 on that continent. By the mid-1990s revenues had dropped by approximately one-third and staffing was reduced by more than 10,000. The number of AAFES facilities had declined from a high of over 17,000 to fewer than 11,000, a figure that included everything from tent stores in temporary field locations to shopping center-sized complexes on 172 of the largest permanent bases. Despite the dramatic changes, the agency managed the transition smoothly and remained profitable, reporting net earnings of $269 million in 1995.

A Focus on Customers

One unique feature of AAFES, compared to its civilian counterparts, was its dedication to serving its customers even if profits suffered. Part of the organization's purpose was to build morale, and serving the off-duty and recreational needs of military personnel was a key part of this mandate. The agency intentionally stocked marginal or money-losing exchanges at far-flung outposts with a wide range of goods to give service personnel more of the comforts of home. Although they made no profit, the exchanges at these locations did not raise their prices to make up the difference. Some 60 percent of AAFES stores fell into this category. Top selling items chain-wide included snacks, beer and tobacco products, along with electronics, sportswear, and athletic shoes.

The agency also provided a wider range of brand and price choices than its civilian counterparts. The customer base served by a PX could range from young enlistees and junior officers all the way up to top brass, and a single AAFES store might need to stock expensive Rolex watches alongside the budget-priced Timex brand. Wives of senior officers were particularly concerned about being able to purchase fashionable clothing, and AAFES made a point of having these items available for them. For budget-conscious shoppers, AAFES stores also offered private brand goods, which included a broad range of items, from health and beauty aids to clothing and photographic film. Total sales of private label items accounted for only about two percent of AAFES's annual revenues, but this figure was expected to grow as the program was expanded and promoted.

In the mid-1990s, AAFES, using information from a data-warehousing program begun earlier in the decade, began to reconfigure its stores based on which types of goods were selling the best. They began to give more space to items like luggage, linens, home decor, and audio recordings. Stores were also being reorganized for their local market's needs based on this data. The buying patterns at a large training-base PX were much different than those of the one located in Homestead, Florida, for example, where 90 percent of the customers were

Key Dates:

1895: U.S. War Department issues General Order 46 establishing stores at army posts.

1919: The abbreviation ''PX'' is first used to refer to the Post Exchange, or base store.

1941: Army Exchange Service is created to reorganize the existing PX system.

1940s: Exchange Service goes to war; catalog ordering is introduced.

1948: Expanding, the organization becomes the Army and Air Force Exchange Service.

1960: Overseas exchanges begin selling luxury goods made in the United States.

1967: AAFES headquarters moves from New York City to Dallas.

1980s: AAFES responds to private-sector competition by upgrading stores and services.

1991: National Guard and Reserve personnel are added to AAFES customer pool.

1996: AAFES catalog goes on-line.

1999: AAFES signs a $1.5 billion phone-service deal with MCI WorldCom.

retirees. To improve its data gathering, AAFES earmarked $50 million to upgrade computer systems in 145 of the largest stores, with such equipment to eventually be installed in every location that generated more than $30,000 per month in sales. AAFES made an ongoing effort to learn directly from its customers. In the front of each store were commander's communication cards on which customers could write questions or complaints. The organization also conducted surveys and focus groups, and each base had a council of spouses—male and female—that met with store managers to discuss their needs.

1990s Success with On-line Catalog Sales

AAFES's catalog had grown by the mid-1990s into a full-color, 500-page volume. Qualified customers worldwide could order through a toll-free phone number, and delivery was free. Catalog sales typically totaled about one percent of overall revenues. In 1996 AAFES put the catalog on-line via its Web site, publicizing the move by printing the Web address on shopping bags, receipts, and in the catalog itself. The response was surprisingly strong, with Internet sales for the first year totaling one-tenth of all catalog orders. By the end of the decade, this amount grew to one-third of the total revenues. In 1998 features were added that allowed customers to access their AAFES-affiliated military credit card information on-line, make payments, and receive e-mail confirmations of payments. AAFES vendors could also check their accounts via the Web, an option that suppliers praised. The successful online catalog led *Information Week* magazine to rank AAFES fourth on its annual ''E-Business 100'' list in 1999.

AAFES stores' distribution of pornographic materials received media attention in 1996 when the House of Representatives passed the Military Honor and Decency Act, which banned sales of pornography on military bases. Income from this category had totaled $12 million for AAFES in 1995. The ban was quickly struck down as unconstitutional, but was later upheld by the Supreme Court. The Pentagon ultimately issued a directive banning some 150 pornographic publications while allowing the stores to continue selling ''softer'' titles such as *Playboy*.

As the 1990s waned, AAFES continued to strike up new partnerships with private-sector companies. In 1999 a $1.5 billion, ten-year deal was signed with MCI WorldCom to provide long-distance, calling card, pay telephone, and other services to AAFES customers worldwide. The following year Booksamillion.com was also granted exclusive rights to sell books to AAFES's 7.5 million customers over the Internet.

As it entered the 21st century, the Army and Air Force Exchange Service continued to provide its customers with a wide range of goods and services at discounted prices, while generating steady profits to fund morale-building recreational programs and facilities. Its mettle had been tested through wartime service as well as during the downsizing of the military following the Cold War, and the organization continued to survive and thrive. As long as Americans served their country in the Army and Air Force, AAFES would continue to be there for them with the goods and services they needed at attractive prices.

Principal Competitors

7-Eleven, Inc.; Best Buy Company, Inc.; Circuit City Group; Costco Wholesale Corporation; J.C. Penney Company, Inc.; Kmart Corporation; The Kroger Company; METRO AG; Sears, Roebuck and Company; Target Corporation; Wal-Mart Stores, Inc.

Further Reading

Baldwin, Pat, ''U.S. Troops Find Retail Oasis in the Desert,'' *Dallas Morning News,* January 13, 1991, p. 1H.

Colley, Richard D. and Evans, Earnest L., ''Let's Go to the PX!,'' *Army Logistician,* May 1, 1997, p. 27.

Crowley, Aileen, ''Military Retailer in Net Boot Camp, *PC Week,* September 15, 1997, p. 88.

Dworkin, Andy, ''Military Service: Oak Cliff Firm Provides Minor Comforts to Overseas Troops,'' *Dallas Morning News,* May 6, 1999, p. 1D.

''Four-Star General Merchandise Sold Here,'' *Chain Store Age Executive with Shopping Center Age,* September, 1984, pp. 119–122.

Goodridge, Elizabeth, ''AAFES: Worldwide Supplier,'' *Information Week,* December 13, 1999, p. 96.

Jackson, William, ''AAFES Phone Service Contract Goes to MCI WorldCom,'' *Government Computer News,* March 15, 1999.

Johnson, Jay L., ''AAFES: A $7 Billion Military Enterprise,'' *Discount Merchandiser,* March, 1996, p. 70.

King, Paul, ''Mess-Hall Era Ending as Name Brands Establish Beachhead on Military Bases,'' *Nation's Restaurant News,* September 6, 1999, p. 47.

Miller, Robert, ''Military Exchange Service Prepares for the Changing of the Guard,'' *Dallas Morning News,* May 18, 1993, p. 3D.

Wilson, Marianne, ''AAFES Storms Retail Mission,'' *Chain Store Age Executive with Shopping Center Age,* June 1, 1991, p. 21.

Witt, Clyde E., ''Multi-Million Dollar Facelift for Exchange Service,'' *Material Handling Engineering,* August, 1988, pp. 47–52.

—Frank Uhle

Atchison Casting Corporation

400 South Fourth Street
Atchison, Kansas 66002
U.S.A.
Telephone: (913) 367-2121
Fax: (913) 367-2155
Web site: http://www.atchisoncasting.com

Public Company
Incorporated: 1991
Employees: 4,200
Sales: $468.3 million (2000)
Stock Exchanges: New York
Ticker Symbol: FDY
NAIC: 331511 Iron Foundries; 331528 Other Nonferrous
   Foundries (Except Die-Casting); 331513 Steel
   Foundries (Except Investment)

Atchison Casting Corporation produces iron, steel, and non-ferrous castings and forgings for customers involved in more than 35 markets. The company's metal castings range in size from a few ounces to 550,000 pounds and are manufactured by 20 operating units. Atchison Casting's subsidiaries are located principally in the eastern half of the United States. Internationally, the company maintains facilities in Canada, Great Britain, and France.

Origins

Atchison Casting was formed during the early 1990s, but the assets the company owned enjoyed a far lengthier legacy. During its first four months in existence Atchison Casting existed in name only, a barren corporate entity organized expressly to acquire a foundry and machine shop in Atchison, Kansas. Once the acquisition was completed, the company gained its first asset and its link to the past.

The Atchison foundry traced its origins to the 19th century and the age of railroads. The foundry began operating in 1872 to supply iron castings to the Atchison, Topeka, and Santa Fe Railroad, indirectly marking Atchison Casting's entry into a market that would support the company more than a century later. In 1906, the foundry's operations were combined with a machine shop, the St. Joseph machine shop. In 1930, another major expansion was completed when a new steel foundry was built in Atchison. In 1956, the Atchison works acquired a company named Rockwell Spring and Axle Company, which later became the defense industry behemoth known as Rockwell International Corporation. Rockwell, with diversified interests that made it one of the largest conglomerates in the world, acquired the Atchison foundry and St. Joseph machine shop to support its valve divisions. Rather than rely on an outside supplier, Rockwell used the Atchison works to produce its own steel castings, a relationship that endured for the ensuing three decades.

Under Rockwell's stewardship, the Atchison operations flourished, benefiting from the vast financial resources of its parent company. Rockwell's commitment to advancing foundry technology turned the Atchison foundry into a leading producer of large carbon and low alloy steel castings. Eventually, however, Rockwell's commitment to the Atchison works began to wane, particularly after the company sold its valve divisions in 1989. The divestiture of the valve divisions was just one of a series of divestitures the company would make in the 1990s, as it sought to tailor itself into an industrial automation company. Early in the decade, the metal castings division became a candidate for divestiture, its fate determined in large part by Rockwell's exit from valve production.

Although it was no longer deemed to be part of Rockwell's business scope by the beginning of the 1990s, the Atchison/St. Joseph metal castings division was not without its admirers. One interested party was an investor group led by Hugh H. Aiken, who worked for an investment firm located in Boston named Riverside Partners, Inc. Aiken and his associates were intent on entering the castings business and acting as a consolidator. The castings industry was highly fragmented, consisting of thousands of relatively small, independent foundries that could be acquired and absorbed by a single corporate entity, thereby creating an organization whose sum would be greater than its parts. Aiken formed Atchison Castings to be such an organization, incorporating the company in February 1991. Several months later, in June, the acquisition of Rockwell's metal castings division in Atchison was completed, giving the company a foundation on which to build.

Company Perspectives:

Atchison manufactures highly engineered metal castings and forgings that are utilized in a wide variety of products, including cars, trucks, gas, steam and hydroelectric turbines, mining equipment, locomotives, passenger rail cars, pumps, valves, army tanks, navy ships, paper-making machinery, oil field equipment, reactor vessels for plastic manufacturing, computer peripherals, office furniture, home appliances, satellite receivers and consumer goods. Having completed nineteen acquisitions since 1991, the Company has established itself as a leading consolidator in the casting industry. As a result of these acquisitions, the Company has the ability to produce castings from a wide selection of materials, including carbon, low-alloy and stainless steel, gray and ductile iron, aluminum and zinc as well as the ability to manufacture parts in a variety of sizes, ranging from small die cast components for the computer industry that weigh a few ounces to mill stands for the steel industry that weigh up to 280 tons. The Company believes that its broad range of capabilities, which addresses the needs of many different markets, provides a distinct competitive advantage in the casting and forging industry.

Much of the 1990s would be devoted to expanding on the base established in Atchison, as the company embarked on an exhaustive acquisition campaign. Its lengthiest spell of acquisitive inactivity occurred following its initial acquisition, a nearly two-year period highlighted by the expansion of the facilities in Atchison. A stainless steel-making plant was installed in January 1992 as part of Aiken's efforts to give the new company a broader footing, both in terms of the types of castings it could produce and the customers it could attract. Customers in the market for shaped metal components essentially had three manufacturing processes from which to choose: forging, fabrication, and castings, each capable of shaping metal according to customer-supplied specifications. Forgings were made by using dies, hammers, or other tools capable of shaping metal through the application of pressure. Metal fabricators fulfilled their customers' needs by welding together individual pieces of metal. Castings were made by pouring molten metal into a mold and waiting for the metal to solidify, which, unlike fabricated metal components, created a seamless metal component. If made properly, castings were generally lighter, stronger, and more corrosion-resistant than fabricated parts and less expensive than forgings, giving Aiken and his management team advantages they hoped to exploit.

The installation of the stainless steel-making plant in early 1992 added casting capabilities that enabled Atchison Casting to diversify its product line and its customer base. Although such internal expansion contributed to growth, Atchison Casting's greatest gains were achieved on the acquisition front, where the company could play out its primary role as a consolidator. Once the company switched into the acquisition mode, it did so with vigor, beginning with its second acquisition, the February 1993 purchase of Amite Foundry and Machine, Inc. Both the foundry and machine shop, located in Amite, Louisiana, were shuttered when Aiken completed the deal, but both facilities were re-opened once Atchison Casting assumed control.

Fueling Expansion with 1993 Public Offering

After acquiring Amite, Atchison Casting's next move shored up its resources for the flurry of acquisitions to follow. In October 1993, the company completed its initial public offering (IPO) of stock, earning $23.3 million in net proceeds, which provided some of the capital required to adopt the posture of a consolidator. Investors were introduced to a company that had carved its niche in the transportation industry, the legacy inherited by acquiring the operations in Atchison. The company specialized in manufacturing train undercarriages, supplying the large steel structures used to support locomotives and mass transit trains. Customers such as General Electric Co. and General Motors Co. relied on Atchison Casting for the fundamental metal components required to manufacture their products, linking the Kansas-based concern with some of the largest manufacturers in the world. These relationships were not lost on investors, who helped provide the financial means for Aiken to diversify his company's customer base further.

New markets opened up for Atchison Casting following its IPO, as acquisitions added new capabilities and new customers. In April 1994, the company paid $14 million for $24 million-in-sales Prospect Foundry, Inc., a manufacturer of ductile and gray iron castings. At the time of the acquisition, the market for ductile iron castings was growing at a faster rate than the steel or gray iron markets, giving Atchison Casting entry into a lucrative market that served customers in the transportation, construction, agricultural, and hydraulic equipment industries. Atchison Casting's capabilities were enhanced two months later, when the company acquired CMI-Quaker Alloy, Inc. from CMI International Inc. The acquisition, valued at approximately $3.5 million, gave Atchison Casting Pennsylvania-based operations that produced stainless and high alloy steel castings for the pump and valve industries. Before the end of the year, the company completed one more acquisition, purchasing Canadian Steel Foundries, Ltd. in December. Aside from strengthening Atchison Casting's capabilities in manufacturing large castings, the purchase of Canadian Steel also gave the company access to hydroelectric and steel mill markets.

By the end of 1994, sales reached $82.5 million, up from the $54.7 million the company recorded during its first year in 1992. Atchison Casting duplicated its acquisition total from 1994, purchasing three companies in 1995. The first purchase of the year occurred in January, when the company acquired Kramer International, Inc., a leading manufacturer of castings for the pump industry. The purchase of Empire Steel Castings, Inc. followed a month later, increasing Atchison Casting's capacity for producing carbon, low alloy, and stainless steel castings. In December 1995, the success of the Prospect Foundry acquisition a year and a half earlier encouraged Aiken to deepen the company's involvement in ductile iron castings. Missouri-based La Grange Foundry, Inc., a producer of smaller gray and ductile iron castings, was acquired, helping Atchison Casting to post $141.5 million in sales for the year.

As Atchison Casting entered its fourth full year of operation, Aiken's shopping spree intensified. The company completed four acquisitions in 1996, beginning with the March 1996 acquisition of G&C Foundry Company, which, like La Grange Foundry, produced smaller gray and ductile iron castings. Next, in September, the company purchased LA Die Casting Inc., a

Key Dates:

1991: Hugh Aiken and investment group purchase Rockwell International's metal casting division.
1993: Atchison Casting converts to public ownership.
1997: A secondary public offering of stock is completed.
1998: First overseas acquisition is completed.
2000: Three Atchison Casting foundries are closed.

producer of precision aluminum and zinc die castings for the computer, communications, and recreation industries. October saw Aiken set his sights north across the border again, where Atchison Casting acquired Ontario-based Canada Alloy Castings, Ltd., a producer of stainless, carbon, and alloy steel castings for, among others, the power generation and pulp and paper machinery markets. Before the end of the month, Aiken agreed to acquire Pennsylvania Steel Foundry and Machine Co., entrenching the company's presence in the northeastern United States, where it operated two foundries gained through the Empire Steel and Quaker Alloy transactions. Pennsylvania Steel, a producer of carbon and high-alloy steel castings, generated $19 million in revenue at the time of the acquisition.

By the end of 1996, Atchison Casting's revenue volume had swelled to $185 million, more than tripling the total recorded after the company's first year in business. Acquisitions fueled the growth, creating a company with nine foundries operating in seven states and in Canada. The acquired foundries steered Atchison Casting into new markets and established relationships with a greatly expanded customer base. When the company commenced business in 1991, it served 12 customers. By 1996, Aiken counted more than 300 customers involved in a variety of markets, including locomotive, farm equipment, military, utility, mass transit, and general industrial.

Late 1990s Acquisitions

Aiken's strategy for the late 1990s was a continuation of the acquisition campaign that had driven the company's growth during the first half of the 1990s. In February 1997, the company acquired Jahn Foundry Corp., a Springfield, Massachusetts-based producer of iron gray castings for the industrial and automotive markets. After completing a secondary public offering of stock in May 1997, Aiken used some of the proceeds to acquire Beloit Corporation's castings division in July 1997. Renamed PrimeCast Inc., the acquisition added four foundries and $31 million in revenue to Atchison Casting's fold. The last acquisition of the year occurred in October 1997, when Inverness Castings Group, Inc., a producer of aluminum die castings, became the company's 15th foundry.

For the first time in its history, Atchison Casting extended its reach overseas in 1998. In April, the company acquired Great Britain-based Sheffield Forgemasters Group Ltd. for $51.5 million. A $177 million-in-sales company, Sheffield gave Atchison Casting entry into European markets and entry into a new market niche, forgings. In May, the company returned to the domestic front with the acquisition of New Hampshire-based

Claremont Foundry, Inc., a producer of steel castings for the mass transit and mining and construction markets. In September, Atchison Casting deepened its involvement in Canada with the acquisition of another Ontario-based company, London Precision Machine & Tool, Ltd. Operator of an industrial machine shop, London Precision served the locomotive, pulp and paper, and mining and construction markets.

By the end of the 1990s, Aiken's acquisition campaign began to wind down. The company completed one acquisition in 1999, the purchase of France-based Founderie d'Autun, but completed no significant acquisitions in 2000. The company had no plans to add to its roster of operating companies in 2001. Instead, Aiken and management team devoted their energies to integrating the acquisitions of the previous nine years, taking the time to efficiently absorb the assets that had pushed annual revenues up to $475 million. As Atchison Casting prepared for the future, its confidence was shaken by the closure of three foundries in late 2000. The Claremont foundry was shuttered in December 2000, followed by the closure of a steel foundry in Pennsylvania and an iron foundry in Wisconsin later in the month. Slackening demand forced the company to shut down the foundries, slowing Atchison Casting's stride as it entered its second decade of existence.

Principal Subsidiaries

Amite Foundry and Machine, Inc.; Canada Alloy Castings, Ltd.; Canadian Steel Foundries, Ltd.; Claremont Foundry, Inc.; Empire Steel Castings, Inc.; Kramer International, Inc.; London Precision Machine & Tool Ltd. (Canada); Pennsylvania Steel Foundry & Machine Co.; PrimeCast, Inc.; Quaker Alloy, Inc.; Sheffield Forgemasters Group Limited (U.K.); Founderie d'Autun (France); The G&C Foundry Company; Jahn Foundry Corporation; La Grange Foundry Inc.; Inverness Castings Group, Inc; LA Die Casting, Inc.

Principal Competitors

AMSTED Industries Incorporated; Grede Foundries, Inc.; Intermet Corporation.

Further Reading

"Atchison Buys Prospect Foundry," *American Metal Market,* April 6, 1994, p. 7.
"Atchison Buys Quaker Alloy," *American Metal Market,* May 12, 1994, p. 2.
"Atchison Casting Agrees to Buy Pennsylvania Firm," *American Metal Market,* October 29, 1996, p. 5.
"Atchison Casting Buys Beloit Unit," *American Metal Market,* July 10, 1997, p. 3.
"Kansas-Based Atchison Casting Completes Purchase of British Company," *Knight-Ridder/Tribune Business News,* April 8, 1998.
"Kansas Foundry Operator Reports Higher Sales for Quarter," *Knight-Ridder/Tribune Business News,* August 15, 1997.
Labate, John, "Atchison Casting," *Fortune,* November 14, 1994, p. 258.
Sacco, John E., "Atchison Casting Closes Two Subsidiary Foundries," *American Metal Market,* December 4, 2000, p. 2.

—Jeffrey L. Covell

Atlas Air, Inc.

<table>
<tr><td>

2000 Westchester Avenue
Purchase, New York
U.S.A.
Telephone: (914) 701-8000
Fax: (914) 701-8001
Web site: http://www.atlasair.com

Public Company
Incorporated: 1992
Employees: 1,255
Sales: $790.5 (2000)
Stock Exchanges: New York
Ticker Symbol: CGO
NAIC: 481112 Scheduled Freight Air Transportation;
    481212 Nonscheduled Chartered Freight Air
    Transportation

</td></tr>
</table>

Atlas Air, Inc. transports cargo for major international airlines on scheduled flights to 101 cities in 46 countries. Atlas is the third largest cargo carrier in the world, trailing Federal Express and United Parcel Service (UPS). Unlike its larger rivals, Atlas only transports cargo from airport to airport, thereby avoiding the expenses required to maintain dispatch centers and ground-handling operations. The company's fleet comprises 22 Boeing 747-200 freighters and ten Boeing 747-400 freighters. China Airlines Ltd. is Atlas's primary customer, accounting for 26 percent of the company's business.

Origins

Atlas was born from the entrepreneurial talents of Michael A. Chowdry, a Pakistan-born émigré who found riches and success in the United States. Chowdry left war-ravaged Lahore, Pakistan in 1970 when he was 15 years old. He fled to London before making a permanent move to the United States, where he was introduced to what would become a lifelong passion for aviation. By the time he was 21 years old, Chowdry was paying for his tuition at the University of Minnesota by flying crop dusters in rural North Dakota and Minnesota. By his late 20s, he

had settled in Denver, Colorado, where he made his living in aviation business, buying and selling landing and takeoff rights at major airports. In 1983, Chowdry was hired as an airline consultant for Frontier Airlines to help the company form Frontier Horizon, a short-haul carrier. The project collapsed, in large part because of the clash between union-organized Frontier Airlines and nonunion Frontier Horizon, but Chowdry's time at Frontier Airlines was far from wasted.

In 1984, Chowdry completed a windfall deal that gave him the capital to begin a career as an aviation entrepreneur. He bought seven Boeing 727 airplanes from Frontier Airlines and sold the aircraft to an air freight company named Flying Tiger. Chowdry made $3.5 million on the deal, his reward for knowing that Flying Tiger was eager to enter the U.S. cargo business. Executives at Frontier Airlines were not aware of Flying Tiger's interest, or else they would have skirted the middleman—Chowdry—and completed the deal on their own. In a matter of weeks, Chowdry was a multimillionaire, well equipped to venture into the business world on his own.

With money gained from the Flying Tiger transaction, Chowdry started Aeronautics Leasing, Inc. (ALI) in 1984. Through ALI, Chowdry leased passenger airplanes to airlines, a business that thrived under his stewardship. Chowdry cultivated an impressive list of customers, leasing aircraft to global carriers such as Pan American Airways, TWA, Continental, SAS, and British Airways. By the end of the 1980s, ALI was recognized as a genuine force in the leasing business, but circumstances would force Chowdry in a different direction, leading him to form the company that would ultimately distinguish him as one of the most successful aviation entrepreneurs of the 1990s.

Chowdry's decision to abandon ALI for a new company, Atlas, was triggered by recessive economic conditions and hostilities in the Middle East. In attempting to explain the reasoning behind Atlas's formation, Chowdry referred to a night he spent in a Hong Kong hotel room. It was August 1991, six months after the Persian Gulf War, and from Chowdry's vantagepoint his future in aviation was clear. His hotel room overlooked Hong Kong's Kai Tak airport, where the effects of the war were evident. Still hobbled by fears of terrorism, passenger traffic was light, adding to the woes of airlines hit

Company Perspectives:

The world's international airlines are generally high-cost carriers that focus principally on their passenger operations. To meet the increasing demand for air cargo transportation, much less expand their own market share, these airlines must either outsource additional cargo capacity or expand their fleet and add further high-cost labor resources and infrastructure. Atlas Air provides a solution to this problem. The Company provides the aircraft and crews to service these airlines, thereby giving the airlines additional cargo capacity without the financial burden of substantial equipment and personnel costs. With a strong sense of commitment, Atlas focuses on its existing customer base and grows with them, as it also adds new clients. In return, the airlines purchase reliable service from a company that acts as if it were part of the airlines' fleet.

especially hard by the global economic decline. Chowdry noticed, however, that cargo-carrying aircraft were queued one behind another, forming a steady stream of landing lights that lit the night and turned Chowdry's mind toward the resilience of the cargo business.

Chowdry's percolating thoughts about freight carriers were organized into concrete plans a few months after his stay in Hong Kong. In 1992, Pan American Airways, battered by the harsh economic conditions of the early 1990s, collapsed, its failure forcing Chowdry to act. Pan American had leased a Boeing 747-200 from ALI, an aircraft that lay idle after Pan American went out of business. In the midst of the economic trough, finding another airline willing to lease ALI's passenger airplane proved difficult, so Chowdry decided to improve the aircraft's marketability by converting it into a cargo freighter. Although there were no immediate offers, the strategy paid off when Chowdry learned that China Airlines needed the capacity of an additional 747 freighter. The airline, however, was not willing to operate the aircraft itself, a qualification that forced Chowdry to create a cargo company to operate his idle 747. Formed in 1992, Atlas became that airline, prompting Chowdry to turn over the management of ALI to a friend and focus all his attention on a new, promising market niche.

As Atlas began operations, Chowdry benefited immensely from the timing of his strategic move. Many of the major airlines were replacing their older aircraft with twin-engine airplanes such as the Boeing 767 and the Airbus A330, opting for smaller, more fuel-efficient aircraft than the four-engine 747s widely in use. The new airplanes were more fuel-efficient than their predecessors were, but they held 50 percent less cargo than the 747s, creating a need for cargo capacity that Chowdry intended to exploit. Hailing Atlas as the "airlines' airline," as quoted in the June 1995 issue of *Air Transport World,* Chowdry fashioned the company as a "wet leasing" operation: Atlas supplied the aircraft, crew, maintenance, and insurance, while its customers, generally non-U.S. airlines, took responsibility for marketing the freighter service, handling the cargo, and paying for the fuel. The company's job started and ended at the airport, eliminating the need for costly ground-handling opera-

tions and dispatch centers and enabling Chowdry to focus on making Atlas a low-cost operator. He believed that the presence of a low-cost cargo hauler would induce airlines to contract out, or outsource, their cargo business. His confidence in his strategy soon was borne out in Atlas's energetic growth.

For its first flight, from Taiwan to the United States, Atlas transported Eddie Bauer polo shirts, Nike shoes, and computer disk drives. Further orders from China Airlines necessitated the purchase of additional 747-200 freighters, as Atlas's fleet of aircraft grew. Not long after establishing a business relationship with China Airlines, Chowdry signed his first European customer to a contract, marking the beginning of Atlas's ties with KLM Royal Dutch Airlines. By the beginning of 1994, coming off of $40.9 million in sales for the previous year, the company had added its fourth 747, with plans to acquire two more aircraft by the year's end. Chowdry was convinced that the expansion of the company's fleet and the extension of its service area would lead to Atlas's domination of the cargo business. Toward this end, Chowdry implemented an accelerated growth plan after giving Atlas its footing, acquiring the newer, more efficient model of the 747-200, which could carry a larger payload over longer routes.

Sparking Expansion with 1995 Public Offering

Part of Chowdry's accelerated growth plan involved selling a portion of the company to the public. In March 1995, when the company took delivery of its seventh aircraft, Chowdry registered with the Securities and Exchange Commission (SEC) for Atlas's initial public offering (IPO) of stock. According to SEC filings, the company planned to offer 3.45 million shares at a proposed offering price of between $14 and $16 per share. From the proceeds, Chowdry planned to use at least $24 million as a down payment on three 747-200 aircraft. The IPO was completed in August 1995, raising $74 million and beginning a period during which the company's stock value soared. Atlas's stock tripled during its first year, as the size of its fleet doubled, something the company had accomplished in each of its four years of existence. By the end of 1996, sales reached $315 million, up from just $40 million three years earlier, and Chowdry, who still owned 59 percent of the company, was vastly wealthy, reportedly worth $670 million on paper.

Much of Atlas's success was credited to the decision to use 747-200 freighters, recognized as the premier international freighter by numerous sources. The company's one glaring miscue during the 1990s, however, stemmed from its use of 747-200s. The company's troubles occurred after it subleased five Federal Express 747-200s in 1996. The airplanes proved to be a drag on the company's earnings in large part because they did not fit Atlas's established maintenance scheme, leading to operating costs that were $1,000 more per hour than had been anticipated. The mistake cost the company dearly, causing its stock value to plummet in half and removing Chowdry's name from *Forbes* magazine's list of the richest Americans.

Late 1990s: The Debut of the 747-400

The setback suffered by Atlas and Chowdry was only temporary. By 1998, the five aging 747-200s were replaced with new 747 models, the longer-range 747-400. Industry observers

Key Dates:

1984: Chowdry forms Aeronautics Leasing, Inc.
1992: Atlas is founded.
1995: Initial public offering of stock is completed.
1996: The addition of five aging aircraft hobbles financial progress.
1997: Atlas signs a purchase agreement with Boeing for ten 747-400 freighters.
2000: Atlas takes delivery of its tenth 747-4000 airplane.
2001: Chowdry is killed in an airplane crash.

were startled by Atlas's decision to use the jumbo 747-400, an aircraft that was exponentially more expensive than the company's workhorse, the 747-200. Moreover, the 747-200 was viewed as the linchpin to the company's remarkable rise during the 1990s, an opinion held both by Atlas executives and industry analysts, making the decision to use a new aircraft model somewhat of a gamble. The gamble paid dividends, however, enabling Atlas to reverse the losses suffered from operating the Federal Express 747-200s. In 1998, the company used five 747-400s in place of the troubled 747-200s and recorded immediate financial gains. Profits nearly doubled in 1998 from the total recorded in 1997, reaching a record high. Tellingly, the increase was achieved without any increase in the size of Atlas's fleet, providing clear evidence of the value of the 747-400s. Referring to the 747-400s, Atlas's executive vice-president, Richard Shuyler, noted the success of the aircraft in a March 1999 interview with *Air Cargo World.* ''In terms of economics,'' he explained, ''there is no doubt in our mind that they are as, if not more, profitable than the 747-200 aircraft. . . . They've been a very good profit generator.''

As Atlas progressed through the late 1990s, industry observers found it difficult to direct any criticism toward Chowdry's well managed, strategically sound, financially fit organization. Sales in 1998 reached $422 million, more than ten times the total collected five years earlier, making Atlas the third largest cargo carrier in the world. Chowdry, who spent his spare time flying his own jet fighter at near supersonic speeds over the Rockies, earned praise from the market niche he had shrewdly mastered. In 1998, he became the youngest person ever inducted into the International Air Cargo Hall of Fame. In 1999, when four more 747-400 freighters were added to the

company's fleet, sales swelled to $637 million, accompanied by record gains in the company's operating profit margin. For the year, Chowdry was selected as the National Ernst & Young Service Entrepreneur of the Year.

By 2000, Atlas's fleet comprised 22 747-200 freighters and ten 747-400 freighters, with new additions set to arrive in the years ahead. Industry forecasts called for the demand for world cargo services to triple by 2020, a demand Chowdry intended to satisfy by adhering to the same strategy that had fueled his rapid rise during the 1990s. Tragically, the remarkable career of the industry's most promising executive ended before the anticipated growth of the early 21st century could be realized. On January 24, 2001, before an interview with the *Wall Street Journal,* Chowdry and a reporter boarded Chowdry's private airplane. With Chowdry at the controls, the airplane crashed into a field in Watkins, Colorado, two minutes after takeoff. There were no survivors. Richard Shuyler, who had joined Atlas shortly after it was formed, was named chief executive officer the day after Chowdry's death. To Shuyler fell the duty of guiding Atlas through the post-Chowdry era and toward the company's promising future.

Principal Subsidiaries

Atlas Freighter Leasing, Inc.; Atlas Freighter Leasing II, Inc.

Principal Competitors

Airborne, Inc.; FedEx Corporation; DHL Worldwide Express.

Further Reading

''A Tidy Bundle in Air Cargo,'' *Business Week,* April 19, 1999, p. 128.
''Bigger, Better,'' *Air Cargo World,* March 1999, p. 6.
''In a Former Life,'' *Inc.,* October 2000, p. 113.
Levere, Jane, ''Extra Lift,'' *Airline Business,* August 1996, p. 46.
Moorman, Robert W., ''The Airlines' Airline,'' *Air Transport World,* June 1995, p. 185.
Ouzounian, Shahe, ''Weight of the World,'' *Flight International,* April 16, 1997, p. 32.
Samuelson, James, ''Flying High,'' *Forbes,* August 12, 1996, p. 84.
Svaldi, Aldo, ''Atlas Air Builds International Empire from Tiny Golden Office,'' *Denver Business Journal,* January 14, 1994, p. 3.
Turney, Roger, ''Chatty Chowdry,'' *Air Cargo World,* April 2000, p. 14.

—Jeffrey L. Covell

Bajaj Auto Limited

Akurdi, Pune 411035
India
Telephone: +91 20 740 2851
Fax: +91 20 740 7397
Web site: http://www.bajajauto.com

Public Company
Incorporated: 1945 as M/s Bachraj Trading Ltd.
Employees: 17,200
Sales: Rs 42.16 billion ($903.36 million)(2000)
Stock Exchanges: Pune Mumbai Delhi London Berlin
    Frankfurt Munich
Ticker Symbols: BAJAJAUTO 490 BJATq.L 893361.BE
    893361.F 893361.MU
NAIC: 336991 Motorcycle, Bicycle, and Parts
    Manufacturing

Bajaj Auto Limited is India's largest manufacturer of scooters and motorcycles. The company generally has lagged behind its Japanese rivals in technology, but has invested heavily to catch up. Its strong suit is high-volume production; it is the lowest-cost scooter maker in the world. Although publicly owned, the company has been controlled by the Bajaj family since its founding.

Origins

The Bajaj Group was formed in the first days of India's independence from Britain. Its founder, Jamnalal Bajaj, had been a follower of Mahatma Gandhi, who reportedly referred to him as a fifth son. ''Whenever I spoke of wealthy men becoming the trustees of their wealth for the common good I always had this merchant prince principally in mind,'' said the Mahatma after Jamnalal's death.

Jamnalal Bajaj was succeeded by his eldest son, 27-year-old Kamalnayan, in 1942. Kamalnayan, however, was preoccupied with India's struggle for independence. After this was achieved, in 1947, Kamalnayan consolidated and diversified the group, branching into cement, ayurvedic medicines, electrical equipment, and appliances, as well as scooters.

The precursor to Bajaj Auto had been formed on November 29, 1945 as M/s Bachraj Trading Ltd. It began selling imported two- and three-wheeled vehicles in 1948 and obtained a manufacturing license from the government 11 years later. The next year, 1960, Bajaj Auto became a public limited company.

Rahul Bajaj reportedly adored the famous Vespa scooters made by Piaggio of Italy. In 1960, at the age of 22, he became the Indian licensee for the make; Bajaj Auto began producing its first two-wheelers the next year.

Rahul Bajaj became the group's chief executive officer in 1968 after first picking up an MBA at Harvard. He lived next to the factory in Pune, an industrial city three hours' drive from Bombay. The company had an annual turnover of Rs 72 million at the time. By 1970, the company had produced 100,000 vehicles. The oil crisis soon drove cars off the roads in favor of two-wheelers, much cheaper to buy and many times more fuel-efficient.

A number of new models were introduced in the 1970s, including the three-wheeler goods carrier and Bajaj Chetak early in the decade and the Bajaj Super and three-wheeled, rear engine Autorickshaw in 1976 and 1977. Bajaj Auto produced 100,000 vehicles in the 1976–77 fiscal year alone.

The technical collaboration agreement with Piaggio of Italy expired in 1977. Afterward, Piaggio, maker of the Vespa brand of scooters, filed patent infringement suits to block Bajaj scooter sales in the United States, United Kingdom, West Germany, and Hong Kong. Bajaj's scooter exports plummeted from Rs 133.2 million in 1980–81 to Rs 52 million ($5.4 million) in 1981–82, although total revenues rose five percent to Rs 1.16 billion. Pretax profits were cut in half, to Rs 63 million.

New Competition in the 1980s

Japanese and Italian scooter companies began entering the Indian market in the early 1980s. Although some boasted superior technology and flashier brands, Bajaj Auto had built up several advantages in the previous decades. Its customers liked the durability of the product and the ready availability of maintenance; the company's distributors permeated the country.

The Bajaj M-50 debuted in 1981. The new fuel-efficient, 50cc motorcycle was immediately successful, and the company aimed to be able to make 60,000 of them a year by 1985. Capacity was the most important constraint for the Indian motorcycle industry. Although the country's total production rose from 262,000 vehicles in 1976 to 600,000 in 1982, companies like rival Lohia Machines had difficulty meeting demand. Bajaj Auto's advance orders for one of its new mini-motorcycles amounted to $57 million. Work on a new plant at Waluj, Aurangabad commenced in January 1984.

The 1986–87 fiscal year saw the introduction of the Bajaj M-80 and the Kawasaki Bajaj KB100 motorcycles. The company was making 500,000 vehicles a year at this point.

Although Rahul Bajaj credited much of his company's success with its focus on one type of product, he did attempt to diversify into tractor-trailers. In 1987 his attempt to buy control of Ahsok Leyland failed.

The Bajaj Sunny was launched in 1990; the Kawasaki Bajaj 4S Champion followed a year later. About this time, the Indian government was initiating a program of market liberalization, doing away with the old "license raj" system, which limited the amount of investment any one company could make in a particular industry.

A possible joint venture with Piaggio was discussed in 1993 but aborted. Rahul Bajaj told the *Financial Times* that his company was too large to be considered a potential collaborator by Japanese firms. It was hoping to increase its exports, which then amounted to just five percent of sales. The company began by shipping a few thousand vehicles a year to neighboring Sri Lanka and Bangladesh, but soon was reaching markets in Europe, Latin America, Africa, and West Asia. Its domestic market share, barely less than 50 percent, was slowly slipping.

By 1994, Bajaj also was contemplating high-volume, low-cost car manufacture. Several of Bajaj's rivals were looking at this market as well, which was being rapidly liberalized by the Indian government.

Bajaj Auto produced one million vehicles in the 1994–95 fiscal year. The company was the world's fourth largest manufacturer of two-wheelers, behind Japan's Honda, Suzuki, and Kawasaki. New models included the Bajaj Classic and the Bajaj Super Excel. Bajaj also signed development agreements with two Japanese engineering firms, Kubota and Tokyo R&D. Bajaj's most popular models cost about Rs 20,000. "You just can't beat a Bajaj," stated the company's marketing slogan.

The Kawasaki Bajaj Boxer and the RE diesel Autorickshaw were introduced in 1997. The next year saw the debut of the Kawasaki Bajaj Caliber, the Spirit, and the Legend, India's first four-stroke scooter. The Caliber sold 100,000 units in its first 12 months. Bajaj was planning to build its third plant at a cost of Rs 4 billion ($111.6 million) to produce two new models, one to be developed in collaboration with Cagiva of Italy.

New Tools in the 1990s

Still, intense competition was beginning to hurt sales at home and abroad during the calendar year 1997. Bajaj's low-tech, low-cost cycles were not faring as well as its rivals' higher-end offerings, particularly in high-powered motorcycles, since poorer consumers were withstanding the worst of the recession. The company invested in its new Pune plant in order to introduce new models more quickly. The company spent Rs 7.5 billion ($185 million) on advanced, computer-controlled machine tools. It would need new models to comply with the more stringent emissions standards slated for 2000. Bajaj began installing Rs 800 catalytic converters to its two-stroke scooter models beginning in 1999.

Although its domestic market share continued to slip, falling to 40.5 percent, Bajaj Auto's profits increased slightly at the end of the 1997–98 fiscal year. In fact, Rahul Bajaj was able to boast, "My competitors are doing well, but my net profit is still more than the next four biggest companies combined." Hero Honda was perhaps Bajaj's most serious local threat; in fact, in the fall of 1998, Honda Motor of Japan announced that it was withdrawing from this joint venture.

Bajaj Auto had quadrupled its product design staff to 500. It also acquired technology from its foreign partners, such as Kawasaki (motorcycles), Kubota (diesel engines), and Cagiva (scooters). "Honda's annual spend on R&D is more than my turnover," noted Ruhal Bajaj. His son, Sangiv Bajaj, was working to improve the company's supply chain management. A marketing executive was lured from TVS Suzuki to help push the new cycles.

Several new designs and a dozen upgrades of existing scooters came out in 1998 and 1999. These, and a surge in consumer confidence, propelled Bajaj to sales records, and it began to regain market share in the fast-growing motorcycle segment. Sales of three-wheelers fell as some states, citing traffic and pollution concerns, limited the number of permits issued for them.

In late 1999, Rahul Bajaj made a bid to acquire ten percent of Piaggio for $65 million. The Italian firm had exited a relationship with entrepreneur Deepak Singhania and was looking to reenter the Indian market, possibly through acquisition. Piaggio itself had been mostly bought out by a German investment

---

Key Dates:

1945: Bajaj Auto is founded.
1960: Rahul Bajaj becomes the Indian licensee for Vespa scooters.
1977: Technical collaboration with Piaggio ends.
1984: Work begins on a second plant.
1998: Bajaj plans to build its third plant to meet demand.
2000: Thousands of workers are laid off to cut costs.

---

bank, Deutsche Morgan Grenfell (DMG), which was looking to sell some shares after turning the company around. Bajaj attached several conditions to his purchase of a minority share, including a seat on the board and an exclusive Piaggio distributorship in India.

In late 2000, Maruti Udyog emerged as another possible acquisition target. The Indian government was planning to sell its 50 percent stake in the automaker, a joint venture with Suzuki of Japan. Bajaj had been approached by several foreign car manufacturers in the past, including Chrysler (subsequently DaimlerChrysler) in the mid-1990s.

Employment fell from about 23,000 in 1995–96 (the year Bajaj suffered a two-month strike at its Waluj factory) to 17,000 in 1999–2000. The company planned to lay off another 2,000 workers in the short term and another 3,000 in the following three to four years.

Principal Subsidiaries

Bajaj Auto Finance Ltd.; Bajaj Auto Holdings Ltd.; Bajaj Electricals Ltd.; Bajaj Hindustan Ltd.; Maharashtra Scooters Ltd.; Mukand Ltd.

Principal Competitors

Honda Motor Co., Ltd.; Suzuki Motor Corporation; Piaggio SpA.

Further Reading

"Bajaj Auto Is Shooting Up the Fast Track," *India Business Intelligence,* June 15, 1994.

"Bajaj Finds New Worlds to Conquer," *India Business Intelligence,* May 3, 1995.

Bose, Kunal, "Buoyant Demand Lifts Indian Vehicle Makers," *Financial Times,* Companies and Finance, June 6, 1996, p. 19.

Dubey, Rajeev, "Can Rahul Bajaj Stymie Piaggio's Re-Entry?," *Business Today,* November 7, 1999, p. 46.

Frost, Tony, "Competing with Giants: Survival Strategies for Local Companies in Emerging Markets," *Harvard Business Review,* March/April 1999, pp. 199+.

Guha, Krishna, "Bajaj Rises Despite Falling Market Share," *Financial Times,* Companies & Finance, May 14, 1998, p. 40.

——, "Bajaj Tools Up for Counter-Attack on Rival Manufacturers," *Financial Times,* Companies & Finance, May 20, 1998, p. 33.

——, "International Competition Hits Bajaj," *Financial Times,* Companies & Finance, October 21, 1997, p. 27.

——, "Motorcycle Group Sees Profits Rise: Bajaj Auto Results Offer Chance to Assess Fight Against Giant Rivals," *Financial Times,* Companies & Finance, May 12, 1999, p. 31.

——, "Producers No Longer the Kings," *Financial Times,* Survey—India, November 19, 1999, p. 6.

——, "Restructuring Corporate India," *Financial Times,* Survey—Investing in India '98, April 28, 1998, p. 2.

——, "Software Services Lead the Charge," *Financial Times,* Survey—India, November 19, 1999, p. 5.

"Indian Motorcycles: Winners All," *Economist,* May 14, 1983, p. 84.

Merchant, Khozem, and Angus Donald, "Bajaj Auto May Purchase 50 Percent Stake in Maruti," *Financial Times,* Companies & Finance, November 25, 2000, p. 22.

Murthy, R.C., "Bajaj Auto Blames Piaggio for Setback," *Financial Times,* Sec. II, Companies and Markets, September 1, 1982, p. 15.

Nair, Geeta, "Bajaj Auto Plans to Foray into Insurance Sector," *Financial Express* (Bombay), July 25, 2000.

Ninan, T.N., "Business Dynasties: Family Groups Face Struggle to Survive," Survey—India '97, *Financial Times,* June 24, 1997, p. 20.

"Pune: Where PhDs Grow on Trees," *Business Week,* Asian ed., February 2, 1998, p. 18.

Vlasic, Bill, "The Little Car That Could Carry Chrysler Overseas," *Business Week,* January 29, 1996, p. 39.

Wagstyl, Stefan, "Bajaj Auto Aims to Maintain Its Dominance—The Indian Scooter Maker Is Capitalising on Economic Liberalisation," *Financial Times,* International Company News, May 13, 1994, p. 26.

—Frederick C. Ingram

Barmag AG

Leverkuser Strasse 65
D-42897 Remscheid
Germany
Telephone: (49) (2191) 67-1366
Fax: (49) (2191) 67-1313
Web site: http://www.barmag.de

Public Company
Incorporated: 1922 as Barmer Maschinenfabrik AG
Employees: 2,730
Sales: DM 662.1 million ($337.8 million) (1999)
Stock Exchanges: Frankfurt/Main
Ticker Symbol: BRG
NAIC: 333292 Textile Machinery Manufacturing

Barmag AG, with a market share of about 40 percent, is one of the world's leading manufacturers of plants, machines, and equipment used to produce and refine synthetic fibers. Yarn-spinning machines, textile machines, and chemical pumps made by Barmag are used to produce fibers with specific qualities such as water- and wind-proof fabrics for outdoor sportswear, and stress-resistant technical yarns for high-speed tires, airbags, and safety belts. Another Barmag specialty is machines that make high-quality fibers for carpets. About one-third of Barmag's sales comes from Asia, another third from Europe, and 27 percent from NAFTA countries. Barmag's main subsidiaries are located in Germany, Switzerland, China, India, Brazil, and the United States. The Swiss Saurer AG, which is one of the world's top makers of textile machines, owns 75 percent of Barmag's stock.

1922–52: The First 30 Years

On March 27, 1922, two synthetic fiber makers—the German Vereinigte Glanzstoff-Fabriken AG and the Dutch N.V. Nederlandsa Kunstzijde Unie Enka—founded a company to supply each of them with the machinery necessary for their operations. The new company was called Barmer Maschinenfabrik AG and was located in Barmen in the German Ruhr, a small town that later became part of Wuppertal. As one of the first of its kind in the world, Barmer Maschinenfabrik began designing and producing machines for the then brand new chemical fiber industry. The company made yarn spinning machines and spinning pumps for Viscose and copper silk. In the following years Barmer Maschinenfabrik added button thread machines and spooling machines to its product line. The company's market expanded so rapidly that the Barmen plant was not able to accommodate the facilities needed for the growing production. In 1925 Barmag acquired an existing production and office building in Lennep and moved its headquarters there.

The year 1935 marked an important milestone for Barmag. In that year the company constructed its first double-strand thread machine. It was based on the principle of turning a thread twice during one full turn of a spindle, a technology that had been known for half a decade. However, Barmag patented in 1930 a special component—the so called Speicherscheibe (a special take-up disk for the new thread)—which made it possible to apply this principle in industrial scale machinery for the first time.

Barmag's invention had a significant impact on yarn spinning technology throughout the world. Another of Barmag's technical hallmarks was its precision spinning pumps. Based on cogwheel technology, these pumps were at the heart of chemical fiber production. The pumps forced the plastic mass through spinning nozzles at high pressure in consistently equal amounts. Out of the nozzles came the popular synthetic fiber threads for Viscose and Acetate. These pumps not only had to meet high precision standards, they also had to withstand the high temperatures and caustic chemicals used to refine or color the thread to which they were exposed.

Barmag's progress was interrupted by World War II. Beginning in 1939 textile machine building was restricted by the German government, and all industry was focused on war production. As many other German companies, Barmag used foreign slave workers to replace its employees who were called to the front, according to German business publication *manager magazin,* citing the American Jewish Committee. Two years after the war was over the company was granted permission from the military government to resume operations. In the economic boom which followed the war, Barmag strove to

---

Company Perspectives:

Our success and our future is supported by several pillars of great importance to Barmag: Customers *give us orders and thereby preserve our jobs.* We, the workforce, *guarantee that orders are filled as quickly as possible, efficiently and with a high quality.* Suppliers *provide us promptly and reliably with necessary tools and machine components.* Shareholders *entrust us with their money which is invested in research and development and new equipment.* "Hier bin ich richtig." *[I'm in the right place here.] This guiding phrase connects us with our customers, suppliers and shareholders at all times. Only when all our business partners are convinced and say "Barmag. Hier bin ich richtig," can we say it too.*

---

make up lost ground in technology development. The company started developing machinery for the new chemical fibers being marketed at the time, such as Nylon and Perlon made from polyamids. It also focused its research and development on technologies that cut costs and enabled the chemical fiber industry to produce higher quality products.

1954–90: Diversification and Going Global

In 1954 Barmag started producing another kind of machine for synthetic fiber production: the texturing machine. When used to make synthetic textiles, the slick spun yarn, called filament, was mechanically fluffed up to make it softer and more comfortable to wear. Barmag's first generation of texturing machines reached a roll-up speed of 100 meters per minute. Models made in the 1990s were able to roll up the synthetic yarn 15 times as fast.

In 1958 Barmag again expanded its production line and started building extruders for the fast-growing plastics processing industry. The company bought a license for these machines from American extruder manufacturer Midland-Ross Corp. An unexpected synergy effect emerged from the new venture. The extruder technology was used to develop much faster machines for spinning synthetic fiber than other common at the time, and older machines were soon replaced by Barmag's spinning extruders. The new technology was used for the rapid spinning of endless synthetic yarn from a bundle of single threads. This yarn was taken up at a rate of up to 8,000 meters per minute with one spindle carrying up to 120 kilograms of yarn. In 1973 Barmag also ventured into hydraulics when it acquired shares in several hydraulics companies. Another new market was entered when the company started making vacuum pumps for the automobile industry.

In the late 1950s Barmag took on a more international focus, opting to introduce its machines to the world markets. This decision resulted in sustained growth and a growing share of exports in its total sales. International subsidiaries were set up to establish a presence in major markets. In 1965 American Barmag Corporation (ABC) was founded in Charlotte, North Carolina. A subsidiary in Brazil was set up in 1973 to bypass Brazilian import restrictions. Another growing market emerged

in the Far East where Barmag's first subsidiary, Barmag Far East Ltd., was established in Hong Kong in 1973. Barmag Far East laid the groundwork for a major expansion into the emerging Asian markets in Taiwan, South Korea, and China.

In 1984 Barmag succeeded in breaking into the Chinese market when it became a preferred supplier for the Chinese synthetic fiber industry, defeating the Japanese competition. Cooperation agreements were signed with three Chinese machine building companies—Shanghai No.2, Wuxi, and Jingwei—for manufacturing polyester yarn spinning and texturing machines. The cooperation later led to two joint ventures with Barmag's Chinese partners. Another Asian country in which Barmag became active was India where the company helped build the synthetic fiber industry. In 1988 a joint venture was founded in the southern India town of Coimbatore. The products of Lakshmi Synthetic Machinery Manufacturers Ltd., in which Barmag held a 30 percent share, were distributed and marketed by Barmag's Bombay-based subsidiary Barmag India.

1991–94: Going Public and Dynamic Growth

In 1990 Barmag changed hands, and Frankfurt-based industrial holding company Aktiengesellschaft für Industrie und Verkehrswesen (Agiv) became the company's new parent. Barmag's former major shareholder, Dutch chemical concern Akzo NV, headquartered in Eindhoven, sold its package of about 85 percent of Barmag shares to Agiv after a strategic decision to concentrate on its core business. However, Agiv quickly decided to lower its Barmag shareholdings to 55 percent. In 1991 Barmag AG offered about one-quarter of its share capital in an initial public offering on the German stock exchanges in Frankfurt and Dusseldorf. At the end of 1991 Barmag took over the former East German Spinn- und Zwirnerei Maschinenbau GmbH in Chemnitz. The new subsidiary was renamed Barmag-Spinnzwirn GmbH and equipped with new machinery.

The year-end results for 1991 showed that Barmag had become the world's leading manufacturer of synthetic yarn-spinning and texturing machines with an average market share of more than 50 percent. These machines accounted for three-quarters of Barmag's total sales that year. Also, despite fierce Japanese competition, Barmag's efforts in China started paying off. In 1991 Barmag had an 85 percent market share in the market for Polyester spinning machines; it served 160 Chinese customers, and had total sales of over DM 200 million. In India business was growing too, with sales between DM 60 and DM 80 million annually. On the other hand, Barmag's plastics processing machine division was not faring as well due to an industry downturn that was created partly by the public discussions on the environmental impacts of plastic packaging. The division's share in total sales slipped below ten percent while hydraulic aggregates for elevators and airplanes accounted for 13 percent.

In 1992 Barmag passed the DM 1 billion sales mark for the first time. Exports had become its most important income source. Some 80 percent of the company's total sales were generated outside Germany. Europe, including Germany, accounted for about one-third of Barmag's sales. Over 50 percent were generated in Asia. Barmag earned about 14 percent of its total sales in the United States. The year 1993 became the most successful in the company's history, due largely to its takeover of Braunschweig-based Ingenieurgesellschaft für Verkehrsplanung und Verkehrssicherung GmbH (IVV), in 1992 and a boom in orders from Asia. Sales totaled DM 1.44 billion, a growth of 22 percent compared to 1992, doubling its results from 1987, in just five years.

However, signs of a less dynamic future growth were on the horizon. Manufacturers of synthetic yarns were becoming more cautious with their new investments. The competition focused increasingly on price, slimming the industry's profits. In the growth markets Korea and Taiwan, Japanese competitors lowered their prices by no less than 20 percent. Furthermore, some of Barmag's Chinese partners indicated there were problems financing the machines they ordered. A new investment program initiated by the Chinese government focused on modernizing the country's infrastructure, drawing funds from other areas of the economy. To secure its strong position in China, Barmag's most important export market, the company actively worked on transforming its agreements of cooperation with its Chinese partners into joint ventures. Barmag raised its share in one Chinese joint venture, founded to deliver assembling and maintenance services for Barmag machines, from 25 to 50 percent. The company also began efforts to establish manufacturing plants in China that would lower production costs.

1995 and Beyond: Reorganization and a New Majority Shareholder

Because of the unfavorable market conditions, Barmag abandoned its hydraulics division in 1995 in order to concen-

trate on its core business. At the end of the year Barmag was DM 105 million in the red. A rigorous restructuring program of the production divisions, including significant downsizing of the work force by about 1,100 employees, was started in 1996. The 1996 year-end results showed first signs of success. While sales dropped by about 30 percent, losses were diminished by 75 percent, amounting to DM 25 million. This success was due mainly to the higher prices Barmag charged for its products, the result of innovative new technologies and higher product quality, but also due to a more selective approach to the orders accepted.

In January 1997 German industrial conglomerate Metallgesellschaft announced that it was interested in taking over a nearly 50 percent share of Agiv AG. Barmag's parent company had met with financial woes during the previous years and had slipped DM 40 million into the red in 1996. This deal threatened Barmag, since Frankfurt-based Zimmer AG, a subsidiary of Metallgesellschaft, was an important customer as well as competitor of Barmag. If the deal went through, Barmag management speculated, it could lose about half of its business. However, the deal fell through. After working hard for a month or so to smooth relations with Barmag's business partners, company executives were able to concentrate on the restructuring program again. After another loss year in 1996, the company further reduced the number of employees, from 3,486 in 1996 to 2,730 in 1999.

In August 1998 parent company Agiv upped its stake in Barmag another 19 percent, acquiring shares held by the Allianz Group and increasing its total shares to 75 percent. However, only one year later, in October 1999, Agiv management announced that it would sell most of their Barmag holdings. A few weeks later the Swiss Saurer Group, the world's largest manufacturer of textile machines, announced that it would be taking over Agiv's 75 percent share in Barmag for DM 318 million.

At the end of 1999 a new Barmag subsidiary was set up in Liberec, Czech Republic, to help lower production costs. The new company was named Barmag Spinning Company Liberec s.r.o. (BSC) and manufactured components that were integrated in spinning machines in Barmag's Swiss subsidiary in Zug. In 2000, Barmag took over Neumünstersche Maschinen- und Anlagenbau GmbH (Neumag), another leading manufacturer of textile machines. Both companies had facilities for synthetic carpet manufacturing and filament spinning equipment. Neumag's filament spinning equipment production was integrated into Barmag. By the end of the 1990s more than 2,000 tons of polymers worldwide were refined per minute by using Barmag-made extruder systems. In 2000 Barmag held a world market share of about 40 percent.

Principal Subsidiaries

American Barmag Corp.; Barmag-Spinnzwirn GmbH; Wuxi Barmag Hongyuan Machinery Co. Ltd. (China; 53%); Barmag Far East Ltd. (Hong Kong; 99.99%); Barmag GmbH (Switzerland); Neumünstersche Maschinen- und Anlagenbau GmbH; KAS Management Services GmbH; Barmag do Brasil Ltda. (Brazil; 99.58%); Shanghai Barmag Machinery Co. Ltd. (China; 51%); BB Engineering GmbH (50%); Beijing Jingma

Chemical Fibre Co. Ltd. (China; 50%); Barmag Spinning Company Liberec s.r.o. (Czech Republic).

Principal Competitors

Atkins Machinery, Inc.; Burlington Textile Machinery Corp.; Speizman Industries, Inc.

Further Reading

''Agiv stockt Beteiligung an der Barmag auf,'' *Frankfurter Allgemeine Zeitung*, August 20, 1998, p. 19.

''Angeschlagene Barmag baut 1100 Stellen ab,'' *Süddeutsche Zeitung*, December 15, 1995.

''Barmag: Abkühlung beim Auftragseingang,'' *Frankfurter Allgemeine Zeitung*, May 3, 1994, p. 20.

''Barmag erwirbt Neumag von Babcock Borsig,'' *Frankfurter Allgemeine Zeitung*, June 14, 2000, p. 22.

''Bei Maschinen von Rezession keine Spur,'' *TextilWirtschaft*, May 19, 1993, p. 85.

''Der Rest der Agiv wird zerschlagen,'' *Frankfurter Allgemeine Zeitung*, October 8, 1999, p. 19.

''Die Barmag kommt wie geplant voran,'' *Frankfurter Allgemeine Zeitung*, December 2, 1996, p. 25.

''Drückeberger?,'' *manager magazin*, February 1, 2000.

''MG-Konzern nimmt die Agiv ins Visier,'' *Süddeutsche Zeitung*, January 14, 1997.

''Saurer kauft die deutsche Barmag,'' *AFX—Swiss*, October 29, 1999.

—Evelyn Hauser

Baron Philippe de Rothschild S.A.

BP 117
33250 Pauillac
France
Telephone: (33) 5 57 75 21 19
Fax: (33) 5 56 73 20 44
Web site: http://www.bpdr.com

Private Company
Incorporated: 1956
Employees: Not available.
Sales: EUR 166.91 million ($150 million) (2000 est.)
NAIC: 312130 Wineries

The Rothschild name is not only associated with high finance, it is also synonymous with the world's finest wines, made by Baron Philippe de Rothschild S.A. The family has controlled its Bordeaux region vineyards for nearly 150 years; since 1922, when Philippe Rothschild took over the vineyard's operations, the Mouton Rothschild name has established itself as one of the world's most sought after labels. Baron Philippe de Rothschild (BPR) First Growth wines typically command more than $100 per bottle, and can reach into the thousands of dollars at auction. This is not only because of the wine in the bottle, but also because of the company's famed labels, which, since 1945, have featured artwork from some of the greatest artists of the 20th century. BPR also produces and bottles premium wines under the labels Château Clerc Milon and Château d'Armailhac. Yet the company's innovative branded wine, Mouton Cadet, is perhaps its most famous, and at any rate most accessible. Featuring Bordeaux grapes blended under BPR's supervision, the company produces some 14 million bottles of Mouton Cadet. BPR also bottles a variety of wines under labels targeted at specific markets, such as the restaurant and mail-order circuits. The company opened an e-commerce capable web site in October 2000. Total wine sales for the entire company topped 22 million bottles in that year. BPR has also extended its production beyond its Bordeaux, France, home. In 1979 the company set up the California joint-venture with Mondavi to produce the premium-class Opus One wine, which produces more than 250,000 bottles of what many consider as one of the world's top wines. The success of the Opus One joint venture has led the company to launch a second joint venture with Chilean producer Concho y Toro to create the French-Chilean label Almaviva, launched in 1998. Both the Opus One and Almaviva joint ventures feature French expertise adapted to local grape varieties. Philippine Rothschild heads BPR; she is the daughter of the late Baron, who died in 1988. She is seconded by Pierre Guinchard, who serves as company CEO. Since 1995, the privately held company has more than doubled its revenues, which are estimated to have topped FFr 1 billion in 2000.

Making Wine History in the 1920s

The Rothschild brothers—Nathan, James, Aemschel, Carl, and Salomon—were sons of Aemschel Rothschild, who had built up a successful merchant and banking business from the family's home in the Frankfurt ghetto. At the end of the 18th century, the elder Rothschild sent his sons to each of the major European capitals of the day to build the family's fortune. Nathan went to England, while James was sent to Paris, Carl to Naples, and Salomon to Vienna. Aemschel remained in Frankfurt. The Rothschilds cooperated closely, establishing their own private courier service, and soon established the Rothschild name as one of the foremost financial families in the world.

Nathaniel Rothschild, son of Nathan, moved to Paris at the beginning of the 1850s. The idea of serving his guests wine bearing his own name appealed to him, and in 1853, Rothschild purchased the Château Brane Mouton (''mouton'' came from the old French word ''mothon,'' meaning hill), in Pauillac, in the heart of the Medoc region, on the French coast near Bordeaux, between the ocean and the Gironde estuary, which by then had already achieved world renown as the site of the world's greatest vineyards. Rothschild quickly gave his own name to his new property, which became known as Château Mouton Rothschild.

The vineyard purchase came just before the first official classification of the Gironde region wines. Unfortunately for Rothschild, the classification, presented on the occasion of the

Company Perspectives:

Since 1933, Baron Philippe de Rothschild SA, located at Pauillac in the Médoc, has been motivated by a constant ambition: to make the world's finest wines, each in its own category, whether the châteaux wines for which it is responsible—the renowned Château Mouton Rothschild, a First Growth, and its distinguished lieutenants, Château Clerc Milon and Château d'Armailhac—or branded wines, like the famous Mouton Cadet.

Universal Exhibition of 1855, was made according to price, not quality. Because wines from the Mouton Rothschild estate sold for slightly less than its famous neighbors—Lafitte, Latour, Margaux, and Haut Brion, which all received First Growth qualification—Mouton Rothschild was subsequently classified as a premium Second Growth wine. Yet neither Nathaniel, nor his son James, who inherited the estate after his father's death in 1870, took an active interest in running the vineyard. Nor did Nathaniel's grandson, Henri, who was to turn over the winery to his youngest son, Philippe, in 1922.

Philippe Rothschild was to revolutionize the Bordeaux wine industry. Coming from Paris, where he had become a well-known patron and friend of the lively art scene in that city, the 20-year-old Rothschild arrived in a region with a business structure unchanged since the 19th century. Rothschild, however, not only proved a more active landlord than his predecessors, he took the running of the Château Mouton Rothschild estate in his own hands—and in doing so, sent a wake-up call to the entire region. From the start, Philippe Rothschild began to challenge the wine classification system, adopting the motto "Premier ne puis, Second ne daigne, Mouton suis" (First I may not be, Second I will not be, Mouton I am).

One of Rothschild's first and boldest moves was to begin bottling his wine at the château itself, breaking with long-standing industry tradition. Until then, wineries sent their wine in casks to wine merchants in the city of Bordeaux, who then undertook the responsibility of stocking the casks for the two-year aging process, before bottling the wines. Although labels had been in use since the middle of the 19th century, they served merely to provide basic information about the wine contained in the bottle—or what, at any rate, was supposed to be in the bottle. Because the châteaux did not bottle their own wines, no one could guarantee the contents of the bottles bearing their names. The system also placed control of the wine industry with the merchants, rather than the châteaux themselves.

Philippe Rothschild changed all this when he decided to add the now-famous mention "Mis en bouteille au château" to his wines. To stock the casks for the two-year aging period, Rothschild commissioned the construction of a storage facility, the so-called "Grand Chai," a 100-meter-long structure that could stock some 1,000 oak casks, and became the inspiration for similar structures in the Bordeaux area as competing vintners adopted Rothschild's idea.

By 1924, Château Mouton Rothschild was ready to release its first self-bottled vintage. For the occasion, Rothschild commissioned popular poster designer Jean Carlu to design a label for the château. Carlu's cubist-inspired label shocked the wine community—Philippe Rothschild was to scrap the label design only two years later—but nonetheless succeeded in calling worldwide attention to the new era of Rothschild wines. In the years leading up to the World War II, the Rothschild château continued to experiment with its wine labels, incorporating the famed "five arrow" motif of the Rothschild family but also a "rams rampant" motif, of two rams, another Rothschild family symbol—butting horns. In the 1930s, Rothschild labels also began to include the number of bottles that had produced in that year's harvest, which proved to be a new marketing success.

Postwar Renaissance

The company's preoccupations with its labels—which was to inspire a new marketing coup in the post-war years—did not interfere with its production of premium quality wine, which continued to achieve accolades as being among the finest wines in the world. Yet Philippe Rothschild's high quality standards were to lead him to striking a new chord with the world's wine community. Dissatisfied with the quality of the 1930 vintage, Rothschild refused to bottle the wine under the château's label. Yet because the wine was nonetheless of good quality, Rothschild created a new name for the wine: Mouton Cadet. The Cadet name, first released in 1932, was later to become a brand name for the wine blended by the company from grapes bought from Bordeaux region producers. The original Cadet vintages, however, were bottled from the family's own vineyards.

Mouton Cadet proved a success and inspired Rothschild to expand the family's vineyard holdings to supply its growing production needs. In 1933, Rothschild acquired neighboring Château Mouton d'Armailhacq, then classified as a Fifth Growth vineyard. With that purchase the company also acquired the wholesaler company Société Vinicole de Pauillac, bringing Rothschild into the distribution arena and providing the basis for what was later to become Baron Philippe de Rothschild SA.

France's capitulation to the Nazi invaders and the installation of the collaborative Vichy government nearly spelled disaster to the Rothschild wine business. The château itself was occupied by the Nazis and made a German headquarters, while the Vichy government placed operations of the vineyard under its agricultural department's control. Philippe Rothschild and his family were captured—Rothschild's wife was killed in a Nazi death camp—but Philippe Rothschild managed to escape, finally joining up to fight with the Free French army under General Charles de Gaulle.

Returning to his château after the war, Rothschild decided to allow his first post-war vintage to celebrate the Allied victory. Rothschild asked friend Philippe Julian to design a new label for the 1945 vintage. Based on Churchill's famed V-sign, the label sparked a new era for Mouton Rothschild. As Philippine Rothschild told *Wine Spectator*, "he wanted to let the world know that Mouton had survived the war."

Rothschild, who had already been among the pioneers in recognizing the marketing potential of a wine's label, now decided that the label for each year's vintage was to feature an

Key Dates:

1853: Nathaniel de Rothschild buys Château Brane Mouton.

1855: Château Mouton Rothschild is classified as second growth.

1922: Philippe de Rothschild takes over operation of château; begins bottling at the château.

1924: The first château-bottled vintage is released.

1933: The company acquires of Château Mouton d'Armailhacq.

1945: The first Mouton Rothschild label featuring artwork appears.

1956: The company is incorporated as Baron Philippe de Rothschild SA.

1959: The Georges Braque label is introduced.

1970: The company acquires Château Clerc Millon.

1973: Mouton Rothschild receives first growth classification.

1979: The company begins Opus One joint-venture with Mondavi.

1988: Philippe de Rothschild dies.

1990: Baron Philippe de Rothschild SA becomes the official company name.

1997: The company launches Almaviva joint-venture with Concho y Toro.

1998: The company purchases Domaine de Lambert.

2000: Sales top FFr 1 billion.

region was reclassified according to the quality of its wines. At long last, Mouton Rothschild was classified among the First Growth growers. Rothschild according changed the company's motto to: "Premier je suis, Second je fus, Mouton ne change" (First I am, Second I was, Mouton does not change).

The growing importance of California wines, which, under such names as Robert Mondavi, had been steadily increasing in quality, led Rothschild for the first time to branch out beyond France. In 1979, Mondavi and Rothschild formed the joint venture Opus One. Bringing French oak casks and wine varieties and Rothschild techniques to California's Napa Valley region, Opus One was designed as a premium quality producer. Indeed, the new winery—led by Mondavi's son Tim Mondavi—quickly became classified among the world's top-quality wines.

Through the 1980s, the Rothschild name gained further renown, especially with the worldwide tour of an exhibition of the Mouton Rothschild label's artwork. That exhibit, which featured the original artwork alongside their label reproductions, was mounted by Rothschild's daughter Philippine, heralding her entry into the company's operations.

Philippe Rothschild died in 1988 at the age of 86. Philippine de Rothschild took over the château's operations, a marked departure from the Rothschild family's male-dominated traditions. Philippine de Rothschild also took over the commissioning of the Mouton Rothschild label artwork, expanding its scope to feature more international artists.

During the 1990s, Mouton Cadet became the company's spearhead into the mass market. Boosted by the Rothschild name, Mouton Cadet quickly became one of the world's top-selling branded wines, with more than 14 million bottles sold each year. By the mid-1990s, the company's sales were topping FFr 500 million. Rothschild continued to look for new international opportunities. The growing maturity of the Chilean wine industry led the company to conclude a new joint-venture agreement, this time with that country's largest vintner, Concho y Toro, to create the premium class Almaviva wine. The first Almaviva vintage was released in 1998, to worldwide acclaim.

In that year, Rothschild acquired a new property, Domaine de Lambert, near Saint-Polycarpe, in the Languedoc region. That purchase marked a departure for the company; it was its first vineyard holdings outside of the Bordeaux region. The company began renovations of its new vineyards in 1999, including replanting much of the vineyard to improve the quality of the traditionally poorly rated Languedoc grapes. The company hoped to be able to release its first Domaine de Lambert vintages with the harvest of 2002. Meanwhile, the company had begun to look even farther afield for future expansion possibilities, considering not only purchases in Italy and Spain, which had their own strong wine traditions, but in India as well. As it entered the 21st century, Rothschild, with sales topping FFr 1 billion, aided by a growing interest in wines in the Asian markets, carried on Philippe de Rothschild's commitment to creating history with wine.

original piece of artwork—commissioned from Rothschild's circle of friends, only some of whom were artists. Yet all received the same payment: five cases from that year's vintage, plus five cases chosen from the Rothschild cellars. The new era of labels proved a publicity coup for the company, which saw its wines gaining steadily in demand, and its prices rising—even when vintages proved disappointing. In 1955, the Rothschild label took on a still more serious role. That year's label featured a design from famed painted Georges Braque. From then on, the Rothschild labels were to become a showcase for the world's top contemporary artists, featuring, among others, drawing and paintings from Joan Miro, Salvador Dali, Henry Moore, Marc Chagall, Pablo Picasso, Andy Warhol, and later artists such as Keith Haring, Balthus, and others.

Diversified Wine Empire for the New Century

The company incorporated as Baron Philippe de Rothschild SA in 1956, yet continued to operate under other names—such as La Baronnie—until the 1990s. The company expanded its production again in 1970, when it acquired another Pauillac Fifth Growth property, Château Clerc Milon. This and the company's other fifth growth châteaux became a central part of the company's increasingly diversified product, as it began to target specific markets, such as the restaurant, specialized retail, supermarket, and other segments, with specific labels.

The company got a major boost in 1973, when, after nearly 50 years of pressure from Philippe Rothschild, the Bordeaux

Principal Competitors

Antinori; Banfi Vintners; Beringer Wine Estates Holdings, Inc.; Bodegas Riojanas, S.A.; Bodegas y Bebidas, S.A.; Cantine Giorgio Lungarotti S.r.l.; The Chalone Wine Group, Ltd.; Constellation Brands, Inc.; E. & J. Gallo Winery; Federico Paternina, S.A.; Golden State Vintners, Inc.; Gruppo Italiano Vini Soc. Coop. a r.l.; Kendall-Jackson Wine Estates, Ltd.; Laurent-Perrier; Marne et Champagne SA; Martini & Rossi S.p.A.; Mercian Corporation; Ravenswood Winery, Inc.; Rémy Cointreau; R.H. Phillips, Inc.; The Robert Mondavi Corporation; Sebastiani Vineyards, Inc.; Taittinger S.A.; Trinchero Family Estates; Vina Concho y Toro S.A.; Willamette Valley Vineyards, Inc.; The Wine Group, Inc.

Further Reading

Buckley, Kathy, "Mouton Rothschild loses a star in annual Ranking," *Wine Enthusiast*, October 6, 1997.

David, Christian, "Mouton-Rothschild saga, ou l'essor d'une PME du vin," *L'Expansion*, October 12, 2000.

Matthews, Thomas, "Mouton-Rothschild withdraws its 1993 artist label," *Wine Spectator*, February 29, 1996.

Matthews, Thomas, "A Love affaire of Art and Life," *Wine Spectator*, May 31, 1995.

Pederson, Rena, "Good Taste a Way of Life at Rothschild," *Dallas Morning News*, December 14, 1997, p. 1G.

—M.L. Cohen

Berlitz International, Inc.

400 Alexander Park
Princeton, New Jersey 08540
U.S.A.
Telephone: (609) 924-8500
Toll Free: (800) 257-9449
Fax: (609) 683-9138
Web site: http://www.berlitz.com

Public Subsidiary of Benesse Corporation
Incorporated: 1989
Employees: 5,718
Sales: $446.2 million
Stock Exchanges: New York
Ticker Symbol: BTZ
NAIC: 6111630 Language Schools

Berlitz International, Inc. is a languages services firm providing language instruction, cross-cultural training, translation services, and publishing products in 50 countries. For language instruction, the company employs its proprietary Berlitz Method, which avoids tedious memorization exercises and grammar drills in favor of a conversational, usage-driven approach to virtually all living languages. Berlitz's publishing division produces pocket-size travel guides and language phrase books, as well as bilingual dictionaries, trade paperback travel guides, and self-teaching language guides from audio cassettes to interactive compact discs. The company's translation services provide technical translation, interpreting, software localization, electronic publishing, and other services that are related to foreign languages.

Maximilian Berlitz Emigrates to America in 1872

Berlitz's origins date back to 1872, when 20-year-old Maximilian D. Berlitz emigrated from Germany to America in 1872 to teach Greek, Latin, and six other European languages. Employing the traditional grammar-translation approach, he served as a private instructor for several years, then, in 1878, accepted a position as professor of French and German at the Warner Poly-technic College in Providence, Rhode Island. The position turned out to be nothing less than immediate ownership of the "college," where he also served as dean, principal, and sole faculty member. In desperate need of an assistant, Berlitz hired Nicholas Joly directly from France, based solely on a letter of application. When Joly arrived in Providence, Berlitz was surprised to learn that his new assistant spoke no English. To make matters worse, Berlitz had fallen ill from the strain of running the school alone and was unable to teach for several weeks. Joly had no choice but to take over and conduct classes strictly in French, instructed by Berlitz to name objects and act out verbs, essentially, to make the best of it. When Berlitz recovered, he discovered that the students had made remarkable progress in French. Berlitz's main tenet of language instruction—the transfer of usage by actually using no language other than the one being studied—thus gained credibility, sparking development and fine-tuning of the young school's trademark pedagogy, the Berlitz Method.

Though Berlitz was convinced that his "direct" method of language instruction was the most effective available, the public and academic community at first viewed it with suspicion. Starting with the first greeting by the instructor, the Berlitz Method dictated that only the target language was to be spoken in class. The method emphasized the spoken word, with students learning to read and write only what they had already learned to say and understand. In the place of formal grammar instruction, students absorbed a grammatical system naturally, by using it. Above all, to develop fluency, students learned to think in the new language, not to translate—to associate new words with objects and ideas, rather than with the distractingly familiar words of their mother tongue. To encourage students in the use of the target language, instructors typically employed question-and-answer techniques to prompt dialogue while expanding vocabulary.

However unconventional, the young company, known as the Berlitz School of Languages, produced results that simply couldn't be ignored. Berlitz opened his first language center in Boston in 1880, followed soon after by centers in New York City and Washington, D.C. He then expanded to other American cities as well as Europe. By the turn of the century, an explosive tourist industry prompted Berlitz to develop travel guides, self-teaching materials, and interpretation services to meet this growing demand. Berlitz died in 1921, but the company he founded, and his method, were carried on by his son-in-law and associate, Victor Harrison. Victor Harrison, Jr., briefly assumed control in 1932, but was replaced by a long-time Berlitz employee, Jacques Strumpen-Darrie, who guided the company for 20 years, before his son, Robert, took charge. The younger Strumpen-Darrie ran Berlitz until his retirement in 1970, even after the company was sold to Macmillan in 1966.

Berlitz Internationalization at Mid-Century

Through both world wars of, the number of Berlitz schools multiplied with growing demand for language skills. After World War II, Berlitz seized emerging opportunities in language training and translation services brought on by multinational companies expanding their business around the world. Such expansion was fueled by the rise of computer information systems starting in the 1970s. With the advent of digitized communication networks, increasing amounts of information could be conveyed almost instantaneously between virtually any points on the globe, intensifying the need—and the market—for effective cross-cultural and cross-linguistic communication. Moreover, the 1980s saw the crumbling of key international trade barriers, as markets in the former Soviet Union, China, and various developing nations increasingly moved toward free trade. Indeed, the company's 1993 annual report described cutbacks in Western European nations that were experiencing economic stagnation. Meanwhile, the company aggressively moved into rapidly growing markets in Central and Eastern European countries, establishing new facilities in the Czech Republic, Slovakia, Poland, and Eastern Germany. A December 5, 1993 article in *The Warsaw Voice* heralded the arrival of a new Berlitz school in Warsaw and plans for another in February, as well as other schools in such cities as Poznan, Cracow, and Gdansk. To exploit global markets in the 1990s, Berlitz also opened new language centers in Brazil, Colombia, and Venezuela, as well as Mexico, where NAFTA brought new language-training needs.

From the 1980s onward, Berlitz's language instruction division increasingly developed options and additions to its classroom instruction facilities. The Berlitz Study Abroad (BSA) Program offered students a complete travel package and the opportunity to study their new language in its country of origin. The Berlitz Jr. program provided special foreign language teaching service for U.S. elementary, middle, and high school students both at schools or camps and at the Berlitz Language Centers. For slightly older students, Berlitz acquired the Language Institute for English (L.I.F.E.) in 1988, providing intensive English instruction, recreation, and accommodations to foreign students on campuses in Boston, New York, Miami, Orlando, San Diego, San Francisco, and Chicago.

Berlitz developed several products and programs to that combined language and social skills. The company also expanded on its popular Cross-Cultural Division, designed to instruct students in business and social etiquette and day-to-day activities to supplement language skills. In 1994, the company acquired Cross-Cultural Consultants of Brooklyn, New York, to ensure a stronger future in that growing market. Led by noted author and lecturer Dean Foster, the division held seminars and briefings designed to sensitize businesses to the intricate social, political, and cultural issues that can determine a company's effectiveness in foreign markets.

In the spirit of a skilled language teacher, the company itself listened to the talk around it and continued to develop linguistic solutions to accommodate changing market trends. Joining forces with the University of Phoenix in 1991, for example, Berlitz put together a custom-designed language program for the McDonnell Douglas Helicopter Company, which wanted the program to enhance its employees' global competitiveness.

In 1995, Berlitz's language-instruction division responded to the needs of contemporary language enthusiasts by introducing Club Berlitz, a network of groups that enabled members to speak the foreign language of their choice with groups of people at similar proficiency levels. Participants honed their language skills while engaging in activities ranging from international dinner parties to cultural evenings, theme events like plays and movies, and study abroad programs. "Club Berlitz reflects the growing interest in the study of language and culture for both business and personal use," said Hiromasa Yokoi, vice-chairman, chief executive officer, and president of Berlitz International in a March 20, 1995 *Business Wire* article.

Berlitz's dedication to world languages for "both business and personal use" spurred the development of two other business segments: publishing and translation. Since the early 1970s, Berlitz Publishing has produced language and travel-related publications recognized internationally for their accuracy and ease of use. By the 1990s, the division was publishing more than 1,000 titles, ranging from a European Menu Reader to inexpensive pocket paperbacks and state-of-the-art interactive CD-ROMs.

To maintain its stature as a premier, single-source provider of language services, Berlitz Publishing continued to develop innovative products into the 1990s. A 1991 joint venture with Sphere Inc. (doing business as Spectrum Holobyte), resulted in the co-development of a language learning game based on CD-ROM technology. The game "El Grito del Jaguar," or "The Cry of the Jaguar," taught users the Spanish language and Mexican culture through an adventurous computer-driven challenge, setting the ground for similar projects in other languages. That same year, Berlitz's parent company, Maxwell Communications Corporation, in conjunction with the European industrial and electronics giant, N.V. Philips, announced a joint venture publishing company, Maxwell Multi Media. The new company planned to produce and sell self-teaching language courses for the home, office, and school using interactive compact disks (CD-I) as well as other formats.

Key Dates:

1878: Maximilian Berlitz founds a language school in Providence, Rhode Island.
1880: Berlitz opens a language center in Boston.
1921: Berlitz dies, leaving his son-in-law in charge.
1966: The company becomes a subsidiary of Macmillan Inc.
1988: Maxwell Communications buys the company from Macmillan.
1989: Berlitz International goes public.
1992: The company is bought by Fukutake Publishing (later known as Benesse Corporation)

New Parentage in the 1990s

In the late 1980s and early 1990s, Berlitz underwent several dramatic reorganizations that seemed to threaten the company's stability. Ultimately, however, they left it in a strong position to enter the 21st century. In 1989, Berlitz's main business divisions—Berlitz Languages Inc., Editions Berlitz, S.A., Berlitz Publications Inc., and other affiliates—were acquired by Maxwell Communication Corporation plc (MCC). The new entity was renamed Berlitz International Inc. With the unexpected death of media magnate Robert Maxwell in late 1991, much of his media empire crumbled and fell into the hands of bankruptcy courts, casting doubt over Berlitz's future. Berlitz, however, insisted that it maintained control of its assets and operated independently of the Maxwell chaos. Two days after Maxwell's death, MCC sold its 56 percent stake in Berlitz for $265 million to Fukutake Publishing Company, Ltd., a leading Japanese publisher specializing in correspondence classes and publication of related materials, which had already purchased a 20 percent stake in Berlitz Japan in 1990. By 1992, Fukutake's share in Berlitz had grown to 67 percent, with the remaining stock held by public shareholders. Fukutake combined its resources with those of Berlitz to provide optimal language services worldwide.

Fukutake planned to boost its services throughout the world, with special emphasis on regions of Asia where Berlitz was not as well positioned. With services in Taiwan (since 1989) and South Korea (since 1991), Fukutake announced plans to begin test-marketing in the People's Republic of China in the mid-1990s. "Economic development and a rise in willingness to learn supplement each other," the company's president said in a November 21, 1994 article in the *Nikkei Weekly*.

The company experienced some lean years during the recession of the early 1990s. Under the management of Mr. Soichiro Fukutake, chairman, and Mr. Hiromasa Yokoi, vice-chairman, CEO, and president, Fukutake took aggressive steps to expand its services in tandem with those of Berlitz, as well as to streamline operations while improving the use of technology in the classroom to increase customer satisfaction. In 1995, the company launched a campaign to maximize its customer services across the board. As part of that effort, in 1995 Fukutake changed its name to the Benesse Corporation. The new name combined the Latin words "bene" and "esse," meaning well being, to drive home the company's commitment to support customers' personal aspirations for a better life, according to company materials.

In 1995, Berlitz launched a campaign to refresh its own identity. The company introduced a new, clean-lined logo and a new, company-wide tagline, "Helping the World Communicate." Berlitz remodeled the retail stores at its language centers and began a new franchising program, its first in more than 35 years. The company was determined to make itself more consumer-friendly as it moved away from its typical office locations to stores. Revenues in 1995 stood at $351 million, a significant increase over 1994's $300 million. Earnings jumped from $900,000 to $2.3 million over the same period.

Berlitz began to reach out in several directions at once. In 1996 it established Berlitz Kids, to enter the children's market, a

Although Berlitz would leave the Maxwell empire within a year, some of the strategy from the Philips venture would contribute to later developments. In 1993, for example, Berlitz Publishing Company signed a licensing agreement with Sierra On-Line Inc., through which Bright Star Technology, a wholly owned Sierra subsidiary, would develop, manufacture, and market a new CD-ROM-based foreign language and culture series called "Berlitz Alive!" Using patented lip-synching technology and animated personal tutors, as well as Berlitz's teaching methodology, Bright Star launched its first foreign-language educational series, "Japanese Alive!," in September 1993. "Combining Sierra's interactive multimedia technology with Berlitz's language content, name recognition, and proven learning methodology opens new markets for our educational products, expanding into adult education and foreign language," said Alan J. Higginson, president of Bright Star Technology, in an August 4, 1993 PR *Newswire* article.

Riding the growing wave of digital media, Berlitz also moved onto the Internet in 1995, as it assumed management of Prodigy Inc.'s Foreign Languages bulletin board. On-line customers could learn about a foreign country, talk in a native tongue, secure translation services, and obtain instant information on all Berlitz products and services.

Into the 1990s, the company's translation segment, Berlitz Translation Services (BTS) maintained its reputation as a world leader in technical documentation translation and software/multimedia localization, as well as full production capabilities in desktop publishing and graphics, audio visual services, and simultaneous and consecutive interpretation.

Founded in 1984, BTS quickly gained an excellent reputation for its accuracy and its ability to integrate linguistic services and versatile project management. Starting in the late 1980s, the translation segment greatly expanded its international scope through a series of acquisitions, including: the Institute for Fagspneg in Copenhagen (June 1989), Able Translations Ltd. in Baldock, England (Fall 1990), Kayer Coll. Technical Translators in Sindelfingen, Germany (December 1990), Nordoc A/S (1991), and Softrans International Limited (1991). By the mid-1990s, the BTS International Network provided translation-related services in more than 37 locations across 16 countries.

move that it had been planning for some time. The goal was to expand from a series of books using fictional characters to offering language-based reference books, games, and CD-ROMs, as well as other ancillary products. To supplement its adult business, in 1997 Berlitz purchased ELS Educational Services Inc., an English-language instruction service, for $95 million. The ELS deal brought with it 25 language centers in the United States and two in England, located mostly on or near colleges and catering to foreign students. To bolster Berlitz GlobalNet's translation business and establish a foothold in Latin America, the company purchased operating subsidiaries, assets, and key personnel of Language Management International, with locations in Brazil and Argentina, as well as the United States and Singapore. In 1999 Berlitz created a new Internet translation service called BerlitzIt that provided timely person-to-person translation that replaced software-translation programs. Not intended to replace its corporate translation and localized services, Berlitz, it was designed for smaller jobs and the general public through an ''off the shelf'' version.

Berlitz Kids joined forces with a powerful partner in 1999 when it reached an agreement with the Children's Television Workshop, creators of *Sesame Street*, to produce *Sesame English,* a 15-minute program using a new Muppet named Tingo to teach children how to speak English. Starting in China, Taiwan, and Japan, where demand for English instruction high, the partners had plans to eventually bring the program to Europe, Latin America, and North America. With possible home sales and Internet distribution of an entire line of Sesame language products, Berlitz was not reticent about projecting a potential $4 billion global market for the partnership, a figure that would be ten times the total revenue Berlitz achieved in 1998. By the spring 2000, *Sesame English* was ready to air in its first markets, to be followed by Germany and Austria in May; Hong Kong, Korea, Thailand, and Israel in July; Puerto Rico in August; Colombia, Mexico, and the United States in September; and Venezuela in October. An equally ambitious rollout to other countries in Latin America, Europe, and Asia was planned for 2001. At the same time, *Sesame Español* was being prepared, with an early 2001 airing date scheduled for the United States.

Its ambitious plans notwithstanding, Berlitz stock dropped by 30 percent in 1999, and the company's yearly results only reinforced investors' concerns. Total revenues rose just 2.3 percent over the previous year, to $446.2 million, with a reported net loss of $13.1 million. In March 2000 the company announced that Yokoi would retire and be replaced by James Kahl, chairman and chief executive officer of Le Petite Academy. Furthermore, the company would be restructured into two divisions: Berlitz Language Services and Berlitz GlobalNET. In January 2001 Berlitz announced an initiative to cut operating expenses by $20 million for fiscal 2001 and by $12 million each year after that. The work force would be trimmed and underperforming operations eliminated. The book-publishing division would also be consolidated with product development and Berlitz Kids.

Despite disappointing financial results, Berlitz retained enviable brand-name recognition. Partnered with an even more recognizable brand of Sesame Street, Berlitz and its children's program still held the potential to float the entire company and launch it into a promising and highly profitable future.

Principal Divisions

Berlitz Language Services; Berlitz GlobalNET.

Principal Competitors

Sylvan Learning Systems Inc.; ALPNET, Inc., Lernout & Hauspie Speech Products; The Translation Group Ltd.

Further Reading

''Berlitz Reaches Accord to Split From Macmillan,'' *New York Times*, December 23, 1992, p. D4.

Bounds, Wendy, ''Berlitz to Realign as Two Divisions; Top Officers to Exit,'' *Wall Street Journal,* March 21, 2000, p. B10.

Bragg, Rebecca, ''How The Berlitz Language Empire Came Into Being,'' *Toronto Star*, February 8, 1992, p. F2.

Cox, James, ''Berlitz Won't Hear of Bankruptcy Talk,'' *USA Today*, December 31, 1991, p. 3B.

Diemniewska, Ewa Kielak, ''The Language Revolution: Berlitz Leading the Charge,'' *Warsaw Voice*, December 5, 1995.

Fay, Natalie, ''Berlitz Japanese; Bright Star Technology's Berlitz For Business Japanese CD-ROM Training Program; Software Review,'' *MacWeek*, August 1, 1994, p. 45.

Imada, Toshihiko, ''Education Firm Burnishes Global Image; Berlitz Parent Fukutake to Adopt New Name,'' *Nikkei Weekly*, November 21, 1994, p. 10.

Lodge, Sally, ''Berlitz Launches Children's Line,'' *Publishers Weekly,* September 9, 1996, p. 40.

Mifflin, Lawrie, ''Berlitz Will Use 'Sesame Street' to Teach English,'' *New York Times*, July 12, 1999, p. 11.

Sears, David, ''Berlitz Interpreter; Data Base of Foreign Words; Software Review,'' *Compute!,* March 1993, p. 122.

Tannenbaum, Jeffrey A., ''Big Companies Bearing Famous Names Turn to Franchising to get Even Bigger,'' *Wall Street Journal,* October 18, 1995, p. B1.

—Kerstan Cohen
—update: Ed Dinger

HARRIS
INTERNET SERVICES   DIRECTORY & DATA SERVICES

Bernard C. Harris Publishing Company, Inc.

3 Barker Avenue
White Plains, New York 10601
U.S.A.
Toll Free: (800) 326-6600
Fax: (914) 287-2144
Web site: http://www.bcharrispub.com

Private Company
Incorporated: 1963
Employees: 2,000
Sales: $100 million (1999 est.)
NAIC: 514191 On-Line Information Services; 51114
    Database and Directory Publishers

In its four decades of existence, Bernard C. Harris Publishing Company, Inc. of White Plains, New York, has grown into America's leading publisher of college alumni directories. Fully exploiting its niche, the family-dominated company also offers similar directory services to trade organizations and other so-called affinity groups, as well as to public and private high schools. To take advantage of the information gathered in its directories, Harris Publishing has developed telemarketing operations that can help clients in fund-raising activities. Embracing new media, Harris offers its directories in a CD-ROM database format in addition to the traditional print version. With the advent of the Internet, Harris Publishing recognized the opportunity to put its core business on-line and now offers a wide range of Internet services. More than just gathering the names and vital statistics of client members, Harris Publishing creates on-line communities in which members can interact and clients can strengthen ties and better serve their constituents.

Creation of Harris Publishing in 1963

In the early 1960s Bernard C. Harris worked for a Chicago company that published regional directories. Teaming with his brother Adrian in New York City he began publishing similar directories in 1963. Their first client was a perfect fit for the start-up publishers: Manhattan College. Close to 80 percent of the school's alumni lived in the vicinity, so that the cost of long distance phone calls was kept to a minimum. Although in the early years Harris Publishing limited its client base to within a 50-mile radius of New York City, the business grew steadily. The concept was simple but effective. At no charge to the school, Harris Publishing would update alumni records and compile the information in directory form. The school would then receive a copy of the information and Harris Publishing would be granted permission to sell the resulting directory to the alumni, who generally were pleased to purchase a resource that allowed them to maintain, or renew, ties with classmates. Harris Publishing also relied on a well-earned reputation for confidentiality. Although it would routinely receive requests from a variety of businesses looking to rent its valuable directory lists, Harris Publishing always declined. To protect client information, the company went so far as to use dummy names on its copyright materials.

Over the years, alumni directories became even more attractive for both colleges and their graduates. With budget shortfalls, more and more schools had to turn to their graduates in fund-raising efforts, and the no-cost information that Harris Publishing provided proved invaluable. Alumni, as well, began to make use of the directories to network with classmates to help further their individual careers.

Relocation and Growth Through the Early 1990s

Harris Publishing not only expanded beyond the immediate area of New York City, it began to publish member directories for clients other than colleges, adding professional schools, technical schools, fraternities, and professional societies to its list of customers. In 1973 the company, numbering eight employees, left its New York City offices to relocate in White Plains, a nearby Westchester County suburb, where the company could more easily expand its operations. Soon staffed at 30, it occupied some 2,000 square feet. By 1981 Harris Publishing would move to a new office building, where it would lease 12,000 square feet for its 100 employees. An additional 100 people worked elsewhere nationwide. With annual sales of $10 million, the company boasted 1,000 clients.

Because it had to process so many records, Harris Publishing embraced the use of computers and their ability to maintain databases. With no extra effort, the company could now offer information to its clients that was sorted alphabetically, geographically, and by class year. Furthermore, Harris Publishing created a Composite Donor Index that would rank potential donors by quantifying economic and demographic information. It highlighted the names of members' employers who offered matching gift programs. Computers were also cost-effective in the procuring of information. After questionnaires, based on school records, were sent to alumni, operators would call to verify information or contact alumni who had failed to reply, as well as to initiate a sales pitch for the final directory that generally took nine months to compile and sold for around $50. Harris Publishing began using an automated phone dialing system that would connect a live operator only when someone answered. The intent was to make just one phone call per household, not only to avoid being a nuisance but to save money. In the late 1980s Harris Publishing was making 14 million calls a year, at a cost of $3 million.

By 1989 Harris Publishing controlled 65 percent of a directory market that was continuing to grow. The company had published close to 2,000 directories for colleges and other organizations, and gross sales stood at $32.5 million. By 1991 revenues neared $40 million and clients numbered almost 4,000. The company employed more than 300 in White Plains and an additional 1,000 across the country.

In the early 1990s Harris Publishing expanded into new but related areas. Harris Select Communication, a telemarketing unit, was created to further assist clients in fund raising. The company set up operations in Austin, Texas; Norfolk, Virginia; Nashville, Tennessee; and Albuquerque, New Mexico. Close proximity to military installations was extremely desirable because of the large pool of spouses of military and civilian defense personnel. The cost of such labor was less than what the company could find in White Plains. Even though the company promised that it would expand its operations in White Plains, in December 1994 Harris Publishing cut its Westchester staff in half, moving manufacturing, technical, and much of its information services to Norfolk.

In the early 1990s Harris Publishing also began to produce directories for high schools, both public and private, as many secondary schools now found themselves, like colleges, turning to graduates to help raise much needed funds. As with its college clients, Harris Publishing did not charge the schools, which would receive the directory's database in electronic form. It was estimated that in the secondary school market between 8 and 18 percent of listed alumni would purchase a directory, which also came in a deluxe cover edition at a higher price. Within a few years, Harris Publishing would be producing close

to 300 new high school directories each year. Total annual revenues for the company reached $74 million in 1994, then made a dramatic 28.3 percent jump the following year when sales reached $95 million. Sales leveled off to $98 million in both 1996 and 1998.

Offering On-line Directories in 1997

After expanding its client base to Canada and the United Kingdom, offering telemarketing services, and turning to nonprint CD-ROMs, while controlling 85 percent of the American college alumni directory market, Harris Publishing seemed to reach a sales plateau. The company was convinced that the key to all future expansion would be the Internet, and it began to invest in the necessary technology and personnel. On-line subscription-based databases were introduced late in 1997. Although Harris Publishing would top $100 million in revenues in 1998, fueled in great part by its new electronic sales, much of the CD-ROM and Internet business came at the expense of its own print product. Rather than positioning itself just as a database publisher, Harris Publishing began to emphasize its ability to provide "communication tools" that could strengthen bonds between organizations and their members, as well as between members themselves. To achieve this end, the company went beyond the mere gathering of member information to creating on-line communities, password-protected web sites where client memberships could interact. Organizations could then efficiently, and inexpensively, post notices and establish resources of information pertinent to the group, send broadcast e-mail messages, provide job placement and recruitment services, and, of course, raise funds. In addition to making use of the web-based directory, members could pay dues on-line and communicate via chat rooms or bulletin boards to maintain social ties as well as to network for career advancement. Members could post resumes as well as establish and maintain mentoring relationships with other graduates. Harris Publishing also took steps to provide e-commerce to the sites, whereby community members could purchase goods and services through direct links. Client organizations and Harris Publishing would then share royalties on the business generated. Harris Publishing formed Alumni Connections Online Community for colleges and Member Connections Online Communities for associations to market its new cyber business. Rather than require clients to carry advertisements, and leaving e-commerce capabilities optional, Harris Publishing elected to charge a fee to create the directory and site and an annual fee on a multiyear contract in order to maintain it. In this way the company could ensure that the site's biographical information would be protected for the sole use of the client and not exploited to generate revenue just to pay for the site. Thus the trust between Harris Publishing and its clients that had been built up over 40 years would continue to serve as a prime asset for the company.

By 2000 Harris Publishing had more than 100 alumni and association Internet directory sites in operation of the nearly 200 clients contracted. Its college clients included The Wharton School at the University of Pennsylvania and Villanova University. Association clients included Kiwanis International, Air Force Association, and the American Society for Public Administration. Harris Publishing clearly had made significant inroads in its new line of endeavor, but the potential business was

Key Dates:

1963: Company produces first alumni directory for Manhattan College.
1973: Operations are moved from New York City to White Plains, New York.
1990: Company begins to sell directories to secondary school market.
1997: On-line directories are introduced.
2000: Harris Internet Services division is formed; company acquires School Days program.

staggering. The nation's 3,606 institutions of higher learning had 53 million alumni, whereas 23,000 national associations had a membership that numbered more than 87 million. The country's 92,000 regional, state, and local organizations were also potential customers. In contrast, the population served by the company's on-line communities totaled only seven million members.

In April 2000 Harris Publishing created a new division, Harris Internet Services, dedicated solely to the running of its on-line business, providing clients with service at every stage of the development process, from concept to the final site. The company added 35 jobs to its White Plains headquarters, including developers, producers, and client support staff. The concept was also refined. Client members would receive e-mail addresses that included the institution's name, despite any change in their Internet service providers. On-line poll and surveys provided instantaneous feedback. Members were provided with tools to help them easily create their own homepages for posting to the Web. The community sites also were designed to incorporate the colors, logos, and other graphics used by the parent organization. Furthermore, the sites were now designed to serve as portals similar to Yahoo!-customized start pages where members could also receive news, weather, sports scores, and stock quotes. E-Commerce also was improved by forging a partnership with an Internet marketer, BATNET1, to provide links to commercial sites.

In May 2000 Harris Publishing announced that it had contracted with the University of Southern California, Santa Clara University, and the University of San Francisco to provide Internet services for the schools' alumni organizations, bringing the number of California schools served to 15. With many of their graduates working in the high-tech or Internet industries, the California schools felt that having an alumni presence on the Web was crucial, a perception that was likely to be duplicated at schools across the country.

Harris Publishing signed a major nonacademic Internet client in November 2000: the Reserve Officers Association (ROA), whose 70,000 members included active, retired, and former officers of the seven U.S. uniformed services. Unlike the academic communities, the ROA site was more politically ori-

ented. The group could keep members more fully informed on the progress of relevant legislation, such as military funding and national security issues, and coordinate member response to bolster ROA's influence on Washington.

Harris Publishing did not forget the traditional format of paper. In November 2000 the company announced that it had acquired the fledgling ''School Days'' business from Harmony Unlimited, which produced free calendars for participating school districts. Limited at its inception to Virginia, the calendars with their targeted audiences were supported by such major advertisers as General Mills, Del Monte, Dole, and Campbell's. Not only were schools able to notify families about important events and scheduling information at no cost, they received scholarship funds. Harris Publishing added two new programs to the School Days Scholarship Calendar. Food for Thought engaged the children, awarding food and/or merchandise coupons for correct answers to monthly questions. The School Funding Tree also paid school districts a percentage of calendar ad revenues. Not only did the School Days calendar business promise great potential nationally for Harris Publishing, it also complemented its high school directory business, strengthening brand awareness and ties between schools and the company.

Over the years, Harris Publishing systematically expanded its business, at first achieving the lion's share of the college alumni directory market, then branching into affinity groups and secondary schools. The company, always open to new technologies, saw beyond the paper used by traditional publishers to take advantage of the CD-ROM format and sought to be an early player in the Internet. This was perhaps its greatest strength going into the next century.

Principal Divisions

Directory & Data Services; Internet Services.

Principal Competitors

infoUSA Inc.; Student Advantage, Inc.

Further Reading

''Bernard C. Harris Adds E-Commerce to Its Net Directories,'' *Electronic Advertising & Marketplace Report,* February 22, 2000, p. 7.
''Bernard C. Harris to Add E-Commerce Capabilities to Its Internet Directories,'' *SIMBA Report on Directory Publishing,* February 2000, p. 12.
Frenette, Liza, ''Publisher Grows by Telling Graduates About Themselves,'' *Across the Board,* June 23, 1989, p. 13.
Lott, Ethan, ''High School Takes College Approach to Alumni Reunions, Fund Raising,'' *Pittsburgh Business Times,* August 26, 2000, p. 30.
Philippidis, Alex, ''White Plains Publisher Expands Its Operations in Virginia,'' *Westchester County Business Journal,* March 4, 1996, p. 15.
——, ''White Plains Publishing Firm to Expand into Cyberspace,'' *Westchester County Business Journal,* May 8, 2000, p. 5.

—Ed Dinger

Bewag AG

Puschkinallee 52
D-12435 Berlin
Germany
Telephone: (49) (30) 2671-0600
Fax: (49) (30) 2671-0605
Web site: http://www.bewag.de

Public Company
Incorporated: 1884 as Städtische Elektricitäts-Werke,
    Aktiengesellschaft zu Berlin (A.G.StEW)
Employees: 6,385
Sales: DM 3.42 billion ($1.67 billion) (2000)
Stock Exchanges: Frankfurt/Main
Ticker Symbol: BEWAG
NAIC: 221112 Fossil Fuel Electric Power Generation;
    221121 Electric Bulk Power Transmission and
    Control; 221122 Electric Power Distribution

Berlin-based Bewag AG supplies Germany's capital city with electricity. With a share of 97 percent in Berlin's electricity market, the company owns and runs 20 power stations in and around Berlin with a capacity of 3,000 MW for electricity and 6,000 MW for heat generation. Bewag also operates an electricity network of 40,000 kilometers and is involved in electricity trading through its subsidiary best energy GmbH. Bewag holds a major share in Berlin-based gas and heat supplier GASAG. Since 1997 Bewag has been partly owned by the American power utility Southern Energy, Inc., which since changed its name to Mirant. The sale of E.ON Energie AG's 49 percent share in Bewag to Hamburg-based electricity company HEW was pending in 2001.

1880s Origins

In 1866 German engineer Werner von Siemens discovered the "electro-dynamic principle," which made possible the construction of "dynamo-machines" that could generate electricity. Not long after that, in 1881, the inhabitants of Germany's capital were startled to see the first electricity-powered tram run in the Berliner Lichterfelde suburb. At the same time the city government set up a "Beleuchtungskuratorium" (illumination-committee) and started experimenting with electrical illumination of Berlin's streets. From 1882 on Potsdamer Platz and Leipziger Strasse were constantly lit.

In the same year, when the first block power station based on plans of inventor Thomas A. Edison went into operation in New York City, German politician and industrialist Emil von Rathenau, backed by several banks, founded a research society called the "Gelegenheits-Gesellschaft" (the opportunity society) for the construction of "Glühlichtanlagen." These electric lightning systems were badly needed in Berlin's numerous theaters, many of which had been devastated by fires started by open gas lighting. Within nine months the company had installed 40 electric lightning systems.

In 1883 the Edison Society agreed to grant Rathenau's company rights to Edison's patents for a license fee. Werner von Siemens' company Siemens & Halske acquired an exclusive right to build dynamo machines, cables, and power lines. In April 1883 the Gelegenheits-Gesellschaft was transformed into Deutsche Edison Gesellschaft für angewandte Elektricität (DEG), "the German Edison Society for Applied Electricity." In January 1884 Bavarian Staatsbaupraktikant Oskar von Miller became DEG's second director. Unlike many other specialists in the field, Rathenau strongly believed in centralized power generation to supply electricity to large areas. Before building a large central power station, however, a smaller one was set up in a cellar at Friedrichstrasse 85 at the corner of Unter den Linden. It was used to illuminate the famous "Kranzler Eck" and "Café Bauer." After lengthy negotiations with Berlin's city government, DEG finally cut a deal in February 1884 obliging it to provide electricity to every customer who signed a three-year contract with the company. DEG was allowed to lay the necessary cables to supply an area of about 800 meters radius around the Fürstenhaus am Werderschen Markt and was required to pay a concession fee from its profits to the city. On May 8, 1884 DEG founded the new subsidiary Städtische Elektricitäts-Werke, Aktiengesellschaft zu Berlin (A.G.StEW), a public limited company that became Berlin's public electricity provider; DEG transferred its concession to the new company. The agreement was adopted soon afterward by many other German municipalities and initiated the sprouting up of public electricity works throughout the country. DEG in turn secured the more profitable business of manufacturing the equipment needed by the Städtische Elektricitäts-Werke to deliver electricity to its customers.

After the legal and economic structure for the company was set up, the first German "Kraftzentrale" (power center) was built on a property in Berlin's Markgrafenstrasse 44. In August 1885 the power station started generating electricity. It was called the "Centrale" and consisted of five "waterpipe-furnaces" and six steam engines with a capacity of 540 kW. At first the Centrale supplied 28 customers with electric light, including two large accounts, the Royal Schauspielhaus theater and the Reichsbank. Only one year later, a second power station was put into operation at the central Mauerstrasse 80, primarily to provide illumination for a large shopping center in Leipziger Strasse and the hotel Kaiserhof, which became Berlin's first hotel with electric light. Two other power stations were built in 1889 at Spandauer Strasse 49 and one year later at Schiffbauerdamm 22. The power stations were connected, using a scale model of several square meters that included all of the streets, which was designed by Edison.

Dynamic Expansion at Turn of the Century

Städtische Elektricitäts-Werke tried its best to accomplish the demanding task of setting up and expanding the necessary infrastructure and of winning over new electricity customers. The company was able to survive, however, only by means of a significant financial infusion from DEG. The major breakthrough came with the help of Deutsche Bank, which at that time had existed only 17 years. On May 23, 1887, the Allgemeine Electricitäts-Gesellschaft (AEG) was founded as the legal successor of DEG. A few months later, on October 1, 1887, Städtische Elektricitäts-Werke was renamed Berliner Electricitäts-Werke (BEW). At the same time AEG, headed by Rathenau, von Miller, and financial specialist Felix Deutsch, agreed to manage BEW for the following ten years. In August 1888 a new concession agreement was finally approved by the city of Berlin. It allowed BEW to expand its reach and to build two more power stations within the city limits. At the same time, however, the city withdrew BEW's exclusive right to install electricity cable in houses and invited other competitors into the market.

After ten years the business had thrived to such a degree that AEG's and BEW's management were split once again. Von Miller left AEG in spring 1890, while Rathenau eagerly promoted the transmission of electricity over long distances. When electricity was still being used primarily for lighting, its much higher impact on the production infrastructure of the whole economy could already be seen on the horizon. In 1889 BEW delivered electricity to the firm Ludwig Loewe & Co. to power motors instead of light bulbs, and only six years later BEW and AEG founded a subsidiary to promote electric motors to small businesses.

Around the turn of the 19th century Berlin greatly expanded its network for the supply of electricity. New high-voltage transmission technology made it possible to move power generation from the city center to the suburbs. In 1896–97 AEG built two power stations, one in the southwestern suburb of Zehlendorf, another in Oranienburg for Berlin's northern suburbs, and Drehstromwerk Oberspree to supply the neighboring southern areas such as Teltow and Niederbarnim. Between 1898 and 1914 several more power stations were set up in and around Berlin: the Berliner Vororts-Elektrizitätswerke, which supplied Tempelhof, Steglitz, and Dahlem in 1898; the Charlottenburg power station in the southwest in 1899; the Städtisches Elektrizitätswerk Charlottenburg in 1900; the Rummelsburg power plant in 1907; the Moabit plant in 1908; Gemeindekraftwerk Steglitz in 1911; and Kreiselektrizitätswerk Oberhavel in the north in 1914. Equipped with this capital-intensive infrastructure, Berlin's electricity industry witnessed a dynamic upswing before the onset of World War I. Electricity production jumped from 425,000 kWh in 1897–98 to two million kWh in 1903–04, a growth of almost 500 percent in only six years. A major advance was smaller and longer-lasting steam turbines, which were also easier to maintain than the piston-steam engines they replaced. The higher capacity also made it possible to introduce electricity-powered industry machinery as well as electric household appliances, which in turn gave the emerging electric industry, but also the electrochemical industry, an enormous boost.

Interruption by Two World Wars

World War I broke out in August 1914 and four months later the 1899 concession agreement with BEW expired. The city government decided to transform the company into a municipal entity. In October 1915 it purchased all of the power stations and other plants from BEW for 132 million marks. The company was renamed Städtische Elektrizitätswerke Berlin (StEW) and its management was overseen by city officials. During World War I the electricity works' primary task was supplying the war industry. It struggled with the growing scarcity of raw materials, fuel, and skilled workers.

Plans to ensure Berlin's electricity supply by means of long-distance power lines from large centralized power generators far away from the city finally were realized after the war's end. As early as 1913 AEG and BEW had acquired large bituminous coal fields around Bitterfeld, almost 100 miles away from the Prussian capital. The acquisition was made primarily to lower dependence on the highly volatile coal prices, but also with the idea of using it to generate energy for Berlin. Within only a year Germany's biggest power station Golpa-Zschornewitz was erected there, which at first supplied only war industry. In winter 1917–18, however, an 80-mile-long high-voltage power line was laid and from June 1918 on electricity was delivered from Golpa-Zschornewitz to Berlin. These deliveries were suf-

Key Dates:

1884: The first German public electricity supply company is founded in Berlin.

1915: The city of Berlin acquires Städtische Elektricitäts-werke Berlin (StEW).

1923: Berliner Städtische Elektrizitätswerke Akt.-Ges. (Bewag) is officially registered as a public stock company.

1934: Berliner Kraft- und Licht-Aktiengesellschaft (BKL) and Berliner Städtische Elektrizitätswerke Akt.-Ges. (Bewag) merge to form Berliner Kraft- und Licht (Bewag) Aktiengesellschaft.

1948: Bewag is split into two companies as a result of World War II.

1952: West Berlin is cut off from other electricity distribution networks.

1979: Ost-Bewag becomes VEB Energiekombinat Berlin (EKB).

1991: Bewag takes over EKB's successor Energieversorgung Berlin AG (EBAG).

1994: Bewag is connected with the network of power company VEAG.

1997: Berlin puts its share in Bewag up for sale; Southern Energy becomes major shareholder.

ficient to meet basic demand, while the smaller, older, and less economical power plants around Berlin supplied only the extra electricity at peak times. As it turned out in the following years, however, this model was not as secure as expected and was abandoned after several power blackouts occurred.

The 1920s brought an unprecedented increase in demand for electricity in Berlin. In 1920 Berlin's surrounding suburbs merged to form "Groß-Berlin" (Greater Berlin). The Städtische Elektricitätswerke's red tape-driven organizational structure did not seem appropriate for the dynamic growth needed to expand the energy supply infrastructure. Thus once again the city brought in professional managers to help run the power plant. On December 8, 1923 the Berliner Städtische Elektricitätswerke Akt.-Ges. (Bewag) was registered officially as a public stock company. All shares remained in the city's hands, but a 50-year lease agreement allowed Bewag to use all of the power generation and distribution facilities of the city. In turn, Berlin received a percentage of the company's revenues.

In the early 1920s Germany was hit hard by hyperinflation. By April 1920 electricity prices had more than quadrupled in comparison with prewar levels. When the inflation spiral started spinning out of control, however, in January 1923 a kWh cost 275 marks; by November it was no less than 420 *billion* Marks. A currency reform eventually normalized the situation and demand for electricity started to rise again. By 1927 half of all Berlin households was connected to the power network; by 1928 the city's elevated trains and subway were powered by electricity.

The next crisis, however, hit even harder. In the aftermath of the New York Stock Exchange crash in October 1929, eco-

nomic depression spread throughout the world. Big cities like Berlin were suddenly faced with high unemployment, and production of and demand for electricity dropped. Faced with high budget pressures, the city took out a loan using the electricity works as collateral. A new holding company, the Berliner Kraft- und Licht-Aktiengesellschaft (BKL), with Bewag as its subsidiary, was set up in 1931. The city of Berlin held a 16 percent share and the banks held 67 percent in the new company. After the Nazis came to power, however, the two companies were merged in November 1934 to form Berliner Kraft- und Licht (Bewag) AG. By the onset of World War II Bewag had become Germany's biggest local power utility.

Division in 1948 and Reunification in 1990

Although most of Berlin's power stations survived the war, more than half of their furnaces and turbines were dismantled by Russian troops, leaving power-generating capacity in the Western sectors of the city at 30 percent of the prewar level. The city was split into two parts and for the next four decades West Berlin became an "energy island." In 1948 Bewag moved its headquarters to the West Berlin Tiergarten district and the Soviet-dominated eastern sector of the city founded its own power utility company, the "Ost-Bewag" (East-Bewag). In April 1948 the British military commander approved the reconstruction of the dismantled Kraftwerk West power station. This turned out to be an extraordinary endeavor, however—beginning on June 24, 1948, the Russian army completely blocked all rail, road, and water connections to West Berlin for almost a year. All the necessary construction material, including furnaces that had been cut into parts with blowtorches and fuels, were flown into the western part of the city by the Western Allies. On December 1, 1949, West Berlin Mayor Ernst Reuter opened the first section of the newly built power station, which was renamed after him, "Kraftwerk Reuter." On March 4, 1952, West Berlin was cut off from the West German power distribution infrastructure. The city's geographical isolation pushed Bewag to set up an energy supply system that was able to provide all the necessary electricity without being connected to a larger network.

Meantime, the East German Ost-Bewag became a government-managed company and rebuilt the power generation and distribution networks in the eastern part of the city. Bewag was hit hard by the two oil price shocks in 1973 and 1979 since the company relied on 25 percent oil as a fuel, compared with only three percent in West Germany, and half of its power generation capacity was oil-based. In the mid-1970s the Soviet Union suggested letting a West German firm build a nuclear power station in Königsberg, Russia and deliver the generated power through Poland and East Germany to West Berlin and West Germany. This plan, however, as well as similar ones, were vetoed by the East German government. On the other hand, Bewag rejected another East German government plan to deliver electricity from a brown-coal power station near Leipzig to West Berlin. It was turned down because of the extraordinarily high prices demanded. In 1978 the Ost-Bewag was renamed VEB Energieversorgung Berlin, which was changed again one year later to VEB Energiekombinat Berlin (EKB).

The city's two power utilities were finally reunited after the sudden fall of the Berlin Wall in 1989. A new company, Energieversorgung Berlin AG (EBAG), was founded to succeed the East German EKB and was—in accordance with an agreement between the East and West German governments—sold to Bewag, effective January 1, 1991. A year later Bewag's claim for restitution was fully accepted. In December 1992 an emergency energy supply connection between the two parts of Berlin ended the city's "energy isolation." Another high-voltage connection with Berlin-based power company VEAG, which supplied electricity to eastern German states, ended West Berlin's isolation in 1994. In the same year EBAG merged with Bewag and two years later the East Berlin company was fully integrated into Bewag again.

Bewag for Sale in 1997

In May 1997 the city of Berlin decided to sell off its 50.8 percent share in Bewag. The city government was under tremendous budget pressure and wanted to lift some financial weight from its shoulders by cashing in on some of its assets. At the same time Germany was awaiting the deregulation of the country's power supply market, which was dominated by a handful of companies. The German antitrust office signaled that it would not approve a deal if only German power companies were involved. After lengthy negotiations a DM 2.9 billion deal was signed by a consortium of three companies. German power suppliers PreussenElektra AG and Bayernwerk AG, which already held ten percent share packages in Bewag, were able to upgrade their shares to 23 and 26 percent, respectively. A new major shareholder was found in Atlanta-based Southern Energy, Inc., which acquired a 26 percent stake in Bewag. Southern Energy was thus the first non-German company to break into Germany's energy supply market. The Americans secured management leadership but agreed to produce a large percentage of electricity for Bewag at Berlin facilities to guarantee jobs in the German capital. The two German parties agreed to hold their shares for at least 20 years. The other 25 percent of Bewag shares were held by smaller portfolio investors.

The next challenge the newly privatized Bewag had to face was Germany's sudden liberalization of the country's energy market, which abolished the supply monopolies of German power companies for determined regions and opened their electricity distribution networks to other energy suppliers for a fee. The reform went into effect on April 29, 1998, and within a year energy prices dropped between 25 and 50 percent for businesses and ten to 20 percent for private customers. To remain competitive in its core market—one that because of its density was very lucrative to other energy suppliers—Bewag intensified marketing efforts. With German telecommunications company MobilCom AG, it founded a joint venture, best energy GmbH, a new subsidiary to expand into new territory through electricity trading. BerlinDat Gesellschaft für Informationsverarbeitung und Systemtechnik GmbH was another joint venture set up with Siemens AG to venture into information service markets. Bewag also made a concerted effort to lower raw material and repair costs. The number of employees was reduced by one third, dropping from 9,800 in 1995–96 to 6,385 in 1999–2000. Despite these measures Bewag's electricity sales dropped by five percent in business year 1999/2000 compared with the previous year, while net earnings went down 15 percent during the same period.

When German electricity giants VEBA and VIAG announced their merger to form E.ON Energie AG in the late 1990s, the German antitrust office ruled that PreussenElektra AG, which was owned by VEBA, and Bayernwerk AG, which was owned by VIAG, had to give up their Bewag shares. They found a potent new shareholder in Hamburg's electrical works HEW, which was majority owned by Swedish electricity company Vattenfall AB. However, Bewag's third shareholder, Southern Energy, which in the meantime had changed its name to Mirant, blocked the deal because it was interested in taking over Bewag completely and believed it had first option on further shares. The case was slated for arbitration in 2001.

Principal Subsidiaries

FHW Fernheizwerk Neukölln AG (75.22%); EnergieSüdwest AG (51%); GASAG Berliner Gaswerke AG (31.58%); BerlinDat Gesellschaft für Informationsverarbeitung und Systemtechnik mbH (74.99%); IPH Institut "Prüffeld für elektrische Hochleistungstechnik" GmbH; EAVV Energie Assekuranz Versicherungs Vermittlungs GmbH (60%); best energy GmbH (50%); Berliner Energieagentur GmbH (33%); EBH Energie-Beteiligungsholding GmbH (25%).

Principal Competitors

E.ON Energie AG; RWE AG; Electricité de France.

Further Reading

"Aufsichtsrat stimmt Verschmelzung zu," *Frankfurter Allgemeine Zeitung,* November 1, 1993, p. 18.

Bahde, Curt, Klaus Bürgel, and Wolfgang Hahn, "100 Jahre Stromverteilung in Berlin," *Elektrizitätswirtschaft,* republished in *VDE 100 Jahre Stromgeschichte,* Berlin, Germany: 1992, p. 48.

"Berlin ist nach 42 Jahren keine Strominsel mehr," *Frankfurter Allgemeine Zeitung,* December 7, 1994, p. 16.

"Berliner Senat stimmt Verkauf der Bewag fuer 2,9 Milliarden DM zu," *Frankfurter Allgemeine Zeitung,* May 14, 1997, p. 19.

"Best energy will innerhalb von drei Jahren eine Mio Kunden haben," *vwd,* December 9, 1999.

Franke, Peter, "Berlin Now Well Connected," *Modern Power Systems,* June 1995, p. 43.

Isles, Junoir, "Learn to Expect the Unexpected," *Modern Power Systems,* June 1997, p. 17.

Matschoß, C., Schulz, E., and Groß, A. Th., *50 Jahre Berliner Elektrizitäts Werke 1884–1934,* Berlin, Germany: VDI Verlag GmbH, 1934.

Tegethoff, Wilm, "100 Jahre elektrizitätswirtschaftliche Energiepolitik in Berlin," *Elektrizitätswirtschaft,* republished in *VDE 100 Jahre Stromgeschichte,* Berlin, Germany: 1992, p. 8.

—Evelyn Hauser

Blacks Leisure Group plc

105 Baker Street
London W1H 1FA
United Kingdom
Telephone: (+44) 20 7616-9222
Fax: (+44) 20 7616-9200
Web site: http://www.blacksleisure.co.uk

Public Company
Incorporated: 1923 as Thomas Black and Sons Ltd.
Employees: 5,581
Sales: £207.83 million ($328 million) (2000)
Stock Exchanges: London
Ticker Symbol: BSLA.L
NAIC: 339920 Sporting and Athletic Goods
    Manufacturing; 421910 Sporting and Recreational
    Goods and Supplies Wholesalers; 451110 Sporting
    Goods Stores; 451 Sporting Goods, Hobby, Book, and
    Music Stores; 422320 Men's and Boys' Clothing and
    Furnishings Wholesalers

Blacks Leisure Group plc is one of the United Kingdom's leading retail sportswear and sporting goods groups and is that market's largest specialty outdoor retailer. The company operates nearly 450 stores under seven company-owned and managed retail chains: through its Sports & Fashion division, Blacks runs the 152-store First Sport chain, the 24-store AV chain, first introduced in 1997, and the company's newest store concept, Pure Women, the company's first attempt to target specifically the women's sportswear and sports fashions category, introduced in 2000. The company's other major division is its Outdoor division, featuring the company's original store format, Blacks Outdoor, with 43 stores, and boosted by the company's acquisition in December 1999 of U.K. outdoor sporting goods leader The Outdoor Group—which brought Blacks Leisure the 199-store Millets chain of family-oriented sporting goods stores and the higher-end Air and youth-oriented Free Spirit retail chains. That acquisition, which added more than 400,000 square feet of selling space, cost Blacks Leisure more than £50 million. Blacks Leisure is cutting back on a third division, Wholesaling, which,

after the sale of the company's Fifa UK license back to Italian parent Fifa International in 2000, is represented by the company's U.K. concession of the popular O'Neill sporting goods and sportswear label. Most of the company's O'Neill-related sales come through sales to third-party retailers, but also through its own retail chains and two company-owned O'Neill branded retail stores. Blacks Leisure has been led since 1989 by chairman and chief executive Simon Bentley—who missed most of the 2000 fiscal year after being hospitalized by a skiing accident. Blacks, which posted revenues of nearly £208 million in 2000, is traded on the London stock exchange.

From Adventurer to Manufacturer in the 19th Century

Thomas Black's adventurous background led him to found the company that later became one of the United Kingdom's leading retail sporting goods and sportswear companies. Born in 1836, Black was already a veteran sailor by the beginning of the 1850s. His experience aboard various British merchant vessels gave him not only a share of adventures—including a brush with pirates in the Greek Islands—but also skill as a sail maker. In 1853, Black joined with others of his ship's crew members to make the journey to Australia, where Black spent two years mining gold during that country's gold rush. With the gold he discovered, Black returned to England—now as a passenger, not a crew member.

Arriving back in England in 1856, Black had not yet slaked his thirst for adventure. His next journey took him to the then-Spanish Guinea, in Africa, where he acted as an ivory agent for Laughland and Brown of London. Black's African adventure soon was ended by illness, and Black returned to the United Kingdom, where he took up the sail maker's trade in Glasgow.

Married in 1861, Black moved to the port city of Greenock on the Clyde, where he set up his own sail making business. The British dominance of the seas provided for a bustling shipbuilding industry—and high demand for Black's sails. Toward the end of the century, however, the shift to steamships brought about steady declines in the sail making industry.

Key Dates:

1861: Thomas Black founds a sail-making business in Greenock.
1905: Thomas Black, Jr., takes over company and initiates tent production.
1918: Company develops its own lightweight tent designs.
1923: Company incorporates as Thomas Black and Sons (Greenock) Ltd.
1948: New production facility in Glasgow is opened.
1967: Company engages in reverse takeover of Benjamin Edgintons Ltd.
1975: Company changes name to Blacks Camping and Leisure Ltd.
1984: Blacks merges with Greenfields plc. and adopts new name soon thereafter: Blacks Leisure Group plc.
1987: Company acquires Howard Sports, Sullivan Sports, and Teesside Sports.
1988: MC Sports and West 8 Sports are acquired; Howard and Sullivan are sold off; the First Sport retail store is launched.
1989: Company acquires U.K. distribution rights to Fila brand.
1995: The first AV store debuts.
1999: Company acquires The Outdoor Group Limited and Sports Shop (Fife) Limited.
2000: Blacks launches the Pure Women retail format; sells off Fila license.

Black died in 1905, leaving the flagging business to son Thomas Black junior. The younger Black, who had had his own youthful adventures in California, had not only inherited his father's business but his sail making skills as well. But with the end of the great sail making era, Black needed to find a new outlet for the company. While in California, Black had discovered a growing new pastime, that of camping. The lead from sail making to tents seemed natural for the company, which promptly turned its production to making a variety of bell-type and large-scale marquee tents. During the First World War the company helped supply tents to the British military, filling orders ranging from field hospital tents to a canvas hangar for the British army's dirigibles.

At the end of the war, camping became a growing leisure activity in the United Kingdom. Black, who was then joined by his two sons, quickly seized on this trend, turning its production to lightweight tents suitable for the leisure camper and becoming one of the first to enter the market. Retail sales steadily became an important part of the company's activities, particularly after the opening of two new showrooms in Glasgow. The company also began adding to its catalog of camping-related items, expanding its Greenock showroom by the beginning of the 1920s. The company changed its name to Thomas Black and Sons (Greenock) Ltd. in 1923.

An important step for the company was the opening of its first London store, on Bury Street, in 1928. The company's success quickly led it to move to larger quarters in the city, before later making London the company's corporate home.

When Thomas Black junior died in 1930, his son D. Crawford Black took over the leadership of the company. During the years leading up to the second World War, the company scored a number of marketing coups that helped build it into one of the United Kingdom's most important tent makers and camping good suppliers. Backing the company's growth was the appearance of its first printed catalog, called "Good Companions," in 1931. The company also achieved renown for a number of events. One of these called for the company to supply nearly 5,000 tents, as well as provisions to bed 14,000 people. Another came in early 1933 when the company supplied camping gear to adventurer Jock Scott—known for his treks, such as one from Greenock to Cape Town, South Africa, or his walk from San Francisco to New York.

World War II saw the company once again turn its production to support the United Kingdom's war effort, manufacturing canvas tents and gear for the military, while also producing sleeping bags—including ones used by Winston Churchill. The company faced disaster in 1941, after a bomb destroyed its Greenock production facility. The company quickly set up temporary quarters and was back in business within a month of the bombing. After the war, the company inaugurated a new manufacturing plant, now in Glasgow, in 1948.

A Retailing Leader for the 21st Century

Blacks was well positioned to take advantage of the growing ranks of camping enthusiasts, as the adoption of new and modernized production techniques freed up more leisure time for more people. In 1953, Blacks broadened its retail capacity with the purchase of City Camp and Sports Ltd., which helped the company extend its activities to the national scale. By the end of that decade, the company was increasingly international, with rising proportions of its sales going to Africa and North America. To support its expansion, Blacks opened its first foreign subsidiary in Canada in 1958. The company added warehouse and distribution facilities in the United States in 1962.

Blacks went on an extended acquisition drive that helped the company take a leading position in its U.K. markets. Among its acquisitions were those of Jackson and Warr Ltd., bringing Blacks a line of ski equipment, in 1962, and, in 1967, the reverse takeover of Benjamin Edgington Ltd. That company had been a longtime rival to Blacks' tent-making business, and the merger of the two companies' operations created one of the leading European tent makers—and official tent makers to the British crown.

In the 1970s, the company merged with Milletts, adding that company's 19 retail stores, which were converted to Blacks stores. The growing importance of retail sales to the company was highlighted by the creation of a dedicated division, with the company's retail name changed from Blacks of Greenock to Blacks Camping and Leisure Ltd. in 1975. Less than a decade later, following the 1984 acquisition of Greenfields plc., the company once again changed its name, to Blacks Leisure Group plc.

The 1980s saw the company step up its retailing arm, while also moving into the wholesaling field. The company, which had long targeted the specialist sports market, made its first entry into the general sporting goods market in the mid-1980s, acquiring two sporting goods chains: Howard, based in north-western England, and Sullivan, based in Liverpool. These acquisitions, made in 1987, were followed quickly by those of Teesside Sports, MC Sports, and West 8 Sports, based in London. Yet the company soon was faced with the need to bring a single face to its new type of retail network. In 1988, the company moved to sell off the Howard and Sullivan properties and instead to concentrate its efforts on the Teesside and West 8 stores. These were regrouped under a new retail sporting goods concept, called First Sport. At the same time, the company boosted its specialist sports retail sales with the acquisition of Alpine Sports, a retailer of ski and outdoor equipment, in 1988.

The first First Sport store opened in August of 1988. The company quickly converted its other retail sporting goods stores to the First Sport format. At the same time, Blacks was developing an interest in wholesaling, acquiring the license to then-popular brand LA Gear in a joint venture in 1988, before acquiring the U.K. distribution license to growing Italian sportswear brand Fila in 1989 and the O'Neill brand in 1991. The company acquired other distribution contracts in the early 1990s, such as the soccer footwear and accessories brand Quasar, fashion brands such as Skechers and Karl Kani, and womenswear's Miss Sam.

The disastrous economic situation of the late 1980s and early 1990s in the United Kingdom quickly caused Blacks' fast-growing empire to wobble. The company was forced to shed a number of money-losing operations, including most of its wholesaling activities, while restructuring its aggressively expanding First Sport chain. The company also invested in its infrastructure, improving its warehousing and distribution facilities and incorporating a new computerized inventory system, while also boosting its training initiatives for its retail staff. Now led by Chairman and CEO Simon Bentley, Blacks slowly rebuilt itself into the mid-1990s.

The company changed the name of its Blacks Camping stores to Blacks Outdoor in 1994 in order to capture more fully the wide range of the outdoor leisure market. The company refitted a number of its Blacks Outdoor stores; at the same time, the company decided to focus its specialist retail efforts on the United Kingdom's city centers, leaving the extra-urban market to rivals such as JJB Sports and JD Sports and closing a number of stores. Blacks' retailing interests were also rapidly expanding to include sportswear and other fashions. In 1995, the company inaugurated a new retail concept, AV, which featured so-called "active lifestyle" brand names. The AV concept caught on quickly, allowing the company to boost the number of AV Stores to 26 by the end of the century.

With the company's sales once again rising steadily, jumping from £68 million and 83 stores in 1996 to nearly £147 million and 183 stores in 1999, Blacks decided to step up the pace. In August 1999, the company acquired Sport Shop (Fife) Limited and its 28 Scotland-based retail stores for £1.1 million

in cash. At the end of that year, Blacks took a giant step when it bought up larger rival The Outdoor Group Limited, which brought the company its 199-store chain of Millets sporting goods stores, the largest chain in the United Kingdom, as well as 24 specialist stores under the Air and Free Spirit signs. The acquisition led Blacks to reorganize its holdings into three new divisions: the Sport & Fashion division included its First Sport and AV stores, and the new Outdoor division included Blacks Outdoor, Millets, Air, and Free Spirit. The third division, Wholesaling, continued to include the company's licensed activities for the O'Neill and Fila brands.

Bentley was forced to sit out most of the 2000 year after a skiing accident left him hospitalized in January 2000. Under an acting chairman and CEO, Blacks set out to absorb its newly expanded empire. The company also initiated a new retail concept, the Pure Women store, featuring women's sportswear and fashions. At the end of the year the company sold off its Fila license back to Italian parent Fila International, which was preparing a major international expansion of the brand.

Returning to work in January 2001, Bentley was faced with sluggish sales due to a mild winter season, as well as a slower-than-hoped-for pace of merging the company's existing operations with its newly acquired holdings. Meanwhile, analysts, long skeptical of the chances of sustained growth for the booming—and rapidly consolidating—sporting goods and sportswear retail sectors, continued to warn of market slow-downs. Blacks Leisure remained confident nonetheless, particularly as its spread of retail holdings gave it a well-balanced position from which to enjoy its leadership role.

Principal Subsidiaries

Blacks Outdoor Leisure Ltd.; Blacks Retail Distribution Ltd.; First Sport Ltd.; The Sports Shop (Fife) Limited; Sandcity Ltd; Blacks Investments Ltd; The Outdoor Group Limited; The Outdoor Groupo (Trading) Ltd.

Principal Competitors

adidas-Salomon AG; Debenhams plc; Harrods plc; JJB Sports plc; John Lewis Partnership plc; Selfridges plc.

Further Reading

Blackwell, David, "Weather Puts the Freeze on Blacks Leisure," *Financial Times,* January 11, 2001.

"Fashion Puts Bounce in Blacks Leisure," *Financial Times,* May 21, 1997.

"Focus: Blacks Leisure," *Guardian,* October 20, 1999.

"Gloomy Day for Clothing Group," *Birmingham Post,* January 11, 2001, p. 24.

Lumsden, Quentin, "Sports Chain Looks Unbeatable," *Independent on Sunday,* August 18, 1996, p. 6.

Potter, Ben, "Blacks Sticks to Expansion Track," *Daily Telegraph,* October 20, 1998, p. 33.

—M.L. Cohen

Boston Professional Hockey Association Inc.

One FleetCenter, Suite 250
Boston, Massachusetts 02114-1303
U.S.A.
Telephone: (617) 624-1900
Fax: (617) 523-7184
Web Sit: http://www.bostonbruins.com

Private Company
Incorporated: as Boston Professional Hockey Association
   in 1952
Employees: 75
Sales: $70.5 million (1999)
NAIC: 711211 Sports Teams and Clubs

The Boston Professional Hockey Association Inc. is the corporation that operates the Boston Bruins, the first U.S franchise in the National Hockey League. Playing in a state-of-the-art arena, the FleetCenter, and enjoying the stable ownership of Jeremy M. Jacobs, chairman and chief executive officer of the highly successful Delaware North Companies, the Bruins are one of hockey's most successful franchises. On the ice, the team has known periods of greatness, and over the last three decades of the 20th century, it was one of the most consistent winners in all of team sports, making the Stanley Cup playoffs 29 consecutive seasons.

Boston Joins the National Hockey League in 1924

The predecessor to the National Hockey League (NHL) was the National Hockey Association (NHA) formed by two rival Canadian "amateur" leagues to prevent themselves from stealing each other's players. Another league, the Pacific Coast Hockey Association (PCHA), was then created, and it promptly began luring away NHA players. Within two years, the champions of the NHA and PCHA were playing for the Stanley Cup, an award originally given to the top amateur hockey team in North America. Disrupted by World War I, the NHA reorganized, and on November 22, 1917 in Montreal's Windsor Hotel, the National Hockey League (NHL) was born. Within a few years the PCHA would merge with the Western Hockey League (WHL), although the enterprise would eventually fail. The Stanley Cup and the business of major league hockey would be the exclusive domain of the NHL—and of Canada.

If the NHL was to thrive, its leaders knew that it had to incorporate larger U.S. cities. The league wanted to add New York and Boston for the 1924–25 season, but the owner of New York's Madison Square Garden, Tex Rickard, was reluctant to invest in ice-making equipment and declined the invitation. The target for Boston ownership was Charles Adams, a grocery-chain magnate who had soured on hockey after sponsoring an amateur team and learning that rival clubs had been making illicit payments to players. The NHL convinced Adams to attend the 1924 Stanley Cup finals between Calgary and the Montreal Canadiens. Excited by the kind of play he witnessed, Adams agreed to pay $15,000 to purchase a NHL franchise and, in the process, brought Boston the distinction of being the first American city in the league.

Adams quickly hired the now-legendary Art Ross as general manager, coach, and scout. Ross was one of the most innovative men to ever be involved in the game. He designed the goal net, introduced the first helmet, standardized the puck, and was the first coach to employ the tactic of removing the goalie in favor of an extra skater when trailing late in the game. He also had an excellent eye for talent, bringing to Boston its first superstar player, Eddie Shore, although he had passed the first time he had the chance to sign the great defenseman.

Aside from hiring a coach, Adams needed a name for his new team, and it had to fit within specific guidelines. Most importantly, the team uniform had to be brown with yellow trim, to match the color scheme of his chain of Brookside Stores. Second, the team name "should preferably relate to an untamed animal whose name was synonymous with size, strength, agility, ferocity and cunning, and in the color brown category." Numerous suggestions came from local newspapers and sports fans. Dissatisfied with all of the choices, Adams finally selected the name Bruins, which had been submitted by his secretary, who ran a Montreal sporting goods store part-time.

Bruins Begin Play in the Boston Garden in 1928

The Bruins began play in the Boston Arena, finishing last in the six-team NHL in their first season. Fan support was strong enough, however, to prompt Adams to spend money to bring in better talent. By its third year in the league, with Eddie Shore now in the lineup, the Bruins made the Stanley Cup finals, losing to Ottawa but firmly establishing themselves with the city of Boston. Following the cup loss, the team would receive 29,000 applications for tickets. Unhappy after four years of paying rent to the Boston Arena, Adams began to explore other accommodations. Rickard, who was looking to establish a string of Madison Square Gardens across the country, signed Adams to a five-year lease for $500,000, and within a year he built an arena on property of the Maine Railroad over Boston's North Station. Always the showman, Rickard opened Boston Madison Square Garden ("Madison Square" would soon be dropped) by having President Calvin Coolidge turn on the lights from the White House by means of a key fashioned out of Yukon gold. The Bruins played their first game at the Garden on November 20, 1928. Although the team lost to the Montreal Canadiens 1–0, it would draw 17,500 patrons, 3,000 more than the new arena was supposed to hold. At the end of the season, the Bruins would also be crowned Stanley Cup champions for the first time in franchise history.

Over the next dozen years, the Bruins would enjoy success on and off the ice, as Weston Adams took control of the team for the family. With Eddie Shore serving as the Garden's primary draw, the team won Stanley Cups in 1939 and 1941 before World War II broke the club's momentum. The Depression years of the 1930s, however, were difficult for other members of the NHL, which went from being a ten-team league split into two divisions in 1930–31 to being a six-team league by the 1942–43 season.

The so-called era of the "Original Six" teams in the NHL was, for the most part, one of stability but little growth, lasting through the 1966–67 season. For the Bruins it was a generation of limited success. WHDH, a Boston radio station, began to broadcast the games, and the team generally made the playoffs, although it lacked the talent to compete for the cup with Montreal, Toronto, and Detroit. Perhaps the lowest point in its history for the Bruins' franchise came in 1950 when the team missed the playoffs, its minor league system was in shambles, and attendance dropped below 6,000 per game. Boston Garden

Arena Corporation purchased a 60 percent interest, and Weston Adams resigned as president to work as a stockbroker. He turned over day-to-day management of the team to Walter Brown. At one point Brown had to borrow money from B&M Railroad to keep the team running. It was in 1952, under Brown, that the Bruins were incorporated as the Boston Professional Hockey Association.

The measure of Bruins' success in the 1950s was simply making the playoffs, a goal that four out of the six teams in the NHL would meet. By 1960, however, even that accomplishment would be beyond the reach of the talent-poor club. During the first seven seasons of the 1960s Boston finished in last place six times. Adams relieved Brown in 1964 and resumed control of the club. The fortunes of the Bruins would begin to change when 33-three-year-old Harry Sinden took over as coach for the 1966–67 season, although the seeds of what was to become another Stanley Cup championship team may have been planted as early as 1960. That was when Bruins' scouts first spotted a 5'2", 110-pound, 12-year old playing in an Ontario bantam tournament. His name was Bobby Orr, and he was destined to become one of the greatest players ever. The Bruins signed him to a contract to play for a Bruins junior team when he was 14, then signed him to a record-breaking NHL contract when he was 18.

Although the Bruins would again finish in last place for the 1966–67 season, Bobby Orr was named rookie of the year, and interest in the team was clearly on the rise. Average attendance was up almost 2,000 per game, and the games were sold out 18 times. The following season, when the NHL expanded from six to twelve teams, the Bruins would finish third in their division and make the playoffs for the first time in eight years, although they would be quickly eliminated by the Montreal Canadiens. Average attendance increased by another 800. The 1967–68 season also introduced what would become something of a New England tradition: WSBK TV 38 telecasts of Bruin games with Don Earle doing play-by-play commentary.

The Bruins finished second in their division in 1968–69 and won their opening-round series before again losing to Montreal. Every home game was sold out, and with good reason. Not only did Orr win his second consecutive Norris Trophy, awarded to the league's best defenseman, he set the record for points and goals in a season by a defenseman. Teammate Phil Esposito won the Ross Trophy as the league's leading scorer, becoming the first in NHL history to record 100 points. He also took the Hart Trophy as the league's most valuable player. The following season the Bruins would tie for the best record in the league and go on to win the franchise's first Stanley Cup since 1941. Although he had brought the cup to Boston after only four years of coaching the team, Sinden was denied a raise by Adams and resigned to accept a business opportunity outside of hockey.

With Tom Johnson as coach, the Bruins would enjoy a splendid regular 1970–71 season, outpacing the league in win and goals scored by a wide margin, only to be upset by the Canadiens in the playoffs. Determined to avenge themselves, the Bruins regained the cup the following season. The 1972–73 season would see the Bruins lose key players to a new rival league, The World Hockey Association (WHA), as well as to NHL expansion teams. As a result, the team would finish second in its division and lose in the opening round of the playoffs. In the meantime, Sinden, after his business venture went bankrupt, coached Canada to victory in the historic 1972 series against the Soviet Union. He was then brought back to the Bruins as general manager, a position he would hold for the next 28 seasons.

The Adams Family Relinquishes Control in 1975

In August 1973 the Boston Garden Arena Corporation merged with the Storer Broadcasting Corporation (owner of WSBK-TV), leaving Storer as the official owner of the team, although Weston Adams remained in charge. The team returned to the Stanley Cup finals in the spring of 1974, but was upset by the Philadelphia Flyers, the first of the expansion teams to win a championship. The 1974–75 season would see the Bruins again fall in the opening round of the playoffs. It would also be the last season the team would be under the control of the Adams family. In 1975 Sportsystems Corporation of Buffalo, New York, would purchase the Boston Garden and the Bruins from Storer Broadcasting for $10 million.

Sportsystems was the business created by three brothers: Charles, Marvin, and Louis Jacobs. As children they shined shoes, peddled newspapers, and sold popcorn in a Buffalo theater and sundries at a minor league baseball park. In 1926 they established Sportservice when they landed the concessions' contracts at minor league ballparks in Buffalo and Syracuse. By 1930 the brothers had gotten their first contract with a major league baseball park, Tiger Stadium in Detroit. In 1939 the brothers formed Sportsystems to run the horse and greyhound tracks that they had acquired. Over the years, Louis Jacobs also owned minor league baseball and minor league hockey teams. His son, Jeremy M. Jacobs, would own the Cincinnati Royals of the National Basketball Association in the 1960s. In 1968 he would become chairman and chief executive officer of Sportsystems, which would eventually be renamed Delaware North Companies Inc. Ten years after purchased the Bruins, direct ownership would pass to Jeremy Jacobs, who would continue to live in Buffalo while Sinden ran the franchise in Boston.

Although the Bruins would not win another Stanley Cup, and the Orr years ended abruptly (due to the defenseman's many crippling knee injuries), the team consistently made the playoffs for 29 years straight. The Bruins lost in the Stanley Cup finals in 1977, 1978, 1988, and 1990. Attendance, however, never matched the Orr years. The Garden, as beloved as it may have been by hardcore Bruins' fans, was far from the ideal venue for a hockey franchise. During the 1988 Stanley Cup finals a game had to be postponed because of a power failure in the building. Furthermore, as player salaries escalated in all professional sports, it was becoming imperative that franchises generate as many revenue streams as possible, especially hockey clubs, which did not command the same level of television money as the other major team sports. Premium seating, both luxury boxes and club seats, were becoming essential to a team's bottom line.

At a cost of $160 million, Jacobs and Delaware North Companies privately financed and built a new arena near the Garden for the Bruins, as well as the basketball team, the Celtics. The FleetCenter opened on September 30, 1995. Maximum capacity was 19,850 people, and the center had 4,000 premium seats and 104 luxury suites (ranging in price from $200,000 to $300,000 per season) and 2,500 club seats (ranging in price from $11,000 to $15,000 per season). Delaware North also provided food service, the sales of which contributed 25 percent of the FleetCenter's annual revenues.

Ironically, the team's success in building a new arena would coincide with the Bruins failure to make the playoffs for the first time in a generation. As management struggled to find new stars to lead the team and the right man to serve as coach, it continued to serve as a model of consistency for the league. Both Jacobs and Sinden remained highly respected and influential leaders of the NHL. In November 2000 Sinden turned over his general manager's position to long-time assistant Mike O'Connell, but remained the team's president. With Jacob's Delaware North as one of the top private companies in the world, there's every reason to expect that his Bruins in their new FleetCenter will eventually recapture the glory they knew in the Boston Garden.

Principal Competitors

Buffalo Sabres; Montreal Canadiens; Toronto Maple Leafs; Ottawa Senators.

Further Reading

Allen, Robin Lee, ''FleetCenter: New Arena Scores with Boston Garden Fans,'' *Nation's Restaurant News,* February 22, 1999, p. 3C.

Booth, Clark, *Boston Bruins: Celebrating 75 Years,* Del Mar, Calif.: Tehabi Books, 1998.

Diamond, Dan et al, *Total Hockey*, Kingston, N.Y.: Total Sports, 1998.

''Sinden Hands Over Bruins' GM Duties to O'Connell,'' *Sporting News,* November 1, 2000.

Vantour, Kevin, *Boston Bruins Book,* Toronto: ECW Press, 1997.

—Ed Dinger

Boyd Bros. Transportation Inc.

3275 Highway 30
Clayton, Alabama 36016
U.S.A.
Telephone: (334) 775-1400
Toll Free: (800) 338-2693
Fax: (334) 775-1432
Web site: http://www.boydbros.com

Public Company
Incorporated: 1956
Employees: 815
Sales: $126.7 million (2000)
Stock Exchanges: NASDAQ
Ticker Symbol: BOYD
NAIC: 484121 General Freight Trucking, Long-Distance,
   Truckload

Boyd Bros. Transportation Inc. is a flatbed trucking company headquartered in Clayton, Alabama. The firm operates in the eastern two-thirds of the country, where it maintains ten regional service centers. Its major terminals are in Clayton and Birmingham, Alabama; Greenville, Mississippi; and Springfield, Ohio; it also has six smaller, satellite service centers in Kentucky; Virginia; Maine; Arkansas; Maryland; and Wisconsin. These service centers permit the company to re-dispatch equipment terminating at one center to another point, recruit drivers, and help drivers get home on a more regular basis. Boyd's principal customers are high-volume, time-sensitive steel and building material shippers who require on-schedule deliveries. The company maintains a fleet of more than 1,100 tractors and 1,450 flatbed trailers. The trucks, equipped with two-way satellite systems and computers, are monitored constantly through the use of Qualcomm communications technology. Qualcomm's OmniTracs allows the company to record various data instantly and provide up-to-the-minute snap shots of a shipment's status, which it makes available to its customers via the Internet. Boyd's wholly-owned subsidiary, Welborn Transport Co., based in Tuscaloosa, Alabama, is a short-haul trucking company specializing in the transport of building

materials to delivery points within a 400-mile range. It maintains several locations in the Southeast, from which it dispatches over 350 company owned or driver owned and operated trucks. With the acquisition of Welborn in 1997, Boyd Bros. became one of the largest flatbed trucking companies in the nation. Although Boyd Bros. is a public entity, chairman and founder Dempsey Boyd still owns about 37 percent of the company. His daughter, Gail B. Cooper, is the firm's president and CEO.

1956–89: A Growing Family Business

In 1956, Dempsey Boyd and his brothers founded Boyd Bros. Transportation Inc. as a small, regional, family-owned flatbed-trucking operation. To a large extent, it would remain under the Boyd family control until the end of the century, despite going public. In 1972, Dempsey Boyd's daughter, Gail B. Cooper, joined the company and worked in various positions that gave her familiarity with all phases of the business. She would eventually become president and CEO of the company, with her father as chairman of the board.

Boyd's initial fleet consisted of three tractors. Its specialty was hauling flatbed, open trailers for customers who needed delivery on time. Most of the freight it hauled consisted of steel products and building materials. It slowly added trucks and regional centers, creating a network that by 1989 had extended its range of operations across the eastern two thirds of the United States. Throughout its development into the early 1990s, Boyd hired its drivers and provided both the tractors and trailers for them to use. That policy would later change.

During its early history, Boyd established its corporate headquarters and principal service center on a 17.9 acre tract in Clayton, Alabama. On this site, it built facilities consisting of some 22,000 square feet of office area, 12,000 square feet of equipment repair space, and three acres of parking area.

1990–96: Going Public and Facing Challenges

Starting in the 1990s, Boyd Bros. began adapting new technologies to its operations. By the end of 1990, the company had installed a Qualcomm provided satellite-based OmniTracs system in each of its tractors. Because it permitted on-the-road truckers and service center dispatchers to establish instantaneous communications, the system greatly improved both the efficiency and quality of the company's operations. It also allowed Boyd to provide customers with up-to-the minute information on the status and anticipated delivery time of their shipments.

Over the next couple of years, Boyd also installed Qualcomm's Sensortracs on-board computer systems in all its tractors. This equipment monitored various kinds of data and generated reports that helped Boyd assess the performance of both its vehicles, particularly their fuel efficiency, and their drivers. The data were also used to assess the effectiveness of the company's driver-training programs.

The company went public in 1994, at which time it boasted a $50 million fleet made up of about 400 tractors and 700 flatbeds domiciled at 12 terminals. The transition caused some adjustment problems. Although Boyd's revenue climbed to $59.1 million from $50.3 the year before, it reported a net loss of $2 million. The next year it fared better. It reduced its employees from 713 to 633, and it restored the profitability it had enjoyed in 1993, despite the fact that, in general, 1995 was a bad year for the trucking industry, which was plagued by a severe economic downswing that forced some companies into bankruptcy. At the end of its 1996 fiscal year, the company had revenues of $65.5 million ($4.5 million short of its projections) and 807 employees. Its net profit margin dropped from 3.4 percent in 1995 to 1.2 percent, with a net income of about $800,00, hence slipping again.

In 1996, in response to the company's faltering, Boyd Bros. began what its CFO Richard Bailey termed an "aggressive restructuring program." The move involved some layoffs and the resignation of Christopher Healy, the company's COO, with whom other executive officers had some "philosophical differences." Baily, who had joined the company as CFO in 1992 and had become a director in 1995, spearheaded the restructuring with the support and help of Gail B. Cooper, who had served as the company's secretary since the 1970s.

According to the company, the mid-decade operations downturn from 1994 to 1996 resulted from Boyd's overemphasis on technology and internal systems. Although this focus added personnel and programs, it led to a decline in productivity and growth. To get back on track, Boyd returned to its basic operation, concentrating on "sales, service, driver retention, and cost control." The move paid off, producing a significant upswing in 1997.

1997 and Beyond: Restructuring

Two major changes came in that same year. First, in June, Boyd started its owner-operator program. At that time it began contracting independent tractor owners to provide service for the company's customers. The program allowed such owner contractors having at least one year's experience to bring their own tractors to Boyd Bros. The company also initiated a lease-purchase program that gave its regular drivers the option of buying their own tractors through a lease-purchase arrangement with the company. Under the program's terms, drivers leased tractors from Boyd and, in turn, leased the use of tractors and their services back to Boyd. Because drivers would have the option of purchasing their leased tractors, Boyd's management believed the program would help reduce driver turnover and improve the company's chances of meeting its growth projections because it would attract additional contractors and safe, professional drivers.

Next, on December 8, 1997, Boyd acquired Welborn Transport, Inc. as an independently operating, wholly owned subsidiary. W. Miller Welborn had established Welborn in 1989 with co-founder Steven S. Rumsey. Its operational hub was Tuscaloosa, Alabama, where it was founded, but it dispatched its short-haul trucks from several southeastern locations. Like Boyd Bros., Welborn trucked building materials such as roofing and sheetrock, but only at an average hauling distance of under 400 miles. When acquired, at a cost of $6.63 million, Welborn had some 330 tractors and over 350 flatbed trailers, with annual sales of over $30 million. However, all but 50 of the tractors were owned by their operators, who were paid by Welborn on a revenue percentage basis. Also, over 50 percent of Welborn's loads were booked through agents rather than directly with their customers, whereas Boyd Bros. traditionally contracted directly with its customers. Still, Welborn's short-haul trucking provided a good complement to the longer trekking done by the Boyd Bros.' fleet of trucks.

The acquisition of Welborn led to further management changes. Initially, W. Miller Welborn joined Boyd Bros. as vice-president. He became acting CEO in July 1998, then CEO in 1998. Later, in 2000, he would become Boyd Bros.'s vice-chairman and vacate his posts as president and CEO, relinquishing these to Cooper.

At the end of 1997, Boyd Bros. had 54 owner-operators and contractors in its programs, but over the next two years that figure increased to 230. Its lease-purchase program permitted experienced drivers to enter the program without any down payment, taking between two-and-a-half and four years to buy the tractor that they drove for the company. Under the terms of their lease contracts, the drivers had the option to purchase the tractors at a fair market value or upgrade into a new tractor.

In 1998, as part of its growth strategy, Boyd Bros. announced plans to construct a $3 million "super terminal" in North Birmingham and began aggressively recruiting truck drivers by increasing pay for experienced drivers. The company

Key Dates:

1956: Company is founded by Dempsey Boyd and his brothers.

1989: W. Miller Welborn founds Welborn Transport.

1990: Boyd Bros. completes installation of OmniTracs system on all its trucks.

1994: Company goes public, trading on NASDAQ as BOYD.

1997: Boyd Bros. initiates owner-operated program and acquires Welborn Transport.

1998: W. Miller Welborn is named CEO.

2000: Company begins trading common stock on NASDAQ SmallCap Market; Gail B. Cooper becomes company president and CEO when Welborn becomes Boyd's vice-chairman.

also announced its intentions of acquiring Ruel Smith Transportation Services, Inc., a privately owned, Houston-based flatbed trucking company, and its affiliate, RSTS Logistics Corp., a marketer of freight brokerage services. Ruel Smith provided both short- and long-haul flatbed trucking services throughout North America, and in 1998 had a fleet of 150 tractors and 164 trailers. The company was profitable and would have immediately enhanced Boyd's earnings. However, in early 1999, the deal fell through when the two companies failed to reach "mutually acceptable terms."

In 1999, Boyd Bros. had record high revenue and earnings, despite a dropping off in the fourth quarter. Its revenue for the year climbed to $133 million, a rise of 13 percent over the previous year, even through in the fourth quarter its earnings per share fell off from 20 cents in the same quarter of 1998 to 12 cents in 1999. Boyd blamed the drop on increased fuel prices, which fluctuated considerably during 1999.

Outside of driver salaries and owner/operator costs, fuel had always been the Boyd Bros.'s greatest expense; thus, like all businesses heavily dependent on the petroleum industry, Boyd was to a large degree at the mercy of that industry's extremely volatile market. That dependency means that it was difficult to make reliable predictions. In 1998, with the newly purchased Wellborn factored into its calculations, one of the company's stated goals was to increase its total revenues to $200 million by 2001, an increase of $123 million over its revenues for 1997. It was an ambitious goal, one that proved too ambitious. In fact, although the company's revenues reached a record high in 1999, in 2000 they fell slightly, down to $126.7 million, and Boyd Bros. incurred a net loss of $1 million. An increased fuel cost was one of the major reasons for the company's slippage.

Boyd Bros. faced not only increased fuel costs but a weakening freight market in 2000, notably a decline in requests for steel shipments. This soft market condition, in addition to fuel costs, reduced the profits for Boyd's owner/operations, some of whom left the company and thereby reduced its fleet of available trucks, particularly at its Welborn division. In the fall of 1999, at its peak, Boyd Bros.' owner/operator programs had around 550 drivers, 270 of whom operated equipment leased from the company. By the end of the fourth quarter of 2000, the number had dropped to 130, a steep decline. The situation began to stabilize near the end of the year, however. Although encouraged by that, Boyd's CEO and president, Gail B. Cooper, cautioned that "challenging revenue and cost conditions will continue to pressure our earnings at least through the early part of 2001." In 2000, hoping to regain profitability over the long haul, the company implemented fuel surcharges and fuel efficiency programs designed to offset rising diesel fuel costs. Boyd Bros. also put in place a program to lower costs in non-driver related sectors. It remained to be seen whether these measures would prove effective in the first few years of the new century.

Principal Subsidiaries

Welborn Transport Co.

Principal Competitors

Heartland Express, Inc.; J.B. Hunt Transport Services, Inc.; Patriot Transportation Holding, Inc.; Schneider National, Inc.; Swift Transportation Co., Inc.; Transtar, Inc.

Further Reading

Bearth, Daniel P., "Boyd Moves Westward with Texas Acquisition," *Transport Topics—Trucking's Electronic Newspaper,* November 9, 1998.

"Boyd Bros. Names W. Miller Welborn President and Chief Executive Officer," *Business Wire,* February 22, 1999.

"Boyd Bros. Repurchases Shares; Company Terminates Ruel Smith Acquisition Negotiations," *Business Wire,* January 8, 1999.

"Boyd Bros. Signs Letter of Intent to Acquire Ruel Smith Transportation Services, Inc. and Its Logistics Affiliate," *Business Wire,* November 3, 1998.

"Boyd Bros. Transportation Announces Management Changes," *Business Wire,* February 17, 2000.

Milazzo, Don, "Boyd Brothers Planning $3M Super Terminals," *Birmingham Business Journal,* August 31, 1998, p. 1.

Schultz, John D., "Boyd Bros., Marten Transport Set Earnings, Revenue Marks in '98," *Traffic World,* February 15, 1999.

Wells, Garrison, "Boyd Bros. Transportation Inc. Undergoes Restructuring," *Knight-Ridder/Tribune Business News,* March 20, 1996.

—John W. Fiero

Bruce Foods Corporation

Bruce Foods Corporation

P.O. Drawer 1030
New Iberia, Louisiana 70562
U.S.A.
Telephone: (337) 365-8101
Toll Free: (800) 299-9082
Fax: (337) 365-5891
Web site: http://www.brucefoods.com

Private Company
Incorporated: 1928
Employees: 1,200
Sales: $187 million (1999 est.)
NAIC: 311421 Fruit and Vegetable Canning; 311422
Specialty Canning

Bruce Foods Corporation, headquartered in New Iberia, Louisiana, is one of the largest, privately-owned specialty food manufacturers in the United States. It or its forerunners have been canning yams (sweet potatoes) and manufacturing and distributing Cajun and Tex-Mex foods for over 70 years, starting long before either Cajun or Tex-Mex cuisines became popular outside Louisiana and Texas. The family company, owned by four generations of Browns, not Bruces, operates four domestic processing plants. These are located in New Iberia and Lozes, Louisiana; El Paso, Texas; and Wilson, North Carolina. In addition, Bruce has an affiliate plant at Kerkrade in The Netherlands. The company currently manufactures over 550 individual products under nine brand names, including Casa Fiesta Mexican Food, "The Original" Louisiana Hot Sauce, Louisiana Gold Pepper Sauce, Cajun King Seasonings and Sauce Mixes, Bruce's Yams, Munch King Canister Snacks, Magic Garden Seasonings, Gravy Gourmet, and Green's of New Orleans Creole Soups. Bruce's products are distributed throughout the United States and in over 100 other countries, and they are carried by most of the major supermarket and grocery chains in its geographical markets both at home and abroad. Altogether, its exports account for about 30 percent of its sales. Over the last two decades, Bruce Foods' successful

growth strategies have earned the company several marketing and exporting awards. However, its primary markets are still in this country, where Bruce products are very widely sold, including, for example, Louisiana Hot Sauce, which can be found in 75 percent of America's supermarkets and, in six-ounce bottles, outsells McIlhenny's two-ounce bottles of Tabasco sauce. Although some of the Browns no longer live in Louisiana, the family has always been proud of its Louisiana heritage and has supported it both at home and abroad.

1928–54: Two Upstarts Combine to Form Bruce Foods

Although its name suggests that Bruce Foods should have some connection to a man or family named "Bruce," the connection has been obscured by time. The company started out in 1928 in New Iberia, Louisiana, as a manufacturer of a single product—a hot pepper sauce. Coincidentally, it was also in that year that J.S. Brown, Sr., formed a company named J.S. Brown and Son Food Brokers, also in New Iberia. Brown was originally a wholesale grocer in that small city, but when forming his new company he became what was then called a "factor," a middleman or buying broker. In those days there was an extra distribution layer in the food industry. Up through the 1940s, factors bought food products from farmers and producers and sold them to regional distributors, who in turn sold them to retail stores. Early on in its history, the company's products were still transported by horse-drawn wagons and paddle-wheel steamers on the Bayou Teche, limiting the range of its business to about a 150-mile radius of New Iberia.

Brown was also the scion in four generations of Browns, the family that has owned Bruce Foods since 1954. His son, J.S. Brown, Jr., entered the business with his father, and together they saw their company both grow and prosper. Among other things, when Louisiana roads improved, the company was able to move goods greater distances. It also expanded its operations. By the 1940s, it maintained a small fleet of trucks and, in addition to its warehouses and offices in New Iberia, it had warehouses in New Orleans, Shreveport, and Jackson, Mississippi. Its markets took in all of Louisiana, eastern Texas, southern Mississippi, and southern Arkansas.

Company Perspectives:

To get anything fresher, you would have to grow it yourself. Our vegetable products, dips, sauces and salsas are prepared and packaged less than 24 hours after the produce leaves the fields. That's the kind of quality you can always expect from Bruce Foods. Our products also boast all-natural ingredients and no preservatives—just as they have since 1928.

J.S. Brown, Jr.'s three sons—Gordon, Norman, and Si (J.S. Brown III)—all joined the company in the 1950s after attending Tulane University and completing military service. They were thus in a position to help their father take the family business in a new direction, necessitated by the fact that large grocery chains were quickly driving both factors and regional food distributors out of business. Accordingly, in 1954, the year that Gordon joined the company, the family made a major investment, buying out Bruce Foods. At the time, Bruce was still primarily a hot sauce producer and bottler, but it had branched out a little, making a few other pepper products as well as a gumbo filé. It was run by J.E. Broussard, a neighbor and friend to J.S. Brown, Sr. Broussard was also a business associate of J.S. Brown and Son, which for years had been brokering Bruce Foods' products. Significantly, the company had begun exporting its specialty foods as early as 1947, an important step for the future of Bruce Foods under the control of the Browns.

1955–80: Development of a Varied Product Line

Having purchased Bruce Foods, and extended the name of that company to include all of their holdings, the Browns quickly sought both to expand and diversify the company through further acquisitions and new product development, strictly within the food processing market. It added canned sweet potatoes and okra to its line when, in 1957, it purchased L.C. Soileau and Son Inc., which operated a canning plant at Lozes, Louisiana, specializing in Southern vegetables.

Wanting to extend the product range of Bruce Foods further, the Browns also bought the rights to other companies' brands. Included were Louisiana Brand Hot Sauce, acquired from a Shreveport company, and the Mexene (Tex Mex) brand line bought from Riviana Foods, a major rice producing company located in Houston. However, it was not until 1972 that Bruce acquired a third plant, one a good distance from its home territory, in the Acadiana region of south-central Louisiana. In that year the Browns bought a potato and sweet potato cannery located in Wilson, North Carolina. The seller was Lance Inc., a manufacturer of crackers and other snacks, which was then divesting itself of some of its diverse interests. The purchase worked out very well for Bruce Foods, which eventually became the nation's largest processor of canned yams.

Although the Mexene brand products had earlier eased Bruce Foods into the Tex-Mex food line, it was not until 1980 that the company jumped into that speciality whole-heartedly. In that year it bought the extensive line of Ashley Mexican Food products and that company's plant in El Paso, Texas, near the Mexican border. Ashley, which had been in business since 1931, had begun producing Mexican foods long before they became widely popular outside Mexico. The business had actually started out as a Mexican restaurant, then evolved into the first company in the United States to can what are now standard Mexican food staples sold north of the U.S.-Mexico border. At the time Bruce Foods made the acquisition, Ashley was owned by the Holly Sugar Corporation of Denver. The Browns were not really looking to enter the Mexican food business at the time—they simply wanted more acreage and another plant for their pepper business—but Holly Sugar was anxious to divest itself of a company that did not readily fit into its business portfolio and made the Browns a deal too good to turn down.

Because Mexican food was just starting a rapid climb in popularity, the timing of the purchase was very fortuitous. Using the brand name "Casa Fiesta," Bruce hoped to help the popularization process, just as it had been doing for its Cajun foods. In fact, the plan worked well. Casa Fiesta branded foods eventually became the company's top selling product line. Casa Fiesta also became the number one brand of Mexican food sold in Europe and by the century's end was beginning to make strong market inroads elsewhere abroad.

1981–90: Sustained Growth Both at Home and Abroad

In the 1980s, Bruce Foods responded to the fluctuating value of the U.S. dollar, rigorous packaging requirements, and tariff barriers abroad by modifying its products to better adapt to new markets while strengthening its presence in its existing markets. When the dollar was strong, it was the company's policy to subsidize prices to get a foothold in new markets, in some places all but giving foods away at cost in order to give foreign customers a chance to acquire a lasting taste for them. It was a strategy that worked well, helping stabilize prices and even increase sales when the dollar weakened.

Its marketing strategies also won Bruce Foods some significant awards. In 1986 the company won a Clio Award for innovative package design as well as the Intermediate Product Award at the Sial Exhibition in Paris. These awards resulted from Bruce's ongoing efforts to develop new products and attractive packaging tailored to individual markets, a concerted plan in which the company had invested millions. As part of its program, Bruce Foods exhibited products in various U.S. pavilions at trade shows in West Germany, France, and Japan.

At about the same time, Bruce Foods took some more innovative steps that revealed its ongoing willingness to adapt to changing technologies. The effort had started early in the 1970s, when the New Iberia pant became the first cannery in the country to use computerized equipment to control its food processing. Later, in 1986, in a joint venture involving the University of Texas at El Paso, the Bureau of Reclamation (an agency of the Department of the Interior), and El Paso Electric Corporation, the company began using the country's first solar pond to produce both pure water and electricity for its El Paso plant. The heavily salinated .83-acre solar pond produced heat from the sun's rays then used it to operate a turbine capable of generating 100 kilowatts of electricity, enough to save the plant about 20 percent of its energy costs.

Key Dates:

1928: Two New Iberia, Louisiana, business are started: Bruce Foods and J.S. Brown and Son Food Brokers.
1931: The Ashley Mexican Food Plant is founded in El Paso, Texas.
1947: Bruce Foods begins exporting its hot sauce.
1954: J.S. Brown, Jr., and his sons acquire Bruce Foods.
1957: Bruce buys its second Louisiana plant from L.C. Soileau and Sons, Inc.
1972: The company buys a North Carolina potato and sweet potato processing plant from Lance Inc.
1980: Company purchases Ashley Mexican Foods.
1990: Bruce Foods earns ''E Star'' Award presented by President Bush and opens its affiliate plant at Kerkrade in The Netherlands.
1997: Chairman Gordon Sandoz Brown dies.

In 1987, because of its programs promoting American products abroad, President Ronald Reagan granted Bruce Foods the prestigious ''E'' Award, a special honor given to select U.S. exporters. In the next year, Bruce Food's president, J.S. (''Si'') Brown III, traveled to Moscow to visit the Soviet World Trade Center, where, in conjunction with Louisiana chef John Folse, Bruce Foods opened a temporary Cajun restaurant called ''Lafitte's Landing East.'' By design, it was only open two weeks for a trade show, but it drew big crowds and enthusiastic reviews. Moreover, Bruce Foods entered an agreement with a Moscow restaurant organization and a West German company to supply the first Mexican food restaurant in Moscow.

Its imaginative and energetic overseas marketing earned additional awards for Bruce Foods. In 1989, it garnered a National Association of Marketing Officials Award for outstanding marketing, and in May 1990 the company was awarded the ''E Star'' Award by President George Bush. Importantly, in the three-year interval between receiving its two ''E'' Awards, the company doubled its exports. By 1990, it was employing 800 workers worldwide, including 85 at its headquarters in New Iberia. In addition to its four U.S. plants, it was completing an ''affiliate'' factory at Kerkrade in the Netherlands, where laws prohibited its outright ownership of the plant. It was selling products on all continents, shipping various items to over 65 countries. One of its customers was the Pope, who liked the company's Cajun gumbo so much that every month Bruce Foods packed up and air-freighted him two frozen gallons of the irresistible, first-you-make-a-roux concoction.

1991 and Beyond: Reflecting the Health-Conscious Era

Throughout the 1990s, Bruce foods reflected the era's focus on health, product quality, and ''alternative foods.'' For example, it took pride in the fact that all of its vegetable products, sauces, salsas, and dips were prepared within 24-hours after their ingredients were harvested, and were packaged with no artificial ingredients. That the National Council of Nutrition named the yam or sweet potato the number one vegetable for health and nutrition gave Bruce Foods a great boost. It was, after all, the nation's leading canner of yams. The company also developed a line of other sweet potato products, including pancake, muffin, and biscuit mixes, all packaged with the Heart Healthy symbol authorized by the American Heart Association.

On May 1, 1997, Gordon Sandoz Brown, company chairman, died. He and his brother, Si Brown, had been the firm's chief executives since the death of their father, J.S. Brown, Jr. In fact, all three sons of J.S. Brown, Jr., had served on a rotating basis as company CEO and president.

Bruce Foods diligently continued to develop its export trade through the 1990s, even during the 1997–99 Asian financial crisis, when most companies watched their export trade falter. Bruce actually increased its foreign market share in those years. According to Si Brown, the company ''had a wonderful 1999.'' Its nets sales had risen in each of the previous three years, and Bruce Foods had become one of the top 100 exporting companies in the United States. Prospects for the new century looked even better.

Principal Competitors

Authentic Specialty Foods, Inc.; B&G Foods, Inc., McIlhenny Farms; Trappey.

Further Reading

''E Award Winning Exporters Bruce Foods Corp.,'' *Journal of Commerce*, September 28, 1990, Foreign Trade Sec., p. 5A.
''Hotter Than Hot Sauce,'' *New Orleans Magazine*, November 1992, p. 70.
Johnson, William, ''Bruce Foods: The Yam What They Yam,'' *Acadiana @ Work*, March 2000, p. 16.
Robinson, Duncan, ''Exporter Invests in Future,'' *Journal of Commerce and Commercial*, September 28, 1990, p. 1A.
——, ''US Exporter Redesigns Label after Losing Lengthy Battle,'' *Journal of Commerce and Commercial*, May 14, 1991, p. 3A.
''Texas Solar Pond Is First in US,'' *Journal of Commerce*, October 17, 1986, p. 7A.

—John W. Fiero

C.H. Boehringer Sohn

Binger Strasse 173
D-55216 Ingelheim
Germany
Telephone: (49) (6132) 77-0
Fax: (49) (6132) 77-3000
Web site: http://www.boehringer-ingelheim.com

Private Company
Incorporated: 1885 as Albert Boehringer, Chemische
    Fabrik, Nieder-Ingelheim a. Rhein
Employees: 26,448
Sales: DM 9.94 billion ($5.07 billion) (1999)
NAIC: 551112 Offices of Other Holding Companies;
    325412 Pharmaceutical Preparation Manufacturing

C.H. Boehringer Sohn is the holding company for Boehringer Ingelheim GmbH, which is among the top 20 international research-based pharmaceuticals manufacturers. The company offers prescription drugs for diseases of the human respiratory, cardiovascular, gastrointestinal, and central nervous systems, cancer, and HIV treatments. Boehringer Ingelheim also makes over-the-counter drugs, veterinary vaccines and antibiotics, and bulk pharmaceutical chemicals. Based in Germany, the group consists of about 140 companies all over the world, including 40 R&D and production facilities in 20 countries. A total of 86 percent of Boehringer Ingelheim's sales comes from abroad. The firm is owned by the Boehringer and von Baumbach families.

Beginnings in the Early 19th Century

It was 1817 when German entrepreneurs Christian Friedrich Boehringer and Christian Gotthold Engelmann set up a chemicals trade and production business in the German city of Stuttgart. They renamed the materials trading company B.F. Balzische Material-Waren-Handlung, which they had bought from relatives, Engelmann & Boehringer and started trading chemicals such as quinine, morphine, and tartaric acid. Engelmann & Boehringer's own chemical products were ether, santonin, and chloroform. After 42 years Engelmann retired as

business partner, leaving Christian Friedrich Boehringer and his two sons Christian Gottfried and Christoph Heinrich as the owners of the firm. Renamed C.F. Boehringer & Söhne, the company employed 15 people in 1859. By 1871 Christoph Heinrich Boehringer was the only surviving member of the three family partners and became sole proprietor of the firm, which moved to Mannheim a year later. When Christoph Heinrich Boehringer died in 1882, his eldest son Ernst took over the company. Ernst Boehringer's younger brother Albert studied chemistry in Munich after an apprenticeship at a Mannheim pharmacy. Inspired by his older brother, Albert acquired a small chemical plant in Lower Ingelheim on the Rhine in summer 1885. On July 31 that facility was officially registered in Bingen as Albert Boehringer, Chemische Fabrik, Nieder-Ingelheim a. Rhein (Chemical Factory, Lower Ingelheim on the Rhine). Boehringer Ingelheim was born.

Starting out with 28 employees, Boehringer Ingelheim produced tartaric acid and salts made using it. The demand for tartaric acid was rising, a result of the invention of baking powder and lemon soda. Taking advantage of this development, Boehringer Ingelheim started making better quality tartaric acid that could be used in the food processing industry. Struggling with high production costs and the growing competition, however, the 1880s were tough years for Boehringer Ingelheim. When Albert Boehringer's brother Ernst died in 1892, the family of his business partner Friedrich Engelhorn became the owner of C.F. Boehringer & Söhne in Mannheim. Albert Boehringer changed the name of his company to C.H. Boehringer Sohn, Chemische Fabrik, Nieder-Ingelheim a. Rhein (Chemical Factory, Lower Ingelheim on the Rhine). To avoid confusion between the two names, the parties agreed to include the locations Mannheim and Ingelheim in the company names.

In the early 1890s Alfred Boehringer started experimenting with citric acid. Rather by accident Boehringer Ingelheim invented a technology for the production of technical grade lactic acid when a fermentation batch for citric acid heated up too quickly and lactic acid bacteria formed in the nutritive solution. Boehringer Ingelheim began mass producing lactic acid with the new technology while further experiments with citric acid were put on the back burner. At the same time, a market had to

Company Perspectives:

Boehringer Ingelheim's corporate vision is founded on five key principles; statements which together form a shared ambition and worldwide commitment. Change is our opportunity: *Without change there can be no progress.* Value will be our competitive advantage: *In a competitive world, we expect our customers constantly to demand more for less.* Innovation in everything will be our challenge: *We will only deliver outstanding value to our customers if we are innovative in everything we do.* Waste is our enemy: *We need to have one of the lowest cost bases in the industry, if we are to deliver outstanding value to our customers.* Our distinctive character is our strength: *We are worldwide and measure ourselves against world class standards. Yet we are also a corporation with family traditions in which people are valued as individuals. Collectively, the principles add up to Value through Innovation, the vision which strengthens Boehringer Ingelheim's business worldwide and keeps it more competitive.*

be developed for the new product, which at the time was practically nonexistent. By 1905, however, the demand was so high that a new production plant was erected. Boehringer Ingelheim's technical grade lactic acid was used for dying leather and textiles while food quality lactic acid was in demand by the food and beverage industries. One example was Chabesco, a refreshing drink that had lactic acid among its ingredients.

Adding Pharmaceuticals in the Early 20th Century

Around 1900 Boehringer Ingelheim expanded its business and started producing basic substances used by pharmacies and in the pharmaceutical industry, such as morphine, codeine, and, later, atropine. It was also in the first years of the 20th century when Albert Boehringer introduced a number of social programs for his staff. Health insurance was introduced in 1902. Apartments for Boehringer Ingelheim employees were built between 1907 and 1909 and a workers compensation program was initiated. Beginning in 1910 the company granted every employee who had worked a specific length of time up to 14 paid annual vacation days and a travel allowance. To make sure that the workers really went on vacation, Albert Boehringer—who knew every employee—insisted that they send him a postcard from their holiday destination. By 1910 the company had acquired a reputation in the region and employed 157 people.

In the second decade of he 20th century Boehringer Ingelheim intensified its activities in the growing market for pharmaceuticals. In 1912 the company started testing a painkiller based on several opium alkaloids. Three years later the drug was introduced to the market under the name Laudanon. Picking up the latest industry trend Boehringer Ingelheim offered the drug pre-packaged and pre-dosed in various forms such as tablets, ampoules, syrup, solution, or powder. Although the product was packaged in Ingelheim, the drug was pressed into tablets and filled into ampoules in another company in Frankfurt/Main. Laudanon was a failure on the market. The specialties working group that had been created to develop the

drug, however, became the foundation for Boehringer Ingelheim's pharmaceutical product division.

When World War I broke out in 1914 Albert Boehringer was required to manage a medical company for the German war economy. His nephew Robert Boehringer successfully managed Boehringer Ingelheim during the war years. It was during this time, in 1915, that the company's research division was started, growing out of Robert Boehringer's cooperation with two cousins of Albert Boehringer: chemistry professor Heinrich Wieland, who in 1927 would receive the Nobel Prize for Chemistry, and pharmacology professor Hermann Wieland. One of the first results of Heinrich Wieland's research was Boehringer Ingelheim's production of bile acid, which started in 1917. In the following years two products were developed based on bile acid—Cadechol and Perichol. The two remedies, which were used to fight chronic cardiovascular damage and angina pectoris, were introduced in the early 1920s. They were followed by the respiratory analeptic Lobelin, which became a huge medical success. Its active ingredient, an alkaloid, was first extracted from the plant lobelia inflata and later chemically synthesized, based on research by Heinrich Wieland.

The 1920s turned out to be difficult for Boehringer Ingelheim. While the German economy was being shaken by the post-World War I hyperinflation, the company issued its own emergency currency. When France occupied the Rhineland in 1923, Albert Boehringer decided to leave Ingelheim and move to Hamburg to set up a second company location. In 1924 the Pharmaceutical Specialties group was moved to Hamburg and a year later production of opiates started in a brand new plant.

World War II and the Postwar Years

The economic downturn at the beginning of the 1930s coincided with a generation change in Boehringer Ingelheim's top management. The founder's two sons—Albert and Ernst—together with the founder's son-in-law Julius Liebrecht, who had entered the company management in the 1920s, took over new responsibilities. Albert Boehringer, who had studied business administration, was given responsibility for the Alkaloid Department, Pharmaceutical Chemicals, and Purchasing. His brother Ernst, a chemist, focused on pharmaceutical specialties, and Liebrecht managed the Acid Department. The three worked together very well and were able to steer the company successfully through the rough waters before and after World War II. Company founder Albert Boehringer died in spring 1939, just a few months before World War II broke out.

The continuing work in the field of pharmaceutical specialties yielded positive results during this period of time, however. To stabilize sales the company started building a brand name by adding "Ingelheim" to all of its pharmaceutical products, such as codeine, caffeine, and theobromine. Packaged in a ready-to-use form such as tablets and ampoules, they became known as the "Ingelheim packs." Boehringer Ingelheim also developed successful brand name drugs, such as the two cough remedies, Codyl Syrup and Acedicon, and the cardiovascular symphathomimetic sympatol. The biggest success was Aludrin, a drug used in bronchial asthma and spastic bronchitis, which was introduced to the market in 1941. One year later Boehringer Ingelheim started making synthetic caffeine using a technology

Key Dates:

1885: Albert Boehringer's company is officially registered.
1900: Boehringer Ingelheim starts making basic chemicals for pharmaceuticals.
1923: Albert Boehringer leaves the occupied Rhineland and sets up shop in Hamburg.
1927: Albert Boehringer acquires Winnenden-based Dr. Karl Thomae GmbH.
1935: A technology for mass producing citric acid based on fermentation with fungi is developed.
1941: Asthma remedy Aludrin is successfully introduced to the market.
1946: Thomae introduces the analgesic Thomapyrin.
1950s: The company's international expansion starts in Europe.
1970: Boehringer Ingelheim's first subsidiary in the United States is founded.
1991: CEO Hubertus Liebrecht dies.
1992: Erich von Baumbach, son-in-law of Albert Boehringer, Jr., becomes CEO.
1998: A new organizational structure is established.
1999: Ben Venue Laboratories in Bedford, Ohio is acquired.

that was developed by company chemists in the 1930s. This made the company independent from imported ingredients for natural caffeine production. In March 1945 Ingelheim was occupied by American troops. Undamaged by the war, however, the company resumed production in May after being forced to close down for two months. To secure the necessary raw materials in those difficult times, a so-called procurement department was established; sometimes bartering baking powder, citric acid, or Ingelheim wine was the only way to obtain the necessary raw materials. After five years of negotiations and petitions, the company finally received a letter in June 1949, confirming that Boehringer Ingelheim had been removed from the list of companies included in war reparations and hence would not be dismantled.

Aside from setting up the old production lines again, the company continued to successfully develop and market new pharmaceutical specialties in the postwar years. The number of employees in the Pharmaceutical Specialties Department grew fivefold from 23 in early 1946 to 125 in 1953. As a result, pharmaceutical sales grew in the following years, from DM 11.6 million in 1950 to DM 23.3 million five years later. In the early 1950s Boehringer Ingelheim started marketing the pharmaceutical products of the American drug maker Chas. Pfizer & Co. in Germany, in particular their new antibiotics Terramycin, Streptomycin, and Tetrazyn. The two companies worked together until the early 1960s when Pfizer established its own German subsidiary. For a short period Boehringer Ingelheim also distributed insulin products from a Danish drug maker after the war. Another venture the company began in those years was its subsidiary Dr. Karl Thomae GmbH in Winnenden, a company with a considerable market share in the market for opiates. It was acquired by Albert Boehringer from chemist Dr. Karl

Thomae in 1927. In 1946 Thomae introduced several special drugs, including the successful analgesic Thomapyrin. Three years later Thomae started producing and distributing pharmaceutical specialties for Swiss drug maker J.R. Geigy. The new activity, which resulted from a close friendship of Geigy manager Dr. Karl Koechlin and the top managers from Boehringer Ingelheim, gave Thomae's business a huge boost.

Building an International Network in the 1960s and 1970s

As early as in the 1930s Boehringer Ingelheim had exported their pharmaceutical specialties to a number of foreign countries, primarily in Europe. Foreign markets did not play an important role for the company after World War II, however, until after the currency reform in Germany in 1948. The first foreign subsidiary that represented a wide range of Boehringer Ingelheim products, the Bender & Co. GesmbH in Vienna, Austria, was established in the 1950s. Bender also expanded business into Eastern Europe and was responsible for Boehringer Ingelheim's pharmaceutical business in Switzerland. In the late 1950s Boehringer Ingelheim established a subsidiary, a research lab, and production plant and bought a plantation in Spain.

During the 1960s and 1970s Boehringer Ingelheim wove together a network of international subsidiaries that spanned the whole world. The company's international expansion always followed the same pattern. First, Boehringer Ingelheim products were marketed by another pharmaceutical company or their agent in a particular country. Next, a company subsidiary was established that mainly channeled scientific information to doctors and hospitals about Boehringer Ingelheim products. When sales reached a certain level, a production plant was set up. Countries where Boehringer Ingelheim established subsidiaries included Portugal, Italy, France, the United Kingdom, Belgium, The Netherlands, Sweden, Denmark, and Greece in Western Europe; Argentina, Brazil, and Columbia in Latin America; Japan, Korea, Taiwan, Philippines, Indonesia, and Thailand in Asia; South Africa, Senegal, and Kenya in Africa; as well as in Australia and New Zealand.

The cooperation with American drug maker Chas. Pfizer & Co. after World War II had provided Boehringer Ingelheim with valuable know-how about American business practice. In the 1950s the two companies worked together in other countries. In the United States Boehringer Ingelheim products were distributed for a long time by Geigy's American branch. In 1970 Boehringer Ingelheim Ltd. was established in the state of New York and later moved to Ridgefield, Connecticut, where the construction of a research center began in the mid-1970s. A Canadian subsidiary was established in Montreal, Québec in 1973 and moved to Burlington, Ontario, in 1978.

Boehringer Ingelheim in the 1980s and 1990s

At the beginning of the 1980s Boehringer Ingelheim had evolved as a research-driven developer and producer, with a worldwide reputation, primarily of prescription drugs for humans. By the end of 1983 Boehringer Ingelheim held 870 patents. This was the result of a systematic investment in research and development activities over several decades. In

1963 the company invested DM 20 million in R&D; 20 years later the number had risen 25-fold to DM 500 million. The number of R&D staff tripled within about the same period of time, from 1,000 in 1963 to more than 3,000 in 1985. About one third of them worked at Boehringer Ingelheim's subsidiary Dr. Karl Thomae GmbH in Biberach, and the others worked in the company's research centers in Vienna, Austria; Kawanishi, Japan; Milan, Italy; and Ridgefield in the United States. Pharmaceutical research concentrated on treatments for cardiovascular, respiratory, and gastroenterological ailments. Some of Boehringer Ingelheim's successful products were Persantin, a coronary therapeutic agent used to prevent the development of thrombosis; Viramune, a drug to fight AIDs; and Sifrol, for the treatment of Parkinson's disease.

Aside from these activities, research was done over the years in other fields such as veterinary pharmaceuticals, baking aids, cosmetics, and pesticides. None of these areas became a major business activity for Boehringer Ingelheim, however, when compared with human pharmaceuticals. As a result, the company withdrew from most of those sectors in the 1980s and 1990s. Its pesticide plant in Hamburg-Moorfleet was closed down after government officials required the installation of environmentally friendlier waste disposal technologies, which would have called for substantial investment. In addition, after a boom in the 1970s and early 1980s the company's sales share from chemical production fell continuously in the 1990s. The production of citric acid was dropped completely in the early 1980s. In 1991, 9.6 percent of Boehringer Ingelheim's total sales derived from chemicals. Half of the company's ten production facilities for chemicals worldwide were closed down in the 1990s. In 1999 Boehringer Ingelheim transferred its marketing activities to the food, cosmetics, and chemical industries to Purac Deutschland GmbH, a subsidiary of Dutch Purac Biochem bv, the world's largest producer of lactic acid.

Another strategic decision for the company was to focus intensively on the world's largest market for drugs—the United States. In part due to more restrictive laws in Boehringer Ingelheim's home country, Germany became the company's third largest market for pharmaceuticals, behind the United States and Japan. Cooperative ventures were begun with La Jolla, California-based Sequana Therapeutics Inc. in genetic asthma research; with Carlsbad, California-based Isis Pharmaceuticals Inc. to develop agents used to treat organ transplant complications; with the two New York-based cancer research institutes Ludwig Institute for Cancer Research and Sloan-Kettering Institute on the development of new drugs against cancer; with Cambridge, Massachusetts-based Cambridge Neuroscience on a drug to treat stroke and brain injuries; and with Genetronics Biomedical Ltd. in San Diego, California, in certain areas of gene therapy. In 1999 Boehringer Ingelheim also acquired Ben Venue Laboratories, based in Bedford, Ohio, which was America's oldest producer of sterile pharmaceutical goods.

The company's new strategic orientation, with focus on prescription and nonprescription drugs for humans and the United States as a strategic market, was accompanied by changes in the organizational structure of Boehringer Ingelheim. Research activities in Germany were concentrated at Thomae in Biberach, and production was carried out primarily in Ingelheim. The company decided to concentrate its European pharmaceutical production in Spain and purchased a large property in Sant Gugat del Valles near Barcelona.

In 1998 Boehringer Ingelheim introduced a new organizational structure. Boehringer Ingelheim KG and Dr. Karl Thomae GmbH were organized under the umbrella of Boehringer Ingelheim Pharma KG. Owned by the third and fourth generation of the Boehringer family, the company announced in the late 1990s that, despite merger-mania, it was not interested in a merger with another big player in the field. Instead, Boehringer Ingelheim intended to continue cooperating on distribution with other pharmaceutical companies, as was already done with leading drug makers such as Glaxo Welcome and Abbott Laboratories.

Principal Subsidiaries

Boehringer Ingelheim GmbH (Germany); Boehringer Ingelheim International GmbH (Germany); Boehringer Ingelheim Pharma KG (Germany); Boehringer Ingelheim Vetmedica GmbH (Germany); Delta-Pharma GmbH (Germany); Pharmaton GmbH (Germany); Pharma Investment Ltd. Toronto (Canada); Boehringer Ingelheim Corp.; Boehringer Ingelheim Pharmaceuticals Inc.; Roxanne Laboratories Inc.; Ben Venue Laboratories Inc.; Boehringer Ingelheim Chemicals Inc.

Principal Competitors

Aventis; Bayer AG; Merck & Co., Inc.

Further Reading

"Boehringer Ingelheim arbeitet mit Sequana," *Frankfurter Allgemeine Zeitung,* June 20, 1995, p. 22.

"Boehringer Ingelheim kauft Ben Venue Labs," *Frankfurter Allgemeine Zeitung,* November 3, 1997, p. 28.

"Boehringer Ingelheim kauft zu," *Frankfurter Allgemeine Zeitung,* August 24, 1996, p. 16.

"Boehringer Ingelheim schafft Pharma KG," *Frankfurter Allgemeine Zeitung,* December 18, 1997, p. 19.

"Boehringer Ingelheim und Isis," *Frankfurter Allgemeine Zeitung,* July 20, 1995, p. 14.

"Boehringer verlegt Produktion nach Spanien," *Frankfurter Allgemeine Zeitung,* September 8, 1995, p. 29.

"Das Auslandsgeschäft wird für Boehringer Ingelheim immer wichtiger," *Frankfurter Allgemeine Zeitung,* May 20, 1994, p. 20.

"Genetronics und Boehringer Ingelh. mit Genforschungs-Kooperation," *vwd,* November 8, 1999.

"Kooperation Boehringer und Purac Biochem auf neuer Basis," *vwd,* June 1, 1999.

100 Years Boehringer Ingelheim 1885–1985, Ingelheim am Rhein, Germany: Boehringer Ingelheim Zentrale GmbH, 1985.

"Umstrittenes Konzept bei Boehringer Ingelheim," *Frankfurter Allgemeine Zeitung,* December 23, 1993, p. 16.

—Evelyn Hauser

Centennial Communications Corporation

3349 Route 138
Wall Township, New Jersey 07719
U.S.A.
Telephone: (732) 556-2200
Fax: (732) 556-2242
Web site: http://www.centennialcom.com

Public Company
Incorporated: 1988 as Centennial Cellular Corporation
Employees: 2,200
Sales: $501.3 million (2000)
Stock Exchanges: NASDAQ
Ticker Symbol: CYCL
NAIC: 513310 Wired Telecommunications Carriers;
    513322 Cellular and Other Wireless
    Telecommunications

In the United States, Centennial Communications Corporation owns and operates cellular systems in two regional clusters that cover six states, three in the Midwest (Michigan, Indiana, Ohio), and three in the South (Texas, Louisiana, Mississippi). It provides mobile wireless communications primarily to small city and rural markets that are next to major metropolitan markets. By focusing on those types of markets, Centennial has become an attractive roaming partner to the larger regional and nationwide wireless operators. Centennial's Caribbean operations are centered in Puerto Rico, where the company provides wireless personal communications services (PCS), as well as wired services over its own fiber-optic and microwave network. As of June 2000, Centennial was the largest all-digital wireless carrier in Puerto Rico, with 181,500 wireless subscribers. In addition, Centennial is the only significant fiber-based competitive local exchange carrier (CLEC) in Puerto Rico and owns its own communications network there with more than 16,000 switched access lines and some 32,000 equivalent lines of dedicated circuits. Its Puerto Rican wireline business offers a broad range of telephone services to commercial, Internet service provider (ISP), carrier, and government customers over its fiber-optic network. Centennial expanded its Caribbean pres-

ence in 2000 with the introduction of wireless services in the Dominican Republic. The company also planned to build a wireless network in Jamaica in 2001. Centennial's controlling stockholders are the investment firm of Welsh, Carson, Anderson & Stowe and an affiliate of The Blackstone Group.

Regional Wireless Services Provider, 1988–97

The company was founded in 1988 as Centennial Cellular Corp. and was originally based in New Canaan, Connecticut. The company grew rapidly and offered wireless personal communications services (PCS) in Indiana, Michigan, Ohio, Louisiana, Texas, Mississippi, Arizona, and California. Its strategy was to obtain cellular licenses in small cities and rural areas that bordered on major metropolitan areas. These less densely populated areas would not attract the investment necessary to build extensive new PCS networks—thus reducing potential competition—while at the same time making Centennial an attractive roaming partner for PCS providers in the nearby major cities.

In the Midwest, the company's cluster in Indiana, Michigan, and Ohio covered portions of three major interstate highways that connected Chicago, Detroit, and Indianapolis. In the South, the company's East Texas and Louisiana cluster covers portions of interstate highway I-10, as well as areas adjacent to Houston, New Orleans, Shreveport, and Baton Rouge. Centennial's Southwest cluster covered Yuma, Arizona, and El Centro, California, and was bordered by Los Angeles to the northwest, San Diego to the west, Phoenix to the east, and Mexicali, Mexico, to the south.

In 1996 Centennial established its Midwest operations headquarters in Fort Wayne, Indiana. At the time, Centennial was the parent company of Cellular One of Fort Wayne. Centennial had annual revenue of nearly $150 million and about 800 employees. Since its 1988 founding, the company had enjoyed a 50 percent annual growth rate. Its rapid growth was due in part to acquisitions and in part to the growing demand for wireless services.

Expanding into Caribbean: 1997–2000

In 1997 Centennial entered the Puerto Rico market as a personal communications services (PCS) provider. The com-

Company Perspectives:

Centennial Wireless is one of the nation's largest independent wireless providers. We provide the latest in digital phones, accessories, features, and services designed to meet your business or personal communication needs. As one of the first cellular companies, Centennial covers nearly 82,000 square miles of service area in six states, and has one of the most comprehensive networks in the country. Our "big area" home calling area is a seamless calling area. Centennial has over 100 stores, retail outlets, and authorized agents to serve you. Since we are a local, regional company, every market has a manager that has the authority to take care of you—our customer. Centennial Wireless offers true value by simply offering a large calling area for a low price. Centennial Wireless, "the big area, small price wireless phone company."

pany chose CDMA (code division multiple access) technology for its system there, in part because the system and all its network interfaces would be defined by industry standards. That would enable Centennial to develop a multivendor network and distinguish it from its competition.

In July 1998 Centennial agreed to be bought by the private investment firm of Welsh, Carson, Anderson & Stowe for approximately $2 billion. The company would continue to operate as an independent cellular phone service company under its current name.

In January 1999 Centennial underwent a recapitalization. As the result of a merger with a new entity formed by Welsh, Carson, Anderson & Stowe, a new group of equity investors acquired a 92.9 percent ownership interest in Centennial. Public stockholders owned the remaining 7.1 percent of the company, with shares trading on the NASDAQ. As part of the recapitalization, the company entered into a $1.05 billion senior term loan and revolving credit facility and issued some $550 million in notes. Also in January, Michael J. Small was named president and CEO of Centennial. He was formerly executive vice-president and CFO of 360 Communications Company, which became a subsidiary of Alltel Corp.

For fiscal year 1999, ending May 31, Centennial reported revenue of $369.2 million, operating income of $16 million, and a net loss of $80.2 million. The loss included recapitalization costs of $52.8 million and an extraordinary loss of $35.1 million, net of taxes. The company's wireless subscriber base increased 41 percent, from 322,200 on May 31, 1998, to 454,100 on May 31, 1999, with about half of the increase attributed to new wireless subscribers in Puerto Rico.

During 1999 Centennial upgraded most of its domestic systems to offer digital services. While its Caribbean systems utilized CDMA digital technology, Centennial's domestic digital services used TDMA (time division multiple access) technology. During fiscal 2000 ending May 31, the company added 133 cell sites domestically for a total of 577 cell sites, and it added 17 cell sites in Puerto Rico for a total of 149 cell sites there.

For 1999 and 2000 Centennial continued to expand in the Caribbean region and to acquire new licenses to complement its domestic areas of service. In August 1999 Centennial acquired Integrated Systems Inc. and Spiderlink Puerto Rico Internet Services for $5.9 million in cash and stock. Located in Puerto Rico, these companies specialized in network design and integration, systems consulting, software design development, and Internet solutions, including Web page design, Web hosting, e-commerce, and related services. In November 1999 Centennial acquired the wireless telephone system in Allegan, Michigan, for $34.7 million in cash and stock.

In January 2000 Centennial acquired a 70 percent controlling interest in All America Cables and Radio, Inc., an international long-distance provider in the Dominican Republic. The acquisition also included a PCS wireless license covering 8.9 million Pops (points of presence). At the end of February 2000 the company changed its name from Centennial Cellular to Centennial Communications to better reflect the integrated communications services that it offered.

In March 2000 Centennial acquired an international gateway switch in Miami, Florida, that was expected to deliver the company's growing outbound traffic from its Caribbean service areas closer to its destination. The company also hoped to attract more southbound calling destined for Puerto Rico, the Dominican Republic, Jamaica, and other areas in the region. In April 2000 the company acquired the wireless telephone system serving Kokomo, Indiana, for $25.6 million in cash.

In May 2000 Centennial agreed to acquire the cable television assets of Pegasus Communications Corp. for $170 million in cash. Pegasus's cable TV systems covered the western part of Puerto Rico and had more than 55,000 subscribers. The acquisition closed in September 2000.

A second Caribbean acquisition in May 2000 involved obtaining a 51 percent controlling interest in Paradise Wireless (Jamaica) Ltd., which had a CDMA wireless license covering 2.6 million Pops. Following the acquisition Paradise Wireless became Centennial Digital Jamaica Ltd. Later in the year Centennial acquired a 60 percent interest in Infochannel Ltd., a leading ISP on Jamaica with more than 6,000 subscribers.

For fiscal year 2000 ending May 31, Centennial reported revenue of $501.3 million, operating income of $155.2 million, and net income of $16.7 million. During the year, the company's wireless subscriber base increased 38 percent, from 454,100 on May 31, 1999, to 626,800 on May 31, 2000.

In July 2000 Centennial entered into an agreement to sell its Southwest cluster, representing 311,000 Net Pops, to Western Wireless Corp. for $202.5 million in cash. It was Centennial's smallest cluster, with service areas in and around Yuma, Arizona, and El Centro, California; its Midwest cluster contained about 3.7 million Net Pops, and its cluster in the South contained about 2.3 million Net Pops.

Also in July Centennial acquired the remaining 74.9 percent of the Lake Charles, Louisiana, wireless license that it didn't own for about $42 million. This market connected the company's existing Louisiana and Texas service areas.

In November 2000 Centennial completed the sale of its limited partnership interest in Sacramento-Valley Limited Partnership to Verizon Wireless for $236 million. The partnership provided wireless telephone service in Northern California and Nevada and was controlled and managed by Verizon Wireless. The sale of Centennial's interest was part of its strategy to monetize investments in companies that it did not control. Under the same strategy, earlier in the year, Centennial realized $48 million from the sale of its 2.9 percent investment interest in a San Francisco Bay-area cluster.

For the quarter ending November 30, 2000, Centennial reported a 25 percent gain in revenue over the same quarter in 1999. Its wireless subscriber base increased by 27 percent, from 525,100 in 1999 to 664,400 in 2000. Domestic cellular subscribers decreased by 12,100, including a loss of 22,600 subscribers from the sale of Centennial's Southwest cluster in Arizona and California. Caribbean wireless subscribers increased 12,500 during the quarter.

Caribbean Initiative

In the Caribbean, Centennial launched its wireless service in the Dominican Republic in October 2000 and obtained a $75 million vendor financing commitment to construct a wireless network in Jamaica. In December 2000 Centennial announced it would acquire the Puerto Rican cable TV company Teleponce for $108 million in cash. Teleponce had more than 37,000 subscribers and passed over 124,500 homes in southwestern Puerto Rico. The Caribbean was becoming an increasingly significant source of revenue for Centennial. For the quarter ending November 30, 2000, total Caribbean revenue was $68.6 million—an increase of 39 percent over the same quarter of the previous year—while domestic wireless revenue for the quarter was $85.8 million. Other significant developments included the acquisition in December 2000 of Com Tech International Corp., which increased Centennial's undersea fiber-optic cable capacity.

Centennial was well positioned to grow in the Caribbean region in 2001. The company planned to build a wireless network in Jamaica and introduce wireless services there, as well as in the U.S. Virgin Islands. In Puerto Rico Centennial was the only fully integrated competitive communications provider, offering PCS, wireless local exchange, fiber-based local exchange and private line, long distance, and Internet access services. The company planned to leverage its dominant position in Puerto Rico to become the leading integrated carrier in the Caribbean region. In the United States Centennial planned to rely on growth from its roaming revenue in the two geographic clusters where it offered wireless services. Having upgraded its domestic network, Centennial was able to offer a full range of digital services.

Principal Divisions

Centennial de Puerto Rico; Centennial Digital Jamaica Ltd.; Centennial Dominicana.

Principal Competitors

Cellular Communications of Puerto Rico, Inc.; Puerto Rico Telephone Co.; Nextel Communications Inc.; AT&T Wireless; GTE Wireless; Verizon Wireless; Sprint PCS Group.

Further Reading

"Centennial Sold," *Telephony,* July 13, 1998.
"Centennial Comm to Buy Puerto Rico Cable TV Firm," *Futures World News,* December 19, 2000.
Graf, Rudy, "Centennial Communications Gives Its Business Case for Deploying CDMA in Puerto Rico," *America's Network,* December 1, 1997, p. 24.
LeDuc, Doug, "Centennial Cellular to Establish Midwest Operations in Kentucky," *Knight-Ridder/Tribune Business News,* August 21, 1996.
——, "Fort Wayne Ind.-Based Telecom Firm to Add Voice-Recognition to Cell Phones," *Fort Wayne News-Sentinel,* October 24, 2000.

—David P. Bianco

Checkpoint Systems, Inc.

101 Wolf Drive
Thorofare, New Jersey 08086
U.S.A.
Telephone: (856) 848-1800
Toll Free: (800) 257-5540
Fax: (856) 848-0937
Web site: http://www.checkpointsystems.com

Public Company
Incorporated: 1969
Employees: 5,017
Sales: $370.5 million (1999)
Stock Exchanges: New York
Ticker Symbol: CKP
NAIC: 334290 Other Communications Equipment
   Manufacturing

Checkpoint Systems, Inc. is one of the world leaders in electronic article surveillance (EAS) technology that tags retail items to prevent shoplifting and employee theft (so-called "shrinkage"). With 42 percent of the global market share in EAS, Checkpoint trails only Sensormatic Electronics and its 45 percent. The longtime rivals employ different technologies, which has caused some friction between the firms, resulting over the years in negative advertisements and litigation. Checkpoint is involved in other areas of security control, including closed-circuit TV and monitoring systems, and access control systems, which determine employee access to restricted areas at specified times. Checkpoint also offers a radio frequency identification (RFID) system that can simultaneously read data from a large number of "intelligent tags" without the need for line-of-sight. The technology has been used to automate toll lanes to ease congestion at bridge and turnpike entrances. Checkpoint employs RFID in its library services, not only to prevent theft but also to control inventory and allow patrons to check out and return materials with self-service equipment. In recent years Checkpoint has expanded beyond the bounds of retail security by offering bar code labeling systems and hand-held pricing systems. With security tagging embedded during the manufacturing process ("source tagging"), Checkpoint's systems are able to provide inventory control as well as security, to track goods from manufacture to point of purchase. Despite the move to diversify its business, however, Checkpoint still relies on EAS systems to account for almost 80 percent of its sales.

Company Origins

Checkpoint was originally incorporated in Pennsylvania in 1969 as a wholly owned subsidiary of Logistics Industries Corporation, a packaging company. Checkpoint first serviced the library market, providing security and control over revolving materials. Logistics' founder, A.E. (Ted) Wolf, recognized that Checkpoint held more promise than the company's main packaging business. In the 1970s Checkpoint expanded into retail security. When the subsidiary reached $3 million in sales in 1977, Wolf spun it off and distributed the company's common stock to Logistics' shareholders as a dividend, in conjunction with a merger between Lydall Inc. and Logistics.

As long as theft was a growth industry, and there was no hope that it would suffer a prolonged slump, companies like Checkpoint were likely to prosper. Costs associated with shrinkage were staggering, amounting to the loss of billions of dollars each year. Studies from 1996 indicated that $21 billion worth of merchandise was stolen from domestic retail operations. Consumers, as a result, were made to pay higher prices, and the government lost up to a $1 billion in tax revenues. Of the $21 billion in stolen merchandise, $9.1 billion was attributed to outside shoplifters, $10.7 billion to employees, and $1.5 billion to vendor representatives on the premises. Furthermore, reducing shrinkage could have a dramatic impact on a company's bottom line. It was estimated that every percentage point eliminated from shrinkage translated into a pre-tax net increase of 33 percent.

Before such studies were conducted, retailers assumed that the vast majority of shrinkage was caused by outside shoplifters. Confronting worker theft and systemic bookkeeping errors thus were avoided in favor of blaming an underclass of habitual thieves. In addition to a skewed understanding of shrinkage, the measures taken to combat shoplifting proved unsatisfactory. Locking merchandise behind glass cases provided security but required hiring a large sales staff to wait individually on customers. Placing products in the open, to stimulate sales, necessitated fixtures and locking devices that would allow the customer to feel the merchandise but not walk off with it. Efforts to make goods even more available to customers, to stimulate impulse buying, would lead to security guards, both uniformed and plain clothes, patrolling catwalks above the floors of department stores, peering through one-way mirrors, or keeping an eye out for shoplifters from lifeguard-like perches. Security companies boasted about the numbers of shoplifters apprehended, but in reality shrinkage in the 1960s and 1970s continued to increase, as did the cost of prevention. Thus retailers were hurt at both ends. The stigma attached to shoplifting also was lessening, with some people justifying it as a ''political act.'' In any case, it was becoming increasingly more difficult to spot a likely shoplifter in the crowd, as well as to assume the trustworthiness of employees, who might see theft as an appropriate remedy to grievances. It was in this environment that electronic article surveillance was developed.

The initial technology of EAS was simple enough, essentially that of radio. A transmitting tag was attached to an item of merchandise that could be removed only by a cashier. If the tagged merchandise was taken from the premises a receiver flanking the entrance would pick up the signal and sound an alarm. The system depended on proper training of personnel, to make sure tags were removed properly, and on maintenance of equipment. Still, the results were impressive, at least until shoplifters found ways to circumvent the system. Security personnel were also too quick to assume guilt when an alarm sounded, which led to a rash of falsely accused customers and costly legal settlements. Retailers learned that the new EAS systems had an elastic zone of detection that could extend well beyond the store's entrance, creating a ''bubble'' that expanded during heavy pedestrian traffic. Alarms could be triggered by nearby racks of tagged items, and angry customers were stopped and searched for no reason. Even when the system caught a legitimate shoplifter, gaining a conviction proved difficult, since that would require a direct observation of the theft. Nevertheless, shrinkage was curtailed substantially and the loss prevention industry was well established.

Changing Leadership in the Early 1990s

The early leader in the EAS business was Sensormatic Electronics Corporation. By 1986 Checkpoint, focusing on drugstores, would be tied for second with Knogo Corporation, but it still lagged well behind Sensormatic. Preparing to step down, Wolf named a former accountant, Gerald Klein, to serve as Checkpoint's senior vice-president of operations, with the un-

derstanding that Klein would take charge when Wolf retired in two years. By 1992, however, with the price of Checkpoint stock virtually unchanged, Wolf removed Klein and resumed control of the company. Wolf vowed to make Checkpoint a more feared competitor, a trait that he found lacking in Klein.

In addition to beefing up the sales force by 50 percent and bringing out new security products, Wolf also initiated a program of global expansion. In 1992 Checkpoint acquired its Canadian distributor, Checkpoint Canada, allowing the company to directly sell its products in the Canadian marketplace. The following year Checkpoint purchased its distributor in Argentina. Checkpoint also moved into the Australia and Mexico markets.

Wolf clearly was determined to grow Checkpoint and challenge Sensormatic for supremacy, not only in sales but technology. The two companies had come to rely on different methods for EAS. Checkpoint was committed to radio frequency (RF) technology, whereas Sensormatic now opted for acousto-magnetic technology, in which alarms were triggered by the vibration of metal in the security tags. Both systems had advantages and disadvantages. RF tags were paper thin and easier to work with, but also led to a high number of false alarms. Acousto-magnetic tags were cumbersome and pressure sensitive, but suffered virtually no false alarms. Both systems also had big name retail customers with heavy investments in their systems who weighed in on either side. Under Klein there was good relations between the two companies; Sensormatic even agreed to distribute Checkpoint RF systems in Europe. But there was a war brewing over which system would become the standard for source tagging in the music industry.

Music retailers, with a younger customer base that was susceptible to the temptation of shoplifting and a product that could be easily concealed, were one of the major users of antitheft devices. Much of the security involved the manufacturers' use of cardboard ''longbox'' packaging. The industry, facing pressure from ecologists, agreed to eliminate the packaging by April 1993. The move to source tagging, embedding the security transmitter directly into the product, was the logical solution to providing product loss security for the new smaller tape cassette and compact disc packaging. Most music retailers, however, used a tagging system that relied on microwave technology, which would not be compatible with source tagging. Furthermore, the microwave system had proven to be easily defeated by shoplifters who used body shielding or foil-lined bags. In preparation for the longbox conversion, the National Association of Recording Merchandisers (NARM) tested EAS systems with the intention of establishing a standard. Of the four participants in the testing (Checkpoint, Sensormatic, 3M, and Knogo), only Checkpoint was wedded to just one technology. The others also offered RF and could more easily adjust if NARM ruled out magnetics in favor of radio. Thus the stakes for Checkpoint were extremely high, even though it was likely that the winner would license its technology to the other companies.

As NARM delayed announcing its decision, Wolf and Checkpoint released a full-page ad in the January 9, 1993 issue of *Billboard* that claimed that certain magnetic deactivation systems could distort the audio quality of audio and videotapes. While Sensormatic was not mentioned in the ad, the acousto-

Key Dates:

1969: Checkpoint is created as subsidiary of Logistics Industries.
1977: Company is spun off as part of a merger between Logistics and Lydall, Inc.
1986: Founder A.E. Wolf names Gerald Klein to succeed him.
1992: Wolf resumes control of company.
1995: Kevin Dowd becomes new president and CEO.
1999: Company acquires Meto AG.

magnetic technology it criticized was proprietary to Sensormatic, and based on NARM criteria it was really the only logical alternative to Checkpoint's RF system. With NARM on the verge of announcing its decision, Sensormatic lost no time in filing suit against Checkpoint for false and misleading advertising, seeking $35 million in damages.

In February 1993 rumors that the NARM subcommittee working on the security question had recommended the Sensormatic system sent Checkpoint stock tumbling, losing a third of its value in two days. In March NARM announced its decision to go with Sensormatic, only to discover through further testing that indeed the system's deactivation process did cause deterioration in the sound quality of some cassettes. Now the price of Sensormatic stock dropped and Checkpoint's was driven up. While Sensormatic rushed out new deactivation devices that it maintained corrected the problem, Checkpoint again trumpeted the studies that led to the company being sued, as it tried to pressure NARM to reopen its process.

The Mid-1990s and Beyond

On June 26, 1993, Sensormatic agreed to drop its suit against Checkpoint, when the two entered a pact agreeing not to criticize one another in their advertisements; also as part of the settlement, however, Sensormatic discontinued its agreement to sell Checkpoint products in Europe. The next month, to forestall a loss in European sales, Checkpoint acquired Dutch makers of security products and services, ID Systems International B.V. and ID Systems Europe B.V.

The NARM controversy, with the stakes so high, was destined to fester. Checkpoint and Target stores, which used Checkpoint systems and sold a great deal of music products, filed suit against NARM. When PolyGram in 1996 began to employ the source tagging standard recommended by NARM, Checkpoint and Target sued the music distributor. PolyGram suspended its operation, with its president, James Caparro, commenting, "We maintain support of source-tagging, but we will not fund the fight on behalf of the entire industry."

In the meantime, Checkpoint continued to grow. Kevin Dowd took over as president and CEO in 1995, with Wolf now serving as chairman of the board. Also in that year the company acquired Eagle Security, its distributor in Norway, as well as Actron Group Limited in the United Kingdom. In 1996 Checkpoint opened a European distribution center in Mechelen, Belgium. Checkpoint moved into the closed-circuit TV (CCTV)

security market in 1995 with the purchase of Alarmex, then over the next two years made further purchases to bolster its position, adding Canada's Vysions Systems, Denmark's Checkout Security Systems, and Belgium's D & D Security.

In April 1997 the suit against NARM was settled out of court. While NARM urged manufacturers to begin placing Sensormatic tags on CDs, it also sent a letter to the six major music distributors requesting that they meet with Target to discuss its concerns, in effect asking them to consider embedding more than one tag or tagging separate batches of CDs with both technologies, a position that NARM had opposed for the 12 years that it had been involved in the question of source tagging. Target had maintained, however, that much had changed in the intervening years: other industries had dealt with the same question of multiple technologies in source tagging. While Checkpoint concurred and urged that market forces be allowed to work, Sensormatic took the position that CDs were not conducive to two tags and that the delays cause by litigation had simply prevented merchants from enjoying the savings that could be realized by better security measures. Even though music companies would pass along the cost of tagging to the retailer, and in turn the consumer, they were clearly in no hurry to implement source tagging, despite everyone's general support of the concept. It was not until 1999 that Sony Music Distribution and WEA announced that they would begin to embed Sensormatic tags in their CDs but would also conduct talks with Checkpoint about accommodations with the company's competing system. They held out the possibility of placing the RF tags on blow-in cards in the CD package or on album artwork.

Also in 1999 Wolf stepped down as chairman of the board of Checkpoint in favor of director David Clark. The company continued to diversify beyond EAS, entering the access control business and working with Mitsubishi on RFID technology. Checkpoint made a major move in 1999 when it purchased the German company Meto AG for $265 million, plus the assumption of $35 million in debt. Not only would the deal double the size of Checkpoint, it dramatically increased its European presence and allowed the company to expand into the bar-code labeling system. The so-called "auto identification" market was estimated to be worth $8 billion to $10 billion a year. According to Dowd, who was quoted by the *Wall Street Journal,* "This transforms Checkpoint from the electronic article surveillance business into retail supply chain management."

Checkpoint also returned to its roots with the introduction of its Intelligent Library System (ILS). Building upon its RFID technology the Checkpoint system would attach a paper-thin, flexible "circulation circuit" label to each item in the library that could then be inventoried rapidly with a hand-held wand without the need for line-of-sight reading. The system also would have the capability of providing ATM-like self-checkout units that printed due date slips. Academic libraries that installed ILS reported that material handling time by staff was reduced by as much as 75 percent.

In little more than 30 years Checkpoint had transformed itself from a subsidiary of a packaging company into a global concern with its own subsidiaries in Australia, Argentina, Brazil, Canada, Denmark, France, Germany, Italy, Japan, Mexico, The Netherlands, Sweden, Norway, Portugal, Spain, Switzerland, and the United Kingdom. Checkpoint had diversified beyond EAS into the broader category of material handling, as well as RFID technology and its myriad of applications (from libraries to toll booths to cattle herds), and other security services (from CCTV to Access Control). These efforts should help insulate Checkpoint from the dangers of being overly committed to its radio frequency EAS format.

Principal Operating Units

Electronic Article Surveillance; CCTV Systems and Monitoring Services; Access Control Systems; Radio Frequency Identification; Bar Code Labeling Systems; Hand-held Labeling Systems; Retail Merchandising Systems.

Principal Competitors

Sensormatic Electronics Corporation; 3M; Knogo Corporation.

Further Reading

Budden, Michael Craig, *Preventing Shoplifting Without Being Sued,* Westport, Conn.: Quorum Books, 1999.

Deogun, Nikhil, "Checkpoint Agrees to Buy Germany's Meto for $265 Million," *Wall Street Journal,* August 11, 1999, p. B4.

Horan, Donald J., *The Retailers Guide to Loss Prevention and Security,* Boca Raton, La.: CRC, 1997.

Jeffrey, Don, "PGD Suspends Source-Tagging; No Longer Target of Lawsuits," *Billboard,* September 7, 1996, pp. 1, 17.

——, "Source-Tagging Suit Settled, But Questions Linger," *Billboard,* April 26, 1997, pp. 1, 17.

Lubove, Seth, " 'Gerry Chose to Be a Very Nice Human Being,' " *Forbes,* March 15, 1993.

Verna, Paul, "Source-Tag Contenders Square Off," *Billboard,* February 6, 1993, p. 37.

—Ed Dinger

CHRISTIE'S

Christie's International plc

8 King Street, St. James's
London SW1Y 6QT
United Kingdom
Telephone: (44) 20 7839 9060
Fax: (44) 20 7839 1611
Web site: http://www.christies.com

Private Company
Incorporated: 1766
Employees: 1,900
Sales: $2.92 billion
NAIC: 453998 Auction Houses

Christie's International plc oversees the operations of one of the world's premier art auction houses. Although the company holds regular auctions worldwide, its principal selling centers are located in London and New York City. Dubbed "the oldest fine arts auctioneers in the world" (rival Sotheby's is 22 years older, but began by selling books), Christie's has been in the business more than 200 years and has set record prices not only for works of art but also wine, scientific instruments, carpet, photographs, cameras, and teddy bears. The company went private in 1998. Soon thereafter, a U.S. Justice Department probe of possible price fixing with Sotheby's rocked the art world and has damaged the fortunes and reputations of both venerable auction houses.

18th-Century Origins

Although documentation on his early life story is somewhat sketchy, it is generally held that James Christie was born in Perth, Scotland, in 1730 to a Scottish mother and English father. After serving briefly as a midshipman in the Royal Navy, he worked for an auctioneer named Annesley as an apprentice in fashionable Covent Garden, London. After a few years, Christie opened his own auction house at Dalton's Print Rooms in the Pall Mall district. These premises also housed what was to become the Royal Academy of Arts. His first auction, on December 5, 1766, which included wine, netted £76, 16 shillings,

and sixpence. This sale was the first recorded in a bound log of sales that has survived more than 200 years.

James Christie excelled at auctioneering. In the early years, he sold many things aside from works of art, including chamber pots, loads of hay, and even someone's suddenly unneeded coffin. All of these were proffered with mellifluous and verbose charm, earning Christie the nickname "The Specious Orator" from satirical cartoonists of the day.

Within only a few years, Christie was handling truly valuable paintings, such as those by Europe's "Old Masters," which he picked up on the fashionable Grand Tour, as well as several by promising American artists. Christie eventually moved his offices (and residence) to 125 Pall Mall, becoming next door neighbors with Thomas Gainsborough, the great British painter, who later (like Sir Joshua Reynolds) painted Christie's portrait. (After changing hands several times, Gainsborough's *Portrait of James Christie* was bought by J. Paul Getty for $26,500 in 1938, Getty's first major painting purchase.)

Moreover, Christie was influential in the promotion of art, displaying the works of new artists at a time when, save the Royal Academy's annual show, there were no other public places to display contemporary works. Many esteemed artists, including Landseer, Rossetti, and Sargent, saw their work pass through the auction house. Increasingly, when an artist who had been helped by a Christie auction passed away, the executors of his estate naturally turned to Christie to sell pictures remaining in the studio.

Christie's reputation as a connoisseur was so esteemed that in 1778 he was called on to sell Sir Robert Walpole's magnificent art collection, which Catherine the Great eventually acquired for £40,000, then a colossal figure. (These pictures were the basis of the Hermitage in St. Petersburg; a few bought by Andrew Mellon made their way to the National Gallery of Art in Washington, D.C.)

Christie's and the London art business as a whole benefited from the emigration of Huguenots from France. After the

French Revolution destroyed Paris as the leading art market, the revolutionary government turned to the nation of shopkeepers, and to Christie's specifically, to dispose of La Comtesse Dubarry's "most superlative" collection of jewels after she was guillotined. The Reign of Terror both removed buyers and flooded the market with paintings, however, making jewelry sales still more important.

Industrial Era Transitions

American tycoons, newly rich from the Industrial Revolution, such as Mellon, Pierpoint Morgan, Vanderbilt, and Kress, began to dominate buying activity in the 19th century. At the same time, Christie's became known as a clearinghouse for country estates, a tradition that has continued for two centuries. Such a sale in 1848, for the Duke of Buckingham's Stowe House, lasted 40 days and realized £77,562. It also brought in a new employee and a future partner, the gatekeeper's son, Thomas Woods, who thoroughly impressed the firm with his knowledge of the house's paintings.

James Christie died in 1803, whereupon management of the company was taken up by his son, James Christie II, and later his two grandsons. In 1823, Christie's moved its headquarters to 8 King Street, where it would remain for more than 170 years. The auction room there known as the "Big Room" is said to have been designed by James Christie in the form of a hexagon to maximize wall space; paintings were hung on these walls all the way up to the ceiling.

In 1831 William Manson joined the firm. Thomas Woods became a partner in 1859, and the firm's name changed to Christie, Manson and Woods. The year 1889 saw the retirement of the last of the Christie family to be associated with the company: James Christie IV. Christie's held the first auction of Impressionist paintings in Britain in the same year.

The Modern Era

After 50 years of passing picture sales on to Christie's in favor of auctioning book collections, Sotheby's management decided to begin auctioning paintings. By 1917, the company was holding regular art auctions. In response, Christie's stopped referring books to Sotheby's, opting to auction such collections themselves. Thus began a competition and rivalry between the two auction houses that would continue into the year 2000.

Although it had begun to broaden its offerings to include books and even fine wines, Christie's focus remained primarily in the picture market. Among its more notable sales during this time was that of the *Portrait of Mrs. Davenport,* by British painter George Romney. The portrait was sold by Christie's for £360,900 in 1926. Other significant sales in the interwar period included the Russian crown jewels, which realized nearly £250,000 in 1927.

Global economic depression and the world wars were devastating to the art market, and in the 1930s talk began to surface of a merger between Christie's and Sotheby's. Nothing came of the discussions, however, and in the race for the top auction house spot, Sotheby's began to gain ground, having been early to establish a presence in the United States.

In 1940, R.W. Lloyd bought a substantial share of Christie's stock and thus became chairman of the company. Under Lloyd, Christie's became a private limited company, and Sir Alec Martin, who had begun working for Christie's at the age of 12 as an office boy, was named managing director. New management faced several challenges. In addition to its financial concerns, Christie's suffered a terrible blow on April 16, 1941, when an incendiary bomb destroyed the interior of the firm's building on King Street; the premises would not be completely rebuilt until well after the war, in 1953. Another wartime inconvenience was the suspension of wine sales, which did not resume until 1966.

Postwar Crisis and Opportunity

Christie's market grew broader yet again after World War II, as art auctions, previously the domain of the upper classes, gained a more widespread appeal. Television cameras began to crowd into auction rooms, and the public began to hear news reports of important art sales and the money they fetched.

In 1958, Christie's was reorganized as Christie, Manson and Woods Ltd: the new company issued £60,000 worth of capital. Ivan O. "Peter" Chance was selected to lead the new company. In order to buy shares owned by Martin and Lloyd (who died in April 1958), the Crown Lease of 8 King Street was sold to the Commercial Union Assurance Co. and leased back to Christie's.

A process of professionalization had begun at Christie's. First, Peter Chance promptly hired consultants to set up a press office at Christie's. Then, the company began focusing on establishing a presence in Europe, becoming the first British auction house to hire a European representative, whom it situated in Rome. Soon offices in other European countries were established, and an American representative was hired. Christie's also began to appoint more specialists in areas such as collectible coins and porcelain. Finally, as competition between Christie's and Sotheby's intensified in the late 1950s, both houses began requiring their managers to read the obituaries daily, looking for estates that might need auctioning. Later, social intelligence gathering would become more sophisticated, all with the end of determining who would control known valuable art collections. Christie's had approximately 150 sales a year in this period.

In 1960 Christie's reported sales of £2.7 million, and the following year that figure had risen to £3.1 million. The company was trailing by a significant margin behind Sotheby's, however, a trend that some analysts attributed to a lack of confidence in Christie's picture department. Nevertheless, Christie's continued to set sales records, recording the highest price paid until then ($27,950) for a Pre-Raphaelite painting, *The Lady of Shalott* by Holman Hunt.

In 1962, as the Cuban missile crisis was simmering, Peter Chance reportedly made a secret trip to Cuba to consider auctioning property seized when Castro had risen to power in 1959. Although a valuation team arrived to catalog the valuables in what was in many ways a febrile environment, no sales materialized from their efforts. In spite of the bold efforts, Christie's lost £6,000 that year, although it sold only slightly less art than the year before. Five years later, Christie's did succeed in establishing a business relationship with the Soviet Union, selling for £65,751 ($193,308) a 1,700-piece porcelain banquet service made for Tsar Nicholas I in 1830.

A couple of notable staff additions helped bolster Christie's ailing reputation in its picture department, as did initial moves to divide the company's departments into areas of specialty. Moreover, the sale of the Cook collection of Old Masters in 1965 proved Christie's was a force to be reckoned with; Rembrandt's *Portrait of Titus* (his son) sold for $2.2 million, a price that surpassed all expectations.

In 1965, Christie's acquired White Bros. Printers for £38,000, a purchase that helped the company to produce its considerable volume of catalogs more efficiently. Interestingly, the company used an old-fashioned letterpress system until 1979, when it converted to offset lithography (which also required using union labor for the first time). In 1980 White Bros. began printing all of Christie's Park Avenue catalogs as well.

To celebrate its 200-year anniversary, Christie's held a tremendous Bicentenary Exhibition in January 1967. About 60 important drawings and paintings that had passed through Christie's rooms over the years were lent back for the display, which raised about £3,000 for the National Art Collections Fund. Together, the works, which included Gainsborough's *Portrait of James Christie,* were valued at approximately $5 million.

During this time, Christie's European operations, based in Rome, were being hindered by Italy's strict art export laws. In response, Christie's established a new subsidiary, Christie's International S.A., which was incorporated in Geneva in 1967 to oversee European business. Switzerland, moreover, did not have the import taxes of Great Britain. A program of international expansion included a host of new Christie's auction houses in Australia, Japan, and Canada, as well as an American headquarters move to a new facility on Madison Avenue in New York.

New Leadership for a New Era

Christie's went public in 1973, strengthened by three years of good results and expansion. Pretax profits had grown tremendously in the prior five years: from £139,000 in 1968 to £1.1 million in 1972. In two years, after practically doubling 1972's profits, Peter Chance announced his retirement as chair of Christie, Manson and Woods, although he would remain chairman of Christie's International plc for two more years.

Jo Floyd took up Chance's former duties just in time to be met by a worldwide economic recession. To cope with dwindling profits in London, both Christie's and Sotheby's introduced a ten percent buyer's premium in the early 1970s. This new policy was not met with enthusiasm on the part of London's art dealers, several of whom began litigation against the auction houses.

In autumn 1974, Christie's acquired Debenham and Coe in South Kensington, for the purpose of handling lower value lots more efficiently than was possible at its King Street facility. At the end of the decade, Christie's bought Edmiston's, a Glasgow auction firm.

In 1977, Christie's opened a New York salesroom in the Delmonico Hotel, a 1920s era skyscraper at 502 Park Avenue. American sales were becoming increasingly important to the British-based firm; by 1983, New York sales had surpassed those from London. In 1978, a second New York showroom, dubbed Christie's East, was opened in a six-story East 67th Street garage. Christie's reputation in America seemed to be cemented when in 1980 Henry Ford II chose the firm to sell ten of his excellent Modern and Impressionist paintings. A painting that had performed so impressively for Sotheby's in 1958, Van Gogh's *Le Jardin du Poete, Arles,* was sold by Christie's for a record $5.2 million (£2.2 million) in London. Overall, the paintings brought in $18.3 million in one evening. Other great sales during this time included that of Coco Chanel's wardrobe, a huge production that earned £43,250 for 40 dresses and brought in an even more impressive amount of good publicity.

In 1987 several records were set at Christie's, for paintings ($39.9 million for Van Gogh's *Sunflowers*), jewels ($6.4 million for a 65-carat pear-shaped diamond), and automobiles ($9.8 million for a 1931 Bugati Type 41 Royale). Christie's marketing efforts, aimed at broader audiences, helped sell large collections, such as the Nanking Cargo, consisting of gold bars and porcelain from a freighter sunk off the coast of Java in 1751. Human interest helped elevate the price to £10 million. Such valuable collections attracted interest from all walks of life, and in 1984 a group of armed robbers stormed into a jewelry auction at King Street, wielding a shotgun and a sledge-hammer. Fortunately, the truly valuable pieces were overlooked.

In 1990 Christie's set a record for furniture; $15.1 million was offered for the Duke of Beaufort's Badminton cabinet. Then, the record for all works of art was broken with Christie's sale of Van Gogh's *Portrait of Dr. Gachet,* which went for $82.5 million. These records represented only the cream of many Modern and Impressionist paintings that Christie's handled during the late 1980s and early 1990s. Christie's was holding approximately 1,400 sales per year in the late 1980s.

Before resigning in 1989, Jo Floyd had secured a new 125-year lease for expanded premises on King Street. Christopher Davidge, whose grandfather had worked as a clerk at the firm, assumed the role of Christie's CEO after becoming managing director four years earlier. Davidge had previously worked his way up the ranks at White Brothers, Christie's printing company. He made effective communications and standardization throughout the organization two of his top priorities. As the art market lapsed into a recession that would last from 1991 to 1995, he also streamlined the staff and aggressively cut commissions to gain sales.

A long-term pattern of competing over market share with Sotheby's—as one firm underpriced the other—would depress profits and lead to stagnant stock prices. Because there was so little art on the market during the slump of the early 1990s, the big sellers were able to negotiate zero commission deals in exchange for their business. Entering new categories of selling, such as rock and roll memorabilia, helped, but did not generate enough profits to offset the loss of commissions from the high-end art market. In March 1995, Davidge announced a new two percent commission on sales of more than $5 million. A few weeks later, Sotheby's followed suit, with the result that neither auction house lost business to the other. Even when Christie's passed Sotheby's in market share for the first time in more than 40 years, its profits were clipped by escalating marketing costs. In 1997 the two rival firms and more than a dozen New York art dealers became the subject of a U.S. Justice Department investigation about possible collusion to depress prices, but the inquiry seemed to peter out, leaving only a patch of bad publicity.

Lacking a majority owner, Christie's also found itself the target of takeover bids. Late in 1997 a Swiss investment bank, SBC Warburg, entered into talks with Christie's about purchasing the firm. The talks eventually stalled, but a short time later, in May 1998, French tycoon Francois Pinault bought Christie's for $1.2 billion. After buying such interests as Chateau Latour wines, Vail Resorts in Colorado, and Gucci, Pinault was known to analyze a new purchase during the first year, then change management. It was a difficult time for Christie's, which was losing employees to Sotheby's and Internet sites looking to sell art and collectibles.

In December 1999, after 34 years with Christie's, Davidge was terminated and replaced by Edward Dolman, the head of the U.S. operation. The next day, Davidge handed Dolman a package of documents that included meeting minutes and handwritten notes of phone conversations that implicated top management of Christie's and Sotheby's in an effort to fix commis-

sion fees. After lawyers reviewed the material, Christie's turned over the information to the U.S. Justice Department. Davidge provided more information to the government, and in exchange for their cooperation both Davidge and Christie's received conditional immunity from prosecution. Sotheby's executives were not so fortunate. While its chairman, A. Alfred Taubman, chose to fight the charges, Davidge's counterpart, Diana D. Brooks, pleaded guilty in October 2000 to conspiracy to fix commission rates for auction customers.

Christie's did not escape unscathed, however. Aside from tarnished images, Christie's and Sotheby's both faced a European Union inquiry and dozens of U.S. class action suits, which eventually would be settled at a cost of $256 million for each firm. Overseas suits looked to haunt the auction houses for years to come. The task of restoring the company's image was daunting enough for Christie's, but perhaps of greater concern was the need to question how the auction business was run in general. Godfrey Barker wrote in the *Wall Street Journal:* "Sotheby's and Christie's are the luxury toys of men who see their real businesses elsewhere. . . . The auction houses are jewel boxes for their wives and fantasy stage sets for the owners themselves, places to meet people beyond their social reach and throw great parties—not companies dedicated to making serious money. . . . It cannot last much longer, though. A revolution is bound to come."

Principal Subsidiaries

Christie's Great Estates, Inc.; Christie's Education; Christie's Fine Art; Christie's Images; Christie's Publications.

Principal Competitors

Sotheby's Holdings, Inc.; Phillips Auctioneers.

Further Reading

"Artful Auctioneering," *Economist,* March 11, 1995.

"Blockage Discount at Issue in Andy Warhol's Estate," *Tax Management: Estates Gifts & Trusts Journal,* January 13, 1994, pp. 55–56.

Barker, Godfey, "At the Court of the Auction Kings—What, Compete Seriously? How Modern, How Declasse," *Wall Street Journal,* March 10, 2000, p. W17.

Brough, James, *Auction!,* Indianapolis: Bobbs-Merrill, 1963.

DuBois, Peter C., "African Icon Brings $1.2 Million," *Barron's,* May 8, 1995, p. 16.

——, "Art Fix," *Barron's,* October 31, 1994, p. 20.

——, "The Art of the Sale," *Barron's,* May 15, 1995, p. 13.

——, "High Contrast," *Barron's,* November 21, 1994, pp. 24–25.

——, "Pretty Picture?," *Barron's,* May 8, 1995, pp. 15–16.

Grey, Sarah, "When the Sky's Not the Limit," *Accountancy,* March 1995, p. 58.

"Hammering Asia," *Economist,* September 17, 1994.

Herbert, John, *Inside Christie's,* New York: St. Martin's Press, 1990.

Huus, Kari, "Art Market: Do I Hear Three?," *Far Eastern Economic Review,* May 12, 1994, pp. 69–70.

——, "Jewellery: East Buys West," *Far Eastern Economic Review,* May 12, 1994, p. 69.

Jaffe, Thomas, "IOCs, How Many Gs?," *Forbes,* May 8, 1995, p. 20.

Jarrett, Ian, "A Gentler Kind of Bear Market," *Asian Business,* March 1995, p. 61.

——, "Zoom In on a Good Buy," *Asian Business,* August, 1994, p. 56.

Lacey, Robert, "A Grand Old Rivalry," *Vanity Fair,* January 1996, pp. 104–18.

Morais, R.C., "Blood and Monet," *Forbes,* November 25, 1991, p. 149.

"The Older the Better," *Economist,* March 5, 1994.

Raslan, Karim, "Art Market: Price Propping," *Far Eastern Economic Review,* March 17, 1994, pp. 44–45.

Richmond, Susannah, "Butterfield Day Founder Swaps Ads for Artefacts," *Campaign London,* January 28, 1994, p. 10.

Rozhon, Tracie, "Fighting for Turf: Sotheby's vs. Christie's," *New York Times,* April 14, 1996, Sec. 9, pp. 1, 10.

Serwer, Andrew E., "Art Dealers Trade Screams for Smiles," *Fortune,* April 17, 1995.

Siobhan, Quin, "An Ethnical Investment," *Resident Abroad,* June 1995, pp. 65–66.

—Frederick C. Ingram
—update: Ed Dinger

Clinton Cards plc

The Crystal Building
Langston Road
Loughton, Essex IG10 3TH
United Kingdom
Telephone: (+44) 20-8502-3711
Fax: (+44) 20-8502-0295
Web site: http://www.clintoncards.co.uk

Public Company
Incorporated: 1968
Employees: 4,300
Sales: £253.64 million ($480.1 million)(2000)
Stock Exchanges: London
Ticker Symbol: CC
NAIC: 45321 Stationery Stores; 45322 Gift, Novelty, and Souvenir Stores

Clinton Cards plc operates the United Kingdom's largest chain of retail greeting card specialty shops. The company has grown steadily since going public in 1988, building its network of shops from just 77 primarily southeastern England stores to nearly 700 stores across the United Kingdom. The company's stores are typically located on the United Kingdom's fashionable "high streets," including its 9,000 square-foot flagship store, the world's largest greeting cards store, located on London's Oxford Street. Clinton Cards also operates more than 23 concession shops within the Debenhams department store chain. A pioneer specialty retailer, Clinton Cards has captured nearly 20 percent of the total market for greeting cards and related gifts items in the United Kingdom, estimated to be between £1 billion and £1.2 billion per year. The United Kingdom is also the world's second-largest greeting cards market, behind the $7 billion U.S. market. However, the United Kingdom boasts the largest number of per capita sales, with an average of 55 cards received per year per person, compared to 45 cards per person in the United States and less than 40 per person in Canada. The largest single percentage of Clinton's card sales come during the Christmas season, which accounts for some 30 percent of all Clinton sales; the company typically posts losses during the first half of the year, relying on the Christmas season for its annual profits. Yet the company has been among the leaders of extending the seasonal nature of its business year-round, building up a strong array of spring sales—which have reached ten percent of sales—from such holidays and events as Valentine's Day, Mother's Day, Father's Day, and Easter. The company has also played a role in creating and promoting "new" holidays, including Secretaries Day, Nurses Day, Bosses Day, Grandparents Day, and days commemorating saints, including Saint George. Together with the traditional birthday, anniversary and "get well" market, these sales account for some 60 percent of Clinton's total card sales. The company is led by founder Don Lewin, his son and managing director Clinton Lewin, and daughter Debbie Darlington, who was appointed to the company's board of directors in 2000. The Lewin family holds 36 percent of the company's shares, which are traded on the London stock exchange.

Specialty Pioneer in the 1970s

Clinton Cards plc was founded by Don Lewin in 1968. Lewin had already been active in the greeting cards industry, working first as an agent selling greeting cards before developing a specialty store concept. Until then, the U.K. greeting cards market operated within a larger retail store format. Lewin guessed that shoppers would be attracted to a store format devoted to an extended range of greeting cards. He named his first store, opened in Epping, Essex, in 1968, after his son, Clinton, then just six years old.

The younger Lewin naturally joined his father's business, starting out in the shop at the age of 15. Over the next decade, the Lewin family began to build the company from the first original store to a network of 77 shops covering most of southeastern England. The Clinton Cards shops were typically located in the country's high streets and featured not only greeting cards but also gifts, stuffed animals, and other items. Helping to fuel sales was the rising trend of character merchandising, as shoppers sought products featuring representations of their favorite television characters.

By 1988, the Lewins were ready to take Clinton Cards on a new growth spurt. In order to finance its expansion, the company sold its stock on the London stock exchange. With the money raised, Clinton Cards began to open new stores, extending deeper into England. The company's growth was also aided by flagging rental prices, the result of the collapse of the U.K. building market in the late 1980s, and a lingering recession. Despite the poor economic climate, Clinton Cards continued to book strong revenue gains. Where other retail sectors suffered from declining consumer spending, the greeting card industry—based around relatively inexpensive purchases—remained a steady seller. Indeed, the United Kingdom's love for greeting cards placed the market as one of the world's strongest, leading the world in per capita sales and second only to the giant United States market in total sales.

Market Leader for the 21st Century

The modern greeting cards had been invented in England in the middle of the 19th century and rapidly grew into a national tradition, celebrating not only Christmas but birthdays and anniversaries as well. ''Get well'' cards soon made an appearance as well. Yet in order to support an industry—and especially a fast-growing chain of retail stores—the greeting card industry continued to look for new reasons for giving and receiving cards. One of these proved to be Valentine's Day, helping to fill the retail lull between the Christmas and Easter holidays. The extension of Ireland's St. Patrick's Day celebration plugged another hole in the calendar, while both Mother's Day and Father's Day holidays helped extend the buying season beyond Easter. Halloween also became an opportunity for sending greeting cards.

In the 1990s, retailers and greeting card manufacturers were joined by other interested parties in the creation of such new holidays as Grandparents Day, Secretaries Day, Bosses Day, and even Nurses Day. At the same time, character merchandising sales were booming, aided by such popular television programs (and the characters based thereon) as the U.S.-based animated comedy ''The Simpsons,'' or the Mr. Blobby sensation that briefly swept the United Kingdom in the mid-1990s. By 1994, Clinton Cards had grown into a chain of more than 275 stores.

The decision of industry giant Hallmark to exit the U.K. retail market in order to concentrate on manufacturing cards gave Clinton Cards a new opportunity for growth. In October 1994, the company bought out Hallmark's chain of 83 U.K.-based stores. The purchase price of £3.5 million, described as a bargain price, extended Clinton Cards' reach across England and into Wales.

The company followed that acquisition with the purchase the following year of another rival greeting card specialist, Carlton Cards. That purchase, for £3.2 million, gave Clinton Cards 112 new stores and extended its reach into 57 new towns across the United Kingdom. The company began a massive conversion program, transforming its new Hallmark and Carlton stores into the Clinton Card format, while also identifying and closing overlapping stores.

Clinton Cards, which now featured Clinton Lewin himself as managing director, continued to build its retail empire through organic growth as well. After topping 450 stores by mid-1997, the company stepped up its new store openings, with its 500th store opened in time for the company's 30th anniversary celebrations in March 1998. At that time, the company announced plans to open another 30 by years' end, with an ultimate goal to run an empire of some 800 stores.

By the end of 1998, however, Clinton Cards found itself revising its goals. In September of that year the company announced its acquisition of rival GSG Holdings, adding to its stable that company's 212-store The Greetings Store, Strand, and Papertree retail chains. As with the company's other major acquisitions, the purchase of GSG Holdings, which cost the company more than £27.5 million, was financed by the company's own cash flow. GSG also helped establish Clinton Cards in Scotland, while reinforcing its total U.K. presence. After the acquisition, the company announced its plans to close up to 50 stores, up to half of which were from the GSG group, in order to reduce its surplus stores and streamline its portfolio. Nonetheless, the company entered 1999 with nearly 700 stores. At that time, the company began converting its new stores to the Clinton Cards format, while at the same time carrying out a renovation program on some 60 of the former GSG stores. Clinton Cards, which continued to seek new acquisition opportunities, announced its intention to continue adding up to 40 new stores per year. Management speculated that organic growth alone could build the chain to more than 1,000 stores.

Clinton Cards had taken the position as the undisputed leader of the United Kingdom's greeting cards market, capturing some 20 percent of the estimated £1.2 billion market. The company continued to benefit from strong character marketing initiatives, such as the sudden boom in ''South Park'' character-based merchandise that swept the United Kingdom in the late 1990s. Meanwhile, Clinton Cards was seeking to launch a new flagship store, settling on London's Oxford Street and completing the store in 1999. At 9,000 square feet of selling space, the new Clinton Card store established a world's record for the largest store devoted to greeting cards sales.

New Directions for the Future

The late 1990s and turn of the century saw the company develop two new retail initiatives. The first was the installation of a number of concession shops in the Debenhams department store chain. The initial trial of four Clinton Card boutique shops proved successful enough to encourage both companies to roll

Key Dates:

1968: Don Lewin founds Clinton Cards.
1977: Clinton Lewin joins the company.
1985: Debbie Lewin Darlington joins the company.
1988: Company is listed on the London Stock Exchange.
1994: Hallmark Cards' U.K. stores are acquired.
1995: Company acquires Carlton Cards.
2000: The Clinton Cards e-commerce web site is launched.

out Clinton Card boutiques across most of the 100-store Debenhams chain, a move which began in 2000. At the same time, Clinton Cards began identifying other potential locations for boutiques shops, such as hospitals and garden centers.

The second new initiative brought the company onto the Internet, when Clinton Cards launched its e-commerce web site in April 2000. The web site enabled customers to personalize their own cards, including wedding invitations, while also establishing a personal reminder calendar for sending greetings. The move was also seen as a defensive one, as some analysts questioned whether web-based and email greetings messages might one day rival traditional greetings cards.

In September 2000, the company brought on a new member to its board of directors; Debbie Darlington, the 32-year-old daughter of Don Lewin, had joined the family business when she was 17 years old. That move sparked criticism from stock analysts, who had already proved wary of the family-run com-

pany. In response, Clinton Cards expanded its board to include two more non-executive directors. Nonetheless, other analysts pointed out that the Lewin family leadership had successfully built the company from a single store to an industry heavyweight in just 30 years. With the new generation already guiding the company's operations, Clinton Cards was ready to help the United Kingdom greet the new century.

Principal Competitors

Blooms of Bressingham Holdings plc; Bogod Group plc; The Boyds Collection, Ltd.; Calendar Club LLC; CelebrateExpress.com, Inc.; DFS Group Ltd.; Factory Card Outlet Corporation; Findel plc; FTD.COM INC.; The Gadget Shop Ltd.; Highway Capital plc; JUSCO Co., Ltd.; King Power International Group Co., Ltd.; William Sinclair Holdings plc.

Further Reading

Blackwell, David, "Product Range Benefits Give Cheer to Clinton," *Financial Times*, January 12, 2001.

Duckers, John, "Low Expectations on High Street Knock Firms Sideways," *Birmingham Post*, January 12, 2001, p. 26.

Kahn, Stephen, "Clinton Chief Plays 'Happy Families' Card," *Daily Express*, September 22, 2000.

Kleinman, Mark, "Clinton Cards Explores In-Store Postal Service," *Marketing*, November 9, 2000, p. 1.

Litterick, David, "Love Rescues Clinton," *Daily Telegraph*, April 5, 2000.

"Poorly Cards Retailer Hopes to Get Well Soon," *Birmingham Post*, September 22, 2000, p. 21.

"Seasonal Greetings," *Investors Chronicle*, October 13, 2000.

—M.L. Cohen

Close Brothers Group plc

10 Crown Place
London EC2A 4FT
United Kingdom
Telephone: (+44) 20 7426-4000
Fax: (+44) 20-7426-4044
Web site: http://www.closebrothers.co.uk

Public Company
Incorporated: 1878
Employees: 1,365
Total Assets: £2.6 billion ($3.7 billion)
Stock Exchanges: London
Ticker Symbol: CBG
NAIC: 523110 Investment Banking and Securities
   Dealing; 522293 International Trade Financing

Small but steady Close Brothers plc is the last independent merchant bank in the United Kingdom. In an era that has seen its competitors gobbled up by the banking industry's global giants, Close Brothers has carved out a strong niche among the United Kingdom's small and mid-sized businesses often neglected by the larger banks. Close Brothers, which is set up as a confederation of some 30 businesses, each with its own management team and board of directors, operates in three primary areas: Merchant Banking, including corporate finance and asset management activities; Asset Finance; and Market-Making. The latter division, led by subsidiary Winterflood Securities, is also the company's rainmaker, contributing more than 60 percent of Close Brothers' 2000 operating profits. The bank boasts 25 years of unbroken profit growth, which, aided by the company's strong market-making presence in the high-technology sector, jumped past £380 million with the boom of so-called "dot.com" companies. Close Brothers is led by Chairman David Scholey, former head of SG Warburg, who joined the bank in 1999, and founding member of the "modern" Close Brothers, managing director Roderick D. Kent.

Gold Fever Beginnings in the 19th Century

The Close family had been prominent bankers for more than 100 years before W.B. Close and his brothers founded their own banking and investment firm in the late 1870s. Englishman James Close had traveled to Sicily, setting up "merchant" operations, a name popularly used by investment and banking firms of the era. In 1856, James Close set up a new business in the Kingdom of Naples—before that city was included in the formation of the modern Italian state. Close was no mere merchant, however. Acting as financial advisor to Neapolitan King Ferdinand II, Close was to be granted the status of cavalier. Upon the death of Ferdinand in 1859, Close retired to his yacht and devoted himself to raising his numerous children.

Among these was William Brooks, known as W.B., the sixth Close child, who was born in 1853. When W.B. was 12 years old, James Close died, and W.B. and his brothers were sent to school in England. W.B. and brothers James and John were all rowing enthusiasts, joining the team at Trinity College at Cambridge; another brother, Frederick, chose not to continue his education, and instead journeyed to the United States to become a West Virginia farmer.

A regatta in Philadelphia brought W.B. to the United States in 1876; while there, W.B. met up with a family from Illinois, who invited him out to tour the prairies of Iowa. The family—W.B.'s future in-laws—had been making a fortune buying up public land and selling parcels to the growing number of settlers moving west in the post-Civil War era. W.B. soon was joined by brother Fred, and, together with James Close, they formed the Close Brothers partnership, based in London.

The brothers hit pay dirt on their first try, buying up nearly 15,000 acres for just US$35,000. At less than US$2.50 per acre, the Close Brothers stood to make a handsome profit and the beginning of a new family fortune. Yet the company already showed itself as an investment house, rather than seeking mere profits. The Closes recruited settlers from the United Kingdom, and then taught the new farmers proper farming techniques for Iowa conditions. Close Brothers even went so far as to set up its own agricultural college.

The partnership opened its first office in Sioux City, then moved to Chicago, where it began to work closely with First National Bank of Chicago as the Close Brothers looked farther afield for their next investment opportunities. The company's British branch also had continued to grow, and in 1888, the partnership formed a subsidiary operation, Mortgage and Debenture Co. Ltd., for its business interest in the United Kingdom. By the end of the 19th century, however, Close Brothers was put to the test. A long depression had devastated its Iowan investment interests, and the Close Brothers struggled.

The great Alaskan gold rush provided the partnership with its next claim to fame. Prospectors rushing to Skagway, Alaska were required to cross the treacherous White Pass to reach the gold-rich Klondike region. In 1897, Close Brothers bought the right to construct a railway to link Scagway to the Yukon region, including building a bridge across White Pass. Close Brothers sent their representatives to Scagway, and construction got under way in 1898.

While in Scagway, the Close Brothers representatives met Michael Heney, a Canadian surveyor with railroad experience, who had recognized the potential for building a railroad linking the Yukon River with the Pacific Ocean and had begun surveying the proposed route. Close Brothers quickly agreed to back Heney's plan. Close Brothers' investment reached some US$7 million over the life of the project, which continued into the years leading up to the First World War.

Transformations in the 20th Century

The White Pass & Yukon Railway gave Close Brothers a degree of fame as a member of the rather exclusive club of railroad magnates at the turn of the century. The company's chief source of revenues continued to come from its Midwest mortgaging business and the railway, but the bank also began loaning to the mining and other industries. Another growing source of income was the company's banking, investment, and lending activity among a select group of private individuals—for the most part from W.B. Close's circle of aristocratic friends. In 1909, Close Brothers added two new partners, W.H.B. Stevens and J.P. Cushing, and reincorporated as a London-based private company. The American operations were incorporated subsequently as a subsidiary to the London firm.

The private company was reincorporated again after the death of W.B. Close in 1923. By then, the company had shut down its Chicago banking operations and its center of activity began to shift to its London banking operations. The appointment of Arthur Martens as chairman in 1934 breathed new life into the bank, which had greatly reduced the scope of its operations in the decade following W.B. Close's death. Under Martens, Close Brothers began developing a new area of investment interest—in the mid-1930s, Martens led Close in establishing the South Western Gas Corporation, a holding company that went on a buying spree, acquiring some 100 small gas and electric utility companies operating in the United Kingdom's then highly fragmented utility industry. South Western Gas became the dominant utility company in its southwestern England region and remained in operation until the nationalization of the United Kingdom's utility industries at the end of the Second World War.

Although Close Brothers continued to control its railroad, it ceded the lease to the United States government during World War II. In the years following the war, the company switched its attention to new investment endeavors. Among these was the formation of Bramalea Consolidated Developments Ltd., set up in Canada to finance the development of a new town, located near Toronto, for a total investment of some $80 million. Close Brothers was also behind the financing of a new type of "floating diamond mine," designed to mine diamonds from beneath the waters off the African coast in the 1960s. That project proved a flop, however. More successful were its investments in more traditional mining, utility, property, and banking projects. In the 1960s, Close Brothers was behind the listing of Purle Brothers Holdings, which later became known as Redland plc.

Arthur Martens's death in 1964 led the company into a new transformation. Martens's successors, including son Fraser Martens, were unable to match the bank's former success, and by the early 1970s Close Brothers was losing money. In 1970, Close Brothers was bought up by Max Maimann, who had fled to England from Austria during the Second World War and who had already launched two successful public companies. Maimann quickly sold off most of Close Brothers' money-losing North American interests—which by then nonetheless represented the majority of the bank's active operations—and restored the banks' profits by 1972. In that year, Maimann sold more than 45 percent of Close Brothers to London & Western Trust.

London & Western Trust had been set up by Michael Morley, James Leek, and other colleagues at merchant bank Samuel Montague. The young team—Morley was just 32 years old—sought for London & Western Trust to be a merchant bank. Acquiring Close Brothers turned out to be London & Western's fastest route to a position in the banking industry. Morley et al quickly revived Close Brothers' diversified interests, developing new property lending and corporate finance activities. The bank soon took on a specialized focus as a lender to smaller companies usually bypassed by larger institutional lenders.

As the United Kingdom's property market headed into slump in the mid-1970s, Morley and his team sought to boost the company's operations into more high-volume activities. London & Western turned to Consolidated Goldfields, a mining industry finance and investment house, seeking to buy out

Consolidated's export finance operation. Goldfields turned Close Brothers down—and instead proposed to acquire London & Western itself. Morley and partners agreed, receiving more than £2.7 million. Morley was appointed head of Consolidated's newly enlarged finance wing, while James Leek took over as head of Close Brothers. Leek left the bank in 1975, placing Rod Kent, who had just completed a degree at the prestigious Parisian INSEAD business school. At the age of 27, Kent was faced with negotiating Close Brothers through the deep recession of the late 1970s.

By 1978, Morley and Kent were joined by two other partners to lead a management buyout of Close Brothers from its Consolidated Goldfields parent. The team attracted a number of institutional investors, including London & Yorkshire Trust and Safeguard Industrial Investments, successfully breaking away from an initially reluctant Consolidated Goldfields. Morley left Close Brothers in 1981, joining rival merchant bank Charterhouse, before returning to Close Brothers in 1985.

By then, Close Brothers had transformed itself, as the small bank went on an acquisition drive to build new product areas. Between 1982 and 1987 the bank acquired a number of companies, including Century Factors, which was renamed as Close Invoice Finance, and then Air and General Finance, a lending company to the aircraft industry. The company also launched its PROMPT insurance premium finance vehicle. Yet Close Brothers' most ambitious move was its reverse-takeover of principal investor, Safeguard, which, valued at £21 million, dwarfed

Close Brothers, which was then valued at less than £4 million. The reverse takeover was finalized in 1984.

The following year, Close Brothers made headlines when it rescued struggling British computer company Acorn Computers and orchestrated that company's acquisition by Olivetti. Close Brothers also was achieving success away from the spotlight, such as advising Caledonia Investments on its £427 million pullout from British & Commonwealth Holdings—effectively rescuing Caledonia's shareholding when B&C collapsed at the end of the decade. Caledonia became a major investor in Close Brothers, building up a 20 percent stake before the 1990s.

Close Brothers continued making acquisitions, expanding its areas of operations. While the merchant bank guided overall strategy, its subsidiary operations remained, in large part, independent, retaining existing management and headquarters. As the United Kingdom headed into a new recession in the early 1990s, Close Brothers was presented with new acquisition opportunities. Among the companies acquired at this time were the soon-to-be-named Close Brothers Investment, a specialist in BES transactions, and Close Consumer Finance, adding automobile financing operations, both acquired in 1991. The following year, Close Brothers added Business Advisory Services.

One of Close Brothers' most significant acquisitions was that of Winterflood Securities, a leading market-maker for small company stocks, which the company bought in 1993. The £19 million purchase price placed Close Brothers in a front spot for the coming explosion of high-technology stock listings. By the late 1990s, the Winterflood operations were to grow to represent some 60 percent of Close Brothers' operating profits. Meanwhile, the company was absorbing another major acquisition, that of the Hill Samuel corporate finance wing of Lloyds TSB Group. Funding Close Brothers' growth was a new rights issue, which raised more than £50 million for further investments. In 1995, Close Brothers boosted its investments side with the launch of Close Fund Management and a new range of trust and fund products dubbed Escalator.

Founding partner Peter Stone left the company in 1998. A year later, the bank lost another of its founding buyout partners when Michael Morley died. The bank found a new chairman in David Scholey, who had served as chairman of SG Warburg before its acquisition by Swiss Bank Corporation. Scholey, with Rod Kent as chief executive, quickly found themselves in the spotlight when a news leak in 2000 revealed that French powerhouse bank BNP-Paribas had approached Close Brothers with an acquisition offer. As the last remaining independent merchant bank in the United Kingdom, many analysts began to wonder for how long Close Brothers would be able to resist future acquisition offers.

Meanwhile, Close Brothers continued to invest in its own growth, acquiring Rea Brothers to boost its fund management wing, and Warrior, a financial services provider to the United Kingdom's armed forces, both in 1999. In 2000, Close Brothers began boosting its international presence, buying 50 percent of France's Dôme & Cie, as well as extending its products with the acquisitions of optical equipment finance house Braemar Finance and the European insurance finance wing of Transamerica Insurance Finance Company, a subsidiary of Transamerica Financial Corporation. Close Brothers appeared determined to maintain its independence into the new century.

Principal Subsidiaries

Air and General Finance Limited; Close Asset Finance Limited; Close Brothers Corporate Finance Limited; Close Brothers Equity Markets S.A.; Close Brothers Investment Limited (98%); Close Consumer Finance Limited (98%); Close Credit Management (Holdings) Limited (99%); Close Fund Management Limited (90%); Close Investment Limited (92%); Close Investment Management (Isle of Man) Limited; Close Invoice Finance Limited (95%); Close Trustees (Switzerland) S.A. (70%); Close Wealth Management Limited (88%); Dôme Close Brothers S.A. (50%); Freyberg Close Brothers GmbH (60%); Mortgage Intelligence Limited (75%); Surrey Asset Finance Limited (83%); Transamerica Insurance Finance Corporation; Winterflood Gilts Limited (95%); Winterflood Securities Limited (95%).

Principal Competitors

3i Group plc; Abbey National plc; Bank of Ireland; Barclays plc; Charles Schwab; Goldman Sachs; HSBC Holdings; Jefferies Group; Legg Mason; Lloyds TSB; Merrill Lynch; Natexis; Royal Bank of Scotland; Schroders; Singer & Friedlander Group; St. James's Place Capital; UBS Warburg.

Further Reading

Buckingham, Lisa, ''The Lament of Rod Kent: A Patriot in Pinstripes,'' *Financial Mail on Sunday,* February 4, 2001.

Bushrod, Lisa, ''Merger Changes Close Strategy to Buy-and-Build,'' *Private Banker International,* June 19, 2000.

''A Different Kind of Gold Rush,'' *Daily Telegraph,* March 7, 2000, p. 39.

Garfield, Andrew, ''Close Brothers Gives Paribas a Speedy Brush-off,'' *Independent,* October 9, 2000, p. 16.

Gomer, Hilaire, ''Old Ways Prove Successful at Close,'' *Daily Telegraph,* March 4, 1999, p. 69.

Trefgame, George, ''Brothers Unite,'' *Private Banker International,* August 9, 1999.

—M.L. Cohen

Concepts Direct, Inc.

2950 Colorful Avenue
Longmont, Colorado 80504
U.S.A.
Telephone: (303) 772-9171
Fax: (303) 682-7140
Web site: http://www.cdir.com

Public Company
Incorporated: 1992
Employees: 520
Sales: $55.5 million (1999)
Stock Exchanges: NASDAQ
Ticker Symbol: CDIR
NAIC: 323119 Other Commercial Printing; 454110
Electronic Shopping and Mail-order Houses

Concepts Direct, Inc. is a direct mail order catalog company that sells personalized paper products, t-shirts, and other casual apparel, home decorative items, gifts, and collectibles. The company's catalog concepts are *Colorful Images, Linda Anderson, Linda Anderson Collectibles, The Music Stand,* and *Snoopy etc.: A Catalog With Character.* Concepts Direct offers goods for sale by mailing catalogs to 11 million customers annually. In addition, each catalog brand has a corresponding Internet site. Other Internet businesses include NewBargains.com, YourCountryStore.com, and an Internet portal for online retailers, called BOTWEB.

Independence From a 1992 Spin-off

Concepts Direct originated in 1987 as the Consumer Products Division of Wiland Services, a database management and information services company serving direct mail merchants. The division sold personalized paper products, such as self-adhesive address labels and stationery with colorful scenes and images, directly to consumers utilizing the company's direct marketing resources. As new products were added, the *Colorful Images* catalog evolved. In addition to 450 different styles of address labels, the product line included self-adhesive lunch bag labels, note pads, pencils, self-inking stamps, and photo coffee mugs. Prices ranged from $5.95 for a set of address labels to $39.95 for a sunflower watch. In less than three years the division neared the $10 million sales mark.

Concepts Direct became an independent company in 1992 when Philip A. Wiland, founder and chairman of Wiland Services, sold the technical services division to Neodata and transformed the direct marketing division into a separate, publicly owned company. With 50 employees, including several key executives from Wiland Services, Wiland planned to develop a mail order catalog company using *Colorful Images* as a base. Concepts Direct started as a money-losing operation despite revenues of $15 million; the company was valued at 52 cents per share.

The sale of Wiland Services allowed Wiland to improve operations and to refine the marketing base at Concepts Direct. The company streamlined customer service and order fulfillment procedures that enabled telephone orders to be filled and posted within 24 hours and mail orders to be filled within 48 hours. Consolidation of different orders for a specific label design into one printing run also improved efficiency. After experimentation with the product line, adding t-shirts, blankets, wind chimes, statuary, and other items, the company identified its market niche and found a more secure customer base. The company attracted primarily female customers, with 95 percent of orders from women at a slightly above average income. The average customer's age, at 45 years old, hid the diverse range, from teenagers to retirees.

In 1994 Concepts Direct sought to expand its business with new products and by prospecting for new customers. In January the *Colorful Images* catalog featured a new line of women's apparel, which became the basis for a new catalog concept, *Linda Anderson.* The personalized paper products remained under the *Colorful Images* line, and gifts, casual clothing for women, and home decorative items sold through the new catalog. Wiland surveyed other retail catalogs to determine competitive pricing and value-oriented products appropriate for the midrange to upscale merchandise. The October 1994 *Linda Anderson* catalog produced a good response, meriting further testing and mailing. In addition, Concepts Direct expanded the

Company Perspectives:

Concepts Direct is focused on serving four critical constituencies: Customers, Employees, Shareholders and our Community. Every decision we make and every action we take is in support of serving these constituents.

Colorful Images catalog from 32 pages at the end of 1993 to 48 pages at the end of 1994. Prospecting for new customers, the company rented a list of potential customers.

By the end of 1994, Concepts Direct had developed a customer database of 4.8 million people. With five mailings per year, the company circulated a total of 16 million catalogs throughout the United States and Canada, although orders arrived from as far away as Japan. The catalogs generated 2,000 telephone orders per day and more than double that during the winter holiday shopping season. The company filled 15,000 to 20,000 orders for personalized address labels, printing 7,000 to 8,000 labels a day on three laser printers. A staff of 140 full-time employees and a temporary holiday staff of 60 employees filled the orders. The return rate hovered from five percent to eight percent, considered a good record for a direct marketing company. Wiland attributed this low return rate to accurate descriptive text and true-to-life, color pictures.

In 1994 revenues reached $20.7 million in 1994, garnering a first profit of $1.5 million. This prospecting produced a positive result, although the higher overhead, as compared with established customer lists, resulted in slower earnings growth. In addition, the overall response to the catalog, from established and new customers, was higher than expected. Demand required the company to hire new employees and train them quickly, while order fulfillment fell behind schedule, prompting the company to pay higher shipping costs for timely delivery. During the fourth quarter—the holiday shopping season when a majority of sales are generated in direct mail businesses—sales increased 73 percent and earnings grew 49 percent.

Mixed Results in the Mid-1990s

Concepts Direct continued to fine-tune and expand its catalog brands in 1995. In January a second test catalog of *Linda Anderson* met with a positive response. The fall issue featured more gift and home decorative items and less apparel, all at lower price points, as well as a brighter catalog presentation. With 1.4 million catalogs circulated in 1995, *Linda Anderson* generated average orders of $69.00. This compared with *Colorful Images'* lower-priced products, which generated average orders of $20.00. The *Colorful Images* catalog was expanded to 80 pages by the October, pre-holiday release. The company more than doubled its catalog circulation to 44 million catalogs in 1995, thereby doubling revenues to $42.2 million.

Expansion and improvements produced mixed results, however. Sales increased 103 percent, causing the company's stock value to more than double from $5.50 per share in December 1994, to $13.55 in December 1995, topping $20 by mid-1996. The company invested in a new computer system and software development to improve order processing and fulfillment, data-base management, purchasing, warehousing, and general ledger capabilities. Implementation and disruption to business operations due to bugs in the system hampered earnings. In addition, a 14 percent postage rate increase and the higher cost of paper stock for catalogs lowered company earnings.

Revenue and earnings grew at a more equal rate in 1996, 21 percent and 30 percent, respectively, through higher customer response in relation to advertising costs. Increases in paper costs prompted the company to cut circulation midyear, but lower prices at the end of the year allowed for a full-scale mailing for the holiday shopping season. Advertising strategies designed to sidestep increasing postage and paper costs included promoting return address labels through newspaper inserts and direct mail cooperative advertising and in magazines. Prospecting catalogs, those delivered to untested customer lists, contained fewer pages, offering the company's key products only. The company launched a new catalog, *Colorful Images Presents Impressions,* in June; uncertain results required further development of the catalog concept.

With new catalogs in development and plans to add 100 new employees, Concepts Direct took steps to expand its operational capacity. Funds from a secondary public offering of stock in May 1997 provided support for expansion. The company purchased a 153-acre lot where it began construction on a 120,000-square-foot facility, combining its warehousing and manufacturing operations, customer service center, and administrative offices at one location.

Concepts Direct successfully launched two new mail order catalog brands. *Linda Anderson Collectibles,* spawned by the success of *Linda Anderson,* featured stuffed animals and figurines. Strong sales of the Boyds Collection, Precious Moments, Hummel, and Charming Tails brands in the original catalog motivated development of direct marketing of collectibles. Concepts Direct launched the catalog with a test mailing to potential customers in fall 1997. Response to the mailing, with average orders at $57, merited further testing and development of the database. Through the circulation of one million catalogs before the Christmas holiday, Concepts Direct obtained 14,000 active customers.

The second successful catalog introduction in 1997 was prompted by the popularity of the Peanuts address labels. Merchandise in *Snoopy, etc: A Catalog With Character* featured images of Charles M. Schulz's popular Peanuts comic strip characters, including Charlie Brown, Snoopy, and Woodstock. Concepts Direct obtained a license to merchandise the products from United Media. Circulation of 1.6 million catalogs in the second half of 1997 generated average orders of $71 from 16,000 active customers.

Success of the two new catalogs generated a 54 percent increase in sales, from $51.1 million in 1996, to $78.5 million in sales in 1997. Net income declined, however, from $1.9 million in 1996 to $1.6 million in 1997. The decline stemmed from one-time costs for prospecting for customers for the two new catalogs, development of the catalogs themselves, increasing paper costs, and investment in infrastructure. Prospecting for customers through catalog circulation, the largest expense of a mail order business, continued to hinder profits, leading to a loss of

Key Dates:

1987:   Company begins as Consumer Products Division of Wiland Services.
1992:   Company is spun into separate company; adopts name Concepts Direct.
1994:   Company launches *Linda Anderson* catalog.
1995:   Revenues double to $42.2 million.
1997:   Company launches *Snoopy etc.: A Catalog With Character*
1999:   Internet commerce commences.

$1.4 million in 1998 on a record $84.7 million in sales. Losses continued into 1999 as the company drastically cut circulation to reduce costs while launching new Internet web sites.

In June 1999 Concepts Direct purchased *The Music Stand* catalog and related assets, including inventory, a customer database, and the brand trademark. *The Music Stand* sold music-related gifts, collectibles, and awards, finding its main customers among teachers and students of music, dance, and theater for 20 years. Concepts Direct merged *The Music Stand* into its operations in Longmont. Sales from the fall catalog issues exceeded expectation.

Focus on Internet Commerce at Turn of the Century

Internet commerce being a logical extension of direct mail merchandising, Concepts Direct continued to invest in its computer infrastructure. Through partnerships with software and hardware developers, the company developed *Enable* to handle all aspects of on-line operations, including hosting web sites for its own catalogs and third party on-line retailers.

In addition, Wiland developed the BOTWEB portal to provide web shoppers quicker access to direct market retailers on the Internet. Short for "Best Of The Web," the BOTWEB portal site provided reviews of e-commerce web sites under 44 product categories, such as apparel, crafts, and pets, including coverage on download time, customer service, and content. Concepts Direct sold advertising only to retailers deemed "Best of the Web." The December 1999 launch involved a 48-page directory of BOTWEB participants mailed to 200,000 customers in December and 400,000 in early January. The site generated revenues from banner advertising and the BOTWEB directory.

Concepts Direct successfully launched its own direct marketing web sites, beginning with LindaAnderson.com in July 1999. Sales improved steadily from $1000 in July to $50,000 in October and $118,000 during November holiday shopping. The company also launched MusicStand.com in November; the site generated $46,000 in sales in its first month. A web site launched in December, iGift.com, provided consumers with a Gift Finder that compiled a product list based on the information about the intended recipient. Users input information about the gift recipient, such as gender, age, interests, and hobbies, as well as about the occasion and desired price range. From more than 7,000 items, mostly for women, Gift Finder presented a list with the most appropriate items at the top. The company

planned to add men's and children's gift items to the product list. In January 2000 Concepts Direct launched NewBargains .com, an online outlet for unsold merchandise from the company's catalogs. The site offered 25 percent to 85 percent discounts on new, undamaged merchandise.

The shift of resources to Internet-based retailing contributed to a net loss in 1999. Sales for the fourth quarter 1999, the holiday shopping season, dropped 30 percent, and sales declined 35 percent for the year. Like many catalog retailers, Concepts Direct had reduced catalog circulation to cut costs, while hoping its Internet presence would counterbalance the reduction. Circulation for *Linda Anderson* was cut 65 percent, and sales for the fourth quarter declined 52 percent. A $2.2 million write-off for the excess inventory resulted in a net loss of $1.7 million for the quarter. Sales for 1999 declined to $55.5 million and net loss increased to $3.6 million. J. Michael Wolfe, president and COO since 1992, considered this a temporary setback as the company repositioned itself through better targeted catalog circulation and through investment in the Internet. In addition, each catalog proved to be profitable for the first time in accordance within certain parameters of operational and administrative costs.

To assist shareholders in differentiating areas of profit and loss, Concepts Direct formed two new subsidiaries to separate on-line activities from its direct mail catalog business. iConcepts, Inc. acted as the umbrella for new brands and new web sites until those businesses became strong enough to form independent subsidiaries. iConcepts provided site hosting, on-line order processing, and database management for Concepts Direct businesses and, in the future, for third parties. J. Michael Wolfe became CEO of Concepts Direct, freeing Wiland, still chairman, to oversee Internet start-ups. Wiland also oversaw the second new subsidiary, BOTWEB, Inc., which handled business related to the web portal.

New web site brands launched in early 2000 included TheBearHouse.com and YourCountryStore.com. TheBearHouse .com sold collectibles proven to be popular brands from the *Linda Anderson's Collectibles* catalog, such as the Boyds Collection and Judith G. The site was a natural extension of the company's microniche program, which targets customers for the sale of specific collectibles. The company planned to offer other collectibles on a web site in development, CollectiblesCity.com. YourCountryStore.com offered 2,300 products in American classic country style, including gifts, home decorations, and collectibles. Concepts Direct also expanded its direct mail catalogs, successfully testing *Colorful Christmas* in late 1999 and *Colorful Spring* and *Colorful Cats* in early 2000.

As financial difficulties continued, Concepts Direct decided to sell 100 acres of undeveloped land next to its Longmont facility. Stock value tumbled to $4.34 per share in August on news of losses and a three-month medical leave for Wiland. Sale of the vacant land and a sale/lease back of the building that autumn raised $15 million in capital for debt reduction, continuing operations, and expansion.

Concepts Direct continued to develop its Internet presence. In November 2000 the company launched SnoopyStore.com in partnership with Charles M. Schulz Creative Associates. ColorfulImages.com generated $50,000 in revenue during its first 16 days, offering personalized paper products, gifts, and t-shirts.

Principal Subsidiaries

BOTWEB, Inc.; iConcepts, Inc.

Principal Competitors

Current, Inc.; Fingerhut Companies, Inc.; Hanover Direct; Lillian Vernon Corporation.

Further Reading

"Cutting Losses by Cutting Circ.," *Catalog Age,* August 1999, p. 8.

Esterson, Emily, "Longmont, Colo., Concepts Direct Labels 1994 a Success," *Knight-Ridder/Tribune Business News,* December 5, 1994, p. 12050243.

"Fourth-Quarter Blues," *Catalog Age,* May 2000, p. 8.

Glairon, Susan, "Longmont Concepts Direct Inc. Stock Plunges Catalog and Internet Retailing Company Cuts Back Spending," *Boulder Daily Camera,* August 3, 2000, p. 1D.

Laughlin, Joyanna, "Concepts Direct Doubles in Size, Invests in Tough Circumstances," *Boulder County Business Report,* June 1, 1996, p. 4.

Locke, Tom, "Concepts Direct Plans Secondary Stock Offering," 1997, p. 6B.

"Mailer Turns Portal," *Catalog Age,* December 1999, p. 5.

McCann, Susan de Castro, "Concepts Direct Will Build New Headquarters in Weld," *Northern Colorado Business Report,* March 1, 1997, p. 2B.

Oberndorf, Shannon, "Mining New Niches," *Catalog Age,* October 1998, p. 6.

—Mary Tradii

The Cooper Companies, Inc.

6140 Stoneridge Mall Road, Suite 590
Pleasonton, California 94588
U.S.A.
Telephone: (925) 460-3600
Fax: (925) 460-3649
Web site: http://www.coopercos.com

Public Company
Incorporated: 1958 as Cooper Laboratories, Inc.
Employees: 1,750
Sales: $197.3 million (2000)
Stock Exchanges: New York Pacific
Ticker Symbol: COO
NAIC: 339113 Surgical Appliance and Supplies
Manufacturing

The Cooper Companies, Inc. is a specialty healthcare company operating in two medical device markets: contact lenses and women's healthcare products. Through its subsidiary, CooperVision, Inc., Cooper Companies develops and markets contact lenses globally, manufacturing soft toric, aspheric, disposable, and colored lenses. The sale of contact lenses accounts for more than 80 percent of Cooper Companies' sales volume, a total drawn chiefly from the sale of soft toric lenses, which correct astigmatism. CooperVision ranks as the leading marketer of soft toric lenses in the United States. Cooper Companies' other business unit, CooperSurgical, Inc., specializes in gynecological instruments and disposable medical products for the women's healthcare market.

Cooper's Origins

Cooper Companies traces its history to the formation of Cooper Laboratories in 1958. Cooper Labs was founded by Parker Montgomery, a 30-year-old, Harvard-educated son of a Boston attorney, who was himself an attorney. Before starting Cooper Labs, Montgomery practiced law on Wall Street, gaining experience he would use in the stewardship of his new company. Although Cooper Labs represented Montgomery's entry into the healthcare equipment and services industry, it soon became apparent that Montgomery's true affection lay in the world of Wall Street finance, in the realm of acquisitions, deal-making, and corporate strategizing. Montgomery's approach directed Cooper Labs onto a direct route for growth, but on several occasions his penchant for accelerating growth via acquisitions led to serious problems. As a result, Cooper Cos. early history—the years of Cooper Labs—included several misadventures, which eventually led to Montgomery's ouster from the company he had started.

Montgomery's first notable miscue occurred during the 1970s. During the decade, he launched an aggressive acquisition campaign, one that proved to be ill timed and overly aggressive. Through a series of acquisitions, Montgomery increased Cooper Labs' sales to nearly $100 million, but a combination of recessive economic conditions and the company's inability to effectively absorb its new assets hobbled the burgeoning concern. "We had the unhappy coincidence of first shooting our own legs off," said Montgomery in the November 7, 1983 issue of *Forbes* magazine, "and then having the economy shoot the rest of us up." The ill-fated acquisition spree weakened the company, its troubles evident in a sharp decline in sales and two years of losses. The situation was set to worsen, but Montgomery was able to arrest the slide by completing a series of divestitures. The company's problems did not end after the asset sales, however. Montgomery's next regrettable move occurred as the 1980s began.

In 1981, Montgomery was in the midst of orchestrating a mammoth deal: two acquisitions that would transform Cooper Labs into a billion-dollar conglomerate essentially overnight. It was, as Montgomery conceded in the November 7, 1983 issue of *Forbes,* "a terrible tactical error." To complete the first half of the deal, Montgomery borrowed heavily, enabling him to purchase Sterndent, a Connecticut-based dental supply company with $250 million in annual sales. Montgomery failed to execute the second half of his masterstroke, the acquisition of a dental distribution company with more than $200 million in annual sales, but the damage had already been done by the Sterndent acquisition. With Cooper Labs' debt towering at $159 million, the prime rate shot up to 21 percent, delivering a

Company Perspectives:

Cooper is a medical device company operating in two attractive specialty markets: contact lenses in the vision care market through CooperVision, and diagnostics and devices used in the physician's office in the women's healthcare market through CooperSurgical. In both these markets, we offer proprietary, patented, and, where possible, differentiated products. At CooperVision, we develop new products and improve manufacturing processes through research and engineering. Our business development activities focus on geographic expansion and, occasionally, product acquisition. At CooperSurgical, we develop new products internally, license innovative technology and attempt to consolidate the highly fragmented women's healthcare market through product and company acquisitions.

crippling blow to the debt-ridden Montgomery. Again, Cooper Labs teetered on the brink of collapse, its interest expense rising to $25 million, or 65 percent of the company's 1982 operating profit. As he had done several years earlier, Montgomery was able to stave off disaster through asset sales. He sold most of Sterndent to Johnson & Johnson, making no profit on the deal. In another attempt to reduce the company's debt, Montgomery sold other parts of Cooper Labs, but he did so in a way that became the talk of Wall Street.

The Roller Coaster 1980s

As part of a strategy that Montgomery called "Project Supernova," parts of two subsidiaries were sold to the public in 1983. In January, he sold 18 percent of CooperVision, a subsidiary with $195 million in annual sales that owned an assortment of contact lens and ophthalmic supply companies. The stake in CooperVision, which figured as the core of Cooper Cos. during the 1990s, was sold at $20 per share, or approximately 27 times the subsidiary's 1982 earnings. In August, Montgomery sold 17 percent of CooperBiomedical, a subsidiary that generated $50 million in sales that developed and sold drugs and research laboratory products. Investors paid 35 times Cooper-Biomedical's 1983 earnings in the offering. Montgomery's spin-offs were part of a trend in which parent companies sold typically less than a third of their subsidiaries to the public, a strategy that generated cash—Montgomery raised $60 million from the partial sale of CooperVision—and piqued investors' interest in the assets of the parent company. "I don't think management can just sit passively and see the price of their stock as being totally outside their control," Montgomery explained to *Fortune* magazine in an August 8, 1983 interview.

Aided by Project Supernova, Cooper Labs recorded a remarkable turnaround from the Sterndent debacle. The company's stock value more than doubled in 1983, profits rose, and annual revenues neared $400 million. At the heart of the recovery was CooperVision, which displayed a vitality that attracted investors and encouraged Montgomery to treat it as his primary vehicle for expansion. In 1983, he set a five-year goal of lifting CooperVision's annual revenue volume to $1 billion, proposing to increase the subsidiary's size fivefold. Toward this end,

Montgomery made an important acquisition several months after selling the 18 percent stake in CooperVision to the public. The subsidiary purchased UCO Optics, a company that had played a pioneering role in the development of contact lenses and whose history was linked to the year Montgomery founded Cooper Labs.

In 1958, the year Cooper Labs began operating, Dr. Stanley Gordon founded the Contact Lens Guild in Rochester, New York. Gordon, who renamed the company Gordon Contact Lenses, Inc. in 1965, was renowned for his expertise in rigid lens design, but his most celebrated work involved the development of soft contact lenses. In 1970, Union Corporation purchased Gordon's company, creating a new company named UCO Optics. The same year the UCO Optics corporate banner was first unfurled, Gordon developed tetrafilcon, which could be used to make a soft, hydrophilic contact lens to replace the hard, hydrophobic contact lenses that many wearers found uncomfortable. After an extensive development phase, UCO Optics used its proprietary tetrafilcon to unveil its Aquaflex brand in 1976, the third soft contact lens to be approved by the Food and Drug Administration (FDA).

The acquisition of UCO Optics by CooperVision added market strength to Montgomery's position in the contact lens industry. Four years before the union was completed in 1983, CooperVision had released Permalens, the first contact lens approved by the FDA for 30-day continuous wear, which, combined with UCO Optics product line, created an enviable foundation on which to build.

The list of CooperVision's eye care assets increased significantly in the years following its stock offering. In 1985, the company expanded its product line to include the Permalens, Permaflex, and Aquaflex brands. The following year, Cooper Companies was adopted as the parent company's corporate title, with CooperVision, housing all the organization's eye care assets, operating as a subsidiary of Cooper Companies.

Montgomery fell short of his five-year sales goal, but by 1988 he had more than tripled the size of CooperVision, increasing its annual revenue to more than $625 million. His work, however, was deemed unsatisfactory by a group of shareholders. Ironically, for someone who had attracted national press by displaying a penchant for asset sales, Montgomery's fall stemmed from his unwillingness to sell assets, a perception held by two sets of brothers, the Singers and the Sturmans. There were three brothers from each family, all of whom had attended the same high school in Westchester County, New York. Collectively, the Singers and the Sturmans controlled 14 percent of Cooper Companies, giving them enough influence to force Montgomery to resign when the brothers threatened to launch a proxy fight. Montgomery stepped down in August 1988, leaving a company he had started 30 years earlier.

With the close of the Montgomery era, a new chapter in the company's history began, arguably the bleakest period in Cooper Companies' existence. Disputes in the boardroom raged in the wake of Montgomery's ouster, as the company's performance—praised several years earlier by numerous analysts—sputtered amid the rancor. The turmoil boiled over after a federal insider trading investigation led to indictments against

Key Dates:

1958: Parker Montgomery founds Cooper Laboratories.
1979: CooperVision introduces Permalens, the first contact lens approved for 30-day continuous wear.
1983: UCO Optics is acquired.
1986: Cooper Laboratories is renamed The Cooper Companies, Inc.
1991: Thomas Bender is hired as chief operating officer.
1998: Company announces the divestiture of Hospital Group of America.

members of the Singer and Sturman families, which led to their removal from the company's boardroom. Saddled with debt and lacking senior management to guide it, the company suffered profoundly. In 1991, the company's stock value plunged to $1 per share, which, together with a $6 million loss for the year, served as the telltale signs of a company in crisis. The company needed a savior to cure its profound problems. In 1991, such an individual joined the ranks of Cooper Companies' senior management, sparking a revival that gathered momentum throughout the 1990s.

New Management, Stability, Growth for the 1990s

Thomas Bender joined Cooper Companies in 1991 as its new chief operating officer. He and fellow executives were forced to take drastic measures to breathe new life into the ailing concern. They shed assets that were underperforming, laid off hundreds of employees, and reduced debt. "It was a tough job," recalled Bender in a January 18, 2000 interview with *Knight-Ridder/Tribune Business News*, addomg "We told employees that what we were doing was something for them long-term—and if we didn't, there wouldn't be anything for anyone."

Cooper Companies emerged from the massive restructuring program as a dramatically smaller company focused on three business segments. What had once been a company with more than $600 million in annual revenue ended 1993 with $92.6 million in revenue, a total collected from its involvement in the mental healthcare market, the vision care market, and the women's healthcare market. Cooper Companies operated in these three business areas through three subsidiaries: Hospital Group of America (HGA), CooperSurgical, and CooperVision. Of the three subsidiaries, two figured in the company's long-term plans. HGA, which owned and operated psychiatric hospitals that provided inpatient and outpatient treatment, was declared a discontinued operation in October 1998. The decision to divest HGA stripped Cooper Companies of roughly $50 million in annual revenue, but Bender, named chief executive officer in 1994, wanted to sharpen the company's focus exclusively on medical devices. Consequently, as the 1990s progressed, CooperSurgical and CooperVision received the bulk of the company's attention and its resources.

CooperSurgical was formed in 1990, the year it acquired Frigitronics, a technology company that produced an assortment of gynecological and ophthalmic products. The acquisition provided CooperSurgical with entry into the women's healthcare

market, a foundation that was strengthened in 1991 with the purchase of Euro-Med, a direct-mail-order business that marketed gynecological instruments. In 1992, CooperSurgical continued to bolster its involvement in women's healthcare by introducing a line of electrical instruments and disposable products to perform LEEP (Loop Electro-surgical Excision Procedure). LEEP, a surgical procedure, enabled physicians simultaneously to diagnose and treat diseases of the cervix. CooperSurgical's stature increased in 1996, when the subsidiary purchased Unimar, a company that generated $6 million in sales of its disposable diagnostic products. Another $6 million-in-sales company was acquired in 1997, when CooperSurgical purchased Marlow. The transaction made CooperSurgical the exclusive distributor of an embryonic transfer catheter that was marketed to fertility clinics in the United States. In 1998, CooperSurgical made further advances when it introduced "Cerveillance," a device the company developed that enabled physicians to document, store, and retrieve digital images of cervix examinations. In its final deal of the 1990s, CooperSurgical acquired the women's healthcare assets of BEI Medical Systems, Inc.

As CooperSurgical increased its presence in the women's healthcare market, CooperVision increased its stature through a series of acquisitions. In 1993, the subsidiary purchased CoastVision, Inc., a manufacturer of toric lenses. Toric lenses are required to correct astigmatism, an irregularity in the shape of the cornea of the eye that causes distorted vision. By acquiring CoastVision, CooperVision entered the toric lens market, which would become the strongest facet of the company's contact lens business. In 1996, CooperVision doubled its contact lens manufacturing capacity, increasing the size of its Scottsville, New York, facility to 38,000 square feet. The following year, a series of important deals were concluded, beginning in February when the company acquired the Natural Touch line of cosmetic lenses from Wesley Jessen Vision Care. In December 1997, the company completed two important international deals. CooperVision acquired a British contact lens manufacturer, Aspect Vision Care, Ltd., and signed a marketing agreement with Rohto Pharmaceuticals, Ltd. to enter the Japanese contact lenses market, the second-largest market in the world. In March 1999, CooperVision received regulatory clearance to market lenses in Japan.

By the end of the 1990s, the expansion conducted through CooperVision and CooperSurgical increased Cooper Companies' revenue volume to $165 million. Between 1993 and 1999, CooperSurgical's sales grew from $14.6 million to $29.3 million, while during the same period CooperVision's sales swelled from $32.6 million to $136 million. Cooper Companies drew much of its strength from its mainstay CooperVision subsidiary, which ranked as the leading manufacturer of toric contact lenses in the United States. The company hoped to become the largest manufacturer of toric lenses in the world by 2000.

Principal Subsidiaries

CooperVision, Inc.; CooperSurgical, Inc.

Principal Competitors

Johnson & Johnson; Bausch & Lomb Inc.; Wesley Jessen VisionCare, Inc.

Further Reading

Cieply, Michael, "Coopernova," *Forbes,* November 7, 1983, p. 231.

"Cooper Signs Definitive Agreement with Focus Healthcare to Divest Meadowwood Hospital; Hospital Group of America Will Close Its Headquarters," *Business Wire,* January 10, 1999, p. 1.

Crabtree, Penni, "Irvine, Calif.-Based Contact Lens Maker Eyes Its Options," *Knight-Ridder/Tribune Business News,* January 18, 2000.

Hicks, L. Wayne, "Marquest Takeover Bid Isn't Dead Yet," *Denver Business Journal,* July 19, 1991, p. 6.

Ketzenberger, John, "Cutting Its Loss: Copper Cos. Sells Anacomp Notes," *Indianapolis Business Journal,* July 2, 1990, p. 5.

Pare, Terence P., "All in the Families," *Fortune,* August 15, 1988, p. 83.

—Jeffrey L. Covell

CORINTHIAN
COLLEGES, INC.

Corinthian Colleges, Inc.

6 Hutton Center Drive, Suite 400
Santa Ana, California 92707
U.S.A.
Telephone: (714) 427 3000
Fax: (714) 427 3013
Web site: http://www.cci.edu

Public Company
Incorporated: 1995
Employees: 2,600
Sales: $1.32 million (1999)
Stock Exchanges: NASDAQ
Ticker Symbol: COCO
NAIC: 61131 Colleges, Universities, and Professional
    Schools

Corinthian Colleges, Inc. is one of the largest companies in the United States involved in for-profit, post-secondary education. In 2000 it maintained 45 colleges in 18 states in its system, with a total enrollment of more than 18,000 students. Corinthian was formed to own and operate schools across the nation that focus on in-demand and highly specialized job skills. The company divides its business among two segments: schools that award diplomas and those that offer degrees. Through Corinthian Schools, Inc., the company offers a variety of diploma programs, with curricula focusing on healthcare, business, and computers and information technology. Corinthian School's colleges operate under a variety of names, including National Institute of Technology, Kee Business College, and Bryman College, a school that offers medical and dental assistant programs in 11 California cities. Through its Rhodes Colleges, Inc., division Corinthian offers programs leading to various academic degrees. Rhodes courses are concentrated in business administration. Schools in the Rhodes division include the nine Florida Metropolitan University campuses, Las Vegas College, Blair College in Colorado Springs and Springfield College in Springfield, Missouri. Most Rhodes students graduate with associate's degrees after two years of study, but bache-lors and masters degrees can be earned in some Rhodes programs. Corinthian Colleges strives to place its graduates in good jobs in their field of training within three months of graduation. The company does not consider its graduates successfully situated until they have worked at least three months in a job for which they have studied.

Mid-1990s Origins

Corinthian Colleges was founded in February 1995. The five founders—David Moore, Paul St. Pierre, Frank McCord, Dennis Devereux, and Lloyd Holland—were executives at National Education Centers, Inc. (NECI), a for-profit operator of vocational schools based in Irvine, California. The plan of the five founders was simple: to acquire schools that were fundamentally sound and with good reputations, but which for one reason or another were performing below their potential.

Between June and December 1996 the group effected a management buyout of NECI, acquiring 16 colleges and uniting them in a new company called Corinthian Schools, Inc. At the time NECI schools were experiencing difficult times and the company was on the verge of shutting down many of its campuses. However, within barely nine months of acquiring the NECI colleges, the new owners effected a financial turnaround. The formerly ailing schools had enrollments that were near capacity, and they began turning a profit ahead of the schedule the founders had set for themselves.

One change Corinthian made was to tighten the focus of the academic programs at the colleges. Before the takeover, students could choose from a full junior college curriculum, including aviation science. Under Corinthian they offered only allied health and computer technology programs, skills much in demand among employers. Securing jobs for its graduates was a prime concern of Corinthian from the beginning. The company's goal was to place 70 percent of its students in jobs within three months of graduation. Each of its colleges employed a full-time placement officer to track each graduate's progress monthly until he or she found a job, as well as for the first three months of his or her employment. Corinthian also offered lifetime employment placement services to its graduates.

Corinthian more than doubled its size in October 1996 when it acquired 18 colleges from Phillips Colleges Inc. Based in Gulfport, Mississippi, at the time Phillips was one of the nation's largest private companies involved post-secondary education. Phillips' decision to sell was related to an audit that revealed sizable student loan violations and left Phillips $107 million in debt to its students, banks, and the federal government. As a result of the loan irregularities, $3.7 million in Phillips' federally guaranteed student loans were frozen by the Department of Education, rendering its schools essentially inoperable. The sale to Corinthian was made as part of the final settlement with the government and a portion of the $30 million received from Corinthian went toward government penalties. The acquisition made Corinthian Colleges at the time the largest private, post-secondary school operator in the United States. Among the schools acquired were two of the oldest private business colleges in the country, Duffs Business Institute in Pittsburgh and Blair College in Colorado Springs.

The purchase broadened Corinthian's presence throughout the nation, adding the eight schools of Florida Metropolitan University, along with other campuses New York, Washington, Nevada, Utah, Oregon, and Missouri. It also gave Corinthian an additional academic focus. Phillips colleges taught business and computer technology courses, along with court reporting, video production, hotel management, and the like. Moreover, they granted bachelors and masters degrees.

As a further consequence of the acquisition, Corinthian underwent a complete corporate restructuring, organizing its schools into two corporate divisions. The schools acquired from Phillips were made part of Rhodes Colleges, Inc. under the corporate umbrella of Corinthian Colleges, Inc. Corinthian Schools also became a corporate division. Rhodes included primarily degree-granting business colleges, while Corinthian Schools were diploma-granting schools that taught allied health and computer technology primarily.

Going Public in the Late 1990s

For the first three years of its existence, Corinthian Colleges was privately owned by the five partners who had founded it. In July 1998, however, they made the decision to go public, in order to repay the sizable debt incurred with the Phillips Colleges acquisition. By that time, the company had added a school and had 35 colleges in 16 states with a total student enrollment of about 14,000. An initial public offering (IPO) was held in February 1999. Corinthian had hoped the stock would garner $16 to $18 a share. 2.7 million shares were sold at $18 each, raising approximately $49 million. Those shares accounted for about 30 percent of the firm's total stock, the rest remaining in the hands of company management. Wall Street reacted favorably to the offering; Corinthian was attractive to investors for a variety of reasons. First, Corinthian's career-oriented schools were seen as the wave of the future. They were highly attractive to students looking for practical knowledge that would lead to secure job prospects. Second, because students enroll for a year at a time—and commit to paying a full year's tuition at the beginning of a school year—income was highly predictable. Moreover, profits for such businesses tended to be a healthy 15 percent.

In March 1999, Corinthian announced that it had received a license from the state of Virginia, as well as national accreditation from the Accrediting Council of Independent Colleges and Schools, for a Kee Business College, which Corinthian would open in Chesapeake, Virginia, on March 25, 1999. Corinthian already operated one Kee campus in Newport News, Virginia. The school offered various allied health programs of eight to ten month duration. In early April of the same year, the company announced the opening of a Houston, Texas, campus of its National Institute of Technology.

In late April 1999, Corinthian made public gains in both enrollment and earnings. Earning were above previously publicized expectations, and the company's student population was up nearly 14.5 percent over the previous spring. As a result, Corinthian shares, which had fallen by 29 percent earlier, recovered. They first reached $16.38, and a day later climbed to $19 a share. The stock had gone as high as $19.75 before the decline began. At the end of the fiscal year in June, when Corinthian announced its results for the year, it looked like the confidence of Wall Street analysts at the time of the IPO had been well-founded. Corinthian's revenues for 1999 had increased nearly 30 percent over 1998, up from $106.5 million to an all-time high of $133 million. That represented a four-year increase in revenues of over 400 percent, from the 1996 figure of $31.5 million. Those gains were accounted for by the rise in enrollment, together with an average 9.7 percent increase in each student's tuition. "Our performance exceeded even our own high internal expectations," said Corinthian CEO and president David Moore in a press release.

During this time, Corinthian announced that it was developing a new Information Technology curriculum for its schools. The first phase was the introduction of a Computer Network Administration program. Students in the program could take courses toward an 18 to 24 month associates degree at National Institute of Technology campus in Southfield, Michigan, or a 12 to 15 month diploma at Corinthian Schools campuses in Colorado Springs, Orlando, or Tampa. A second phase of the IT curriculum, the Microsoft Office User Specialist (MOUS) program, was initiated later the same year. Programs in Internet Engineering, Programming, and Corporate Training were being developed at the same time.

Corinthian Colleges also undertook a partnership with Embark.com, an Internet site that provided information and services on higher education. Corinthian's presence on Embark

Key Dates:

1995: Company is founded as Corinthian Schools, Inc., and acquires 16 colleges from National Education Centers, Inc.
1996: 18 colleges are acquired from Phillips Colleges, Inc., and company is renamed Corinthian Colleges.
1998: Company goes public.
2000: Corinthian acquires Georgia Medical Institute, as well as four schools from Educorp, Inc.
2001: Grand Rapids Educational Center, Inc. is acquired.

.com would enable prospective students and guidance counselors to access information on schools and to apply to Corinthian electronically through Embark's Enrollment Services Systems. Embark.com boasted over one million hits monthly, which Corinthian believed would translate to much higher visibility for its schools, while at the same time lower administrative costs.

2000 and Beyond

Corinthian Colleges made significant additions to its roster of schools in 2000. Final approval from the state of Texas enabled the company to open its new National Institute of Technology school in Houston. At the same time it completed a deal to purchase for an undisclosed price the Harbor Medical College, an allied health school in Torrance, California. In April the company acquired the three campuses of the Georgia Medical Institute in Atlanta. The school had some 830 students and annual net revenues of $6 million at the time of the purchase. In May 2000 Corinthian finalized a lease agreement that enabled it to open a new branch campus of the Florida Metropolitan University (FMU) in Jacksonville, Florida. FMU was one of the first campuses at which students could study in Corinthian's Internet distance learning program. In June 2000 Corinthian purchased all the assets of the Academy of Business Inc. from owner The Tesseract Group. Tesseract, a company in Phoenix that ran private and charter schools, had lost some $14 million over the previous two years. It was faced with the prospect of posting a $700,000 bond with Arizona education authorities in order to renew the license of the school—which operated under the name Academy of Business College—as well as to cover by cash or a letter of credit half of the $1.7 million in federal funds the business school received in 1999. Corinthian did not disclose the amount of the deal which gave the company its first foothold in the Phoenix area.

By the summer of 2000 Corinthian Colleges was operating 46 schools in 18 states with a total enrollment of approximately 20,000 students. New acquisitions were the backbone of Corinthian's growth strategy. According to the company's head, David Moore, it evaluated some 50 potential acquisition targets every year, and seriously considered about ten of those. The company made huge financial strides in fiscal year 2000. In August 2000 it announced that revenues rose 28 percent from 1999 levels to $170.7 million. Company earnings more than tripled, from $4.5 million in 1999 to $15.4 million the following year.

In July 2000, anticipating the good results, Credit Suisse First Boston upped its 18-month price target for Corinthian stock from $35 to $40 a share. Wall Street didn't seem to be paying attention at first; by July Corinthian stock was at just over $23 a share, and that was down from a high of $27.25. It jumped again following the announcement of the yearly results in August, however, and reached $55 a share by early September. Stock prices dropped again later in the month, by nearly 20 percent when the company announced that its executives and some major institutional investors would release about three million of their own shares for public trading in a secondary stock offering. The stock was offered to the market in October 2000 for $50 a share. Just a day later the shares had risen to $54. In November, Corinthian's stock was strong again. Its value had increased fourfold since the spring, reaching $65.63 per share. The company's board of directors announced that a two-for-one split of Corinthian common stock would take place in mid-December. After the split, the company had some 23 million shares available for trading.

Beginning in October 2000, Corinthian Colleges made more substantial additions to its portfolio of schools. First it acquired four colleges from Educorp, Inc. Located in Los Angeles, Whittier, Ontario, and Long Beach, California, the schools had about 1,400 students enrolled primarily in allied health programs. Just days after the Educorp acquisition, Corinthian purchased the two campuses of the California Training Academy. The information technology and business schools added about 500 students to Corinthian's total student body. Later, in January 2001, the company opened a branch campus in Rancho Cucamonga, California. By the start of 2001, Corinthian had record numbers of students in Internet-based distance learning courses. 1,276 students were enrolled 28 different courses offered via eleven Corinthian campuses. The company planned to add 18 courses and five additional campuses, as well as the possibility of earning associates and bachelors degrees online by the middle of 2001. Moreover, at the beginning of February the company purchased the Grand Rapids Educational Center Inc. for approximately $3.1 million. The acquisition included three Michigan campuses in Grand Rapids, Kalamazoo, and Merrillville, with about 460 students altogether. Corinthian planned to merge its campus in Wyoming, Michigan, into the Grand Rapids campus. Early in 2001, the company announced plans to open new schools in Dearborn, Michigan, and one in Skokie Illinois. The Skokie campus would be Corinthian's first in the Chicago area.

Principal Divisions

Corinthian Schools, Inc.; Rhodes Colleges, Inc.

Principal Competitors

ITT Educational Services Inc.; Apollo Group, Inc.; DeVry Inc.

Further Reading

"Corinthian Colleges' Income Nearly Doubles; Revenue Up 32%," *Los Angeles Times,* August 31, 2000, p. C3.
"Corinthian Colleges Raises $48.6 Million In Stock Sale," *Los Angeles Times,* February 5, 1999, p. C6.

Dessoff, Alan L. ''Private Lessons,'' *Techniques: Making Education & Career Connections,* October 1996, p. 29.

Earnest, Leslie, ''Corinthian Colleges Gets Off to Good Start on Initial Offering,'' *Los Angeles Times,* February 6, 1999, p. C1.

Huettel, Steve, ''Calif. Firm Buys Tampa College,'' *Tampa Tribune,* October 18, 1996, p. 1.

Kelleher, James B., ''Santa Ana, Calif.-Based Vocational School Operator Performs Well,'' *Orange County Register,* July 1, 2000.

''Tesseract Sells Business College,'' *Arizona Republic,* May 5, 2000, p. D7.

—Gerald E. Brennan

CTS Corporation

905 West Boulevard North
Elkhart, Indiana 46514
U.S.A.
Telephone: (219) 293-7511
Fax: (219) 293-6146
Web site: http://www.ctscorp.com

Public Company
Incorporated: 1896 as Chicago Telephone Supply
   Company
Employees: 9,000+
Sales: $866.5 million (2000)
Stock Exchanges: New York
Ticker Symbol: CTS
NAIC: 334415 Electronic Resistor Manufacturing;
   334417 Electronic Connector Manufacturing; 334419
   Other Electronic Component Manufacturing

Established in 1896 to make telephones and switchboards, CTS Corporation has become a leading manufacturer of passive electronic components and electronic assemblies. The company has fine-tuned its direction to meet demand in the communications equipment, computer equipment, and automotive markets, among others. In the 1920s and 1930s it was the growing demand for radios that inspired CTS to supply radio parts and its engineers to develop a new resistor that lowered the cost of radios. During World War II the company developed a special precision potentiometer for radar units that gave the Allies their first capability to perform night bombing missions, thereby shortening the war. When the demand for television sets exploded in the late 1940s, CTS supplied the needed resistors. When the U.S. government mandated emissions control standards for automobiles in the 1970s, CTS developed throttle position sensors and other sensor products for automobiles. More recently, CTS has redefined itself by acquiring the wireless components business of Motorola Inc. in 1999, and has become a leading supplier of electronic components for wireless handsets and other wireless devices.

Early History: 1896–1920

The company now known as CTS Corporation was founded in Chicago in 1896 by A.J. Briggs and his son, George, as Chicago Telephone Supply Company. It was established to make magneto-driven telephones and switchboards, which were sold either to telephone companies or to end consumers. The company quickly built a reputation for quality and product reliability by issuing certificates guaranteeing trouble-free service for the telephone equipment it manufactured.

Needing larger facilities for its work force of 250 employees, the company moved 100 miles east to Elkhart, Indiana, in 1902. That city gave CTS a new building on a railroad spur in exchange for promised jobs and wages. For the next 18 years CTS would manufacture some 175,000 telephones and hundreds of switchboards.

Serving Commercial and Military Markets: 1920–80

In the 1920s CTS redirected its efforts from telephones to radios. The radio communications market was emerging in the early 1920s, and by 1922 half of CTS's sales came from radio parts, including jacks, plugs, headphones, antenna switches, and rheostats for home radio receivers. During the 1930s CTS evolved from a manufacturer of finished products to a manufacturer of components. During the Great Depression CTS developed a more cost effective, stable carbon composition resistor that helped lower the cost of radios. CTS's custom variable resistor controls became the cornerstone of its business for the next 50 years. By 1941 CTS was the largest producer of variable resistor products in the world. During World War II the company supplied the U.S. Army with remote field sets. It also developed the RLB, a precision potentiometer for radar units that enabled night bombing. Peacetime RLB applications included air traffic safety, weather forecasting, and medical diagnosis.

CTS continued to develop the technology and products required by the radio market and the emerging television market in the 1940s and 1950s. Between 1946 and 1950 the number of television sets manufactured in the United States went from 6,000 to 7.5 million. Each set required from six to ten variable resistor components, and CTS supplied many of them.

Company Perspectives:

CTS Corporation designs, manufactures and sells a broad line of electronic components and electronic assemblies, primarily serving the electronic needs of original equipment manufacturers (OEMs). CTS product lines serve major markets around the world, which principally include communications equipment, automotive and computer equipment— with a wide range of technologies and capabilities. CTS' growth in global markets is served by worldwide operations.

The company also provided technology and products for commercial and military applications. In 1958 CTS engineers developed Cermet, a more stable resistance element that met the demand of miniaturized applications for military use. In 1960 the company officially changed its name to CTS Corporation, formally adopting the name by which is was generally known by the public. In 1962 CTS began trading its stock on the New York Stock Exchange. The next year CTS entered the data processing market by adapting Cermet technology to produce thick film fixed resistor networks, which became common components of computers during the 1960s. CTS met the demand for miniaturization of consumer electronic products by manufacturing hybrid mircocircuits. In 1968 CTS established a manufacturing operation in Taiwan to serve the offshore production facilities of North American-based OEMs. This helped the company further expand its product applications in international markets.

The company's broad technology base opened new markets, which in turn required CTS to develop complementary technologies involving new materials and manufacturing processes. In addition to military and automotive applications in the 1960s and 1970s, CTS was also supplying components for the consumer electronics market. At the beginning of the 1970s CTS recorded dramatic sales increases to the home entertainment market, due in part to the explosive demand for color television sets. As the decade progressed, however, imported TV sets began gaining market share at the expense of domestically produced sets. Overwhelming competition from Japanese manufacturers eventually forced CTS to abandon the consumer electronics market by the end of the 1970s.

When the U.S. government mandated automobile emissions control requirements in the early 1970s, CTS developed throttle position sensors. CTS began developing and redirecting its production focus to provide components and assemblies for custom under-the-hood and chassis sensor applications. In 1979 CTS opened a manufacturing facility in Singapore, primarily to remain competitive in supplying components for car radios.

Expansion Brings Challenges: 1980s

CTS remained a well-established supplier of components for data processing, instruments and controls, and communications markets. The early 1980s saw a two-year economic recession that hit U.S. high-tech manufacturing companies especially hard. In June 1983 CTS acquired California-based Micro Peripherals, Inc., a leading manufacturer of floppy disk drives for computers. By 1984 CTS had sustained significant losses in its floppy disk drive business and decided to divest Micro Peripherals. In January 1985, 15 months after acquiring Micro Peripherals, CTS found a buyer for the subsidiary in Vista Technologies, Inc., a marketing start-up based in Westwood, California.

A shareholder suit brought against CTS in early 1986 by Dynamics Corporation of America (DCA) noted that CTS's acquisition of Micro Peripherals had resulted in pretax operating losses. The suit also noted that the company's entry into the printed circuit board (PCB) business in late 1981 and early 1982 also resulted in quarterly losses. In its suit, DCA held CTS's chairman, president, and CEO Robert D. Hostetler responsible for the ''ill-conceived'' acquisitions.

At the time DCA, which already had a substantial equity stake in CTS, was making a hostile tender offer for one million CTS shares at $43 per share for the purpose of taking control of the company. If successful, DCA would own 27.5 percent of CTS. Although DCA's tender offer was successful, an Indiana law governing hostile takeovers allowed CTS to refuse voting rights to stock acquired in a hostile takeover. In a lawsuit that went all the way to the U.S. Supreme Court, CTS's position was upheld, and DCA failed to gain voting rights for the one million shares it had acquired as a result of its hostile tender offer.

CTS initially responded to DCA's tender offer by looking for a ''white knight,'' a company that would make a friendly takeover of the company. When that failed, CTS stock fell back into the $30 range. Then, in December 1986, AVX Corp. offered the equivalent of $35 a share. When DCA countered with a $37.50 offer, AVX withdrew. However, the sale of CTS stalled when DCA decided that $37.50 a share was too high a price. In March 1987, CTS and DCA reached an agreement to end their differences, with the result that DCA would have a significantly expanded role in decision-making at CTS. CTS's board of directors was restructured, with DCA gaining three of the board's seven seats. As part of the agreement Hostetler resigned as president and CEO, after having been replaced as chairman by George F. Sommer, who assumed the additional duties of president and CEO.

Later in 1987 CTS closed its PCB business, which was responsible for most of its operating losses. While the telecommunications market was flat, where AT&T and Northern Telecom were major customers, the company was enjoying strong sales for its data processing and automotive components. By 1989 CTS returned to profitability, reporting revenue of $262 million and net income of $14.3 million.

Refocusing in the 1990s

By the 1990s CTS was focused on providing passive electronic components to original equipment manufacturers (OEMs) in the automotive, data processing, and communications industries. It also continued to offer products in the instrument and control, defense, and consumer markets, including products on the Advanced Tactical Fighter and space applications with the Jet Propulsion Laboratory.

In the automotive market CTS's core product was its resistive contacting throttle position sensing device, which used the company's proprietary position-sensing technology. Other products developed for the automotive market included exhaust emission gas recirculating sensors, pintle position sensors, fuel pedal sensors, actuators for electronic throttle controls, and suspension shock height sensors. The company also manufactured seat position sensors, accelerometer assemblies for air bag release systems, thick film substrates for fuel level sensing, and resistor networks for speedometers, cruise control, and engine control.

CTS celebrated its 100th anniversary in 1996. Under the leadership of chairman, CEO, and president Joseph P. Walker, who assumed these roles in 1988, CTS had focused on improving its manufacturing processes. CTS called its improvement process a "A Journey to Excellence." The company began by addressing manufacturing excellence, including engineering, then added sales, marketing, and human resources, to achieve a level of operational excellence throughout the organization.

In 1997 CTS acquired DCA, which had continued to hold a significant equity stake in CTS since its failed takeover attempt ten years prior. Under the terms of the agreement, CTS began a cash tender offer for 50 percent of DCA's stock at $55 per share. Following the acquisition, DCA would continue to operate as a division of CTS, with Joseph Walker remaining as the chairman, CEO, and president of the combined company.

With the U.S. economy gaining momentum, CTS had a good year in 1997. The company enjoyed particularly strong demand in its automotive and microelectronic segments. Moreover, its manufacturing improvement process was also resulting in more control over manufacturing and operating expenses. In late 1997 CTS completed its acquisition of DCA and reached an agreement to sell DCA's Waring Products Division, which manufactured appliances under the Waring brand, to Conair Corp. Other DCA divisions integrated into CTS included IERC, which made heat sinks, and Reeves-Hoffman, which made crystals and oscillators. Following the acquisition CTS formed a task force to study DCA's remaining businesses, which included small appliances, power and controlled environmental systems, and fabricated metal products and equipment, to see if they should be sold, closed, or integrated into CTS.

Following CTS's solid financial performance in 1997, Bear, Stearns & Co., Inc. initiated coverage of CTS stock in 1998. Analysts noted that the company's growth rate was due in part to three industry trends: electronic component integration, man-

ufacturing services outsourcing, and increasing automotive electronic content.

In September 1998 CTS announced it would acquire the Component Products Division (CPD) of Motorola, Inc.'s Automotive, Component, Computer, and Energy Sector. This operation manufactured ceramics, quartz, oscillator, lead zirconate titanate (PZT), and surface acoustic wave (SAW) components primarily for the telecommunications market.

By the end of 1998 CTS had 18 manufacturing facilities located around the world, including Canada, Mexico, Scotland, Singapore, Taiwan, and China. During that year it opened an Interconnect Systems facility in Hudson, New Hampshire, which became ISO 9001 certified in 1999. CTS's Automotive Products division accounted for about 30 percent of the company's 1998 revenue.

Assuming Leadership in the Wireless Market in Late 1990s

Once CTS completed its acquisition of Motorola's CPD unit, wireless communications products would account for about 40 percent of CTS's annual revenue. After the acquisition was completed in early 1999, CPD became CTS Wireless Components Inc. and the parent gained a portfolio of some 300 high technology patents globally as well as manufacturing facilities in China, Taiwan, and the United States. Also during this time CTS completed the divestiture of most of the non-core businesses of DCA, while DCA's frequency products and thermal management product lines were fully integrated into CTS's core business.

Later in the year CTS reorganized some of its business units as part of its plan to concentrate on the communications market. *Electronic Buyers' News* named CTS as the best-managed company in the passive electronic components industry in its October 18, 1999, issue. The company's stock was also picked by *Bloomberg's Personal Finance Magazine* as one of the top 100 hot stocks for 1999.

As a result of its acquisition of Motorola's CPD unit, CTS enjoyed an 83 percent increase in revenue, from $370 million in 1998 to $677 million in 1999. The acquisition transformed CTS and positioned it as the largest manufacturer of electronic components for wireless applications in North America. The company was now a global leader for supplying components to the fast-growing mobile wireless industry and would pursue a strategy of globalization to enhance that position.

In early 2000 CTS formed a RF (radio frequency) Integrated Modules business unit as part of CTS Wireless Components. The RF unit, based in West Lafayette, Indiana, would offer complete RF sections of a cellular phone as an integrated module. By May the CTS Wireless Components Business Group had been restructured into four business units: CTS RF Integrated Modules, CTS RF Crystal and Oscillator Products, CTS RF Ceramic and SAW Filter Products, and CTS Piezoelectric Products. CTS's new wireless components business and its core passive electronic components business were complementary, because they both relied on quartz crystals, oscillators, and other frequency control devices.

As part of the company's globalization strategy, CTS announced several initiatives in Asia in the first half of 2000. The CTS Wireless Components Group formed a strategic partnership with Kyocera Corp. of Japan to develop quartz crystal and other frequency control products primarily for cell phones and other wireless applications. In addition, CTS opened a branch sales office in Seoul, Korea, to focus on developing and selling wireless components to manufacturers of cell phones, pagers, and other mobile wireless devices. CTS also opened a new Interconnect Systems manufacturing facility in Tianjin, China, to support the communications infrastructure market. The new facility would operate as a manufacturing and distribution center for CTS Interconnect Systems' backpanel and high-level systems integration business, with an initial manufacturing focus on supporting the expanding wireless base station market.

For 2000 CTS reported a 28 percent growth in revenue with record sales of $866.5 million. The company's net earnings of $83.8 million also established a record high. CTS was ranked 16th among *Business Week's* "The Info Tech 100" in June 2000 and seventh on the magazine's list of the world's most profitable Info Tech companies. In January 2001 CTS appointed Donald K. Schwanz as president and COO. Joseph Walker would continue as the company's chairman and CEO. Schwanz came to CTS from Honeywell, and his immediate task at CTS would be to deal with the overall economic slowdown forecast for 2001.

Principal Subsidiaries

CTS of Canada Ltd.; CTS Corporation U.K. Ltd.; CTS Singapore Pte. Ltd.; CTS Components Taiwan Ltd.; CTS (Tainjin) Electronics Co. Ltd. (China); CTS Wireless Components Inc.

Principal Operating Units

CTS Automotive Products Division; CTS Interconnect Systems; CTS Reeves Frequency Products; CTS Resistor/Electrocomponents; CTS RF Integrated Modules; CTS RF Ceramic & SAW Filters; CTS RF Crystal & Oscillator; CTS Piezoelectronic Products.

Principal Competitors

BEI Technologies Inc.; Pioneer-Standard Electronics Inc.; Tyco International Ltd.

Further Reading

Alper, Alan, "Product Cycles, Predatory Prices, Bane of Floppies," *Electronic News,* October 1, 1984, p. 21.

Baljko, Jennifer L., "Joseph P. Walker Creates Strong Management Team to Lead CTS' Metamorphosis," *Electronic Buyers' News,* December 21, 1998, p. 82.

Bernstein, Corinne, "Best-Managed Companies," *Electronic Buyers' News,* October 18, 1999, p. 26.

"CTS Corp.," *Indianapolis Business Journal,* January 4, 1999, p. 30.

"CTS Corp.," *Microwave Journal,* February 2000, p. 64.

"CTS Corporation," *Indianapolis Business Journal,* June 25, 1990, p. 33A.

"CTS, Dynamics in Merger Pact," *Electronic News (1991),* May 19, 1997, p. 62.

"CTS Gets the Nod from Bear Stearns," *Electronic Buyers' News,* August 10, 1998, p. 34.

"CTS, Motorola in Quartz Deal," *Electronic News (1991),* January 4, 1999, p. 10.

"CTS Mulls Dynamics' Future," *Electronic Buyers' News,* April 20, 1998, p. 38.

"CTS Offers Turn-Key Solutions," *Electronic News (1991),* November 9, 1998, p. 46.

"CTS Plant Deemed ISO 9001-Compliant," *Electronic Buyers' News,* September 13, 1999, p. 38.

Dobie, Maureen, "Acquisition Sends CTS's Revenue Soaring," *Indianapolis Business Journal,* May 22, 2000, p. 6B.

Dunn, Darrell, "CTS Agrees to Buy Motorola's CPD Unit for About $240 Million," *Electronic Buyers' News,* September 21, 1998, p. 106.

"Dynamics-CTS Merger Backed," *American Metal Market,* August 8, 1997, p. 3.

Holt, Daniel J., "CTS: A Customer Focused Company with a 100 Year History," *Automotive Engineering,* September 1966, p. 145.

Jaffe, Thomas, "And Then? And Then?," *Forbes,* April 20, 1987, p. 126.

Levine, Bernard, "CTS, Kyocera Partner in Frequency Control," *Electronic News,* April 10, 2000, p. 54.

"Maker of Waring to Merge with CTS," *HFN: The Weekly Newspaper for the Home Furnishing Network,* May 19, 1997, p. 6.

Marcy, Steve, "Supreme Court Ruling Upholds Takeover Rules," *Oil Daily,* April 29, 1987, p. 2.

Murphy, Mary Ann, "CTS' Resistor Recipe Mixes Old, New," *Electronic Buyers' News,* October 16, 2000, p. 86.

"The News-Sentinel, Fort Wayne, Ind., Winner's Circle Column," *Knight-Ridder/Tribune Business News,* February 1, 2000.

Rappleyea, Warren, "DCA Bids Challenge AVX Offer for CTS," *Electronic News,* December 22, 1986, p. 6.

Richtmyer, Richard, "CTS Acquires, Invests—and Grows," *Electronic Buyers' News,* February 8, 1999, p. 40.

——, "CTS Restructures as Part of Communications Focus," *Electronic Buyers' News,* August 23, 1999, p. 8.

——, "Pricing Pressure Weighing Down Sector Stocks," *Electronic Buyers' News,* October 25, 1999, p. 16.

Riser, Joseph D., "CTS to Exit Floppies; Sets $20M Charge," *Electronic News,* September 24, 1984, p. 1.

Silverman, Elizabeth S., "High-Tech Stocks after the Fall," *Fortune,* October 3, 1983, p. 231.

Simpson, Cam, "Elkhart, Ind.-Based CTS Corp Does Well for Investors in 1997," *Knight-Ridder/Tribune Business News,* August 4, 1997.

"Takeover Hurdle; a Ruling Backs State Regulation," *Time,* May 4, 1987, p. 74.

Vinton, Bob, "DCA in Hostile Bid to Hike CTS Stake to 27%," *Electronic News,* March 24, 1986, p. 39.

——, "DCA May Go to Court to Get CTS Voting Rights," *Electronic News,* June 1, 1987, p. 6.

"Vista Tech Agrees to Buy Micro Peripherals," *Electronic News,* January 21, 1985, p. 30.

—David P. Bianco

The Daiwa Bank, Ltd.

2-1, Bingomachi 2-chome
Chuo-ku Osaka 540-8610
Japan
Telephone: +81-6-6271-1221
Fax: +81-6-6268-1337
Web site: http://www.daiwabank.co.jp

Public Company
Incorporated: 1918 as Osaka Nomura Bank
Employees: 7,315
Total Assets: $7.46 billion (2000)
Stock Exchanges: Tokyo
Ticker Symbol: 8319
NAIC: 52211 Commercial Banking

Following a 1995 scandal in its New York branch office that resulted in a massive fine and a ban on operating in the United States, The Daiwa Bank, Ltd. is returning its focus on its core domestic business, as well as transforming itself into a "super-regional" bank of Asia. The Daiwa Bank is unique among Japanese financial institutions in that it is licensed to conduct both trust and regular banking operations. Daiwa is therefore able to offer a wider range of in-house services and to emphasize a number of diverse and more profitable operations as market conditions change. In an environment such as Japan, where a bank's fortunes are normally tied to a narrow range of financial products, Daiwa has clearly enjoyed greater mobility and flexibility over the years, giving it a distinct competitive edge.

Early 20th Century Origins

The Daiwa Bank was founded in Osaka, Japan's first major industrial and commercial center, by Tokushichi Nomura, a shrewd entrepreneur and talented venture capitalist. Daiwa came into existence in 1918 as the Osaka Nomura Bank. It was created largely to take advantage of the new capital Japan had amassed from foreign commercial ventures and domestic industrialization. In many cases, the Osaka Nomura Bank arranged financing that enabled small but promising companies to expand and prosper under often-difficult economic conditions.

One of the bank's operations, the securities division, experienced such growth both in volume and in profits that it was run almost as a separate entity. Finally, in 1926, the division was spun off to create Nomura Securities, one day Japan's leading securities company. The following year "Osaka" was dropped from the bank's name to give it a closer identification with Nomura Securities and to dispel the impression that its business was limited to Osaka.

Nomura (later Daiwa) would continue to maintain a close relationship with Nomura Securities, which acted as the bank's sole underwriter. (Daiwa Securities, a competitor of Nomura, was in no way related to the Daiwa Bank.) Nomura became a major shareholder of the Daiwa Bank, and, though Daiwa eventually divested itself of its interests in Nomura, the two companies maintained many parallel interests through an informal arrangement.

While the Nomura Bank had developed interests all across Japan, in 1929 it was appointed the sole banking agent of the Osaka prefectural government. It continued, therefore, to be associated with the Osaka establishment, leading it to be viewed with some suspicion in the more dynamic rival commercial center of Tokyo.

Japanese industry grew spectacularly during the 1930s as Japan began to mature as an industrial power. One of the most important factors in Japan's industrialization was the rise to power of militarists who favored the creation of larger, centrally directed firms. During World War II these militarists permitted, or directed, the Nomura Bank to absorb the operations of its affiliate, the Nomura Trust Company, in 1944. It was as a result of this somewhat awkward centralization scheme, coming at a time when the war was placing increasing hardships on the Japanese economy, that the bank began to operate both trust and regular banking services.

After the war, the Allied occupation forces enacted a variety of laws aimed at decentralizing Japanese industry. Many companies were divided into smaller ones, and many were forbidden to use their prewar names. Unlike some competitors, the Nomura Bank was not split up. It was also permitted to continue both trust and regular banking services, though it was forced to

---

Company Perspectives:

Daiwa Bank is currently making the transition to a Super-regional Bank with strong ties to the Kansai region. As we move into the 21st Century, the guiding principle throughout the Bank's scope of operations will continue to be to retain the confidence and trust of its customers.

---

change its name. In 1948 it became Daiwa Bank (*Daiwa* means "great harmony" in Japanese).

Postwar Expansion

In addition to expanding its domestic network, Daiwa established a foreign department in 1948, and the following year was authorized as a foreign-exchange bank. It took Daiwa several years to open overseas offices. Unlike its competitors Mitsubishi and Sanwa, which had merely to reopen their American and European offices, Daiwa entered these markets with Japanese clients who were attempting to expand overseas. Daiwa opened representative offices in New York in 1956 and in London in 1958. The bank also gained a stronger presence in the Tokyo market during this time, taking over seven offices there that had been operated by the Bank of Tokyo. It was an important acquisition for Daiwa, as Tokyo had become the center of Japanese commerce.

Daiwa began pension-trust banking in 1962. It was the first Japanese bank to manage pensions, a business that later proved both stable and profitable. Daiwa was also the only bank allowed to maintain branch offices inside the Diet—the Japanese parliament. The bank established a second office there in 1962, creating one for the Upper House and one for the Lower House. This presence gave Daiwa an intimate knowledge of government activities and a more privileged role in government finance.

Japan experienced a powerful export-led economic expansion during the late 1950s and the 1960s. Daiwa experienced similarly rapid growth as a banker and financial agent for Japanese exporters. However, it was from the pension market that Daiwa experienced the bulk of its growth. The Japanese, without a social security program, had a great propensity to save, and their employers generally maintained conservative pension and insurance practices. During the following decade, the bank opened more overseas offices, in Los Angeles in 1970, Frankfurt in 1971, Hong Kong in 1976, and Singapore in 1979. Although shaken by the Arab oil embargo in 1973 and 1974 and the Iranian Revolution in 1979, Daiwa avoided serious reverses. Some losses were incurred and, predictably, growth slowed, but by 1980 the bank's pension trust surpassed ¥1 trillion, and only four years later the fund exceeded ¥2 trillion.

Beginning in 1952 the gradual deregulation of Japanese financial institutions caused occasional shocks in the banking community. One trend, however, that became especially acute in the 1980s was the narrowing spread between lending and deposits—as a result of increased competition. The Japanese banking community in general began to promote fee-based services. Daiwa took the matter a step further, attempting to cover all the bank's expenses with revenues from fee income alone. In the event that spread-based operations became unprofitable, the bank could more easily maintain growth.

Daiwa established a new trust headquarters in 1985 to reinforce its position in trust banking, promote fee income, and demonstrate its ability to accommodate the increasingly diverse needs of Japanese society. As an example, Daiwa became involved in land trusts, a type of real estate-asset management. The bank's most important land trust was the Chuokan project, operated on behalf of the Osaka prefectural government.

The man most responsible for Daiwa's successful exploitation of fee-based services was Sumio Abekawa, who was named president in 1984. He replaced Ichiro Ikeda who, despite tremendous personal sacrifice, had been unable to shake Daiwa out of a period of stagnation. Daiwa resumed a higher rate of growth during the mid-1980s, and began to prepare for the ensuing decades as a more aggressive and confident institution.

However, it was Daiwa's entry into securities trading in the 1980s that would lead to a scandal with longtime repercussions. Daiwa, like most Japanese banks, made its profits through lending, but failed to implement appropriate oversight procedures when it turned to high-volume securities trading. The Japanese business culture encouraged management to place far more emphasis on trust in subordinates than on oversight. Because books had to be kept in English for offices in the United States, Japanese bankers were even more dependent on employees fluent in English. Furthermore, while European and U.S. banks were employing computer systems to monitor trades, Daiwa was still working with paper documents. In September 1995 the world would learn just how ill-prepared Daiwa was to deal in securities, when officials reported that one of its New York bond traders, Toshihide Iguchi, had embezzled funds and altered bank records in order to conceal 11 years of losses than amounted to $1.1 billion. Iguchi was not only a trader, he was in charge of oversight in his office. What began as an effort in 1984 to conceal a $200,000 loss on the U.S. government-bond market spun out of control, as Iguchi raided accounts belonging to customers to finance further trading in order to recoup his mounting losses. He then forged documents to make it appear that the customer accounts were still intact.

This coming less than a year after the notorious Barings Bank collapse caused by nearly $1.4 billion in losses by Nick Leeson, it was easy at first to paint Iguchi simply as a rogue trader who had deceived Daiwa. As more facts came out, however, the bank's management became more mired in scandal. It was revealed that Iguchi confessed to his conduct in a letter to management in July, yet Daiwa waited nearly ten weeks before reporting the information to U.S. officials, and only then after the urging of their U.S. attorneys, who along with the accountants had been kept in the dark about the problem.

In October 20, 1995, Iguchi pleaded guilty in Manhattan federal court to six counts of fraud, but he also testified that even after he confessed his conduct to Daiwa, he was asked to continue to forge bank records to conceal his losses. Daiwa, despite knowledge to the contrary, told the U.S. Federal Reserve that it still held $600 million in government securities that Iguchi had already sold to conceal his losses. Iguchi also testified that in 1989 and 1992 Daiwa management misled state and

Key Dates:

1918: Company founded as Osaka Nomura Bank.
1948: Company's name is changed to The Daiwa Bank, Limited.
1956: A New York office is opened.
1962: Daiwa begins to offer pension-trust banking services.
1995: Bank fined $340 million and forced to close U.S. offices.

federal regulators when it maintained that the bank's trading operations were moved uptown to keep it separate from the oversight function of record-keepers. Although the traders did change offices, the separation of functions simply did not exist. Unconnected with the Iguchi losses, another impropriety also came to light through court proceedings. Daiwa's New York office used a corporate shell in the Cayman Islands to absorb some $97 million in losses incurred between 1984 and 1987.

The general manager of Daiwa Bank's New York office, Masahiro Tsuda, was also indicted and would eventually plead guilty to a single conspiracy count. The bank itself would plead guilty to 16 fraud charges and agree to pay one of the largest fines ever imposed in the United States, $340 million. Daiwa was also expelled from the country. In Japan the bank faced a $1.4 billion suit from shareholders, as well as restrictions placed on it by Japan's Ministry of Finance.

Daiwa, unlike Barings, was never in danger of collapse. Losses of $1.1 billion represented only eight percent of it capitalization, but its reputation was severely tarnished. Trust customers in particular had to be reassured that their funds were being properly administered. Daiwa closed four overseas offices and returned its focus to retail and trust banking. In September 2000 Daiwa was still enduring the impact of the New York scandal when a Japanese court ruled on the shareholder suit. A number of former and current management officials were ordered to pay $775 million in damages to shareholders for failing to properly oversee Iguchi's trading. How long the cloud would hang over Daiwa was uncertain.

With some 180 offices total, in Japan, China, Indonesia, Singapore, South Korea, Thailand, as well as the United Kingdom, Daiwa set about controlling the damage of its U.S. entanglements. The company upgraded its computer systems, and, in an uncharacteristic move for a Japanese firm, turned to an outside company, IBM, to complete the work. In essence Daiwa was recasting itself as a regional bank with a limited overseas presence. Toward that end, it explored opportunities for joint venture with Japan's Sumitomo Trust, acquired assets of the Japanese Namihaya Bank when that bank failed, remained one of the country's top business lenders (committed in particular to supporting the activities of the ailing Tokyo Mutual Life Insurance Company), and continued to manage the trusts and pensions of Japan's largest companies.

Principal Subsidiaries

Daiwa Bank, Canada; Daiwa Bank (Capital Management) Ltd. (U.K.); Daiwa Overseas Finance Ltd. (Hong Kong); Daiwa Fiananz AG (Switzerland); Daiwa BK Financial Futures Singapore Pte. Ltd.; Daiwa Finance Australia Ltd.

Principal Competitors

Sumitomo Trust and Banking Co., Ltd.; Yasuda Trust and Banking Co., Ltd.; Chuo Mitsui Trust and Banking Co., Ltd.; Sanwa Bank, Ltd.; Asahi Bank, Ltd.

Further Reading

Kashiwagi, Akiko, "Daiwa Officials Fined Millions; Japanese Executives Held Accountable in Landmark Case," *Washington Post,* September 21, 2000, p. E2.

Leung, James, "Daiwa Transforms Itself," *Asian Business,* February 1999, pp. 34–36.

Mulligan, Thomas S., "U.S. Charges Japanese Trader with Bank Fraud," *Los Angeles Times,* September 27, 1995, p. 1.

Norihiko, Shirouzu, "Daiwa Scandal Creates Fallout for Tokyo," *Wall Street Journal,* September 28, 1995, p. A16.

O'Brien, Timothy L., "Daiwa May Have Condoned Earlier Loss," *Wall Street Journal,* November 8, 1995, p. A15.

"Wall Street Shokku," *Economist,* September 30, 1995, p. 83.

—update: Ed Dinger

Datascope Corporation

14 Phillips Parkway
Montvale, New Jersey 07645
U.S.A.
Telephone: (201) 391-8100
Toll Free: (800) 288-2121
Fax: (201) 307-5400
Web site: http://www.datascope.com

Public Company
Incorporated: 1964
Employees: 1,200
Sales: $298.8 million (2000)
Stock Exchanges: NASDAQ
Ticker Symbol: DSCP
NAIC: 334510 Electromedical and Electrotherapeutic Apparatus Manufacturing; 339112 Surgical and Medical Instrument Manufacturing; 339113 Surgical Appliance and Supplies Manufacturing

Datascope Corporation is a leading maker of medical devices for cardiac patients. The company pioneered the manufacturing of intra-aortic balloon pump systems and catheter technology. Intra-aortic balloon pumps are used in various types of coronary surgery, where the balloon catheter acts as the pumping device within the patient's aorta. Datascope's intra-aortic balloon pumps and catheters are used in the treatment of acute heart failure, irregular heart rhythm, cardiac shock, and in openheart surgery and coronary angioplasty. About 40 percent of the company's sales come from its Cardiac Assist division, which develops and manufactures intra-aortic balloon pumps and catheters. Datascope has three other principal divisions. Its Patient Monitoring division manufactures devices used in hospitals to keep track of patients' vital data, including blood pressure, temperature, cardiac output, blood oxygen saturation, airway carbon dioxide, and concentration of anesthetic. This division generates about 35 percent of Datascope's sales. The company operates another division, Collagen Products, to market its VasoSeal line of arterial sealant devices. The VasoSeal is a collagen-based plug that is used to seal arterial punctures and prevent bleeding. Patients undergoing angioplasty or other sim-

ilar procedures end up with a puncture wound in the leg where the catheter was inserted. Datascope's VasoSeal products reduce the time needed to stop bleeding from this puncture. The division also manufactures other products used to stop bleeding during surgery. Datascope's fourth division is run as a subsidiary company, InterVascular Inc. InterVascular makes knitted and woven polyester-coated grafts used to replace diseased arteries. InterVascular Inc. derives almost 60 percent of its sales from overseas markets, with strong sales in France, Germany, Italy, Belgium, and Japan. Datascope is headquartered in New Jersey, and operates several manufacturing and research facilities in that state. Datascope's InterVascular subsidiary also operates a manufacturing plant in La Ciotat, France.

Early Years

Datascope was founded in 1964 by Lawrence Saper. The company made high-tech medical diagnostic equipment. It went public in 1972, and its stock began trading on the Nasdaq exchange. The company was small, but by the mid-1980s, it was the market leader in both patient-monitoring equipment and cardiac-assist devices. Its two principal products were intra-aortic balloon pumps, which accounted for about half its sales, and patient monitors. The company's net profits rose and fell, but sales grew steadily. Datascope began the 1980s bringing in just over $31 million in sales, and passed $50 million in 1985. Sales topped $100 million in 1988, and climbed annually into the early 1990s. Despite the small size of the company, it eventually became notable for its profitability. A specialist in high-tech stocks interviewed in *Barron's* on January 12, 1987, picked Datascope as one of the best health care stocks around, noting in particular that the company's research and development gave it a consistent stream of valuable new products. By 1990, Datascope commanded from 60 to 70 percent of the intra-aortic balloon market. Its biggest competitors were Aries Medical Inc. and Kontron Instruments Inc. While Kontron suffered from quality-control problems that led to a temporary shutdown, Datascope continued to do well. Sales grew to over $113 million in 1990, and then to over $120 million in 1991. The company came up with new patient-monitoring products in the early 1990s. Although the initial versions were troubled by software problems, they had advantages over competitors' products because of special safety features.

Company Perspectives:

Datascope Corporation manufactures proprietary products for clinical health care markets in interventional cardiology and radiology, anesthesiology, cardiovascular and vascular surgery, emergency medicine and critical care.

New Products in the Early 1990s

By 1991, Datascope was still leading the intra-aortic balloon pump market, but sales were slowing. Its products were used to support the heart during heart surgery, and the market seemed to have matured. The company set its sites on another, similar market, by developing a catheter for angioplasties. The balloon angioplasty catheter was used to clear clogged arteries in a procedure that was an alternative to the traditional heart bypass operation. This market was expected to grow rapidly and be worth about $400 million already in 1991. Datascope invested heavily in a new catheter, called Integra, and another called Micross-sl. But the angioplasty catheter market was highly competitive, and Datascope may have come to it too late. In 1992, the company announced that it was giving up on development of an angioplasty catheter and concentrating its efforts on other product lines.

Its most promising product was the VasoSeal. In 1991 Datascope announced that this new device would debut in Europe and was expected to get approval for the United States market soon. Already expert in the intra-aortic balloon, Datascope found a need for a device for what was essentially the other end of the coronary operation. Doctors inserted intra-aortic balloons through a catheter inserted in the patient's femoral artery. The balloon was pushed through the patient's bloodstream until it reached the proper position in the aorta, and surgery could proceed. After the surgery, the balloon was withdrawn through the catheter, and the catheter removed. Then a nurse or technician would apply pressure to the resulting puncture wound in the leg. It usually took some 20 minutes before the wound caused by the catheter stopped bleeding, and then the patient had to be immobilized for hours, and usually not allowed to walk for some time. VasoSeal worked to plug the puncture wound with collagen derived from cows. The device needed only about five to eight minutes of pressure from a nurse or technician before bleeding stopped. It was absorbed into the body in about six weeks. The worldwide market for the device was expected to be large; an estimated 2.5 million arterial catherizations were performed annually across the globe. In dollar terms, the worldwide market was estimated to be worth from $250 to $350 million. Critics claimed that the VasoSeal was not medically necessary. It was expected to cost upwards of $100 per use, and a low-tech solution—manual pressure on the wound—already existed. Nevertheless, Datascope was confident it had discovered a new niche market, and the company's share price more than tripled from the end of 1990 to late 1991.

Growth in International Sales

VasoSeal was approved for use in Europe years before it became available in the United States. Datascope worked hard during the early 1990s to increase its sales in Europe and abroad. Working with overseas customers also taught the company some things about handling changing domestic conditions. During the early 1990s, Datascope's Cardiac Assist division in particular aggressively pursued foreign markets, opening four new sales offices and adding 20 people to sell Datascope's catheter balloons and pumps abroad. According to the division's sales manager, Ken Waters, quoted in *Sales and Marketing Management,* from August 1995, price was more of an issue in medical markets outside the United States, because hospitals usually operated under some form of managed care or national health insurance. Datascope's sales force had to do more than demonstrate that their product worked. They had to persuade and educate customers to overcome barriers against new technology that might be costly. The overseas sales force became versed in selling to hospital administrators and financial officers, whereas the domestic force was focused more on selling directly to cardiologists. Waters considered his sales team's experience with overseas markets valuable preparation for changes in the domestic market, as doctors themselves began to have less say in hospitals' financial decisions. By 1996, foreign sales accounted for more than 20 percent of Datascope's total revenue.

Increasing Competition in the Late 1990s

Price was a certainly a factor in Datascope's sales abroad, but it was also becoming more of an issue in domestic sales. Though the company maintained strong market share, competition forced it to lower prices for its intra-aortic balloon pumps. The company also cut into its profit margin by spending heavily on research and development for its second core business, patient monitoring. Datascope did see overall sales gains through the mid-1990s, continuing a long pattern of growth. Sales passed $150 million in 1992, and by 1995, the company brought in $195.7 million. Sales for 1996 went up to over $211 million. By 1996, about half the company's sales came from its Cardiac Assist division, and about 40 percent from its line of patient monitoring devices. Most of the remainder of its sales came from its vascular graft products. But VasoSeal finally got approval from the Food and Drug Administration (FDA) in late 1995, and it was the only product of its type for sale in the United States. FDA approval was granted at first only for use in coronary angioplasty and a related procedure, angiography. But the potential market was large, as nearly a million Americans underwent these procedures annually. In early 1997, the FDA approved more uses for VasoSeal, allowing it to be used to seal puncture wounds caused by certain radiology procedures. Datascope's stock jumped 14 percent on the news of the FDA's widened approval.

Though VasoSeal was first to reach the U.S. market, it was not the only such product. At least two other American companies made and sold devices for sealing arterial punctures in Europe and were aiming for the domestic market as well. Kensey Nash, of Exton, Pennsylvania, had a similar product called AngioSeal, which got FDA approval for sale in the United States in August 1996. AngioSeal worked using collagen in combination with a plastic plug manipulated with a tube and string. Perclose, a Menlo Park, California, company co founded by a well-known cardiologist, marketed an arterial sealing device that allowed a physician to suture the wound shut

Key Dates:

1964: Lawrence Saper founds the company.
1972: Datascope becomes a public company.
1988: The company's annual sales top $100 million.
1991: The company announces its new VasoSeal product for sale in Europe.
1995: VasoSeal gets FDA approval for use in United States.

with flexible needles. Perclose became a subsidiary of the health care conglomerate Abbott Labs in 1999. Kensey Nash was a small company with a record of losing money, but its stock, like Datascope's, jumped at news in 1997 of FDA approval of wider use for its device. By 1997 AngioSeal was bringing Kensey Nash about $6.4 million annually. Nevertheless, Datascope was ahead of the game. It was bringing in about $8 million in its first year of selling VasoSeal, and sales increased dramatically over the following years. The worldwide market for VasoSeal and its competitors' products was potentially huge. The estimated dollar value placed on that market rose, varying from $400 million to as much as $1.3 billion.

By the late 1990s, Datascope was comfortably situated with four growing business divisions. In 1999, the company announced plans to spend $16 million on new facilities. Some of its laboratory and warehouse space was outdated, so it built a state-of-the-art facility in Mahwah, New Jersey. By 2000, Datascope had seen ten straight years of double-digit sales and earnings growth. Overall sales were close to $300 million for 2000. Its Cardiac Assist division accounted for about 40 percent of total sales, less than in earlier years, but the company believed its market still had room for growth, particularly in Europe. Sales of patient monitors also continued to increase, jumping ten percent in 2000. Datascope had a line of portable, battery-powered bedside monitors that led the market for their type. International sales were also particularly strong for this division. The company's Intervascular, Inc. subsidiary did almost 60 percent of its sales overseas. Its profits were sometimes mixed because of currency fluctuations, but this division too seemed to be expanding. In 2000 Datascope acquired a 30 percent equity in a German company, AMG GmbH, which distributed stent products (tubes used inside blood vessels in coronary operations). Datascope planned to market AMG's stents through its own sales force in Europe, and to have AMG sell VasoSeal in Germany. Datascope's Collagen Products division, which marketed VasoSeal, was its real success story. Sales for the unit leapt over 30 percent in 2000. The company brought out VasoSeal ES, a second generation product, and readied a third generation, VasoSeal EZ, for clinical trials in 2001.

Datascope had grown almost exclusively through developing its own products, and it had little debt. It continued to bring out new lines and to invest heavily in research and development. For 2000, over 40 percent of its sales came from products the company had developed in the past three years. It continued to expand its sales of its core line of intra-aortic balloon pumps in spite of years of warnings about softening conditions in that market. And its patient monitors continued to be market leaders.

With the great promise of its collagen product line, the company seemed poised for more gains in years to come.

Principal Divisions

Cardiac Assist; Patient Monitoring; Arterial Puncture Sealing; Vascular Grafts.

Principal Subsidiaries

InterVascular, Inc.; Datascope Belgium S.p.r.l.; Datascope B.V. Hoevelaken (Netherlands); Datascope S.A.R.L. (France); InterVascular S.A.S. (France); Datascope GmbH (Germany); InterVascular GmbH (Germany); Datascope Italia s.r.l; Datascope Medical Co. Ltd. (United Kingdom).

Principal Competitors

Abbott Labs; Kensey Nash Corporation.; Agilent Technologies.

Further Reading

Benway, Stuart J., "Datascope Corp." *Value Line,* Edition 1, Part 3, March 22, 1991, p. 215.

"Datascope Corp.," *Wall Street Journal,* July 21, 1992, p. B3.

"Datascope Corp.: FDA Clears Sale of Seal for Use in Heart Surgery," *Wall Street Journal,* October 3, 1995, p. B4.

"Datascope Corp.: FDA Requests More Data to Finish VasoSeal Review," *Wall Street Journal,* December 11, 1992, p. B6.

"Datascope Corp.: Stock Rises 14% as FDA Approves New Product Use," *Wall Street Journal,* January 8, 1997, p. A12.

"Datascope Unveils Device Used to Seal Arterial Punctures," *Wall Street Journal,* April 30, 1991, p. B4.

Gianturco, Michael, "A Play on Catheterization," *Forbes,* December 30, 1996, p. 146.

Hower, Wendy, "A Dream Team Revives Kontron Instruments," *Boston Business Journal,* October 22, 1990, p. 6.

Keenan, William Jr., Royal, Weld F., and Campanelli, Melissa, "Bravo, Bravo!," *Sales and Marketing Management,* August 1995, p. 35.

Key, Sandra W., and Daniel J. DeNoon, "Datascope Plans to Enter Life Science Research Market," *AIDS Weekly Plus,* November 3, 1997, p. 23.

Lazo, Shirley, "Speaking of Dividends," *Barron's,* December 2, 1991, p. 42.

Lowenstein, Roger, "Medical Gear Maker Datascope Draws Crowd, But Doubters Cite Hospital Cost Pressures," *Wall Street Journal,* July 11, 1991, p. C2.

"New Device Stops Bleeding Faster," *FDA Consumer,* January-February 1996, p. 2.

Oppenheim, Mitchell A., "Datascope Corp." *Value Line,* Edition 1, Part 3, September 18, 1992, p. 215.

Plante, Thomas R., "Datascope Corp.," *Value Line,* Edition 1, Part 3, September 13, 1996, p. 213.

Shook, David, "Montvale, N.J.-Based Medical Device Manufacturer to Move 350 Workers," *Knight-Ridder/Tribune Business News,* February 1, 1999.

Stark, Karl, "FDA Approves Pennsylvania Firm's Artery-Repairing Tool for Wide Use," *Knight-Ridder/Tribune Business News,* August 12, 1997.

"The Growing Might of Midcap Stocks," *U.S. News & World Report,* November 18, 1991, p. 98.

Welling, Kathryn, "High on Tech," *Barron's,* January 12, 1987, pp. 11, 27–32.

—A. Woodward

Debevoise & Plimpton

Debevoise & Plimpton

875 Third Avenue
New York, New York 10022
U.S.A.
Telephone: (212) 909-6000
Fax: (212) 909-6836
Web site: http://www.debevoise.com

Partnership
Founded: 1931 as Debevoise & Stevenson
Employees: 1,750
Sales: $269 million (1999)
NAIC: 54111 Offices of Lawyers

Debevoise & Plimpton is one of the United States' major law firms. Clients such as American Airlines, the Democratic National Committee, the National Football League, and *The New York Times* receive advice from the Debevoise firm on intellectual property, tax, litigation, mergers and acquisitions, and other legal specialties. Although the firm has relatively few foreign offices, its far-flung international practice makes Debevoise & Plimpton a major player in the globalization of the world's economy. It also is a leading provider of pro bono services to those with limited resources.

Origins

In 1931 Eli Whitney Debevoise and William Stevenson, two associates at the New York law firm of Davis Polk & Wardwell, decided to form their own partnership. Two years later, Francis Plimpton joined them, and in 1936 Robert G. Page became the fourth name partner.

Initially the new partnership received work from some of New York City's large law firms, including Davis Polk & Wardwell, Sullivan & Cromwell, and Milbank Tweed. Its early work for Phelps Dodge increased until it became their first corporate client. The firm's bankruptcy work for Kreuger & Toll in 1932 also helped it get started. The partnership also represented the Southwestern Bell Telephone Company in one of the first public stock offerings issued under the newly enacted Securities Act of 1933.

Starting in the Depression years, lawyers at the young firm did considerable reorganization work for the Florida East Coast, Central of Georgia, Norfolk Southern, New Haven, and Erie railroads, and also public utilities such as American Power & Light and General Gas & Electric. The 1930s also marked the beginning of the firm's service for the St. Joe Lead Company that had mines in Missouri and New York State and also for the Consolidation Coal Company that eventually became the nation's major bituminous coal company. In 1937 the John Hancock Mutual Life Insurance Company came to the partnership to request assistance in a private securities placement, a new form of financing that was developed to avoid the strict requirements of public securities. Similar work for other insurance companies became a prominent part of the law firm. By 1940 the partnership gained as clients the investment counsel firm of Scudder, Stevens & Clark and also Tampax Inc., later renamed Tambrands Inc.

During World War II, the law firm lost several lawyers as they left to support the war effort. For example, Stevenson left to head the Red Cross. Although Debevoise remained with the firm, he spent many hours as the chairman of an Alien Enemy Hearing Board in New York City. At the time, because the firm's attorneys were not specialists, they were able to handle work left by those who had joined the military. After the firm merged in 1943 with Hatch, McLean, Root & Hinch, it had 13 lawyers. At the end of 1944, the number had grown to 19 lawyers, increasing further as veterans returned in 1945.

Postwar Practice

In 1948 the young law firm gained American Airlines as a major client when it decided to move its headquarters to New York City from Washington, D.C. As the airline's general counsel, the firm earned at least $150,000 in annual income, and American Airlines remained a client for several decades.

In the early years of the Cold War, firm partner Edward C. McLean defended Alger Hiss in what D. Bret Carlson called "undoubtedly the most publicized matter ever handled by the firm." Accused in 1948 by Whitaker Chambers of transmitting government documents to the Russians in the 1930s, Hiss demanded a public trial to defend himself. Although he was never

Key Dates:

1931: Firm is founded in New York City.
1936: Firm becomes Debevoise, Stevenson, Plimpton & Page.
1943: Firm merges with Hatch, McLean, Root & Hinch.
1947: Firm becomes known as Debevoise, Plimpton & McLean.
1949: Firm's client Alger Hiss is convicted of perjury in a well-publicized case.
1964: Paris office is opened.
1976: Barbara Robinson becomes the firm's first female partner.
1981: Firm is renamed Debevoise & Plimpton on its 50 anniversary.
1982: Firm opens its Washington, D.C., office.
1991: A book based on oral history interviews of firm lawyers is published.
1994: Firm's first Asian office in opened in Hong Kong.
1997: Moscow office is formally opened in December.

convicted of spying, in 1949 he was convicted of perjury in a controversial case during the second Red Scare.

After World War II, the firm's reputation increased from its partners' work in government, higher education, and business. Phelps Dodge Corporation chose Page as its president in 1947. Debevoise became counsel to the high commissioner of West Germany in 1951 and served as the acting deputy high commissioner in 1952 and 1953. Stevenson was the American ambassador to the Philippines and later became the president of Oberlin College. In the 1960s Presidents Kennedy and Johnson appointed Plimpton as ambassador to the United Nations. In 1956 the law firm represented The Ford Foundation when it completed its first public offering of stock of the Ford Motor Company. According to George Lindsay, in the firm's history, "That was the largest financing that had ever been held up to that time and was replete with new inventions in the law," and thus involved complex negotiations among the company, foundation, and Ford family members.

In 1959 Debevoise & Plimpton became general counsel for the First National City Trust Company that administered the pension fund of the affiliated First National City Bank, later renamed Citibank. In 1961 the law firm moved its offices to a new building at 320 Park Avenue constructed for the bank and trust company. After the trust company merged with and became a department of the bank, the law firm continued as its general counsel. Meanwhile, Debevoise & Plimpton represented the Rockefeller family in various matters, including the transition of Rockefeller Institute into Rockefeller University and the family's real estate dealings through the Rockefeller Holding Company.

Growth of the Firm in the 1970s and 1980s

In 1980 the firm accepted a request by Chrysler to serve as its lead counsel in its struggle to survive financially. Following the Arab oil embargo of 1973, many Americans chose small foreign cars that used much less gas than did American cars. Thus, Chrysler lost market share, acquired a large inventory of unsold cars, and received over 400 loans from American, Canadian, Japanese, and European banks and other entities by the end of the decade.

In 1979 Congress had passed a law guaranteeing loans to Chrysler, but the automaker had to adhere to strict requirements for the law to be implemented. Debevoise partners, with the help of more than one-fourth of all its associates, helped Chrysler understand the complex federal law and then restructure its old loans and gain new ones. Although its operations were disrupted by a major fire in Debevoise's New York office, the firm finally helped Chrysler avoid bankruptcy and eventually recover in what James B. Stewart described in 1983 as "the largest corporate rescue mission ever attempted." The firm continued to do work for Chrysler on other matters in the years to come.

In 1982 Debevoise & Plimpton joined the growing number of law firms with offices in Washington, D.C. The number of lawyers in the nation's capital increased from 11,000 in 1972 to 45,000 in 1987.

In the 1970s and 1980s, Debevoise & Plimpton grew rapidly. From its origins with 2 lawyers in 1931, it had grown to employ 102 in 1970. By 1980 it employed 147 lawyers, and then in the 1980s it grew even faster, reaching a total of 368 lawyers at the end of 1990. Important corporate clients at the time included Prudential, Aetna, John Hancock, Equitable Mutual Life, Mass Mutual, American Airlines, KLM Royal Dutch Airlines, St. John Minerals, Continental Corporation, Cooper Laboratories, Wheelabrator Frye, and Kelso and Company. The firm also represented the Ford, Russell Sage, and Hartford Foundations and Columbia and Princeton Universities.

Debevoise & Plimpton's growth was part of a general trend that transformed many law firms. In the late 1970s two major developments spurred the changes. First, the U.S. Supreme Court ruled that professional restrictions on advertising violated the First Amendment's free speech provision. That led to more lawyers and other professionals openly soliciting clients. Second, legal journalism changed dramatically with the publication of two new periodicals, *The National Journal* and *The American Lawyer*, both of which covered the internal management practices and finances of law firms. With such data available, and attorneys becoming more aware of salaries and opportunities elsewhere, lateral hiring increased significantly in the 1980s as large law firms added literally hundreds of lawyers to their ranks. Intense competition for top talent, more formal management methods, the use of public relations experts, and the use of management consultants were also part of the transformation of America's large law firms.

Practice in the 1990s and Beyond

In 1992 Debevoise & Plimpton represented Infinity Broadcasting Corporation when it became a public corporation. In 1996 the law firm helped the broadcasting corporation acquire TDI Worldwide, Grannam Holdings, and Alliance Broadcasting, then assisted Infinity when it was in turn acquired by Westinghouse Electric Corporation.

The law firm began to take on more work representative of the Information Age. Starting in 1994, it helped the Internet service provider CompuServe deal with the U.S. Patent and Trademark Office's rules concerning online intellectual property rights. Around 2000, the firm was involved in other major developments related to digital technology and the Internet. It represented *The New York Times*, Time Inc., and *Newsday* in *Tasini v. New York Times*, an important case that dealt with publishers' rights to disseminate their work online. Its media and technology practice also served clients such as the National Football League, the National Basketball Association, Dow Jones, Reuters, *The Washington Post*, *Times Mirror*, CNN, and *USA Today* that were concerned about the proper role of the Internet.

Like several other law firms, Debevoise & Plimpton cut the number of attorneys that it employed during the economic downturn of the early 1990s, decreasing from 397 attorneys in 1992 to 376 in 1993, when 307 worked in New York and the rest in branch offices in Washington, D.C., Paris, Los Angeles, London, and Budapest. According to *Of Counsel* of May 3–17, 1993, Debevoise & Plimpton assisted the Mexican telephone company Telmex and Bancomer, a large Mexican bank, when they were transformed from government to private businesses. The firm also participated in developing the oil and natural gas resources of Russia's Sakhalin Island and in the privatization of the Prague Ruzyne International Airport. Later the firm closed its offices in Los Angeles and Budapest and opened its Moscow office.

In a 1996 survey by the Volunteers of Legal Service, Debevoise & Plimpton was one of the top New York law firms for pro bono work; it was one of only four New York firms that averaged 91 to 110 hours per lawyer and had increased its pro bono totals from 16,085 hours in 1995 to 30,714 hours in 1996. Debevoise & Plimpton's pro bono activities ranged from international human rights and poverty law cases to prisoners' rights, civil rights, and various environmental, educational, arts, and other nonprofit concerns.

The firm's Washington, D.C., office, with about 30 lawyers in the late 1990s, operated differently from other firms. From that office's 1982 beginning, "We had an odd-duck philosophy," said partner Ralph Ferrara in *Of Counsel* on October 18, 1999, explaining that the firm did not do legislative work for its corporate clients. He also said, "Washington lawyers do trade regulatory work. . . . We do [Securities and Exchange Commission] stuff, but it's not regulatory, it's disclosure." The Debevoise office represented financial, telecommunications, and other business clients in arranging mergers and dealing with complex litigation. For example, in the 1990s it helped insurance companies like New York Life and John Hancock deal with unprecedented class actions filed by policyholders.

In 1999 Debevoise & Plimpton provided counsel in over 135 mergers and acquisitions worth more than $435 billion. Merger and acquisitions clients included: 1) the Jim Henson Company (Jim Henson was the creator of the Muppets) when it was purchased by EM.TV & Merchandising AG; 2) Lawrence Dolan in his purchase of The Cleveland Indians; 3) Chrysler in its $38 billion merger with Germany's Daimler-Benz. Fashion house Prada, LG Electronics, GlobeNet Communications, and AXA Financial, Inc. also used the Debevoise firm during 1999.

The firm's litigators in 1999 won victories for Gap Inc. in a copyright/trademark case, General Electric in both British and U.S. courts, and Showa Aluminum Corporation in a patent trial. It also represented American Home Products Corporation, American Express, Citibank, MetLife, the Council for Tobacco Research, and American Lawyer Media in litigation cases.

According to *The American Lawyer*, Debevoise & Plimpton was ranked as the nation's 37th largest law firm in 1999, based on its annual gross revenues of $269 million. Its revenue per lawyer was $670,000, which placed it at number 13 nationally, and its profits per partner of $1.225 million ranked the firm as number eleven in the United States. With an 80 percent increase in its profits per partner since 1990, the firm was considered one of the "Winners of the Nineties." Debevoise & Plimpton also was the nation's 18th most prestigious law firm, according to a survey of 4,800 lawyers published in 2000 in the third edition of the Vault.com *Guide to the Top 50 Law Firms*. These statistics and surveys indicated that Debevoise & Plimpton was well prepared to confront the numerous legal challenges of the new millennium. However, the firm needed room to expand, so it planned to move its New York headquarters in summer 2001 to newly built offices at 919 Third Avenue.

Principal Operating Units

Corporate; Tax; Litigation; Trusts and Estates.

Principal Competitors

Davis, Polk & Wardwell; Skadden, Arps; Sullivan & Cromwell.

Further Reading

Carlson, D. Bret, *Debevoise & Plimpton: The Autobiography of a Law Firm,* New York: Debevoise & Plimpton, 1991.
Cherovsky, Erwin, *The Guide to New York Law Firms,* New York: St. Martin's Press, 1991, pp. 74–78.
Dean, William J., "Pro Bono Digest: Law Firm Activities," *New York Law Journal,* July 9, 1997.
"Debevoise & Plimpton [profile]," *Of Counsel,* May 3–17, 1993, p. 138.
Jaskunas, Paul and D.M. Osborne, "Cashing in on Cyberspace," *Am-Law Tech,* summer 1996.
"Lawyers Reveal All in New Guidebook to Top Law Firms," *Business Wire,* August 29, 2000.
Malkani, Sheila V. and Michael F. Walsh, *The Insider's Guide to Law Firms,* 2d ed., Boulder, Colo.: Mobius Press, 1994, pp. 347–350.
Merelman, Diana, "Dealmaker," *American Lawyer,* September 1996.
Pearlman, Laura, "Opening Doors," *American Lawyer,* March 1999.
Stewart, James B., "Chrysler: Debevoise, Plimpton, Lyons & Gates," Chapter 5 in *The Partners: Inside America's Most Powerful Law Firms,* New York: Simon and Schuster, 1983, pp. 201–44.
Tripoli, Lori, "Ralph Ferrara Pioneers a New Breed of DC 'Inside Outside'," *Of Counsel,* October 18, 1999.

—David M. Walden

Delta Air Lines, Inc.

Hartsfield International Airport
Atlanta, Georgia 30320
U.S.A.
Telephone: (404) 715-2600
Fax: (404) 715-1400
Web site: http://www.delta.com

Public Company
Incorporated: 1934 as Delta Air Corporation
Employees: 81,000
Sales: $15.89 billion (2000)
Stock Exchanges: New York
Ticker Symbol: DAL
NAIC: 481111 Scheduled Passenger Air Transportation;
481112 Scheduled Freight Air Transportation; 481219
Other Nonscheduled Air Transportation

Delta Air Lines, Inc. is one of the largest and most successful air carriers in the United States. Originally founded as a crop dusting service in 1924, Delta was led for 40 years by an agricultural scientist and pilot named Collet Everman Woolman. Until his death in 1966 Woolman dominated the operations of Delta. In this sense he was similar to his three major competitors, Eddie Rickenbacker at Eastern, Juan Trippe at Pan Am, and Howard Hughes at TWA. Expansion through acquisition characterized the era that followed. Then, in the 1990s Delta adopted an aggressive business strategy in order to retain market share in an increasingly competitive airline industry. The new strategy was an enormous success, and in 2000 Delta enjoyed a net income of more than $1 billion and carried a record 117 million passengers. Entering the new century the airline had extended its route network to serve 221 cities in 48 states, and an additional 118 cities in 47 foreign countries.

From Crop Dusting to Passenger Transport

The history of Delta may be traced to 1924, when Collet Everman Woolman and an associate joined a conversation with some Louisiana farmers who were concerned about the threat to their crops from boll weevils. Woolman knew that calcium arsenate would kill the insects, but the problem was how to effectively apply the chemical. Having learned to fly the boxy "flying jennys" during World War I, Woolman considered dropping the chemical from an airplane. He engineered a "hopper" for the chemical and later perfected the system, and then began selling his services to farmers throughout the region. As a result, the world's first crop dusting service, named Huff Daland Dusters, was born.

In 1925 Woolman left the agricultural extension service to take charge of the duster's entomological work. In 1928 the crop dusting operation broke away from its parent company to become Delta Air Service. Woolman continued his crop dusting business across the South and expanded into Mexico and South America. The company began to diversify by securing air mail contracts, and in 1929 inaugurated passenger service between Dallas and Jackson, Mississippi. Later, routes to Atlanta and Charleston were added.

Delta began its climb to prominence when the U.S. government awarded it an airmail contract in 1930, remaining in business even during a temporary but costly suspension in the airmail contract system in 1934. By 1941, the company, now called Delta Air Corporation, would be awarded three more airmail contracts. During World War II, Delta, under contract to the War Department, devoted itself to the allied war effort by transporting troops and supplies. Delta returned to civilian service in 1945 and entered an age of growth and competition never before seen in the airline industry.

The Growth of Air Travel After World War II

On May 1, 1953 Delta merged with Chicago and Southern Airlines and continued to prosper as a major regional trunk carrier through the 1950s and 1960s. In June 1967 Delta merged with Delaware Airlines and officially adopted the name Delta Air Lines.

Delta's exposure to the northeast part of the country increased with the acquisition of Northeast Airlines on August 1, 1972. In July 1976 Delta purchased Storer Leasing, a move that added several jets to the existing fleet of about 200. Recognizing the value of high technology, Delta formed two computerized marketing subsidiaries, Epsilon Trading Corporation in 1981 and Datas Incorporated in 1982, to coordinate and sell more passenger seats on all Delta flights.

Delta's consistent growth could be partially attributed to its successful transition of leadership. In the early days of commercial air transport airlines were run by individuals who would be better described as aviation pioneers first and as businessmen second. At American, Eastern, Pan Am, TWA, and Delta, these men established what could be described as almost dictatorial operations, retaining their posts as long as possible. Many of these leaders were majority stockholders who categorically refused to share their power or prepare successors to operate the company after them. For many airline companies, when the chairman did eventually die, there was a difficult period of readjustment to the new management.

The departure of Delta's Woolman, however, was not surrounded by difficulties. He suffered a heart attack in his late 60s and was forced to relinquish some of his duties to Delta's board members. As Woolman's health deteriorated the board members gradually assumed more of his duties until his death at age 76. Although Woolman's absence was deeply felt at Delta, business continued as usual, and the airline was able to make a smooth transition to a more modern, corporate style of collective management. Under the new consensus-style management, Delta quickly became recognized for having one of the best planning and management teams in the airline industry. The company also earned a reputation for being on very good terms with its employees, treating its workers as family. By maintaining pay and benefits above the unionized competition, Delta was able to keep the majority of its employees non-unionized.

Although the company did not invent it, Delta was the first airline to widely employ the so-called "hub and spoke" system, in which a number of flights are scheduled to land at a hub airport within approximately 30 minutes, enabling passengers to make connections for final destinations conveniently and quickly. By the early 1990s the "big push," as it was called, was occurring about ten times a day at the Atlanta hub. Delta was also operating hubs at Dallas-Fort Worth, Boston, Memphis, and Cincinnati.

On the whole, Delta's management style remained conservative throughout the 1970s. While it boasted one of the most modern jetliner fleets in domestic service, the company developed a reputation for purchasing new planes only after they had been proven, often in a costly way, at other airlines. This "wait-and-see" policy saved the company a large amount of money. Only after competing airlines had used the Lockheed 1011 for several years did Delta purchase the plane, and Delta began replacing its fleet of Boeing 727s with the 757, 767, and MD-88 in the late 1980s, later than most, with the intention of using these technologically advanced and fuel efficient planes for at least 20 years. This 15-year strategy for flight equipment and support facility planning was typical of Delta. According to the vice-chairman and chief financial officer at the time, Robert Oppenlander, "Success is based on the long term maintenance of a technical edge, which is cost efficiency."

Delta also became known for having the most conservative balance sheet in the industry. With a debt-equity ratio that was consistently below one to one (meaning that their debts were usually outweighed by their net worth), the company was able to do most of its financing internally. This conservative approach was aptly summed up in a statement by the late chairman W.T. Beebe: "We don't squander our money on things like goofy advertising."

A New Business Strategy for the 1980s

In the 1980s, however, Delta assumed a more aggressive corporate personality, as its commitment to internal growth became increasingly threatened by a general trend in the industry toward external growth. Throughout the 1980s, Delta became relatively smaller, as companies such as TWA, Texas Air, and Northwest expanded through mergers. In order to remain competitive, in 1986 Delta announced its intention to take over the Los Angeles-based Jet America; however, the $18.7 million deal never materialized. Later that year Delta went ahead with the $680 million purchase of another air carrier based in Los Angeles: Western Air Lines. As Delta's chief executive officer, David Garrett, explained, "For a merger to be worthwhile, two plus two has to equal seven." Enlarged by Western's hubs in Los Angeles and Salt Lake City, Delta management was able to make that kind of math work, in spite of initial difficulties integrating Western's unionized work force into Delta's system.

In 1987 Ronald W. Allen, who rose through the ranks of Delta's personnel administration department, was named the airline's CEO. An aggressive and outgoing business person, Allen proved willing to make larger and riskier investments. Shortly after taking office, for example, he negotiated a $15 million dollar deal for Delta to become the official airline of Walt Disney World.

In the late 1980s and early 1990s, recession, rising fuel prices, and war in the Middle East all contributed to declining passenger traffic and inflated costs. Thanks in part to its financially solvent status, Delta weathered the industry troubles comparatively well, despite a 1991 operating loss of $450 million. Small, financially weak, and regional airlines were hardest

Key Dates:

1924: Huff Daland Dusters, a crop dusting operation, is founded.
1929: Delta inaugurates passenger flights between Dallas and Jackson, Mississippi.
1953: Delta merges with Chicago and Southern Airlines.
1967: Delta merges with Delaware Airlines, becomes Delta Air Lines.
1972: Delta acquires Northeast Airlines.
1986: Delta acquires Western Air Lines.
1994: Delta's Leadership 7.5 program is launched, seeking to dramatically restructure and streamline operations.
2000: Total number of passengers carried during the year reaches an all-time high of 120 million.

hit by the trouble; Delta was one of the prime beneficiaries of the failure in January 1991 of Eastern Airlines, which like Delta had a significant portion of its routes in the southeastern United States. After Eastern's demise, Delta flew over 80 percent of traffic out of Atlanta.

In 1991 Delta made a major move toward becoming an international player by purchasing a $1.7 billion package of assets from Pan Am, outbidding chief rivals American and United. The package, which included the assumption of $668 million of liabilities, gave Delta a hub in Frankfurt, Germany, dozens of European routes, including flights from Miami and Detroit to London, a New York shuttle route, and 21 Airbus A310s. As with the purchase of Western, the deal was viewed by some in the industry as a departure from Delta's traditionally conservative business stance, and possibly too costly a purchase. Delta management, however, termed it a necessary stop in a consolidating purchase-or-be-purchased airline market: "We think it is a very conservative move," Allen told *Fortune* magazine, adding, "To have missed this opportunity would have been the risky course."

Delta appeared to have adapted well to the expansion-oriented market. Whereas Delta fliers used to joke that, though you might not know whether you would go to heaven or hell when you died, you would definitely have to change planes in Atlanta, the airline's customers could now fly to Europe via its Frankfurt hub, or to Latin America via Miami. As it adapted to the aggressive and expanding modern market, Delta strove to maintain its policies of good labor relations and attention to service. Delta's employees were still among the highest paid in the industry and, like founder C.E. Woolman, Allen sometimes rode on Delta flights to interact with passengers. Indeed, *Forbes* magazine queried in a 1988 headline: "Is Delta too nice for its own good?" At the time, however, its emphasis on people seemed not to have crippled Delta.

Record Profits, New Problems: Heading into the Twenty-First Century

By 1992 it became clear that the financing agreement with Pan Am had come at a bad time for Delta. The general eco-

nomic recession and continued high fuel prices, combined with the weight of Pan Am's heavy debt, resulted in net losses of $506 million for fiscal year 1991. In an effort to lower costs, Delta was forced to reduce its work force by five percent, in addition to implementing wage freezes and salary cuts. At the same time, the company was eager to integrate Pan Am's extensive European routes into its system, hoping to restore itself to profitability by improving its position as an international carrier. However, the lingering effects of the recession, as well as the recent Gulf War, had precipitated an overall decline in commercial air travel. To counteract this trend, Delta announced reductions of 45 percent on transatlantic fares at the onset of the summer 1992 season, resulting in record traffic of 8,511,966 passengers in August. In April 1993, in an effort to increase its share of transpacific air traffic, Delta launched new non-stop flights between Los Angeles and Hong Kong.

Initially, the stronger emphasis on overseas routes paid off for the company, leading to profits of $60.4 million in the first quarter of fiscal 1993, compared to a net loss of $125.2 million for the first quarter of the previous year. Inspired by this success, Delta strove to further expand its international presence by entering into code-sharing agreements with a number of foreign carriers in 1994, including Virgin Atlantic, Vietnam Airlines, and Aeromexico. Code sharing allowed an airline to purchase tickets from its rivals and resell them to its own customers, providing greater scheduling flexibility and control over prices. While some considered the practice deceptive, by the mid-1990s it had become prevalent throughout the airline industry, with the number of code-sharing partnerships reaching 389 by 1996. For its part, Delta established 14 such contracts with other airlines between 1992 and 1996.

Another wave of heavy losses in the first three months of 1994 forced the company to undertake a more drastic cost cutting scheme, and in April Delta launched its Leadership 7.5 program, a restructuring initiative designed to streamline operations. The goal was implied in the program's name; Delta hoped to reduce the cost of flying to 7.5 cents per mile, per seat, with an overall aim to cut operating expenses by $2 billion over a three year span. The reorganization called for a reduction of 20 percent of the company's work force, a realignment of its domestic route system, and a discontinuation of some of its less profitable European routes. These drastic measures brought quick results, and the company was able to claim a net profit of $251 million for the fourth quarter of fiscal 1995.

Delta's impressive financial comeback was not without costs to its reputation as a "family" corporation. The reduction of the company's customer service team resulted in a significant increase in passenger complaints, and by 1997 Delta dropped to last place in on-time rankings among the ten leading U.S. airlines. The decline in customer service was hardly unique to Delta. Overall, the annual number of airline passengers in the U.S. jumped to 640 million in 1999, compared to 453 million in 1991, with the ratio of seats filled reaching an all-time high of 71.3 percent. Overcrowding, frequent delays, and poor service resulted in a substantial increase in the numbers of complaints lodged with the Department of Transportation in 1999, prompting Congress to consider legislation that would impose stricter regulations on the airlines' business practices.

The airline industry also faced a number of labor disputes at the beginning of the new century. The expiration of the Delta pilots' contract in May 2000 was followed by several months of unproductive negotiations. When the impasse dragged into December, the pilots retaliated by refusing voluntary overtime during one of the airline's busiest seasons, forcing Delta to cancel 3,500 flights over the course of the month. The new year brought little relief, and another 1,700 cancellations followed in the first ten days of January 2001. While the company enjoyed net profits of $897 million in 2000, and saw its total number of passengers reach an all-time high of 120 million, it was clear Delta still faced several unresolved issues, both with customer service and labor, as it continued on its quest to become the nation's leading airline.

Principal Subsidiaries

ASA Holdings, Inc.; Atlantic Southeast Airlines; Delta Technology, Inc.; Comair Holdings, Inc.; WORLDSPAN, L.P. (40%)

Principal Competitors

AMR Corporation; Southwest Airlines Co.; UAL Corporation.

Further Reading

Banks, Howard, "Is Delta Too Nice for Its Own Good?," *Forbes,* November 28, 1988.

Brelis, Matthew, "For Airlines, Forecast Is Still a Gloomy One," *Boston Globe,* January 20, 2001.

Harrington, Jeff, "Sky-High Frustration," *St. Petersburg Times*, February 27, 2000.

Ho, Rodney, "A Closer World: Airlines Extend Their Reach by Selling Tickets on Each Other's Flights," *Atlanta Journal and the Atlanta Constitution,* March 19, 1996.

Huettel, Steve, "Delta Seeks a Steady Course," *Tampa Tribune*, April 7, 1997.

Laibich, Kenneth, "Delta Aims for a Higher Altitude," *Fortune,* December 16, 1991.

Lewis, David W., and Wesley Philips Newton, *Delta: The History of an Airline,* Athens: University of Georgia Press, 1973.

——, "The Delta-C & S Merger: A Case Study in Airline Consolidation and Federal Regulation," *Business History Review* (Boston), 1979.

Maxon, Terry, "Burdened by Expense of Pan Am Move, Delta Air Lines Adjusts to Lean Times," *Journal of Commerce,* August 19, 1992.

Reed, Dan, "Delta's Dawn: New Delta Executives Redefining Airline's Once-Stodgy Image, Boosting Bottom Line," *Fort Worth Star-Telegram,* January 24, 1999.

Thurston, Scott, "Delta Joining Dogfight over Latin America," *Atlanta Journal and the Atlanta Constitution,* April 5, 1998.

——, "High Expectations: With Profits Back, Delta Focusing on Image and Service," *Atlanta Journal and the Atlanta Constitution,* March 9, 1997.

——, "New CEO Gives Delta a Brisk Shake," *Atlanta Journal and the Atlanta Constitution,* December 28, 1997.

—John Simley
—updates: James Poniewozik, Stephen Meyer

Deutz AG

Deutz-Mühlheimer Strasse 147-149
D-51057 Köln
Germany
Telephone: (49) (221) 822-0
Fax: (49) (221) 822-3525
Web site: http://www.deutz.de

Public Company
Incorporated: 1864 as N.A. Otto & Cie
Employees: 6,693
Sales: DM 2.46 billion ($1.26 billion) (1999)
Stock Exchanges: Frankfurt/Main
Ticker Symbol: DEZ
NAIC: 335312 Motor and Generator Manufacturing;
    333611 Turbine and Turbine Generator Set Unit
    Manufacturing; 333618 Other Engine Equipment
    Manufacturing; 33312 Construction Machinery
    Manufacturing; 333131 Mining Machinery and
    Equipment Manufacturing

Deutz AG is one of Germany's leading manufacturers of diesel and gas engines for the global market. The Deutz product range includes liquid and air-cooled high-speed diesel and gas engines with a performance of four to 7.4 kilowatts (kW) which are used in cars, tractors, ships, turbines, compressors, and pumps, to name but a few. Deutz is the main supplier of diesel engines for Swedish auto maker Volvo AB. The company's industrial plant business division is organized under the umbrella of KHD Humboldt Wedag and builds industrial plants for the cement, mining, and aluminum industry. Deutz has sales and service offices all around the world. Deutsche Bank owns a 25 percent share in Deutz, while Volvo holds a ten percent stake.

Beginnings in 1864

In 1860 Jean-Joseph-Etienne Lenoir, a versatile inventor from Belgium-Luxembourg, built an internal combustion engine powered by household gas. Nicolaus August Otto, a German businessman with a knack for technical inventions, was intrigued by Lenoir's idea. However, Otto had a different vision. Based on Lenoir's principle, he ultimately wanted to burn a liquid fuel so he could use his engine in vehicles. While working as a traveling salesman for a Cologne-based wholesale trade company, 29-year old Otto started experimenting with an engine based Lenoir's model in 1861. He discovered that the process could be improved significantly when the air and fuel mixture was compressed before it was burnt. This observation led to the idea of a process divided into four phases: intake, compression, combustion, and exhaust. Otto then discovered that the pressure generated by the combustion process was very powerful and hard to control. He refined his technology using atmospheric air pressure to generate power. In 1863 Otto started testing his ''atmospheric gas engine'' in a workshop in Cologne and secured several national and international patents.

On February 9, 1864, Eugen Langen observed Otto's machine. Only a few weeks later, on March 31, the engineer and owner of a sugar factory signed a contract with Otto to set up the engine factory N.A. Otto & Cie. Backed up by his father and other businesspeople he knew, Langen provided the necessary funds to get the business up and running, while Otto contributed the machinery (in which he had already invested) and his innovative technical insight to further refine the technology. The small workshop of N.A. Otto & Cie in Cologne's Servasgasse became the breeding ground for the world's motorization. In 1867 Otto and Langen presented their atmospheric gas engine at the Paris World Fair where it was awarded a gold medal for the most economical propulsion machine for small business. One year later, three atmospheric gas engines were shipped to the United States. An important business relationship was established in the following year when Manchester-based Crossley Brothers acquired a manufacturing license of Otto's invention for England. In 1869 businessman Roosen-Runge from Hamburg provided additional funding, and a brand-new factory was built in Cologne's Deutz suburb on the east bank of the Rhine River. In 1872 the company was transformed into a public share company and was renamed Gasmotoren-Fabrik Deutz AG. At that time, German engineer Gottlieb Daimler joined the company as engineering director.

Otto worked continuously to refine his technology and finally in 1876 reached a breakthrough. The following year, he

Company Perspectives:

Focus on the Customer. *DEUTZ has been a reliable and independent supplier for more than 130 years, one with ultra-modern engines, a comprehensive range of services, and a global service network. Because of our many years of experience we know our way around the world of our customers and know what matters to them. Successful action requires not only capital, good employees, and innovative ideas and products, but also loyal customers. They are the most important asset for the long-term success of our company. We therefore direct our every action towards making our customers successful in their markets. The customer is and always will be the strictest measure of our efforts. ''Knowing it's DEUTZ''—our customers can rely on that, all over the world.*

received a German patent for his versatile, new four-stroke engine with compression, and the company started marketing the new engines under the brand ''Otto's neuer Motor'' (Otto's New Motor). The bright economic prospects of Otto's invention, however, attracted the attention of several potential competitors who began challenging Otto's patent. In the meantime, Otto worked on an ignition process that would allow his motor to run on liquid fuel. In 1884 he invented low voltage magnetic ignition.

During this time, Daimler left Deutz after several differences of opinion led to tensions between him, Otto, and Langen. For one thing, Daimler was more interested in building more powerful, fast running engines than in the small and cheap ones Langen requested him to produce.

After producing a total of 2,649, the company ceased production of the atmospheric gas power machines. In 1886 the German central court *Reichsgericht* rescinded part of Otto's patent. The inventor never really recovered from the bad news, feeling his reputation severely damaged. He died in 1891 at age 59 in Cologne. Four years later Deutz's co-founder Eugen Langen passed away.

Diversification in the Early 20th Century

During the 20 years following Otto's death, motor technology improved significantly. New combustion processes, electric ignition, and other improvements made gas and petroleum powered motors more efficiently and safely, expanded their performance and, in turn, increased their potential applications in industry, transportation, and agriculture. At the beginning of the 20th century Deutz had become a company with international connections. By 1886 the company was operating production plants in Vienna, Austria, Milan, and Italy, as well as in Philadelphia, and had business contacts in France and Russia. For the next few decades, Deutz focused on diversifying its product range and grew by means of a number of acquisitions. Deutz's Philadelphia plant, the Otto-Gas-Engine-Works AG started producing Otto-motor-powered locomotives as early as 1894. Two years later the first model for use in the mining industry was introduced.

Another German inventor, Rudolf Diesel, had as significant an impact on Deutz's development as Otto. Diesel had invented another type of motor and offered his patent to Deutz in 1892. Eugen Langen was concerned that the technology would not work and refused to manufacture the engines. Diesel found an interested partner in Heinrich Buz, Director of Maschinenfabrik Augsburg, where many changes were made from the initial concept. When the first functioning diesel engine was built in Augsburg in 1897 Deutz entered a licensing agreement with German manufacturer MAN AG to build the engine. Only two motors of the first series were finished and one of them, shipped to the United States, was the first diesel engine to be put into operation there. Deutz started experimenting with the second one and within a year developed its own model without the cross head that Diesel's design used.

In 1901 Deutz canceled the expensive licensing agreement with MAN after that company issued another license to the Petersburg-based firm Nobel and hopes for huge export business with Russia dimmed. After Diesel's patent expired in 1907, Deutz started the mass production of diesel engines and soon developed new models, such as a three-cylinder 75 PS motor for ships, and the 450 PS engine for the Berlin-Friedenau power station. In 1911 Deutz introduced the first diesel motor without a compressor which the company built in different variants with one to four cylinders and performance ranging from 16 to 500 PS.

After experiments to develop a locomotive that could be used in agriculture were not immediately successful, the company ventured into automobiles. In 1907 Deutz hired famous auto engineer Ettore Bugatti and made plans to build cars in Berlin. Several Deutz-Bugatti car models were developed and built in Cologne. However, the obstinate inventor was not willing to pay as close attention to the technical constraints of economical mass production as Deutz expected. In 1909 Bugatti left Deutz to set up his own business. The last Deutz-Bugatti cars were made in 1912.

New Leadership and the World War I Era

After Eugen Langen's death, Deutz was left without a strong leader for almost a decade. New energy came from Adolf and Arnold Langen, two of his eight sons, who entered the company at the beginning of the new century. Adolf Langen soon became technical director and focused on modernizing the company's product lines. Arnold Langen started working for the family business in 1903 and in 1919 became General Director. He successfully focused on modernizing the company's technical and organizational processes and in the years before 1914 led the company to new highs. Arnold Langen was also able to maintain the atmosphere of a family business at a time when many large companies were becoming impersonal conglomerates.

In 1906 Peter Klöckner was elected to the Deutz board of directors. Members of the Langen family had become acquainted with Klöckner through their joint work at the board of directors of the Schaaffhausenscher Bankverein in Cologne, the leading bank for industry in the Rhineland. The 43-year old member of a ship-building family in Koblenz had a reputation as an experienced troubleshooter and manager of big companies. Soon Klöckner became the driving force behind Deutz's

Key Dates:

1864: N.A. Otto & Cie. is founded in Cologne, Germany.
1869: The company is renamed Langen, Otto & Roosen.
1872: Company is transformed into a public share company and is renamed Gasmotoren-Fabrik Deutz AG.
1921: Cooperation with Motorenfabrik Oberursel starts and name is changed to Motorenfabrik Deutz AG.
1930: Company merges with Maschinenbauanstalt Humboldt AG and Motorenfabrik Oberursel to become Humboldt-Deutzmotoren AG.
1938: The company is integrated into Peter Klöckner's conglomerate and renamed Klöckner-Humboldt-Deutz AG (KHD).
1953: KHD becomes independent again.
1992: KHD AG is transformed into a management holding company.
1997: The company is renamed Deutz AG.

further development. A forward-looking man, Klöckner envisioned his own industrial empire; Deutz became part of his plan. When he entered the company in 1907 Klöckner acquired ten Deutz shares; by 1914, however, he owned 7.6 percent of the total share capital, while the Langen family owned about 13.8 percent and the Otto family 10.3 percent.

By Deutz's 50th anniversary in 1914, its motors for use in industry, agriculture, and in small ships had earned the company an international reputation. It employed a work force of more than 4,000. Diesel motors made up roughly one-third of the company's sales, and about half of the company's production was exported. Deutz's smaller diesel motors became especially popular and were also produced for the United States in Philadelphia. However, up until World War I, the company struggled with slow payments from its customers, and its total accounts receivable more often than not equaled its total sales.

The war hit the company unexpectedly in August 1914. Sales dropped by 40 percent in that business year. For several reasons Deutz did not initially receive many orders for the German war effort. Later the company started making shells and still later locomotives for the military. Finally, the company began producing Argus motors for airplanes but ceased production right after the war ended.

Becoming Part of the Klöckner Concern in 1938

In 1919 Klöckner became vice-president of Deutz board of directors. Two years later Deutz took advantage of an opportunity to work with Motorenfabrik Oberursel near Frankfurt/Main, one of the company's main competitors. Deutz took over the production of all motors that matched the company's existing product line while a new production line of middle-sized two-stroke diesel motors, especially for ships, was started in Oberursel. Since the company's product range by far exceeded gas motors, Gasmotoren-Fabrik Deutz was renamed Motorenfabrik Deutz in 1921.

The costs of further technological development and company expansion exceeded the means of the founding families.

Peter Klöckner financed a part of the expense with the necessary capital infusions. By May 1922 he owned almost 30 percent of Deutz, and after the tidal waves of hyperinflation had receded Klöckner had become the company's majority owner, and he took over as president of Deutz's board in 1924. The year before, Klöckner had reorganized all his firms under the umbrella of Klöckner-Werke AG, and this group included five ore mines, two big foundries, and three iron and steel production plants. In 1924 Deutz entered an agreement with Maschinenbauanstalt Humboldt AG, which had fallen into financial trouble. After several years in the red, Humboldt, with partner Deutz, turned a small profit once again in 1929. While orders for motors were on the rise at Deutz, Humboldt specialized again on its core business: machines and equipment for processing coal, ore, and minerals.

Finally, on October 21, 1930, the three companies—Deutz, Humboldt, and Oberursel—merged to form Humboldt-Deutzmotoren AG. Two years later, in the middle of a severe company crisis caused by the worldwide economic recession, the plant in Oberursel was shut down temporarily. However, as a result of Klöckner's initiative, Deutz managed to survive by accepting large orders from the Soviet-Russian government that kept the company going for two to three years. After the serious crisis of the early 1930s was overcome, Dr. Arnold Langen retired in 1936.

In the meantime Deutz started another venture into vehicles—this time into trucks. In July 1933 Deutz management decided to build a model series of 50 trucks. Negotiations to collaborate with other firms—such as Büssing, Adler, and Opel—failed, and a potential takeover of Hansa-Lloyd's truck division was deemed too financially risky. However, when Ulm-based truck and fire extinguisher maker C.D. Magirus was willing to cooperate in 1935, Klöckner did not hesitate to affiliate with the company, and Deutz took that company over the following year. Finally, in 1938 Klöckner integrated Humboldt-Deutzmotoren AG into his empire. In that year the company was renamed Klöckner-Humboldt-Deutz AG (KHD).

Dynamic Expansion Follows World War II

By 1938 Deutz had become Germany's largest diesel engine manufacturer. After the consolidation into KHD, Klöckner's group ranked among Germany's top corporations and employed 18,000 people. When World War II began in fall 1939, Deutz was not a first choice for the production of war materiel, as its motors were too small for military ships and tanks. Deutz did begin producing bigger motors for the German Marines and later an artillery tractor for the German Army. Demand for the fire extinguishers made in Ulm rose as German cities began suffering Allied air raids. Peter Klöckner did not live to witness the destruction of his plants; he died on October 5, 1940.

After World War II Peter Klöckner's son-in-law, Dr. Günter Henle, joined the Deutz top management. About three-quarters of Deutz production facilities were destroyed. The Oberursel plant, which survived the bombings, was dismantled and the production halls taken over by American troops. In mid-1945 Deutz was allowed to resume the production of motors and replacement parts for civil use, but only a few months later the permit was withdrawn. For the next few years the Occupation

Forces allowed Deutz to make scarcely any motors. The Humboldt plant in Kalk repaired railway bridges and produced machinery and replacement parts for mining equipment.

Things finally changed for the better with the currency reform in West Germany in 1948 after which the German economy gradually normalized again. Deutz went back to making the air-cooled diesel motors that the company first developed at the request of the German military. In contrast to the mostly water-cooled models on the market, the air cooled version was able to function securely under extreme conditions, such as very high and very low temperatures. Deutz had started mass production of air-cooled diesel motors in 1944 and resumed it in 1949. By 1954 the company had made some 100,000 of them in Cologne and Ulm. Due to unparalleled enthusiasm among all its employees to rebuild the company, Deutz exceeded its prewar results in 1951. That year the company had 15,700 people on its payroll and generated DM 292 million in sales.

The following three decades were characterized by continuous growth, mainly through acquisitions and international expansion. In 1953, as dictated by the plan of the Occupation Powers for the reorganization of the Klöckner companies, Klöckner Werke became Klöckner & Co., and the merger agreement with Deutz was annulled, making Klöckner-Humboldt-Deutz (KHD) independent once more. However, Klöckner & Co. continued to hold a major share in KHD.

Also that year a cooperation agreement was signed between KHD and Mainz-based Vereinigte Westdeutsche Waggonfabriken AG, a manufacturer of railroad cars. Six years later that company merged with KHD. Other acquisitions included that of combine harvester maker Maschinenfabrik Fahr AG in Gottmandingen in 1968; a majority share in Bochum-based industrial equipment manufacturer WEDAG Westfalia Dinnendahl Gröppel AG in 1969, which was taken over in 1973; and the takeover of large engine maker Veorde in Dinslaken in 1971. In 1975 KHD's Magirus truck manufacturing arm was merged into IVECO, a joint venture with Italian car maker Fiat, and sold off to Fiat five years later for about DM .5 billion. In 1985 Deutz acquired a majority share in Motoren-Werke Mannheim AG (MWM), a manufacturer of a full range of water-cooled motors.

Deutz's international activities included the establishment of subsidiaries in the United Kingdom, Australia, Morocco, the United States, and Argentina during the 1950s, in Japan in 1963, and in Singapore in 1970. Exports reached 40 percent of sales in 1964 and continued to grow during the following decades. In 1985 Deutz took over of the agriculture equipment arm of American competitor Allis-Chalmer Corporation and founded Deutz-Allis Corporation in Milwaukee, Wisconsin.

Struggling in the Mid-1980s and 1990s

In its 125th anniversary year, 1989, Deutz was represented in 135 countries around the world and had working agreements with 25 companies in 16 countries. The company was the world's top manufacturer of air-cooled diesel engines and was involved in various activities in addition to motors, including the development of tractors, aircraft technology, industrial equipment and plants for the chemical, raw materials, and food processing industries, and small power generators. However, the following decade turned out to be a turbulent chapter in the company's history.

The Deutz horizon began to darken in 1987 when the company slipped into the red for the first time. Stagnation in various segments of the world market that began in the mid-1980s were mirrored in the company's continuously shrinking sales and profits. The North American market for farm equipment which had been suffering a serious crisis dropped significantly again after a severe drought in 1987. The financially pressured governments in many countries shifted their orders away from new plants and equipment, opting instead to modernize the existing infrastructure. Demand for processing plants from OPEC countries also started drying up. At the same time, production, development, and organizational costs for Deutz's diverse portfolio had gone through the roof. After it reported a loss of DM 285 million in 1987, Deutsche Bank took over the share majority from the Henle family, Klöckner's heirs. The company entered a long period of restructuring in 1988, first under the leadership of Kajo Neukirchen, an experienced troubleshooter who later became CEO of Metallgesellschaft AG. During these years the number of Deutz employees melted from about 27,000 in 1986 to 13,000 in 1991.

The company was divided into strategic business divisions in 1989, and the production subsidiaries Deutz Argentina S.A. and Deutz-Allis in the United States, together with other subsidiaries, were sold off. By 1990 the company was out of the red. That year an organizational and production renewal program was developed and carried out over the following years. KHD AG became the management holding company for its nine legally independent business divisions. A brand-new state-of-the-art DM 600 million production plant opened in Cologne-Porz in 1993. However, sales started dropping again because of a recession in the machine building industry, and the capacity of the new facility turned out to be overly optimistic. In 1994 the agriculture business division which made tractors and farm machines, Deutz-Fahr, was sold to make up for new losses amounting to DM 300 million in that year.

In December 1995, as the financial picture for Deutz had begun to clear, a fire destroyed several buildings at Deutz Service International. Early the next year, it became evident that Deutz subsidiary KHD Wedag AG had produced huge losses in connection with three cement plants it had built in Saudi Arabia, and had manipulated financial reports to mask the disappointing results. Deutz was headed for bankruptcy were it not for a concerted effort and financial backing from the company's shareholders, especially Deutsche Bank AG, the state North-Rhine Westphalia, the city of Cologne, its employees (who agreed to cut their wages, salaries, and pensions), and from sales of company assets.

The company was renamed Deutz AG and restructured again to focus on its engine business. The group's subsidiaries were integrated into Deutz AG, and KHD was liquidated. The only exceptions were Motoren-Werke Mannheim AG which remained legally independent until 1998, and the two subsidiaries of the Industrial Plant division, KHD Humboldt Wedag AG and INDUMONT GmbH, which were slated for sell off. In 1998 the company's fate seemed to turn around again when

Swedish auto maker Volvo AB signed a contract with Deutz, making it Volvo's main supplier of diesel motors for construction equipment, trucks, buses, marine, and other applications. In turn, Volvo bought a ten percent interest in the company. Another contract was signed with Berlin-based Adtranz DaimlerChrysler Rail Systems GmbH in January 2001. To honor N.A. Otto, the man who had laid the foundations for Deutz, and his impact on the worldwide automobile industry, the inventor was inducted into the Automotive Hall of Fame in Detroit in October 1996.

Principal Subsidiaries

Deutz Corporation; KHD Humboldt Wedag AG; DEUTZ ENERGY GmbH; Humboldt Wedag Inc.; KHD Guss GmbH; DEUTZ MWM Fahrzeugmotoren GmbH; DEUTZ Canada Inc. (Canada); KHD Deutz of America Corporation; Ad. Strüver KG (94%); Humboldt Wedag ZAB GmbH); Motoren-Werke Mannheim AG (99.9%); Maschinenfabrik Fahr AG (99.8%); HUMBOLDT-LOTZ Elektrotechnik GmbH; HUMBOLDT-ZAB Zementanlagenbau GmbH; Erz- und Kohleflotation GmbH.

Principal Competitors

Cummins Engine Company, Inc.; Detroit Diesel Corporation; ThyssenKrupp AG.

Further Reading

''Das Unternehmergespräch,'' *Frankfurter Allgemeine Zeitung*, August 26, 1996, p. 14.

Garding, Christoph, et al, ''KLÖCKNER-HUMBOLDT-DEUTZ; Neues Milliardengrab am Rhein,'' *Focus*, June 3, 1996, p. 214.

Goldbeck, Gustav, *Kraft für die Welt*, Dusseldorf, Germany: Econ-Verlag GmbH, 1964, 293 p.

Hallensleben, Jutta, ''Konzentration aufs Wesentliche,'' *HORIZONT*, December 11, 1997, p. 26.

Hohmeyer, Ursula, ''Der Traum, die Nummer 1 zu werden.... Chronik des Niedergangs des Klöckner-Humboldt-Deutz-Konzerns (KHD),'' *Süddeutsche Zeitung*, May 29, 1996.

Osenga, Mike, ''A First Look at the Deutz-Volvo Deal,'' *Diesel Progress North American Edition*, September 1998, p. 36.

Peterek, Irmgard, ''Deutz schliesst Rahmenvertrag mit ADtranz ab,'' *vwd*, January 24, 2001.

''Sand im Getriebe,'' *Focus*, December 11, 2000, p. 284.

''Vom Glanz der Vergangenheit ist nichts geblieben,'' *Frankfurter Allgemeine Zeitung*, May 30, 1996, p. 18.

—Evelyn Hauser

easyJet Airline Company Limited

easyLand
London Luton Airport
Bedfordshire LU2 9LS
United Kingdom
Telephone: +44 8706 000 000
Fax: +44 1582 44 33 55
Web site: http://www.easyjet.com

Public Company
Incorporated: March 1995
Employees: 1,400
Sales: £263.69 million ($385.8 million) (2000)
Stock Exchanges: London
Ticker Symbol: EZJ
NAIC: 481111 Scheduled Passenger Air Transportation

EasyJet Airline Company Limited is a no-frills airline based in London. The carrier apes the Texas-based low-cost pioneer Southwest Airlines to the extent of placing that company's mission statements on its boardroom wall. Its fares are often one-third of those of state-sponsored airlines like British Airways. Direct selling is a key part of controlling costs; the corporate URL is painted on the sides of its jets in its unmistakable trademark orange.

Orange Origins

Stelios Haji-Ioannou, the son of a Greek Cypriot shipping tycoon, came to England in 1984. After studying at the London School of Economics, he earned a masters degree in business at City University. Stelios then went to work for his father, who, in 1992, loaned him $50 million to set up his own company to transport refined petroleum products. He was 25 years old at the time.

Stelios (who enjoined people to use his easier first name instead of his confusing last name) began thinking about aviation when Virgin Atlantic's Greek franchisee approached him to invest in a London-Athens route. Instead, Stelios decided to start his own airline. His father loaned him £5 million ($7.7 million) to fund the venture.

The search for successful business models led Stelios to the United States and Southwest Airlines and its principle of price elasticity. Southwest lowered fares to the extent that it attracted people who would not have otherwise traveled by air. It competed as much with buses as it did with other airlines.

At first, easyJet operated a paper airline. It contracted British World Airlines to fly and maintain its two leased Boeing 737s (the model of choice of Southwest Airlines), which it packed with 148 seats a plane. Other early providers of planes and pilots included Monarch Airlines and Air Foyle.

EasyJet's base in London was low-rent Luton Airport, formerly used only by charter operations. (A large part of easyJet's strategy was the use of secondary airports, but not as out-of-the-way as those served by the Irish discount carrier Ryanair.) EasyJet first linked London with Glasgow (beginning November 10, 1995) and Edinburgh (two weeks later) via two leased planes. Aberdeen was added in January 1996.

Soon after, easyJet ventured into Europe, competing against British Airways (BA) and KLM in Amsterdam. EasyJet focused on short-haul routes, where European fares, mile per mile, were often twice those of their American counterparts, with the aim of halving its competitors' fares. The ideal market for easyJet was one that could support eight to ten flights a day and was operated by two state-owned carriers.

Among easyJet's earliest routes were ones to Geneva and Zürich. Stelio capitalized on the Swiss connection by buying a 40 percent stake in TEA Switzerland, a failing charter airline that was renamed easyJet Switzerland.

Some have suggested the company spent all its revenues on advertising in the beginning. Billboards proclaimed the £29 ($43) London-Scotland fare "as cheap as a pair of jeans." It was one-tenth the price charged by British Airways. Television ads directed customers to call the company's reservations number (0990 29 29 29; it was also painted on all their planes) and book flights with their credit cards, bypassing travel agents. In fact, easyJet's own reservationists were paid by commission only (80p per seat). Direct selling was an important part of the equation; the Internet quickly became the company's preferred booking medium.

EasyJet was notoriously lean on service. There was no catering; the company even charged passengers for soft drinks and snacks. There were no cancellations or refunds; easyJet sold only the number of seats on the plane.

Simplification, frugality, and friendliness were three keys to easyJet's strategy. "Easy come, easy go" was its motto. The dress code reflected this casual (yet fast-paced) attitude. Cabin crews wore jeans and orange sweatshirts. Neckties were banned for all personnel except pilots, although the company did eventually upgrade its employee uniform somewhat.

Orange, easyJet's distinctive corporate color, covered everything, including the mass of hangar-like buildings (a gift from Luton Airport) known as "easyLand" that served as easyJet's headquarters.

Marketing described the corporate culture as "brutally transparent"; employees in all areas of the paperless offices shared all types of information (apart from payroll). The company scanned all its documents into a computer system accessible to all employees.

By introducing price competition to a market driven by freebies (such as frequent flier miles) and previously oriented towards business travelers, easyJet stimulated traffic in the markets it entered, much as Southwest Airlines had done in the United States. However, *The Economist* observed, easyJets carried their share of proverbially thrifty Scottish businessmen.

A More Mature Image in 1996

EasyJet grew up quickly. In March 1996, Stelios hired New Zealander Ray Webster as easyJet's new managing director. By this time, he told *Air Transport World,* the founder had determined that the market was responding and was committed to buying new aircraft and expanding the business.

Stelios had visited ValuJet (later known as AirTran) in Atlanta before setting up his own airline (note the similarity in company names); its example had prompted him to outsource most operational functions in the beginning. However easyJet did not use as many different vendors as the ill-fated American airline, which suffered a devastating crash in May 1996. EasyJet also was not growing at the same explosive rate.

To promote confidence in the passengers leery of cut-rate airlines, easyJet's advertising began featuring a more mature image in mid-1996. The ads explained why it was possible to reduce fares without compromising safety. Gone was the cartoon airplane, replaced by a butcher trimming fat, an analogy for "the virtually fat-free airline."

Within its first year, easyJet had added service to Barcelona, Nice, and Amsterdam. The expansion, however, was not completely smooth for the orange upstart. Stelios complained in the courts and in the media of a number of obstructions, beginning with KLM Royal Dutch Airlines trying to keep it out of Amsterdam's Schiphol Airport via alleged predatory pricing. An easyJet in-flight magazine (quoted in *Air Transport World*) reported the following line from an internal KLM memo: "We have to stop the development and growth of easyJet."

At the end of 1996, easyJet was operating four jets. By this time, British Airways (BA) CEO Bob Ayling was offering to buy the company. When that failed, BA began setting up its low-cost subsidiary that would be known as Go Fly Limited (Go).

With the liberalization of the European air transport market, several other new airlines had joined the fray, including Ryanair of Ireland and Britain's Debonair. EasyJet had been rumored to be discussing a merger with Brussels-based Virgin Express as BA, through Operation Blue Sky, was preparing to launch Go.

In 1997, easyJet turned a profit of £2 million on a turnover of £50 million. By the next year, the Haji-Ioannou family had invested a total of $90 million in the company, which had ordered a dozen new Boeing 737s worth £500 million.

Stelios and a few of his staff booked seats on the first Go flight. Although Go CEO Barbara Cassani sent Stelios a personal note welcoming him aboard, her gesture was overpowered by easyJet's ensuing publicity coup. Stelios and a few colleagues boarded the plane wearing orange boiler suits and completely hijacked the media attention. During the flight, they handed out 148 vouchers for free flights on easyJet to their fellow passengers. The easyJet web site later invited visitors to predict Go's annual losses (which amounted to £22 million in its first full year). Theatrics also turned up aboard easyJet planes, recorded by the British reality-based television program, *Airline.*

In the next couple of years, Stelios extended the easy brand into other family-owned companies separate from easyJet's corporate structure, including easyRentacar and easyEverything Internet cafés, which were popular in Britain due to the relative dearth of personal computers. Stelios had global aspirations for the cybercafés—one opened in New York City in November 2000.

A Public Offering in 2000

EasyJet posted a profit of $33 million for the 2000 fiscal year, ended in September. A quarter of company's stock was floated on the London Stock Exchange on November 15, 2000. Shares were offered exclusively to institutional investors in an offering that raised £190 million ($275 million); most of this was earmarked for 32 new Boeing 737s. In the first day of trading, the share price rose impressively.

<table>
<tr><td colspan="2">

Key Dates:

</td></tr>
<tr><td>**1995:**</td><td>easyJet is founded by Stelios Haji-Ioannou.</td></tr>
<tr><td>**1996:**</td><td>The company starts its first service to the Continent (London-Amsterdam).</td></tr>
<tr><td>**1997:**</td><td>British Airways launches its low-cost competitor, Go.</td></tr>
<tr><td>**2000:**</td><td>A quarter of easyJet's shares are floated on the London Stock Exchange.</td></tr>
</table>

BA began offering Go for sale in November 2000, which may have seemed an attractive investment for Stelios if only for its base at Stansted Airport. Luton, then in the hands of Barclays Bank, was at the time trying to triple its landing fees. After donning his infamous orange boiler suit and publicly cutting up his Barclays card, Stelios challenged the rate hike in court. (He had attempted to buy Luton himself in 1997, but the local council declared a conflict of interest.)

EasyJet began services to several destinations from a new Amsterdam hub in January 2001, creating its fourth hub after Luton, Liverpool, and Geneva. The company, which then operated a fleet of 19, had more than 30 brand new Boeing 737s scheduled for delivery through 2003.

Often compared to Richard Branson in his struggle with British Airways, Stelios fashioned himself a champion of the common man à la Sir Freddie Laker. "You must never underestimate the importance of being seen as the little guy against the big guy," he told *Airways* magazine, which noted the easyJet catchphrase, "the web's favorite airline," a play on BA's motto.

Principal Subsidiaries

easyJet Switzerland (40%).

Principal Competitors

Go Fly Ltd.; Ryanair Holdings plc; Virgin Express.

Further Reading

Bentley, Stephanie, "EasyJet Seeks to Merge with Virgin," *Marketing Week,* January 8, 1998, p. 7.

Bowes, Elena, and Laurel Wentz, "Like a Virgin," *Advertising Age,* November 27, 2000, pp. 1, 16.

Bowman, Louise, "What You See Is What You Get," *Airfinance Journal,* February 1998, pp. 44–47.

Crump, Eryl, "EasyJet Makes Success Look Easy," *Airways,* January/February 2000, pp. 35–42.

Curtis, James, "No-Frills Airline: No-Frills Culture," *Marketing,* July 9, 1998, pp. 24–25.

"EasyJet: Affordable as a Pair of Jeans," *Airways,* November/December 1996, pp. 25ff.

"EasyJet IPO Hits Highs as Rival Comes on to the Market," *Airfinance Journal,* December 2000, p. 12.

"EasyJet Out to Prove It Can Make Aggressive Growth Target," *Euroweek,* November 3, 2000, p. 17.

Feldman, Joan M., "Easy Does It on EasyJet," *Air Transport World,* January 1997, pp. 64–65.

Lee, Julian, "EasyRider," *Marketing,* August 7, 1997, p. 13.

Lennane, Alexandra, "Do Not Pass Go," *Airfinance Journal,* March 1998, p. 14.

Levy, Mike, "Making It All Look Easy," *Director,* August 1999, p. 80.

Michaels, Daniel, and Kay Larson, "Low-Cost EasyJet Hopes IPO Will Fly Smoothly Through Market Turbulence," *Wall Street Journal,* November 6, 2000.

Rigby, Rhymer, "Cheap and Cheerful," *Management Today,* August 1997, pp. 52–54.

Rogers, Danny, "EasyJet Plans Belfast Dogfight," *Marketing,* May 21, 1998, p. 1.

——, "No Anorak Required," *Marketing,* October 8, 1998, p. 22.

Rothnie, James, review of *Nuts! Southwest Airlines' Crazy Recipe for Business and Personal Success,* in *Marketing,* July 13, 2000, p. 22.

Senter, Al, "Let Battle Commence," *Director,* February 1998, pp. 34–39.

Shifrin, Carole A., "EasyJet Uses Southwest as Frills-Free Model," *Aviation Week & Space Technology,* April 21, 1997, p. 42.

"An Upstart Takes Wing," *Economist,* July 13, 1996, p. 69.

—Frederick C. Ingram

Ecology and Environment, Inc.

368 Pleasant View Drive
Lancaster, New York 14086-1397
U.S.A.
Telephone: (716) 684-8060
Fax: (716) 684-0844
Web site: http://www.ecolen.com

Public Company
Incorporated: 1970
Employees: 800
Sales: $69.9 million (2000)
Stock Exchanges: American
Ticker Symbol: EEI
NAIC: 541330 Engineering Services

One of the earliest companies dedicated to the problem of environmental conservation and enhancement, Ecology and Environment, Inc. (E & E) is based in Lancaster, New York, with regional offices throughout the United States and active subsidiaries in Costa Rica, Venezuela, Brazil, Chile, Germany, Russia, Kazakhstan, and China. The company also has representation in 20 other countries. Focusing on the engineering and scientific consulting side of the industry, rather than direct waste clean up or disposal, E & E is also involved in the entire range of macro-environmental problems, including acid rain, ozone depletion, global warming, biodiversity, and mass deforestation. E & E creates teams of specialists from more than 70 disciplines, depending on client requirements, to provide environmental impact assessments; industrial hygiene and occupational health studies; infrastructure planning; solid, hazardous, and mixed waste management, as well as analytical laboratory and field monitoring services. Since its creation in 1970, E & E has been highly dependent on federal contracts, awarded mostly by the U.S. Environmental Protection Agency (EPA) and Department of Defense (DoD). In recent years E & E has made an concerted effort to diversify its business.

1960s Pollution Laws Spark Creation of E & E

A case can be made that the rise of the modern environmental movement can be traced to Rachel Carson's 1962 book, *Silent Spring*, which brought to public attention the dangers of the indiscriminate use of synthetic chemicals, especially pesticides employed in agriculture. In fact, Carson infused the everyday word "environment" with new meaning when she wrote, "The most alarming of all man's assaults upon the environment is the contamination of air, earth, rivers and sea with dangerous chemicals, from the moment of conception until death." The public outcry to the charges in *Silent Spring* was so intense that even before the book was officially published, President Kennedy promised an investigation. Congress established 13 committees to address environmental problems. The first Clean Air Act was passed in 1963, the first Clean Water Act in 1965. The environmental movement gained even broader support in 1969 when an oil platform off the coast of Santa Barbara, California, blew out and spilled 235,000 gallons of black crude oil over 30 miles of beaches in an affluent community.

On April 22, 1970 the first Earth Day was celebrated by some 20 million Americans. Although greeted with skepticism from both the political left and right, Earth Day at the very least established a loose, nationwide coalition of committees that could provide organization to the environmental movement. The coordinating organization, Environmental Action, grew into a Washington, D.C., presence, with offices and a full-time staff of lobbyists. Perhaps the most important event of 1970, however, came in December, when President Nixon signed into law the creation of the Environmental Protection Agency, the first time that a single, independently budgeted entity would be responsible for monitoring and enforcing the nation's environmental protection laws.

One week before Earth Day 1970, four men trained in engineering, physics, and biophysics formed Ecology and Environment, Inc. to work in the environmental consulting business. Gerhard Neumaier, a mechanical engineer and physicist; Frank Silvestro, a biophysicist; Ronald Frank, a mechanical engineer and biophysicist; and Gerald Strobel, a licensed professional civil/sanitary engineer, had worked together on environmental issues at the Cornell Aeronautical Laboratory (later Calspan) in Buffalo, New York. When Congress in 1969 passed the National Environmental Policy Act (NEPA), they anticipated a demand for consulting firms that could provide specialists in a combination of fields, all related to environmental science and engineering, who would conduct the impact assessments that government would now require. Because the emphasis at Calspan was on defense work and automobile crash testing, the four men decided to form their own company to pioneer the new environmental industry. Initially they operated out of an office above a carpet store.

Most of E & E's early business was done locally in the Buffalo area and involved waste-water and water-pollution control. Soon after, the company became involved in the energy industry, opening an office in Houston, Texas, to work with natural gas exploration and pipeline transmission firms. It landed its first major contract in 1974 with the Department of Interior to act as its environmental monitors during the design and construction of the $8 billion, 800-mile Trans-Alaskan pipeline, the largest private construction project ever undertaken. In the same year, E & E became the environmental consultant for the consortium building the Northern Border Pipe Line that would deliver natural gas from Alberta, Canada, to the midwestern United States.

National concern about the environment continued to grow in the 1970s. A 1977 study estimated that 95 percent of the country's river basins were polluted. A little-known Niagara Falls, New York, neighborhood nicknamed Love Canal gained notoriety because of the unusually high rate of birth defects, miscarriages, cancer, epilepsy, and other diseases that plagued the community. A controversy turned into a scandal when it was learned that city officials had concealed the fact that the community had been built on land that had served as a chemical waste dump for the area's largest industry, Hooker Chemical Company. As a result, the environmental movement took on a new face, that of the "angry mom," a force that politicians ignored at their own peril. Only weeks before leaving office, President Carter in 1980 signed the Comprehensive Environmental Response, Compensation, and Liability Act, which would become commonly known as the "Superfund." The $1.6-billion appropriation, funded in part by taxes on petroleum and other chemicals, was intended for the cleanup of toxic-waste sites and oil spills.

In the late 1970s E & E received an EPA contract to establish Technical Assistance Teams (TATs) to support the agency's Oil and Hazardous Substances Spill Emergency Response program. The company was required to open offices in Washington, D.C., as well as the nine other cities where EPA had regional offices. E & E's multidisciplinary teams of engineers, scientists, and technical specialists responded to spill emergencies whenever there was federal intervention. E & E received another major EPA contract to provide Field Investigation Teams (FITs) to assist it with Superfund activities involving uncontrolled and abandoned hazardous waste sites,. Although the company profited from its EPA contracts, E & E found it increasingly difficult, despite its sound reputation, to generate business within the chemical industry because of its close ties to EPA's regulatory function. The result would be an over-dependence on federal contracts, making the company susceptible to government budgetary constraints. In 1982 the company was forced to lay off employees whom it would later rehire as these specialties again became needed.

As early as the mid-1970s, E & E made attempts to break into foreign markets. Although an effort in Japan failed, the company was able to land consulting assignments on industrial park development in Bolivia and water supplies in Caracas, Venezuela. In 1979 E & E became the environmental consultant to the Saudi Arabian Royal Commissioner for Jubail and Yanbu. It would open subsidiaries, as well as establish affiliations with foreign specialists, until E & E had a presence in almost 30 countries around the world.

Environmental Movement Hampered in the 1980s

The environmental movement and industry suffered a general setback during the early years of the Reagan administration, as EPA went a year without a new administrator. According to Hal K. Rothman in his book, *Saving the Planet:* "The Reagan administration also worked to curtail EPA's reach. . . . Enforcement standards were set so that the $1.6 billion Superfund would not be spent. This meant that the agency generally did not pursue law enforcement, instead resorting to sometimes fruitless negotiation with polluters. . . . Later, in 1986, Reagan signed Executive Order 12580, which gave the Department of Justice the right to disapprove any EPA enforcement action against a federal facility. The Justice Department held that the executive branch entities could not sue each other, effectively ending EPA's ability to enforce its mandate on federal lands."

An outraged Congress held hearings that revealed that the Pentagon itself recognized 4,611 contaminated sites at 761 military bases, many of which posed grave threats to local communities. In October 1986 Congress re-authorized the Superfund cleanup program, allocating $9 billion for the next five years. E & E received major contracts from the Department of Defense in connection with the clean up of hazardous wastes cause by munitions and fuels, as well as environmental impact studies on base closings that would result from the termination of the Cold War. Established players like E & E were now challenged by hundreds of start-ups companies, and soon investors recognized the potential for growth in the industry.

In June 1987 E & E filed an initial public offering of one million Class A common shares of stock with the Securities and Exchange Commission and began trading on the American Stock Exchange. With some of the $15 million raised in the offering, E & E purchased 85 acres of an abandoned golf course in Lancaster, New York, and built an environmentally friendly headquarters. More than 90 percent of the property would serve as a game preserve.

For the next few years E & E showed steady growth in revenues and profits. It signed another major four-year contract with the EPA in August 1990 that was worth $111.3 million. In July 1991 it signed a $15 million contract with the Army Corps of Engineers to assist in the clean up of civil works and military facilities in California, Arizona, Colorado, Nevada, and Wyoming. However, also in 1991, E & E suffered a setback when its FIT contract with the EPA expired.

In 1992 the price of E & E's stock tumbled, as the industry in general suffered from a sluggish economy. With the election of President Bill Clinton and Vice President Al Gore, who was well known for his support of environmental concerns, it was generally assumed that the environmental services industry would enjoy renewed growth. E & E in particular felt good about the news that Carol Browner would head the EPA. When she served as Florida's top environmental official, E & E was the state's largest contractor involved in waste problems caused by underground storage tanks. E & E anticipated that its work on military sites would also increase and was optimistic about the potential of its overseas' work, especially in China, where the company already had two projects.

E & E Endures a Downturn in the Mid-1990s

E & E's profits grew during the first two years of the Clinton Administration, but the 1994 Republican takeover of the Congress soon had a chilling effect on the environmental services industry. Congress proposed deep cuts in the budget of the EPA and its Superfund projects. Because of uncertainty about Congressional intent to reauthorize environmental legislation, there was concern that both federal and state agencies and private sector firms might postpone, or cancel altogether, the cleanup programs that would have normally gone forward. The military, because of interventions in Somalia, Kuwait, and Haiti, opted to shift money away from environmental projects. By August 1995, after three rounds of layoffs, E & E had trimmed its staff by 17 percent. The price of its stock was down 43 percent from a high in 1994. Its laboratory business found itself in an increasingly competitive market, as 1,400 firms began to go through a period of consolidation. Even when E & E received five contracts from the EPA, potentially worth more than $200 million, the company found itself a collateral victim of the prolonged budget fight between the president and Congress that precipitated the notorious ''government shutdown.'' Heavily reliant on federal contracts, E & E would continue to suffer even after the

impasse was resolved. It would report declining results in eleven out of twelve quarters, finally reaching bottom in 1997.

E & E began to seriously look at diversifying its business. As early as 1995 it investigated the possibility of getting involved in shrimp farming, hoping to use its expertise to increase yield and bring to market an environmentally friendly product that could command a premium price. Negotiations, unfortunately, failed on two separate deals. E & E also engaged in talks with a California real estate manager to create a venture that would clean up properties with minor environmental problems that depressed values, in order to resell at a profit.

As the economy picked up, E & E began to recover as well. Companies made plans to expand, requiring site preparation and clean-up work. With more cash on hand, businesses were also more willing to address environmental problems. Furthermore, E & E's efforts to diversify began to show progress. In January 1998 the company became involved in reviving the shellfish industry in the Narragansett Bay in Rhode Island that had both pollution and over-harvesting had damaged. Under the $400,000 contract, E & E would raise up to 50 million clams in a nursery, then transplant them in the bay. The company also formed a finance group to arrange financing for development projects such as the cogeneration plants it had developed in China.

The company finally purchased a shrimp farm in 1999, paying $1.89 million for a 90 percent stake in a Costa Rican operation. E & E also became involved in providing support for companies installing fiber optic systems that require environmental permits. In addition the company began to sell expertise to corporations and law firms engaged in risk-based decisions, as well as litigation that involved health-related and economic/property devaluation claims. It sought to diversify further via selective acquisitions of consulting firms. In 1999 E & E acquired a controlling interest in an environmental consulting company in Chile, as well as a Colorado firm, Walsh Environmental Scientists and Engineers.

E & E's traditional government work also picked up at the end of the 1990s. The company signed a three-year contract with the U.S. Army Corps of Engineers to work on hazardous waste and related clean-up projects; a new deal with the EPA to support cleanups of oil, petroleum, and hazardous waste in western Pennsylvania and West Virginia; and three new Superfund contracts. E & E won a contract with the Illinois Department of Transportation to do site assessment work. It entered into an agreement with Urbitran Corporation to work with the New York City Department of Sanitation in anticipation of the 2002 closing of existing landfills. E & E also received a contract from the U.S. Minerals Management Service to assess the environmental effects on the Gulf of Mexico from floating production, storage, and offloading vessels (FPSOs) that transfer oil to smaller shuttle tankers for delivery to port.

Internationally, investments in the environment looked especially promising in eastern Europe, where many countries were becoming concerned after decades of unchecked pollution. With a 30-year reputation as a leader in its field, and still operated by its four founders, E & E looked to position itself as a true global concern with a broad range of related businesses that would no longer be overly dependent on the patronage of one federal agency.

Principal Subsidiaries

Ecology and Environment Engineering, Inc.; E & E Drilling and Testing Co. Inc.; Ecology and Environment, Limited.

Principal Competitors

American Ecology Corporation; The IT Group Inc.; Waste Management, Inc.

Further Reading

Archer, Jules, *To Save the Earth,* New York: Penguin, 1998.

Dowie, Mark, *Losing Ground,* Cambridge, Mass.: MIT Press, 1995.

"E & E Celebrates Silver Anniversary," *The Bear Facts: The Newsletter for the Employees of Ecology and Environment, Inc.,* Summer 1995, pp. 1–3.

Robinson, David, "E & E Exploring New Ventures," *Buffalo News,* January 19, 1996, p. B6.

Rothman, Hal K., Saving the Planet, Chicago: Ivan R. Dee, 2000.

Rubin, Debra K., "Countries and Companies Make Cleanup a Priority," *Engineering News Record,* July 3, 2000, pp. 50–1.

—Ed Dinger

84 Lumber Company

Route 519
Eighty Four, Pennsylvania 15384
U.S.A.
Telephone: (724) 228-8820
Fax: (724) 228-4145
Web site: http://www.84lumber.com

Private Company
Incorporated: 1956
Employees: 4,500
Sales: $1,800 million (1999)
NAIC: 44411 Home Centers; 44419 Other Building
   Materials Dealers

84 Lumber Company is a family-run company that has grown from being a no-frills provider of lumber and building supplies that catered almost exclusively to the do-it-yourself market to becoming a preferred vendor of professional contractors. In recent years the company began to export its products, posting impressive sales figures in nine countries, including China, Japan, and Germany. Its new 84 Plus store format also has positioned 84 Lumber to compete in the home improvement category dominated by such major players as Home Depot. Even as it pursues an aggressive program to build new 84 Plus outlets, the company also is converting traditional stores to the concept.

Company Origins

The history of 84 Lumber is primarily the story of entrepreneur Joseph A. Hardy, Sr. After military service in World War II and earning a degree in industrial engineering at the University of Pittsburgh, Hardy went to work for the family jewelry company, Hardy & Hayes. Although proving to be a top salesman, at the age of 31 he left to start his own business, entering the building materials supply business at the suggestion of a friend. In 1952 he started Green Hills Lumber, which fared so well that by 1956 Hardy partnered with his two younger brothers and a friend to build a new "cash-and-carry" lumber yard at a location that would be convenient to home builders in the tri-state area of Pennsylvania, West Virginia, and

Ohio. The property on which Hardy settled was located near a small town 20 miles south of Pittsburgh called Eighty Four. The town (at least according to the most likely of many competing legends) was named in honor of Grover Cleveland's presidential election in 1884. In any case, Hardy liked the sound and decided to name his new lumber yard after the small town. The number 84 would provide the basis for the company's marketing and graphics for the next 50 years.

Hardy's business philosophy consisted primarily of "nothing fancy." He soon became renowned for his frugal approach to sales and management. As he built more stores, he continued to pay cash for land and facilities that, typically, had no heating or air conditioning systems since that would have increased overhead costs. Hardy's example sent a message to company employees, whom he preferred to call "associates" in order to foster a sense of family working toward a common goal. The plain, no-frills stores conveyed the company's commitment to keeping costs down for its target market of skilled do-it-yourselfers and small contractors. Hardy told *Do-It-Yourself Retailing* magazine, "We want the pickup truck crowd. We want the guy who backs his truck up, smashes the bumper into the loading dock and says, 'Let's get going'."

Hardy continued as owner and president of 84 Lumber for almost 30 years, working in the lumber yards, visiting each store, and talking with the associates. Although he strove to maintain his image as a small town, small business owner, his interests were diversifying during this time. He acquired real estate in several states and began collecting artwork, including paintings by Norman Rockwell, Pablo Picasso, and Andy Warhol. In 1983, Hardy spent $170,000 to purchase an English lord's title and an additional $58.1 million to acquire and renovate Nemacolin, a 550-acre retreat in southeastern Pennsylvania. Hardy's daughter Maggie took charge of the resort, which soon featured a spa, five restaurants, and a golf course.

Expanding and Diversifying in the 1980s

While Hardy focused on new interests and enterprises, the character of 84 Lumber changed as the stores began to stock nonlumber items in order to compete with such home improvement superstores as Home Depot, which were taking market share away from lumber yards. The company also ordered a 200-store expansion. Rapid expansion and diversification of products, however, resulted in a drop in earnings from $52 million in 1987 to less than half of that two years later. Hardy responded by slowing his expansion plans and even closing some stores. Furthermore, Hardy's oldest son, Joe Hardy, Jr., who had served as executive vice-president and had run the company for several years, was found to be in the early stages of multiple sclerosis. When his father decided that his son was not up to the task of running the company, Joe, Jr., left in anger to run his own real estate development company. A rapid succession of top executives at 84 Lumber ensued, and the company continued to lose its focus, targeting "yuppie" consumers rather than its traditional market of contractors and do-it-yourselfers.

In 1990, chief operating officer Jerry Smith joined 84 Lumber. In an effort to refocus the company, he drafted a mission statement clarifying the goals and values of the company and communicating its character to associates, vendors, and consumers. The mission statement said, in part, that "84 Lumber is dedicated to being the low-cost provider of lumber and building products to residential builders, residential remodelers, and dedicated do-it-yourselfers, while adding value to our products through trained, knowledgeable and motivated associates." The company further hoped to gain an edge through personalized service, inventory maintenance and competitive prices, and growth and strong leadership. Associates began carrying laminated business card sized copies of the mission statement in their pockets, and messages posted throughout company buildings and in an employee newsletter reminded associates of company goals and plans.

Modernizing in the 1990s and Continuing Success into the 21st Century

In 1991, Hardy reclaimed a more active role as head of the company and designated his daughter Maggie as his heir-apparent to the company presidency. He halted the expansion plans and recommitted the company's merchandising efforts to the lumber business. But the increasing number of home improvement superstores was still an impediment to 84 Lumber's growth. Hardy's response was to diversify into do-it-yourself home and kitchen design centers. In 1991, 84 Lumber opened 24 new kitchen design centers, which featured state-of-the-art computer technology for designing kitchens and baths.

In its approach to materials purchasing, 84 Lumber opted to switch to a centralized system for its hundreds of lumber yards during this time. The company had tried unsuccessfully to implement such a system in the mid-1970s, but had quickly

returned to regional and store purchasing. Regional buying had allowed more market awareness since inventory could be tailored to the specific store in response to customer demand and new markets. This splintered purchasing structure, however, also meant loss of bulk-buying power. Furthermore, the lack of coordination with company headquarters also meant dead inventory in stores and wide discrepancies in prices each region or store paid for its products. When company management decided to institute centralized purchasing, it also moved operations, accounts payable, and sales from the store and regional levels and centralized them at company headquarters. A team of "purchasing managers" was formed from former store managers familiar with operations at the store level. Purchasing managers developed expertise in specific product categories. Vendors had not been in the habit of making site visits to 84 Lumber stores, but with the new arrangement, they were encouraged to train 84 Lumber sales associates and aid them in merchandising. Stores adopted vendor suggestions for improving efficiency.

The company also invested in new computer technology to upgrade communications and information management, so that each night, daily sales data from each store could be sent to the company headquarters by telephone modem. This daily information became the basis for purchasing. The operations department could now keep in close communication with each store through biweekly bulletins and telephone calls twice a day. The company made communication with store managers a priority, making sure that they were kept up-to-date on any changes or additions to product lines. Despite the centralization of many functions, company executives maintained that store managers and associates still had significant input into product and promotion decisions.

The company continued to purchase wood in the United States and in Canada. About one-third of its stores were served by railroad, some with direct rail service right to the yard. Other 84 Lumber stores were supplied through reload centers, where freight from a rail car was loaded onto trucks or further rerouted by rail. This latter practice allowed the company to reduce inventory at a single 84 yard by splitting railcar loads among several yards rather than sending an entire carload to one yard. The reload centers also allowed the company to send both lumber and plywood to its lumber yards. A reload center in Aurora, Illinois served 84 Lumber yards as far east as Ohio and as far south as St. Louis, Missouri; Charleston, West Virginia; and Charlotte, North Carolina.

In 1992, 84 Lumber launched a new concept entitled 84 Affordable Homes Across America, a line of do-it-yourself homebuilding kits. Hardy was willing to double the company's long-term debt to $80 million to back the new enterprise, which consisted of 30 home models in a price range of $39,900 to $59,900 (not including the cost of the lot). Included in the price were all the supplies necessary for the structure itself as well as the costs of excavation, plumbing, wiring, and heating.

In 1991, Hardy turned over 40 percent of the 84 Lumber stock to Maggie. Within two years she would be named president. At 27 years old, she faced a tough challenge replacing her father. She had no college degree and her only management experience was at the Nemacolin Woodlands Golf, Spa, and Conference Center. Hardy maintained, however, that Maggie, the youngest of his five children, displayed more of an aptitude and interest in business than her older siblings. In fact, since the age of five she had spent time with her father on the job and over the years accompanied Hardy at new store openings and on-site inspections. She worked for a time in her early twenties at the Bridgeville, Pennsylvania store to become familiar with every-day operations at 84 Lumber.

Maggie was not afraid to wield her power. She terminated a number of managers that her father had brought in to run the company; she was unhappy with their buttoned-down look and attitude, which conflicted with the traditional 84 Lumber shirts everyone else wore at headquarters. The following year, the 84 Lumber Company pursued an extensive training and develop-ment program, requiring every associate to attend the ''84 Uni-versity'' program to learn about new products and sharpen their sales skills. In 1992, 84 Lumber opened a new management training center and dormitory in Eighty Four, Pennsylvania, and throughout the year store managers and other employees from all over the country attended three-day training sessions.

Under Maggie, 84 Lumber reached the $1 billion plateau in annual sales. Much of the success was due to a renewed com-mitment to contractor sales, which at 25 percent of the com-pany's business would climb over the ensuing five years to account for 75 percent. The purchasing executives also antici-pated a shortage of materials in 1993 and took steps to make sure that 84 Lumber had inventory. Many of its competitors were left short. Building on this success, Maggie would lead 84 Lumber to record-breaking sales for the next six years, topping $1.8 billion in 1999.

In 1998, 84 Lumber established an International Sales Divi-sion to export building materials, including complete home packages. Shipping primarily from the Port of Baltimore, the company supplied nine countries located in Europe, Asia, and South America. In the first year, the company totaled $300,000 in sales. The following year saw even better results, as interna-tional sales reached $2.7 million, or a 900 percent increase over the previous year.

In 1999 the company also took major steps to increase its domestic business. 84 Lumber introduced a new design center called Maggie's Building Suggestions Showroom, a 17,000-square-foot facility located in Pittsburgh. The interactive center, geared toward homeowners, builders, designers, and architects, featured a showroom with hundreds of home products and decor, as well architectural consulting services, multimedia conference rooms, and staff designers. In 1999, 84 Lumber opened two Installed Sales Centers and announced plans to open several more. The centers would then support outlets on a regional basis. Builders would be able to leave blueprints, materials list, sketches, or just ideas at a local 84 Lumber Store, which would then forward the information to the Installed Sales Center, which would estimate the materials and cost. Within 48 hours a delivery could be made to a contractor's site. The company also instituted a 30-day price guarantee that allowed builders to lock in a price and take delivery as needed without incurring any extra charges.

Perhaps the biggest change, one that would have the most impact on 84 Lumber in the future, was the introduction of its new ''84 Plus'' store—a radical departure from the company's traditional warehouse approach. Aimed at the contemporary do-it-yourselfer, the suburban SUV rather than the rural pick-up truck customer, the 20,000-square-foot, consumer-friendly units devoted half of their space to a hardware store that offered an expanded line of supplies and a showroom that showcased kitchen, bath, door, and window displays. In December 1999 the company announced that it planned to open 50 84 Lumber Plus stores each year for the next three years, as well as begin converting old units to the new format. If the building program is a success, 84 Lumber will boast 500 stores and be well positioned to continue its pattern of increasing sales.

Principal Competitors

Carolina Holdings; Home Depot, Inc.; Payless Cashways; Sutherland Lumber.

Further Reading

Aeppel, Timothy, ''The Favorite,'' *Wall Street Journal,* April 24, 1997, p. A1.
''Business Brisk at 84 Lumber Co.'s New Convenience Store Proto-type,'' *Do-It-Yourself Retailing,* April 1999, p. 23.
Johnson, Walter E., ''Life at 84 Lumber,'' *Do-It-Yourself Retailing,* February 1992.
Mallory, Maria, ''The Lord of 84 Lumber Co. Is Back Behind the Counter,'' *Business Week,* June 22, 1992, pp. 80–81.
Stern, Gabriella, ''More Daughters Take the Reins at Family Busi-nesses,'' *Wall Street Journal,* June 12, 1991, p. B2.
''Two Views of Decentralized Purchasing,'' *Building Supply Home Centers,* November 1989, pp. 52–56.

—Wendy J. Stein
—update: Ed Dinger

The Emirates Group

Airline Centre
P.O. Box 686
Dubai
United Arab Emirates
Telephone: 971-4-2144444
Web site: http://www.emirates.com

State-Owned Company
Incorporated: 1985
Employees: 6,500
Sales: AED 5.59 billion ($1.52 billion) (2000)
NAIC: 481111 Scheduled Passenger Air Transportation;
481112 Scheduled Freight Air Transportation; 488119
Other Airport Operations; 488999 All Other Support
Activities for Transportation; 56152 Tour Operators

The Emirates Group is composed of airport services provider DNATA (the Dubai National Air Transport Association) and Emirates Airlines. Owned by the government of Dubai and based at the busiest airport in the Middle East, Emirates has flourished under the sheikdom's "wide open skies" policy, in spite of the restrictions placed on it by other countries. The airline, renowned for its luxurious in-flight service, was unique among long-haul airlines in that it had not joined a global alliance such as the Star Alliance or oneworld by the beginning of the new millennium.

Origins

Dubai, a fishing village at the southern end of the Arabian Gulf, has grown to become one of the leading trade centers of the Middle East, fueled at first by pearls, then petroleum. The Beni Yas tribe assumed control of the town around 1830. The Maktoum family led the tribe throughout the 19th and 20th centuries. Dubai became one of seven sheikdoms in the United Arab Emirates, which was formed in 1970.

As the British pulled out of Dubai in the late 1950s, Sheikh Saeed Al Maktoum decreed an open seas, open skies, and open trade policy, to develop the country into a regional crossroads for trade and tourism. He also required all government agencies to make a profit. The country was aiming to eliminate its dependence on its finite oil reserves within 50 years.

The Dubai National Air Transport Association (DNATA) was formed in 1959. By the mid-1980s, DNATA had grown to 2,500 employees. In addition to providing support services at Dubai Airport, the company served as sales agent for 26 airlines. Dubai had been used as a stopover on routes between Europe and the Far East since the days of Imperial Airways (precursor to British Airways), which landed its flying boats there en route to Australia. Its open skies policies kept its airport among the busiest in the region.

Gulf Air began to cut back its service to Dubai in the mid-1980s. As a result, Emirates Airlines was conceived in March 1985 with backing from Dubai's royal family, whose Dubai Air Wing provided two of the airline's first aircraft, used Boeing 727s. (An Airbus A300 and Boeing 737 were two others.) Because of Dubai's unique political structure, wrote Douglas Nelms in *Air Transport World,* Emirates could be described as both government-owned and privately held, though most considered it state-owned. It was required to operate independent of government subsidies, however, apart from $10 million in start-up capital.

Maurice Flanagan was named managing director of the new airline. Formerly of the Royal Air Force, British Airways, and Gulf Air, Flanagan had been seconded to DNATA in 1978 on a two-year assignment as assistant general sales manager.

Chairman was Sheikh Ahmed bin Saeed Al Maktoum, nephew of the ruler of Dubai. Only 27 years old in 1985, he had graduated from the University of Colorado just four years earlier (his degree was in political science and economics). Sheik Ahmed also became chairman of Dubai Civil Aviation and DNATA itself. Although he lacked any direct experience in the airline industry, Sheikh Ahmed embraced his new role, learning to fly a variety of aircraft along the way. As Lisa Coleman duly noted in *Chief Executive,* he was indeed experienced in one area that would be the new airline's defining trait: luxury. From the beginning, Emirates boasted a tradition of providing the best creature comforts available at 40,000 feet.

The first flight, Dubai-Karachi on October 25, 1985, was a Pakistani connection in more ways than one. The airline leased the aircraft, an Airbus 300, from Pakistan International Airlines. Bombay and Delhi were the other two earliest destinations. From the beginning, Emirates flights carried both passengers and cargo.

Emirates was profitable within nine months. During its first year, it carried 260,000 passengers and 10,000 tons of freight. Gulf Air, part owned by the much more wealthy neighboring emirate Abu Dhabi, had previously dominated air traffic in the region. Its profits fell more than 30 percent during the first year of its new rival's operations, however, prompting Gulf Air to drop its privatization plans. The next year, Gulf Air posted a loss.

In its second year, Emirates also posted a loss, before setting out on decades of profitable growth. One reason for the success of Emirates was its aggressive marketing. Another was the high level of in-flight service in its new Airbus aircraft, which it outfitted with generously spaced seating.

In 1986, Colombo, Dhaka, Amman, and Cairo were added to the route network. Emirates launched daily nonstop service to London (Gatwick) on July 6, 1987 with two new Airbus A310s. This complemented the overnight flights British Caledonian was sending to and from Dubai. Other destinations added in 1987 were Frankfurt via Istanbul, and Male (Maldive Islands). Emirates lacked a regional feeder network since most of its neighboring countries were shareholders in rival Gulf Air.

This impressive early growth came as the region was experiencing a business downturn, with the Gulf War a contributing factor, and the subsequent laying off of expatriate workers—both bad news for the air travel industry. In its second year, competitors accused Emirates of starting a price war. The airline countered that its lower fares were stimulating traffic, not stealing it from its rivals. By the end of 1987, Emirates was serving 11 destinations.

"The Finest in the Sky" in the 1990s

Emirates Sky Cargo, which operated as a separate entity, carried 25,000 tons of freight in fiscal 1989. In the early 1990s, a number of Asian firms began using Dubai as a warehousing center for European deliveries. Emirates expanded its route network into the Far East in 1990, serving Bangkok, Manila, and Singapore. Hong Kong was added in 1991. Emirates added Paris, Rome, Zurich, and Jakarta in the summer of 1992.

About the same time as it was extending its reach into Asia, Emirates was courting long-haul business travelers. Calling itself "the finest in the sky," the airline toned down its Arabic identity for a more "corporate" feel, positioning itself as a competitor to global carriers such as British Airways and Singapore Airlines.

Emirates was one of the world's fastest growing airlines. Revenues increased by about $100 million a year, approaching $500 million in fiscal 1993. It carried 68,000 tons of cargo and 1.6 million passengers that year. The Gulf War, ironically, had benefited Emirates by keeping other airlines out of the area. Emirates was the only airline to continue flying in the last ten days of the war, although it had to cover increased insurance premiums and higher fuel costs (flying around the war zone added an extra ten hours to flights).

A partnership agreement with US Airlines entered in the fall of 1993 allowed Emirates to offer around-the-world service. It had previously inked cooperation agreements with Cyprus Airways.

By 1994, 60 international airlines were flying to Dubai. Emirates was connecting 32 destinations with its 15 aircraft. It was the sixth largest of eight Middle East carriers. Despite its small size, the airline had accumulated numerous awards by lavishing attention and money on passenger and cargo service. It was the first airline to install personal video systems in all seats, for example. Flight attendants celebrated special occasions with in-flight cakes and Polaroid cameras. Passengers flying first class were served six-course meals on Royal Doulton china.

Emirates took in $643.4 million in the fiscal year ending March 30, 1994. Income increased more than eightfold, to $24.4 million. The young airline had 4,000 employees and carried two million passengers a year between 34 destinations with a fleet of 18 Airbus aircraft.

Seven state-of-the-art Boeing 777s worth $1 billion were on order since 1992 to satisfy long-range ambitions. They began to arrive in the spring of 1996. One of the planes was used on a new service to Australia (Melbourne) via Singapore. Emirates placed a large order with Airbus later in the year. In spite of the large capital expenditures, the Dubai government had laid out only $50 million since the airline's inception.

A total of 92 air carriers were serving Dubai in the mid-1990s. Emirates was able to flourish, however, in spite of restricted markets abroad and intense competition at home. The Dubai government had been promoting the country as an escape from European winters with great success, much to the benefit of Emirates. (Dubai's summertime weather was grueling, with Fahrenheit temperatures and relative humidity readings in the 100s.) Abroad, its route network was expanding in the Pacific and Africa.

In 1997, Emirates was flying a dedicated freighter to Amsterdam, a point not on its network of passenger routes, in cooperation with KLM Royal Dutch Airlines. It carried about three million passengers during the year. The growing cargo business accounted for 16 percent of the airline's revenues.

Emirates opened a unique, $65 million training center in January 1997. It was built in the shape of an airplane. The airline was then able to provide advanced simulator training for its crew members—who represented 50 different nationalities—and flight and maintenance personnel from around the world. In the

Further Reading

"Air Lanka Finds a Friend in Emirates," *Airfinance Journal,* May 1998, p. 12.

"Airline Competition in the Gulf: The Strength of Emirates," *MidEast Markets,* September 28, 1987.

Allen, Robin, "Dubai: Paradox Wrapped in a Conundrum," *Financial Times,* December 13, 2000, p. 2.

"Cargo Key for Emirates," *Aviation Week & Space Technology,* May 19, 1997, p. 48.

Coleman, Lisa, "Ahmed bin Saeed Al Maktoum," *Chief Executive,* March 1995, p. 29.

"Dermot Mannion," *Airfinance Journal,* December 1999, p. 44.

"Desert Storms," *Airfinance Journal,* September 1996, pp. 38–41.

Done, Kevin, "Airbus Wins First Order for A3XX Super Jumbo," *Financial Times,* May 1, 2000, p. 1.

"Dubai: The Gulf's Gateway to the World," *Asian Business,* July 1991, p. 59.

"Emirates Plays the Finance Game," *Airfinance Journal,* September 1996, pp. 40–41.

"Emirates Tries 'Humorous' Ad Campaign," *Marketing Week,* January 21, 1999, p. 8.

Flottau, Jens, "Emirates Updates Its Fleet Planning," *Aviation Week & Space Technology,* November 20, 2000, p. 47.

Fox, Harriot Lane, "Emirates Tries Corporate Ploy," *Marketing,* November 25, 1993, p. 15.

Gostelow, Mary, "Can Emirates Fill the Gulf?," *Director,* July 1987, pp. 69–72.

Kingsley-Jones, Max, and Andrew Doyle, "Emirates Is Looking at Airbus Replacements," *Flight International,* July 3, 1996.

Lennane, Alexandra, "Opportunity Knocks," *Airfinance Journal,* May 1999, pp. 39–41.

Michaud, Paul, "Letter from Dubai," *Marketing,* February 10, 1994, p. 7.

Nelms, Douglas W., "Emirates' Open-Trade Routes," *Air Transport World,* February 1998, pp. 83–87.

——, "Genii from the Desert," *Air Transport World,* March 1994, p. 95.

O'Toole, Kevin, "Emirates' Pilot," *Flight International,* March 26, 1997.

Phelan, Paul, "Growing Ambitions," *Flight International,* December 11, 1996.

"Profit for Dubai-Based Airline," *MidEast Markets,* October 27, 1986.

Shane, Bob, "Emirates: An Oasis of Hospitality and Excellence," *Airliners,* January/February 2001, pp. 43–47.

Shifrin, Carole A., "Dubai Training Center Extends Emirates' Reach," *Aviation Week & Space Technology,* May 19, 1997, p. 44.

——, "Emirates Slows Rate of Expansion," *Aviation Week & Space Technology,* May 19, 1997, p. 42.

——, "State-of-Art Maintenance Center Readied for Emirates Group," *Aviation Week & Space Technology,* May 19, 1997, p. 46.

—Frederick C. Ingram

Key Dates:
1959: Dubai National Air Transport Association (DNATA) is formed.
1985: Dubai forms its own airline: Emirates.
1993: Emirates forms partnership with United Airlines.
1997: New training and maintenance centers open.
1998: Emirates buys a 40 percent stake in Air Lanka.

fall of 1997, a new air-conditioned maintenance center allowed the group (which consisted of Emirates Airlines and DNATA) to solicit third-party contracts in that capacity as well.

A record group profit of AED 371 million was achieved in 1997–98. Emirates executives planned a slowdown in the airline's growth in the late 1990s to stabilize its expansive route network.

In May 1998, Emirates paid the Sri Lankan government $70 million for a 40 percent stake in Air Lanka. Emirates received almost full management rights as the Sri Lankan flag carrier was in debt and operating at a loss and had needed new capital to upgrade its fleet.

A new, lighthearted advertising campaign launched in January 1999 enjoined travelers to "Be good to yourself. Fly Emirates." One ad aired in Britain featured a business class passenger calling his dog with the on-board phone.

Emirates signed on in May 2000 as the first launch customer for the Airbus A3XX, designed to be the largest civil aircraft ever built. Emirates justified purchasing the 481- to 656-passenger super jumbo to maximize its use of scarce takeoff and landing slots at crowded airports like London's Heathrow. The airline planned to order up to a dozen of the planes, with the first to be delivered in 2006.

Toward the end of 2000, Emirates was planning to start ultra-long-haul service to the East Coast and West Coast of the United States as well as nonstop flights to Australia and Argentina. Traffic continued to grow at an impressive clip (20 percent) in 1999–2000, and Emirates executives planned to sustain that.

Principal Divisions

Emirates; Dubai National Air Transport Association (DNATA).

Principal Competitors

Gulf Air; British Airways plc.

Encyclopaedia Britannica, Inc.

310 South Michigan Avenue
Chicago, Illinois 60604-4202
U.S.A.
Telephone: (312) 347-7000
Toll Free: (800) 747-8513
Fax: (312) 347-7399
Web site: http://corporate.britannica.com

Private Company
Incorporated: 1943
Employees: 390
Sales: $168 million (1999 est.)
NAIC: 51113 Book Publishers; 51121 Software
　Publishers

Encyclopaedia Britannica, Inc., has published one of the world's finest encyclopedias for more than two centuries. The *Britannica* is respected throughout the world for its combination of breadth and thoroughness in its treatment of everything from the Punic Wars to quantum mechanics, and many of its articles, written by outstanding scholars in their respective fields, are masterpieces of compact erudition unlike anything else in the field of learning. Encyclopaedia Britannica, Inc., markets the *Britannica* in more than 100 countries around the world and is also the parent company of Merriam-Webster, Inc., publishers of the famed dictionaries. The popularity of personal computers and the Internet have had a profound impact on the company, which now relies largely on sales of CD-ROM versions of the *Encyclopaedia* and the subscriptions of online educational users to stay afloat. Since its purchase in 1996 by financier Jacob Safra, the company has dropped its home sales program and has put the encyclopedia online for free via the advertising-supported Britannica.com, a sister company.

18th Century Origins in Scotland

The *Encyclopaedia Britannica* was first published between 1768 and 1771 "by a society of gentlemen in Scotland, printed in Edinburgh for A. Bell and C. Macfarquhar, and sold by Colin Macfarquhar at his printing office in Nicolson-street," as the First Edition's title page informed its readers. The idea of uniting in a single publication all aspects of human knowledge went back at least to Roman times, but it was in the 18th-century, the Age of Enlightenment, that encyclopedias in the modern form began to appear in Europe. The French *Encyclopedie,* first published in 1751, became the symbol of French radical humanism and generated international controversy for its allegedly blasphemous philosophy, but there is no evidence that the creators of the *Encyclopaedia Britannica* were directly inspired by the fame of the *Encyclopedie* (which in fact was begun as a translation of an earlier work by the Englishman Ephraim Chambers).

Andrew Bell, a prosperous engraver of Edinburgh, and printer Colin Macfarquhar were convinced that the English-speaking world could use a reference work featuring substantial treatises on the arts, sciences, and trades combined alphabetically with shorter entries defining important terms and concepts. The two men engaged William Smellie, a 28-year-old scholar at the University of Edinburgh, as general editor of the First Edition of their proposed *Encyclopaedia Britannica,* which was published and sold in 100 parts between 1768 and 1771. The *Encyclopaedia* contained 2,659 pages, including articles borrowed from such luminaries as Benjamin Franklin (on electricity) and John Locke (on human understanding). The editors themselves wrote many of the shorter articles, while the longest pieces ("Surgery" and "Anatomy") were treatises of well over 100 pages each. The new encyclopedia sold well, and its editors began immediate preparations for a second, much larger edition.

James Tytler succeeded Smellie as editor of the Second Edition, which was published between 1777 and 1784 in ten volumes totaling 8,595 pages and 340 copperplates engraved by Bell. The Second Edition was among the first encyclopedias to include articles on history and biography, two subjects which have since become standard. It was followed by a Third Edition of 18 volumes completed in 1797, edited by Macfarquhar and George Glieg, later a bishop and Primus of the Scottish Episcopal Church. (Macfarquhar died in 1793 at the age of 48, "worn out," as later publisher Archibald Constable put it, "by fatigue and anxiety of mind.") By this time the *Britannica* was well known and widely sought after; the Third Edition sold between

10,000 and 13,000 copies and is said to have returned the substantial profit of £42,000 to Andrew Bell, its sole proprietor after the death of Macfarquhar.

Bell remained the owner and manager of the Britannica until his own death in 1809, after which his heirs sold the company's stock and copyrights for £13,500 to Archibald Constable, an Edinburgh publisher. Constable was an able promoter and manager, and under his direction the Britannica made important advances in the quality of its writing and increased sales both in Great Britain and the United States. Constable's Fifth Edition of 1817 was criticized as little more than a reprint of Bell's Fourth, but soon afterward a six-volume Supplement appeared which cemented the reputation of the *Britannica* as the premier encyclopedia of the English-speaking world. Constable was the first *Britannica* publisher to solicit new articles from the leading scholars and artists of his day, and among the contributors to the Supplement and the Sixth Edition, both completed in 1824, were such distinguished men of letters as William Hazlitt, Walter Scott, David Ricardo, and Thomas Malthus. Constable died in 1827, before he could make a start on the planned Seventh Edition.

The 1800s: The A & C Black Era

Copyrights to the essays were bought at auction by Adam Black, an Edinburgh bookseller, who collaborated with his relative Charles Black and their sons to publish the Britannica for the next 70 years as A & C Black Ltd. The Seventh Edition, edited by Macvey Napier, appeared between 1830 and 1842 and included a set of introductory essays intended to describe the progress of human knowledge since medieval times in four fundamental classifications: metaphysical, moral, and political philosophy; mathematics and physics; chemistry; and zoology, botany, and mineralogy. Similar attempts to organize all knowledge under a handful of rubrics had been common among encyclopedists, but the increasing scope and complexity of science in the 19th century discouraged the *Britannica* from making any further efforts in this direction. Indeed, so rapid was the progress of scientific and historical knowledge in the age of Charles Darwin and Karl Marx that by the 1860s the children of Adam Black were eager to publish a totally new *Britannica* in tune with the startling changes of their age.

The resulting Ninth Edition (completed in 1889) has since been acknowledged as one of the most impressive collections of scholarship ever produced, its articles written by outstanding experts in every domain of the arts and sciences. Thomas Henry Huxley, the distinguished biologist, served as general advisor for the scientific articles; typical of the contributors' excellence was the example of Prince Pyotr Kropotkin, the famed Russian

political theorist, who wrote his essay on "Anarchism" from his prison cell in Clairvaux, France.

The Ninth Edition sold about 10,000 sets in Great Britain between 1875 and 1898, but it found a far larger market in the United States, where its authorized publisher, Charles Scribner's Sons, sold no fewer than 45,000 sets during the same period. Unfortunately, international copyright laws had not been agreed upon between the two countries, and several hundred thousand other, pirated *Britannicas* were sold in the United States, many of them incomplete or mutilated. Such marketing problems discouraged the Black family, which in 1897 agreed to turn over promotion of the *Britannica* to an American company led by Horace E. Hooper and Walter M. Jackson. The two men negotiated an agreement with the *Times* of London whereby that paper—the most respected in England, but also in financial trouble—would advertise, sell, and receive commissions for the latest reprint of the Ninth Edition. Although the scheme appeared improbable to many Englishmen, it succeeded in keeping the *Britannica* alive until Hooper and Jackson could purchase all copyrights and plates of the encyclopedia in 1901, thus bringing the symbol of England's cultural dominance into U.S. hands at about the same time as the Empire lost its economic and political leadership to the United States.

Hooper and Jackson formed companies in both the United States and England to market their unique product. Both men were experienced publishers and booksellers, and in their efforts to find outlets for the Britannica they were aided in no small measure by the genius of Henry Haxton, a freewheeling advertising executive who devised all manner of ad campaigns, games, and contests to generate popular interest in the formerly staid Britannica. After the publication in 1902 of a revised and supplemented version of the Ninth Edition marketed as the Tenth, Horace Hooper began work in earnest on a completely new Eleventh Edition. His enthusiasm was not matched by Walter Jackson, and the two men gradually dissolved their partnership, but the Eleventh Edition sailed on under the editorial guidance of Hugh Chisholm in London and Franklin Hooper (the brother of Horace) in the United States. To reassure London bankers of the new edition's salability, Horace Hooper negotiated an arrangement with Cambridge University by which the latter would lend its prestigious name to the encyclopedia in exchange for a degree of editorial control and royalties on sales. Suitably impressed, London financiers provided the capital needed to support publication of the 29 volume Eleventh Edition in 1910 and 1911. Among its contributors were Matthew Arnold, R.L. Stevenson, and Alfred North Whitehead, and, like the Ninth Edition, the Eleventh would be long remembered as a treasure of world scholarship. The edition was the first to be dedicated to the U.S. president as well as the British monarch, and the first to be printed by the large U.S. printing firm of R.R. Donnelley and Sons. Despite its wealth of distinguished contributors and the imprimatur of Cambridge University, sales of the Eleventh were slowed by World War I, and the Britannica found itself once again in severe financial difficulty.

Changing American Owners in the Early 1900s

U.S. marketing provided the solution again, this time via the retailing giant Sears, Roebuck & Co. Horace Hooper had long been the friend and golfing partner of Julius Rosenwald, the president of Sears and a well known philanthropist in his own right. Rosenwald took an interest in the fortunes of the *Britannica,* and in 1915 Sears agreed to market a new, less expensive version of the Eleventh Edition designed to appeal to the middle-class buyer throughout the English-speaking world. Sales remained weak, however, and in 1920 Sears bought Encyclopaedia Britannica Company outright, retaining Horace Hooper as publisher and his brother Franklin as editor in New York, with Hugh Chisholm remaining London editor. Sears's purchase of the *Britannica* was a philanthropic gesture rather than a business decision, as it was clear by this time in its history that the encyclopedia would be chronically short of cash. Indeed, after three years of operation Sears reported a loss of $1.8 million at the Britannica and in 1923 sold the company back to the widow of Horace Hooper (who had died in 1922) and her brother, William J. Cox.

The Twelfth and Thirteenth editions were published in 1922 and 1926, but these were merely reprints of the Eleventh edition along with supplementary material. Since the publication of the Eleventh edition in 1910, the shape of western civilization had been profoundly altered by World War I, and in the late 1920s William Cox began the laborious process of raising the $2.5 million needed for a completely rewritten Fourteenth Edition. Rosenwald and Sears offered to contribute a million dollars if

the University of Chicago could be persuaded to take over the role of general editor formerly filled by Cambridge. Chicago—and later Harvard—refused, however, and Sears was saddled with nearly all of the new Edition's cost, resuming ownership in 1928 just prior to publication. Sales were good until the Great Depression paralyzed economies around the world; it became obvious that the *Britannica* would require radically new marketing techniques if it were not to prove a permanent liability for Sears. After the death of Julius Rosenwald in 1932, the company replaced William Cox as president with Elkan H. ''Buck'' Powell, a Sears secretary and treasurer.

Powell completely restructured Britannica. On the sales side, he scrapped the attempt to market the encyclopedia via Sears outlets and instead built a nationwide network of sales representatives who went door to door and also staffed booths at conventions, shopping centers, and the like. Of greater importance was Powell's decision to publish the *Britannica* continuously by revising a portion of its articles each year, thus keeping the entire work in print and relatively up to date at the same time. Previously, the financial health of the encyclopedia had been made unpredictable by its long publication cycle, which over a 15- to 30-year period called first for a massive editorial effort with virtually no sales, followed by an intensive sales program with no need for editors, until the growing obsolescence of the current work made a new edition necessary and the cycle began again. Powell recognized that such a pattern was inherently inefficient and in 1938 introduced the new system of continuous revision and publication, which has remained in effect ever since.

Although sales picked up during the 1930s under Powell's leadership, Sears chairman General Robert E. Wood was not comfortable with the company's ownership of the Britannica. In 1941 a vice-president of the University of Chicago named William Benton suggested that Sears again try to interest the University in running the Britannica. Benton was the remarkable co-founder of the advertising agency Benton and Bowles; after amassing a comfortable fortune he retired in 1935 (at the age of 35) and soon became active at the University of Chicago. Believing passionately in the importance of the *Britannica,* he urged the University to accept General Wood's offer to give it the company's stock, but the University's board of trustees balked at the financial risk. Benton thereupon offered to put up needed working capital if the University would agree to lend its name and editorial advice to the venture. An agreement was reached in 1943 by which Benton acquired two-thirds of the stock in a new company, Encyclopaedia Britannica, Inc., of which he became chairman, while the University received one-third of the company stock, a royalty on sales, and an option to buy another third of the company. Robert Maynard Hutchins, president of the University of Chicago, was named chairman of the Board of Editors of the Britannica, but the University assumed neither financial responsibility nor managerial control of the company.

1950–90: New Products and Acquisitions

In 1938 Britannica had begun publishing the *Britannica Book of the Year* (later called the *Britannica World Data Annual*), a yearly synopsis of world events, and in 1952 it brought out the 54-volume *Great Books of the Western World*. Edited by

Hutchins and Mortimer Adler, who also wrote its two-volume index known as the *Syntopicon,* the Great Books attempted to trace the development of Western thought from the ancient Greeks to Sigmund Freud by collecting 443 critically important texts by 74 different authors. Britannica revised the *Great Books* in 1990 to include many 20th-century authors as well. In 1943 Britannica branched into the world of film with the acquisition of ERPI, a division of Western Electric that owned the nation's largest collection of films for the classroom. Known first as Encyclopaedia Britannica Films, Inc., the company became Encyclopaedia Britannica Educational Corporation in 1966 and eventually expanded into filmstrips, video, and laserdisc technology as well as conventional films and reference books for school markets.

Under the continued leadership and financial support of William Benton, Encyclopaedia Britannica, Inc., was able to buy out the University of Chicago's share of stock in 1952 and begin preparations for the radically new Fifteenth Edition that would appear in 1974. Not only did Encyclopaedia Britannica survive, but thanks to the generosity of Benton it became the parent company of a host of other reference publishers, including Merriam-Webster, publisher of the famous dictionaries by that name, and F.E. Compton Company, fellow makers of encyclopedias. Encyclopaedia Britannica, Inc., went international in 1957 with the publication of the 16-volume *Enciclopedia Borsa* in Spanish, a joint venture that would later distribute Britannica products throughout Latin America under the name Encyclopaedia Britannica Publishers. Britannica went on to publish native-language encyclopedias in countries including Japan, the People's Republic of China, France, Italy, and Korea, all of them after 1974 under the management of Encyclopaedia Britannica International. The latter oversaw all of Britannica's foreign business, which by 1990 included offices in 130 countries and operating companies in 17 countries.

William Benton died in March 1973, just before the Britannica's new Fifteenth Edition was published. *Britannica 3,* as the new edition was christened, incorporated the most radical changes in the encyclopedia since its founding 200 years before. *Britannica 3* was composed of a ten-volume *Micropaedia* for handy reference use, a 19-volume *Macropaedia* for reading in depth, and a one-volume *Propaedia,* or guide to the encyclopedia's use. This hybrid creation was the subject of a front page article in the *New York Times* and caused considerable debate between those readers who preferred the traditional format and those who favored the innovative Fifteenth Edition. In 1985 a two-volume index was added, as well as other refinements. Britannica launched an extensive public relations campaign to promote its experiment; the results were excellent as measured by sales, but dissatisfaction with the *Britannica 3* was more widespread than the parent company would likely admit.

Succeeding Benton as publisher and chairman of Encyclopaedia Britannica, Inc., was Robert P. Gwinn, a University of Chicago graduate, member of the board of directors of Encyclopaedia Britannica, and at that time chairman of Sunbeam Corporation. It was Gwinn who decided on the division of the company's operations into Encyclopaedia Britannica USA (later EB North America) and Encyclopaedia Britannica International in 1974, in addition to the Merriam-Webster, Compton's, and Educational divisions. Under the leadership of Gwinn, Encyclopaedia Britannica, Inc., increased total revenues every year between 1974 and 1990 (with the single exception of 1980), with sales more than doubling during the 1980s alone. A large portion of the parent company's revenue was contributed by Encyclopaedia Britannica North America, which sold the *Britannica* in thousands of display booths located at shopping malls, fairs, trade shows, and rail terminals, among other venues; its representatives also visited private residences upon appointment.

In 1980 all shares of Encyclopaedia Britannica, Inc., were transferred to the William Benton Foundation of Illinois, created as a non-profit supporting organization of the University of Chicago. By placing Encyclopaedia Britannica, Inc., in the hands of a foundation, the Bentons hoped to ensure the company's long-term independence, both in its editorial philosophy and as a financial entity protected from hostile takeovers. Robert Gwinn was also named chairman of the Benton Foundation.

In 1985 a revised version of the Fifteenth Edition (with the number of articles in the *Macropaedia* reduced from 4,200 to only 681) was published. Subsequently, Britannica Software (later Compton's New Media, Inc.) was formed as a separate division to work on the design of educational computer programs. The company also acquired two reading skills enterprises, American Learning Corporation and Evelyn Wood Reading Dynamics, and in 1990 published a revised and expanded *Great Books of the Western World,* including six additional volumes and 20th-century authors. The year 1989 saw release of *Compton's Multi-Media Encyclopaedia,* a version of that encyclopedia transferred to CD-ROM. Encyclopaedia Britannica, Inc. also created a new Far Eastern Pacific Region in its international division, and in 1990 announced that it was embarking on a joint venture with Soviet publishers to produce a Russian-language encyclopedia. Sales for the year peaked at $650 million, with nearly 120,000 encyclopedia sets sold in the United States alone.

The 1990s: Falling Sales and Unique Solutions

The early 1990s saw sales of encyclopedia sets plummet, however. The U.S. economic downturn and increasing competition from cheap CD-ROM versions took a heavy toll. In 1994 Encyclopaedia Britannica's sales were reported at $453 million, with only some 51,000 bound sets sold in the United States. That same year the cash-starved company sold its Compton's interests to The Tribune Company.

Britannica responded slowly to the changes brought by the new technology. An online subscription-based version was launched in 1993 for institutional users, and the company belatedly introduced a CD-ROM version of its encyclopedia at the unrealistic price of nearly $1,000. The increasingly bleak financial picture soon led the University of Chicago to seek outside investors or a buyer. Before one could be found, it was announced that more than 70 percent of the company's 91 U.S. sales offices would be closed, forcing layoffs of several dozen employees.

In January 1996 Jacob Safra stepped in to purchase Encyclopaedia Britannica. The reclusive Lebanese banker led a group that reportedly paid $135 million for the company, less than half its estimated value. He immediately called for a restructuring, with layoffs of more than 120 people including many of the company's top administrators. Encyclopaedia Britannica Educational Corporation was also put up for sale. Soon afterwards the home sales force was completely dismantled, with 140 additional employees losing their jobs along with 300 independent contractors. An attempt was made to sell encyclopedia sets through bookstores, with a cheaper, slimmed down version introduced when initial sales proved slow. The public remained largely uninterested, however, given the wide availability of inexpensive CD-ROM encyclopedias such as Microsoft's *Encarta,* which was often included for free with new computer purchases. Britannica quickly began cutting the price of its own CD-ROMs, eventually reaching a low of $85 for a disc that included the entire 44 million words along with illustrations and hypertext links between subjects. The company's Web site was also overhauled and offered to the public for a fee, with some unique information added that was not in the print or CD-ROM versions. A free site, Britannica Internet Guide (later eBlast), was created that offered other information and links to recommended sites.

Finally recognizing the need to seriously compete with the growing multitude of ad-supported free information sites, the company launched a new Internet service in 1999 called Britannica.com. Safra set up a separate company to operate this Web site, which was introduced in October. The site contained the complete Encyclopaedia Britannica and again added unique articles such as biographies of pop culture figures not available elsewhere. Britannica.com also served as a sales site for Encyclopaedia Britannica CD-ROMs and the company's other publications, including the still available print version, which was now being offered on the installment plan for the first time ever. The largest advertising campaign in Britannica history was created to announce the site's launch.

When an estimated ten million users attempted to access Britannica.com on its opening day, it crashed repeatedly, and after several days of continued problems it was shut down. Restarted a few weeks later with upgraded capacity, it functioned more smoothly, but usage leveled off after the original barrage. A company executive bravely stated that he hoped it would be profitable by 2002, but analysts were not quite so optimistic. Just one year after being formed, Britannica.com laid off 20 percent of its work force and sought further ways to cut costs. Meanwhile, the subscription-only Britannica Online was continued as a separate operation aimed at educational users.

Stunned by the changes brought on by the computer revolution, Encyclopaedia Britannica struggled to find its niche in the information-rich 21st century. The company continued to offer expensive sets of printed books for sale via the Internet, but its CD-ROM, now priced at less than one-tenth of the bound version, was by far the better seller. With the complete text available for free via the Internet, and fierce competitors such as Microsoft on the attack, it was hard to predict what the future would hold for this venerable institution.

Principal Subsidiaries

Encyclopaedia Britannica North America; Encyclopaedia Britannica International; Merriam-Webster, Inc.

Principal Competitors

Franklin Electronic Publishers, Inc.; Grolier, Inc.; Harcourt General, Inc.; Havas SA; Houghton Mifflin Co.; The McGraw-Hill Companies, Inc.; Microsoft Corp.; Pearson plc; Random House, Inc.; Simon & Schuster, Inc.; The Thomson Corporation; Time, Inc.; Tribune Company.

Further Reading

Atkinson, Dan, ''US Recluse Saves Britannica,'' *Guardian,* December 20, 1995, p. 2.
''Britannica.com Arrives, Belatedly: Encyclopedia Seller Bets Future of Brand on Ad-supported Web Site,'' *Advertising Age,* May 10, 1999, p. 24.
Edwards, Cliff, ''Now: A 'Micropaedia' Britannica,'' *AP Online,* June 1, 1998.
——, ''Roadkill? Britannica Nearly Flattened on Info Highway,'' *St. Louis Post-Dispatch,* May 15, 1996, p. 8C.
Haase, Roald H., *The Story of Encyclopaedia Britannica,* Chicago: Encyclopaedia Britannica, Inc., 1990.
Jones, Tim, ''Venerable to Vulnerable: Encyclopaedia Britannica Trying to Survive in the Age of Technology,'' *Newsday,* November 26, 2000, p. F8.
Ollove, Michael, ''Turning the Pages,'' *Baltimore Sun,* January 10, 2000, p. 1E.
Parr, J., ''Low Tech Lives,'' *Forbes,* November 17, 1986.
Reid, Calvin, ''Britannica.com Fires 75,'' *Publishers Weekly,* November 27, 2000, p. 12.
Whiteley, Sandy, ''Hard Times: Encyclopedia Publishing in the 1990s,'' *American Libraries,* July 1, 1995, p. 640.

—Jonathan Martin
—update: Frank Uhle

Ethan Allen Interiors, Inc.

Ethan Allen Drive
P.O. Box 1966
Danbury, Connecticut 06813-1966
U.S.A.
Telephone: (203) 743-8000
Fax: (203) 743-8298
Web site: http://www.ethanallen.com

Public Company
Incorporated: 1932 as Baumritter Corp.
Employees: 8,090
Sales: $856.2 million (2000)
Stock Exchanges: New York
Ticker Symbol: ETH
NAIC: 337122 Nonupholstered Wood Household
     Furniture Manufacturing; 337121 Upholstered
     Household Furniture Manufacturing; 44211 Furniture
     Stores; 44221 Floor Covering Stores; 442299 All
     Other Home Furnishings Stores

Ethan Allen Interiors, Inc. is the holding company for Ethan Allen, Inc., which manufactures and retails quality home furnishings, offering a full range of furniture and decorative accessories through more than 300 Ethan Allen Galleries (including more than 30 abroad). Ethan Allen products are available only through these dealers and through the company's web site. As of 2000 the company directly operated 78 stores, including its flagship stores in New York City, and in Danbury and Stamford, Connecticut. In an industry characterized as highly fragmented, Ethan Allen maintains a national presence by branding its products and retail stores with the same name. The company also is distinguished by its vertical integration of operations, overseeing the design, manufacture, distribution, display, and marketing of Ethan Allen furnishings. Ethan Allen operates more than 20 manufacturing facilities in the United States, as well as three saw mills and 11 distribution facilities. Roughly 90 percent of Ethan Allen products are made domestically, at its own plants.

Debut in the Depression

The history of Ethan Allen may be traced to the 1930s. In 1932, The Baumritter Corp., a housewares sales agency, was founded by two New Yorkers, Theodore Baumritter and his brother-in-law, Nathan S. Ancell. The worst year of the Great Depression was hardly an auspicious time for such an undertaking, and at the end of the year the partners were in the red by $3,000—more than they had put into the firm. According to a 1965 *Home Furnishings Daily* article, people out of work and struggling to make ends meet had little thought for the plaster gnomes, trellises, and garden swings manufactured by Baumritter.

"Looking back, I suppose 1935 was our crucial year," Ancell told Earl Lifshey in the interview for *Home Furnishings Daily.* Ancell continued, "We had managed to survive the depths of the Depression and began to make a little headway. But I could see no real future for the kind of drop-shipment jobbing business in which we were engaged. We were nothing but a middleman. I concluded—and Ted agreed completely—that if we were going to build our destiny we would have to control all the elements with which we were working."

Thus, in 1936, the partners bought a furniture factory, a bankrupt plant in Beecher Falls, Vermont, which a federal agency sold to them for $25,000. Ancell and Baumritter did not realize at the time that the factory's machinery dated from 1917 and was belt-driven. Nevertheless, it was not long, Ancell continued, "before we fell hopelessly in love with Vermont and with what New England represents historically," and the partners remained committed to the idea of furniture manufacturing. Recognizing the market potential for Early American furniture, a style mostly untapped in the industry, the partners put together a group of 28 pieces of Early American furniture, naming it for Ethan Allen, whose Green Mountain Boys fought to make Vermont the nation's 14th state. The furniture was first unveiled in 1939, but only to selected buyers who would be willing to

---

Company Perspectives:

At Ethan Allen, we're dedicated to providing you superior quality home furnishings at a good, honest value. We support our innovative Classic and Casual indoor and outdoor furnishings with a commitment to service that goes beyond the expected. These principles, set over 67 years ago, remain at the forefront of everything we do and that's why today 'everyone's at home with Ethan Allen.'

---

display it properly in stores. This marked the beginning of the company's exclusive franchise policy.

Expanding the Furniture Experience in the 1960s

Through their observations, Ancell and Baumritter found that the typical furniture wholesale buyer focused primarily on price, while the typical customers, at the time, women, were more concerned with decorating techniques and customer service than price. The solution, they believed, was to offer correlated groupings of classic furniture from which a woman could select the specific pieces to solve her particular furnishing problem. Within the company's Early American decorating scheme, the customer could add to her furnishings and complete a room not just in a matter of months or a year, but several years later if she chose. By the mid-1960s, the Baumritter Corp. had a 1,600-piece line of Ethan Allen traditional Early American furniture: the biggest single group, by a very wide margin, of furniture made by any manufacturer in the world.

For Ancell, the company was selling ''thoughts,'' not ''things,'' an ''environment—not furniture.'' He told Lifshey, ''In this business we are dealing primarily with a series of very emotional products that are purchased and used in a very emotional manner primarily by the female of the species.'' Referring to the home as ''the cornerstone and the hallmark of our civilization,'' Ancell suggested the female buyer looked for ''protectiveness, for warmth, for orderliness'' in her furnishings, and ''it's at that point that she must have some place to go and some people with whom she can confidently talk and rely upon to safely guide and assist her in doing the job herself.''

The policy of Baumritter Corp. was to reinvest every dollar of profit into the enterprise. By 1962 the company had 14 furniture factories in the East, and that year it acquired Kling Factories, Inc., which owned three furniture-making plants near Jamestown, New York. The Kling Colonial group of about 350 pieces and Viko line of about 150 steel furniture pieces supplemented the Ethan Allen line. In addition to furniture, the company made lamps, painted wooden accessories, and decorative wall hangings.

By the mid-1960s there were around 700 Ethan Allen dealers in the United States, with others in Canada, Australia, France, Belgium, The Netherlands, and Switzerland. Baumritter management invoked a careful selection process before licensing a dealer for their furnishings. Potential store sites were researched carefully for sufficient levels of population, retail activity, average-income levels, and upper-income levels, and the prospective area would be studied not only on the ground

but from the air. A dealer would be selected on the basis not only of financial considerations but understanding of the Ethan Allen program and willingness to dedicate himself to it. If selected, dealers then owned and operated the store themselves. The average store size at the time was 16,000 square feet, and about one-quarter of the dealers accounted for three-quarters of sales volume.

In 1970 the company acquired the Volckman Furniture Manufacturing Co. of Morrison, Illinois, through an exchange of stock. This purchase added to the production of Ethan Allen upholstered living room furniture. Also in that year Ancell, the company's president, became chairperson, replacing Baumritter, who retired. In early 1972 the Baumritter Corp. changed its name to Ethan Allen Industries and moved its headquarters from New York City to Danbury, Connecticut.

That year, Ethan Allen began supplementing (and eventually phasing out) its regular franchised dealers with a network of 200 owner-managers of ''showcase galleries.'' These outlets, concentrated in shopping centers of well-heeled suburban areas, were producing 72 percent of total sales volume, which rose to $70 million in 1971 from $43 million in 1965. The owner-managers invested $65,000 to $125,000 to build the stores but were not required to sign contracts with Ethan Allen or pay franchise fees; they owned their inventory, unlike regular franchised dealers. By 1982 there were some 350 such galleries in the United States, of which 20 were owned by Ethan Allen itself.

In June 1972 Ancell announced plans to expand into furniture styles other than Early American, as well as into producing broadloom carpeting, oriental rugs, wallpaper, and draperies. Also during this time, the company, which had launched its first national print advertising campaign around 1951, developed its first series of nationwide television ads.

Changing Ownership in the 1980s and Early 1990s

In 1979 Ethan Allen agreed to be acquired by Interco Inc., a St. Louis-based conglomerate. The transaction, which called for an exchange of stock originally valued at about $130 million and later at $150 million, was completed in 1980, with Ethan Allen continuing as an Interco subsidiary headed by Ancell. Over the next eight years annual sales grew from $230 million to $600 million.

Ancell was succeeded as president in 1985 and as chair and chief executive in 1988 by M. Farooq Kathwari, who had formed a joint venture with Ethan Allen to develop products in 1973 and had joined the company as a vice-president in 1980. Under Kathwari, Ethan Allen, Inc. became independent again, when a management group headed by Kathwari purchased the company from Interco for about $385 million in a leveraged buyout in 1989. Ethan Allen was made a wholly owned subsidiary under a company incorporated as the Green Mountain Holding Corp., which would become Ethan Allen Interiors, Inc. in the early 1990s. Ethan Allen Interiors then went public, completing its first public offering in March 1993 by raising $156.9 million through the sale of common stock. A secondary public offering completed in November 1993 raised nearly $40 million. In July 1994, J.K. Castle controlled 11.9 percent of

1932: Company is founded in New York as Baumritter & Co.
1936: Company purchases first manufacturing plant; launches Ethan Allen brand name.
1969: Firm is renamed Ethan Allen, Inc.
1980: Ethan Allen is acquired by Interco, Inc.
1985: M. Farooq Kathwari becomes president.
1989: Kathwari and other managers and investors take company private, break with Interco.
1993: Ethan Allen Interiors, Inc. becomes public company.

Ethan Allen's common stock, and Kathwari held 10.5 percent. Long-term debt came to $144.5 million.

Transforming Image in the 1990s

The dynamic Kathwari was quick to change the direction of the company. At the time, the Ethan Allen network included more than 100 retailers across the United States, and little consistency was maintained in store projection, interior display, merchandise mix, and advertising. Kathwari personally visited the stores and found that not only was the style of the furniture out of date, but the retail environment was unappetizing. Peggy McLinden, head of store planning for the firm, recalled in an April 6, 1998 article in *Forbes* that Ethan Allen's "old stores looked like museums. Sometimes customers couldn't find their way back to the front door." Kathwari took over the running of some underperforming stores and instituted measures to change the product mix and its presentation. Between 1992 and 1997, almost every Ethan Allen store underwent renovation and redesign, resulting in a chain of light, airy stores exhibiting much more contemporary wares than the old Early American line.

Kathwari had been updating Ethan Allen's product line since the early 1990s. Company research had shown that the Early American style was no longer popular, and the company worked hard to bring a range of new styles into its showrooms. The new styles included American Impressions, introduced in 1991, which included straight-line pieces made of solid cherry inspired by Shaker furniture and the designs of Frank Lloyd Wright. This line soon became the fastest growing new product in the company's history. A second contemporary line, American Dimensions, was introduced in 1992, accenting geometric shapes. After that came Country Crossings, featuring rustic-looking maple furniture; Legacy, based on Italian architecture styles; and the ultra-contemporary Radius, offering sleek styles recalling those of the 1960s. In addition, a choice of 2,000 fabrics was offered for upholstery. Perhaps more notably, Ethan Allen was transformed from strictly a furniture retailer into a total home furnishings source, offering textiles, wall decor, bedding, lamps, and other decorative items to its customers.

Kathwari made other changes as well. Two factories were closed, others were retooled for new styles, and plants were added to produce such home furnishings as pillows, bedspreads, mirrors, and clocks. Quality control was improved and the company's 300 delivery vans were replaced by larger, less fuel-thirsty vehicles. Moreover, annual week-long courses for salespersons were given at "Ethan Allen College," established at company headquarters. In addition, Kathwari cracked down on its dealers, many of whom had not been observing the requirement to sell Ethan Allen products exclusively.

An aggressive advertising campaign was launched in the fall of 1991 to attract younger customers conditioned to think of Ethan Allen as the choice of their parents. By mid-1992 only one-eighth of displayed Ethan Allen furniture was Early American. Classical yet contemporary storefronts began to replace the familiar white-column facades. Prices fell, with queen size beds, for example, dropping from an average price of $1,000 to $700 or $800. The new approach was apparently paying off; in 1993 sales grew by 9.5 percent, and between July 1993 and April 1994 sales were up 20 percent in stores open a year or more. Moreover, for fiscal 1994, the company's net sales rose 13.8 percent to reach $437 million.

A new advertising campaign for 1994 featured nationwide television commercials with the theme, "Everyone's at home with Ethan Allen." In an interview, the company's vice-president of advertising remarked, "The tag line invites a broader group of consumers to respond to our advertising, from older, empty-nesters to young people starting out. It says, 'Find your place within our spectrum of styles and price points.'" The TV spots were supplemented with print ads and radio commercials featuring consumers varying widely in life-styles and attitudes. A concurrent $45 million marketing program included a new logo, advertising, direct mail, merchandising, store displays, and signs. The target market was people between 25 and 54 with household incomes greater than $35,000.

These moves were meant, in part, to help combat the heavy load of debt the company assumed in becoming an independent, which resulted in four years of red ink. In going public, Ethan Allen offered 48 percent of the common stock at $18 a share. By February 1994 the company's common stock was selling at $32 a share, but it had dipped as low as $19.50 during the year. At the close of 1994 the company turned its credit card operations over to GE Capital Corp. under a long-term agreement.

The changes the company had made put it in a good position for growth. In the mid-1990s, the furniture industry as a whole grew at around five percent annually. Ethan Allen had increased store traffic by about 25 percent by the middle of the decade, and the company's revenue grew by ten percent in both 1996 and 1997. More than 30 percent of the company's total sales in the mid-1990s was provided by Ethan Allen's string of company-owned stores. There were 65 by 1998, including three that were personally supervised by Kathwari himself. New ideas for products or management techniques were tried out in the company-run stores first, allowing Ethan Allen a vital laboratory for studying customer needs and responses.

Ethan Allen also set its sights on international expansion in the mid-1990s. By 1995, the company had 28 stores located outside the United States, including stores in Japan and the Middle East. These overseas branches contributed only four percent of the company's total sales in 1995. But Kathwari planned to expand the company's presence overseas, hoping to bring stores to Europe. Ethan Allen opened new stores in Japan, operating them under an agreement with a Japanese furniture retailer. Previously, Ethan Allen had sold its furniture in a few Japanese department stores, but the new arrangement tripled the company's floor space in that country. Ethan Allen also revamped its store in Jeddah, Saudi Arabia in 1995.

Other new directions for the company included the launching of a children's furniture line, internet retailing, and expansion into the lower end of the market. The market for children's furniture was promising in the late 1990s, as demographic projections showed the number of children under 14 in the United States would rise significantly over the next ten years. Retail sales for the total kids' market had grown as much as 400 percent between 1980 and 1997, and total sales were more than $4 billion. Ethan Allen brought out its E.A. Kids line in 1998, featuring four main product groupings. In 2000, Ethan Allen began selling directly to customers through its web site. Because the Ethan Allen brand was so well known, and already supported with national advertising, the expansion into e-commerce seemed a logical extension. The web site allowed consumers to browse through Ethan Allen's product line, apply for on-line financing, and buy on-line. Ethan Allen also built a computer network between its existing stores and its distribution facilities and service centers. It was hoped this would speed communication and allow for better customer service and more efficiency. Ethan Allen also began looking for new ways to lure less affluent customers at the beginning of the 2000s. Its customers were typically between the ages of 35 and 60, and in middle- to upper-income brackets. Over the course of the 1990s, Ethan Allen had brought its prices down about 15 percent, and 90 percent of its products had been redesigned. The overall effort was aimed at bringing in younger customers. Since younger customers were usually budget-conscious, the company brought out a new financing program in 2000, to help people pay for their furniture. Called Simple Finance, it allowed people to pay in installments, with an average credit line of $16,000. In 2000 President Kathwari also told investors that the company was considering bringing out a new, moderately priced line of furniture. This was just in the planning stages, but reflected the company's overarching strategy of shedding its old, stuffy image and appealing to younger, thriftier consumers.

Principal Subsidiaries

Ethan Allen, Inc.; Ethan Allen Manufacturing Corp.; Andover Wood Products.

Principal Competitors

Lifestyle Furnishings International Ltd.; Furniture Brands International Inc.; Klaussner Furniture Industries Inc.; La-Z-Boy Inc.; Homelife Furniture Corporation.

Further Reading

Adamson, Guy, "Kids Now at Home with Ethan Allen," *HFN,* December 7, 1998, p. 29.

Barmash, Isadore, "New Lines and New Life for Furniture Maker," *New York Times,* October 6, 1991.

Buchanan, Lee, "Ethan Allen Will Sell Furniture Online," *HFN,* August 2, 1999, p. 18.

Elliott, Stuart, "Advertising," *New York Times,* January 10, 1994, p. D7.

"Ethan Allen Breaks with Tradition," *Business Week,* June 10, 1972, p. 22.

"Ethan Allen Revising Operations in Japan as Part of Expansion," *Wall Street Journal*, November 16, 1995, p. B5.

"Ethan Allen Tries to Shed Its Colonial Past," *New York Times,* November 28, 1992, pp. 33, 41.

Goldbogen, Jessica, "Ethan Allen Reinvents Itself," *HFN,* May 29, 2000, p. 20S.

——, "Ethan Allen Seeks Thriftier Customers," *HFN,* February 21, 2000, p. 4.

Lifshey, Earl, *The Baumritter Story,* New York: Baumritter Corp., 1965.

Marcial, Gene G., "Fresh Looks and New Fans for Ethan Allen," *Business Week,* August 2, 1993, p. 78.

Power, William, "Ethan Allen Sets Table in Bid to Slash Debt," *Wall Street Journal,* January 29, 1993, p. C2.

Roush, Chris, "Rearranging the Furniture at Ethan Allen," *Business Week,* July 11, 1994, p. 102.

Sansoni, Silvia, "Do As I Do," *Forbes*, April 6, 1998, p. 82.

Schonfeld, Erick, "Bring Out the Love Seats," *Fortune,* July 10, 1995, p. 209.

Singer, Penny, "The Changing Face of Furniture Making," *New York Times,* November 6, 1994.

Stangenes, Sharon, "A Revolutionary Look," *Chicago Tribune,* July 26, 1992, Sec. 15, p. 3.

"Tradition with a Twist," *Sales and Marketing Management,* April 1994, p. 24.

—Robert Halasz
—update: A. Woodward

Fabbrica D' Armi Pietro Beretta S.p.A.

Via Pietro Beretta, 18
25063 Gardone Val Trompia
Brescia
Italy
Telephone: 030.8341.1
Fax: 030.8341421
Web site: http://www.beretta.com

Wholly Owned Subsidiary of Beretta Holding, S.p.A.
Founded: 1526
Employees: 1,900
Sales: $233.1 million (1999)
NAIC: 332994 Small Arms Manufacturing

Fabbrica D' Armi Pietro Beretta S.p.A., maker of James Bond's trusty .25 caliber Beretta pistol, is the oldest manufacturing firm in the world. Amazingly, a single family has controlled the company throughout its history, which has spanned from ancient guilds to computerized robotics. In 1985, Beretta won a hotly contested bid to replace the Colt .45 in the U.S. arsenal. However, sporting arms comprise about three-quarters of Beretta's production; most of these are exported.

16th Century Origins

The home of Fabbrica D'Armi Pietro Beretta S.p.A. is the village of Gardone, in the center of the northern Italian valley known as Val Trompia. Iron ore in the hills of northern Italy made the area an iron-working center from the Middle Ages.

Bartolomeo Beretta was born in 1490. The earliest documentary evidence of his forge is a contract from the Doges of Venice, dated October 3, 1526, for 185 "arquebus" barrels. (The harquebus was a type of musket so heavy it had to be propped up with supports. Beretta's first product was quite a contrast to the handguns for which it later became known.)

The operation may well pre-date the year 1526 from which the company counts its anniversaries. In his extensive history, *The World of Beretta*, R.L. Wilson cites an 1860 account of a flood in the Mella Valley, which indicated the forge "bore the date AD 1500 carved on its lintel." Since medieval custom dictated that only sons of master craftsmen could become masters themselves, it is also quite possible that Bartolomeo was not the first Beretta to make gun barrels.

Bartolomeo had a son, Jacomo, and a grandson, Giovannino, who became a master gun barrel maker. Another grandson, Lodovico, established a gun lock fabrication trade.

At the middle of the 16th century, Val Trompia had 50 mines, eight smelteries, and 40 smithies. It produced 25,000 guns a year, mostly for export, as well as various other types of iron and steel goods. (During the war between Venice and Turkey in 1570, production more than tripled to 300 weapons per day.)

Giovanni Antonio Beretta designed his own breech-loading cannons in 1641, but it is unclear whether they were ever built. In the late 1600s, the Beretta clan was involved in a deadly feud with the Chinellis that saw one of their members, Francesco Beretta, sentenced to four years of military service. In 1698, the Berettas were the second largest barrel producer among 33 in Gardone, making 2,883 barrels, mostly for long arms.

The Venetian senate sporadically banned the export of gun barrels throughout the 16th and 17th centuries. When it was allowed, high duties slowed sales. The artisans involved in the highly specialized business of making gun barrels were vulnerable to these downturns. During these times, the Republic of Venice went to great lengths to prevent the export of technology.

New Rules in the 19th Century

The guild system began to collapse in the 18th century under pressure from merchants. Interestingly, one of Francesco Beretta's sons, Giovanni, was a merchant. Gardonese muskets began to wane in popularity in the 1750s, putting more pressure on the guilds to accept the merchants' economic terms. When Napoleon took over Venice in 1797, the French outlawed the "antidemocratic" guild system. For the next dozen and a half years, the Berettas made barrels to supply a new firearms factory in nearby Brescia, which produced 40,000 guns a year.

Austria provided a market for military guns after Napoleon was defeated in 1815. The same year, Pietro Antonio Beretta toured Italy, making connections with gun dealers. In 1832, he gave the firm the name it has carried for more than a century and a half: Fabbrica d'Armi Pietro Beretta. After his death, Pietro's son Giuseppe toured abroad in search of business connections and helped the family operation to produce complete firearms for the first time.

Whereas the previous century had been dominated by military production, in the 1850s Giuseppe Beretta focused the factory on producing fine sporting guns. The company was making at most 300 guns a year through 1860. Twenty years later, annual production had increased to as many as 8,000 guns a year. Beretta was also marketing, via catalog, guns made by other manufacturers, including Colt, Remington, Smith & Wesson, and Winchester.

Beretta again began making military firearms after the unification of Italy in 1861. In 1899, Giuseppe saw to the construction of the Beretta Hotel in Gardone to accommodate the many foreign visitors the world-renowned factory was receiving.

20th Century Expansion

The second Pietro Beretta has been credited with guiding the firm into the modern era. The 20th century was a time of incredible growth. At the time of Giuseppe Beretta's death in 1903, the company had 130 employees and a single 10,000-square-foot factory. By 2000, it would occupy 75,000 square feet of space in Gardone and another 50,000 square feet on other sites in Italy, Spain, and the United States (Maryland).

This Pietro Beretta, who succeeded Giuseppe, soon established a hydroelectric plant on the Mella River to supply the factory with its own source of power. During World War I, it developed new arms to use with existing ammunition, designed largely by the firm's intrepid inventor, Tullio Marengoni. By the end of the war, Beretta was making more than 4,000 units of Marengoni's Model 1915 automatic pistol a month for the Italian Army. Marengoni is also said to have designed the world's first true submachine gun. Employment at Beretta had more than doubled during World War I, to 1,000 workers.

Beretta bought out the Fabbrica d'Armi Lario near Como in the late 1920s, bringing its machinery to Gardone. Wilson's

extensive company history reported that the fascism of the 1930s did not take root in Val Trompia due to Beretta's close relations with employees.

The company made military arms for the Italian government during World War II until the Germans occupied the plant in 1943. As the war ended, the Nazis held Pietro Beretta hostage until he was freed by partisans. After the war, Beretta was associated with the Beretta-Benelli-Castelbarco automobile. For some years the company also owned MI-VAL, a motorcycle manufacturer.

In the early 1950s, Beretta registered the distinctive three-arrow device that appears on its guns. In much the same way that Enzo Ferrari had adopted the prancing horse of the Italian aviator Baracca for his cars, the Berettas used the personal trademark of the flamboyant Italian poet Gabriele d'Annunzio as their corporate trademark.

Pietro Beretta died on May 1, 1957, leaving control of the company in the hands of his sons Pier Giuseppe, who became board chairman, and Carlo. The company was heading to new levels of international fame. In the 1960s, Ian Fleming's famous fictional spy James Bond clutched a .25 caliber Beretta pistol in novels and films. "How could one have such ties with an inanimate object?," he asked in *Dr. No.*

Pier and Carlo directed the internationalization of the company's marketing and production. Beretta distributorships were established in Greece, Great Britain, and France between 1961 and 1971 to open up new markets in sporting arms. The company's Brazilian affiliate began building revolvers in 1971; Beretta sold this unit to Forjas Taurus S.A. in 1980 after shifting its focus to the United States.

Entering the United States in 1977

Beretta U.S.A. was founded in 1977, when Beretta acquired a bankrupt gun factory near Washington, D.C., that had previously had a contract to service its products. Beretta's Model 92 nine-millimeter pistol, one of the most widely produced firearms in history, had been introduced two years earlier; this was the gun that would soon land Beretta a massive military contract and thousands of smaller deals to supply law enforcement agencies.

Beretta won a hard-fought contract to replace the Colt .45 in 1985. The U.S. military had decided to reduce the number of different types of weapons in its arsenal and wanted a new handgun that could fire standard NATO nine-millimeter rounds.

The deal raised Beretta's profile considerably in the United States. Its pistols continued to appear in Hollywood movies such as *Lethal Weapon*. Law enforcement agencies around the country began ordering the commercial version (92-F) of the Beretta Model 92 nine-millimeter handgun, appreciating its ability to fire 15 shots before reloading, versus the eight-round capacity of most large caliber pistols. Civilians also bought them; the pistol retailed for about $600. Smaller .22 caliber pistols sold for $200.

In the United States, Beretta was forced to defend its centuries old brand name. It sued General Motors after GM

Key Dates:

1526: The Beretta forge receives its earliest known contract.

1698: The Berettas are the second largest gun barrel producer in Gardone.

1797: Napoleon takes over Venice and outlaws the guild system.

1832: The name Fabbrica D'Armi Pietro Beretta is adopted.

1880: Production reaches 8,000 guns a year.

1903: Pietro Beretta begins to guide the firm into the modern era.

1917: Employment reaches 1,000.

1957: Pier and Carlo Beretta become the company's new leaders.

1985: Beretta wins a contract to supply the U.S. military with nine-millimeter pistols.

2000: Beretta seals deals to buy three other gunmakers.

appropriated the name for the Chevrolet Beretta car in 1987. Eventually, the two worked out a settlement; GM agreed to give $500,000 to the Beretta Foundation for Cancer Research and Treatment and was allowed to keep using the name on its automobile.

The brand name was extended with permission to the Beretta Sport line of high-end clothing and accessories introduced in 1988. However, the company sued five Japanese firms for manufacturing toy guns displaying its name and trademark without permission. (Beretta had licensed these to only one Japanese toy gun maker, Western Arms.) The company also faced the problem of bootleg production, such as that which had begun in the Philippines.

Ugo Gussalli Beretta became president of the company in 1993 after the death of his uncle Giuseppe. He had been managing director since 1981. In spite of the large and prestigious U.S. military handgun contract, the commercial market in America (which included law enforcement agencies) gave Beretta its fastest area of growth, rising about 30 percent a year. In 1998, Beretta added a retail outlet in Buenos Aires to its galleries in New York City and Dallas.

As the *Financial Times* noted, the very lethality of guns made them unique in the legal environment. Their very potential for harm was what made them useful. Beretta was thus the target of a few high profile lawsuits, though not on grounds of defective manufacture.

The family of a 15-year-old California boy killed while playing with a semiautomatic Beretta pistol unsuccessfully sued the company in 1998, alleging a design flaw contributed to the death (since a round remained in the chamber after the clip was removed). Moreover, three companies, including Beretta USA,

were ordered to pay more than $500,000 in damages to a New York shooting victim in 1999. At the same time, 20 major cities in the United States were considering a tobacco industry-style lawsuit to hold gun manufacturers liable for the medical costs of people injured in gun-related crimes. Some suits accused the industry of negligent distribution. They alleged gun makers sold arms to ''straw purchasers'' whose only intention in buying them was to resell them to criminals.

Expanding in 2000

In early 2000, Beretta bought the remaining shares in Benelli Arms S.p.A., another venerable Italian gunmaker. In March of that year, it bought an 86 percent share in Aldo Uberti & Co., s.r.l., a $15 million a year replica gunmaking business founded in 1959. With a corporate umbrella company in place to oversee its subsidiaries, Beretta Holding next acquired Sako Ltd., a Finnish maker of hunting and sports rifles, from Metso Corporation in January 2001. Sako had net sales of about FIM 150 million a year.

The best opportunities for future sporting arms sales seemed to lie in the former Soviet Republic. China and Turkey were two other emerging markets being courted. Beretta was also supplying U.S. armed forces with a combat shotgun. Beretta had survived for five centuries by exploiting the advantages of each successive technological shift. Craftsmen in the old world style still customized and engraved Beretta's finest firearms by hand. Mastering information technology was Beretta's adaptive challenge at the beginning of the Millennium.

Principal Subsidiaries

Meccanica Del Sarca, S.r.l.; Beretta USA Corporation—Cougar Corp.; Benelli Armi S.p.A.; Benelli USA Corporation; Franchi S.p.A.

Principal Competitors

Browning Arms; Colt's Manufacturing Company, Inc.; Sturm, Ruger & Company, Inc.

Further Reading

''The Arsenals of Progress,'' *Economist,* March 5, 1994, p. 5.

Edgecliffe-Johnson, Andrew, and Patti Waldmeir, ''Handgun Industry Faces Legal Onslaught,'' *Financial Times,* June 8, 1999, p. 5.

Lent, Ron, ''Gun Maker Wins Product-Liability Case,'' *Journal of Commerce,* November 19, 1998, p. 12A.

Morin, Marco, and Robin Held, *Beretta: la dinastia industriale più antica al mondo,* Chiasso, Switzerland: Acquafresca editrice, 1980.

Morozzi, Justin, ''Rest, Work and Play by the Gun,'' *Financial Times,* April 19, 1997, p. 4.

Shelsby, Ted, ''Beretta Targets Booming Commercial Firearm Market,'' *Los Angeles Times,* July 10, 1990, p. D7.

Wilson, R.L., *The World of Beretta: An International Legend,* New York: Random House, 2000.

—Frederick C. Ingram

Faiveley S.A.

143 Boulevard Anatole France
Carrefour Pleyel
F-93285 Saint-Denis Cedex
France
Telephone: (+33) 1 48-13-65-00
Fax: (+33) 1-48-13-66-47
Web site: http://www.faiveley.com

Public Company
Incorporated: 1916 as Etablissements Louis Faiveley
Employees: 1,837
Sales: EUR 226.56 million ($203.85 million)(2000)
Stock Exchanges: Euronext Paris
Ticker Symbol: FAI Sicovam: 5314
NAIC: 336510 Railroad Rolling Stock Manufacturing

Faiveley S.A. is one of the world's top four suppliers of equipment to the railroad industry. The company is worldwide leader in three core markets, those of automatic door systems, passenger train air conditioning systems, and pantographs—the devices used to convert power from third rails for use by trains. Grouped under the company's Faiveley Transport subsidiary, this division represents 80 percent of the company's annual sales of more than EUR 226 million. Based in France, Faiveley has been one of the first of the world's railroad equipment makers to go global, with well-established operations in Spain, Portugal, Brazil, and Italy, joined by the company's more recently formed Japanese, American, United Kingdom, and Chinese operations. In all, exports account for more than 60 percent of the company's sales. If Faiveley continues to be known and highly regarded for its cutting-edge technology—which also includes specially designed ''black boxes'' for trains and ecologically friendly air conditioning systems—the company is hoping to become equally known for its plastics divisions. Launched in 1992, Faiveley had expanded its plastics operations to account for some 19 percent of its sales, helping to balance out the company's more cyclical railroad business. Faiveley's plastics division, operating through subsidiaries

Grand-Perret, VPI-Verchère, Sepal, and Rhône Moulage Industrie, produces primarily small plastic parts for the cosmetics, textile, automotive, and other industries. Traded on the Euronext Paris stock exchange, Faiveley continues to be majority controlled by the founding Faiveley family. François Faiveley, holding 62 percent of the company's voting rights, and better known for being the guiding force behind the family's famed Burgundy wine production, is also company chairman. CEO Robert Joyeux, named to his post in 1999, is helping to lead a reorganization of the company as it struggles to confront a shrinking and more competitive railroad market.

Pantograph Specialist in the 1920s

Faiveley began as a small electro-mechanical workshop opened by Louis Faiveley in 1919, in Saint Ouen, in France's Indre-et-Loire region. Etablissements Louis Faiveley, as the company was then called, quickly became a railroad equipment specialist producing new generation, electro-mechanic parts for France's changing railroad system. In 1923, Faiveley debuted its first pantograph—the device that connects electric-driven trains to the third rail, converting the electric power for use by the locomotive. The pantograph played a crucial role in the ability of a train to develop speed, and Faiveley's early commitment to research and development helped the company spur France's railroad to greater speed achievements.

The availability of electric power to trains, and especially passenger trains, introduced a wide range of possibilities to constructors, enabling trains to become not only quicker, but also more comfortable. Faiveley branched out into designing and producing door systems in 1930. By 1935, Faiveley already counted among France's leading railroad equipment and systems producers. The company reincorporated, becoming a joint stock company, while remaining wholly controlled by the Faiveley family.

The destruction of much of France's rolling stock during World War II was to provide new opportunities for the company. In the immediate postwar years, as the country began to rebuild its train system, Faiveley expanded its production range to include another important part of the new era passenger train,

Key Dates:

1916: Etablissements Louis Faiveley is founded.
1923: Company introduces first pantographs.
1935: Company starts production of door systems.
1946: Faiveley launches electric heating systems.
1955: First single-arm pantograph is introduced.
1965: Company begins building automatic door systems.
1972: Faiveley introduces very-high-speed pantograph.
1982: Company opens Canadian subsidiary.
1988: Transport operations are grouped under Faiveley Transport subsidiary.
1990: Faiveley helps establish new train speed record at 515.3 kilometers per hour.
1992: Company acquires Grand-Perret.
1994: Company is publicly listed on Paris stock exchange.
1999: Company introduces black boxes for trains; a restructuring plan begins.

that of electric heating systems. Faiveley began production of this line of products in 1946.

Meanwhile, the company continued to enhance its pantograph system. In 1955, the company helped to establish a new train speed record, as a Faiveley-equipped train topped 331 kilometers per hour. In that year, also, Faiveley introduced the world's first single-arm pantograph. This innovation helped the company build its position as world leader in railroad system pantographs.

Internationalization in the 1970s

Faiveley continued to build on its reputation as a technological leader in its sector. In 1961, the company turned toward the burgeoning electronics industry, creating its own research and development team for adapting electronics applications to the railroad industry. The result was a new line of electronic switching devices. At the same time, Faiveley had branched out from its core railroad equipment market to begin equipping the new generation of rubber-wheeled Paris Metro cars.

In the mid-1960s, Faiveley sought to apply its automatic door mechanisms to other markets, particularly the building market. The company's first building doors were produced by 1965. In 1968, the company launched a new subsidiary specifically for its building door systems production, Faiveley Automatismes. By then, Faiveley had made its first move into the international market, launching a subsidiary in Madrid, Spain in 1966.

The 1970s were to prove an era of increasing international presence for the company. In 1976, the company opened a Brazilian subsidiary, Equipfer, quickly becoming a leader of that large and growing market. Two years later Faiveley launched a subsidiary in Italy as well. France remained Faiveley's most important market, however. After taking part in the French railroad system SNCF's launch of a new series of Corail railroad coaches in 1970, the company also was chosen to supply equipment for a new generation of Métro trains, the MF77. Faiveley's commitment to cutting-edge technology once

again showed when it introduced its very-high-speed pantograph in 1972. The company also was preparing to debut its first electric automated door systems, a market segment that was to become one of its most successful.

Faiveley also attempted to enter the North American market, launching subsidiary operations in the United States and Canada. Its railroad activities in the U.S. market remained limited, however, until the late 1990s. The company's fortunes were stronger in its European base, particularly as the company continued to increase its scope of operations. In 1984 the company bought up Saint Gobain subsidiary Air-Industrie's transport division, giving it operations in passenger train air conditioning systems. In that same year, Faiveley acquired the tachometry activities of Matra subsidiary Interelec. Together with the company's other transportation-related activities, these subsidiary operations were brought under a newly created umbrella subsidiary Faiveley Transport.

Faiveley Transport was in at the ground floor of a new revolution in railroading. The company helped equip the new line of TGV trains ("trains à grande vitesse" or high-speed trains) commissioned by the SNCF. Faiveley's pantograph designs were to play a significant role in the achievement of a new train speed record—515.3 kilometers per hour set by the TGV Atlantique line in 1990. By then, the company was seeking to enter new markets, with mixed results. An attempt to enter the Japanese market was thwarted in 1987, when Faiveley saw the production of its equipment designs for the Shinkansen 300 line taken over by a Japanese constructor. Faiveley instead began to develop a new strategy based on diversification. As a company representative told La Tribune, "Not being cautious enough, we let the production run get away from us."

Diversified Manufacturing for the 21st Century

The company moved its headquarters to Saint-Pierre-des-Corps in 1991. In that year, it invested in expanding its electronics production facilities, building a new plant in La Ville-aux-Dames. The following year, Faiveley determined to gain a measure of protection against the cyclical nature of its core industry and especially the growing awareness that the railroad market was soon to tighten, with the privatization of most of Europe's formerly government-run railroad systems and the introduction of more severe pricing restrictions and heightened competition among equipment suppliers. At the same time, the SNCF's heavy investments in launching the TGV trains were coming to an end, and spending was expected to diminish through the middle of the decade.

In 1992, the company took its first step toward building a new pole of operations, when it acquired plastics product maker Grand-Perret. Founded in 1875, Grand-Perret had first entered the plastics industry with the purchase of an injection press in 1948. The Grand-Perret acquisition was to be the first of several companies that added some FFr 200 million to the company's sales, which by then neared FFr 800 million.

In 1993, Faiveley moved to concentrate its activities around its historic core of railroad and transportation equipment and its brand new plastics division, selling off its Faiveley Automatismes subsidiary. At the same time, the company made a new, more successful attempt to move into the Japanese market, which had become one of the world's strongest markets for the new generation high-speed trains. This time Faiveley went in with a partnership with one of Japan's largest railroad equipment makers, forming the Nabco-Faiveley Ltd. joint venture and winning a contract to supply some 3,000 electronically controlled automated door systems—a first for Japan, which until then had seen only hydraulic systems—for the country's train system. That year, Faiveley launched its U.K. subsidiary, placing itself in a position to capture a share of that market as the British Rail system was being privatized.

Faiveley began to prepare for a more ambitious expansion in the late 1990s. In 1994, the company went public, selling some 30 percent of its shares on the Paris stock exchange. The Faiveley family, now led by François Faiveley, nonetheless retained solid control of their company's stock. The listing enabled the company to pay down debt and to go on a bit of a spending spree, especially to boost its plastics division.

In 1995, the company acquired VPI-Verchère Plastiques Industriels, founded in the 1930s and originally focused on products using bakelite, before turning to thermo-injected plastics. The following year, Faiveley added the operations of Rhône Moulage and Sepal, Ltd. Both Lyon-area companies had been led by Horst Bilger, who remained CEO of these operations after their acquisition by Faiveley. These two companies added another FFr 100 million to Faiveley's annual sales, which by then had topped FFr 1.3 billion. By the end of the decade, plastics had risen to nearly 20 percent of Faiveley's total sales.

Although the company continued to book steady gains in annual turnover, its acquisition binge gave it a nasty case of indigestion in the late 1990s. Chiefly responsible for the company's profits drop was its 1995 acquisition of German railroad air conditioning specialist Hagenuk Fahrzeugklima, from parent company Siemens, for FFr 120 million. The purchase gave Faiveley an important foothold into the German railroad equipment market, Europe's largest, as well as the leading position worldwide in the air conditioning segment. Yet Hagenuk and its subsidiary operations were in dire need of restructuring. By 1997, the acquisition had begun to drain Faiveley's profits, and the company was forced to post a net loss for 1998.

The result was a restructuring of Faiveley's management as well, as François Faiveley stepped in to take the chairman's seat, dismissing Alain Bodel, who had been the architect of the group's expansion since the 1980s, and appointing Robert Joyeux as CEO in his stead. The company embarked on a restructuring of its operations on a wider scale, including cutting out some 40 percent of its German workforce and a number of jobs from its French manufacturing facilities as well. Faced with a shrinking market, especially shrinking margins in its traditional European base, Faiveley stepped up its international expansion abroad. In 1997, the company launched a new subsidiary in the United States, Faiveley Rail Inc., based in Pennsylvania. The company also boosted its activities in the Asian markets. The Hagenuk acquisition, while proving a temporary burden, also had given it a subsidiary in China, Shanghai Hagenuk Refrigerating Machine Co. Ltd., which held some 50 percent of that potentially vast market. The company also opened a subsidiary in Hong Kong.

Faiveley's continued investments in research and development kept the company at the leading edge of its industry. The company debuted its innovative "black box" systems, similar to those used in airplanes, adapted to the needs of railroads. This product received a warm welcome, particularly from Italy's rail system, which put in an order for nearly 2,500 boxes, worth more than FFr 240 million. Faiveley's German arm, meanwhile, completed a new generation air conditioning system commissioned by the German rail system, based on cycled air, eliminating the highly polluting systems typically found in trains. Still held at more than 62 percent by the Faiveley family, the company looked forward to equipping the world's trains in the 21st century.

Principal Subsidiaries

Faiveley Transport; Sofaport; Faiveley Española S.A. & Transequipos; Faiveley Italia Spa; Faiveley UK Limited; HFG-Hagenuk Faiveley Gmbh (Germany); HFG-Shanghai Hagenuk Refrigerating Machine Co. Ltd (China); Faiveley Far East Ltd. (Hong Kong); NFL-Nabco Faiveley Ltd. (Japan); Equipfer Faiveley Ltda (Brazil); Faiveley Rail Inc. (U.S.).

Principal Competitors

ALSTOM; AMSTED Industries Inc.; Ansaldo Signal N.V.; Bombardier Inc.; Bunzl plc; Siemens Corporation; Wabtec Corporation.

Further Reading

Bonneau, Cécile, "Faiveley Transport se remet sur les rails," *L'Usine Nouvelle,* September 14, 2000.

Carrot, Jérémie, "Faiveley plonge dans le rouge," *La Tribune,* July 20, 1999.

De Jaegher, Thibaut, "Les bôites noires de Faiveley équiperont les trains italiens," *L'Usine Nouvelle,* July 6, 2000.

"Faiveley s'introduit au second marché le 8 septembre," *Les Echos,* August 23, 1994, p. 12.

"Faiveley veut développer son pôle plasturgie," *Les Echoes,* July 5, 1996, p. 12.

Farhi, Stéphane, "Ferroviaire Faiveley cherche à se diversifier," *L'Usine Nouvelle,* September 1, 1994.

Lambert, Xavier, "Les équipementiers français s'imposent au Japon," *La Tribune,* January 11, 1995.

—M.L. Cohen

Farm Family Holdings, Inc.

344 Route 9W
Glenmont, New York 12077
U.S.A.
Telephone: (518) 431-5000
Fax: (518) 431-5975
Web site: http://www.farmfamily.com

Public Company
Incorporated: 1996
Employees: 469
Total Assets: $1.1 billion (1999)
Stock Exchanges: New York
Ticker Symbol: FFH
NAIC: 524126 Direct Property and Casualty Insurance
Carriers

Farm Family Holdings, Inc. is a holding company that was formed in 1996 as part of a plan to convert Farm Family Mutual Insurance Company from a mutual property and casualty insurance company to a stockholder-owned company. Headquartered in Glenmount, New York, the principal subsidiaries of Farm Family (Farm Family Casualty Insurance Company and Farm Family Life) were sponsored originally by the Farm Bureau organizations of several northeastern states in the 1950s. Farm Family continues to maintain close ties to the Farm Bureau organizations. It pays an annual $15 fee per Farm Bureau member for the right to utilize Farm Bureau membership lists in ten of the 12 states in which the company operates and the authority to use the Farm Bureau names and service marks in connection with the marketing of the company's insurance products. Farm Family and the New York Farm Bureau also share office space, and the chairman of the board of directors of Farm Family Holdings, Clark W. Hinsdale III, is also the president and a director of the Vermont Farm Bureau. A majority of Farm Family directors are directors or executive officers of Farm Bureau organizations. Membership in a Farm Bureau organization is a prerequisite for purchasing coverage with Farm Family Casualty, but membership generally can be sought by anyone with an ''interest'' in agriculture.

Farm Bureau Movement Origins in the Early 1900s

The history of Farm Family Holdings is very much a part of the Farm Bureau movement and the dozens of insurance companies created by the state organizations that today generate some $6.5 billion in annual revenues. The first county farm bureau was established in 1911 in the Binghamton, New York Chamber of Commerce to sponsor an extension agent from the U.S. Department of Agriculture. The tag ''bureau'' soon was applied to state farming organizations. By 1919, 500 members representing state farm bureaus (or representing states that were in the process of organizing) gathered in Chicago to form a national organization that would become the American Farm Bureau Federation (AFBF). More commonly, the organization became known as the Farm Bureau.

From its inception, the Farm Bureau faced the question of what was to be its focus: education or commerce. According to Orville Menton Kile in his book *The Farm Bureau Through Three Decades,* ''Those who favored active business operations wanted heavy fees and a big budget; the advocates of the purely educational type of organization not only felt that a big fund was not needed, but that its existence would be a constant temptation to embark upon commercial pursuits.''

One of the earliest commercial ventures pursued by individual state farm bureaus was auto insurance, as a ''service to member'' operation. The pioneer in this field was the founder of State Farm Insurance, George Mecherle of Bloomington, Illinois. He created a mutual insurance company for rural and small town drivers who in the early 1920s were paying higher premiums even though they had fewer accidents than drivers in more urban areas. By linking insurance rates to risk levels, Mecherle was able to offer significantly lower premiums than his competitors. He also signed agreements with state farm bureaus, which would receive a fee for each of their members who purchased policies. Some state farm bureaus took Mercherle's lead and formed their own mutual auto insurance companies: Ohio in 1926, Illinois in 1927, and New Hampshire in 1928. Not only did insurance generate revenue for the farm bureaus, it acted as an inducement for membership.

In the words of an early Farm Bureau insurance executive, Murray Lincoln, quoted in *Dollar Harvest,* ''When we first

> ## Company Perspectives:
>
> *Over the years, Farm Family has earned a solid reputation, with an established tradition of trust. Farm Family agents are insurance professionals who recognize that personal service is the key to meeting individual and business concerns.*

started our insurance company, it never dawned on me that we would ever insure anyone but farmers. But once we started insuring farmers other than Farm Bureau members, we found that we simply could not keep out the barber in the small town, the grocer, the gas station attendant, the shopkeeper, or any other type of small businessman. Finally, as our company grew, we had to throw out the window the concept of restricting our insurance only to farmers.'' Expanding in a similar manner, state Farm Bureaus began sponsoring insurance companies that also sold fire, casualty, and life insurance policies.

Affiliation with the Farm Bureau proved to be a powerful selling tool. According to *Dollar Harvest,* ''When a Farm Bureau insurance agent knocks on the door in many areas of the country, he immediately has the respectability of the organization working for him. If the man or woman who answers the door is not a member himself, perhaps his father was, or maybe his son is active in a 4-H club which meets in the Farm Bureau building. In any case, the image is not the same as that presented by other insurance companies, and image is all-important in the sale of insurance.'' Because so many county agricultural agents also sold Farm Bureau memberships and Farm Bureau products, the private state Farm Bureau organizations gained quasi-governmental status. Many people even assumed that the Farm Bureau was in fact a government agency. Across the country, Farm Bureau insurance companies flourished. The Ohio Farm Bureau Mutual Automobile Insurance Company founded in 1926 would, 30 years later, elect to drop ''Farm Bureau'' and coin a new corporate name to expand into states that already had Farm Bureau insurance companies. The name chosen was Nationwide Insurance.

Launching the Farm Family Insurance Companies in 1953

In 1953 the Farm Bureaus of seven northeastern states sponsored the creation of the Farm Family Life Insurance Company. Then on April 21, 1955, with the help of AFBF, the Farm Bureaus of New York, New Jersey, Delaware, West Virginia, Connecticut, Rhode Island, Vermont, New Hampshire, Massachusetts, and Maine sponsored what would become the lead entity of the Farm Family Insurance Companies: Farm Family Mutual Insurance Company, incorporated under the laws of the state of New York. On November 16, 1956, Farm Family Mutual began business, working together with Farm Family Life and sharing office facilities with the New York Farm Bureau in Glenmount, New York. In 1988 Farm Family Life created a subsidiary, United Farm Family Insurance Company, to serve as a reinsurer for Farm Family Mutual.

The reputation of the Farm Bureau and its network of businesses was tarnished in 1967 when ranking New York Congress-

man Joe Resnick, chairman of a subcommittee of the House Agriculture Committee, began to question the practices of the Farm Bureau. After his House colleagues refused to look further into the Farm Bureau, Resnick held his own public hearings across the country. After his death, his aide Samuel R. Berger, who would become National Security Adviser to President Clinton, compiled the information for publication in *Dollar Harvest.* Berger charged, ''The Farm Bureau is far more than simply an organization of farmers, as it so often claims. The nation's biggest farm organization has been quietly but systematically amassing one of the largest business networks in America. . . . The Farm Bureau empire now spans the economy: from insurance to oil, from fertilizer to finance companies, from mutual funds to shopping centers. . . . The Farm Bureau claims it is in business simply to provide 'services to its members.' But the Farm Bureau business activities now clearly dominate the organization. . . . Over the years the farmer has increasingly become customer, not constituent to the Farm Bureau.'' In short, Berger claimed, ''The Farm Bureau has become a giant, self-serving bureaucracy,'' and ''Membership has become little more than a device through which Farm Bureau products are sold.''

Despite the unwelcome notoriety, the Farm Bureau and its affiliated businesses, such as the Farm Family insurance companies, continued to prosper. The largest line of business for Farm Family was auto insurance, comprising about 40 percent of the group's total. The company's ''flagship product,'' and second largest line, would become its ''Special Farm Package '10','' which combined personal, farm, and business property and liability insurance for farm owners and other agricultural related businesses. In 1983 Farm Family Life entered the flexible premium/benefit market with its Family Universal Life Policy. United Farm Family expanded beyond reinsurance to engage in limited, direct underwriting operations in 1993.

In November 1995, the Farm Family Insurance Companies reached a turning point when the chief executive officer of the group, Philip P. Weber, announced that Farm Family Mutual would convert from a mutual property and casualty insurer into a stockholder-owned company. Although the company had been growing, to reach the next level Farm Family Mutual contended that it needed access to additional capital that was difficult for a mutual to raise. To accomplish the demutualization plan, a holding company was formed, Farm Family Holdings, Inc. Policyholders, who legally were the owners of Farm Family Mutual, then would receive shares of common stock in the holding company, pending a review by the New York State Insurance Department and approval from policyholders. Farm Family Holdings then planned to make a public offering of its stock. What would happen to Farm Family Life and United Farm Family was not addressed at the time, but at a later date Weber indicated that he hoped to eventually bring the sister companies into the fold.

Farm Family faced some opposition to its conversion plans during the only public hearing held in April 1996. Whereas Weber testified that the conversion would provide immediate benefits to policyholders, those opposed to the plan complained that the policyholders' meeting was scheduled during planting season and also expressed concerns that the best interests of policyholders might conflict with the best interests of stock owners. The Center for Insurance Research, a consumer watch-

Key Dates:

1919: Farm Bureau is established as a national organization.
1926: Ohio State Farm Bureau begins selling insurance.
1953: Northeastern Farm Bureaus establish Farm Family Life Insurance.
1955: Farm Family Mutual Insurance Company is established.
1988: United Farm Family is created as a subsidiary of Farm Family Life.
1996: Farm Family Mutual converts to stock ownership and becomes a subsidiary under newly created Farm Family Holdings, Inc.
1999: Farm Family Life and United Farm Family are purchased by Farm Family Holdings.
2000: Agreement is reached to sell Farm Family Holdings to American National Insurance Department.

dog group, sent a letter to state regulators claiming that Farm Family's management would profit personally from the conversion. Nevertheless, on May 1, New York State Superintendent of Insurance Edward J. Muhl approved the demutualization plan, stating that it was fair and equitable and in the best interests of policyholders.

Demutualization and 1996 Creation of Farm Family Holdings

A special meeting for policyholders of Farm Family Mutual was scheduled for June 17, 1996, to vote on the plan. It passed with 93 percent of the policyholders approving demutualization, with some 22,000 policyholders voting either in person or by proxy. Farm Family officials characterized the support as "overwhelming," and critics maintained that "7 percent against indicates a degree of policyholder cynicism." As part of the conversion, Farm Family Mutual changed its name to Farm Family Casualty Insurance Company and became a subsidiary of Farm Family Holdings.

In the midst of turbulent stock market conditions, Farm Family Holdings made a public offering of its stock in July 1996 and fell short of the expectations it expressed in papers filed with the Securities and Exchange Commission. Hoping to raise $54.3 million at $22 per share, the company actually raised $39.4 million at $16 per share. Trading on the New York Stock Exchange, however, Farm Family stock began to rise steadily in price.

In December 1996 Farm Family initiated moves to reduce expenses and make the company more competitive in the insurance marketplace. It offered early retirement to more than 60 employees, a plan that after an outlay of $600,000 would save the company as much as $225,000 a year. The company also changed retirement benefits to tie them closer to the company's profitability. Furthermore, Farm Family announced that it was looking into offering mutual funds and related financial products.

Almost 15 percent of Farm Family shares was sold in February 1997 to two of the country's largest investment companies:

Franklin Resources of San Mateo, California (eight percent), and Fidelity Management and Research Co. of Boston (6.36 percent). A spokesman with the Center for Insurance Research was quick to suggest that, as predicted, policyholders were losing control of their company. By the time Farm Family held its first annual meeting since converting from mutual to stock ownership, another large block of shares, 6.67 percent of the total, was sold to Gotham Partners L.P. and an affiliate. Other large holders of Farm Family stock included Crabbe Huson Small Cap Fund and the Crabbe Huson Group Inc. of Portland, Oregon, with 7.4 percent, and W.R. Berkley Corp. of Connecticut, with 5.18 percent. During this time, the price of Farm Family stock climbed from its initial $16 per share to almost $23 per share.

At the annual meeting a stock option plan for employees was approved, with executives allowed to buy 215,000 shares at no less than 85 percent of the stock's fair market price, in order to create financial incentives for management (officers and directors held less than 12,000 shares in the company). Weber alone would receive an option on 75,000 shares. The stock option plan for other employees did not include discounts. In addition, papers filed in connection with the meeting indicated that Weber's base salary increased by 18.75 percent over the previous year and that the directors awarded him a $114,000 bonus in connection with the initial public stock offering.

By October 1997 the price of Farm Family stock had risen to a 52-week high of $30.75. In December the company announced a tentative agreement to purchase Farm Family Life and its subsidiary United Farm Family for $37.5 million, pending approval from stockholders and members of several Farm Bureaus that were stockholders of Farm Family Life. It would be another 18 months before the transaction was finalized and all the Farm Family insurance companies could be brought together under the publicly traded holding company.

Farm Family reported 1997 profits of $18.9 million on revenues of $173.7 million, a significant improvement over 1996 when the company reported a $6.9 million profit on $146.9 million. In the proxy statement released before its April 1998 annual meeting, it was revealed that four investors now owned 28 percent of the company's stock, with the largest block, nearly ten percent, held by the FMR Corp. of Boston. The filing also indicated that Weber's total compensation was up 28 percent over the previous year, increasing from $403,090 in 1996 to $518,815 in 1997.

On January 1, 1998, the reinsurance agreement between Farm Family Casualty and United Farm Family was terminated. United Farm Family then expanded its direct underwriting operations, selling the product portfolio of Farm Family Casualty in Maryland and Pennsylvania, increasing Farm Family's reach from ten states to 12. It was not until April 1999 that the acquisition of Farm Family Life and United Farm Family was finalized.

In February 1999, Farm Family reported that 1998 earnings were up 6.7 percent over the previous year. It also continued cost-cutting measures, including the reduction of its extended earnings program for sales agents. Although the price of its stock dropped almost four percent during the first few months of

1999, it made a dramatic gain, almost 11 percent, when in July it was announced that Farm Family would be added to the Russell 2000 Index of small-capitalization of stocks.

Profits declined slightly in 1999 compared with 1998, due to a one-time accounting change. Excluding that increase, Farm Family's operating income increased by 34 percent over the previous year. In April 2000, Farm Family held its annual meeting, and shareholders elected a new director to the company's board: Edward J. Muhl, the former New York State Superintendent of Insurance, who four years earlier had approved Farm Family's plan to demutualize.

Also in April 2000, charges against the Farm Bureau resurfaced on the CBS television show "60 Minutes." The implication of the story was that Farm Bureau–affiliated insurance companies conflicted with the Farm Bureau's tax-exempt status and that the group was more concerned about the plight of large agribusinesses than with family farms. In addition, Defenders of Wildlife, an environmental group founded in 1947 that was bitterly opposed to some of the policy positions of the Farm Bureau, issued a white paper called "Amber Waves of Gain," intended to be an update of *Dollar Harvest*. The report was especially critical of Farm Bureau–affiliated insurance companies such as Farm Family: "In many states, the nonprofit farm bureaus also own all or most of the stock of the insurance companies. And those stocks pay dividends to the state organizations. The farm bureaus also benefit from using insurance customers to inflate their membership members, since everyone who buys a policy must join the bureau. The insurance companies also benefit from the alliances. . . . state farm bureaus have lobbied hard for limits on medical malpractice damage awards. And AFBF is pushing for privatization of Social Security, which could bring a profit windfall to insurance company and financial investment firm ventures. Relating any of those issues to agriculture is a far stretch, but they certainly affect the Farm Bureau's bottom line."

In November 2000, Farm Family and American National Insurance Co. announced a merger, pending approval from the state Insurance Department and Farm Family shareholders. The $280 million transaction would make Farm Family a subsidiary of the larger Texas-based American National, allowing it to offer its agricultural insurance products in 46 states. Weber,

who would serve as CEO of the American National subsidiary, said, "It's a tremendous, tremendous opportunity for an organization like us." He assured Farm Family customers that they would continue to work with the same agents and, as a result of the merger, also could expect a wider variety of products. Also as a result of the merger, according to SEC filings, Weber would received a $2.8 million cash payment for unexercised Farm Family stock options and, 18 months after the merger, would be in line to receive a $1.8 million retention payment. Concerning the proposed merger, the chairman of Farm Family's board, Clark W. Hinsdale III, commented, "We didn't need to do this for any pressing reason, other than where we need to go in the future."

Principal Subsidiaries

Farm Family Casualty Insurance Company; Farm Family Life Insurance Company; Farm Family Financial Services, Inc.; Rural Agency and Brokerage, Inc.

Principal Competitors

State Farm Insurance Companies; Merchants Group Inc.; Erie Indemnity Co.; Allstate Corporation.

Further Reading

Aaron, Kenneth, "Merger Extends Insurer's Reach," *Times Union,* November 2, 2000, p. E1.

Berger, Samuel R., *Dollar Harvest,* Lexington, Mass.: Heath Lexington Books, 1971.

"Consumer Watchdog Attacks Farm Family Plan to Go Public," *Times Union,* April 24, 1996.

Defenders of Wildlife, "Amber Waves of Gain," white paper, April 2000.

"Defenders of Wildlife Report: Farm Bureau Hurts Those It Claims to Help," *U.S. Newswire,* April 10, 2000.

"Farm Family CEO Defends Plan to Shift to Stock Company," *Times Union,* April 3, 1996, p. B9.

—Ed Dinger

Fleury Michon S.A.

BP1
Route de la Gare
85707 Pouzauges Cedex
France
Telephone: (+33) 02 51 66 32 32
Fax: (+33) 02 51 65 82 33
Web site: http://www.fleurymichon.fr

Public Company
Incorporated: 1934
Employees: 3,084
Sales: EUR 365.37 million ($311.83 million) (2000)
Stock Exchanges: Euronext Paris
Ticker Symbol: FLE
NAIC: 311 Food Manufacturing 311991 Perishable Prepared Food Manufacturing

Located in the Vendée, in the northwestern region of France, Fleury Michon S.A. produces self-service delicatessen and other packaged meat products, such as patés, and ready-to-cook meals for the Fremch consumer supermarket and restaurant markets. With sales at EUR 365 million in sales, Fleury Michon is one of France's leaders in its industry and counts among the most well-known brand names. Not content to have found its way to the consumer's stomach at home, Fleury Michon has launched two other initiatives: the first is a vending machine, much like those that sell canned soft drinks, that provides ready-to-eat meals in only 60 seconds. Aimed at businesses with 50–100 employees, as well as at such locations as passenger trains, the vending machines were launched in 2000. Fleury Michon has also launched its own restaurant concept, Graine d'Appétit, where diners can choose among Fleury Michon's packaged meals—the same ones sold in supermarkets—that the buyer then heats and serves at home. The first Graine d'Appétit in Nantes has met with strong success, with per-day sales tripling those at a typical supermarket. Future Graine d'Appétit restaurants are being planned for Paris, London, and Frankfurt. The company also provides salads for the Quick fast-food restaurant chain. Fleury Michon went public at the beginning of 2000, listing on the Euronext Paris secondary market. The company is paying increasing attention to the international market. Fleury Michon is already present in Poland, the Czech Republic, and Hungary, where it operates a string of 50 "French-style" fast-food restaurants. While these restaurants bear little relation to the company's French products, Fleury Michon hopes to use its growing brand recognition to launch its lunch meats and packaged meals in these countries. Meanwhile, the company is entering partnership agreements in Italy and Spain to import its products to these countries. These activities should help boost the share of international sales in the company's revenues, which stood at just four percent in 1999. The primary revenue generator for the company remains its packaged meats, which account for 55 percent of sales, with prepared meals accounting for 40 percent of sales. Fleury Michon is led by Yves Gonnord; the company continues to be majority controlled by the founding families.

Butcher in the 1920s

Established in 1926 by brothers-in-law Pierre Fleury and Gustave Michon, the Fleury Michon company originally operated as a butcher in its Vendée region. In 1934, the pair extended their retail operations to include delicatessen meats, dried sausages, and other prepared meats. Fleury Michon saw an opportunity to expand its operations in the late 1940s, as it began to produce custom-cut delicatessen products. The company turned to new production methods, beginning its conversion from artisan to industrial food producer.

A boost to the company's growth came in the late 1950s. In 1957, Fleury Michon was the first in France to offer prepackaged cold cuts. The company's sausages and hams quickly found their way on a growing number of grocer's shelves. The development of France's supermarket—and then massive hypermarkets—in the 1960s helped spur demand for Fleury Michon's products. The company responded in 1964 with the launch of a new line of self-service packaged foods. By the end of the 1960s, the company built a new factory, in Chantonnay, to support its future expansion.

Fleury Michon was quick to recognize changing consumer food habits, even in France, where the three-hour lunch remained something of a tradition. As more and more women joined the workforce, families found themselves with less time to prepare meals. Fleury Michon anticipated this trend with the launch of a line of fresh, precooked, self-service meals, offering an attractive alternative to the frozen dinner. Launched in 1974, the company's packaged meals were to take the company into a new direction at the beginning of the next decade. Meanwhile, as it closed out the decade, Fleury Michon entered another promising market, that of providing fresh-cooked meals to the restaurant market.

Brand Name Specialist in the 1980s

At the beginning of the 1980s, Fleury Michon prepared to take its operation to a grander scale. The company defined an ambitious strategy of redefining its operations. Abandoning the last of its butchering operations, while also exiting a number of other sectors, including conserves and slaughtering, the company determined to place its future in its two fastest-growing segments, that of packaged delicatessen meats and prepackaged meals to the supermarket and restaurant markets, aiming to achieve leadership status in both product categories. Leading the company's charge into the future was Yves Bonnord, who had entered the company in 1961 after marrying the granddaughter of one of the company's founders. Bonnord took over the company's leadership from his father-in-law in 1981.

The following year, the company launched an entirely new line of fresh, pre-cooked self-service meals in France's supermarkets and hypermarkets. Supporting the rollout of the "new" Fleury Michon was a sponsorship contract with Philippe Poupon, one of France's champion sailboat racers. The Fleury Michon-Poupon partnership helped build Fleury Michon into one of the best-known brand names in the country. The company also continued to build its infrastructure to support its growing sales. In 1983, the company inaugurated a new state-of-the-art sausage production line in Chantonnay, giving its one of the most modern such facilities in Europe.

Fleury Michon struck a marketing coup in 1987 when it entered a collaboration agreement with renowned French chef Joel Robuchon (the only chef in the world to have patented a cooking process). Together with Robuchon, the company began creating a new series of recipes, finding immediate success with the French consumer. At the same time, the company was investigating a new market—that of surimi, a crab-flavored fish product made popular in Japan. In 1990, the company became one of the first in Europe to open its own surimi production facility. The following year, the company opened four new production facilities to support its growing sales, in Vernoux en Vivrarais, Boffres, Villefranche de Rouergue, and Auzances. Fleury Michon was also preparing to open a new 10,000-square-meter facility in Monifaut that was to give a huge boost to the company's production capacity.

International in the 21st Century

In 1991, the company took its first step outside of France, when it opened its first "French-style" fast-food restaurant in Cracow, Poland. Although the restaurant had little direct relation to the company's main products, Fleury Michon hoped nonetheless to popularize its brand name in Eastern Europe. The success of the first restaurant led the company to expand the concept into a chain of more than 40 restaurants in Poland, before moving into the Czech Republic and then Hungary, later in the decade. These operations nevertheless remained a small part of the company's overall sales.

In 1992, Fleury Michon attempted to take itself to a new level when it acquired the Olida company, and its Cochonou brand, beating out a number of larger competitors, including Nestlé's Herta subsidiary. The acquisition doubled Fleury Michon's size overnight and gave it Olida's strong position in the market for dried sausages. Yet Olida, losing some one million francs per day, nearly sank Fleury Michon. After struggling to turn around Olida's troubled operations, Fleury Michon's losses mounted to nearly FFr 300 million less than a year after the acquisition. At last, Gonnord was forced to admit, to *Capital*: "We didn't realize that was no possible synergy between our two companies."

Loaded with debt, Gonnord began to consider opening the family-owned company to outside investors. At last, in 1993, the company sold off most of the Olida operations, including the Cochonou brand name, and reorganized its operations to focus almost exclusively on its delicatessen and packaged-meal products. The company also revised its marketing program, ending its long relation with Poupon (the company continued a limited sponsorship of Poupon, however) to focus its advertising efforts on the television and other media markets. Fleury Michon also continued its industrial investment program, spending some FFr 300 million to modernize its production, logistics, and distribution facilities.

The company's investments continued into the mid-decade, with the inauguration of a state-of-the-art computerized logistics system at Fleury Michon's Pouzauges site. The company also transferred its surimi production to a new facility in Mouilleron, while moving its de-boning facility to Montifaut. The company also began a series of small-scale acquisitions, including a bakery operation, specialized in pizzas and quiches for private label brands, renamed as Société Albigeoise de Panification, and high-end delicatessen meats producer Henri Le Hir.

Joining the company in 1995 was Frédérick Bouisset, who had previously worked for Nestlé and Bongrain, two of Fleury Michon's top competitors. Bouisset was charged with leading the company into new markets. One such market was found through a 1996 agreement with Weight Watchers to make "lite" salads for the diet-product specialist. The company entered a similar agreement in 1999 to provide salads for fast-food chain Quick, headquartered in Belgium and one of the leaders in the French fast food market. In 1997, Fleury Michon also launched a new line of food products featuring the Joel Robuchon name. Within months after its launch, the first of the Robuchon-devised products, a duck paté, had captured one-third of its market.

Toward the end of the decade, the company—which had been recognized as one of France's leading brand names—began to eye means for bringing its name and products to its European neighbors. In 1998, the company entered a production and distribution agreement for southern Europe with the companies Navidul in Spain and Beretta in Italy. The first of Fleury Michon's meals for the Italian market were launched in the year 2000. The company was meanwhile focusing on the quiche and pizza business, selling off its shares in Société Albigeoise de Panification to the United Kingdom's Hazlewood Foods in 2000.

At the same time, Fleury Michon was entering another new promising market, catering, and particularly the fast-food and lunch segments, albeit taking a different approach to these growing segments—as average French lunch times had dropped from one hour in the mid-1980s to just 35 minutes in the 1990s. In 1998, the company began development of a vending machine capable of serving one of its meals in just 60 seconds. By 2000, the company was ready to launch its vending machine, targeted at companies with between 50 and 100 employees—larger companies tended to have their own cafeterias or other food services, while smaller companies could not generate the volume sufficient to pay back the purchase cost of the machine. The company also hoped to place the machines in other high-traffic areas, such as passenger trains and food markets; the machine also seemed an ideal companion to the offices of the "startup" sector, given the typical fast-pace and long working hours of these businesses.

Industry analysts greeted another Fleury Michon initiative with enthusiasm as well. At the beginning of 2000, the company opened its first fast-food restaurant, Graine d'Appétit, in the city of Nantes. Calling the concept "assisted self-service," the new restaurant featured the variety of Fleury Michon meals—the same found in supermarkets—which a diner could then purchase and have prepared and served at a table. The first Graine d'Appétit was an instant success, quickly tripling the daily volume of sales of a typical supermarket. Fleury Michon began plans to roll out the Graine d'Appétit concept in Paris, while also taking the restaurant outside of France, with initial plans to open restaurants in London and Frankfurt.

To support this new expansion, Fleury Michon finally went public in 2000, listing the company's stock on the Euronext Paris Secondary Market. Although the original founding families continued to control 68 percent of the company's stock, Fleury Michon was preparing nonetheless for a different kind of revolution. In 2000, Yves Bonnord, preparing for his retirement in 2001, announced his intention to name Frédérick Bouisset as his successor, marking the first time in the company's history that Fleury Michon will not be led by a member of the founding families. Yet as architect of much of Fleury Michon's expansion in the second half of the 1990s, Bouisset seemed certain to maintain the company's tradition of strong growth into the 21st century.

Principal Divisions

Fleury Michon Charcuterie; Fleury Michon Traiteur; Fleury Michon Logistique; Fleury Michon Poland; Fleury Michon Czech Republic; Fleury Michon Hungary.

Principal Competitors

Nestlé S.A.; Bongrain S.A., Madrange S.A.; Martinet S.A.; Bonoduelle S.A.

Further Reading

Guélaud, Claire, "Les Filières du Bocage," *Les Echos,* July 1, 1997, p. 72.

Legrand, Constance, "Fleury Michon Ose le Distributeur Automatique de Plats Chauds," *Les Echos*, May 5, 2000, p. 75.

Piétralunga, Cédric, "Les Recettes Gnantes de Fleury Michon," *Capital*, July 2000, p. 46.

—M.L. Cohen

Follett Corporation

2233 West Street
River Grove, Illinois 60171-1895
U.S.A.
Telephone: (708) 583-2000
Toll Free: (800) 621-4345
Fax: (708) 452-9347
Web site: http://www.follett.com

Private Company
Incorporated: 1894
Employees: 8,000+
Sales: $1.42 billion (2000 est.)
NAIC: 451211 Book Stores; 42292 Book, Periodicals and
Newspaper Wholesalers; 51121 Software Publishers;
45321 Office Supplies and Stationery Stores; 334113
Computer Terminal Manufacturing

The Follett Corporation operates the largest chain of college and university bookstores in North America, sells books and audiovisual materials to elementary and high schools and libraries, and provides library automation software and consulting services. Augmenting the company's 625 stores, a national online textbook ordering site was launched in 1999. Headquartered in a suburb of Chicago, the company has been owned by members of the Follett family for over four generations.

19th-Century Origins

Follett family members were born and bred under the auspices of the printed word, a passion passed down through four generations from Follett's founder, Charles W. (C. W.) Follett. The history of the Follett Corporation may be traced to 1873, with a home-based bookstore located in Wheaton, Illinois. The homeowner and proprietor was the Rev. Charles M. Barnes, a scholarly man who used his private library as his initial inventory.

In 1901, 18-year-old C.W. Follett met and fell in love with Edythe Benepe, a Chicago reporter. Before the two could marry and begin a new life, however, Follett needed to find gainful employment in the Chicago area. He found a job with Charles Barnes, who hired him for a week to help move his bookselling business to another location in Chicago. After his week was up, Follett stayed on and worked as a stock clerk and salesman, learning the book business from the inside out while working alongside Barnes's son, William.

Though Barnes's tiny bookstore had grown rapidly since its homespun beginning in Wheaton, it had floundered in 1893 when the country was rocked by a recession. Needing capital, Barnes had turned to his wife's family and given up controlling interest. Subsequently, when the founder's son William Barnes married Blanche Wilcox, her father invested in the company, making the Wilcox family large shareholders. By 1899, the Barnes bookselling enterprise had bounced back from losses during the recession with sales in excess of $237,000. In 1902, just a year after C.W. Follett had joined the company, Charles Barnes retired, leaving William and William's father-in-law, John Wilcox, to mind the store. The business thrived under the direction of Wilcox and the younger Barnes until 1917, when William decided to relocate to New York to form a partnership with a gentleman named Noble. While the Barnes and Noble venture went on to make bookselling history, C.W. Follett was given an opportunity to pursue his own bookselling dreams.

When William Barnes left the company, Follett bought his shares and the bookstore was subsequently renamed J.W. Wilcox & Follett Company. In the preceding years, Follett had become head stock clerk and then made sales calls throughout the Midwest and beyond, so he was well-prepared for his new role. Wilcox died in 1923, and Follett purchased the Wilcox family's shares and shortened the company name to Wilcox & Follett.

Diversification Under a New Generations of Folletts

C.W. and Edythe Follett welcomed their first child in 1904, a son named Dwight. Three more sons soon followed: Garth, Robert, and Charles ("Laddie"). In the 1920s, Follett's four sons joined the business and pushed the company into new fields. Garth started a wholesale business to serve libraries, which later became known as Follett Library Resources; Robert began a business wholesaling college textbooks, out of which grew Follett Campus Resources and Follett College Stores; Dwight created an elementary textbook publishing operation. Charles "Laddie" Follett, the youngest son, worked within

Company Perspectives:

Follett Corporation is the foremost provider of materials, technology and ideas to the education marketplace. On campus, in schools and in public libraries around the globe and via the limitless realm of cyberspace, Follett enables students, educators and administrators to capitalize on the explosion in information access. Through our various operating units, we serve students, parents, bookstores, teachers, and professors, as well as publishers, school administrators, school and public librarians and consumers—every one with a vested interest in advancing learning skills and enhancing the educational experience.

Wilcox & Follett's core business. For the remainder of the 1920s and into the 1930s, the company continued to grow and diversify its bookselling; even the Great Depression did little to stem its expansion.

Over the next two decades, a third generation of Folletts began joining the company, helping to fuel its continued growth. These family members included: Charles R. Follett, Sr., Garth's son, who built the company's library wholesaling business and eventually retired; Ross C. Follett, Laddie's son, who eventually headed up Follett Library Resources; Kent A. Follett, Laddie's eldest son, who would head up Follett Educational Services; and Richard A. Waichler, who married Dwight Follett's daughter Nancy and would eventually serve as vice-president of operations.

On December 19, 1952, C.W. Follett passed away at age 69, after 51 years in the book industry. Eldest son Dwight Follett was tapped to succeed his father. During the 1950s, three new family members who would eventually converge in the executive suite joined the company.

First, Dwight's eldest child and only son, R.J.R. Follett, started his career as an editor for Follett Publishing Company in 1951 after graduating from Brown University and taking postgraduate courses at Columbia University. Like his grandfather before him, R.J.R. learned the business by holding a myriad of positions, including copywriter, designer, editor-in-chief, marketing manager, and salesman, eventually rising to the corporation's executive offices. Second, P. Richard Litzsinger's association with the Folletts began with his 1954 marriage to Dona Lucy Follett (granddaughter of C.W. and daughter of Robert D.). After graduating from the University of Missouri with a double degree in accounting and finance and a three-year stint as an air force officer, Litzsinger began working at Follett in its retail stores division. Finally, Richard M. Traut joined the company in 1958, following his graduation from West Point and military service. While in the military, Traut married Charron, granddaughter of C.W. and daughter of Robert. Traut began his career with Follett in its textbook wholesaling division in 1958.

During this time, the company created a corporate parent and distinct subsidiaries with officers for each, and then relocated the entire operation to 1000 West Washington Boulevard in Chicago. At the time, the company was comprised of a retail division, a publishing company, and three wholesaling arms that dealt with libraries, colleges, and elementary, and high

school (El-Hi) markets. Follett's varied enterprises were only temporarily housed under one roof, however. Growth soon propelled several subsidiaries into the nearby suburbs.

Success With Books for Children in the 1960s

Follett made publishing history by developing the first racially integrated textbooks as well as the first textbook program for educationally disadvantaged children. Another milestone, its "JUST Beginning-to-Read" series, featured small-formatted books with lively illustrations and straightforward prose (often retelling classic fairy tales). This series proved very popular with teachers and first-time readers.

By the 1960s, Follett's three young leaders were on the move. Litzsinger was named Follett's retail stores supervisor in 1962; within four years he was president of Follett's college stores division. On the wholesale side of the business, Traut was named assistant general manager in 1965, and he would eventually take the reins of Follett Campus Resources as president in 1974. In 1968, R.J.R. Follett was named president of the publishing company and continued his own writing and publishing efforts. In 1977, R.J.R. succeeded his father, Dwight Follett, as chairman of the board, and Litzsinger was appointed president and CEO. This year also marked the founding of Apline Guild, an Oak Park-based publisher established by R.J.R. to produce business- and finance-related titles.

In 1977, Dwight Follett retired as president, and Litzsinger was named president and chief executive officer. Dwight remained as chairperson until 1979, when he was succeeded by son R.J.R. Follett. In 1982, Follett decided to shift gears slightly, selling its publishing division. "In the future, there will be room only for large publishing companies covering a broad spectrum with strong sales support, or for small companies filling a specialized niche," Follett told *Publishers Weekly* in December 1982, shortly before the sale. "Medium-sized companies are not going to be around," he added. Rather than run aground as a well-intentioned, medium-sized publisher (1982 revenues exceeded $13 million), Follett Publishing Company—a leader in social studies texts and critically acclaimed children's books—was sold to the Esquire Education Group in 1983.

Expanding the Bookstore Chain in the 1980s–90s

Using funds from its divestitures, Follett bought a chain of 35 college bookstores. With the acquisition of other bookstore management businesses, including Campus Services, Inc. and Brennan College Services, Follett became the country's largest operator of college bookstores.

The second generation of Litzsingers joined Follett in 1978, when Dick's son Mark arrived after completing his schooling at Texas Christian University. Beginning as a retail stores management trainee, the younger Litzsinger managed college bookstores at the University of Illinois at Champaign and Northwestern University before leaving retail to become director of corporate development. In 1989, Christopher Traut, Richard's son, came to Follett from Vanderbilt University and worked in the software division. In 1991, when Follett Collegiate Graphics was on the drawing board, Mark Litzsinger left his corporate post to head up the new division. Chris Traut then left Follett Software Company and replaced Mark as director of corporate

Key Dates:

1873: Rev. Charles Barnes founds a small bookstore in his Wheaton, Illinois, home.

1893: Barnes sells controlling interest in the store to his wife's family.

1901: Barnes hires 18-year old C.W. Follett to work in his new Chicago location.

1917: Barnes' son William sells his stake in the company to C.W. Follett.

1923: Follett purchases additional shares; company renamed Wilcox & Follett.

1930s: Company expands into book publishing and wholesaling.

1940s: Follett begins publishing children's books.

1952: C.W. Follett's son Dwight assumes control of the company upon his father's death.

1977: Dwight Follett retires and hands reins to his son R.J.R. Follett.

1983: Follett Publishing Company division sold to Esquire Education Group.

1999: Launch of efollett.com, an Internet-based textbook sales site.

development in 1992. Todd Litzsinger, Mark's brother, also worked for Follett, as midwestern regional marketing director for CAPCO, within the graphics division.

As the 1980s came to a close, Follett's college and El-Hi divisions continued to thrive by staying one step ahead of their competition. Using computers long before they were mainstream (starting in 1952 with an IBM punch-card sorting system), Follett eventually revolutionized the book industry with its software applications. The systems gave libraries and schools the ability to place and track orders and take inventory of their holdings with the touch of a button. In 1989, Follett introduced Tom-Tracks, a fully computerized college bookstore system for textbooks. By 1994, Follett had installed Tom-Tracks in over 500 other bookstores nationwide. Additionally, the company introduced FIRSTsystem (Follett Integrated Retail Systems Technology), a state-of-the-art, point-of-sale system for college bookstores that was fully integrated with an accounts payable system. The year 1989 also marked R.J.R. Follett's retirement as chairman. Richard M. Traut succeeded R.J.R., while P. Richard Litzsinger remained president and CEO.

Six Strong Divisions By the Mid-1990s

By 1995, after several incarnations and name changes, the Follett Corporation's six divisions were: Follett Educational Services, Follett Library Resources, and Follett Software Company, all of which catered to elementary and secondary school markets; and Follett Campus Resources, Follett College Stores, and Follett Collegiate Graphics, which served colleges and universities across the country.

The company's largest division was the bookstore chain. Follett College Stores (FCS), located in Elmhurst, Illinois, was the country's largest operator of college bookstores. With more than 450 stores in 46 states and Canada by 1995, FCS's nearly seven decades of experience in the field met the needs of over 200,000 faculty members and upwards of three million students. Follett's stores carried not only textbooks and stationery supplies, but popular sidelines like computer software, clothing, and music. The number of bookstores subsequently grew to 625 just five years later. Most were at smaller colleges, but also included were locations at such universities as Notre Dame, Purdue, and Mississippi State.

Follett Campus Resources (FCR), the company's second-largest division, had been run by George Carr since 1994, when he succeeded Richard M. Traut, who became chairman. Located in River Grove, FCR served 3,000 U.S. college bookstores (a number of which were managed by its sister division, Follett College Stores) in 1994, as both a wholesaler of new and used textbooks and as a provider of software applications for college store management via its automated textbook software system. FCR's used book services offered students discounted prices on their textbooks, and its retail systems helped college store managers operate more effectively and efficiently. FCR also produced the Follett Blue Book, the industry's premier wholesale pricing guide for more than 60 years, which featured over 90,000 available titles and was updated 11 times each year.

Follett Educational Services (FES), formerly Wilcox & Follett, was the oldest of the company's divisions, dating back to 1873, and was overseen by Kent A. Follett (grandson of C.W. Follett, son of Laddie). By 1994 FES had become the largest El-Hi provider of used textbooks and new workbooks in the industry, with more than 23,000 customers nationwide. FES's state-of-the-art automated inventory and tracking system contained upwards of 20,000 titles and holdings in excess of two million books. With its "zero-defects policy," FES gave schools the chance to save money and be environmentally conscious at the same time. FES had more than quadrupled in size over the preceding decade, to occupy a 65 percent share of the market.

Follett Library Resources (FLR), having serviced elementary and secondary school libraries for more than 50 years, entered both the high school and public library marketplace in the mid-1990s. Headed up by Ross C. Follett (the eldest son of Laddie), FLR was the largest distributor of books, videos, and CD-ROMs to elementary and high school libraries in the country. Supported by a growing selection of over 65,000 precatalogued titles available to its more than 45,000 clients (roughly 40 percent of the market), FLR delivered comprehensive processing and cataloguing services, automated bibliographic data, and a professional staff with the expertise to help school libraries select titles and build collections.

Follett Software Company (FSC) operated from offices in McHenry, Illinois, with Charles Follett, Jr. (son of Charles R. and great-grandson of C.W.) as president. This division had been founded in 1985. With annual sales topping $21 million in 1994 (up from 1993's $16 million), FSC was experiencing incredible growth as a provider of automated management systems to 20,000 school and smaller public libraries. FSC's ongoing research produced trademarked DOS programs including AlliancePlus, CardMasterPlus, CirculationPlus, Sneak PreviewsPlus, and TextbookPlus, as well as MacCatalog and MacCirculation Plus for Macintosh computers.

Follett Collegiate Graphics (FCG), was founded in 1992 and run by Mark Litzsinger. Taking full advantage of a void in the production of customized "coursepack" anthologies after the departure of the industry leader, Kinko's, FCG secured a substantial share of the $250 million national anthology market, which accounted for ten to 15 percent of the college textbook market. While FCG's subsidiary CAPCO (Custom Academic Publishing Company) handled copyright clearance and centralized printing operations for anthologies, a software program called CAPNET monitored the assembly process and paid the appropriate royalties. CAPCO was a joint venture with BMI Systems Inc., a Canon dealership in Oklahoma City. With the anthology market expected to top $500 million by 1997, FCG was exploring several alternatives to traditionally printed materials, including multimedia applications. In the latter half of the 1990s the division was renamed Follett Custom Publishing and expanded. Follett also bought out co-owner BMI Systems.

In 1998 the company's divisions were further reorganized and grouped into three larger business units. These were: the Elementary/High School Group (Follett Educational Services, Follett Software, Library Systems & Services); the Library Group (Book Wholesalers, Inc., Follett Audiovisual Resources, Follett Library Resources); and the largest, the Higher Education Group (the college bookstores, course pack publishing, CourseWorks and FirstSystem software systems, publishing and distribution of the Follett Blue Book and other promotional and marketing services). During the latter half of the 1990s the company also made several acquisitions, buying used book dealer Western Textbook Exchange and young adult book distributor Book Wholesalers.

1999 and Beyond

Follett was also experimenting with new bookstore concepts, opening a redesigned $4 million outlet in the fall of 1997 at the University of Illinois. The store featured a two-story "cyberwall" of television sets, an in-store café, Internet-connected computer stations for customers to "surf" on, plus clothing, music and software for sale. The café was designed in partnership with Lettuce Entertain You Enterprises, and Kinko's Copies was involved with the creation of an in-store publishing and copying center. Input also came from the designer of Planet Hollywood's theme restaurants, Associates in Architecture and Design, Ltd. A $5 million deal was signed the following year to build a new store at the University of Texas.

With the rise of the Internet, Follett began creating Web sites for many of its individual bookstores which allowed students to order course books ahead of time, avoiding the inconvenience of standing in line at the start of a semester. They could simply arrive at the store to find them already assembled, pay for them, and be on their way. Professors could also send the stores lists of their required texts over the Web. By the end of the 1990s several new startup companies, including VarsityBooks.com and BigWords.com, had launched online textbook sites that advertised discounts of up to 40 percent off list price. Follett responded in January 1999 with its own nationally advertised site, efollett.com. In addition to discounted prices, the new operation capitalized on the company's core store locations, offering students the convenience of easy pickup and returns at existing Follett stores. Efollett was also able to offer a steady stream of less expensive used textbooks drawn from the stores, which the competitors could not.

As the new century began, Follett continued on in solid shape. The combination of college bookstores, wholesaling, coursepack publishing, software and consulting services was a strong one, and the addition of an online sales site and splashy new bookstore designs brought the company completely up to date.

Principal Divisions

Book Wholesalers, Inc.; Follett Audiovisual Resources; Follett Educational Services; Follett Higher Education Group; Follett Library Resources; Follett Software Company; Library Systems & Services

Principal Competitors

Baker & Taylor Corporation; Barnes & Noble, Inc.; Borders Group, Inc.; Chapters, Inc.; D&H Distributing Company, Inc.; Data Research Associates, Inc.; Ecampus.com, Inc.; Educational Development Corporation; Ingram Industries, Inc.; Kinko's, Inc.; Nebraska Book Company, Inc.; Varsity Group, Inc.; Wallace's Bookstores.

Further Reading

Beiser, Karl, "CardMaster Plus," *Computers in Libraries,* May 1993, pp. 50–51.

Berss, Marcia, "A Family Affair," *Forbes,* March 27, 1995, p. 136.

Borden Jeff, "A Textbook Case: Campus Titan Follett Takes on Online Upstarts," *Crain's Chicago Business,* February 8, 1999, p. 3.

"Charles W. Follett" (obituary), *New York Times,* December 20, 1952, p. 17.

Christianson, Elin, review of *How to Keep Score in Business: Accounting and Financial Analysis for the Non-Accountant* by Robert Follett, *Library Journal,* August 1978, p. 1,504.

"The 500 Largest Private Companies in the U.S.," *Forbes,* December 5, 1994, p. 208.

Freeman, Laurie, "Bookstore Contract Boosts Revenues," *School Planning and Management,* January 1, 1997, p. 20F.

"General News: Follett Software Redesigns Products," *Online,* January 1994, p. 81.

"Leading Private Firms," *Crain's Chicago Business,* December 28, 1992, p. 5; December 26, 1994, p. 11.

"Management: Textbook Strategic System," *PC Week,* January 23, 1989, p. 48.

Miller, Cyndee, "Marketing Textbooks to the MTV Generation," *Marketing News,* October 13, 1997, p. 1.

"Projected Sale of Baker & Taylor to Follett Corp. Called Off," *Publishers Weekly,* June 27, 1994, p. 13.

Schmeltzer, John, "Used Books 101—A Course on Profit," *Chicago Tribune,* September 25, 1994.

St. Lifer, Evan, and Rogers, Michael, "Follett Ready to Finalize Deal for Baker & Taylor," *Library Journal,* June 15, 1994, p. 12.

"Software News: Follett Introduces Library Applications for the Macintosh," *Online,* January 1993, pp. 68–70.

Unsworth, Tim, "Tales from Chicago," *Publishers Weekly,* October 14, 1988, p. 44.

"The Week: Esquire, Inc. to Acquire Follett Publishing Division," *Publishers Weekly,* December 24, 1982, pp. 18–19.

—Taryn Benbow-Pfalzgraf
—update: Frank Uhle

Frankel & Co.

111 East Wacker Drive
Chicago, Illinois 60601-4507
U.S.A.
Telephone: (312) 552-5000
Fax: (312) 552-5400
Web site: http://www.frankel.com

Wholly Owned Subsidiary of Publicis Groupe S.A.
Incorporated: 1962 as Abelson-Frankel
Employees: 850
Sales: $95 million (2000 est.)
NAIC: 54181 Advertising Agencies; 54186 Direct Mail
    Advertising

Frankel & Co. is one of the leading marketing services firms in the United States. The company plans and executes marketing and promotional campaigns for a variety of top clients such as McDonald's, United Airlines, Frito-Lay, Visa, and the U.S. Postal Service. Notable Frankel successes include the creation of the McDonald's Happy Meal and Visa's "Read Me a Story" charitable campaign. Founded in 1962 by Bud Frankel and Marv Abelson, the company was sold in 2000 to French advertising giant Publicis Groupe S.A.

1960s Beginnings

The history of Frankel & Co. can be traced to 1962, when two men met while working in the promotion department of Kling Studios in Chicago. Bernard "Bud" Frankel had studied marketing at the University of Buffalo before moving to Chicago and working as a media representative for Concrete Publishing Co. Migrating to Kling, he took a position as an account representative. There he met production manager Marv Abelson, with whom he would work after Robert Snyder & Associates bought the company. Frankel later left for a job at William A. Robinson, Inc., where he was disappointed to find that his creative suggestions were being ignored. Looking for a better situation, he called Abelson and suggested the two form an independent promotions agency. Abelson-Frankel was soon established in Chicago to perform sales promotion work. Early clients of the new firm included electronics manufacturers Zenith and Admiral.

Within a year, Abelson-Frankel's offices were moved to a new location, and in 1965 the company hired a new creative director, John Forbes. The firm's business grew steadily throughout the 1960s. In 1969, Abelson-Frankel responded to the socially conscious atmosphere of the times by developing the first so-called "worthy cause" promotion. Instead of the usual prizes or coupons, client Clark Gum donated 2.5 cents to charity for each empty pack mailed in by the public. By this time the firm of Abelson-Frankel had more than 20 employees.

Another important relationship for Abelson-Frankel was begun in 1973 when Illinois-based fast food giant McDonald's Corporation engaged the company's services. A major success was achieved for the burger company three years later when a promotion tied to the Olympic games, "When the U.S. Wins, You Win," brought in record numbers of customers. McDonald's patrons were given a game piece that represented a particular Olympic event, and if the United States won that event, patrons could redeem the token for free food.

In 1979 Frankel staffers came up with a promotion that would have even more impact on the McDonald's bottom line and would soon enter the lexicon of American popular culture. This was the Happy Meal, a child-targeted combination of food and a giveaway toy that was an instant success with the public.

1980s: A Name Change to Frankel & Co.

In 1981 co-founder Marv Abelson left the firm to start a new company, Abelson-Taylor, which focused on healthcare clients. His ownership stake was bought by Bud Frankel, and the firm's name was changed to Frankel & Co. At the same time, a move to new headquarters on Wacker Drive was made. The company now had more than 100 employees and annual revenues of $5.7 million.

Bud Frankel's approach to the business was to focus on thoroughness. He felt that for his firm to best serve its clients, a working knowledge of the full range of a company's operations was necessary. To this end, Frankel staffers would study a client

Company Perspectives:

Smart brand marketing begins with an idea. At Frankel, we view our clients as partners, with the shared goal of delivering memorable, energized ideas into the global marketplace and making contact with consumers in the most effective way. Every time consumers connect with your products or services, it's a moment for selling. Whether it's breaking through the clutter at the point of sale, expanding your brand into the digital realm or creating one-to-one relationships with your customers, Frankel will help maximize every opportunity to attach meaning and value to your brand. A partnership with Frankel brings dedication and commitment to your business needs. We recruit the smartest and most creative people in the marketing industry. Right from the start, you will be confident that your brand is in the best hands and that it will enjoy an enduring relationship with consumers.

from top to bottom before planning a promotion. For McDonald's, this meant that many Frankel staffers attended that company's famed "Hamburger U" and even drove trucks and made sales calls. As Frankel told *Advertising Age,* "You can't design something without being intimately involved [and being] sensitive to the needs of the trade. . . . It's essential to know everything we can and we've spent a lot of time learning the client's business." Some companies were hesitant to allow complete access to all areas of their operations, and it occasionally took a certain amount of persuasion to convince the owners of the value of this approach.

During the 1980s Frankel & Co. continued to grow and add clients. In 1986 the company opened a branch office in Southern California. New relationships were established with Ford Heavy Trucks in 1986 and United Airlines and Federal Express in 1987. A popular promotion would later bring United together with McDonald's, via the "Friendly Skies Meal" that featured a burger, chips, and a toy.

Bud Frankel, who had been serving as president and CEO, turned over the presidency to Jim Mack in 1988. The following year saw Frankel & Co. named *Advertising Age* magazine's "Agency of the Year," and Bud Frankel become the first person inducted into the Council of Sales Promotion Agencies' Hall of Fame. The *Advertising Age* honor was based on three recent Frankel campaigns. These included a direct mail business builder for Federal Express, a proof-of-purchase redemption plan for Scott Paper that rewarded schools with free equipment, and a campaign for Visa called "Our Treat" in which the credit card firm paid for randomly selected purchases of its cardholders. The latter promotion required Frankel staffers to handle a number of specialized tasks, including the creation of proprietary computer software as well as establishing relationships with the numerous banks that issued Visa cards. Frankel & Co. took care of all of these details for its clients, who had now grown to include such major names as Ameritech, Hallmark Cards, G. Heileman Brewing Co., Kellogg Co., and Planter's Nuts.

The promotion marketing business had changed dramatically in the nearly three decades since the company was founded. New consumer products as well as variations on older ones were being introduced at a rapid pace, and advertising "clutter" was raising the bar for marketers' attempts to reach their targets. Consumers were also continually becoming more sophisticated and were increasingly able to either see through hype-filled ad campaigns or to ignore them altogether. Additionally, recent technological changes had made managing promotions much more complicated, while simultaneously offering myriad new channels for communication. The development of the free-standing newspaper insert full of colorful ads and coupons, television "watch and win" sweepstakes, telemarketing campaigns, couponing systems that utilized checkout scanner data, and more all came into existence during Frankel's first 30 years. In the early 1990s, the Internet was not yet a factor, but it too would add many new wrinkles in just a few short years. In addition to these changes, the overall goal of promotions marketing had evolved from simply drumming up more business to functioning as an essential part of a company's overall brand-building and market share boosting mix.

Continued Growth in the 1990s

In 1991 vice-president David Tridle was named co-president and chief operating officer, with Bud Frankel stepping back to serve as chairman. The following year the company celebrated its 30th anniversary and reached record sales of $22.4 million. Many more clients were added to the fold including Target Stores, Nestlé, and Hunt-Wesson. Frankel now employed more than 250 people.

In 1993 the company launched a campaign in conjunction with Baxter Healthcare that targeted patients in hospitals. Seven million coupon booklets were distributed as part of a standard admissions kit that Baxter handed out across the United States. The coupons were for health-oriented products made by companies such as Colgate-Palmolive. The admissions kits had previously contained free samples of such items as soap and hand lotion, but this was the first time that coupons were included.

The following year Frankel became the "agency of record" for Eastman Kodak's promotions of film, cameras, and photofinishing. In 1995 both Microsoft Corp. and the U.S. Postal Service engaged Frankel to work on promotional campaigns. At this time the company also opened a full-service office in San Francisco which employed a staff of 15. Initially devoted to working for one client only—Visa—the office soon took on other assignments. Frankel also hired Editel-Chicago president Richard Mandeberg to serve as vice-president for electronic marketing, spearheading the company's ongoing efforts to integrate existing marketing techniques with the Internet, CD-ROMs, and interactive display kiosks to create new promotional opportunities.

With Frankel's sales growth consistently in the 30 to 40 percent-per-annum range for several years running, in 1996 the time seemed ripe to go public. However, after announcing plans to make an initial stock offering, the company postponed it indefinitely, citing unfavorable market conditions. In the meantime, a new contract was signed to do promotion work for General Motors' Oldsmobile division. Frankel was first charged with creating a "buzz" around the launch of the carmaker's new Intrigue sedan. Tactics included a "Whose Intrigue"

Key Dates:

1962: Bernard ''Bud'' Frankel and Marvin Abelson found a promotions agency in Chicago.
1969: Company's Clark Gum ''worthy cause'' promotion is first to donate money to charity.
1973: McDonald's Corporation becomes a client.
1976: Olympics-themed promotion for McDonald's proves a huge success.
1979: Frankel helps McDonald's launch the Happy Meal.
1981: Marv Abelson leaves firm; name is changed to Frankel & Co.
1989: Frankel & Co. named Agency of the Year by *Advertising Age*.
1991: David Tridle takes over as CEO from Bud Frankel.
1995: A full-service office is opened in San Francisco.
1997: Southfield, Michigan, office opens following receipt of the Oldsmobile account; the Siren Technologies subsidiary is formed to produce digital display systems.
1998: Company is restructured into Frankel & Co. and New Ventures units.
1999: Oldsmobile drops Frankel; Southfield office is closed.
2000: Publicis Groupe S.A. purchases company.

sweepstakes at movie theaters, in which filmgoers guessed the manufacturer's identity to enter a three-car giveaway. Starbucks Coffee Co. stores in ten markets were also utilized in the campaign, with attractive models giving out free cups of coffee along with postcards simply listing a toll-free phone number under the tagline ''Compliments of Intrigue.'' Other efforts included radio ads, billboards, and the projection of huge images of the cars at night on buildings in 16 cities. In 1997 Frankel opened an office in Southfield, Michigan, to help facilitate the Oldsmobile work. By this time the company was also assisting other GM divisions, including Cadillac.

Late 1990s: A New Subsidiary is Formed

Continuing to explore new methods of message delivery, Frankel launched a subsidiary called Siren Technologies in the summer of 1997 to produce a digital advertising display system for retail outlets. The flat-screen system was developed by a team led by Richard Mandeberg, and the company hired Tony Dillon, previously head of technology development for McDonald's, to run the new unit. Early users of the devices were McDonald's restaurants in the Chicago area, which showed video clips of food products to hungry customers who were waiting in line. The installation cost was put at between $5,000 and $20,000 per location. Advantages of the new technology included savings in development time and reduced labor costs in the field. Though Siren's first assignments all came from Frankel, it was not restricted to work generated by the parent company.

Another new technology-based campaign, this time from Frankel itself, was a CD-ROM produced as a cross-promotion for Compaq Computers and Atlantic Records. The giveaway item utilized an Anita Baker music video to promote four different Compaq models. The disc also featured TV comedian Paul Reiser, whose Atlantic label music CD was highlighted.

In 1998 Frankel added Frito-Lay to its roster of clients, initially focusing on that company's recently acquired Cracker Jack brand as well as the WOW! low-fat snack and Planet Lunch snack pack lines. Frankel subsequently terminated its relationship with Kraft Foods at Frito-Lay's request, due to the Pepsico unit's discomfort over Kraft's competitor status. Billings for Frito-Lay were estimated at $100 million, substantially more than what Kraft generated. Near the end of the year Frankel & Co. announced a restructuring into two business units. The first retained the Frankel name, while the second, dubbed New Ventures, performed development tasks.

The following spring Oldsmobile shifted the company's promotions work to its ad agency, Leo Burnett of Chicago. The ailing automaker was trying to cut costs in a bid to stay competitive, but the effort was futile, as GM shut down the nameplate the next year. Frankel's Southfield office had few other major accounts, and was later dismantled. Despite the setback, annual sales continued to grow, reaching a record level of $95 million during the year.

2000 and Beyond

In January 2000 Frankel & Co. was sold to Publicis Groupe S.A. of France, a leading European advertising company. Publicis had recently been aggressively expanding into the United States, with four other U.S. firms acquired during the previous year. The company's founder, now 70, had owned two-thirds of the firm, with 15 others splitting the remainder. The sales price was estimated at $140 to $150 million.

The deep pockets of Publicis would enable Frankel & Co. to pursue its Vision 2003 plan, which consisted of investment in technology projects, international expansion, and increasing revenues and billings by a sizable margin. Frankel & Co. would continue to operate independently, keeping its name and identity intact. The company was now ranked by *Promo* magazine as the sixth largest promotional agency in the United States Management changes following the sale were minor, and founder Bud Frankel stayed with the company as chairman.

As it adapted to the change in ownership, Frankel & Co. remained focused on its clients' needs and its goals for the future. The company's thorough yet sensitive approach to its work and its use of cutting edge promotional solutions continued, while the financial backing of new owner Publicis would enable it to develop still more ways to get its messages across. With founder Bud Frankel still on board, the firm neared its 40th anniversary in solid shape, and the road ahead looked bright.

Principal Subsidiaries

Digital Marketing@Frankel; Siren Technologies.

Principal Competitors

Bcom3 Group; Cyrk, Inc.; Gage Marketing Group; The Interpublic Group of Companies, Inc.; Modem Media, Inc.; Omnicom Group, Inc.; Snyder Communications, Inc.; Total

Research Corp.; True North Communications, Inc.; WPP Group plc.

Further Reading

"Agencies: Frankel Goes Global Via Publicis," *Promo*, February 1, 2000.

"Agencies: The Long and Winding Road," *Promo*, March 1, 2000.

DeSalvo, Kathy, "Mad About a CD-ROM," *Shoot*, September 19, 1997, p. 32.

Ellison, Sarah, "French Ad Firm Publicis to Expand in U.S., Buy Marketing-Services Firm," *Dow Jones Business News*, January 11, 2000.

"Frankel & Co. Company Profile," *Promo*, June 7, 1997, p. 50.

"Frankel at 35: The Founder and the Next Generation Map Frankel's Growth," *Advertising Age*, August 11, 1997, p. C12.

"Frankel at 35: The Frankel Years," *Advertising Age*, August 11, 1997, p. C2.

"Frankel Divides to Conquer," *Adweek*, October 5, 1998, p. 4.

"Frito-Lay Krafts Frankel Exit," *Adweek*, March 29, 1999, p. 2.

Green, Norma, "Field Fits Frankel to a Tee," *Advertising Age*, September 12, 1988, p. S-6.

Halliday, Jean, "Olds Fires Promotions Agency," *Automotive News*, April 26, 1999, p. 51.

——, "Promotion is Key for Oldsmobile's Launch of Intrigue: 'Buzz Tactics' Range from TV to Movie Tie-Ins," *Advertising Age*, June 30, 1997, p. 38.

Hume, Scott, "Frankel Honored as Agency of the Year," *Advertising Age*, December 18, 1989, p. 30.

Miller, Craig, and Paul Nolan, "Promotion Marketing: Withstanding the Test of Time," *Potentials in Marketing*, January 1, 1993, p. 5.

Ratny, Ruth L., "Innovative New POP System Saves Time," *Chicago Sun-Times*, July 29, 1997, p. 40.

—Frank Uhle

Furniture Brands
I N T E R N A T I O N A L

Furniture Brands International, Inc.

101 South Hanley Road
Saint Louis, Missouri 63105
U.S.A.
Telephone: (314) 863- 1100
Fax: (314) 863-5306
Web site: http://www.furniturebrands.com

Public Company
Incorporated: 1911 as International Shoe Company
Employees: 10,700
Sales: $2.11 billion (2000)
Stock Exchanges: New York
Ticker Symbol: FBN
NAIC: 337121 Upholstered Household Furniture
Manufacturing; 337122 Nonupholstered Wood
Household Furniture Manufacturing; 337125
Household Furniture (except Wood and Metal)
Manufacturing

Furniture Brands International, Inc. is the largest manufacturer of residential furniture in the United States. Its subsidiaries include Broyhill Furniture Industries, Inc., Lane Company, Incorporated, and Thomasville Furniture Industries Inc. Its Thomasville subsidiary operates more than 100 retail furniture stores. Furniture Brands also sells its goods through partnerships with leading regional furniture retailers such as Havertys and Mathis Brothers. The corporate name was changed to INTERCO Inc. from International Shoe Company in 1966. Until the mid-1990s, the company operated two major shoe subsidiaries, Florsheim and Converse. These are now separate companies, and the name was changed again in 1996 to reflect the company's sole line of business.

Beginning the 20th Century as a Shoe Conglomerate

The corporation was organized in 1911 as the International Shoe Company (ISC) by the consolidation of Roberts, Johnson & Rand Shoe Company and the Peters Shoe Company, both of Saint Louis, Missouri. The company built a reputation for manufacturing quality footwear in basic styles in the low-to-medium price range.

The early years of ISC were under the direction of the Johnson brothers, Jackson and Oscar, and their cousin, Frank C. Rand, son of Henry O. Rand, one of the two financial backers of the firm. John C. Roberts was the other backer. The Johnsons and the Rands, from Mississippi, had moved to Memphis, Tennessee, in 1892 to organize the Johnson, Carruthers & Rand Shoe Company. They sold out in 1898 and moved to Saint Louis to organize a new shoe concern. Jackson Johnson served as president of the newly formed company, then as president of ISC until 1915, and finally as chairman until his death in 1929. It was his vision and entrepreneurial drive that led to the formation of the International Shoe Company. He was succeeded briefly as president of ISC by his younger brother, Oscar Johnson, who died suddenly in 1916. Frank C. Rand guided the company as president from 1916 to 1930, and as chairman from 1930 to 1949. He joined the firm as a stock clerk after graduating from Vanderbilt University in 1898 and rose to vice-president ten years later. Rand was the guiding force behind the tremendous growth of the corporation during the 1920s as well as the survival of the company during the difficult years of the Great Depression.

The corporation benefited from production demands that came with the outbreak of war in Europe. In 1916 orders came from the War Department as the United States prepared for its involvement in the war. Military orders placed with the shoe industry in general were huge. The importance of shoes as war material was demonstrated when, in 1917, the War Department was forced to take over the Hamilton Brown Shoe Company of Saint Louis when it was idled by a strike.

In 1921 ISC was restructured and chartered in Delaware. At that time it had 32 shoe factories in Missouri, Illinois, and Kentucky and had recently acquired the three tanneries of Kistler, Lesh & Co. as part of the long-range goal to achieve full vertical integration. In May 1921 ISC acquired W.H. McElwain Company of Boston, with ten shoe factories, two tanneries, and four shoe-material factories, all in New Hampshire. It was a profitable manufacturer that was experiencing serious labor problems. The company had approximately 5,000 workers and in the previous year had raised wages by ten percent and reduced the work week to 48 hours. McElwain's factories had been organized by the United Shoe Workers. The company experienced some difficulties in the recession of 1920–21 and proposed a wage reduction of 22 percent, which was unacceptable to the union. A strike of all McElwain plants was called in January 1921. The sale of the company to nonunionized International Shoe in the spring of 1921 was, in part, a means of resolving this labor dispute.

The merger of ISC and McElwain was challenged by the Federal Trade Commission as a violation of the Clayton Antitrust Act. The commission argued that the combined companies would lessen competition and create a monopoly in shoe manufacturing. The company's position was that no substantial competition had existed between the two companies, and that the McElwain Company was in such financial straits that sale or liquidation were the only options. The commission's order that ISC divest itself of its McElwain holding was, in 1930, reversed by the Supreme Court. The newly merged companies had combined annual sales of $130 million and could produce 120,000 pairs of shoes daily.

During the 1920s, with minor exceptions, sales and profits increased regularly. In 1927 the corporation increased its authorized common stock to provide its stockholders with a four-for-one split. A dividend of $2 was declared on the new stock, and by January 1928 the corporation was reporting a net income of $4.55 per share.

Profitability was achieved in part at the cost of good labor relations. ISC was not unionized. It tended to control production by means of layoffs of workers. The company also attempted to reduce wages periodically, proposed by management as a means of lowering shoe prices and thereby gaining steady employment for its workers. Although unorganized, workers in the factories did resist this strategy but with limited success.

The year 1929 was ISC's best to that date. Sales and profits reached new highs, and dividends were increased by 50 percent to $3.00 per share. That year it produced 54.73 million pairs of shoes, the largest output ever by a single firm. ISC had not missed a dividend payment from its founding 17 years earlier, and by 1929 it had made millionaires of 38 members of the firm. The economic collapse that came at the end of the 1920s would affect the business, but ISC was a well-managed firm, and it was to remain profitable through most of the Depression years. During those difficult years ISC did as most others; it periodically laid off workers and cut wages and salaries when necessary. It also cut the price of its product line and kept most of its factories operating, although at a reduced level. In 1932 the corporation reported a 9.72 percent rate of return on investment, as compared with 19.29 percent in 1929. The rate of return rose

to 13.53 percent by 1935. On occasion the corporation found it necessary to increase production, as it did in mid-1931. Some of the New Hampshire plants were placed on an overtime schedule. The spurt in demand was attributed to lower-priced footwear, and the relative absence of labor problems was the reason for increasing production at the New Hampshire factories.

The most difficult times for ISC came in the late years of the Depression. In 1937 ISC raised workers' wages twice for a total of ten percent, only to be forced to rescind the increase the following April, of 1938, when the economy again declined. In July of that year ISC reported six-month earnings of 19¢ per share—the lowest earnings of the Depression era. Nonetheless, it had survived the worst of the Great Depression and had emerged as a strong company and a major force in the shoe industry. ISC did well enough in 1939 to divide $600,000 in bonus money among workers earnings less than $50 per week. In the final report for fiscal 1939, ISC reported that sales in dollars were the highest since 1930, and that production and shipments surpassed any year since 1929.

Management of ISC remained rather stable throughout these years. In 1939 William H. Moulton, who had assumed the office in 1930, retired as president of ISC and was succeeded by Byron A. Gray. Both had joined the corporation in the days of the Roberts, Johnson & Rand Shoe Company, Moulton in 1908 and Gray in 1909. Frank Rand continued as chairman and remained the dominant force in management.

Production by ISC for World War II began in the first half of 1940 as preparedness gained momentum. In July 1940 the U.S. Army let out for bid a contract for 452,028 pairs of service shoes. Of the 13 companies that bid, only ISC had the production capacity to bid on the entire order and came in with a low bid of $2.48 per pair. By the end of 1940 ISC had approximately 30,000 employees, primarily in the Midwest and New England. Contracts throughout the war kept the company's plants operating at close to full capacity. In 1943 the Boston Quartermaster Depot awarded contracts for 7.2 million pairs of service shoes—the largest single order—1.34 million pairs to be manufactured by ISC. From early 1940 to January 1945, ISC supplied the government with 33 million pairs of shoes.

Government contracts were awarded to ISC despite opposition from organized labor. The company was not highly regarded among labor organizers or sympathizers, dating back to 1913, when it was accused by the Illinois Vice Commission of encouraging vice among its women employees because of ISC's unwillingness to pay decent wages. Until the labor legislation of the New Deal era made such practices illegal, ISC used a variety of strategies to prevent its workers from organizing unions. By 1940 a number of ISC's plants had been organized, but the company was involved in litigation with the National Labor Relations Board over its noncompliance with an order to allow workers in the Hannibal, Missouri plant to organize. In late 1940 labor representatives objected to ISC receiving a War Department contract for 620,000 pairs of shoes. The issue was resolved politically, but it did encourage ISC to work out its labor problems.

The capacity of the corporation had grown enormously during the 1940s and was not limited to war production. Consumer

Key Dates:

1911: Company is founded in St. Louis as International Shoe Company.
1952: Company acquires Florsheim Shoes.
1959: Company launches International Retail Sales division.
1966: Name is changed to INTERCO Inc.
1979: Company acquires furniture-maker Ethan Allen.
1988: Company defends itself against hostile takeover attempt.
1991: Company enters Chapter 11.
1992: Reorganized company emerges from Chapter 11; Apollo Investment Fund owns 60 percent.
1996: Name is changed to Furniture Brands International.

demand for shoes increased with the improving economy during the war years, and the production of shoes was limited only by the supply of raw materials. In 1944 government business constituted 36 percent of ISC's dollar volume and 27 percent of its production. That year ISC manufactured 53.92 million pairs of shoes—surpassing for the first time the production level of 1929. By the end of World War II, International Shoe had approximately 32,000 employees in 67 shoe factories, subsidiary plants, and tanneries located in Missouri, Illinois, Kentucky, New Hampshire, Arkansas, West Virginia, North Carolina, and Pennsylvania. Plant capacity was significantly more than 200,000 pairs of shoes daily. By 1950 ISC had added an additional 3,000 employees and increased capacity to 70 million pairs annually. Its tanneries could process 3.5 million hides annually, and, in addition, the company manufactured rubber heels, cements, containers, and ten million yards of textiles for shoe linings.

Postwar Acquisitions and Diversification

The death of Frank C. Rand in 1949 marked a significant turning point for ISC. His presence had been felt for 31 years as president. It was primarily at his direction that ISC grew through vertical integration, expansion, and the acquisition of other shoe manufacturing firms. Two of his sons would assume the presidency of the firm, Edgar E. Rand in 1950 and Henry H. Rand in 1955. Although the Rands would continue to have a significant role in the firm, nonfamily management would determine the future of ISC, and growth would take on different characteristics. The acquisitions in 1952 of the Florsheim Shoe Company, a manufacturer of better-quality men's shoes founded in 1892, and in 1954 of Savage Shoes, Ltd., the largest shoe manufacturer in Canada, were the last sizable acquisitions of shoe manufacturers until the mid-1980s. In 1958, however, ISC acquired its first offshore manufacturer, the Caribe Shoe Corporation of Puerto Rico. The firm was small, with a daily capacity of 3,500 pairs of juvenile shoes, but it foretold of the future. Six months later ISC closed permanently a plant in Chester, Illinois that had been operating since 1916 and manufacturing approximately 5,000 pairs of juvenile shoes daily.

Additions for the rest of the decade were in shoe retailing operations, and in 1959 ISC formed a new division, International Retail Sales. As a result of this expansion, by 1960 ISC had controlling interest in approximately 800 retail outlets, as compared with 275 in 1955. This was a response to the implications of low-priced imports. ISC moved quickly to ensure the continued profitability of the firm by expanding its retail operations and by diversifying into other product areas. The drive to diversify was guided by Maurice R. Chambers, who had joined ISC in 1949 as a divisional sales manager and who was elected president of the firm in 1962. He was the first person to reach this position who was neither with the original Roberts, Johnson & Rand Shoe Company nor a member of the Rand family. Under his direction, ISC moved aggressively to expand operations outside the continental United States and to acquire companies in areas other than shoe manufacturing or retailing. Chambers's strategy was to seek out well-managed and profitable companies with strong brand identification and, once acquired, to leave the management team intact. Between 1964 and 1978 ISC acquired 21 separate companies, and with the exception of Central Hardware in 1966, all were apparel manufacturers or retailers. The acquired companies were given operating freedom, and some of these units went on to acquire additional firms in related areas of business, adding to the overall growth of ISC. The company was markedly successful in acquiring thriving firms with good product lines, and it became a role model for other firms seeking to ensure profitability through acquisitions. In 1966 in keeping with its broader base as a diversified apparel maker, footwear manufacturer, retailer, and department store operator, the International Shoe Company adopted the corporate name INTERCO.

During the 1960s there were significant changes in INTERCO's core business. Within a year of Chambers taking office, the company permanently closed six manufacturing facilities (more closings were to come) and set up a special division to import a full line of footwear from Italy. The plant closings reduced overall production capacity approximately 12 percent and were part of a major effort to streamline and upgrade facilities to meet the surge of import competition. This strategy, coupled with diversification, kept INTERCO profitable despite the fact that by the mid-1970s imports had taken more than 44 percent of the domestic shoe market. By the early 1970s INTERCO's apparel and general merchandise subsidiaries were generating approximately 56 percent of sales and 47 percent of profit. By 1974 INTERCO had become a billion dollar corporation with ten consecutive years of record sales and earnings.

Moving into Furniture in the 1980s

The expansion and diversification of the late 1960s and the 1970s had created a firm with three major operating divisions. The apparel manufacturing group consisted of 11 apparel companies, with 62 manufacturing plants and 13 distribution centers. The general retail merchandising group operated 856—owned or leased—retail locations in 29 states. The footwear manufacturing and retailing group operated 874 shoe stores and leased shoe departments in 43 states and in Mexico, Canada, and Australia; and it managed 24 factories and ten distribution centers. A major addition to the footwear group was made with the acquisition in 1986 of Converse, a Massachusetts-based manufacturer of athletic footwear founded in 1908.

A new direction was begun in 1979 when INTERCO agreed to the acquisition of Ethan Allen Inc. for cash and stock totaling $130 million. Ethan Allen, begun in 1932 as a home furnishings jobber, was a fully integrated manufacturer and retailer of furniture and accessories. With the acquisition in January 1980, Ethan Allen's 24 factories and more than 300 retail showcase galleries became the core of INTERCO's fourth operating group in furniture and home furnishings. That same year, in August, INTERCO agreed to the acquisition of Broyhill Furniture Industries for cash and notes totaling $151.5 million. At the time of the acquisition, Broyhill, located in western North Carolina, was the largest privately owned furniture manufacturer in the world. The acquisition added 20 manufacturing facilities to the furniture and home furnishings group.

The largest acquisition in furniture and home furnishings came in 1987 when INTERCO gained control of the Lane Company at a cost approaching $500 million. Lane, based in Altavista, Virginia, was founded in 1912 as a maker of cedar chests, and through growth and acquisition expanded into a full-line manufacturer of furniture in the medium to upper price ranges. With the addition of Lane's 16 plants, sales of the furniture and home furnishings group approached 33 percent of INTERCO's total sales.

The primary architect of the merger and acquisition drive, Maurice R. Chambers, relinquished day-to-day control of the company in 1976, but continued as a major force as a director and as chairman of the executive committee until his retirement in 1981. His successor as CEO, William L. Edwards, Jr., continued Chambers's policies. In early 1981 and in anticipation of Chambers's retirement, INTERCO restructured as part of a plan to develop younger managerial talent within the company. John K. Riedy was moved up to the vacant position of vice-chairman and was succeeded as president and chief operating officer by Harvey Saligman. Then 42 years old, Saligman had been president of Queen Casuals, an apparel manufacturer founded by his grandfather and acquired by INTERCO in 1976. The move was propitious in that Riedy and Saligman were in place when Edwards died unexpectedly in June 1981. Riedy was elected chairman and CEO, positions he would hold until his retirement in June 1985. His successor in these offices, Saligman, would lead INTERCO into the most tumultuous period of the company's existence.

Damaging Hostile Takeover Attempt in 1988

The acquisitions of Converse in 1986 and Lane in 1987 were an integral part of the reorganization of INTERCO devised by Harvey Saligman. Of the four operating groups in the company, footwear manufacturing and retailing and furniture and home furnishings were the two most profitable and appeared to offer the most promise for the future. Beginning in 1985, Saligman's long-term strategy was to emphasize footwear and furniture and to divest the company of less profitable operations in apparel manufacturing and retailing. INTERCO's overall performance and stock price in the mid-1980s did not meet expectations and showed no sign of an immediate turnaround. Saligman's restructuring strategy came at a time when heavily leveraged hostile takeovers of undervalued companies were rampant. INTERCO was a prime candidate. Because the company owned well-known brand names, INTERCO was regarded by takeover specialists as worth more broken up than as a conglomerate.

At the annual meeting in June 1985, while reporting a first quarter net income decline of 42 percent, INTERCO amended its bylaws to create obstacles in the event of a hostile takeover bid. Additional similar action was taken at a board meeting several months later and again the following spring. At the same time INTERCO was proceeding with the divestment or closing of apparel manufacturing firms, including Saligman's family firm, Queen Casuals, and unprofitable retail operations. The acquisitions of Converse and Lane were negotiated at this time. It appears that these acquisitions contributed to a liquidity problem and a lowering of the value of the company's stock, which may have made the company more vulnerable to takeover. In May 1988, a firm hired by INTERCO to watch its stock reported that someone was buying up a chunk.

Anticipating a takeover bid, Saligman and INTERCO retained the services of an investment banker, Wasserstein Perella & Company, in July 1988. The firm's advice and handling of a takeover challenge, however, eventually helped bring INTERCO to bankruptcy. A bid for INTERCO came later that same month from a group of investors led by Steven M. Rales and his brother Mitchell Rales, of Washington, D.C. The initial bid of $2.26 billion, approximately $64 per share, was followed within days by an increased offer of $2.47 billion, or approximately $70 per share. INTERCO's stock had increased by $8.375 to $67.75 a share in response to the first bid, and to $72.50 with the second bid.

INTERCO rejected both bids and took defensive measures to retain its independence. The Rales group had acquired 8.7 percent of INTERCO's stock before making the bid. It had the resources to pursue the takeover battle, and it indicated that its intent was to sell off all INTERCO assets with the exception of the furniture manufacturing group, which would be retained. Financing and direction of the hostile bid was being provided by Drexel Burnham Lambert. With INTERCO shares trading above the hostile offer, management was encouraged to pursue defensive measures. Wasserstein Perella was authorized to provide confidential financial data to potential friendly merger partners, and Goldman, Sachs & Co. was employed to seek purchasers for the planned divestment of the apparel manufacturing group.

In mid-September the Rales group extended and increased its offer to INTERCO shareholders, but the bid appeared to be in serious trouble. Drexel Burnham Lambert was charged by the Securities and Exchange Commission (SEC) with insider trading, a charge that eventually would lead to the downfall of that company. Drexel, unable to raise sufficient funds from outside investors, was obliged to provide more than $600 million of its own money to support the bid. To counter the Rales bid, INTERCO's board approved a $2.8 billion restructuring and special dividend plan that was valued at $76 a share in cash and debentures. The plan would be financed by the sale of assets, including the possible sale of Ethan Allen, the core of the furniture group. In October INTERCO declared a dividend of $25 per share and declared its intent to sell securities in the open market with the proceeds to go to stockholders. In effect, INTERCO was taking on an enormous amount of debt to make the company less attractive to a hostile raider. The Rales group increased its bid to $74 a share and indicated the possibility of an additional increase if it was able to gain access to IN-TERCO's confidential financial data. By early November approximately 93 percent of INTERCO shares had been tendered to the Rales group, but it was prohibited from purchasing the stock because of legal proceedings instituted by INTERCO in the Delaware courts. The Rales group brought matters to a head by establishing a firm deadline for negotiations with IN-TERCO's board. At the deadline it canceled the offer to purchase shares. Within weeks Rales sold its stake in the company and took a profit of $60 million on its three million shares.

The withdrawal of the bid did not release INTERCO from its obligation to restructure the firm, and it proceeded with its plans to pay special dividends of cash and securities to shareholders. INTERCO went ahead with the sale of assets, disposing of major units in apparel manufacturing, retailing operations, and Ethan Allen in the furniture group. This was being done in the midst of a declining bond market, which affected the value of the restructured company. The expectation was that the recapitalized firm would give shareholders a total value of $76 a share. By July 1989 the total value was estimated to be $61 and the stock of the restructured firm, which had been expected to trade at approximately $10, was trading for less than $3 per share. The sale of assets never reached the projected level, falling far short of the amount needed to service the company's obligations. By the early months of 1990, INTERCO stock was trading at less than 50¢ per share, and company bonds were trading in the range of three percent to 25 percent of face value.

In March 1989 Richard B. Loynd was named president and chief operating officer. Loynd had led a leveraged buyout of Converse and was chairman of that firm when it was acquired by INTERCO. In August, Harvey Saligman, who had initiated the restructuring of the firm and who uncompromisingly resisted the hostile takeover, stepped down and Loynd became chief executive officer of the firm. Saligman noted that IN-TERCO was entering a new phase of development and that Loynd's experience in leading a company in a highly leveraged environment would be beneficial.

In and Out of Bankruptcy in the 1990s

The company that Loynd led into the 1990s was far different from the INTERCO of a few years earlier. The company that had grown in relatively small increments over an extended period of time, and had done so with a minimum of debt, began the 1990s with a negative net worth of almost $1 billion. It had narrowed itself down to the two operating groups, footwear manufacturing and retailing and furniture and home furnishings, with some peripheral assets slated for divestment. The Rales brothers' failed bid for INTERCO was one of the biggest deals of the takeover craze of the 1980s, and the company was crippled by the debt it had taken on. The firm had sold off its assets at far less than it had projected. Sales declined for the company overall, and in January 1991, INTERCO filed for bankruptcy. INTERCO went into Chapter 11, which allowed the company to continue to operate while it planned for a way to satisfy its creditors. At the time, it was the fifth largest bankruptcy case in U.S. history. INTERCO continued to sell off what it could as it struggled to reorganize. By mid-1992, the company had shed all of its retailing and apparel divisions, leaving it with four key components—Broyhill Furniture Industries and the Lane Company for furniture, and Converse and Florsheim in its shoe division. INTERCO predicted it would make its first profit in five years for fiscal 1993. The company emerged from Chapter 11 in August 1992, with a new majority owner, the Apollo Investment Fund Ltd. Apollo was a New York-based investment firm that specialized in troubled companies, and it was headed by Leon Black, formerly of Drexel Burnham Lambert. Of course, it was Drexel that had backed the Rales brothers' bid for INTERCO, setting up the events leading to the bankruptcy. Apollo gained about 60 percent of IN-TERCO's stock and got slots for about half the seats on the board.

In mid-1994, INTERCO announced plans to slim down its core business even further. It indicated that it would spin off both its shoe companies, Converse and Florsheim. Accordingly, in 1996 the company changed its name to Furniture Brands International, showing its new exclusive focus on furniture. Richard Loynd stepped aside as CEO in 1996. He was succeeded by Mickey Holliman, who previously had headed the company's Action Industries subsidiary. Holliman had built up Action Industries from a maker of recliners to the leading manufacturer of so-called motion furniture, a growing niche. Holliman declared that Furniture International would work on entering new markets and building market share in the furniture industry. As a slimmed-down company focused on just one general market, furniture, the company seemed to do well. By the end of 1999, Furniture Brands was reporting its fifteenth straight quarterly earnings gain in a row. Furniture Brands included three major furniture manufacturers—Broyhill, Thomasville, and Lane. These were some of the strongest brand names in the furniture industry. Furniture Brands entered a relationship with a major furniture retailer, Havertys, in the late 1990s, getting that chain to set aside about half its floor space for Furniture Brands' lines. Both companies gained by the relationship. Sales for both Havertys and Furniture Brands increased, as the retailer was given priority service and quick delivery of orders.

By 2000, Furniture Brands seemed to have recovered from the shocks it underwent as INTERCO. Yet the furniture industry was cyclical, somewhat tied to the housing and construction markets. By the end of 2000, retailers in many industries were worrying about a possible recession, and Furniture Brands advised that its earnings would fall because higher fuel costs were holding back consumer spending. Nevertheless, the company ended 2000 with record sales and earnings, holding just a few percentage points above 1999's healthy figures. The company considered moving into retailing as a way of enhancing its distribution. Its Thomasville subsidiary already had a significant presence in retail, operating approximately 130 freestanding stores. As the economy threatened to slow in 2001, and a key vendor, Heilig-Myers, ran into financial trouble, Furniture Brands announced that it would consider launching retail stores of its own under the Lane and Broyhill names. Other growth was expected to come through close relationships with major regional furniture retailers such as Havertys.

Principal Subsidiaries

Broyhill Furniture Industries, Inc.; The Lane Company, Incorporated; Thomasville Furniture Industries Inc.; Action Industries Inc.

Principal Competitors

Ethan Allen Interiors Inc.; La-Z-Boy Inc.

Further Reading

Buchanan, Lee, ''Furniture Brands Mulls Expanding Distribution,'' *HFN,* August 7, 2000, p. 4.

——, ''Haverty's Growth Outpaces Competition,'' *HFN,* February 14, 2000, p. 1.

''Clayton, Mo.-Based Furniture Company Posts 15th Straight Quarterly Rise,'' *Knight-Ridder/Tribune Business News,* October 26, 1999.

Feurer, Rosemary, ''Shoe City, Factory Towns: St. Louis Shoe Companies and the Turbulent Drive for Cheap Rural Labor, 1900–1940,'' *Gateway Heritage,* Fall 1988.

''Holliman Is CEO of Action's Parent,'' *HFN,* October 7, 1996, p. 4.

INTERCO: A Review, Saint Louis, Mo.: INTERCO, 1981.

Jereski, Laura, ''Fiction In, Fiction Out,'' *Forbes,* December 9, 1991, p. 292.

Leonard, John W., ed., *The Book of St. Louisans: A Biographical Dictionary of Leading Living Men of the City of St. Louis,* Saint Louis, Mo.: St. Louis Republic, 1906.

Lloyd, Mary Ellen, ''Rate Rises, Energy Costs Hurt Furniture Firms,'' *Wall Street Journal,* October 16, 2000, p. B16.

Nunn, Henry Lightfoot, *Partners in Production: A New Role for Management and Labor,* Englewood Cliffs, N.J.: Prentice Hall, 1961.

——, *The Whole Man Goes to Work: The Life Story of a Businessman,* New York: Harper, 1953.

Patterson, Gregory A., ''Interco Plans Spinoff of Florsheim and Public Offering of Converse Stake,'' *Wall Street Journal,* August 25, 1994, p. A9.

Quick, Julie, ''Back in Step?,'' *St. Louis Business Journal,* February 3, 1992, p. 1A.

——, ''Leon Black—Ready to Snare Interco,'' *St. Louis Business Journal,* June 22, 1992, p. 1.

Sahm, Cathy, ''Creditors at Odds on $185 Million Loan,'' *St. Louis Business Journal,* February 25, 1991, p. 1A.

—George P. Antone
—update: A. Woodward

Getronics NV

Donauweg 10
1043 AJ Amsterdam
The Netherlands
Telephone: (+31) 20 586-1412
Fax: (+31) 20 586-1568
Web site: http://www.getronics.com

Public Company
Incorporated: 1887 as Elektronische Fabriek NV
    (Groeneveld, Van der Pol & Co.)
Employees: 34,713
Sales: EUR 4.29 billion ($3.88 million) (2000)
Stock Exchanges: Euronext Amsterdam
Ticker Symbol: GTN
NAIC: 541512 Computer Systems Design Services;
    54161 Management Consulting Services

The Netherlands' Getronics NV is European leader and one of the world's top five providers of Information & Communications Technology (ICT) services, active in two primary fields of Business Solutions and Consulting, and Systems Integration and Networked Technology. The company offers its corporate clients a full array of ICT services, ranging from strategy consulting to systems implementation, integration, and management; Getronics also offers customers full outsourcing services. Getronics' leap into the top five came with its $2 billion acquisition of American computer pioneer Wang Global in 1999, nearly tripling the company's size and adding Wang's North American market strength. The company followed the Wang acquisition, the largest of a long string of acquisitions made during the 1990s, with a takeover of Olivetti's financial software subsidiary Olivetti Ricerca, boosting Getronics' activity in the financial sector, its largest area of revenues at 35 percent of its total sales. A truly global company, with operations in some 150 countries and nearly 35,000 employees, Getronics' is a contender for a position as industry leader among IBM, EDS, Hewlett Packard, and ICL/Fujitsu. In 2000, Getronics shed some EUR 970 million worth of noncore operations—including a producer of automated teller machines and Spanish computer distribution business Diode—to complete its transformation to

a pure-play services provider. The company has plans to break into the industry top three by 2003, promising to double its turnover every three years at the beginning of the new century. Getronics is led by President and CEO Cees G. van Luijk. The company's shares are traded on the Euronext Amsterdam stock exchange as part of the leading AEX index.

Technology Pioneer in the 19th Century

Before becoming an ICT services superstar at the end of the 20th century, Getronics already had established a long history as a technology services provider. The company's origins lay in the creation, by Dutch firm Groeneveld, Van der Pol & Co., of a new subsidiary, Elektrotechnische Fabriek NV., in 1887. This company began business as an installer of control and technical equipment for various industries, including the shipbuilding industry and the newly growing utilities networks.

Groeneveld added to its technology interests in the 1950s when it created Technisch Verkoop Kantoor Groenpol, a sales and distribution subsidiary for industrial products ranging from microswitches to steam turbine components and systems. Groeneveld then combined its sales and distribution wing with its Elekrontechnische Fabriek installation and services unit to form a new company, Groenpol NV., which was then spun off as a separate, public company in the 1960s.

In 1968, Groenpol merged with Geveke NV, a public company that had similar operations in The Netherlands. The new company, which retained a listing on the Amsterdam stock exchange, was named Geveke & Groenpol NV. Despite the merger, the two companies' former operations continued to be run as separate businesses.

Geveke & Groenpol was taken over by Steenkolen Handelsvereniging (SHV) in 1970, which removed the company from the Amsterdam stock exchange. SHV also split up Geveke & Groenpol operations into their installation and sales and distribution components, creating the sales group Groenpol Industriële Verkoop (Groenpol Industrial Sales) under SHV's Groep Technische Handel distribution division.

SHV led its new subsidiary operations beyond The Netherlands, setting up subsidiary operations in Belgium and France.

As part of this expansion, the company changed its Groenpol Industriële Verkoop unit's name to Geveke Electronics. By the early 1980s, however, SHV agreed to spin off Geveke into a separate company through a management buyout led by Anton Risseuw, with SHV retaining a position as a minority shareholder. The leveraged buyout was completed in 1983.

Geveke reorganized its operations, combining all of its subsidiary operations under the Geveke Electronics International NV parent company. By 1985, Geveke was prepared to go public again, taking a new listing on the Amsterdam stock exchange.

Acquiring Leadership in the 1990s

Geveke proved itself a new and aggressive contender in the booming market for information and communications technologies. The company began a long string of acquisitions that boosted it from a modestly sized distributor of computer-related technologies to a global ICT powerhouse by the end of the century. One of the company's earliest acquisitions was that of Electric Engineering, which brought Geveke a telematics installation operation in 1986.

Two years later, Geveke stepped up the pace of its acquisitions, bringing in Datex, which became the company's Getronics Software Solutions subsidiary and added software services and consulting operations, and Gematica, which launched the company into Spain with a network and computer systems maintenance subsidiary. The company also built up its distribution arm, purchasing XTEC Computer Systems, which distributed ICT systems, and Klaasing Electronics, giving Geveke a new computer components distribution business. In 1988, the company changed its name to emphasize its commitment to fast-growing electronics industry, becoming Getronics NV.

By the late 1980s, Getronics had captured a leading share of the computer maintenance. Yet Getronics remained a small company, especially compared with the industry's traditional leaders such as IBM and EDS. Posting just NFL 55 million in 1989, Getronics' share price, at around $25 per share, made it a potential target for a takeover. Instead, Getronics intensified its own takeover activity, hitting the acquisition once again as the new decade got under way. After acquiring the information consulting services of Synergie Consultancy in 1990, the company stepped up the pace the following year, acquiring Vanandel, giving it closed mobile communications networks capacity, Computer Uitwijk Centrum, adding automatic data processing operations, and Koning and Hartman, a distributor and servicer of data networks and telecommunications systems.

In choosing its acquisitions, Getronics sought factors such as whether the proposed purchase would produce high value-added activities or improve Getronics' scale. New candidates

for the growing Getronics group of companies were Datatraffic, which offered payment solutions and related financial services applications, acquired in 1992 and renamed as Getronics Transaction & Card Systems. That same year the company expanded its computer maintenance wing with the addition of Computer Service Holland, while strengthening its growing ICT business with the Intercai Holding joint venture with KPN Telecom.

These and other acquisitions helped the company build up a network of operations through much of western Europe. The company attempted to fill in some of its geographic gaps, adding ICT services in the Norwegian market with the addition of Cinet, which covered a range of services from systems integration and workplace automation to network and systems management. By the mid-1990s, Getronics had successfully built a position as one of the leading providers to the ICT market in Europe.

The company enhanced that position with the purchase of 50 percent of The Netherlands' Raet in 1995. Raet gave the company important capabilities in the human resources and payroll fields. It also placed the company in conjunction with government-owned Roccade, the former accounting service of the Dutch government, which had joined Getronics in the Raet acquisition. In 1996, Getronics acquired the remaining 50 percent from Roccade—in part in preparation for a proposed purchase of Roccade itself. As Risseuw described the Raet acquisition to *De Telegraaf*, "When we took over Raet together with Roccade in 1995, the business was without any future."

Getronics had been placed on the fast-track toward acquiring Roccade when it was granted the right to make a bid for the company in 1995. Acquiring Roccade would have allowed Getronics to become one of the heavyweights in the steadily growing ICT industry. Instead, after two years of negotiations, the deal fell through and the former government service appeared likely to fall into the hands of a foreign company. Risseuw did not hide his disappointment, saying: "We're dealing here with a government that only wants to see money."

The proposed Roccade acquisition also prevented the company from bidding for another company then coming onto the sales block. Olivetti had split off its automation services division, Olsy, as a separate company and put it up for sale in 1995. With its interests tied up in the proposed Roccade purchase, Getronics was forced to allow Olsy to go to another bid. Wang Global, formerly known as Wang Laboratories, which had risen from bankruptcy in 1992, finally acquired Olsy in 1998.

After acquiring a majority interest in Business Management Group in 1997, the company acquired Ark, of Norway, in an effort to improve its relatively weak penetration into the Scandinavian market. Yet that market was to prove a difficult one for Getronics to crack and the company, despite conquering the rest of Europe, remained a minor player in Scandinavia. In 2000, the company sold much of its Scandinavian operations to Norway's Merkatildata, in exchange for an 11 percent share in that company. Germany also presented a difficult market for the company. Meanwhile, Getronics had greater success elsewhere, such as Spain, where it added to its ICT operations when it acquired Grupo CP, a software solutions and consulting business. That same year, Getronics also added the human resource specialists IBM/Asap.

By then, Risseuw was already leading the company in discussions with a new potential acquisition target. Negotiations continued into 1999, despite Risseuw's retirement at the beginning of that year. It was left to newly named President and CEO Cees G. van Luijk to make the announcement in June 1999 that Getronics had agreed to acquire Wang Global for US$2 billion. The acquisition boosted the company's projected sales to some US$4.5 billion by 2000, with a global workforce of some 35,000.

Wang Global had nearly ceased to exist at the beginning of the 1990s. Formerly known as Wang Laboratories, that company had been among the early leaders in the pioneering computer industry. An Wang, who had immigrated from China to complete a PhD at Harvard University, had established his company in 1951 with just US$600 in savings. Wang's company at first sold memory components for computer systems, then began producing calculators. After going public in 1967 and adopting the name Wang Laboratories, the company moved into the office automation segment. Wang soon established itself as a leading company in this new industry, a position assured when it designed the first word processing systems. By the early 1980s, Wang had moved into designing and manufacturing ''mini-computers''—which were still the size of a closet, despite their name—and became one of the foremost names in office computing at the time.

Yet Wang had failed to recognize the rise of the personal computer market, which not only replaced the need for its cumbersome minicomputers but also took over its word processing market. By the beginning of the 1990s, Wang's market had dried up and, in 1992, the company filed for bankruptcy. Emerging from bankruptcy a year later, Wang had acquired new management and a new business plan, reinventing itself as a software services and digital imaging company called Wang Global. Although it sold off its digital imaging wing to Eastman

Kodak in 1997, Wang Global succeeded in its resurrection, gaining a strong share of the U.S. market while reinforcing its worldwide presence. The company went on an acquisition spree, including the purchase of Olys from Olivetti, which more than doubled Wang Global's size and gave it a strong share of the European and Asian markets as well.

Getronics' and Wang Global's operations proved highly complementary, reinforcing Getronics' existing operations in key areas, while giving the Dutch company an entry into the United States, a market it had ignored, in large part, until then. Now a global powerhouse (also known as Wang Getronics in the North American market) that counted itself among the top five in its industry, behind leaders IBM, EDS, Hewlett Packard, and ICL/Fujitsu, Getronics prepared itself for still stronger growth. Following on the Wang Global acquisition, Getronics added another Olivetti unit, Olivetti Ricerca (it had already acquired 20 percent through Wang Global). These purchases enabled Getronics to refocus itself wholly on its ICT services activities. In 2000, the company announced its intention to sell of a number of its distribution and hardware businesses, now deemed noncore, in a series of sales and management buyouts. Completed at the beginning of 2001, the selloffs represented some EUR 970 million of Getronics revenues.

After nearly tripling its revenues in the final years of the 20th century, Getronics appeared to have only just begun. Indeed, following the 1999 acquisitions of InterEdge, a web design specialist, BMG, another ICT and strategy consulting group, and the acquisition of Brazil's Connect in 2000, van Luijk declared that the company's ambitions now called for Getronics to join the world's top three ICT groups by 2003, with plans to double its revenues every three years.

Principal Divisions

Systems Integration & Networked Technology Systems; Business Solutions & Consulting.

Principal Competitors

International Business Machines Corporation; Accenture; Atos Origin; Bull SA; Cap Gemini SA; Electronic Data Systems Corp.; ICL/Fujitsu; Logica plc; Misys plc; Sema plc; Unisys Corporation.

Further Reading

Blenkinskop, Philip, ''Getronics Buys Wang Global,'' *Reuters,* May 4, 1999.
''Dutch Company Getronics Scoops Up Wang for $2 Billion,'' *InfoWorld,* May 10, 1999.
''Getronics, Merkantildata to Link Ops,'' *Reuters,* April 17, 2000.
''Getronics Net Surges, Splits Shares,'' *Reuters,* March 3, 2000.
''Getronics waant zich in startblokken wereldtop,'' *De Telegraaf,* March 4, 2000.
Scannell, Tim, ''Desinvesteringen Getronics afgerond,'' *De Telegraaf,* January 26, 2001.
''Wang Global Agrees to Buyout Offer,'' *Computer Reseller News,* May 10, 1999, p. 37.

—M.L. Cohen

Gordon Food Service Inc.

333 50th Street S.W.
P.O. Box 1787
Grand Rapids, Michigan 49501
U.S.A.
Telephone: (616) 530-7000
Toll Free: (800) 968-4872
Fax: (616) 2261-7600
Web site: http://www.gfs.com

Private Company
Incorporated: 1946
Employees: 4,400
Sales: $2.15 billion (2000)
NAIC: 42241 General Line Grocery Wholesalers

Gordon Food Service Inc. (GFS) is the largest family-owned food service distributor in the United States and provides hospitals, restaurants, college dormitories, hotels, and other institutions with a wide variety of foods, beverages, and paper products. Marketed primarily in a territory that extends from Michigan's Upper Peninsula to southern Ohio and Indiana, and from Chicago to Cleveland, GFS's product line includes national brand names as well as products carrying its own GFS label. Having introduced new operations, technologies, and training methods that have since been adapted in other organizations, GFS is regarded as an innovator in the food service industry.

Company Origins

GFS traces its origins to the turn of the 20th century when Isaac Van Westenbrugge, a 23-year-old Dutch immigrant living in Grand Rapids, Michigan, borrowed $300 from his brother to start up a business providing dairy products to local grocers. Van Westenbrugge and his wife maintained a barn in back of their house for storing their merchandise, which they inspected by hand for freshness. Delivering cheese, butter, and eggs in a horse-drawn wagon to Grand Rapids stores, Van Westenbrugge became a successful businessman known for his commitment to high-quality products and dependable service. Eventually he

was able to rent business space in the wholesale food district of Grand Rapids.

Within a few years, Van Westenbrugge sought to expand and, quitting his delivery business, entered a partnership in general grocery wholesaling. This venture ultimately dissolved in 1913, however, when he and his partner could not agree on product lines and expansion policies. Van Westenbrugge then began a new business in his original field of dairy product distribution, carrying the standard eggs, cheese, and butter, while adding new products on occasion, such as "renovated" butter—made in the summer and re-churned for freshness in the winter—and Blue Ribbon brand margarine. Van Westenbrugge was able to provide quicker service this time, having replaced his horse and wagon with two rebuilt delivery trucks.

In 1916 an industrious young man named Ben Gordon, a classmate of Van Westenbrugge's daughter Ruth, began working part-time for Van Westenbrugge after school and on Saturdays loading and unloading the trucks. Gordon soon left to serve in the army during World War I, and when he returned in 1918, he moved to Indiana to pursue an opportunity with the Nucoa Nut Butter Company. Nucoa manufactured an inexpensive butter substitute made with coconut oil, a popular alternative during the war years when the price of butter rose to more than a dollar a pound. Gordon invested $1,500 to establish a sales and distribution office for Nucoa in Terre Haute, but after less than a year, as the war ended and butter prices plummeted, the venture failed, and Gordon returned to Grand Rapids. He began working for Van Westenbrugge again, this time as first assistant. Later that year Gordon married Ruth Van Westenbrugge.

Over the next ten years, the company began to deliver a wider variety of food products, introducing Philadelphia Cream Cheese, Rival Dog Food, Best Foods Mayonnaise, and several other items on its routes. The business grew rapidly, and in 1932 Kraft cheeses were added to the product line. In 1935 Gordon bought into Van Westenbrugge's business, and the name was subsequently changed to Gordon-Van Cheese Company. Two years later Gordon's brother Frank, having left his position as the manager of an A&P grocery store to work at Gordon-Van, was put in charge of opening and managing a new branch in Traverse City, Michigan.

The Gordon-Van Cheese Company went out of business in 1941 when it was purchased by Kraft. As part of the deal, Ben and Frank Gordon were employed by Kraft as general managers, but within a year they sought to return to their roles as independent food distributors. At this time, however, Ben was unable to participate in a competitive business venture, because of an injunction from Kraft. Therefore, Frank saw to the daily operations of their newly formed company, Gordon Food Service, while Ben went to work for the Office of Price Administration as a food price specialist. When Ben was able to rejoin Frank in the business in 1946, GFS was in full operation, servicing retail outlets in Grand Rapids, Kalamazoo, and Traverse City with a fleet of seven trucks. That year Gordon Food Service was incorporated, with Ben Gordon as president and Frank Gordon as treasurer.

In 1947 Ben's oldest son, Paul, a college graduate and World War II veteran, joined GFS as a salesperson. That year, the company opened a fourth sales center and warehouse in Lansing. The following year, the company's headquarters and main warehouse in Grand Rapids moved into a new facility that featured refrigerated storage space for frozen food products. Frozen foods became the focus of GFS's sales push in the 1950s. Among the first frozen foods the Gordons distributed was a new item becoming popular in restaurants at the time, french fries. By the end of the decade, GFS had employed two salespeople, and the company's concerns began to shift from merely selling to providing "food service," a new concept that came to denote broader and more thorough service to larger, institutional markets. Rather than arriving at a retail establishment with a supply of products for the merchant to choose from, as had been the norm at GFS, the new GFS sales staff began spending certain days taking advance orders and other days delivering.

Shifting Emphasis and Leadership: The 1960s–70s

By 1960 GFS was redefining its business as a food service distributor with a product line consisting mainly of frozen foods. The company had profited from the need for a local frozen food distributor in southwestern Michigan. With limited freezer space, Grand Rapids operators were forced to place small frozen food orders frequently. Because orders had to be brought in from Detroit or Chicago, many stores had difficulty stocking enough frozen food to meet customer demands. GFS was positioned to step in to fill this need and others. Throughout the 1960s the company expanded its sales staff as well as its product line, which came to feature grocery and disposable items.

In 1962 GFS built a new 54,000-square-foot headquarters and warehouse in Grand Rapids. This building would be expanded several times over the next ten years, eventually becoming the largest distribution facility of its kind in the country at 400,000 square feet. In its first year of operation the warehouse was also the site of the first annual trade show—featuring informational seminars and booths highlighting new food products—held by GFS. During this time, Ben and Frank began preparing to turn the company over to the next generation of Gordons. In 1965 Paul Gordon was made president of GFS, Ben became the company's chairperson, and Frank stepped in as vice-president. John Gordon, Ben's younger son, who had joined the company in 1953 as the manager of the Traverse City operation, was appointed secretary-treasurer.

GFS became fully committed to the food service industry in the mid-1970s when it discontinued the last of its accounts with retail establishments. Marketing mainly to restaurants, hotels, and schools in western Michigan, the company had around 4,000 steady customers by 1974 and achieved $36 million in annual food service sales that year. Realizing that GFS drivers had a great deal of contact with customers, the company changed the title of driver to "sales serviceman" and provided this staff with special training in customer relations and sales. In recognition of this commitment to customer service as well as its continued growth and success, GFS received the first annual "Great Distribution Organization" award from the trade magazine *Institutional Distribution* in 1974.

New Technology and Product Lines: Late 1970s–80s

Years of technical innovation and expansion followed for GFS. Committed to exploring newer and more efficient means of keeping records and filling orders, the company transferred much of this information onto microfiche in 1977. The microfiche price books and customer records, along with handheld viewers, allowed sales representatives to carry much of the information they needed with them in a briefcase or pocket when calling on customers. In 1980 the company's Grand Rapids warehouse was among the first of its kind to become automated when a computerized order selection and sorting system was installed for its warehouse products.

Given its rapidly expanding territory, GFS soon needed more distribution space than its Grand Rapids facility could provide. In 1985 the company broke ground for a second distribution center in Brighton, Michigan, intended to service the eastern half of its territory. The 40-foot-high, $15 million facility was slated for completion in August of the following year, but was delayed due to an accident in which several 400-foot-long racks of processed food crashed to the floor. No one was injured, but the building suffered water damage. Nevertheless, the Brighton Distribution Center opened only a few months later than expected. Run by the same mainframe computer that controlled the Grand Rapids warehouse, the highly mechanized Brighton center featured automatic inventory selection machinery and nearly 20,000 feet of conveyor belts that carried products directly into GFS delivery trucks.

Key Dates:

1897: Original eggs and butter delivery business is begun.
1942: Family business is reorganized and renamed by brothers Ben and Dan Gordon.
1946: Gordon Food Service is incorporated.
1962: Company opens a new headquarters and warehouse in Grand Rapids.
1965: Paul Gordon becomes president as a second generation takes control of the business.
1985: A second major distribution center is opened in Brighton, Michigan.
1991: Paul Gordon's son, Dan, is named president.
1994: Company reaches $1 billion in annual sales.

The GFS product line also expanded during the 1970s. Noting that increasingly health-conscious Americans were selecting more meals from restaurant salad bars and purchasing more raw vegetables from grocery stores, GFS began marketing fresh, precut vegetables to customers interested in saving preparation time. By 1989 the company offered more than 100 different vegetable items. Also added to the GFS menu were ethnic foods, as the popularity of Chinese, Mexican, Cajun, and other cuisines increased in the Midwest. Furthermore, in addition to its already wide variety of canned goods, meats, dairy products, frozen foods, and main dish items, the company expanded its line of disposables, including paper napkins and silverware, as well as other nonfood food items, such as coffee machines and soap dispensers.

By 1991 nonfood products accounted for nearly 20 percent of the company's sales. Another ten percent of GFS sales was attributed to GFS Marketplace Stores located in Michigan, Indiana, and Ohio. GFS began the cash-and-carry retail outlets in 1979 primarily to service the emergency needs of customers. They also became the primary supplier for smaller customer who preferred pickup rather than delivery. GFS Marketplace Stores soon began to serve individuals and groups planning to host large gatherings or events. The 26 Marketplace stores offered complete lines of meats, seafoods, desserts, vegetables, and other items, such as coffee cups and stir sticks, economically priced in bulk quantities. Sales staff were available to help the customer plan an event, offering advice on how much food should be purchased or how to most successfully meet an already planned budget. Nonetheless, the bulk of GFS's business remained in commercial markets. In addition to its traditional customers—hotels, restaurants, country clubs, nursing homes—the company also gained large sales from supermarkets wishing to use a food service distributor to stock their delis and salad bars. In 1987 GFS reported $530 million in sales from an estimated 10,000 active accounts. The following year it was given the Great Distributor Award for a second time.

GFS credited its success to the high quality of its products, the innovations it effected in food service industry, and the dedication of its employees. Aside from providing its staff with state of the art equipment and facilities, GFS educated its sales force through ongoing and comprehensive training programs. Furthermore, the company offered several incentive plans, including profit-sharing and individual performance awards. *Institutional Distribution* reported in 1988 that the average GFS sales representative handled 55 accounts translating into a yearly sales figure of $2.9 million. Hoping to achieve an increase in sales of 15 percent every year, GFS equipped its sales force with laptop computers. This allowed sales associates to access information about product availability, food preparation instructions, and menu suggestions.

Further Growth in the 1990s and Beyond

By 1991 GFS sales reached $800 million, and the company had become the eighth largest food service distributor in the country, offering more than 10,000 products to its 10,000 customers. At the beginning of the year Paul Gordon's son, Dan (who had joined GFS in 1972), took over the presidency and Paul became the company's chairperson. Under Dan Gordon, the company saw more expansion. Purchasing a 20-acre lot on Clay Avenue around the corner from its corporate headquarters, the company erected a $35 million, 16-million-cubic-foot warehouse and distribution center that featured 32 receiving docks, a five-mile-long system of conveyor belts, and computer-controlled machinery to stack cases of food and track them as they were shipped. The Clay Avenue Distribution Center was completed in 1993.

GFS went international in 1993 when it purchased the Ontario and Quebec divisions of Maple Leaf Food Service from Maple Leaf Foods Inc. The result was Gordon Food Service Canada, a venture that eventually would be augmented by the purchase of two additional family owned food service distributors to make it the second largest food service distributor in Canada. Four primary distribution centers were established to service the market. GFS would top $1 billion in yearly sales in 1994, but once the full benefit of the Canadian operations were realized, the company's revenues would jump to $1.657 billion for 1997.

Early in 1998 GFS opened a major new state-of-the-art distribution facility occupying 50 acres of land in Springfield, Ohio. The warehouse, with it 20 million cubic feet of capacity and ceilings that at points reached 110 feet high, was even larger than the flagship Grand Rapids facility and was designed to carry some 7,000 items. It would service a 250-mile radius, sending out 200 truckloads a day to a territory that included northern Kentucky, Indiana, central and southern Ohio, western Pennsylvania, and parts of West Virginia. GFS anticipated that the Ohio center, once fully operational around 2002, would do $500–$600 million in business. The company's total warehouse capacity now reached 1.5 million square feet.

GFS Marketplace Stores also grew at fast clip, going beyond its original purpose to serve as satellite distribution centers to compete with supermarkets and the rash of wholesale clubs that became popular with consumers. Like the clubs, GFS charged no membership fee. With the opening of a Rockford, Illinois outlet in December 2000, the number of GFS Marketplace stores reached 77.

GFS continued its commitment to technology. Not only was the inventory of all its distribution centers maintained by a centralized system, the sales force had immediate access to the information via laptop computers, along with advanced order entry capabilities. For its customers GFS also created and supported GFS Plus, software that featured sophisticated food service management tools to allow customers to control inventory and order products, as well as plan recipes and menus. Furthermore, GFS made available the NutriQuest software, which could provide nutritional analysis of the GFS products used in the recipes.

GFS entered a new century ranked number 74 in the *Forbes* Private 500 with more than $2 billion in annual sales, still very much an independent, family-run company. There has been no decline in fortunes that beset many companies when its founder has turned over the reins. For more than a hundred years the family business has enjoyed even greater prosperity with the advent of a new generation. There is nothing to indicate that GFS will not continue to enjoy healthy growth in the foreseeable future.

Principal Divisions

Gordon Food Service; GFS Marketplace.

Principal Competitors

McLane Foodservice, Inc.; Costco Wholesale Corporation; Alliant Exchange, Inc.; U.S. Foodservice.

Further Reading

Bologna, Michael J., "GFS Credits Its Customers, Employees for Inspiring High-Tech Center," *Grand Rapids Press,* May 19, 1991.

"The Great Distributor Organization Award: Gordon Food Service," *Institutional Distribution,* July 1988, pp. 74–280.

Hulm, Trevor, "Major Collapse Delays Opening of Warehouse," *Ann Arbor News,* August 7, 1986.

"Maple Leaf Foods Reaches Sales Agreement," *Nation's Restaurant News,* January 1, 1994, p. 70.

Salkin, Stephanie, "Gordon Launches New Ohio Operation," *Voice of Foodservice Distribution,* June 1998, p. 20.

—Tina Grant
—update: Ed Dinger

Groupe Go Sport S.A.

17, avenue de la Falaise
38360 Sassenage
France
Telephone: (+33) 4 7628 2020
Fax: (+33) 4 7628 2099
Web site: http://www.go-sport.fr

Public Subsidiary of Groupe Rallye S.A.
Incorporated: 1976 as Société Alpine de Sport
Employees: 4,500
Sales: FFr 4.35 billion ($621 million) (2000 consolidated)
Stock Exchanges: Euronext Paris
Ticker Symbol: 3292.PA
NAIC: 451110 Sporting Goods Stores

Groupe Go Sport S.A. is one of the leading sporting goods retailers in Europe. With a 16 percent market share in its home country of France, Go Sport is that country's second largest sporting goods retailer, yet remains far behind dominant player Decathlon, a member of the Auchan group, which has captured 50 percent of the total sporting goods retail market. Where Decathlon realizes the largest part of its sales with its own-label goods, Go Sport has established itself as a seller of major brand names, while also promoting its own labels, Go Sport, for its sporting goods, and Wannabee, for its sports-related clothing. Go Sport's own label sales account for less than 20 percent of its sales. To counter the strength of Decathlon—which has been accused by both Go Sport and rival Intersport of abusing its position of dominance in the French market—Go Sport has announced its intention to step up its number of new store openings to as many as 30 new stores per year. Targeting primarily midsized cities, the average Go Sport has roughly 1,500 square meters of selling space. Go Sport also has been targeting international growth since the late 1990s, moving into Poland in 1999 and Hungary in 2000, with plans to expand into other international markets in the early years of the new century. Go Sport also is present in Belgium and Spain. With 70 percent of its shares held by Groupe Rallye—which also holds

54 percent of the French hypermarket and supermarket group Casino and 100 percent of American footwear retailer Athlete's Foot—Go Sport completed a takeover of another Rallye subsidiary, the sporting shoe chain Courir, at the end of 2000. The newly enlarged company had consolidated sales of FFr 4.35 billion ($621 million) and a network of more than 252 stores, including 107 Go Sport stores, which contributed FFr 3.35 billion, and 140 smaller Courir stores, adding nearly 740 million. The merged company also included several Moviesport stores, a sports clothing chain created by Courir in the late 1990s. Some analysts have viewed the merger of Go Sport and Courir as a prelude to a possible spin-off by Rallye, as that group, in the wake of the Promodes-Carrefour merger of 1998, eyed a potential merger with Auchan. Groupe Go Sport is led by CEO Charles Setboun.

Sporting Goods Alternative in the 1980s

A growing interest in physical fitness and in leisure sports in France in the 1970s saw the rise of a growing number of sporting goods specialist retailers, including the creation of the Decathlon chain, associated with the Mulliez family of the Auchan retail empire. Auchan was not alone in its interest in sporting goods: a number of other of France's hypermarket and supermarket chains also set out to stake a claim to the fast-growing market for sporting goods and related articles. Among them was the Genty-Cathiard group, originally founded in the 1920s, and Docks de France, which had been one of France's leading hypermarket groups until its absorption by Auchan in 1994. A number of other retail groups joined the sporting goods market in the 1980s, including the appliance specialist Darty, and the FNAC chain.

Yet it was the Mulliez family who had been among the first to recognize the new potential of the sporting goods market, which was helped especially by France's newfound interest in such activities as jogging and aerobics, the rapid democratization of skiing and other winter sports, and growing numbers of hiking and bicycling enthusiasts. The country's other supermarket groups found themselves in the position of playing catch-up to the Mulliez-Auchan group. Genty-Cathiard's entry into sporting goods came in 1976, when it created a specialized

Company Perspectives:

With its know-how and financial health, and a market growing by 5 percent each year, the group Go Sport is able to consecrate itself on an intense development both in France and internationally. The perspectives are for 13 to 18 points of supplementary sales in 2000 and for 20 to 30 new stores each year starting from 2001.

subsidiary, Société Alpine de Sport, and launched a chain of sporting goods stores under the Team 5 name. One year later, Docks de France prepared its own entry into the booming sporting goods market, creating the Go Sport store concept.

The first Go Sport opened in Paris in 1978. The success of the initial store encouraged Docks de France to expand its sporting goods division, adding new stores in Paris and then in other major cities in France, while also moving across the Belgium border in 1980 to open its first store under its new Go Sport Belgique subsidiary. During the same period, Genty-Cathiard also had been building its sporting goods interest, notably through its Team 5 chain. The Team 5 signage also was exploited by another group, SEGMAS, which built up its own network of six stores before merging into Genty-Cathiard operations in 1983. At the same time, Docks de France returned to its supermarket core, selling off its growing Go Sport chain—which had reached 11 stores in the early 1980s—to Genty-Cathiard.

The acquisition of the Go Sport chain led Genty-Cathiard to merge all of its sporting goods interests into a single subsidiary, with Société Alpine de Sport, SEGMAS, and the Team 5 store name giving way to Go Sport in 1984. The newly formed Go Sport group now boasted 25 stores, making it France's largest network of sporting goods stores. Yet that lead was only temporary, as the Auchan group built up the Decathlon chain's dominant position before the end of the decade.

Under Genty-Cathiard, Go Sport saw a slow but steady expansion into the mid-1980s, with the company's concentration remaining on the French market. Yet the company continued to build up its interests in Belgium, which saw five Go Sport stores by the end of 1986. In that year, Genty-Cathiard placed Go Sports stock on the Paris Bourse's secondary market. The public offering gave Go Sport the financing to pursue a newly aggressive expansion program.

In 1987, Go Sport was presented with new opportunities for growth when both FNAC, which had opened FNAC Sport sporting goods stores in Lyon and Paris, and Darty, which, under its subsidiary Société de Diffusion Sport et Loisirs, had built up a chain of 11 Sparty sporting goods stores, decided to exit the sporting goods market. The acquisition of these new stores, coupled with the acquisitions of southern France-based sporting goods specialist Sports Sud and the Team 5 stores operated by the Société Nouvelle de Sport, enabled Go Sport to boost the number of its stores to 54—including 50 in France. Those stores soon were joined by a new store—and an entirely new market—by the end of 1987, when Go Sport entered the huge—and hugely competitive—U.S. market.

The first Go Sports store in the United States was joined by a second in 1988, and a third—and last—store in 1989. By then, Go Sports had made a number of other expansionist moves, including the acquisition of 50 percent of the group SPAO, a distributor of sporting goods in the Rhone-Alps region, in 1988. Go Sport took full control of SPAO in 1989, adding the company's ten stores to its growing network. The company also attempted a new international market in 1989, launching its first Go Sport in Spain. A second Spanish store was to open the following year. Genty-Cathiard's sports interests, meanwhile, had expanded beyond the Go Sport name, when it acquired the Courir chain of 16 retail sports footwear stores, established at the beginning of the 1980s.

Playing Catch-Up for the New Century

Go Sport's rapid expansion through the 1980s had left it in financial disarray as the decade came to a close. By 1989, the company's losses mounted to FFr 127 million on sales of FFr 1.1 billion. Genty-Cathiard, which had remained relatively modest-sized in a distribution climate marked by the rise of just a few giant retail groups, such as Auchan, Rallye, Carrefour, Leclerc, and others, itself bowed to the pressures of the highly competitive French retail scene when it agreed to be acquired by the Rallye group in 1990. Rallye, which had acquired control of the successful U.S. sports footwear specialist Athlete's Foot, placed Go Sport and Courir under its Sports division.

Under its new ownership, and now led by André Crestey, Go Sport was given a thorough reorganization. As Crestey described Go Sport's condition to *La Tribune:* "The stores were in bad shape, the personnel were unmotivated, and there was no enterprise-wide strategy to guide the various names." The company closed down a number of its underperforming French stores in 1990 and 1991. With new management in charge of Go Sport, the Go Sport name became the sole name for the company's entire chain, replacing the various stores' names inherited through acquisitions and kept in place under Genty-Cathiard. These moves helped Go Sport cut its losses, down to FFR 53 million in 1990 and to just FFr 8 million in 1991. By 1992, after the company sold off its Spanish and U.S. stores, Go Sport was once again able to show profits, of FFr 20 million. More store closings followed into the mid-1990s, now accompanied by a number of new store openings and the remodeling of a large number of existing locations. The company's chain now was stabilized at 75 stores in France and six stores in Belgium by the middle of the decade.

Accompanying the company's revamp of its retail network was a number of strategic capital investments, including the construction of a new distribution facility in Amiens, the opening of a new central buying facility, and the modernization of the company's computer technology. By the end of 1995, Go Sport had boosted its annual sales past the FFr 2 billion mark. With all of the company's stores now operating under the single Go Sport name, the company stepped up its employee training efforts, boosting the number of services stores offered to clients while also helping employees achieve a greater professionalism. Go Sport also began preparing to introduce its own brands—a formula that had helped Decathlon become France's dominant sporting goods specialist.

Key Dates:

1976: Genty-Cathiard forms Société Alpine de Sport and launches sporting goods store Team 5.
1977: Docks de France launches Go Sport.
1980: First Go Sport store is opened in Belgium.
1983: Genty-Cathiard acquires Go Sport and SEGMAS.
1984: Merger of Société Alpine de Sport, SEGMAS, and Go Sport under Go Sport name.
1986: Go Sport lists on Paris Bourse secondary market.
1987: Company acquires FNAC Sport and Sparty; opens first store in the United States.
1988: Company acquires SPAO.
1990: Genty-Cathiard is acquired by Groupe Rallye.
1992: Company sells off U.S. and Spain stores.
1995: Central purchasing facility and new distribution facility opens.
1999: Company enters Poland and, soon thereafter, Hungary.
2001: Go Sport and Courir merge.

The remodeling of the Go Sport chain took on greater steam in the late 1990s as the company completed the remodeling of more than 70 of its stores between 1996 and 1997, as well as expanding more than ten of its sites into a new, larger-scale format. The company also once again began opening new stores, with three new stores in 1996, six more in 1997, and seven more, including a new Belgium site, in 1998. That year also saw the company's sales jump as Go Sport reaped the benefits of France's hosting of the Soccer World Cup, which culminated in France's victory. The company also quickly began reaping the advantages of its inhouse labels—Wannabee and Go Sports—which swiftly rose to account for some 20 percent of the company's sales.

Go Sport's modest expansion moves in the late 1990s were to give way to a far more aggressive approach at the end of the decade, as the company vowed to begin expanding by as many as 20 to 30 new stores each year, starting with the 2001 year and targeting especially France's mid-sized cities, long neglected by the group. Part of the company's new expansion strategy was an increasing interest in international development. In 1999, the company moved into a new market when it opened three stores in Poland. Eastern Europe remained a target for the company's growth, as Go Sport entered the Hungarian market with a store in Budapest. At the same time, the company announced its intention to step up its international expansion, suggesting that it would enter at least one new foreign market each year. Spain and Italy were identified as potential expansion targets.

Supporting the company's growth was the opening of a new distribution facility in Valence in 2001. By then, Go Sport had been expanded in a new way when the company announced its intention to acquire its Rallye sister subsidiary Courir. Although analysts were somewhat skeptical about the promised synergies to be gained by the merger—since the Go Sport and Courir retail concepts differed greatly, not only in terms of merchandise but also in terms of the size of the stores—the merger boosted Go Sport, now renamed as Groupe Go Sport, to a solid place as France's number two sporting goods specialist chain, with nearly 250 stores and nearly FFr 4.4 billion in annual sales.

The company nonetheless remained far behind the French market leader Decathlon, a fact that gave rise to speculation that the Go Sport-Courir merger might only be a prelude to a future spin-off of the Rallye's French-based sporting goods wing. The merger of Promodes into Carrefour in 1998 created a new retail distribution heavyweight not only in France but on the international marketplace as well. In the race for survival in the quickly consolidating global retail landscape, Rallye and Auchan were tipped as likely merger partners—which in turn would necessitate a spin-off of Go Sport to avoid the creation of a Go Sport-Decathlon monopoly of the French sporting goods market. Both Rallye and Go Sport continued to deny any such plans as the new century got under way. While the French distribution market waited for the new wave of retail consolidation, Go Sport, now led by Charles Setboun, remained committed to its newly aggressive expansion plans.

Principal Subsidiaries

Go Sport S.A.; Courir S.A.; Go Sport Les Halles SNC; Club Sport Diffusion SA (Belgium); Go Sport International SAS; Les Buissieres SAS; Grand Large Sport SAS; Go Sport France SAS; Go Sport Diversification SAS; Go Sport Polska SP Z OO.

Principal Competitors

Athlete's Foot Group Inc.; Decathlon S.A.; GIB S.A.; Intersport International Cooperation; Venator Group, Inc.

Further Reading

Boudet, Antoine, ''Go Sport modifie ses structures pour accélérer son internationalization,'' *Les Echos,* June 22, 2000, p. 25.
Chauveau, Julie, ''Go Sport part à la conquête des villes moyennes,'' *La Tribune,* February 2, 1999.
Chevallard, Lucile, ''La fusion des filiales Rallye, Go Sport et Courir, laisse les analystes sceptique,'' *Les Echos,* September 6, 2000, p. 28.
Megnan, Geraldine, ''Go Sport retrouve la forme et le goût de la compétition,'' *La Tribune,* November 10, 1995.

—M.L. Cohen

C A S A
SABA

Grupo Casa Saba, S.A. de C.V.

Paseo de la Reforma 215
Mexico City, D.F. 11000
Mexico
Telephone: (525) 284-6600
Fax: (525) 284-6665
Web site: http://www.autrey.com

Public Company
Incorporated: 1937 as Botica Americana, S.A.
Employees: 5,572
Sales: 13.15 billion pesos ($1.38 billion) (1999)
Stock Exchanges: Mexico City New York (for American
   Depositary Receipts)
Ticker Symbols: SAB; ATY
NAIC: 42221 Drug, Drug Proprietaries and Druggists'
   Sundries Wholesalers; 42241 General Line Grocery
   Wholesalers; 551112 Offices of Other Holding
   Companies

Grupo Casa Saba, S.A. de C.V. is a holding company whose core business is the wholesale distribution of pharmaceutical products. Casa Saba is the largest distributor in Mexico of such products. It also distributes food products, health and beauty aid products, and perfume. The company distributes its products nationwide, to pharmacies, supermarkets, and department, convenience, and grocery stores. For more than a century the enterprise was owned and run by members of the Autrey family, and for more than 50 years it was known as Casa Autrey (House of Autrey). It was sold in 2000 to Grupo Xtra, the holding company of Isaac Saba Raffoul, one of Latin America's richest men.

Tampico Pharmacist and Distributor: 1892–1944

Newspaper and magazine articles—presumably based on Autrey family accounts—have described Adolfo Prescott John Autrey as the descendant of an ancestor who came to America from France with the Marquis de Lafayette to fight in the Revolutionary War and whose own descendants settled in Alabama to grow cotton. According to these accounts, after the Civil War the family drifted to Texas and then to Mexico, where Adolfo Autrey became the first to receive an oil drilling concession and to refine petroleum in Mexico. A scholarly book, however, describes this man as A.G. Autrey, an Irish-American chemist and reputed inventor of Angostura bitters. He emigrated to Mexico after the Civil War and bought a property in Papantla, Veracruz, in 1870, where he drilled for oil, although he was not the first to do so. He also built a small refinery to produce kerosene, which he sold to local markets. Autrey married, adopted Mexican citizenship, and after his wells dried up, moved to the port of Tampico in the state of Tamaulipas, where in 1892 he established a pharmacy called the Botica Americana.

Following a major strike in 1901, the Huesteca area of northern Veracruz and southern Tamaulipas became the center of the nascent Mexican oil industry, and Tampico became a boom town. A.G. Autrey had missed out on black-gold riches, but Tampico—hot, humid, and insanitary—was an ideal location to manufacture and sell medicines to the companies and their employees involved in extracting petroleum, refining it, and transporting the products. Botica Americana became Autrey y Autrey in 1896, presumably when the founder's son, Adolfo Alejandro Autrey Rena, joined the firm. The latter Autrey and his brother-in-law Gilo Davila de la Garza administered the business during the difficult years of the Mexican revolution that followed the overthrow of President Porfirio Diaz in 1911. During this period the enterprise had to contend with a change in money every time a new revolutionary band took control of the port. By the 1920s, however, stability was returning to Mexico, and Tampico prospered as never before.

Adolfo Autrey Rena's oldest child, Adolfo Eduardo Autrey Davila, was educated in the United States and graduated from the Philadelphia School of Pharmacy in 1925, following which he joined his father and uncle in the family business. During the 1920s the firm produced 80 percent of the medicines it sold, but by 1940 competition from drug manufacturers and laboratories had reduced this proportion to only 30 percent. Accordingly, Botica Americana—as the firm was renamed on its incorporation in 1937—became a small-scale wholesale distributor of medicines as well as a retailer and manufacturer. In 1941 the company purchased Drogueria Azteca, S.A., a small drug dis-

Company Perspectives:

Casa Saba's mission is to anticipate the requirements of our customers, suppliers and commercial partners in order to meet or exceed their value expectations when distributing and commercializing products or services. To expand our markets and create new relevant ones. To strengthen efficiency and technology and recognize our employees as the most important resource in order to achieve the company's highest profitability and its competitiveness.

tributor based in Mexico City, renaming itself Casa Autrey, S.A. in 1944, when the businesses officially merged. Autrey Rena remained proprietor of Botica Americana in Tampico until 1944, when the store closed following a labor dispute.

Nationwide Wholesaler: 1948–92

Casa Autrey dedicated itself to wholesaling drugs just at the right moment, because the industry was dominated by Germans who lost their foothold when Mexico declared war on Germany in 1942, six months after the United States entered World War II. But the business also entered its most difficult moment because of a recent decree—the imposition by the Mexican government of a price ceiling on medicines. The Mexican business magazine *Expansion* later quoted Autrey Davila in these words, "Owing to the price regulation on medicinal products ... the margins received by manufacturers have been reduced to such an extent that the business is in grave danger of a serious blow to its operations. ... In order to confront the situation now existing, it is necessary to make up in volume the lack of profit in each operation. In order to obtain greater volume of sales, it is necessary to augment capital."

Autrey Davila was as good as his word. In 1948 Casa Autrey established two lines of distribution: one for Mexico City, the other for the rest of the country. Its list of suppliers grew steadily larger and included Johnson & Johnson, Eli Lilly & Co., Roussell Uclaf, and Bristol-Meyers Co., to name just a few. In 1958 the business opened its first branch, in Monterrey, followed by four others in the next dozen years. By 1970 Casa Autrey was the largest of the 66 pharmaceutical distributors in Mexico. Distributors handled 90 percent of the annual 4 billion pesos ($320 million) in sales to pharmacies, typically taking a 23 percent markup from the manufacturer's price. Casa Autrey claimed to take only 18 percent and to offer discounts. It was employing more than 1,400 people and, according to Autrey Davila, had grown by an average of about 12 percent a year over the last 30 years.

By this time Casa Autrey was providing more than 16,000 products to about 6,500 of Mexico's 7,500 pharmacies. Interviewed by *Expansion,* Autrey Davila observed, "Half these products didn't exist 10 years ago. As a result, one of the most serious problems of distribution stems from the constant progress that the pharmaceutical industry has attained in recent years. We have to be very alert to changes ... and to alert our clients so that they don't keep ordering obsolete products." Without distributors such as Casa Autrey, he went on to say, pharmacies would be overwhelmed by the task of choosing products from 450 laboratories with a presence in Mexico. "We don't think of ourselves as selling medicine but as selling service."

Casa Autrey at this time employed a network of 200 sales agents who visited an average of 25 pharmacies, sometimes as often as twice a day. They not only took orders but also instructed the personnel about the tendencies of the market and the appearance of new products. "The laboratory," Autrey Davila continued, "can't estimate the volume of sales for a new drug. But we've already made the promotion. . . . We do special promotions above all in medications of a popular character or cosmetics." In this way, he added, the agents acted as marketing consultants, ensuring that the pharmacies did not select merchandise that would not sell well. Casa Autrey also extended 30- to 60-day credit to its customers, receiving 30-day credit itself from its suppliers.

Once an order was placed in Mexico City, it would be received in 95 percent of all cases at the warehouse early the next morning. The first trucks would depart in little more than two hours. A second shift of delivery vehicles would be sent out in the afternoon to important customers. Outside of Mexico City, orders would be filled and delivered in two days. The warehouse typically received 5,000 orders a day, with more than 12,000 items. A subsidiary, Laboratorios Azteca, S.A., was producing medications on a small scale, such as salves and bronchial syrups. Two of Autrey Davila's sons joined the company in 1964 and the other two in 1974, all of them after completing postgraduate studies in the United States.

In 1982 Casa Autrey transformed itself into a holding company that, in 1986, was renamed Organizacion Autrey, S.A. de C.V. The firm automated its distribution facilities and, in 1994, had 40,000 square meters (about 430,000 square feet) of warehouse space, more than 33,000 square meters (about 355,000 square feet) of shelf space, 4,723 meters (15,495 feet) of chutes and belts, and two Austrian-made robots handling more than 110,000 units a day of such high-demand items as Kodak film, cold remedies, and prescription drugs. In order to earn larger profits, Organizacion Autrey began distributing merchandise not subject to price controls in 1989, when it added nonprescription pharmaceutical products, usually sending them to supermarket chains, department stores, and local wholesale establishments. (Price controls on domestically manufactured pharmaceutical products began to be lifted the following year.) Also that year, it became the exclusive distributor of M&M and Mars chocolates in Mexico. By 1992 it had negotiated similar deals with Procter & Gamble Co. and Eastman Kodak Co. The company was renamed Grupo Casa Autrey in 1992 and made its initial public offering on the Mexico City and New York stock markets in 1993, selling 27 percent of the stock at $17 a share for a total take of $73 million. The value of the stock nearly doubled within a year. The sale of more stock in 1996 cut the Autrey family's share of the company to 60 percent.

Public Company: 1993–2000

Casa Autrey's sales reached about $843 million in 1994. Its net income was about $23.5 million. It was now distributing more than 200 foreign products and had added clients such as Lysol Brands (household products), Brown & Williamson To-

---

Key Dates:

1892: A.G. Autrey, a chemist, establishes a pharmacy in Tampico.
1941: Now chiefly a distributor, the company moves to Mexico City.
1970: Mexico's biggest drug wholesaler, Casa Autrey is distributing more than 16,000 products.
1993: Grupo Casa Autrey makes its initial public offering of stock.
2000: The company is purchased by Isaac Saba Raffoul and becomes Grupo Casa Saba.

---

bacco Corp., Duracell Inc. (batteries), and Gillette Co. (razors). Although supplying small retailers such as drugstores remained its staple business, it also was distributing products to one-quarter of all Mexico's supermarkets and big general merchandisers such as Cifra, S.A. de C.V. and Wal-Mart Stores Inc. Autrey trucks, based at 19 distribution centers, were delivering to points as far as 200 miles in any direction and making 30 to 40 deliveries in a single day.

Autrey Davila died in 1990. His eldest son, Adolfo Autrey Maza, was chairman of the board in the 1990s, and another son, Sergio, was director general (president). It was the two other sons, however—Carlos and Xavier—who were credited with redirecting the firm into other fields. They purchased the brokerage subsidiary (renamed Bolsa Mexico) of Grupo Financiero Bancomer, S.A. de C.V. in the early 1990s and used this vehicle to purchase stakes in Transportes Aeromar, Mexico's first regional airline; Minera Real del Monte; Mexico's largest steel manufacturer, privatized Altos Hornos de Mexico, S.A.; Grupo Financiero Inverlat, S.A.; Multibanco Comermex; and Satellites Mexicanos (Satmex), a satellite-communications system. Carlos ran the financial interests, Xavier the mining and steel businesses, and Sergio the telecommunications interests such as Satmex. The Autrey family was believed to be worth close to $1 billion.

Net profits dropped in 1995 as Mexico entered a severe recession and many of Casa Autrey's pharmacy accounts defaulted on their bills or went out of business. Nevertheless, Casa Autrey began distributing books and magazines that year after purchasing Publicaciones Citem, S.A. de C.V. The following year it purchased Uno a Uno, S.A. de C.V. (formerly Tecnografix S.A. de C.V.) and began distributing office supplies to corporate customers. This area was expanded in 1998, when the company acquired Papelera General, S.A. de C.V., a regional wholesale distributor of office supplies. In 1997 Casa Autrey purchased a competitor, Drogueros S.A. Analysts questioned the rationale for acquiring this distributor of pharmaceutical products, perfumes, cosmetics, beauty aids, school supplies, foods, and sweets, but the purchase enabled the company to stay No. 1 in sales in its field in the face of a challenge from Nacional de Drogas, S.A. de C.V. (Nadro). Publicaciones Citem had added distribution of Warner Bros. In addition, 20th Century Fox contributed movie videotapes to its offerings, and Casa Autrey was now distributing such food brands as Danone, Kraft, Pringles, and Uncle Ben's, plus household products such as Mop & Glo.

Although Grupo Casa Autrey's net sales recovered in subsequent years and its net income increased in 1996, the following year net income fell slightly, and in 1998 it dropped sharply to a disappointing 93.87 million pesos (in constant pesos as of the last day of 1999, or the equivalent of $9.87 million), representing less than one percent of its net sales of 11.79 billion constant pesos ($1.24 billion). The Drogueros acquisition was a drag on Casa Autrey's profits, and such nonpharmaceutical products as candy bars proved to be low-margin goods. The Autrey family's portfolio was doing even worse. The family lost control of Inverlat in 1996. By 1999 Altos Hornos and Aeromar were in difficulty. Grupo Casa Autrey's shares were trading at one-fourth the 1994 peak price.

Altos Hornos, which was held through Grupo Acerero del Norte—50 percent owned by the Autreys—was unable to meet payments on $1.8 billion in debt in 1999 and was sold to Grupo Imsa, S.A. de C.V. Grupo Casa Autrey pledged to restructure its debts after its bankers queried loans and guarantees totaling $140 million to two closely held Autrey family firms. Before the year was out, the Autreys had signed a letter of intent to sell the company for an estimated sum of more than $300 million to Grupo Xtra, the holding company of Isaac Saba Raffoul. The son of a Syrian-born Jewish dry goods peddler, he also had large holdings in flour milling and real estate.

Grupo Casa Autrey's finances improved slightly in 1999, with net income of 247.22 million pesos ($25.99 million) on net sales of 13.15 billion pesos ($1.38 billion). Sales, by product, consisted of pharmaceuticals, 80 percent; health and beauty aids and other products, 12 percent; publications, four percent; office products, two percent; and food products, two percent. The company had a branch in Mexico City and 19 other Mexican cities. There were 24 distribution centers with a total of 1.36 million square feet of warehouse space. The company's 725 trucks and vans filled 4.38 million orders during the year. It was buying pharmaceutical products from more than 81 laboratories and manufacturers. Among the products it was distributing on an exclusive basis in Mexico were Coppertone suntan lotion, General Mills granola bars, and Auriga Plasticos blank cassette tapes and diskettes. It was the leading distributor of weekly magazines in Mexico and was offering more than 650 titles from 400 publications. In all, the company was distributing 21,000 different products.

The sale of Grupo Casa Autrey was completed in February 2000. Publicaciones Citem was sold to Sergio Autrey and Papelera General to Adolfo Autrey. Saba Raffoul became chairman of the board. Manuel Saba Ades was appointed chief executive officer and a vice-president. The assistant CEO and two other vice-presidents also were members of the Saba family. The company was renamed Grupo Casa Saba. The new administration reduced the company's fleet of executive passenger cars from 350 to 150 and centralized the operation of the distribution centers with a Baan software system. An Internet-based business-to-business network was established to link 700 suppliers throughout the country. A business-to-consumer network, estabien.com, was to be established as a joint venture with Grupo Televisa S.A., which was to provide advertising for the system. Casa Saba's sales growth was expected to come close to eight percent in real terms in 2000, and its share of the Mexican pharmaceutical distribution market was said to have risen from 26 to 29 percent by one count (and 24 to 27 percent by another).

Principal Competitors

Grupo Corvi, S.A. de C.V.; Marzam, S.A. de C.V.; Nacional de Drogas, S.A. de C.V.

Further Reading

"Adolfo E. Autrey Davila," *Expansion,* April 13, 1994, pp. 31–33.

"Carlos Autrey Maza," *Expansion,* June 10, 1992, p. 55.

Dolan, Kerry A., "Drugstore Cowboy," *Forbes,* August 12, 1996, p. 16.

"Un enlace entre 500 y 6,500," *Expansion,* February 10, 1971, pp. 52–55.

Huerta, Eduardo, "El que mucho abarca . . . ," *Expansion,* October 8, 1997, pp. 71–72, 75–77.

"Latin America's Model IR Program," *Institutional Investor,* May 1995, p. 88.

Millman, Joel, "Mexican Billionaire Enjoys Good Timing," *Wall Street Journal,* August 22, 1997, p. A10.

——, "Mexican Family Attempts a Comeback," *Wall Street Journal,* May 3, 1999, p. A16.

——, "Mexico's Group Xtra to Buy Casa Autrey in Effort to Revive Drug Wholesaler," *Wall Street Journal,* November 17, 1999, p. A19.

——, "Pipeliners," *Forbes,* September 12, 1994, pp. 218, 220.

Ocasio Melendez, Marcial E., *Capitalism and Development: Tampico, Mexico 1876–1924,* New York: Peter Lang, 1998, pp. 100, 121.

Thurston, Charles W., "Mexico's Saba Builds Up Drug Distribution Network," *Chemical Market Reporter,* October 16, 2000, p. 22.

—Robert Halasz

Grupo Cydsa, S.A. de C.V.

Avenida Ricardo Margain Zozaya 325
San Pedro Garza Garcia, Nuevo Leon 66220
Mexico
Telephone: +52 8 152 4500
Toll Free: (888) 848-5117
Fax: +52 8 152 4813
Web site: http://www.cydsa.com

Public Company
Incorporated: 1945 as Celulosa y Derivados, S.A.
Employees: 10,652
Sales: 7.73 billion pesos ($813.89 million) (1999)
Stock Exchanges: Mexico City
Ticker Symbol: CYDSASA
NAIC: 551112 Offices of Other Holding Companies;
    325211 Plastics Material and Resin Manufacturing;
    326122 Plastics Pipe and Pipe Fitting Manufacturing;
    32511 Petrochemical Manufacturing; 325998 All
    Other Miscellaneous Chemical Product
    Manufacturing; 313111 Yarn Spinning Mills; 31323
    Nonwoven Fabric Mills

Grupo Cydsa, S.A. de C.V. is a Mexican holding company that, through its subsidiaries, manufactures in four areas: chemicals and plastics, fibers and textiles, flexible packaging, and water-treatment plants. Its products include acrylic fibers, yarns, textiles, and textile products, and polyvinyl chloride (PVC) resins and products, including pipes, fittings, and irrigation systems. Cydsa has more than 20 subsidiaries and manufacturing plants in eight Mexican cities. It exports its products to more than 50 countries.

Chemicals, Plastics, Packaging, and Fibers: 1945–80

Celulosa y Derivados, S.A., better known by the acronym Cydsa, was established in Monterrey in 1945 to manufacture rayon. Miguel G. Arce Santamarina, an engineer who had been working as a superintendent for a Mexico City rayon plant, organized the company after he left his previous employer when it was acquired by Celanese Mexicana, S.A. "Simply put," he later told the Mexican business magazine *Expansion,* "I didn't want to work for a foreign enterprise." Ten investors put up the initial capital of 500,000 pesos ($103,250). Among them was Andres G. Sada of the powerful combine of the Sada and Garza families known as the "Monterrey Group." The company lost money until September 1948, after which it was never in the red again, according to Arce Santamarina, who later became director general of the company.

Cydsa started making rayon cord for automobile tires in 1947 and viscose rayon for the manufacture of clear cellulose film in 1955. It added a chlorine and caustic-soda plant in 1958 and a carbon bisulfide plant in 1959. In 1961 it formed a partnership with Allied Chemical Co. to produce coolants under the Genetron name. In 1965 Cydsa established a packaging and wrapping plant, and with the French firm Rhone-Poulenc S.A., which made acrylic yarn. The company purchased a second chloride and caustic-soda plant in Pajaritos, Veracruz, owned by Petroleos Mexicanos (Pemex) in 1967. Between 1965 and 1969, Cydsa's sales grew, on average, by 34 percent a year, while net profits averaged a gain of 26 percent. Management sought an annual return of 20 percent and to pay a dividend of 12 percent.

By 1971 Grupo Cydsa consisted of 16 companies in Mexico and one in Costa Rica. Its three divisions—chemistry, synthetic fibers, and films and packaging—had combined annual sales of 1 billion pesos ($80 million). The plants in Monterrey and Guadalajara manufactured synthetic fibers consisting of six types of nylon and rayon, three of polyester, and two of acrylics. Polyester and acrylic fibers were being marketed under the Terlenka and Crysel names, respectively. This division was second only to Celanese Mexicana in quantity of synthetic fibers produced in Mexico, but Arce regarded the market as almost saturated.

Cydsa's more than 20 basic chemical products, with special emphasis on refrigerants and propellants, hydrofluoric acid, and potassium salts, were accounting for only about 20 percent of Cydsa's sales. Arce Santamarina, however, considered the company's future in petrochemicals as practically unlimited. The company was building new plants to produce sodium sulfide and hydrosulfide, plus caustic potash and potassium carbonate, of which Cydsa would be the first Mexican producer. Petrocel S.A. had been established in 1970 to produce DMT and TPA for use in filaments of synthetic fibers, especially polyester. Cydsa had signed a number of technical-assistance and joint-venture pacts with foreign companies. In addition to its ties with Allied and Rhone-Poulenc, it had established agreements with Morton Salt International of the United States, AKZO N.V. of the Netherlands, and British Cellophane Ltd. With B.F. Goodrich Chemical Corporation, Cydsa in 1971 acquired a controlling interest in Policyd, S.A. de C.V., a producer of polyvinyl chloride resins.

In 1973 Cydsa began offering its shares on the Mexico City stock exchange. That year Andres Marcelo Sada Zambrano, eldest son of Andres G. Sada, succeeded Arce Santamarina as director general. Educated as a mechanical engineer at the Massachusetts Institute of Technology, he had worked for Cydsa for 20 years, most recently as director general of its synthetic-fiber division. A year later, he was named Cydsa's chairman of the board as well. By 1975 Cydsa had added plastics and international divisions, and in that year, as a joint venture with the German firm Bayer AG, it opened a plant for the manufacture of toluene di-isocyanate (TDI), the only one in Latin America for this product used by the plastics industry. Sales in 1974 came to $2.485 billion pesos ($198.8 million), and employment reached 8,214. The Crysel plant in Guadalajara for the manufacture of acrylic fibers was the largest in Latin America, and the PVC plant in Mexico City the largest of its kind in the country.

Seeking New Areas of Growth: 1980–92

Cydsa's sales reached 8.62 million pesos (about $376 million) in 1980. The following year it acquired Plasticos Rex, S.A. de C.V., which was manufacturing PVC pipe and connectors and pressurized drip-irrigation systems. In 1982, however, world oil prices suddenly dropped, ending a decade-long Mexican boom. Overspending, both public and private, had resulted in debts that could not be met and Cydsa, like other enterprises, spent much of the decade trying to put its finances into order. By 1985 its sales had passed 130 billion pesos (about $420 million), and in 1987 it ranked tenth in sales among reporting Mexican companies (compared to 18th in 1974). The company acquired full ownership of Policyd—by now the leading PVC producer in Latin America—in 1988 and established a division for environmental services in 1990, represented by its subsidiary Atlatec, S.A. de C.V. This division's focus was on the design and production of water treatment plants, as well as on consulting.

Cydsa's efforts in the latter field had originated with the design and construction, in Monterrey in 1956, of the first water-treatment plants for industrial reuse in Mexico. Other companies and municipal bodies in northern Mexico subsequently hired Atlatec for this purpose. In Nuevo Laredo, for example, Atlatec constructed the largest wastewater-treatment plant in Mexico, 70 percent financed by the U.S. federal government. Between 1978 and 1987 Cydsa tried to change its internal culture and attitudes with regard to environment and safety, eventually adopting a master plan to deal with its problems in complying with the Mexican government's standards for air, water, and hazardous waste. Where environmental changes were not economically feasible, the company later closed plants making carbon disulfide, sulfuric acid, and rubber chemicals. Cydsa also converted from diesel- and bulk-oil fuels to natural gas to heat its steam generators.

By 1990 Sada Zambrano had been succeeded as director general of Cydsa by his close collaborator, Fernando Sada Malacara. His task in the early 1990s was to address the decline in profits that began in 1988, even though sales rose to 2.69 billion new pesos ($892.24 million) in 1991. Sada Malacara turned the company's focus from intermediate to consumer products by means of vertical integration and especially to exports, which had declined from a peak of 29 percent of company sales in 1987 and 1988. One measure taken toward this end in 1992 was to acquire Grupo San Marcos, owner of 12 textile plants. This consortium was Cydsa's leading Mexican consumer of acrylic fibers and yarns and the nation's leading manufacturer of acrylic products such as bedspreads, blankets, towels, tablecloths, and curtains. Cydsa also invested about $100 million in Masterpak, its holding company for the packaging division, in order to acquire machinery and reconvert its plants—which specialized in cellophane and bio-oriented polypropylene films—to more sophisticated products, such as toothpaste tubes and folding cartons. With negotiations that culminated in the North American Free Trade Association (NAFTA), underway, he looked to the United States and Canadian markets in founding a manufacturer of acrylic sweaters and forming a joint venture with Royal Plastics Group Ltd. to produce window frames.

Cydsa also divested itself of enterprises that didn't offer great opportunities for growth and profit. Accordingly, it sold its participation in companies such as Novaquim, a producer of specialty chemicals, and Plasticos Laminados, manufacturer of PVC and polyurethane laminates. It also closed the installations of Quimica Organica de Mexico, which was producing agrochemicals in Mexicali, Baja California. ''We analyzed in depth all our businesses as they exist now,'' Sada Malacara told Javier Martinez Staines of *Expansion,* ''and projected the future of each one in candid discussions. We found we had products that even if profitable today, wouldn't be in a totally competitive environment.'' Cydsa management was concerned, for example, about company manufacturing plants that consumed large quantities of electricity. In some of these facilities, electricity—more expensive than in the United States or Canada—represented 40 percent of all general operating costs.

Mixed Results: 1993–99

Although Cydsa's profits increased slightly in 1992 (on lower sales), in 1993 the company recorded a net loss of 41.3 million pesos ($13.1 million). The following year Tomas Gonzalez Sada succeeded Sada Malacara as director general and Sada Zambrano as chairman of the board. The drastic fall of the peso in late 1994 turned what would otherwise have been a profit for the year into a loss, but in 1995—in spite of a severe recession in Mexico—Cydsa registered the first of three consecutive years of profit. Exports were now accounting for about one-quarter of all sales, with acrylic fibers; yarns, blankets, and sweaters; PVCs; and flexible packaging films leading the way. Crown Crafts, Inc. had become the commercial agent for San Marcos products in the United States and Canada. To free funds to pay down debt and finance priority enterprises, Cydsa sold Bonlam, S.A. de C.V., a producer of nonwoven fabrics; Colombin Bel, S.A. de C.V., a manufacturer of polyurethane foam; and Genetec, S.A. de C.V., its agency for the exclusive distribution of Macintosh computers in Mexico, in 1994. Accordingly, the number of employees dropped from about 12,000 to about 10,000.

A sister enterprise, Vitro Corporativo S.A. de C.V., sold its 49.9-percent holding in Cydsa (valued at $250 million) in return for the proceeds from 47.6 million of its own shares, or 13.2 percent, that was held by Gonzalez Sada and his family. The Gonzalez Sada shares themselves were sold the next year. (Tomas Gonzalez Sada was a cousin of Federico Sada Gonzalez, the chief executive officer of Vitro.)

Cydsa lost money in both 1998 and 1999 on lower sales. Of the company's net sales of 7.73 billion pesos in 1999 (as adjusted for purchasing power on the last day of the year, and equivalent to $813.89 million), chemicals and plastics accounted for 47 percent; fabrics and textiles for 30 percent; packaging for 19 percent; and water-treatment plants for four percent. Exports came to 25

percent of sales. A solid profit of 171.17 million pesos ($18.02 million) in fabrics and textiles was more than obliterated by a loss of 519.3 million pesos ($54.66 million) in chemicals and plastics, and the company as a whole registered a net loss of 143 million pesos (about $15 million). The long-term debt came to 4.29 billion pesos ($448.7 million).

The products of the chemical division in 1999 were chlorine, caustic soda, sodium hypochlorite, hydrochloric acid and derivatives; refrigerant, foams, and propellant gases; toluene diisocyanate; refined salt and salt with lemon for cocktails; polyvinyl chloride, homopolymer and copolymer, suspension and dispersion resins; PVC pipes and fittings, irrigation systems, and polyethylene pipes and tanks for water storage; and chemical products for water treatment. The packaging division's products were regenerated cellulose film, bio-oriented polypropylene film, printed and laminated films, and folding cartons. (Masterpak, the holding company for the packaging division, sold its Celorey plant for regenerated cellulose film to UCB Films, Inc. in 2000.) The environmental division was designing, constructing, and financing industrial and municipal water-treatment plants, offering environmental consulting and laboratory services, and operating and maintaining water and wastewater systems and water-treatment plants.

The fibers division was manufacturing acrylic fibers for textile products and rayon textile and industrial filament. The yarn spinning and apparel division was producing acrylic yarns, acrylic blends with both natural and synthetic fibers, fancy yarn, knitting specialties, sewing threads, sweaters, and knitted garments. The home textile division was manufacturing blankets, bedspreads, comforters, quilts, throws, bedroom sets, towels, tablecloths, rugs, and curtains.

Principal Subsidiaries

Atlatec, S.A. de C.V.; Celulosa y Derivados, S.A. de C.V.; Celulosa y Derivados de Monterrey, S.A. de C.V.; Derivados Acrilicos, S.A. de C.V.; Hometex Products, Inc. (United States); Industrias Cydsa-Bayer, S.A. de C.V. (60%); Industrias Quimica del Istmo, S.A. de C.V.; Masterpak, S.A. de C.V.; Operadora de Servicios de Agua, S.A. de C.V.; Plasticos Rex, S.A. de C.V.; Policyd, S.A. de C.V.; Quimica Ecotec, S.A. de C.V.; Quimobasicos, S.A. de C.V. (51%); Sales del Istmo, S.A. de C.V.; San Marcos Textil de Mexico, S.A. de C.V.; Ultracil, S.A. de C.V.

Principal Operating Units

Chemical; Environmental Services; Fibers Division; Home Textiles; Packaging; Yarn Spinning and Apparel.

Principal Competitors

Alfa, S.A. de C.V.; Celanese Mexicana, S.A. de C.V.

Further Reading

"Frente y vuelta," *Expansion*, May 14, 1975, pp. 115–16, 199.
"La formula quimica de una integracion corporativa," *Expansion*, April 7, 1971, pp. 17–18, 20–22, 24, 26.
"La hombre de 'Expansion,'" *Expansion*, February 5, 1975, pp. 26, 28, 30.

Leal, Alba, ''Andres Marcelo Sada Zambrano,'' *Expansion,* April 26, 1995, pp. 22–23, 25.

Martinez Staines, Javier, ''El camino se hace al andar,'' *Expansion,* May 12, 1993, pp. 48, 52, 55.

——, ''El llamado de la integracion,'' *Expansion,* September 16, 1992, pp. 48–53.

''La nueva feria de San Marcos,'' *Expansion,* June 8, 1994, pp. 57–58, 61.

Rotman, David, ''Grupo Cydsa,'' *Chemical Week,* December 8, 1993, p. S8.

''Tomando valor,'' *Expansion,* June 21, 1995, pp. 66, 68.

Torres, Craig, ''Mexico's Sada Family Scraps Its System of Cross-Holdings to Stay Competitive,'' *Wall Street Journal,* December 10, 1997, p. A19.

—Robert Halasz

Elektra ⚙

Grupo Elektra, S.A. de C.V.

Avenida Insurgentes 3579
Mexico City, D.F. 14000
Mexico
Telephone: (525) 629-9000
Toll Free: (800) 021-3535
Fax: (525) 629-9200
Web site: http://www.elektra.com.mx

Public Company
Incorporated: 1950 as Grupo Empresarial Fenix S.A. de
   C.V.
Employees: 18,500
Sales: 11.47 billion pesos ($1.21 billion) (1999)
Stock Exchanges: Mexico City New York
Ticker Symbols: ELEKTRA; EKT
NAIC: 44211 Furniture Stores; 443111 Household
   Appliance Stores; 443112 Radio, Television and
   Other Electronics Stores; 44814 Family Clothing
   Stores; 551112 Offices of Other Holding Companies

Grupo Elektra, S.A. de C.V. is Latin America's largest specialty retailer and consumer finance company. It sells consumer electronic products, household appliances, and furniture through its Elektra and Salinas y Rocha stores and clothing through its THE ONE outlets. These products are also available through the Internet. Grupo Elektra's stores also offer such financial services as consumer credit, electronic cash transfers, extended warranties, home mortgages, and savings accounts. Grupo Elektra claims as its target customers the 83 percent of the Mexican population with monthly household income between $400 and $2,600 in 1999. Controlled by Ricardo Salinas Pliego, the group cross-markets its goods and services by means of other Salinas-controlled companies, including TV Azteca (two national networks), Unefon (wireless telephone service), Movil@access (pagers), Radiocel (radiocommunications equipment), and Todito.com (an Internet portal).

Elektra and Its Origins Before the 1990s

The origin of Grupo Elektra lies in the Monterrey furniture-manufacturing business that was opened in 1906 by Benjamin Ricardo Salinas Westrup and his brother-in-law, Joel Rocha, with the goal of selling the goods on discount. Some years later, it added mattresses to its products and developed into a holding company that produced kitchen appliances as well. It also, in the 1930s, implemented a formula new in Mexico: sales on credit. By 1943 the firm was being run by Salinas's son and Rocha's nephew Hugo Salinas Rocha. In that year the firm introduced its first department store, in Monterrey. It proved so successful that two years later the company introduced a second department store, in Mexico City.

In 1950 Salinas Rocha opened a business manufacturing radio sets, which he named Elektra. Two years later, his son Hugo Salinas Price became chief executive officer of the company. He made it Mexico's first television manufacturer and opened the first of its retail outlets in 1957, also introducing credit sales. There were six stores in 1958. This new enterprise opened a breach with his Rocha cousins, and in about 1960 Salinas Rocha and Salinas Price were expelled from their posts in Salinas y Rocha, although retaining a stake in the department store chain.

The Elektra chain grew to 12 in 1968 and 88 in 1980. This expansion was financed by banks, and in 1982 they held 52 percent of the company's stock, while the Salinas family held only 20 percent. When oil prices dropped sharply in the early 1980s, the peso lost 80 percent of its value against the dollar in two years. Elektra fell into, or close to, bankruptcy in 1982, for its sales were in pesos, while its debts were in dollars. While Salinas Price restructured Elektra's debts, his son Ricardo Salinas Pliego was taking an increasing part in managing the stores. The recent graduate of Tulane University's business school invested in a computer system after spending a day with Sam Walton, founder of Wal-Mart Stores Inc. Computerization of the stores allowed each one to operate with only six employees and provided instant information about sales, expenses, and inventory. Elektra also reduced prices and the number of lines of merchandise that the stores carried.

<table>
<tr><td>

Company Perspectives:

Our mission is to maintain our ability to offer customers affordable goods at a fair price, and to win their loyalty through service. We achieve this goal through continuing growth in neighboring stores, adding new accounts and increasing our market share.

</td></tr>
</table>

Even more important to Elektra's renewed growth, according to Salinas Pliego, who became president of the chain in 1987, was the decision to offer warranties on merchandise. Although this was not new in Mexico, the chain's extension of the concept to low-priced goods was truly revolutionary. Elektra's customers, Salinas explained in 1990 to Jorge A. Monjaras Moreno of the Mexican business magazine *Expansion,* were "humble people, of few resources. . . . But in a market so large, there are always people who have money," and they had the same expectations of quality as upper- and middle-class shoppers. "Among the readers of *Expansion,*" he added, "no one knows Elektra. But the chauffeur or the secretary know it well, because they are those who shop here," drawn by radio commercials declaring that no one could undersell the chain. Sales grew from 21 billion pesos ($23 million) in 1986–87, to $650 billion pesos ($249 million) in 1989–90, while the number of stores increased from 55 to 250 during this period.

By product, Elektra's sales at this time consisted of television, audio, and video, 65 percent; appliances, 18 percent; computers, seven percent; telephones, five percent; and furniture, five percent. Elektra held 30 percent of the national market in electronic products. About 40 percent of the electronics goods sold by the chain bore the Elektra trademark. Almost all of these products were made in Mexico until 1986, after which they were still assembled there, but with foreign parts. (Furniture and appliances were all made in Mexico.) At first, foreign companies were not interested in supplying Elektra with parts, but Salinas went to South Korea to convince companies such as Goldstar Co., Ltd., Daewoo Corp., and Samsung Electronics Co., Ltd. that Elektra would be a reliable partner for this function. Salinas told Monjaras Moreno that his chain now enjoyed the luxury of picking and choosing among suppliers. "It has to be an article well priced and dedicated to the popular market," he said. "We don't handle elitist products. Finally, the supplier must have sufficient capacity, because the volumes we deal with are very great."

Elektra's computer division also was proving successful at this time. IBM-compatible computers, sold under the Elektra name, were being assembled in Mexico from imported parts and being sold to customers of limited means. Salinas said, "Our clients are going to continue opting for the service and warranties that we offer them, above all because a computer requires a lot of technical knowledge in order to repair it." The telecommunications division was offering multiline telephone equipment, fax machines, and modems, all at low prices to attract trade from small and medium-sized businesses. Elektra also was seeking to sell trunking radiocommunications equipment for taxi fleets and delivery trucks, as well as digital beepers.

Consumer Credit Fueling Elektra's Growth: 1991–96

Between 1981 and 1987 the cost of living doubled, on average, each year in Mexico, forcing Elektra to suspend its credit program—not for the first time—in the latter year and substitute a layaway plan. In 1991 Elektra once again resumed extended credit to low-income people. This service cost them dearly, for they were required to make weekly payments (which drew them back in the stores to make more purchases) for 26 weeks and were charged what amounted to annual interest rates of 60 to 90 percent. In addition to the merchandise itself, the applicant had to offer collateral in the form of his or her own real estate or that of a co-signer. These customers had little option except to do without, for few qualified for bank credit cards. Within three years, more than half of Elektra's sales were on credit. Even so, the company did not approve credit applications lightly; in 1994 it employed 1,100 investigators to validate the information given by making house calls and checking salaries, reporting back within 24 hours. As a result, the default rate was so low that in 1997 Elektra became the first company in Latin America to issue securities backed by accounts receivable.

Elektra was still not truly nationwide in 1990. It was planning to open stores along the border with the United States, with a goal of 300 stores by the end of the year and 500 in 1993, the year Salinas Pliego moved up to chairman of the board. Although Elektra did not meet this goal, there were 400 stores at the end of 1995. "Visiting the average Elektra store is still like walking into a Mom-and-Pop appliance business," Mark Stevenson wrote that year for *Business Latin America,* "with one or at most two models of each item. Often located in neighborhoods where streets are yet to be paved, Elektra shops—almost always rented locations—are frequently the first businesses to enter many newly settled areas in ever-expanding Mexico City. Open-front set-ups and sticker prices listing weekly payments of as little as $6 on television sets draw a healthy crowd." Elsewhere, Elektra stores were generally somewhere near the "municipal market, where they sell chickens and fruit and so forth," as Salinas told Stevenson. Stores ranged in size from 2,000 to 7,000 square feet in traditional format to the 12,000 to 15,000 square feet in the MegaElektra format introduced in 1993.

The company made its initial public offering in December 1993 under the name Grupo Elektra, selling seven percent of its stock for $65 million. When Salinas launched TV Azteca in 1993, he used a $204 million bank loan to Elektra to help finance the purchase of the broadcasting network, which in turn used unsold air time to advertise Elektra's products. In 1996 Elektra spent $107 million for an indirect 14.5 percent stake in TV Azteca, through its 36 percent share of Comunicaciones Avanzados, S.A. de C.V., the broadcasting company's controlling shareholder. By the fall of 1997 this stake in TV Azteca had increased to 20 percent, but in 2000 Elektra sold it back to Comunicaciones Avanzados for about $400 million.

Elektra's sales rose from $1.46 billion new pesos ($458.73 million) in 1993 to $1.82 billion new pesos ($518.74 million) in 1994. Its net profit rose from 114.9 million pesos ($36.5 million) in 1993 to 192.9 million pesos ($55.1 million) in 1994. At the end of the latter year there were 586,000 active credit

Key Dates:

1950: Elektra is organized to manufacture radio sets.
1957: The first Elektra retail store is opened.
1980: The Elektra chain has reached 88 stores.
1991: Elektra resumes credit sales to its predominantly low-income clientele.
1996: Grupo Elektra purchases Hecali, a clothing store chain.
1999: Grupo Elektra acquires the Salinas y Rocha chain.

accounts, and nearly 70 percent of total sales were on credit. The chain's data bank held more than two million names.

A lucrative operation that Elektra introduced in 1994 was its "Money Within Minutes" remittance service, a joint venture with Western Union. Some 362,000 electronic transactions that year received in Elektra's stores yielded $100.5 million in payments made to south of the border and a profit of $4.4 million—thanks to its half of Western Union's eight percent transfer fee. Moreover, every recipient picking up money at an Elektra store was a potential merchandise buyer. "We know that approximately 17 percent of the people who receive money purchase something in the store afterward," Elektra's chief executive officer, Pedro Padilla Longoria, told *Discount Merchandiser* in 1995. "Money Express," a similar service for electronic cash transfers within Mexico, was introduced in 1996.

With only 20 percent of its debt in foreign money, Elektra was not badly hurt by the peso devaluation of December 1994. The chain dealt with the ensuing recession by orienting the product mix toward lower-priced products and extending the terms on the loans it was providing for big-ticket purchases. Sales dropped by only five percent in 1995. The number of Elektra stores reached 458 at the end of the year, when Grupo Elektra acquired 72 percent of Grupo Hecali, S.A., a clothing retailer with 40 stores, increasing this share to 88 percent the following year. Hecali accounted for five percent of Grupo Elektra's sales in 1996.

More Expansion and Cross-Marketing: 1997–2000

Elektra became, in 1997, the first major Mexican retailer to open stores abroad, introducing five in Guatemala and four in El Salvador. By late 1998 this number had increased to 22 and 10, respectively. There were also 18 stores in the Dominican Republic, 11 in Honduras, and ten in Lima, Peru. Elektra introduced photo-development and savings account services to its stores in 1997. The following year Salinas Pliego launched a low-cost fixed wireless telephone company named Unefon, S.A. Elektra's role, in return for three percent of Unefon's revenues, was to offer space in its stores for Unefon's sales and payment collection.

Salinas Pliego regained control of the Salinas y Rocha chain cofounded by his great-grandfather when Grupo Elektra purchased 94.3 percent of bankrupt Grupo SyR in 1999 for $77.7 million. Elektra kept the chain's 86 appliance stores but sold ten of its 11 department stores to El Puerto de Liverpool, S.A. de C.V., a department store chain that paid $27 million. Salinas y

Rocha was offering roughly the same merchandise mix as Elektra, but with a greater emphasis on furniture and to a more upscale customer. Elektra immediately invested $50 million in a program to remodel the Salinas y Rocha stores and negotiated more time to pay its suppliers, who were owed nearly $480 million pesos (about $50 million) in 1997. One of the most attractive aspects of the acquisition for Elektra was Salinas y Rocha's tax losses of $310 million, which Elektra amortized over three years. The Salinas y Rocha chain continued to operate under its name and under a separate administration until 2000, when Grupo SyR was absorbed by Grupo Elektra. Since Salinas y Rocha was still losing money, the fusion allowed Elektra to lower its tax rate.

Grupo Elektra's net income fell to its lowest level in years in 1998, but the following year it increased this profit by nearly threefold, earning net income of 780 million pesos ($105.5 million) on net revenues of 11.47 billion pesos ($1.21 billion). During 1999 the Hecali chain was renamed THE ONE. At the end of the year there were 598 Elektra stores in 320 Mexican cities, of which 366 were MegaElektra stores. Of the 232 others, 50 were Bodegas de Remates remainder outlets. Some 99 more Elektra stores were in the Dominican Republic, El Salvador, Guatemala, Honduras, and Peru. The number of THE ONE stores had grown to 159, and there were 90 Salinas y Rocha units, for a total of 946. Grupo Elektra was maintaining five distribution centers in Mexico and one each in the other five Latin American countries. Of the group's merchandise store sales, Elektra accounted for 86 percent, THE ONE for eight percent, and Salinas y Rocha, six percent.

Grupo Elektra had 812,676 credit accounts in 1999, and credit sales constituted 59 percent of its merchandise revenues that year. Interest earned on credit offered yielded 2.39 billion pesos ($251.92 million), or 21 percent of the group's revenues. Grupo Elektra's revenues from electronic money transfers came to 347.6 million pesos ($36.67 million), its share of $641 million from Money in Minutes and $139 million from Money Express. In alliance with Banca Serfin, the group was offering savings accounts to its customers. Also available were pagers and pager service contracts from Biper, radiocommunications trunking equipment from Radiocel, and wireless phones from Unefon—all of them Salinas-controlled enterprises.

In 2000 Grupo Elektra established a five-year strategic alliance with Todito.com, S.A. de C.V., a leading Internet portal and marketplace for Spanish speakers. Todito began opening kiosks in Elektra stores to sell low-cost computers equipped with Todito's Internet connection service. It also was offering computer classes in Mexico's largest chain of computer stores. The bundled hardware, software, and service sold for an average of about $1,000. Qualified Elektra customers were able to purchase Todito's packages through the chain's credit program. Also in 2000, Grupo Elektra began marketing home mortgages in its stores, in alliance with three other companies.

Salinas family members owned 63 percent of Grupo Elektra in 2000 according to one count; about 70 percent according to another. The following year Grupo Salinas was established as the umbrella body for holdings controlled by the Salinas family or in which the family held substantial investments. In addition to Grupo Elektra and TV Azteca, this grouping included

Movil@access (formerly Biper), Todito.com, Unefon, and Telecosmo, a newly formed high-speed wireless Internet access company. Grupo Salinas said that while each was under independent administration, the companies generated important synergies among themselves, conferring competitive advantages in their respective lines of business.

Principal Subsidiaries

Elektra Comercial, S.A.; Elektrafin Comercial, S.A.; Salinas y Rocha, S.A.; THE ONE, S.A.

Principal Competitors

Ceteco Holding N.V.; Coppel, S.A. de C.V.; Famsa; Singer Mexicana, S.A. de C.V.; Viana.

Further Reading

Arantzatzu Rizo, "Salinas y Rocha," *Expansion,* August 18, 1999, pp. 115–16, 119–21.

Cano, Araceli, "Desenlistaran a Salinas y Rocha de la BMV," *El Financiero,* January 4, 2001, p. 17.

Dolan, Kerry A., "The Salinas Touch," *Forbes,* November 1, 1999, pp. 129–30.

Estrada, Ivette, "Elektra: Abonando las finanzas," *Expansion,* July 5, 1995, pp. 64–65.

Friedland, Jonathan, "The New Protector," *Wall Street Journal,* May 8, 2000, p. R11.

Millman, Joel, "Mexican Retailer's Move Pummels Stock," *Wall Street Journal,* April 9, 1996, p. A15.

Monjaras Moreno, Jorge A., "Quien dice que no hay mercado?," *Expansion,* September 12, 1990, pp. 74–77, 80.

Palmeri, Christopher, "Shotguns and Airwaves," *Forbes,* June 6, 1994, pp. 50–51.

Pellet, Jennifer, "Grupo Elektra: Creative Retail South of the Border," *DM/Discount Merchandiser,* August 1995, pp. 24, 26, 28, 30, 81.

Pozas, Ricardo, and Luna, Matilde, eds., *Empresas y los empresarios en Mexico contemporaneo,* Mexico City: Editorial Grijalbo, 1991, pp. 337–54.

Stevenson, Mark, "A Formula for the Masses," *Business Latin America,* August 14, 1995, pp. 6–7.

Torres, Craig, "Mexican Rivals Heed Elektra's Expansion," *Wall Street Journal,* September 30, 1997, p. A19.

——, "Mexico's Grupo Elektra Pays Steep Price for Self-Deals," *Wall Street Journal,* July 13, 1994, p. A10.

Wright, Jeffrey, "Hold the Salsa," *Business Mexico,* October 1998, pp. 26–29.

—Robert Halasz

GWR group

GWR Group plc

PO Box 2345, 3B2 Westlea
Swindon SN5 7HF
United Kingdom
Telephone: +44-118-928-4314
Fax: +44-118-928-4310
Web site: http://www.gwrgroup.musicradio.com

Public Company
Incorporated: 1981 as Wiltshire Radio
Employees: 804
Sales: £102.3 million ($163.7 million) (2000)
Stock Exchanges: London
Ticker Symbol: GWG
NAIC: 5131 Radio and Television Broadcasting

Fast-growing GWR Group plc is the United Kingdom's leading commercial radio station group—in terms of number of radio stations owned; the company also has reached the government-imposed cap of 15 percent market share. GWR's flagship station is nationally operating Classic FM, which commands its classical music category with an average of some six million listeners, beating out rival BBC Radio 3. The company, which owns 63 percent of a partnership, also holds the United Kingdom's first national license for digital radio. The company launched its Digital One digital radio service in November 1999 with a bouquet of ten stations. Although digital radio sales remained slowed by high prices, as much as £800 ($1,200) for a home system, the company expects that more than 80 percent of the United Kingdom's homes will have digital-capable radios by 2005 as prices come down. In addition to its national services, GWR also holds more than 40 local radio stations throughout the United Kingdom, covering the gamut of radio formats. More than 98 percent of GWR's sales come from its U.K. home market. As the company continues, however, to press the British government to abandon the market caps imposed on commercial radio stations (which do not apply to government-owned BBC Corporation), GWR has gone overseas to look for growth. The company's primary international station is in Australia, but it also owns stations in Austria,

Finland, Holland, South Africa, Poland, Hungary, and Bulgaria. After taking over the radio holdings of the Daily Mail and General Trust (DMGT) media group in June 2000, GWR announced its intention to sell off some of its other radio stations to comply with government rules. The deal, which took the form of a shares swap, gave Daily Mail and General Trust a 27 percent holding in GWR. Led by founders Ralph Bernard, the group's CEO, and HPJ Meakin, its chairman, GWR also has made inroads onto the Internet, launching Internet-based broadcasting of its Classic FM station, while also offering free Internet access to its Classic FM listeners. At the end of 2000 the group also announced its interest in moving into pay television, with plans to reformat DGMT's arts station under the Classic FM format. Supporting its stations, the company set up a nationally operating sales office, Opus. The company posted revenues of more than £102 million in 2000.

Commercial Radio Revolution in the 1980s

Britain's radio waves remained controlled by government-run British Broadcasting Corporation until the 1970s when the first local licenses for commercial radio were awarded. Although the national market remained a government monopoly until the early 1990s, local radio stations quickly flourished, and the United Kingdom radio market was to feature some 150 local station licenses by the early 1980s and some 200 stations by the early 1990s.

Yet the United Kingdom's radio market was to remain limited in its impact. The focus on the local market meant small, revenue-poor stations, often owned by local celebrities or businesses, or institutions such as churches and schools. The results were generally amateurish stations unable to attract major advertisers. An equal hurdle to the commercial radio market was strict ownership rules put in place by the government, which included various ownership caps and restrictions: no single group could own more than 20 local stations or have more than 15 percent of all available licenses; owners of local newspapers were prohibited from owning more than 20 percent of any overlapping stations, while owners of national newspapers were limited to 20 percent ownership of any local radio stations. Another restriction was a requirement that companies broadcast simultaneously on both AM and FM bands. Such limitations prevented the formation of radio-oriented companies large enough to provide the technology advances needed by the radio market or broad enough audiences to attract major advertisers.

Among the new radio station owners were Henry Meakin, who had been behind the founding of media group Advent Communications in the late 1960s, and Ralph Bernard, who had held various radio positions, including a post at Sheffield's Radio Hallam, since the mid-1970s. Meakin acquired the license for Wiltshire Radio, starting the company's operations in 1981. He was joined for the launch of Wiltshire Radio by Bernard the following year. Meakin and Bernard quickly added a second local station. Yet their ambitions were to take their company to a national scale.

In 1985, Wiltshire Radio merged with Radio West, a failing station in Bristol's local market. The company now changed its name to GWR. In 1987, GWR acquired another station, Plymouth Sound. That same year, the company went public, taking the name GWR Group Plc. Meakin took the chairman's position and Bernard became CEO and, according to many, the visionary behind GWR's growth.

The United Kingdom's radio market had begun to transform itself by the end of the 1980s. A number of larger groups was building increasingly stronger market positions. Among these groups were Capital Radio, Emap, Scottish Media Group, and the Daily Mail and General Trust group. Pressure to pass new legislation governing the country's radio waves had been building up through the decade. A first step toward the more liberalized market of the 1990s came with the publication of the *Peackock Review of Broadcasting,* which recommended a number of changes, including the splitting of the AM and FM bands—enabling station license holders effectively to double their number of stations.

Other changes were in store as the government prepared the Broadcasting Act in 1990, which created a new licensing board, the Radio Authority, and provisions for the first national commercial radio licenses. The passage of this act—which nonetheless left most of the ownership restrictions in place—sparked a much-needed consolidation of the radio industry, as the industry's larger players raced to position themselves at the top of the market. GWR proved among the most aggressive of the new

industry leaders; by 1989, the company already had added two more stations, in Reading and Bournemouth. At the same time, GWR was making plans to win one of the proposed new national licenses to be awarded by the Radio Authority.

Radio On in the 1990s

GWR's entry into national radio came in 1992, when Classic FM took to the air. GWR had taken a 17 percent share of Classic FM and made no secret of its ambition to gain full control of the classical music broadcaster. That year saw a true outbreak of acquisition fever among the contenders for the United Kingdom's commercial radio market. By 1994, most of the country's 200 licenses were controlled by just six companies, including GWR, Metro, Capital Radio, Emap, Scottish Radio, DMGT, and Chiltern. These larger groups were helping commercial radio reach respectability—and profitability—and a number of fronts. The creation of the Radio Advertising Bureau by the big six gave commercial radio greater appeal to major advertisers. GWR was also to join with Capital Radio to form the Media Sales and Marketing advertising sales group. The larger groups also were able to invest in new technology, not only for their broadcasts, but also to link advertisements across the different radio stations in each group. These developments sparked the first strong revenue growth across the industry, sending most of the groups' profits soaring into triple-digit growth.

GWR's stake in Classic FM gave it a share of the increasingly strong market for national advertising revenues. By 1993, national advertising already had captured more than half of all radio revenue (and more than two-thirds by the end of the decade). Meanwhile, GWR had built up a portfolio of 20 local radio stations. The company also had gained two important shareholders: Capital Radio, with 20 percent of GWR, and DMGT, which owned nearly as much. Such cross-holdings among the major radio groups sparked a wave of consolidation moves through the mid-1980s. They also provided GWR with the opportunity to gain full control of Classic FM at the end of 1996.

The Classic FM acquisition, which gave the company a six million-strong national audience, helped the company's revenues soar from just £31 million at its September year-end in 1995 to more than £77 million at its new year-end in March 1997. At the same time, GWR brought its advertising sales in-house, creating the national advertising sales division Opus. The company meanwhile continued to build up its share of the local market, acquiring 30 percent of London New Radio, then paying nearly £4 million to acquire Radio Wyvern, of Hereford. This last acquisition, however, caused the company to top the station ownership limits, forcing it to sell part or all of a number of other stations. Yet the Radio Wyvern acquisition was seen as a strategic move for the company, giving GWR ''a strong geographic fit with the group's existing operations in the surrounding area,'' as Meakin told the *Independent.*

Bumping up against ownership restrictions had brought GWR to extend its acquisitive interests overseas, and the company began building up radio station portfolios in such countries as Australia and New Zealand, Austria, and other western European countries, while also eyeing the potentially lucrative markets in the former Eastern bloc countries. Nonetheless, the United Kingdom was to remain the company's chief source of revenues, representing more than 98 percent of its sales at the end of the century.

That market was set to grow still more. In 1998, GWR led a group of investors to win the United Kingdom's first national digital radio license—the company was uncontested in the bidding. The new radio service, which promised ten stations, included Classic FM and two other national radio stations, Virgin and Talk Radio, broadcasting digital quality sound, with a degree of interactivity (such as being able to tailor programming to listener preferences) that analog radio was unable to offer. GWR bet that digital radio would rise to become a major force in the U.K. radio market; the committed accepted, however, that its Digital One service might remain unprofitable for seven years or more. Hampering the penetration of digital radio was the high cost of digital-capable sets, with car radios costing upward of £500 and home sets up to £800. Increases in programming and consumer interest in high-technology was expected to fuel demand, in turn enabling prices to drop to a target of £100. GWR's majority position in Digital One was expected to cost it up to £3 million per year for the next several years.

Digital One began broadcasting at the end of 1999. By then, GWR had moved onto the Internet as well, launching Classic FM in a web-based format. The company also set up its own free Internet service for Classic FM listeners. The company began to extend its presence on the Internet the following year, forming a new Internet investment subsidiary, ecast ventures, and also launching the Musicradio.com portal site offering access not only to Classic FM, but also to its local stations and digital-only stations through the Internet.

Meanwhile, GWR continued acquiring new radio stations, making seven purchases through 1999, including Orchard FM, based in Somerset, Gemini FM, and 97 FM Plymouth Sound. In 2000, GWR strengthened its ties with shareholder and longtime collaborator DMGT when it agreed to acquire that company's DMG Radio division. The deal gave GWR eight new radio licenses in the United Kingdom, as well as operations in Australia and Hungary in exchange for an increase in DMGT's holding in GWR to slightly less than 27 percent. The deal was expected to herald a new period of closer collaboration between the two companies, leveraging DMGT's media resources with GWR's broadcasting clout. GWR announced its intention to enter the pay-TV market, applying the Classic FM format to DMGT's arts-oriented television channel.

Sales of digital radios began to rise steadily by the beginning of 2001, as prices began to fall. Meanwhile, the company's flagship Classic FM continued to post new listening audience records, attracting more than six million listeners for a total weekly hour rate of 48.7 million. The company, meanwhile, was awaiting a new Government White Paper for the new century, expected to loosen the country's ownership restrictions. With backing from many within the government, GWR hoped to make new acquisitions to increase its already strong position in its home market.

Principal Subsidiaries

GWR Radio Services Ltd.; Classic FM plc; Beacon Broadcasting Ltd; Wiltshire Radio plc; GWR (West) Ltd.; Thames Valley Broadcasting plc; Two Counties Radio Ltd; Chiltern Radio plc; Leicester Sound Ltd; Mercia Sound Ltd; Mid Anglia Radio plc; Radio Trent Ltd; Radio Broadland Ltd; Suffolk Group Radio plc; Radio Wyvern plc; Orchard Media Ltd; Plymouth Sound Ltd.; ecast ventures.

Principal Competitors

BBC Corporation; Scottish Radio plc; Capital Radio plc; SMG Plc; Chrysalis Group plc; Virgin Group Ltd; Emap plc.

Further Reading

Barrie, Chris, "Radio Attempts to Reinvent Itself, But Will We Tune In?," *Observer,* December 13, 1999.

Counsell, Gail, "Stay Tuned for Radio Takeovers," *Independent,* April 13, 1994, p. 18.

Horsman, Mathew, "GWR Tunes into Radio Wyvern with Pounds 3.9m Bid," *Independent,* January 1, 1997, p. 13.

Hughes, Chris, "GWR Will Be Back After the Break," *Independent,* November 8, 2000, p. 24.

McCann, Ralph, "Radio Cashes In on Classics Boom," *Independent,* June 17, 1998, p. 7.

O'Connor, Ashling, "GWR Buys Daily Mail Group's Radio Assets," *Financial Times,* June 14, 2000.

Teather, David, "GWR Plans Brand Extension into Pay-TV," *Guardian,* May 27, 2000.

Thackray, Rachelle, "GWR Finds the Rights Wavelength," *Independent on Sunday,* November 1, 1998, p. 25.

—M.L. Cohen

Hagemeyer N.V.

Rijksweg 69
1411 GE Naarden
The Netherlands
Telephone: (+31) 35-695-76-11
Fax: (+31) 35-694-43-96
Web site: http://www.hagemeyer.nl

Public Company
Incorporated: 1904
Employees: 18,841
Sales: EUR 6.41 billion ($6.45 billion) (1999)
Stock Exchanges: Euronext Amsterdam
Ticker Symbol: HGM
NAIC: 421620 Electrical Appliance, Television, and Radio Set Wholesalers

Hagemeyer N.V., inheritor of the great Dutch trading houses of the 19th century, is reinventing itself for the 21st century. The company, which operates as a holding company for a vast array of subsidiaries located all over the world, is shedding its consumer products distribution wing to concentrate around a new core of business-to-business products and services. Consumer products accounted for approximately one-fourth of Hagemeyer's revenues at the end of the century. Among the businesses sold off by the company at the turn of the century were Freetime Group's consumer angling division, the largest supplier of fishing equipment and related products in Europe; Case Logic, a leading marketer of cases for personal stereo and compact discs; Polly Logic, a maker of business gifts and related products; and Hagemeyer's two-thirds ownership of car rental agent Avis, which Hagemeyer sold to Avis Europe in January 2000. The company also is exiting the information technology distribution market. In November 2000, the company announced its plan to sell off its fast-growing Tech Pacific subsidiary, which is a leading supplier of computer hardware products to the Pacific Rim and Asian markets. The company also merged its Codis computer hardware distribution operations into a joint venture with Getronics NV. A steady diet of acquisitions will nonetheless assure continued growth to Hagemeyer's revenues. At the end of

2000, the company announced its acquisition of Almacenes de Baja y Media (ABM), the Spanish market's leading electrical distributor. Part of the company's decision to reorient its operations stem from the collapse of its South American retail subsidiary Ceteco, which foundered on the region's late 1990s economic crisis. Yet Hagemeyer has a long tradition of reinventing itself and adapting to current business realities. The company has been led by Rob Ter Haar since 1999. Hagemeyer trades on the Euronext Amsterdam stock exchange.

A Modern Trading House at the Turn of the Century

The Golden Era of Dutch trading was already some centuries past at the end of the 19th century, particularly as the British merchant houses gained control of the world's shipping lanes and dominated colonial trade. Yet the Dutch trading houses remained a strong force in world trade, especially between The Netherlands and its own colonies. Changing market conditions, however, were forcing a number of trading houses to exit such principal markets as the Dutch East Indies (Indonesia), leaving the field open for newcomers more willing and able to adapt to modern trade arrangements.

These newcomers included brothers Anton and Johan Hagemeijer (the "ij" was pronounced roughly like a "y"). Sons of an Amsterdam watchmaker, the Hagemeijer brothers traveled to Surabaya, in Indonesia, in the 1890s, beginning careers as bookkeepers in the colonial offices of other trading houses. Their career as independent traders began at the turn of the century, when Anton Hagemeijer, then 26 years old, traveled back to The Netherlands to marry. During his stay in The Netherlands, Hagemeijer agreed to receive a consignment of 24 cheeses from Alfensche Kaashandel, a cheese merchant located in Hagemeijer's wife's village of Alphen aan den Rijn, to be sold on commission. The consignment arrived in February of 1901 and sold at a profit. By March of that same year, with the arrival of a new consignment of cheeses, Hagemeijer was no longer working on commission, but in a joint venture with Alfensche Kaashandel.

Anton soon was joined by elder brother Johan in the growing new trading venture. By September of that year, Hagemeijer's ledgers recorded not only sales of cheeses, but a variety of other

Company Perspectives:

Hagemeyer N.V. is committed to creating value for shareholders. The primary focus of the Group's financial performance will be improvement in economic value generated, as measured by the excess of net operating profit after tax less a charge for the capital invested in the Group. To achieve this, the Group's strategy will target the following: manage the Group on a more focused basis thereby creating critical mass and opportunities for synergies and improved returns on the capital already invested in the businesses; allocate capital to acquisitions and investments which support the more focused strategy and lead to an improvement in economic value; withdraw from businesses which fit better with a third party and reinvest the proceeds in core businesses to create economic value; manage the Group's finances and capital structure to minimise the cost of capital whilst maintaining a strong balance sheet.

products, such as cigars, kapok, and even china—finding ready customers among the colony's luxury-starved European settlers. The Hagemeijer brothers soon quit their bookkeeper jobs to devote themselves full-time to their expanding business. By 1903, the business had grown to include a long list of items sailing to Indonesia from The Netherlands, including clocks, traveling bags, fabrics, ink, and wine, as well as continued imports of cheeses. Whereas the cheese imports remained a joint venture, the rest of the Hagemeijers' trade was entirely at their own risk. By then, however, the company already was booking some 60,000 guilders in revenues—a figure that doubled a year later.

The Hagemeijer brothers formally joined in business in 1904, establishing Hagemeijer & Co. in Surabaya. Soon after creating the business, Anton returned to Amsterdam to oversee the new company's growing purchasing operations, which were most likely handled by the brothers' father until then. A feature of the company was its willingness to trade in branded goods— a niche left untouched, for the most part, by its more established competitors. Hagemeijer not only acted as a distributor for well-known brand items, it also developed its own brands for its Indonesian market for a range of bulk goods. By the end of the first decade of the new century, Hagemeijer & Co.'s sales had topped NFl 1 million.

At the outbreak of the First World War, Hagemeijer's sales already had doubled, topping NFl 2 million, with profits of some NFl 200,000. The company's concentration on importing and wholesaling activities, and its focus on Indonesia, left it mostly untroubled during the war. Indeed, the company, which had entered the war with a capital of NFl 800,000, emerged from the war years with a capital that had more than quadrupled. The Netherlands' neutral position during the war enabled the company to continue operating from its main Amsterdam purchasing office, but also to open new purchasing agents, such as in Manchester, England, and extend its Indonesian distribution operations by opening a new branch in Medan.

The company lost one of its founders when Johan Hagemeijer died in October 1918. At that time, the company was reincorporated as a limited liability company, with shares divided equally between Anton Hagemeijer and his brother's widow. At the same time, the company adopted a new spelling for its name—Hagemeyer—because the "ij" character was not always available on typewriters of the day. The company's main East Indies operation was by then transferred to Batavia.

Recovering from Crisis in the 1920s

If Hagemeyer had prospered during the war, it was quickly caught up in its aftermath. The disruption of large parts of international trade had caused large-scale warehousing of merchandise and commodity items. The end of the war re-opened international trade. The market was now flooded with items, resulting in a vast price collapse that wiped out many of Hagemeyer's competitors, including a number of The Netherlands' oldest trading houses. Hagemeyer's own low levels of stock helped protect it from the worst of the market collapse. Yet it soon was forced to close a number of its branch offices and by 1921 the company's losses nonetheless mounted to some NFl 500,000. After posting losses again the following year, all of the company's shares were taken over by its creditor bank, a move that enabled Hagemeyer to remain in business and under Anton Hagemeijer's leadership. Control of the company later was transferred back to the Hagemeijer family, as the market quickly recovered in the early 1920s.

The company now sought to protect itself by restricting its activity almost entirely to shipments based on firm client orders, instead of allowing the company's far-flung buying agents to make purchases from the company's own funds. The company's growing presence in the relatively small Indonesian markets gave it a new boost in a rapidly changing market. Manufacturers increasingly granted market monopolies to distributors, giving trading houses such as Hagemeyer exclusive importing rights to a particular market. Hagemeyer successfully gained a strong list of clients and product markets for its Indonesian base, including Procter & Gamble, the Camel cigarette concession of Reynolds, Burroughs Wellcome & Co. beauty products, Willem II cigars, and Lijempf dairy products.

Hagemeyer, like most of the world's international trading houses, was hard hit by the Great Depression, which also had as a result a growing number of import and export restrictions. Nonetheless, by the late 1930s, the rebuilding of much of the world economic scene gave the company hope for renewed growth. To capitalize on the potential for expansion, Hagemeyer went public in 1937, listing on the Amsterdam stock exchange. Yet, just three years later, the company faced a new crisis, as The Netherlands was invaded by the German army.

The German takeover of The Netherlands sealed off the company's Netherlands operations from its main Indonesian branch. Shortly after the takeover, the Amsterdam branch had succeeded in building up a large stock; it was with this stock that the company's Netherlands' office managed to survive the war, even turning a small profit, while carefully avoiding collaborating with the Nazi occupier. Company founder Anton Hagemeijer, however, had been less careful. Hagemeijer had been in Manchester, England during the invasion of The Netherlands and, therefore, found himself classified as a German enemy. Meanwhile, the Dutch government in exile discovered

Key Dates:

1900: Anton and Johan Hagemeijer begin importing activities.
1904: Business incorporates as Hagemeijer & Co.
1918: Company reincorporates as limited liability company Hagemeyer & Co.
1921: Bank takes over company's shares.
1937: Hagemeyer is listed on Amsterdam stock exchange.
1950: Operations in New Guinea are established.
1952: An office in the Congo is opened.
1958: Hagemeyer acquires Handelmaatschappij v/h JF Sick & Co.
1965: Company acquires Amsterdamse Leder Maatschappij.
1969: Company acquires Indola.
1982: First Pacific acquires majority shareholding.
1988: Company enters U.S. specialty foods distribution market.
1995: Company acquires Borumij Wehry.
2000: Company acquires Almacenes de Baja y Media.

that Hagemeijer had been a major donor to the NSB, the Dutch Nazi party. Leadership of the company's Indonesian operations was placed under Hagemeyer's Batavia office, while Anton Hagemeijer fled to the United States.

The Japanese invasion of Indonesia put an end to Hagemeyer's activity in 1942. The Japanese capitulation in 1945 only brought a brief moment of renewed hope for the company, as nationalists proclaimed the republic of Indonesia, sparking a bitter four-year war ultimately lost by The Netherlands. Sensing that trade opportunities were to become extremely limited in the new Indonesian state, Hagemeyer already had begun to take steps to shift the focus of its operations. In 1950, the company was granted a one-year import and export monopoly for The Netherlands' New Guinea colony. Hagemeyer also began to develop operations in Singapore as well. By 1956, Hagemeyer decided that its New Guinea and Singapore operations were profitable enough for the company to exit the increasingly restrictive Indonesian market. An attempt to sell the company fell through, however, in that year.

Nonetheless, the company's expansion moves helped protect it when all Dutch companies operating in Indonesia were placed under Indonesian government control. Hagemeyer's position as a pure trading house helped buffer the company's losses; meanwhile, it stepped up its international expansion, targeting other Asian markets, but also looking toward the African continent. Hagemeyer had opened its first agent office in Congo in 1952; in 1958, the company acquired Handelmaatschappij v/h JF Sick & Co., giving it operations in Ghana, Nigeria, and Cameroon as well. In 1957, the company had turned also to the Dutch colony of Surinam, hoping to enter the South American market.

Transforming for a New Century

By the 1960s, Hagemeyer faced a new market reality—the growth of the jet airplane industry enabled manufacturers to come into closer contact with their customers, eliminating much of the market for the world's trading houses. Political unrest, as much of the world's colonies clamored for independence, led Hagemeyer to refocus its activities on its European home. By the early 1970s, some 70 percent of the company's activity came from Europe, compared with just 21 percent at the start of the 1960s. Where Hagemeyer had formerly imported European goods to Asia, it now began importing Asian goods, and especially Japanese products, into Europe. Among the company's important customers was the Matsushita group, which manufactured under such brand names as Panasonic.

Yet manufacturers increasingly moved to take over their own marketing and distribution activities in the 1970s. This climate led Hagemeyer into transforming itself from a pure import-export concern to a diversified manufacturer, a move the company began in 1965 with the acquisition of leather goods maker Amsterdamse Leder Maatschappij. This was to prove the first of a long series of acquisitions, including the 1969 acquisition of Indola, a diversified maker of cosmetics and pharmaceuticals, as well as electrical appliances. The company's manufacturing operations quickly proved disastrous, however. By the mid-1970s, the company, which continued in its struggle to achieve profitability with its manufacturing wing, gave up on new acquisitions. The deepening recession at the beginning of the 1980s brought new woes for the company, which slipped into losses. Rescue came, ironically, from Indonesian giant First Pacific, which gained majority control of Hagemeyer in 1982.

The arrival of Andrew Land as CEO and chairman helped Hagemeyer reestablish itself on the world scene. Land steered the company from a modestly sized, overly diversified and struggling company of just NFl 700 million in 1985 to a focused holding company posting more than NFl 12 billion by the end of the century. Land led Hagemeyer into building up a successful specialty foods importing arm in the United States, starting in 1988. The following year, the company acquired JW Bernard & Zn., bringing it into the wholesale electrotechnical business—which was to grow to become one of the company's primary businesses by the late 1990s.

The company, which existed primarily as a small head office guiding a growing empire of more or less independently operating subsidiaries, focused on building itself through acquisition, while being careful to buy only companies with profitable operations. Not all of the companies' acquisitions were successful, however, such as its purchase of Allwave, meant to mark an entry into retailing in 1989; the company sold off the Allwave chain of stores in 1992.

In 1995, Hagemeyer reached an agreement to acquire Borsumij Wehry, one of the oldest and formerly largest of The Netherlands' trading houses. The acquisition gave Hagemeyer the Ceteco South American retail operation, giving the company a stake in that continent for the first time. At the same time, Hagemeyer began to look into entering the fast-growing Asian computer market, acquiring computer hardware distributor Tech Pacific in 1997. The following year, as that market sank into economic turmoil, First Pacific sold off its 40 percent holding in Hagemeyer.

The extension of the Asian crisis into the Latin American market brought Hagemeyer its own headaches, as the company's Ceteco retail subsidiary, which operated extensive credit operations, found itself hit not only by the economic crisis but also by a series of natural disasters. Ceteco finally was forced to declare bankruptcy, bringing Hagemeyer its first losses in some 15 years.

The Ceteco collapse and the retirement of Andrew Land provided the moment for a new transformation for the company. Joining Hagemeyer now was Rob Ter Haar, who was given a mandate to revise the company's strategy. Ter Haar immediately announced the company's decision to sell off its consumer goods distribution operations and instead concentrate around a new core of business-to-business services. As part of its new orientation, the company also shed much of its only recently acquired computer businesses, including most of Tech Pacific in 1999. Instead, the company has increased its focus on business-to-business distribution, especially its strong electrotechnical wing. That operation was strengthened at the end of 2000 with the acquisition of Almacenes de Baja y Media, the Spanish market's leading distributor of electrical products. The transformed Hagemeyer, celebrating its 100th anniversary, looked forward to carrying on its trading house Heritage through the new century.

Principal Subsidiaries

Elektroskandia AB (Sweden); Elektroskandia AS (Norway); Elektroskandia Oy (Finland); Elektroskandia Ltd. (Russia); Elektroskandia AS (Estonia); Elektroskandia SIA (Latvia); UAB Elektroskandia (Lithuania); Elektroskandia Logistics (Shanghai) Co. Ltd. (People's Republic of China); Elektro Technischer Großhandel ETG J. Fröschl & Co. GmbH & Co. KG (Germany; 83.4%); Brück Elektrofachgroßhandel GmbH & Co. KG (Germany; 83.4%); Heberlein & Probst Elektro-Großhandlung GmbH & Co. (Germany; 83.4%); Heberlein & Probst GmbH & Co. (Germany); J.Fröschl & Co. Prag S.R.O. (Czech Republic; 83.4%); Newey & Eyre Ltd. (U.K.); Dunlop & Hamilton (U.K.); Newey & Eyre Specialist Cables (U.K.); Newey & Eyre Data Networking (U.K.); Nationwide Lamps (U.K.); Ross Electrical (U.K.); Lerwick Engineering Supplies & Services (U.K.); BLM Electrical Supplies (U.K.); A&A Security Technologies Ltd. (U.K.); Barron Control Group Limited (U.K.); Newey &

Eyre (C.I.) Ltd. (Guernsey); Newey & Eyre (Jersey) Ltd.; Eastern Electrical (Republic of Ireland); Bernard B.V.; Cable Support B.V.; Schweitzer Elektrogrosshandel GmbH (Austria); ELIN Elektrohandel GmbH (Austria); Winterhalter + Fenner AG (Switzerland); ElectroLAN SA (Switzerland); Tristate Electrical & Electronics Supply Company, Inc. (U.S.); Vallen Corporation (U.S.); Encon Safety Products, Inc. (U.S.); Vallen Safety Supply Company (U.S.A.); Lion-Vallen L.P. (U.S.; 50%); Century Sales & Services, Ltd. (Canada; 50%); Vallen Safety Supply Company, Ltd. (Canada; 62%); Proveedora de Seguridad Industrial del Golfo, S.A. de C.V. (Mexico; 90%); Vallen-Acetogen Safety Chile S.A. (Chile; 50%); Gen-Weld Safety Equipment Company Limited (Ireland); Stokvis Tapes en Lijmen B.V.; Peco Tapes B.V.; Qualitape N.V. (Belgium); Stokvis Danmark A/S (Denmark); Stokvis Finland Oy, Nummela; Stokvis Valorem S.A. (France); Stokvis Technische Klebebänder GmbH (Germany); Stokvis Tapes (U.K.) Ltd.; Norway Stokvis Tapes Norge AS; Sweden Garco AB; Van Wijk & Boerma Pompen B.V.; Van Wijk & Boerma Firepacks B.V.; Wynmalen & Hausmann B.V.; Pelle Services B.V.; Nemaasko B.V.; Diko Trading B.V.; Bouwmachines Hoogerheide B.V.

Principal Competitors

Anixter International Inc.; Consolidated Electrical Distributors Inc.; Graybar Electric Company, Inc.; Hughes Supply, Inc.; Legrand SA (France); Pameco Corporation; Premier Farnell plc; Thomas & Betts Corporation; Tyco International Ltd; WESCO International, Inc.; Wolseley plc.

Further Reading

"Hagemeyer Optimistic on Recovery," *Nation (Thailand)*, February 12, 1998.
"Hagemeyer wil kerngroep Tech Pacific afstoten," *De Telegraaf*, November 25, 2000.
Huisman, Rob, "Hagemeyer vaart wel by rechtlijnige flexibiliteit," *De Telegraaf*, May 24, 1997.
Jonker, Joost, and Keetie Sluyterman, *At Home on the World Markets*, Utrecht: SDU Uitgeves, 2000.
Puntasen, Jim, "Hagemeyer koopt Spaanse marktleider in distributie," *De Telegraaf*, December 15, 2000.

—M.L. Cohen

Haworth Inc.

1 Haworth Center
Holland, Michigan 49423
U.S.A.
Telephone: (616) 393-3000
Toll Free: (800) 344-2600
Fax: (616) 393-1570
Web site: http://www.haworth-furn.com

Private Company
Incorporated: 1948 as Modern Products Inc.
Employees: 10,000
Sales: $1.58 billion (1999 est.)
NAIC: 337211 Wood Office Furniture Manufacturing;
    337214 Office Furniture (Except Wood)
    Manufacturing; 337127 Institutional Furniture
    Manufacturing

Haworth Inc. is the second largest manufacturer of office furniture in the United States. Its principal competitors are Steelcase, Inc., the industry leader, and Herman Miller, Inc., and all three are Michigan companies. Haworth makes a huge range of furniture, from low-end lines sold at mass merchandisers like Office Depot to award-winning showcase design selections. Some of its brand names are Haworth, United Chair, Anderson Hickey, and Globe. Brands stemming from its European operations include Castelli, Comforto, Ordo, and Seldex. The company originated prewired movable office panels and successfully sued its larger rival Steelcase for patent infringement involving this product. Haworth began growing through acquisitions in the late 1980s and now has a host of subsidiaries in North America and in overseas markets. The company has manufacturing and sales operations in more than 70 countries worldwide. In addition to its strong presence in Europe, Haworth operates a sales and service division in Hong Kong to serve the Pacific Rim countries and has an extensive sales network throughout South America and the Middle East. Haworth is privately held by members of the Haworth family.

From Hobby to Business: 1940s–70s

Haworth began as a hobby for its founder, Gerrard W. Haworth, a graduate of Western Michigan University and the University of Michigan, who began teaching industrial arts in a Holland, Michigan high school in 1938. Hoping eventually to help finance college educations for his children, Haworth sought to supplement his income by beginning a part-time woodworking business out of his garage. Over the next ten years, his craftsmanship was recognized, and the number of orders he received for wood products grew.

Hoping to turn his passion for woodworking into a full-time profession, Haworth approached a local bank for a loan in 1948. Having had no prior business experience, however, he was rejected as too great a risk. Undaunted, Haworth mortgaged his home and accepted a $10,000 loan from his father, and, once obtaining the money he needed to begin business, he quit his teaching position, purchased secondhand shop equipment, and founded Modern Products. During its first two years, the company employed six woodworkers at a small plant in Holland and received orders for a wide variety of products, but in 1951 Modern Products won a contract that would determine the course of its business.

That year Haworth was approached by an architect who had designed an office partition to be used at the new United Auto Workers (UAW) union headquarters in Detroit. Haworth accepted the job of producing the partitions, and he set about planning the prototype. Referred to as a "bank partition," the product measured 66 inches high, consisting of 43 inches of wood and 12 inches at the top made of glass. The prebuilt partitions were well received at the UAW headquarters, and, speculating that other companies might also be interested in them, Haworth decided to focus his business on their production.

Business boomed over the next ten years, growing 30 to 40 percent annually, sometimes more, and in 1959 Modern Products became a national manufacturing concern. In 1961 the company moved to larger facilities, and during this time, Haworth's teenage son Richard began working at Modern Products, sweeping floors and operating some of the machinery. In

Company Perspectives:

Haworth Inc. is a leading designer and manufacturer of office furniture with a global reputation for innovative, high-quality products and services. International design magazine FX *states, 'Haworth seems to have a genuine intellectual lead among its influential peers. Such extreme thinking demonstrates a thoughtfulness and willingness to push boundaries.'*

1964, having graduated from Western Michigan University with a Bachelor's degree in business, Richard became an assistant sales manager at Modern Products, working at a plant in his hometown of Holland. Within two years he was promoted to vice-president for research and development, but soon was obliged to leave the company for service in the U.S. Army. When Richard returned to Modern Products in 1969, his father relied on him to help develop a new type of office furniture product.

During the 1960s, competitor Herman Miller, Inc. of Zeeland, Michigan had introduced the innovative Action Office System, consisting of movable panels, shelves, cabinets, and desktops that could be rearranged to create workstations and open spaces to accommodate a variety of floor plans. Richard countered with the development of a unique movable panel insulated with carpeting to reduce noise and help ensure privacy. Modern Products began manufacturing these new panels in 1971, and the following year the company's sales were estimated at $6 million.

Over the next few years Richard Haworth became increasingly interested in panel design. Christopher Palmeri, in an article in *Forbes,* stated that Richard's colleagues remembered him "anonymously visiting competitors' showrooms and taking their furniture apart" to learn more about panel construction. During this time he devised a method of installing electrical wiring inside panels that would exert a tremendous influence on the industry. Modern Products' prewired panels, introduced and patented by Richard Haworth in 1975, could be easily snapped together and eliminated the client's need to pay extra for electricians to wire office spaces. The new line of these panels, called Uni-Group, was a huge success, and that year sales increased sharply to around $10 million, while the number of people employed at Modern Products grew to 136.

Rapid Rise in the 1980s

Also that year the name of the company was changed to Haworth Inc., and a new corporate headquarters was established in Holland. In 1976 G.W. Haworth stepped aside, becoming chairperson and naming his son president. Richard Haworth oversaw years of phenomenal growth at Haworth Inc. Not only did the office systems and furniture industry as a whole become more profitable in the 1980s, but Haworth consistently grew at a rate more than two times the industry average. In 1980 Haworth set up a European division after reportedly spending nearly $30 million to acquire West German chair manufacturing company Comforto GmbH. By 1986 Haworth had become the country's third largest office furniture manufacturer; its sales exceeded $300 million, and its staff of 2,600 was producing office chairs, filing cabinets, and fabrics, in addition to the popular panels. Three years later, the company opened a showroom in London and estimated that nearly ten percent of its sales was generated in foreign countries.

During its expansion, Haworth became involved in a legal dispute with industry giant Steelcase, Inc. that would last more than 15 years. Steelcase had begun marketing a panel similar to Haworth's prewired panel in the late 1970s. Claiming that Steelcase had infringed on his patent, Richard Haworth sought compensation from the company in the early 1980s. Steelcase argued, however, that its prewired systems were developed by its own staff and brought into question Haworth's right to the patent. So in November 1985 Haworth filed a civil lawsuit against Steelcase. The case was tried in a Michigan court, and in May 1988 a U.S. District Court judge ruled in favor of Steelcase. In January 1989, however, the decision was overturned by the U.S. Court of Appeals, which found several errors in the Michigan court's interpretation of the case and ruled that Haworth's rights as patent holder had been infringed upon. The case was not definitively settled until 1997, when the U.S. District Court for western Michigan ordered Steelcase to pay Haworth damages of $211.5 million. This was deemed one of the largest patent litigation judgments in U.S. history. Richard Haworth filed a similar suit against Herman Miller, Inc. in 1992, declaring in *Forbes* that although litigation leads to bad will between the companies, "we believe we have to protect what we invest in."

The late 1980s was a difficult time for the office systems industry. Aggressive discounting and the increased sale of used office equipment led to a "shakeout" of the industry's smaller companies and to decreased earnings for Steelcase, Herman Miller, and Haworth. Nevertheless, Haworth continued to gain market share, and in 1990 it purchased the Mueller Furniture Company, a Holland-based manufacturer of wooden tables and chairs. In December of that year *Industry Week* magazine compared Haworth to an "overachieving younger sibling, who's content not just to catch up, but to overtake big brother's lead."

During this time, Haworth's unique corporate philosophy attracted attention in the business community. Referring to employees as "members," Haworth espoused a participative management style, in which all members were required to spend one hour per week brainstorming ways in which Haworth could better serve the customer. During busy periods, the company paid members overtime for this one-hour commitment. Characterizing its approach as "customer-driven," Haworth produced a creed for its members that, in the words of Richard Haworth, "put profit last on purpose because we believe profits are a result of doing the right thing, focusing on quality, our customers, and giving our employees freedom to do what's right."

In response to customer needs for a more open, interactive workspace than the paneled workstations provided, Haworth introduced new products in the 1990s. Conference tables were developed that could be easily rearranged to form circles, U-shapes, or individual tables, as were panels of lower heights made of transparent materials. Furthermore, Haworth made available adjustable-height work surfaces. The Trakker adjust-

Key Dates:

1948: Company is founded by Gerrard Haworth.

1976: Name is changed to Haworth Inc.; company introduces prewired office panels.

1986: Company becomes third largest in U.S. office furniture industry.

1997: Haworth wins more than $200 million in patent infringement case against Steelcase.

able table, for example, contained a computer memory that could be programmed to adjust the table to as many as 19 different heights. The computer could be set to periodically remind users to adjust the table in order to lessen their chances of stress injuries.

Acquisitions in the 1990s

Haworth had begun a run of acquisitions with its purchase of Comforto in the 1980s. The 1990s saw a marked increase in Haworth's size, as it bought up office and business furniture makers across the world. It concentrated on low- to middle-priced office furniture manufacturers, buying up or investing in a dozen companies between the late 1980s and 1993. Some of the companies it bought included Mueller Furniture Company, Kinetics, and Lunstead, all acquired in 1990. In 1993 Haworth purchased Globe Business Furniture, a domestic manufacturer of seating, institutional furniture, and ready-to-assemble office furniture. Globe was headquartered in Hendersonville, Tennessee and had estimated sales of more than $100 million for 1992. It sold its products through catalogs, warehouse clubs, and office superstores, and so it gave Haworth entry into these mass market distribution channels. Haworth picked up GSP Manufacturing in 1994, a maker of upholstered wood office furniture located in Tijuana, Mexico. Then in 1995 Haworth purchased Office Group America, of Leeds, Alabama. Office Group had sales of $150 million for 1995 and consisted of two units, Anderson Hickey and United Chair. All of the added subsidiaries put Haworth's total sales up to $1.2 billion by 1995. That year it did better than its close rival Herman Miller, Inc., giving Haworth the number two ranking in the office furniture industry.

By 1995, Haworth was deriving about 30 percent of its sales from overseas. The company hoped to push that figure to 50 percent over the next five years. Foreign acquisitions were key to Haworth's growth strategy. The company realized that many of its major customers operated globally. It had contracts with firms like Motorola and Sun Microsystems, and these companies were likely to want Haworth to work with them in overseas locations. Richard Haworth developed a lengthy process of getting to know possible acquisition targets. He explained his system in an article he authored for the January/February 1995 *Mergers & Acquisitions,* detailing how his firm worked for five or six years sometimes with companies it hoped to buy, moving cautiously toward formal acquisition talks. However, for Haworth, the long period of getting to know the target company paid off.

Haworth boasted rapidly accelerated revenues by 1996. Over the preceding five years, sales at Haworth almost doubled, while the overall business furniture market increased by only 30 percent. Haworth's operating margins were also better than its close competitors'—it had operating margins of ten percent, versus eight percent for Herman Miller and six percent for Steelcase. The slew of acquisitions had given Haworth a complete line of office furniture across all price ranges, but it had a good concentration of low- to medium-priced lines. The company worked hard to keep manufacturing prices down, to be able to continue to keep prices below its competitors. Although Haworth almost quadrupled in size over the early 1990s, the percentage it spent on sales, administrative, and other expenses went down significantly. The company also was known for lowering its prices in order to undercut competitors. A New York furniture distributor quoted in a May 1996 *Forbes* article described Haworth's policy thus: "If Miller and Knoll are offering 65% off on a project, Haworth says 71%." By 1996 Haworth boasted that it won 65 percent of all new contracts it bid on.

In the late 1990s and into the next decade, Haworth worked on developing innovative products. It established a research and development group in the late 1990s to work on ergonomically designed furniture and office space. Haworth not only looked to design more comfortable chairs and desks, but strived to design work spaces that helped workers concentrate and reduced stress. Haworth also invested in new computer software, using a system that enabled customers to view virtual workspaces on the screen so that changes could be previewed. The system also tallied estimated costs.

Haworth's acquisitions did not slacken as the company moved into the 21st century. In 2000 Haworth acquired a majority interest in a Canadian maker of laminate office furniture, Group Lacasse. Haworth also bought another Canadian company that year, Smed International. Smed, based in Calgary, with sales in Canadian dollars of $192 million, agreed to be bought by Haworth rather than accept another hostile offer. The Smed acquisition was expected to boost Haworth's sales so that it would surpass its rival Herman Miller for the number two spot in the office furniture industry.

Principal Subsidiaries

Comforto GmbH (Germany); Mueller Furniture Company; Lunstead, Inc.; Kinetics, Inc.; Ordo S.A. (France); Anderson Hickey Co.; Globe Business Furniture; First Source Furniture Group.

Principal Competitors

Steelcase, Inc.; Herman Miller, Inc.

Further Reading

Adams, Larry, "Blockbuster Deals Usher Out 1995," *Wood & Wood Products,* February 1996, p. 62.

Benson, Tracy E., "America's Unsung Heroes," *Industry Week,* December 3, 1990, pp. 12–22.

Brown, Christie, "You Say 65% Off, They Say 71%," *Forbes,* May 20, 1996, p. 164.

Crawley, Nancy, "Haworth, No. 3, 'Tries Harder,'" *Grand Rapids Press,* October 12, 1986.

——, "Reuther Order Gave Haworth His Start," *Grand Rapids Press,* October 12, 1986.

Garau, Rebecca, "Design with the Body in Mind," *HFN,* December 22, 1997, p. 22.

Geran, Monica, "Haworth in Chicago," *Interior Design,* January 1988, pp. 223–24.

Girard, Kim, "Want to See That Desk in 3-D?," *Computerworld,* April 6, 1998, p. 55.

Haworth, Richard, "The Mid-Sized Firm as a Global Acquirer: Haworth Inc.," *Mergers & Acquisitions,* January-February 1995, p. 31.

"Haworth to Acquire SMED," *Wood & Wood Products,* February 2000, p. 15.

"Haworth's International Initiative," *Industry Week,* February 15, 1993, p. 26.

Marks, Robert, "Haworth Acquires Globe," *HFD,* September 27, 1993, p. 21.

McClenahen, John S., "Global Citizen: Commitment to People and Community," *Industry Week,* January 4, 1993, pp. 31, 34.

Palmeri, Christopher, "Smart Boy," *Forbes,* May 11, 1992, p. 146.

Radigan, Mary, "Haworth Recalls Years of Growth for WMU Club," *Grand Rapids Press,* February 24, 1993.

Schrodt, Anita, "Material Handling Innovations Showcased: Mich. Furniture Manufacturer Is Customer-Driven Company," *Journal of Commerce,* February 23, 1989.

Sullivan, Elizabeth, "G.W. Haworth: Inside Track," *Grand Rapids Business Journal,* March 29, 1993.

"Sweet Justice," *Forbes,* January 27, 1997, p. 14.

Yue, Lorene, "Michigan Firms Aim to Adjust, Enlarge Work Spaces," *Knight-Ridder/Tribune Business News,* October 19, 2000.

—Tina Grant
—update: A. Woodward

Helmsley Enterprises, Inc.

230 Park Avenue, Room 659
New York, New York 10169
U.S.A.
Telephone: (212) 679-3600
Fax: (212) 953-2810

Private Company
Incorporated: 1938 as Dwight, Voorhis & Helmsley
Employees: 3,000
Sales: $1 billion (1999 est.)
NAIC: 53112 Lessors of Nonresidential Buildings (except Miniwarehouses); 53111 Lessors of Residential Buildings and Dwellings; 53121 Offices of Real Estate Agents and Brokers; 72111 Motels (Except Casino Hotels) and Motels

Beleaguered as it has been since Leona Helmsley's 1989 indictment and eventual conviction and imprisonment on charges of tax fraud, Helmsley Enterprises, Inc. is still one of the largest real estate companies in the country. Through a labyrinth of subsidiaries, it owns some nine million square feet of commercial space and more than 5,000 apartments, as well as the 2,600-room Helmsley Hotel chain and a large development site in Fort Lee, New Jersey. A significant portion of this empire is situated atop some of the priciest land in the country, namely Manhattan. The company's most prestigious cash cow is the Empire State Building, which it leases and manages but does not own. After Harry Helmsley's death in 1997, about half of the company's real estate has been sold, bringing in an estimated $2.5 billion. Nine individual properties sold for more than $100 million apiece between 1997 and 2000.

Until the late 1980s, the crown jewel of the Helmsley fold was the inordinately lush 55-story Helmsley Palace (since renamed The New York Palace), located at Madison Avenue and 50th Street. Ironically, this was one of the few Helmsley properties not solely owned by Helmsley founder Harry Brakmann Helmsley and his wife, Leona, whom he married in 1972. Because of this, and because of what even the mainstream media have called Leona Helmsley's ''Queen of Mean'' tactics,

the Palace became the Achilles' heel that brought about Leona's downfall.

The genius behind the phenomenal success of Helmsley Enterprises was Harry Helmsley. In its pre-gossip column, pre-tabloid, pre-Leona days, the Helmsley name was synonymous with the best, biggest, and brightest in New York real estate. The word, handshake, and vision of Harry Helmsley was what the company's development was founded upon.

Rise of Harry Helmsley in the 1930s and 1940s

Helmsley was born in the Bronx, New York, in 1909 to a family of modest means. Following graduation from high school in 1925, he obtained a job with the small Manhattan real estate brokerage of Dwight, Voorhis and Perry, serving first as a mail room clerk for $12 a week. The brokerage specialized in buying, selling, leasing, and managing buildings in low-rent neighborhoods. Helmsley was soon elevated to the role of rent collector in the Hell's Kitchen district. ''That's how he learned the city from the street up,'' recalled a Helmsley-Spear Inc. executive in a 1988 *Crain's New York Business* article.

Around the time of the 1929 stock market crash, Helmsley began free-lancing; that is, although he had no money of his own and his firm had none to spare, he began snatching up prime foreclosed properties by convincing banks the investments were sound and that he would manage the properties for them. During the 1930s Dwight, Voorhis benefited enormously from Helmsley's negotiating and managerial talents, and by the end of the Great Depression the young realtor was both a partner and chief spokesman for the firm, whose name was changed to Dwight, Voorhis & Helmsley and then Dwight-Helmsley, Inc.

Helmsley took his first major stride toward self-made billionaire status in 1938 when he assumed ownership—rather than management—of his first property, a ten-story office building on East 23rd Street between Fifth and Madison avenues. The property was scheduled to foreclose, and Helmsley used that informational leverage to acquire the $100,000 mortgage for a mere $1,000 down payment (all that Helmsley then had). *New York* contributor Nicholas Pileggi quoted Helmsley on the circumstances of the deal: ''The mortgage at the time was 3 percent, and it cost me $3,000 a year . . . and I remember I had a hard time, but I was confident that I would be able to turn the building around. I was in the management business. . . . I watched the building's expenses, such as fuel, electricity, and the payroll. I made sure that there wasn't one extra man on the staff. One extra employee could cost $3,000 in those days, and that made the difference as to whether I could pay the mortgage.'' Shortly after World War II, Helmsley sold the building for $165,000. He had built his nest egg and earned himself a reputation as a fair, though tight-fisted, operator.

Even before the sale, Helmsley was busy leveraging his abilities and testing his hunches through several other deals. According to Richard Hammer in *The Helmsley's: The Rise and Fall of Harry and Leona,* ''His goal was to build Dwight-Helmsley into a major force in New York real estate and in the process turn himself into a mover and a shaker.'' Foreseeing a postwar boom in the midst of World War II, Helmsley began to seek out bargain properties located close to Grand Central Station and other major commuter terminals. As before, he lacked the cash necessary to purchase them, but he discovered that he could retain part-ownership in exchange for signing away his five percent commission. Helmsley further sweetened these deals by contracting for the management of the buildings, which ensured him and the firm—now essentially owned by him—an ongoing stream of income.

Big Player After World War II

In 1949, wrote Jeanie Kasindorf in *New York,* ''Harry Helmsley entered the big time.'' The impetus was Helmsley's meeting with Lawrence Wien, a highly successful real estate lawyer. Wien had become an expert at the tax and legal strategies of buying and selling properties. What he lacked was the knowledge and experience that Helmsley so obviously possessed, that of selecting the choicest pieces of New York real estate and negotiating the best possible prices. Wien offered Helmsley an informal partnership that amounted to a pioneering venture in real estate syndication, which later became a common practice in the hybrid form of the Real Estate Investment Trust, or REIT.

Real estate syndication involves assembling groups of passive investors to buy properties otherwise unaffordable by the principal investors, with the ultimate goal of seeking a high rate of return for all involved. During the next 30 years, Wien and Helmsley created nearly 100 such syndicates, with Helmsley putting up little if any of his own money while generally reaping high profits and lucrative management fees. One of the most complex—and certainly the most famous—of the Wien-Helmsley deals was the sale-and-leaseback of the Empire State Building involving Prudential, which eventually was completed in 1961.

Two other realtors in the Dwight-Helmsley firm, Alvin Schwartz and Irving Schneider, also were making a name for themselves and the company in the New York market. Around the time that Helmsley began teaming with Wien, Schwartz left the firm to join Spear and Company, which specialized in managing office buildings and was owned by Schwartz's uncles. In 1955 Helmsley was flush with syndication revenues and seized an opportunity to reunite with Schwartz, whom he valued, by purchasing Spear and Company for half a million dollars.

Helmsley renamed the expanded concern Helmsley-Spear, which within a decade or so would become one of the city's foremost brokerages. Helmsley himself won early recognition in 1958 when he was named Realty Man of the Year by his peers. Helmsley-Spear (later subsumed by Helmsley Enterprises) gained its prominence by first acquiring the well-respected Charles F. Noyes Company, which was used to expand Helmsley's portfolio in lower Manhattan. The later purchase of Brown, Harris, Stevens was equally important, for this venerable firm brought Helmsley into the arena of rental and cooperative apartment sales and management. Well-publicized legal battles, however, that arose from Helmsley's repeated attempts to convert residential complexes, such as the Parkchester in the Bronx, into condominiums later soured the mogul on this real estate area.

In the Hotel Business in the 1970s and 1980s

After fashioning Helmsley-Spear into the largest real estate management company in the United States by 1970, Helmsley turned his attention to the luxury hotel business, to which he had first been exposed years back when he purchased the St. Moritz with Wien. Despite his unquestionable achievements, Helmsley was still known disparagingly in real estate circles, according to Milton Moskowitz in *Everybody's Business: A Field Guide to the 400 Leading Companies in America,* ''as a frugal operator, a landlord who would 'take a schlock property and run it as a schlock property forever'.'' In an effort to undo this reputation and to build something from the ground up, Helmsley announced his plans to open the Park Lane Hotel, which was to be the first new luxury hotel built in New York City in a decade. On the heels of the Park Lane's hugely successful opening came Helmsley's divorce from his first wife and his marriage to Leona Roberts, an ambitious New York realtor who already had made her first million and had been hired by Helmsley to work at Brown, Harris, Stevens.

Leona allegedly exerted an enormous and increasingly detrimental influence over Helmsley, who up until that time was a retiring Quaker unaccustomed to palatial living or, for that matter, underhanded business dealings. Although he was still being hailed in 1980 by *New York* magazine as ''by far the most successful real-estate man in New York today,'' with an estimated $5 billion empire, Helmsley was nearing the end of his reign. It was this same year that Leona was installed as president of Helmsley Hotels.

In her new position, Leona Helmsley oversaw the construction of Helmsley Palace, which Harry financed through a limited partnership with Leperq, deNeuflize and Company. The initial estimated cost of the Palace was $73 million, but Leona's numerous embellishments, and a layer of hidden costs that unduly benefited such Helmsley subsidiaries as Deco Purchasing Company (nominally headed by Leona's son from a former marriage), brought the total to $110 million by the time of its opening in 1981. When Harry Helmsley sought an additional $20 million from the Leperq investment group to help cover the overrun, he was met with firm rejection. In 1983 the Leperq group won a $3.5 million judgment against Helmsley for excessively high commissions charges related to Deco. Ironically, this same year Leona became chief executive of all Helmsley hotel operations.

In a devastating critique, Tom Shachtman commented in *Skyscraper Dreams: The Great Real Estate Dynasties of New York:* "Leona's vision involved spending, not creating, and her business decisions were principally negative. Once she took the empire in hand, there were no purchases of outstanding properties, but a considerable decline in the maintenance of those Helmsley properties in New York and Miami that were not her main focus, and a steady exodus of competent middle-rank employees from Helmsley-Spear (the brokerage hub of the empire) who felt that the organization Harry Helmsley had created no longer had a future." The impotency of the Helmsley empire was noticeably hinted at in a 1983 *Forbes* article, which mentioned Harry's grandiose but long-unimplemented plan to top the 1,454-foot Sears Tower of Chicago with a new skyscraper in his own beloved Manhattan.

Improprieties in the Early 1980s

Were it not for the Helmsleys' purchase of Dunnellen Hall, an $8 million country estate outside Greenwich, Connecticut, all might have been well. The purchase date of June 20, 1983 marked the beginning of a massive scheme, orchestrated by Leona, to defraud minority shareholders in the Palace and other Helmsley properties. In essence, the Helmsleys financed all of the remodeling of the estate, which approached astronomical proportions, through existing Helmsley subsidiaries. In addition, from 1983 to 1985, as the Leona Helmsley trial would later uncover, the Helmsleys evaded more than $4 million in state and federal income taxes. Many cited unadulterated greed as the reason for the scheme, but the amount the Helmsleys appeared to have gone to such great lengths to save paled in comparison to the actual taxes of more than $240 million the couple paid to the government during roughly the same period.

Whatever the case, the aging Harry Helmsley was declared unfit to stand trial in 1989. Following a final appeal of her conviction, Leona began her prison term on April 1, 1992. Meanwhile, as an abbreviated *Forbes 400* notice dated October 18, 1993 put it: "Harry still collecting receipts on empire while marking time, but estimated worth over $1 billion." Meanwhile, a dispute between the investors in the New York Helmsley Palace finally led to that building being placed in receivership and sold for $202 million in 1993.

The Empire After Helmsley's 1997 Death

At that time, no clear successor to the Helmsley empire had been named, especially given the untimely death of Leona's son, Jay Panzirer. At one point, Schwartz and Schneider were said to have retained the option of buying Helmsley-Spear upon the death of Helmsley, but the Helmsley estate, according to *Forbes* and insiders, was to go to the Quakers. Leona Helmsley was freed from prison in February 1994, after having served eight months in a federal prison, plus several months at a halfway house and in her own home under house arrest. Harry Helmsley remained in frail health. In 1996, when he was 87, his long-time partners Schwartz and Schneider sued Helmsley and Leona, alleging that Leona's management had bilked money from Helmsley-Spear, leaving that company unable to pay the millions of dollars it owed them. Harry Helmsley was apparently too ill to personally manage his business, and the relationship between Leona Helmsley and her husband's partners was described in the *New York Times* (May 8, 1996) as a "standoff." The Helmsley portfolio included many aging buildings suffering from lack of maintenance, but the legal tangles of the strained ties between the Helmsleys and their partners made simple sale of assets difficult.

Then Harry Helmsley died in January 1997, leaving Leona his real estate portfolio in its entirety. Six months after his death, Leona announced that the Helmsley property was for sale. She settled the lawsuits against her with Schneider and with Peter Malkin, the son-in-law of Lawrence Wien. In 1997 Schneider and Schwartz took over Helmsley-Spear, and Leona was no longer involved in its management. But Malkin and Schneider continued to disagree, leading to another lawsuit by Malkin over improper management of the Empire State Building. The real estate investment bank Eastdil organized the sale of the Helmsley buildings that were not encumbered by lawsuits. The list of available properties was headed by the chain of 13 Harley hotels, followed by several notable Manhattan buildings such as 140 Broadway and the Graybar Building, which was located over Grand Central Terminal. Many of the other buildings were nondescript office buildings or commercial spaces, some in poor repair. Eager buyers took over the properties and in some cases spent millions on renovations. The new owner of 140 Broadway, Silverstein Properties, spent more than $60 million on renovations on the building Harry Helmsley developed in the 1960s. Included in the new decor was a 20-foot-long black granite memorial to Helmsley, which Leona had requested.

By 2000, about half the Helmsley properties had been sold, bringing in an estimated $2.5 billion. Vornado Realty Trust paid $410 million in 1998 for 1 Penn Plaza and also paid $165 million for 770 Broadway. The Starrett-Lehigh Building at 601 West 26th Street sold for $152 million in 1998. The new owners then spent $22 million on renovations. A group of apartment buildings on the Upper West Side went for $122 million in 2000. By that year, Helmsley had sold a total of nine buildings for more than $100 million each, and many more for lesser prices. Leona Helmsley continued to live in the Helmsley Park Lane in Manhattan and the Helmsley Sandcastle in Sarasota, Florida. Although the 2,600-room hotel chain was hers to sell, her personal attachment to her homes made this sale unlikely. Other properties were not easy to dispose of because of the complicated ownership structure. For instance, the Fisk Building at 250 West 57th Street in midtown Manhattan had 15 partners in its original ownership structure. Getting the heirs and remaining players to agree on terms of sale would have been a formidable feat. As for the Empire State Building, by 1997 it remained clouded by Peter Malkin's lawsuit against Helmsley-Spear. Although Mrs. Helmsley had a majority interest in the building's operating sublease, other partners had to agree to the sale. Malkin hired a private detective firm to investigate mismanagement of the building, as part of his attempt to dislodge Helmsley-Spear from its management contract. What seemed to be personal animosity between Malkin and Irving Schneider, who was 80 years old in 2000, looked like it would hinder smooth resolution to problems at the historic building. So it remained in the Helmsley portfolio.

By 2000, Leona Helmsley herself had reached the age of 80. That year, the position of chief operating officer of Helmsley Enterprises went to Patrick Ward, a 47-year-old former optometrist. Ward quickly made changes at the company, such as hiring new managers for some of the company's hotels, the Park Lane and the Carlton. Helmsley Enterprises still owned vast amounts of property, despite the scores of buildings that had already been sold. The future of the company seemed to rest on the disposition of the legal quarrels between co-owners of its properties. Given the age of the principal players, it also looked like heirs and successors might be the ones to resolve the future of the remaining Helmsley empire.

Principal Competitors

Vornado Realty Trust.

Further Reading

Amster, Robin, "Helmsley Conviction Should Have Little Impact on Hotel Empire," *Travel Weekly,* September 21, 1989, p. 30.

Bagamery, Anne, " 'I Notice Everything'," *Forbes,* March 16, 1981, p. 164.

Barnfather, Maurice, "Has Success Spoiled Harry Helmsley?," *Forbes,* July 20, 1981, p. 94.

Brandt, Harris, "Did Leona's Ad Persona Win Her a Trip Up the River?," *Advertising Age,* April 27, 1992, p. 32.

Dunlap, David W., "Dividing Harry Helmsley's Empire," *New York Times,* November 26, 2000, Sec. 11, p. 1.

Grant, Peter, "Helmsley's Friend," *Wall Street Journal,* December 6, 2000, p. B14.

——, "Inside the Bitter Battle for Helmsley Buildings," *Wall Street Journal,* May 3, 2000, p. B14.

Hammer, Joshua, "Once Upon a Time It Was All Harry's," *Newsweek,* August 21, 1989, pp. 50–51.

Hammer, Richard, *The Helmsley's: The Rise and Fall of Harry and Leona,* New York: New American Library, 1990.

"Harry Brakmann Helmsley," *Forbes 400,* October 18, 1993, p. 156.

"Harry Helmsley in 'Let's Make a Deal,'...," *Nation's Business,* October 1980, pp. 55–58.

Kasindorf, Jeanie, "Leona and Harry: Money and Love," *New York,* October 3, 1988, pp. 41–49.

"Mr. Empire State Strikes Back," *Forbes,* April 11, 1983, pp. 180–81.

Moskowitz, Milton, ed., "Helmsley," *Everybody's Business: A Field Guide to the 400 Leading Companies in America,* New York: Doubleday, 1990, pp. 130–31.

Pacelle, Mitchell, "Once-Great Helmsley Property Portfolio Suffers Strains of Age and Neglect," *Wall Street Journal,* May 8, 1996, pp. B1, B4.

Pierson, Ransdell, *The Queen of Mean: The Unauthorized Biography of Leona Helmsley,* New York: Bantam Books, 1989.

Pileggi, Nicholas, "The Men Who Own New York," *New York,* May 19, 1980, pp. 26–33.

Selwitz, Robert, "Queen Ousted; Helmsley Palace on the Market," *Hotel & Motel Management,* October 5, 1992, pp. 1 and 21.

Shachtman, Tom, *Skyscraper Dreams: The Great Real Estate Dynasties of New York,* Boston: Little, Brown and Company, 1991.

Slatin, Peter, "Sale of Queen Leona's Portfolio Will Illustrate a Big Shift in Property Ownership; Cash Is Preferred," *Barron's,* November 17, 1997, p. 59.

Sommerfield, Frank, "Inevitable Fall," *Crain's New York Business,* May 23, 1988.

Teinowitz, Ira, "Helmsley Not Talking About Ads," *Advertising Age,* December 18, 1989, p. 44.

Waters, Harry F., "A Queen on Trial," *Newsweek,* August 21, 1989, pp. 46–51.

Winters, Patricia, "Leona Exits Helmsley Ads," *Advertising Age,* February 26, 1990, pp. 4 and 59.

—Jay P. Pederson
—update: A. Woodward

**The Science of Caring
for Companion Animals** ™

Heska Corporation

1613 Prospect Parkway
Fort Collins, Colorado 80525
U.S.A.
Telephone: (970) 493-7272
Toll Free: (800) 464-3752
Fax: (888) 437-5215
Web site: http://www.heska.com

Public Company
Incorporated: 1988 as Paravax
Employees: 463
Sales: $51.2 million (1999)
Stock Exchanges: NASDAQ
Ticker Symbol: HSKA
NAIC: 325412 Pharmaceutical Preparations
  Manufacturing; 339112 Veterinarians Instruments and
  Apparatus Manufacturing; 42210 Drugs and
  Druggists' Sundries Wholesalers; 541710
  Biotechnology Research and Development
  Laboratories or Services

The Heska Corporation is involved in biotechnical research for the development of vaccines and related diagnostic products for companion animals. The company manufactures health care products for dogs, cats, and horses and markets them to veterinarians. Products include treatments for fleas, heartworms, allergies, dermatitis, and viral infections. Heska also manufactures and distributes diagnostic and monitoring devices to veterinarians.

1980s Origins

Dr. Robert Grieve and Barr Dolan founded Heska in 1988 as Paravax, a name that reflected the company's intention to develop vaccines to treat parasites in companion and farm animals. Dolan provided funding as a venture capitalist with Charter Ventures, while Grieve provided expertise as professor of parasitology at the College of Veterinary Medicine at Colorado State University (CSU) in Fort Collins. With three employees, Paravax applied biotechnology—molecular biology, biochem-

istry, immunology, and genetic engineering—to the prevention and control of parasitic diseases, such as heartworm, transmitted by mosquitoes, and dermatitis, skin allergies caused by flea bites. Up to this time, most animal vaccine development addressed only viral and bacterial infections. Paravax intended the parasite vaccines to hinder the spread of disease much like rabies and distemper vaccines hinder those viruses. Dolan established Paravax in Mountain View, California, but the company relocated to Fort Collins in 1991 to be in closer contact with Grieve and to be closer to research facilities at CSU.

The first years at Paravax focused on research and development. Methods involved dissecting insects and removing the ovaries and salivary glands of fleas and the intestines of mosquitoes, to map the genetic codes and identify the amino acids that controlled digestion or reproduction. By cloning protein compounds that stopped digestion or reproduction, the company hoped to develop a genetically engineered vaccine that either killed the parasite or at least halted reproduction.

In October 1990 Paravax signed a research, development, and licensing agreement with Maboy Corporation, a subsidiary of Bayer USA, Inc., to create a vaccine for the prevention of toxoplasmosis in cats. The vaccine design aimed to reduce the excretion of the eggs of toxoplasma gondii, the protozoa that causes the disease, in cat feces. While the disease occasioned mild discomfort in cats, it was potentially harmful to pregnant women, as a cause of miscarriages and birth defects, and to people with immune disorders. Under the agreement Maboy financed the research and took responsibility for marketing the product when it gained approval from the U.S. Department of Agriculture (USDA). Paravax handled research and development and received a royalty based on sales. Also, in June 1991 Paravax received a $50,000 Small Business Research Grant from the National Institute of Health for research on the toxoplasmosis vaccine.

As biotechnical research continued, the proceedings compelled Grieve to leave his position at CSU and join Paravax as chief scientific officer in 1994. The following year Paravax changed its name to Heska, a Lakota word meaning ''white mountain,'' reflecting the company's location near the Rocky Mountains. With $10.63 million in venture capital—$10 mil-

213

lion from Volendam Investeringen NV and $630,000 from Charter Ventures—Heska continued its research and development, began efforts for marketing and sales, and started to acquire technology and products.

The company signed a licensing agreement with Atrix Laboratories in April 1995 to develop a periodontal treatment for companion animals. Atrix agreed to develop a sublingival product using its ATRIGEL Drug Delivery System. The implant released antibiotic doxycycline over several days to kill periodontal-causing bacteria. Atrix took responsibility for laboratory studies and production, and Paravax took responsibility for clinical testing in dogs and cats and for marketing and distribution worldwide.

Research and development on vaccines for companion animals expanded and progressed. Diseases addressed included Bartonella henselae, known as cat scratch fever and caused by the scratch of a infected cat's claw. Though generally not a fatal disease, it has been fatal to people with damaged immune systems. Heska completed development of a vaccine to kill fleas or hinder reproduction. The vaccine contained an antibiotic that the flea absorbed when it bit into an animal; the antibiotic bonded with digestive or reproductive proteins in the flea. All animal testing of products took place at CSU and followed the university's animal welfare guidelines.

During 1996 Heska doubled its research staff and facilities, increasing staff to more than 200 and adding two buildings to existing facilities, for a total of five facilities in the Fort Collins area. Increased spending on research accompanied this expansion, from $6.4 million in 1995 to $14.5 million in 1996 and $20.3 million in 1997.

Eight Years of Research Yields First Revenues

By 1996 the company had obtained government approval for several products and prepared for market production. Heska acquired Diamond Animal Health, a federally licensed biological and pharmaceutical manufacturing facility in Des Moines, Iowa. Assets included 166,000 square feet of operating space on 34 acres of land. Their Introductory products included many innovations, such as the first vaccine to prevent heartworm, the first vaccine for flea control, and the first vaccine for toxoplasmosis. The company also completed development of vaccines for cat scratch fever, equine influenza, feline leukemia, and feline immunodeficiency virus, as well as products to diagnose, prevent, and treat flea allergy dermatitis. Immunotherapy treatment sets, specific to each allergy, covered prescriptions for several injections with higher dosages during the course of the treatment, strengthening the immune response of the pet over the months.

In 1996 Heska's first revenues from products sales reached $15.6 million, for a total of $17.5 million in revenues, including funds received for sponsored research. This represented a very substantial increase; comparatively, in 1995 the company earned revenues of $4.7 million from royalties and $2.2 million from sponsored research.

Heska sought to expand through acquisitions in the United States and Europe in 1997. Heska entered the European animal health care market by providing veterinarian diagnostic services through its own laboratories. Hence, the company acquired Bloxham Laboratories Limited in the United Kingdom and attained production capacity when it purchased an interest in CMG Centre Medical des Grands' Places S.A. in Switzerland. The company established Heska AG to manage operations in Europe from Basel, Switzerland.

Acquisitions in the United States included Astarix, which specialized in allergy research and development, and Center Laboratories in Port Washington, New York, which provided a licensed manufacturing facility for allergy immunotherapy products. Heska acquired an interest in Sensor Devises, Inc., manufacturer and distributor of monitoring instruments, such as for monitoring pulse rate or respiration of animal patients under anesthesia. Renamed Heska Waukesha, Heska obtained complete ownership of the company in March 1998. Overall acquisitions increased Heska's staff to 500 employees, with 300 at research laboratories and administrative offices in Fort Collins and the balance at all other facilities.

Heska became a public company in July 1997 with an initial offering of stock at $8.50 per share, though the original asking price ranged from $14.00 to $16.00 per share. The offering raised $45 million for continued research, development, manufacturing, and marketing efforts. New products at this time included diagnostic products for heartworms in cats and a chewable dietary supplement to treat hypothyroidism in dogs.

Heska's strategy for expansion in 1998 involved alliances with other animal health and medical research companies. An exclusive agreement with iSTAT Corporation gave Heska the rights to market a portable blood analyzer and cartridges used to detect blood gases and electrolytes in animals with respiratory disease, renal disease, and disturbance of the central nervous system, or for monitoring animals under anesthesia for long periods of time. The product complemented Heska's existing line of monitoring instruments and diagnostic products.

Heska sought cooperative agreements with other health researchers to increase their technological options in product development. An agreement with Iomai Corporation involved evaluation of that company's proprietary Transcutaneous Immunization Technology for possible use in a painless, "no-needle" vaccine delivery systems for cats, dogs, and horses. Heska paid an option fee for an exclusive license in which Iomia would receive license fees, milestone payments, research funding, and royalties. Also, in a license agreement with Vaxcel Inc., Heska gained the rights to a microencapsulation technology for the development of oral vaccines.

In July 1998, the USDA approved Heska's breakthrough Solo Step FH, a feline diagnosis kit for heartworm infection completed in one step. The point-of-care product allowed veterinarians to diagnosis the disease using three drops of the cat's blood, obtaining results in five to ten minutes. Heska also

Key Dates:

1988: Paravax is founded to develop vaccines for animals.
1991: The company relocates to Fort Collins, Colorado.
1995: The company is renamed Heska.
1996: The company obtains its first revenues from direct sales of products.
1997: The company makes its initial public offering of stock.
1999: The management restructures the company to increase its profitability.
2000: Heska introduces the ALLERCEPT Detection System.

received six patents from the U.S. Patent and Trademark Office in September. The patents involved a novel vaccine delivery system for recombinant canine herpes virus, a flea allergen treatment, and four heartworm antigens.

In late 1998 Heska's pursuit of collaborative partnerships culminated in several cooperative agreements. An agreement with the National Jewish Medical and Research Center in Denver gave Heska access to the intellectual property for new treatments of cancer in companion animals. In exchange Heska agreed to make research milestone payments and to pay royalties. Heska hoped to treat tumors with a local injection of genes to induce a stronger immune system response from the pet. GeneMedicine Inc. allowed Heska to evaluate proprietary catonic lipid and polymer-based DNA formulation and delivery technologies. Research with the technology involved medicines for cancer-infectious diseases, utilizing therapeutic proteins or to stimulate the immune system in helpful ways. An agreement with Phytopharm plc involved the evaluation of a botanical compound with the potential for an exclusive license. Through a distribution agreement with Novartis Agro KK Heska gained the right to evaluate selected veterinary products from Novartis Animal Health in exchange for allowing Novartis to market certain Heska products in Japan, including heartworm diagnostic kits, periodontal treatments, and feline viral vaccines.

Striving for Profitability in 2000

After ten years in operation, Heska had not yet made a profit and decided to restructure the company to reduce overhead in an attempt to step toward the founding goal to be profitable in 2000. Heska eliminated or deferred research projects as research costs peaked at $25.1 million in 1998. In late 1998 the company eliminated 70 positions in Fort Collins, primarily research and development personnel, for an $8 million expense reduction in 1999. Leadership changes accompanied the restructuring. Fred Schwarzer, CEO since 1993, became chairman of the board, and Grieve became CEO effective January 1, 1999. The following August Heska announced its consolidation of diagnostic and monitoring equipment operations in Waukesha, Wisconsin, with facilities in Fort Collins and Des Moines, thereby reducing staff by 40 and closing the Wisconsin facility for a $2 million annual savings. Heska also discontinued products with low volume sales and low profit margins and narrowed its focus to veterinary products for companion animals.

Heska's research and development efforts continued to bear fruit. In 1999 the company launched a single-step diagnostic test and monitoring product for heartworm infection in dogs, HESKA Solo Step CH. The company received four patents in October, two for novel flea allergens and two for use of high affinity Immunoglobulin E (IgE) receptor alpha chain to detect IgE levels in cats and dogs. A total of 12 patents were issued in 1999 for a cumulative total of 42 patents, with 93 patents pending and related international patent filings. Heska also received USDA approval of Flu Avert I.N., an equine influenza vaccine, and began selling the product to veterinarians in December 1999. The nasal mist proved to be effective for up to six months in clinical tests, more effective than existing equine flu vaccines.

Heska's efforts to become profitable produced mixed results. Revenues increase 29 percent over 1998, at $51.2 million in 1999, and net loss decreased from $44.3 million in 1998 to $35.4 million net loss in 1999. While Heska paid some debt, its accumulated deficit reached $152.6 million in 1999. A public offering of 6.5 million shares, at $2.06 per share, to institutional investors in December 1999, raised $13.3 million for continued operations.

In its efforts to become profitable, Heska divested intellectual property and several facilities. The company sold its canine periodontal treatment, PERIOceutic Gel, to Pharmacia & Upjohn Animal Health, a company that already held a large share of the market for dental products for companion animals. In addition to receiving payment for worldwide sales and distribution rights, Heska received royalties based on sales of the product. Heska also sold two subsidiary units, Heska UK, a diagnostic laboratory serving veterinarians, and Centre Laboratories in Port Washington, New York, which produced allergy testing agents for humans and pets. Alk-Abello purchased the manufacturing facility and other assets for $6.4 million and agreed to supply Heska with allergen extracts and immunotherapy treatment sets. Alk-Abello also licensed Heska's intellectual property for recombinant allergens for human treatments, agreeing to pay royalties for product sales.

In 2000 Heska launched several health care products for cats. HESKA Feline ImmuCheck Assays tested the serum level of antibodies for feline panleukopenia virus, feline herpesvirus, and feline calicivirus. The diagnostic products assisted veterinarians in deciding the level of vaccination for these diseases by determining the strength of a cat's own immune response. Also, in cooperation with Ralston Purina, Heska developed a cat food for diabetic cats, DM-Formula. Under the CNM brand Ralston Purina marketed the cat food to veterinarians.

As Heska focused its research, development, and marketing activities on diagnostic and treatment products for companion animals, the company began to license intellectual property for use in human therapeutic applications, receiving fees and royalty payments in exchange. In an exclusive agreement, Circassia licensed certain small cat allergen peptides, and obtained the option to license house dust mite, ragweed, rye grass, and dog allergen peptides for human applications. Meiji Milk Products Co. of Tokyo licensed Japanese pollen allergens from Heska for human treatments in Japan.

In fall 2000 Heska presented research results for its ALLERCEPT Detection System, a technology for the diagnosis of allergies in companion animals. The test measured the level of IgE from a small blood sample; high levels of IgE indicated the presence of allergens. The test also identified the particular allergen from a panel of pollen, grass, mold, and insect allergens. Before ALLERCEPT, allergen testing involved great discomfort to the pet, requiring the veterinarian to shave a patch of skin and administer several injections. This form of testing entailed subjective evaluation. The ALLERCEPT test made detection and treatment easier and more effective while it addressed a primary reason that people take their pets to the veterinarian.

Strategic alliances continued to be an important avenue of growth and development. Heska entered into a collaborative effort with Valentis, Inc. through the license of a gene delivery system and DNA manufacturing technology. Heska applied the technology to the treatment of canine cancer hoping that clones of immune stimulators administered directly into cancerous tumors would reduce tumor growth and prevent the spread of cancer in other areas of the body. The company paid a license fee and agreed to make milestone payments, and to pay royalties from sales of the final product.

A distribution agreement with Novartis Animal Health in January 2001 involved giving Novartis exclusive rights to sell Heska's E-Screen Test in Europe. E-Screen Test prescreened dogs for allergens through a general test of IgE levels before the ALLERCEPT system tested for specific allergens. Production took place at CMG Heska allergy products facility in Fribourg, Switzerland.

Principal Subsidiaries

CMG-Heska Allergy Products S.A. (Switzerland); Diamond Animal Health, Inc.

Principal Competitors

American Home Products; Aventis; Bayer AG; Merial Ltd.; Novartis Animal Health; Pfizer, Inc.; Scherring-Plough Corporation; Pharmacia & Upjohn, Inc.; IDEXX Laboratories, Inc.

Further Reading

Aguilar, John, "Fort Collins Company Takes Lead in Pet Health," *Denver Post*, July 24, 2000, p. E1.

"Alliance Between Heska Corporation and Ralston Purina Results in Nutritional Product," *PR Newswire*, July 28, 2000.

Cornelius, Coleman, "Going through the Woof: Fast-Rising Fort Collins Firm Keeps Pets Healthy, Owners Happy," *Denver Post*, January 5, 1998, p. E1.

Day, Janet, "Paravax Itching to End Fleas," *Denver Post*, July 23, 1995, p. G1.

Gellici, Janet, and Arthur Harrison, "Paravax Developing Vaccine Against Ticks," *Denver Post*, October 9, 1992, p. C1.

"Heska and Novartis Enter into European Distribution Pact," *PR Newswire*, January 3, 2001.

"Heska Announces Completion of Public Offering," *PR Newswire*, December 3, 1999.

"Heska Announces Cost Reduction and Restructuring Plan," *PR Newswire*, December 2, 1998.

"Heska Corporation Granted Four Patents for Allergy Products," *PR Newswire*, October 13, 1999.

"Heska Granted Six Patents for Novel Vaccine Delivery System, Flea Allergens and Heartworm Antigens," *BIOTECH Patent News*, September 1, 1998.

"Heska Launches In-Clinic Canine Heartworm Diagnostic Test in U.S.," *PR Newswire*, January, 1998, p. 2559.

"Heska Launches In-Clinic Feline Heartworm Test in U.S.," *PR Newswire*, July 27, 1998.

Lenthe, Sue, "Leaner Heska Corp. Focuses on Future, Cuts Center Company on Core Products," *Northern Colorado Business Report*, October 20, 2000, 2B.

Wood, Carol, "Heska Doubles Work Force," *Northern Colorado Business Report*, December 1, 1996, p. 1A.

—Mary Tradii

HOLNAM

Holnam Inc.

6211 North Ann Arbor Road
P.O. Box 122
Dundee, Michigan 48131
U.S.A.
Telephone: (734) 529-2411
Toll Free: (800) 831-9507
Fax: (734) 529-5368
Web site: http://www.holnam.com

*Wholly Owned Subsidiary of Holderbank Financière
Glaris, Ltd.*
Incorporated: 1981
Employees: 5,200
Sales: $1 billion (1998 est.)
NAIC: 212321 Construction Sand and Gravel Mining;
32731 Cement Manufacturing; 32732 Ready-Mix
Concrete Manufacturing

Holnam Inc. is the largest cement manufacturer in the United States. Its parent company, the publicly traded Swiss company Holderbank Financière Glaris, Ltd., is the world's largest manufacturer of cement. Holnam operates 14 manufacturing facilities and more than 70 distribution terminals across the United States, and it has the capacity to produce more than 12 million tons of cement and mineral components annually. Besides cement, the company manufactures and markets mineral components such as fly ash and granulated blast furnace slag, which can be added to concrete and cement products, and it also manufactures a line of masonry products. Holnam was originally formed as a subsidiary of Holdernam Inc., a wholly owned subsidiary of Holderbank Financière Glaris. Beginning in March 1990 a succession of mergers and acquisitions made Holnam the largest cement company in North America. Holnam controls about 13 percent of the U.S. cement market, the leading share.

Holnam produces and delivers more than ten million tons of cement, the primary ingredient in concrete, each year. To produce cement, varying amounts of limestone, shale, clay, iron ore, and sand, are ground and mixed and then burned in a kiln where temperatures range from 350 to 3,400 degrees Fahrenheit. The resulting substance, known as clinker, is then mixed with gypsum and ground into the fine, gray powder that is cement, which may be mixed with sand, gravel, and water to produce concrete. The basic Portland cement, said to have the qualities of a particular building stone quarried on the British Isle of Portland, is available in several strengths suited for various applications in sidewalks, highways, building foundations, dams, and retaining walls. Holnam's masonry cements, including Rainbow brand custom color masonry cement, are used in both stone and stucco constructions, including walls, chimneys, manholes, and catch basins. Other construction needs are filled with Portland Pozzolan cement, which contains volcanic ash. Finally, Holnam also produces concrete mixtures for mass pourings as well as fly ash admixtures that serve to strengthen concrete by incorporating fly ash, a man-made by-product resulting from the combustion of coal.

Swiss Roots Early in the 20th Century

Holnam Inc. was first developed as a holding company for the U.S. interests of Holderbank, the world's largest producer of cement products and related services. Holderbank originated with a Swiss cement company called the Aargauische Portlandcement-Fabrik Holderbank-Wildeggbegan, founded in 1912 by Ernst Schmidheiny. The company was a success, and increased production capacity and earnings enabled it to acquire its rival, the Rheintalische Zementfabrik of Ruthi, in 1914. Beginning in the 1920s, the founder and his son expanded the company beyond Swiss borders, acquiring the Nederlandse Cement Industrie and the Ciments d'Obourg in Belgium, as well as constructing plants in Egypt and in Greece. To control its growing international empire, the company regrouped its interests in 1930 under an umbrella company known as Holderbank Financière Glaris Ltd.

The companies that would eventually comprise Holnam originated as early as 1953, when Holderbank founded its first North American enterprise, St. Lawrence Cement Inc., in Canada. Within two years, the first of St. Lawrence's cement plants was completed in Beauport, Quebec. The company's second plant, in Mississauga, Ontario, was established in 1956 and would become Canada's largest cement plant. St. Lawrence eventually gained a third plant in Canada and two more in the northeastern United States.

Holderbank's first U.S. venture, the Dundee Cement Company in Dundee, Michigan, was formed in 1958, becoming fully operational two years later. Like St. Lawrence, Dundee continued to expand under Holderbank's supervision. Its second plant in Clarksville, Missouri, on the Mississippi River, was completed in 1967 and featured the world's largest cement kiln, which measured 760 feet long and 25 feet in diameter and could accommodate 1.4 million tons of clinker a year. In 1978, Dundee acquired the Santee Portland Cement Corporation of Holly Hill, South Carolina, which marketed cement and mortar exclusively in the southeastern states. Dundee's final acquisition, the January 1990 purchase of Northwestern States Portland Cement Co., located in Mason City, Iowa, provided the company with another large facility.

In 1986 Holderbank reportedly paid nearly $110 million for a 66 percent interest in the struggling Denver-based Ideal Basic Industries. Ideal maintained nine plants in the mid-central, western, and southwestern regions of the United States, allowing Holderbank to explore new markets. Soon after the purchase, renovations were begun on Ideal's obsolete production facilities. Holderbank reportedly absorbed an extra $5.7 million increase in interest charges to renovate the Fort Collins, Colorado, plant alone. Ideal continued to struggle, however, posting a $24.1 million loss on sales of $245 million in 1989.

With the acquisition of Ideal, Holderbank gained a commanding 14 percent market share in the United States, ahead of its foreign competitors Blue Circle Industries of the United Kingdom and Lafarge Coppée of France. Furthermore, employing superior, highly cost-effective production techniques to gain a market advantage over rival U.S. cement makers, Holderbank had established a significant presence in North America during the building boom of the 1980s. However, recognizing the dependence of the cement industry on both business cycles and the construction industry, and becoming aware of the threat of a worldwide economic downturn, Holderbank began to consolidate its global activities for greater profitability toward the end of the 1980s. In 1988, preparing to consolidate and reorganize its U.S. companies, Holderbank contributed its interests in St. Lawrence, Dundee, and Ideal to Holnam Inc., a corporate shell established nine years earlier as a subsidiary of Holdernam Inc., Holderbank's U.S. arm.

A New Holnam for the 1990s

Two years later Holnam had been recreated, through mergers and acquisitions, as the country's largest cement manufacturer. First, in March 1990, Dundee and Ideal merged under the name Holnam Inc., which was then listed on the New York Stock Exchange. In the transaction, Holderbank acquired the remaining 34 percent interest in Ideal and retained 89.3 percent of Holnam's outstanding common stock, with minority shareholders owning the remainder. Holnam remained a direct subsidiary of Holdernam.

In its new form Holnam was comprised of Ideal Basic Industries, Dundee Cement Company with its subsidiaries Santee Cement Company and Northwestern States Portland Cement Co., and a 60 percent interest in St. Lawrence Cement, whose stock was traded separately on the Montreal and Toronto exchanges. The company established headquarters in Michigan, and Mark von Wyss, who had served as president at Dundee since 1971, became Holnam's president and chief executive officer. Peter Byland was named chairperson, a position in which he also served at St. Lawrence.

In the months immediately following the merger Holnam continued to expand. In August 1990, the company purchased the United Cement Company, whose facility represented the only cement plant in Mississippi, for approximately $60 million. Two months later the company paid approximately $2 million for Diversified Manufacturers, Inc. (DMI), an Alabama-based producer of masonry cement and stucco. C-Cure of Florida, a business similar in scope to DMI, was purchased by Holnam in March of the following year. During this time Holnam reorganized, providing a central management structure for manufacturing, transportation, distribution, and marketing.

Financially, Holnam experienced difficulties during the first two years after the merger. Although revenues in 1990 reached one $1 billion, and the company was ranked in the Fortune 500 list, Holnam sustained an overall loss of $28 million. A downturn in the construction industry as well as higher costs for fuel and pollution control equipment were cited as principal reasons for the heavy losses. The following year sales fell to $979 million as the company posted a net loss of $95 million. Furthermore, for the first time ever, St. Lawrence also reported losses. Analysts noted, however, that the economic recession during this time caused similar losses to be realized by Holnam's competitors throughout the industry.

Environmental issues also played a major role in Holnam's operations in the early 1990s. Public concern over Holnam's cement kilns arose in several areas of the country, when the company applied for permits to burn chemical wastes to fuel their kilns. Referring to the proposal as a ''win-win situation,'' Holnam maintained that besides providing the company with an economical alternative to burning coal or oil, it offered the country a safe and practical means to dispose of municipal and industrial waste, thereby reducing the need for landfills and conserving the natural resource of coal. Objections were raised both by local residents and environmentalists, who feared that the chemicals released into the air during the burning would be hazardous to plant and animal life in the area. Although protestors in Colorado convinced Holnam to abandon plans to burn

Key Dates:

1912: Ernst Schmidheiny founds Aargauische Port-landcement-Fabrik Holderbank-Wildeggbegan.

1930: Swiss holdings are organized under Holderbank Financière Glaris, Ltd.

1953: Holderbank opens first North American subsidiary.

1958: Dundee Cement Co. is founded.

1978: Dundee acquires Santee Portland Cement Corporation.

1981: Holdernam Inc., a subsidiary of Holderbank, forms its own subsidiary, Holnam Inc.

1986: Holderbank acquires majority interest in Ideal Basic Industries.

1990: Holnam created out of Dundee and Ideal; becomes largest U.S. cement maker.

wastes at the LaPorte and Fremont County kilns, subsequent research did not conclusively find the burning to be dangerous. Holnam did receive permission from other state regulatory agencies, and by the end of 1991 kilns in California, Alabama, Michigan, Missouri, and other locations began burning paint thinners and dry cleaning solvents for fuel. Others, including the Seattle operation, burned shredded tire scraps. Yet Holnam was unable to resolve other environmental problems so economically. The Dundee plant reportedly spent $17 million on controlling the emissions from its smokestacks, while another $2 million was spent to clean up the plant in Mason City, Iowa.

In 1991, forming a committee to work in cooperation with a consulting firm, Holnam studied the market, seeking ways to make the company profitable. Deciding to streamline its operations, the company closed its Denver offices as well as some of its bulk distribution terminals, maintaining its shipping fleet of five tugs, 75 barges, and 397 railroad cars. Renewing its commitment to its core products, Holnam introduced bagged cement and mortars into its Wisconsin, Missouri, Michigan, and Ohio markets, setting up new warehouses in the Midwest and promoting the products through new packaging and advertising.

During this time, the company terminated its relationship with BoxCrow Cement Company, a Texas-based company whose business and assets Holnam had acquired with an option to purchase before the merger in 1989. As part of the original agreement, the company had extended working capital loans to BoxCrow. By 1991 these loans totaled over $30 million, and BoxCrow was still experiencing cash flow problems and weak sales. Believing it unlikely that BoxCrow would be able to repay the loans, Holnam cut its losses by terminating the agreement. In another reorganization move, Holnam's Swiss parent decided to buy back all the company's outstanding stock. By February 1994, Holderbank Financière Glaris had acquired 100 percent of Holnam, and it operated the company as a private subsidiary.

Increasing Production in the Late 1990s and After

In its relatively new role as the country's leader in cement production, Holnam continued to seek out ways of making operations more efficient and cost-effective, while exploring new, related product lines. The company had a range of facilities across the United States, and it began spending money in the mid-1990s to make upgrades and improvements. One of its largest projects was the upgrade of its Devil's Slide plant in Morgan Canyon, Utah. The plant had been built in 1948, and Holnam planned to spend around $100 million on new, state-of-the-art equipment that would double the plant's capacity. Plans to improve the facility got underway in 1996. That year, Holnam also made a key acquisition. It bought the granulated blast furnace slag business of a company called Koch Minerals. This gave it production facilities in Weirton, West Virginia, and in South Chicago. Holnam had marketed slag, which could be used as a cement additive, for five years. The acquisition of Koch's slag assets assured Holnam a source for this mineral product.

Demand for cement in the United States continued to boom in the late 1990s, and Holnam added production to other plants. In 1999, the company announced it would spend approximately $200 million to build an addition to its existing plant in Florence, Colorado. The addition would make the finished plant one of the largest in the country. Like many of Holnam's other facilities, the Florence plant had a long history. It had been producing cement since 1898. The plant had been expanded once in 1948 and again in 1974. Colorado was a major market for cement. The state was estimated to need 2.3 million metric tons of cement in 1999, but total production capacity locally was only 1.7 million metric tons. When Holnam finished its work in Florence, that plant alone was expected to be able to supply 1.9 million metric tons. Holnam also looked at plans in 1999 to double the capacity of its cement plant in Holly Hills, South Carolina. The company also neared completion of upgrades at a large plant in Midlothian, Texas, and tripled capacity at its Chicago plant for slag-bearing cement. Next, the company considered building what would be one of the world's largest cement factories on land it acquired near the Mississippi River in Ste. Genevieve County, Missouri. The new plant was to mine limestone from a rich vein under the 3,900-acre site, and a kiln would produce some four million tons of cement. In working to persuade local officials of the need for the huge facility, Holnam explained that its plants were all producing at capacity, yet the U.S. still needed to import cement.

Principal Subsidiaries

Braswell Concrete Products, Inc.; Braswell Industries; Braswell Sand and Gravel Co., Inc.; Graysonia, Nashville & Ashdown Railroad; Ideal Concrete; Kevaland Corp.; Kevaland Texas Corp.; St. Lawrence Cement Inc.

Principal Competitors

Lafarge Corporation; Southdown, Inc.; Cemex, S.A. de C.V.; Heidelberger Zement AG; Blue Circle Industries plc.

Further Reading

"Holnam, Inc.," *Concrete Products*, December 1999, p. 41.

"Holnam Inc. to Buy Koch Operation," *Pit & Quarry*, June 1996, p. 15.

"Holnam Oversubscribed," *Private Placement Report*, December 14, 1998, p. 2.

Jones, Lara, "Cement Producer Planning $100 Million Upgrade of Morgan County Plant," *Enterprise/Salt Lake City*, March 25, 1996, p. 3.

Kohler, Jeremy, "One of the World's Largest Cement-Making Operations May be Built in Ste. Genevieve," *St. Louis Post-Dispatch*, April 27, 2000, p. JC1.

Mitchell, Jerry, "Chem Waste, Holnam Linked: Joint Venture to Supply Kiln Fuel," *Mississippi Business Journal*, January 11, 1993, p. 1.

Raabe, Steve, "Cement Plant to Expand in Colo.," *Denver Post*, February 2, 1999, p. C2.

Seebacher, Noreen, "Cementing a Spot on the Fortune 500," *Detroit News*, April 15, 1991.

Wernle, Bradford, "Dundee is Home to New $1 Billion Company," *Crain's Detroit Business*, March 26–April 1, 1990, pp. 1, 47.

—Tina Grant
—update: A. Woodward

Howard Hughes Medical Institute

400 Jones Bridge Road
Chevy Chase, Maryland 20815-6789
U.S.A.
Telephone: (301) 215-8500
Fax: (301) 215-8937
Web site: http://www.hhmi.org

Non-Profit Organization
Chartered: 1953
Employees: 3,000
Total Assets: $12 billion (1999)
NAIC: 813211 Grantmaking Foundations

The Howard Hughes Medical Institute (HHMI) is one of the largest private medical research organizations in the world. In the United States, only the federal government spends more money for medical research than the nearly $500 million received by some 330 HHMI scientists annually. The Institute's scientists conduct research in six broad areas: genetics, immunology, cell biology, neuroscience, structural biology, and computational biology. HHMI is also a major supporter of science education, awarding nearly $100 million each year to elementary and high schools, graduate and undergraduate institutions, zoos, and museums.

Benefactor Background

The Howard Hughes Medical Institute owes its existence to a drill bit, patented by Howard Robard Hughes, Sr., in 1909. Within a decade, three quarters of the world's oil wells used that bit, and the Hughes Tool Company was a profitable enterprise.

In 1924, 19-year-old Howard R. Hughes, Jr., inherited the majority share of the Hughes Tool Company and quickly bought his relatives' shares to gain control. A year later he wrote a will calling for the creation of a research institution "the objects and purposes of which shall be the prosecution of scientific research. . . . [It] shall be devoted to the search for and development of the highest scientific methods for the preven-

tion and treatment of diseases." It would be 25 years before Hughes took any specific steps toward that goal.

In the meantime, he set about making a name for himself. He went into the movie business in 1926 and later bought RKO Studios. In 1932, he created a division of the Hughes Tool Company to design airplanes. The Hughes Aircraft Company was born in a hanger in Burbank, California, rented from the Lockheed Aircraft Corporation. Over the next 15 years, Hughes designed such wonders as the H-1 racer, in which he set a transcontinental air record (nine hours and 27 minutes from Los Angeles to Newark), the power-driven landing gear, improved machine guns used in World War II, and the "Spruce Goose," the largest plane ever to fly. He also created Jane Russell's uplift bra for his movie "The Outlaw." In 1936 he invested $15 million in Transcontinental and Western Air, a failing rail and air service, which he built into Trans World Airlines.

Moving into Medical Research: 1950s

Hughes again turned to the topic of medical research while recuperating from extensive injuries after the 1946 crash of his XF-11 experimental photo-reconnaissance plane. At the urging of Alan Gregg of the Rockefeller Foundation, Hughes chose a decentralized research model that would affiliate with university medical schools rather than distribute grants to individuals or institutions. In 1951, Hughes named six physician-scientists as Howard Hughes Medical Research Fellows, paying their salaries himself.

In December 1953, Hughes chartered the Howard Hughes Medical Institute as a public charity, with himself as the sole trustee. At the same time he chartered the Hughes Aircraft Company and transferred all 75,000 shares of stock to HHMI, with a portion of the company's profits to be used to support the Institute's research. However, the complicated transaction left HHMI saddled with $18 million in debt and no endowment. Thus, in its first decade, it had to pay back to Hughes Tool Company (thus to Howard Hughes) most of the money it received from Hughes Aircraft. During 1954, HHMI's first full year of operation, it received less than $45,000 to spend on research. Through 1963, that amount came to less than $5 million.

221

According to Joel Brinkley in a 1986 *New York Times* article, the entire transaction was a tax dodge. The U.S. Air Force was threatening to cancel its contracts with Hughes Tool Company, whose subsidiary, Hughes Aircraft, was making parts for military aircraft. The Pentagon was satisfied when a charity became the owner of the defense contractor, and Hughes turned over corporate decision making to an appointed manager. The IRS was less sanguine, and in 1955 found that HHMI was "merely a device for siphoning off otherwise taxable income." That decision held for less than two years. In 1957, shortly after Hughes gave Donald Nixon, the vice-president's brother, an interest-free loan of $205,000, the IRS declared HHMI a tax-exempt charity.

Meanwhile, the Institute selected Miami, Florida, as its headquarters. A Medical Advisory Board, headed by Hughes' personal physician, appointed 12 Hughes Fellows in the first year of operation, paying them grants of up to $9,000. A Scientific Advisory Board was formed in 1956.

By 1957, HHMI had 47 investigators working at eight different university medical centers, including Harvard, Yale, the University of Miami, Johns Hopkins, and the University of Southern California. Their research encompassed a wide variety of fields, including biochemistry, cardiac surgery, crystallography, endocrinology, enzymology, immunology, microbiology, organ transplantation, and physiology. In 1959, HHMI established its first Institute laboratory—microbiology at the University of Miami. However, little was heard from the Institute for the next two decades, and the Medical Advisory Board never heard from Howard Hughes after the mid-1950s. In the 23 years between its founding and Hughes' death in 1976, HHMI provided some $63 million to support scientific research, on average less than $3 million a year.

1976: Where There's Not a Will . . .

Hughes' death, without a valid will, initiated a long, convoluted court battle over his estate. Heirs, trustees, and executives fought over Summa Corporation, the holding company for Hughes Airwest, Hughes Helicopters, and the tycoon's real estate holdings, casinos and hotels. Texas claimed he was a resident; the State stood to gain $355 million in inheritance tax. Nevada's claim (with no inheritance tax) was supported by Summa Corp. and the relatives.

The big prize was Hughes Aircraft, with over $1 billion in annual sales. HHMI held all the stock, but Howard Hughes had not designated anyone to succeed him as trustee. Who would control the Institute, and thus Hughes Aircraft? Who would pick the new trustees to replace Howard Hughes? By default, the decision fell to the State of Delaware, where Hughes Aircraft was incorporated.

As the case slowly moved through the Delaware Court of Chancery, HHMI's budget began to grow, from $4 million in 1975 to $15 million in 1978. The staff also increased. Headquarters moved into a 12-acre estate in Coconut Grove, Florida, and the Scientific Advisory Committee was reconstituted as the Scientific Review Board, becoming more active in reviewing scientific progress.

1984–87: "A Complete Reformation"

Following Hughes' death, the Institute gradually organized its research agenda into four areas: genetics, immunology, cell biology, and neuroscience. HHMI spending continued to increase—to $18 million in 1981, $39.5 million in 1982 and $56 million in 1983.

In January 1984, the judge in Delaware ruled that the Attorney General of Delaware could choose four members of the new board of trustees, the Institute could choose four, and the new board would then choose a ninth member. The result was a group that included a Hughes relative, the president of the University of Chicago, a long-time Hughes employee, the retired chairman of Morgan Stanley & Co., and the former chairman of DuPont. At its first meeting, the board selected one of its members, Donald S. Fredrickson, a distinguished researcher and former director of the National Institutes of Health, to become HHMI's first full-time president. As a consultant to HHMI, Fredrickson had revamped the process for selecting researchers, replacing reliance on the "old-boys' network" with a rigorous search process. He had also designed the new position of president.

Still, the Institute was involved in a battle with the IRS going back over a decade. Under the federal tax laws, a not-for-profit medical research organization had to spend the equivalent of 3.5 percent of its assets annually on medical research in conjunction with a hospital. The issues with the IRS included not only HHMI's net worth but whether it was a charity or a foundation, and if the latter, whether HHMI labs at MIT and CalTech, which were not affiliated with a hospital, should be included in that formula.

Fredrickson set about to resolve these issues with the IRS as well as to smooth relations with the medical schools where HHMI had labs. In 1985, HHMI sold Hughes Aircraft to the General Motors Corporation for more than $5 billion, making HHMI the largest private foundation in the country. In 1986, HHMI moved from Florida to Bethesda, Maryland, and in 1987 the Institute reached a settlement with the IRS.

The sale of Hughes Aircraft finally established HHMI's net worth, determining the amount that must be spent annually on medical research. Under the settlement, HHMI made a direct payment of $35 million to the federal government and agreed to spend $500 million in the next decade on top of the 3.5 percent of assets going to medical research. In 1988, the Institute's operating budget was $230 million.

1987–2000: Moving Outside the Laboratories

The next 13 years would be a period of tremendous growth, diversification, and achievement. Leading the Institute was

Key Dates:

1924: Howard Hughes inherits the Hughes Tool Company.
1925: Early Hughes' will provides for the creation of an institution to support medical research.
1932: Hughes starts the Hughes Aircraft Company and begins research on military aircraft.
1951: First Howard Hughes Medical Research Fellows appointed.
1953: Howard Hughes Medical Institute (HHMI) and Hughes Aircraft Company chartered, with HHMI owning all the shares of the company.
1976: Hughes dies.
1985: HHMI sells Hughes Aircraft Company to General Motors Corporation for $5.2 billion.
1987: HHMI and the IRS reach settlement on tax status; HHMI initiates science education grants program and begins Affiliated Investigator Program.
1991: Institute first sponsors research outside the United States.
1993: HHMI inaugurates new headquarters in Chevy Chase, Maryland, and awards first grants to informal educational institutions, such as zoos and museums.
2000: Thomas Cech assumes presidency of HHMI.

Purnell W. Choppin, who became president in 1987. The IRS agreement meant HHMI was now free to move into areas beyond laboratory research. Science education was the area the Institute chose to concentrate on outside the laboratory.

HHMI established a grants program for graduate, undergraduate, and precollege science education that grew into the largest private science education initiative in U.S. history. At the graduate level, HHMI established three fellowships for graduate students in the biomedical sciences. At the undergraduate level, grants were made to colleges and universities to update science courses, curricula, and laboratories; to engage undergraduates in research projects; to create faculty positions in emerging areas of science; and to strengthen science outreach programs to elementary, middle, and high school students and teachers. Between 1988 and 1999, the Undergraduate Biological Sciences Education Program awarded more than $425 million to 224 universities and colleges.

During the 1990s, the grants program expanded to unique national research organizations and medical schools as well as to what the Institute called ''informal educational institutions'' such as science museums and aquariums. In 1991, HHMI sponsored research outside the United States for the first time, providing five-year grants to biomedical scientists and funding for conferences and workshops.

The Institute also undertook its own education activities. In 1990, it began publishing a series of reports, including *Blood: Bearer of Life and Death* and *Seeing, Hearing, and Smelling the World*, to bring research results to the general public, particularly to science teachers. It also pushed for safety in its own laboratories, establishing an Office of Laboratory Safety, and developing a training video entitled *Practicing Safe Science*, which it made available to academic and research institutions around the world. In 1993, the Institute opened its new headquarters in Chevy Chase, Maryland. The 22.5-acre campus, with offices, libraries, meeting rooms, and housing for visitors, quickly became a center for mectings and conferences on issues in biomedical sciences.

The bulk of HHMI's annual spending, however, was used to employ research scientists called ''investigators.'' The influx of money from the Hughes Aircraft sale did not alter HHMI's original decentralized structure of employing biomedical researchers (as well as technicians and junior scientists) at major academic research institutions and stocking laboratories. The funds did allow HHMI to increase the number of researchers and labs, especially those in emerging fields such as structural biology and computational biology. During Choppin's tenure, HHMI's endowment grew to nearly $12 billion.

Investigators did not apply directly to HHMI. Rather, scientists were recommended by their institution and then underwent a rigorous selection process. The scientists were hired by HHMI for five to seven years and remained on the faculty of their host institution, where they could continue some teaching or administrative work (up to one-quarter of their time). In 1988, the Institute employed 130 investigators at 33 research centers and universities. By 1992 that number had nearly doubled, to 223 scientists in 53 institutions, and by the late 1990s there were 330 investigators at 72 sites.

With its vast amount of money, HHMI could move into a field quickly, providing resources for projects no one else, including the National Institutes of Health, could or would finance. In the mid-1980s it added structural biology to its existing four areas of concentration (genetics, cell biology, immunology and neuroscience), and spent $3.2 million to build an X-ray beam line at the Brookhaven National Laboratory on Long Island exclusively for researchers in that field.

In the area of genetics, in 1986, the Institute helped organize several international meetings. It also supported several computerized databases available to any scientist, augmenting a government database. These efforts led to the creation of the human genome project, mapping and analyzing the estimated 100,000 genes in the human body.

Hughes investigators were the elite of the biomedical world. They were well paid, and their research requirements were supported comfortably. HHMI did not tell them what to research, only that they were expected to break new ground and to produce. Their work was evaluated for refunding every five years.

The process had its questioners, however. Some thought the investigators would have received significant funding even without HHMI. Others cited jealousies created among non-Hughes researchers at affiliated research centers.

2000 and Beyond

In 2000, Thomas R. Cech (pronounced ''check'') became the third president of the Institute. Cech, a Nobel chemistry laureate and HHMI investigator since 1988 at the University of

Colorado in Boulder, appeared to be looking at ways HHMI could be more adventurous. One consideration, according to a 1999 *New York Times* article, was to cap the number of investigators at 350 and to finance special initiatives in emerging fields such as using computer programs to locate genes in the genome (bioinformatics) and figuring out what the genes do (functional genomics). He also moved to allow investigators to take their Hughes award with them if they moved to another institution.

Early in 2001, HHMI announced plans to build a $500 million research complex and conference center across the river in Virginia. ''We wanted to make a place that in 2031, people will say, 'There's something we'd like to do and here's a place—and the space—to do it,'' an Institute spokesperson explained to the *Washington Post.*

As a powerhouse in biomedical research, HHMI would hardly be recognized by its founder. The Institute, through its support for top-notch, pioneering research, has contributed significantly to the advancement of basic biomedical research. Through its fellowships and science education efforts, it is creating a pipeline of biomedical scientists, some of whom may well become Hughes investigators.

Principal Competitors

National Institutes of Health.

Further Reading

''Biomedical Heavyweights,'' *Science*, October 8, 1999, p. 216.

Brinkley, Joel, ''The Richest Foundation,'' *New York Times*, March 30, 1986, Sec. 6, p. 32.

Footlick, Jerrold K., and Martin Kasindorf, ''The Hughes Legacy,'' *Newsweek*, December 27, 1976, p. 63.

Haney, Daniel Q., ''Howard Hughes Institute Dispenses Big Money to a Lucky Few,'' *The Associated Press*, October 24, 1992.

Hedgpeth, Dana, ''Loss of Two Research Firms Worries Leaders,'' *Washington Post,* February 22, 2001, p. T6.

''The Heritage of a Silent Billionaire,'' *Business Week*, April 19, 1976, p. 38.

Marshall, Eliot, ''Hughes Network Expands by a Big Leap,'' *Science*, May 23, 1997, p. 1,189.

Matthews, Tom, et. al., ''The Secret World of Howard Hughes,'' *Newsweek*, April 19, 1976, p. 24.

Schrage, Michael, and Nell Henderson, ''Hughes Institute Woos Sciences' Best and Brightest,'' *Washington Post*, August 4, 1986, p. F1.

Thompson, Larry, ''The Howard Hughes Medical Institute: Buying the Best in Science,'' *Washington Post,* December 12, 1988, p. Z12.

''A Twentieth Century History,'' Chevy Chase, MD: Howard Hughes Medical Institute, 1999.

Wade, Nicholas, ''A New Criterion for Howard Hughes Medical Institute: Adventure,'' *New York Times*, Decemer 28, 1999, p. F3.

''Who Will Call the Shots at Hughes Aircraft?,'' *Business Week*, September 13, 1976, p. 56.

—Ellen D. Wernick

HYLSAT MEX
Hylsamex, S.A. de C.V.

Munich 101
San Nicolas de los Garza, Nuevo Leon 66452
Mexico
Telephone: 52 8 328 2828
Fax: 52 8 331 1885
Web site: http://www.hylsamex.com.mx

Public Subsidiary of Alfa, S.A. de C.V.
Incorporated: 1943 as Hojalata y Lamina, S.A.
Employees: 7,715
Sales: 13.65 billion pesos ($1.43 billion) (1999)
Stock Exchanges: Mexico City; NASDAQ (for American Depositary Receipts)
Ticker Symbols: IIYLSAMX; NYLMB YP
NAIC: 21221 Iron Ore Mining; 331111 Iron & Steel Mills

Hylsamex, S.A. de C.V. is Mexico's second-largest steel manufacturer. Its products include flat steel, bars, rods, pipes, coils, and wire, used primarily for the construction, auto-parts, and home-construction industries. The company also has subsidiaries for scrap processing, freight services, and steel distribution. In addition, Hylsamex owns iron-ore mines and holds stakes in a mining consortium, a power-generating company, and a steel producer in Venezuela. It participates in strategic partnerships with more than ten companies, including United States' and German firms. Hylsamex is a subsidiary of Mexico's largest industrial conglomerate, Alfa, S.A. de C.V.

Visa Subsidiary: 1943–74

Members of the Monterrey-based Sada, Garza, and Muguerza families became Mexico's first significant industrialists early in the 20th century. The holdings of this interrelated extended family, known informally as Grupo Monterrey, were divided in 1936. One of the two, Valores Industriales S.A., known by the acronym Visa, founded Hojalata y Lamina S.A., known by the acronym Hylsa, in 1943. Hojalata y Lamina referred to sheets or plates of flat-rolled steel, a product needed by Visa's brewery for its bottle caps during World War II, when U.S. firms—the former source of supply—diverted shipments to the war effort.

Hylsa was founded with an original investment of 203 million pesos (about $42 million) by members of the Muguerza, Sada Muguerza, and Garza Sada branches of Grupo Monterrey. Camilo Garza Sada was named chairman. At first the company made only flat sheets of steel (4,300 tons in 1945), but that year an electric (rather than open-hearth) furnace was installed, and it also began making its own steel bars. The labor force grew from the original 16 to 560 in 1950. A sister enterprise, Cia. Minera Las Encimas, was established in 1951 to exploit iron deposits in Pihuamo, Jalisco. Hylsa's facilities, still not large enough to meet the ambitions of its owners, were modernized in 1953 with U.S. and Mexican government loan guarantees. That year another electric furnace, plus trimming and finishing mills, was installed.

Hylsa's steel production still depended on scrap iron as its basic material, but the principal provider, the United States, had restricted its export. At this time only blast furnaces could convert iron ore into the raw material needed for steel. The search by Hylsa for a cheaper method led to the construction of a pilot plant to produce sponge iron by direct reduction of iron ore. The method tried was costly and did not produce enough of the material, but a new process developed in 1957 under the direction of company engineer Juan Celada proved successful on an industrial scale. The HyL process, which involved exposing iron-ore pellets to natural gas, was patented, and by 1980 rights had been sold in more than 50 countries. A facility was put into service with a capacity of 200 tons of sponge iron a day. A second such installation was added in 1960, and by 1974 there were four.

Aceros Alfa Monterrey, S.A. was established in 1954 to use Hylsa's steel for the production of pipe. Aceros de Mexicano, S.A. was created in 1957 to make corrugated-steel bars for reinforcing concrete. In 1959 Hylsa—the largest privately owned steel company in Mexico—produced 238,095 metric tons of steel products (18 percent of the national total), compared to only 34,750 tons in 1950. The company acquired a plant at Apodaca, near Monterrey, in 1963 to produce bars, corrugated rods, wire, and light structural shapes from flat-rolled sheets. This was supplemented in 1969 by a new plant at Xoxtla, Puebla, operated by a new subsidiary, Hylsa de Mexico, S.A. In all, parent Hylsa's steel production came to 24 percent of the national total in 1970. The company also opened Mexico's first plant for iron-ore pellets that year, in the state of Colima. In 1972 it purchased a rebar facility that was the first continuous-casting plant in Latin America.

Seven Fat and Seven Lean Years: 1974–88

Grupo Monterrey was broken up again in 1974, this time into four parts. One of the four, Grupo Industrial Alfa, S.A. (later simply Alfa, S.A.) received Hylsa, Empaques de Carton Titan, a packaging company, and 25 percent of the television broadcasting company Televisa S.A. Originally Hylsa constituted two-thirds of Alfa's assets. As Alfa's steel division, it was divided into three parts. Hylsa proper was responsible for mining and the transformation of iron ore into basic steel. Aymax was established for specialized steel products. Hyl was in charge of technology and services with regard to the HyL process. Soon after, Galvak became the company's galvanizing and coated-products division.

In 1975 Hylsa was still Mexico's second-ranking producer of steel and had revenues of 2.18 billion pesos ($174.4 million). Two years later it passed 1 million metric tons of output for the first time. Production reached 1,512,000 tons in 1981, just before world oil prices nosedived and, as a result, Mexico's overheated economy crash-landed. Interest on Hylsa's debt (95 percent of it in dollars) came to 21 percent of its sales in 1983. It had to shoulder Alfa's debts as well as its own, and its financial and operating costs were increasing twice as fast as the rate of inflation. By early 1987 Hylsa owed more than $1 billion, but since at least 90 percent of its sales were domestic, it was earning depreciated pesos rather than dollars. Hylsa's debt, which included $300 million in overdue interest, had reached $1.21 billion owed to 68 lenders in 11 countries by the spring of 1988, when about 70 percent of the foreign creditors accepted in exchange for debt owed by the company a package of cash and the Mexican government's own debt. The other foreign lenders

and Mexican banks agreed to extend loan repayments over 15 years and also received 21 percent of Hylsa's common stock. This agreement reduced the amount due to $574 million. Meanwhile, as the Mexican economy slowly recovered, Hylsa's sales increased from 150.82 billion pesos (perhaps about $485 million) in 1985 to 2.4 trillion pesos ($853 million) in 1988.

Recovery in the 1990s

In 1995 Hylsa opened the first Mexican steel minimill, located just outside Monterrey. The $400 million facility had an annual capacity of 730,000 metric tons of flat-rolled steel and was considered the most advanced in the world for producing thin-slab sheets. Thin-slab production was considered far more advanced and efficient technologically than ingot steel. The company also spent about $260 million between 1988 and 1992 to upgrade its pipe- and long-products operations. In addition, in 1991, the wire and rod division purchased three facilities from rival Altos Hornos de Mexico, S.A. for $42 million. Taking the name Hylsamex in 1992, when the company's divisions were integrated into the subsidiary rather than parent company Alfa, the company began offering its stock in Mexico City and New York in 1994.

In 1997 Hylsamex took a 30 percent share in Consorcio Siderurgia Amazonia, Ltd., a group of Latin American steel producers that purchased 70 percent of Venezuela's CVG Siderurgica del Orinoco (Sidor), the last major government-owned steel producer in the hemisphere, for $1.2 billion. Hyslamex soon raised this stake to 35 percent. But a drop in world oil prices depressed Venezuela's economy the following year, and Hylsamex's share of Sidor's losses in the first quarter of 1999 alone came to $46 million.

Hylsamex spent $1.6 billion on capital projects in the 1990s, replacing 78 percent of its installations. Following the inauguration of the thin-slab-casting minimill, which was established with the participation of the German firm SMS Schloemann-Siemag AG, a $140-million expansion, completed in 1999, doubled its capacity to 1.5 million metric tons. In 1998, Galvak's capacity was increased from 240,000 to 400,000 annual tons of galvanized and coated steel and other products, the division signed an agreement with AK Steel Holding Corp. to supply each other with products for distribution in their respective markets, and the HYL Technology Division installed a new direct-reduction facility.

Hylsamex's Raw Materials Division included two Colima mines, at Alzada and Manzanillo, and 51 percent of a mining consortium at Pena Colorada. They turned out a combined total of 3.2 million metric tons of pelletized iron ore in 1999. The output was shipped by rail to Hylsamex's production plants for conversion from ore into iron by direct reduction. The San Nicolas de los Garza plant, just outside Monterrey, housed the Flat Production Division, whose main installations were the thin-slab minimill, and the older mill, which had a capacity of one million tons a year and was converted from producing five-ton ingots to ten-ton ones in 1996. The Flat Products Division sold 1.7 million metric tons of steel in 1999, of which 200,000 tons were exported. The Bars and Rod Division, with plants at Xoxtla and Apodaca, sold 976,000 tons. The Tubular Products Division, located at San Nicolas de los Garza, sold 168,000 tons.

Established in 1995, Acerex was the company's processing joint venture with Worthington Steel Co. After the installation of a middle-gage slitter it cut to length 250,000 tons in 1999. Galvak turned out 466,000 tons of products from San Nicolas de los Garza. Hylsamex's share of Hylsabek, the joint venture with Belgian steelmaker N.V. Bekaert, S.A. for wire and wire-related products organized in 1992, was sold at the end of 1999 for about $11.5 million. A new unit called Galvacer was created in 1999 to enhance Hylsamex's participation in products of high aggregate value. It was composed of Galvak, Galvamet (Galvak's joint-venture unit for making insulated panels), the Tubular Products Division, and a unit devoted to small- and medium-sized Mexican customers that sold 103,000 tons of steel products in 1999. Galvacer's task was to market a number of products, including hot- and cold-rolled sheets of steel, galvanized and coated steel, insulated panels and constructive systems, various kinds of pipes, and structural frames.

President and chief executive officer of Hylsamex since 1995, Alejandro Elizondo was chosen 1999 Steelmaker of the Year by the U.S. trade publication *New Steel*. The company-organized Industrial Union of Hylsa Workers was representing its employees. As of 2000, there had never been a strike at Hylsa. Employees and their families belonged to Nova, an association in Monterrey that provided medical services and recreational facilities such as basketball courts, soccer fields, and swimming pools. Nova also provided banking services such as loans and saving plans and offered cultural activities such as plays and concerts.

Hylsamex was solidly profitable in the late 1990s. It sold a record 2,849,000 metric tons of steel products in 1999. Net sales came to 13.65 billion pesos ($1.43 billion). Net income was 716 million pesos ($74.9 million). The long-term debt at year's end was 10.88 billion pesos ($1.38 billion). In September 2000, the company closed its ore mines, the Xoxtla plant, and two of the three in the Monterrey area because of the soaring price of natural gas. Hylsa was especially vulnerable because the direct-reduction process requires large amounts of this fuel. The company was paying an all-time high of $7 per million cubic feet of gas, compared to about $2 at the beginning of the year, thereby increasing its total production costs per ton of steel by 65 percent.

Principal Subsidiaries

Exan Corporativo, S.A. de C.V.; Galvak, S.A. de C.V.; Hylsa, S.A. de C.V.; Hylsa Latin, L.L.C. and associates; Promotora Azteca, S.A. de C.V.

Principal Operating Units

Acerex; Bar and Rod Division; Flat Products Division; Galvak; HYL Technology Division; Raw Materials Division; Tubular Products Division.

Principal Competitors

Altos Hornos de Mexico, S.A. de C.V.; Grupo Simca, S.A. de C.V.; Imsa Acero, S.A. de C.V.

Further Reading

"Arde HYLSA?" *Expansion,* September 26, 1984, pp. 43+.

Bagsasrian, Tom, "More Thin Slabs and Galvanized at Hylsa," *New Steel,* March 1999, pp. 36–37.

Balcerek, Tom, "Steelmakers Adjust to Free Market Forces," *MBM/ Metal Bulletin Monitor,* February 1993, pp. 24–25.

Blumenthal, Karen, "Hylsa's Debt of $1.2 Billion Is Restructured," *Wall Street Journal,* May 4, 1988, pp. 4.

Cedillo, Juan, "La nueva encrucijada," *Expansion,* February 17, 1993, pp. 53–54.

Flores Vega, Ernesto, "Alfa y la guerra de los cinco anos," *Expansion,* April 15, 1987, pp. 56.

——, "Despues de la reestructuracion . . . ," *Expansion,* October 26, 1988, pp. 46, 48–50.

Haflich, Frank, "Hylsamex Hikes Sidor Stake," *American Metal Market,* March 6, 1998, p. 12.

"La industria siderurgica en Monterrey: Hylsa," in Mario Cerutti, ed., *Monterrey: Siete Estudios Contemporaneos,* Monterrey: Universidad Autonoma de Nuevo Leon, 1988, pp. 55–95.

Millman, Joel, "High Natural-Gas Prices Put Squeeze on Mexico's Fox," *Wall Street Journal,* December 11, 2000, p. A34.

Novo, Salvador, *Man, Steel and Time,* Monterrey: Grupo Acero Hylsa, 1968.

Parisi, Anthony J., "Mexico Promotes Steel Process," *New York Times,* April 2, 1979, pp. D1, D4.

Ritt, Adam, "A Mini-Mill Technology Leader," *New Steel,* August 1999, pp. 18–20, 23, 26, 28–29.

——, "Where Minimills Should Be," *New Steel,* August 1999, p. 2.

Toledo Beltran, Daniel, and Francisco Zapata. *Acero y Estado.* Mexico City: Universidad Autonoma Metropolitana, 2 vols., 1999.

—Robert Halasz

Industrias Bachoco, S.A. de C.V.

Avenida Tecnologico 401
Celaya, Guanajuato 38010
Mexico
Telephone: (524) 618-3500
Toll free: (800) 943-9715
Fax: (524) 611-6502
Web site: http://www.bachoco.com.mx

Public Company
Founded: 1952
Employees: 11,215
Sales: 5.64 million pesos ($595.2 million)
Stock Exchanges: Mexico City New York (for Associated
    Depositary Receipts)
Ticker Symbols: BACHOCO; IBA
NAIC: 11221 Hog & Pig Farming; 11231 Chicken Egg
    Production; 11232 Broilers and Other Meat Type
    Chicken Production; 11234 Poultry Hatcheries;
    311615 Other Animal Food Manufacturing; 551112
    Offices of Other Holding Companies

Industrias Bachoco, S.A. de C.V. is a holding company whose Bachoco, S.A. de C.V. is Mexico's leading poultry producer and one of the world's top ten chicken producers. As a vertically integrated producer, Bachoco has operations that include preparing feed, breeding, hatching, and growing chickens, and processing, packaging, and distributing chicken products. The company also produces eggs and swine. It transports and sells its products to both wholesalers and retailers. Industrias Bachoco has more than 600 facilities, including breeding and growing farms, feed plants, processing plants, and cold-storage facilities and warehouses.

First the Egg, Then the Chicken: 1952–88

Henry Robinson Bours emigrated from Holland to Mexico at the beginning of the 20th century. Alfonso, Javier, Enrique, and Juan—sons of Henry's eldest son, Alfonso—were residents of Ciudad Obregon, Sonora, engaged, in the 1940s, in various businesses, such as wheat and sorghum cultivation, the production of fertilizers, and the sale of automobiles and agricultural machinery. Business was poor, however, and one Friday afternoon the only way that Enrique could meet his payroll was because his wife suddenly provided an unexpected cache of savings accumulated by selling eggs to the neighbors from the family's corral of chickens. This seemed like such a good idea that the Robinson brothers decided to add egg production to their roster of businesses. (Of their four farms at the end of the 1940s, the most important was near Navojoa, in an area called by the Indians *bachoco,* meaning "place where water passes.")

At an early point in Bachoco's history the Robinson brothers made a decision to specialize in brown eggs, which have no nutritional value superior to white ones but command a price premium from Mexican shoppers. By the mid-1960s egg production had become the main family business, and by the 1970s the brothers had withdrawn from the others to give their full attention to this endeavor. In time the state of Sonora became too small a market for Bachoco and also insufficient for its feed requirements, particularly sorghum and corn, and so the company opened a plant in Los Mochis, Sinaloa. In 1971 the Robinsons opened their first poultry operation, in Culiacan, Sinaloa. Three years later they extended their operations from northern to central Mexico by opening a second poultry processing plant in Celaya, Guanajuato. By about 1977 Bachoco's chicken sales had outstripped its egg sales.

By the mid-1970s it was clear that Mexican chicken growers and egg producers were unlikely to survive unless they consolidated and thereby achieved economies of scale. Chicken producers, according to the president of the National Union of Poultry Cultivators, were paying higher prices for feed while constrained by the federal government from passing on their costs of production. In addition, he said, poor-quality chickens and eggs were being smuggled into the country from California and Texas and sold at very low prices. During the ensuing years the union tried, without success, to persuade the government to limit American imports of chicken. The government, however, favored a level of imports sufficient to keep chicken prices from rising significantly and, therefore, to keep the product affordable for Mexico's poor. (A 1997 *Wall Street Journal* article said that despite growing incomes and chicken's low price relative to other meats, per-capita poultry consumption in Mexico historically had been less than a third of U.S. consumption and only about half of consumption in the rest of Latin America.)

Bachoco proved to be one of the survivors of the shakeout. According to Enrique Robinson, the company's chairman of the board, one reason was that the enterprise was careful not to take on more debt than it could handle. In this way it had the resources to acquire other producers when they fell into difficulties. In addition, he had noted that aviculture moved in cycles, with high prices stimulating production to the point where the inevitable surplus resulted in a drop in prices. Bachoco's response was to hold back production until prices recovered. Interviewed for the Mexican business magazine *Expansion* in 1994, Robinson described the company as, by tradition, "extremely conservative, its shareholders preferring to use its own cash flow for growth" rather than to borrow funds.

By 1988 Bachoco was Mexico's leading producer of chicken, with more than ten percent of the production reported that year by the 52 members of the producers' union. The company was also first in chicken purchases, however, with more than ten percent of the total reported. Only 14 percent of its chicken sales came from its own breeding farms; the rest were from chickens produced by other growers and sold to Bachoco. Nevertheless, by 1992 the company owned 159 farms and rented 63 more, with an inventory of six million hens derived from the Hisex stock imported from Holland.

Still Growing in the 1990s

Bachoco was planning to make its initial public offering in 1992, but its performance that year was not satisfactory. Although sales rose by ten percent, net profit fell by 52 percent, mainly because of higher prices for its raw materials, particularly imported ones. The company's debts rose to 47 percent of its capital. As a result, Bachoco reorganized its operations to reduce its production and administrative costs. One of these measures was to move corporate headquarters from Ciudad Obregon to Celaya. "Given that the major part of the business is in the center of the country," Robinson (who did not make the move) explained to *Expansion,* "there arrived a moment in which there wasn't much sentiment to have our offices so isolated from our principal markets and centers of operation. In addition, this has allowed our executives to make more contact with the market, which allows them to react faster." He added, "We have succeeded, with the same resources, to augment our production substantially. This has resulted in a very important reduction in our expenses." One example he cited was an

increase in the speed of the Celaya plant's production line from 8,520 to 9,300 chickens an hour.

Bachoco's reorganization was a resounding success. In 1992 it reported net sales of 1.05 billion new pesos (about $338.1 million) and net income of 39.4 million new pesos (about $12.7 million). These totals grew the following year to 1.22 billion new pesos (about $387.3 million) and 184.8 million new pesos (about $58.7 million). The company's debt fell to 27 percent of its capital. The nearly fivefold increase in profits opened some eyes and rated the company a cover story in *Expansion,* which put Bachoco in first place on its list of the ten top enterprises of the year. Robinson told the magazine, "The goals that we have, as in all businesses, are to be more efficient, to utilize our assets better, to lower our production costs, to better our systems of distribution, to reach all corners of the country with a better product."

Industrias Bachoco processed and sold almost 165 million chickens in 1993, an increase of about ten percent over the previous year. Chickens represented 73.5 percent of the company's total sales and 20 percent of the national market. It was particularly strong in the nation's northwestern and north-central states, plus the Federal District (Mexico City). As Robinson forecast, the company in 1994 acquired a third processing plant in Tecamachalco, Puebla, to establish a presence in southern and eastern Mexico and challenge Univasa, one of its main rivals. A fourth processing plant was acquired in Lagos de Moreno, Jalisco. Egg production accounted for 17 percent of the company's sales (and made it the nation's second-ranking producer) but was considered a secondary opportunity for growth by the company because Mexican per-capita consumption of eggs was already higher than the U.S. figure. "The principal opportunity is chicken," Robinson told *Expansion.* "We are seeing a very important increment in its consumption per person, given that continually, by the efficiency achieved in its production, it can be provided to the consumer at prices ever more accessible. This is not the case for the consumption of red meat, which in some places has fallen and in others remains static." The company's three percent share of the national swine market made it one of Mexico's most important producers, however. Bachoco also was distributing to supermarkets frozen chicken and turkey sausage that was being imported but sold under the Bachoco name.

The capital flight of late 1994 that led to a drastic devaluation of the peso before the end of the year and a consequent severe recession in 1995 resulted in a sharp drop in chicken prices and consumption. This marked a crucial moment in the consolidation of the industry, with big producers such as Bachoco augmenting their share of the market by purchasing smaller producers. By 1998 the company held 21 percent of the market. Industrias Bachoco made its initial public offering in 1997, selling about one-sixth of its outstanding shares, both on the Mexican stock exchange and on the New York Stock Exchange, in the form of American depositary receipts. After selling shareholders received their proceeds, the company's management retained more than $40 million to expand production and thus meet the challenge of U.S.-based rivals such as Tyson Foods Inc., the world's biggest chicken processor, and Pilgrim's Pride Corp., Mexico's second-ranking broiler producer. "Our strategy is to increase market share through opportunities rising from the continuing consolidation of the indus-

Key Dates:

1952: The company is founded in Ciudad Obregon, Sonora.
1971: Bachoco establishes its first poultry operation, in Culiacan, Sinaloa.
1974: A second processing plant opens in Celaya, Guanajuato.
1992: Bachoco moves corporate headquarters to Celaya.
1994: The company acquires its third and fourth processing plants.
1997: Industrias Bachoco becomes a public corporation by selling stock.
1999: The company acquires Grupo Campi, S.A. de C.V., Mexico's fourth largest poultry producer.

try," Enrique Robinson told Joel Millman of the *Wall Street Journal.* "We will continue to evaluate possible acquisitions."

Working in Industrias Bachoco's favor was a growth in Mexico's chicken consumption that was outstripping even its rapidly growing population and by 1998 constituted a market exceeding $3 billion a year. In spite of the growth of U.S. competition, Mexico remained the world's fifth largest producer of chicken and the fourth largest of eggs. In addition, Bachoco increased its volume of chicken sold by more than 55 percent from 1995 to 1999, compared with an increase of 18 percent in overall Mexican chicken production during this period. Millman reported, however, that "many marginal producers already have been picked off" and that the remaining producers "would have a hard time duplicating a formula that fueled farm growth in the U.S.: raising birds by independent contractors. That frees producers from tying up capital and management talent and has proved successful in places like Brazil and Thailand. It is almost unheard-of in Mexico." By the terms of the North American Free Trade Association (NAFTA), duties on imported poultry products began to fall in 1999 and were due to end entirely in 2003, thereby enhancing opportunities for increased sales by Bachoco's U.S. competitors.

Bachoco in 1999–2000

In 1999 Bachoco sold some 415,700 metric tons of chicken (about 254.8 million chickens), a 17 percent increase over the previous year and about 23 percent of all Mexican chicken production. Sales of chicken products accounted for 87.5 percent of the company's net sales of 5.64 billion pesos ($595.2 million). Bachoco was the third largest producer of table eggs in Mexico, with a total of 67,500 metric tons, or about 88.4 million dozen eggs, and 3.7 percent of the market. Eggs accounted for nine percent of the company's net sales. Sales of swine, which Bachoco was selling on the hoof to meat packers for the production of pork products, came to 9,500 metric tons and accounted for nearly two percent of net sales. The remaining portion of net sales was made of miscellaneous poultry-related products. Net income came to 813.7 million pesos ($85.8 million).

During the year Industrias Bachoco maintained 87 chicken-breeding farms, 306 broiler grow-out farms, 15 egg incubation

plants, 52 egg production farms, a swine-breeding farm, ten swine grow-out farms, and eight feed plants. The company believed itself to be the largest producer of animal feed in Mexico. Bachoco maintained processing plants in Celaya, Culiacan, Lagos de Moreno, and Tecamachalco, and 42 cold-storage facilities and warehouses. From there the goods were sent to wholesale distributors, supermarkets, and food service operations. Of Bachoco's chicken production, some 64 percent consisted of rotisserie chickens, which went directly to retailers, and public market chickens, which generally had no wrapping or identification and were sent to wholesalers. Another 20.5 percent consisted of supermarket broiler chickens (plus chicken parts and eggs) distributed to retailers and wholesale clubs. Nine percent consisted of live chickens shipped primarily to wholesalers.

Shortly before the end of 1999, Industrias Bachoco purchased Grupo Campi, S.A. de C.V., Mexico's fourth largest chicken producer, for 1.21 billion pesos ($126.59 million). This brought the consolidated company's share of Mexican chicken production to 31 percent and its share of egg production to six percent. The number of chicken-breeding farms increased to 111, the broiler grow-out farms to 439, and the egg incubation plants to 17. At the end of the year Bachoco's debt was 1.98 billion pesos ($206.92 million), of which 92 percent was in U.S. dollars. This figure represented an increase of more than 200 percent and a rise in the ratio of net debt to capital from 11 to 28 percent. Short-term liabilities grew by 147 percent in terms of foreign exchange. Industrias Bachoco's 1999 sales and income figures were, in constant prices, inferior to those of 1997 and 1998. The company blamed this result on an oversupply of goods in the Mexican market, leading to a fall in prices. According to *Tendencias,* a Mexican periodical, imports from the United States totaled 218,000 metric tons, far exceeding the quota of 64,000 established by NAFTA. For the first nine months of 2000, Industrias Bachoco reported an increase of 2.6 percent in sales over the same period in 1999, before taking into consideration the Campi acquisition.

Bachoco, S.A. de C.V. accounted for 99.99 percent of Industrias Bachoco's consolidated revenues in 1999. Induba, S.A. de C.V. was established in 1999 to hold investments in other companies. There were eight other consolidated operating subsidiaries. Enrique Robinson Bours was still chairman of the board in 1999. Family trusts owned 84 percent of the parent company's shares.

Principal Subsidiaries

Bachoco, S.A. de C.V.; Induba., S.A. de C.V.

Principal Competitors

Pilgrim's Pride Corporation; Tyson Foods Inc.; Univasa.

Further Reading

"Un asunto muy cacareado," *Expansion,* March 3, 1982, pp. 32–33.
"Elevo Bachoco sus ventas 49%, pese a la competencia," *El Financiero,* December 14, 2000, p. 32.
"Jose Eduardo Robinson Bours," *Expansion,* June 10, 1992, p. 64.

Leon Leon, Maria Josephina, *Situacion actual de la avicultura pro-duccion de carne,* Mexico City: Instituto Technologico Autonomo de Mexico, 1990.

Manley, C. Conrad, "Mexican Poultrymen Face Difficult Problems," *Journal of Commerce,* May 6, 1975, p. 7.

Millman, Joel, "Mexican Poultry Processor Girds for Foreigners," *Wall Street Journal,* September 19, 1997, p. A8.

Monjaras Moreno, Jorge A., "El huevo o la gallina?," *Expansion,* July 6, 1994, pp. 35, 38–41.

"Piedras en el camino de avicultores," *El Financiero,* December 29, 2000, p. 19.

Ramirez Tamayo, Zacarias, "Un pollo de pelea," *Expansion,* March 11, 1998, pp. 17 +

—Robert Halasz

International Dairy Queen, Inc.

7505 Metro Boulevard
P.O. Box 39286
Edina, Minnesota 55439
U.S.A.
Telephone: (952) 830-0200
Fax: (952) 830-0480
Web site: http://www.dairyqueen.com

Wholly Owned Subsidiary of Berkshire Hathaway, Inc.
Incorporated: 1962
Employees: 700
Sales: $460 million (2000)
NAIC: 722211 Limited-Service Restaurants; 31152 Ice
    Cream and Frozen Dessert Manufacturing

International Dairy Queen, Inc. licenses, services, and develops over 5,900 Dairy Queen stores in the United States, Canada, and numerous foreign countries, including Austria, Slovenia, China, Oman, and Guam. In addition to selling its famous dairy desserts, many of the stores also sell hamburgers, chicken, hot dogs, and a variety of beverages. The company also owns Karmelkorn Shoppes, Inc., a franchisor of over 30 retail stores that sell popcorn, candy, and other items, as well as Orange Julius, a franchisor of some 400 stores which feature blended drinks made from orange juice, various fruits, and fruit flavors. In 1998 International Dairy Queen was purchased by Warren Buffett's Berkshire Hathaway Inc.

1920–40: A Good Idea in Search of an Audience

The founders of Dairy Queen, J.F. "Grandpa" McCullough and his son Alex, originally established the Homemade Ice Cream Company in 1927. Located in Davenport, Iowa, the two men sold a variety of ice cream products throughout the Quad Cities area (which includes Moline and Rock Island, Illinois, and Bettendorf and Davenport, Iowa). In order to expand their operations, during the early 1930s the McCulloughs moved their business to Green River, Illinois, and purchased a former cheese factory in which they located their ice cream mix plant.

When the McCulloughs made ice cream at their plant in Green River, it was a complicated process. Butterfat, milk solids, sweetener, and stabilizer were first combined, then mixed, and finally put into a batch freezer where the combination was chilled, given a specific amount of air (technically called "overrun"), and flavored. The product was denser and richer than most ice creams, with less overrun. When the temperature reached 23 degrees Fahrenheit, a spigot was opened in the freezer and the soft ice cream flowed into three-gallon containers. The containers were covered with lids, frozen at minus-ten degrees Fahrenheit, and delivered to customers. When an ice cream store was ready to serve the product, the ice cream was put into a dipping cabinet and the temperature increased to five degrees Fahrenheit.

The ice cream was frozen solid, not for the pleasure and enjoyment of the customer, but for the convenience of the manufacturer and store owner. Yet the elder McCullough had known for a long time that ice cream at colder temperatures numbed the tastebuds and resulted in a much less flavorful product; soft, fresh ice cream drawn from a spigot at approximately 23 degrees Fahrenheit tasted best. He began to wonder if there was some way to dispense semi-frozen ice cream that kept its shape but soon realized that the batch freezers in use during the 1930s were unsuitable. An entirely different type of freezer was required and, moreover, every ice cream store that wished to dispense the new product would have to purchase at least one of the new freezers. Faced with these difficulties, Grandpa McCullough decided to give up the idea as impractical.

After a few years, however, Grandpa McCullough was still thinking about soft ice cream, and he convinced his son that they should find out whether or not the product would capture people's tastebuds. They asked one of their customers, Sherb Noble, if he would arrange a special offering of soft ice cream at his store in Kankakee, Illinois. With an advertisement of "All you can eat for 10 cents," the sale was held in early August 1938. Using an ordinary commercial batch freezer, the men put the soft ice cream into five gallon containers and then hand-dipped the product into 16-ounce cups. In two hours, Noble and the McCulloughs dished out over 1,600 servings. A short time later, another sale of soft ice cream was offered at Mildred's Ice

Company Perspectives:

The DQ tradition you grew up with is continuously growing as new locations are opening in both new and existing markets. Our brands—Dairy Queen, Orange Julius and Karmelkorn—have very high favorable consumer awareness. Most importantly, we thrive because of our hardworking franchisees. The vast majority of our locations are franchised—we own and operate very few stores. We are strong believers in franchising, unlike many of our competitors who operate a significant number of their own stores. While we have grown over the years and adapted to changing market conditions, IDQ Companies' family of fast food concepts have remained rooted in the tradition of DQ quality and customer satisfaction.

Cream Shop in Moline. The response from the public was the same. With such overwhelming success, the McCulloughs began searching for the type of freezer that would make dispensing soft ice cream a reality.

The McCulloughs approached two manufacturers of dairy equipment and asked if they would be interested in designing a machine that dispensed semi-frozen dairy products into dishes or ice cream cones. The first manufacturer immediately rejected their proposal, and the second firm, Stoelting Brothers Company in Kiel, Wisconsin, thought the idea lacked potential. With nowhere else to go, the McCulloughs seemed to arrive at a dead end. However, one day while Grandpa McCullough was casually paging through the want ads in the *Chicago Tribune* he noticed an advertisement for a continuous freezer that would dispense soft ice cream. The ad had been place by Harry M. Oltz.

Oltz and the McCulloughs met in the summer of 1939. Having already received the patent for his freezer in 1937, Oltz extended the production rights to his new partners, as well as rights for the exclusive use of the freezer in Illinois, Wisconsin, and all the states west of the Mississippi River. According to the agreement, Oltz kept exclusive rights to use of the freezer in all states east of the Mississippi and would receive continuous royalties based on the number of gallons of soft serve ice cream processed through all the dispensing freezers produced under the patent. Oltz then moved to Miami, Florida, and established AR-TIK Systems, Inc., a firm that would find stores to serve soft ice cream in the eastern United States. Meanwhile, the McCulloughs returned to the Stoelting Brothers and reached an agreement with them to manufacture a soft-serve ice cream freezer for their own company.

1940: Dairy Queen is Born

The first Dairy Queen store opened in Joliet, Illinois, on June 22, 1940. Jointly owned by the McCulloughs and Sherb Noble, the store was managed by Jim and Elliot Grace. By the end of the summer, the store had grossed $4,000, and Noble decided to buy out the McCulloughs' interest in that store. On April 1, 1941, the McCulloughs opened another store in Moline and once again contracted the Graces to manage it for them. Additional stores were opened in Aurora, Illinois, and Davenport, Iowa, and by the

end of 1942 there were a total of eight Dairy Queen businesses in operation. However, with the advent of World War II, manufacturing materials used for building the freezers were reassigned to the war effort. Without new freezers, no new stores were able to open for the duration of the war.

Despite the inability of the McCulloughs to open more stores, they remained active. During the war, father and son sold rights to would-be store owners to use the Dairy Queen freezer and mix, and develop businesses in certain geographical areas of the country. Since they both suspected that the popularity of Dairy Queen would be brief, it was more sensible to the McCulloughs to sell territories outright rather than to arrange an ongoing royalty system. All profits were up front, and if the product lost its appeal there was no fear of losing any income. Unfortunately, the McCulloughs' method of contracting the development of new territories was extremely informal— sometimes scribbled on a napkin, paper sack, or daily newspaper—and this led to a host of problems later on.

Impressed with the long lines at the Dairy Queen store in Moline, Harry Axene, a sales manager for a farm equipment company, approached Grandpa McCullough and soon became a 50–50 partner in the mix company. He also purchased the territory rights for Illinois and Iowa at a price of $12,000. By the end of the war, Axene had purchased the remaining interest in the mix company and, more importantly, had seen the future of Dairy Queen in franchising. In November 1946, Axene organized a meeting with 26 potential investors at the LeClaire Hotel in Moline. Excited about organizing a national Dairy Queen franchise system, Axene introduced the idea of selling territories based on a royalty system where territory store owners would pay Axene an initial fee plus an ongoing royalty fee for the soft serve mix. Even though no formal organization resulted from this meeting, interest in Dairy Queen stores grew at a tremendous pace. With only eight stores in operation at the end of the war, by the end of 1946 there were 17, and by the end of 1947 there were over 100 Dairy Queen stores operating throughout the United States.

In 1948, Axene arranged for 35 store owners and territory operators to meet in Minneapolis with the purpose of establishing a national organization. In December of the same year, the first official meeting of the newly incorporated Dairy Queen National Trade Association (DQNTA) was held in Davenport, Iowa. Organized as a not-for-profit corporation, with C.R. Medd as its first president, national offices were soon established in the city. The DQNTA was created in order to standardize cones, plastic goods, and all other materials used in Dairy Queen stores, along with coordinating all the various kinds of advertising for Dairy Queen products. By the early 1950s, membership in the DQNTA had grown to nearly 900 dues-paying members.

An Expanding Menu in the 1950s

There were 1,400 Dairy Queen stores open for business in 1950, and up until that time the menu was limited to sundaes and cones for immediate consumption, or pints and quarts to take home. When supermarkets began to sell ice cream at low prices and when air conditioning and television began keeping people home on sultry summer evenings, sales in Dairy Queen stores across the country began to suffer. In order to keep attracting customers, most stores responded to requests for an expanded menu. In 1949, milkshakes and malts were made available, and banana splits were added in 1951. Toppings for sundaes were expanded to include hot fudge, chocolate, strawberry, pineapple, butterscotch, and other flavors. Take home novelty products were also introduced, including the Dilly bar, a soft-serve, chocolate-dipped confection with a wooden tongue depressor inserted for the customer to hold while eating.

During the 1950s, Dairy Queen stores were also challenged by the emergence of fast food outlets that offered hamburgers, hot dogs, french fries, and various soft drinks. Since these outlets served full meals, they remained open the entire year; Dairy Queen stores were put at a disadvantage since they were boarded up for most of the winter season. In order to stay competitive, store operators in different parts of the country began to offer various food products, from bowls of chili to pork fritters. Yet the lack of a standardized menu brought complaints from customers, until the Brazier system of broiled burgers, hot dogs, barbecued beef, french fries, and onion rings was introduced in 1958. With the introduction of this system, the quality control and standardization of meat products helped to increase profits for store owners.

Though the DQNTA had been formed in 1948 to standardize products and services for store operators, its not-for-profit status rendered it unable to enforce any of its policies. As a result, the DQNTA was reformed in 1955 and made a for-profit corporation. Renamed the Dairy Queen National Development Company, its members gave it more latitude and authority to implement uniform products, operating practices, standards, and services to all Dairy Queen stores, though it had no franchising rights. Relocating its offices to St. Louis, Missouri, the new

company immediately initiated a consumer research program and lobbied for a standardized mix formula for all soft serve products.

After years of involvement, the family members who had started Dairy Queen slowly left the company. Grandpa McCullough had retired during the late 1940s, while his son retired in 1953. Harry Oltz also retired during the late 1940s, while his son Hal continued the family's involvement with the Dairy Queen system. Harry Axene presented the idea of an automatic continuous freezer to the Dairy Queen store operators convention in 1949, but when his proposal was rejected he severed ties with the system and formed the Tastee Freeze business, which he operated on the Pacific coast for 20 years. Only Alex's son, Hugh, remained to look after the McCullough family interests during the 1950s, and by 1960 trouble was brewing on the horizon.

1960s: Legal Troubles Lead to a Change in Ownership

Harry Oltz's patent on his continuous freezer expired in 1954, and a number of store operators refused to continue paying royalties. Hugh McCullough responded with a lawsuit to prove that franchisees were not only paying royalties for use of the freezer, but for use of the trade name. The dispute became even more complicated when a group of store owners who had acquired their territory and franchise rights from Harry Axene filed suit to prove that people who had purchased territory rights from Axene had the right to use the Dairy Queen name because it was Axene and not the McCulloughs who owned the rights.

As the legal battles dragged on and on in the courts, Hugh McCullough grew more and more weary, and finally agreed to sell all his holdings and the rights to the name Dairy Queen. For $1.5 million in cash, McCullough relinquished his claim to all territory and trade name rights. Thus in March 1962, a new corporation, International Dairy Queen, was formed by a group of investors led by Burt Myers, who served as chairman of the board, and Gilbert Stein, who became president.

Headquartered in Minneapolis, management immediately created a wholly-owned subsidiary, American Dairy Queen Corporation, to take care of trademarks, collect royalties, and sell store franchises. More importantly, the new management quickly cleared up all the remaining lawsuits and established undisputed ownership of the name Dairy Queen. In addition, management inaugurated a standardized food program, implemented a national advertising and marketing program, created a national training school, imposed product uniformity at over 60 percent of Dairy Queen stores, revised contracts to cover percentages of sales rather than gallons of soft serve mix, and increased the number of employees in the national office from five to 125.

During the mid-1960s, International Dairy Queen consolidated its domestic operations by purchasing the franchising rights of Harry Oltz's AR-TIK Systems, including seven southeastern states, and by securing the development rights for territories in numerous states. The confusion over who owned territory in what state, and whether fees were outstanding or not, was due to the McCulloughs' tendency during the early years to sell territories and prospective store locations in a haphazard manner. Management's intention was to provide more effective services and standardize products by ironing out these problems. At the same time, management launched an aggressive acquisition strategy by purchasing interests in franchise operations within the recreation industry. A ski-rental firm in Denver was bought first, and was soon followed by a franchise for camping equipment.

1970s: Further Leadership Changes and a Return to Profitability

The company's consolidation of operating territory and its acquisition strategy proved costly, and a $2 million loss was forecast for fiscal 1970. With a growing cash flow problem that made it a potential takeover target, company management decided to accept the overtures of a new investment group. Headed by men who were part of the development of National Car Rental System, Inc., the group offered $3 million in cash with $2 million in credit to provide financing for working capital and expansion needs. In return, the investors assumed both majority interest and effective control of International Dairy Queen. Bill McKinstry became executive committee chairman and chairman of the board of directors and Harris Cooper was named president.

McKinstry's and Cooper's reorganization strategy had immediate effects. By discontinuing one of the company's divisions, closing 16 accounting and regional offices, and standardizing operating procedures and product lines, International Dairy Queen soon became profitable once again. In 1972, the company began trading its stock on the over-the-counter market; during the same year, its stock price increased from $1.50 per share to $22.75.

In May 1972, the first Dairy Queen store was opened in Tokyo. While 75 stores were operating outside the United States and Canada in 1976, more than 150 stores in Barbados, Guatemala, Iceland, Japan, Panama, Puerto Rico, Trinidad, the United Arab Emirates, and Hong Kong were operating by the end of the decade.

International Dairy Queen's total revenues in 1979 amounted to $956 million; as the system celebrated its 40th anniversary in 1980 total revenues came to $1.2 billion. Within the fast food industry, Dairy Queen ranked fifth in total sales volume behind McDonald's, Kentucky Fried Chicken, Burger King, and Wendy's; the company ranked third in total number of stores behind McDonald's and KFC. In the United States, Dairy Queen had 4,314 stores in operation, with 365 in Canada, 123 in Japan, and over 30 in eight other foreign countries.

In 1976, McKinstry was replaced as chairman by John Mooty, who worked well with President Cooper. Due to a sudden fall in stock prices during the mid-1970s, Mooty implemented a stock repurchasing plan to provide more stability for the company. By the early 1980s, International Dairy Queen had used nearly $40 million to buy back two-thirds of its outstanding shares on the stock market. At the end of the decade, the performance of the stock was widely regarded as one of the best; an individual who had invested $10,000 in Dairy Queen stock in 1980 would have a portfolio worth $470,000 in 1990.

1980s–90s: New Products and Restaurant Chains

Under Mooty's and Cooper's stewardship, International Dairy Queen had introduced both the Peanut Butter Parfait and Fudge Brownie Delight, both of which were highly successful novelty products. However, it was the introduction of the Blizzard, a concoction of soft-serve ice cream blended with candy, cookies, or fruit, that secured Dairy Queen's ranking as the number one treat chain during the 1980s. In 1985 alone, the year it was introduced, the Blizzard achieved sales of over 100 million units. Along with the success of the Dairy Queen stores, the company's purchase of Golden Skillet, a chain of fried chicken restaurants; KarmelKorn Shoppes, Inc., a 60-year-old popcorn and candy franchise; and Orange Julius, a franchise selling fruit-flavored blended drinks and various snack products, secured the parent's position as the eighth ranked fast food chain in the United States. International Dairy Queen also purchased 60 percent of a staffing agency, Firstaff, Inc., in 1989.

As the company entered the 1990s, John Mooty remained chairman of the board of directors and Mike Sullivan had replaced Cooper as president. Slow domestic growth and international expansion continued. Within the United States, the company was developing opportunities to open stores in shopping malls, office complexes, railroad stations, airports, and other non-traditional markets. In the international arena, the company initiated development programs in Thailand, Cyprus, Kuwait, Oman, Taiwan, and Indonesia, and planned a major campaign to open stores in Western and Eastern Europe.

In 1994 a dispute with franchisees surfaced when a group of store owners filed suit against International Dairy Queen, alleging that their efforts to develop alternative sources of food and paper supplies had been thwarted by the parent company. Two years later the case was granted class-action status by a federal court.

Continuing to test new marketing concepts, in 1996 the company unveiled a new, smaller prototype store in Caledonia, Minnesota. The "1500 Series" store, only 1,500 square feet in size, had half the capacity of a typical 90-seat restaurant and a smaller kitchen area. The intent was to develop a store that was appropriate for markets of 2,500 people or less. Franchisee interest was reportedly strong. The following year the company sold its 60 percent interest in Firstaff to AccuStaff, Inc. of Florida, and also jettisoned its long-time advertising agency, Campbell Mithun Esty, replacing it with Grey Advertising of New York.

Late 1990s Acquisition by Berkshire Hathaway

The biggest news of 1997 came in the fall, when it was announced that the company would be sold to Berkshire Hathaway Inc. of Omaha, Nebraska. Investment guru Warren Buffett controlled Berkshire, which would pay $585 million in stock and cash. Owners of Dairy Queen shares grumbled that the amount was low, but the deal was approved by voting stockholders and finalized in early 1998. The sale had been spurred by the death of Rudy Luther, a Twin Cities-based car dealer who owned 15 percent of Dairy Queen. When Luther's heirs decided to sell his stake, Buffett was approached. Having previously sought to buy the entire company, he refused to take only a portion and renewed his earlier offer, which was now accepted. Buffett pledged to be a "hands off" owner, and no major management or structural changes were planned.

Grey Advertising delivered the company's biggest promotional campaign ever during the summer of 1998. A new tag line, "Meet me at DQ," and an emphasis on the chain's hometown feel were features of the $25 million push. The first television spots were scheduled to run in the United States and Canada beginning in July.

In 2000 the six-year-old lawsuit with franchisees was finally settled. International Dairy Queen agreed to contribute $5 million per year for six years to the store owners' national advertising fund, while also giving the Dairy Queen Operators' Cooperative $6 million to help ensure availability of alternate sources of food and supplies. The court-approved settlement was hailed by all sides as a fair one. At the end of the year CEO Michael Sullivan stepped down and became chairman of the board, with chief financial officer Chuck Mooty taking over the top position. Mooty, age 39, was the son of John Mooty, who was named chairman-emeritus.

Turning the corner into the 21st century, International Dairy Queen was facing the future with renewed vigor. The deep pockets of Warren Buffett and an experienced team of leaders provided the proper conditions for continued success. The company's ongoing international expansion was further extending the reach of one of the most recognizable advertising symbols in the world: "The Cone with the Curl on Top."

Principal Subsidiaries

American Dairy Queen Corporation; KarmelKorn Shoppes, Inc.; Orange Julius of America.

Principal Competitors

A&W Restaurants, Inc.; AFC Enterprises, Inc.; Ben & Jerry's Homemade, Inc.; Burger King Corporation; Carvel Corporation; Checkers Drive-In Restaurants, Inc.; CKE Restaurants, Inc.; CoolBrands International, Inc.; Friendly Ice Cream Corporation; Jack In The Box, Inc.; McDonald's Corporation; Sonic Corporation; TCBY Enterprises, Inc.; Triarc Companies, Inc.; TRICON Global Restaurants, Inc.; Wendy's International, Inc.

Further Reading

Feyder, Susan, "Auto Dealer's Death Influenced IDQ's Decision to Sell," *Star-Tribune Newspaper of the Twin Cities Mpls.-St. Paul,* November 22, 1997, p. 1D.
Gibson, Richard, "Buffett is Scooping Up Dairy Queen in a Deal that Has Sent Some Investors into Meltdown," *Wall Street Journal,* November 5, 1997, p. C4.
Kalstrom, Jonathan, "Sullivan Treats Franchisees Right," *Minneapolis-St. Paul CityBusiness,* May 12, 2000, p. 29.
Kramer, Louise, "Dairy Queen Touts Hometown Feeling in $25 Mil Campaign," *Advertising Age,* June 1, 1998, p. 4.
Otis, Caroline Hall, *The Cone with the Curl on Top: The Dairy Queen Story, 1940–1980,* Minneapolis, Minn.: International Dairy Queen, Inc., 1990.
Shalhoup, Mara, "Federal Anti-Trust Lawsuit Against Dairy Queen Settles in Macon, Ga.," *Macon Telegraph,* March 24, 2000.
Tellijohn, Andrew, "CEO-To-Be Has DQ in his Blood," *Minneapolis-St. Paul CityBusiness,* August 25, 2000, p. 1.

—Thomas Derdak
—update: Frank Uhle

Jarvis plc

Frogmore Park
Watton-at-Stone
Hertford SG14 3RU
United Kingdom
Telephone: (+44) 1920-832800
Fax: (+44) 1920-832832
Web site: http://www.jarvisplc.com

Public Company
Incorporated: 1846
Employees: 6,742
Sales: £669.1 million ($1 billion) (2000)
Stock Exchanges: London
Ticker Symbol: JRVS
NAIC: 23 Construction; 233320 Commercial and
   Institutional Building Construction; 234990 All Other
   Heavy Construction

CEO Paris Maoyedi has transformed Jarvis plc from a tiny, money-losing construction firm in the early 1990s to one of the United Kingdom's leading facilities management and infrastructure services firms. Between 1995 and 2000 alone the company's revenues have soared from less than £80 million to near £670 million. The company's steady profit gains have contributed to one of the United Kingdom's most successful stock advances during the decade, as Jarvis's share price has soared from as little as five pence to near as high as 700 pence at times. The most significant feature of the "new" Jarvis—the company's prehistory dates back to the 19th century—is its leading share of the United Kingdom's railroad maintenance and infrastructure services market, built up through a series of acquisitions after the breakup and privatization of former government monopoly British Rail in the early 1990s. The company holds a number of key Railtrack contracts worth more than £700 million, including a five-year £250 million contract awarded in February 2000. In early 2001 the company was on the fast track toward winning a new £50 million maintenance contract for the United Kingdom's east coast mainline railway. At the same time, Jarvis has been making inroads in capturing a

strong share of the European roads and airport maintenance activities, a market the company entered with its 1998 acquisition of Streamline Holdings. Jarvis, through its Accommodation Services division, is also a strong contender in the market for public sector construction and facilities management projects, particularly under the Private Finance Initiative (PFI) program, set up in 1992 to encourage the building and management of public sector facilities by private sector companies. Jarvis has captured a strong share of PFI-financed projects, included a £170 million contract for the design, construction, and long-term management of the Ministry of Defence's Army Foundation College, awarded in September 2000.

Express Train to Transformation in the 1990s

Jarvis plc was a small and struggling publicly held construction firm that had been hit hard by the building bust in the United Kingdom in the late 1980s. Originally established in 1846, the company—which had achieved a market capitalization of only about £10 million—collapsed along with the construction market and by the early 1990s was posting annual losses of more than £5 million. The company might have faded out completely if it had not caught the attention of construction industry veteran Paris Maoyedi in 1994.

Iranian-born Maoyedi (his original first name was Parviz, but he had it changed to Paris to make it easier to pronounce) had come to England as a student in the late 1950s, then married and remained in the United Kingdom to begin a distinguished career with construction firm AMEC plc at the start of the 1960s. Maoyedi went on to a number of top management positions within AMEC, before leaving that company in the 1980s to take a top role with another firm, Walter Lawrence, as it was preparing to enter the housebuilding market. Seeing a future in accommodation services, Maoyedi left Walter Lawrence in 1988 and decided to found his own company, Team Services, to specialize in student dormitories.

Rather than take Team Services itself public, given the disastrous construction climate of the late 1980s, when the building boom that had marked the United Kingdom during that decade suddenly turned to bust, Maoyedi found a back door to a public listing. Jarvis plc had been hard hit by the collapse of the building market and had seen its share price slide below five pence per share. Maoyedi approached his partners in Team Services with the idea of performing a reverse takeover of Jarvis, thereby enabling Team Services to go public under the Jarvis name. The two companies entered talks, but Jarvis's partners decided not to pursue the takeover. Instead, Maoyedi went ahead and formed a joint venture company with Jarvis, investing his personal funds into the £1 million venture.

That joint venture did not go far. Instead of pursuing the joint venture, Jarvis, by then leaking more than £5 million per year and facing being cut off by its creditor bank, offered Maoyedi the CEO's position at Jarvis. Maoyedi was reluctant to accept the offer. As he told the *Daily Telegraph:* "I didn't exactly jump at the idea." Jarvis won him over, finally, after giving Maoyedi the power to replace the company's board of directors. Maoyedi joined Jarvis at the end of 1994. His first success at the company was in convincing its bank creditor to add another £1.5 million to the company's overdraft, saving the company from failure. Maoyedi helped restructure the company, refocusing its operations on competing for higher-margin contracts in the design-and-build and space management segments. Maoyedi also sent the company out after a new type of contract, funded by the Private Finance Initiative of the British government to encourage the private sector to take over the construction and management of various public works projects, including schools and hospitals. By the end of 1995, Jarvis had returned to profitability, posting some £500,000 in pretax profits on more than £76 million in sales.

Jarvis might have remained a relatively small construction company had Maoyedi not recognized the opportunities waiting in the proposed breakup and privatization of the nearly 50-year-old government-held U.K. railroad monopoly British Rail. The breakup called for the division of British Rail maintenance and infrastructure facilities wing into some 11 separate companies (which later merged down to just six companies). Maoyedi led Jarvis in a bid for one of these companies, Northern Infrastructure Maintenance Company, or NIMCO, which was responsible for maintenance and renewal operations on more than 4,000 miles of track in the northern England region. Jarvis paid just £9 million for NIMCO and suddenly transformed itself from a small construction group to a company with nearly 4,000 employees. The company inherited more than £350 million in contracts extending over five years, while gaining control of about one-fifth of the new railway infrastructure market.

The NIMCO acquisition caused Jarvis's long-dormant stock to wake up as Jarvis now appeared a strong player in a new and vital market. By the end of 1996, the company had booked the second strongest share price gain on the London stock exchange, when its share price soared by more than 500 percent. While the company worked to integrate its new division, contin-

uing a payroll slimming exercise begun under British Rail to reduce the NIMCO division to fewer than 3,000 employees, Jarvis's share price began to climb. Its new market clout placed Jarvis in the position to consider further expansions to its new arm. By the end of its next fiscal year (the company changed its year-end to March 31) the company's sales had risen to more than £261 million, with more than £6 million in retained profits.

In 1997, Jarvis made its next moves to capture the lead of its new market. In May of that year, the company paid £4.9 million to buy a 50 percent share, plus an option to acquire full control for an additional £5 million, of Scotland-based Relayfast, a rail engineering and maintenance company formed out of the British Rail privatization. Less than a month later, Jarvis was prepared to take its rail division to the next level. In June 1997, the company raised some £62 million in a rights issue in order to acquire another of the British Rail spin-off companies, Fastline, and to acquire the remaining 50 percent of Relayfast.

Yet the rights issue nearly failed, as Jarvis and its share price were hit hard by a Railtrack decision that placed a temporary ban on contracts to Jarvis because of alleged overpricing made by the NIMCO division before its takeover by Jarvis. That dispute was quickly resolved, with Railtrack and Jarvis forming a joint venture, Alliance, to oversee the handling of contracts between the two companies. The dispute, however, caused a sharp drop in the company's share price, leaving the bulk of the rights issue in the hands of its underwriting companies. Jarvis's underwriters were nevertheless to profit handsomely as Jarvis's share price later tripled in value. When Jarvis at last succeeded in merging its new Fastline and Relayfast operations into its railway maintenance division, the company had gained the leading share in its market, with more than 60 percent of the country's railway system under its responsibility. The company was buoyed further by the award of three contracts for three years each from Railtrack, worth some £290 million in December 1997. These contracts helped boost the company's revenues, which topped £355 million, with net profits of more than £17 million for the year ending March 31, 1998.

"Europe's Biggest" for the 21st Century

With its rail operations at their limit in the United Kingdom—the Fastline acquisition had already prompted calls for intervention from the United Kingdom's Mergers and Monopolies Commission—Jarvis now looked to extend itself into becoming what Maoyedi described to the *Daily Telegraph* as "Europe's biggest integrated infrastructure maintenance company for transport."

In May 1998, the company announced a friendly takeover of Streamline Holdings. Worth nearly £184 million, the stock and cash deal gave Jarvis entry into a new area of operations, that of road and airport maintenance, not only in the United Kingdom, but across Europe as well, while also boosting its U.K. railway maintenance business. Streamline had been a part of Shell until the early 1990s, when it was spun off as part of a management buyout and then taken public in 1996, and had built a position as Europe's leading road maintenance company. Streamline had only recently entered the airport maintenance field, an area Maoyedi pledged to develop further. The Streamline acquisition

Key Dates:

1846: Jarvis construction company is founded.
1994: Paris Maovedi becomes CEO of Jarvis.
1996: Company acquires NIMCO.
1997: Company acquires Fastline and Relayfast.
1998: Company acquires Streamline Holdings.
1999: Company acquires Trafiroad.
2000: Company sells roofing and building products subsidiaries.
2001: Company is chosen preferred bidder for £50 million east coast mainline maintenance contract.

was to help boost Jarvis's revenues to more than £605 million by the end of its 1999 fiscal year.

Yet Jarvis entered 1999 under a cloud, as its railway workers, more than 60 percent of whom belonged to the RMT union, joined an industrywide strike to protest attempts to change their contracts. To trim its payroll costs, Jarvis sought to eliminate the long-standing provision for overtime pay on weekend and overnight shifts—the very times when Jarvis was able to conduct its railway maintenance operations. The dispute was to last more than ten months, and was finally resolved with a compromise, with Jarvis agreeing to raise base salaries in exchange for an end to overtime pay. This, and a new dispute with Railtrack, helped to depress the company's earnings in 2000, despite a rise in revenues to more than £669 million for the year.

The new dispute with Railtrack, which continued to press for lower prices from its railway maintenance bidders, highlighted Jarvis's need to reduce the weight of its railway maintenance activities on its revenues. The company's road maintenance division continued to show promise and was to be boosted by the acquisition of Trafiroad NV, of Belgium, which also brought the company Trafiroad's Netherlands operations. The deal, worth up to £8.5 million, was to be carried out in two stages, with the first tier giving Jarvis 75 percent of Trafiroad in exchange for 1.65 million shares in Jarvis, worth more than £3.7 million. The second phase to acquire the remaining shares of Trafiroad was scheduled to be completed before 2002. The company also added to its European road maintenance network with France's Prosign, which was that country's leading maker and applier of road paint and other road marking products.

While building up its railway and road operations, Jarvis was also stepping up its growth into another direction, that of facilities management, as the company continued to benefit from the PFI program. In February 2000, Jarvis joined with the Halifax Group to win contracts to build and manage the Army Foundation College, a project with an ultimate worth of more than £435 million. In September of that year, the company won another large-scale contract with the award of a £230 million contract to upgrade and maintain eight public schools.

As the company focused on its public works construction and management wing, it exited a number of noncore areas, selling off a roofing subsidiary early in 2000, then receiving £20 million for a building products subsidiary in October 2000. Entering 2001, Jarvis was lifted again by the announcement that it had been chosen preferred bidder for a new Railtrack contract, worth £50 million, which was expected to give Jarvis access to maintenance work on the United Kingdom's east coast mainline railway for the first time. At the same time, the company announced that it had won a 25-year contract worth nearly £100 million to develop, build, and manage the new site for the prestigious Jews Free School.

Principal Subsidiaries

Jarvis Facilities Ltd.; Jarvis Fastline Ltd.; Jarvis Construction (U.K.) Ltd.; Jarvis Newman Ltd.; Jarvis Training Management Ltd.; Jarvis Projects Ltd.; Jarvis Workspace FM Ltd.; Jarvis Property Company Ltd.; Jarvis Estates Ltd.; Jarvis International Ltd.; PRismo Ltd.; Techspan Systems plc; On Track Plant Ltd.; Jarvis Traffic Systems Ltd.; Jarvis (Barnhill) Ltd.; Prosign SA (France); Enterprise Foulon SA (France); Veluvine BV (Netherlands); Wolff GmbH (Germany); Oric SA; Trafiroad NV (Belgium); Trafiroad BV (Netherlands); De Moor NV (Belgium).

Principal Competitors

ABB Ltd.; AMEC plc; Amey plc; Balfour Beatty plc; Bechtel Group, Inc.; Bouygues S.A.; Serco Group plc; Tarmac plc.

Further Reading

de Aenille, Conrad, ''The Little Rail-Equipment Makers That Could,'' *International Herald Tribune,* May 23, 1998.
Casciato, Paul, ''Jarvis Hit by Railtrack Dispute,'' *Reuters,* June 22, 1999.
Cave, Andrew, ''Jarvis Profits Treble as Rail Acquisitions Bear Fruit,'' *Daily Telegraph,* December 9, 1997.
Gallioni, Alessandra, ''Jarvis Soars as Rail Row Settled,'' *Reuters,* August 16, 1999.
Osborne, Alistair, ''Calm Driver of the Jarvis Express,'' *Daily Telegraph,* July 4, 1998, p. 31.

—M.L. Cohen

John Menzies plc

108 Princes Street
Edinburgh EH2 3AA
United Kingdom
Telephone: (+44) 131 225-8555
Fax: (+44) 131 226-3752
Web site: http://www.johnmenzies.co.uk

Public Company
Incorporated: 1906 as John Menzies & Company Ltd.
Employees: 7,680
Sales: £1.39 billion ($2.09 billion)(2000)
Stock Exchanges: London
Ticker Symbol: MNZS
NAIC: 42292 Book, Periodical, and Newspaper
   Wholesalers; 49211 Couriers

After more than 150 years as a retailer, John Menzies plc (Menzies is pronounced "Mingus") has redefined its role for the 21st century. The company is in the process of shedding all of its retail activities in order to become one of the world's top-three logistics and distribution groups. Toward that end, the company has divested its chain of more than 230 John Menzies bookstores and also seeks a buyer for its 220-store chain of Early Learning Centre children's toys and games stores. John Menzies is also exiting the volatile entertainment distribution market, announcing its intention to end its long-standing distribution agreement with Japan's Nintendo, which had given John Menzies, through subsidiary THE Games, exclusive distribution rights to Nintendo products in the United Kingdom. The company is also selling off its Total Home Entertainment (THE) subsidiary, which distributes videos and music, in a management buyout. What remains of the holding company is a logistics and distribution group. The company's Menzies Wholesale is a leading distributor of magazines and newspapers to the U.K. market and represents the largest share of the company's sales. The company also remains committed to expanding its Aviation Services division, which includes subsidiaries Menzies Transport Services, Menzies World Cargo, and Menzies Aviation Support Services. The acquisition of U.S.-based Ogden Ground Services for $118 million in 2000 has transformed Menzies into one of the world's leading independent and international logistics experts.

19th Century Wholesale Empire

After serving as an apprentice bookseller in Edinburgh and then working in London for bookseller and publisher Charles Tilt, John Menzies returned to Edinburgh in 1833 to establish his own shop at 61 Princes Street. The limited nature of bookselling during that period—booksellers acted as agents for a limited number of publishers—and the great distance between Edinburgh and London in the pre-railroad United Kingdom led Menzies to expand his bookselling operation to acting as a wholesaler. One of Menzies' first customers was Charles Tilt. Other London publishers quickly assigned their Scottish business to Menzies. Among these was Chapman & Hall publishers, then bringing out the first weekly installments of a novel called *The Pickwick Papers*. The success of that Charles Dickens novel helped Menzies wholesale business become the major part of his growing operations.

Menzies had also been quick to seize on two other growing trends. He was one of the first to sell newspapers, such as the *Scotsman,* over the counter. Menzies also received the wholesale contract for the periodical *Punch,* which would become one of the most important magazines in the English-speaking world in its time. In 1855, Menzies added more newspapers sales to his lists—the *Daily Express* and the *Daily Mirror*—and sought other newspaper distribution opportunities. The most important of these came with the growing importance of the railroad in 19-century Scotland. Railroad stations were being served by a new type of retailer, the newsstand, and in 1857 Menzies acquired the newsstand concessions for many of Scotland's railroads and their stations, though he missed out on the country's two largest stations in Edinburgh. Menzies was to acquire the stands at both of these stations by early in the next decade.

The growing importance of Menzies' wholesale trade and of his newsstands operations led him to exit the retail bookselling market in 1859, when he closed the company's Princes Street location. At the same time, Menzies opened a new, larger wholesale facility. Wholesale remained the company's major source of revenues, representing more than three-quarters of the company's sales by 1860, a percentage that only increased in the following decades. Nonetheless, the newsstands represented a key feature of the growing Menzies company, offering what was to become a strategic distribution network.

While Menzies' sons, John and Charles, were destined to take over the family-run operation, Menzies, in 1867, prepared for his eventual succession by reforming the business as a partnership with three of his employees. The company's willingness to promote from within remained a hallmark until well into the 20th century. The new partnership, called John Menzies and Company, prepared to extend beyond its Edinburgh focus when it opened its first wholesale warehouse in Glasgow in 1868.

By the time of Menzies' death in 1879, his company had become one of Scotland's principal book, magazine, and newspaper distributors. Sons John and Charles took over the lead of the company and proved indefatigable workers, extending and strengthening the company's wholesale business throughout all of Scotland. The brothers continued to lead the company into the 1930s.

The company formally incorporated as John Menzies & Company Ltd. in 1906. In the early decades of the new century, Menzies began branching out from its distribution business, which itself was helped out by the arrival of the first reliable gasoline-driven vans and trucks. The company also began a foray into publishing, which did not last long. More successful for the company was its diversification beyond newsstands, an occasion offered by its acquisition of tobacconist Finlay's in 1922. Many of the Finlay tobacco stands were located not only in the same train stations but often alongside the Menzies newsstands. The combination of the two activities was a natural. Toward the end of that same decade, Menzies returned to its founding business; in 1928 it acquired Elliott's book shop on Edinburgh's Princes Street, down the block from the original Menzies location. The Elliott's acquisition became only the first of many new Menzies stores, to the point where, by the end of the century, Menzies had become one of the United Kingdom's preeminent book retailers.

Major Postwar Growth

The 1930s were marked by the Great Depression, which cut into the company's newsstand sales in particular. Paradoxically, the outbreak of World War II, despite the damage the company suffered from the Nazi bombing raids, represented a boom time for Menzies, as people eagerly snapped up newspapers to remain current with events. When Charles Menzies died, he was

succeeded by his widow, Helen, who guided the company into the 1950s. In 1951, John Maxwell Menzies, great-grandson of founder John Menzies, took over as company chairman.

By that time, Menzies had branched out from railroads, opening its first airport-based newsstand in Edinburgh's Turnhouse airport. The company also launched its first mobile newsstand. Menzies, now turning over some £10 million in revenues per year, had also been building up its chain of retail book stores, with seven stores by the beginning of the 1950s. By 1958, as Menzies celebrated its 125-year anniversary, the company had opened or acquired another 19 stores and was on its way to becoming one of the United Kingdom's pre-eminent booksellers.

The nationalization of Britain's railway system in 1953 largely left Menzies dominance of the Scottish newsstand market in place. Sharing the newsstand market in the United Kingdom were Easons in Ireland, and Wymans and WH Smith in England. John Menzies soon extended its dominance into England, when, in 1959, it acquired publicly-held Wymans. Menzies added Wymans' 78 retail book stores, 200 newsstands, and a strong London-based wholesaling business to its holdings. By the beginning of the 1960s, Menzies, now reincorporated as John Menzies (Holdings) Ltd., was operating more than 350 newsstands. Yet that figure was destined to shrink over time as British Rail engaged on a massive streamlining program that closed many of the country's rural and underused train stations.

The company meanwhile had been stepping up its wholesale wing, acquiring Pickles, in Leeds, and Belfast-based wholesaler Porter. The following year, the company acquired Horace Marshall & Son. Ltd. Also that year, the company went public. Menzies remained controlled by the Menzies family, which had retained some two million of the 2.5 million issued shares. The family's grip on the company's ownership was slowly to dwindle over the following decades, though family members would remain major shareholders into the 21st century.

While its wholesale wing, with more than 90 branches throughout the United Kingdom, and its retail store operations, with more than 160 shops by the mid-1960s, continued to grow, Menzies newsstands were taking on lesser importance. A major part of the newsstands' decline was the shrinking numbers of railway passengers, as more and more people opted for buses and their own cars. Yet, the growth of Menzies retail and wholesale business helped propel the company's sales to £50 million by 1970. Just ten years later, the company's sale were to climb past £200 million.

Transforming for the New Century

In the 1980s, Menzies began to branch out from its core books and newspapers distribution activities. In 1980, the company acquired Terry Blood (Records) Ltd., which formed the core of the company's later Total Home Entertainment subsidiary. That acquisition launched Menzies into the wholesale music distribution market. By the end of the decade, after its acquisition of Wynd-Up Records in 1989, that division was to become the market leader.

Key Dates:

1833: John Menzies opens a book store in Edinburgh.
1835: Menzies begins a book wholesale business.
1857: The first of the company's newsstands are opened.
1859: Menzies exits the retail book store market.
1867: The partnership John Menzies and Company is formed.
1879: Sons John and Charles take over leadership of company.
1906: Company incorporates as John Menzies & Company, Ltd.
1922: Company acquires U.K. tobacconist chain Finlay's.
1948: Menzies opens its first airport newsstand.
1951: John Maxwell Menzies, great-grandson of the founder, takes over the company's reigns.
1962: Menzies goes public on the London exchange.
1985: Company acquires the Early Learning Centre chain.
1989: Menzies enters the wholesale courier services market.
1993: Menzies acquires Air Marketing Services Group and forms Air Menzies International.
1995: Concorde Express is acquired.
1998: Company begins exiting the retail business.
2000: Menzies acquires Ogden Ground Services and restructures the logistics division as Menzies Aviation Services.

Menzies expanded into other areas in the 1980s as well, starting with a purchase of Children's Books (Rudgeley) Ltd., in 1981, which gave the company wholesale activities in children's books, toys, and games. In 1985, Menzies added the acquisition of the Early Learning Centre chain of U.K. stores specializing in toys and games for very young children. Menzies quickly expanded Early Learning Centre internationally, opening shops in Holland before preparing an expansion into the United States. At the same time, Menzies was building up an internationally operating distribution business in library supply and commercial stationery products with the purchases of Lonsdale Universal plc and Cambridge Jackson, both in 1982. Despite these diversification moves, the company book wholesaling unit remained a central focus and was boosted by the acquisition of Hammick, a wholesale and retail bookseller in 1987. The following year, Menzies further expanded its retail empire when it acquired the Martin Retail Group. The addition of that company's nearly 70 retail stores doubled the company's existing presence in England.

Yet, as the 1990s were beginning, Menzies was preparing the first step of what was to become an entirely new direction. This came in 1989 when the company acquired Scan International Group, giving the company an international wholesale courier service. The company extended its new Transport Services division with the freight handler Cargosave in 1990. In 1993, after the acquisition of Air Marketing Services group, Menzies reorganized its growing division into a new subsidiary, Air Menzies International. The company became the United Kingdom's leading independent wholesale express air courier and air-freight consolidator. This division continued to grow in 1995, after Menzies acquired Concorde Express, based at Lon-

don's Heathrow Airport, where it provided cargo handling, contract labor, and cargo transport services.

In the mid-1990s, Menzies caught on to the growing market for video games when it acquired a 37 percent share of Funsoft, the leading European distributor of games software. It then created a new subsidiary, THE Games, which captured the exclusive distribution rights to Nintendo products—including the massively popular Gameboy and Nintendo 64 systems—in the United Kingdom and Ireland. The company's retail operations also celebrated an agreement to place some 70 Menzies stores in the London Underground.

Yet the retirement of John Menzies and the appointment of David Mackay as the company's CEO—the first time someone outside of the Menzies family had been appointed to direct the company—signaled the beginning of a new era for Menzies. Recognizing that Menzies was unable to compete in a new retailing climate that included new numbers of competitors—particularly with the loss of the newsstands' monopoly on newspaper sales—Mackay promised a restructuring of the company's operations. By 1998, Mackay had outlined the company's intentions. In that year, he announced the decision to exit retailing. First, the company sold off its chain of John Menzies retail shops to rival WH Smith for £68 million in March 1998, and then it announced its intent to sell the struggling Early Learning Centre chain. That chain had yet to find a buyer by the end of the year 2000. At the beginning of 2001, however, the company announced the end of it's the subsidiary, selling the main subsidiary in a management buyout while closing the THE Games division after Nintendo's decision not to renew its distribution contract. (Both companies were among several under investigation for taking part in an alleged price-fixing cartel for the European market.)

The company's exit from retailing coincided with its decision to regroup around its core wholesale distribution wing while stepping up the expansion of its logistics services division. The company reached a partnership agreement with Lufthansa's Airport and Ground Services subsidiary to form the joint venture London Cargo Centre, based at Heathrow, in 1998. When that partnership was extended to the Manchester and Birmingham airports as well, its name was changed to Menzies World Cargo.

By the end of the year 2000, Menzies' new direction was evident and gaining support from analysts. In November 2000, the company completed an acquisition of Ogden Ground Services, based in the United States and one of that country's leading aviation services companies. The Ogden acquisition, worth £74 million ($108 million), established Menzies as the world's number three aviation logistics services groups. The acquisition also led the company to change the division's name to Menzies Aviation Group. As Menzies entered the new century, it pledged to continue its transformation, particularly with the promise to build up its logistics arm as an equal counterpart to its far-larger wholesale division.

Principal Divisions

Menzies Wholesale; Menzies Aviation Group; Menzies Transport Services; Menzies World Cargo; Menzies Aviation Support Services; Early Learning Centre; Total Home Entertainment (THE).

Principal Competitors

Advanced Marketing Services, Inc.; Société Air France; Airborne, Inc.; Alpha Airports Group; ASDA Group Limited; Baker & Taylor Corporation; FedEx Corporation; Hays plc; Publishers Group Incorporated; Tesco PLC.

Further Reading

Griffin, Rob, ''Menzies Out of the Game,'' *Guardian*, December 9, 2000.

''Reinventing John Menzies,'' *Independent*, July 8, 1997, p. 21.

Snoddy, Julia, ''Menzies to Dump Loss-Making Early Learning Centre,'' *Guardian*, January 24, 2001.

Turpin, Andrew, ''John Menzies Looks to the Skies,'' *Scotsman*, January 24, 2001.

—M.L. Cohen

Jones Apparel Group, Inc.

250 Rittenhouse Circle
Bristol, Pennsylvania 19007
U.S.A.
Telephone: (215) 785-4000
Fax: (215) 785-1228
Web site: http://www.jny.com

Public Company
Incorporated: 1975
Employees: 22,350
Sales: $4.14 billion (2000)
Stock Exchanges: New York
Ticker Symbol: JNY
NAIC: 31523 Women's and Girls' Cut and Sew Apparel
    Manufacturing

Jones Apparel Group, Inc. is a leader in the apparel industry. The company designs and markets a broad array of men's, women's, and junior's sportswear as well as moderately priced suits, dresses, and casualwear. Its clothing is sold under its original Jones New York label, as well as the labels Evan-Picone, Rena Rowan, Saville, Todd Oldham, Nine West, Easy Spirit, Enzo Angiolini, Bandolino, and Napier. Licensed brands include Lauren by Ralph Lauren, Ralph by Ralph Lauren, and Polo Jeans Company. The company also markets costume jewelry under the Tommy Hilfiger brand licensed from TH Corporation. Jones Apparel Group was one of the fastest growing companies in the U.S. apparel industry during the late 1980s and early 1990s. Federated Department Stores Inc. and Mays Department Stores Co. are Jones's biggest customers.

Late 1970s: Creating Inexpensive, Designer-Inspired Clothing

Jones Apparel Group was founded by Sidney Kimmel as a division of Grace & Co. in 1975. A 20-year veteran of the women's clothing industry, Kimmel recognized a potentially lucrative void in the marketplace that he could fill by designing and marketing a line of clothing that mimicked extremely expensive designer fashions. Hoping to appeal to the middle-income market of working women, Kimmel decided that his apparel would be high in quality yet affordable.

By the time Kimmel started his Jones venture, he had already proven himself in the women's clothing industry. The son of a Philadelphia taxi driver, Kimmel had dropped out of college in the early 1950s to work in a knitting mill. Hard work and high energy, as well as his knack for developing and bringing to market popular clothing designs, earned Kimmel a top management spot at the mill by the 1960s, and he eventually became president of Villager, Inc., a top designer and manufacturer of women's sportswear.

Eager to build his own apparel line, Kimmel left Villager in 1969 to join W.R. Grace & Co. A diversified conglomerate, Grace & Co. was seeking to branch out into women's clothing and chose Kimmel to head up the new division. Kimmel brought with him his girlfriend, Rena Rowan, who had worked for him at Villager as a knitwear designer. Shortly after moving to Grace & Co., Kimmel and Rowan hit upon their idea of creating inexpensive, designer look-alike clothing.

During this time, however, Grace's management decided their company didn't belong in the fashion business. Seeking a smooth way out of the undertaking, Grace jettisoned its new Jones division in 1975, selling it to Kimmel and Gerard Rubin, a Grace accountant. Kimmel and Rubin were pleased to get the business, along with its liabilities, for a relatively small cash investment. The two partners incorporated Jones Apparel Group, Inc., in Pennsylvania, and their staff soon consisted of Rowan and several other former Grace employees.

While there was no mistaking Kimmel's acuity in the fashion trade, his knowledge of finance was limited, as he recalled in the December 21, 1992 issue of *Forbes:* "I didn't know how to read a balance sheet." Even Rubin was unable to steer the fledgling company clear of fiscal distress, and, during its first five years of business, Jones Apparel was burdened by debt and short on cash. Nevertheless, Kimmel pursued an aggressive growth agenda, beginning several new labels and licensing the rights to other clothing lines.

Company Perspectives:

There are many ways in which Jones Apparel Group is differentiated as an industry leader. One important way is by our extremely efficient and dynamic infrastructure. This infrastructure permits the leveraging of the company's strengths in design, merchandising, sourcing, and distribution to successfully execute aggressive growth initiatives. Ideas from the Jones Apparel Group and merchandising teams are innovative and fresh, incorporating the daily lifestyle of today's consumer as opposed to chasing fashion trends. Those teams interact closely with retail coordinators who work closely with consumers on the retail selling floor. Consumer reaction is reported back and incorporated into styling to constantly develop and improve styling for future seasons. Jones Apparel Group products are known for consistency and quality of fit. This reputation reflects the hard work of our production and quality control teams who work diligently behind the scenes with a network of experiences contractors to ensure adherence to uncompromising production and quality values. Finally, the Jones Apparel Group distribution team executes a seamless delivery of product from our distribution centers covering more than 3 million square feet to the retail selling floor. This collaborative effort ensures the complete satisfaction of our customers.

1980s: Jones Gains on its Industry Peers

The company did achieve a relatively high degree of success, particularly during the 1980s. Kimmel found a strong demand for many of his products among women who appreciated style and quality but didn't have a lot of money to spend on expensive designer wear. The Jones New York line, which featured career sportswear, suits, and dresses, was especially successful; for $100 to $300, women were able to purchase professional and casual wear that looked and felt like name brands selling for twice the price or more. Moreover, Kimmel was able to profit by outsourcing the manufacturing of his clothes to both U.S. and overseas producers. That tactic allowed Jones to focus on designing, marketing, and distributing its products, while at the same time bypassing hefty capital investments in manufacturing facilities.

Jones also gained on its industry peers by implementing the latest productivity-enhancing technology. Indeed, while many U.S. apparel producers succumbed to fierce foreign competition during the decade, Jones thrived. In 1981, for example, Jones became one of the first apparel designers in the United States to start using a computer-aided design (CAD) system and to employ a systems manager, Maureen Behl, in its design department. The new system saved large sums in wasted fabric, because it allowed designers to lay patterns out on a facsimile of the fabric (a process called marking), like pieces of a puzzle, before transferring the design and cutting the actual fabric.

CAD also slashed labor costs related to grading (shrinking a standard-size garment design to make other sizes). "There's really no comparison," Behl commented in the September 24, 1993 issue of *Philadelphia Business Journal*. "Doing it manually, it could take a day to do the marking and grading for one pattern. Now it takes a few hours." The improved turnaround time associated with the CAD system allowed Jones Apparel to provide better customer service. On short notice, Jones designers could get a sample of a design to a client within hours, and then quickly alter the computerized pattern to suit the client's needs.

Besides its keen market niche, low-cost manufacturing strategy, and advanced design program, Jones benefited from economic and demographic trends as well during the mid-1980s. Generally healthy business expansion bolstered the demand for professional and casual wear in the United States. More importantly, the number of working women in the nation increased dramatically during the decade. As a result, the demand for suits and career sportswear flourished, and the discretionary income available to women in Jones' key markets increased. Furthermore, diversifying into a range of apparel aimed at a variety of niche markets, the company purchased the rights to other clothing lines, including Gloria Vanderbilt Jeans, and thus enjoyed demand growth for products outside its core Jones New York line. By the mid-1980s, with annual sales of over $250 million, Jones had become the leading supplier of moderately-priced women's apparel, marketing its lines through retail establishments and catalogs throughout North America.

Faltering, Reorganizing, and Recovering in the Late 1980s

Kimmel continued to pursue new markets in an effort to increase sales, despite warnings from company accountants that Jones Apparel was growing too quickly. Moreover, Kimmel also engaged in several business deals that soured. Chief among such mishaps was his purchase of the marketing rights to Murjani's Gloria Vanderbilt. Kimmel neglected to secure any control over manufacturing costs, pricing, inventory, or delivery of the jeans for which Gloria Vanderbilt was famous, thus undermining his savvy marketing initiatives. That deal alone cost Kimmel $20 million by the late 1980s, severely crimping the company's profitability.

Largely as a result of the failed Murjani transaction—but also because of the heavy debt Jones had accrued during its start-up and rampant growth—Jones Apparel was on the verge of bankruptcy by 1987. As cash flow dried up and the cofounders were forced to spend much of their time putting out financial fires, sales and earnings plummeted. Sales topped $260 million in 1986, but Jones posted a distressing net loss of $4.6 million. In 1987, moreover, sales plunged 32 percent, to $177 million, for a net loss of $6 million.

Rather than seizing and liquidating the company, creditors offered Kimmel and Rubin an alternative. Kimmel and Rubin agreed to a strict reorganization plan designed to shore up the Jones balance sheet and restore the flailing company's profitability. To keep control of the operation, Kimmel and Rubin were forced to drop most of the labels Kimmel had licensed during the 1980s as add-ons to its core apparel lines. They also agreed to lay off many of their employees, scrap most of the companies 17 scattered divisions, and liquidate a major warehouse. Finally, both Kimmel and Rubin had to put their personal assets on the line by guaranteeing $8 million in loans made to the company. The aim of the shake-up was to help Jones Apparel Group focus on its most successful product line, Jones

New York. The company also retained a few of its more profitable complementary brands, such as Christian Dior.

Jones reported a small profit as it wrapped up its reorganization in 1988, and, the following year, the company began to focus heavily on promoting and streamlining its Jones New York line. Weary from Jones' financial woes, Rubin bailed out of the concern in 1989, selling his ownership interest to Kimmel. Unfortunately for Rubin, his departure marked the start of revenue and profit growth at Jones that would continue into the mid-1990s. Indeed, as the United States sank into a recession, demand for Jones New York apparel escalated. Many buyers abandoned expensive designer labels in favor of Jones' more practical attire; the Jones version of the Giorgio Armani suit, for example, sold for only $240, or about $1,200 less than the Armani.

Kimmel augmented Jones' improved market appeal during the late 1980s with increased advertising and a new emphasis on cost control. Furthermore, he began to stress financial stability, working to pare the company's debt load and tighten its customer credit policies. As demand surged and operating costs fell, Jones Apparel posted a 25 percent sales gain in 1989, to $212 million, as net income soared to nearly $13 million. In 1990, moreover, income approached $30 million from revenues of $290 million. That year, to further reduce the company's liabilities, Kimmel took Jones Apparel Group public. By early 1993, the company's debt had been almost entirely eliminated, and Kimmel still personally owned about 45 percent of the corporation.

Early 1990s: Expansion into Complementary Markets

Kimmel's financial recovery in the early 1990s was regarded in the business community as miraculous. Having faced the prospect of losing his company and much of his personal

fortune, Kimmel and his company rebounded, earning $185 million in cash during the 1991 stock offerings and reporting a net worth of nearly three-quarters of a billion dollars in the early 1990s. Expansion at Jones Apparel continued unabated, moreover, as Kimmel boosted Jones New York sales and extended the company's reach into complementary markets. Importantly, in 1991, Jones introduced its Rena Rowan for Saville line. Designed by and named after the woman who had driven the design success of the Jones New York line since 1970, the Rena Rowan line was priced slightly lower than the Jones New York apparel line. By 1993, Rena Rowan clothing was accounting for about 15 percent of Jones' total receipts and was expected to lead sales growth into the mid-1990s.

In addition to making a bid for the lower-priced casual sportswear and dress market with the Rena Rowan line, Jones Apparel also expanded the Jones New York line, seeking to take advantage of four major niche markets: career sportswear, casual sportswear, suits, and dresses. Its Jones New York Sport line, created to penetrate the market for knit weekend and leisure sportswear, was bringing in about 20 percent of Jones Apparel revenue by 1993 and was expected to contribute much more in the future. Other additions to the Jones New York line included: Jones & Co., which offered "career casual" clothing to augment the Sport group; Jones New York Dress, which featured more casual business attire; and Jones New York Suits, a line of higher-priced career apparel. Jones also purchased the rights to use the Evan-Picone brand name in 1993 for $10.5 million in cash. This move illustrated its intent to break into the market for women's rainwear, coats, footwear, intimate apparel, hosiery, handbags, and other accessories.

The company's prudent growth strategy continued to pay off in 1991 and 1992. Sales rose to $334 million in 1991 and then to $436 million one year later. Net income, moreover, rose more than 50 percent between 1990 and 1992 to over $41 million. Jones Apparel's solid profit growth reflected its huge profit margins, which, at about ten percent, were double the industry average. Income gains were also the result of Kimmel's cultivation of diverse distribution channels. For example, Jones began aggressively selling its merchandise through factory outlet stores in the early 1990s, opening more than 100 stores in outlet malls throughout the United States. By 1993, sales from the high-margin outlets had surpassed $55 million. Although department stores still made up more than 60 percent of company sales in the early 1990s, Jones had beefed up its distribution channels to encompass more than 8,000 locations in North America, including its direct mail catalog centers.

Late 1990s: Sustained Growth and Acquisitions

Going into the mid-1990s, Jones Apparel sustained its impressive growth rate. Sales increased 24 percent in 1993 to $541 million, from which nearly $50 million in net income was gleaned. Importantly, the company's core market niches were expanding steadily, while its major competitors were losing ground. Part of Jones Apparel's success came from taking advantage of the trend in the late 1990s toward more casual wear at work and home. Jones updated its Evan-Picone lines, and by 1996 had launched Jones Sport, Jones & Co., Jones New York Country, Jones Studio, and Jones Jeans. In 1995, its sales of casual wear nearly doubled to amount to about 65 percent of its total sales of $776 million.

In 1996, Jones Apparel, which posted sales of $1.02 billion that year, introduced its licensed designer label, Lauren by Ralph Lauren. The line proved remarkably successful—so much so that Jones jettisoned its high-end Christian Dior license to concentrate on more moderately priced clothes. During this period, Jones Apparel also expanded into corollary arenas. A partnership with Madison Maidens resulted in Jones New York Intimates, which debuted a line of sleepwear, robes, loungewear, bras and panties in early 1995. Jones New York Neckwear for men followed in 1996.

Major department stores continued to serve as the primary outlet for Jones Apparel merchandise, accounting for about 75 percent of company sales. However, in 1996, it opened a flagship Jones New York store in Montreal. Two years later, targeting an older customer than competitors Polo, Hilfiger, or Nautica, Jones Apparel introduced its first menswear line, hiring Joe Heiss, founder of the J.J. Farmer sportswear brand, as president of the division. The company also purchased Sun Apparel Inc., sportswear designer and manufacturer of the Polo label, licensed from Ralph Lauren for $217 million. Sun purchased the worldwide rights to the Todd Oldham trademark in 1999 in a move to develop a stronger presence in the junior market.

In 1999, Jones Apparel purchased the Nine West Group, a leading maker of women's shoes, for $1.4 billion. The deal did not please Jones Apparel shareholders; Nine West had been in financial straits following slumping sales and an SEC investigation into its accounting practices, and had cut two-thirds of its work force since 1997. Moreover, Nine West shareholders maintained that the company would not fit well into the Jones Apparel structure and that better offers may have been ignored. Jones Apparel's share price fell following announcement of the Nine West acquisition, but Jones moved quickly to make Nine West profitable again. It immediately shuttered Nine West's Kentucky and Indiana plants, eliminating slightly more than 500 workers, and closed a plant in the Dominican Republic that had employed more than 1,000. The company also began plans to shut down nearly 250 unprofitable Nine West stores.

In 2000, Jones acquired Victoria & Co. for $90 million, a company whose brands represented 20 to 45 percent of the market share in retail fashion jewelry. Kimmel, in an August 2000 *Women's Wear Daily Accessories Supplement* article voiced the company's optimism about the purchase, saying that it provided "a new dimension to our corporate strategy of offering ... complete head-to-toe dressing with trusted brand names." In a separate agreement with Polo Ralph Lauren, Jones became the direct supplier the Lauren and Ralph lines in Europe, Israel and the Middle East.

As the company celebrated its 30th anniversary, designer Rena Rowan retired from active service, and Jones celebrated record revenues of $4.14 billion. According to Kimmel, in a February 2001 press release, Jones Apparel's core competencies in apparel, footwear, accessories and costume jewelry provided "the foundation to build complete lifestyle brands serving a wide berth of consumers in a wide range of income levels and shopping destination preferences."

Principal Subsidiaries

Camisas de Juarez, S.A. de C.V.; Jones Holding Company; Jones Investment Co., Inc.; Melru Corporation; Sun Apparel Inc.; Nine West Group, Inc.; Victoria & Co.

Principal Competitors

Bernard Chaus Inc.; Ellen Tracy, Inc.; St. Johns Knits International Inc.; Liz Claiborne, Inc.

Further Reading

Armstrong, Michael W., "Jones Apparel Seeks $58 million from IPO," *Philadelphia Business Journal,* April 22, 1991, p. 5.
Berry, Kate, "Jones Apparel's Sidney Kimmel," *Investor's Business Daily,* September 3, 1996, p. A1.
Breskin, Ira, "Jones Apparel Still Expanding But Retains That Classic Look," *Investor's Business Daily,* February 14, 1997, p. B14.
Card, Wesley R., "Jones Apparel Group, Inc. Reports Record Sales and Earnings for 1992," *PR Newswire,* February 10, 1993.
Davis, Jessica, "At Textile, Students Learn Computerized Design," *Philadelphia Business Journal,* September 24, 1993, p. 1.
——, "Jones Apparel After Acquisition," *Philadelphia Business Journal,* May 3, 1993, p. 6.
Furman, Phyllis, "Jones, Like Liz, Outfitted to Grow," *Crain's New York Business,* March 16, 1992, p. 35.
Longley, Alice Beebe, *Company Analysis: Jones Apparel,* New York: Donaldson, Lufkin & Jenrette, May 11, 1994.
Jones, John A., "Jones Apparel Group Fits Casual, Designer-Label Trends," *Investor's Business Daily,* March 27, 1996, p. B12.
Moukheiber, Zina, "Close Call," *Forbes,* December 21, 1992, p. 194.
Much, Marilyn, "At Jones Apparel, Material Gains Are By Design," *Investor's Business Daily,* September 11, 1992, p. 3.
Newman, Jill, "Victoria's Secret: What's in Store for Victoria & Co. Under the Umbrella of Jones Apparel Group?," *Women's Wear Daily,* August 2000, p. 8.
Pachuta, Michael J., "Jones Apparel Gets a New Look with Acquisition of Nine West," *Investor's Business Daily,* July 1, 1999, p. A19.
Peterson, Melody, "The Markets: As Jones Apparel and Nine West Plan Nuptials, Some Investors Already Want an Annulment," *New York Times,* March 12, 1999, p. C6.

—Dave Mote
—update: Carrie Rothburd

Lafuma S.A.

B.P. 60
26140 Anneyron
France
Telephone: (+33) 4 75 31 31 31
Fax: (+33) 4 75 31 57 26
Web site: http://www.lafuma.fr

Public Company
Incorporated: 1930
Employees: 1,232
Sales: EUR 132.3 million ($113.7 million) (2000)
Stock Exchanges: Euronext Paris
Ticker Symbol: LAF
NAIC: 339920 Sporting and Athletic Goods
    Manufacturing

Lafuma S.A. is one of the world's top ten manufacturers of outdoor-oriented clothing, shoes, and accessories, including backpacks, sleeping bags, tents and other camping paraphernalia, and equipment for rock climbers, mountain climbers, and the like. Headed by Philippe Joffard, grandson of one of the company's founders, Lafuma has built a strong portfolio of brands, led by flagship retail consumer-oriented brand Lafuma. In 1999, the company reorganized its brand operations around three core areas: Mass Market, featuring the Lafuma brand; Technical, including Millet, Rivory, and One Sport; and Hunting/Fishing, featuring the boots and clothing of Le Chameau and La Dunoise. Well known in its European home market—the company is the leading producer of backpacks and camping equipment in Europe and in France, number two leading manufacturer of hiking and mountain climbing clothing, and the second largest manufacturer of specialized boots—Lafuma is looking to expand into the United States, where the company's competition includes such industry heavyweights as Timberland and Columbia. Lafuma also has targeted Japan and other Asian markets for its turn of the century growth. Since the late 1990s the company has made strong progress toward the internationalization of its revenues. In 2000, foreign sales represented nearly half of the company's total sales of more than EUR 132 million. Lafuma also has branched out into retail, opening its first store in Hong Kong and three more stores in France.

Backpack Innovators in the 1930s

The Lafuma brothers, Victor, Alfred, and Gabriel, started up a business manufacturing canvas bags in 1930 in Anneyron, in the Drôme region of France. Among the Lafuma brothers' products were backpacks, and it was this category that was to provide the company with its initial success. In 1936, Lafuma created the first backpack with a metal frame. The invention of this product coincided with a new social innovation—the French government had enacted legislation providing for paid holidays. Camping quickly became a favorite holiday among French families. Lafuma's backpacks also were quickly adopted by the French military, and the French military services remained one of Lafuma's principal clients into the 1950s.

After the military ended its orders for backpacks, Lafuma was forced to look elsewhere to boost its sales. The company expanded beyond its backpacks to manufacture tents, camping beds, and other camping equipment, remaining a principal supplier of these products to its French market. The booming French economy, the implantation of the automobile, and the appearance of an entirely new leisure activity in postwar France provided Lafuma with new generations of camping and hiking enthusiasts in the 1950s and 1960s.

The Lafuma brothers had either died or retired by the beginning of the 1970s, leaving their company's direction to others, although Lafuma was still wholly owned by their three families. Despite branching out into other products, Lafuma's core product remained its backpack, which itself remained more or less unchanged from its original design. Yet the company's competitors had been steadily developing the market for backpacks, introducing new designs, technologies, and materials. The lack of new innovation in the small, family-owned company's backpack design nearly led to Lafuma's disappearance. By the early 1980s, the company's backpacks had been outclassed by its competitors and the company was on the verge of bankruptcy.

Yet Lafuma was rescued from oblivion in 1984, when Philippe Joffard, grandson of founding brother Gabriel

A GROWTH STRATEGY: Based on the probability of a favourable market and a group comprising one of the most attractive brands and product offering in Europe, our development plan gives priority to 2 areas: 1. An organisation in 3 sectors representing a complete, complementary and synergetic offer. 2. Organic growth by increasing the product offering and international operations.

Lafuma—and holder of one-third of the company's shares—agreed to take over the direction of the company. Joffard, who had been working for a noted management consultant firm in Paris and was then just 29 years old, began his new career by filing for bankruptcy.

Joffard's plan for rescuing the company included cutting out 84 of the company's 450 employees, which earned the company a week-long strike, during which Lafuma's workers occupied its headquarters. The two sides ended up agreeing on an innovative compromise, when workers agreed to accept a 35-hour work week averaged across an entire year and thus adaptable to peak production periods.

With this human relations problem settled, Joffard turned to transforming the company itself. Through the mid-1980s, Joffard recreated Lafuma's in-house culture, adding a new design department as well as marketing and especially market research personnel to spark a new era of innovation. The company adopted new and lighter-weight materials to a modernized range of backpack designs, taking into account changes in the marketplace. Lafuma also sought to develop new product categories, striking gold with its development of a new breed of school bag for France's student population, introduced in 1985. Adding padded straps and using lightweight materials and youth-oriented designs, as well as technical innovations such as reflective strips, the company's satchel-like designs quickly captured a leading share of that growing market. By the 1990s, buying a new school bag had become an essential part of the country's yearly back-to-school ritual, and Lafuma's ten percent market share gave it sales of some 250,000 bags per year in France alone.

Lafuma again extended its product range in 1986, when it brought its technical expertise to bear on related markets, creating a line of sleeping bags and tents. To support this new operation, the company opened a new subsidiary, Context, in Tunisia, marking the first time Lafuma had moved beyond France for its production.

Joffard also recognized that, to build the company into an international competitor, Lafuma needed to expand its operations. Rather than taking the family-owned company public, Joffard rallied most of the family of shareholders and convinced them to open up its capital to outsiders for the first time. This took place in 1987 when the company sold shares to Axa and Siparex.

Building the Outdoor Market in the 1990s

Lafuma was beginning to benefit from a growing new trend in the late 1980s that was to result in the creation of an entirely new retail category in the 1990s. The so-called Outdoor market developed around the rising numbers of hiking, rock climbing, mountaineering, and other outdoor enthusiasts. With more and more people taking to the hills in their leisure time, demand for Lafuma's backpacks, which were steadily regaining their reputation for innovation and quality, was once again taking off. The company extended its backpack and outdoor products operations with the acquisition of rival Pamir, in 1987. This was to be the first of a number of highly targeted acquisitions made by the company in the 1990s.

The majority of Lafuma's sales continued to come from France, while it steadily gained a leading share of the European market as well. In 1988, the company made the first steps to broaden its global reach, opening a commercial subsidiary in the United States. The following year, the company opened a sales office in Hong Kong as well. By 1990, Lafuma had topped FFr 200 million in annual sales. In that year, the company opened its capital again; by the time of its public offering in 1997, the Lafuma family reduced shareholding position to slightly less than 50 percent.

In 1992, Lafuma made a new acquisition, taking it into an entirely new category. In that year, the company added Mac, a specialist in technical clothing for the "adventure sports" market. This move gave Lafuma an important entry into the lofty realms of the mountain climbing circuit, which in turn was to improve the company's image among consumers as a maker of "serious" outdoor gear. At the same time, Lafuma boosted its manufacturing capacity with a new subsidiary in Hungary. This subsidiary opened a production facility for the company's high-end backpack and Gore-Tex clothing designs. Lafuma had been among the first to adapt the Gore-Tex material to its clothing products.

When the company discovered that consumers also were convinced that Lafuma manufactured its own line of sportswear—which until the early 1990s, it did not—the company decided to launch itself into this category as well. The Lafuma brand outdoor clothing line was introduced in 1993.

As the Lafuma brand name came to be more and more closely associated with outdoor activities, the company formed a joint venture company, Lafprom, charged with developing licensed products using the Lafuma brand. In this way, Lafuma was able to associate its name with a wider variety of related products, without having to invest its own capital in product development and manufacturing.

An Outdoor Leader for the 21st Century

In just a decade, Joffard had succeeded in transforming the company from a failing family-owned company into a fast-growing global contender for a leadership spot in the booming global Outdoor market. The company's product development had become one of its strongest arms, receiving up to three percent of revenues to add to and constantly redevelop and redesign its product range, enabling the company to take the forefront of technical developments in its industry. By 1994, Lafuma sought to boost its expansion further by seeking a listing on the Paris stock exchange.

Yet the company placed the listing on hold to digest two important new acquisitions made in 1995. The first of these was the purchase of Millet, in February 1995 (the company was to buy out the Millet license holder in Hong Kong in 2000, giving it full control of its new subsidiary). Millet, a manufacturer of high-end backpacks, helped expand Lafuma's range and provide a key element in the company's new multibrand strategy for the second half of the 1990s. Three months later, in May 1995, the company announced its acquisition of bootmaker Le Chameau, giving the company a new brand and two new product categories: boots for the outdoor enthusiasts, such as the hunting and fishing markets, and boots for professional use. These two acquisitions helped boost the company's annual sales to nearly FFr 460 million for 1995–96, representing a jump of some 30 percent in one year. More significant, Lafuma's profits also were growing, with profits of FFr 14.3 million representing a gain of nearly 57 percent over the previous year.

Lafuma succeeded in merging the Millet and Le Chameau acquisitions by 1997, enabling it to make its public offering at last, listing on the Paris Bourse's secondary market in May of that year. The company's insistence on a public listing was based on its increasing interest in expanding its international activity. As Joffard told *La Tribune:* "A quoted company definitely has a more serious image in the American and Asian markets." The company turned once again to the acquisition trail, now buying up Rivory & Joanny, a specialist in rope manufacture for climbing apparatus. Despite the fact that this acquisition made Lafuma the market leader of the category, the company sold off its newest acquisition after little more than a year as it redeveloped its growth strategy on finished products.

That strategy, now firmly focused on developing Lafuma as a multibranded Outdoor products company, brought a new acquisition and line of products into Lafuma's expanding portfolio. In 1998, the company made new acquisitions, including Charles Dubourg and its hunting clothing line, the La Dunoise brand of hunting and fishing clothing and accessories, and One Sport, a manufacturer of boots and shoes and other products for rock and cliff climbing.

In 1999, Lafuma restructured its operation around three primary divisions while rebranding its product range to its major brands. The first, and largest, revenue generator was its Mass Market division, represented by its Lafuma brand. The second division was its Technical division, led by the Millet brand name and including its One Sport range. The third division was its Hunting/Fishing division, which was regrouped under the Le Chameau brand name.

By the end of 1999, Lafuma was boosting its new brand strategy with the addition of a new line of Lafuma shoes. The company also opened its first retail store in Hong Kong. The success of that opening led the company to open three new Lafuma stores in France, with plans to expand the retail chain worldwide. The company's international growth became its primary focus at the turn of the century, as Lafuma, which by then ranked among the world's top seven Outdoor specialists, sought to deepen its penetration in the U.S. and Asian markets. The acquisition of Millet Asia in 2000, which completed the company's control of that brand name (which had long been a top seller to the Japanese market), gave it a still stronger springboard from which to build its brand name in that and other Asian countries. Philippe Joffard, who himself had developed a passion for mountaineering after taking over the company's direction, expected to lead Lafuma to new heights in the 21st century.

Principal Subsidiaries

Context (Tunisia); Lafuma Hungary; Lafuma Hong Kong; LWA (Belgium); Lafuma America; Lafuma GmbH (Germany); Lafuma BV (Netherlands); Lafuma UK; LAFPROM (49%); PAMIR; Millet One Sport; Rivory & Joanny; Cousin Rivory SNC; Le Chameau; Caoutchoutiere des Zenatas (Morocco).

Principal Competitors

Aigle SA; Berghaus; Columbia Sportswear Company; Decathlon SA; Helly-Hansen; K2; North Face; Lost Arrow; Orvis Company; Patagonia Inc.; Peak Performance; Pentland Group Ltd.; REI; Schieffel; Timberland; VF Corporation.

Further Reading

Berger, P.L., "Lafuma se positionne dans les sept premiers mondiaux de l'outdoor," *Classe Export,* November 1999.

Ghiulamila, Juliette, "Parcours Philippe Joffard," *L'Usine Nouvelle,* April 28, 1994.

Guy, Marie-Stéphane, "Le groupe Lafuma parie sur ses trois marques," *La Tribune,* November 29, 2000.

Guy, Marie-Stéphane, "Lafuma rachete Millet Asie," *La Tribune,* April 12, 2000.

Saget, Estelle, "Philippe Joffard relance Lafuma en Bourse," *L'Expansion,* February 20, 1997, p. 13.

Tournier, Pascale, "Lafuma premier de cordée," *Capital,* October 1998, p. 16.

—M.L. Cohen

Lechters

Lechters, Inc.

1 Cape May Street
Harrison, New Jersey 07029
U.S.A.
Telephone: (973) 481-1100
Fax: (973) 849-6197
Web site: http://www.lechtersonline.com

Public Company
Incorporated: 1975
Employees: 6,100
Sales: $420 million (2000)
Stock Exchanges: NASDAQ
Ticker Symbol: LECH
NAIC: 442299 All Other Home Furnishing Stores

Lechters, Inc. is the leading specialty retailer of housewares in the United States. The company operates more than 500 stores, which sell a wide variety of kitchenware and other practical devices. More than 400 of its stores are known as Lechters; others are called Lechters Kitchen Place, and the company runs off-price stores under the names Famous Brands Outlet/Lechters Houseware Outlet and Cost Less Home Store. In addition, the company planned to introduce the name Think-Kitchen for several stores and its web site beginning in 2001. Lechters started as a store designed for shopping malls and expanded dramatically throughout the 1980s. As overall mall business slowed, however, Lechters began to seek other places for its stores, opening outlets in cities and in outdoor strip shopping centers.

Failure, Then Success, as a Mall Chain in the 1970s

Lechters was founded in 1975 by Albert Lechter. The company ran housewares departments in leased space in two Valley Fair discount stores in New Jersey. The discount stores were owned by Donald Jonas, who had run a variety of retail outlets since entering the field in 1947 at age 18.

In 1977, Jonas and Lechter decided to team up to open their own separate housewares store. Because many conventional department stores had shrunk or eliminated their housewares departments, the two businessmen felt that there was a gap in the market that they could fill with their store. In addition, they wanted to offer their goods in malls. Although these locations generally concentrated on clothing, shoes, and jewelry stores, Lechter and Jonas felt that their merchandise would also find a market there.

The two opened their prototype store in a mall in Rockaway, New Jersey. This store proved a complete failure. Not yet fully versed in the nature of their business, Lechter and Jonas had rented a large space, 6,500 square feet, in a far corner of the mall where there was very little foot traffic. In addition, relying on Jonas's experience in the clothing business, they had stocked their store with seasonal goods, such as picnic baskets in warm weather and holiday-themed kitchenware. When customers failed to buy the products at the appropriate time, they had to be marked down severely in order to be sold at all.

After two years, Lechter and Jonas had realized that they needed to adjust their formula. In 1979, Jonas bought out the bulk of Lechter's holdings in the company, and the two tried again. The second Lechters prototype was smaller than the first, with just 4,500 square feet. The company stocked this store with 4,000 different timeless, basic housewares, which never needed to be discounted.

By specializing in housewares, Lechters filled the gap between department stores, which offered a small selection of higher-priced items, and discount and variety stores, which considered housewares just one small part of a much larger variety of offerings. In addition, the company was moving into an area that had no dominant national retailer in place. Although housewares on the whole were not high-priced items, Lechters found that it could make money on a steady turnover of small, less expensive goods. The company instituted an everyday low-price policy, which matched the offerings of the discount stores and did not rely on special sales or promotions to bring customers into the stores.

Growth in the 1980s

By the end of the year, the new Lechters store had become profitable, and Jonas moved to expand his concept to other malls. The company grew rapidly in the early 1980s, in an effort to

> **Company Perspectives:**
>
> *We provide useful, reliable and fun products and ideas that will make your experience in the kitchen and while dining more enjoyable and hassle free. The "experience" encompasses: shopping for the kitchen, mealtime planning, food preparation, cooking, serving, dining, clean-up and storage.*

preempt any competitors who might decide to join Lechters in the niche it had created. By the end of 1980, Lechters had opened 30 stores in malls. By 1984, the company was expanding at a rate of 40 percent per year. In 1985, 83 Lechters stores had been opened. By the mid-1980s, Lechters' management was confident that they had a hot retail concept on their hands, and the company moved aggressively to capitalize on its success.

In 1986, Lechters raised $11 million in a private placement of stock, and the company used these funds to fuel even more rapid expansion. In the next three years, the company's number of stores more than doubled, to reach 297. In 1988, sales reached $120.7 million, and, in the following year, they grew to $150 million. The company's growing revenues and earnings were driven by the ever larger number of Lechters outlets taking their place in malls around the country.

In 1989, Lechters moved out of malls into the cutthroat retail environment of Manhattan for the first time. The company made this move with trepidation. "We weren't sure how people in Manhattan felt about Rubbermaid and cake plates," a Lechters' vice-president later told *HFD,* a trade journal. The high density of customers, the relatively high income of the population, and the lack of any real competition, however, made Lechters executives feel that the risk was worth it. The company shortly discovered that its experiment had been a success, as Lechters' Manhattan store began to turn in revenues twice as high as those of stores in suburban malls.

To fund further expansion, Jonas sold 35 percent of Lechters to the public in 1989. This offering of stock raised $53 million. Of this sum, $31 million was used to buy out previous investors and insiders, and the rest was dedicated to funding Lechter's growth. To direct this expansion, Lechters recruited seven senior executives from top retailers around the country in the late 1980s.

These managers were brought in to help Lechters move to the next stage of its development. The company had successfully invented and refined its concept, and it had rapidly expanded its format to a large number of locations. By the end of the 1980s, however, it was necessary for Lechters to invest in systems and controls to enhance the profitability of its existing operations.

Evolving Retail Concepts in the Early 1990s

By January 1990, these operations comprised 280 separate Lechters stores. The company's sales had grown at a compound rate of 43 percent over the last five years. In that time, Lechters had come to dominate its housewares category, retailing gadgets, gifts, and frames, as well as basic cookware. Despite this

success, one worrisome note was the company's reliance on new store openings for growth. Sales increases at individual stores had been minimal, rising just $20 per square foot over a two-year period.

In addition, the company experienced some difficulty with its Kitchen Place outlets. Along with its trademark stores, Lechters had moved into the burgeoning discount mall category, opening 13 Kitchen Place units. These stores were bigger than the typical Lechters and sold similar products at slightly lower prices. In its initial guise, this concept did not contribute strongly to Lechters' earnings, so the company revamped the idea to see if it would fly in strip malls. The new Kitchen Place store was envisioned as a more aggressively promoted, high-tech outlet, with lower prices and a higher profile. The company tested out this idea in a Price Club Plaza in North Haven, Connecticut.

In an effort to improve operations at its flagship chain, Lechters turned its attention to the consistency of its merchandise and to its distribution system. The company began testing new computers for sales and inventory control and also began to diagram more precisely where items should be displayed in each store. Without such planning, displays in Lechters' small stores sometimes became haphazard and disorganized. In addition, the company moved to pare down its offerings in some categories, after discovering that it had twice as many versions of some items as it needed. With these steps, the company hoped to position itself as a slightly more upscale retailer, with an average purchase slightly higher than its standard $6.

As part of this program, Lechters aggressively expanded its presence in Manhattan. In May 1990, the company opened a New York outlet, its 319th overall, and then in June a fourth Manhattan store was brought on line. By the end of the year, Lechters had a total of 364 units open. In an effort to reduce costs, the company also had started to import its products directly from overseas manufacturers. Lechters' sales for 1990 totaled $187.6 million.

As mall traffic began to slow, Lechters looked to a variety of store formats for further growth in 1991. The company had expanded its initial concept to include the Kitchen Place strip mall store, of which it planned to roll out 20 to 25 in the course of the year. In addition, Lechters resurrected a discount mall store called Famous Brands Housewares Outlets and introduced a mall "superstore," which was much larger than a regular Lechters. The Kitchen Place stores and the Famous Brands Outlets were to feature the same merchandise and price levels in different settings. Famous Brands merchandise also would be supplemented by excess inventory from manufacturers like Rubbermaid and Ekco.

Lechters' superstores had 50 percent more space than the regular stores. In their initial tests, in A&S Plaza in New Jersey and Newport Center in Jersey City, the Lechters superstores reported sales that grew by 50 percent when their size was expanded. New products offered in the bigger spaces included a wide variety of home decorations, such as ceramics, lamps, dried flowers, and brass and pewter objects.

In July 1991, Lechters rolled out a new prototype for its traditional stores, which featured more subtle shelving, wider aisles, and a bigger open space at the front of the store. In this way, the company hoped to relieve the crowding present in many of its smaller locations. In a test on Staten Island, these changes increased sales volume by 40 percent.

In addition to these changes, Lechters also planned to expand its urban operations by opening three more Manhattan stores and a first location in downtown Chicago. At the major intersection of 57th Street and Broadway in Manhattan, Lechters opened a two-level, 8,000-foot superstore. Called the ''Lechters Home Store,'' this outlet featured an expanded selection of merchandise. Despite Lechters' moves into the city and into strip malls, more than 80 percent of the company's revenues still derived from stores in malls by the end of 1992.

In January 1993, Lechters' sales reached the $234 million mark and earnings were at $13 million. This growth came despite a generally slowed economy. Rather than depress Lechters' earnings, the downturn appeared to have enhanced them, as people began to eschew expensive restaurant outings to eat more at home, which prompted them to buy more housewares.

Although Lechters' sales figures showed strong growth, trouble loomed on the horizon, as traffic in malls continued its steady drop. To counteract the effect this decline would have on its business, Lechter located just 20 of the 65 stores it opened in 1993 in malls. Despite this measure, the company reported falling profits in the first quarter of 1993, even though sales had risen. This trend continued throughout the year, and the company ended 1993 with sales up $44 million to $350 million and profits down $4.3 million, to $11.1 million. This drop was attributed to weakness in the company's product selection and low levels of customer recognition. Without noticing it, Lechters had failed to establish any clear identity for the company in the public's mind.

To redress these problems, Lechters revamped its product presentation and increased the amount of information presented to customers, so that the store would become easier and more efficient to use. As part of this program, Lechters implemented a computerized ticket-scanning system at all of its cash registers. Lechters also opened its first distribution center in 1993, to serve its 100 west coast stores. Located in Las Vegas, this facility included 155,000 square feet of storage space. By the end of the year, the company's number of stores had reached 567, and Lechters executives estimated that there was room for at least 500 more stores in the years to come. Dominating a market niche that it had pioneered, Lechters looked forward to expanding its operations throughout the late 1990s.

Revamping in the Late 1990s and Beyond

Instead, the retailer was forced to pull back. Lechters' earnings slid, declining quarter after quarter, and the company was forced to come up with a strategy to turn itself around. Employee turnover was extremely high, and something was clearly amiss with the housewares chain. In 1994, Lechters brought in Dutch-born Steen Kanter as vice-chairman and chief executive. Kanter had been behind the success of the Swedish furniture and housewares chain Ikea, and he was thought to have the kind of merchandising savvy that could pull Lechters back from the brink. Kanter began to reorganize the Lechters stores, primarily by focusing them on kitchen items and removing housewares such as picture frames and storage units that belonged in other rooms of the house. Kanter cut the number of skus (shelf-keeping units) each store carried from about 18,000 to only 4,200. Some categories had been cluttered because there were too many choices. For example, before Kanter's reorganization, Lechters carried 15 kinds of colander. This number was soon reduced to seven. Customer surveys and focus groups showed that the store layout was confusing. So the company redesigned its stores. Another part of Kanter's strategy was to expand Lechters' private label business and offer a more complete cookware line. Plans for new store openings were put on hold.

The company hoped to see results of its reorganization by early 1996. Instead, Lechters continued to flounder. Sales at both its full-price Lechters store division and at its off-price division decreased. The company went back on some of its earlier decisions, faced with continuing poor results. In focusing more exclusively on cookware and kitchen items, the chain had lost some of its higher-margin items. Picture frames and storage units had been banned, but were brought back, and placed in the front of the store. Meanwhile, the company's competitors chipped away at Lechters' leading position. When the chain began, it was the first of its kind, but by 1997 it had major competitors in Bed Bath & Beyond, Linens 'n Things, and HomePlace. Department stores and discount stores also carried many of the same housewares as Lechters. An article in *Discount Store News* from April 1, 1997 quoted several analysts who were still disappointed with the ''new'' Lechters. Although the housewares market as a whole was doing well, Lechters' ''stores are not differentiated enough,'' complained one Wall Street analyst. Another analyst quoted in the same article also declared that Lechters did not seem unique. Despite the changes of the mid-1990s, the chain still lacked a clear identity.

By mid-1997, the chain had 648 stores total. Of these, 484 were the full-price Lechters Housewares, and 164 were its Famous Brands Housewares Outlets. A year later, the company announced that it would close as many as 70 underperforming stores. Most of these were mall stores. Its urban sites and strip mall stores did better on the whole than its mall locations, and Lechters did plan to open more of these. However, overall, the chain was shrinking, not growing. At the start of fiscal 1998, the company announced again that it had a new focus, and again, this was the kitchen. Lechters resolved to bring in ''trend right'' products, meaning new, fresh items that hit current fads. The company resolved to push national brands, while continuing to promote its three private labels. Lechters had three private lines, one for its cookware, one for frames, and one for storage products, and it hoped to derive 40 percent of its sales from these. The chain continued to close stores in the late 1990s, so that by 2000 it had barely more than 500 stores total. Sales continued flat, despite management's continued exertions to bring the company back to its former profitability. In late 2000, the company announced that its cofounder, David Jonas, would be succeeded as CEO by David Cully, a former Barnes and Noble executive. In December 2000, Cully remarked to *HFN*, an industry journal, that "If we don't change both boldly and quickly, there will be no more Lechters." This was the most dire pronouncement yet. Cully's plan relied on Internet technology to bring customers into the store. The company planned to open an e-commerce site called ThinkKitchen, followed by prototype ThinkKitchen stores featuring computer terminals to link to the web offerings.

Principal Subsidiaries

Lechters New York, Inc.; Lechters N.Y.C., Inc.; Lechters New Jersey, Inc.; Lechters California, Inc.; Lechters Texas, Inc.; Cooks Club, Inc.; Regent Gallery, Inc.; Lechter Investment Corporation.

Principal Divisions

Lechters Housewares; Famous Brands Housewares Outlet.

Principal Competitors

Bed Bath & Beyond Inc.; Linens 'n Things, Inc.; HomePlace of America, Inc.

Further Reading

"An Open and Shut Case: Lechters Closing Some Units," *HFN,* March 9, 1998, p. 4.

Croghan, Lore, "Lechters: Just Like Ikea?," *Financial World,* June 6, 1995, p. 24.

Duff, Mike, "Vendors and Competitors Keep Eye on Lechters as New Formats Develop," *Discount Store News*, November 22, 1999, p. 4.

Erlick, June Carolyn, "Lechters Takes Manhattan," *HFD—The Weekly Home Furnishings Newspaper,* March 14, 1994.

Garbato, Debby, "Lechters New Manhattan Store Bows," *HFD—The Weekly Home Furnishings Newspaper,* June 29, 1992.

Gilbert, Les, "Lechters Fills Vacuum," *HFD—The Weekly Home Furnishings Newspaper,* January 22, 1990.

——, "Lechters Speeds Up Expansion," *HFD—The Weekly Home Furnishings Newspaper,* November 11, 1991.

——, "Lechters to Expand with Superstores Concept," *HFD—The Weekly Home Furnishings Newspaper,* May 4, 1992.

Guttner, Toddi, "You Can't Say No to Opportunity," *Forbes,* November 23, 1992.

Kehoe, Ann-Margaret, "Lechters' Game Plan: Heat Up the Kitchen," *HFN,* March 23, 1998, p. 32.

Nicksin, Carole, "Lechters Thinks Up a Turnaround Strategy," *HFN,* December 4, 2000, p. 1.

Thau, Barbara, "Lechters' Reincarnation," *HFN,* September 13, 1999, p. 1.

Wilensky, Dawn, "Wares and Woes Under One Roof," *Discount Store News,* April 1, 1997, p. 19.

—Elizabeth Rourke
—update: by A. Woodward

The Leslie Fay Company, Inc.

1412 Broadway
New York, New York 10018
U.S.A.
Telephone: (212) 221-4000
Fax: (212) 221-4245

Public Company
Incorporated: 1984
Employees: 444
Sales: $197.4 million (2000)
Stock Exchanges: NASDAQ
Ticker Symbol: LFAY
NAIC: 31523 Women's and Girls' Cut and Sew Apparel Manufacturing

The Leslie Fay Company, Inc. sells its career, evening, and social occasion dresses and its sportswear through leading department and specialty stores nationwide. The company's moderate-priced brands include Leslie Fay, Leslie Fay Haberdashery, Joan Leslie, and Reggio, while its better-priced brands include David Warren, Rimini by Shaw, Outlander Sportswear, and Hue. Leslie Fay is a licensee for Liz Claiborne and Elisabeth dress labels and Cynthia Steffe label. The company has operated continuously since 1947 despite entering bankruptcy protection from 1993 to 1995.

1947–82: A Family-Run Business With a Distinctive Style

Leslie Fay was founded in 1947 by Fred Pomerantz, who had produced dresses for the Women's Army Corps during World War II. The company was named for his daughter and offered department stores substantial profit margins for carrying the company's line of stylishly conservative women's wear. Pomerantz was a colorful figure in the New York garment district; he reportedly had a liking for gambling, and people on the street knew when he was at work because his distinctive Rolls-Royce was parked outside the company's Broadway offices.

Leslie Fay went public in 1952. From 1959 until April 1982, the business was called Leslie Fay Inc. Pomerantz's son John became president of the company in 1972. He had joined the company in 1960, right after he graduated from the Wharton School with a business degree. John continued to run the company much as his father had run it. When other companies were turning to computers in the early 1980s to help keep track of daily sales at stores around the nation and were using market testing to determine whether its styles would sell, Leslie Fay continued to make deals with a handshake and telephone stores weekly for sales figures, unlikely business practices for a public company of its size. Practices such as these may have worked for a smaller company, and it may have worked before the 1980s, a decade of takeovers and business opportunism.

Major changes in the 1980s

In 1982, Leslie Fay was taken over through a leveraged buyout for $58 million and became a private company operating under the name The Leslie Fay Company. In 1984, in another leveraged buyout, the company became known as The Leslie Fay Companies, Inc. This time, management and outside investors paid $158 million to buy out the investors from the 1982 takeover. The leveraged buyout by managers and investors brought John Pomerantz and his wife, Laura (also a company official), 1.7 million shares of stock, or a 8.7 percent share, for which they paid $162,000—a bargain at only nine cents a share. In 1986, the company went public again, however, with management and institutional investors still controlling 55 percent of the outstanding shares.

The fashion industry in general was enjoying a period of prosperity in the mid-1980s, and Leslie Fay was growing fast. Leslie Fay and other garment industry companies, though, were subject to the ups and downs of fashion, and Leslie Fay watched its stocks rise and dip, from $18 per share in 1986, down to $9 in 1989, and then up to the upper teens again by the early 1990s.

Leslie Fay acquired several companies during the end of the 1980s, buying the assets and trademarks of Albert Nipon, Inc., for $8.3 million and Mary Ann Restivo, Inc., for $5.3 million in 1988. It also assumed Mary Ann Restivo's $3.9 million in liabilities. In 1989, Leslie Fay acquired Non-Stop Fashions, Inc., and NS Petites Inc.

All of these changes signaled a new era for Leslie Fay, which had awakened to the need to transform its image. It had received feedback from upscale stores, which were long-time customers, that Leslie Fay apparel was too drab and matronly. Leslie Fay responded to the criticism by bringing in new designers. It also adopted a new marketing approach, following the lead of Calvin Klein and Liz Claiborne by opening boutiques within department stores. Pomerantz convinced 500 retailers to install the boutiques, even though there were doubts that Leslie Fay's $100 dresses could generate enough sales to justify the expense.

Leslie Fay also updated its marketing by talking directly to consumers through fashion shows and videotapes and by inviting consumers to talk directly to the company through a toll-free phone number. It also launched an $8.5 million ad campaign. The new approach paid off, and Leslie Fay left behind its production-oriented approach to become a sophisticated, consumer-driven dress manufacturer. In 1990, sales revenues were at the company's all-time peak of $859 million, triple what they had been only ten years earlier.

Because Leslie Fay had a strong brand name, it phased out some labels and replaced them with a Leslie Fay label. It also sought to broaden its base by licensing the use of its name for coats, shoes, lingerie, and children's clothing, so that the company would become known as a manufacturer of a broad assortment of moderately priced clothing.

Early 1990s: Lagging Sales Turn to Losses

In 1991, Leslie Fay sold its Head Sports Wear division to Odyssey International Group in order to focus on women's apparel. Leslie Fay received $47.5 million in cash and non-interest-bearing notes for the division that carried ski, tennis,

and golf apparel for men and women. Pomerantz used the proceeds from the sale to reduce the company's bank debts.

In June 1992, Leslie Fay announced it would acquire Hue International, a hosiery firm with 1991 sales of $35 million. Hue sold colorful legwear for women, including tights, socks, kneesocks, bodywear, and leggings. Leslie Fay anticipated that the purchase of this company would give it entry into a segment of the apparel market that it had not previously reached.

Despite positive changes through acquisition, Leslie Fay needed to stimulate lagging sales. The company had a reputation for creating pressure to meet profit goals, but 1992's profit goals were particularly ambitious because of an unhealthy economy and a 20-year decline in dress sales, a disquieting trend for Leslie Fay because they depended on dress sales for one-third of its total sales. The company also faced serious problems with retailers' and consumers' negative responses to its apparel lines. Specifically, Leslie Fay fashions were criticized by some as over-priced and old-fashioned. Department stores had been cutting back on orders, in part because they were having a hard time selling Leslie Fay fashions specifically, in part due to serious competition from discount and outlet stores. Leslie Fay's marketing strategy, however, still centered around department stores, some of which were filing for bankruptcy, including key Leslie Fay customer, Macy's.

Management announced a long-term marketing strategy that included reducing prices on its dresses by at least ten percent in the fall of 1992. Dresses and pantsuits, which had sold for $89 to $139 each, were lowered $10 to $20. Leslie Fay felt the price reduction would not hurt the company because it would sell more dresses before marking them down. It announced that it would reduce the number of styles it made and also planned to discontinue its Mary Restivo label. The Mary Restivo division had losses of $2.9 million on sales of $5.5 million.

In September 1992, when fall orders had not picked up, Pomerantz ordered price cuts across the board on all future orders. The company also began offering retailers rebates or markdown money of millions of dollars if they had to slash prices on Leslie Fay apparel to move their inventory—a common practice in the industry, though Leslie Fay's were uncommonly high rebates. Retailers and other businesses in the industry were surprised; the expected response to slow sales was to cut production. Instead, the company would have to sell more merchandise, albeit at more attractive prices, to make money.

The plan appeared to succeed at first. Despite the recession that had hit the national economy and the garment industry, 1992 appeared to be a favorable year for Leslie Fay with profits of $23.9 million. Pomerantz and others received substantial bonuses based on the company's reported $23.9 million profit. Pomerantz alone received $2.2 million. Leslie Fay announced plans to replace its Breckenridge, Joan Leslie Evening, and Outlander labels with one new label, Theo Miles. The Theo Miles brand was intended to compete in the $2 billion better-price market against the leader Liz Claiborne. Laura Pomerantz, who had been a senior vice-president, was named to a newly created post as executive vice-president over the company's better brands, including the new Theo Miles label. She already headed the Albert Nipon and Leslie Fay Evening lines.

Then, in late January 1993, Pomerantz learned that the company's books had been doctored to inflate pretax profits by $81 million from 1990 to 1992. According to reports, Pomerantz had not paid close attention to the financial operations of the company, which were not even housed in the New York headquarters, but were instead located in Wilkes-Barre, Pennsylvania. News of the discrepancies sent Leslie Fay stock plunging from 12 and three-eights in January to five and one-quarter per share by the beginning of March. Several stockholders initiated lawsuits against the company.

In fact, analysts had heard rumors of declining sales in July 1992. The company noted that orders for the fall season were down, but shortly thereafter the company forecast earnings for 1992 higher than those for 1991. Pomerantz had also offered to buy back up to a million shares of Leslie Fay stock, a move that showed his own optimism about the company and reassured Wall Street.

Pomerantz said he knew nothing about the overstated profits or doctored books, which in 1996 proved to be the work of the company's chief financial officer. Pomerantz and the other company officials returned their bonuses shortly after the 1992 losses were revealed. According to the *Wall Street Journal,* the misleading figures were chiefly an overstatement of the number of garments manufactured, coupled with an understatement of the manufacturing cost of each item. Leslie Fay's strategy of cutting prices instead of production could "inflate phantom profits."

The *Wall Street Journal* noted that such accounting practices were not uncommon among small, private companies in the industry. However, Leslie Fay had grown into a large public company, and for a business its size to play the small company game, the results were disastrous. According to ex-employees, in order to meet profit goals, invoices were backdated and recorded as revenue even though the money had not been received. The financial department might have survived this practice if the market had remained strong, but the recession hurt performance, as did poor response to the company's merchandise. It became impossible to cover a shortfall with revenue from the next quarter as sales dropped.

The Late 1990s: Bankruptcy and Turnaround

The company entered bankruptcy protection two months after the disclosure of accounting improprieties. In response to the news, some of traditional department stores cut their orders, but others remained loyal. In fact, the company did gain a client, when J.C. Penney began to sell Leslie Fay products beginning in 1994. In October, Leslie Fay axed its Theo Miles line, and Laura Pomerantz left the company. Before year's end, it shut four of its five U.S. plants, eliminating 1,050 jobs, but hired another 600 workers at its last remaining plant after a garment worker union strike. That plant closed the following July. Leslie Fay reported an operating loss of $27 million in 1994 and a net loss of $159 million.

Management announced plans in January 1995 to emerge from Chapter 11 by focusing on its core dress and sportswear businesses—Leslie Fay Dress, Leslie Fay Sportswear, Outlander, and Castleberry—and selling or spinning off its biggest money maker, Sassco Fashion, while disposing of its retail store division. Sassco had contributed about half the company's 1994 revenue of $535 million. Arthur Levine, who headed Sassco, and who had sold it to Leslie Fay 15 years earlier, stepped forward with an offer to buy the unit back, but was unable to come up with the necessary financing. Despite its internal difficulties, Leslie Fay dominated *Women's Wear Daily's* "Fairchild 100," with five of the industry's top 10 recognized brands. The company reported an operating profit of $1.2 million on net sales of $445 million in 1995.

In January 1996, another buyer for Sassco stepped forward, but Leslie Fay decided instead, in March 1996, to spin off the division and distribute 80 percent of 3.4 million new shares of Leslie Fay to its creditors. Creditors were to take 80 percent of Sassco's shares, while the division's management, including Arthur Levine, received 20 percent. The company finally emerged from bankruptcy in mid-1997 with the distribution of its equity into two newly formed entities: The Leslie Fay Company, Inc. and Sassco Fashions Ltd.

Despite falling to third position in the Fairchild 100 for 1997, Leslie Fay continued to generate profits for the next several years: a gross profit of $30 million on net sales of $132 million in 1997; a gross profit of $36 million on sales of $152 million in 1998; and a gross profit of $49 million on net sales $197.4 million in 1999. In 1997, the company relaunched its Haberdashery Sportswear label; it also reintroduced Leslie Fay Evenings and launched a moderate suit line in 1998. That year, Leslie Fay also acquired The Warren Apparel Group Ltd., a privately owned, New York City-based manufacturer and wholesaler of women's career, social, and evening dresses.

Perhaps more importantly, in 1999, the company obtained the license to the Liz Claiborne Dresses and Elisabeth Dresses labels, and sold the license for its Outlander Sportswear better knitwear label to Regent International. It also sold the license to its Leslie Fay trademark to Bruscan, Inc. for a line of women's shoes. In 2000, the company purchased the assets of Cynthia Steffe, Inc., a designer of sportswear for the young contemporary market.

The pared-down Leslie Fay had pulled off an impressive turnaround. Consumer demand for the Leslie Fay name remained strong, and the company had won back space on department store floors. Shares in the company began trading again in December 1998. In 2000, in a change of leadership, John Ward, who had been with the company since 1989, replaced John Pomerantz as chief executive of the company. Leslie Fay had not yet recaptured its former industry dominance, but the company had by now proved its staying power.

Principal Operating Units

Leslie Fay Dress, Leslie Fay Sportswear, Outlander.

Principal Competitors

Bernard Chaus, Inc.; Donna Karan Co.

Further Reading

Agins, Teri, "Leslie Fay Says Irregularities in Books Could Wipe Out '92 Profit; Stock Skids," *Wall Street Journal,* February 2, 1993, p. A4.

——, ''Loose Threads: Dressmaker Leslie Fay Is an Old-Style Firm That's in a Modern Fix,'' *Wall Street Journal,* February 23, 1993, p. A1.

Berton, Lee, and Teri Agins, ''Shareholders Sue Leslie Fay Following Disclosure of Accounting Investigation,'' *Wall Street Journal,* February 3, 1993, p. B2.

Curan, Catherine, ''Dressed Down: Leslie Fay Produces Fatter Returns After Paring Back to Get Fiscally Fit,'' *Crain's New York Business,* February 15, 1999, p.1.

Lesly, Elizabeth, ''Who Played Dress-Up with the Books?,'' *Business Week,* March 15, 1993, p. 34.

Turfa, Pamela, ''Clothing Maker The Leslie Fay Co. Enjoys Financial Rebound,'' *Times Leader,* May 7, 1998, p.

—Wendy J. Stein
—update: Carrie Rothburd

Madison Gas and Electric Company

133 South Blair Street
Madison, Wisconsin 53703
U.S.A.
Telephone: (608) 252-7000
Fax: (608) 252-4714
Web site: http://www.mge.com

Public Company
Incorporated: 1896
Employees: 700
Sales: $274.1 million (1999)
Stock Exchanges: NASDAQ
Ticker Symbol: MDSN
NAIC: 221122 Electric Power Distribution; 221112 Fossil
   Fuel Electric Power Generation; 221119 Other Electric
   Power Generation; 22121 Natural Gas Distribution

Madison Gas and Electric Company (MGE) is a relatively small power company that has remained independent and profitable in the face of rapid changes and consolidation in the energy industry. MGE provides electrical power to a base of about 250,000 customers in Madison, Wisconsin and surrounding areas and provides natural gas to approximately 340,000 customers in seven Wisconsin counties. MGE's home territory includes the University of Wisconsin, and MGE has long held that Madison's unique economy makes the company virtually "recession-proof." In the late 1990s, southeastern Wisconsin was one of the most vibrant regional economies in the nation, and MGE likewise did well. In 1995 Standard & Poor's ranked the company second in the United States for its competitive position, and MGE also had ranked second nationwide among electric utilities in 1993 for financial stability. The company generates power through fossil-fueled plants and also has developed a wind power program. MGE sold its 18 percent share in the Kewaunee, Wisconsin nuclear power plant in 1998.

19th-Century Beginnings

Madison Gas and Electric was formed out of two smaller companies in 1896. M.E. Fuller and Emerson McMillin were jointly the first presidents of the new utility, which merged Madison's existing electric company, Four Lakes Light and Power, with Madison City Gas Light and Coke Co. The new company was headquartered on Main Street and served a population of just 17,000 people. At the time of the company's founding, gas was used for Madison's streetlights, and to light some stores and homes. It was just beginning to be used as heating oil, replacing wood. The city had an electric trolley system, and some commercial and residential buildings also were lit by electricity. But electric lighting surpassed gas by the end of the century. In 1899, the new utility became a subsidiary of a larger firm, American Light and Traction Company. Three years later, MGE built the first gas engine electricity generating station in the country. This replaced an earlier plant, which used steam-driven dynamos. By 1915, the company returned to using steam, freeing up gas for use as fuel.

The city of Madison grew, and MGE with it. Madison was not only the state capital, but home to the state's public university, and so its population included a high proportion of government and education workers who had a fairly high standard of living. By 1920, Madison's population had reached 31,000, and MGE had to build more power generating capacity. It installed a 5000 kilowatt turbo-generator in 1923 and, in 1928, enlarged its electric plant again. The company also enlarged its gas works. By 1930, Madison had added another 25,000 people, and more and more customers were using appliances. When the company began, street lighting and the trolley system had been the major uses of gas and electricity. By 1930, residential customers enjoyed electric lighting, as well as electrically powered home appliances such as vacuum cleaners and washing machines. Most houses were equipped with a gas water heater and a gas range, and the use of gas for heating became more and more common throughout the 1930s. MGE encouraged the use of electric appliances. In the mid-1930s company operatives set out for rural areas around Madison to demonstrate different appliances, and the company itself sold appliances until the mid-1970s. MGE also put out a newsletter, *Today's Home,* that promoted such products as the gas refrigerator. In the late 1930s, despite the Depression, MGE spent almost $2 million on construction. By 1942, the company served 24,000 electric meters and 18,500 gas meters, and the city of Madison had grown to roughly 74,000 people.

Company Perspectives:

As a community-based energy company, MGE will: provide quality service at competitive rates; meet all of our customers' gas, electric and related energy needs; earn a reasonable return for investors; maintain the highest standards of corporate citizenship and fair treatment for all employees.

Postwar Development

Just before the close of World War II, in 1944, MGE broke away from its parent company, American Light and Traction. Madison voters rejected a plan for the city to take over the utility and, instead, the company was taken public. The demand for both gas and electricity increased rapidly over the next decade. Residential use of electricity came close to doubling, and use of gas doubled and then some. MGE had to plan ahead to meet the accelerating demand for its products. Starting in 1949, MGE began buying natural gas from a pipeline in Michigan. Natural gas was cleaner burning than manufactured gas, so this change was good for the environment. The company also had begun installing devices to collect airborne ash from its boilers at its electrical plants in the late 1940s. Despite continued updating of its equipment, MGE was able to keep prices low. In the mid-1950s, Madison was ranked as having one of the lowest electric rates in the United States. MGE had to limit the amount of natural gas heating it could provide, however, because it could not get all the gas it could sell. By 1960, the utility resolved this problem when the Michigan pipeline brought in additional sources for gas. MGE added gas service areas to the north and west of Madison around that time. The company also added on to its main electricity generating station, boosting its total capacity by about 25 percent. MGE's service territory totaled almost 200 square miles around this time, up from just 25 square miles, encompassing only downtown Madison, when the company started out. Throughout the 1960s, MGE added nearby communities to its service territory. Some of these small towns were hotly disputed between MGE and a rival power company, Wisconsin Power and Light, later in the company's history.

Rate Hikes and Stock Sales in the 1970s

MGE continued to add new customers throughout the 1970s. Its customer base grew at a little less than three percent a year, and sales and revenues for both the electric and gas divisions of the company increased annually. The company was part of a consortium of power companies that built a nuclear power plant in Kewaunee, Wisconsin beginning in 1967. That plant started operating in 1974 and provided about 26 percent of MGE's electric generating capacity by the end of the decade. In 1974 MGE began burning refuse-derived fuel at some of its Madison generating plants, in a recycling project it entered with the city. This unique program lasted until the early 1990s, when concerns about toxic emissions shut it down. The company bought almost half of its power from a coal-fired generating plant that it partly owned, Columbia Energy Center. Although MGE's sales and revenues increased steadily, the company paid heavily for construction during the decade. The firm borrowed money,

owing $16 million by 1975. More than half of its funds came from borrowed sources, putting the utility over the limit set by its state regulatory body, the Public Service Commission. The utility was closely regulated by this state agency, which had to be appealed to for rate hikes. In 1972 and then twice in 1975, MGE sold stock to raise cash to retire debt. The company also repeatedly asked the Public Service Commission to approve rate increases. MGE raised its electricity rates three times between 1974 and 1976, bringing them up by more than 50 percent in the process. The Public Service Commission had to balance the needs of MGE's customers for affordable power with the desire of its stockholders for enjoyable profit. The company wanted to be allowed a profit level of 15 percent, to keep MGE attractive to investors. The Public Service Commission, which also regulated other area utilities including Wisconsin Power and Light, often compromised with MGE, not granting all of its wishes. The commission also mandated other changes, such as making the utility switch to a so-called time-of-use rate, where customers were charged different rates according to time of day. This allowed customers a cheaper electricity rate for drying their clothes after midnight, for example, but MGE complained about the cost of installing new and more sophisticated meters.

Another financial factor affecting MGE in the 1970s was inflation. Because of the time-consuming process of appealing for rate hikes, it was often months or years before the company could raise the price of its services enough to keep up with inflation. MGE executives complained about the burden of regulation, feeling that in some situations the Public Service Commission's recommendations did not help either the company or the public. Yet MGE acknowledged that some regulation was desirable. Lack of regulation would be chaotic.

Takeover Battle in the 1980s

MGE continued to benefit from its relationship with Michigan Wisconsin Pipe Line (Mich-Wis), the pipeline company that supplied it with natural gas. The oil embargo in the 1970s had encouraged domestic oil exploration, and Mich-Wis was active in searching out natural gas in the continental United States. Through its parent company, it was a partner in the Alaskan pipeline, and it also obtained natural gas from offshore Louisiana, Texas, and other states. Mich-Wis promised MGE a plentiful supply of natural gas for the early 1980s, as more of its exploration paid off. In the mid-1980s, oil costs began to sink, and interest rates also went down, making for excellent cash flow and profits for the utility industry in general. But because the level of profit was regulated by government bodies, utility companies had to find something to do with excess cash, lest they be asked to lower rates to consumers. Bigger power companies began buying smaller ones. An article in the May 19, 1986 *Business Week* speculated that MGE might be an attractive takeover target by its larger neighbor, Wisconsin Power and Light. The magazine was correct, although the bid did not come in until three years later.

Wisconsin Power and Light (WPL) also was headquartered in Madison, and its service area in southern and central Wisconsin totally surrounded MGE's. While MGE supplied the lucrative, economically stable Madison metropolitan area, with its university, hospitals, state government, and industries, WPL furnished gas and electricity to 35 counties, covering more than 600 cities and villages. WPL had about three times as many electricity customers as MGE. It owned nine small generating plants and had part or whole interest in several large ones, including a share of more than 40 percent in the Kewaunee nuclear plant. WPL was nearly as old as MGE, founded in 1917, and altogether about three times as large as its rival. The two companies competed directly over some of the small towns on the outskirts of Madison where their territories overlapped. WPL had been interested in a merger with MGE for several years, but finally made an unsolicited offer in the spring of 1989. The deal was to be a stock swap, with no cash changing hands. The final bid was valued at around $268 million, with WPL offering 1.75 of its shares for each MGE share. Although questions remained over whether WPL could afford the premium it was offering to get the smaller company, and whether the excess cost eventually would be passed to the utility's customers, MGE's board and shareholders overwhelmingly rejected the offer. On May 31, MGE conveyed to WPL that its bid was too low for any further consideration, and no further talks on the merger went forward.

Battles for Deregulation in the 1990s

The soured takeover bid did nothing to help relations between MGE and its much larger rival. Both companies fought for the small communities that straddled both their territories, apparently letting workers go in 1990 to keep costs and, therefore, rates down. A bigger battle than that over towns like Black Earth was over deregulation of electrical utilities. WPL and other large power companies were in favor of looser regulations inside Wisconsin, allowing more direct competition between providers. MGE wanted a cautious approach to deregulation, fearing adverse effects to the state's economy. WPL and other firms hired lobbyists in the mid-1990s to push the state legislature and the Public Service Commission toward freeing up restraints on competition. MGE also hired a lobbyist to handle its side of the story and joined a consortium of other municipal utilities, electric co-ops, and labor and environmental groups to ask the PSC to go slow. But things became more fierce in 1996, when WPL announced that it would pursue an unusual three-way corporate merger. The new company, which became Interstate Energy, later renamed Alliant Energy Corp., put together WPL, IES Industries, and a third firm, Interstate Power Company. Soon after, Wisconsin Energy Corp., based in Milwaukee, merged with the Minneapolis-based Northern States Power Co. to form Primergy Corp. Primergy became the tenth largest

utility in the nation. In response to the mergers around it, MGE took out newspaper ads featuring "Big Boris," a pig who claimed to crave "Radical Electric Deregulation." Big Boris claimed that deregulation would let the "big guys" get all the electricity they wanted and the ad's readers, presumably residential customers or little guys, would get only the leftovers. WPL responded with ads portraying MGE as a dinosaur. Both firms became more embroiled in state politics, backing opposing candidates for the Madison area representative to congress. In 1996 the state Public Service Commission adopted a proposal to open up the utility industry to competition, but it ordered a 32-step plan that would be enacted over the next three to seven years. So although it seemed that things would change, it would not be as abrupt as MGE had perhaps feared.

MGE geared for change, but nevertheless it found itself in a strong position. In a 1996 presentation to stockholders, MGE Chairman David Mebane told his audience that the company had frozen or reduced rates since 1991, at the same time achieving historic financial highs. MGE was one of only four utilities in the country to receive the highest credit rating from the New York investment firm Bear Stearns, and the company's return to investors over the first half of the 1990s was more than twice the industry average. The company had acquired two small subsidiaries in the 1990s, Great Lakes Energy Corp., known as Glenco, and American Energy Management Inc., of Chicago. In 1997 MGE announced that these two subsidiaries would form a joint venture with National Gas and Electric, a Houston company, to investigate marketing natural gas and energy services in the Great Lakes region. Another change MGE made was to sell off its part ownership in the Kewaunee nuclear plant. It sold its 17.8 percent share in 1998, to the Wisconsin Public Service Corp.

In 1999, MGE had total revenues of more than $274 million, a rise of almost ten percent over 1998. Earnings also rose. The firm's annual report boasted that the vibrant and diverse economy of the Madison area made it "virtually recession-proof." The strengths of its small service area continued to be one of MGE's major advantages. Supplies of electricity tightened statewide in the late 1990s, and MGE responded by improving its own generating capacity in 1999. In 2000, the company turned on an 83-megawatt gas-fueled generating plant that upped its total generating capacity by 14 percent. The company made additional plans for more improvements over the next few years. MGE also began making electricity from wind power, catching a trend that had advanced rapidly nationwide beginning in the late 1990s. MGE ended the first quarter of 2000 with the highest per share earnings in its history. MGE's Chairman Mebane assured shareholders that MGE was a safe, secure investment that was not prone to take risks. MGE seemed much smaller in 2000, since its nearest neighbors had grown so much, but Mebane downplayed the possibility of a merger or takeover. He envisioned the company remaining a municipal utility that would continue to do well in the thriving Madison-area economy.

Principal Subsidiaries

Great Lakes Energy Co.; American Energy Management Inc.

Principal Competitors

Alliant Energy Corp.

Further Reading

Bergquist, Lee, "Wisconsin Utilities Enlist Top Lobbying Talent for Deregulation Battle," *Knight-Ridder/Tribune Business News,* February 23, 1995.

Hawkins, Lee, "Wisconsin's MGE Expects to Remain Strong Despite Deregulation," *Knight-Ridder/Tribune Business News,* May 7, 1996.

Holley, Paul, "Two Utilities, Two Philosophies, Same City: Watch the Sparks Fly," *Business Journal-Milwaukee,* July 6, 1996, p. 24.

Imrie, Robert, "Electricity Drawn with the Wind," *Capital Times* (Madison, Wis.), December 12, 2000.

Marcial, Gene G., "Small Utilities May Be Worth Plugging Into," *Business Week,* May 19, 1986, p. 134.

Newman, Judy, "MGE: A Place to Hide?," *Wisconsin State Journal,* May 10, 2000, pp. 1E, 2E.

——, "Strategy for Electric Demand Is to Find Savings," *Wisconsin State Journal,* June 4, 2000.

O'Keefe, John, "MGE Will Sell Common Stock," *Wisconsin State Journal,* August 9, 1975.

——, "PSC Backs MGE Hike," *Wisconsin State Journal,* November 13, 1975.

Radford, Bruce W., "Hog Wild in Wisconsin," *Public Utilities Fortnightly,* January 1, 1996, p. 4.

Seppa, Nathan, "Power Plays at MGE," *Wisconsin State Journal,* February 25, 1990.

"WPL Holdings' Revised Bid Is Rejected as Inadequate," *Wall Street Journal,* June 1, 1989, p. A12.

—A. Woodward

Masco Corporation

21001 Van Born Road
Taylor, Michigan 48180
U.S.A.
Telephone: (313) 274-7400
Fax: (313) 374-6135
Web site: http://www.masco.com

Public Company
Incorporated: 1929 as Masco Screw Products Company
Employees: 42,500
Sales: $6.3 billion (1999)
Stock Exchanges: New York
Ticker Symbol: MAS
NAIC: 33711 Wood Kitchen Cabinet and Countertop
    Manufacturing; 326199 All Other Plastics Product
    Manufacturing; 33251 Hardware Manufacturing;
    332913 Plumbing Fixture Fitting and Trim
    Manufacturing

Masco Corporation is the world's largest faucet manufacturer as well as the leading U.S. cabinet manufacturer. The company manufactures hundreds of building specialty and home improvement products, including kitchen appliances, whirlpools and spas, bath and shower tubs and enclosures, residential and commercial locks and hardware, venting systems and ventilating products, electrical outlet boxes, and water pumps. Masco Corporation's best-known product is the single-handled Delta faucet, developed and promoted in the 1950s by the company's founder, Alex Manoogian. Masco's 20 lines and 250 styles of cabinets include stock, semi-custom, and custom cabinetry for the replacement/remodeling and new construction markets.

Origins as a Screw Machine Business in 1929

In 1920 Alex Manoogian, at the age of 19, immigrated to the United States from Smyrna, Turkey, fleeing political persecution and danger that threatened him as a Christian Armenian in Moslem Turkey. After holding several odd jobs in Bridgeport, Connecticut, including brief employment in a screw machine business, Manoogian came in 1924 to Detroit, Michigan, where he worked in a screw machine business and learned about metalworking for automobile components. In 1929, six weeks after the stock market crash, he founded Masco Screw Products Company with two partners, Harry Adjemian and Charles Saunders, who left during the first year. They began with a few thousand dollars, several used screw machines, and a truck— less than $33,000 in assets. "Masco" was derived from the first letters of the partners' last names plus "co" for company.

The automobile industry was still young and largely untested, and Masco's initial years were difficult. Hudson Motor Car Company was the first customer, with a $7,000 contract, but Masco could not yet afford to pay salaries. Manoogian was sales manager, estimator, foreman, press operator, and repairman.

The first plant was located on the fifth floor of an old building, with a furniture manufacturer on the floor below. Soon after business began, oil from the Masco machines leaked through the floor, ruining newly upholstered furniture. Manoogian was able to remain in business by arranging extended payments for the furniture damage.

During the 1930s, Masco worked mainly with Chrysler and had contracts with Ford, Graham Page, Spicer Manufacturing, and Budd Wheel. Since Masco produced parts to the specifications of these firms, the company did not distinguish itself through product design and, instead, focused on providing excellent service.

In 1931 Manoogian brought his family to the United States and married Marie Tatian. In 1934 his brother Charles joined the company, followed a few years later by another brother, George. By 1936, all sales were to the automotive industry and had increased almost fourfold since the first year, to $234,000. In 1937, Masco went public, its shares selling for $1 on the Detroit Stock Exchange.

Later in 1937, the plant caught fire. Fortunately, snow that had accumulated on the roof of the building melted and poured over the heavy machinery, reducing the fire's damage. Although Masco was in business again three months later, this was the one year in its history when the company lost money.

Like most U.S. metalworking companies during World War II, Masco worked exclusively for the defense industry. In 1942, its sales reached $1 million and continued to increase for two years. When the war ended in 1945, sales declined as Masco returned to manufacturing for the automotive industry, and three years later, Masco offered more stock to the public. The sale of 13,000 shares generated the capital to buy the Ford Road Plant in Dearborn, Michigan, which then became the company headquarters.

In 1950, just after the Korean War began, Masco resumed production for the defense industry. Although sales increased, profits remained flat, due to the payment of wartime excess-profits taxes. Masco began work on a new kind of artillery-shell timing mechanism, a precision-made part that demonstrated the company's expertise in metalworking. Chrysler asked Masco to bid on a contract that required a new metalworking technique called cold extrusion, one unfamiliar to Masco engineers. Soon the company was producing satisfactory parts by cold extrusion. In 1953, when wartime contracts ended, Masco could not afford to continue developing the new technology and did not resume using cold extrusion until 1967.

The Launch of Delta Faucet in 1954 Proves Pivotal

The year 1954 was a turning point for the company when Alex Manoogian won a small contract to manufacture parts for a new type of faucet being produced in California. At the time, Masco was still an automotive parts manufacturer with little experience in plumbing fixtures. The unusual design of this faucet was its single handle, which controlled both cold and hot water. Unfortunately, the faucet, nicknamed by plumbers "the one-armed bandit," did not operate properly, and orders for it ceased. Because of his metalworking expertise, Manoogian detected the deficiencies in the faucet and redesigned it. He paid the original owners for licensing rights to produce and market his own version. At first, he formed a separate company to protect Masco if the new faucet did not sell. He tried to interest plumbing manufacturers in marketing the faucet, but they claimed there was no market for it. Eventually, Manoogian transferred the rights to Masco, which produced and marketed

the Delta faucet. Sales increased rapidly, topping $1 million by 1958. In 1959 Masco bought a separate plant in Greensburg, Indiana for faucet manufacturing. That year also, Manoogian's son, Richard, graduated from Yale University and helped launch the new faucet operation.

From the beginning of his career, Richard Manoogian led the company toward expansion. He engineered Masco's first major acquisition in 1961, that of Peerless Industries, Inc., a manufacturer of plumbing products, to widen Masco's production capabilities. In the same year, Masco closed its Dearborn plant and moved automotive parts production to Ypsilanti, Michigan. The faucet sector, which continued with steady success, offset the cyclical nature of the automotive industry. By 1962, Delta faucet sales reached $7 million and accounted for more than half of Masco's sales. By then, Masco Screw Products Company was an inappropriate name for a supplier to both the automotive and construction industries and the name was changed to Masco Corporation. In 1962, Masco acquired Mascon Toy Company, a manufacturer of toy telephones and play furniture, but Mascon was sold in the late 1960s, because of its low profit margins and its incompatibility with Masco's other interests.

Later in 1962, Masco was placed on the American Stock Exchange, and Smith Barney, the investment banking firm, accepted Masco as a client, opening new sources of financing. Masco began an aggressive plan of acquisition and diversification spearheaded by Richard Manoogian.

In 1962 Masco acquired Steel Stamping Company, and in 1964 it acquired Nile Faucet Corporation, broadening its capabilities in the automotive and plumbing parts sectors. Over the next few years, as the construction industry flourished, the company began to expand its product line, acquiring Auto-Flo Company and Auto-Flo Corporation, which produced air-handlers, such as ventilators, and furnaces, and Gibbs Automatic Molding Company, a plastics firm.

Masco headquarters moved in 1967 to new facilities in Taylor, Michigan. The company began using the technique of cold extrusion, a process that resulted in greater structural strength and improved energy efficiency. In 1968, Masco acquired the Burns Companies, which manufactured components by cold forging and by automatic screw machines, followed by a series of acquisitions in the metalworking industry throughout 1970, including Punchcraft, Inc., Molloy Manufacturing Company, Century Tool Company, Keo Cutters, Inc., and Commonwealth Industries.

In 1968 Richard Manoogian was made president of Masco, and Alex Manoogian became chairman of the board. Masco had become a major manufacturer of plumbing products for the kitchen and bathroom, with sales of $5.5 million. In 1969, Masco was listed on the New York Stock Exchange.

Acquisitions Continue in the 1970s and 1980s

During the 1970s, Masco's two main markets, the automobile industry and the construction industry, fared badly in the country's recession. American automobile companies faced increasing foreign competition. Inflation and high interest rates caused a 34 percent decline in the number of new homes by 1974.

Key Dates:

1920: Alex Manoogian immigrates to the United States.
1929: Masco Screw Products Company is formed.
1937: Masco begins selling shares on the Detroit Stock Exchange.
1954: Masco launches the Delta Faucet.
1961: Masco acquires Peerless Industries, Inc.
1968: Richard Manoogian becomes company president.
1984: Masco Industries Inc. is formed.
1993: Masco Industries becomes MascoTech Inc.
1996: Masco sells furniture unit to Furnishings International, Inc.
2000: Masco sells remaining interest in MascoTech to Heartland Industrial.

Nevertheless, Masco earnings continued to grow at an average of 20 percent per year. Masco had become the leading supplier of many household items, and it continued to diversify. Plumbing products for do-it-yourself home improvement continued to do especially well, and renovation and replacement accounted for more than half of Masco's faucet sales by 1975. In 1972 Masco began to market a new faucet design, a double-handled faucet called the Delex, based on the same rotating-ball principle as the Delta. Masco continued to introduce new models over the next few years, and by 1975 had increased its market share to 22 percent.

In 1971 Masco entered the communications business when it acquired Electra Corporation, which manufactured scanning monitor radios. That year Masco began to manufacture parts for trailers and other recreational vehicles with its purchase of Fulton Company in 1971 and Reese Products in 1973. In 1972 Masco bought several small manufacturing companies for its automobile sector, and in 1973 it bought American Metals Corporation.

In 1973 Masco made its first foreign acquisition with Holzer and Company, a West German manufacturer of air-handlers. That same year, Masco entered the petroleum equipment sector, acquiring 47 percent of Emco, a Canadian manufacturer of oil pipes and plumbing hardware. Foreign sales in 1973 accounted for four percent of the company's total, increasing one year later to seven percent.

Between 1973 and 1974, when the automobile and construction industries hit their worst slump of the decade, Masco's stock value plummeted from 46 times earnings to a multiple of 20, although sales were up 23 percent and earnings were up 22 percent.

In 1975, Manoogian took advantage of the growing market for citizens band (CB) radios and acquired Royce Electronics. CB sales continued to soar at the beginning of 1976, but, by the end of the year, the supply of CBs exceeded demand. When the federal government expanded the available channels from 23 to 40, the 23-channel radios became virtually obsolete. Royce's sales plummeted from $53 million to $17 million, and the company suffered $1 million in losses. Masco sold 51 percent of Royce in 1976 and its remaining shares in 1977.

Nevertheless, the company remained in the communications sector. Electra continued to make scanning monitor radios and other electronic products. In 1976 Masco sued RCA Corporation, Teaberry Electronics Corporation, and Sanyo Electric Company for infringing on Electra's patents for scanning radio receivers. Sanyo produced the radios in Japan for the other two companies, but Masco required that firms sign a licensing agreement to sell the scanners. The case was settled in court when Sanyo agreed to pay Electra royalties under a new licensing agreement.

Masco continued to penetrate the petroleum equipment market in 1976, acquiring A-Z International Companies and Grant Oil Tool Company, both manufacturers of drilling tools, as well as Dansk Metal and Armaturindistri of Denmark. Masco also created Forming Technology Company, a firm with technologically advanced equipment that produced larger metal components swiftly and economically. In 1977, Masco acquired Walker McDonald Manufacturing Company and R & B Manufacturing Company, producers of petroleum equipment, and, in 1978, Rieke Corporation, which made closures for oil drums and other large containers. In 1979 Masco purchased Jung-Pumpen, a West German maker of sump pumps, and Arrow Specialty Company, a maker of engines and engine repair parts.

During the late 1970s, Masco began to advertise its faucets on network television. In a March 16, 1981 interview with *Forbes,* Richard Manoogian stated, ''Everybody thought we were crazy. . . . They told us that the only time you buy a faucet is when your old one leaks.'' Masco realized that there was a steady consumer demand for the product and continued to expand its line of faucets. By 1980, Masco had increased its market share to 28 percent.

In 1980, while automobile production slowed 24 percent, Masco worked with car manufacturers on design, to create additional car parts. In 1981, while the housing industry was in its worst state since the mid-1970s, Masco's sales in that sector continued to grow. Masco's products in the home improvement area were not subject to extreme economic swings, and the home improvement sector was growing faster than the industrial one.

Masco continued to expand in 1980, acquiring AlupKompressorenPressorun, a West German maker of air-compressors, Lamons Metal Gasket Company, and Arrow Oil Tools, a manufacturer for the petroleum industry. In 1981 Masco introduced a nonceramic toilet, which used much less water and was insulated to muffle the sound of flushing.

Diversification continued in 1982. Masco acquired two small companies that made valves and related products for the oil industry, as well as Evans-Aristocrat Industries, which made steel measuring tapes. That same year it also purchased Baldwin Hardware Manufacturing Company, which made hardware for builders, and Marvel Metal Products, manufacturer of steel work stations for the office.

The year 1982 was the first since 1956 that earnings for operations did not increase, because of the effects of the recession. Masco's sales in the cold extrusion industry declined 17 percent, primarily because of the depressed automobile and construction industries.

In 1983 Masco acquired Brass Craft Manufacturing Company, a maker of plumbing supplies. Building and home improvement product sales were up more than 50 percent to $500 million, because of profitable acquisitions and steady faucet sales. At the same time, decline in oil prices spurred a drop in petroleum equipment sales.

Industrial Businesses Spin-Off in 1984

For many years, the cyclical industrial sectors—petroleum and construction equipment and automobile parts—had lowered Masco's overall yearly results, even though total annual sales had continued to grow. In 1984 Richard Manoogian spun off Masco's industrial businesses into a separate, publicly held company, Masco Industries Inc. (MI). This change gave Masco Corporation a firmer identity as a home improvement and building products company, enabling it to focus on that sector. While the move allowed both companies to expand more quickly, it also gave Masco Corporation continued access to MI's metalworking technology. Richard Manoogian became CEO of the new company, and its headquarters remained in Taylor, Michigan, with Masco Corporation. Masco Corporation distributed 50 percent of MI stock to shareholders as a dividend and retained the other half, worth about $50 million. A year later, Masco ownership of MI decreased to 44 percent.

In the restructuring, the two companies formed Nimas Corporation as a vehicle to facilitate Masco's leveraged buyout of NI Industries, a large diversified company. NI Industries manufactured many building products, including Thermador cooking equipment, Weiser locks, Waste King appliances, Artistic Brass faucets, and Bowers electrical outlet boxes (Masco's first entry into the electrical equipment business). NI also produced several automobile and defense products. Masco paid $483 million for the company; using Nimas allowed Masco Corporation and MI to make an expensive acquisition without placing the debt on either company's balance sheet.

During the next few years, MI focused on developing its manufacturing technology and expanding through acquisitions, investing more than $1 billion. As a result, yearly earnings suffered, although sales increased from $545 million in 1984 to $1.7 billion in 1989.

Erwin H. Billig became president of Masco Industries in 1986. Between 1986 and 1989, MI diversified into architectural products, acquiring manufacturers of steel doors, door frames, metal office panels, security grills, sectional and rolling doors, and similar items. By 1989, it had become one of the largest U.S. producers of steel door products. MI also entered a new sector of automotive parts in 1986, acquiring several manufacturers of components such as windshield wiper blades, roof racks, brake hardware repair kits, and front-wheel-drive components. MI focused on establishing its own niches in the market, which continued to expand as the need for replacement parts for longer lasting automobiles increased. MI production of customized goods for the defense industry, including cartridge casings, projectiles, and casings for rocket motors and missiles, declined in the late 1980s, as the U.S. government began to decrease defense spending.

After the creation of MI, Masco Corporation continued its expansion, acquiring, in 1984, Trayco and Aqua Glass, both kitchen-and-bathroom-products manufacturers with sales of about $70 million. At the same time, Masco phased out its Electra personal communications products, a market no longer suited to the company's criteria for growth.

In 1985 Masco acquired Merillat Industries, a manufacturer of cabinets, and Flint and Walling Water Systems, which made water pumps. Masco also introduced the largest faucet selection in the history of the plumbing industry. Wayne B. Lyon became president of Masco in 1985, and Richard Manoogian served as chairman and CEO of both Masco Corporation and Masco Industries.

In the early 1980s, Richard Manoogian saw a great potential for growth abroad and acquired the Berglen group of companies, which distributed faucets in the United Kingdom, and 25 percent of Hans Grohe, the top European hand-shower manufacturer. Because of disadvantageous foreign currency rates, sales in dollars in Europe had remained stagnant for several years, but European sales in domestic currencies were thriving.

In 1986 Masco filed lawsuits against several plumbing suppliers—Waxman Industries, Keystone Franklin, and Radiator Specialty Company—for infringement on the Delta faucet trademark. The following year, Masco's competitors agreed to mark packages more clearly, following the trademark specifications. It was the first of several trademark infringement cases involving the Delta name.

Expanding into Furniture in the Late 1980s

Masco moved into the furniture industry in 1986, acquiring Henredon Furniture Industries and Drexel Heritage Furniture and, one year later, Lexington Furniture Industries. The three companies represented about $700 million in sales. Masco also acquired Walkins Manufacturing Corporation, a producer of spas, and Fieldstone Cabinetry.

In 1987 Masco purchased Marbro Lamp Company and Hueppe Duscha, a West German maker of shower equipment. Masco also issued 1.2 million shares to finance its acquisition of La Barge Mirrors; two new furniture companies, Hickorycraft and Alsons Corporation; and Marge Carson, Inc., a manufacturer of plumbing products. By 1988 furniture sales accounted for about 25 percent of the company's $2.9 billion sales, and Masco continued to expand, acquiring American Textile Company and the Robert Allen Companies.

In 1988, MI transferred nine of its smaller businesses to TriMas Corporation, a publicly traded spin-off, primarily a manufacturer of industrial fasteners. Two years later, Masco Corporation sold TriMas its recreational vehicle accessories and its insulation products businesses. Initially, Masco held a 19 percent (by the mid-1990s reduced to four percent) stake in TriMas, and MI held a 48 percent stake (by the mid-1990s 37 percent).

In 1989 earnings declined, and Masco Corporation's stock sold at discounted rates, due to investor uncertainty about the future of the home improvement sector. Consequently, the company repurchased four million of its common shares in

1989, and, in 1990, the board voted to repurchase up to ten million additional common shares.

Expansion continued in 1989, as Masco bought Universal Furniture of Hong Kong, its largest overseas acquisition. Foreign sales, mainly in Canada and Europe, accounted for about 13 percent of Masco's total revenues. In 1990 Masco bolstered its cabinetry operations through the acquisition of KraftMaid Cabinetry, Inc.

Refocusing on Home Improvement and Building Products in the 1990s

Masco's move into furniture turned out to be a major mistake. Part of the problem was bad timing, as the furniture industry in 1988 entered into a deep recession, which it did not pull out of until 1992. However, furniture also simply turned out to be a bad fit for Masco, unlike the company's move into cabinetry, a product sector that was much more closely aligned to such Masco mainstays as faucets than was furniture. Following its move into cabinet making, Masco had been able to achieve manufacturing efficiencies, thus improving upon the businesses it acquired; furniture manufacturing, however, was less sophisticated and thus did not lend itself to the kinds of management techniques Masco typically used. Furthermore, Masco had great difficulty marketing its furniture lines, whereas it had been able to sell its cabinets through many of its existing channels.

By the early 1990s the company's furniture group was a major drag on company earnings. Despite this, Masco continued to increase its investment in furniture by making additional acquisitions, including the mid-1994 purchase of Berkline Corp., a Tennessee-based maker of recliners and upholstered family room furniture that had sales of $165 million in 1993.

Meanwhile, Masco also felt the effects from a troubled Masco Industries, which was suffering from the effects of the early 1990s recession, a downturn that hit the auto industry particularly hard. Prospects had improved by 1993 thanks to a restructuring and an improving economy and Masco took advantage of MI's stronger position by reducing its stake in its sister company that year to 35 percent. Also in 1993, MI changed its name to MascoTech Inc. By 1997 Masco Corporation had further simplified its holdings by reducing its MascoTech stake to 17 percent, with the prospect of completely eliminating this noncore holding by the turn of the century.

An even more important divestment occurred in 1996 when Masco sold its furniture unit. In June of the previous year, the company had decided to sell the unit, finally concluding that it would be unable to turn the unit around and that it would be best for Masco Corporation to return to an exclusive focus on home improvement and building products. Masco had been unable to increase the furniture unit's operating profits, which had ranged from three to six percent, nowhere near the 15 to 20 percent generated by the company's other operating units. In November 1995 Masco announced that Morgan Stanley Capital Partners would buy the furniture unit for nearly $1.2 billion, but in January of the following year the deal was abandoned without explanation. Then, in August 1996, Masco sold the troubled unit to an investment group, Furnishings International Inc., with proceeds exceeding $1 billion, $708 million of which was cash.

As part of the agreement, Masco gained a 15 percent stake in Furnishings International. Masco soon used a large portion— about $550 million—of the cash it gained to reduce its long-term debt, which had been fairly high.

Following its abandonment of furniture, Masco made several acquisitions that extended its existing products lines in brand-name and geographic terms. In 1996 three European companies with combined 1995 sales of $140 million were acquired: The Moore Group Ltd., a leading U.K. maker of kitchen cabinets; Horst Breuer GmbH, a German manufacturer of shower enclosures for the do-it-yourself market; and E. Missel GmbH, a leading German manufacturer of proprietary specialty products for the new construction, remodeling, and renovation markets. In March 1997 Masco acquired Franklin Brass Manufacturing Company, a California-based maker of bath accessories and bath safety products, and LaGard Inc., another California company, which was an electronic lock manufacturer. Later in 1997 two more cabinetry companies were acquired: Liberty Hardware Manufacturing Corporation of Boca Raton, Florida, a maker of cabinet hardware; and Texwood Industries, Inc., a leading maker of kitchen and bath cabinetry based in Duncanville, Texas. Masco expanded further outside the United States in July 1997 when it acquired The Alvic Group, a leading Spanish manufacturer and distributor of kitchen and bath cabinetry, and The SKS Group, a leading German maker and distributor of roller shutters and aluminum balcony railing systems.

As the new century approached, with its ill-fated furniture adventure more or less behind it and its holding in MascoTech substantially reduced, Masco Corporation appeared ready to reclaim some of its past glory. Newly committed to its core home improvement and building products businesses, the company was likely to continue to seek out targeted acquisitions both at home and abroad to strengthen its already commanding position.

Heading into the 21st Century

In 1997 one of Masco's lesser known subsidiaries emerged as a major source of revenue for the corporation. Considered a minor acquisition when it was obtained in 1994, Vapor Technologies Inc. assumed a more prominent role in company operations in 1995 with the release of Brilliance, an anti-tarnish and anti-rust metal finish. By 1997 Masco was applying the innovative finish to a number of its faucets and locks. The financial results were impressive, as faucet sales rose from $757 million in 1996 to over $900 million in 1997; the following year, Masco announced plans to expand its line of Brilliance faucets from 60 models to 2,000. The company also began exploring the possibility of wider applications for Brilliance, and use of the versatile finish on light fixtures, lamps, and other brass furnishings eventually helped boost sales of Masco's brass products by 300 per cent. Overall the company enjoyed record profits for 1997, with net income reaching $382.4 million, compared to $295.2 million in 1996.

A number of key overseas acquisitions in 1998 helped bolster the company's share of the European home furnishings market. In March Masco acquired Vasco Corporation, a Belgian manufacturer of hydronic radiators and heat convectors, key components of heating systems in the majority of European homes. A similar manufacturer, Brugman Radiatorenfabriek B.V. in Holland, was purchased in July, and in November the company acquired the British bath fixture company Heritage Bathrooms. During this period the company also made an effort to establish a stronger niche in the Japanese home furnishings market, establishing Masco Japan Ltd. in February 1998. The Japanese market showed significant room for growth, with over a million new houses being built annually, and a faucet, cabinet, and lock market estimated at $7.2 billion. In the midst of these new ventures Masco sold its Thermador subsidiary to Bosch-Siemens in June, signaling the company's formal exit from the appliance manufacturing business.

The year 1998 again brought record earnings, with net profits exceeding $475 million. In 1999 the company embarked on a major acquisition campaign, beginning in March, when it purchased Spanish household and kitchen equipment manufacturer GMU. A series of key acquisitions came in April, with Faucet Queen, Inc., A & J Gummers, The Cary Group, and Avocet Hardware (U.K.) entering the Masco fold. Masco completed its largest purchase in September, when it acquired five companies with combined yearly sales of over $1.5 billion. The companies—which included Arrow Fastener Company, Behr Process Corporation, Inrecon, Mill's Pride, and Superia Radiatoren N.V. of Belgium—expanded Masco's role as a major supplier to Home Depot, and business with the home furnishings chain was expected to rise from $500 million in 1998 to $1.5 billion in 2000. In May 1999 Masco also entered into a strategic alliance with Pulte Corporation, which made Masco subsidiaries Merillat Industries and Quality Cabinets the primary cabinet suppliers for the homebuilder through 2002.

While the company continued to enjoy record profits in 1999, with net earnings nearly reaching $700 million, a decline in the home furnishings business was approaching. A combination of decreased sales and high energy costs resulted in low share value for the company's stock, and profits for 2000 and 2001 were expected to be lower than previously projected. The company was also hit by unfavorable exchange rates during this period, with a strong U.S. dollar resulting in lower international earnings. In an effort to phase out its less profitable holdings, in August 2000 the company sold its remaining interests in MascoTech to Heartland Industrial for $2 billion. In general, however, the slight economic slump did not deter the company from continuing to pursue its aggressive acquisition strategy. In January 2000 Masco acquired Danish firm Tvilium-Scanbirk, a leading manufacturer of ready-to-assemble shelving, cabinetry, and other furniture products in Europe, and a major supplier for Staples. In May the company acquired Masterchem Industries, a specialty paint products company, and Glass Idromassaggio, an Italian manufacturer of bathtubs, shower enclosures, and whirlpools; in November it purchased BSI Holdings and Davenport Insulation. While Masco's profits for 2000 may not have topped the $700 million mark, as it forged ahead into the new century the company could still boast a significant share of the home furnishings market.

Principal Subsidiaries

A&J Gummers, Ltd. (U.K.); Alfred Reinecke GmbH & Co. KG (Germany); Alma Küchen Aloys Meyer GmbH & Co. (Germany); Alsons Corporation; The Alvic Group (Spain); American Metal Products; American Shower & Bath Corporation; Aqua Glass Corporation; Arrow Fastener Company; Avocet Hardware, plc (U.K.); Baldwin Hardware Corp.; Behr Process Corporation; Berglen Group, Ltd. (U.K.); Brass Craft Mfg. Company; Brugman Radiatorenfabriek B.V. (Holland); BSI Holdings, Inc.; The Cary Group; Cobra Products, Inc.; Computerized Security Systems; Damixa A/S (Denmark); Davenport Insulation; Delta Faucet Co.; E. Missel GmbH (Germany); Faucet Queen; Fieldstone Cabinetry, Inc.; Franklin Brass Mfg. Co.; Gale Industries, Inc.; Gamco (General Accessories MFG. Co.); Gebhardt Ventilatoren GmbH&Co. (Germany); Ginger; Glass Idromassaggio S.p.A. (Italy); GMU-XEY (Spain); Grumal (Spain); Heritage Bathrooms, PLC (U.K.); Horst Breuer GmbH & Co. (Germany); Hüppe GmbH&Co. (Germany); Inrecon, L.L.C.; Jung Pumpen GmbH & Co. (Germany); KraftMaid Cabinetry Inc.; La Gard, Inc.; Liberty Hardware; The Marvel Group; Masterchem Industries, Inc.; Melard Manufacturing Corp.; Merillat Industries, Inc.; Mill's Pride; Mirolin Industries Corporation; Moores Furniture Group Ltd. (U.K.); Newteam Limited (U.K.); Peerless Faucet Company; Rubinetterie Mariani S.p.A. (Italy); SKS (Stakusit Bautechnik GmbH) (Germany); StarMark, Inc.; S.T.S.R. (Italy); Superia Radiatoren, NN (Belgium); Texwood Industries, L.P.; Tvilum–Scanbirk A/S (Denmark); Vapor Technologies Inc.; Vasco plc (Belgium); Watkins Manufacturing Corporation; W/C Technology Corporation; Weiser Lock, Inc.; Zenith Products Corporation.

Principal Competitors

American Standard Companies Inc.; Fortune Brands, Inc.; U.S. Industries, Inc.

Further Reading

Barkholz, David, "Masco's Furniture-Biz Pullout Could Be Costly," *Crain's Detroit Business,* June 26, 1995, pp. 1, 26.

Bodipo-Memba, Alejandro, "Taylor, Mich., Bathroom Fixture Maker Braces for Lower Profits in 2000, 2001," *Detroit Free Press,* October 5, 2000.

Koselka, Rita, "Resetting the Table," *Forbes,* March 16, 1992, pp. 66–67.

McCracken, Jeffrey, "Masco's Little Deal Dazzles: Anti-Tarnish Technology Shines Across Wide Array of Products," *Crain's Detroit Business,* October 27, 1997.

——, "Masco Talking Acquisitions," *Crain's Detroit Business,* February 1, 1999.

Masco Corporation: A Tradition of Excellence for 65 Years, Taylor, Michigan: Masco Corporation, 1994.

Masco 50: The First Fifty Years 1929–79, Taylor, Michigan: Masco Corporation, 1979.

Palmeri, Christopher, "Keeping Good People," *Forbes,* May 24, 1993, pp. 50–51.

Parker, Jocelyn, "Taylor, Mich.-Based Construction Material Firm Swallows Five Companies," *Detroit Free Press,* September 2, 1999.

Reingold, Jennifer, "The Masco Fiasco: Masco Corp. Was Once One of America's Most Admired Companies. Not Anymore," *Financial World,* October 24, 1995, pp. 32–34.

Salomon, R.S., Jr., "Can an Old Boss Learn New Tricks?," *Forbes,* July 29, 1996, p. 102.

Stopa, Marsha, "Masco at Home in Mexico," *Crain's Detroit Business,* July 10, 1995, pp. 1, 24.

—René Steinke
—updates: David E. Salamie, Stephen Meyer

Mervyn's California

22301 Foothill Boulevard
Hayward, California 94541
U.S.A.
Telephone: (510) 727-3000
Toll Free: (800) 637-8967
Fax: (510) 727-5770
Web site: http://www.mervyns.com

Wholly Owned Subsidiary of Target Corporation
Incorporated: 1949 as Mervyn's
Employees: 32,000
Sales: $4.09 billion (2000)
NAIC: 44812 Women's Clothing Stores; 44811 Men's
    Clothing Stores; 44815 Clothing Accessories Stores;
    44819 Other Clothing Stores; 44815 Clothing
    Accessories Stores; 44813 Children's and Infants'
    Clothing Stores; 45211 Department Stores

Mervyn's California, owned by retail giant Target Corporation, operates 267 department stores in 14 states. Whereas most of Mervyn's stores are located in California and Texas, the company also operates outlets in Arizona, Colorado, Idaho, Louisiana, Michigan, Minnesota, Nevada, New Mexico, Oklahoma, Oregon, Utah, and Washington. Mervyn's is a middle-market promotional department store offering moderately priced name-brand and private label casual apparel and home fashions.

Company Origins

Mervyn's was founded in 1949 in San Lorenzo, California by Mervin Morris, who took the advice of an architect who told him that exchanging the "i" in his first name for a "y" would add flair to the department store that he named after himself. The centerpiece of Mervyn's merchandise was a line of private-label family apparel, which Morris sold in season at prices higher than a discount retailer's but still below what his customers would pay for similar goods in other department stores. With the help of two full-time employees, Mervyn's sales reached $100,000 in its first year of business.

1960s and 1970s: Innovative Marketing and a Focus on Value

Morris relied on rapid inventory turnover to secure profits, maintaining a loyal customer base by ensuring that Mervyn's products represented good value. Innovative advertising also helped keep Mervyn's in the public eye. For many years, it was the only retailer in California to publish its own tabloid advertisement. The tabloid, which was distributed in the stores and through the Sunday newspapers, pushed weekly promotions and helped establish Mervyn's reputation as a value-oriented retailer.

This emphasis on providing customers with value, rather than on offering a luxurious shopping experience, was an unusual concept at a time when the full-service department store was still the standard in general merchandise retailing. It proved profitable, however, and Morris gained a reputation as a pioneer in the industry. By the early 1970s, the company was in a position to expand considerably. In 1971, it went public, raising $5.4 million over the counter to retire all of its outstanding debt. Then, between 1972 and 1978, Mervyn's nearly quadrupled in size, opening 31 stores, all of them in California and Nevada. In 1977, the company earned $11.8 million on sales of $264 million.

1978 Acquisition by Dayton Hudson

Mervyn's success attracted the interest of Dayton Hudson, a midwestern retailer known primarily for operating the upscale Dayton's and Hudson's store chains. Both Dayton's and Hudson's had venerable histories as big city department stores. Hudson's began as a haberdashery established in Detroit in 1881 by Joseph L. Hudson, who was looking for a way to rebuild his fortune after going bankrupt in the panic of 1873. In 1954, the company built Northland, then the largest shopping center in the United States, in suburban Detroit. Dayton's was founded in Minneapolis in 1902 by George Dayton, a former banker. In 1956, the company built Southdale, the world's first fully enclosed shopping mall, in Minneapolis. In 1962, Dayton's created two subsidiaries that would prove highly successful, the Target chain of discount retailers, and the B. Dalton chain of bookstores.

Dayton's went public in 1966 and three years later acquired Hudson's, which was then still privately owned. Dayton Hudson promptly expanded by acquiring shopping malls and specialty retailers. Despite this aggressive course of expansion, however, the company was not well known outside the upper Midwest. With its B. Dalton stores well established in California, Dayton Hudson sought to introduce its department stores on the West Coast and, in 1978, the company acquired all 55 Mervyn's stores in a stock swap valued at nearly $300 million.

Mervin Morris became a director at Dayton Hudson, and his family became one of the company's largest stockholders as a result of the deal. John Kilmartin replaced Morris as CEO of Mervyn's, overseeing a period of impressive growth. Backed by Dayton Hudson's financial resources, Mervyn's embarked on a remarkable course of expansion. By the mid-1980s, the chain was operating 148 stores. In 1984, Mervyn's opened nine stores in Texas—its first adventure outside the western United States—and posted a $223.3 million profit on sales of more than $2 billion. The following year, Mervyn's contributed 37 percent of Dayton Hudson's operating profit. Impressed with this success, Dayton Hudson planned to allocate approximately half of its capital investment budget from 1986 through 1990 for new Mervyn's stores.

Mervyn's was highly regarded in the retail industry in the mid-1980s, when many of its competitors for the mid-range department store customer were floundering. During this time, many of Mervyn's rivals retooled themselves, adopting many of Mervyn's best ideas. Most notable, J.C. Penney abandoned its old identity as a full-line department store and like Mervyn's, focused on apparel and soft goods. Moreover, competitors began publishing their own tabloid advertisements, imitating the marketing tactic Mervyn's had used for decades. Perhaps most important, several retailers across the retailing spectrum began selling department store-quality goods at discounted prices. Faced with increased competition, Mervyn's business began to taper off, particularly when factory outlet stores started becoming popular.

Late 1980s and 1990s: Competition and Financial Instability

Perhaps led by a false sense of security, Mervyn's made no aggressive moves to stay ahead of the competition. Dayton Hudson executives later admitted that they did not pay close enough attention to their star performer. Mervyn's profits sank sharply in 1986 and remained depressed in 1987, despite continuing strong revenues. Earnings at Dayton Hudson sank correspondingly, and speculation surfaced in the financial press that

the company might become a takeover target as a result of this weakness.

During this period, Mervyn's centralized its buying operations that previously had been split between its stores in the West and its fledgling stores in Texas. Consolidating buying operations in California speeded up inventory replenishment and cut costs. The chain also contained costs by focusing more of its resources on product quality control and by installing checkout scanners to help manage inventory, among other things.

More important, though, Mervyn's began to recalibrate its merchandise lines. Since low prices and good values no longer made Mervyn's unique, in an era when Kmart became the largest retailer in the United States and intramural rival Target prospered, the company had to find a way to distinguish itself once more. The chain responded by focusing its attention even more closely on apparel, which had been responsible, in large part, for founder Morris' success in the first place. ''We dropped toys, infants' furniture and draperies because we couldn't be dominant in them without sacrificing potential in our core businesses,'' Walter Rossi commented. Even within its apparel lines, Mervyn's sacrificed variety to concentrate on its best-selling items. For instance, it pared in half the number of women's blouses that it offered, leaving only the most popular ones.

Mervyn's also responded to heavy price competition from its rivals by trying to upgrade the quality of its clothing, even when that meant raising prices slightly. One of the chain's most popular clothing lines was its men's and women's sweat clothes. Mervyn's sweats, however, tended to shrink substantially in washing and did not have a reputation as high-quality garments. Mervyn's decided to size them more generously and upgrade the fabric and the sewing, even though it meant a price increase of nearly 20 percent. To compensate for the price hike, Mervyn's offered a broader range of colors and more fashionable designs.

As a result of these changes, Mervyn's sales and profits slightly rebounded in 1988 and 1989. In the 1990s, however, the chain's recovery stalled, hurt by the sharp downturn in the California economy. Sales flattened out during the first half of the decade, and profits dropped sharply from $284 million in 1991 and 1992 to $179 million in 1993. During this time, Rossi was succeeded as CEO by Joe Vesce, and then Mervyn's received five new top executives, including three transfers from Target.

Mervyn's struggle continued into the mid-1990s. Dayton Hudson's 1993 annual report characterized Mervyn's performance as disappointing, and that year Moody's announced that it was considering lowering Dayton Hudson's debt rating due to Mervyn's financial problems. Some analysts were skeptical as to Mervyn's ability to overcome its losses and began to speculate as to whether or not its parent would sell off the faltering retailer.

Late 1990s: A New Name, A New Image

As part of a plan to bolster its merchandise image, the company changed its name to Mervyn's California in 1995. Management hoped the new, brighter logo and casual, fun image would appeal to consumers who had been disenchanted with the old look. The store also received a modest face-lift by

Key Dates:

1949: Mervin Morris establishes Mervyn's in San Lorenzo, California.
1971: Company goes public.
1978: Dayton Hudson acquires Mervyn's.
1984: Nine stores open in Texas and company revenues exceed $2 billion.
1986: Profits begin to falter due to increased competition in the industry.
1993: Mervyn's continues to post disappointing sales figures.
1995: Company changes its name to Mervyn's California.
1996: More than $100 million in expenses are cut and 127 positions are eliminated.
1997: Bart Butzer is named president.
1999: Mervyn's web site is launched.

moving its cash registers to the front of stores and hanging new ad banners in the aisles. In 1996, the company established the Mervyn's California/Women's Sports Foundation Scholarship Fund, which rewarded academic and athletic excellence. At the same time, however, parent Dayton Hudson was growing weary of Mervyn's poor performance and cut its expense budget dramatically. Its merchandising department was hit hardest, with 127 positions eliminated.

In 1997, Mervyn's closed its stores in Florida and Georgia in an attempt to lower company costs and improve sales. The company began to see a light at the end of the tunnel as the California economy began to rebound. Bart Butzer, a regional senior vice-president with Target, succeeded Paul Sauser as Mervyn's president and began an aggressive merchandising campaign. In 1998, financial numbers appeared to be on the rise and Dayton Hudson approved store renovation plans, feeding money into its expense budget that had once been severely cut. Although the parent company had faith that the department store could overcome its tarnished financial past, it warned that if its performance remained inconsistent, it would have to take action to maintain shareholder value.

An Uncertain Future in the New Millennium

In early 2000, Dayton Hudson changed its name to Target Corporation to reflect the fact that the Target stores accounted for more than 75 percent of company business. Under the direction of Butzer, Mervyn's continued to push its casual and fun image and the company's merchandise mix continued to change

in order to remain competitive. The company also delved into e-commerce under the leadership of Target Direct, a unit created to oversee electronic retailing and direct marketing efforts. Butzer remained focused on securing sales and creating innovative marketing plans. In August 2000, stores in California offered two days of tax-free shopping in an attempt to lure back-to-school shoppers.

By January 2001, however, Mervyn's attempts to secure consistent financial results were deemed unsuccessful as the company reported a 2.4 percent decrease in sales during the holiday season. The retail industry as a whole began to struggle as consumer confidence faltered and spending started to decline. While some analysts speculated that Target Corporation would eventually rid itself of the department store, others stated that it would hold on to it because Mervyn's provided cash to fund Target Corporation's stock re-purchase program. The company introduced a new marketing slogan, ''Mervyn's Begins with Me,'' in early 2001 with a goal of attracting female shoppers. Mervyn's executives remained positive that the company was on the right track but as consumer spending and confidence slipped, the department store's future remained uncertain.

Principal Competitors

American Retail Group Inc.; J.C. Penney Company Inc.; The TJX Companies Inc.

Further Reading

Barmash, Isadore, ''A Turnaround at Dayton Hudson,'' *New York Times,* May 28, 1989.

''DH Wants More From Mervyn's,'' *WWD,* October 14, 1998, p. 14.

Hammond, Teena, ''Mervyn's on the Mend,'' *WWD,* March 23, 1998, p. 6(1).

Harris, Pat Lopes, ''Hayward, Calif.-Based Department Store Chain Fights for Survival,'' *Knight-Ridder/Tribune Business News,* January 4, 2001.

Heller, Laura, ''DH Strategy Uses Divisions to Feed Target, Drive Profit,'' *Discount Store News,* April 19, 1999, p. 55.

McKinney, Melonee, ''Dayton Hudson Changing Corporate Name to Target; Discount Change Now Accounts for 75 Percent of Corporate Revenues, Pretax Profits,'' *Daily News Record,* January 14, 2001, p. 2.

''Mervyn's Gets the Ultimatum to Improve,'' *Discount Store News,* April 1, 1996, p. 46.

''Mervyn's Outlines Plans to Cut $200M in Expenses,'' *Daily News Record,* February 6, 1996, p. 8.

''Mervyn's Sales Slump,'' *San Francisco Business Times,* January 12, 2001, p. 9.

—Douglas Sun
—update: Christina M. Stansell

Metropolitan Baseball Club Inc.

Shea Stadium
123-01 Roosevelt Avenue
Flushing, New York 11368
U.S.A.
Telephone: (718) 507-6387
Toll free: (800) 972-1808
Fax: (718) 507-6395
Web site: http://www.nymets.com

Private Company
Incorporated: 1962
Employees: 200
Sales: $125.6 million (1999 est.)
NAIC: 711211 Sports Teams and Clubs

The New York Mets, legally known as the Metropolitan Baseball Club Inc., have known sporadic success in their four decades of existence, with two world championships to their credit and two other appearances in the World Series. The Mets generally play in the shadow of their cross-town rivals, the New York Yankees, only on occasion eclipsing the more storied franchise in media attention. Like the Yankees, the Mets are one of the most financially powerful clubs in Major League Baseball and now aggressively compete for the top free agent players that come onto the market. Enjoying stable management, the Mets have rebounded from a stretch of disappointing results in the early 1990s to emerge as a team looking to match the Yankees and the Atlanta Braves, its main competitor in its division, as consistent winners.

The 1957 Departure from New York

The birth of the Mets is also the story of two departures, that of the New York Giants and the Brooklyn Dodgers. The Giants joined the National League in 1883 and played their home games at the Polo Grounds near Harlem. The Dodgers joined the National League in 1888. It was not until the Western League declared itself to be a major league (changing its name to the American League) and challenged the supremacy of the National League, that the Yankees (then known as the High-landers) began play in the city in 1901. The Giants, winning pennants and championships under the leadership of the legendary John McGraw, were the toast of the town until the 1920s when Babe Ruth would revolutionize the game of baseball and launch the Yankees to unparalleled success. The Dodgers, meantime, were generally ignored, except in Brooklyn where they forged a deep bond with the residents of the borough.

By the 1950s the Dodgers were perennial winners, generally outshining the Giants and facing the Yankees in the World Series year after year. But a number of factors were converging that would eventually lead to both National League teams departing New York. For 50 years, Major League Baseball had been limited to 16 teams located in ten cities, none of which were further west than St. Louis. With the advent of air travel and the rise of new population centers, there seemed to be no reason to limit Major League Baseball to its traditional confines. The less popular teams in two-team cities, struggling to draw fans and remain solvent, saw relocation as a matter of survival. The first to move was the Boston Braves' franchise, which in 1953 relocated to Milwaukee where the club soon led the league in attendance. The next year, the St. Louis Browns moved to Baltimore to become the Orioles; and in 1955 the Philadelphia Athletics moved to Kansas City. All three enjoyed new or renovated municipal facilities. Teams like the Giants and the Dodgers were left to play in outdated ballparks in declining neighborhoods. The Giants found themselves increasingly more reliant on their interborough rivalry with the Dodgers to boost attendance. The team remained profitable, mostly due to television revenues that were second only to the Dodgers in the National League. Although somewhat better off than the Giants, the Dodgers still could not match the Milwaukee Braves in attendance. The Dodgers' owner, Walter O'Malley, knew that the Braves would soon translate attendance into the cash that could build a ballclub that would surpass the Dodgers. His fears proved legitimate, as the Braves would win the World Series by 1957.

O'Malley's dream was to escape Ebbets Field and its crowded neighborhood for a domed stadium in downtown Brooklyn where a number of subway lines and a terminal for the

Key Dates:

1957: New York Giants and Brooklyn Dodgers relocate.
1960: The National League awards an expansion team to New York.
1962: The Mets begin league play.
1964: Shea Stadium opens.
1969: The Mets win their first World Series.
1975: The original owner, Mrs. Joan Whitney Payson, dies; her daughter, Mrs. Lorinda de Roulet, assumes control.
1980: The de Roulet family sells the team to Fred Wilpon and Nelson Doubleday, Jr.
1986: The Mets win their second World Series.
2000: The Mets lose to the Yankees in the first ''subway'' World Series in 45 years.

Long Island Railroad met. He was willing to pay for the new park; all he said he needed from the city was help in acquiring the necessary land at a reasonable price, via eminent domain. That help could only come from two men: Mayor Robert Wagner and Robert Moses, the autocratic head of parks, highways, and urban renewal. Of the two, Moses was arguably the more powerful. While mayors came and went, Moses stayed, bolstered by his ability to raise money independently by issuing bonds through the Triborough Bridge Authority. Moses thwarted O'Malley's plans at every turn. His dream was to make Flushing Meadows in Queens a true ''Central Park'' of the five boroughs, as well as a lasting tribute to himself. Only there would he allow a new stadium for the Dodgers to be built. O'Malley felt that if his team played in Queens, they would no longer be the Brooklyn Dodgers. Instead, he opted to relocate to a new territory that offered immense potential: Los Angeles. According to some accounts, he also convinced Giants owner Horace Stoneham to move his club to San Francisco in order to keep alive their rivalry and to make road trips more convenient for the other teams in the league. When the Dodgers left Brooklyn, O'Malley was vilified, and the borough suffered a blow from which it would never truly recover. The Giants were not offered the ballpark in Queens, and their fans seemed to accept the loss of their team with little emotion. When the Giants Board of Directors voted to move to San Francisco, financier M. Donald Grant, who held a minority interest, cast the only dissenting vote. Earlier, he had helped a wealthy friend and Giants fan, Mrs. Joan Whitney Payson, to purchase a single share of stock for sentimental reasons. Both were destined to play a major part in the history of the Mets.

With an election looming, Mayor Wagner in October 1957 announced the formation of a committee to immediately return National League baseball to the city. The group of citizens was headed by attorney William Shea. Using the lure of a new stadium in Flushing, Shea at first tried to land an established club, but Philadelphia, Pittsburgh, and Cincinnati declined the offer. Furthermore, the National League seemed content to remain an eight-team league, seemingly uninterested in being represented in the nation's largest media market. Shea then tried a different tactic. He decided to form a third major league: the Continental League.

Returning to New York in 1962

In all likelihood the Continental League and its proposed eight teams was never more than a paper organization, but it proved to be a creditable enough threat to Major League Baseball, especially when Shea induced 80-year-old Branch Rickey, a venerable baseball executive, to serve as president. The Continental League eventually dissolved when the majors agreed to absorb four of its franchises. Thus Houston and New York were slated to begin National League play in 1962.

To find backers for the New York entry in the Continental League, Shea had turned to wealthy Long Islander Dwight F. ''Pete'' Davis, whose family was responsible for the Davis Cup tennis competition. Davis in turn brought in Mrs. Payson and Mrs. Dorothy J. Killiam, a wealthy Canadian sportswoman and Dodger fan. Each of the three controlled 30 percent of the team, with lesser amounts owned by G. Herbert Walker and William Simpson. Soon Mrs. Payson would buy out her partners, so that she owned 80 percent of the new franchise. She arranged for Grant to look after her interests.

Originally named president of the franchise, Grant became chairman of the board and led a search for someone to take over day-to-day control of the club. He turned to George M. Weiss, who had assembled the great Yankee teams of the 1950s and who had recently been eased out by management. As part of the terms of his ''retirement,'' Weiss was unable to become general manager of another major league team for five years, so instead Grant named Weiss to be president, a move that would not endear the franchise with the Yankees, especially since the Yankees had to continue to pay a man who was now trying to compete for their fans. The Yankees also were not pleased with the announcement that their ex-manager, Casey Stengel, would manage the new club. As colorful a figure in all of baseball, the 72-year-old Stengel was a sportswriter's delight and virtually guaranteed press attention.

Everything about the club, in fact, was big news, worth backpage spreads in the city's tabloids, especially the selection of a nickname for the club. Sportswriters were invited by Mrs. Payson to a cocktail party at her Manhattan apartment to select the ten finalists in a nickname contest. They chose: Continentals, Skyliners, Mets, Jets, Meadowlarks, Burros, Skyscrapers, Rebels, NYBs, and Avengers. Although Mrs. Payson preferred the Meadowlarks, the fans chose Mets, with Skyliners a close second.

More important than picking a name, however, was finding a place to play in 1962 and signing players to fill the roster. It would take two years for the new Queens ballpark to be completed, and the Yankees refused to share Yankee Stadium. The only option was the decrepit Polo Grounds. Weiss lured away another Yankee employee, James K. Thomson, who had been stadium manager at both Ebbets Field and Yankee Stadium, to restore the old grounds to playing condition. Many of the players made available to the Houston Colt .45s and New York Mets were reclamation projects of their own. After seeing the names in the expansion pool, Houston almost boycotted the draft. The Mets opted for former Dodger and Giant players who were more likely to help at the gate than build a foundation for long-term success. The result would be years of futility, but successful futility. The Amazing Mets, as Stengel called his team, would perfect the role of lovable losers and within three years would outpace the Yankees in attendance.

Much of the spike in attendance was a result of the 1964 opening of Shea Stadium, which at the behest of Mayor Wagner had been named after the attorney who was instrumental in bringing the National League back to New York. Shea Stadium cost $20 million to build and seated 55,300 for baseball and 60,000 for football. Although the Mets shared the facility with the New York Jets football team, baseball took precedence.

After years of poor results, the Mets began a rapid climb to respectability in the late 1960s, proving especially adept at developing young pitching talent. In 1969 the ''Miracle Mets'' would climb from the bottom of the standings the previous season to win the National League pennant, then upset the highly favored Baltimore Orioles to win the franchise's first World Series. The Mets would make a second Series appearance in 1973, but would lose the championship to the Oakland Athletics. For the next dozen seasons the team would not seriously challenge for the pennant, finishing last in its division as often than not. In the mid-1970s baseball was undergoing a revolution. After years of suppressed salaries, due to restrictive contracts, players won the right to negotiate with clubs for their services through free agency. The Yankees embraced the new system and bought high-priced talent that would bring two more World Series championships to the Bronx. Despite the advantage of playing in a big market, however, the Mets only made token efforts at signing free agents.

The Mets also underwent a change in ownership. In 1975 Mrs. Payson died and control of the club passed to her husband, Charles Shipman Payson, who had little interest in baseball and turned the team over to a daughter, Mrs. Lorinda de Roulet, who was named president of the Mets. Granddaughters Bebe and Whitney de Roulet also would become involved in the management of the team, but essentially Grant continued to make the major decisions. Hopelessly out of step with the changes in the game, however, the Mets struggled on the field and saw attendance steadily decline. Finally Grant was forced out, and in January 1979 Mrs. de Roulet became the first woman owner to be directly involved in the running of a major league baseball team when she was named the club's new chairman of the board. The Mets made gestures at playing the free agent game, but little came of it. The team barely escaped finishing in last place for the third straight season and saw attendance plunge to an all-time low of 788,905. The newspapers began to report rumors of investors groups that were looking to buy the team. Then on November 19, 1979, Mrs. de Roulet and her family announced that they were selling the Mets and that a three-person committee would screen the bids.

New Ownership in 1980

Over the course of the next two months some 20 rival groups bid against one another for the right to own a team that had become a chronic loser of both games and money. The Mets' greatest asset was the city in which it played. In the end the team would fetch a record $21.3 million, 25 percent more than any previous sale of a major league franchise. The new owners were Fred Wilpon, a real estate developer, and Nelson Doubleday, Jr., of the family-owned Doubleday publishing house, plus a coalition of minority shareholders. It was the inclusion of Doubleday when the auction was already under way that gave Wilpon the edge in buying the Mets. Although Doubleday controlled 80 percent of the club, Wilpon, who owned ten percent, would run the daily affairs of the team.

To revive the fortunes of the Mets, Frank Cashen was hired as executive vice-president and general manager. He had spent ten years in the front office of the highly successful Baltimore Orioles, and another three as administrator of baseball for Commissioner of Baseball Bowie Kuhn. Cashen patiently rebuilt the Mets, developing young players, trading wisely, and judiciously adding free agent talent. After finishing last in their division in 1982 and 1983, the Mets finished second in 1984 and 1985. In 1986 the team would win its division, as well as the National League pennant, then defeat the Boston Red Sox in the World Series to earn the second championship in franchise history.

The Mets of the late 1980s were the top team in New York. With the financial clout that comes with playing in a large market, the club also looked as if it was poised to dominate all of baseball for the foreseeable future. Injuries, off-field controversies, and free agent signings that did not pan out, however, would lead to another stretch of frustrating results. A chronicle of the Mets' 1992 season would be titled, *The Worst Team Money Could Buy.* The Yankees, meanwhile, were building a new dynasty, and the Orioles were building Oriole Park at Camden Yards, a retro-ballpark that was ushering in a new era of enhanced revenues for those franchises that could entice local governments to build new facilities that produced entire seasons of soldout games and additional income from luxury suites.

Cashen restored the talent level of the Mets in the mid-1990s. In 1997 the team would enjoy its best season in seven years. Also in October 1997 the team announced plans to build a new stadium, an idea that had been floated for a decade. This ballpark, to be built a mere 100 feet from Shea, would be a 40,000-seat tribute to Ebbets Field, but with a retractable roof and the requisite luxury boxes. The cost, most of which would be picked up by city taxpayers, was estimated to be $450 million. The facility would be ready for opening day, April 2001.

But by the fall of 2000 the Mets were no closer to having a new stadium than they were in 1997, although the team on the field was vastly improved. The Mets won the National League pennant and made the club's first appearance in the World Series in 14 years. It also would be the first ''subway series'' in a generation, as the two New York baseball teams would meet for the first time in postseason play. It would be the Yankees who would prevail, taking their third World Series in a row, but the Mets and their hefty payroll looked prepared to remain a stiff challenge for years to come.

Whereas *Forbes* estimated in 1998 that the Yankees were the most valuable franchise in Major League Baseball, the Mets ranked only 12th. Every team above them by 2001 was playing in new stadiums, with the exception of the Yankees. For the Mets to realize the potential worth of the franchise, the question of Shea Stadium had to be addressed. During the 2000 World Series, Wilpon was once again sounding hopeful about building a new ballpark that could be ready for play in 2004. Shea, under Wilpon's plan, could be converted into a football-only stadium.

Mets co-owner Doubleday, however, stated a preference for rebuilding Shea, at much less expense than the $700 million to $1 billion it was now estimated to cost for a new stadium. With the Yankees and other area sports teams also seeking government assistance in building new facilities, the future of the Mets' hopes for a new home, and the enhanced wealth that came with it, was far from certain.

Principal Competitors

Atlanta National League Baseball Club, Inc.; YankeeNets L.L.C.; The Philadelphia Phillies.

Further Reading

Bock, Duncan, and John Jordan, *The Complete Year-by-Year N.Y. Mets Fan's Almanac,* New York: Crown, 1992.

Botte, Peter, ''Doubleday Would Rather Rebuild Than Build,'' *Daily News,* October 25, 2000.

Caro, Robert, *The Power Broker: Robert Moses and the Fall of New York,* New York: Vintage Books, 1975.

Frommer, Harvey, *New York City Baseball: The Last Golden Age, 1947–1957,* San Diego: Harcourt Brace Jovanovich, 1992.

Honig, Donald, *The New York Mets: The First Quarter Century,* New York: Crown, 1987.

Klapisch, Bob, and John Harper, *The Worst Team Money Could Buy,* New York: Random House, 1993.

Lang, Jack Frederick, *The New York Mets: Twenty-Five Years of Baseball Magic,* New York: H. Holt, 1987.

''Reports Say Shea's Days Are Numbered,'' *St. Louis Post-Dispatch,* April 22, 1993, p. 3D.

Sullivan, Neil J., *The Dodgers Move West,* New York: Oxford University Press, 1987.

Thorn, John et al., *Total Baseball,* Kingston, N.Y.: Total Sports, 1999.

—Ed Dinger

Mikohn Gaming Corporation

920 Palms Airport Drive
Las Vegas, Nevada 89119
U.S.A.
Telephone: (702) 896-3890
Toll Free: (800) 336-8449
Fax: (702) 896-2461
Web site: http://www.mikohn.com

Public Company
Incorporated: 1986 as Mikohn Inc.
Employees: 822 (1999)
Sales: $106.9 million (1999)
Stock Exchanges: NASDAQ
Ticker Symbol: MIKNE
NAIC: 339999 All Other Miscellaneous Manufacturing;
   713290 Other Gambling Industries

Mikohn Gaming Corporation designs, manufactures, and distributes a variety of casino games, gaming jackpot and tracking systems, and interior and exterior signage for the casino industry. Mikohn's products include several table games, such as Caribbean Stud and Progressive Blackjack, as well as branded table games and slot machines based on Hasbro board and dice games, including Monopoly and Yahtzee. The company is also an industry leader in the design of interior displays, for stand-alone games or for clusters of progressive jackpot games in casinos. Mikohn holds gaming licenses for over 150 gambling jurisdictions worldwide.

1980s Origins

Mikohn Gaming, originally incorporated as Mikohn Inc. in 1986, pioneered the technology for "progressive jackpot systems" used by casinos for managing clusters of slot machines and other gaming machines. The software Mikohn developed allowed casino managers to determine the amount of a jackpot and frequency of payoff based on player participation at connected machines. Moreover, signage utilizing light-emitting diodes (LED) displayed the current jackpot amount, while at-tracting consumer attention with flashing, traveling, and other types of moving displays, as well as animated and graphic displays of red, green, and yellow lights. The company's Mystery Jackpot software set jackpots based on a schedule, while Bonus Jackpot software allowed for random jackpots in addition to the regular payout.

After five years in business the company was reporting a profit of $54,324 on $5.8 million in revenues. By November 1993 Mikohn was prepared to go public, with an initial offering of three million shares offered at $15 per share. Under the leadership of David J. Thompson, named president and CEO of the company in 1988, Mikohn used the proceeds from the offering, some $40 million, to support continuing research and development, to fund capital expenditures, to pay debt, and for strategic acquisitions.

Through acquisition Mikohn hoped to integrate game technology development with sign and lighting operations to create new progressive gaming machines with spectacular visual displays that would attract attention in an already active casino environment. Toward that end, the company acquired Current Technology Systems, another jackpot systems manufacturer, as well as three large distributors, Casino Signs in Las Vegas, and Casino Signs Pty Ltd. and Club Casino Products Pty Ltd., both based in Sydney, Australia. For the November 1994 acquisition of John Renton Young Lighting & Sign, Mikohn paid $4 million and stock, plus 90 percent of the appraised real estate value of facilities in Nevada, New Jersey, and Mississippi. Young Lighting designed and installed both interior and exterior lighting systems and signs for the gaming industry. Acquisitions increased revenues at Mikohn to $57 million in 1994, while the company's net income reached $6.4 million.

Next, CEO Thompson prepared to take Mikohn global, suppling the international market for its products by establishing sales offices and manufacturing facilities abroad. The acquisitions of Casino Signs and Club Casino Products had given Mikohn a foothold in Australia, and the company expanded and upgraded facilities there. Mikohn also opened a sales office in Amsterdam, Mikohn Europe, BV, and completed construction on a sign manufacturing and assembly plant there in 1995. Mikohn formed a joint venture, Mikohn South America, S.A., and opened a 60,000 square foot plant in Lima, Peru. In 1996 the company opened a sales and service office in Buenos Aires, Argentina.

Mikohn's strategy for growth and development during this time involved obtaining exclusive rights to distribute certain casino games or gaming-related technology. In 1994 Mikohn acquired the rights to CasinoLink, an accounting and player-tracking system. CasinoLink assisted casino managers in the design of promotions (such as rewarding customers for game play recorded on player identification cards), discerning maintenance needs, and serving as a form of security and identification for customer credit. The system debuted in two casinos in Las Vegas in early 1995.

Mikohn acquired the exclusive rights to distribute the Caribbean Stud poker game which used progressive jackpot controllers and displays. The company also purchased the patent rights of the ''Flip-It'' coin-pusher slot games for $1.5 million. Assets included an inventory of 200 machines already in place at 50 casinos throughout Nevada. Mikohn next obtained approval to install Flip-It slots in casinos in Mississippi as well.

Mikohn's product development began to focus on security-related technology and acquisitions. In September 1994 Mikohn acquired TransSierra Communications, provider of security, surveillance, and communications to the gaming industry. In 1995 Mikohn acquired the rights to manufacture, market, and distribute SafeJack, which incorporated surveillance technology into Black Jack game tables. SafeJack provided a small monitor which displayed the play of the table to the dealer. A camera read each card as dealt and indicated a winning hand on the monitor by flashing a light near that hand. Bally's Hotel & Casino in Las Vegas tested the product before Mikohn obtained regulatory approval from the Nevada Gaming Control Board in 1996. Mikohn also acquired the rights to develop, manufacture, and market TableLink, a player tracking system for table games.

In 1995 Casino Excitement, Inc., Mikohn's sign and lighting subsidiary, introduced its MikohnVision sign technology, a low-voltage, low-energy-use display. Designed to provide attention-getting signage for the casino industry, MikohnVision furnished bright, vivid lighting for real time wording changes, graphics, animation, and video clips in 16.5 million colors. The company installed the first MikohnVision sign at Players Island Resort, Spa, and Casino in Mesquite, Nevada. The company's national recognition received a boost when conglomerate ITT Corporation ordered a MikohnVision display for placement in New York's Times Square. In Las Vegas the Stratosphere Tower and the Sahara Hotel and Casino installed MikohnVision signs in 1996 and 1997, respectively.

Legalized Gaming in the Mid-1990s

Approval of legalized gambling throughout the United States in the mid-1990s expanded the potential market for Mikohn's products. Gaming legislation passed in Mississippi in 1994 and for riverboat gambling in the Midwest in 1995 and 1996. Several new casinos opened on Native American reservations in 1996 and 1997. In anticipation of new business Mikohn expanded its manufacturing facility in Gulfport, Mississippi, in 1995. The construction project more than doubled the plant's size, from 12,000 square feet to 30,000 square feet.

As its facilities and holdings grew, Mikohn also embarked on a restructuring program, consolidating some administrative, manufacturing, and distribution positions, closing some facilities in Nevada, Missouri, and Mississippi, and discontinuing production of older products. These changes reduced the Mikohn work force by 16 percent and reduced annual payroll by $5 million. Mikohn experienced a loss of $6.5 million in 1995, which it attributed to writeoffs related to restructuring. While 1996 revenues reached $91.4 million, research and development costs for SafeJack, MikohnVision, CasinoLink and new slot machine products resulted in a net profit of only $612,000.

In 1996 Mikohn introduced its new SuperLink technology, which provided casino managers with real time data on individual slot machines, clusters of machines, or small groups of progressive slots scattered throughout the casino floor. The first SuperLink installation occurred at Monte Carlo Resort & Casino on the Las Vegas Strip. Mikohn also won a $4.5 million contract to provide SuperLink and jackpot systems, as well as casino signs, for the new Station Casino in Kansas City. The Mohegan Sun casino and resort, on the Mohegan Indian reservation in Connecticut, held its grand opening in October 1996 and contracted for Mikohn's new SuperLink progressive jackpot system as well as signage and graphics displays. A $2.4 million contract with Horseshoe Gaming LLC in 1997 included the SuperLink progressive jackpot system as well as signage and graphics displays at its casino in Robinsonville, Mississippi.

Both CasinoLink and SuperLink proved popular. Canadian gaming businesses took a strong interest in CasinoLink, and Mikohn signed a $1.8 million contract with the British Columbia Lottery Corporation for management of slot machines at existing charitable gaming operations. Several casinos in Australia and Europe also installed the CasinoLink system, including multi-site monitoring from a central location. Holland Casino used CasinoLink to monitor slot machines at ten locales throughout The Netherlands from one central location.

Continuing to focus on new technologies, the company introduced its patented MoneyTime slot bonus jackpot system. MoneyTime was designed to create further excitement on the casino floor by generating random, surprise jackpots, apart from the normal slot payouts. The MoneyTime system operated through linked machines in limited areas, and machines were distinguished by special themes, flashing lights, music, and sound effects when a player won the jackpot. By April 1998, Mikohn had connected MoneyTime software to 478 machines in 11 casinos in Nevada, New Mexico, Mississippi, and Connecticut. MoneyTime, along with SafeJack, was named among the top 20 innovative products or services by *Casino Journal* for 1998.

```
┌─────────────────────────────────────────────────┐
│              Key Dates:                          │
│                                                  │
│ 1986:  Company is founded.                       │
│ 1993:  Mikohn goes public on the NASDAQ exchange.│
│ 1994:  The CasinoLink accounting and player      │
│        tracking system is introduced.            │
│ 1996:  MikohnVision display is installed at New  │
│        York's Times Square.                      │
│ 1998:  Mikohn acquires Progressive Games and its │
│        proprietary Caribbean Stud table game.    │
│ 1999:  Company begins development of table games │
│        and slots based on popular Hasbro games.  │
└─────────────────────────────────────────────────┘
```

Mikohn planned to expand its capacity to combine casino gaming and surveillance technologies with the purchase of Progressive Games, Inc. (PGI) for $35 million cash. PGI's proprietary game, Caribbean Stud poker, was a popular product, allowing players to place a side bet on the progressive jackpot; a player with a flush or higher won from the jackpot. PGI obtained most of its revenues from game licensing, with Caribbean Stud available in over 300 casinos worldwide. Licensing revenues in 1997 reached $11.5 million, while the sale of game equipment garnered $1 million. Through Mikohn's purchase of PGI, which would become Mikohn's Progressive Game Division, Caribbean Stud machine placement increased by eight percent; 80 new orders for the game were placed within a month of completion of the acquisition in September 1998. Mikohn also purchased two distributors of Caribbean Stud, P&S Leasing Corp. in Mississippi, and P&S Leasing LLC in Louisiana.

Mikohn's game security technology was enhanced through a joint development with Harrah's Entertainment. Mikohn purchased the U.S. rights to Harrah's Total Track player tracking and accounting technology and then combined the technology with its own SafeGames technology. Mikohn and Harrah's planned to install the technology at up to 100 tables at Harrah's casinos nationwide.

While the market for gaming equipment stalled in 1998, large-scale casino development in Las Vegas offset the effects, and Mikohn won several large lighting and sign contracts. A $1 million contract with the Aladdin Casino and Hotel on the Las Vegas Strip involved the use of MikohnVision on a double-sided sign some 50 feet high and 37 feet wide to attract attention during and after reconstruction of the facility. A $3 million contract with the Mirage Resorts' new Bellagio Hotel and Casino resulted in an even larger Mikohn sign, 200 feet high and 85 feet wide. The contract also included 250 minor directional signs for areas outside the casino floor and 280 casino signs. Completed in late 1998, the signs were designed by Mikohn to complement the casino's Italian styling.

Mikohn also provided signage and equipment to the new Mandalay Bay Resort & Casino, which opened in spring 1999. In addition to Mikohn's Colossus and Mini Bertha sign machines, Mandalay ordered oversized slot machines, which Mikohn manufactured through an exclusive license with International Game Technology.

Sales of Mikohn's CasinoLink system, particularly as a supplementary system to existing gaming infrastructure, continued strong in the late 1990s, particularly in Canada. Moreover, the company's CasinoLink contract with Casino Municipale di Venezia in Italy proved important to Mikohn's European operations, due to its prominence in a central location.

New Design Opportunities in the Late 1990s

Mikohn gained its most comprehensive design opportunity through a $1.8 million contract with the renowned City Tattersall's Club in Sydney, Australia. Tattersall's gave Mikohn complete creative freedom to design a casino room as well as to design and manufacture the slot machines for it. Mikohn went with a Mardi Gras in Rio de Janeiro theme. Adapting the latest technology, fixtures included 15 animatronic characters which spoke to one another as well as to passers by; sound effects, dancing, and detailed movements enhanced the display. Mikohn completed the project in December 1999.

Mikohn launched two new poker games, Wild Aruba Stud, a poker game with deuces wild, and Tre' Card Stud, a three-card stud poker game. Both games offered progressive jackpots for side bets, which added to the excitement. The games debuted at the Grand Casinos in Biloxi, Gulfport, and Tunica in late 1999 and in Las Vegas in early 2000. Mikohn also installed its first "electronic pit" at the Grand Casino in Biloxi. The game pit included eight Progressive Black Jack tables, two Tre' Card Stud tables, and two Monopoly Poker Edition tables, all linked to three progressive jackpots.

The late 1990s also saw Mikohn's entrance into developing and distributing several new casino games based on popular board and dice games through an exclusive license agreement with Hasbro, Inc. Monopoly Poker Edition, the first branded specialty table game, allowed players to win up to 125 times a bet by matching railroad, utility, house or hotel property cards dealt from a deck of 50 cards. Community Chest and Chance cards acted as wild cards, while token cards, such as the iron, the hat, etc., gave the player a no-lose pass if the card matched the player's betting spot. Players had the option for an extra side bet of one dollar for the progressive jackpot. In addition to installing the game in Biloxi, Mikohn conducted field tests at Circus Circus in Las Vegas as part of the approval process in Nevada.

Mikohn also developed slot machines and a poker-style table game based on Hasbro's Yahtzee dice game. The table game used five oversized electromechanical dice and allowed for two rerolls. Players tried to match the numbers on the dice, with five of a kind—Yahtzee—being the big winner. The Yahtzee series of slot games included Yahtzee Bonus, Yahtzee Take a Chance, and Yahtzee Video. By October 2000 the company had contracts for 2,000 of the slot machines and had installed 1,500 machines.

Also in October 2000, Mikohn began distribution of a slot game based on Hasbro's Battleship game, the Battleship All Aboard Slot video game. The game incorporated strategy and skill elements, allowing a player eight chances to fire missiles at ships positioned on a grid similar to that of the original Hasbro game. *Casino Journal* placed the Battleship All Aboard Slot video game among the top 20 innovative gaming/service products for 2001. Mikohn next began to develop slot games based on Ripley's Believe It or Not! and Hasbro's Clue, a murder mystery board game.

Passage of a bill allowing gambling on Native American reservations in California provided a new outlet for Mikohn's products. Soon thereafter, the Barona Casino near San Diego signed a $1 million equipment contract with Mikohn calling for ten Mini Bertha slot machines and electronics and visual displays. By October Mikohn had contracts with 16 casinos for 344 proprietary games, including new branded slots and progressive table games.

Mikohn introduced the TableLink player-tracking and accounting system in 2000. Similar to CasinoLink and SuperLink, TableLink was the first tracking system designed for such table games as blackjack, draw poker, and *pai gow* poker. Using a computer microchip, embedded in each gaming chip, which transmitted radio signals, TableLink's capabilities included automated bet recognition and calculation of win/loss per player. TableLink was installed at Harrah's in Tunica, Mississippi; the Motor City Casino in Detroit; Casino de Genting in Malaysia; and Crown Casinos in Australia.

Despite declines in net income in 2000, largely attributed to start-up expenses associated with its new LED technology for video displays such as that installed in Times Square, Mikohn management remained optimistic. Specifically, CEO Thompson cited strong sales (as demand for its Yahtzee and Battleship casino games in particular continued to grow) and the increasing potential for sales growth in California.

Principal Subsidiaries

Casino Excitement, Inc.; MCG, Inc.; Mikohn Australasia Pty., Ltd (50%); Mikohn Europe, B.V.; Mikohn International, Inc.; Mikohn Nevada Progressive Games, Inc.; Mikohn South America, S.A. (50%); TransSierra Communications.

Principal Divisions

Mikohn Games; Mikohn Systems.

Principal Competitors

Alliance Gaming Corporation; International Game Technology; Anchor Gaming.

Further Reading

Busby, Charles, ''Mikohn Gaming Corp. Starts Work on Southeast Expansion,'' *Sun Herald,* February 23, 1995, p. 1995.
——, ''More Observations from the World Gaming Congress & Expo in Las Vegas,'' *Sun Herald,* October 29, 1995.
Edwards, John G., ''Casino Data Profits Down; Mikohn Gaming Shows Loss,'' *Las Vegas Review-Journal,* November 1, 1995, p. 9E.
''Harrah's, Mikohn Ink Deal,'' *International Gaming and Wagering Business,* July 1998, p. 16.
''Mikohn Gaming Corp. Completes Restructuring Program,'' *S&P Daily News,* October 31, 1995.
''Mikohn Gaming Corp. Enters Agreement to Acquire Designers, Installers of Lighting Systems,'' *S&P Daily News,* June 30, 1994.
''Mikohn Gaming Corp. Reaches Agreement to Acquire Casino Signs in Sydney, Australia,'' *S&P Daily News,* December 14, 1993.
''Mikohn Gaming Corp. Registers for Initial Public Offering,'' *S&P Daily News,* November 2, 1993.
''Mikohn is Expecting to Report 90% Jump in 4th Quarter Net,'' *Wall Street Journal,* February 17, 1995, p. B4.
''Mikohn's Income Drops,'' *Las Vegas Review-Journal,* November 11, 2000, p. 3D.
Simpson, Jeff, ''Mikohn Predicts Rosier Numbers,'' *Las Vegas Review-Journal,* April 26, 2000, p. 7D.
''Technology for the Future,'' *International Gaming & Wagering Business,* 1996, p. 207.

—Mary Tradii

Mississippi Chemical Corporation

3622 Highway 49 East
P.O. Box 388
Yazoo City, Mississippi 39194-0388
U.S.A.
Telephone: (662) 746-4131
Fax: (662) 746-9158
Web site: http://www.misschem.com

Public Company
Founded: 1948
Employees: 1,514
Sales: $485.2 million (2000)
Stock Exchanges: New York
Ticker Symbol: GRO
NAIC: 325311 Nitrogenous Fertilizer Manufacturing;
    325312 Phosphatic Fertilizer Manufacturing; 325188
    All Other Basic Inorganic Chemical Manufacturing;
    32512 Industrial Gas Manufacturing; 325998 All
    Other Miscellaneous Chemical Product and
    Preparation Manufacturing

Although it was originally formed as a farmers' cooperative, Mississippi Chemical Corporation is now a multi-million dollar public corporation traded on the New York Stock Exchange. Its home is Yazoo City, Mississippi, located between the hills of the central part of the State and its southern, soggy-bottom Delta area. Through its subsidiaries, the company produces and markets the three essential crop fertilizers necessary for high-yield agriculture: nitrogen, phosphorus, and potassium (potash). Its principal, wholly-owned subsidiaries are MissChem Nitrogen, L.L.C., which produces nitrogen products in Yazoo City; Triad Nitrogen, L.L.C., which manufactures nitrogen in Donaldsonville, Louisiana; Mississippi Potash, Inc., which produces potash fertilizer at its two mines and refineries in Carlsbad, New Mexico; and Mississippi Phosphates Corporation, which makes phosphate fertilizer in Pascagoula, Mississippi. Mississippi Chemical also has a stake in Farmland MissChem Limited, a joint-venture producer of ammonia, a nitrogen fertilizer, in the Republic of Trinidad and Tobago. In addition to fertilizers, Mississippi Chemical makes and distrib-

utes industrial-market products. Its anhydrous ammonia, carbon dioxide, nitric acid and standard potash products are all employed in industrial applications, including such end products as acrylics, adhesives, animal feed, carpet fibers, melamine, polymers, resins, rocket fuels, and water treatment chemicals.

1947–51: Origins as a Farmers' Cooperative

In the wake of World War II, both a booming economy and a population surge in the United States created a significant shortage of fertilizers, particularly nitrogen products. By the end of the hostilities, because nitrogen had been used in the manufacture of bombs and ammunition, reserves in both the United States and Europe were almost completely depleted. American farmers desperately needed nitrogen to achieve maximum yields from the limited acreage the federal government permitted them to plant. In 1947, under the leadership of Owen Cooper, director of the Mississippi Farm Bureau, a group of about 600 farmers urged the board of the Farm Bureau to study the feasibility of creating a farmer-owned nitrogen fertilizer plant.

After approving the project, a Farm Bureau board committee initiated the most extensive stock sales drive in Mississippi's history, a necessary step in financing the plant's construction. The goal was to raise $4 million. Meanwhile, confident that the necessary funds would be raised, on October 27, 1948, farmers and farm leaders from six southern states formally organized and chartered Mississippi Chemical as a cooperative and, in November, hired Cooper as CEO and president. The new 22-member board selected Yazoo City as the site for the new plant.

The $4 million target was not reached, but by the end of the drive in 1949, some 7,000 Southern farmers had bought $3.25 million worth of stock, or about 81% of the goal. The shortfall was made up by a $750,000 bond issue approved for Mississippi Chemical by Yazoo County voters. However, before construction could begin, the company had to secure a $3.4 million loan from the U.S. Reconstruction Finance Corporation. The loan was approved in February, 1950, and construction of the Yazoo City facility began.

The facility was completed in 1951, making Mississippi Chemical the world's first cooperative to build a nitrogen production plant. By March of that year, the company had pro-

Company Perspectives:

Mississippi Chemical Corporation has fostered a culture that is best described as doing the right thing. A strong commitment to workplace safety, environmental stewardship and a commitment to do what we'll say we'll do are also part of the company-wide ethic. This well-established corporate culture may be our most important export.

duced its first ton of ammonium nitrate fertilizer and, by the following July, had made its first ton of ammonia. The first products were made using outside sources of ammonia, but in order to produce final fertilizer products economically, two manufacturing facilities were needed: a nitric acid plant and an anhydrous ammonium plant. In tandem, these would provide the fertilizer ingredients without reliance on outside providers. The ammonia plant offered some problems, but by the summer of 1951 it was online, and before the year was out, the company had sold 41,000 tons of ammonium nitrate and 10,000 tons of ammonia to its farmer-shareholders.

1952–72: Growth Under the Leadership of Cooper

After getting the first nitrogen and ammonia production plants on line in 1951, Mississippi Chemical set out both to expand and to diversify. Guided by Cooper, the company undertook some investment ventures and initiated some new projects.

Most importantly, between 1952 and 1972, the company set up a network of delivery terminals across the South. It also increased its output of chemicals, building new plants, notably the $12 million Kellogg ammonia plant built at Yazoo City in 1966. In that same year, Cooper and LeRoy Percy formed Mississippi Action for Progress, the first-of-its-kind partnership of black and white businessmen. Two years later, in 1968, the company completed its new headquarters building in Yazoo City.

In 1970, Mississippi Chemical and First Mississippi Corporation entered into a joint venture, starting up Triad Chemicals Inc., with each partner owning a 50 percent share. The two parties had historic links, for it was the same group of Mississippi businessmen that had helped start Mississippi Chemical in 1948 that founded First Mississippi Corporation in 1957. Triad, a $40 million nitrogen urea complex located in Donaldsonville, Louisiana, soon began producing nitrogen fertilizers.

Two years later, in 1972, the company put into operation its Pascagoula, Mississippi, double-contact sulfuric acid plant—the world's largest at the time. Its output, plus that of the complex at Donaldsonville, helped Mississippi Chemical reach a significant milestone in that same year: combined sales topped $100 million for the first time in the company's history.

1973–93: Growth and Diversification under New Leadership

In 1973, Owen Cooper stepped down, leaving his positions as president and CEO to Thomas C. Parry. Prospects at that juncture, the company's 25th anniversary, looked good. Parry and Mississippi Governor Bill Waller announced plans for a

$43 million expansion program geared to increase the annual nitrate production in Yazoo City by 150,000 tons (up to 555,000 tons) and the annual NPK (nitrogen/phosphorous/potassium) output of the plant in Pascagoula by 200,000 tons (up to one million tons). Much of the expense involved arose from mandatory compliance with new EPA air and water standards. Among other things, the company had to build a waste water treatment plant at Pascagoula, which, when completed in 1976, had cost Mississippi Chemical $22 million.

In was also in 1973 that Mississippi Chemical adopted its new slogan: "We Make Things Grow." It could have appended the words, "including us," at least in the next year, when, for $20 million, it purchased the nation's oldest and largest potash reserve and mine, located in Carlsbad, New Mexico. It followed that up in 1975 with the purchase of some large phosphate rock deposits near Wauchula, Florida. Both these acquisitions reflected the company's policy of buying reserves of raw materials for use in future fertilizer production.

By 1978, the combined operations of Mississippi Chemical's plants reached a 2.5 million ton capacity mark, 30 times the amount that its first plant in Yazoo City could produce in 1951. The value of its assets had also climbed from the company's original $10 million capitalization to $350 million. Two years later, in the 1980–81 period, the company reached the most successful stretch in its history, with revenues of $395 million and patronage earnings of $53.6 million. Thereafter, though, the company entered a difficult period.

The mid-1980s were tough on the fertilizer industry in general. By 1986, when Owen Cooper died, there was a farmer debt crisis that was cutting deeply into fertilizer demands. In addition, much cheaper fertilizer produced in the crumbling Soviet Union was driving market prices down to unprofitable levels.

Mississippi Chemical's worst year was 1987, when it lost over $40 million. The bottom-line realities forced Parry to downsize the company. He ordered the lay off of hundreds of employees, closed the large Pascagoula, Mississippi plant, and dropped company plans for phosphate mining in Florida. Because Mississippi Chemical too easily fell prey to the vicissitudes of unstable commodity trading, Parry also sought to diversify the company's interests. Accordingly, in 1986 the company entered the newsprint business, opening Newsprint South in Grenada, Mississippi, a Mississippi Chemical subsidiary, and in 1987 began construction of its state-of-the-art newsprint mill.

Conditions improved somewhat at the beginning of the 1990s. Demands for nitrogen and potash increased, again reaching profitable levels. At that time, Mississippi Chemical was able to reopen its Pascagoula facility. Its newsprint business was struggling, however, and, in 1994, the year after Parry retired as president, the company sold it.

1994 and Beyond: Going Public and Facing Challenges

Parry was succeeded by Charles O. Dunn as the company's president and CEO. One of Dunn's first tasks was to oversee the transition of Mississippi Chemical from a farmer-owned cooperative into a public company. The conversion was made in

Key Dates:

1948: Mississippi Chemical Corporation is organized as a farmers' cooperative under the leadership of Owen Cooper.

1950: Company becomes first cooperative in the world to build its own nitrogen fertilizer plant.

1966: Mississippi Chemical completes construction of high-tech ammonia plant in Yazoo City.

1970: Company enters joint venture with First Mississippi Corporation, establishing Triad Chemicals Inc.

1972: Company's annual sales climb over $100 million for the first time; double-contract sulfuric acid plant starts production in Pascagoula.

1973: Cooper retires and is succeeded by Thomas C. Parry.

1986: Founder Owen Cooper dies; subsidiary, Newsprint South, Inc., is formed.

1987: Company begins construction of Newsprint South's state-of-the-art newsprint mill.

1993: Parry retires and is succeed by Charles O. Dunn as CEO and president.

1994: Mississippi Chemical is reorganized as a publicly held company and begins trading on NASDAQ; company sells Newsprint South.

1996: Company begins trading on the New York Stock Exchange; buys two potash mines in New Mexico.

1998: Company starts up joint venture with Farmland Industries, Inc., an ammonia manufacturing plant in Trinidad and Tobago.

2000: Company buys IMC-Agrico Company's granular urea plant in Faustina, Louisiana.

August 1994, when the company made its initial public offering of stock, selling five million shares for a total of about $75 million. Initially the stock was listed on NASDAQ, but in 1996 it switched over to the New York Stock Exchange.

It was also in 1996 that the company began a $130 million expansion of its nitrogen fertilizer plant in Yazoo City and acquired Eddy Potash and New Mexico Potash from Trans-Resources of New York. Both acquisitions were potash mining operations in the same area of New Mexico. In an effort to increase its profits from the operation, Mississippi Chemical altered its plans for Eddy Potash. The company concentrated all of Eddy's mining activity on recovering high-grade potash, a move that accelerated the mine's depletion. As a result, the next year, facing declining profits, the company shut down Eddy's mining operations altogether.

Also in 1996, the company entered into an agreement with First Mississippi Corporation to purchase First Mississippi's fertilizer operations. The deal was designed as a tax-free "Morris Trust" transaction that occurred in two stages: first, the chemical operations of First Mississippi would be spun-off to shareholders as a publicly traded company; second, the remaining fertilizer assets of First Mississippi would merge with Mississippi Chemical. The total price tag in stock and cash would come to about $300 million. The sale was completed in

1997, the year in which Mississippi Chemical also announced the planned expansion of its Pascagoula facility, with the projected rise in its annual diammonium phosphate output to 900,000 tons. In the next year, 1998, in a joint undertaking with Farmland Industries, Inc., Mississippi Chemical began production at its 1,850 metric ton per day ammonia plant in the Republic of Trinidad and Tobago, its first venture outside the United States.

However, the company had to face some serious problems towards the end of the decade, including a natural disaster. In 1998, Hurricane George, causing extensive damage, forced the closing of the company's Pascagoula phosphate plant for several weeks, a shutdown that resulted in a net loss of almost $1 million. Still, the biggest problems were increasing production costs at a time when market demands were declining and surpluses were mounting, threatening a glut and driving prices down. The situation was fairly grim in 1999 and 2000, and the company had little choice but to resort to curtailed production and temporary shutdowns. Ammonia prices in 1999 dropped 25 percent below the previous year, and fertilizer consumption by mid summer had slid five percent below the demand at the start of the year. In August, Mississippi Chemical responded by cutting back production at its Triad Nitrogen number-two ammonia plant in Donaldsonville. In 2000, the company also reduced production at its number-three ammonia plant in Yazoo City and shutdown production at its number-four plant for an indefinite time.

Despite the market conditions, the company continued to plan for better times. In fact, in April 2000, at an undisclosed price, it bought IMC-Agrico Company's granular urea plant located in Faustina, Louisiana, barely a mile away from Mississippi Chemical's ammonia and urea production facilities in Donaldsonville. The acquisition increased the company's granular urea output capacity to 810,000 tons. The fact that it shut down the operations of the Faustina facility within a couple of months argues that Mississippi Chemical was investing more for the future than the present, hoping for a much improved market in the beginning years of the new century. It faced serious problems, though, one being swelling production costs driven by a tremendous increase in the price of natural gas, its principal fuel. The good news was that the price of natural gas had begun to moderate by March of 2001.

Principal Subsidiaries

MissChem Nitrogen, L.L.C.; Mississippi Phosphates Corporation.; Mississippi Potash, Inc.; Triad Nitrogen, L.L.C.

Principal Competitors

CF Industries, Inc.; Agrium Inc.; IMC Global Inc.; Potash Corporation; Terra Industries Inc.

Further Reading

Adams, Jarret, "Mississippi Chemicals Shuts Ammonia Plant in Ailing Market," *Chemical Week*, July 21, 1999, p. 15.

Friedman, William, and Wiggins, Kevin, "Fertilizer Mergers: The Field Narrows," *Chemical Week*, October 16, 1996, p. 35.

Henry, Brian, "MissChem Acquires FirstMiss' Fertilizers," *Chemical Marketing Reporter*, September 2, 1996, p. 3.

Jones, Kevin, "Newsprint Mill Losses Reaching Critical State," *Mississippi Business Journal*, November 16, 1992, p. 1.

McFarland, Jr., Robert, "Mississippi Chemical Corporation: Making Things Grow for 50 Years," *Delta Business Journal Online*, October 1998.

"1990 Captain of Industry," *Mississippi Business Journal*, August 13, 1990, p. 1.

Prichard, Jo G., *Making Things Grow: The Story of Mississippi Chemical Corporation*, Oxford: University Press of Mississippi, 1998.

Seewald, Nancy, "Terra Settles Suit with Mississippi Chemical," *Chemical Week*, August 16, 2000, p. 12.

—John W. Fiero

Mitsui Mutual Life Insurance Company

1-2-3, Ohtemachi, Chiyoda-ku
Tokyo 100
Japan
Telephone: 813-3211-6111
Fax: 813-3215-1580
Web site: http://www.mitsui-seimei.co.jp

Mutual Company
Incorporated: 1927
Employees: 23,776
Total Assets: $19.43 billion (1998)
NAIC: 524113 Direct Life Insurance Carriers

Among the top life insurers in the world, Mitsui Mutual Life Insurance Company for years also has ranked sixth among its Japanese competitors in premium income, contracts in force, and assets. Along with The Mitsui Trust & Banking Company and Mitsui Marine and Fire Insurance Company, Mitsui Mutual functions in the banking and finance sector of the Mitsui Group, one of Japan's largest and most powerful corporate combinations. Mitsui Mutual maintains close relationships with other members of the Mitsui Group and with its Japanese competitors. Mitsui Mutual's ties to other Japanese insurers are so close that they have sometimes been referred to as a cartel. Severe economic problems in Japan in the 1990s, however, has revealed some serious structural flaws in the industry, as two major insurers collapsed and one other became subject to statutory restrictions. Mitsui Mutual, with its credit rating downgraded, began efforts to convert to a stock form of ownership in order to gain access to capital and maintain solvency.

17th-Century Roots

Launching a company in Japan usually requires some degree of acceptance by the companies already in that field. A new company seeks a niche—a business specialty that it can develop within a group of competitors. Mitsui Mutual has focused on customer service-oriented products from the start, but the company began to change its traditional approach in the 1970s.

During the 1970s and 1980s Mitsui Mutual initiated product and investment changes that expanded its business, notably pioneering international group life insurance. Despite some retrenchment in overseas investment to cope with worldwide and domestic market fluctuations, the indications are that the next decade will see Mitsui Mutual expand further, especially in the European and Southeast Asian markets.

Mitsui Mutual is a relative newcomer among the companies in the Mitsui Group, which dates back to the rise of the merchant class in Japan in the last half of the 17th century. Like other samurai warriors, head of the family Sokubei Mitsui had become a chonin, a merchant, when times changed. He established a soy and sake brewery, which he passed on to his son Takatoshi. Takatoshi Mitsui expanded the business to include a dry goods store named Echigoya in honor of an ancestor, a pawnshop, and a currency exchange that later became a bank. The Mitsui corporate symbol, a circle (the heavens) surrounding a well-frame (the earth), which contains the mitsu (mankind), is said to have been suggested by a dream Takatoshi Mitsui's mother had. The symbol may have seemed grandiose when applied to Echigoya in 1676, but time seems to have borne out this largeness of vision. With the opening of Japan to Western trade, cultural, and business influences in the late 19th century, the Mitsui Group was already firmly established in manufacturing, finance, and other types of enterprises. The Mitsui Bank was a major commercial bank when the Banking Act of 1882 formalized a niche system for the banking industry, creating banks for specific types of business. Major banks, such as the Mitsui Bank, became cores of financial combines known as zaibatsu.

Formation of Mitsui Mutual in 1927

The Mitsui Group had become a powerful springboard for launching new businesses by 1927, when Mitsui Mutual Life came into being. The group's long tradition of successful enterprise was a substantial advantage for a company hoping to win public trust. The tradition of private savings is strong in Japan. By the same token, insurance has been a popular form of savings since the 1890s, when the first modern forms were introduced into Japanese commerce.

Recovery from a post-World War I recession and from the Great Kanto Earthquake of 1923 were well under way in 1927, but the feeling of personal and financial vulnerability remained even as business and industry gained momentum between wars. The market for life insurance grew with the influx of industrial workers into factory towns and retail and other business employees into the cities. It grew even faster as preparations for war progressed in the 1930s.

The niche that Mitsui Mutual realized it could fill was the need for an increased emphasis on individualized types of insurance and customer service. Strict government regulations imposed the same system of premium rates and rates of return on all insurance products. A prospective insurance customer would base a choice not on the prospect of direct financial returns but on such factors as the company's stability, length of service, investment policies, and attention to personal needs.

Although Mitsui Mutual's positioning proved effective in promoting growth, the company, like other Japanese companies, suffered with Japan's defeat in World War II. The prewar Mitsui zaibatsu had been the oldest and largest industrial group in Japan. Its holding company had been owned by 11 households of the Mitsui family, controlling 294 major companies, but not even the powerful Mitsui companies could retain their overseas holdings through war and defeat—and by the war's end their domestic markets were in shambles.

Business began anew after World War II. The zaibatsu were no longer operative; the occupation authorities replaced them with a new, antimonopolistic philosophy that encouraged competition in the market.

The former zaibatsu, however, began efforts to reunite their companies, not as zaibatsu, but as keiretsu—a network of closely associated companies with noncontrolling financial interests in one another. Mitsubishi and Sumitomo were among the first former zaibatsu to develop keiretsu—and the advantage this gave them is evident in their leading positions today. Mitsui lagged behind, in part because of an affinity for the new concept of opportunity for individual companies to compete and in part because of the reluctance of some of its larger companies to rejoin. Toshiba, for example, formerly a member company, decided to form its own keiretsu.

During the 1950s and 1960s, as the nation's domestic economy resurged, Mitsui succeeded in reuniting a number of its former member companies and added new groups of companies, expanding not only in numbers but in the range of types of its business concerns. Although the Mitsui Group has never regained the topmost leadership position, the conglomerate has remained a leader. Mitsui Mutual continued to play a large role in insuring other members of the Mitsui Group.

With the economy's recovery, the market for insurance responded positively to Mitsui Mutual's individualized, "self-designed" insurance product approach. Individual and group life insurance products proliferated during the decades of rapid economic growth after the war.

The investment policies pursued by Mitsui Mutual up to the 1970s had always been conservative and closely tied to the fortunes of the domestic economy. The company was a major institutional investor. In 1972 Mitsui Mutual was ready to strike out in a new direction: overseas investment. By 1988 Mitsui Mutual's investments in overseas securities reached close to $6 billion. The company concentrated its investments mainly in Europe and North America, with some activity in Southeast Asia. Mitsui Mutual also struck out in another direction in the 1970s, broadening its financial services. The company's conservative lending policies have provided Mitsui Mutual with a solid base for expansion. In 1978 the company began an international lending program, the success of which has contributed to a shift in the emphasis of Mitsui Mutual activity to the international scene. The company also added consumer lending through special policyholder cards that expedite loans for individuals, and subsidiaries offer investment advice and mortgage securities. As a pioneer in international group insurance in the 1970s, Mitsui Mutual established a network of agreements with more than 200 insurance companies in 40 countries around the world. Among its business partners are Aetna Life and Casualty Company in the United States and Assicurazioni Generali in Italy. The company also has agreements with three leading European reinsurance companies.

Late 1980s Retrenchment

Mitsui Mutual's success brought some problems, however. In the 1980s, when Japan's economy reached the height of prosperity, insurance company income began to overflow the capacity of domestic opportunities for profitable investment. Even though the government had liberalized its strict control of the insurance business, Japanese insurers with excess cash to invest followed Mitsui Mutual's example in placing their investment money in overseas real estate developments and other types of long-term overseas investment prospects.

Other surprises were in store as the decade came to a close. The stock market crashed in 1987, monetary value fluctuations ensued, and by the fall of 1990 the Japanese market showed about a 15 percent loss overall. Mitsui Mutual Life Insurance Company, like other insurers, was quick to put a hold on immediate investment programs and, for the moment, retrench.

For the long haul, however, company president Koshiro Sakata intended to expand overseas operations, adding to the staff in international administration while carefully monitoring the risks. A tool that was expected to contribute to expansion abroad was the investment index model developed by the company in 1986 that has helped the company maintain one of the highest yield levels in the industry since it was put into use to manage funds for variable life insurance policies.

The 1990s, however, would prove to be a troubling period, not only for Mitsui Mutual but for the insurance industry and the Japanese economy in general. In April 1996 a revised Insurance Business Law went into effect in Japan to reduce government regulation, with the expectation that insurers would have more freedom to engage in global financial activities. Instead of entering a period of unprecedented prosperity, the industry, crippled by a weak economy, quickly witnessed what had once been unthinkable: Nissan Mutual Life, Japan's 16th largest life insurer, went bankrupt. The failure sent shock waves across the industry. A year later Toho Mutual would also collapse. The faith of policyholders was tested; and because Japanese policyholders had no regulatory or industry mechanisms to protect the value of their policies, faith was all that maintained the traditional bond between policyholders and the life insurers. Deregulation also brought new players into the life insurance business, so that policyholders, whose loyalty was eroding, had more options. In effect, too many companies began to chase an ever-shrinking premium pool, as it was estimated that within two decades one quarter of the Japanese population would be older than 65.

Underlying structural flaws in the insurance industry became apparent. Mutuals in Japan were run essentially as nonprofits, with most of the profits returned to policyholders. The companies also had a limited ability to increase capital. As long as the Japanese economy remained robust, insurers could count on increasing unrealized gains on domestic stocks to provide the necessary capital to offer higher dividends to policyholders. With the price of securities depressed, insurers were unable to meet the level of promised benefits and could only turn to commercial lenders for an infusion of cash.

Challenges in the Late 1990s and Beyond

In 1998 Mitsui Mutual experienced a second consecutive year in which it signed fewer contracts. Premium revenues dropped ten percent, and the company's total assets fell by 7.2 percent. Because of Mitsui Mutual's relatively weak earnings profile and capital position, Standard & Poor's lowered the credit rating of the insurer. The insurer was forced to turn to the Mitsui-affiliated Sakura Bank for a $424 million bailout.

Mitsui Mutual looked for ways to improve its position. There was talk of reviving the *zaibatsu,* with Mitsui Mutual forging a union with other Mitsui financial entities under the wing of a holding company. Another, more likely, possibility was converting from a mutual form of ownership to stock, which would allow the insurer to raise capital through a public offering. The tax laws did not provide for conversion, but the Ministry of Finance supported demutualization, and Mitsui Mutual and other insurers hired advisers to begin the process.

As Mitsui Mutual awaited new legislation that was expected, eventually, to allow demutualization, it began to sell insurance products over the Internet. It received an infusion of $1.2 billion dollars in cash from Sakura Bank and other Mitsui Group companies. The establishment of the Life Insurance Policyholders Protection Corporation of Japan to create a safety net for policyholders also helped to quell consumer fears. Therefore, despite Mitsui Mutual's recent struggles, the insurer—given the strengths of its ties to the Mitsui Group—appears to have a positive long-term forecast.

Principal Subsidiaries

Mitsui Seimei America Corporation (U.S.); Mitsui Life Investment Luxembourg S.A.; Mitsui Life Investment Bahamas Company, Ltd.; Mitsui Life Asset Management America Corporation (U.S.); Mitsui Seimei Investment Jersey Ltd. (U.K.); Mitsui Life International London Ltd. (U.K.).

Principal Competitors

Nippon Life Insurance Co.; Dai-Ichi Mutual Life Insurance Co,; Sumitomo Life Insurance Co.; Maiji Life Insurance Co.; Yasuda Mutual Life Insurance Co.

Further Reading

"Completion of Safety Net Stimulates the Reorganization of Life Insurance Industry," Norinchukin Research Institute, September 2000.

"Japan Insurance Digest 2000," New York: Standard & Poor's, 2000.

Prindl, Andreas R., *Japanese Finance: A Guide to Banking in Japan,* New York: John Wiley & Sons, 1981.

Reischauer, Edwin O., *Japan, the Story of a Nation,* Tokyo: Charles E. Tuttle Co., 1971.

Shimbun, Asahi, "Dismal Results for Insurance Firms," *Financial Times,* June 10, 1999.

—Betty T. Moore
—update: Ed Dinger

Monsoon plc

87 Lancaster Road
London W11 1QQ
United Kingdom
Telephone: (+44) 207 313-3000
Fax: (+44) 207 313-3020
Web site: http://www.monsoon.co.uk

Public Company
Incorporated: 1973
Employees: 1,802
Sales: £154.4 million ($231.8 million) (2000)
Stock Exchanges: London
Ticker Symbol: MN
NAIC: 448120 Women's Clothing Stores

Monsoon plc is a leading women's clothing and accessories retailer in the United Kingdom, operating three retail store concepts. The company's flagship retail store is its chain of some 150 and growing Monsoon clothing stores, nearly all of which operate in the United Kingdom and Ireland. Monsoon has built up a loyal following in its core U.K. market, which represents more than 90 percent of company sales, with its Asia-inspired designs and colors offering customers what Monsoon calls "delux bo-ho chic." Monsoon's fastest-growing chain is its Accessorize retail store and in-store boutique formats featuring home designs and other goods inspired by the company's clothing collections. Launched in the mid-1980s, Accessorize has overtaken the Monsoon chain in number of store openings, reaching more than 130 stores; many Monsoon stores also feature Accessorize in-store boutiques. Accessorize generates some 40 percent of the company's annual sales. Monsoon's third store concept is Monsoon Home, launched in 1999. The company plans to open a series of stand-alone stores under this format, as well as including Monsoon Home boutiques in its larger stores. To accommodate its growing variety of goods, the company has been moving a number of its key stores to new and larger locations. In a difficult retail climate, Monsoon also has been attempting to shore up sales growth by refining the Monsoon format, cutting back on the number of items available

in order to increase the stores' clarity. The company also has suggested that it intends to double its network of U.K. stores by 2002. At the same time, Monsoon has been targeting an ambitious international expansion in order to secure its future growth, favoring a franchising concept over extending its company-owned stores. The company intends to achieve this foreign expansion through lower-risk franchise agreements, in a number of primarily smaller European markets, including Greece, Iceland, and Malta. In October 2000, the company set up a joint venture with the United States' Charming Shoppes to bring the Monsoon and Accessorize names to that market. The company is seeking similar franchise and partnership agreements in order to enter the larger European retail markets as well. Monsoon continues to be led by founder, chairman, and majority shareholder Peter Simon and managing director John Spooner.

Hippie Retail Magnate in the 1970s

Peter Simon began his retail career as a fishfinger salesman at a stall in the Portobello Road market in London during the waning days of the Woodstock era. A self-described hippy, Simon was also a traveler, and it was during a trip to India that Simon decided to turn toward the retail clothing market. Returning from that trip, Simon brought with him a supply of clothing. The quick turnover of brightly colored designs encouraged Simon to look for more clothing fashions from the eastern and Asian markets. On a trip to the island of Gobo, near Malta, Simon discovered the "shoat," a cross between a sheep and a goat. Working with locals, Simon began producing coats made of the shaggy wool and importing them to his London stall.

Sales of the shoat coats inspired Simon to quit the marketplace and open a full-fledged retail shop in Beauchamp Place in the Knightsbridge area of London in 1973. Simon chose the name of Monsoon for his company, recalling his own birth during a monsoon in Sri Lanka. In addition to the shoat coats, the new store featured other clothing items imported from primarily Asian sources. The company also began designing its own fashions, sticking to Asian-inspired designs and natural materials, while developing its own distinctive styles and colors and incorporating techniques ranging from embroidery and batik to beading. The company caught on with London customers, and Monsoon began opening new stores, at first in London and then later throughout the United Kingdom and Ireland.

Changing fashion trends led the company to adapt, moving its growing number of stores into a more up-market bracket and evolving its clothing into more sophisticated designs. The company was later to describe its fashions as ''deluxe bo-ho chic.'' Yet the company's ethnic-inspired origins remained the centerpoint of its designs and retail ambiance. At the same time, Monsoon remained committed to using natural fibers, while also being among the first retailers to adopt stricter requirements from its producers for their working conditions.

Monsoon's growth led Simon to expand the company's management, bringing in Andrew May, who became the company's finance director, in 1981, and John Spooner, who joined the company in 1984, becoming managing director. Monsoon was ready to extend its retail offerings with a new retail concept. Launched in 1984, Accessorize offered a new product range, featuring home furnishings, accessories, and jewelry, incorporating Monsoon's ethnic-inspired design feel. The first Accessorize opened in Covent Garden Plaza in London. Its quick success among shoppers led Monsoon to open more Accessorize stores, while adding Accessorize boutiques into some of its Monsoon stores.

The second Accessorize opened in 1986, on famed London fashions street Carnaby St. After adding several more Accessorize stores in the London area, the chain was ready to follow the Monsoon retail chain into other markets in the United Kingdom. In 1992, the company opened an Accessorize store in Manchester, its first outside of London. In that same year, the company proved the flexibility of the Accessorize format when it opened a shop at Gatwick airport. By then, the company's Monsoon chain had neared 60 stores.

International Expansion for the 21st Century

Monsoon's mood was buoyant in the early 1990s, despite the extended economic recession of the period. In 1992 the company prepared a new and massive expansion program that was to transform the company into a leading retailer in the United Kingdom. Monsoon stepped up its rate of store openings, boosting both Monsoon and Accessorize formats. The latter received extra attention from Monsoon, with the company

opening some 16 Accessorize stores per year starting with the 1992 year. Parallel to the company's expansion was the sale by Simon of two-thirds of the company's shares to an investment trust, Sycamore Trust, based in Malta.

Into the mid-1990s, Monsoon continued to build up its retail empire. The Monsoon chain continued to lead the company's revenues, as the number of stores reached 84 in the United Kingdom. Monsoon also made its first international moves, opening company-owned stores in the United States, Iceland, Gibraltar, Australia, and a number of European markets. By 1996, the company had 13 foreign stores, a number that was to nearly double in less than a year. Accessorize's growth paralleled the Monsoon chain, reaching 52 stores by mid-1996. The company also had seen steady gains in sales growth, reaching £62.1 million for 1996, and had more than a decade of unbroken growth in its profits.

Monsoon then announced that it would seek a listing on the London stock market by the end of the 1996 summer. The purpose of the listing, which was to take the form of a placement among institutional investors, was to enable the company's majority shareholder, Sycamore Trust, to cash in on some of its shares. Simon himself was not selling any of his remaining one-third of the company's shares. Yet the listing quickly derailed. Claiming that it was unable to determine the identity of the beneficiaries of the initial public offering (IPO)—as Sycamore Trust refused to give out information about itself—the IPO's broker, BZW, pulled out of the proposed listing, amid Simon's assertion that he had no connection with Sycamore Trust. Nevertheless, Simon admitted to the *Daily Telegraph,* ''Myself and my family were not beneficiaries. But there were certain circumstances under which me and my family could have benefited from it.''

Monsoon continued expanding both of its retail networks as it prepared a new attempt at a stock listing. By the end of 1997, the company had boosted the Monsoon chain to 127 stores, including 24 foreign stores, while the Accessorize chain jumped to 76 stand-alone stores and another 103 Accessorize boutiques located within most of the Monsoon stores. With sales continuing to increase, jumping from £79.56 million in 1996 to £107.9 million in 1997, and with net profits growing to £15 million, Monsoon was ready to try again for a public offering.

The company finally came to the London stock exchange in 1998, after the Sycamore Trust's stake in the company was acquired by trusts set up in Guernsey by Simon and his family. Now holding 96 percent of Monsoon, Simon raised eyebrows anew when he admitted that the listing was being made despite the fact that Monsoon was not seeking to raise new capital for expansion—its growth, traditionally, had been financed organically. Many analysts complained that, as the *Daily Telegraph* suggested, Simon had ''failed to come up with a convincing reason for selling his shares.'' Others proposed that Simon, worried about possible downturns in the retail climate, hoped to cash out on some of his shares while the retail market was still at its peak. Undaunted by these criticisms, the company's flotation went ahead, fetching a premium price of 198.6 pence for each of the 44.6 million shares on offer—worth about 25 percent of the company, and, at a massive multiple of 18, valuing the company at nearly £350 million. Simon's gain from the offering, which

Key Dates:

1972: Peter Simon begins selling ethnic clothing.
1973: First Monsoon retail store opens.
1984: Company launches Accessorize stores.
1986: Second Accessorize store opens.
1992: Company steps up store expansion; opens first international stores.
1998: Company floats shares on the London Stock Exchange.
2000: Company forms joint venture with Charming Shoppes in the United States.

took the form of a placement among institutional investors in February 1998, was valued at £88 million.

Less than one year later, Monsoon's shares had dropped some 75 percent of their value. While the company's share fortunes were battered by a growing pessimism about the United Kingdom's retail climate (many feared the advent of a new recession as economic crises rocked the Asian, Russian, and South American economies) Monsoon itself added to its troubles at the end of its 1999 year when it announced its first profits slip in 13 years. Despite growing sales, to £132 million, the company's profits had dropped to £20 million, from £27 million one year earlier.

To improve its sales, Monsoon set out revitalizing its stores, streamlining the Monsoon stores' product offering to add more clarity for its customers. The company also began a series of moves to transform its clothing designs, moving toward higher quality tailoring and closer-fitting garments, while also extending its range of sizes to attract a wider customer base. After rolling out its first Monsoon Home the company also began targeting international expansion of both the Monsoon and Accessorize brand names as a company priority. Seeking to avoid the costly capital investment necessary to establish its own stores internationally, however, Monsoon announced its intention to seek partners for its existing foreign stores and to concentrate future international growth through franchise and partnership agreements. A first Accessorize store, which opened in Athens, Greece, showed the company's international promise, outperforming all of the company's U.K. stores.

Monsoon attempted to bring its successful retail formula to the World Wide Web in 2000, opening an e-commerce-capable web site. The company hoped to build up yearly sales to that of one of its bricks-and-mortar stores. Yet the site's sales quickly proved a disappointment, as the company recognized that its customers preferred the physical experience of in-store shopping. By the beginning of 2001, the company announced that it was pulling the plug on its e-commerce operation, using its web pages instead as a promotional site.

Nevertheless, Monsoon closed its 2000 year with renewed growth in its net profits and continued revenue gains. By the beginning of 2001, the company was promising to continue to build up its strong Monsoon and Accessorize brands, doubling its number of stores in the United Kingdom and Ireland over the next two or three years. At the same time, Monsoon hoped to establish its two brands as leading retail names throughout the world. A major part of this goal got under way in October 2000 when the company formed a joint venture with the United States' Charming Shoppes to open 20 Monsoon branded stores in the U.S. market.

Principal Subsidiaries

Monsoon Holdings Ltd; Monsoon Accessorize Ltd.; Monsoon of London Pty Ltd (Australia); Monsoon Coordination Services Ltd (Hong Kong); Monsoon Twilight Inc. (U.S.); Monsoon SARL (France); Monsoon Accessorize ApS (Denmark); Brands Exploitation Ltd (Malta).

Principal Competitors

Arcadia Group plc; ASDA Group Limited; Debenhams plc; The Great Universal Stores plc; Harrods Holdings; House of Fraser plc; James Beattie plc; John Lewis Partnership plc; Marks and Spencer plc; Matalan plc; N Brown Group plc; New Look Plc; NEXT plc; Otto Versand Gmbh & Co.; Selfridges plc; Storehouse plc.

Further Reading

MacAlister, Terry, ''Monsoon Launches in US,'' *Guardian,* August 1, 2000.
Menary, Steve, ''Monsoon Outlines Fresh Strategy to Revive Sales,'' *Financial Times,* January 26, 1999.
''Monsoon Postpones Pounds 250m Flotation,'' *Financial Times,* July 11, 1996.
''Monsoon Pours in Millions to Extend Reign,'' *Birmingham Post,* January 23, 2001, p. 19.
''Monsoon Rains Supreme,'' *Scotsman,* August 1, 2000.
''Monsoon Sees Strong Sales Growth at Xmas,'' *Investor's Chronicle,* January 22, 2001.

—M.L. Cohen

Moore-Handley, Inc.

3140 Pelham Parkway
P.O. Box 2607
Pelham, Alabama 35202
U.S.A.
Telephone: (205) 663-8011
Toll Free: (800) 633-3848
Fax: (205) 663-8229
Web site: http://www.moorehandley.com

Public Company
Incorporated: 1881 as Moore & Handley Hardware
    Company
Employees: 492
Sales: $167.2 million (1999)
Stock Exchanges: NASDAQ
Ticker Symbol: MHCO
NAIC: 42171 Hardware Wholesalers; 42182 Farm and
    Garden Machinery and Equipment Wholesalers;
    42172 Plumbing and Heating Equipment and Supplies
    (Hydronics) Wholesalers; 42161 Electrical Apparatus
    and Equipment, Wiring Supplies, and Construction
    Material Wholesalers; 42131 Lumber, Plywood,
    Millwork, and Wood Panel Wholesalers; 42133
    Roofing, Siding, and Insulation Material Wholesalers

Moore-Handley, Inc. is the nation's third-largest independent building-materials wholesaler. It is a full-service distributor of a wide array of hardware and building supplies, including hand and power tools; paint and paint sundries; builders' hardware and materials; lumber, plumbing and electrical supplies; lawn and garden tools and equipment; fastening tools; heating and cooling equipment; locks and home security devices; fasteners, cordage, wire and chain, fencing, automotive and mobile home and recreational vehicle parts, and home housewares and appliances. It also offers special support services, including advertising and promotional campaign services and materials, retail-store installation and design services, and computerized inventory control systems. Under the name "Hardware House," it also provides a store identification program and additional promotional aid. Additionally, it offers similar programs under the "Pro" trade name. The company maintains a state-of-the-art, 500,000 square foot distribution facility in Pelham, a suburb of Birmingham, Alabama, the city of its corporate headquarters. It also maintains 20,000-square-foot redistribution facilities in Ocala, Florida, and Winston-Salem, North Carolina. Its customers include retail home-improvement centers, hardware stores, building material dealers, combination stores, and a select number of mass merchandisers. Most of its current 1,500 customers are located in Alabama, Florida, Georgia, Kentucky, Louisiana, Mississippi, North Carolina, South Carolina, Tennessee, Virginia and West Virginia. In 1999, none of its clients accounted for more than 1.6 percent of the company's net sales, indicating that its business is securely spread across its customer base. A fair portion of Moore-Handley is owned by its employees, including CEO William Riley, who owns about 20 percent of its stock.

1880s Origins and Development Through the 1960s

The Alabama-based business which would evolve as Moore-Handley, Inc. came into being in 1882 as Moore, Moore & Handley, named after its founders James D. Moore, Benjamin F. Moore, and W.A. Handley. James Moore had moved to Birmingham that year, though he and Handley had been business partners in an earlier venture, a rural country store in Randolph County, Alabama, where Moore, for several years a teacher, had helped found Roanoke Institute. He and his partners proved to be both shrewd and lucky, and the early record of the new company was unusual for "its rapidly enhancing fortunes and daring enterprise."

The company was created as a wholesale hardware business at the outset, but the good fortune of the partners initially came from real estate investments. In 1884, after already having moved twice, the company bought property for $15,000 from which they made a considerable profit. They built the Metropolitan Hotel on a portion of the land, rebuilt it after a fire, and then sold it for $175,000. Also, from rents and the sale of a portion of the property they garnered revenues great enough to capitalize their business at $100,000 when they incorporated it as the Moore &

290

Handley Hardware Company in 1888. The company would move again in 1903, six years before Handley died. Just before his death in June 1909, the partners reincorporated the business with a capital of $500,000. Thereafter, Moore-Handley emerged as "one of the great mercantile houses in the South." Through the next several decades, Moore-Handley developed into a chain of hardware and building supply stores located throughout the southeastern part of the United States. It was also a distributor of industrial and electrical supplies and machine tools.

1968–80: New Parent Company Focuses on Homecrafter Division

In 1968, Union Camp Corporation, a major lumber producer and manufacturer of paper and corrugated board, purchased Moore-Handley for about $10 million. Its principal reason for acquiring the company was its interest in vertical integration. It planned to convert Moore-Handley's company-owned lumber yards into product outlets, thereby not only producing lumber but directly marketing it as well. Industry gurus at the time were touting the "homecenter" concept, convinced that it would become to the 1970s and 1980s what the giant discount-store concept had been to the 1960s. The idea was to develop Moore-Handley's rural lumber yards into homecenters. Accordingly, Union Camp hired consultants and drew up plans for transforming Moore-Handley's lumber yards into Moore-Handley Homecrafter centers operating under a new Homecrafter Division. W.W. French III, whose family had guided the development of Moore-Handley for several decades, remained as the company's president and CEO.

Union Camp elected to concentrate on the Homecrafter Division. It sold Moore-Handley's Electrical Division to Westinghouse and allowed its Steel and Coal Divisions, already performing poorly, to decline further. By the mid-1970s, over 60 percent of Moore-Handley's revenue was generated by the Homecrafter Division. In 1974, Moore-Handley was operating 42 stores, with each long-established store logging annual revenues of between $2.5 million and $3.5 million. At the time, about 65 percent of their sales were made to contractors and most of the remainder to weekend, do-it-yourself enthusiasts. Meanwhile, the Wholesale Division's customer base was dwindling as more and more mom-and-pop hardware operations were failing, unable to compete with much larger chain stores.

Although by 1980 the Moore-Handley Homecrafters outlets increased to 50 locations in six states and had annual sales

between $125 million and $130 million, the division could not offset Moore-Handley's operating expenses. Union Camp's solution was to sell all the company's assets except the Homecrafters Division. Officially, the divestment was justified as part of Union Camp's renewed commitment to its core paper, packaging, and chemical business.

1981–90: Going Public and Refocusing on Wholesale

The remaining divisions and assets were bought by William Riley and a group of investors. Riley reorganized and reincorporated the company in 1981. He wanted to revamp Moore-Handley, returning to its earlier concept as a wholesale distributor of building supplies and tools to independent retailers. The new focus was on the distribution facility in the Pelham suburb of Birmingham.

In 1986, a year in which its revenues reached $85 million, Moore-Handley elected to go public. In that same year, the company sold the assets and businesses of its Industrial Supply and Machine Tool Divisions for about $2.06 million, and in the following year purchased certain assets and the primary inventory of the wholesale hardware division of Pleasant Hardware Company for $2.25 million in cash. Although in 1988 it reacquired Moore-Handley Machine Tool & Industrial, Inc. for about $170,000, it shortly sold it off again.

At the end of 1994, the directors of the company, who were also its principal owners, indicated that the growth path Moore-Handley had taken in the 1980s had become untenable and that in the late 1980s and early 1990s the company had taken steps to rectify the situation. Previously, Moore-Handley's policy had been to increase revenues by adding sales personnel and expanding its customer base without sufficient regard for quality. By 1986, the customer base had swelled to about 4,000. However, analyses later indicated that the company's operating costs more closely paralleled the size of its customer base than any other single factor. It acknowledged that its business customers faced stiffening competitive pressure from Home Depot and similar chains, forcing them to price their goods more competitively in order to survive. The result was that Moore-Handley began cutting its customer base down to size. It was already reduced to 2,400 customers by 1989, and over the next five years would be thinned down to 1,200. In the same period, its sales climbed to $136 million, up 46 percent.

1991 and Beyond: Modernization and Struggle for Profitability

However, between 1991 and 1994, the company's investment in automation, rather than saving money, actually increased its cost of doing business. First, in 1991, it installed a bar-code-driven sorting and routing conveyor for its central warehouse; and even though sales reached $123.6 million, the company had a net loss of $1 million.

In 1993 and 1994, the company followed with the installation of additional hand-carried bar-coding controls at select locations in the warehouse and in the delivery system. These were the initial steps needed to develop an efficient computerized warehouse management and delivery system, but the installations increased warehouse expenses to an unacceptable

---

Key Dates:

1882: Company is founded as Moore, Moore & Handley.

1888: Firm is incorporated as the Moore & Handley Hardware Company.

1968: Union Camp Corporation purchases Moore-Handley.

1980: Union Camp divests assets of Moore-Handley—except the Homecrafters Division—to a group of investors.

1981: Moore-Handley is reincorporated in Delaware.

1986: Company goes public.

1987: Company acquires certain assets of Pleasants Hardware Company.

1996: 50,000 square-foot mezzanine is added to company's distribution facility.

1997: Moore-Handley enters a marketing alliance with PPG Industries.

---

degree, despite the fact that their operation helped reduce errors, resulting in a higher degree of customer satisfaction and a lower percentage of returns or credit charge-backs. Sales were improving, resulting in net profits, though only marginally.

Furthermore, in the mid-1990s the company hit something of a slump. Sales stagnated and produced bottom-line losses. The first red-ink year was 1996, when Moore-Handley reported a net loss of $1.07 million, although the loss was partly explained by disruptions caused by a warehouse modernization project which drove the company's net income down by about $1.5 million. According to Riley, the changes were being made ''in an effort to make the company as low cost and high quality a distributor as possible.'' The show piece in the changes was the addition to the 488,000-square-foot Birmingham warehouse and distribution facility of a 50,000-square-foot mezzanine strictly limited to individual-item picking. Stocked in accordance with the turnover rate of items sold in it, the new addition was designed to allow customers to pick out single items as quickly and efficiently as possible. However, Moore-Handley paid the bottom-line price during the mezzanine's construction; it disrupted operations and drove 1996 warehouse and delivery costs up by more than $2 million over the previous year.

During the last few years of the century's final decade, Moore-Handley struggled to regain the profitability lost in 1996. To turn its bottom line figures black again, the company invested substantially in warehouse retrofitting, employee training, and a renewed commitment to computerization. Among other things, in 1997, when revenues dropped off slightly from the previous year, the company entered into a marketing alliance with PPG Industries. Under the agreement, Moore-Handley would sell a full-line of DIY (do-it-yourself) products under exclusive Lucite WallCare and HouseCare names and promote the sale of other PPG products. It was also in 1997 that Emery H. White resigned as Moore-Handley's CEO and president. Michael Gaines, a former Grossman's Inc. executive who

joined Moore-Handley earlier in the year, replaced him as president.

In 1998, the company discontinued issuing its printed catalog, thereafter relying solely on its electronic sales catalog, dubbed SalesHelper and first introduced in 1992. In 1999, it also added paint store and industrial-commercial clients, a diversification that increased its account base to about 1500 customers.

During the first year and a half of the turn-around efforts, the cost of the retrofitting, training, and installation of new computers and electronic communications kept the bottom line red, but after a net loss of $1.4 million in 1997, the company's performance began improving. Total revenue, which had flattened out between 1995 and 1997, rose significantly in 1998 and again in 1999, reaching $167.2 million that year, up almost 13 percent from the company's 1997 revenue of $145.7 million. In 1998, it eked out its first net profit since 1995, even though it still had to pay out $500,000 in construction costs carried forward from the 1996 revamping of its warehouse.

A major factor in the change was Moore-Handley's improved efficiency. For example, order-picking errors that had been averaging between four and five per 1,000 improved to less than one per 1,000 after the installation of a radio-frequency picking system. Plans also called for other improvements, including another modification of the company's SalesHelper tentatively called Sales Helper Lite. When it went online in 2000, it allowed Moore-Handley's key customers to place orders directly from the company's warehouse. Riley believed that the company's CD-ROM catalogs would be of greater benefit to Moore-Handley's customers and ultimately preferable to e-commerce and online purchasing. Just how much the company's improved efficiency and its CD-ROM modus operandi would benefit its sales in the long run remained to be seen.

Principal Competitors

American Builders & Contractors Supply Co. Inc.; Builder Marts of America, Inc.; Cameron Ashley Building Products, Inc.; PrimeSource Building Products, Inc.

Further Reading

Allison, David, ''Big Hardware Distributor Cries Foul Play,'' *Atlanta Business Chronicle*,'' April 22, 1991, p. 8A.

''A Formula That Differs from Home Centers,'' *Discount Merchandiser*, August 1974, p. 33.

Gonzalez, Jason, ''For Moore-Handley, Change Has a Price,'' *National Home Center News*, November 24, 1997, p. 6.

''Moore Handley Returns to Profitability after a Tough Three Years,'' *National Home Center News*, April 3, 2000.

''Moore-Handley to Offer Exclusive Line of Paint and to Distribute Company Catalogs on CD-ROM Only,'' *Do-It-Yourself Retailing*, December 1997, p. 27.

Toriello, Monica, ''Moore-Handley Ready to Fly after Weathering Storm,'' *National Home Center News*, June 21, 1999.

Washburn, Don, ''Moore-Handley Reports '96 Losses,'' *Home Improvement Market*, April 1997, p. 24.

—John W. Fiero

N M Rothschild & Sons Limited

New Court, Saint Swithin's Lane
London EC4P 4DU
United Kingdom
Telephone: (+44) 171 280 5000
Fax: (+44) 171 929 1643
Web site: http://www.nmrothschild.com

*Wholly Owned Subsidiary of Rothschilds Continuation
Holdings AG*
Incorporated: 1799
Employees: 725
Total Assets: £7.22 billion ($10.38 billion) (2000)
NAIC: 523110 Investment Banking and Securities Dealing

United Kingdom banker N M Rothschild & Sons Limited is one of the last remaining of the great family-controlled banking dynasties established in the 19th century. Dwarfed by its larger, public rivals, Rothschild nonetheless remains a mythical name in the banking world. N M Rothschild provides banking and treasury financing services, treasury metals, and resource banking, including a central position in the world bullion markets, investment banking services (together with its joint-venture partnership with ABN AMRO), and risk management services. Since the 1990s, N M Rothschild has been taking steps to consolidate the operations of the various and far-flung Rothschild financial operations, most of which operate as subsidiaries under the Rothschild family-controlled Rothschild Continuation Holdings AG, established in Switzerland in the early part of the 20th century to protect the family's ownership of its banking empire. N M Rothschild has also been working in close cooperation with the—independent—Paris branch of Rothschild banking interests, Rothschild & Cie, led by David de Rothschild, who also functions as deputy chairman of N M Rothschild and is the heir-apparent to chairman and long-time leader Evelyn de Rothschild.

Founding a Banking Dynasty in the 18th Century

The Rothschild banking dynasty began in Frankfurt, Germany's, Jewish ghetto in the mid-18th century when patriach Meyer Aemschel Rothschild set up a small antiques business. Rothschild's interests quickly expanded to include textiles, and then financial interests. Among the Rothschild family's clients was the Elector of Hesse-Cassel; providing asset management services to the Elector was to give the family the capital to develop itself as one of the world's great banking families. As the century drew to an end, the now-wealthy Rothschild sent four of his five sons (the oldest remained in Frankfurt) to settle in Europe's capital cities to develop the family's fortunes.

Nathan Rothschild traveled to Manchester, England, where he set out to develop the family's textiles business. Born in 1777, Nathan Rothschild grew to become the main force behind the growth of the Rothschild dynasty—even his brothers referred to him as the "commanding general" of the family's interests. Rothschild quickly built up a successful commercial trade, expanding from textiles into a variety of products. At the same time, Rothschild began operating as a moneylender, and it was this latter activity that captured his greatest interest. By 1806, Rothschild decided to set up a full-fledged financial services firm in London and opened his first offices in that city in 1808. The following year, N M Rothschild opened at its New Court location, which remained the firm's home into the 20th century. By 1811, Rothschild sold off his Manchester operations to concentrate fully on his banking interests.

The Rothschild brothers remained a close-knit family, cooperating extensively as they built the different branches of the family's empire. A primary factor in the Rothschild's success was Nathan Rothschild's inauguration of a private courier service. The ability to share information quickly among the major European capitals was a distinct advantage to the Rothschilds, particularly given the great political and industrial upheavals of the period.

The Napoleanic Wars provided Nathan Rothschild with the foundation of the dynasty's wealth. By providing funds to the allies and funding Wellington's army, Rothschild became largely responsible for the victory at Waterloo. The brothers' courier service operated so efficiently that Nathan Rothschild received news of Napoleon's defeat a full day before the British government. The family's financial backing of the war effort led them to become the official bank for many European governments and royal families—the family's financial clout even extended to the Vatican, which turned to the Rothschilds for a loan in 1830. N M Rothschild came to the British government's

---

Company Perspectives:

N M Rothschild & Sons is committed to the pursuit of excellence and for this reason concentrates on sectors and markets in which commitment and expertise are more vital than numbers. Where it chooses to compete, the bank ranks with the very best. Its influence and reputation flow from the quality of its people and the standing of its clients. This, combined with a culture that values pragmatic innovation, integrity, and intellectual rigor above all else, has resulted in a reputation for ground-breaking ideas that are functional as well as imaginative.

---

aid again in 1825 when it provided a loan to the Bank of England that prevented the collapse of the entire British banking system. At this time N M Rothschild also began pursuing interests outside of the United Kingdom and Europe, establishing operations in Brazil. Less successful for the family was its attempt to enter the United States; the lack of a significant Rothschild presence in North America was to come to haunt the company in the 20th century as the balance of financial power shifted to the United States.

The next generation of Rothschilds—which had by then been granted noble status, adding the "de" to the family name—took over the family empire in the mid-1800s. Nathan Rothschild himself had died in 1836. The family came to play a primary role in the building of Europe's railway system, transforming the continent and the United Kingdom and driving the Industrial Revolution. With N M Rothschild providing much of the financial backing, the Rothschild brothers helped inaugurate the railway systems of Austria, France, and Belgium. Highlighting the banking group's importance to the British government was the appointment of N M Rothschild as head of the Royal Mint Refinery in 1852, a position the company held for more than 100 years.

New glory came to the family after it helped organize the early repayment of France's indemnity to Prussia after the Franco-Prussian war in 1871. N M Rothschild in turn proved central to Britain's foreign interests when it provided a £4 million loan to the government to acquire a controlling share of the Suez Canal. In South Africa, Rothschild helped cement the De Beer family's control of the world's diamond interests; the bank also provided funding for Britain's first telephone companies in the 1890s.

Fading Fortunes in the 20th Century

If the Rothschild name had become synonymous with European finance in the 19th century—and remained one of the leading financial names worldwide—N M Rothschild was nevertheless to lose much of its prominence during the 20th century. Its inability to establish a strong position in the United States market, the appearance of new, larger rivals and the lack of cohesion of succeeding generations placed the company in a more marginal position. Losing out to its United States rivals during World War I, the family was devastated during World War II, which saw much of its operations captured by the Nazi regime. By then, the family had already moved to protect most

of its assets, setting up the Switzerland-based holding company, Rothschild Continuation Holdings. With 75 percent controlled by the Rothschilds (with the N M Rothschild branch holding some 50 percent), Rothschild Continuation Holdings was later to provide an umbrella for the gradual consolidation of the various Rothschild family interests, begun at the close of the century.

Although unable to regain its former glory as a financier to kings, Rothschild remained a force in the financial world, redefining itself as a quality financial services partner rather than emphasizing quantity. Rothschild continued to play a leading role in industrial development, such as its creation of the British Newfoundland Corporation, which was formed in 1852 to develop timber, mining, and hydroelectric power interests in a 60,000-square-mile area in that Canadian province. N M Rothschild continued to expand its international operations, opening subsidiaries in Australia and in Guernsey in the 1960s, and then in Hong Kong, Singapore, and Chile in the 1970s.

N M Rothschild restructured itself as a private limited company in 1970. The Rothschild family's interests then came under the leadership of Evelyn Rothschild, whose guidance of N M Rothschild continued into the 20th century. Often criticized for his conservative leadership of the banking firm, Rothschild nonetheless helped prevent the company from investing too heavily in the South American markets and maintained a cool head during the frenzied British financial market of the late 1980s. The company also carefully avoided the diversification moves—granted during the British financial reforms in that decade—that brought about the downfall of many of its fellow family-owned financial firms. Indeed, by the mid-1990s, with the collapse of Baring and Warburgs, N M Rothschilds remained one of the last of the world's great independent, family-operated financial firms.

Consolidating for the 21st Century

N M Rothschild found plenty of work in the great wave of British privatization that swept the country during the late 1980s. The company was involved in a number of the country's most ambitious privatization programs, including the £5.6 billion privatization of British Gas in 1986, the exit of the British government from British Petroleum in 1987, and the privatization of the United Kingdom's water and sewage industry in 1989. At the same time, N M Rothschild, while remaining true to its family-owned and independent status, nonetheless made moves to establish itself as a globally operating entity capable of competing with the financial industry's heavyweights. As such N M Rothschild bolstered its international presence, consolidating its United States operations under the single Rothschild Inc. entity, based in New York, in 1981 and establishing separate Canadian operations with its Rothschild Canada Inc. subsidiary. The firm also opened offices in Germany and Italy at the end of the decade.

During the 1990s, N M Rothschild began making stronger moves to draw together the various elements of the Rothschilds' empire. One of the last of these was the highly successful Paris-based banking arm, Rothschild & Cie., which retained its independent status. This business, led by David de Rothschild, had been created in the mid-1980s as France's banking industry shrugged off the ill-fated nationalization of the country's

Key Dates:

1765: Meyer Aemschel Rothschild establishes his business in Frankfurt, Germany.

1798: Son Nathan M. Rothschild opens business in Manchester.

1808: N M Rothschild opens a London office.

1814: Rothschild provides funding for Wellington's army.

1815: Company backs the English, Dutch, and Prussian allies at Waterloo.

1825: Rothschild provides backing to prevent collapse of Bank of England.

1871: Rothschild organizes French repayment of war indemnity.

1875: The loan for the British acquisition of Suez Canal is provided by Rothschild.

1931: Company helps save the troubled Austrian Creditanstalt.

1941: Rothschild Continuation is formed as a holding company to ensure continuity of family involvement in banking.

1967: Establishes N M Rothschild & Sons (Australia).

1970: Rothschild incorporates as private limited company.

1973: Offices in Hong Kong and Singapore are opened.

1979: An office in Chile is opened.

1982: Company creates Rothschild Incorporated in the United States.

1986: Rothschild backs British Gas privatization.

1989: Offices in Germany and Italy are opened; Rothschild Canada Inc. subsidiary is established.

1995: An office in Shanghai, China, debuts.

1998: 200th anniversary of Nathan Mayer Rothschild's arrival in England.

commercial banking system under the Socialist government in the early 1980s. The former Banque de Rothschild had been nationalized in 1982. Two years later, Baron Guy de Rothschild and son David took the compensation they had received—about 80 million—and started a new investment banking firm, Paris-Orleans Finance. It was not until 1986, however, that the French Rothschilds were granted a new banking license and the right to restore the family's name to their bank, as the French banking industry once again became privatized.

David de Rothschild quickly took the lead in rebuilding Rothschild & Cie, transforming it into a new French financial powerhouse and one of the driving forces behind many of the country's largest business deals through the next decade. When Evelyn de Rothschild began to look toward consolidating the family's banking interests, he tapped David de Rothschild to become N M Rothschild's deputy chairman in 1992, establishing his younger cousin as his heir apparent. That position was reinforced in 1996, when N M Rothschild engaged in a restructuring of its global operations, reorganizing its businesses around five main product lines: resource banking and treasury operations; investment banking; asset management; development capital; and private banking and trust management services. At the same time the Rothschild operations set up a group investment banking committee charged with coordinating the global financial business of the Rothschild empire. David de Rothschild was named as

head of the new committee. Also in that year, N M Rothschild established a joint venture with Dutch bank ABN AMRO to compete for contracts in the world's equity markets. By 1999, that venture—ABN AMRO Rothschild—was completing deals worth more than $125 billion per year.

In the late 1990s, N M Rothschild's client-intensive approach paid off as the group became an important player in the booming European market for mergers and acquisitions. The firm took part in such important deals as the launch of EADS, the European aerospace group created from the merger of France's Aerospatiale, Spain's CASA, and Germany's DASA. N M Rothschild was also an advisor on the massive restructuring of Deutsche Telekom, valued at more than $15 billion; the firm also backed England's National Grid Group in its $8.9 billion takeover of Niagara Mohawk Holdings in the United States, while playing a supporting role in the takeover of Mannesmann by Vodaphone, worth more than $200 billion.

As the company celebrated more than 200 years of operations at the heart of the world's financial markets, N M Rothschild continued to explore new frontiers. In 1999 the company announced its plans to extend the ABN AMRO Rothschild joint venture to cover the lucrative market for initial public offerings in the United States. Closer to home, N M Rothschild announced its intention to establish subsidiary operations in Birmingham, England, to bring the company closer to the region's growing market of small and mid-sized companies. That subsidiary was expected to begin operations in early 2001.

Principal Subsidiaries

ABN AMRO Rothschild (50%); Banco BICE (Chile); N M Rothschild & Sons Ltd.; N M Rothschild & Sons (Australia) Ltd.; N M Rothschild & Sons (Hong Kong) Ltd; Rothschild Bank AG (Switzerland); Rothschild Europe BV (Netherlands); Rothschild GmbH (Germany); Rothschild Japan KK; Rothschild North America, Inc. (U.S.).

Principal Competitors

ABN AMRO Holding N.V.; AXA Financial, Inc.; The Bank of Tokyo-Mitsubishi Ltd.; Barclays PLC; Citigroup Inc.; Credit Suisse Group; ; Deutsche Bank AG; Dresdner Bank AG; The Goldman Sachs Group, Inc.; ING Groep N.V.; J.P. Morgan Chase & Co.; Lazard LLC; Lehman Brothers Holdings Inc; Merrill Lynch & Co., Inc.; Morgan Stanley Dean Witter & Co.; Salomon Smith Barney Holdings Inc.; UBS AG.

Further Reading

Cunningham, Sarah, "A Patrician in the Nescafe World," *European*, May 16, 1996, p. 36.

Moutet, Anne-Elisabeth, "The Crown Prince at the House of Rothschild," *European*, October 31, 1996, p. 23.

N M Rothschild & Sons, London: N M Rothschild, 1999.

Rodgers, Peter, "Rothschild Dynasty Plans Global Shake-Up," *Independent*, October 1, 1996, p. 16.

Rossant, John, and Stanley Reed, "The Rothschilds Are on a Roll," *Business Week International*, December 11, 2000, p. 64.

——, "Rothschild Has Big Plans for Branch," *Birmingham Post*, December 21, 2000, p. 17.

—M.L. Cohen

New York Stock Exchange®

New York Stock Exchange, Inc.

11 Wall Street
New York, New York 10005
U.S.A.
Telephone: (212) 656-3000
Fax: (212) 656-2126
Web site: http://www.nyse.com

Non-Profit Company
Incorporated: 1971
Employees: 1,500
Operating Revenues: $735.5 million (1999)
NAIC: 52321 Securities and Commodity Exchanges

Founded in 1792 amid the budding financial enterprises of lower Wall Street in New York City, the New York Stock Exchange, Inc. (NYSE) has evolved into one of the world's foremost securities marketplaces. It is the oldest and largest stock exchange in the United States, and one of the most important world-wide. The NYSE currently operates as a not-for-profit corporation, run by a board of directors and its 1,366 members. About 3,000 companies, both domestic and foreign, are listed on the NYSE. These companies have a combined market capitalization of $15 trillion. The NYSE runs a floor-based trading system, where members called specialists are assigned to particular stocks. The specialist is charged with maintaining a fair and orderly market for the assigned stocks. The system requires human beings on the trading floor, but it is also highly automated, and has the capacity to process about ten billion shares a day. Changes in information technology in the late 1990s led to increasing competition from the NASDAQ (National Association of Securities Dealers Automated Quotation) exchange and from alternative electronic brokerages. NYSE announced plans in the late 1990s to transform itself into a public company, though by 2001 no definite date for the change had been set. The NYSE makes most of its revenue from fees on listings and on trading and market data.

Late 1700s Origins

The NYSE took shape in New York City in the 1790s, where merchants and brokers held public auctions and negotiated

deals in and around the landmark Tontine Coffee House at the corner of Wall and Water Streets. New York proved a particularly rich market for the government securities which had helped fund the Revolutionary War. As New York commerce evolved, the budding securities market grew accordingly in complexity and scope. On May 17, 1792, two dozen brokers signed the "Buttonwood Agreement," founding the Exchange on lower Wall Street. They agreed to avoid public auctions, to collect minimum commissions on federal bonds (public stock), and to "give preference to each other" in their trading deals.

Following the War of 1812, the stock market experienced unprecedented growth. Increased trade with Britain transformed New York into the leading American port. Private and commercial banks proliferated. Key brokers decided to establish a steady forum—with a fixed location and regular hours—and on March 8, 1817, they adopted a constitution and the name "New York Stock & Exchange Board" (NYS&EB).

The NYS&EB was governed by distinct rules and procedures. Members were elected on the basis of a ballot-style election process. The exchange followed rules regarding sales and delivery procedures, commission rates, and business ethics. Stipulations also controlled absenteeism, distractions during bidding, and even the wearing of hats. Daily trading consisted of members bidding on securities from designated seats, while the president "called" out each stock or bond.

The stock market fed off a flow of new capital from the 1820s to the 1830s. Trading of federal securities financed the construction of roads, bridges, canals, and municipal water, sewerage, and lighting systems. New laws brought governmental charters within closer reach of young companies. Consequently, trading volume at the NYS&EB rose from an average of 100 shares per day in 1827 to 5000 shares per day in 1834. By the late 1830s, however, the securities market followed the overall economy into a slump. British cutbacks in American investment, rampant speculation in land and securities, and the 1836 closing of the federally-chartered Second Bank of the United States culminated in the Panic of 1837. Though it lost the momentum it had gathered in the 1820s and early 1830s, the NYS&EB managed to survive until the down cycle reversed in 1843.

Among the many new issues listed at the Board, railroads accounted for particularly high trading volume in the mid-1800s. Though the first railroad issue—Mohawk & Hudson Railroad—was listed on the Exchange in August of 1830, the rail frenzy reached its pinnacle in the 1850s and 1860s. By the early 1850s, the NYS&EB listed over ten rail companies.

In 1863, the Board changed its name to the New York Stock Exchange (NYSE) and began construction of its first permanent building. Designed by John Kellum, in the Italian Renaissance style, the new space accommodated expanded business. The second-floor Board Room was designed to seat the elected members with assigned places from which they negotiated the stock call, held three times daily.

With the end of the Civil War, intense capitalization of American industry spurred unprecedented growth in stock trading and the emergence of new and competing exchanges. In 1869, the NYSE joined forces with two key competitors: the Open Board of Brokers and select representatives from the Government Bond Department. These mergers were accompanied by administrative and organizational changes that would effect the shape of the NYSE over the following century. Trading volume rose substantially to over $3 billion in securities, a figure that was managed by a body of 1060 members, up from 533 before 1867. On October 23, 1868, memberships were made salable, with prices averaging between $7,000 and $8,000. Continuous trading replaced the "call" system.

Innovations in the Late 19th Century

The latter half of the nineteenth century brought numerous technological advances. Communications between brokers, investors, and different exchanges were catapulted by the development of the telegraph in 1844, the completion of a transatlantic cable in 1866, and, eventually, the development of the telephone, which reduced trading time from roughly 15 minutes to less than sixty seconds after 1878. The NYSE also benefited from the 1867 introduction of the first stock ticker. In order to control accuracy and fair distribution of trade information, the NYSE established its own New York Quotation Company to gather transaction data and distribute it systematically to ticker companies.

Despite efforts to control trading, a combination of financial buccaneering and broad economic influences disrupted the securities market in the late 1860s and early 1870s. Reckless gold speculation in 1869, including an attempt by Jay Gould and James Fisk, Jr., to corner the gold market, prompted the U.S. government to sell some of its supplies, precipitating a sharp break in gold and other securities on September 24. The investor calamity earned the name "Black Friday." In September 1873, the failure of Jay Cooke & Company sparked another major market break that closed NYSE offices for ten days and scared the securities industry until the end of the decade.

By the 1880s, the scope and trading volume of the NYSE reflected the rise of large corporations and industry-wide trusts. The Exchange created an "Unlisted Department" through which shares were traded until a company qualified for regular listing (the department was abolished in 1910). On December 15, 1886, the exchange traded a record 1.2 million shares. When trading volume reached three million shares in April of 1901, plans were drafted for expanded offices. Completed in 1903, the new Exchange building was designed by George B. Post in the classical-revival manner. To embellish the white marble facade, J.A. Ward sculpted the figures of "Integrity Protecting the Works of Man."

In the early 1900s, the NYSE saw the rise of oil and steel industries and the tremendous financial clout of such magnates as John D. Rockefeller, Henry Clay Frick, and John Pierpont Morgan. On October 23, 1907, monetary inflation and speculation caused a run on banks and a rapid decline in stock prices. Containment of the crisis was largely attributed to Morgan, who organized a consortium of major banks to hold up the market with a subscription of over $25 million. The Panic of 1907 had almost abated when World War I broke out in the summer of 1914, with foreign exchanges closing down in droves. By July, the NYSE stood as the last major exchange to absorb worldwide investor panic. It suspended trading until December 14. When it reopened, military procurements stimulated renewed trading energy that carried the NYSE prominently into the 1920s. To finance the war, large issues of United States Liberty Bonds were traded, attracting new investors.

After the war, the American economy was powered by retail chain stores and massive holding companies which accounted for rapid expansion in new issues, greater volume of trading, and increasing value of listed shares. The NYSE took several measures to maintain order amid the flux of new activity: the Stock Clearing Corporation was established on April 26, 1920, to facilitate transfers of cash and stock between members, banks and trust companies; Exchange membership was increased from 1100 to 1375 in 1929; and the trading floor was physically expanded and updated to handle higher volume. While the market value of all NYSE listed stocks was $27 billion in 1925, it jumped to approximately $90 billion by 1929.

In the late 1920s, financial optimism persisted despite signs of weakening markets in agriculture, real estate, and construction. On October 24, 1929, however, the market underwent its first sharp break, known as "Black Thursday." One week later, on October 29, 1929, the market crashed. Stock prices dropped 11.7 percent and volume soared to a record 16,410,000 shares. The Dow Jones Industrial Average dropped from 386 to 41.

Regulation and Reorganization During the Depression and After

The United States Congress passed corrective legislation, of which the Securities Act of 1933 and the Securities Exchange

---

Key Dates:

1792: Formal founding of the exchange.
1817: Exchange adopts the name New York Stock & Exchange Board (NYS&EB).
1863: Name changed to the New York Stock Exchange (NYSE).
1903: Exchange moves to its 11 Wall Street location.
1938: NYSE names its first president.
1971: Organization is overhauled, and the NYSE becomes non-profit corporation.
1987: Membership in the NYSE reaches a record price of $1.5 million.
2001: Exchange begins all trading in decimals.

Act of 1934 directly influenced the NYSE. The 1933 Act mandated the registration of all new issues of securities with the Federal Trade Commission (FTC) and the full availability of all pertinent information to investors. The later Act created the Securities and Exchange Commission (SEC) to monitor price manipulation, speculation, and unfair practices in all securities exchanges. On October 1, 1934, the NYSE registered with the SEC as a national securities exchange. The NYSE initiated substantial organizational change with the June 30, 1938, election of its first full-time paid president and chief executive officer, William McChesney Martin, Jr. Martin restructured the Exchange's Governing Committee and its entire committee system, and paved the way for stricter self-regulation.

After weathering World War II and assisting the federal government in the sale of seven giant defense loans, the NYSE entered the 1950s with a plan to gain the confidence of new investors. In June 1953, the Exchange admitted its first member corporation, Woodcock, Hess & Co., expanding on rules that had limited memberships to partnerships. In January 1954, the Exchange inaugurated a Monthly Payment Plan, in which stocks could be purchased with regular payments. And in February of that year, the push to broaden public ownership fostered a print and radio campaign of public education with the theme: "Own Your Share of American Business."

Starting in the 1960s, a virtual revolution in automated data-processing, information, and communication technology effected every level of Exchange activity, from trading practices to regulation and industry-wide organization. In December 1964, the "black box" ticker was replaced with a 900-character-per-minute model. The old pneumatic tube system was replaced with computer cards. The Market Data System (MDS), completed in December of 1966, used the latest computer technology to integrate the ticker system, the NYSE Common Stock Index and stock-clearing operations. A joint venture between the NYSE and the American Stock Exchange resulted in the 1972 establishment of the Securities Industry Automation Corporation (SIAC), which provided consulting and development services in automated systems for the entire industry. Improved systems utilized by the NYSE also included the 1976 Designated Order Turnaround (DOT) system to electronically route trade information between the Exchange and member firm offices (the improved SuperDOT system followed), and a computerized Stock Watch system to monitor price fluctuations in listed stocks.

Starting in the early 1970s, major organizational changes affected the NYSE and the securities industry at large. In 1970, public ownership of member firms was approved. Then in February of 1971, the Exchange again called on William McChesney Martin, Jr., to overhaul its constitution, rules, and procedures. Changes following Martin's recommendations were numerous: the NYSE was incorporated as a not-for-profit organization; in July 1971, member corporations began listing their stock; alternative listing standards attracted foreign-based corporations, and qualified foreign-based brokers were invited to apply for membership; electronic-access memberships were added to physical memberships to expand broker-dealer participation in NYSE markets; and the fixed commission system was abolished in May 1975. In addition, the Board of Governors was replaced by a Board of Directors in July 1972; by 1993, the Board consisted of 12 public members, 12 industry members, and two NYSE officers, the chair/CEO and the president/chief operating officer.

Market Innovations in the 1980s

With the Securities Acts Amendments of 1975, Congress enacted further changes. A full consolidated tape was introduced to electronically collect and report trades in NYSE listed stocks from all markets in which they occurred. The 1978 inauguration of the Intermarket Trading System (ITS) used computers to connect the NYSE to six other stock exchanges: the American, Boston, Cincinnati, Midwest, Pacific, and Philadelphia. A Composite Quotation System and National Clearance and Settlement System enabled brokers to do comparative shopping between different markets. Those markets grew in number to include, among others, the over-the-counter (NASDAQ) market after 1982.

In the 1980s, the NYSE was influenced by three main trends: the rise of options and financial futures markets; the proliferation of non-Exchange instruments such as limited partnerships, penny stocks, and junk bonds; and the surge of computerized information delivery systems, giving industry professionals unprecedented power to manipulate the market in what the press often called "market games." The first trend was manifest in the August 7, 1980 opening of the New York Futures Exchange (NYFE). All three trends contributed to a bullish market throughout the early 1980s.

The September 21, 1987, record price of $1.15 million paid for a NYSE membership reflected confidence in the market's strength. Nevertheless, less than six months later the market experienced a sudden downturn. On October 19, 1987, the Dow Jones Industrial Average dropped 508 points, followed a day later by the highest volume day of 608,148,710 shares at the NYSE. In order to reduce record stock-market volume, on October 20 the NYSE curbed the use of its electronic order-delivery system, forcing many traders to turn away orders. The overall turmoil and tremendous loss to investors earned the name "Black Monday." The overall crisis became known as the Crash of 1987.

The Crash of 1987 prompted energetic discussion and planning toward regulatory overhaul of the nation's financial industry. While strategies differed, general consensus supported the basic objectives of national market system legislation: fair competition between market participants; economically efficient and fast execution of customer orders; public access to market information; and the opportunities for investors to interact without broker participation. The exact means of arriving at these objectives remained a subject of heated and ongoing debate. One plan proposed a $1 billion superfund, created with capital advanced by large member firms. In a *New York Times* editorial on October 21, 1987, Lawrence H. Summers suggested that the stock index futures market should be regulated out of existence, as it "increased market volatility by creating huge selling pressure following market declines." Edward A. Kwalwasser, executive vice-president of the NYSE Regulatory Group, proposed a general regulatory structure that would apply the same rules to all securities execution systems. He argued that different regulations too often applied to different trading systems.

Indeed, from the 1980s on, the NYSE faced growing competition by off-exchange trading in NYSE-listed securities. Customers were increasingly drawn to so-called third-market firms for several reasons: they had no exchange fees to pay, they outperformed regional exchanges, and they could execute orders at incredible speeds, often within seconds. Yet critics cited important disadvantages as well: third-market firms permitted their brokers/dealers to funnel order flow to sources of liquidity that might undermine the primacy of the investor and the capital raising function. In an April 1993 hearing on the future of the Stock Market, NYSE CEO William Donaldson defended the Exchange against the encroachment of dealer markets. He noted that "the fragmented nature of dealer markets combined with flexibility in the time a trade can be reported makes trade reporting in the dealer market inherently unreliable." Praising the NYSE's combination of computer automation with on-floor communication, Donaldson added that "It's only at the point of sale where we believe that human intelligence and competitiveness must be brought together in executing an order."

In January 1992, the NYSE began a year-long series of programs and events in observance of its bicentennial. It also continued its fight to retain any further slippage in its market share, adding policies like the "clean-cross rule" allowing large institutional investors to cross block orders on the floor without interference from smaller public orders. In addition, the NYSE continued to develop international contacts: in November of 1986 it led a Wall Street delegation to China for a symposium on financial markets; in November of 1988 it opened an office in London to facilitate European access to U.S. capital markets; and in October of 1990 the NYSE established an exchange program with the Soviet (now C.I.S.) Ministry of Finance and Gosbank, the state bank.

Increasing Competition in the Late 1990s and Beyond

The long bull market of the 1990s was good for the NYSE, yet the overall growth of the stock market also helped fuel the company's principal competitor, NASDAQ, and promoted many alternative electronic trading systems. These alternative systems (known as ECNs, for electronic communication networks), such as Instinet Corp. and Bloomberg Tradebook, used advanced communication technology to allow institutions to trade among themselves, cutting out the middleman. These were increasingly viewed as low-cost alternatives to traditional trading. By the mid-1990s, the ECNs accounted for close to four percent of orders in securities listed on the NYSE, up from just over one percent in 1991. As for NASDAQ, it was known as the haven of technology stocks, and by and large it was technology that was thought to account for the long season of prosperity in the U.S. stock market. It became increasingly important for the NYSE to distinguish itself from NASDAQ and its competitors, and to sell itself as the best stock exchange. The principal difference between NASDAQ and the NYSE was the floor trading system. NASDAQ did not have the member specialists who tracked each listed stock, but dealt through so-called market makers, who handled all trades electronically. Different market makers might quote different prices for the same stock, depending on their inventory.

In 1995, Richard Grasso became chairman of the NYSE, and he moved swiftly to bolster the exchange against its rivals. The NYSE struggled to woo firms away from NASDAQ, it reached out to companies just going public, and it set its sights on overseas companies. Many firms went to NASDAQ with their initial public offerings (IPOs), because of that exchange's lower bar for capitalization. Under Grasso, the NYSE tried to capture more of the young companies just going public. The NYSE had 74 IPOs in 1995, and increased that number to 117 the next year. This was still slight compared to 730 IPOs on NASDAQ for 1996. In the mid-1990s the NYSE opened an office in Menlo Park, California, near the heart of Silicon Valley, in order to be closer to many of the up-and-coming technology firms. Over the next few years, NYSE made overtures to about 600 companies listed on NASDAQ, hoping to get them to switch. Companies that made the move included the computer company Gateway 2000 and the internet provider America Online, and both NASDAQ and the NYSE competed heavily for new foreign listings. Here too, NASDAQ had a distinct advantage throughout the 1990s because of its less stringent entrance requirements and its reputation as the place for technology sector stocks. However, by 1999, the NYSE had 28 new foreign listings, and in 2000 it gained 32 (compared to 63 and 86 for NASDAQ). To make itself more amenable to foreign markets, the NYSE allowed trading in 16ths (instead of only in eighths) in 1997, and by 2001 had phased out fractions, to trade in decimals. The move to decimals brought the NYSE in line with other world stock exchanges. The stock exchange also announced plans to float itself as a public company, perhaps in 1998. However, these plans were put off, apparently because the NYSE had trouble defining its business model.

The NYSE spent heavily on advertising in the late 1990s, doubling its budget from $7 million to $14 million between 1996 and 1997. It tried to build on the prestige of its long history, which again set it apart from NASDAQ and newer electronic competitors. Nevertheless, talk of the moribundity of NYSE, with its antiquated floor-trading system, persisted through the end of the century. The close of 2000, however, saw a collapse of many of the high-flying new technology firms, and the NASDAQ dropped 40 percent. Moreover, the threat of alternative electronic trading sites seemed to be weakening. NYSE's Grasso argued that the proliferation of new trading venues meant a host of new, and usually hidden, middlemen, who didn't always work to the best interests of the investor. The NYSE had a massive weapon against the ECNs, which was its liquidity. It traded a billion shares a day, while even the largest of the ECNs sometimes traded only in the hundreds of shares after hours. In 2000, Grasso announced the NYSE would soon unveil several new electronic trading tools, giving investors on NYSE the same instantaneous trading the electronic communication networks offered. One was called Network NYSE, and it allowed investors to either work with a broker or to send orders electronically directly to the stock exchange. MarkeTrac was a web-based program that represented the NYSE trading floor in real time, showing "hot spots" of trading activity, and allowing investors to make instantaneous trades. In a sense, NYSE was positioning itself as the best of both worlds—both the staid, old-fashioned, and mighty stock exchange and the quick, cutting-edge, electronic network. Though by early 2001 it was too soon to tell what would happen to the struggling technology sector, it looked like NYSE had not been brought down by its electronic rivals.

Principal Subsidiaries

New York Futures Exchange (NYFE).

Principal Competitors

London Stock Exchange plc; National Association of Securities Dealers Inc. (NASDAQ); Instinet Group LLC; E*Trade Group, LLC.

Further Reading

Anders, George, Cynthia Crossen, and Scott McMurray, "Big Board Curb on Electronic Trading Results in Halt at Stock-Index Markets," *Wall Street Journal,* October 21, 1987, p. 3.

"The Battle for Efficient Markets," *Economist,* June 17, 2000, p. 69.

"Can the Big Board Police Itself?" *Business Week*, November 8, 1999, p. 154.

"Demolition on Wall Street; The NYSE Is Gloomy Because the NYSE Is Gloomy," *Economist,* February 4, 1987, p. 81.

"E*Trade Moves to NYSE, So Is Nasdaq Losing Out?" *Investment Dealers' Digest,* January 29, 2001.

"Excerpt of the Hearing of the Telecommunications and Finance Subcommittee of the House Energy and Commerce Committee," *Federal News Service,* April 14, 1993.

Fadiman, Mark, *Rebuilding Wall Street,* Englewood Cliffs, N.J.: Prentice Hall, 1992.

Feinberg, Andrew, "Blown Away by Black Monday," *New York Times Magazine,* December 20, 1987, pp. 39, 67–71.

Gardner, Deborah S., *Marketplace: A Brief History of the New York Stock Exchange,* New York: NYSE, 1993.

Jones, Alex S., "Caution in the Press: Was It Really a 'Crash'?" *New York Times,* October 21, 1987.

Metz, Tim, *Black Monday: The Catastrophe of October 19, 1987 and Beyond,* New York: William Morrow, 1988.

Schmerken, Ivy, "Off-Exchange Trading Chips Away at NYSE Volume," *Wall Street & Technology,* December 1992, p. 42.

"Stock in a Stock Exchange?" *Business Week,* September 27, 1999, p. 151.

Summers, Lawrence H., "In the Wake of Wall Street's Crash," *New York Times,* October 21, 1987.

"Text of Testimony Prepared for Delivery by Edward A. Kwalwasser, Executive Vice-President Regulatory Group, NYSE, Before the Telecommunications and Finance Subcommittee of the House Energy and Commerce Committee," *Federal News Service*, May 26, 1993.

Vinzant, Carol, "Wall Street Taking Another Look at Decimals," *Washington Post*, February 13, 2001, p. E1.

Wagley, John, "The Battle for Overseas Listings," *Investment Dealers' Digest*, October 2, 2000.

Weinberg, Neil, "The Big Board Comes Back from the Brink," *Forbes*, November 13, 2000, p. 274.

Woolley, Suzanne, "The Booming Big Board," *Business Week*, August 4, 1997, pp. 58–63.

—Kerstan Cohen
—update: A. Woodward

NINE WEST.

Nine West Group, Inc.

Nine West Plaza
1129 Westchester Avenue
White Plains, New York 10604
U.S.A.
Telephone: (914) 640-6400
Toll Free: (800) 999-1877
Fax: (914) 640-3499
Web site: http://www.ninewest.com

Wholly-Owned Subsidiary of Jones Apparel Group, Inc.
Incorporated: 1977 as Fisher Camuto Corporation
Employees: 15,600
Sales: $1.92 billion (1999)
NAIC: 316214 Women's Footwear (Except Athletic)
Manufacturing; 448210 Shoe Stores; 316219 Other
Footwear Manufacturing

Nine West Group, Inc. is a leading designer, developer, and marketer of women's casual and dress footwear, offering a full selection of women's shoes in three retail price ranges, from $25 for a pair of shoes to $150 for a pair of leather boots. The three market segments of the U.S. women's shoe market in which Nine West competes are classified by industry terms as "better," "upper moderate," and "moderate." Nine West has realized considerable success in both wholesale and retail operations, and the company's footwear is available through department, specialty, and independent stores nationwide, in addition to the company's own retail outlets. The company's nationally recognized brands include Enzo Angiolini, Calico, Spa, and Westies. In 1999, in the wake of slumping sales and an SEC investigation of the company's accounting practices, Nine West was purchased by Jones Apparel Group, Inc., becoming a wholly-owned subsidiary.

The Women's Shoe Market in the 1970s and 1980s

The company commenced operations in May 1977, when Jerome Fisher and Vincent Camuto incorporated a wholesale women's shoe business named Fisher Camuto Corporation. The company was a logical extension of business ties the two founders had formed nearly a decade earlier with manufacturers in southern Brazil, where costs associated with production were relatively low. Specifically, raw materials were abundant in Brazil, labor was cheaper, and capital expenditures were minimal. Fisher Camuto Corporation's utilization of Brazilian manufacturing facilities and personnel was a boon to the company, a hallmark of its success, and one not to be underestimated in understanding the history of the company's growth.

As the relationship with factory managers in Brazil matured and facilities there became more sophisticated, Fisher Camuto Corporation grew. The company generated $9 million in sales within its first year of business, a total that increased to more than $300 million over the course of the next decade. Although its design and marketing operations were based in the United States, and manufacturing was performed abroad, the Fisher Camuto Corporation nevertheless managed to maintain a production schedule commensurate with those of other U.S.-based shoe designers and manufacturers. Moreover, Fisher and Camuto proved adept at adjusting the company's designs to suit rapidly changing fashion trends.

In 1988, Fisher and Camuto formed Jervin Inc., a name derived by combining the first three letters of their first names. Jervin was established as a private-label concern engaged in arranging, on an agency basis, the sale of unbranded, or private-label, women's footwear manufactured in Brazil to retailers and wholesalers. The following year, when the company's annual sales were $338.7 million, Fisher and Camuto attempted to acquire the footwear division of U.S. Shoe Corporation, the assets of which had already aroused the interest of several other companies. A bidding war ensued, with Merrill Lynch Capital Partners emerging as the leader. Although Fisher and Camuto were willing to better Merrill Lynch Capital Partners bid of $422.5 million, U.S. Shoe Corporation's financial adviser, Merrill Lynch Capital Markets, claimed that the terms of a binding contract between U.S. Shoe and Merrill Lynch expressly forbade U.S. Shoe from providing the wholesaler with any confidential material or allowing it to participate in the bidding process. Rebuffed, Fisher and Camuto were forced to turn their attentions elsewhere.

Key Dates:

1977: Jerome Fisher and Vincent Camuto form the Fisher Camuto Corporation.
1988: Jervin Inc. is formed.
1991: Nine West Group Inc. is formed.
1993: Nine West begins selling shares on the New York Stock Exchange.
1995: Nine West acquires U.S. Shoe Corporation.
1997: SEC launches investigation of Nine West accounting practices.
1999: Nine West is acquired by Jones Apparel Group.

Nevertheless, over the next three years, Fisher and Camuto's company embarked on a period of prodigious growth. From 1989 to 1992, annual sales climbed from $338.7 million to $461.6 million, while net income increased more than 60 percent, from $14.3 million to $38.2 million. These increases were particularly impressive given the business environment at the time. The late 1980s and early 1990s were deleterious years for women's specialty apparel and footwear retailers, as overall sales had declined dramatically during a recession that stifled the nation's economy.

New Concepts in Shoe Retail: The 1990s

By the end of the 1980s, Fisher and Camuto's company was involved in both the wholesale and retail markets of the women's shoes business. On December 31, 1991, these concerns—Fisher Camuto Corporation, Fisher Camuto Retail Corporation, and Espressioni, Inc.—merged to form a new company, which was soon renamed Nine West Group Inc. Preparing to go public, Fisher and Camuto merged Jervin Inc. into the Nine West Group, of which it became a division in 1992. Once this transaction was completed, Nine West became a public corporation in early February 1993, selling shares of common stock on the New York Stock Exchange.

By this time, Nine West was operating 236 retail and outlet stores as well as designing and marketing branded and private-label shoes to more than 2,000 department, specialty, and independent store customers. Of its five nationally recognized brands, its Nine West brand was the most successful, having been redefined and repositioned in 1989 to compete in the $50 to $65 price range. The company's more moderately priced Calico brand represented its most traditionally styled shoe, typically selling for between $40 and $50. Nine West's Westies brand, sold only by independent retailers, competed in the under $40 market segment, while the Enzo Angiolini brand, the company's designer label, comprised leather shoes priced between $65 and $80. The company's fifth brand, 9 & Co., was created to attract a younger clientele and featured a line of junior footwear priced below $50, which was sold through the company's new retail store concept, also named 9 & Co.

In the wholesale side of its business, Nine West distributed private-label shoes to a host of large, nationally recognized customers, including J.C. Penney Company, Sears, Roebuck & Co., Thom McAnn Shoe Company, and Kinney Shoes. Design,

manufacturing, and sales operations of the private-label footwear were overseen by Nine West's Jervin division. The company's branded shoes were distributed to several of the largest department stores in the country, including The May Department Stores Company, R.H. Macy & Co., Federated Department Stores, Nordstrom, and Dillard Department Stores.

Nine West's success was largely dependent on its use of Brazilian manufacturing facilities. While these factories had initially manufactured 200 pairs of shoes per day for Fisher and Camuto, the production level had increased exponentially, reaching 130,000 pairs of shoes per day in 1993. During this time, the industry in Brazil employed a work force of over 39,000 and maintained cost-efficient factories, which operated their own tanneries. Moreover, through manufacturing arrangements with 25 independent Brazilian shoe manufacturers, which produced Nine West shoes in 40 factories, Nine West was able to deliver design specifications and receive completed products in an eight-week period, giving the company a supplier network that ranked among the best in the U.S. shoe industry.

Buoyed by this established supply network, Nine West capitalized on a fashion trend away from sneakers toward heavier, sturdier shoes, a trend widely embraced by younger consumers in late 1993 and early 1994. The shift in consumers' tastes caught several of the country's large athletic shoe manufacturers—Reebok International Ltd., Nike, Inc., and L.A. Gear, Inc.—by surprise, and their sales figures declined. However, Nine West and some other companies, such as Timberland Co., an outdoor apparel and shoe company, experienced a surge in profits. Nine West's stock price, which initially sold for $17.50 per share, shot up to more than $34 by the fourth quarter of the company's 1993 fiscal year.

As Nine West planned for the future, it focused on becoming a greater retail force in the U.S. shoe industry, a market segment that represented a $14 billion business in 1993. Toward this end, in 1994, the company planned to open 20 Enzo Angiolini stores, prompted by heightened consumer interest in elegant footwear. By 1997, Nine West's management hoped to derive half of its sales from the retail segment of its business, which during the mid-1990s recorded one of the highest sales-per-square-foot averages in the U.S. shoe industry at $555 per-square-foot a year. With more than 325 retail stores and its established wholesale business supplying more than 5,500 storefronts with women's shoes, Nine West expected to garner a greater share of the U.S. retail and wholesale market.

Highs and Lows in the Late 1990s

By the mid-1990s, however, prospects for the U.S. shoe industry were bleak. A glut of shoe products, combined with the rapid proliferation of retail outlets nationwide, drove sales forecasts down to two or three percent. Compounding the problem for shoe manufacturers was a recent practice among retailers and department stores of developing their own private-label products. To counter this trend, Nine West began opening a number of new boutiques in upscale urban areas, most notably in Union Square, San Francisco, in November 1994. At the same time, in an effort to diversify its product line, Nine West acquired LJS Accessory Collections, Ltd., a manufacturer of women's accessories, in January 1995.

In March 1995 Nine West finally acquired U.S. Shoe for $600 million. The deal doubled the size of the company and made Nine West the nation's third largest shoe manufacturer. More significant than this growth, however, was the acquisition of U.S. Shoe's major brands, which included Amalfi, Evan-Picone, and Bandolino. Particularly valuable was the Easy Spirit line of shoes, which saw $200 million in sales in 1994, and accounted for all of U.S. Shoe's $35 million profits. By the end of 1995 Nine West could boast 35 percent of all women's shoes sold in department stores, as well as 17 percent of the specialty footware market. Contrary to industry forecasts, Nine West's future seemed bright.

In November 1996, the company moved back to New York, taking advantage of a number of financial incentives, such as tax breaks and electricity savings, to relocate to White Plains. The year 1996 was another strong year for the company, with sales of $1.6 billion, an increase of 33 percent over the previous year, and net profits reaching $95 million. Riding the momentum of this continued success, the company embarked on a new publicity strategy, in the hopes of changing its image from that of a manufacturer of affordable shoes into a major "fashion brand." In 1996 the company reached a licensing agreement with Calvin Klein, whereby Nine West would assume responsibility for the operation of 20 CK Shoe boutiques, and an ambitious advertising campaign, featuring photographs by Herb Ritts, was launched in early 1997. Meanwhile, the recently-acquired accessories business was doing far better than expected, with sales reaching $45 million after only two years.

This growth came to an abrupt halt in May 1997, however, when the SEC announced its intention to launch an investigation into Nine West's accounting practices, in particular its manner of reporting sales. The company's initial reluctance to report this development to its shareholders only made matters worse; when a press release became unavoidable the company's stock dropped 18 percent. By December the stock had fallen 45 percent from the year's high, and in 1998 the company was forced to cut production from five million to three million units, resulting in the closing of two factories and 100 retail stores, and nearly 1,000 job cuts. More problems followed in early 1999, when a number of independent Nine West store owners filed an anti-trust suit against the company, alleging that it was engaging in unfair pricing practices with major department stores.

It was in the midst of these difficult times that the Jones Apparel Group tendered a substantial offer for the company, and an acquisition, worth $885 million, was announced in March 1999. While the proposed deal did not sit well with some Jones Apparel investors, in light of Nine West's ongoing legal difficul-

ties, the merger went through in June, and Nine West became a wholly-owned subsidiary. In the wake of the consolidation, the shoe manufacturer was forced to close three plants and lay off 1,900 workers, or 21 percent of its work force. After Jones entered into a settlement agreement with the Nine West Store owners in March 2000, it seemed the shoe company was once again on an even keel, and analysts were projecting sales for the newly-combined businesses to rise as high as $4.18 billion for the coming year, with profits increasing by 20 percent.

Principal Competitors

Brown Shoe Company, Inc.; Kenneth Cole Productions, Inc.; Candies, Inc.; Etienne Aigner, Inc.; Maxwell Shoe Company Inc.

Further Reading

Gault, Ylonda, "Dressing to the Nines: Nine West Is a Shoe-In for Investors," *Crain's New York Business*, April 14, 1997.

Getler, Warren, "Insiders Often Dump Shares Long Before Concerns Enter Bankruptcy, Study Says," *Wall Street Journal*, July 7, 1993, p. A5.

Goldman, Abigail, "Jones Apparel in $885-Million Deal to Buy Nine West," *Los Angeles Times*, March 3, 1999.

Grant, Peter, "State Snares 1,400 Jobs; Conn. Loss White Plains Gain," *Daily News* (New York), November 15, 1996.

Hoffer, Richard, "Wayne Weaver," *Sports Illustrated*, December 13, 1993, p. 64.

"Jones Apparel Completes Nine West Group Acquisition," *Women's Wear Daily,* June 16, 1999, p. 2.

"Jones Apparel Says Schwartz Will Leave Its Nine West Group," *Wall Street Journal Abstracts,* January 12, 2000, p. C21.

Marcial, Gene G., "Nine West Has Put On Its Dancing Shoes," *Business Week*, May 31, 1993, p. 79.

"Market Basket," *Women's Wear Daily*, May 24, 1994, p. 8.

"Nine West Group," *Fortune*, May 3, 1993, p. 73.

Pereira, Joseph, "Footwear Firms Hit by Fashion Change, Face Disappointing Quarterly Earnings," *Wall Street Journal*, January 17, 1994, p. A5.

Petersen, Melody, "A Good Fit Is Starting to Pinch; Nine West Tries to Fend off Investigations and Debt," *New York Times*, December 6, 1997.

——, "Bringing 'Em to Heel: Shoe Stores Say Nine West Unfairly Fixes Prices," *Los Angeles Daily News,* January 16, 1999, Bus. Sec.

Reilly, Patrick M., "Nine West Group Prepares for Return of Sleek Footwear," *Wall Street Journal*, March 11, 1994, p. A4.

"U.S. Shoe Corp.," *Wall Street Journal*, March 15, 1989, p. C6.

—Jeffrey L. Covell
—update: Stephen Meyer

⬙ NOVARTIS

Novartis AG

Lichtstrasse 35
CH-4002 Basel
Switzerland
Telephone: (41) 61-324-1111
Fax: (41) 61-324-8001
Web site: http://www.novartis.com

Public Company
Incorporated: 1996
Employees: 67,653
Sales: CHFr 35.80 billion ($22.21 billion) (2000)
Stock Exchanges: Zurich New York
Ticker Symbols: NVS (NYSE); NOVN (SWX)
NAIC: 325412 Pharmaceutical Preparation
    Manufacturing; 541710 Research and Development in
    the Physical, Engineering, and Life Sciences; 621511
    Medical Laboratories; 541380 Testing Laboratories

Novartis AG was founded in 1996 with the merger of Ciba-Geigy Ltd. and Sandoz Ltd. Based in Basel, Switzerland, Novartis is an international leader in the development and marketing of pharmaceuticals and nutrition products, in addition to operating a number of research institutes dedicated to the study of gene therapy. Although the controversy surrounding the emergence of genetically-modified foods in the late 1990s compelled the company to spin off its agribusiness holdings in 1999, entering the 21st century Novartis was poised to become a major player in the booming U.S. pharmaceuticals market, with a number of potential ''blockbuster'' drugs ready to be launched in 2001–2002.

The History of Ciba-Geigy

In the early years of the 20th century, the world's strongest chemical industries were in Germany, the United States, and Switzerland. German companies, fearful of losing their leading position to rapidly advancing American firms, openly colluded and coordinated business strategies. After World War I the German companies formed a cartel, the notorious IG Farben. In order to remain competitive with the Germans, the three largest Swiss chemical companies, Ciba Ltd., J.R. Geigy S.A., and Sandoz Ltd., formed a similar cartel called Basel AG. This trust lasted from 1918 to 1951. By 1970, however, market conditions led Ciba and Geigy to merge, forming one of the world's leading pharmaceutical and specialty chemical companies.

Geigy was the older of the two companies—one family member was in the drug business as early as 1758. Through several generations, the Geigy family had married into the prosperous silk manufacturing establishment in Basel and then became established in the dye trade in 1883. Only a few years later, the Geigy family set itself apart from other dyers in Basel by embracing newly discovered synthetic dying processes.

Several years earlier, in 1859, a French silk weaver named Alexander Clavel moved to Basel, where he established a dyeworks called the Gesellschaft für Chemische Industrie im Basel, or Ciba. In 1884 Clavel abandoned silk dying for a more lucrative trade in dyestuff manufacturing. Ciba gained a reputation for Fuchsine, a reddish purple dye, and Martius yellow.

By 1900 Ciba was the largest chemical company in Switzerland. With a major alkali works located at Monthey, it was one of the only Swiss manufacturers of inorganic dyes. Ciba, however, started a limited diversification into the pharmaceutical business with the introduction of an antiseptic called Vioform. Between 1900 and 1913 net assets quadrupled while profits nearly tripled. During this period, Geigy remained steadfastly committed to organic dye production; some of the dyes were still derived from coal tar.

Early in the century both Ciba and Geigy established factories in Germany, due in part to a labor shortage in Switzerland, but also to avoid enforcement of environmental laws designed to reduce pollution in the River Rhine.

Until World War I, German chemical companies dominated the world dye trade with a 90 percent market share. Those companies, including BASF, Hoechst, and Bayer, could easily have run Swiss competitors out of business through price competition; they had proven their ability to hold back the American chemical industry in its infancy. Instead, Ciba and Geigy developed practices that would permit international expansion while not provoking the Germans. Central to this strategy was the abandonment of bulk dye production (a German specialty) in favor of more expensive specialty dyes.

In time, the German companies developed a vested interest in the survival of their Swiss counterparts. Eighty percent of the raw materials used by the Swiss companies came from Germany. In eliminating Swiss competitors, the German companies would eliminate customers whose capacity they could not economically absorb. Furthermore, competition among German companies to fill a sudden void left by the Swiss could have destabilized the careful balance maintained by the cartel. As Swiss companies became acclimated to the German system, they were granted certain privileges, such as an exclusive right to export to Germany. Cooperation between Swiss and German companies also took the form of an occasional profit-sharing pool, as the one that existed between Geigy, Bayer, and BASF for black dye.

The onset of World War I in Europe in 1914 severely upset the equilibrium that had existed between Ciba, Geigy, and their German counterparts. Unable to secure raw materials and chemical intermediaries from German suppliers, factories in Basel were forced to suspend dye production. The Swiss later negotiated an agreement with the British, who had been dependent on German dyes and were unprepared for their trade embargo. The British agreed to supply the Swiss with raw materials on the condition that Swiss dyes would be sold preferentially to Britain. While Swiss factories in Baden were seized by the German government, the Swiss were free to export to the lucrative (and formerly German) markets in Britain and the United States and to establish factories in France and Russia.

Ciba's profits increased dramatically, from SFr 3 million in 1913 to SFr 15 million in 1917. While the end of the war reopened world markets, it also found the industry in a severe state of overcapacity. By 1921 Ciba's profits had fallen to SFr 1 million. At this time the German companies decided to reform their cartel, this time under the aegis of a large holding company called IG Farben. Ciba, Sandoz, and Geigy were invited to join IG Farben but, true to Swiss neutrality, elected instead to form their own cartel, Basel AG.

Basel AG, founded in 1918, was fashioned after IG Farben. The group consisted of Ciba, Geigy, and Sandoz—virtually the entire Swiss chemical industry. The agreement mandated that all competition between the three companies would cease, technical knowledge would be freely shared, and all profits would

be pooled. Ciba would receive 52 percent of the group's profits, while Geigy and Sandoz would each be entitled to 24 percent. Any sales between the companies were to be invoiced at cost, raw materials would be purchased jointly, and the manufacture of any product would be assigned to whichever company could produce it at the lowest cost.

From the cartel's inception, Geigy's weak market position was a source of tension for its partners. Geigy still produced vegetable dyes, which were gradually losing market share to organic dyestuffs. Despite Sandoz's contention that it was being forced to subsidize Geigy, Basel AG remained stable. In fact, it was considered more successful than the larger and more powerful IG Farben. All three firms invested their profits into a broader range of chemical interests, including chemicals and pharmaceuticals. By 1930 these divisions contributed more than one quarter of the group's profits. A joint venture between Sandoz and Geigy led to the establishment of the Cincinnati Chemical Works, a subsidiary that gave Basel AG a tariff-free foothold in the American market.

In 1929, placing profit before independence, Basel AG joined with IG Farben to create the Dual Cartel. French dyemakers joined the group shortly afterwards, forming the Tripartite Cartel. In 1932, with the addition of the British cartel Imperial Chemical Industries, the group was again renamed the Quadrapartite Cartel. This pan-European cartel existed until 1939, when World War II forced its dissolution.

Due to the secrecy characteristic of Swiss firms, little is known about Basel AG's activities during the war; the company had subsidiaries in both Allied and Axis nations. At one point, Ciba angered its partners by placing its shares in Cincinnati Chemical Works under the custody of an American trust. Apparently fearing the eventual seizure of those shares by the alien property custodian, Geigy and Sandoz protested in American courts but were unable to retrieve Ciba's shares.

In 1939 Dr. Paul Mueller, a researcher with Geigy, discovered the insecticidal properties of DDT. Originally thought safe enough to be sprayed directly on refugees to eradicate lice, DDT was considered a ''wonder chemical.'' Research during the war led to the development of several ethical drugs, including Privine, a treatment for hay fever, and Nupercaine, a spinal anesthetic used in childbirth. The companies also developed drugs for treatment of high blood pressure and heart disease.

After the war Ciba notified Geigy and Sandoz that as a result of U.S. antitrust laws, the 1918 agreement could not be respected among subsidiaries in the United States. Geigy made a similar declaration regarding American assets in 1947. Two years later Sandoz again raised the issue of cross-subsidization and proposed that the cartel be dissolved. Geigy opposed the motion, but Ciba, unwilling to abandon its lucrative markets in the United States, eventually sided with Sandoz; the postwar environment no longer justified cartelization for self-protection. Basel AG was finally dissolved in 1951.

Geigy's poor financial performance called into question its survivability outside the cartel. During the 1950s, however, the full market potential of DDT was realized. Suddenly profitable, Geigy expanded its market in agri-chemicals by introducing a corn herbicide called triazine.

Key Dates:

1859: Alexander Clavel founds silk dyeing works in Basel, Switzerland.
1886: Kern & Sandoz is formed.
1898: Geigy is founded in Grenzach, Germany.
1911: Sandoz Chemical Company Ltd. begins operations in England.
1917: Arthur Stoll creates Pharmaceutical Department at Sandoz.
1918: Ciba, Sandoz, and Geigy form Basel AG cartel.
1929: Basel AG joins IG Farben to form Dual Cartel.
1935: Geigy begins producing insecticides.
1939: Dr. Paul Mueller discovers insecticidal properties of DDT.
1949: Geigy launches anti-rheumatic drug Butazolidin.
1951: Basel AG is dissolved.
1958: Sandoz launches neuroleptic drug Melleril.
1964: Sandoz forms research center in East Hanover, New Jersey.
1970: Ciba and Geigy merge to form Ciba-Geigy Ltd.
1974: Ciba-Geigy Ltd. acquires Funk Seeds International.
1980: Ciba-Geigy Ltd. forms biotechnology unit.
1987: Ciba-Vision is formed.
1996: Ciba-Geigy and Sandoz merge to form Novartis AG.
1999: Novartis divests seed and crop protection holdings.

Both Ciba and Geigy grew steadily during the 1950s. Between 1950 and 1959, Ciba's sales grew from SFr 531 million to SFr 1.02 billion, and Geigy's grew from SFr 260 million to SFr 738 million. By 1960 both Ciba and Geigy were diversified manufacturers, competing directly in pharmaceuticals, dyes, plastics, textile auxiliaries, and agricultural and specialty chemicals. Each year Geigy's sales grew stronger, until in 1967 the company overtook Ciba.

Although older than Ciba by 25 years, Geigy maintained a more youthful image. While Ciba sold itself as the company "where research is the tradition," Geigy recruited engineers with the slogan, "future with Geigy." But in 1970, while Ciba and Geigy personnel were quibbling over their respective talents, the leaders of both companies were discussing a possible merger.

The idea to merge was first raised when the two companies jointly established a factory at Toms River, New Jersey. With increasingly difficult conditions in export markets—particularly the United States—officials of the two companies began to explore the benefits of combining their textile and pharmaceutical research; Geigy's strength in agricultural chemicals complemented Ciba's leading position in synthetic resins and petrochemicals.

Ciba and Geigy were both in excellent financial condition. However, some of the same market conditions that had led them to form Basel AG in 1918 were once again prevalent. Competition against German companies in export markets had intensified. But it was as a defense against emerging petrochemical industries in oil-rich Persian Gulf states that the merger was most attractive.

The largest obstacle to a merger between Ciba and Geigy was U.S. antitrust legislation. Antitrust sentiment in the United States was so strong that federal prosecutors vowed to block the merger in Switzerland if it threatened to restrain American trade in any way. In order to win approval in the United States, Ciba agreed to sell its American dyeworks to Crompton and Knowles, and Geigy consented to turn over its American pharmaceutical holdings to Revlon. Despite further challenges, including one from consumer advocate Ralph Nader, the merger was approved.

Mechanically, the merger consisted of a takeover of Ciba by Geigy. This was done to minimize tax penalties amounting to SFr 55 million. Geigy's chairman, Dr. van Planta, assumed the chairmanship of the new company, with Ciba's chairman, Dr. Kappeli, serving as honorary chairman.

As promised, the Ciba-Geigy merger has proven "synergistic." The more profitable but less diversified Geigy has benefited from Ciba's research capabilities. Ciba, on the other hand, has profited from Geigy's more modern approach to marketing and management. In the United States, the company's American subsidiary passed the one billion dollar sales mark in 1978, and doubled that figure only six years later. The company's worldwide sales that year were SFr 17.5 billion, 30 percent of which came from U.S. operations. Despite a 14 percent drop in profits between 1978 and 1980, Ciba-Geigy has maintained strong annual sales growth since 1981; profits as a percentage of sales was 8.1 percent in 1985.

In contrast to its impressive performance on the balance sheet, Ciba-Geigy has suffered a few problems with its public image. In the mid-1970s a Ciba-Geigy product marketed in Africa as an ordinary analgesic produced a horrifying side-effect: the loss of large pieces of flesh. In addition, its plant at Toms River discontinued production of Posgene in response to a Greenpeace campaign that warned the community of a possible accident similar in magnitude to the tragedy in Bhopal, India.

Troubles at Toms River continued; in 1982 the plant was added to the U.S. Environmental Protection Agency's (EPA) list of "Superfund" cleanup sites when more than 120 chemicals were discovered in local groundwater. Then, in 1984, investigators found a leak in the ten-mile conduit leading from Ciba's facility. The company discontinued dye, resin, and additive production at Toms River in 1986 and pleaded guilty to one charge of illegal waste disposal in March 1992. The corporation paid more than $60 million in fines and landfill and groundwater cleanup costs and agreed to make donations to New Jersey state conservation projects. The Toms River experience, combined with tightening European Community pollution regulations, helped convince Ciba-Geigy to cite the environment as one of its focuses.

Environmentalism became one of the cornerstones of Ciba's "Vision 2000" strategy, a long-term plan to balance the economic, social, and environmental objectives of the company. The company logo was shortened to just "ciba," but the formal name remained unchanged. The corporation was reorganized from functional/geographical units into 14 separate businesses with autonomous research and development, production, and marketing divisions. Ciba's businesses could be grouped into three basic areas: healthcare, agriculture, and industry.

The company considered its Pharma, Plant Protection, and Additives divisions its primary businesses. Pharma, the single largest operating unit, ranked among the world's top five pharmaceutical concerns. The corporation's leading product was Voltaren, an anti-rheumatic. Ciba's Pharma unit also claimed the second most popular smoking cessation patch, Habitrol (known as Nicotinell outside the United States). Habitrol encountered stiff competition in the 1990s, but was launched in France and Canada in 1992 and received over-the-counter status in the United Kingdom and Italy that year. One problem with transdermal nicotine patch sales was that the product created a self-defeating market: if the treatment worked, patients would eventually end the therapy; if the patches were ineffective, smokers would not buy them. Ciba-Geigy purchased the Dr. R. Maag plant protection business from Hoffman-La Roche in 1990 and achieved majority ownership of Bunting Group's plant protection business in 1992.

Ciba-Geigy's Self Medication, Diagnostics, and Ciba Vision units were recognized by the corporation as growth enterprises. Self Medication was expanded with the 1992 acquisition of Fisons' North American business, and the purchase of Triton Diagnostics buttressed the Diagnostics group. Ciba Vision's contact lenses, lens care products, and ophthalmic medicines ranked number two worldwide.

Ciba-Geigy's Seeds and Composites units were considered long-term investments. In 1990, the company announced that it had successfully inserted marker genes into corn cells that produced fertile plants and passed the new traits on to viable seeds. The company thereby entered the race to genetically engineer plants with the most attractive traits.

The core industrial businesses of Ciba-Geigy in the early 1990s included Textile Dyes, Chemicals, Pigments, Polymers, and Mettler Toledo scales. The leading market positions of these businesses allowed them to function as "cash cows" for research and development in other areas. For example, Ciba's textile dyes, additives, and Mettler Toledo units ranked number one worldwide in their respective categories.

Ciba's reorganization included the divestment of its Flame Retardants and Water Treatments Chemicals businesses, valued at approximately $100 million. The units were sold to FMC Corp. in 1992. Ciba-Geigy's sales and profits increased steadily in the late 1980s and early 1990s, exceeding SFr 22 billion in revenue and SFr 1.52 billion in profits in 1992. The majority of Ciba's sales, 36 percent, were made in European Community countries. Overall European sales comprised 43 percent of the total, while North America contributed 32 percent, Asia constituted 13 percent, and Latin America made up seven percent.

In 1992, Ciba-Geigy was one of the five largest chemical companies in the world. While it was widely diversified within the industry, it maintained a steady emphasis on sophisticated chemicals—pharmaceuticals, plastics, pigments, or pesticides.

The Emergence of Sandoz Ltd.

In 1886 two Swiss men, Dr. Alfred Kern and Mr. Edouard Sandoz, established a company in Basel in order to manufacture and sell synthetic dyes. Thirty years earlier the English chemist, William Henry Perkin, while trying to synthesize quinine from coal tar, came up with a purple dye instead. Two years later a Frenchman used a similar process to produce a magenta dye, and a new industry was born, ending the reliance upon purely animal, vegetable or mineral dyes. The new dyes were more brilliant than the old and lasted longer. They worked better on synthetic fabrics and they allowed for the development of new dye colors. It was an industry that many recognized as potentially very profitable.

Dr. Kern was 36 when the business was formed and was well known as a chemist specializing in dyestuffs trade. The two men purchased 11,000 square meters on the west bank of the Rhine River, built a manufacturing plant, and registered their business under the name of Kern & Sandoz, beginning work on the July 1, 1886. They had ten workmen and a 15-horsepower steam engine, and a certainty that they would succeed. There were some early setbacks: the dyes they originally had intended to produce, including Auramine, Victoria Blue, and Crystal Violet, required a process originated by Kern and an old partner, but that partner would not release his patent rights; another dye, Alizarine Blue, caused a reaction kettle to explode.

The company managed not only to survive but to expand. Kern developed new dyes and Sandoz traveled extensively, searching for more customers and markets for their products. In five years, from 1887 to 1892, their production increased from 13,000 kilograms of six different types of dyes to 380,000 kilograms of 28 dyes.

In 1893 the company began to change considerably. Dr. Kern collapsed and died of heart failure and, though Sandoz tried to run the company himself, two years later he was compelled to retire from active management for health reasons. In 1895 Sandoz and Company was converted into a limited company called Chemische Fabrik vormals Sandoz (Chemical Works formerly Sandoz) with a share capital of two million francs and with Edouard Sandoz as the first chairman of the board. At this point, the company was fortunate in its selection of managers and chemists to replace the founders; it was these people who, over the next 30 years, provided the company with direction and enabled it to expand. On the technical side, Arnold Steiner and Melchior Boniger developed and produced new products such as sulphur and azo dyes. Two talented sales managers, Werner Stauffacher and Georg Wagner, built a worldwide sales organization that expanded up to and even through World War I.

Although the company was fortunate in the appointment of its managers, it had many misfortunes, particularly from 1903 to 1909 (known among insiders as the "seven lean years") when serious consideration was given by members of the board to the possibility of a merger or even liquidation. Prices for manufactured goods kept falling while those for raw materials increased. There were very expensive patent litigations with competitors as well. However, by 1910 profits began to increase again, reaching one half million francs in 1913, the year after the company's shares first appeared on the Basel Stock Exchange.

World War I, and Switzerland's isolation, resulted in some intriguing, and later profitable, opportunities for Sandoz. Germany prohibited all exports and, as a means to this end, blocked transit traffic so that everything from fuel to raw materials was in short supply. Wood, transported to Sandoz's plant in horse drawn carts, was used instead of coal throughout the war. Intermediates, which had formerly been imported, were now blocked, but buyers somehow managed to get those purchased in England and the United States into Switzerland. The company's own chemists were able to produce the others. After the war, the world chemical market that had formerly been dominated by the Germans was soon open to competition.

Sandoz profited under these circumstances. It purchased the Rothaus estate in Muttenz, just in case land was needed for expansion. In 1918, to circumvent the protectionist legislation in other countries which, in turn, inhibited Sandoz's international expansion, Sandoz, Ciba, and Geigy formed the Association (Interessengemeinschaft) of Basel Dyestuff Manufacturers. They used this association primarily to establish jointly owned factories in many countries, although they also pooled profits to ensure that none of the members would be forced to declare bankruptcy. The original charter of the Association was for 50 years, but it was amicably dissolved after 33.

In 1911 Sandoz established its first subsidiary in England, and in 1919 established another in New York. In Switzerland the technical departments were restructured by Dr. Hermann Leeman (later president of the company from 1952 to 1963). The previous organization had been a system under which any chemist might be assigned to work simultaneously in research, manufacturing, and application. According to the restructuring, these three functions became separate departments, with the addition of a patent department.

A difficult period was again experienced during the early 1920s, when a crisis in the textile industry caused a recession in the dependent dyestuffs industry. The work force was at first put on part-time employment, but in 1921 nearly 30 percent of the employees had to be laid off. By 1929 business had been severely affected. However, partly due to the protection afforded by the Association, and partly to the company's lead in research and development, Sandoz was able to set up numerous subsidiaries around the world providing a protective network against the failure of any one subsidiary. More significantly, the company embarked on a program of diversification into chemical agents for use by the textile, leather and paper industries, and later for the agricultural industry. Research in these areas produced industrial cleansers, soaps, softening agents, mercerizers, bleaches and, after World War II, fungicides, herbicides, insecticides, and rodenticides.

The most interesting part of the company's diversification program began with the establishment, under Dr. Arthur Stoll, of a pharmaceuticals department. Already well-known for his work on chlorophylls, Dr. Stoll now became world famous for the development of a process for the isolation and for the discovery of the importance of ergotamine, an alkaloid of the rye fungus called ergot. The products developed from ergotamine were numerous and sold steadily, so that the pharmaceuticals department gave stability to the company's sales.

When World War II started, Sandoz Ltd., as it had been named in 1939, was financially secure with fully stocked warehouses, production sites and sales agencies throughout the world. Transportation of supplies would not be the problem it had been during the previous war, as supplies were now stocked near company plants. Fuel alone remained a problem. Mr. Leeman was credited with having advised the purchase of an old brown-coal mine. This purchase was finalized and, mining 18,000 tons of fuel for itself during the war, the company had solved its fuel problem. As soon as the war was over the Muttenz site was put to use, with a large plant for chemical and agrochemical production being built there. Little is known of Sandoz's contribution, if any, to either side's war effort, but from 1933 to 1948 company profits increased from SFr 48 million to SFr 253 million.

The international postwar expansion did not exclude Sandoz. The company's only difficulty involved increasing production to keep pace with demand. In 1949 Professor Stoll was promoted to managing director. New headquarters were built which altered Basel's skyline. In addition, automation was introduced in the production facilities. And in 1964 annual sales surpassed one billion francs for the first time. Each of the three divisions, including dyes, pharmaceuticals, and chemicals, prospered individually. The dyes division created dyes for the new plastics, paints and synthetic fibers now in demand, as well as the new foron dyes for polyester, and dyestuffs for mass dyeing.

The developments within the pharmaceuticals division caught the world's attention. Sandoz concentrated heavily on its recently discovered synthetic compounds for the treatment of mental illness and migraine. Most of the products developed were based on ergotamine and included such drugs as Methergin, which stopped post partum hemorrhage, and Gynergen, which when injected early enough relieved the pain of migraine headaches. Certainly the most famous of these drugs was Delysid, also called LSD 25. In 1961 the company's *Jubilee Volume* proudly reported the drug's ability to cause "disturbances in the perception of space and time, depersonalization and color hallucinations" and that "it was destined to play a great role in experimental psychiatry." Research in the hallucinogen called mescaline, derived from the Mexican peyote cactus, and in psilocybin, derived from certain mushrooms, was also aimed at producing drugs which might be used in conjunction with psychotherapy and, in particular, psychoanalysis.

Although the use of Delysid was strictly controlled, and issued only to authorized research centers, within 15 years of its discovery in 1942 it was being produced illegally all over America and Europe as a "recreational drug." The consequences of a large number of people across the Western world experiencing what the *Jubilee Volume* referred to as "model psychosis" from LSD had yet to be fully understood. The company quickly curtailed its research into hallucinogens, but it would always be remembered as the company which "invented acid."

The late 1960s and early 1970s continued to be a period of growth for the company; sales doubled from SFr 1.97 billion to SFr 3.61 billion. The massive size of the company required further organizational revisions. As a result, an executive committee took over management. In 1968 the dyes and chemicals divisions were amalgamated and a new agro-chemical division was created. The company's diversification also continued during this time. In 1967 a merger with Wander Limited of Berne added a nutrition department. Two years later, the takeover of

Durand & Huguenin eliminated a neighboring competitor in dyes manufacturing. A hospital supply business was acquired and its activities combined, during 1976, with those of Rhone-Poulenc in a joint venture. These acquisitions and mergers were engineered by one of the few nonchemist presidents of the company, Carl Maurice Jacotett, a lawyer's son from Neuchatel who had studied theology and philosophy before going into business. During his short presidency, from 1968 to 1976, the work force increased from 6,345 to over 33,000 people, making Sandoz one of the world's largest pharmaceutical companies.

The oil crisis of 1973, and the consequent rise in prices for raw materials and energy, dramatically affected Sandoz and other manufacturers who could not possible raise the prices of products high enough to cover costs. In 1975 a five year recession began, which led to another review of company structure, this time to reduce overhead and streamline organization. A steady reduction in the number of personnel and a firm control of wage increases helped to decrease losses. Continued diversification and acquisitions soon increased both equity and profit. Sandoz entered the seed business with the acquisition of Rogers Brothers and Northrup King Company (U.S.A.) and Zaadunie B.V. (Netherlands). In 1982 Wasa (Sweden) was acquired, Sodyeco and Zoecon (U.S.A.) in 1983, and Master Builders (U.S.A.) in 1985, the last introducing the company into yet another market, that of chemicals for the construction industry.

By 1975 a department of ecology and safety had been set up in Basel to establish and supervise guidelines throughout the company and its holdings. An effort to develop products with low environmental impacts was also initiated. However, Sandoz received bad publicity for an environmental disaster at one of its Basel plants. Near the end of 1986, when the company was celebrating its centennial, a large amount of toxic chemicals spilled into the Rhine River killing fish and shore life from Switzerland through West Germany to The Netherlands. Sandoz entered 1987 with sales over SFr 8 billion, profits over SFr 500 million, and an equity of more than SFr 4.5 billion.

The 1996 Merger of Ciba-Geigy and Sandoz

As international drug markets continued to expand rapidly in the 1990s, pharmaceutical companies realized that multi-national conglomerates, with diverse operations and worldwide resources, would dominate the future of the industry. Ciba-Geigy and Sandoz were not blind to this trend, and in early 1996 the two companies announced their intention to form a new corporation, Novartis AG. At the time it was the largest merger in history, with the combined value of the two companies exceeding $70 billion. The goal of Novartis—the name was derived from the Latin *novae artes*, or "new skills"—was to become a world leader in the field of "life sciences." With the merger, Ciba and Sandoz were creating the world's largest supplier of crop-protection products, and the second largest pharmaceutical company.

The size and scope of the deal, however, raised concern among regulatory agencies, both in Europe and the United States. Because many of the two companies' principal operations overlapped, particularly in the pharmaceutical, crop protection, and animal health sectors, the European Union (EU) launched an in-depth probe into the merger in May 1996. In July the EU approved the deal, on the condition that the companies divest a number of their animal health and agricultural chemicals interests, in addition to using the new company's considerable influence to insure competition in the field of gene therapy. To gain Federal Trade Commission (FTC) approval in the United States, the company shed a large portion of Ciba's dominant share of the U.S. crop protection market, while providing further reassurances of competitiveness in the future gene therapy business. To this latter end, the company reached a licensing agreement with rival Rhone-Poulenc Rorer for certain gene therapy patents, and in December 1996 Novartis AG was officially incorporated.

The new company's focus was on biotechnology, and the wide range of applications for genetic research. The FTC projected that the market for gene therapy, while still insubstantial in the late 1990s, had the potential to reach $45 billion by 2010, and Novartis was intent on becoming a dominant player in this burgeoning industry. The future growth of the industry, however, was far more promising in the United States. Patent procedures for biotechnology inventions were complicated and expensive in the European Union, with costs approaching $120,000 per patent, compared to $13,000 in the United States. Fearing that this discrepancy would inevitably drive the majority of biotech research to the United States, the European Chemical Industry Council (Cefic) issued a directive in May 1997 that called for the simplification of patenting procedures. While the EU eventually adopted many of the industry's recommendations, the effort encountered strong resistance from the public, which remained wary of genetic research in the wake of the scare over "mad cow disease" in the early part of the decade. To help assuage these fears, the EU passed a law in September 1997 requiring that all seed and food products carry labels stating whether or not they contained genetically-modified materials.

In the midst of this controversy, Novartis was searching for ways to establish a stronger research presence in the United States. In April 1998 the company announced plans to build a research institute in San Diego dedicated to the study of human genes; a second lab, devoted to plant genetics, was announced in July. At the core of the company's human gene research was the imminent completion of the Human Genome Project; the company wanted to move beyond the mapping of genes, to devote itself to the study of how genetic material functioned. At the same time, the company's plant research remained focused on the development of genetically-modified, herbicide-resistant crops. Novartis remained a worldwide leader in this field, becoming the first company to sell genetically-modified white corn seeds in the United States in May 1998. In June, its Bt-11 modified corn was approved for sale by the European Union.

The late 1990s witnessed a dramatic shift from Europe to the United States in the pharmaceutical industry. Part of the problem again involved more stringent regulatory policies in Europe, where pricing standards were strictly governed, and there were few incentives for innovation. The States were also quicker to realize the massive growth potential of so-called "lifestyle drugs" like Viagra and Prozac, an area where the European firms were lagging behind. In the hopes of seizing a sizable piece of the booming U.S. market, Novartis Pharmaceuticals devoted itself in the latter half of the 1990s to the development of a number of potential "blockbuster" drugs, including

Zelmac, an irritable bowel medicine, and Visudyne, a treatment for macular degeneration, the most common cause of blindness in people over 50.

Unfortunately, a series of setbacks struck the Novartis agribusiness sector in the late 1990s. The company's initial success with its genetically modified crops was hit hard by a report released in the United States in May 1999, which claimed that pollen from genetically-modified corn was responsible for wiping out large populations of Monarch butterflies. The EU quickly suspended approval processes for genetically-modified seeds pending further investigation, and agribusiness stocks plummeted. With public skepticism over genetically-modified food still a powerful force at the turn of the century, Novartis decided to divest its agribusiness holdings in order to focus on the pharmacological and therapeutic applications of biotechnology, and in late 1999, the company's seed and crop protection operations merged with a British-Swedish company to form Syngenta.

A restructuring of the company's pharmaceutical operations followed in July 2000, and by the early part of the new century the company was poised to launch eight new drugs, including Starlix, which treated Type-2 diabetes, and Femara, a breast-cancer treatment. With the merger of pharmaceutical giants Glaxo-Wellcome and SmithKline Beecham in December 2000, the success of Novartis's potential blockbuster drugs, in particular Starlix and Zelmac, seemed even more critical to its future as an international leader in the pharmaceutical industry.

Principal Subsidiaries

Syngenta AG (Switzerland; 61%); Wesley Jessen VisionCare, Inc. (U.S.); SyStemix, Inc. (U.S.); Gerber Products Company (U.S.); Genetic Therapy, Inc. (U.S.); Novartis Pharmaceuticals Corporation (U.S.).

Principal Operating Units

Novartis Pharma AG; Novartis Generics; Novartis Consumer Health; Ciba-Vision; Novartis Animal Health.

Principal Competitors

Merck & Co., Inc.; Aventis; AstraZeneca plc; Pfizer Inc.

Further Reading

Buckley, Neil, ''More on Gene-Modified Food,'' *Financial Times* (London), July 25, 1997.

Capell, Kerry, with Heidi Dawley, ''Healing Novartis,'' *Business Week*, November 8, 1999.

Enri, Paul, *The Basel Marriage: History of the Ciba-Geigy Merger*, Zurich, Switzerland: Neue Zurcher Zeitung, 1979.

Fisher, Lawrence M., ''Two Deals Extend the Financial Frontiers of Gene Therapy,'' *New York Times*, January 14, 1997.

Ford, Peter, ''Wary Europe Enters Biotech Age,'' *Christian Science Monitor*, June 10, 1998.

Gebhart, Fred, ''Skin Patch Makers Fight to Be No. 1 in War on Nicotine,'' *Drug Topics,* January 20, 1992, p. 26.

Graham, David E., ''Plant Genetics to Grow Here: Swiss Company Announces $600 Million Biotech Lab,'' *San Diego Union-Tribune*, July 22, 1998.

Hall, William, ''Sandoz and Ciba to Sell Part of U.S. Business,'' *Financial Times* (London), August 29, 1996.

Hunter, David, ''Ciba-Geigy: Back to the Roots for Renewed Growth,'' *Chemical Week,* June 21, 1989, p. 21.

Kirschner, Elisabeth, ''Ciba-Geigy and New Jersey Settle Toms River Battle,'' *Chemical Week,* March 11, 1992, p. 14.

Lichtenstein, William, ''The Toms River Experience,'' *Chemical Engineering,* April 1991, p. 45.

McCarthy, Joseph L., ''Alex Krauer: Ciba-Geigy,'' *Chief Executive,* July/August 1992, p. 20.

Michaels, Adrian, ''Novartis Hopes New Drugs Will Boost US Sales,'' *Financial Times* (London), February 15, 2001.

Morris, Gregory D., ''Ciba-Geigy Enters the $1.5 Billion/Year Corn Biotech Race,'' *Chemical Week,* September 12, 1990, p. 12.

Shon, Melissa, ''Nicotine Patch Market Takes a Fall, But Why?,'' *Chemical Marketing Reporter,* September 14, 1992, p. 5.

Wilsher, Peter, ''The Feeling Grows That Going Green Is Good for Business,'' *Management Today,* October 1991, p. 27.

—updates: April S. Dougil; Stephen Meyer

Otis Elevator Company, Inc.

One Farm Springs Road
Farmington, Connecticut 06032
U.S.A.
Telephone: (860) 676-6000
Toll Free: (800) 676-5111
Fax: (860) 676-5111
Web site: http://www.otis.com

Wholly Owned Subsidiary of United Technologies
Corporation
Incorporated: 1867 as Otis Brothers & Co.
Employees: 63,000
Sales: $6.2 billion (2000)
NAIC: 333921 Elevator and Moving Stairway
Manufacturing

Otis Elevator Company, Inc. is the world leader in the manufacture, maintenance, and service of elevators, escalators, moving walkways, and other horizontal transportation systems. After more than a century in business, Connecticut-based Otis has more than 1.2 million elevators and escalators in operation, controlling about 22 percent of the world's elevator market. Almost 80 percent of the company's business is done overseas. Since 1975 Otis has been a subsidiary of United Technologies Corporation (UTC), a conglomerate that also owns Pratt & Whitney and Carrier. Otis contributes approximately 23 percent of UTC's annual sales.

Development of the Safety Hoist in 1852

Although vertical hoisting devices date back as far as the construction of the pyramids in Egypt, they all contained the same drawback: if the supporting rope or cable snapped, the platform plummeted to the ground. Vermont-born Elisha Graves Otis, a mechanic living in Yonkers, New York, invented the first safety hoist in 1852. He attached saw-toothed rachet bars to each of the four side guide rails and placed a wagon spring on top of the platform. When the lifting cable was attached to the upper bar of the spring, the pull from the heavy platform made the spring taut enough to keep it from touching the rachet bars. If the cable snapped, the tension on the spring would be released, and each end would engage the ratchet bars, locking the platform in place and preventing it from falling.

Armed with two unsolicited $300 elevator orders, Otis opened his own factory in Yonkers on September 20, 1853. The following year he demonstrated his invention at the Crystal Palace Exposition in New York City. By the end of 1856 he had sold more than 40 elevators, all for use in carrying freight. The next year he installed the first passenger elevator—with a completely enclosed car—in a five-storied New York retail building. A classic Yankee tinkerer, Otis developed his elevator design without a drawing board, blueprint, or prototype model, illustrating his invention only to the degree required for a Patent Office application. But his talents did not extend to business. When Otis died in 1861 of "nervous depression and diphtheria," he left an estate of only $5,000, counterbalanced by $8,200 in debts.

Otis's two sons, Charles and Norton, took over the business, which became known as Otis Brothers & Co. Between them they amassed 53 patents for elevator design and safety devices. By 1872 the company had built more than 2,000 steam-powered elevators and taken in more than a million dollars. In 1878 Otis introduced a faster, more economical hydraulic elevator. During 1880–81 the company received orders to install elevators in the Capitol, the White House, and in the Washington Monument. The year 1889 marked the introduction of the first successful direct-connected electric-powered elevator and the exhibition of the first escalator—the term was an Otis trademark until 1950—at the 1900 Paris Exposition. In 1903–04 Otis introduced the gearless-traction electric elevator, a design that remains essentially unchanged today.

The Otis Elevator Co. was formed in 1898 from the $11 million merger of Otis Brothers & Co. and 14 other elevator companies. This proved so powerful a combine that in 1906 the company had to agree to stop collusive bidding and other restraints of trade. Otis started buying established firms overseas as early as 1902. By 1912, when net income came to $883,317, the company owned seven factories in the United States and by 1924 had subsidiaries in Canada, Germany, Italy, and Belgium. To

Company Perspectives:

Over 22,000 Otis mechanics maintain one million elevators, escalators and moving walks worldwide. They are supported by a comprehensive range of maintenance, communications and service dispatching networks which remain unmatched in the industry. Indeed, Otis remains very much a global company. Its products are offered in more than 200 countries and territories, and Otis maintains manufacturing facilities in the Americas, Europe, Asia and Australia, and engineering and testing centers in the U.S., Japan, France, Germany and Spain.

offset slow sales during recessions, Otis began selling contracts to service and maintain its installations in 1922. Net income reached nearly $8.4 million by 1929 before dipping sharply with the advent of the Great Depression. The company lost money for the first time in 1933 and 1934, yet continued to pay out dividends, an unbroken tradition since 1903.

1931: Otis Elevators in the Empire State Building

The first third of the century saw constant improvements in Otis elevators. In 1915 the company introduced a self-leveling device that allowed the elevator platform to stop exactly at floor level. A push-button system introduced in 1924 made stops and speed automatic rather than at the option of the operator. When the Empire State Building was completed in 1931 and became the world's tallest building, its Otis elevators were capable of a record speed of 1,200 feet per minute. The following year Otis installed the first double-deck elevator in a Wall Street office tower; it featured eight double-decked cars that stopped at two floors at the same time.

During World War II Otis filled military orders. The war generated not only orders for elevators, but also for rangefinders and tank and aircraft engine components. Defense contracts continued to be important during the Korean War era, accounting for 22 percent of Otis's business in 1953.

Even before World War II push-button elevators were common in apartment houses, private residences, and small office buildings for many years. In 1948 Otis introduced the improved Autotronic system for commercial installations. Electronic controls were sufficient to operate the cars, and a computer directed a bank of cars to handle traffic most efficiently. Two years later Otis introduced Autotronic elevators that could function without an attendant. By 1956 the position of elevator attendant was no longer a job with a rosy future; every major commercial building using Otis elevators wanted Autotronic equipment. Unlike the earlier push-button models, these elevators were large, fast, and could change speeds and adjust their schedules to suit traffic demands, bypassing floors when fully loaded. Moreover, Otis projected an annual saving of $7,000 per car in labor costs. In 1956 it did some $20 million worth of conversion work from manual to automatic.

Despite these developments, the decade following World War II was a period of some stagnation for Otis. Although net sales passed $90 million in 1948 and approached $120 million

by 1954, net income fell from $12.1 million to $9.6 million. In 1952 Otis's share of the nation's new elevator business dropped to an unusually low 40 percent due to high prices. The company had to cut its operating margin from 20 to 11 percent to regain market share from its competitors. Other problems identified with making elevators were the cyclical nature of the construction industry and growing suburbanization, which in this period was characterized by ranch-style homes and single-story shopping centers.

To jump-start its flagging business, Otis began to diversify. Its first outside acquisition since 1898 was the purchase of Transmitter Equipment Manufacturing Co. (Temco) in 1953. Temco, which held a contract to make electronic pilot trainers, became Otis's defense and industrial division. The following year, Otis bought forklift truck manufacturer Baker-Raulang Co., which became its truck division. Toward the end of 1955 Otis began producing automatic bowling pinsetters. None of these ventures would prove profitable over the long run: Temco was a poor performer and actually lost money in 1963; Baker lost money every year but one between 1955 and 1961; and after a strong start the pinsetter operation fell into the red and was sold in 1963. Between 1955 and 1968 Otis's net sales increased fourfold, from $121 million to $481 million, but its net income rose only from $11.9 million to $22.1 million during the same period.

In 1968, a year after Otis installed 255 elevators and 71 escalators in New York City's newly completed World Trade Center, the company held nearly half the U.S. elevator market. It continued to look to other areas for profit, however. In a 1968 *Forbes* article, President Fayette S. Dunn explained: "Elevator prices are down. With everyone trying to increase their market share, we just can't make the money on contracts we should." Between 1967 and 1970 Otis acquired five companies involved in materials handling: York Manufacturing Co., a maker of large lift trucks; Moto-Truc Co., producer of smaller lift trucks; West Coast Machinery, manufacturer of postal and in-plant vehicles, golf carts, and personnel carriers; Euclid Crane & Hoist Co., builder of hoists and cranes; and Saxby, S.A., a French manufacturer of hoists and cranes. In 1969 the company established the Diversified Systems Division to apply elevator and escalator technology to automated automobile-parking, container-handling, and warehouse systems.

The company also was actively engaged in designing and manufacturing automated horizontal moving systems. Otis's "Trav-O-Lator" moving walkways were engineered to carry people, horizontally or on an incline, quickly and comfortably at airline terminals and other points where large numbers of people had to be moved without congestion. By 1973 Otis had passed $800 million in sales. Maintaining plants in 17 countries, and dependent on overseas operations for 37 percent of its net income, Otis's share of the elevator market in low-rise buildings had increased from 19 percent to 30 percent in five years. Earnings had risen every year since 1968. The backlog of orders in March 1973 was $1.1 billion, an all-time high. Net sales reached a record $1.1 billion in 1974—more than half of which was generated overseas—and net income a record $43.5 million. Among its foreign operations in 1975 were five special glass-walled observation elevators for the world's tallest free-standing structure, Toronto's 1,815-foot-tall CN Tower.

Key Dates:

1852: Elisha Graves Otis invents first safety-hoist elevator.
1861: Otis dies; two sons take over business.
1889: First electric-powered elevator and escalator are introduced.
1898: Otis Elevator Company is formed.
1975: United Technologies Corporation buys company.
2000: Gen2 belt-driven elevator is introduced.

Otis's rapid expansion overseas was not without hazards. In 1976 the company revealed to a federal agency that it estimated it had made between $5 million and $6 million in improper payments during the past five years, some of them to foreign government officials and employees. These payments were made in connection with installations in large buildings where government involvement was substantial and bribery and kickbacks were allegedly normal procedures. In 1975, 65 percent of Otis's $752.7 million in new orders had come from foreign sources.

United Technologies Purchases Otis in 1975

In October 1975 United Technologies Corporation (UTC) made a cash offer of $42 a share for more than 55 percent of Otis's stock, which was trading for $37.63 a share at the time. UTC's motivation was to end its heavy dependence on military contracts at the end of the Vietnam War. Otis's management at first resisted the offer but dropped its opposition in November after UTC agreed to pay an additional $2 per share and buy up all of Otis's common stock. The cost was estimated at $276 million. The untendered shares were exchanged for shares of a new convertible preferred United Technologies stock under a 1976 merger.

Otis continued to grow as a UTC subsidiary. Sales volume passed $1.5 billion in 1980, $2 billion in 1986, $3 billion in 1989, and $4 billion in 1990. The flagship Yonkers factory, parts of which dated back to 1868, was deemed obsolete and abandoned in 1983. An elevator test tower and engineering center was completed in Bristol, Connecticut, four years later. This exceptionally slender, 383-foot, 29-story, $20 million structure was just 54 feet across but accommodated 11 elevators and an escalator. The structure, which helped Otis develop models that rode more smoothly, operated more efficiently, and broke down less often, was its first North American test tower; others were located in France, Italy, Japan, Spain, India, and China.

Otis unveiled its "Elevonic 101" system—the first elevator control system using microprocessors to control every aspect of elevator operations—in 1979. The Elevonic 401, introduced in 1981, was the first control system with synthesized speech, information display, and security systems. It dispatched cars in response to variations in building traffic as they occurred. The Elevonic 411 system, introduced in 1990 for gearless elevators, was capable of modifying its software-based dispatching rules for more responsive elevator service. When linked to a new computerized control system, it enabled building managers to coordinate the performance of up to 64 elevators.

New artificial intelligence software patented by Otis in 1993 used "fuzzy logic" to estimate how many people were waiting for elevators at a given moment in office buildings or hospitals where several elevators were operational and traffic patterns changed throughout the day. The program tracked traffic flow by compiling information about time elapsed between stops at the same floor, the number of buttons pushed by people boarding a car, and the car's changing weight load. It then combined this data to arrive at an estimate of the number waiting and decided which car to send—not necessarily the closest one. The first Otis elevator system incorporating fuzzy logic modules was installed at the Hyatt Osaka Regency Hotel in Osaka, Japan, which opened in 1994.

OTISLINE, a computerized, 24-hour-a-day dispatch service for mechanics, was introduced in 1983 to aid the world's largest elevator service workforce. In 1985 an Otis people-mover system was introduced to connect Harbour Island and downtown Tampa, Florida. People movers also were installed by Otis in Serfus, Austria, and Sun City, South Africa. In 1992 the company completed a similar "horizontal elevator" in the new Tokyo international airport at Narita, Japan. Like the Florida shuttle, it combined elevator and Hovercraft technology, transporting a total of 9,800 standing passengers and their luggage 900 feet between two terminals each hour. One-car trains moved at 13 miles an hour on a half-inch cushion of air.

In 1984, when Otis accounted for 20,000 of the 100,000 elevators sold in the world each year, the company signed a joint venture to build elevators in China; a decade later, it had three Chinese joint venture plants. In 1990 Otis renewed a relationship with Russia in which it had not engaged since providing Czar Nicholas II with three elevators in the early part of the century. By the end of 1992 Otis had formed four Russian and one Ukrainian joint ventures to manufacture, install, and maintain elevators and was maintaining about 20 percent of the elevators in these two countries by 1994. It opened its first major manufacturing plant in Southeast Asia—in Malaysia—in 1993. The following year, the U.S. government lifted its trade embargo with Vietnam and Otis negotiated two joint ventures with Vietnamese companies to sell, install, service, and maintain elevators throughout that country.

Otis had 24 percent of the world market for elevators and escalators in 1990, twice as large a share as its nearest competitor. By then the company had installed 1.2 million elevators. However, it was not resting on its laurels. Its president, Karl Krapek, told a correspondent for the London-based magazine *Business,* "We are one of the few American industries that can compete long-term and successfully against the Japanese. There are very few left: jet engines, helicopters, and elevators. Boy, we have to do that. And we will do that." By late 1992 Otis had raised its market share in Japan to 13 percent, compared with three percent 20 years earlier.

With the end of the cold war, Otis replaced aircraft engine manufacturer Pratt & Whitney as UTC's largest income producer. UTC lost money in 1991 and 1992, mainly because of Pratt & Whitney's problems. To cut costs the company modernized manufacturing techniques. Otis was one of the UTC units to abandon standard assembly-line production in favor of worker teams that assembled products from start to finish. UTC claimed that by giving workers more responsibility it reduced mistakes and eliminated downtime. As an example, the company noted that workers at an Otis plant in France were, in 1993, turning out a top-selling elevator in five days, compared with five weeks in 1991.

In 1994 Otis's revenues of $4.64 billion comprised nearly 22 percent of UTC's total revenue, while its operating profits of $421 million were more than 27 percent of the parent company's total. It held 23 percent of the world market in new elevator equipment in 1994 and was selling about 39,000 elevators and escalators annually. Otis also serviced about 790,000 elevators and escalators. Two-thirds of its approximately 66,000 employees were field installers and mechanics averaging 15 years of company experience. Installation and maintenance accounted for 61 percent of Otis's revenue in 1992 and an even greater proportion of company profits.

Otis continued to thrive in the mid-1990s, although the meltdown of the Asian economy in 1997 threatened the company's well being. Otis was forced to restructure its Asian Pacific business. Approximately seven percent of the region's workforce was cut, and other cost-saving measures were taken. In addition, Otis consolidated operations in other parts of the company, reducing engineering centers from 19 to six and closing its European headquarters. In all, Otis shed 1,100 jobs or 1.6 percent of its total work force.

Otis, determined to maintain its position as industry leader, was not afraid to embrace change. In what at first glance might seem an incongruous marriage for a traditional manufacturer, Otis turned to the Internet in 1999. The company announced that it had teamed with IBM and Next Generation Network to bring the Internet to its elevator cars. The new service, called e*Display, would feature flat-panel screens that displayed full-motion, full-color displays of information (news, weather, sports, and entertainment), which would be provided by an Internet hook-up and change every five to ten seconds. There would be no audio, which tests had indicated would be too intrusive. Not only would the system be able to provide building owners with a way to efficiently and inexpensively broadcast important notices to occupants, it promised to be a boon to advertisers. Elevator riders tend not to make eye contact or engage one another and were likely to find the screen a welcomed distraction. It was estimated that the average employee in an office building used the elevator six times a day, with each trip lasting 45 seconds, but what was especially attractive to advertisers was the demographics of the riders. Depending on the office building, advertisers could target some of the highest paid professionals, who had the ability to immediately get on-line and buy a product. Advertisements could be tailored for the type of tenants that occupied a particular building. Within two or three years Otis hoped to sell more than 10,000 screens at the cost of $5,000 each. Furthermore, it would share in advertising revenues. Otis also announced two further Internet initiatives. E*Direct allowed new customers to shop for elevators and escalators on-line. e*Service provided customers with an Internet capability of monitoring the performance of their elevators and escalators, taking advantage of Otis's computer-based system diagnostics and performance measurements.

More important than its entry into e-business was the introduction in 2000 of the Gen2 elevator system, which the company boasted was the first major advance in lift technology in nearly 150 years. Gen2 elevators were intended for buildings that ranged from two to 20 floors, a market that accounted for 75 percent of new elevators sold each year. Gen2 elevators used steel belts encased in polyurethane. Because the belts were far more pliable than steel cables, the traction sheave above the elevator was only one-fifth as large, and the size of the motor could also be reduced so that the entire drive mechanism could be installed inside the elevator shaft. As a result there was no longer a need for a machine room (in some cases, an entire floor) devoted to elevators, thus saving builders money and creating the potential for more rental space. The Gen2 elevators, offered at first in The Netherlands, Austria, and Switzerland, became the company's fastest selling new elevator product in its history. Otis also looked to expand the technology to high-rise buildings.

The future for Otis seemed secure, but where would it go from here? Perhaps the answer is space. When NASA speculated in August 2000 about the possibility of building an elevator that would carry passengers into space, Otis was eager to accept the challenge, claiming that if the technology on which the company was currently working was applied to the project, a space elevator could be constructed within ten years. The multi-deck ''car'' would be hoisted 22,000 miles above Earth to a point in space known as ''genosynchronous orbit'' via a thin diamond fiber. It sounded fantastic—as, likely, did the concept of the elevator more than 150 years ago.

Principal Operating Units

L.I.S. and Canada; Latin America: North Europe; South Europe; Central and East Europe; South and Central Asia; Japan.

Principal Competitors

Schindler Holding Ltd.; ThyssenKrupp AG; KONE Corporation.

Further Reading

Drain, Sharon Cramer, ''A Mechanic Gave the World a Lift,'' *American History Illustrated,* November 1987, pp. 42–50.

''For Otis: More Electronics,'' *Business Week,* October 17, 1953, pp. 119–20.

''Going Down, Please,'' *Time,* November 24, 1975, p. 92.

''How Otis Gets the Business,'' *Fortune,* July 1954, pp. 100–03, 124, 126.

''How to Make Mistakes and Still Prosper,'' *Forbes,* May 1, 1964, p. 35.

Jacobs, Karen, ''Elevator Maker to Add Commercial Touch,'' *Wall Street Journal,* December 7, 1999, p. B8.

——, ''Otis Elevator Creates Design for Efficiency,'' *Wall Street Journal,* February 7, 2000, p. A35C.

Jackson, Donald Dale, ''Elevating Thoughts from Elisha Otis and Fellow Uplifters,'' *Smithsonian,* November 1989, pp. 211–18.

Kleinfield, N.R., ''Otis's '29 Stories Full of What-Ifs,' '' *New York Times,* July 2, 1989, p. III4.

Lawless, John, ''Mighty Otis Stays on Top,'' *Business,* November 1990, pp. 131–32, 134.

McManus, Terry, ''Advertisers View for the Eyes of Elevator Riders,'' *Advertising Age,* February 21, 2000, p. 44.

"Otis Goes on an Acquisition Ride," *Business Week,* June 6, 1970, pp. 132, 134.

"Otis—Going Up!," *Financial World,* May 9, 1973, p. 12.

Pinder, Jeanne B., "Fuzzy Thinking Has Merits When It Comes to Elevators," *New York Times,* September 22, 1993, pp. D1, D9.

Shipman, Alan, "Otis Seizes the High Ground," *International Management,* November 1992, pp. 50–52.

Smart, Tim, "UTC Gets a Lift from Its Smaller Engines," *Business Week,* December 20, 1993, pp. 109–10.

"Twinkle, Twinkle, Little Star, Was That an Elevator Car?," *Canadian Corporate News,* October 26, 2000.

"Why Go Outside?," *Forbes,* May 15, 1968, p. 82.

—Robert Halasz
—update: Ed Dinger

Palm Harbor Homes, Inc.

15303 Dallas Parkway, Suite 800
Addison, Texas 75001
U.S.A.
Telephone: (972) 991-2422
Fax: (972) 991-5949
Web site: http://www.palmharbor.com

Public Company
Incorporated: 1977
Employees: 4,700
Sales: $777.47 million (2000)
Stock Exchanges: NASDAQ
Ticker Symbol: PHHM
NAIC: 321992 Prefabricated Wood Building Manufacturing

Palm Harbor Homes, Inc. is one of the largest producers of manufactured homes in the United States. The company manufactures single and multisection homes at 16 manufacturing facilities, marketing its products under the brand names Palm Harbor, Keystone, Masterpiece, River Bend, and Windsor Homes. Customers choose from more than 150 floor plans, and nearly all—90 percent—customize their homes either structurally or decoratively. Excluding land, the average retail price of a home manufactured by Palm Harbor is $58,000, with a typical home containing between two and five bedrooms, a living room, family room, dining room, kitchen, and two or three bathrooms. Palm Harbor sells its homes through independent retailers and through company-owned retail centers, which display furnished and landscaped homes. The company operates 133 superstores in 17 states. A vertically integrated company, Palm Harbor sells homeowners' insurance to its customers through a subsidiary, Standard Casualty Company, and offers financing through another subsidiary, CountryPlace Mortgage, Ltd.

Origins

Palm Harbor was founded on the last day of 1977 by a veteran of the manufactured housing industry. Lee Posey had 21 years of experience in the industry when he started Palm Harbor, having spent the previous ten years as president of Redman Industries, Inc., based in Dallas, Texas, one of the country's largest manufactured housing concerns. When Posey left Redman Industries in 1977, he enjoyed a short reprieve before entering the fray again, this time by starting his own business from scratch. Posey enlisted the help of four colleagues; they pooled their savings and obtained a small loan from a venture capital firm to start Palm Harbor.

With the capital, Posey and his supporters purchased two manufacturing facilities, thus entering the manufactured housing industry just as it was recovering from the recessionary and inflationary economic conditions of the 1970s. Industry-wide sales for the broadly defined mobile-home industry fell to $2.5 billion in 1974 after exceeding $4 billion in 1972. Companies such as Posey's Redman Industries, which, along with three other manufacturers, controlled 30 percent of the market, were devastated by the downturn, as unit shipments plunged 42 percent. The industry began to recover in 1976, two years before Palm Harbor began operations, presenting manufacturers with market conditions that were, at least in one respect, better than they had been before the downturn. During the mid-1970s, the price of a conventional new home leaped 61 percent, making the far less expensive manufactured home an attractive alternative.

As he established Palm Harbor, Posey could take comfort in the improving conditions, but there were other, perhaps more important, developments underpinning his newest foray into the industry. The mobile-home industry, which first emerged during the 1920s to provide housing to migratory workers, had developed into a multibillion dollar business, spawning subsidiary industry segments such as the manufactured home segment that Palm Harbor occupied. The decisive point in the mobile-home industry's evolution occurred during the mid-and late 1950s, when manufacturers realized that mobility was not the primary selling point of their products. Instead, affordability swayed consumers to purchase what was marketed as a "home on wheels." Once they had realized that their business had less to do with the automotive industry and more to do with the construction industry, manufacturers tailored housing designs to match homebuyers' needs. Manufactured homes such as those made by Palm Harbor were mobile in the sense that

Company Perspectives:

Under the direction of Lee Posey, who has been in the industry since 1956, management's thrust has been dedicated to assuring that the customer is satisfied with a quality product and that the associates at Palm Harbor Homes feel this is the best job they have ever had. This commitment has worked—as the demand for manufactured housing in the United States soared, Palm Harbor has stayed on the leading edge of innovative design, construction, and marketing while empowering its employees with the tools and responsibility they need to achieve even beyond their own expectations.

sections of the house were transported to the customers' land, but once constructed on site, the homes were permanently fixed in place, like a conventional home.

During Palm Harbor's formative years, the company grew by using its profits to fund capital expansion projects. As such, the company expanded through internal means, adding new manufacturing capacity only after the success of existing facilities warranted expansion. Toward this end, the company enjoyed a rousing start to its corporate life. Profits enabled Posey to establish two more manufacturing facilities in 1981, one in Austin, Texas, and another in Plant City, Florida. An additional plant was constructed alongside the Plant City facility in mid-1985, followed by the debut of another manufacturing plant in Boaz, Alabama, in December 1986.

The conclusion of Palm Harbor's first decade of physical expansion also marked the company's entry into the retail side of the business. In 1986, Palm Harbor co-founded Newco Homes, Inc., a retail operation in Texas that sold manufactured homes. The move into retail represented the company's first attempt at developing a synergistic presence in manufactured housing. Ultimately, Posey wanted to control every aspect of the relationship between Palm Harbor and its customers, a goal that he would vigorously pursue during the 1990s. In the interim, Newco served as the testing ground for Palm Harbor's future in retail, while Posey concentrated on the manufacturing side of his business. Once the manufacturing operations were in order, he began to delve into complementary business areas, creating a highly efficient, vertically integrated manufactured housing concern.

Quality Control Measures Adopted in 1988

As Palm Harbor entered its second decade of business, manufacturers of a different ilk were experimenting with a new management practice and enjoying great success. Total Quality Management (TQM), a program that embraced statistical quality control methods, was credited for significant performance improvements at some of the country's largest manufacturing operations. Companies such as Ford, Motorola, and General Electric had adopted TQM standards and recorded marked improvements, piquing the interest of all types of manufacturers.

The excitement swirling around TQM carried over into the housing industry, but in that industry in general, it proved difficult to use the system to eliminate the variables that com-

promised quality. Much of the production work was subcontracted, performed by workers who were beyond the direct control of a single managerial team or one presiding company. Not so at Palm Harbor, where the actual production work took place in a controlled environment. Accordingly, the company began implementing TQM measures in 1988, starting at the two adjacent manufacturing facilities in Plant City, Florida. Through TQM, Posey and his second-in-command, Larry Keener, soon discovered a problem with quality control that was eroding customer satisfaction. In the October 2000 issue of *Professional Builder*, Keener explained: "We learned that most of the set-up contractors employed by our retailers do a pretty good job on the 'rough set,' which is putting the sections together on-site, getting them level, and making sure they are structurally anchored and 'weathered in.' But they were doing a very poor job on interior finishing. And that's the stuff our customers sit and look at every day."

Posey and Keener focused their efforts on altering the quality control methods covering the final detailing work, a stage in the construction process referred to as "field completions." It took nearly four years to revamp field completions in Florida and another four years before the entire company had adopted the new quality control methods. Eventually, the company developed a network of factory-trained technicians who performed field completions, but by the time the operations in Florida had conformed to the new standards, Posey was ready to branch out into new areas. In 1992, the company began to vertically integrate its operations, beginning with the decision to develop a full-fledged retail arm to its operations. Based on the experience with Newco, which operated roughly a dozen stores, Posey decided to complement the company's reliance on independent retailers with a network of wholly owned superstores.

1995 Public Offering Spurs Diversification and Expansion

To help finance Palm Harbor's diversification into retail, Posey turned to Wall Street, filing with the Securities and Exchange Commission in 1994 for the company's initial public offering (IPO). At the time of the filing, Palm Harbor ranked as the fourth-largest builder of manufactured homes in the country, supported by 12 manufacturing facilities and 20 company-owned superstores in more than two dozen states. With the proceeds from the IPO, Posey intended to add manufacturing plants in Arizona, Oregon, and Idaho, and to open between 12 and 24 retail centers. The IPO was completed in July 1995, followed by a secondary offering three months later in October, which gave the company more than $20 million for the expansion of its retail and manufacturing operations.

The mid-1990s also saw Palm Harbor gain control over additional aspects of the manufactured housing business. In July 1995, concurrent with the company's debut on the NASDAQ exchange, Palm Harbor began offering installment financing to its customers, providing the service through a subsidiary named CountryPlace Mortgage, Ltd. Less than a year later, in May 1996, the company acquired Standard Casualty Company, an underwriter of property and casualty insurance for owners of manufactured homes. The addition of these two subsidiaries turned Palm Harbor into a full-service operator and

---

Key Dates:

1977: Posey and four associates found Palm Harbor.
1986: By co-founding Newco Homes, Inc., the company enters the retail segment of the manufactured housing industry.
1988: Total Quality Management is applied to manufacturing plants in Florida.
1995: Palm Harbor converts to public ownership.
1996: Palm Harbor begins offering homeowners' insurance.
2000: The number of company-owned retail centers reaches 133.

---

added new streams of revenue to a company that was growing at the fastest pace in its history. The manufacturing side of its business was bolstered by the acquisition of a production plant in Georgia in April 1996 that became the company's 15th manufacturing facility. On the retail front, Palm Harbor opted to purchase all of Newco, making the company a wholly owned subsidiary. In August 1996, the company purchased the 58 percent of Newco it did not already own, giving Palm Harbor full control over Newco's 19 retail centers.

As Palm Harbor entered the latter half of the 1990s, the manufactured housing market was growing at a record pace. Posey had kept up with the expanding market by greatly increasing the size and scope of Palm Harbor's capabilities, and the company's stature had swelled exponentially. In 1992, when management embraced the idea of developing its own retail arm, Palm Harbor sold 4,848 homes. In 1996, after more than doubling its manufacturing capacity, the company sold 12,175 homes, which, increasingly, were sold at company-owned retail centers. Although the company continued to add independent retailers to its distribution network, Posey's emphasis during the late 1990s was on increasing the number of company-owned superstores.

The last years of the 1990s brought unprecedented growth to Palm Harbor, substantiating the diversification into financing, insurance, and marketing. Palm Harbor's 16th manufacturing facility, located in Arizona, began shipping houses in August 1997, enabling the company to post record totals for sales, net income, and earnings per share for its 1998 fiscal year. By March 1998, after opening 40 superstores during the previous twelve months, Palm Harbor operated 94 retail centers, which accounted for the majority of the homes the company sold during the year. In 1999, Palm Harbor again achieved record totals in sales, net income, and earnings per share, selling 15,628 homes during the year. The number of the company's superstores rose to 120, accounting for 10,766 of the homes sold during the year.

The consecutive years of record financial totals ended in 2000, as demand within the manufactured housing market began to slacken. Palm Harbor's shipments declined for the first time in years, dropping to 14,301. Despite the downturn, the company increased its store count to 133 by the end of its fiscal year, while the number of independent retailers selling Palm Harbor homes dropped from 300 to 200. Looking ahead, Posey and Keener, who was promoted to chief executive officer in 1997, planned to continue opening new stores and further solidify the company's retail operations. Short-term plans called for the opening of between 15 and 20 new stores in 2001.

Principal Subsidiaries

CountryPlace Mortgage, Ltd.; Standard Casualty Corporation; Palm Harbor Finance Corporation; Palm Harbor G.P., Inc.; Better Homes Systems, Inc.; Palm Harbor Investments, Inc.; Palm Harbor Holding, Inc.; Standard Insurance Agency, Inc.; Palm Harbor Homes I. L.P.; First Home Mortgage Corporation; Palm Harbor Insurance Agency, Inc.; Magic Living, Inc.

Principal Competitors

Champion Enterprises, Inc.; Fleetwood Enterprises, Inc.; Oakwood Homes Corporation; Schuler Homes, Inc.; M/I Schottenstein Homes, Inc.; Crossmann Communities, Inc.

Further Reading

Brober, Brad, ''Assembled Living,'' *Puget Sound Business Journal,* March 17, 2000, p. 21.

Keefe, Robert, ''Strict Regulations, Weather Hurting Sales of Manufactured Homes in Florida,'' *Knight-Ridder/Tribune Business News,* August 29, 1995.

Lurz, Bill, ''Ultimate Quality Control,'' *Professional Builder,* October 2000, p. 76.

Mabray, D'Ann, ''Palm Harbor Aims to Raise $25M in IPO,'' *Dallas Business Journal,* May 27, 1994, p. 1.

''Manufactured Homes Now Carry Energy Star Label Due to Heat Pumps,'' *Air Conditioning, Heating & Refrigeration News,* April 6, 1998, p. 8.

Shilling, A. Gary, ''Home Sweet Factory-Built Home,'' *Forbes,* February 12, 1996, p. 181.

—Jeffrey L. Covell

Papetti's Hygrade Egg Products, Inc.

1 Papetti Plaza
Elizabeth, New Jersey 07206
U.S.A.
Telephone: (908) 354-4844
Toll Free: (952) 851-7249
Web site: http://www.michaelfoods.com/papettis.htm

Wholly Owned Subsidiary of Michael Foods Inc.
Founded: 1908
Employees: Not Available
Sales: $300 million (1998 est.)
NAIC: 112310 Chicken Egg Production

A subsidiary of Michael Foods since 1997, Papetti's Hygrade Egg Products, Inc. of Elizabeth, New Jersey, is the world's largest egg products producer. Third and fourth generations of the Papetti family are still involved in the running of the 100-year-old company that "breaks" approximately 18 million eggs a day (more than 25 percent of all eggs broken in the United States). Papetti's sells the machine-separated eggs—either as whites, yolks, or blended together—to food service, industrial, and retail markets. The company also manufactures extended shelf-life liquid eggs and specialty products such as prepared omelets and egg patties.

Emergence of American Poultry Industry After the Civil War

Laying a large number of eggs is contrary to the instincts of game birds, but many thousands of years ago man discovered that taking an egg from a nest would induce a hen to lay a compensatory egg, a process that could be repeated for an extended period of time. Chickens were, therefore, domesticated and bred for eggs as well as meat. They were brought to America by European settlers and were raised on almost every farm, mostly for family consumption. Excess products were sold in town or exchanged for goods at the general store. Chickens also were commonly kept by people in town. It was not until the post–Civil War era that a large-scale poultry industry began to develop.

The Papetti family became involved in poultry in 1908 when for $3,000 Antonio De Stefano purchased a dairy farm in Elizabeth, New Jersey. His daughter, Santina De Stefano-Papetti, ran the poultry and fresh egg business. (Traditionally, raising chickens was considered women's work. As the poultry industry grew, however, men began to exert more and more control.) To make extra money, her sons, Anthony and Arthur, would break surplus eggs by hand, and in the process they established a trade with local bakers. What would begin as a sideline to a sideline of the family business would evolve one day into a mainstay.

As Papetti's egg business took shape, the poultry industry began to undergo significant changes in the 1920s. Poultry science programs were instituted at American colleges, as the small-farm chicken enterprises run by women and children gave way to large organizations. Hatcheries gained wide use in the 1920s, as did research facilities funded by the major feed companies: Ralston Purina, Quaker Oats, and General Mills' predecessor, Larrowe Milling. In 1934 Kimber Farms was established in Fremont, California, to engage in genetic research to develop chickens for desirable traits, such as the ability to lay a large number of eggs. Vaccines also were developed to cope with the results of not only the chickens' compromised immune systems caused by genetic hybridization, but also the spread of disease caused by the increasingly more crowded conditions under which chickens were kept. Battery cages arranged in rows and tiers became standard in the 1940s, as did the practice of using confinement sheds for broiler chickens. These practices were in many ways a response to the increased demand for poultry and eggs that would be the result of red meat rationing during World War II. Many dairy barns were then converted to the factory system to meet the new market for fresh eggs and broiler chickens after the war.

As with many industries, poultry underwent vertical integration. Single companies, such as Tyson and Perdue, began to acquire all sectors of production: breeder and commercial flocks, eggs, hatcheries, feed mills, medications, slaughter, processing, and delivery. Small farmers were contracted to maintain the chickens at great expense with little reward and less security.

319

Company Perspectives:

Papetti's breaks over 18 million eggs per day to make products including extended shelf-life liquid eggs (Table Ready), dried and frozen yolks, whites and blends, hard-cooked eggs, egg substitutes and specialty egg products such as prepared omelets and egg patties.

Papetti's Focus on Egg Products in the 1950s

During the 1950s, the Papetti family left the chicken and fresh egg business and moved entirely into the eggs products business. The company now bought the eggs that it broke, using machines to separate the whites from the yolks. After undergoing a pasteurization process, the whites and yolks would be sold to food manufacturers, either separately or as a blend. Customers could supply the company with the required formula for its product, then Papetti's would mix the proper blend of yolks and whites. In the case of ice cream producers, Papetti's added the required amount of sugar. Because of the seasonality of some products, Papetti would find itself with a surplus of yolks. The company would then pack and freeze the yolks for later sale to the ice creamer makers who needed more yolks than whites. It also searched for new foods in which to use surplus whites and yolks. As Papetti's egg products business grew, it opened egg-breaking facilities in Pennsylvania and Iowa and created a large fleet of delivery trucks.

Consumers' egg-eating habits slowly changed after World War II and would have an impact on all facets of the poultry industry. Per capita consumption dropped from 400 eggs to 321 eggs by 1960. In 1990 consumption would stand at only 234 eggs per capita. In 1961 eggs accounted for 61 percent of revenues generated in the chicken business, but by 1975 broiler chicken sales outpaced eggs. Egg revenues would fall below 25 percent of revenues by the early 1990s. Much of the decline was due to Americans' shift away from a big breakfast, but there were also health concerns. In 1990 there were more than 2,000 cases of food poisoning and at least two deaths caused by salmonella poisoning, which is passed from the hen to the egg even before the shell is formed. Some of the large restaurant chains began to substitute pasteurized liquid eggs for fresh eggs, but the liquid variety was not as flavorful or versatile. Concern about the high level of cholesterol found in eggs was another troubling issue with consumers, who were becoming increasingly more fearful of heart disease.

Pappetti's and its competitors began to look for ways to allay consumer concerns, as well as to save money by extending the shelf life of liquid eggs. In the late 1980s Papetti's and Michael Foods both introduced extended shelf-life products. Michael Foods sued Papetti's and other companies over patent infringement, litigation that would linger for several years while the rival companies battled on other product fronts. In essence, everyone was looking for one process that would kill salmonella, reduce cholesterol levels, and extend shelf life. Whoever could combine those attributes in a good-tasting, liquid egg product would stand to generate a great deal of business from large institutional food service companies, restaurants, hospitals, and schools.

In 1991 Bon Dente International Inc. announced that it had developed a method of pasteurizing eggs in the shell called Hyperpasteurization. By forcing oxygen into the eggs at high pressure, the new process would kill off Salmonella enteritidis. It could also be applied to liquid eggs, which sparked the interest of Papetti's and the other egg product companies. In addition, attempts were made to create a cholesterol-stripped egg to supercede cholesterol-free egg products that did not use yolks (which contains most of an egg's cholesterol). In the early 1990s a Pennsylvania company began to sell C.R. Eggs, produced by chickens fed on kelp, with the promise that the eggs could help lower cholesterol levels. By 1991, however, the eggs were pulled from the shelves when it was learned that they contained extremely high levels of iodine. A liquid alternative seemed to be the only viable way to produce cholesterol-free (or reduced) eggs. The question was how to include the yolks in the product.

Michael Foods would be Papetti's main competitor in extended shelf-life and cholesterol-free egg products. The company was a 1987 spin-off from North Star Universal, a Minneapolis-based conglomerate. Unlike Papetti's, Michael Foods was a publicly traded company, making its management extremely responsive to the fluctuating price of its stock. In the late-1980s, Michael Foods licensed a process from North Carolina State University that killed salmonella and other bacteria and made it possible to refrigerate liquid eggs for several weeks. Employing this method, Michael Foods began to sell a product it called Easy Eggs. But when sales were less than expected, Michael Foods' stock dropped and two disgruntled shareholders sued the company, claiming that it misled investors about the potential of Easy Eggs. Michael Foods would next apply a process that extracted 90 percent of the cholesterol from yolks that were then recombined with the whites. The resulting product was called Simply Eggs. Papetti's would respond with its version, called Better'n Eggs.

The eggs products industry in the early 1990s would engage in a period of intense litigation. Michael Foods sued Papetti's and Bartow Food Company over patent infringement regarding the North Carolina State process. Cargill, to preempt a suit against its Sunny Fresh Eggs entry in the extended shelf-life product line, sued Michael Foods, maintaining that the North Carolina State process was not original. As a result of the Cargill filing, Michael Foods' stock was affected adversely. In November 1992 the courts ruled against Papetti's in the Michael Foods suits, and the company entered into a consent order, agreeing to refrain from using the extended shelf-life process licensed by Michael Foods.

While Papetti's appealed the court's decision, it strengthened its position in the refrigerated egg product business by acquiring for $9 million the Worthington Foods' product line as well as its egg-processing equipment in the company's Zanesville, Ohio plant. Worthington decided to drop out of the volatile egg products business, opting to focus on vegetarian meat substitutes. Its egg business, which accounted for about $8 million a year in revenue, would now contribute to the bottom line of Papetti's.

In 1995 the U.S. Federal Court of Appeals upheld the earlier patent infringement case, and Michael Foods' stock soared on news of the ruling. Arthur Papetti, president of Papetti's, discounted the importance of the court's decision, maintaining that all that Michael Foods had gained was a chance to return to the patent board. Less than two weeks later an examiner for the U.S. Patent and Trademark Office would reject a number of claims that were made in the two patent applications involving the process for extending the shelf life of liquefied eggs. Stock for Michael Foods would again tumble.

Papetti's and Michael Foods Merger in 1996

After several years of litigation and uncertain business conditions, Michael Foods and Papetti's decided that both sides would be better off if they joined forces. In July 1996, in a move that would resolve all litigation between the two companies, Michael Foods agreed to acquire Papetti's for approximately $85 million in stock and cash. The Papetti family would continue to run the company as a wholly owned subsidiary of Michael Foods. At the time of the deal, Papetti's was generating about $300 million in annual sales. The transaction, following government review, would be finalized in February 1997. Not only would there be a savings on legal costs, the combination of Michael Foods and Papetti's would consolidate costs in a number of areas, including cost of goods, distribution and freight, supplies and packaging. Michael Foods would also re-merge with its parent company, North Star Universal, with Michael Foods becoming the surviving entity. This combination, plus the Papetti's deal and other aggressive acquisitions, would propel the price of Michael Foods stock to new heights in 1997.

The Egg Products Division of Michael Foods consisted of Papetti's and another subsidiary, M.G. Walbaum Company, which along with producing egg products maintained more than 12 million hens in production. In 1999 the Division would control more than 40 percent of the U.S. egg products market, generating some 60 percent of Michael Foods' sales and contributing to 80 percent of the company's operating profits. The Egg Products division was able to achieve a six percent operating profit increase over the previous year, despite a seven-year low in egg pricing.

The outlook for Papetti's, and the poultry industry in general, depended on several factors mostly related to the consumer's evaluation of the product. The poultry industry had received increasing criticism about its practices. For years, moreover, animal rights activists complained about the conditions under which chickens have been kept and the methods employed to produce eggs. Government and academic scientists also began to question whether the care of chickens might cause disease that could spread to humans. While a movement to improve the conditions of all farm animals took hold in Europe, American activists shifted their attention from producers to the major buyers of chickens and eggs. In 2000 the McDonald's restaurant chain, responded to public pressure (generated in part by a popular animated film, *Chicken Run,* which compared a chicken farm to a prisoner of war camp) by announcing guidelines for the care of chickens that it expected to be followed by the companies that supplied it with the 1.5 billion eggs its restaurants bought each year. Whether the McDonald's edict was an indication of widespread consumer concern about chicken and eggs remained to be seen. If consumer confidence in fresh eggs was adversely affected, it was still uncertain what impact might be felt by egg products producers like Papetti's. Moreover, as a subsidiary of a larger concern with an enormous investment in laying hens, Papetti's might realize gains that would simply be offset by losses elsewhere in Michael Foods. In the end, as always, the consumer would decide.

Principal Competitors

Cargill Inc.; Cutler Eggs; Nulaid; Rose Acres.

Further Reading

Davis, Karen, *Prisoned Chickens, Poisoned Eggs: An Inside Look at the Modern Poultry Industry,* Summertown, Tenn.: Book Pub. Co, 1996.
Etter, Gerald, ''Business of Breaking Eggs All It's Cracked Up to Be,'' *Houston Chronicle,* April 25, 1990, p. 4.
Hinge, John B., ''Pasteurization of Eggs in Shell Holds Promise,'' *Wall Street Journal,* August 19, 1991, p. B3.
''Michael Foods Inc.: Federal Court Supports Firm in Dispute Over Egg Patents,'' *Wall Street Journal,* November 16, 1992, p. B4.
Smith, Page, and Daniel, Charles, *The Chicken Book,* Athens, Ga.: University of Georgia Press, 2000.
Witmer, Mark D., ''Papetti's Agrees to Consent Order,'' *PR Newswire,* December 23, 1992.

—Ed Dinger

Pella Corporation

102 Main Street
Pella, Iowa 50129
U.S.A.
Telephone: (515) 628-1000
Toll Free: 800-847-3552
Fax: (515) 628-6070
Web site: http://www.pella.com

Private Company
Incorporated: 1925 as Rolscreen Company
Employees: 6,755
Sales: $900 million (1999 est.)
NAIC: 321911 Wood Window and Door Manufacturing

Pella Corporation is a leading manufacturer of windows and doors, specializing in high-end products. Based in Pella, Iowa, the company operates five manufacturing plants in its home state, as well as another window manufacturing facility in Gettysburg, Pennsylvania. Pella sells its products through a network of Pella Window Stores and Pella Windowscaping Centers throughout the United States. Its least expensive product line is also available at selected lumberyards and building material retailers, including the Home Depot chain stores. The company also operates three subsidiary companies. Cole Sewell Corporation, in Clear Lake, Iowa, is a leading manufacturer of storm doors. Pella's Viking Industries subsidiary makes lower-end vinyl windows and sells primarily in the western United States. Pease Industries, of Fairfield, Ohio, is Pella's third subsidiary company, a manufacturer of entry doors. Pella Corporation is privately owned by the family of founder Pete Kuyper. The company changed its name from Rolscreen in 1992.

Starting Off With a Unique Product in the 1920s

Rolscreen was founded by P.H. ''Pete'' Kuyper and his wife Lucille. They purchased a small company in 1925 that, one year earlier, had started manufacturing unique roll-up windows. In 1926 they moved the company to Pella, their home town, and set up shop. The original operation consisted of a three-person

workforce headed by Kuyper. The company soon was forced to expand as a result of surging demand for its ''Rolscreen'' window screens. Kuyper's manufacturing operations more than doubled by the end of the 1920s.

Despite economic hardship during the Depression era, Rolscreen continued to grow. In 1934, in fact, Kuyper introduced his second product—high-quality venetian blinds. Three years later he started selling his patented deluxe casement window, a steel-framed casement with a wood interior, divided windowpanes, exterior wash feature, and removable insulating glass. As demand for all of Rolscreen's premium products swelled, the company expanded nationwide. By the mid-1930s Rolscreen had established sales offices in 24 U.S. cities and 15 foreign countries. During the late 1930s Kuyper's sales were particularly brisk, mostly because of orders for its unique casement windows. Rolscreen eventually sold more than one million of those units.

Rolscreen shifted gears beginning in the early 1940s, switching from private-sector manufacturing to building windows for defense-related construction. Government purchases during World War II proved a significant boon to the company, and the postwar housing shortage kept its factories running at full tilt. Demand was so great, in fact, that a temporary mill was established in Pella during 1948 and 1949 to process raw lumber. As the postwar economy and population boomed during the 1950s and 1960s, company sales climbed rapidly as architects and builders increasingly turned to the manufacturer for high-quality building components.

Postwar Expansion

Rolscreen met surging markets with a flurry of new products. In 1950, for example, the company created the Pella multipurpose window, which could be used as either a casement or awning. Likewise, Kuyper introduced the Pella wood folding door in 1952. That was followed in 1957 by the Pella twinlite window, one of the first window systems to offer efficient insulating glass as an option. Among other new products, Pella introduced the first removable wood windowpane divider in 1958, the first of many new industry products for the company.

Also during the late 1950s, the popular Pella wooden sliding glass doors were introduced. By the early 1960s those items emerged as a popular design element in many newer homes. Significant product introductions during the 1960s included: folding wood partitions; patented double-hung windows that pivoted for easy washing; wood casement windows; and the first low-maintenance aluminum clad window, which enjoyed immediate acceptance in the homebuilding industry. One of Rolscreen's most important innovations was its "Slimshade" blinds—which featured blinds positioned between the exterior and removable interior glass panes, thus reducing cleaning and maintenance requirements.

The company's growth—even during the Great Depression—was due to a steady stream of product innovations as well as Kuyper's quality strategy. Indeed, from the company's inception Kuyper displayed a commitment to his goal of producing the highest quality products available. Although Pella windows and doors were often more expensive than competing brands, Kuyper found a ready market among designers and builders of quality homes. The company eventually earned a reputation as one of the top window and door producers in the United States. "Our philosophy was, if you built a better product, then somebody would come buy it," explained a company representative in *Fortune* in 1993.

The Pella brand sustained its reputation for quality while the company continued to broaden its distribution network and introduce new products. In 1970, for example, Rolscreen introduced its successful line of low-maintenance clad casement windows, which included later add-ons like pivoting windows and clad sliding glass doors. The organization also introduced popular French sliding glass doors in 1979 and a line of sunrooms and skylights in 1980, reflecting a trend toward more openness and natural lighting in homes.

As a result of savvy innovation and quality strategies, Rolscreen enjoyed solid long-term profit gains. Following World War II and through most of the 1980s, the company increased sales at an average rate of nine percent annually while relying on internal financing and a minimal debt load. The company's employees were rewarded with a generous profit-sharing plan and virtually no layoffs. Although a downturn in construction hampered growth in the late 1970s, housing markets recovered in the 1980s and the Pella brand continued to boost revenues.

Pella's gains were also a result of its strong distribution network. It focused on the high-margin, top end of the construction industry. Through its network of about 80 distribution centers, the company focused on upscale homeowners, professional designers, and builders of high-quality homes, rather than on the lower-profit mass consumer market. Pella profited from the support of independent distributors that were motivated to sell its products, and Pella distributors benefited from being the primary local suppliers for some of the best products available.

Pella continued to benefit from its established distribution network during the 1980s. In addition, it opened the first Pella Window Store to sell its products to upscale retail buyers. The chain proved extremely successful and spiraled to about 370 in number by the early 1990s. The company also continued to introduce new products and to improve internal operations. It expanded its production facilities with a new plant in Carroll, Iowa, and brought out new products such as vented skylights; specially coated, energy efficient windows; and stronger wooden doors that closely simulated solid wood.

With thousands of workers churning out windows and doors in high volume, Pella's manufacturing plants in the 1980s barely resembled its shops of the 1930s and 1940s. But the company's goal was to ensure that every component that left the factory had a handcrafted look. Pella continued to manufacture most of its own hardware and fittings, and even manufactured many of its production machines. Quality and productivity were achieved with high-tech manufacturing and quality control systems. For example, new designs were tested with optical (laser) equipment to ensure that they matched perfectly with blueprints.

In a Rut in the 1980s

Because of its superior quality, Pella had firmly established itself as a top producer in the door and window industry by the late 1980s. The U.S. economy began to slow in 1988, however, and the high-end market tailed off. Pella's profits flattened. The company had experienced market downturns before, but management (Kuyper had since retired) sensed that this slowdown was different. Indeed, the building supplies distribution market began shifting during the 1980s to favor producers that could market lower-priced products geared for the larger mass consumer market. As a result, Pella's customer base became increasingly narrow compared with the overall building supply market.

Of paramount concern to Pella management was the rapidly proliferating market consisting of home renovators, small contractors, and do-it-yourselfers. Those segments had grown quickly, particularly during the late 1980s, and were expected to supply the majority of growth in home construction markets through the end of the century. Most of those customers did not buy through Pella Window Stores or through Pella's chain of independent distributors. Instead, they often bought from various low-cost suppliers, including the many rapidly growing home and hardware supercenters that were opening up around the nation. Even many of those that were familiar with Pella viewed its products as unaffordable.

Recognizing the need for a major change in its strategy, Pella hired a consulting firm to study its dilemma and make suggestions. The analysis contended that Pella had become too complex, and that it was manufacturing too many products for too small a market niche. The study suggested that the company broaden its target market to include the giant middle-market. To

Key Dates:

1925: Company is founded as Rolscreen.
1934: Rolscreen introduces line of venetian blinds.
1957: Company introduces double-glass Twinlite windows.
1988: Company's long profitability slows appreciably.
1992: Name is changed to Pella Corporation; company restructures using Japanese management technique called *kaizen*.

do that, it would have to reduce the complexity of its offerings and focus on reducing production costs so that it could compete with other manufacturers on price.

Reshaping the Company in the 1990s and Beyond

Between 1990 and 1993 Pella spent $35 million restructuring its operations and reshaping its marketing and distribution strategy. The company reevaluated each of its products and jettisoned those that did not contribute significantly to the bottom line. Pella also redesigned many of its major products in an effort to make them simpler and more cost-effective to manufacture. It rearranged the products into three groups, or series: Designer, Architect, and Proline. The Designer Series consisted of Pella's more contemporary offerings, and the more expensive Architect Series was made up of traditionally styled items. Both were sold through Pella Window Stores and wholesale distributors.

The Proline series represented Pella's attempt to penetrate the blooming renovation/do-it-yourself market. Proline windows and doors were designed to be marketed through the proliferating giant home-supply chains such as Builder's Square and Home Depot. Proline components offered fewer options and were designed to be easier to understand and install. They were generally priced at about ten percent to 20 percent less than components sold in the designer series. Although they were less expensive, the company said that the components were similar in quality. To ease distributors' fear of competition from the Proline Series, Pella gave them a percentage of all Proline products sold in their territory. Pella also trained them in servicing and installing Proline goods.

In addition to reorganizing its product lines, Pella instituted a number of measures aimed at further improving productivity; Pella's Carroll plant already had been recognized as one of the nation's most efficient manufacturing facilities by *Industry Week Magazine*. To gain efficiency, Pella adopted a Japanese worker-management process known as *kaizen*. Some Pella executives were introduced to kaizen in 1992, at a point when Pella seemed to be losing ground to its competitor Andersen Corporation and to products sold through the big-box home center stores. Convinced that kaizen would help them change the company, the executives hired the TBM Consulting Group to guide Pella through the process. Using kaizen sessions to focus on problems and quick, if imperfect, solutions, almost every aspect of the way Pella did business changed. One kaizen session looked at the way Pella's core product, double-hung

windows, were made. Within a few months, workers and managers cut the amount of space used to make the windows by three quarters. Gradually other changes were implemented, so that the factory no longer made standard products for inventory, but was able to fill orders as they came in. The factory was reconfigured so it could make different sized windows (mixed production) at once, instead of making batches of the same thing. Pella also reduced the number of suppliers it used and cut its lumber inventory. The fallout of the efficiency efforts was that the time necessary to fill orders at the company dropped from ten to five days, while productivity in some areas increased 25 percent. Pella had been notoriously late in filling orders, but by the late 1990s that had changed. By 2000, Pella delivered 98.5 percent of its orders on time. Custom orders that formerly took five weeks to fill now took two. Pella's improved service allowed its dealers to operate more efficiently as well. They were able to reduce markups because they needed less space, less inventory, and fewer employees.

Pella's efforts to market its lower-end products also paid off. Its Proline series was the least expensive of Pella's three market divisions, yet Proline windows were at the high end of the price range at home center stores. Pella's competitor Andersen also had tried to sell its windows through Home Depot in the early 1990s, without raging success. But Pella pleased Home Depot by shipping direct from its factories to Home Depot's distribution centers and by making its Proline on a two-day production schedule, giving the store time to restock between weekends. According to *Fortune* magazine (November 13, 2000), Pella's sales to home center stores including Home Depot probably reached $100 million annually by the end of the 1990s.

In the late 1990s, Pella began a series of key acquisitions. In 1997, the company purchased Cole Sewell Corporation. Cole Sewell was another Iowa company, and one of the leading manufacturers of storm doors in the United States. The next year, Pella purchased a company in Portland, Oregon called Viking Industries. Viking made vinyl windows, considered a lower-end product than Pella's, and sold them primarily in the West. In 1999, Pella made one more acquisition, the door manufacturer Pease Industries. Pease, of Fairfield, Ohio, had founded the steel door industry in the 1960s and was the dominant player in the entry door market in the United States. Pella ran all three of its new companies under their own names, as wholly owned subsidiaries. The acquisitions enhanced Pella's product line in a logical way, since all three made leading brands in related market categories.

Pella underwent significant change in the 1990s, revamping almost every aspect of the way it did business. It improved efficiency enormously, opened new factories, and entered new markets with its Proline and with the products brought by its acquired subsidiaries. The company began working with advertising giant Young & Rubicam in the late 1990s to project a different image. The company wanted its brands to be seen as belonging to a class of high-end home products, so that Pella was not just the best in windows but the best of the best. In an interview with *Adweek* (January 20, 1997), Pella's marketing director Jerry Dow explained, ''We're competing with Sub-Zero refrigerators, Jacuzzi tubs, and Kohler faucets,'' not just other door and window manufacturers like Andersen. Clearly, the company had its sights set high. Evidence showed that it was succeeding. Sales grew an estimated 50 percent over 1999, leading to an estimated total sales figure of around $900 million. Pella remained dedicated to its kaizen process, telling *Fortune* (November 13, 2000) that it was still working on making changes, so that every year its products would get better. Pella demonstrated throughout the 1990s that it could improve itself, and it seemed likely that it would carry out its innovations into the next decade as well.

Principal Subsidiaries

Cole Sewell Corporation; Viking Industries; Pease Industries.

Principal Competitors

Andersen Corporation; JELD-WEN, inc.; Atrium Companies Inc.

Further Reading

Henkoff, Ronald, ''Moving Up by Downscaling,'' *Fortune,* August 9, 1993, p. 72.

Kasler, Dale, ''Pella Corp. Takes Goods from Boutiques to Payless,'' *Des Moines Register,* March 21, 1993.

Koenig, Karen Malamud, ''Pella Pulls the Shades Over Poor Quality,'' *Wood & Wood Products,* October 1991, p. 71.

Levine, Stephen, ''Y&R Acquires $10 Mil. Account,'' *Adweek,* January 20, 1997, p. 4.

Schwalm, Eric, and David Harding, ''Winning with the Big-Box Retailers,'' *Harvard Business Review,* September–October 2000, pp. 26–30.

Siekman, Philip, ''Glass Act: How a Window Maker Rebuilt Itself,'' *Fortune,* November 13, 2000, p. 384.

Wilson, Marianne, ''Window Shopping Made Easy at Pella,'' *Chain Store Age Executive,* April 1996, p. 96.

—Dave Mote
—update: A. Woodward

Philadelphia Suburban Corporation

762 West Lancaster Avenue
Bryn Mawr, Pennsylvania 19010-3489
U.S.A.
Telephone: (610) 525-1400
Fax: (610) 645-1061
Web site: http://www.suburbanwater.com

Public Company
Incorporated: 1886 as Springfield Water Company
Employees: 945
Sales: $257.3 million (1999)
Stock Exchanges: New York
Ticker Symbol: PSC
NAIC: 221310 Water Supply and Irrigation

Philadelphia Suburban Corporation (PSC) is one of the largest investor-owned water utilities in the United States. With a region spanning five states and serving nearly two million people, PSC is a leader not only in supplying water, but also in water treatment. PSC's largest shareholder is the French company Vivendi/U.S. Filter, the largest water company in the world. From its earliest days as the Springfield Water Company in the 1880s, PSC has strongly believed in growth through acquisition. Yet the genesis for the company was a group of engineering professors at Swarthmore College in suburban Philadelphia—professors who wanted primarily to create a supply of running water for their homes.

Early Days: Bringing Water to the Suburbs

Philadelphia in the 1870s was one of the most important cities in the United States. Formerly a seat of government and culture, it was now also emerging as a key industrial city. Well into the 20th century, Philadelphia was known as the "Workshop of the World." The land outside the city, however, was still primarily rural. Gradually, that began to change as more people flocked to the city. Wealthier people wanted to live in large houses surrounded by open space, and they looked to the farmland of Delaware and Montgomery counties.

As the population expanded, people realized that they needed safe and steady supplies of water. Wells and cisterns were unreliable under the best circumstances, and with more people to serve they became even more so. Both the growing suburban communities and the still plentiful farms wanted a source of water that they could rely on—easy to access and free of disease. The city of Philadelphia had its own well-known municipal system for water supply, the famed Fairmount Water Works. Fairmount's plant filtered the water of the Schuylkill River and stored it in a reservoir located at the present site of the Philadelphia Museum of Art. The city purchased land along the river that later formed the basis for Fairmount Park, the largest municipal park in the world.

The outlying towns and villages saw the benefits of having a similar system, but the city of Philadelphia was prohibited from extending its water mains beyond the city boundaries. Several towns made attempts to transport water to their communities, but this was not cost-effective. In the mid-1880s, a group of engineering professors teaching at Swarthmore College, located in the township of Springfield, devised a way to get running water from a nearby spring to their homes.

After selecting a spring, they had a small pumping station built. Pipes were laid from the pumping station directly to the professors' homes. Not surprisingly, as their neighbors found out what these enterprising engineers had done, they also wanted running water. The demand became strong enough that the professors had to expand their original idea. They received a charter to supply water to the public and they incorporated on January 4, 1886 as the Springfield Water Company.

Late 1800s–1930s: Rapid Expansion

It was not long before the small spring could not keep up with the growing demand for water. Springfield began looking for new sources, but it lacked adequate funding and experience. Help came from the American Pipe Manufacturing Company. This Philadelphia-based firm, which specialized in water works, realized that Springfield's logic was sound, and the two companies entered into a contract. American Pipe would provide pipe to connect Springfield's customers to new water supplies. Also,

Company Perspectives:

Philadelphia Suburban Corporation's strategy for success is growth, primarily through acquisition. PSC believes that only through growth can water companies meet the needs of their customers. These needs include clean and safe drinking water, a steady supply even during drought, and good overall service. By acquiring other companies and consolidating the industry, PSC hopes to create, in its words, "one unit more powerful than the sum of its parts."

an American Pipe executive was named to Springfield's board, whose meetings were moved from the Swarthmore campus to American Pipe's offices in Philadelphia. With the help of American Pipe's clout and expertise, Springfield was able to launch into a period of steady expansion. There were two primary benefits to expansion. First, it gave the company more territory and thus a larger customer base. Second, it gave Springfield access to more sources of water, without which there would be no company at all.

In June 1892 Springfield purchased six new companies recently established by American Pipe. A week later, Springfield purchased its first independent and actively functioning water company, the Ridley Park Cold Spring company, for $37,500. Over the next two decades, Springfield added some two dozen small companies, extending its reach beyond Delaware County into Montgomery and Chester Counties. This involved the laying of new pipe and the construction of new pumping facilities. For a period of about 30 years, Springfield was actually allowed to provide water to a neighborhood within Philadelphia's city limits. After the Oak Lane Company was chartered to provide water to the Philadelphia suburb of Cheltenham, the nearby Oak Lane neighborhood in Philadelphia decided that its residents wanted running water as well. In 1894 the city of Philadelphia passed an ordinance giving Springfield the right to provide water within the city, with the city retaining the right to take over the piping at any time (after paying a price determined by arbitration). The city exercised this option in 1926.

All of this benefited Springfield and also American Pipe (which eventually acquired a controlling interest in Springfield). Springfield's expansion took on new significance in 1905 when the Pennsylvania General Assembly took away the right of "eminent domain" from public water companies. Eminent domain allows public agencies to take private land (for adequate compensation) when such acquisition is deemed in the public interest. Because Springfield had already developed a large network of water sources, it was able to continue its growth and expansion despite the new law. Laws passed in 1907 took still more rights away from water companies, making growth through purchase and acquisition less practical. Instead, Springfield turned to long-term leases as a means of consolidating water supplies.

Springfield continued to grow, building new pumps and plants and delivering water to more customers. World War I mobilized the country when the United States entered in 1917,

and after the war life returned to normal relatively quickly. In the 1920s, Clarence Henry Geist became interested in Springfield. Geist had made a fortune buying up water companies—so much so that he was nicknamed the "Water Boy." He acquired American Pipe's controlling interest in Springfield on January 1, 1925 and was named president. Two other men joined Springfield at Geist's invitation: Harold Schutt, a savvy businessman whom many called a financial genius; and Carleton Davis, an engineer who specialized in constructing dams and reservoirs.

Geist saw room for significant expansion in Springfield, which in April 1925 formally changed its name to Philadelphia Suburban Water Company. When he assumed control the company serviced just over 45,000 customers, with 752 miles of water main carrying more than 12 ½ million gallons per day. His first move was to create a play with the financiers at Drexel & Company that allowed for the issuance of Philadelphia Suburban bonds to raise money. The money raised by the sale of these bonds went toward major improvements that allowed more water to be pumped and filtered more efficiently. Aided by Schutt's business acumen and Davis' engineering skill, Geist moved quickly. A year after he had taken control of the company, there were more than $6 million worth of permanent additions.

Widely regarded as a colorful character, Geist was not known for his finesse. Despite his business success, he was never accepted into Philadelphia society—a society that viewed non-natives as outsiders and wealthy non-natives as parvenus. His three daughters married into prominent families from Philadelphia's Main Line, which allowed him to gain a sort of vicarious acceptance.

The stock market crash of 1929 and the subsequent Great Depression slowed down growth at Philadelphia Suburban, but there was still activity—and Geist cut no jobs. New reservoirs were dug, new filters were installed, new water pipes were laid. By the mid-1930s the economy was starting to do better, and people were looking forward to stronger growth.

Geist did not live to see this renewed growth, however. He died suddenly on June 12, 1938. Schutt replaced him as president. He knew he had large shoes to fill, but his experience and knowledge helped him to effect a smooth transition. Schutt was a strong leader, like Geist; he was equally shrewd, and equally irascible. But he led the company successfully for more than two decades.

The War and Postwar Years

World War II had an impact on businesses throughout the United States, and utilities were clearly no exception. One of the biggest challenges was finding people to replace the men who went into the Armed Forces. Philadelphia Suburban, like many companies, turned to women during the war years to fill jobs. Usually they worked as meter readers. Although there was much less growth at Philadelphia Suburban during the war years, business was still strong; in 1943, the number of customers and the gallon-per-day output were nearly double what they had been when Geist took over the company 18 years earlier. Just before the war some 180 employees of Philadel-

Key Dates:

1886: Springfield Water Company chartered to provide water to Swarthmore residents.
1892: American Pipe Manufacturing Company establishes six water companies, which are acquired by Springfield in its first expansion.
1892–1910: Rapid expansion through Delaware, Montgomery, and Chester Counties.
1925: Clarence Geist purchases Springfield and becomes president; company changes name to Philadelphia Suburban Water Company.
1930: Expansion continues despite Depression.
1938: Geist dies and is replaced by Harold Schutt.
1968: Philadelphia Suburban Corporation (PSC) created as umbrella company for Philadelphia Suburban Water and other utilities.
1971: PSC makes its debut on New York Stock Exchange.
1981: Non-water utilities spin off into separate company.
1992: PSC launches renewed growth-through-acquisition strategy.
1999: PSC merges with Consumers Water Company.

phia Suburban became members of the International Brotherhood of Firemen, Oilers, Powerhouse Operators and Maintenance Men. The union entered into a formal agreement with the company in 1947.

The postwar years were years of growth, particularly in the suburbs. Although suburban Philadelphia's housing boom was somewhat slow getting started, by the late 1940s the customer base was increasing. To keep pace with the growing demand, more pipes were laid. To ensure that the water would continue to be safe and clean, new pumping facilities and filtration plants were built. By 1950, the company was serving 476,584 customers. Water was carried through some 1,417 miles of pipe. Around this time the company also began a small advertising campaign to educate the public about the procedures involved in providing clean, safe water to suburban homes.

Throughout the 1950s the growth continued. Despite—or perhaps, because of—the size and scope of Philadelphia Suburban by then, major changes in the weather created relatively little impact in service. A severe rainstorm in 1950 knocked down many trees and did some damage, but it also added 700 million gallons to the company's reservoirs. A drought in 1952 caused some trouble but almost none of the company's customers experienced a change in service. Even Hurricane Diane, which caused severe flooding in the region and disabled a major pumping station, did relatively little long-term damage overall.

In 1959, Schutt sold the outstanding shares of Philadelphia Suburban (then held by trustees and heirs of the Clarence Geist estate) to an investment group headed by Clint and John Murchison of Texas. This marked a major change in the company's structure. Although there had been immense growth over the past several decades, there had always been a family atmosphere. With the new investment group as owners, the company was made more professional and more modern in its outlook.

Some employees were uneasy at first, but under the leadership of the new president, Thomas Moses, the transition was a smooth one. Employees liked the fact that they were being informed much better about the company's progress and goals. Moses was well-liked, but he came with responsibilities to the Murchisons that left him less time than he wanted to devote to the company. He stepped down in 1962 and was replaced by James Ballengee, whose background was not in water but in law. By this time, Philadelphia Suburban had more than 187,000 customers and distributed 56 million gallons per day.

New Structures, Same Focus

The next few years were plagued by a drought situation that affected water supplies in much of the Northeast. Philadelphia Suburban continued to deliver and continued to grow during those years. In 1968, the company's Board of Directors voted to create the Philadelphia Suburban Corporation as a holding company for the water company and other utilities. Three years later, PSC became a public company; it first traded on the New York Stock Exchange on July 22, 1971.

A year later, PSC suffered its greatest weather crisis to date: Tropical Storm Agnes. The rains came so fast and so heavily that June day that there was little anyone could do but wait. Water submerged much of one of PSC's largest processing stations and the local electric utility cut off all electricity for safety reasons. An all-out effort by PSC's employees kept damage to a minimum and service was restored in a relatively short time. Even with the outages, it was estimated that less than three percent of PSC's customers were affected.

Throughout the 1970s growth at PSC continued. During those years the Federal government was enacting new regulations, many through the Environmental Protection Agency. Although PSC was sometimes painted with the same broad brush as other utilities when activists argued in favor of more regulation, its reputation for superior service, long-range planning, and commitment to its customers served it well. Also, the company worked hard to educate its customers about water and water conservation efforts, using everything from inserts in water bills to plant tours for schoolchildren to provide information.

In 1981, PSC's non-water utilities were spun off into a separate company, and PSC concentrated on water. This allowed each new company to be more focused and concentrate on industry-specific issues. Growth continued through the 1980s and into the 1990s. Between 1991 and 1999, the company increased its customer base by 35 percent to 319,000 customers. Drought conditions and severe storms like Hurricane Floyd took their toll, but again, PSC was able to deal with the weather in a way that had minimal impact on its customers. In 1999, PSC made its most significant acquisition in recent history when it paid $273.3 million for Consumers Water Company (CSC), the sixth largest in the country. (PSC also assumed $190 million in debt.) With customers in five states (Pennsylvania, Maine, Ohio, Illinois, and New Jersey), CSC added more than a quarter million customers to PSC. More than 100 years after its founding, PSC was still able to focus on a simple, basic concern. In the company's 1999 annual report, chairman, president, and CEO Nicholas DeBenedictis wrote that PSC "is continually exploring water-related opportunities that will grow or complement our core business of providing efficient and high quality water service.''

Principal Subsidiaries

Philadelphia Suburban Water Company; Consumers Water Company.

Principal Competitors

American Water Works Company, Inc.; United Water Resources.

Further Reading

Pennsylvania Department of Environmental Resources, *Use Water Wisely,* Harrisburg: Pennsylvania Department of Environmental Resources, 1990.

''Philadelphia Suburban Corporation Acquires Consumers Water Company.'' *Wall Street Journal,* June 30, 1998, p. A9.

Sacchetti, Jerry A., ed., *Reflections on Water: A Centennial History of Philadelphia Suburban Water Company,* Bryn Mawr, Pa.: Philadelphia Suburban water Company, 1986.

—George A. Milite

Pogo Producing Company

5 Greenway Plaza
P.O. Box 2504
Houston, Texas 77252-2504
U.S.A.
Telephone: (713) 297-5000
Fax: (713) 297-5100
Web site: http://www.pogoproducing.com

Public Company
Incorporated: 1970
Employees: 161
Sales: $498 million (2000)
Stock Exchanges: New York Pacific
Ticker Symbol: PPP
NAIC: 211111 Crude Petroleum and Natural Gas
Extraction

Pogo Producing Company is engaged in the exploration, development, and production of natural gas both domestically and at selected onshore sites in Canada and Hungary and offshore sites in the Gulf of Thailand and in the United Kingdom and Danish sectors of the North Sea. Its major regions in the United States are Louisiana and Texas, both onshore and offshore, and onshore in New Mexico. By century's end, Pogo's proven hydrocarbon reserves stood at the highest point in the company's history. In toto, it had proven reserves of almost 80 million barrels of oil, condensate, and natural gas liquids and 374.7 billion cubic feet of natural gas. Altogether, Pogo had an interest in 900 oil wells and 250 natural gas wells. Additionally, it had an interest in 102 federal and state lease blocks in the Gulf of Mexico, making up nearly 30 percent of its proven reserves of oil and natural gas. Domestically, the company owns about 226,000 gross leasehold acres in major oil and gas producing areas onshore, approximately 734,000 gross acres in the Gulf of Thailand, 778,000 gross acres in Hungary, 114,000 gross acres in Canada, and 194,000 gross acres in the combined U.K. and Danish sectors of the North Sea. The company also has an investment in offshore production pipelines in the Gulf of Mexico and about a one-fifth interest in a gas processing plant.

1970s Origins Through the 1980s Oil Boom

Pogo Producing was established in 1970 as part of the Pennzoil Company, then under the control of William C. Liedtke, Jr., and John Hugh Liedtke. In the 1950s, the Liedtke brothers, in a partnership with George Bush and John Overbey, founded the Zapata Drilling Co. in Midland, Texas, and in 1963 they gained control of Pennzoil. The pair were the co-founders of Pennzoil Products Co. and Pogo Producing. ''Pogo,'' an acronym for ''Pennzoil Offshore Gas Operators,'' indicates the earliest focus of the company. At the time that Pennzoil spun off Pogo Producing in 1977, William Liedtke became CEO and president of Pogo. He had served as president of Pennzoil from 1967 until the restructuring turned Pogo into a separate entity.

From the start, Pogo Producing bid competitively with other companies in government sale of leases in federal waters in the Gulf of Mexico off the Texas, Louisiana, and Mississippi coasts. It was through obtaining these leases that Pogo created its reserves of natural gas, condensate, and oil, its ''bank'' from which to draw as demand required. According to Paul Van Wagenen, who later replaced Liedtke as Pogo's CEO and president, ''Back in the '70s, people like Bill Liedtke were big, big bidders for oil and natural gas reserves. They pursued them with vigor. They had enough foresight to not only bid judiciously and aggressively, but they also had a knack for getting the contracts for drilling quicker than the competition.''

Thus Pogo fared well during the oil boom of the 1970s and early 1980s, and at one point, 1983, had to fight off a takeover attempt by Northwest Industries, which in 1981 had acquired a 20 percent interest in Pogo. The takeover attempt turned into a heated court battle when Northwest and Pogo squared off over the total value of Pogo's proven reserves, which, Pogo's accountants asserted, Northwest had deliberately undervalued in order to improve its earnings. Matters soon turned moot, however; the motivation drained from both sides when the oil recession hit and Pogo no longer held the boom-time promise.

1984–91: Emerging from Heavy Debts

In fact, when the petroleum industry faced the big market surplus of the mid-1980s, Pogo quickly became burdened with heavy debts. The market price of gas plummeted, eliminating profits and dimming prospects for growth. The glut and cheap prices left the company struggling for profitability. Between 1987 and 1989, a very volatile period in the industry, its revenues dropped from $140.85 million to $121.12 million, although in 1988 sales rose temporarily to $156.43 million. In the same period, its net income fell from $16.43 million to a loss of $5.59 million, and its total assets dropped from $565.51 million to just under $420.9 million.

Over these years and into the early 1990s, Liedtke and his associates took some draconian measures to reverse the company's downward slide. In the five-year stretch between 1986 and 1991, Pogo reduced its debt from a crushing $515 million to a much more tenable $217 million. It also trimmed its work force from 245 to 101, a belt-tightening necessity common enough in the petroleum industry. The reduced debt load permitted the company to increase its shareholders' stock value. By 1990, the approximate market value of the company's outstanding shares had reached $159.65 million. Its revenues had climbed to $132.4 million, producing a net income of $18.2 million.

Even while struggling to recover, Pogo had gone about the necessary business of replacing its exhausted reserves. In 1989, with recovery not yet on the corporate horizon, it entered into a limited partnership arrangement with Pogo Gulf Coast, Ltd. As a general partner with Pogo Gulf Coast, Pogo Producing was responsible for investing up to $60 million for exploration in both federal and state waters in the Gulf of Mexico. The company would own a 40 percent interest in all properties leased by the limited partnership. All together, by April 1990, Pogo Gulf Coast had acquired 11 federal leases and purchased an interest in two others. As a result, Pogo Producing entered the spring of 1990 owning outright or holding an interest in 104 leases in federal jurisdictions off Gulf state coasts.

Signs that Pogo's fortunes were further on the upswing came in 1991, the year that William Liedtke died. Despite a drop in revenues to $124.4 million, the company had made enough progress in its turn-around efforts to ensure its ability to replace its used reserves. By the summer of that year, its reserves had reached about 19 million barrels of oil and condensate and 218

billion cubic feet of natural gas. Further, with its greatly reduced debt load, the company intensified its competitive bidding for gas and oil reserves, its principal means of replacing those either depleted or abandoned as insufficiently productive.

1992–2000: New Challenges and Robust Growth

When Liedtke died, he was succeeded as CEO by Paul G. Van Wagenen, who, like his older mentor, had come to the company with a legal background. He had joined Pogo in 1979 as its first in-house legal counsel. He was appointed vice-president and general counsel in 1982 and senior vice-president in 1986. As general counsel, he had played a very vital role in protecting Pogo's interests in the industry-wide "take-or-pay" disputes in which many gas buyers were forced to honor long-term purchase contracts with gas producers. In 1990, Liedtke, fighting a losing battle with cancer, had named Van Wagenen chief operating officer and president, in effect passing operational control of Pogo to the younger man before succumbing to his illness.

During the remainder of the 1990s, Pogo compiled an enviable record in replacing its oil, gas, and carbon condensate reserves, its key to achieving higher production levels and growth. Between 1992 and 1999, it replaced an annual average of 185 percent of what it produced and sold. Despite this excellent record of replacing its depleted reserves, Pogo had a couple of lean years, particularly in 1995, when its revenues dropped to $157.6 million and its net income to $9.2 million. On paper, 1998 looked much worse. On revenues of $202.80 million, the company had a net loss of almost $43.1 million, or about $1.14 per share. However, most of the loss resulted from Pogo's debt assumptions in its merger with Arch Petroleum Inc. of Fort Worth, a major acquisition.

Arch, incorporated in 1980 as Sparkman Producing Co., had originally been a wholly-owned subsidiary of Sparkman Energy, but changed its name to Arch Petroleum, Inc. in 1985, two years after it had been spun off by Sparkman. Its core interests were in gas transmission and marketing as well as exploration and development. It started growing very quickly in the early 1990s. From producing revenues of just $7.2 million in 1992, Arch saw its sales surge to $68 million in 1995, an increase of 950 percent. Much credit for the surge went to its transmission system and its excellent marketing capabilities. In 1996, predictions were that by 2000 it would triple its annual revenues, principally through acquisitions and improved output resulting from enhanced technology. Despite its success, Arch went largely unrecognized by Wall Street, and its stock remained undervalued, making it a good merger target. Pogo took the bait, picking up Arch for a fixed exchange of one share of Pogo common stock for each 10.4 shares of Arch common stock and one share of Pogo common stock for each 1.04 shares of Arch preferred stock, a deal valued at about $115 million. Included in Pogo's acquisition was its assumption of Arch's debt service of about $48.5 million and some production payment obligations. Under the terms of the agreement, Arch Petroleum became a wholly owned subsidiary of Pogo operating under that company's name, not as a separate entity.

In any case, in 1999, Pogo again turned things around. From revenues of approximately $275.1 million, it earned a net income of $22.1 million. It was also leaner and tougher, in part because by the closing years of the century, the need for greater efficiency in time and cost had encouraged oil and gas exploration and production companies to outsource construction management services to independent construction management teams (CMTs). Pogo followed suit. In the Gulf of Thailand, Pogo contracted Paragon Engineering Services Inc. to complete two of its Gulf of Thailand pre-production projects, giving Paragon considerable authority in the process. It was Paragon's responsibility to create cohesive, accountable, and effective CMTs from diverse groups of project members. From conceptual design to production start-up, the CMTs directed the first phases of the work. Such outsourcing has allowed and should continue to allow Pogo to maintain its primary focus on its special strengths: reservoir and geophysical interpretation, drilling, and production. It has also abrogated Pogo's need to maintain, at considerable cost, a sizable staff of engineers.

Towards the end of 2000, Pogo Producing acquired Noric Corporation in a $630 million, evenly split stock and cash deal. The New York-based Noric was the privately owned parent company of North Central Oil Corporation, a Houston-based oil and gas exploration company much like Pogo. Pogo also assumed Noric's $120 million debt. Part of Noric's attraction for Pogo was its record of successful reserve replacement, unbroken for 17 years.

With the Noric acquisition, Pogo Producing increased its oil and gas reserves by about 63 percent, notably its onshore natural gas holdings in the United States. Given the sharp rise in the price of natural gas that started in that year, it was a timely acquisition, a fact stressed by Pogo's chairman, Paul Van Wagenen, who noted that the investment provided "the right commodity—natural gas—at the right price in the right place." It increased Pogo's natural gas reserves from 847.4 billion cubic feet to 1.38 trillion cubic feet, accounting for 61 percent of the company's total reserves. By combining the operations of the two companies, Pogo expected to cut the costs of both by about 40 percent, but the downside would be an unspecified number of layoffs. The merger increased Pogo's equity value to about $1.3 billion.

As a result of the merger, Pogo claimed a 2001 capital spending budget of around $350 million and a cash flow of $405 million. Between them, the two merging companies had generated a combined $132.5 million discretionary cash flow in 1999. Pogo, which for years had advanced primarily through its international operations, gained a new momentum in the domestic market thanks to its acquisitions near and at the turn of the century.

Principal Subsidiaries

Arch Petroleum Inc.; Industrial Natural Gas LC; Pogo Offshore Pipeline Co.

Principal Competitors

Anadarko Petroleum Corporation; BP Amoco plc; Conoco Inc.; Exxon Mobil Corporation; Royal Dutch/Shell Group; Texaco Inc; USX-Marathon Group.

Further Reading

Coghlan, Keeley, and Paul Merolli, "Pogo Snaps up North Central for $750 Million," *Oil Daily*, November 21, 2000.

Davis, Michael, "Houston-Based Oil, Gas Exploration Firm to Buy New York Company," *Knight Ridder/Tribune Business News*, November 20, 2000.

Dwyer, Steve, "Pogo Chairman Van Wagenen to Continue Rich Legacy of Mentor," *National Petroleum News*, June 1991.

Hill, Matthew, Harold Walling, and Stephen Brunner, "Outsourced Construction Management Enhances Offshore Projects," *Oil and Gas Journal*, November 8, 1999, p. 74.

Konrad, Walecia, "Take Your Fees and Come Out Fighting," *Forbes*, July 18, 1983, p. 98.

"Pogo Producing Company Completes Arch Merger," *Business Wire*, August 17, 1998.

"Pogo Producing Co.," *Oil Daily*, April 23, 1990, p. 5.

Share, Jeff, "Transmission Pushing Arch Toward $250 Million Company," *Pipeline & Gas Journal*, April 1996, p. 41.

—John W. Fiero

Qiagen N.V.

Spoorstraat 50
5911 KJ Venlo
The Netherlands
Telephone: (+31) 77 320-8400
Fax: (+31) 77 320-8409
Web site: http://www.qiagen.com

QIAGEN GmbH
Max-Volmer-Straße 4
40724 Hilden
Germany
Telephone: (+49) 2103 29 12000
Fax: (+49) 2103-29-22000

Public Company
Incorporated: 1984
Employees: 1,200
Sales: $144 million (1999)
Stock Exchanges: NASDAQ Frankfurt
Ticker Symbol: QGENF
NAIC: 541710 Research and Development in the
    Physical, Engineering, and Life Sciences

Biotech pioneer Qiagen N.V.—the holding company is based in The Netherlands but the company's main operations and headquarters are in Hilden, Germany—is providing the picks and shovels for the 21st century's genetics gold rush. The world leader in such fields as ultrapure DNA and RNA extraction and single nucleotide polymorphism (SNP) screening, Qiagen dwarfs its nearest competitors, and is said to be seven times larger than all of its primary competitors combined. This is because Qiagen, led by founder and CEO Metin Colpan and CFO Peer Schatz, holds the patent for a revolutionary and proprietary resin-based DNA extraction process developed by Colpan in the early 1980s that has since become a standard throughout the world. Qiagen has successfully leveraged and extended that technology to offer a wide array of more than 250 products, primarily in the form of consumable "kits" to more than 150,000 customers worldwide. Qiagen also sells complete

robotics systems enabling automated DNA extraction using its kits, freeing up valuable laboratory time and manpower. The company's technology, which has been used in such infamous circumstances as the O.J. Simpson murder trial and the testing of Monica Lewinsky's dress stains, has helped reduce DNA extraction times from several days to just two hours, allowing for large-scale production of the ultrapure DNA and RNA necessary for the booming genomics—the application of genetic research to the health field—industries. Qiagen, which posted $144 million in revenues in 1999, expects to see its sales jump to as much as $1 billion as the market for its products booms in the early years of the new century. The company trades on the NASDAQ and Frankfurt secondary market stock exchanges.

DNA Extraction Pioneer in the 1980s

Extracting the pure DNA from bacteria or from cells of human or animal tissues was a tedious and even dangerous process in the early 1980s, requiring the handling of toxic and extremely harsh chemicals and involving several days to complete. Yet the availability of large and reliable quantities of pure DNA and RNA was a requirement for the building of the nascent biotechnology field, then just gathering steam with the launch of the human genome project and other genetic breakthroughs being made at the time. Among those working in genetics technology in the late 1970s was Turkish-born Metin Colpan.

Colpan had come to Germany at the age of six with his parents, who were part of the wave of "guest workers" entering Germany in the 1960s. Colpan was to consider this background as an important part of his later success, giving him the flexibility to meet the ever-changing demands of the biotechnology industry. As Colpan told *Business Week:* "I have no problem orienting myself to foreign surroundings." Colpan went on to complete a Ph.D. in chemical engineering at the University of Darmstadt. Colpan's Ph.D. thesis was to provide the foundation for his later success. By the late 1970s, Colpan had become convinced of the need for new methods and technologies for extracting the pure nucleic acid needed for genetics research. Colpan's thesis detailed the development of a silica resin based

Company Perspectives:

The QIAGEN goal is to offer customers high-quality, innovative products that provide maximum convenience and reliable results, backed by excellent technical and customer service. Most QIAGEN products are available in ready-to-use kit format, and are supplied with comprehensive handbooks which include information about both the technology and the protocols. If more information is needed, the QIAGEN Technical Service teams are available to provide helpful advice about QIAGEN products and most molecular biology procedures.

anion-exchanger that could separate out nucleic acids from cells more rapidly than the traditionally time-consuming and more dangerous chemical methods.

Completing his thesis in 1983, Colpan applied for a U.S. patent for his technology (which he received in 1987). Colpan then made the rounds of Germany's pharmaceutical industry seeking financial backing to implement his resin-based technology from such firms as Roche and Bayer. Yet, as Colpan told *Forbes,* these companies thought him ''too entrepreneurial.'' Colpan's fortunes were to change in 1984, however, after a one-hour meeting at the Frankfurt airport with Moshe Alafi, a prominent California-based investor in the newly appearing biotechnology sector. Alafi, who had been among the earliest investors in such biotechnology pioneers as Biogen and Amgen, agreed to provide Colpan with a letter of commitment. With Alafi's backing, Colpan was able to raise some $3 million to launch his company.

Colpan joined with three other partners to launch Qiagen N.V., a Netherlands-listed company with operational headquarters based in Hilden, Germany in 1984. The company claimed the distinction of being the first venture capital-backed German company. His resin-based anionic-extraction technology also was set to revolutionize the biotechnology industry. In 1986, Qiagen introduced its first ready-to-use plasmid kit, which offered customers all the materials and equipment needed for the company's breakthrough nucleic acid cleansing process.

Yet the company, which remained the exclusive manufacturer of Colpans Anion-Exchange Resin, quickly ran into trouble. Part of the company's troubles came from its eagerness to adapt its product to a broad variety of applications, targeting a range of industries from agricultural products to veterinary research laboratories, spreading the company too thin. Another factor in the company's initial growing pains could be found in the hostile climate toward genetic research in Germany during the mid-1980s. Reeling from the forced shutdown of another company's insulin production facility, the country's biotechnology sector took the better part of a decade to regain its assurance. Meanwhile, Qiagen found itself shunned by its potential German customers.

Facing the brink of financial failure, Qiagen turned its attention to the booming U.S. market for biotechnology, which was quickly capturing the lead in what many began to see as the gold rush for the 21st century. Rather than compete in the end-

products sphere, such as in drug development and gene therapies, which required years of costly research with no guarantee of success, Qiagen remained focused on providing what it liked to call ''the picks and shovels'' of the new gold rush. As Peer Schatz, who was named the company's CFO in 1993, told the *Financial Times:* ''You know in the gold rush it was the Levi Strausses and Wells Fargoes that made the money, not the gold diggers. We think genomics will equal significant growth for Qiagen without having to compete with our customers.''

Gathering Strength in the 1990s

Qiagen was finding more and more customers for its revolutionary technique. The company also worked closely with its customers—it was later to claim that its customers represented all of the researchers active in the field throughout the world—a strategy that bore fruit especially in enabling the company to spot new trends in biotechnology research. A contract in 1991 for a large-scale order of DNA led the company to become one of the earliest entrants in developing products for gene therapy applications, a biotechnology segment that was to become one of the fastest growing by the end of the decade. By the end of that year, the company was profitable, while still posting less than $10 million in total sales.

The arrival of Peer Schatz as CFO in 1993 helped the company put an end to its shaky financial condition. The Austrian-born and U.S.-educated Schatz helped Colpan redefine the company's strategy, narrowing its sights—and its resources—on the market for genetics research. The company's new business plan helped the company focus not only its research and development resources but its sales and marketing budget as well. At the same time, the company continued to expand its array of products as it adapted its patented technology to the needs of the various branches of biotechnology research.

In 1995, Qiagen launched a new line of so-called BioRobot workstations. The BioRobot was intended to automate a number of the steps in the DNA purification process, freeing up researchers' time. Although the company's automated equipment remained a sideline to its main consumable products business, Qiagen continued to develop new automated equipment across a wide range of laboratory processes.

By 1996, Qiagen had turned the corner, posting more than $50 million per year, for profits of more than $5 million. The company had successfully positioned itself as the world leader in its product niche, raising its kits—which cost customers between $50 and $2500 each, while returning margins of up to 70 percent to Qiagen—to an industry standard. As Schatz described the company product to *Business Week:* ''We're the Post-Its of the biotech industry.''

Qiagen went public in 1996, taking a listing on the NASDAQ stock exchange, an offering that allowed two of the original four partners to cash out. Qiagen was to see its stock soar, boasting one of the highest price-to-earnings ratios (reaching 295 by the end of the decade) in its market, and valuing the company at some $6 billion. The NASDAQ offering was followed by a secondary offering on the Frankfurt Stock Exchanges Neuer Markt in 1997.

Key Dates:

1983: Metin Colpan completes Ph.D. thesis.
1984: Colpan founds Qiagen.
1986: First ready-to-use plasmid kit is developed.
1993: Peer Schatz is named as CFO.
1995: First BioRobot is marketed.
1996: Public offering is made on NASDAQ exchange.
1997: Secondary offering is made on Frankfurt exchange.
1998: Company acquires Rosys Instruments AG; launches Japan subsidiary.
1999: Company acquires Rapigene Inc.; forms PreAnalytiX joint venture.
2000: Company acquires Operon Technologies Inc.

The public offerings gave Qiagen the financing to begin expanding its operations into new biotechnology areas. One of the company's first moves was to expand its automated process capacity with the acquisition of Rosys AG, based in Switzerland, which the company combined into a new subsidiary, Qiagen Instruments AG. That subsidiary produced a new successor to the original BioRobot in 1999 and continued to develop automated instruments for the biomedical research laboratory. In 1998, Qiagen launched a new subsidiary in Japan, Qiagen KK, helped by the company at 60 percent.

Recognizing the growing maturation of its core plasmid market, Qiagen began making steps to gain expertise in other fast-growing and complementary biotechnology areas. At the end of 1999, the company acquired a new product area when it bought Seattle-based Rapigene, bringing Qiagen that company's Masscode screening technology for single nucleotide polymorphisms (SNP). The addition of Rapigene, which saw its name changed to Qiagen Genomics Inc., gave the company a strong entry into the booming genomics market.

Qiagen also was forming a number of strategic partnerships and alliances, joining with such other companies as Evotec, Zeptosens, Affymetrix, and others. In 1999, the company joined with Becton, Dickinson and Company to create the joint venture partnership PreAnalytiX in order to create standardized systems for nucleic acid collecting, stabilizing, and cleansing.

With its sales nearing $145 million in 1999, Qiagen turned to the new century with confidence—forecasting a rise in its revenues to as much as $1 billion by the year 2005. Aiding this growth was a continued series of strategic alliances and new acquisitions. In June 2000, the company paid $110 million in stock to acquire California-based Operon Technologies Inc., a maker of synthetic DNA and other synthetic genetic materials used for pharmaceuticals testing. With the biotechnology sector set to revolutionize much of medical care and the pharmaceutical industry in the 21st century, Qiagen was well positioned to maintain its position as a leading player in the biotech boom.

Principal Subsidiaries

QIAGEN GmbH (Germany); QIAGEN Inc. (U.S.); QIAGEN Ltd. (England); QIAGEN AG (Switzerland); QIAGEN SA (France); QIAGEN Pty. Ltd. (Australia); QIAGEN Inc. (Canada); QIAGEN Instruments AG (Switzerland); QIAGEN Genomics Inc. (U.S.); QIAGEN K.K. (Japan; 60%); Rosys Inc. (U.S.; 50%); QIAGEN North American Holdings Inc. (U.S.); QIAGEN Sciences Inc. (U.S.); Operon Technologies Inc. (U.S.).

Principal Competitors

APBiotech Inc.; Beckman Coulter, Inc.; Bio-Rad Laboratories, Inc.; Celltech Plc.; Cepheid; Ciphergen Biosystems, Inc.; Genometrix Incorporated; Genset S.A.; Innogenetics S.A.; Invitrogen Corporation; Neurosearch AB; Millipore Corporation; Packard BioScience Company; Stratagene Holding Corporation; Visible Genetics Inc.

Further Reading

Behr, Peter, "Genetics Company Favors Md., Germantown May Get Qiagen Plant," *Washington Post,* November 19, 1999, p. E01.

"CEO Outlines Qiagen's Sales and Marketing Strategies," *Wall Street Transcript,* December 18, 2000.

Firn, David, "Qiagen in Deal to Buy Operon," *Financial Times,* June 13, 2000.

Karnitschnig, Matt, "The 'Post-Its' of the Biotech Industry," *Business Week International,* July 17, 2000, p. 26.

Moukheiber, Zina, "Gold Digger," *Forbes,* November 1, 1999, p. 408.

"Qiagen to Reach $1 bln in Sales in 2005," *Reuters,* April 6, 2000.

Van der Pas, Marijn, "CEO Highlights Qiagen's Competitive Advantages," *Wall Street Transcript,* January 10, 2001.

—M.L. Cohen

Rayovac Corporation

601 Rayovac Drive
Madison, Wisconsin 53711-2497
U.S.A.
Telephone: (608) 275-3340
Fax: (608) 275-4577
Web site: http://www.rayovac.com

Public Company
Incorporated: 1906 as the French Battery Company
Employees: 3,380
Sales: $703.9 million (2000)
Stock Exchanges: New York
Ticker Symbol: ROV
NAIC: 335911 Storage Battery Manufacturing

Rayovac Corporation is the third leading U.S. manufacturer of alkaline storage batteries and the market leader in other battery categories such as hearing aid, computer backup, heavy duty, lantern, and keyless entry. It also manufactures flashlights and other miscellaneous items. The company has played a leadership role in the U.S. battery industry since the early 1900s. After lagging behind Gillette's Duracell and Energizer Holdings, Rayovac enjoyed a rebirth in 1996 when the Thomas H. Lee Group purchased the company and changed management. The company has been publicly traded since 1997.

Company Origins

Rayovac's roots reach back to 1906, when entrepreneurs James B. Ramsay, P.W. Strong, and Alfred Landau joined forces to create the French Battery Company. Ramsay, the leader of the operation, was 35 years old at the time and had already established himself as a successful businessman. His gumption, in fact, was evident early; he convinced the University of Wisconsin to admit him when he was a junior in high school, and subsequently became the only person to graduate from the institution who did not have a high school diploma. After college, Ramsay moved to Medford, Wisconsin, where he started a lumber company and later was elected mayor of the

town. He sold the thriving business when he was 35 years old and returned to Madison in search of a new challenge.

After Ramsay returned to Madison, Strong, an old friend, approached him about a business opportunity. The dry cell battery had been invented in the 1800s in France and demand for the technology was beginning to grow in the United States by the early 1900s. Strong was aware of a man in Chicago named Alfred Landau who was manufacturing batteries in his attic and selling them locally. Cursory research convinced Ramsay that it was a good investment. So, in 1906 the three men initiated the French Battery Company. They started with $30,000 working out of Landau's Chicago attic. ''The company just happened,'' Ramsay noted in company annals, ''as did the history of the fellow who grabbed such a hold of the bull's tail that he couldn't let go.''

Landau's crude manufacturing operation soon outgrew his attic so the men moved the company to a small building in Madison in March 1906. But orders continued to pour in, many of them unsolicited, and the entrepreneurs were overwhelmed with new accounts. Just three months after they had started the company, sales had far surpassed even their most ambitious projections. In the summer, they moved the operation into a two-story brick building with the help of 12 more investors who supplied about $60,000 in new capital. By that time the company was employing 24 workers. During its first year, the French Battery Company churned out 37,000 battery cells, most of which sold for about 13 cents apiece. To boost revenues, Ramsay hired L.H. Dodge as the company's first salesman in January 1907. He added three more salesmen in the summer of that year.

Ramsay and his cohorts were operating a bare bones operation: They owned one roll-top desk, a typewriter, and about $314 worth of lab equipment going into 1907. But they had invested heavily in inventory in anticipation of growing demand. Unfortunately, some of the materials were found to be unreliable after many batteries had been shipped. Disappointed buyers demanded refunds and the struggling upstart began losing money. Infuriated investors demanded that Landau, who was serving as the official head of the company, resign. Landau returned to France, and Ramsay kept the operation going, although another investor was appointed president. By the end of 1907, the company's books showed a total deficit of $50,000 for the two years of operation. Nevertheless, Ramsay remained committed to the company's success.

To replace Landau's technical expertise, Ramsay called on Dr. Charles F. Burgess, the founder of the chemical engineering department at Ramsay's alma mater. Burgess was intelligent and a perfectionist. He was immediately intrigued by Ramsay's enthusiasm about the operation, despite his belief that the French Battery Company was producing the worst battery on the market. Burgess invested in the company and helped it to upgrade its products. Within a year he believed that the company was offering the best dry cell available in the United States. The company struggled for a few more years, narrowly escaping bankruptcy, before posting its first profit in 1910. Enthusiasm about the surplus was negated, however, by a fire that wiped out French's factory. Significantly, though, French began selling a pivotal new flashlight battery that eventually would bring big profits.

French recovered from the fire and achieved steady profits between 1913 and 1920, despite another fire that virtually leveled the company's new factory in 1915. Burgess became increasingly involved in, and vital to, the company during those years and was elected vice-president in 1915. After the 1915 fire, however, relations between Burgess and the company deteriorated. Burgess departed in 1916 to start his own enterprise, although he allowed French to continue manufacturing products under his patents. Burgess was succeeded by his top assistant, Otto E. Ruhoff. Despite management turbulence, French recorded record profits in 1916 of $62,410 from sales of $889,880. That year, moreover, marked the last one in which the company would generate less than one million in sales. Ramsay was elected president of the company in 1918.

Company Survival Through Two World Wars and the Great Depression

Battery sales boomed during World War I because of huge orders from the United States and allied governments. By 1919, the company had established sales branches throughout much of the nation and as far west as Kansas City. An economic downturn in 1920 stalled growth, and wary executives shuttered the company's recently constructed New Jersey manufacturing plant. But the downturn was short-lived. Spurred by new applications for batteries, particularly the radio, demand spiraled during the 1920s and French prospered. French's line of successful batteries was expanded to include Ray-O-Vac (radio batteries), Ray-O-Lite (flashlight cells), and Ray-O-Spark (ignition batteries). Sales topped $3 million in 1923 and production facilities were expanded to meet demand for French's patented batteries. At the peak of activity in the 1920s, when unsolicited orders poured in from around the globe, the company was employing 1,300.

Explosive demand growth during the mid-1920s was driven primarily by the radio, the use of which necessitated batteries. Battery manufacturers were stunned, therefore, when Dr. Samuel Rubin invented technology that made the plug-in electric radio possible. The discovery capped French's growth spurt and even pummeled sales and profits during the late 1920s and early 1930s. Revenues plunged from $4.1 million in 1928 to just $2.1 million in 1933. The industry shakeout left only a dozen beleaguered battery manufacturers intact, one of which was French. Ramsay resigned in 1929, deciding "to make way for a younger man." He remained on the company's board until his death in 1952 at 83 years of age. Ramsay was succeeded by Bill Cargill, an aggressive, flamboyant general manager described by others as larger than life.

In part as a result of Cargill's sheer energy and charisma, the French Battery Company survived the Great Depression relatively unscathed. Because of the name recognition of its Ray-O-Vac battery, the company officially adopted that name in the early 1930s. Ray-O-Vac's fortunes began to turn in the middle and late 1930s, in part as a result of new innovations that boosted sales. Interestingly, in 1933, Ray-O-Vac's research team, led by the talented Art Wengel, developed the first portable radio with high fidelity reception. The radio was so small that it could be carried around in a suitcase-style box. In 1937, moreover, Ray-O-Vac patented the first wearable vacuum tube hearing aid. Despite global economic malaise, Ray-O-Vac's sales steadily surged to an impressive $5 million annually by 1936 and continued to grow to more than $8 million by 1941.

In 1939, Ray-O-Vac's Herman R.C. Anthony invented the leak-proof "sealed in steel" dry cell battery, which played an important role during World War II, as Allied troops used the batteries to power flashlights, radios, walkie-talkies, mine detectors, signal lights, bazookas, and other gear. The company's workforce soared from about 1,500 to more than 14,000, including many women and elderly men. Ray-O-Vac's manufacturing facilities, considered war plants, were patrolled by armed military guards. In some of its plants, battery making was discontinued in favor of production of parts for military gear and weaponry. The government purchased an astounding 23 million units of just one type of leak-proof battery during the war, and Ray-O-Vac operated the largest battery plant in the world—the ten-building Signal Battery complex in Milwaukee.

Batteries were rationed to the public during the war, so the loss of government orders following the war was partially replaced by increased consumer demand. After a brief period of reorganization, the company began growing in the wake of the postwar population and economic boom. In an effort to bring some order to the sprawling organization, Cargill realigned Ray-O-Vac in 1946 into six divisions: Lighting Division; Manufacturers Battery Company, which produced radio batteries and related items; Canadian Division; Specialty Battery Division; Export Division; and Research and Development Division. Although sales and profits swelled throughout the late 1940s and into the 1950s, the reorganization eventually proved inefficient. Nevertheless, Ray-O-Vac continued to innovate and set new records. It sold more than 100 million leak-proof batteries in 1946, for example, and in 1949 Ray-O-Vac's Dr. W. Stanley Herbert introduced the breakthrough "crown cell" alkaline battery for hearing aids. Also in 1949, the company introduced its hugely popular Sportsman flashlight.

International Expansion and Diversification: 1950s–70s

Ray-O-Vac shipped its billionth leak-proof battery in 1950. Two years later, Cargill, in ill health, retired and was replaced by Don Tyrrell. Just a few days after the transfer of power, the company's founder, Ramsay, died. Ray-O-Vac was already operating on several continents going into the 1950s. But Tyrrell stepped up international efforts. Notably, he helped to engineer an agreement with a Japanese company to import and distribute Ray-O-Vac products. Ray-O-Vac soon was producing and distributing batteries throughout the Orient. Sales in that region augmented increased efforts in Europe and South America, among other regions. At the same time, Tyrrell spearheaded a diversification effort. Ray-O-Vac's first purchase was Wilson, a safety products company that it bought in 1955. Other acquisitions followed.

The battery industry was transformed during the late 1950s and 1960s by the introduction of the transistor in 1956. The transistor replaced energy-consuming vacuum tubes, thereby making devices smaller and more energy-efficient. The invention created a plethora of new market opportunities for companies that were willing to take risks. Elmer Ott succeeded Tyrrell

as president in 1957. He continued to diversify the company and to prepare for growth in the popularity of the transistor. Also in 1957, Ray-O-Vac merged with the Electric Storage Battery Co. (ESB), a leading manufacturer of industrial and automotive "wet" batteries. At the time, ESB's sales were $102 million annually—roughly two and a half times as great as Ray-O-Vac's. Ray-O-Vac effectively became a division of ESB. ESB was particularly interested in tapping into Ray-O-Vac's international network, which by the late 1950s spanned 100 different nations and accounted for nearly 25 percent of profits. The Ray-O-Vac name became so well known overseas, in fact, that it was often exploited (illegally) by foreign companies—a humorous example was "Ray-O-Vac Leak Proof Fish Sauce" in China.

In an attempt to adapt to a world increasingly dominated by transistors, Ray-O-Vac introduced a number of low-voltage, miniature battery products during the 1960s, including penlight batteries and super small button batteries. In addition, Ray-O-Vac became a leader in battery-powered lighting systems and devices, including fluorescent camping lanterns, miniature disposable flashlights, and long-lasting boat lamps. Meanwhile, international expansion continued with the development of manufacturing facilities in Iran, for example, and expanded operations in Latin America. Ray-O-Vac was generating annual revenues of about $55 million by 1965, for the first time surpassing World War II sales figures. The company also made national headlines in 1965 because of one of its employees, Doc Swenson. Doc turned 100 in 1965. He had worked for Ray-O-Vac since 1916 and continued to work 40-hour weeks until the age of 90, after which he cut back to 20 hours weekly. Doc, who missed only one-and-one-half days of work during his career, died shortly after his 100th birthday.

After 44 years of service to Ray-O-Vac, Ott passed the torch in 1967 to Owen Slauson. Under Slauson's direction, Ray-O-Vac aggressively automated its manufacturing operations and continued to pursue global diversity with new factories in the Dominican Republic, Mexico, Africa, Peru, Korea, and other places. In the United States, Ray-O-Vac built a $2 million Engineering and Development Center in Madison, Wisconsin. Innovations stemming from research in the facility included the first heavy-duty all zinc-chloride battery, which was introduced in 1972 and doubled the life of existing general purpose batteries. The company also continued to diversify by acquiring, among other ventures, fishing tackle companies, plastic and rubber manufacturers, and mining operations. Unfortunately, most of the acquisitions languished and became a drag on Ray-O-Vac's bottom line. In 1979, ESB, which was purchased by INCO Ltd. in 1974, reunited Ray-O-Vac's domestic and international operations and selected Benno A. Bernt as president of the group.

New Leadership in the 1980s and 1990s

By the early 1980s, Ray-O-Vac was generating about $175 million in annual sales. Ray-O-Vac's attempts at geographic diversity and product innovation, however, belied serious structural problems that plagued the company during the 1970s and early 1980s. Indeed, Ray-O-Vac was the undisputed leader of the U.S. battery industry during the 1950s. During the 1960s and 1970s, though, it lost its edge and gradually succumbed to the challenge of competitors like Everready Battery Co. and

Duracell Inc. Ray-O-Vac's share of the battery market plunged during the period from 35 percent to a measly six percent. Some critics blamed Ray-O-Vac's parent companies for the slide. Others pointed to internal problems that resulted in outdated packaging and stale product offerings in comparison with other battery producers. Most important, Ray-O-Vac executives failed to aggressively pursue the emerging market for alkaline batteries, which quickly became the industry standard. Going into the 1980s, sales were falling, Ray-O-Vac was laying off workers, and major long-term customers were dropping the Ray-O-Vac line.

Enter Thomas and Judith Pyle, a husband-and-wife team with experience selling toiletries, sewing patterns, makeup, and wigs to personal care and consumer products companies. The Pyles, with two other investors, purchased Ray-O-Vac (they changed the name to Rayovac Corporation) from INCO in 1982. The 44-year-old Pyle and his wife became chairman and co-chairwoman and Pyle named himself president and chief executive. They eventually bought out the other two investors and virtually owned the company. The Pyles combined their consumer marketing savvy with Rayovac's untapped manufacturing potential and were able to bring the company back from the edge of disaster. Under their direction, Rayovac introduced a steady stream of innovative products and marketing initiatives. In 1984, for example, the company unveiled its successful WORKHORSE premium flashlight with its ultrabright bulb and lifetime warranty. Likewise, they started selling "Smart Packs" of six to eight batteries instead of the usual two.

The Pyles' strategy was based on experience gleaned from their previous work with consumer products. Judith Pyle called their tactics "nichemanship," meaning that every product, particularly new ones, had to incorporate features, designs, and prices focused tightly on a specifically targeted group of customers. Second, new products had to be truly innovative, as opposed to "me-too" entries into the crowded marketplace. To that end, Rayovac introduced products like the successful Luma 2, the first flashlight with its own emergency backup system; if the batteries failed, a separate lithium-powered system could be activated. Similarly, the Loud 'n Clear hearing aid, unveiled in 1987, represented a breakthrough in hearing-aid zinc battery technology. In the late 1980s, moreover, Rayovac began using the Checkout Pack Merchandising System. That system featured shrink-wrapped battery packages that could be stacked rather than hung on conventional pegboard displays and a new gravity-fed display rack designed for use at checkout counters.

In addition to introducing new products, the Pyles also updated Rayovac's packaging and aggressively sought to recover customers who had dropped their lines. They barraged lost customers in Wisconsin, for example, with letters asking them to start selling Rayovac products again. The effort boosted market penetration in the state from 20 percent to 70 percent within a few years. Meanwhile, Rayovac shuttered some non-performing operations and expanded through acquisition. During the 1980s, the company's acquisitions included, in 1983, certain Timex battery operations in the United Kingdom; in 1988, Raystone Corp., a manufacturer of battery cells; in 1989, Crompton Vidor, a U.K. producer of consumer batteries and flashlights; and the Tekna line of high-tech flashlights. The

Pyles also initiated an aggressive quality improvement program designed to improve operations at every organizational level.

The net result of the Pyles' efforts was that Rayovac's sales rose to $270 million in 1987, reflecting growth of nearly 15 percent in 1985 and 1986. Furthermore, the company's share of the U.S. retail battery market reached 12 percent. Between 1987 and the early 1990s, Rayovac's revenues topped $450 million. Innovations in the early 1990s included: a new alkaline computer clock battery; a line of ultra-tough flashlights; a WORKHORSE fluorescent lantern; and the Renewal battery, the first reusable, long-life alkaline battery that could be used 25 times or more and was environmentally safe. Nevertheless, Rayovac realized only sluggish growth in the early 1990s, growing at a rate of only one to two percent. Rayovac signed sports megastar Michael Jordan to support the rechargeable product in a long-term endorsement contract in April 1995, a move that the company hoped would have a major impact on its market share.

Even Jordan's charisma, however, could not reverse the company's fortunes overnight. For too many years the company's competitors, Duracell and Energizer, had been more aggressive in advertising and marketing their products on a global scale. In September 1996 a Boston-based buyout firm, Thomas H. Lee Group, purchased 80 percent of Rayovac with the intent of taking the company public. Brought in to run the business and serve as chairman and chief executive was David A. Jones, who had significant management experience with Electrolux Corporation, The Regina Company, and Thermoscan, Inc.

Jones's goal was to revitalize the Rayovac brand by updating the company's marketing, advertising, and distribution strategies, as well as expanding product lines and growing through strategic acquisitions. The first major order of business, however, was to take the company public. In November 1997 Rayovac sold 6.7 million common shares of stock at $14 each, raising nearly $94 million, the net proceeds of which were earmarked to repay debt. Also in 1997 Jones introduced the first major product launch under his watch: the Maximum alkaline line of batteries. Aklaline accounted for $2.5 billion of a $4.6 billion U.S. battery market. Jones opted to position Maximum as a value-based alternative to the premium-priced Duracell and Energizer batteries, standing out from the competition by selling at ten to 15 percent less while offering the same performance. Other new products launched under Jones included keyless entry batteries and medical batteries for the home health care market. At the same time, Rayovac increased it efforts to improve its U.S. distribution. When Jones took control, Rayovac batteries were found in 36,000 stores. Within 18 months 50 major chains were added, boosting distribution by 40 percent. An additional 100,000 stores that did not carry Rayovac were identified and targeted. Jones also hired a new advertising agency, fattened the advertising budget, and launched a national campaign that utilized Michael Jordan for the entire company, not just the rechargeable line. The results would be immediate, as alkaline sales jumped dramatically.

Late in 1997 Rayovac added to its overseas presence when it acquired BRISCO GMBH in Germany and BRISCO B.V. in Holland, assemblers and distributors of hearing aid batteries in Europe. Rayovac would take an additional step to increase its world market share with the acquisition of ROV Limited, a move that allowed penetration into Mexico, Latin America, and much of South America. In 1998 Rayovac bolstered its position in the rechargeable battery market by acquiring Direct Power Plus, a New York company that offered a full line of rechargeable batteries and accessories for cellular phone and video camcorders. Early in 2001 Rayovac reinforced its image as a leading innovator in the industry when it announced a major new product launch: the first one-hour Nickel Metal Hydride battery charger for the batteries used by such high-drain devices as digital cameras.

All of the changes that Jones instituted, including ongoing cost-cutting measures, would result in 16 consecutive quarters of record sales. Sales for 2000 were $703.9 million, an increase of 25 percent over 1999's record $564.3 million; net income of $38.4 million was up 59 percent compared with $24.1 million in 1999. As the company neared its centennial, Rayovac was poised to realize an even more successful future.

Principal Subsidiaries

ROV Holding Inc.; Rayovac Europe B.V.; Rayovac (U.K.) Limited; Rayovac Latin America Ltd; Rayovac Canada Inc.

Principal Competitors

Energizer Holdings Inc.; Duracell; Ultralife Batteries Inc.

Further Reading

Gribble, Roger A., ''Workers Essential to Rayovac Quality,'' *Wisconsin State Journal,* February 14, 1993, Bus. Sec.

Kueny, Barbara, ''Flashlights of Innovation Illuminate Rayovac's Bottom Line,'' *Business Journal-Milwaukee,* May 27, 1991, p. 13S.

McDonald, Martha, ''CEO David Jones Steering Rayovac into New Century,'' *Twice,* June 29, 1998, p. 38.

Millard, Pete, ''Look at the Source: Wisconsin Companies Are Developing Technologies to Solve Environmental Problems,'' *Corporate Report Wisconsin,* March 1994, p. 23.

Phillips, Sharon, ''Market Leading Technology—Unique Niche Strategy,'' *Wall Street Corporate Reporter,* June 22–28, 1998.

''Reviving Primary Cells,'' *Machine Design,* March 9, 1995, p. 131.

Ruble, Kenneth D., *The Rayovac Story,* Madison, Wisc.: North Central Publishing Company, 1981.

Tracewell, Nancy, ''Enterprising Companies Build for Future During Recessions,'' *Business Journal-Milwaukee,* December 28, 1987, p. B4.

Weiner, Steve, ''Electrifying,'' *Forbes,* November 30, 1987, p. 196.

—Dave Mote
—update: Ed Dinger

Renaissance Learning Systems, Inc.

2911 Peach Street
Wisconsin Rapids, Wisconsin
U.S.A.
Telephone: (715) 424-3636
Fax: (715) 424-4242
Web site: http://www.renlearn.com

Public Company
Incorporated: 1986
Employees: 700
Sales: $83.6 million (1999)
Stock Exchanges: NASDAQ
Ticker Symbol: ALSI
NAIC: 51121 Software Publishers

Renaissance Learning Systems, Inc. is the leading provider of reading software for Kindergarten through 12th grade students in the United States and Canada. Its software products are used in approximately 50,000 classrooms across North America. The company's principal product is a software program called Accelerated Reader, which was invented by founder Judith Paul for use by her own children. The software tracks students' reading ability and comprehension through computerized tests based on thousands of books. Students earn points based on the length and difficulty of the books they have mastered. The product is marketed directly to teachers. Renaissance Learning also offers Accelerated Math, Perfect Copy, which tests writing skills, Surpass, a test-preparation software kit, and several other software packages. All are designed to allow teachers to track individual students' progress, so that teachers can focus their classroom time more precisely on individual needs. Through its subsidiary, the School Renaissance Institute, the company also trains teachers and other education professionals in how to use its software. The program trained nearly 80,000 educators in 1999 alone. Other subsidiaries include Humanities Software and IPS Publishing. Renaissance Learning is based in Wisconsin Rapids, Wisconsin. More than 70 percent of the company's stock is in the hands of founders Judith and Terrance Paul. Until 2000, the company was known as Advantage Learning Systems, Inc.

Deriving a Business from a Family Project in the Mid-1980s

Judith Paul came up with the idea for Renaissance Learning's key software product as a result of her dissatisfaction with the way her children were being motivated to read in school. Paul had a degree in education from the University of Illinois and was actively engaged with the educational careers of her four children in the mid-1980s. Her children's school offered prizes such as pizza to students who read a lot of books. But the school program did not differentiate between students who read difficult, lengthy books and students who read as many easy books as they could simply to win the prize. Teachers also did not have an accurate means to keep track of reading comprehension. Students could claim that they had read a book, and the teacher would not know if they actually had, or if they had understood it. Paul also was alarmed that many classic books that she had read in her own childhood were not being read at school, perhaps because they were too challenging. So she made up a program for her own children, which included a recommended reading list containing many classics of children's literature and a point system based on difficulty and length of each book. Her children earned points for books read, scoring higher for reading the more challenging ones. In addition, they did not receive their points until they passed a multiple choice test about the book, which Paul designed.

Word of Paul's program got to a nearby Catholic school, and teachers there offered to pay Judith Paul to let them adopt her system. Paul's husband Terrance, then president of Best Power Company in Necedah, Wisconsin, helped formalize his wife's reading program by translating it into computer software. In 1986, the Pauls founded a company they called Advantage Learning Systems to develop and market their reading software. The software eventually was named Accelerated Reader, and they marketed directly to teachers by mailing brochures to names on mailing lists they procured. The company's marketing material was heavy with testimonials from teachers who had liked the software. Sales also grew as word-of-mouth spread the

---

Company Perspectives:

Our primary purpose is to accelerate learning on a world-wide basis for all children and adults of all ability levels and ethnic and social backgrounds.

---

virtues of Accelerated Reader. The company first operated out of the Pauls' home in Port Edwards, Wisconsin. Later Judith Paul ran it out of a building that had formerly housed a supermarket.

Advantage Learning operated differently from many other educational software companies by marketing directly to teachers. Most other firms sold to entire school districts, but Advantage Learning aimed at individual teachers, convincing them that they could keep track of individual students' needs and spend their teaching time more wisely by using the reading software. The basic Accelerated Reader program sold for less than $400 and included testing and comprehension software for a list of 150 to 200 books. Teachers pleased with the success of the program convinced other teachers to buy Accelerated Reader, and teachers with the basic package often moved on to buy software for more or different books. Buoyed by raves from satisfied teachers, Accelerated Reader found its way into classrooms all across the country. By 1992, Advantage Learning had annual sales of $3.2 million.

That year, Terrance Paul joined Advantage Learning full time. He had been involved in a difficult struggle with Best Power, a family-run company, over whether to take the firm public. Paul wanted to keep Best private, and he was finally let go with a $1 million settlement. He turned his energies to Advantage Learning and helped the company manage its rapid growth in the 1990s.

Quick Rise in the 1990s

Advantage Learning quickly became a leading force in the educational software market as Accelerated Reader gained popularity. The number of computers in classrooms across the country grew, and pressure on schools and teachers to raise reading levels remained strong, so Accelerated Reader had a naturally expanding market. In the early 1990s, there were few other products that competed with it. Sales and income for the company increased decidedly, year by year. By 1993, Advantage Learning decided it needed to find a way to train teachers better in how to use its products. It launched a subsidiary company in Madison, Wisconsin that year, called the Institute for Academic Excellence. (When the parent company's name changed in 2000 to Renaissance Learning, the subsidiary changed its name to School Renaissance Institute) The subsidiary began with only three employees, whose job was to study the effectiveness of Renaissance Learning's products. The Institute staff conducted research on Accelerated Reader and other software programs and contributed articles to education periodicals like the *School Library Journal*. The Institute recruited former teachers and school administrators and trained them to lead workshops in the use of Renaissance Learning's software programs. Within four years, the Institute had around 85 em-

ployees, and it had trained tens of thousands of teachers at seminars across the United States. The seminars ran from one to three days, and the price ranged from slightly more than $100 to about $550. By 1996, the Institute for Academic Excellence accounted for more than 20 percent of the parent company's revenue.

Renaissance Learning also grew through acquisition. In 1996, it purchased a small publisher of math software in Vancouver, Washington, called IPS Publishing. The firm specialized in math assessment software. Renaissance Learning planned to mimic its success with Accelerated Reader by putting out a math assessment package, so this acquisition fit in with its goals. The deal was estimated to have cost the company around $6 million.

Sales for 1996 rose to $22.4 million, up from $3.2 million just four years earlier. Net income in 1996 was $4.2 million, and the company's market still seemed to be expanding. By 1996, Accelerated Reader had found its way into approximately 26,000 schools, which represented 21 percent of all the Kindergarten through 12th grade schools in the United States. Accelerated Reader still accounted for almost 70 percent of Renaissance Learning's sales. Satisfied customers continued to come back for more software, as in 1996 alone nearly 80 percent of Renaissance's new customers made subsequent purchases from the company. Spending by schools on educational software continued to grow nationally, with estimates projecting 15 percent growth annually in the market in the years leading into the new millennium. So Accelerated Reader seemed a secure mainstay for its makers. Renaissance also brought out new software. A new product, debuted in September 1996, was a reading assessment software program called S.T.A.R. This software allowed a teacher to assess a student's reading level in as little as ten minutes. Teachers found this useful and time-saving, especially in cases where a new student arrived at school long before transcripts and past reading achievement scores showed up.

In 1997 the company decided to launch a public offering. It had a formidable track record, with sales and net income rising in double-digit increments yearly, and predictions of 40 percent annual growth over the next three to five years. Judith and Terrance Paul were still the only stock holders, and they planned the public offering in part to be able to pay themselves back money they had loaned the company. The company also had incurred debt for construction. Renaissance also wanted cash in order to bring out new products. It planned to bring out its new Accelerated Math software in 1998, and it also considered putting out versions of its reading software in other languages and marketing its English language products overseas. Being a public company was seen as an advantage when dealing with overseas markets, where education spending was likely to come under the purview of government ministries. The Pauls sold 20 percent of their company in the September 1997 public offering. The shares quickly rose from $16 to more than $26 a few weeks later.

By 1998, the company seemed to have convinced the stock market that it was a good bet. Renaissance had revenues of $50 million, but market capitalization of more than 17 times that, or $862 million by the end of 1998. Investors perhaps understood

Key Dates:

1986: Company founded by Judith and Terrance Paul.
1993: Subsidiary, Institute for Academic Excellence, founded.
1997: Company goes public.
2000: Name changed from Advantage Learning Systems to Renaissance Learning Systems.

that education software had a growing customer base as the use of computers in schools increased. Accelerated Reader boasted a market share of 30 percent of Kindergarten through 12th grade schools in the United States and Canada by 1998, and it was clearly a strong product. But being the leader in software was always a risky business, as computer products were easy to imitate. Scholastic Corporation began marketing a similar reading software tool, called Electronic Bookshelf, which threatened Accelerated Reader. Scholastic already held ten percent of the total educational software market, and it reached students and teachers directly through its book clubs. Fear of Scholastic's encroachment apparently spooked investors, and Renaissance's stock went through rapid swings in 1999. However, the company continued to exhibit a fantastic growth rate of more than 60 percent. In addition, Accelerated Reader and Accelerated Math fit in with many people's ideas of the way to ensure that kids became academically proficient: the software offered a form of quality control through its continuous testing. The need for more testing and more feedback seemed a given of mainstream educational debate. So the market for Renaissance's products did not look like it would wither any time soon. The company continued to reap the benefit of word-of-mouth endorsements of its products, too. The principal of a troubled school in Chicago was quoted in *Forbes* (March 22, 1999) explaining how she promised her students she would kiss a pig if they racked up a certain point total on Accelerated Reader by the end of a year. Her students surpassed the goal she had set, she kissed the pig, and the school went off probation. Stories like this were great publicity for Renaissance.

Renaissance introduced nine new software products in 1999 and acquired three new software firms. Sales in 1999 reached $83.6 million, with earnings of more than $17 million. By the end of 1999, the company had firmed up plans to use the internet to sell its products. It began selling its quizzes over the Web in November 1999 and began working on on-line versions of some of its educator training courses. In 2000, the company began offering software designed to help teachers prepare students for standardized tests. The software, called Surpass, first focused on the Texas Assessment of Academic Skills, and then expanded to cover major assessment tests in other states. Surpass was somewhat different from other test preparation software, in that it had students take tests on paper, just as they

would for an actual statewide assessment test. The program was meant to tutor students in test-taking skills, not the math and reading skills the standardized tests assessed.

By 2000, the company found its various software programs in more than 50,000 schools. It had developed beyond its core product, Accelerated Reader, to offer a panoply of reading, math, and test-taking programs. Through its teacher training subsidiary, the company had trained more than 200,000 people since its inception. Growth had been strong ever since the firm began in Judith Paul's home, and market conditions seemed favorable to the company for some time to come. According to *Kiplinger's Personal Finance* (November 2000), industry analysts who followed Renaissance's stock predicted the company would see long-term profit growth of 35 percent a year. Education was a major theme in the 2000 presidential election, and it seemed probable that education spending on technology and software would continue to grow during the new Bush administration.

Principal Subsidiaries

Humanities Software; IPS Publishing; School Renaissance Institute.

Principal Competitors

Scholastic Corporation; Sylvan Learning Systems, Inc.

Further Reading

"ALS Enters Test-Prep Market," *Heller Report on Educational Technology Markets,* July 2000, p. 7.

Bergquist, Lee, "Educational Software Maker Advantage Learning Systems Inc. Plans IPO," *Knight-Ridder/Tribune Business News,* March 4, 1997.

——, "Software Makes Mark in Classroom," *Milwaukee Journal,* November 16, 1997, pp. 1,5.

Fitch, Stephane, "Back of the Class," *Forbes,* November 30, 1998, pp. 364–65.

Newman, Judy, "Shareholders to Assess Wisconsin Educational-Software Firm's Performance," *Knight-Ridder/Tribune Business News,* April 18, 2000.

——, "Wisconsin Entrepreneur Motivates Students to Improve Reading Skills," *Knight-Ridder/Tribune Business News,* October 9, 1997.

——, "Wisconsin Rapids, Wis.-Based Educational Software Firm's Stock Recovers," *Knight-Ridder/Tribune Business News,* July 2, 1999.

——, "Wisconsin Rapids, Wis.-Based Software Maker Acquires Canadian Firm," *Knight-Ridder/Tribune Business News,* January 3, 2000.

Upbin, Bruce, "Instant Feedback in the Classroom," *Forbes,* March 22, 1999, pp. 68–72.

Wiser, Justin, "Investing 101: It's Academic," *Kiplinger's Personal Finance Magazine,* November 2000, p. 82.

—A. Woodward

Richton International Corporation

767 Fifth Avenue
New York, New York 10153
U.S.A.
Telephone: (212) 751-1445
Fax: (212) 751-0397
Web site: http://www.richton.com

Public Company
Incorporated: 1913 as Cohn & Rosenberger
Employees: 700
Sales: $218.2 million (1999)
Stock Exchanges: American
Ticker Symbol: RHT
NAIC: 421830 Industrial Machinery and Equipment
  Wholesalers; 221310 Water Supply and Irrigation
  Systems

The Richton International Corporation is a diversified services company that completely reinvented itself in the early 1990s. For decades the company was dedicated to the manufacture and distribution of costume jewelry and, later, fashion accessories such as ski wear, handbags, and fur coats. Richton's CEO, Fred R. Sullivan, sold off the company's interests in 1992 and turned to a completely different line of business a year later. Today, Richton's main enterprise is Century Supply, a wholesale distributor of irrigation products that serves irrigation and landscape contractors and golf courses, as well as the general public. In addition, Century sells outdoor lighting and decorative fountain equipment, accounting for seven percent of sales. Richton has also created a fast-growing technology group that provides computer network consulting, design, and installation; network management and support; technical-services outsourcing; hardware maintenance; and some equipment sales.

Richton's Connection to Jewelry Dates Back to 1901

If there are any founding fathers of Richton, given the company's radical shift in business, they would be Emanuel Cohn and Carl Rosenberger, who in 1902 opened a small shop on Broad-way in New York City to sell personal accessories and inexpensive jewelry, some of which they made themselves. In 1913 they formed a corporation called Cohn & Rosenberger to manufacture costume jewelry. Originally marking their items with "CR," Cohn and Rosenberger switched in 1919 to the "Coro" brand name, combining the first two letters of the partners' last names. Offering a large number of inexpensive items, Cohn and Rosenberger became a major manufacturer of costume jewelry by the mid-1920s, employing more than 2,000 people. Despite the onset of the Depression, in 1929 the firm opened a factory in Providence, Rhode Island, which at the time was a major center of the jewelry industry. After World War Two, the factory employed 3,500 and was the largest costume jewelry factory in the world. Whereas much of their merchandise could be found in five-and-dime stores, Cohn and Rosenberger's developed upscale lines of costume jewelry retailing at a much higher price in specialty shops. The first, called Francois, was introduced in 1937 but was soon pulled from the market. Its successor, Corocraft, proved popular, and today its pieces are highly collectible.

In 1943 Cohn and Rosenberger, Inc. was reincorporated as Coro, Inc. A small operation opened in England in 1946, employing 18 people, and began full-scale manufacture in the 1950s. Coro created another superior line of costume jewelry to replace Corocraft called Vendome, which also began production in the 1950s, although it wouldn't gain popularity until the 1960s. At the height of its success, Coro had showrooms in New York, Chicago, Los Angeles, Dallas, San Francisco, Toronto, and Montreal.

Cohn & Rosenberger Becomes Richton International in 1969

In 1969 a group of investors led by Franc Mario Ricciardi, the president of Kidde, Inc., bought Coro and reincorporated the company in Delaware as Richton International. The CEO of Kidde at the time was Fred R. Sullivan, who would eventually join Richton's board. Ricciardi sought to aggressively expand beyond jewelry, bringing other fashion-related businesses into the Richton fold. In 1970 the company bought Oscar de la Renta International, Maximillian Fur, Coret Accessories, Bond Street Ltd., Ronay Handbags, Aspen Skiwear, Valerian S. Rybar, Inc.,

Dan Grossman Furs, and Chic-Maid. Two years later Richton acquired Don Rancho, Inc., which it renamed Richton Sportswear. After a period of rapid expansion, Richton then underwent a gradual contraction. In 1973 Richton sold off Dan Grossman Furs. A year later it sold Maximillian Fur and Oscar de la Renta. Aspen Skiwear and Richton Sportswear were sold off in 1983. The company tried to enter a different line of business in 1984 when it acquired a 23.4 percent interest in a nutrition company, Bio-Nutronics, Inc., but mostly Richton was shedding its interests. In 1987 certain assets and trademarks of the Bond Street division were sold for cash. The U.K. subsidiary of Richton was sold off in 1988.

Early in 1987, Kidde, still under the control of Sullivan, purchased more than 150,000 shares of Richton's stock, giving it 5.8 percent of the total. In a Securities and Exchange Commission filing, Kidde maintained that it did not have a plan formulated to seek to acquire control of Richton, yet added that its position "should not be considered to be that of a passive investor." Ricciardi insisted to the press that he knew of no plan for Kidde to gain control of the company. In November 1987 an investor group led by Robert P. Adler, holding 6.9 percent of Richton's stock, indicated that it might seek control of the company. After talks with Richton about a possible acquisition failed to produce an agreement, Adler's group did not foreclose on the possibility that it might make a tender offer or even initiate a proxy contest. In January 1988, Richton's directors approved a shareholder rights plan commonly used by companies to defend against a takeover, although they denied that the move was in response to any particular threat. As it turned out, Ricciardi would maintain control of Richton for the few months that remained in his life. He died in May 1989, and Sullivan assumed firm control over the company, buying 48 percent of Richton's stock. Another 35 percent would be owned by FRS Capital, in which his son owned a majority interest.

Richton's new CEO was 75 years old with an illustrious career already behind him. Sullivan went to work for the Monroe Calculating Machine Company in 1934 at the age of 20, making $14 per week as a clerk. He attended college at night for ten years, earning a B.A. from Rutgers and an M.B.A. from New York University. By 1953, at the age of 39, he become president and proved to be a shrewd judge of acquisition targets, transforming Monroe into a diversified business equipment company. When Monroe merged with aerospace-giant, Litton Industries, Sullivan served as senior vice-president with Litton for three years before leaving in 1964 to become president of Kidde, where he had been a director on its board.

At the time, Kidde was struggling with its primary business, home fire extinguishers. Flexing his muscles as a conglomerate builder, Sullivan reached out in any number of directions, buying dozens of companies in an effort to build up Kidde. He bought a New Jersey stationery firm, a Massachusetts gunsmith, a California crane company, a Detroit hospital company, and a Mississippi clock manufacturer. Eventually Kidde would boast around 100 separate operating units. In addition to a wide range of fire and security products, Kidde would sell such diverse products as golf clubs, airplane seats, toys, camping supplies, billiard equipment, archery equipment, Farberware appliances, hydraulic cranes, Jacuzzi whirlpool baths; products for offices; products for the automotive, defense, and trucking industries; as well as supplying Globe uniformed guards and temporary employees. In short, Sullivan moved with his sense of the country's economic and sociological trends, thinking in terms of customer markets instead of product lines, with the result that Kidde's stock rose steadily, peaking in the early 1980s, with sales in excess of $2 billion.

Kidde's fortunes, however, began to suffer in the mid-1980s, when an expansion into oil and gas exploration was hit hard by a collapse in energy prices that also crippled Grove Crane, the company's hydraulic crane operation. Later in 1985 Kidde sold off its building supply and banking equipment units for about $300 million. Holding only three percent of Kidde's stock, Sullivan was vulnerable to a possible takeover. As Sullivan neared the age of 73 in the summer of 1987, he announced that he was holding talks with two companies about selling off some or all of Kidde's assets, fueling speculation that he was getting ready to retire.

Distraught about the situation at Kidde, Sullivan reportedly confided in a friend, Edward R. Downe, Jr., a businessman and son-in-law of Henry Ford II, at Downe's Southampton estate during a weekend visit in June. Unwittingly, as far as the record indicates, Sullivan set off an insider stock-trading scheme that would surface a few years later, when he was running Richton, and rock New York high society. Also present at Downe's house was cosmetics magnate Martin Revson and David Salamone, a London-based partner of Downe, who then passed on the information about Kidde to Steven A. Greenberg, a New York financial public-relations executive. On Monday, Downe began to buy ten of thousands of Kidde stock through an offshore account, as did Revson, Salamone, Greenberg, and others they tipped off. In August Kidde announced that it was being acquired by a British firm, Hanson plc, for $1.7 billion. The price of Kidde's stock soared, and the inside traders quickly sold their interests, netting more than $3 million. Because the men bought the stocks just before a major corporate announcement, then sold them shortly thereafter, government regulators were alerted to possible illegal activity. Once the name of Downe's offshore entity was identified, it was only a matter of time before the scheme unraveled. For the next two years, however, the ring of insider traders would act on additional tips that they procured about possible acquisition targets.

In the meantime, Sullivan no longer ran Kidde. Following the death of Ricciardi two years later, he found himself well past typical retirement age yet with control of Richton International, a holding company that operated a struggling jewelry and fashion accessories business. For the next three years Sullivan took steps to reduce costs and improve sales but to little effect. In the summer of 1992, even though he had not been involved in any illicit stock trading, he found himself caught up in the embarrassment of an insider trading scandal that rivaled the cases of Ivan Boesky and Michael Milken, due more to the celebrity of the participants than the amount of money involved. Sullivan agreed to settle the SEC allegations by paying a penalty of $58,000 unconnected to the Kidde transaction. He had been accused of telling Downe about the sale of a subsidiary of Tyler Corporation, on whose board he sat. Sullivan, in a statement through his attorney, maintained that he settled the action to avoid the burden or expense or distraction of litigation, but did not admit or deny liability in the matter.

Richton Sells Off Coro Inc, in 1992

Five months later Sullivan sold Richton's operating subsidiary, Coro Inc., to a new company incorporated in Aruba called Coro International A.V.V. Thus, Richton had jettisoned its origins, the costume jewelry business created by Emanuel Cohen and Gerald Rosenberger at the beginning of the century. Sullivan retreated from public attention, and Richton essentially lay dormant for most of the following year. Then in October 1993, when Sullivan was 79 years old, Richton acquired Century Supply Corporation, a distributor of irrigation equipment and landscape supplies.

Century was founded in 1970, operating out of a single location in Berkley, Michigan. By the time Richton acquired the company, it was already a thriving regional business with 29 branches generating $43 million in annual sales. Under Richton's management, Century would accelerate its growth to become a leading distributor. As he had done so many times with Kidde, Sullivan successfully picked a line of business with high growth potential. Landscape irrigation was becoming an important part of the U.S. general construction industry, affiliated with residential and commercial properties, public parks, sports fields and stadiums, highway medians, and especially golf courses where new construction was steady, and old courses were looking to upgrade watering facilities. By 2000, it was estimated, more than $40 billion would be spent annually on landscape products and services.

Because poor weather could adversely affect business, expansion into new regions could mitigate the impact of climactic conditions on sales. Century began to purchase existing stores or open new branches at a steady pace. By the end of 1995 it had grown to 41 outlets, increased to 54 in 1996, 65 in 1997, 85 in 1998, and by the end of 1999 Century had 128 branches operating in six regions that, stretching from coast to coast, included 32 states, Canada, and the Caribbean basin.

In 1995 Richton moved into another promising area of business—computer network design, installation, and sup-port—when for $5 million it bought CBE Technologies. Operating in the Massachusetts, Maine, and Rhode Island markets, CBE was a value-added reseller of Novell and Banyon Computer networking systems, and provided maintenance services for computer and business machines. Its customers included both Fortune 1000 corporations and mid-size companies that were either converting to more sophisticated technology or needed outside expertise to maintain their new equipment.

As it had done with Century, Richton began to expand the technology side of its business, both in locations and services offered. In 1996 CBE acquired three existing operations in Maine, New York, and Los Angeles. In February 1999 Richton acquired Creative Business Concepts (CBC), an Irvine, California, company that performed work similar to that of CBE, but served a new region, the southwest. The Costa Mesa CBE office was consolidated with CBC, with the combined unit working out of CBC's Irvine facilities. In October 1999 CBE acquired Corporate Access, Inc. of Andover, Massachusetts, a computer value-added reseller of computer hardware, software, and peripheral products. The two acquisitions in 1999 doubled the size of Richton's technology group, with sales increasing to $40 million.

Investors and independent observers did not overlook the success of Richton International in its new lines of endeavor. Richton ranked No. 4 in the second edition of Gene Walden's book, *The 100 Best Stocks to Own for Under $25*. In October 2000, *Forbes* listed Richton for the third straight year as one of the ''200 Best Small Companies,'' because of its 34 percent average sales growth and 33 percent average return on equity over the previous five years. *Forbes* also listed Richton as one of eleven small businesses to watch, praising Sullivan for his business sagacity. With its chief executive now 86 years of age, Richton International faced some uncertainty about its future leadership as it entered a new century. Yet, no matter who stood at the helm, whether Richton sold costume jewelry, ski wear, irrigation supplies, or computer services, the corporation seemed destined to carry on.

Principal Subsidiaries

Century Supply Corporation; CBE Technologies, Inc.; Creative Business Concepts, Inc.

Principal Competitors

Environmental Industries Inc.; PW Eagle, Inc.; Toro Company.

Further Reading

Cera, Deanna Farneti, *Jewels of Fantasy,* New York: Abrams, 1992.

Glanston, Eileen, ''Eleven to Watch,'' *Forbes,* October 30, 2000, pp. 194–218.

Lambert, Wade, Jonathan M. Moses, and Laurie P. Cohen, ''High-Society Figures Accused of Insider Trades,'' *Wall Street Journal,* June 5, 1992, p. C1.

Miller, Michael W., ''Low-Key Tycoon Gets Wall Street Fever,'' *Wall Street Journal,* July 14, 1987, p. 1.

Tolkien, Tracy, *A Collector's Guide to Costume Jewelry,* Ontario, Canada: Firefly Books, 1997.

—Ed Dinger

Robertet SA

37, avenue Sidi-Brahim B.P. 100
06130 Grasse Cedex
France
Telephone: +33-493403366
Fax: +33-493706809
Web site: http://www.robertet.fr/us

Public Company
Incorporated: 1850
Employees: 923
Sales: EUR 154.4 million ($140 million) (1999)
Stock Exchanges: Euronext Paris
Ticker Symbol: RBT
NAIC: 325199 All Other Basic Organic Chemical
    Manufacturing

Robertet SA is one of the world's top ten developers of flavor and perfume additives and ingredients. Throughout its history the company has emphasized the natural ingredients sector, leaving synthetic products to its competitors. Based in Grasse, France, the self-proclaimed perfume capital of the world, Robertet realizes some 80 percent of its sales on the international market. The United States alone accounts for more than 40 percent of Robertet's sales, which topped the symbolic FFr 1 billion mark (EUR 150 million) for the first time in 1999. The company's operations are conducted through three divisions: Raw Materials, Perfumery, and Flavorings. Perfumery represents the company's historical activity, and it continues to account for 38 percent of Robertet's annual sales. The company supplies the ingredients that go into the perfume creations of many of the world's great perfumes and scents. Food and beverage flavorings, a market the company entered in the 1970s, has become its chief revenue generator, accounting for 41 percent of its annual sales. This division is particularly active in the United States, where the company has made a number of major investments to support its operations. Since 1999, the company has opened facilities in Piscataway and Plainfield, New Jersey, as well as a production facility in Mexico. The company's third division, Raw Materials, supplies ingredients to the cosmetics industry for products such as soaps, shampoos, and other beauty products, as well as air fresheners. Even though Europe and North America account for the majority of the company sales, Robertet has earmarked the Asian market for future growth and has begun a series of investments in that part of the world, with the opening of production facilities in India scheduled for mid-2001 and the opening of a manufacturing plant in China scheduled for 2002. Robertet, listed on the Euronext Paris stock exchange, remains nonetheless controlled by the founding Maubert family, who own more than half of the company's shares, led by Philippe Maubert.

Scenting the 19th Century

France's Grasse, in the Côte d'Azur region not far from its more famous neighbor Cannes, captured the heart of the world's perfume industry in the 18th century when the perfume-maker's trade was officially recognized by the Parliament of Provence. Grasse originally had been a leather and tanning center, well known for its gloves, before more and more perfume-makers, attracted by the region's climate, especially its flowers, settled in Grasse. By the mid-1900s, the village and surrounding areas had become the country's foremost producer of perfumes and perfume ingredients; it became an important center of flower farming as well.

The development of the perfume industry brought a need for greater quantities of base ingredients. Among those setting up shop to provide these ingredients were François Chauvé and his nephew, Jean-Baptiste Maubert. Opening their factory in 1850, Chauvé and Maubert concentrated on extracting scents from the region's flowers and plants.

The company was acquired by Paul Robertet in 1875, who commissioned Gustave Eiffel to design a new factory on the Avenue Sidi Brahim, which was to become the company's home for more than 125 years. Robertet gave his name to the company, which incorporated as Robertet in 1914; Jean-Baptiste Maubert, meanwhile, led the company's fragrance operations. The company received national recognition in 1900, when Robertet's natural fragrances were awarded the gold medal at the Universal Exposition in Paris. This achievement was to help the company find a new class of clients among the nation's premier perfume-makers.

Jean-Baptiste Maubert's son, Maurice Maubert, was quick to capitalize on the company's growing name, bringing the company such important names as Guerlain and Chanel. Maurice Maubert took over the company's operations in 1923 and led Robertet until 1961. Under Maurice Maubert, Robertet began positioning itself at the forefront of the perfume industry's technical innovations, developing its own extraction processes, such as its "Incolore" process, which the company debuted in 1935.

Even as the perfume industry began adopting new, synthetic ingredients, Robertet remained dedicated to natural fragrance ingredients—which were much more difficult to obtain and, therefore, more expensive. The company's research turned not only to developing new types of fragrances, but also to increasing the purity of its fragrances and the efficiency of its extraction process. Robertet was to achieve another breakthrough when it debuted its "Butaflors" extraction process in 1950.

The company, which now included Maurice Maubert's sons Jean and Paul, began to look to diversifying its products. In 1953, the company began producing perfume bases. The company, which until then had focused on the French perfume market, also began expanding internationally, adding clients across Europe. After Maurice Maubert died in 1961, sons Jean and Paul took over its operations and stepped up both its international growth and its diversification into other product areas.

Entering the United States in the 1980s

Robertet took a new direction in 1964 when it began producing food flavoring ingredients. As Olivier Maubert, grandson of Maurice Maubert, explained to *Les Echos:* "At the beginning, the perfume and flavorings industries were cousins. Going from scent to taste did not present a major problem and the basic extraction techniques for floral essences (distillation, infusion, concentration) could be equally applied to compositions of fruits, vegetables and spices." The company's move into food ingredients was to prove a major source of its growth, especially as the consumer market turned from cooking with basic food ingredients to heating up a fast-growing array of prepared foods. Yet industrialized food preparation methods, while providing convenient and easily preserved and packaged meals, were responsible for eliminating much of the taste of the foods

they contained. Companies like Robertet stepped in to provide flavoring ingredients to help restore some of that lost flavor.

After diversifying into flavorings, Robertet began a new era of expansion. In 1966, the company acquired fellow French company Cavallier. Robertet also stepped up its international growth, setting up subsidiary operations in the United States, Argentina, Brazil, Mexico, and England. In addition to its commercial and manufacturing operations, Robertet, now led by Jean Maubert, began creating worldwide research and development operations, opening laboratories, as well as sales offices, in Japan, Switzerland, Italy, Germany, and Singapore. Leading the company's research effort was its inauguration of a new state-of-the-art production facility in the company's Grasse headquarters. Meanwhile, the company's dedication to natural scents and flavorings gave it a strong lead as "natural" became a potent marketing force in the 1970s.

The next generation of the Maubert family was represented by Philippe, Christophe, and Olivier, who took over the company's operations at the beginning of the 1980s. The family-owned company prepared to step up its activity. In 1984, Robertet went public with a listing on the Paris Stock Exchange's Secondary Market. Yet the Maubert family carefully maintained a majority of the shares and direction of the company. The listing enabled the company to look to expansion in the U.S. market. In 1986, Robertet acquired the United States' Jay Flavors, giving it a manufacturing base in the United States and a number of that country's major food producers as its clients. In 1990, the company changed its U.S. subsidiary's name to Robertet Flavors.

Food and beverage flavorings helped to drive the company's sales into the new decade. This operation was boosted by the creation of a joint venture operation, Champarome, with beverage makers Marie Brizard, Joker, and Idianova. The company, which had remained focused primarily on the U.S. and European markets, stepped up its presence in Japan when it launched a team to develop flavors specifically for that and other Asian markets in 1990.

Even though flavorings had grown to represent a significant portion of the company's sales, Robertet continued to boost its historic fragrance activities. In 1992, the company created a new subsidiary in Italy, Robertet Fragrances. The following year, Philippe Maubert was named the company's president. At the same time, Robertet expanded its U.S. operations with the acquisition of Novarome Inc., a perfume ingredients specialist based in New Jersey, which was then renamed and placed under the company's Robertet Fragrances subsidiary operations. The company also continued to invest in its Grasse location, expanding its research facilities in 1994.

Robertet's revenues rose quickly in the 1990s as both the perfume and flavorings industries proved recession proof. From revenues of FFr 550 million in 1992, the company saw its sales grow steadily, reaching FFr 780 million in 1995 and nearly FFr 900 million by 1998. As the company was preparing to celebrate its 150th anniversary in 2000, it forecasted that it would break the FFr 1 billion mark for the first time. Yet the company bested its own provisions, topping the FFr 1 billion mark a full year earlier than expected in 1999.

Key Dates:

1850: François Chauvé and Jean-Baptiste Maubert found perfume ingredients factory.
1875: Paul Robertet buys company and opens a new factory on Avenue Sidi-Brahim.
1900: Robertet receives gold medal at the Universal Exhibition in Paris.
1923: Maurice Maubert takes over as company director.
1935: Company develops ''Incolores'' extraction process.
1950: Company introduces new ''Butaflors'' extraction process.
1953: Company begins perfume base products operations.
1961: Jean and Paul Maubert become company leaders.
1964: Company enters flavor additives business.
1984: Robertet goes public.
1986: Company acquires Jay Flavors (United States).
1987: Company creates Champarome joint venture with Marie Brizard, Joker, and Idianova.
1990: Jay Flavors becomes Robertet Flavors.
1993: Philippe Maubert becomes president; company acquires Novarome (United States).
2000: Company opens Perfumery plant in the United States.
2001: Manufacturing plant begins operations in India.

Robertet continued to invest heavily as it turned to the new century. The company opened a new $25 million plant in Piscataway, New Jersey, to support its growing U.S. flavorings activities; a year later the company also opened a new factory in Plainfield for its fragrances operations. By then Robertet also had launched a new production facility in Mexico. Meanwhile, Robertet began making plans to increase its presence in the Asian markets, announcing its intention to open a production facility in India in mid-2000 and a production facility in China in 2002 or 2003. Despite its international growth—with foreign sales representing nearly 84 percent of the company's total sales—Robertet remained true to its Grasse origins. In 2000, the company began a FFr 30 million expansion of its Grasse production base.

Principal Subsidiaries

Robertet Inc.; Robertet Flavors; Robertet Fragrances Inc.; Robertet Uk Ltd; Robertet Gmbh; Robertet Deutschland; Robertet Sa (Switzerland); Robertet Espana; Robertet Italia Srl; Robertet Sa (Poland); Robertet De Mexico; Robertet Do Brasil; Robertet Argentina; Robertet Japon; Robertet Sea S.E.A. (Singapore); Robertet Vietnam; Claman (Pty) Ltd (South Africa); Robertet Turquie.

Principal Competitors

Adams Extract; Bayer AG; Bush Boake; Calchauvet SA; Laboratoire Monique Remy SA; Human Pheromone Sciences; IFF; Kerry Group; L'Oréal SA; Mane SA; McCormick Inc.; Millennium Chemicals; Sensient; Unilever; Wrigley Inc.

Further Reading

Basset, Françoise, ''Robertet dépasse le milliard de francs,'' *Parfums Cosmétiques Actualités,* February/March 2000, p. 39.
Bovas, Michel, ''Des arômes Robertet pour les Etats-Unis,'' *La Tribune,* June 21, 1999.
''Case Study: Robertet Flavors,'' *Food Logistics,* November/December 1999.
Goddard, Peter, ''The Science Behind the Scent,'' *Toronto Star,* January 11, 2001.
''L'aromaticien Robertet met le cap sur l'Asie,'' *La Tribune,* October 17, 2000.
''Robertet SA fête ses 150 ans avec un chiffre d'affaires de 1 milliard de francs,'' *La Tribune,* June 27, 2000.
Robinson, Alan, ''Avec le développement de la cuisine rapide, Robertet joue la carte de l'agroalimentaire,'' *Les Echos,* April 21, 1993, p. 2.

—M.L. Cohen

ROHDE&SCHWARZ

Rohde & Schwarz GmbH & Co. KG

Mühldorfstraße 15
D-81671 München
Germany
Telephone: (49) (89) 4129-0
Fax: (49) (89) 4129-12-164
Web site: http://www.Rohde-Schwarz.com

Private Company
Incorporated: 1933 as Physikalisch-technisches
   Entwicklungslabor Dr. Rohde & Dr. Schwarz
Employees: 5,000
Sales: DM 1.6 billion ($800 million) (2000 est.)
NAIC: 33422 Radio and Television Broadcasting and
   Wireless Communications Equipment Manufacturing;
   334515 Instrument Manufacturing for Measurement
   and Testing Electricity and Electrical Signals; 334419
   Other Electronic Component Manufacturing

Rohde & Schwarz GmbH & Co. KG is Europe's top maker of electronic test and measurement equipment. The company is also among the world's leading manufacturers of professional radio systems used in ground stations, ships, and aircraft. Another Rohde & Schwarz product line includes a complete range of equipment for analog and digital audio and TV broadcasting. Finally, the company offers automatic radio-monitoring and frequency management systems—such as receivers, direction finders, signal analyzers, and antennas–used by national and international authorities. Berlin-based Rohde & Schwarz SIT GmbH develops crypto products and systems for information security in electronic data processing systems used by industry and government. Rohde & Schwarz products are developed and manufactured at the company's three German production plants in Memmingen, Teisnach, and Cologne, as well as in the Czech Republic. The company maintains sales offices in more than 70 countries around the globe and cooperates with Beaverton, Oregon-based maker of test and measurement products Tektronix Inc. in North America and with Tokyo-based manufacturer of semiconductor test systems Advantest Corporation in Japan. The private business is owned by the Rohde and Schwarz families.

Two Physicists Set Up Shop in 1933

It was late in the autumn of 1929 when two third-year physics students met in Jena University's physics department. Lothar Rohde, who had studied at Cologne University, and Hermann Schwarz, who came to Jena from Munich University, were both working on dissertations with Jena's physics professor, Dr. Esau. Both students were awarded their doctorates in 1931—Rohde on the discharge of electrical charges in gases at very high frequencies and Schwarz on the measurement of electrical currents at very high frequencies. At the time, during worldwide economic depression, the job market was difficult, so the two young physicists continued to work in university labs. After a number of joint experiments, Rohde and Schwarz developed their first measurement instrument—an interference measurer with a large wavelength range for laboratories—and publicized their work in a professional journal.

In 1932 they met their first potential client, an engineer from Hermsdorf-Schomborg-Isolatoren-Gesellschaft (Hescho), a company that developed industrial ceramics. The company was looking for a measurement instrument that could measure frequencies of one to 100 megaherz (MHZ) to demonstrate the electric characteristics of their materials. Rohde and Schwarz were able to provide exactly what they were looking for. Hescho promised to give the two physicists more assignments, and there were other signs that high-frequency measuring instruments were a promising market niche.

Rohde and Schwarz took a gamble in August 1933 and set up their own research laboratory. Although Berlin was the German capital of the electric industry at that time, the two physicists set up their firm in Munich; Schwarz was a native Bavarian, and Rohde's parents lived there too. They set up shop in an apartment in Munich's *Thierschstraße* and established the Physikaltechnische Entwicklungslabor Dr. Rohde & Dr. Schwarz (PTE). Equipped with some used furniture and laboratory equipment, they started development work on three condenser sorting machines for Herscho. Besides themselves and the mechanic who accompanied the two men to Munich, three craftspeople from the immediate neighborhood were a part of the early operation.

Thriving During the 1930s

To promote their business, Rohde & Schwarz published essays about their measurement technologies and instruments in professional journals and exhibited them at the Leipzig Spring Fair at Hescho's booth. Their first assignment from abroad came in 1934 from an English company that ordered one of the measurement instruments they had publicized. Another surprise was a Bavarian government authority that ordered a one kilowatt (kW) shortwave transmitter. In the following years business flourished. By 1937 PTE was employing 40 people. In summer of that year the company acquired a building at Munich's Tassiloplatz which provided enough space to house the laboratories, workshops, and warehouses. Up to 1937 PTE's promotional literature consisted of typewritten flyers with photos of the different instruments glued on. By 1938, however, the company's price list included about 100 items. That year an office was set up in Berlin to maintain contact with the capitol's many government and industrial institutions.

When World War II broke out in September 1939, PTE employed about 100 people. The company which had earned a reputation as a specialty firm for high-frequency measurement technology was renamed Rohde & Schwarz. Soon the company was struggling to keep up with its growing order load as a vendor of measurement instruments for the German war industry, especially in the area of radio and communication technology. The good news was that many Rohde & Schwarz employees did not have to serve in the German army. The company was even able to request more personnel. Quartzkeramik, another subsidiary specializing in quartz ceramics, was set up in Stockdorf in 1939. By 1941 the company had 260 employees on its payroll.

During the war the Nazi administration requested that Munich enlarge its eastern train station. Because Rohde & Schwarz was located on property needed for the construction project, the company acquired a large piece of land on the edge of the city where they planned to relocate the business. However, as the war gradually moved back into Germany, the construction project was postponed then forgotten, and Rohde & Schwarz was able to stay at Tassiloplatz. Its new property eventually became the core of the company's complex of plants built in the following decades.

War and Reconstruction Years 1942–52

Between 1942 and 1943 several of the company's facilities were partially destroyed in bombings. In 1944 Rohde & Schwarz purchased a knitting factory in Memmingen and took over its 60 employees who were trained for assembling and soldering jobs. Another 60 jobs were transferred from other company locations to Memmingen. The factory was managed by Meßgerätebau GmbH (MB), a subsidiary founded in 1942 which was activated in 1944. MB manufactured serial measurement instruments primarily, in particular radio-observation-receiver "Samos." The development department was moved to Wolznach in the same year. When the Allied army marched into Bavaria in 1945, Rohde & Schwarz employed about 600 people, its subsidiary MB about 200.

In mid-1945 the American military government allowed Rohde & Schwarz to resume its business operations. The first order was placed by the Americans themselves who wanted the company's subsidiary Quartzkeramik to adjust their quartz stock to new frequency channels. Another important service contract was signed with the U.S. Air Force for maintaining and repairing radio receivers in their central warehouse in Europe located in Erding near Munich. The U.S. Signal Corps delivered walkie-talkies by the ton, which Rohde & Schwarz disassembled, conserved, function-checked, and repaired. In the following years the company also started developing and manufacturing radio amplifiers, intercoms, and even auto radios. In 1948, the year of the West German currency reform, Rohde & Schwarz employed 400 people in Munich and 80 in Memmingen.

After the war, mid- and long radio bands were reallocated in Europe at a conference in Kopenhagen in 1947, documented in the "Kopenhagener Wellenplan." As World War II's loser, Germany also lost most of its middle-wave frequencies; the country was not even allowed to send a representative to the conference. As a result, Germany did not have enough available frequencies to satisfy the country's radio listeners, especially in the evening hours. Dr. Rohde participated in the discussions about possible alternatives and advocated the idea of broadcasting in the ultra-short wave band, between 87 to 100 MHZ, a frequency not restricted in the international treaty. Within a few months Rohde & Schwarz developed and built Europe's first FM transmitter for the Bavarian radio station Bayerischer Rundfunk. However, only the few people in Germany who had a car radio from the United States with an FM receiver were able to listen to the station. To promote the new technology in Germany, Rohde & Schwarz developed sample receivers and sent them together with the documentation to electronics manufacturers Grundig and Nürnberg and gave them away to opinion leaders. The brilliant sound quality convinced the industry, which soon started building FM receivers. Rohde & Schwarz won several new clients for its new broadcasting technology, among them British and American military radio stations in Germany.

Dynamic Growth After 1949

The 1950s and 1960s became a period of unprecedented growth for the German economy. At the same time the demand for radio and telecommunication technology increased significantly. For Rohde & Schwarz this translated into annual growth rates of 40 to 50 percent. After several trade show presentations in 1949 and 1950 in Germany as well as in Italy and Turkey, Rohde & Schwarz was approached by many firms and independent sales people interested in selling the company's products. Besides cooperating with such partners, the

Key Dates:

1933: Physikaltechnische Entwicklungslabor Dr. Rohde & Dr. Schwarz (PTE) is established in Munich.
1938: PTE develops the world's first portable quartz clock.
1949: Rohde & Schwarz establishes the first VHF FM radio station in Europe.
1964: The company sets up Europe's first air-traffic noise monitoring system.
1966: Company becomes known as Rohde & Schwarz GmbH & Co. KG.
1971: Friedrich Schwarz becomes company's third CEO in history.
1985: Co-founder Dr. Lothar Rohde dies.
1992: Cooperation agreement is forged with Japanese measurement instrument maker Advantest Corp.
1993: Cooperation with Tektronix Inc. in the United States begins.
1995: Co-founder Dr. Hermann Schwarz dies.

both in their 60s—stayed actively involved in the company's management.

Two trends determined the direction measurement technology took in the 1960s. First, new digital technology in connection with electronic data processing led to more powerful and precise measurement instruments which were also easier to use. Second, system integration became increasingly important. One of the first such systems Rohde & Schwarz developed was a noise monitoring system developed in 1964 for the Rhine-Main airport in Frankfurt. A year later a weather satellite receiving station was delivered to the central office of the German weather services in Offenbach. Bigger projects followed in the late 1960s. In 1969 Rohde & Schwarz delivered equipment for the German satellite project AZUR. To realize the million dollar plus deal, Rohde & Schwarz specialists were sent to the polar circle to set up and test the stations. In 1971 the company supplied the central German ground satellite station system in Lichtenau near Weilheim with antennas. By means of these projects, the company gained valuable know-how for large projects in the areas of systems development and project management.

company opened its own sales offices. Between 1952 and 1960 Rohde & Schwarz offices opened in Hanover, Karlsruhe, Cologne, and Hamburg. The company's repair shop in Cologne developed into a production plant in the early 1960s. In addition to Deutsche Bundespost, the German Post Office, the radio broadcast industry, and the airport security administration, the new West German army, the Bundeswehr, became a fourth big account. Rohde & Schwarz products also sparked interest outside Germany. In 1950 the company exported one third of its total measurement instrument production to 24 different countries. By 1961 Rohde & Schwarz products were being shipped to most of western Europe, South Africa, India, the United States, and Mexico.

During the same period, the company once again broadened its product range. Encouraged by the success of its radio broadcast stations, beginning in 1952 Rohde & Schwarz developed transmitters and receivers for other uses such as telegraphy and telephone communication in the 100W to 20 kW range. The new television technology opened new growth possibilities. Rohde & Schwarz developed measurement technology and added UHF-TV broadcasting and receiving technology later on. The company also developed new professional communication devices and systems for flight security crews at airports. In 1957 the first automatic VHF-guidance system developed by Rohde & Schwarz was installed at Munich's Riem airport. In 1958 the company introduced oscillography-measurement stations.

Within 30 years Rohde & Schwarz had become Europe's biggest manufacturer of electronic measurement instruments. The company had about 3,000 people on its payroll. Sales had grown at a rate of 25 percent annually since 1950 and from 1963 to 1973 they doubled once again. To ensure further growth, between 1969 and 1970 the company acquired two large properties in Munich's Mühldorfstrasse and in Teisnach in the Bavarian Forest. Hermann Schwarz' son Friedrich became the company's third principal in addition to its two founders who—

Modernization and Innovation After 1973

Despite the slowdown in the German economy that began at the end of the 1960s Rohde & Schwarz was able to double its sales again in the ten years between 1973 to 1983. This was mainly due to new product developments in which electronic components replaced work-intensive fine mechanics and used modern production methods. An automated component assembly line started putting together CAD-designed circuit boards in the Memmingen plant beginning in 1979. A modern high-shelf warehouse made the distribution of parts and shipping of products easier and more efficient at the company's Munich plant in 1982.

The company's significant investment in product development gave it a leading position in the new field of automated testing systems for the broadcasting industry and the military. All airports in Germany and many in other countries were equipped with Rohde & Schwarz guidance beacons that featured many independent channels and an interface that connected them to monitors and radar stations. Rohde & Schwarz radio beacons with their unprecedented accuracy of 0.1 degrees were also used to guide traffic through the Ärmelkanal and along the German North Sea coast. In 1982 the company organized "the world's largest guidance beacon show" at Munich-Riem airport which was attended by 400 experts from all over the world. Most Bundeswehr aircraft were equipped with Rohde & Schwarz radios in the 1970s and 1980s. The company also installed radio networks in embassies.

On July 25, 1985 co-founder Dr. Lothar Rohde passed away after a short illness. When he was asked about the event that most impressed him, on his 75th birthday in 1981, Rohde recalled: "It was the friendship with Hermann Schwarz. The reconstruction after the war was only possible because of the complete mutual trust and understanding between two friends." Dr. Hermann Schwarz turned 80 in 1988. For the next seven years he remained involved in the business, continuing to go to his office almost every day. Schwarz died in November 1995.

Strategic Partnerships in Global Markets: Late 1990s

Trends began to take shape in the 1980s that fundamentally changed the world economy, and they accelerated during the 1990s. Europe opened its borders and became a free trade zone with few boundaries; markets were deregulated and government-owned companies were privatized throughout much of the industrialized world; Asian and Latin American countries opened up their economies; the Soviet Union and the Warsaw Pact were dissolved; and globalization set in. For Rohde & Schwarz this translated into fewer orders from government institutions (which instead postponed investments), the breakdown of important markets in Eastern Europe, and increased international competition. CEO Friedrich Schwarz focused on intensive efforts to speed up innovations and at the same time make product development more efficient. Research and development investments at the company represented 23 percent of total sales in the 1980s. In 1991 the company initiated the project *Halbe Zeit zum Markt* (HZM) (''to the market in half the time''), which cut the time needed from the first product idea to its introduction in the market in half. In 1980 an office was set up in Silicon Valley to learn about the latest trends in semiconductors and to promote Rohde & Schwarz technology in the Californian high-tech Mecca. This led to a closer cooperation with Wilsonville,Oregon-based Tektronix Inc., a manufacturer of test and measurement products, that began in August 1993. Tektronix agreed to help Rohde & Schwarz market and distribute their measurement instruments in North America while Rohde & Schwarz did the same for Tektronix in Eastern Europe, the Middle East, and some countries in the Mediterranean. A year before Rohde & Schwarz had entered another agreement with the Japanese maker of measurement instruments, Advantest Corporation.

For the second half of the 1990s Rohde & Schwarz focused on growth markets such as mobile telecommunication, digital radio and television, and data security. In 1996 the company formed a consortium called Tetracom together with German telecommunications firm DeTeWe and Simoco International Ltd. to cooperate in the area of professional mobile telecommunication. Based on a European standard, they developed the new ''Tetra'' technology, for digital streamlined radio communication for organizations with security functions such as the police, fire departments, and disaster prevention and management groups. In 1997 the company was chosen by British satellite communication company ICO Global Communications (later known as New ICO) to develop technologies for so-called dual-mode cell phones which were able to communicate with terrestrial as well as satellite-based signals. Another assignment, this one for Rohde & Schwarz's Berlin subsidiary SIT, came from the German data security authority. The request was for a ''D-channel filter,'' a device that could shield the ISDN-based telecommunication of government agencies between Bonn and Berlin from being monitored by spies. In 1999 Rohde & Schwarz was chosen to equip the Spanish DVB-T television network with transmitting technology which was used in many new digital TV networks such as in England, Finland, and the United States. In 2000 the city of Hamburg asked Rohde & Schwarz to establish a mobile radio network to be used by security, transportation, and courier services. As a worldwide leader in mobile communication measurement systems and digital radio communication, family-owned Rohde & Schwarz seemed well positioned for the future as a specialty firm in the global communications market.

Principal Subsidiaries

Rohde & Schwarz Meßgerätebau GmbH; Rohde & Schwarz Vertriebs-GmbH; Rohde & Schwarz International GmbH; Rohde & Schwarz Engineering and Sales GmbH; R&S BICK Mobilfunk GmbH; Rohde & Schwarz FTK GmbH; Rohde & Schwarz SIT GmbH.

Principal Competitors

Agilent Technologies, Inc.; Teradyne, Inc.; Thales.

Further Reading

''Digitaler Bündelfunk 'Tetra' soll 1998 lieferbar sein,'' *Deutsche Verkehrszeitung,* December 17, 1996.

Habermann, Albert, ''Geschichte des Hauses Rohde & Schwarz. 1. Jahrzehnt 1933–1943,'' *Zeitzeichen,* February 1996, p. 10.

Habermann, Albert, ''Geschichte des Hauses Rohde & Schwarz, Teil 2,'' *Zeitzeichen,* June 1996, p. 11.

——, ''Geschichte des Hauses Rohde & Schwarz, Teil 3,'' *Zeitzeichen,* October 1996, p. 8.

''Hermann Schwarz,'' *Frankfurter Allgemeine Zeitung,* November 15, 1995, p. 26.

Huber, Franz Reinhold, ''Geschichte des Hauses Rohde & Schwarz, Teil 4,'' *Zeitzeichen,* February 1997, p. 8.

——, ''Geschichte des Hauses Rohde & Schwarz, Teil 5,'' *Zeitzeichen,* June 1997, p. 3.

——, ''Geschichte des Hauses Rohde & Schwarz, Teil 6,'' *Zeitzeichen,* October 1997, p. 8.

Ludsteck, Walter, ''DYNASTIEN, AUSSENSEITER, NEWCOMER: Familien Rohde und Schwarz Vom Zwei-Mann Labor zur High-Tech-Schmiede,'' *Süddeutsche Zeitung,* December 4, 1993.

1933–1993; 60 Years Rohde & Schwarz, Munich, Germany: Rohde & Schwarz GmbH & Co. KG, 1993, 15 p.

''Satellitenkommunikation; Dual-mode-handys Schon Bald In Sicht; Rohde & Schwarz Erhaelt Referenzmesstechnik-auftrag,'' *Elektronik,* September 2, 1997, p. 30.

Schöne, Bernd, ''Weltweiter Lauschangriff,'' *Süddeutsche Zeitung,* November 5, 1999, p. V2/6.

Schwarz, Dr. Hermann, ''Die Geschichte der Firma Rohde & Schwarz,'' *Neues von Rohde & Schwarz,* Fall 1983, p. 4.

Wessel, Claudia, ''Umstrittene Entlassungen bei Rohde und Schwarz,'' *Süddeutsche Zeitung,* December 14, 1993.

—Evelyn Hauser

Royal Canin S.A.

RN 113 - BP 4
30470 Aimargues
France
Telephone: (+ 33) 4 66 73 64 00
Fax: (+ 33) 4 67 83 40 20
Web site: http://www.royal-canin.com

Public Company
Incorporated: 1970
Employees: 1,161
Sales: EUR 425.2 million ($497 million) (2000)
Stock Exchanges: Euronext Paris
Ticker Symbol: REX (Sicovam: 003153)
NAIC: 311111 Dog and Cat Food Manufacturing

Royal Canin S.A. pampers your pet—and its bottom line. The Gard, France-region company is the European leader and one of the world's largest manufacturers of premium pet food products. Royal Canin specializes in dry food products for dogs and cats. The company produces more than 40 types of dry dog food and 20 types of dry cat food, developed for a variety of ages, weights, sizes, and other factors. Focusing on the high-end range of pet foods has enabled the company to achieve strong margins while capturing nearly 20 percent of its core European market. Royal Canin's distribution effort focuses on sales through pet store specialists and veterinarians, avoiding competition with lower-priced pet foods found at supermarkets. Nearly 80 percent of its sales come from Europe, including 40 percent outside of France. In 2000, the company boosted its European position with the acquisition of James Wellbeloved, boosting its position to number three in the U.K. market. The United States represents a fast-growing market for the company, which generates more than 12 percent of the company's sales; another major focus market for the company is South America. Royal Canin has three manufacturing facilities in France, a plant in Rolla, Missouri, and a factory each in Brazil and Argentina, giving the company a total production capacity of more than 500,000 tons per year. Royal Canin also invests heavily in its research and development, with research centers in France, the United States, and Brazil—the company has its own ''focus group'' of some 250 dogs and 80 cats to market test its products. Royal Canin is led by Henri Lagarde, chairman, and Alain Guillemin, managing director. The company, which trades on the Euronext Paris stock exchange, posted more than EUR 450 million in 2000, of which its nutritional products category represented EUR 240 million.

Vet to Pet Food in the 1960s

The pet food market was more or less underdeveloped in the 1960s. Pet ownership remained a fairly recent phenomenon, especially in Europe, and the perception of dogs and cats as full-fledged members of a family had only begun to become common since the 1950s. New technologies were introducing more leisure time. At the same time, birth rates were declining and, as families in the industrialized Western countries became smaller, dogs and cats came to take up more prominent positions in the family. This trend was especially evident in France, where the number of domestic animals rose dramatically in the years following World War II.

In the 1960s, veterinarian Jean Cathary, operating a practice in Aimargues, near Montpellier, in France's Gard region, saw rising numbers of patients with skin and fur problems. Cathary recognized that these problems and other pet health conditions were the result of improper nutrition—stemming from the habit of feeding table scraps to animals. The pet foods then available were scarcely more appropriate, tending in large part toward so-called ''wet'' canned foods. In the mid-1960s, Cathary decided to treat the cause of his patients' skin problems by developing his own pet food recipe, based on cereals. Far from any industrialized production method, Cathary cooked up his pet food himself, using an oven installed in his garage. Cathary's recipe successfully cured his patients' skin problems—and launched Cathary into a new business.

By 1967, Cathary had given a name to his recipe—Royal Canin—and the following year Cathary closed his practice to concentrate entirely on producing pet foods. After importing cereal-making equipment from the United States, Cathary began distributing his foods through breeders and other veterinarians. A number of his former clients—the owners, not the dogs—also became Royal Canin salespeople. By 1970, Cathary was ready to begin production on a larger scale. The company incorporated as Royal Canin S.A. and opened its first manufacturing facility in Aimargues. European distribution began almost immediately, and the company quickly set up its Royal Canin Iberica subsidiary in Spain.

Yet the company remained too small and lacked the capital to invest in true industrial production facilities. In 1972, Cathary sold the company to animal feed giant Guyomarc'h; Royal Canin complemented Guyomarc'h's concentration on livestock. With this financial backing, Royal Canin was able to transform its production facilities. The company also established its first research center, in Brittany in 1973, which was to enable it to develop new pet food products with a real scientific basis. Royal Canin's staff included noted animal specialists such as Dr. Daniel Cloche, who became director of the company's research facility and who was one of the pioneers in researching bone-related disorders and diseases among dogs.

In the mid-1970s, Royal Canin bought a second production facility, in Cambrai, in the north of France. The company also developed a product geared specifically toward the market for professional dog breeders. This brand, CLUB, helped to firmly establish the company in this growing and important distribution channel, since people who bought pedigreed dogs tended to stick to the same foods and brands as the breeders and also tended to buy higher-end pet foods. Breeders and veterinarians, but also the dog owners, appreciated Royal Canin's focus on dry food formulas—which were lighter weight, easier to store, and less expensive than wet foods.

The pet food market built rapidly through the 1970s. Despite its relatively small size—compared with giants such as Ralston Purina, Colgate (selling the Hills brand), and Nestlé (Friskies and Fido)—Royal Canin successfully imposed itself on the market, building up a European market share that was to reach ten percent by the end of the 1980s. The company's European expansion was helped by the establishment of subsidiaries in Belgium and Germany in the 1970s and in Italy and Sweden in the 1980s. The company also added subsidiaries in The Netherlands and Denmark, before looking farther abroad.

By the end of the 1970s, Royal Canin's research had pinpointed the cause of a major problem among large-breed dogs, which were prone to a number of bone diseases and disorders. Making the connection between the diet of large-breed puppies—which tended to have longer growth periods than smaller dogs—and the development of their bone structure, Royal Canin began developing a breakthrough dog food formula designed especially for the crucial growth period of large-breed dogs. In 1980, Royal Canin introduced its new food, called AGR, the world's first large-breed-specific puppy food. The company also began developing dietary cat foods as well. New product lines, developed in conjunction with Rhone-Menieux and noted veterinary professor Dr. Grandjean, were launched under the Canistar and Felistar brand names.

High-End Focus for the Turn of the Century

The company's marketing helped reinforce its position as the dog food of professionals. The company's distribution remained wholly focused on a circuit of professional breeders and veterinarians. At the same time, Royal Canin began working with other dog professionals, including competitor dog sled racers and others, creating high-energy food formulas and developing dietary and other research programs to identify and address issues and illnesses specific to competitive dogs. Another successful Royal Canin product introduction came with its line of Cynotechnical foods, marketed exclusively to breeders. The company also developed new lines of products for specific size, weight, age, and other categories.

Toward the end of the 1980s, Royal Canin began to step up its expansion. Growth came from several fronts. The most important was its entry into the U.S. market, the world's largest single domestic pet food market representing some 50 million dogs and 60 million cats. Rather than build its U.S. business from scratch, Royal Canin looked to acquire an established manufacturer. The company found this partner with the acquisition of Pet Foods Plus, based in Missouri.

Pet Foods Plus had started business at the beginning of the 1980s as Farmer's Energy, originally to develop ethanol-based fuels when that market seemed to hold promise. A side product of its corn-based fuel production was the launch of an animal foods business using the leftover, protein-rich cereal byproducts. After the ethanol-based fuel market failed to materialize, the company switched to its pet foods business, selling at first to the private label market. Farmer's Energy then acquired Con Agra's pet food operations, including brand names Bow Wow and Kasco, changing its name to Piasa. Its acquisition by Royal Canin in 1987 marked the French company's entry into the U.S. market. Royal Canin quickly strengthened its U.S. presence with another acquisition, Wayne Pet Foods, the following year, then forming the Pet Foods Plus Inc. subsidiary. The new subsidiary gave the company a second research center as well as a manufacturing presence in its new market, enabling it to avoid costly overseas shipping.

After entering the North American market, Royal Canin turned south, opening a subsidiary and manufacturing operation in Brazil in 1990. The South American market represented a potential client base of more than 80 million pets—most of which continued to be fed table scraps. Sensing the possibility

Key Dates:

1966: Jean Cathary develops own dog food.
1968: Jean Cathary starts up Royal Canin.
1970: Company incorporates as Royal Canin S.A.
1972: Guyomarc'h acquires Royal Canin.
1973: Company establishes first research center.
1980: Cynotechnical and AGR product lines are launched.
1988: Company acquires Pet Foods Plus (U.S.A.).
1990: Company launches RCCI and RCFI product lines; establishes Brazilian subsidiary.
1997: Company lists on the Paris stock exchange; acquires Lawler (Argentina).
1999: Company acquires Crown Pet Foods Ltd. (U.K.).
2000: Company acquires James Wellbeloved (U.K.); U.S. subsidiary changes name to Royal Canin USA Inc. and launches Royal Canin brand in U.S. market.

of building up a brand-loyal customer base, Royal Canin continued to reinforce its presence, adding a research facility and, in 1997, a second factory in Argentina. The company also added to its European presence, opening a subsidiary in Nugat, Germany. These moves coincided with the launch of a new range of dietary programs featuring high-nutrition products. Marketed directly to the consumer market, the Royal Canin Cynotechnique International (RCCI) and Royal Canin Felinotechnique International (RCFI) brands marked a turning point in the company's strategy, as it began to emphasize its high-margin premium products.

At the same time, however, the company found itself under new ownership, when giant French bank Paribas acquired Royal Canin's parent Guyomarc'h. Yet, under its new parent, the company quickly landed in trouble. In the early 1990s, Royal Canin had attempted a diversification drive, starting up wholesale and retail activities, while also turning to the supermarket circuit to distribute its products. Royal Canin briefly attempted to enter other product categories as well. But the company's earnings began to drain away as it propped up its newly diversified operations. At the same time, it was confronted with difficulties in the supermarket distribution channel where the company's products were lost among an array of competitor products—many of which featured prices many times lower than Royal Canin's brands.

Facing shrinking profits, Royal Canin shed its noncore operations and returned its focus to its pet foods. Leading the company's turnaround was newly appointed chairman Henri Lagarde, former head of French appliance leader Thomson Electromenager. Lagarde changed the company's marketing and product development strategy. Whereas high-end, high-margin products represented only a tiny portion of the company's revenues—just one percent in 1991—Royal Canin placed its bets on gradual changes in the consumer market. More and more consumers were turning toward—and sticking with—high-end products. The company, which remained one of the only pet food manufacturers to produce solely dry foods, also was being aided by increasing consumer awareness of the

health benefits of dry foods over wet foods and industrial foods over table scraps.

The company also shifted its marketing and distribution focus away from the supermarket circuit to appeal to the specialist retail pet store circuit and garden and hardware centers, many of which featured large pet departments, while also continuing to target breeders and veterinarians. As Lagarde told *Capital,* "The secret of our growth? Client fidelity. A master who starts with our dry foods for puppies moves onto the adult range and then the senior." Meanwhile, the company turned resolutely to the high-end range of pet food products, upgrading its factories to convert their output to the company's premium quality lines. Royal Canin once again was building market share, capturing 18 percent of the total European market and 36 percent of the French market by the end of the decade. The company was also a thoroughly international company, generating more than 60 percent of its sales outside of France.

Paribas nearly sold off Royal Canin, for FFr 1 billion, in 1995. Lagarde convinced the parent company to hold onto its struggling subsidiary, even when, the following year, Nestlé made an offer of up to FFr 2 billion. Instead, Lagarde convinced its parent to take Royal Canin, listing on the Paris Bourse's secondary market in 1997. With 43 percent of the company placed on the market, Royal Canin's value shot up to more than FFr 4.5 billion. With the money raised from the offering, the company went on a shopping spree, buying up Argentina's Lawler in 1997, then boosting its presence in the United Kingdom—Europe's leading market—with the purchases of Crown Pet Foods Ltd. in 1999 and James Wellbeloved in 2000. These acquisitions gave the company the number three position in the United Kingdom market for high-end cat and dog foods.

Meanwhile, the company was investing heavily in its production capacity, modernizing all of its European facilities, including a FFr 100 million upgrade of its Cambrai facility, while doubling the size of its Brazilian operation. The company also launched a well-received line of nutritional products that took into account factors such as pet size, age, weight, activity levels, and medical status. In 2000, Royal Canin also officially arrived in the United States. After trading under the Pet Products Plus name and brand names since the late 1980s, the company's subsidiary formally adopted the Royal Canin USA Inc. name and the company rolled out its Royal Canin brand name for the first time. Royal Canin turned toward the future with a solid position as a global leader in the fast-growing premium pet food segment.

Principal Subsidiaries

Royal Canin Argentina; Royal Canin Benelux (Belgium); Royal Canin Do Brasil; Royal Canin Denmark; Royal Canin Iberica SA (Spain); Royal Canin Italy; Royal Canin Nederland; Royal Canin Sverige AB (Sweden); Royal Canin USA Inc.; Tiernahrung Gmbh & Co. KG (Germany).

Principal Competitors

Ralston Purina Company; Doane Pet Care Company; H.J. Heinz Co.; Nestlé S.A.; Procter & Gamble Company; Colgate-Palmolive Inc.

Further Reading

Bialobos, Chantal, ''Le sacre de Royal Canin,'' *Capital,* December 1999, p. 50.

Marsetti, Manuel, ''Royal Canin opte pour le haut de gamme,'' *Usine Nouvelle,* December 12, 2000.

Pauly, Franck, ''Royal Canin patit de son succes,'' *La Tribune,* October 25, 2000.

Triouleyre, Nicole, ''Ralston Purina vient chasser sur les terres de Royal Canin,'' *La Tribune,* October 28, 1999.

—M.L. Cohen

SCP Pool Corporation

109 Northpark Boulevard
Covington, Louisiana 70433-5001
U.S.A.
Telephone: (504) 892-5521
Fax: (504) 892-0517
Web site: http://www.scppool.com

Public Company
Incorporated: 1980 as South Central Pool Supply
Employees: 1,110
Sales: $669.8 million (2000)
Stock Exchanges: NASDAQ
Ticker Symbol: POOL
NAIC: 42191 Sporting and Recreational Goods and
    Supplies Wholesalers; 551112 Offices of Other
    Holding Companies

SCP Pool Corporation, headquartered in Covington, Louisiana, is the world's largest independent distributor of swimming pool supplies and kindred products, primarily marketed to swimming pool builders and remodelers. Through its wholly-owned subsidiary, South Central Pool Supply, Inc., it also provides supplies and services to retail stores and swimming pool repair and maintenance companies. The corporation, the leading consolidator in its industry, offers a full line of pool products, including non-discretionary pool-maintenance supplies, such as chemical replacement parts, packaged pools, and swimming pool building kits; and pool equipment, such as cleaners, filters, heaters, pumps, and lights. As of February 2001, the company was distributing over 52,000 national brand and private label products to over 28,000 customers from its 160 service centers located in 35 states, the United Kingdom, and France. In 2000, the company was ranked 79th on *Fortune*'s list of Fastest-Growing Companies.

1980–92: Slow and Steady Growth of SCP Pool

SCP Pools was founded in 1980 by Louisiana native, Frank J. St. Romain. The company opened as a small pool supply and construction company, then called South Central Pool Supply. Its only service center was located in Metairie, a New Orleans suburb. The new company did not actually open for business until the pool season began in the early spring of 1981.

At the time he started the company, St. Romain had been working in the pool business for over 20 years. Part of that time he was in the employ of Seablue Corporation, a Dallas-based company. When a conglomerate bought out Seablue, St. Romain and two associates, Maurice Van Dyke and William R. "Rusty" Sexton, left the company to pursue other options. The three men became partners in South Central and its chief executives, with St. Romain serving as CEO and president, Sexton as chairman of the board, and Van Dyke as CFO.

For its first dozen years, South Central grew at a deliberate, moderate rate. It opened only one new location every year or two as it slowly developed its network of service centers in the south central area of the United States. As SCP Pool's president, Manuel J. Perez de la Mesa would later note, the company's expansion took a "modest form" because, being a private company, "it had limited access to capital." It was a rock solid company, though. It logged an annual growth in both revenues and profits since it first opened its door and, in fact, would continue to do so into the next century. According to Perez de la Mesa, "virtually all the earnings and whatever could be borrowed was used to fund the growth."

1993–94: New Parentage and Accelerated Expansion

However, its growth did not really start accelerating until after 1993, the year in which the company was purchased in a leveraged buyout by Code Hennessey & Simmons Limited Partnership (CH&S), a venture capital firm located in Chicago. It was CH&S's plan to use South Central Pool Supply as a platform company and, primarily through acquisitions, more aggressively expand its network. It began pursuing that strategy in January 1994, when it acquired certain assets of Aqua Fab Industries, Inc., including eight service centers in the Midwest and southeast sections of the country. Although SCP would subsequently close three of these units, consolidating them into existing service centers, the purchase substantially increased

Company Perspectives:

SCP Pool Corporation's mission is to provide exceptional value to its customers and suppliers, in order to provide exceptional return to its shareholders, while providing exceptional opportunities to its employees. . . . As the leading distributor in the industry, SCP Pool Corporation's strategies are to promote the growth of the industry and the growth of its customers' businesses and to continuously strive to operate more effectively.

SCP's operations and initiated the company's dynamic growth. SCP's annual sales also began their mercurial rise in 1994, growing to $102 million, up from $67.2 million in 1993 and $54.1 million in 1992. Thereafter, the company would average an annual increase in sales of $81.1 million, taking its gross revenues in 2000 to $669.8 million.

1995–98: Going Public and Continued Expansion

In 1995, SCP Pool went public. The revenues raised by its initial public offering (IPO) were used to retire the company's debt and provide the borrowing capability to further accelerate growth, both through new acquisitions and the opening of new service center locations. In the same year, SCP started its buying spree in earnest. In February, it acquired all the outstanding capital stock of Orcal Pool Supplies, Inc., which added nine service centers to the company's growing count. It followed that with the March purchase of certain assets of Aqua Chemical Sales and Delivery, Inc., primarily its inventory and a single Illinois service center. Later in the year, in October, the company acquired certain assets of Crest Distribution, a division of Aman Enterprises, Inc. Included were two service centers, located in Oregon and Washington, and their inventories. Next, in November, SCP Pool purchased the capital stock of Steven Portnoff Corporation, which added a service center in Scottsdale, Arizona, to its count. Finally, in December, the company acquired certain assets of Pool Mart of Nevada, Inc., a Portnoff affiliate with a service center in Las Vegas.

The result of its aggressive acquisition strategy was that by 1996 SCP had 44 service centers in operation nationwide; and it had just begun. In that same year, the company entered an agreement with Great Lakes Chemical, swapping its chemical and packing affiliate, Alliance Packaging, for BLN, the distribution arm of Great Lakes' subsidiary Bio-Lab, located in Decatur, Georgia. Great Lakes indicated that the swap would allow Bio-Lab to concentrate on its primary business: the manufacturing and packaging of chemicals for swimming pools and spas. The arrangement brought 39 service centers into SCP's burgeoning network and greatly expanded its geographical presence, particularly in Florida.

In 1997, the success of SCP encouraged Code Hennessey & Simmons to sell off half its interest in the company, moving its venture capital elsewhere. SCP was doing well without it, partly because of its track record as a public company. In December 1997, it made a second public stock offering, issuing 1,350,000 shares of common stock for the primary purpose of raising funds for additional, already planned acquisitions. At the end of the year, the company purchased the swimming pool products businesses of Pacific Industries, Inc., a subsidiary of the large, international conglomerate, Cook Group plc. Pacific, which was part of the Specialty Mouldings sector of Cookson's Plastic Division, entered a long-term supply agreement with SCP, whereby it would make a sizable portion of SCP's polymer pool products, including panels, braces, steps, liners, and other items used in building in-ground, vinyl pools. In 1996, before SCP bought it, Pacific had revenues of $59 million, with a net profit of about $3 million. The acquisition price for SCP was about $21 million.

Expansion continued through 1998. In January, SCP acquired certain assets of Bicknell Huston Distributors, Inc., a swimming-pool supplies wholesaler with 11 service centers in six northeastern states. The aggregate price tag of about $21 million was financed by the SCP Pool stock offering at the close of 1997. In February 1998, SCP also bought certain assets of Valve Engineering Acquisition Company, a privately-owned swimming pool supplies distributor located in Glendale, California. The deal boosted the number of SCP's centers in that state to 14 and increased its greater Los Angeles market presence. At the time of the purchase, SCP had 85 service centers spread through 30 states and was distributing over 34,000 national brand and private products to around 23,000 customers. Among other achievements in 1998, SCP had broadened its geographical market range to Pennsylvania, New Jersey, New York, and New England, where, previously, it had lacked a presence. At the end of 1998, Code Hennessey & Simmons cut loose from SCP Pool altogether, distributing the remaining balance of its interest in the company to its fundholders.

1999 and Beyond

St. Romain retired early in 1999, when chairman Rusty Sexton succeeded him as CEO. Sexton also served briefly as interim president, the position to which Perez de la Mesa was almost immediately elected. At the time of his appointment, Perez de la Mesa, who also assumed the job of COO, was serving as vice-president of operations of Watsco, Inc., an independent, wholesale distributor of residential central air conditioners, heating systems, and industrial and commercial refrigeration products located in Coconut Grove, Florida. Prior to working for Watsco, he had held management positions with Fresh Del Monte Produce N.V., RJR Nabisco, and IBM.

The changes at the top did not slow SCP's expansion one iota. In 1999, it completed four more acquisitions. In January it purchased certain assets of Benson Pump Company and the capital stock of Pratts Plastics Limited. Benson, operating in 16 states, had maintained 20 service centers. SCP consolidated the operations of 15 of these into existing service centers and closed one of the remaining five. Pratts, a British company, had just one service center, located in Essex, England.

SCP's international expansion into Europe continued towards the end of the year, when it also purchased substantially all of the assets of Garden Leisure Products, a privately-owned distributor of pool supplies based in West Sussex, England, and the capital stock of Jean Albouy, S.A., a distributor of pool equipment and supplies located in Rodez, France. This last marked SCP's first foray into the French market. It was also the company's fourth acquisition in Europe since August 1998.

In 1999, the company also entered into a strategic partnership with Advanced Data Exchange, then called The EC Company. Advanced Data Exchange was a provider of Internet business to business transaction/exchange services "for buyers and digital marketplaces who are or will conduct significant transaction volume with small and mid-market suppliers." The partnering agreement electronically enabled SCP's mid-market supply chain, improving its inventory management; reducing its paper handling, procurement, and carrying costs; increasing its sales; and improving its communication with its suppliers.

SCP's aggressive growth continued in 2000 and into 2001. In August 2000, it acquired the assets of Superior Pool Products, Inc., a subsidiary of Arch Chemicals, Inc., a corporation headquartered in Norwalk, Connecticut. Like SCP, Superior was a distributor of swimming pool equipment, parts, and supplies. In 1999, through its distribution network, consisting of 19 service centers in California, Arizona, and Nevada, Superior had sales in excess of $80 million.

Next, in December 2000, SCP purchased the assets of Pool-Rite, Inc., a privately-owned distributor of pool equipment with two service centers in the greater Miami area. In 1999, its net sales were approximately $6 million. The company had also announced the opening of a new service center in Fort Lauderdale, Florida. The acquisition of the three service centers marked SCP's initial entrance into the expansive, South Florida "Gold Coast" market, the second largest in the nation. These acquisitions helped increase SCP's sales for 2000 by $100 million, up to $669.8 million, an 18 percent increase over its 1999 revenue.

The expansion seemed almost non-stop at the century's end. In February 2001, SCP announced that it had agreed to purchase all the assets of the pool division of Orlando, Florida-headquartered Hughes Supply, Inc., including a network of 31 service centers in the eastern part of the country. The Hughes division, in operation since 1995, had revenues of about $120 million in 2000, which would add substantially to the surging revenues of SCP.

Its flurry of acquisitions at the beginning of the new century argued that SCP Pool was a company still very much on the move and one that remained determined to be so. Noting that the year 2000 was SCP's 20th consecutive year of increased sales and profit growth, company chairman W.B. Sexton remarked, "We are very pleased with how SCP has evolved and the growth opportunity that exists for SCP and the swimming pool industry." What kind of growth? Well, as Perez de la Mesa wrote in a March 1, 2001 letter addressed to SCP's fellow industry stakeholders, "there are over *60 million* households in the U.S. that have the backyard space and income to own a swimming pool that don't." So far, he continued, "that means that we, as an industry, have captured barely ten percent of our potential market." Succinctly put, the market water seemed just right for jumping in, and SCP was doing just that—with a very big running start.

Principal Subsidiaries

South Central Pool Supply, Inc.

Principal Competitors

Arch Chemicals, Inc.; Fort Wayne Pools; Great Lakes Chemical Corporation.

Further Reading

"Arch Chemicals Enters Agreement to Sell Superior Pool Products to SCP Pool Corporation," *Business Wire*, June 19, 2000.

"Fortune's 100 Fastest-Growing Companies in America," *Fortune,* September 4, 2000, pp. 118+.

Kirtland, Chad, "Louisiana Entrepreneur of the Year Finalist: William R. "Rusty" Sexton," *New Orleans City Business,* June 17, 1996, p. A19.

"President of SCP Pool Outlines Corporate Vision," *Wall Street Transcript,* May 24, 1999.

"SCP Enters South Florida with Three Service Centers, *Business Wire*, December 4, 2000.

"SCP Pool Corporation Acquires 19 Additional Service Centers; Acquisition Expected to Increase market Penetration," *Business Wire*, August 1, 2000.

"SCP Pool Corporation Acquires 31 Additional Service Centers; Acquisition Expected to Increase market Penetration," *Business Wire*, January 22, 2001.

"SCP Pool Corporation Reports Record 1997 Results; Net Income Per Share Increases to $1.07 Versus $0.70," *Business Wire*, February 17, 1998.

—John W. Fiero

Shaklee Corporation

4747 Willow Road
Pleasanton, California 94588
U.S.A.
Telephone: (925) 924-2000
Toll Free: (800) 7420-5533
Fax: (925) 924-2280
Web site: http://www.shaklee.com

Wholly Owned Subsidiary of Yamanouchi Pharmaceutical
Incorporated: 1956
Employees: 1,850
Sales: $419 million (1999)
NAIC: 45439 Other Direct Selling Establishments; 45411
    Electronic Shopping and Mail-Order Houses; 325411
    Medicinal and Botanical Manufacturing

Shaklee Corporation, a subsidiary of Yamanouchi Consumer Inc., is a major producer and distributor of nutritional supplements, personal care products, and household products. Shaklee products are largely developed in-house and are sold through a multilevel marketing system in the United States and worldwide by a team of fiercely loyal independent contractors. In recent years, Shaklee distributors began establishing web sites, allowing consumers to purchase Shaklee products over the Internet. In addition to its consumer products activities, Shaklee owns a subsidiary, Bear Creek Corporation, that in turn owns some of the more popular names in catalog sales, including gourmet foods seller Harry and David and flower purveyor Jackson & Perkins.

1915–55: The Early Work Life
of Dr. Forrest Shaklee

Shaklee bears the name of its founder, chiropractor Dr. Forrest Shaklee. Shaklee was born in Iowa in 1894. After a vigorous youth, part of which he spent as a traveling carnival performer, he studied chiropractic and established a practice of his own in Rockwell City, Iowa, in 1915. Nine years later, he

moved to Mason City and opened a health care facility which he named the Shaklee Clinic. During this time, he came to believe that conventional chiropractic wisdom was too narrow, and that diet and nutrition were crucial to overall good health. "Too many of the people who came in for treatment appeared to me to be overfed and undernourished," he would later say. He began studying current scientific research on nutrition and experimented with developing his own nutritional supplements.

In 1929, however, a fire destroyed the Shaklee Clinic. Instead of rebuilding, Shaklee moved to the West Coast with his wife, Ruth, and their two sons. They eventually settled in Oakland, California, where Shaklee opened a new practice. In 1941, Ruth Shaklee died after being struck by an automobile, and shortly thereafter Shaklee's sons both enlisted in the armed forces. Left alone, Shaklee closed his practice and retired to a ranch in an isolated part of northern California.

Shaklee emerged from this self-imposed exile in 1945, selling his ranch and returning to Oakland. He resumed part-time practice as a chiropractor and nutritionist, but also began a second career as a motivational speaker. In personal appearances, local radio broadcasts, and four books published in 1951, he expounded a philosophy based on the power of positive thinking, which he called "thoughtsmanship."

1950s–60s: Sales through
Independent Distributorships

In 1955, Shaklee resolved to combine his motivational philosophy with his years of experience as a nutritionist. Together with his two sons, Forrest Jr. and Raleigh, he founded Shaklee Products, which was officially launched in 1956. Drawing on talents they had developed in their previous careers, Forrest Jr. handled the accounting and managed the day-to-day operations of the company, while Raleigh, a former insurance salesman, took charge of marketing operations. Their father directed research and development. The company's first product was a protein-lecithin supplement of Dr. Shaklee's own invention, which they sold under the name Pro-Lecin Nibblers. Later in 1956, it added Herb-lax, a herbal laxative. The next year, it introduced Vita-Lea, a multivitamin, multimineral supplement in tablet form that would quickly become one of the company's mainstays.

Dr. Shaklee's concept of "thoughtsmanship" entered Shaklee Products' operations through its sales force. Rather than hire a permanent sales staff, the company decided from the outset to recruit independent contractors and offer them a series of lucrative incentives that would reward them in proportion to the sales that they generated. It was a system that one loyal Shaklee saleswoman later described as "unstructured" and requiring highly self-motivated participants—a system that was wholly in keeping with Dr. Shaklee's belief in self-motivation and his own persuasive powers. In their first attempt to recruit a sales force, the Shaklees placed an ad in the *Oakland Tribune* asking interested readers to attend an introductory meeting. Six people answered, and all six signed on as distributors.

Shaklee distributorships spread quickly, so that the company was well established throughout California by the end of the decade. This required a grueling travel schedule from all three Shaklees, father and sons, who wanted their distributors to meet all of them personally. At the same time, the company continued to introduce new products and to branch out from the field of dietary supplements. In 1960, Basic-H Concentrated Organic Cleaner, a soap-free, biodegradable cleaning solution, made its debut after Dr. Shaklee experimented with ways to help the wife of a distributor with sensitive skin. Soon thereafter, the company introduced a line of skin care products made from natural ingredients.

In the early 1960s, the Shaklee gospel began to find an even larger audience. In 1962, a Shaklee customer who had moved from San Diego to Minnesota established the company's first distributorship outside of California, selling mostly Basic-H. Shortly thereafter, a Massachusetts family whose grown son had discovered Basic-H while living in Minnesota established the first Shaklee distributorship on the East Coast. In the early 1970s, Shaklee recruited its first Spanish-speaking distributors.

1970s: Astounding Growth

The 1970s saw astounding growth for Shaklee. Annual sales skyrocketed from $20 million to more than $300 million by decade's end. In 1971, the company opened a new research facility, the Forrest C. Shaklee Research Center, in Hayward, California. The company changed its name to its current form in 1972 and went public the next year. In 1976, Shaklee established two subsidiaries, Shaklee Japan and Shaklee Canada, to handle some of its foreign distributorships. During this time, the Shaklees themselves began to play less important roles in the company as it evolved from a family-run organization into a major corporation. Even so, the Shaklee family continued to own a substantial portion of the company's stock. Dr. Shaklee himself continued to be wildly popular among his salespeople (a company staff attorney once attested that "if we didn't have a bodyguard around him [at company conventions], they'd tear his clothes off")and was still vigorous enough at the age of 85 to break ground on the company's new manufacturing facility in Norman, Oklahoma, in 1979. The next year, the company moved its headquarters to a new complex in San Francisco.

At about the same time, however, Shaklee found itself at the center of a nasty and highly publicized controversy. In 1978, the company sued former distributors Franklin and El Marie Gunnell for more than $1.6 million, charging that the Utah couple had illegally defamed Shaklee's products and interfered with its business relationships after signing on with a rival company. The dispute was made all the more bitter by the fact that the competitor in question was Enhance, a health food company that had been founded by Robert J. Wooten shortly after he resigned as chairman and president of Shaklee in 1976.

In 1981, a Salt Lake City jury decided in favor of Shaklee after a six-week trial, but awarded it a judgment so small that it did not even cover the company's legal fees. The evidence showed that the Gunnells had indeed made outrageous claims about Shaklee's products, but also revealed information about one Shaklee product that the company had hitherto concealed. Company documents subpoenaed for the trial showed that in 1973 Shaklee discovered that the alfalfa it was using to make alfalfa tablets—then something of a fad in health food circles—was tainted with salmonella bacteria. The company began treating its alfalfa with ethylene oxide (ETO), despite the fact that the fumigant, used mainly to sterilize medical instruments, had been banned by the U.S. Department of Agriculture as a suspected carcinogen. In 1977, the Shaklee finally burned its alfalfa supply and stopped making alfalfa tablets. However, it had never revealed that it had treated its alfalfa with ETO. After the trial, the jury foreman said that "most of the jurors felt that Shaklee had lied about its products."

The 1980s: Turnaround Follows Hard Times

The first half of the 1980s proved to be a difficult time for Shaklee, and not just because of the negative publicity that came out of the Gunnell case. Profits declined as, ironically, economic prosperity in the United States drew many Shaklee distributors who preferred secure employment back into the conventional job market. At the same time, changing demographics affected the company's sales force; as the female homemakers who had used Shaklee distributorships as a second household income began to seek careers outside the home, the company turned more and more to men to distribute their products. In 1985, the company suffered a great loss when Dr. Forrest Shaklee died at the age of 91.

Shaklee soon began to pull out of its difficulties, however. In 1984, it received a publicity boost when it was named Official Nutrition Consultant to the United States ski team that competed at the Winter Olympics in Sarajevo. In 1986, it found a way around its distribution problems when it acquired Bear Creek Corporation, which was well known for the luxury fruit baskets and confections sold through its Harry and David mail order catalogue. By the end of the decade, Shaklee began selling its own products through the Harry and David catalogue.

Sales turned back up in the second half of the 1980s, drawing the attention of the investment community. In March 1989, Minneapolis-based investor Irwin Jacobs launched a $40-per-share tender offer for Shaklee. Jacobs's bid was not entirely welcome, especially among Shaklee salespeople, who feared that a hostile takeover would bring radical changes in corporate culture and destroy the intimate, family-like feeling that had bred loyalty between the company and its sales force. Some distributors even considered making a counter-offer.

Two weeks after Irwin Jacobs began acquiring Shaklee stock, however, a white knight appeared in a rather unlikely form. In mid-March, Shaklee agreed to be acquired by Yamanouchi Pharmaceutical, a large Japanese drug company with a substantial presence in that country's competitive market for anti-ulcer medication. Yamanouchi's offer came as a surprise to Shaklee management and industry analysts, as Yamanouchi had acquired Shaklee Japan in February but had given no sign of being interested in acquiring its parent company. Yamanouchi's financial package was valued at $395 million, or $28 per share plus a $20 per share one-time dividend to Shaklee shareholders. As part of the deal, Yamanouchi also bought out Raleigh and Forrest Shaklee, Jr., who owned 28 percent of Shaklee stock between them.

Yamanouchi's move was part of a general trend affecting Japanese pharmaceutical companies. Faced with worldwide consolidation in the pharmaceutical industry, Japanese companies began to expand overseas in the late 1980s, entering into joint sales, production, and research ventures with foreign drug companies. Acquisition of smaller American and European

companies was seen by analysts and Japanese drug executives alike as a way of gaining quick access to important foreign markets. Nonetheless, some analysts familiar with the Japanese pharmaceutical industry questioned the wisdom of Yamanouchi's move, saying that Shaklee offered the company few obvious strategic advantages, neither strengthening its research operations nor building its overseas distribution network. Whatever the wisdom of Yamanouchi's move, Shaklee continued to grow and to expand its overseas operations. In 1992, it created Shaklee Mexico, and, in 1994, it established Shaklee Taiwan.

In 1994 the company loaded its calendar with events commemorating the 100th anniversary of the birth of Dr. Forrest Shaklee. The company had surmounted a number of challenges over the years—not just the alfalfa scandal of 1981 and Irwin Jacobs's hostile takeover bid in 1989, but also continual skepticism from different sectors of the scientific community about the efficacy of high-dosage nutritional supplements.

New Directions in the Late 1990s

By the late 1990s, Shaklee was looking forward again. The company's 1996 sales had reached almost $4 billion, and the following year the company broke ground with a *kiko-shiki* ceremony on the first part of a three-phase construction project expanding its manufacturing facility in Oklahoma. The facility, once completed in 1998, became Yamanouchi's first U.S.-based pharmaceutical manufacturing plant. Yamanouchi-Shaklee Pharma, the new pharmaceutical division, was spun off in 1999, as Yamanouchi Pharma Technologies Inc., a separate entity.

Also with its parent Yamanouchi, Shaklee also entered into an agreement in 1997 with Stanford University to build a new research center in the Stanford Research Park that specialized in developing and commercializing new delivery technology for nutritional and active pharmaceutical compounds as well as conventional solid dosage forms of new drug compounds. The new Yamanouchi-Shaklee Pharmaceutical Research Center, opened in November 1997, began a close creative and financial relationship between Yamanouchi and Stanford University and forwarded Yamanouchi's plans for expanding into healthcare products.

In an unforeseen diversification in 1997, Shaklee joined with AT&T to sell the latter's phone services directly to consumers through Shaklee's 500,000 independent sales agents. Other new agreements included securing the rights to Cosmederm Technologies proprietary anti-irritant for a new anti-aging treatment product. With this anti-irritant, Shaklee then introduced a skin care line known as Enfuselle. In 1999, the company began marketing a new nutritional system called Shaklee Basics, which became available in 2000 via Shaklee.net, a web presence designed to allow the company's independent sales agents to build their own e-business sites.

Shaklee Corporation officially opened new corporate headquarters in Pleasanton, California, in March 2000. The 106,400-square-foot administrative building was surrounded by nearly ten acres preserving the area's native ecosystem; plans were being made to build a special demonstration garden of herbs from around the world on the grounds. In September, Shaklee built a new distribution warehouse in Ohio and saw a change in leadership, as Masakatsu Inoue was appointed president and chief executive officer. Throughout it all, Shaklee's loyal and enthusiastic sales force, unusual even by the standards of direct sales, remained true believers, famous for using the products that they sold with an exclusivity that bordered on fanaticism.

Principal Subsidiaries

Bear Creek Corporation.

Principal Divisions

Shaklee Manufacturing Center; Shaklee Research Center; Shaklee Mexico; Shaklee Japan; Shaklee Taiwan.

Principal Competitors

Herbalife International Inc.; Avon Products Inc.; General Nutrition Companies, Inc.; Amway Inc.

Further Reading

Brenner, Nancy, *Shaklee: The Enduring Dream,* San Francisco: Shaklee Corporation, 1995.

Chase, Marilyn, ''For Shaklee Faithful, Selling Is Believing,'' *Wall Street Journal,* March 9, 1989.

Emert, Carol, ''Shaklee Merging Two Offices: Company to Build Offices in Pleasanton,'' *The San Francisco Chronicle,* June 7, 1997, p. D1.

Hill, G. Christian, ''Japan's Yamanouchi to Acquire Shaklee for $395 Million, Thwarting Jacobs' Bid,'' *Wall Street Journal,* March 14, 1989.

''Shaklee Corporation Announces New President and CEO,'' *Business Wire,* September 15, 2000.

''Shaklee to Break Ground for World Headquarters,'' *Business Wire,* May 28, 1998.

Zonana, Victor F., ''Health Products Firm Used Toxic Substance, Ex-Distributor Claims,'' *Wall Street Journal,* January 21, 1982.

—Douglas Sun
—update: Carrie Rothburd

Simpson Thacher & Bartlett

425 Lexington Avenue
New York, New York 10017-3954
U.S.A.
Telephone: (212) 455-2000
Fax: (212) 455-2502
Web site: http://www.simpsonthacher.com

Partnership
Founded: 1884 as Simpson, Thacher & Barnum
Employees: 1,500
Sales: $434 million (1999)
NAIC: 54111 Offices of Lawyers

Simpson Thacher & Bartlett consistently ranks as one of the world's great law firms. It serves large corporate clients, smaller startup companies, foundations, government entities, and individual clients. Its legacy includes representing important corporate clients in the railroad, utility, banking, and other industries. Because it helps clients deal with taxation, antitrust, financing, mergers and acquisitions, litigation, intellectual property, and other concerns, it is a full-service law firm that can deal with virtually any legal specialty. Unlike some of its major rivals, the Simpson law firm operates only a few branch offices, and the large majority of its lawyers work out of its New York headquarters. At the same time, its extensive international practice makes it a major influence in the global economy, in part because of cooperative agreements with foreign law firms.

Origins and Early Practice

On January 1, 1884, three former clerks of the law firm of Alexander & Green formed their own law firm called Simpson, Thacher & Barnum in lower Manhattan. John Woodruff Simpson had graduated from Amherst College in 1871 and attended Columbia University Law School for two years before joining Alexander & Green. Both Thomas Thacher and William Milo Barnum had graduated from Yale and Columbia University Law School before working for Alexander & Green.

The new law firm at first represented a variety of businesses, such as mining, gas, and telegraph companies, along with indi-

viduals who needed help in lawsuits, estates, and wills. Then, starting in 1885, it spent more time helping railroads that were reorganizing during a period of consolidation of a very fragmented industry. Early clients included the New Orleans, Baton Rouge & Vicksburg, the Ohio Central, the Baltimore & Ohio, and the New York, West Shore and Buffalo railroads, plus locomotive manufacturers.

The Simpson law firm in 1895 assisted the Brooklyn Union Gas Company in its set-up and acquisition of seven other local gas companies. This process of uniting several small utilities companies into one significant provider was a common trend in many American cities around the turn of the century.

Around 1900 the partnership served several companies that eventually became the International Silver Company. The firm in 1901 helped the Union Bag and Paper Company start up, and it remained a client for many years. In 1901 the firm also participated in the American Can Company's consolidation and helped found the American Locomotive Company. In 1904 Philip Bartlett became a name partner when William Barnum retired. The firm in 1905 participated in the Northern Securities litigation in which the railroad monopoly was broken up by the federal government under the 1890 Sherman Antitrust Act.

As the firm's lawyers gained experience, they represented a greater variety of clients. A book published on the firm's centennial notes: ''By 1911 the firm represented companies manufacturing or dealing in such varied articles as terra cotta, shoes, shock absorbers, bread, plate glass, tires, and men's clothing.''

In the 1920s, as foreign trade increased, Simpson Thacher began developing an international practice to assist its clients. It also began serving investment banks that helped finance steamship lines, New York Harbor dry docks, dairies, and other diverse businesses. The partnership in 1921 helped start one of New York City's first cooperative apartments to meet the increased housing demand as a multitude of immigrants arrived through Ellis Island.

Although the firm's practice generally declined in the 1930s, it did pick up clients from bankruptcy, reorganization, and real estate work during the Depression. In 1937 partner Whitney North Seymour, at the request of the American Civil Liberties

Company Perspectives:

We believe that the talent of our associates is considerable, as we consistently attract the nation's top law students. Associates and partners alike demonstrate commitment to communities as well as clients, making substantial and ongoing pro bono contributions across a breadth of not-for-profit issues and organizations. The Firm values these efforts, much as we value good judgment, creativity and efficiency in client matters. With more than five hundred fifty lawyers practicing in seven offices around the world, we strive to demonstrate these values and excellence as firm-wide characteristics.

Union, argued successfully in the U.S. Supreme Court case Herndon *v.* Lowry "that a black communist could not constitutionally be punished for insurrection when charged with inducing others to become members of the Communist Party," according to Conrad K. Harper in the law firm's 1984 retrospective.

In 1935 the federal government passed the Public Utility Holding Company Act that had long-term legal consequences for Simpson Thacher clients. Representing Electric Bond and Share Company, the firm challenged the new law's constitutionality, which in 1938 was upheld by the U.S. Supreme Court. In the 1940s and 1950s the law firm spent much time representing Electric Bond and Share in front of the Securities and Exchange Commission and dealing with lawsuits against the holding company from its subsidiaries and other parties.

Meanwhile, the firm's client Radio-Keith-Orpheum Corporation received much publicity during its reorganization that lasted from 1936 until after the United States entered World War II. About the same time, Simpson Thacher worked on the reorganization of the Wabash Railway that was completed in 1951. During the war, the firm helped its clients gain war-related contracts for a variety of weapons and parts. In the 1940s Edwin Weisl joined Simpson Thacher and brought in as new clients Lehman Brothers and Paramount Communications, then called Gulf & Western.

Postwar Practice

After the war ended, the firm continued defending corporations accused of antitrust violations. One notable case was Ferguson *v.* Ford Motor Company. More than 30 Simpson Thacher lawyers helped Ford on this case that ran from 1948 to 1952, when it was finally settled.

In 1952 Simpson Thacher became general counsel to Manufacturers Trust Company, which led to the hiring of many experienced lawyers from the firm of Newman & Bisco. In 1953 the firm represented the newly created New York City Transit Authority when it took over facilities formerly operated by New York City.

Starting in 1952, the Simpson law firm played a key role in the early years of developing peaceful uses for atomic energy. It participated in complex contracts and financing involving the Ohio Valley Electric Corporation (OVEC), its subsidiary Indiana-Kentucky Electric Corporation, several sponsoring private utilities, 39 institutional investors, the Atomic Energy Commission, several other federal agencies, Congress, and also seven state regulatory commissions. Eventually two large plants were built that provided 18 billion kilowatt-hours annually.

In 1969 Simpson Thacher became "the first major law firm to make an African-American attorney a partner," according to *The Insider's Guide to Law Firms*. Litigator Conrad Harper, the former president of the New York City Bar Association, remained with Simpson Thacher until he accepted a State Department position in the early 1990s.

In the booming economy of the 1980s, stimulated by a reduction in federal tax rates, Simpson Thacher grew and prospered. It went from 325 lawyers in 1987 to 448 in 1990, and its gross revenue almost doubled in only three years, from $103 million in 1986 to $201 million in 1989. In addition to its long-term client Manufacturers Hanover Trust, the law firm also served Atlas Corporation, General Motors, and Burmah Oil.

Simpson Thacher & Bartlett was one of the few major law firms, all headquartered in New York, that benefited from the numerous mergers and acquisitions of the 1980s. For example, in 1988 the firm represented investment bank Wasserstein, Perella & Co. that was assisting Philip Morris in a $11.4 bid to take over Kraft.

The partnership in 1989 served as the main law firm for Kohlberg Kravis Roberts & Company when it spent $25.3 billion in a leveraged acquisition of RJR Nabisco Inc. The financing for what the *Wall Street Journal* on February 10, 1989 called "the largest corporate acquisition ever" was completed when at least 150 lawyers and others gathered in a Simpson Thacher conference room.

In 1984 the firm self-published a book to mark its one hundredth anniversary. However, the volume contained little detailed information on the firm's history. The one exception was an essay on the career of Whitney North Seymour, who practiced from 1923 to 1983 at Simpson Thacher & Bartlett, except for 1931 to 1933 when he served as the U.S. assistant solicitor general. A leader in the civil rights movement, Seymour's contributions included being president of the American Bar Association, the American Bar Foundation, and the Institute of Judicial Administration during the 1960s.

Practice in the 1990s and Beyond

Cyrus R. Vance, among the most famous Simpson attorneys, continued to practice law in the 1990s. He had joined the firm after World War II and served as President Lyndon Johnson's deputy secretary of the Defense Department. In 1967 Vance helped mediate an end to the Detroit riots. Vance also served as President Carter's secretary of state, and in the early 1990s he worked to try to bring peace to Yugoslavia. Called the "ultimate troubleshooter" by *Time* in 1992, Vance in 1994 was chosen to mediate the bankruptcy reorganization of R.H. Macy & Company.

In the 1990s Simpson Thacher & Bartlett opened new offices to better serve its clients. Partner Paul B. Ford founded the

Key Dates:

1884: Simpson, Thacher & Barnum is formed in New York City.
1904: The name is changed to Simpson, Thacher & Bartlett.
1938: Firm represents the Electric Bond and Share Company.
1969: Firm becomes the first in the United States to name an African American partner.
1989: Firm represent Kohlberg Kravis Roberts & Company in its $25.3 billion acquisition of RJR Nabisco.
1990: The firm's Tokyo office is opened.
1996: The firm opens its Los Angeles office.
1999: The Palo Alto office is opened.

firm's Tokyo office in 1990 when the Japanese economy was strong. Later in the decade several other American law firms closed their Japanese offices when the Tokyo stock market stagnated, and the yen weakened, but Simpson Thacher kept its office open, based on a belief in the long-term strength of the Japanese economy.

In 1993, 421 of Simpson Thacher & Bartlett's 436 attorneys were based in New York City. Its London office had nine attorneys, while the Tokyo office included three attorneys. The firm also had three attorneys in its Columbus, Ohio office, started because its client American Electric Power Company was headquartered in Columbus. Other notable clients at that time were General Electric, Travellers Insurance, Seagrams, Ford, Barclays Bank, Matsushita, and Lehman Brothers.

In the 1990s American law firms chose different strategies as they opened or expanded their London offices. Some firms chose to hire English lawyers, while others, like Simpson Thacher, staffed their London offices with American lawyers. "Our perspective has been that UK firms have needed some US capability, not that the US firms need an English capability," said Simpson Thacher partner Rhett Brandon in the December 1995 *International Financial Law Review*. (A third option, a trans-Atlantic merger, was demonstrated in 2000 when London's Clifford Chance merged with a New York law firm and also a German firm.)

Simpson Thacher & Bartlett in the 1990s played a major role in consolidating American banks. For example, in 1991 it represented C&S/Sovran Corporation; Manufacturers Hanover Corporation; First Hawaiian, Inc.; and Norwest Corporation in various deals. In 1992 the firm's long-term client Manufacturers Hanover merged with Chemical Bank. According to *The Insider's Guide to Law Firms,* the Simpson law firm "was temporarily shaken by the merger because Chemical Bank continues to use its counsel, Cravath, Swaine & Moore." But by 1994 Simpson Thacher was "reportedly primary counsel to Chemical and handles all aspects of the bank's securities offering work."

The Simpson law firm represented Chemical Banking Corporation when it announced in August 1995 that it was merging with Chase Manhattan Corporation. According to Simpson Thacher partner Lee Meyerson in the July 1996 *Corporate Finance,* the merger created "the largest banking organization in the US (by a wide margin) and one of the largest in the world."

In other merger and acquisition (M&A) work, the Simpson law firm in 1995 represented Glaxo plc in its purchase of Wellcome plv, a $15 billion transaction; The Seagram Company in its $8.8 billion sale of E.I. duPont de Nemours stock; and Matsushita Electric Industrial Company when it sold 80 percent of MCA Inc. to Seagram for $5.7 billion. Other 1995 clients in transactions worth at least $1 billion included ITT, Kemper, Yucaipa, Frontier, Ingersoll-Rand, National Gypsum, and MCI Communications.

Other examples of Simpson Thacher & Bartlett's M&A work included advising KN Energy Inc. in its 1997 acquisition of gas pipeline company MidCom Corporation from Occidental Petroleum for $3.49 billion. In 2000 the Simpson firm represented the telecommunications company Global Crossing when it acquired IPC Communications and its subsidiary 1Xnet.

Business Week, in the February 28, 2000 issue, ranked Simpson Thacher as the top mergers and acquisitions law firm based on its $893.3 billion worth of deals in 1999. Eight of the top ten firms were based in New York City. As of September 30, 2000, Simpson Thacher & Bartlett was ranked second in its M&A work, with its $553.4 billion in deals exceeded by only Sullivan & Cromwell with $753.8 billion.

Meanwhile, the firm opened its Los Angeles office in 1996 to serve the entertainment industry and other clients. In 1999 the partnership opened its Silicon Valley office in Palo Alto, California to serve the growing number of Internet and high-technology businesses. That office's clients included Agilent Technologies, Andersen Consulting, CNET, Drugstore.com, iSyndicate.com, NBC Internet, Intel, and investment banks working with high-tech companies. By 2000 the Palo Alto branch had expanded to about 30 lawyers.

Following successful litigation against the tobacco industry, gun manufacturers in the late 1990s began to be sued for the many deaths and injuries resulting from handgun use. The manufacturers turned to some of the nation's largest law firms for assistance. For example, Colt's Manufacturing Company in 1999 asked Simpson Thacher for legal counsel.

The American Lawyer in its annual rankings of the nation's highest grossing law firms in 1999 listed Simpson Thacher & Bartlett as number 12 based on the firm's $434 million in 1999 revenue. The firm also was listed as one of the "Winners of the Nineties" based on its 87 percent growth of profits per partner since 1990. That impressive track record indicated Simpson Thacher & Bartlett was well prepared for the challenges of the new millennium.

Principal Competitors

Cleary, Gottlieb, Steen & Hamilton; Davis Polk & Wardwell; Wachtell, Lipton, Rosen & Katz.

Further Reading

"American Law Firm Upbeat Over Japanese Economic Outlook," *Mainichi Daily News* (Tokyo), April 1, 1997, p. 1.

Baldo, Anthony, "Richards Layton Top M&A Law Firm in US in 1991," *Investment Dealers' Digest,* May 25, 1992, p. 15

Barrett, Paul M., and Milo Geyelin, "Big National Law Firms Leap to Help Gun Industry as It Fights Suits by Cities," *Wall Street Journal,* July 14, 1999, p. B7.

Cherovsky, Erwin, "Simpson Thacher & Bartlett," in *The Guide to New York Law Firms,* New York: St. Martin's Press, 1991, pp. 183–186.

Cohen, Laurie P., "Takeover Boom Is Expected to Benefit Usual Small Circle of Wealthy Law Firms," *Wall Street Journal,* October 25, 1988, p. 1.

Lipin, Steven, "Legal Eagle Makes Firm One of Top M&A Advisers," *Wall Street Journal,* June 1, 1995, p. C1.

Lipin, Steven, and Peter Fritsch, "KN Energy to Buy Occidental's MidCon–Deal, Valued at $3.49 Billion, Will Create Behemoth in Pipeline Industry," *Wall Street Journal,* December 19, 1997, p. A,3:1.

McNatt, Robert, "Top 10 M&A Law Firms," *Business Week,* February 28, 2000, p. 6.

Malkani, Sheila V., and Michael F. Walsh, ed., "Simpson Thacher & Bartlett," in *The Insider's Guide to Law Firms,* 2d ed., Boulder, Colo. Mobius Press, 1994, pp. 419–22.

Meyerson, Lee, "Home Teams Have the Edge in US Bank Mergers," *Corporate Finance* (London), July 1996, p. 49.

Reilly, Patrick M., and Laura Jereski, "Vance Is Named as a Mediator in Macy Case," *Wall Street Journal,* February 23, 1994, p. A3.

Roberts, Gwenan, "No Holds Barred in the City," *International Financial Law Review,* December 1995, p. 20.

"Simpson Thacher Advises on Financial Network Deal," *International Tax Review,* April 2000, p. 9.

Simpson Thacher & Bartlett: The First One Hundred Years, 1884–1984, New York: Simpson Thacher, 1984.

Talbot, Strobe, "The Ultimate Troubleshooter," *Time,* March 9, 1992, p. 37.

Waldman, Peter and George Anders, "KKR Completes Buy-Out of RJR Without Fanfare—Sound of No Corks Popping Greets History's Largest Corporate Acquisition," *Wall Street Journal,* February 10, 1999, p. 1.

—David M. Walden

rent a car

Sixt AG

Dr.-Carl-von-Linde-Strasse 2
D-82049 Pullach
Germany
Telephone: (49) (89) 74444-222
Fax: (49) (89) 74444-282
Web site: http://www.sixt.com

Public Company
Incorporated: 1912 as Sixt Autofahrten und Selbstfahrer
Employees: 1,864
Sales: DM 4.82 billion ($2.49 billion) (1999)
Stock Exchanges: Frankfurt/Main
Ticker Symbol: SIX3
NAIC: 44112 Used Car Dealers; 532111 Passenger Car
   Rental

Sixt AG is Germany's number one car rental company and it continues to expand into all of Europe. The company maintains about 440 offices in its home country and about 700 in other countries, primarily in Europe, but also in Australia, New Zealand, Tunisia, and Morocco. Focusing on the business traveler, Sixt works with a number of airlines including Deutsche Lufthansa, and hotel chains such as the Hilton Group. Sixt is also one of Germany's largest used car dealers. About one-third of the company's sales come from car rentals, while the remainder is generated from used car sales. Sixt is also active in car and equipment leasing as well as in e-commerce. Descendent of company founder Martin Sixt, Erich Sixt, manages the business and owns 67 percent of Sixt AG.

Origins in 1912

When the automobile became fashionable among well-to-do passengers and drivers, German auto-lover Martin Sixt came up with the idea for a business. In 1912 he founded ''Sixt Autofahren und Selbstfahrer.'' It was one of Germany's first rental car companies, based in Munich. Targeting British noblemen and rich Americans, Sixt rented his four Mercedes and three Luxus-Deutz-Landaulets for a day at a time and offered customized tours

with a company driver. However, only two years later, at the onset of the World War I, the German Army confiscated his vehicles. After the war was over, Sixt acquired a piece of property in the city of Munich at Seitzstrasse 11, from which he gradually expanded his business. He ran his business according to three basic principles: 1. Have the right cars; 2. Offer perfect service to the customer; 3. Minimize administrative costs.

In 1927 Martin Sixt's 20-year-old nephew Hans Sixt took over the business. He added two new principles to the Sixt business philosophy: creativity and innovation. Two years after he took over, the new owner decided to stop using foreign cars, given the difficulty of finding replacement parts. Instead, Sixt chose to use the domestic Mercedes brand and soon built a 20-car fleet. The worldwide economic boycott against Nazi-Germany which was preparing for a war in 1938 resulted in a significant downturn for the rental car business. A year later the Sixt fleet was once again confiscated by the German army to be used on the battlefields of World War II.

As the war was coming to an end, company founder Martin Sixt was overcome by the destruction of his life's work by Allied bombings. He died in May 1945. The following year Hans Sixt started from scratch with a Mercedes 230 Landaulet which survived the war hidden in a barn in upper Bavaria. Sixt was fortunate enough to get a taxi license and chauffeured the members of the American occupation forces through Munich in his seven-seat limousine. Hans Sixt called his new service the Export Taxi and soon offered it to business people and VIPs. The next Sixt innovation was a fleet of Radio Taxis, equipped with radio gear from the United States, introduced in 1948. Three years later the company, called ''Auto Sixt,'' was founded as a rental agency for motorists who wished to drive themselves around. Hans Sixt was also active in car dealerships and gas station businesses. As Germany entered the economic boom of the 1960s, the business started to thrive once again. In 1966 Sixt opened offices at Munich and Frankfurt airports. The Hans Sixt era ended with the company's expansion into car leasing in 1967. Two years later he brought his son Erich into the business and withdrew from management for health reasons. However, before he died in August 1998 at age 89, Hans Sixt saw his company grow into a DM2 billion business.

Erich Sixt Changes the Rules in the 1970s and 1980s

Erich Sixt entered the family business at age 25—after dropping out of college—and fundamentally changed the German car rental industry for good. In the 1960s the industry was characterized by high prices and limited service. Renting a car was something for wealthy people. Erich Sixt had a different vision: renting a car should be affordable for anyone. To free the rental car business from its image of exclusivity, Sixt offered his customers ''a Mercedes for the Volkswagen rate'' of DM66 per day, a very low price at that time. From the very beginning Sixt used provocative advertising campaigns to attract attention and gave his primarily British and American competitors headaches with his flexible prices—which were always a little lower than theirs. ''Rather to Sixt than too expensive'' was another popular slogan which Sixt was soon forbidden to use by the rigid German antitrust authorities.

In 1969 the German car rental market was dominated by seven notable national and international players while some 2,000 local businesses competed for the crumbs. When Erich Sixt took over the company management in that year, the Sixt fleet consisted of 100 cars. One year later the company started renting trucks. Another important Sixt strategy was to obtain significant rebates from car makers for the brand-new cars purchased and then rent the cars for only a few months, up to a year. Not only was the company able to offer its customers the latest models, after a few months of being rented, the cars were still new enough to be sold off for good prices without needing many repairs.

Sixt founded its own used car dealership, Autoland Central Garagen GmbH, which became another important profit center. In the early 1970s Erich Sixt was looking for software to help manage the dynamic growth of the company. However, he was not able to afford the prices charged for customized programming at that time. So he picked up a book about computer programming and wrote the code himself, which at the time was still entered by punching holes into paper cards.

The year 1977 marked another important step for Sixt. In that year the company opened offices at all major German airports. More important, the company entered a licensing agreement with American car rental giant Budget Rent a Car. As a result, Sixt car rental locations were included in Budget's worldwide network listings. To reflect the importance of the alliance, the Budget logo became part of the Sixt logo in 1982 when the company was renamed Sixt Autovermietung GmbH. In 1979 Sixt acquired another license for Germany from Carey-Limousine-Service and was listed in the world's leading chauffeured limousine service network. One year later Sixt entered the leasing business and founded Auto Leasing GmbH (ASL) together with the Dusseldorf-based Disko Group. Later, in 1988, Sixt founded its own leasing arm Sixt Leasing GmbH. By 1982 Sixt was number eight among Germany's rental car companies. In 1986 the company was renamed Sixt AG and went public in Germany which raised some additional capital for further expansion. However, Erich Sixt remained majority shareholder of his company.

New Era of Expansion Begins in 1990

At the beginning of the 1990s Sixt AG had all it took to tackle market leader interRent Europcar Autovermietung GmbH. With over DM 1 billion in sales and 238 rental offices Sixt had worked its way up to Germany's number two rental car company. The opening of the Berlin Wall offered new business opportunities. In 1990 15 Sixt rental stations opened in the former East Germany. The company also profited from the huge demand for used cars in the new eastern German states. In that year Sixt AG's revenues from used car sales were higher than from car rentals. Overall, that year the company's revenues grew by 40 percent for used car sales and by 47 percent for car rentals. In addition to the higher demand that followed German reunification, Sixt worked for a higher market share by using unusual offers to distinguish itself from competitors. Sixt customers were able to rent a Harley Davidson, a Porsche Cabrio, as well as a heavy duty flat-bed truck. Another new vehicle made available by Sixt was the so-called ''conference-mobile,'' a mobile office that included a computer, fax machine, and telephone. Sixt also broadened its leasing services. Besides cars, Sixt Leasing also offered financing for heavy machinery and even equipment for dental practices. The company's so-called ''Vario-Leasing'' allowed customers leasing a car to sign one contract and change the car several times during the term of the lease.

An important part of the company's marketing strategy during this time was provocative ad campaigns that won many advertising industry awards for their creativity. For example, when American competitor Avis was using the slogan ''We try harder,'' Sixt headlined ''Don't try harder, try Sixt.'' Another ad featured the English Queen in her coach of state with the headline ''If she had booked at Sixt she could have had a Mercedes.'' The German news magazine *Der Spiegel* was only willing to run the ad if Sixt agreed to buy the entire English print run if outlets refused to carry it. Sixt refused and placed the ad in other publications.

Not all of Erich Sixt's ambitious plans were successful. His idea of adding hotels for business travelers to his service portfolio never got off the ground. Sixt bid unsuccessfully for the former East German Interhotel chain. Moreover, economic recession in Germany took hold in 1992, and the car rental market decreased significantly for the next three years. Sixt was especially hit hard in the company's core business, putting it under financial pressure. Interest rates went up while prices for used cars went down. The average waiting time to sell used cars doubled. At times the used cars Sixt had for sale clogged the neighboring streets around the company's used car dealerships. At the same time that money was tight, interest debt went up by 30 percent amounting to DM 52 million. Sixt stock lost ground, and the company's capital base began to diminish.

Key Dates:

1912: Martin Sixt founds rental car company Sixt Auto-fahrten und Selbstfahrer.
1927: The founder's nephew Hans Sixt takes over the company.
1946: The business starts from scratch after World War II.
1969: Erich Sixt enters the family business.
1977: License agreement with American rental car company Budget Rent a Car is reached.
1986: Sixt goes public and becomes Sixt AG.
1988: The company enters the leasing business.
1996: The first Sixt office opens at Vienna airport.
1997: Sixt Travel division is founded.
1999: The company enters a cooperative agreement with Dollar Rent a Car.
2000: Sixt opens electronic commerce platform for cars and travel.

Confronting this situation, Erich Sixt restructured his empire. Sixt AG became a management holding company while the car rental business was organized under the umbrella of Sixt GmbH & Co Autovermietung KG. Sixt sold off his 50.2 percent share in ASL to minority shareholder KG Allgemeine Leasing, taking away two-thirds of the total leasing sales of DM 300 million, to gain needed cash and more control over the business.

Partnerships and Innovation Spur Growth in 1994

In the 1990s competition among car rental companies grew stiffer. Within only two years the number of firms competing in the German market went down from 1,400 to 1,100. To regain strength, Sixt AG looked for new business partners in the travel industry. In 1994 the company entered an agreement with the leading German air carrier Deutsche Lufthansa, becoming a partner in that company's Miles & More program. Customers who rented a Sixt car earned frequent flyer miles, and Lufthansa customers were able to rent a car when checking in at the airline counter. Lufthansa's CEO became president of the Sixt board of directors. By the end of 1994 Sixt AG had become Germany's number one car rental company in sales; the company credited much of its success to the alliance with Lufthansa. Sixt also succeeded in targeting business commuters, who accounted for 60 percent of the company's total sales compared with 35 percent on average in the industry. After the company opened several booking offices at high speed ICE rail stations, Sixt began working together with German railway company Deutsche Bahn AG.

Another cooperation agreement was signed in 1997 with Germany's top automobile club ADAC. The club, which offered various on-the-road services for motorists, had entered the car rental market in 1991 with its subsidiary ADAC Autovermietung München GmbH and had started cooperating with Sixt competitor Europcar. ADAC members could reserve rental cars via an ADAC phone number but rented the car from one of 450 Europcar rental stations. To expand its network ADAC entered a second agreement with Sixt and gained access to the company's 326 stations at the time. In this way private travelers not otherwise targeted heavily, were referred to Sixt. However, like Europcar, Sixt had to offer its services at fixed prices. Another area of cooperation with ADAC was in providing replacement cars following accidents to ADAC members; replacement cars could be ordered via a 24-hour-emergency line.

Besides its strategic partnerships Sixt also kept the stream of its own innovations flowing. In 1996 the company introduced its Sixt SelfService Centers in big city airports where customers were able to rent a car without having to deal with a clerk behind a counter. At the Sixt "Car-Express-Automat" a customer could rent his car before departure at an automate, using a credit card or Sixt member card, and—after arrival—pick up the key for his rental car at a Sixt key safe. Not only did waiting in line become obsolete, but the company also saved on personnel. Another experiment was started in the same year together with Deutsche Bahn. Environmentally-conscious individual travelers could rent an InnerCity E-Mobil, a Renault "Clio" equipped with an electric motor, at Munich and Frankfurt/Main ICE train stations. The electric car could be reserved when purchasing an ICE ticket at a train station and was picked up at the Sixt office after arrival in Munich or Frankfurt. The electric cars, with a maximum speed of 95 kilometers an hour, ran for about 90 kilometers with a full battery which could be reloaded at any power outlet. As an additional incentive, the E-mobile could be parked for free in several Munich inner city park houses.

Last but not least Sixt continued to create award-winning advertising campaigns with its Hamburg-based agency Jung von Matt. Distinct and eye-catching ads were placed in Germany's renowned weekly news magazine *Der Spiegel*. One popular ad featured a picture of Social Democrat candidate for chancellor, Gerhard Schröder, and the headline "Sixt has cars for people who don't yet know where they want to go." Among others, the Sixt campaign won the award from Art Directors Club of Europe.

Massive International Expansion in the Late 1990s

In the second half of the 1990s Sixt AG started expanding aggressively into other countries around the globe. In 1996 the first Sixt rental station opened at Vienna airport. The following year, the company expanded into France and Great Britain. In France Sixt set up a joint venture with Paris-based Eurorent S.A. with over 100 rental stations in France. In Great Britain Sixt acquired European Car Rental, a small player in the British market with eight offices and a 1,000-car fleet. In 1998 Sixt offices opened at major airports in Ireland and Italy, Spain and Portugal, Malta and the Netherlands, the Czech Republic and Hungary, Morocco, and New Zealand. Central booking offices were also established in the United States, Canada, and Australia.

At the same time Sixt set up new airline partnerships such as with the British Airways "Executive Club," United Airlines' "Mileage Plus" program, the "Frequence Plus" program of Air France, KLM's "Flying Dutchman" mileage program. A notable partner from the hotel industry was finally found in the American Hilton group.

However, there was at least one party who was not so happy with Sixt's massive international expansion: its license partner

Budget Rent A Car. In spring 1997 Budget canceled its license agreement with Sixt AG. Budget accused Sixt of having breached their contract by not referring rental car bookings from abroad to Budget and questioned the validity of the sales numbers Sixt reported to the American partner. Sixt in turn said it understood that the agreement was only valid for customers who were booking a car for abroad from Germany, and referred customers in other European countries to their own rental stations. Sixt also pointed out that the company referred 87,000 customers to Budget in 1996 while only 59,000 referrals came the other way around. Sixt paid DM 6.6 million in license fees to Budget in that year. However, in April 1999 the Oberlandesgericht Munich found Sixt AG guilty and ordered the company to bear the cost of the lawsuit and to pay damages to Budget. In February 2001 Sixt lost the appeal when the German Bundesgerichtshof rejected the revision Sixt had asked for. However, in the meantime, in 1999, the company signed a cooperation agreement with another major American company, Dollar Rent a Car, which went into effect in March 2000. At that time, the company also acquired British rental car company United Kenning Rental Group.

Erich Sixt's latest venture was as Germany's virtual auto dealer, establishing the e-commerce platform e-Sixt. Already some ten percent of all Sixt rental car business was done over the Internet; by 2003 the company expected to realize DM 300 million selling cars, auto parts, flight tickets, and insurance policies over the Internet. Sixt planned to use its four-million customer database to market the new service. In spring 2000 Erich Sixt told *Süddeutsche Zeitung* writer Karl-Heinz Büschmann that information technology was one of his responsibilities and that he spent many hours daily on the Internet. At age 55, he did not plan to withdraw from his business. "I don't sell," Sixt said. "The business is my life. It's my hobby. I wouldn't know what else to do."

Principal Subsidiaries

Sixt Autoland Central Garagen GmbH; Sixt GmbH & Co Autovermietung KG; Sixt Leasing AG; Sixt Travel GmbH; e-Sixt AG; Sixt Eurorent SAS (France); Sixt plc (U.K.); Sixt AG (Switzerland); Sixt G.m.b.H. (Austria); Sixt B.V. (Netherlands).

Principal Competitors

Accor; Avis Europe plc; The Hertz Corporation.

Further Reading

"AUTOVERMIETER; Drunter und drüber," *Focus,* January 18, 1993, p. 168.

"Bahn AG und Sixt starten Pilotprojekt in Muenchen," *Süddeutsche Zeitung,* April 17, 1996.

Büschemann, Karl-Heinz, "Wir stehen vor einer richtigen Revolution," *Süddeutsche Zeitung,* March 6, 2000, p.23.

Diekhof, Rolf, "Frontalangriff auf leisen Sohlen," *Werben und Verkaufen,* June 16, 1995, p. 64.

"Hans Sixt," *Frankfurter Allgemeine Zeitung,* January 28, 1997, p. 18.

Pellikan, Leif, and Reinhard Röde, "World Wide Sixt," *Werben und Verkaufen,* June 9, 2000, p. 120.

Riefler, Dagmar, "Immer auf der Überholspur," *Werben und Verkaufen,* September 20, 1996, p. 100.

Sixt, Erich, "Die bessere Idee," *Werben und Verkaufen,* October 27, 1995, p.185.

"Sixt greift nach dem Spitzenplatz," *Süddeutsche Zeitung,* June 15, 1991.

"Sixt unterliegt im Streit mit Budget," *Frankfurter Allgemeine Zeitung,* April 16, 1999, p. 18.

"Sixt verliert endgueltig Prozess gegen Budget," *Frankfurter Allgemeine Zeitung,* February 15, 2001, p. 22.

"Sixt will das Eigenkapital weiter aufstocken," *Frankfurter Allgemeine Zeitung,* January 20, 1993, p. 19.

"Sixt: Wir muessen sogar Kunden ablehnen," *Frankfurter Allgemeine Zeitung,* June 28, 1995, p. 17.

"Sixt zweiter Mietwagen-Partner des ADAC," *Süddeutsche Zeitung,* June 17, 1997.

Taylor, Roger, "European Car Rental Deal Drives Sixt's UK Ambitions," *Financial Times,* October 10, 1997, p. 24.

Trapp, Carolina, "Handfeste Werbung fuehrt Sixt zum Erfolg," *HORIZONT,* February 21, 1992, p. H13.

Winkelhage, Johannes, "Der Konkurrenz schlaflose Nächte bereiten," *Frankfurter Allgemeine Zeitung,* August 29, 1998, p.49.

"Wogen zwischen Sixt und Budget glaetten sich," *Süddeutsche Zeitung,* May 6, 1997.

—Evelyn Hauser

Skoda Auto a.s.

Vaclava Klementa 869
293 60 Mlada Boleslav
Czech Republic
Telephone: +420 326 811 111
Fax: +420 326 811 921
Web site: http://www.skoda-auto.com

Wholly Owned Subsidiary of Volkswagen AG
Incorporated: 1895
Employees: 20,300
Sales: CZK 110.41 billion ($2.87 billion)(1999)
NAIC: 336111 Automobile Manufacturing

Skoda Auto a.s., also known as Skoda Automobilova a.s., has been making cars for more than a century. Skoda is the Czech Republic's largest company in terms of revenues, producing about ten percent of the country's exports. Small volumes of Skoda's Felicia model are being assembled in Poland and Bosnia, and other manufacturing ventures are being pursued in India, China, and other countries. In spite of its pioneering heritage, the company reputation for quality suffered tremendously during the years it operated under Soviet control. Volkswagen AG began investing in Skoda in 1991, hoping to capitalize on the Czech Republic's long industrial tradition and labor costs one-tenth of those in Germany. Skoda led Volkswagen's late 1990s success story (alongside the VW, Audi, and Seat brands).

19th Century Origins

The Skoda story begins the week of Christmas 1895. While carolers everywhere were celebrating Czechoslovakia's patron saint, King Wenceslas, a mechanic named Václav Laurin and a bookseller named Václav Klement began to make their first bicycles, adopting the brand name "Slavia."

The Laurin & Klement company had progressed to motorcycle manufacture by 1899. Their first automobile, the Voiturette, appeared in 1905, with a V-2 engine producing seven horsepower. The company soon became, according to company liter-ature, an international success. By 1910, a new model, the ENS, was boasting 50 horsepower.

Laurin and Klement formed a joint stock company in 1907. The company merged with Skoda, a Pilsen industrial firm, in 1925, bringing an end to the Laurin & Klement brand. Production shifted to the Czech town of Mladá Boleslav. As early as 1930, the merged entity was known as the Skoda-Car Industry Joint-Stock Company. Its Skoda 420 model was marketed internationally after the Great Depression.

During World War II, the Hermann-Göring-Werke group took over Skoda, and its production was directed towards the German military effort. During this time, its factory at Mladá Boleslav produced weapons and heavy vehicles. One of the vehicles was the Skoda RSO-Radschlepper OST, which featured a tractor constructed by Ferdinand Porsche.

The Soviet Era

After the war, the car unit split from the Pilsen industrial concern whose name it shared while taking on the cumbersome Soviet title of Skoda AZNP (National Enterprise of Car Factories). It then became sole manufacturer of passenger cars in Czechoslovakia. Its Skoda 1101/1102 Tudor series was stylistically and technologically similar to the prewar Skoda 420.

Designs such as the Skoda 1200, Spartak, Octavia, and Felicia graced the streets of Prague during the Cold War. (As its name hints, the Octavia was the company's eighth model.) However, during this time Skoda's technology began to lag behind that of the West, in spite of the introduction of a revamped model, the Skoda 781 Favorit, which replaced the Estelle, the butt of many auto jokes. Over a million Favorits would be produced in a new factory completed in 1987. In 1989, the last of the Estelles were brisk sellers in Britain due to their low sticker prices beginning at $5,390.

As the Soviet Bloc crumbled, Skoda began to operate in a free market environment after 1989. Like most Soviet automobiles, Skoda's had problems with reliability, fit, and finish. In fact, the company removed its nameplate from its cars until

Company Perspectives:

We offer top-quality products and services—because we are always thinking of our customers. Our explicit goal is to not only meet customer expectations but to exceed them. This philosophy can also be seen and felt close up in the Skoda Auto Brand Experience. Whether in the new Skoda Auto Customer Centre, the Skoda Auto Museum in Mladá Boleslav, the future Skoda Pavilion in Wolfsburg's ''Autostadt'' or the permanent exhibit on the Lindenkorso in Berlin, visitors will experience a unique symbiosis of the power of innovation and living tradition. And visitors to these centres will also find forums, which promote a dialog between Skoda Auto and its guests.

1993, when it introduced Volkswagen-inspired improvements in the Favorit.

The Czech government felt the debt-laden company needed a foreign industrial partner to survive, and by the end of 1990 it had chosen Volkswagen to be that partner.

Privatization in the 1990s

On April 16, 1991, Skoda Automobilova a.s. began operating as Volkswagen's fourth branch, after VW, Audi, and Seat. Volkswagen bought an initial 31 percent stake in the company for DM 620 million, which would increase to a 70 percent shareholding by 1995, at a total cost to Volkswagen of DM 1.4 billion. (Volkswagen also bought the BAZ car factory in neighboring Slovakia, which it used for small batches of niche-produced Volkswagen models such as four-wheel drive Golf hatchbacks.) Skoda reported annual revenues in 1991 of CZK 15 billion (about $390 million).

Volkswagen simultaneously acquired co-ownership rights of the distinctive Skoda winged arrow logo, which had been the property of the Skoda Plzen engineering company since the end of World War II. The Czech government paid Skoda Plzen more than CZK 250 million ($8 million) for the right to have Volkswagen use the trademark on cars. (The logo was updated with new colors in 1993. The name ''Skoda Auto'' was printed in white around a black circle, said to symbolize the company's long heritage. The green of the winged arrow within symbolized contemporary concern for environmental issues.)

Volkswagen immediately took measures to streamline Skoda's production process. The central planning mentality of Skoda's workers had to be retooled to bring them in line with Western standards of efficiency and quality. Skoda's productivity improved in the year following the Volkswagen acquisition, although profits took a bit longer to achieve. By the end of 1992, the company was making 860 cars a day, versus 560 at the beginning of the year, according to the *Financial Times*. Skoda managed to turn a profit ($42.8 million) in 1992. Revenues, meanwhile, had risen dramatically to $1.1 billion.

Volkswagen invested about DM 360 million ($240 million) in Skoda's Czech plants in its first two years of cooperation. A planned total investment of DM 8 billion ($5 billion) for the

decade was aimed to double capacity to 460,000 cars a year by the mid-1990s. Skoda employed 17,000 workers at this time; due to the expansion, this would increase to 20,000 during the decade. They were paid an average monthly salary of $260 each in 1993. Not surprisingly, automotive suppliers flocked to the Czech Republic, chasing Volkswagen's business.

At the time, more than half of all Skodas sold in the European Community were going to Germany, particularly the eastern provinces, where they undersold similar Volkswagen models by 20 percent. Another important market was the United Kingdom, which imported about 10,000 of the vehicles a year. Skoda Automobile UK was established to import cars for this region in 1993.

Overcoming the poor reputation of Skoda and other Eastern Bloc products would be a monumental challenge. One Skoda official estimated there were 100,000 Skodas on British roads in the early 1990s, each one a testament to inferiority. (Intriguingly, a marketing study quoted by the *Financial Times* found their owners loved the cars despite the jokes. Getting non-owners to try the cars was the challenge.) Volkswagen's association with the company gave its new claims of quality credibility. Skoda spent about £11 million on advertising in 1993 and 1994 to persuade potential U.K. customers to give the brand a chance.

Volkswagen scaled back its original investment plans in mid-1993 after sustaining huge losses at its Seat division in Spain. A modified agreement signed six months later committed Volkswagen to investing DM 3.75 billion in Skoda through 1998, with the aim of boosting production to 300,000 cars a year by 2000. Skoda lost CZK 4.26 billion in 1993 on revenues of CZK 35 billion.

Ten thousand workers staged brief work stoppages to protest plans to lay off 800 employees in late 1994. The *Financial Times* reported growing hostility towards foreign investments in the Czech Republic, such as that of Air France in Czechoslovak Airlines.

In November 1994, Skoda replaced the Favorit with its new Felicia model. A million of them would be produced by April 1996. Some Felicias were assembled at Volkswagen's Polish plant, and, beginning in late 1996, under license in Belarus and Smolensk. Ventures in India, Egypt, and China were also being considered.

A New Level of Competition in 1996

Skoda revived the Octavia name for a new mid-size model that debuted in the fall of 1996. Priced from DM 22,950 ($15,200) in Germany, the Octavia was Volkswagen's answer to low-priced Asian marques. Interestingly, the vehicle was Skoda's first to offer an automatic transmission.

The launch of the Octavia, according to *Automotive Components Analysis,* marked the first time that Skoda ever had two models in production at the same time. Volkswagen had built a new, thoroughly modern DM 500 million factory next to the existing one in Mlada Boleslav to accommodate the Octavia's assembly line. Its efficiency was said to rival Japan's most productive facilities. Czech President Vaclav Havel remarked on its abundance of natural lighting, including glass walls at

Key Dates:

1895: Laurin & Klement begin making bikes.
1905: The partners' Voiturette automobile debuts.
1925: L&K merge with the Skoda industrial firm.
1943: Germans take over the plant.
1945: Skoda Auto begins producing cars for the proletariat.
1991: Volkswagen AG acquires management control.
1996: A new mid-size model wins praise.
2000: Volkswagen buys Skoda's remaining shares.

opposite ends, saying, "it would be wonderful if all production halls looked like this. It is a beautiful plant, truly modern, truly appealing." Reflecting the lower cost of labor in central Europe, the new facility was not highly automated. Skoda also had another, smaller plant in Vrchlabi.

Volkswagen stressed commonality of platforms between its four divisions in order to achieve maximum economies of scale. However, as many of the components were made in high-cost Germany, they seemed to have the potential of diluting the wage savings available via Seat and Skoda. The *Financial Times* reported that the Octavia shared a significant fraction of its parts with versions of the Audi A3 and the VW Golf then in development. Many of these parts arrived at the Skoda factory already assembled in subunits, such as the front-end module, which included the bumper, lights, and radiator.

Worldwide sales grew about 25 percent in 1996. Increases were most remarkable in central Europe. In neighboring Slovakia, sales rose 90 percent to 23,035 units; they leapt 102 percent to 15,840 in Poland. The Czech Republic itself remained a vibrant market, with 87,400 cars sold in 1996, up 21 percent.

Annual sales approached CZK 106 billion in 1998. A thoroughly redesigned Felicia was launched in February, and new versions of the Octavia soon followed. A four-wheel drive model appeared in March 1999. In April of that year, Skoda opened its new Design Center, which accommodated 160 employees. In May its new coal-fired SKO-ENERGO s.r.o. power station at Mladá Boleslav began operations.

Skoda spent £12 million to promote the Octavia in the United Kingdom. Although it maintained some of the best owner loyalty rates in the business and had been under Volkswagen ownership for nearly a decade, Skoda still had a challenge getting prospects to give their cars a chance.

Skoda broke ground for a factory in India in January 2000. The company rolled out its new Fabia hatchback three months later. Its new post-VW quality standards led some observers to regard the Skoda Octavia as a potential competitor for premium marques such as Ford Motor Company's Volvo unit. Volks-

wagen finally worked out an agreement to buy the remaining 30 percent of Skoda in May 2000, paying DM 650 million.

Principal Subsidiaries

Skoda Auto Deutschland (Germany); Skoda Auto Polska S.A. (Poland); Skoda Auto Slovensko s.r.o.

Principal Competitors

Adam Opel AG; Fiat S.p.A.; Ford Motor Company; Honda Motor Co., Ltd.; Mitsubishi Motors Corporation; PSA Peugeot Citroën S.A.; Renault S.A.; Toyota Motor Corporation.

Further Reading

Anderson, Robert, "Skoda Drives VW's Success Story," *Financial Times,* Survey—*Financial Times* Auto, March 1, 1999, p. 4.

Boland, Vincent, "Job Cuts Spark Strike at Skoda," *Financial Times,* October 18, 1994, p. 2.

Bollag, Burton, "VW Reaches Accord for Skoda Stake," *New York Times,* Section 1, April 20, 1991, p. 33.

Brown, Kevin, "A Cure Is Found for the Mundaneness of Making Things," *Financial Times,* Survey—Guide to the New Millennium, December 6, 1999, p. 16.

Done, Kevin, "Drive for Fresh Credibility," *Financial Times,* Survey—Czech Industry & Finance, May 14, 1997, p. 5.

Frost, Tony, "Competing with Giants: Survival Strategies for Local Companies in Emerging Markets," *Harvard Business Review,* March/April 1999, p. 119.

Genillard, Ariane, "Skoda Smoothes Out the Bumps," *Financial Times,* September 23, 1992, p. 26.

Griffiths, John, "Companies in Clash Over Skoda Shake-Up," *Financial Times,* January 5, 1993, p. 8.

Lloyd, John, "Cultural Resolution," *Financial Times,* Comment & Analysis, January 5, 1999, p. 18.

Madden, Normandy, "Czech Carmaker to Restage Stunt," *Advertising Age,* September 11, 1995, p. 6.

McClure, Richard, "Baby, You Can Drive My Skoda!" *Independent* (London), May 19, 1995, p. 22.

"No More Cuts in Skoda Investment, Piech Promises," *Finance East Europe,* May 6, 1994.

Siler, Charles, "Skoda Rides VW's Prestige; Automaker Turns UK Lemons into Lemonade," *Advertising Age,* October 17, 1994, p. I21.

Simonian, Haig, "Octavia Becomes VW's Spearhead in Budget Car Battle," *Financial Times,* Companies and Finance, October 1, 1996, p. 23.

"Skoda: The Production Line Story," *Automotive Components Analysis,* November 1996, pp. 13+.

Stevenson, Richard W., "In a Czech Plant, VW Shows How to Succeed in the East," *New York Times,* June 22, 1993, p. A1.

Summers, Diane, "Skoda's Sales Drive Is No Joke," *Financial Times,* May 12, 1994, p. 11.

Trickett, Eleanor, "Marketer Takes the Joke Out of Skoda," *Campaign,* Campaign Direct: Profile of Chris Hawken, July 16, 1999.

"VW are Winners as Skoda Deal is Rewritten," *Finance East Europe,* January 6, 1995.

—Frederick C. Ingram

Smithway Motor Xpress Corporation

2031 Quail Avenue
Fort Dodge, Iowa 50501
U.S.A.
Telephone: (515) 576-7418
Toll Free: (800) 247-4972
Fax: (515) 576-8794
Web site: http://www.smxc.com

Public Company
Incorporated: 1972 as Smithway Motor Xpress, Inc.
Employees: 1,800
Sales: $199 million (2000)
Stock Exchanges: NASDAQ
Ticker Symbol: SMXC
NAIC: 484121 General Freight Trucking, Long-Distance,
    Truckload

Smithway Motor Xpress Corporation is a truckload motor carrier that operates throughout the United States and Canada. It ranks as one of the Midwest's three largest carriers and one of the country's top 100 carriers. In addition to its Fort Dodge, Iowa headquarters, Smithway operates 24 terminals and three sales offices in Iowa, Minnesota, Ohio, Colorado, California, Alabama, Illinois, Kansas, Michigan, Missouri, Nebraska, Oklahoma, South Dakota, Wisconsin, and Texas. Although it has mostly flatbed trailers, it offers a full-service diversified fleet with a growing number of van and single-drop trailers. It manages a mixed tractor fleet that is about half company owned and half owned by independent operators. It transports steel, construction materials, dry van items, heavy machinery, and a variety of other products. Smithway grew rapidly in the 1990s, becoming a public corporation in 1996 and acquiring eight companies between 1995 and 1998. Based on several awards from the Truckload Carriers Association and other groups, Smithway is considered one of the nation's safest and best managed trucking firms. It is still a family-owned firm, with most of its stock owned by the Smith family, who founded the company in 1958.

Origins and Early Years

Smithway began in 1958 when Harold C. Smith and his son William G. Smith purchased Acme Transfer, Inc., an Iowa corporation. In their early years, the new owners operated the company as a local carrier in and around Fort Dodge.

The small company began expanding in the summer of 1972 when it gained a contract to transport wallboard for Fort Dodge's gypsum mills. In November 1972 the company's name was changed to Smithway Motor Xpress, Inc. At about the same time, it acquired Park Transportation Company, a failed St. Louis-based steel carrier that added to Smithway's flatbed fleet and its geographic range.

By the mid-1970s Smithway had routes in 11 states and ran terminals in Fort Dodge and Granite City. Jack Thiessen wrote that in the 1970s Smithway ''became the largest noncontract gypsum carrier based in Fort Dodge.'' With additional terminals in Minneapolis; Chicago; Joplin, Missouri; and Hennepin, Illinois, Smithway passed the $10 million annual revenue mark at the end of the decade.

In 1980 Smithway moved into new offices in Fort Dodge. It spent $100,000 to destroy its old one-story office and then build a new two-story headquarters that housed administrative offices, accounting, and room to add computers in the future. This project doubled the company's office space by adding 2,000 square feet.

By 1982 Smithway transported goods in 27 states and operated 20 terminals. It employed 310 people, who received an annual payroll of $6.9 million. In 1984 William G. Smith became the firm's new president, while Harold C. Smith remained as board chairman as the firm continued to grow. Annual sales reached $28 million in 1984.

In the 1980s Smithway Transportation Brokerage, Inc. (STB), an affiliated firm, was started to use the services of other carriers. By 1998 more than 5,000 carriers helped Smithway meet its customers' needs. Each broker carrier had to meet certain standards set by STB.

Smithway's mission is to develop long-term partnerships with our shippers by providing innovative, responsive, high quality transportation services, while providing our employees the opportunity to realize the full potential of their careers and creating maximum value for our shareholders.

In the 1970s and early 1980s Smithway specialized in moving building and construction materials. In 1984 William G. Smith, as Smithway's new president, began to serve new kinds of customers with different freight needs. He also began to organize what the company called the Smithway Network of offices and other facilities in different communities, usually near customers' plants. This expansion and diversification allowed Smithway in the mid-1980s to gain contracts as the core carrier for some large corporations.

The trucking industry changed considerably after Congress deregulated it in 1980. Trucking companies began to consolidate in the more competitive atmosphere. By 1990 Smithway operated a fleet of more than 400 modern tractors and approximately 500 flatbed trailers from its 25 terminals. By September 1990 it had remodeled its Fort Dodge offices, added a new computer system, and constructed a new terminal in Oklahoma City, Oklahoma. Although the company had grown considerably as the nation's economy expanded in the 1980s, its major growth was still ahead.

Business in the 1990s and Beyond

Smithway in 1991 had $49.8 million in total revenue and $502,000 in net income. The company reached $59.9 million total revenue and $1.1 million net income in 1993 and then $69.2 million total revenue and $3.1 million net income for 1994.

In the 1990s Smithway added three high-tech systems as part of its overall strategy. In July 1993 it started using Spectrum software to improve its freight selection and loading process. Later it added the Qualcomm communication and tracking system to its own tractors and offered it for leasing to its independent drivers. This satellite-based system allowed the company to know exactly where its trucks were at all times and also made it unnecessary to stop and find a telephone in order to contact headquarters. Third, it used Electronic Data Interchange technology to link its headquarters to its customers, providing them instant information on truck positions and expected arrival times.

On January 17, 1995 the Smithway Motor Xpress Corporation was incorporated under Nevada law. It was formed as a holding company to acquire the stock of three companies: Smithway Motor Xpress, Inc.; Smithway Transportation Brokerage, Inc.; Wilmar Truck Leasing, Inc.; and also Smith Leasing's net assets. This was a preliminary step in planning for the initial public offering (IPO) on the NASDAQ on June 27, 1996.

From the IPO stock price of $8.50 a share, in January 1997 Smithway's stock sold at about $9 per share. James Peltz in the *Los Angeles Times* wrote that Wall Street seemed to be ignoring Smithway's sound financial performance, while many other trucking companies did poorly in 1996. He pointed out that Smithway had one of the trucking industry's highest pretax profit margins, almost nine cents per sales dollar, according to a study of 57 trucking companies by Market Guide Inc. Yet at the same time, Smithway had the lowest stock price-to-earnings multiple, just 9.5, on its previous 12 months' performance. Smithway had $93.7 million total revenue and $3.9 million net income in 1996.

Smithway in the second half of the 1990s acquired eight companies. First, in June 1995 it acquired Pittsburgh, Kansas-based Van Tassel, Inc., which emphasized flatbed services for the most part. In January 1996 Smithway acquired McPherson, Kansas-based Smith Trucking Company, a dry van carrier. It acquired Marquardt Transportation, Inc., another flatbed carrier, in October 1996. With headquarters in Yankton, South Dakota and a small Stockton, California facility, Marquardt added to Smithway's ability to haul heavy machinery and manufactured products. A fourth acquisition occurred in February 1997 when Smithway acquired a small Fort Dodge, Iowa flatbed carrier called Pirie Motor Freight, Inc. Royal Transport, Ltd., a flatbed trucking company based in Grand Rapids, Michigan, was acquired in September 1997. That gave Smithway "a regional niche specializing in heavy loads hauled primarily on multiple axle trailers," according to the firm's 1997 10-K Annual Report. At the end of 1997 Smithway, through internal growth and its acquisitions, employed 519 drivers and 234 others and worked with 447 independent drivers.

Smithway acquired East West Motor Express, Inc. of Black Hawk, South Dakota in 1998. A regional flatbed and dry van carrier, East West added 225 trucks to the Smithway fleet. George K. Baum rated Smithway stock a "buy" following that deal. In the April 13, 1998 *Barron's,* Baum said the East West acquisition "increases Smithway's customer and geographic diversification and provides operating synergies. It has consistently demonstrated an ability to achieve revenue gains from acquisitions."

In August 1998 Smithway completed its acquisition of Enid, Oklahoma-based TP Transportation, which had $4 million in annual revenue from owning 34 tractors pulling only flatbed trailers. The following month Smithway completed acquisition of JHT, Inc. of Cohasset, Minnesota. JHT used 185 tractors, half company owned and half driver owned, which served only the dry van market. Its 1997 annual revenue was more than $24 million. The acquisitions of JHT and TP Transportation brought Smithway's total fleet to more than 1,450 power units or tractors.

In the late 1990s, Smithway's average haul length gradually increased, according to its 10-K Annual Reports. It went from an average haul length of 568 miles in 1996 to 609 miles in 1997, 659 miles in 1998, and 678 miles in 1999. At the end of 1999 Smithway operated 2,783 trailers, 844 company-owned tractors, and 689 tractors owned by independent contractors.

In 1999 Smithway began a lease purchase program that gave its drivers the option to purchase a new Peterbilt 379 tractor after a 42-month period. "We found that many drivers want to have their own truck, but do not have the means to buy one," said Smithway's Director of Maintenance Andy Nesler in a press release December 8, 1999. "Drivers are the backbone of the industry. We want to keep them happy." In addition, Smithway sold used tractors such as 1996 and 1997 Peterbilts, Kenworths, Volvos, and Freightliners.

Smithway won several awards in the 1990s. For example, the Iowa Motor Truck Association (IMTA) honored Smithway in 1993 as the safest motor carrier of its size in the state. Smithway President William Smith served as a board member and chairman of the IMTA, which had been started in 1942 to promote lobbying, safety issues, and public relations for the state's trucking industry. The American Trucking Association in 1997 honored Smithway as one of the nation's top ten best-managed for-hire truckload companies in the flatbed category, which led to a feature article about Smithway in the January 1998 issue of *The Trucker*. The nonprofit Iowa-Illinois Safety Council in 2000 honored Smithway with an award for its 1999 accident prevention program, which reduced the number of injured employees recorded by the U.S. Occupational Safety and Health Administration (OSHA). The award came at a time when many were concerned about highway accidents caused by truck drivers, whether from lack of sleep or other causes.

After its expansion through eight acquisitions, Smithway in 1999 announced plans to build a new corporate headquarters in the Industrial Park just north of its existing offices in Fort Dodge, Iowa. The company reported on its web site that the $3 million facility of at least 40,000 square feet would double the size of its office space. "We want to maintain our corporate headquarters in Fort Dodge," said William G. Smith, the company's president, CEO, and chairman, in the April 16, 1999 *Fort Dodge Messenger*. "This is where we started. This is where the base of our people live now. We have offices across the country, but we've elected to stay home."

Smithway's 1999 operating revenue increased more than 20 percent for the third straight year. From 1997 operating revenue of $120 million, it increased to $161.4 million in 1998 and then $196.9 million in 1999. Its 1999 net earnings, however, were $3.9 million, a 30.8 percent decrease from 1997 net earnings of $5.7 million.

Smithway's 2000 operating revenue increased to $199.0 million, but it posted a net loss of $1.99 million, the first loss in its

history. "The trucking industry, Smithway included, operated in a very difficult business environment in 2000," said Smithway President, CEO, and Chairman William G. Smith in a February 6, 2001 *PR Newswire*. "For the entire year, we faced high fuel prices, a depressed used truck market, a declining number of owner-operators, and slowing freight demand." In addition, three important Smithway customers declared bankruptcy.

Smithway's stock value peaked in 1998 at about $17.50 per share but then declined in 1999 and 2000. For example, on August 4, 2000 it was sold at $2.875 per share. As of February 8, 2001, Smithway's stock sold for just $1.875 per share.

At the start of the new millennium, Smithway shipped a variety of freight, including construction materials such as wallboard, lumber, structural steel items, and roofing materials. It also transported packaged foods, commercial air conditioners, irrigation components, locomotive engines and parts, manufacturing and container steel, oversized tires, and construction and other heavy equipment. In 1999 its three largest freight categories were dry van (34 percent), steel (27 percent), and building materials (16 percent).

Smithway benefited from a generally healthy American economy in the 1990s. In addition, some manufacturers with their own trucks decided to have firms like Smithway take care of their transportation needs and thus save about 25 percent on shipping costs, according to a study by the American Trucking Associations Foundation. The most efficient carriers, of course, were the biggest trucking companies, which offered savings due to economies of scale and more capital for improved equipment and better drivers. The small trucking companies simply could not afford to compete with the major players.

All trucking companies in early 2001 faced some major challenges, including higher fuel costs, serious driver shortages, and the general economic slowdown. Smithway, with its modern fleet and seasoned management, seemed well prepared for the rough road ahead, but whether or not it would return to profitability remained to be seen.

Principal Subsidiaries

Smithway Motor Xpress, Inc.; East West Motor Express, Inc.; SMSD Acquisition Corp.; New Horizons Leasing, Inc.

Principal Competitors

Intrenet; J.B. Hunt Transport Services Inc.; Werner Enterprises, Inc.

Further Reading

Arndt, Michael, "Transportation," *Business Week,* January 8, 2001, p. 130.
Burkhart-Patrick, Michele, "Smithway Will Build $3 Million Office in FD," *Fort Dodge Messenger,* April 16, 1999.
Felton, John Richard, and Dale G. Anderson, editors, *Regulation and Deregulation of the Motor Carrier Industry,* Ames, Iowa: Iowa State University Press, 1989.
Hughes, Barbara Wallace, "Truck Association Offers a Unified Voice for Members," *Fort Dodge Messenger,* May 16, 1994.
"New Offices at Smithway Are Completed," *Fort Dodge Messenger,* June 14, 1980.

Peltz, James F., ''Wall Street, California; Not Even Semi-Attractive; A Few Trucking Stocks Show Promise, Analysts Say, But Most Can't Be Expected to Deliver. And for the Longer Term, the Industry's Outlook Is Mixed,'' *Los Angeles Times,* January 28, 1997, p. D5.

''Research Reports,'' *Barron's,* April 13, 1998, pp. 57–59.

Schulz, John D., ''1 Down, 1 to Go,'' *Traffic World,* October 12, 1998, p. 24.

''Smith President,'' *Fort Dodge Messenger,* December 16, 1984.

''Smithway Continues Growth in U.S.,'' *Fort Dodge Messenger,* September 25, 1990.

''Smithway Motor Has 60 Percent Growth in Year,'' *Fort Dodge Messenger,* September 30, 1982.

''Smithway Moves Construction Industry,'' *Fort Dodge Messenger,* September 29, 1984.

Thiessen, Jack, ''Smithway Motor Xpress, Inc.,'' in *A Tribute to Trucking,* Windsor Publications, 1990.

—David M. Walden

Staten Island Bancorp, Inc.

15 Beach Street
Staten Island, New York 10304
U.S.A.
Telephone: (718) 447-7900
Fax: (718) 980-6011
Web site: http://www.sisb.com

Public Company
Incorporated: 1997
Employees: 1,005
Sales: $308.5 million (1999)
Stock Exchanges: New York
Ticker Symbol: SIB
NAIC: 551111 Offices of Bank Holding Companies

Staten Island Bancorp, Inc. is a holding company that was created in 1997 to facilitate the conversion of the Staten Island Savings Bank from a federally chartered mutual savings bank to a federally chartered stock savings bank. For most of its history, dating back to its original charter in 1864, the Staten Island Savings Bank served a limited community. It was not until 1995 that the bank ventured beyond the shores of Staten Island to do business in Brooklyn. Staten Island Bancorp, through its subsidiary SI Bank & Trust, now operates several branches in New Jersey and looks to make further inroads into that market. The bank also has expanded into other areas of the country through the mortgage business. Its subsidiary, Ivy Mortgage, has offices in 25 states. Another subsidiary, American Construction Lending Services, Inc. (ACLS), offers residential construction loans throughout the United States. Nevertheless, Staten Island Bancorp remains committed to the community-oriented approach that made the Staten Island Savings Bank so successful.

Origins in the Early 1800s

The origins of Staten Island Bancorp reach back to the savings bank movement that began in Europe in the second half of the 18th century when small savings organizations were formed in Germany and Switzerland for the benefit of the working class, who were able to earn a higher return on their money by pooling together their small deposits. Although its depositors could withdraw money only upon reaching a certain age, making the plans akin to a pension, these early organizations became a model for British social thinkers who wanted to eradicate poverty. Rather than reward idleness through the giving of alms, the upper classes in England preferred to create savings and annuity plans that they hoped would promote the virtues of thrift, industry, and sobriety. The first self-sustaining savings bank was founded in Scotland in 1810, and the concept spread with such evangelical zeal that by 1818 there were 465 savings banks in the British Isles.

It was inevitable that the mutual savings bank movement would reach the United States. The first New York mutual began operations in 1819, again fortified by the belief that thrift among the laboring class would cure any number of social ills—as well as keep down taxes. By the Civil War there would be 25 mutual savings banks in Manhattan, Brooklyn, and Queens. In the beginning, mutuals were open several hours a week only, and many shared offices with insurance companies and commercial banks (where many of the mutuals deposited their funds). With the passing years, however, mutual savings banks operated less like organs of charity and more like regular businesses. Hours were expanded greatly and full-time managers were hired. Mutuals began to advertise in the newspapers, and they raised interest rates to lure away customers from their competitors. Mutual savings banks that had been created to serve workers now eagerly accepted deposits from businessmen. The Civil War only served to accelerate the transition from part-time, quasi-charitable activity to highly competitive industry.

Charter for Staten Island Savings Bank in 1864

Compared with Manhattan and Brooklyn, Staten Island was rustic, with no financial institutions of any kind. Even when it became one of the five boroughs that would be consolidated together in 1898 to form ''Greater New York,'' Staten Island would for decades remain essentially a rural enclave. It was in this sequestered environment, albeit in the shadow of Manhattan, that the Staten Island Savings Bank was chartered by a special Act of the State Legislature on April 7, 1864 (it would

380

Company Perspectives:

SI Bank & Trust will continue to be a strong financial services company committed to improving shareholder value, while delivering the highest quality products and services responsive to the changing needs of our consumer and business markets. As we grow, we will consistently strive to give extraordinary service to our customers by providing our employees with the means and opportunities to make full use of their skills and capabilities. These commitments to our shareholders, customers, and employees will enable the Company to maintain a level of profitability necessary to remain independent for the benefit of the communities we serve.

---

not begin actual operations until June 1867). Local leaders, headed by Francis George Shaw, founded the bank in the spirit of forwarding the public good, as had the earlier mutuals. Like its predecessors, Staten Island Savings Bank also started small. It conducted its business in a single room that was furnished by the bank's trustees, who would not be reimbursed for the expense for several years. Deposits at the end of the first year totaled only $13,957.

The Staten Island Savings Bank grew slowly but steadily over the years. In 1892 it moved to a new location and began to rent more and more rooms, until 1923 when the bank purchased the building and two adjoining properties, and built a new office that today continues to house a branch office. When its new home was completed in 1925 the assets of the Staten Island Savings Bank neared $15 million. The first branch office opened in 1929, followed by another in 1937, at which point assets reached $21,500,000. By 1950 the amount had more than doubled, reaching $47,333,000, as more branch offices began to open to serve the expanding population of Staten Island. In 1961 the assets of the Staten Island Savings Bank topped the $100 million mark. By 1973 the bank had added two more branches and its assets had grown to $277 million. The bank exceeded the $500 million level in 1980.

In 1983 the Staten Island Savings Bank merged with the Richmond County Federal Savings and Loan Association, the oldest such institution on the island, thus adding three more offices, which allowed the bank to cover nearly all of Staten Island. To provide service to the fast growing community of New Springville, the bank opened its 13th branch office in 1989, and by now its assets had grown to $836 million. Named to lead the Staten Island Savings Bank into a new era was Harry P. Doherty, who became president and chief operating officer in 1989. A year later he would be named chairman and CEO. Doherty began working at the bank in the mid-1960s after serving in the Marines. A management trainee, he first gained experience in the internal audit department, where he worked for several years before becoming chief auditor. He then transferred into finance, became a cashier, and rose to the level of senior VP cashier before being named to head the bank.

In 1990 a further consolidation of the traditional local banking community took place with the dissolution of the Nassau Federal

Savings and Loan Association, which allowed Staten Island Savings Bank to acquire three more branches. Two of the offices originally had contained the Edgewater Savings and Loan Association, and the third had been the office of Prudential Savings and Loan. Edgewater and Prudential were among the island's oldest financial institutions. With the addition of these branches, Staten Island Savings Bank topped $1 billion in assets.

In the world of mutuals, Staten Island Savings Bank was a true success story. Although the philanthropic nature of its origins had long since given way to the realities of business, the bank was able to remain true to its community-oriented vision yet still prosper. The same could not be said for other mutuals, which began to suffer in the 1970s from rising interest rates. Committed to long-term, low-yielding mortgages, many mutuals lacked the flexibility to adapt to such adverse economic conditions. By the mid-1990s, mutuals were becoming a dying breed. At the end of 1972 there had been 1,817 federally chartered mutual savings banks; by the end of 1996 only 653 would remain.

Many mutuals converted to a stock form of ownership. Instead of being owned by the community through its customers, converted mutuals now would have to answer to shareholders, with the result that a longer-term approach would give way to a quarterly results-oriented approach, and sometimes the interests of customers and shareholders would be at odds. Staten Island Savings Bank, operating in a community with growth that was limited by its shoreline, tried to expand its business and hedge its bets against the volatility of interest rates by offering commercial services. It enjoyed limited success, mostly because its main competitor, Gateway State Bank, was doing a better job. When Doherty learned in late 1994 that Gateway had hired an investment banker and might be available for purchase, he approached his board about acquiring the commercial bank. Although no mutual bank had ever bought a stock institution, the board was willing to move forward. The New York State Banking Department initially dismissed the idea, only to conclude a short time later that there was nothing in the state statutes to prevent such a transaction. By March 1995 the Staten Island Savings Bank had completed a definitive agreement to purchase Gateway, and by August the $58 million deal was completed. The Staten Island Savings Bank, therefore, added $320 million in assets, bringing its total to $1.7 billion. The deal also brought with it five offices and a Trust Department that gave Staten Island entry into a new line of business. A branch office in Bay Ridge, Brooklyn, just across the Verrazona Bridge, became the bank's first location off Staten Island. Although the bank's business model was changing to accommodate both consumers and business customers, Doherty insisted at the time that the Staten Island Savings Bank would remain a mutual.

Formation of Staten Island Bancorp in 1997

A year after acquiring Gateway, Doherty announced that the Staten Island Savings bank was converting to a stock institution. To accomplish the conversion, a holding company named Staten Island Bancorp (SIB) was incorporated in Delaware. In December 1997 an initial public offering of stock was made, and Staten Island Bancorp began trading on the New York Stock exchange.

Key Dates:

1864: Staten Island Savings Bank chartered by state.
1867: Bank begins operations.
1983: Bank merges with Richmond County Federal Savings and Loan Association.
1995: Bank acquires Gateway BanCorp.
1997: Staten Island Bancorp (SIB) formed; bank converts from mutual to stock ownership under SIB.
1999: SIB acquires First State Bank, expands into New Jersey.
2000: Banking subsidiary changes name to SI Bank & Trust.

With the money raised from the public offering, SIB began to expand and diversify its business. It formed a mortgage company subsidiary (SIBMC) in 1998 to purchase the Ivy Mortgage Corp., based in Branchburg, New Jersey, with a network of branch offices and correspondents in 21 states. SIBMC elected to continue operating under the Ivy Mortgage name. Also in 1998, SIB created the SIB Investment Corporation (SIBIC) for the purpose of managing certain investments of the bank. It then created the Staten Island Funding Corporation for the purpose of establishing a real estate investment trust that would be run as a wholly owned subsidiary of SIBIC.

Early in 1999 SIB formed American Construction Lending Services, Inc. (ACLS) after being approached by experienced lenders in the residential construction loan business who were looking to create a start-up. ACLS would lend money to builders, who would in turn transfer a new home to the owner. ACLS would then sell the loan in the marketplace. The venture would in effect give SIB the ability to generate higher-yielding, short-term loans in a rapidly growing segment of the residential construction lending business.

Later in 1999 SIB acquired First State Bancorp, Inc. and First State Bank, a New Jersey commercial bank worth $374 million with six branches serving Monmouth and Ocean Counties. The deal was an important step for SIB, not only to reach westward into New Jersey but to grow its traditional business: deposits. The possibilities were limited for further growth on Staten Island (and to a lesser extent, Brooklyn). Most activity would simply be a shifting of accounts from one bank to another. Certain parts of New Jersey, however, offered true growth potential.

Five years removed from the Gateway State Bank transaction, SIB had undergone so many changes, both in product lines and geographic markets, that management felt it was time to change the name of its banking subsidiary, Staten Island Savings Bank. The words "savings bank" was too limiting, and the association with Staten Island meant little to New Jersey customers. A compromise was found in the name SI Bank & Trust, which more accurately described the business while retaining some name recognition for its Staten Island customers.

SIB continued its efforts at diversification in January 2000 when it formed SIB Financial Services to sell life insurance. In October 2000 SI Bank & Trust signed an agreement to purchase four New Jersey branches from Unity Bancorp. Three were located in Union County and one in Middlesex County. The deal brought the total number of New Jersey branches to ten. Doherty also announced the bank's intention to open another three facilities in New Jersey in the near future.

With assets standing at $5 billion (as of June 2000), its business far more diversified than when it had been strictly a mutual savings bank, and a geographic reach that now extended nationwide, SIB entered 2001 poised for continued growth, yet harboring some concerns. Doherty told the *Wall Street Corporate Reporter* in an October 2000 interview, "The biggest challenge ahead of SIB is execution, which is paramount. If we trip and fall in any of the areas where we are trying to execute strategies for expansion into Brooklyn and New Jersey or are unable to find marriages with other institutions, we won't have the ability to expand our base and grow the balance sheet. We need to be able to duplicate what we are doing successfully on Staten Island in our new markets in both Brooklyn and New Jersey and that is just what we are doing."

Principal Subsidiaries

SI Bank & Trust; SIB Investment Corporation; SIB Mortgage Corp.; Staten Island Funding Corporation; American Construction Lending Services, Inc.

Principal Competitors

HSBC USA; Independence Community Bank; Richmond County Financial.

Further Reading

Bird, Anat, "Super Community Banking: A N.Y. Mutual Finds Ideal Partner in Commercial Bank," *American Banker,* June 7, 1995, p. 7.

"Does Mutuality Offer Longevity," *USBanker,* January 1996, p. 10.

Fosse, Lynn, "Leading Community Bank," *Wall Street Corporate Reporter,* October 16–22, 2000, pp. 1–4.

Nixon, Brian, "A Match Made on Staten Island," *America's Community Banker,* October 1995, p. 28.

Olmstead, Alan L., *New York City Mutual Savings Banks, 1819–1861,* Chapel Hill: University of North Carolina Press, 1976.

"Staten Island Bancorp," *Wall Street Transcript,* June 14, 1999, pp. 1–6.

—Ed Dinger

Stewart's Beverages

Snapple Beverage Group
709 Westchester Avenue
White Plains, New York 10604
U.S.A.
Telephone: (914) 397-9200
Toll Free: (800) 964-7842
Web site: http://www.drnk.com

Division of Snapple Beverage Group
Incorporated: 1987 as Cable Car Beverage Corporation
Employees: 100 (1999 est.)
Sales: $35 million (1999 est.)
NAIC: 31211 Soft Drink Manufacturing

Stewart's Beverages is best known for its premium soft drinks that evoke a nostalgic experience through such old-fashioned flavors as Root Beer, Cream Ale, Grape, Cherries N' Cream, Orange N' Cream, Key Lime, and Ginger Beer. Offering its soft drinks in long necked or barrel-shaped glass bottles, Stewart's also markets a line of gourmet diet sodas under the S brand name. An independent company under the parentage of conglomerate Triarc Companies Inc. until June 2000, Stewart's was spun off as a part of the Snapple Beverage Group, which became a wholly owned subsidiary of Cadbury Schweppes plc in October 2000.

Origins

While the history of Stewart's Beverages may be traced through the formation of the Cable Car Beverage Corporation in the 1980s, the history of the original Stewart's root beer reaches back to 1924, when a schoolteacher named Frank Stewart decided to make some extra income by selling root beer. Stewart perfected a recipe and opened a stand in his hometown of Mansfield, Ohio, at which he sold mugs of Stewart's root beer. The beverage remained a popular fountain drink for 66 years, during which time a franchise of Stewart's Drive-Ins was born with outlets in the Midwest and Mid-Atlantic United States.

Stewart's root beer was not bottled for mass consumption until 1990, when the Cable Car Beverage Corporation acquired the bottling rights. Cable Car had undergone several corporate transformations and had its origins in the reorganization of Great Eastern Energy Corp., a Denver-based oil and gas exploration and production company. Great Eastern sold its oil and gas properties in 1984 and hired consultant Samuel M. Simpson to examine other business opportunities. After studying over 100 businesses, Simpson steered the company toward the food and beverage industry. The company was renamed Great Eastern International Inc., and Simpson was named vice-president of the company. (He would eventually become CEO.) Great Eastern entered the food and beverage business with the support of its parent company, ATS Resources, Ltd., of Australia, and with funds from a private offering of stock. Simpson and other officers of the company formed Capvest Limited as their shareholding entity.

In 1986 Great Eastern purchased Quinoa Corporation of Boulder, Colorado, a natural foods company involved in importing quinoa, a highly nutritious South American grain. The company sold whole grain quinoa and quinoa flour under the brand name Ancient Harvest to health food stores and grocers, primarily in Colorado and Southern California. Quinoa Corporation intended to distribute the grain, grown in Peru, Bolivia, and Mexico, nationally and internationally.

Great Eastern's 1986 revenues, $93,873, were derived solely from the Quinoa Corporation. After its first full year under Great Eastern's parentage, in June 1987, the company reported $453,427 in revenues with a net loss of $790,432. Private label bulk sales accounted for 30 percent of revenue. In fall of 1987, the company introduced three new quinoa products, flat and spiral shaped dry pasta and wheat-free dry pasta.

Great Eastern's entry into the beverage business began with the June 1987 acquisition of Sheya Brothers Distributing, Inc., a Denver-based distribution company that focused on all-natural premium juice and soda beverages, flavored and unflavored seltzers, and carbonated and non-carbonated mineral waters. The company served retail stores in Denver and Colorado's other main cities along the front range of the Rocky Mountains.

The August 1987 acquisition of Old San Francisco Seltzer, Inc. (Old SF) complemented the Sheya Brothers acquisition. Old SF marketed naturally flavored and naturally sweetened seltzer waters. Most bottling and distribution was conducted by independent companies; Old SF sold the concentrated flavor syrup for mixture with seltzer water to regional bottlers under its licensing agreements. Old SF also used contractors for bottling and distribution. The products sold in grocery stores, convenience stores, and liquor stores in the United States and western Canada.

Simpson soon realized, however, that the company's scope had become too broad. An 82 percent share of the company's interest in the Quinoa Corporation was divested in June 1988, as total net losses for the year reached $1.4 million on revenues of $3.2 million. As Great Eastern did not have an outside line of credit and depended on funds from operations and from its parent company, Capvest (which had acquired a majority interest in Great Eastern in 1987), the sale of Quinoa Corporation allowed Great Eastern to concentrate its limited resources in one business.

New Focus and Name in 1987

In streamlining operations, Simpson organized the company under the new name Cable Car Beverage Corporation. He also began hiring a management team with experience in the beverage industry. James Lutz, formerly general manager of Royal Crown Bottling, joined Cable Car as vice-president of sales in 1988, while James Fox, brand director for Coors Light, joined the company as senior vice-president of sales the following year.

While searching for opportunities to expand, Cable Car cultivated its existing businesses. The company expanded distribution of San Francisco Seltzer (as it was renamed) in Canada through a ten-percent stake in San Francisco Beverages, an independent bottler. Through that deal, Cable Car received a five-percent gross royalty on that company's sales of the product. In June 1989 Sheya Brothers acquired Arrowood Distributing Company, a beer distributor in the Denver metropolitan area.

Cable Car's greatest inroads in the beverage industry, however, were realized when Simpson approached Stewart's Restaurants to produce, bottle, and distribute Stewart's brand root beer. By that time, Stewart's Restaurants was franchising some 70 Stewart's Drive-In Root Beer stands in New York, New Jersey, Ohio, Pennsylvania, and West Virginia. After six months of discussions with Michael Fessler, owner of Stewart's Restaurants, Simpson obtained an exclusive licensing agreement in July 1989.

Cable Car supported expansion into branded beverages with private and public securities offerings in October 1989 and June 1990, raising a net total of $2.3 million. In addition to develop-

ing the Stewart's root beer brand, the company acquired Aspen Mineral Water Corporation in November 1989. Cable Car added unsweetened flavorings to the product line and repackaged it for sale beginning in August 1990.

After nearly a year in development, Cable Car launched Stewart's Original Root Beer in spring 1990. Cable Car packaged the soda in old-fashioned, long neck, amber bottles with the Stewart's logo fired on in white ceramic. Initial test marketing took place along the East Coast, particularly in New Jersey, where a proven customer base for Stewart's root beer already existed. Marketed for the premium beverage category, the 12-ounce bottles sold for approximately one dollar each, primarily at delicatessens and convenience stores. Using San Francisco Seltzer's method of selling beverage concentrates to bottler-distributors, Cable Car sold 200,000 cases of Stewart's Original and Diet root beers in 1990. Sales of Stewart's beverages surpassed 500,000 cases in 1991.

Still, Cable Car operated at a loss as development of its branded product lines and the process of establishing a customer base kept expenses high. For the year ended June 1990 the company reported losses of $1.16 million on sales of $7.4 million, with 79 percent of sales originating from the distribution business. As the company's marketing programs produced results and the company adjusted overhead expenses in accordance with actual need, Cable Car realized a 64 percent increase in sales to $12 million for June 1991, and its net loss was reduced to $0.5 million.

Stewart's Original Root Beer was distributed in 13 states in 1991, and this figure was expanded to 26 the following year. Moreover, Cable Car began to penetrate the grocery store market, which accounted for less than 20 percent of sales. Most sales involved single bottles, including a 32-ounce "jug" introduced in 1991 and designed to stimulate take-home sales. A private offering of stock in November 1991 and its oversubscription fulfillment in January 1992 raised $1.1 million in capital for continued expansion. Simpson became the majority shareholder, with a 15 percent stake in the company. In 1992 *Inc.* magazine ranked Cable Car the 30th fastest growing public company in the United States.

1990s: The Rise of Stewart's Bottled Soft Drinks

In partnership with Stewart's Restaurants, Cable Car developed two new soda flavors. In May 1992 the company launched Stewart's brand cream ale, diet cream ale, and ginger beer, a non-alcoholic beverage with a strong ginger zest. Advance orders of the products were higher than expected. Cable Car also signed a new licensing agreement with Stewart's Restaurants to market Stewart's beverages as a fountain product in 15 states. To oversee these operations, Cable Car formed a new subsidiary, Fountain Classics, Inc.

Development of its branded beverages prevented Cable Car from expanding its distribution subsidiary. Subsequently, Shey Brothers was spun off, merging with AMCON, a wholesale distributor of groceries and health and beauty care products through eight states in the Midwest and Upper Great Plains. The Omaha-based company intended to continue Sheya Brothers' distribution in Colorado. The merger involved a stock exchange

Beverage Company, which held distribution rights for the City and County of San Francisco.

Key Dates:

1924: Stewart's root beer is invented.
1987: The Cable Car Beverage Corporation is established.
1989: Cable Car obtains a licensing agreement to bottle Stewart's root beer.
1991: Company sells 500,000 cases of Stewart's Original Root Beer.
1992: Cable Car introduces Stewart's Cream Ale, Diet Cream Ale, and Ginger Beer.
1994: Annual sales of Stewart's Original Root Beer exceed one million cases.
1997: Triarc Companies acquires Cable Car Beverage.
1999: Triarc spins off Stewart's as part of the Snapple Beverage Group.
2000: Cadbury Schweppes plc acquires the Snapple Beverage Group, including the Stewart's division.

with distribution of AMCON stock to Cable Car shareholders. Sheya Brothers had accounted for two-thirds of Cable Car's revenues, so the spinoff resulted in much lower revenues on Cable Car's balance sheet. In 1994, the first fiscal year to end December 31, Cable Car recorded revenues of $8.2 million and its first net income of $721,695.

Cable Car launched several new branded products in 1995. Stewart's Country Orange 'N Cream debuted in May 1995 and quickly became the company's second best seller. The company expanded its Aspen brand with Aspen Spring Water, a non-carbonated spring water, and Aspen Extreme, a line of non-carbonated, fruit flavored sports drinks. At the behest of New England distributors, Cable Car developed a line of unsweetened seltzers. The company tested Fountain Classics Seltzers in eight New England markets during the summer 1995. Also, the debut of a 16-ounce, barrel-shaped bottle of root beer attracted new business and increased sales.

In 1996 Cable Car introduced Diet Orange 'N Cream, Classic Key Lime, and Old-Fashioned Cherries 'N Cream sodas under the Stewart's name. Stewart's had in fact become so popular that Cable Car opted to sell off its Aspen Water and San Francisco Seltzer operations, which helped finance further development of the successful Stewart's brand. At this time Stewart's beverages were available in 40 states through over 200 distributors.

New Parentage in the Late 1990s

In November 1997, conglomerate Triarc Companies completed its acquisition of Cable Car in a stock exchange valued at $31 million. Over the previous four years Triarc had acquired Snapple Beverages, Mistic Brands, and Royal Crown Cola, as well as a chain of Arby's Restaurant franchises. Triarc allowed Cable Car, renamed Stewart's Beverages in 1999, to operate without changes or interference as a subsidiary of Snapple Beverages. Triarc intended to create a functionally integrated company, acquiring Millrose Distributors of New Jersey, the second largest distributor of Stewart's products, and California

Stewart's continued to expand as the fastest growing super-premium soda in the United States. Under Triarc ownership, Stewart's distribution had expanded to all 50 states, as well as to Canada and the United Kingdom. Sales increased 13 percent in 1998 and 17 percent in 1999. While single-bottle "cold vault" sales in convenience stores and delicatessens comprised 75 percent of revenues, Stewart's attained a two percent market share of the market for packaged premium beverages in convenience stores, grocery stores, and mass merchandisers.

In 1999 Stewart's celebrated the 75th anniversary of Stewart's Root Beer with special promotions that emphasized the nostalgic appeal of drinking an ice-cold root beer in the summertime, particularly at a baseball game. A national promotion involved a drawing for trips to the World Series and the All-Star baseball games, while local promotions supported Little League baseball.

Stewart's continued to develop nostalgic yet unique soda flavors. The company introduced Classic Grape Soda in 1998 and Peach Soda in 1999. Triarc supported production of the new beverages with a $5 million construction project, building a dedicated production line for Stewart's beverages at the Millrose bottling facility. The new line allowed the company to refine operations and logistics in a manner that accommodated growth in volume.

In May 2000 Stewart's launched "S", a line of low-calorie, gourmet flavored soft drinks and the first line of gourmet diet sodas on the market. Available in Black Raspberry, Orchard Peach, Ruby Red (grapefruit), Vanilla Cream, and Wild Cherry flavors, the S beverages were packaged in sleek bottles etched with an "S" in white. Stewart's sweetened the lightly carbonated beverages with sucralose and Ace K, artificial sweeteners that they believed tasted better than the popular aspartame. After test marketing in California, Stewart's initiated distribution in 35 markets, mostly in the Midwest and Mid-Atlantic states. Distribution channels included Safeway, Kroger, and Albertson's grocery store chains, as well as 7-11 stores in California and Florida. A four-pack of 11-ounce bottles sold for anywhere from $3.29 to $3.50, while individual bottles sold at delis and convenience stores ranged in price from 99 cents to $1.49.

In 2000, after only seven years in the beverage industry, Triarc decided to spin off its soft drink businesses. Toward that end, it reorganized the premium beverage companies—Snapple, Mistic, and Stewart's—and the line of soft drink concentrates—Royal Crown Cola, Diet Rite, RC Edge, and Nehi—under the Snapple name. Headquarters of the various operations were to be merged at Snapple's offices in White Plains, New York. Snapple announced its intention to go public in June 2000, but Triarc sold the company to London-based Cadbury Schweppes plc, a private company, for $1.45 billion the following October.

Cadbury Schweppes maintained that the Snapple Beverage Group would remain a stand-alone company, with Snapple, Mistic, and Stewart's serving as its brand names. Simpson, who had built Stewart's Beverages into the fastest growing premium soft drink company, and had remained as CEO of Stewart's during its tenure with Triarc, left shortly after the Cadbury Schweppes acquisition. New leadership took over in December 2000, as John L. Belsito was named president of the Snapple Beverage Group. Though its corporate identity was once again being restructured, Stewart's root beer and other soft drinks remained popular and widely available.

Principal Competitors

Hansen Natural Corporation; National Beverage Corporation; Ferolito, Vultaggio & Sons; Pyramid Breweries Inc.

Further Reading

Ashanti, Elana, ''Snapple Owner Cable Car New York Company Adds Stewart's Brand to its Beverage Business,'' *Denver Post*, June 25, 1997, p. 2.

Faulhaber, Patricia, ''Distinct Refreshment,'' *U.S. Distribution Journal*, July 1999, p. 38.

Goldman, Lea, ''Thirsty for Growth,'' *Forbes*, October 30, 2000, p. 158.

Hein, Kenneth,. ''Shakeups Loom after Snapple, SoBe Buys,'' *Brandweek*, January 8, 2001, p. 37.

Leib, Jeffrey, ''Cable Car Spinning Off Distributor into Merger,'' *Denver Post*, September 30, 1992, p. 7C.

Locke, Tom, ''Soda Marketer's Sales are Anything But Flat,'' *Denver Business Journal*, may 29, 1992, p. 1.

Martin, Claire, ''Micro-Bottlers Hit a Gold Mine with Root Beer,'' *Denver Post*, September 3, 1992, p. 1E.

MacArthur, Kate, ''S Finds Niche as Diet Gourmet Soda,'' *Advertising Age*, May 15, 2000, p. 32.

Orozco, Stacie, ''Stewart's Root Beer Drive-Ins Wants to Get A-Head in Florida,'' *South Florida Business Journal*, September 1, 2000, p. 3.

Prince, Greg, ''Maybe S,'' *Beverage World*, March 15, 2000.

——, ''Yesterday, Today, & Tomorrow,'' *Beverage World*, March 15, 2000.

''Soda Bottle Slakes Thirst for Sophistication,'' *Packaging Digest,* July 2000, p. 27.

''Stewart's Grape Soda Drawing on Nostalgia,'' *U.S. Distribution Journal*, March 1999, p. 58.

''Stewart's Root Beer Still Rockin' at 75,'' *U.S. Distribution Journal*, May 1999, p. 96.

Theodore, Sarah, ''What a PEACH,'' *Beverage Industry*, January 2000, p. 18.

Vasquez, Beverly, ''Stewart's shakes up pop culture,'' *Denver Business Journal*, April 16, 1999, p. 3A.

''With Cable Car Rolling In, Maybe Triarc Should be Called Quadarc,'' *Beverage World*, August 15, 1997, p. 18.

—Mary Tradii

Swedish Match AB

Rosenlundsgatan 36
SE-118 85
Stockholm
Sweden
Telephone: (46)-8-658-02-00
Fax: (46)-8-658-62-63
Web site: http://www.swedishmatch.ch

Public Company
Founded: 1917 as The Swedish Match Company
Employees: 10,000
Sales: $1.22 billion (2000)
Stock Exchanges: NASDAQ Stockholm
Ticker Symbols: SWMAY SWMA
NAIC: 312229 Other Tobacco Products Manufacturing;
 325998 All Other Miscellaneous Chemical Product
 and Preparation Manufacturing; 339999 All Other
 Miscellaneous Manufacturing.

Based in Stockholm, Swedish Match AB is the leading global manufacturer of matches and the third-largest manufacturer of disposable lighters. The company also markets an array of tobacco products other than cigarettes. It produces pipe tobacco and snuff, chewing tobacco, cigars, tobacco rolling papers, and filters. Some of its well-known brands include Cricket lighters, Swan matches, White Owl cigars, and Red Man, Durango, and Beech Nut chewing tobacco. During the early 1900s Swedish Match became one of the first companies to achieve a truly global presence. Its products are still sold worldwide, with particularly strong markets in Europe and North America. The United States, Germany, France, and the Netherlands are Swedish Match's top markets.

1890s Origins and Early Plans for Global Dominance

Ivar Kreuger founded Swedish Match. Ivar Kreuger was an internationally renowned industrial magnate and a controversial figure who was regarded as a scoundrel by some. He was born in 1880 in Kalmar, a city in southern Sweden. His family owned and operated a match factory that his grandfather had started. The match industry was relatively young when the company was founded; matches had been produced commercially only since the early 1800s, but a large market had developed since matches were commonly used at that time to light kerosene lamps and gas stoves. By the late 1800s the Swedish match industry was employing 7,000 workers and producing about 40,000 tons of matches annually.

The early Swedish match industry was dependent on international suppliers and buyers. Aspen wood, for example, was supplied primarily by Russia. Chemicals such as potassium chlorate, phosphorus, and paraffin were purchased mostly from Great Britain and Germany. Similarly, Germany and England were the greatest export markets for Swedish matches. In fact, Sweden exported about 85 percent of the matches it produced. World War I disturbed the import and export dynamics because supplies were cut, and some countries imposed restrictive trade barriers. Nevertheless, by the time Ivar Kreuger entered the business, the foundation for his international empire had been established.

When Ivar Kreuger began his operations in the early 1910s, Sweden had assumed a global leadership role in the match industry. That lead was largely attributable to technological breakthroughs. In 1884 Gustaf Eric Pasch of the Swedish Royal Academy of Science invented the safety match. It utilized red phosphorus (instead of more toxic yellow phosphorus), which was applied to a striking surface rather than the match head. The result was a much safer match. Early match-making machines—what we now term lighters—had emerged as well.

Kreuger exhibited little interest in his family's enterprise as a young man. His business cunning and penchant for overseas adventure, however, were evident from an early age. As a boy Kreuger stole final term papers from the principal's office and sold copies to students for the equivalent of five cents apiece. After his schooling, in which he studied engineering, Ivar traveled the globe, taking jobs in South Africa, Canada, Germany, and the United States. His brother, meanwhile, operated the family's struggling match business. Unfortunately, the match industry at the time suffered from the growing popularity of

---

Company Perspectives:

Swedish Match produces and markets an extensive range of snuff, chewing tobacco, cigars, and pipe tobacco, as well as matches and disposable lighters. Swedish Match core business focuses on its broad and deep knowledge of snuff and chewing tobacco (smokeless tobacco) and cigars and pipe tobacco (brown tobacco). These products constitute what are known as niche tobacco products or OTP (Other Tobacco Products). Swedish Match shall strengthen its position as a leading, global player in the area of niche tobacco products, particularly in the European and North American markets.

---

electric lighting. Only the increasing number of cigarette smokers, who were major purchasers of matches, prevented further damage to the industry.

Kreuger returned to Sweden when he was 28 years old. He and a fellow engineer, Paul Toll, started a real estate and construction company. Kreuger & Toll was successful, but Kreuger was soon sidetracked by opportunities related to the family business.

The Swedish match industry was highly consolidated by that time. One giant company, Jonkoping & Vulcan, controlled 75 percent of the market, and the Kreugers were one of a few small players still competing. Kreuger was intrigued by the challenge of overcoming Jonkoping's dominance. But he also had greater designs—he believed that he could parlay Sweden's technological advantages into global dominance of the match industry.

Kreuger's business savvy, although ethically questionable, was undeniable. During the early 1910s he managed to bring together most of the remaining Swedish match companies, including his family's, into a single organization called United Match Factories. Kreuger artificially inflated the value of United, making it look as though his company had much more capital than it actually possessed. He used that artificial value to back his takeover of Jonkoping in 1917, thus effectively establishing a monopoly in his home country. When World War I ended a year later, he shifted the focus of his newly formed holding company, The Swedish Match Company, to the European mainland.

During the 1920s Kreuger embarked on an aggressive acquisition campaign, striking deals and snapping up match factories all over Europe. Although his business acumen was revered at the time, his bid for industry dominance would later earn him a reputation for chicanery. For example, it was discovered that he sent secret agents to companies in which he had an interest. The undercover proxies made extremely low offers to buy the enterprises. Kreuger followed these agents in and offered a higher— though still low—price. The practice allowed him to snag new factories at deflated prices. In addition, he often secretly purchased interests in competitors in an effort to avoid national restrictions related to monopolies and foreign ownership.

By the late 1920s, the industrious Kreuger had amassed a huge match-manufacturing network. He controlled a significant share of the match business in Hungary, Yugoslavia, and other East European countries and acquired major stakes in leading British and American match companies. Kreuger also built new factories in countries like India. More importantly, Swedish Match effectively claimed control of the match industries in Norway, Denmark, Holland, Finland, and Switzerland. The company also diversified into other business areas during this time. By the end of the 1920s, in fact, Kreuger controlled a telecommunications company, a pulp and paper enterprise, and a mining company that owned the third-largest gold deposit in the world.

Kreuger's empire churned out 2.8 million cases of matches annually by 1929, making up about 40 percent of total world match output. But leadership in the match industry was only part of the Swedish Match story to that point, for Ivar Kreuger's international reputation grew significantly after the conclusion of World War I. Kreuger used part of his massive fortune to make loans to needy national governments battered by the war. Although many of the loans were used to secure permission for Swedish Match to develop a monopoly in the borrower's country, many observers nevertheless viewed Kreuger's postwar lending to financially troubled governments as magnanimous. By 1930 Kreuger had doled out more than $350 million in loans to a dozen different countries.

In less than a decade, Kreuger had built one of the largest international companies ever created. His business acumen had achieved legendary status. Hundreds of millions of dollars flowed through his diverse holdings of companies, which were organized under four divisions: Swedish Match; Kreuger & Toll; International Match (New York); and Continental Investment (Liechtenstein). Kreuger's enviable reputation as a socially conscious business leader continued to grow, particularly after he made a celebrated $30 million loan to Germany to help it pay war reparations. That move earned him the title of "the savior of Europe" from some politicians at the time.

Nevertheless, neither his success nor his reputation saved him. Kreuger shocked the global financial community when he shot and killed himself on March 12, 1932. His suicide in his Paris bachelor apartment capped the end of his two-year effort to keep his collapsing empire glued together. The previously hidden weaknesses of Kreuger's mammoth enterprise were exposed following the global financial meltdown spurred by stock market crashes around the world. As the value of his companies plunged, Kreuger's personal liabilities ballooned past the $250 million mark, and his companies were unable to meet their obligations. Kreuger took desperate measures, even going so far as to forge $142 million worth of Italian government bonds and promissory notes. Kreuger himself forged the signatures needed on the notes, but misspelled the names. The ruse failed, and Kreuger's reputation was damaged.

It was later discovered that Kreuger's dynasty was built partially on overvalued assets and deceptive accounting practices. Although his business acumen was undeniable, Kreuger had consistently engaged in questionable reporting practices in an effort to expand his holding company. "Throughout his bizarre career," wrote Robert Shaplen, author of the 1960 biography *Kreuger,* "Kreuger alone supplied the figures for the books of his various companies, and he mostly kept them in his head.'' Backing that assertion was Allen Churchill's *The Incredible Ivar Kreuger,* who noted that a former secretary of Kreuger's claimed that Kreuger once dictated the text of the annual reports for his four companies in a single afternoon: ''I accounted for it by the fact that I had often been told that he was a genius,'' she explained.

To Kreuger's credit, he was a highly intelligent businessman and financier. Many of his defenders contend that, although his dealings may appear shady in retrospect, at the time many of his activities represented the norm. Shaplen's biography related the following excerpt from a statement made by Kreuger to Bjorn Prytz, a Swedish tycoon and diplomat: ''In olden times, the princes and everyone would go to confession because it was the thing to do, whether they believed it or not. Today the world demands balance sheets, profit-and-loss statements once a year. But if you're really working on great ideas, you can't supply these on schedule and expose yourself to view. You've got to tell the public something, and so long as it's satisfied and continues to have faith in you, it's really not important what you confess.''

Picking Up the Pieces After Krueger

Teams of attorneys, bankers, and accountants labored for four years sorting out Kreuger's affairs and divvying up the remains of his companies after his death. The Price, Waterhouse accounting firm finally calculated that Kreuger had inflated the earnings of his companies by more than $250 million between 1917 and 1932. Millions of dollars were never accounted for, and Ivar's brother, Tortsen, was sent to jail for 18 months. After his release, Tortsen spent much of the remainder of his life trying to prove that Ivar was murdered. Tortsen's story fell on deaf ears, and the company was wrested from Kreuger-family control.

The Wallenberg family of Sweden came to the rescue of Swedish Match. In an agreement that involved a transfer of $15 million from Stockholm to New York, Jacob Wallenberg was able to gain control of the injured enterprise. The company lost its monopoly contracts with foreign governments and was diminished in size and strength. Nevertheless, Kreuger had amassed massive holdings in the match industry that allowed Swedish Match to sustain its market leadership.

Following World War II and throughout the mid-1900s, Swedish Match tried to expand its match business. Swedish

Match purchased the Cricket disposable cigarette lighter division of Gilette in the mid-1980s, a purchase that—combined with its own Feudor and Poppell lighter brands—gave Swedish Match a hefty 15 percent of that global market. The company's entrance into the cigarette lighter business illustrated how much Swedish Match had changed since Kreuger's reign. Indeed, in an effort to squelch competition from lighter manufacturers, Krcuger had succeeded in getting some countries to ban the use of lighters in public—those laws lingered on the books for several years in a few nations.

Diversified Company in the 1980s

By the late 1980s matches made up less than 25 percent of Swedish Match's global sales. Still, the company remained the largest manufacturer of matches in the world and continued to improve its position in the world market. In 1980, for example, Swedish Match bought out Universal Match, the largest producer of matches in the United States. In 1987 it acquired Britain's second-largest match manufacturer, Wilkinson Sword. The latter purchase gave Swedish Match control of a leading 25 percent of world match markets. Going into the early 1990s, Swedish Match employed more than 25,000 workers globally and generated annual revenues of more than $17 million, about $250 million of which were attributable to U.S. sales.

The company also diversified into several other arenas. Swedish Match company purchased Tarkett, making it the second largest manufacture of floor coverings in the world by the late 1980s. Swedish Match also acquired cabinet makers Marbodal and HTH, and door maker Sweedor, which made it the biggest producer of doors in Sweden. Other acquisitions included forays into packaging material and razor blade industries.

In 1988, Swedish Match was acquired by Stora Kopparbergs Bergslags AB, a diversified company and among the largest forestry companies in Europe. Stora reportedly paid SKr 5.9 billion for Swedish Match, in its efforts to enhance its line of raw materials with consumer products businesses. Stora's parentage was short-lived, however, as Swedish Match was sold to Volvo in 1990.

Focusing on Niche Tobacco Products in the Late 1990s

Volvo held on to Swedish Match for only a few short years, before that company decided to jettison most of its non-automotive subsidiaries. Volvo eventually spun Swedish Match off to its shareholders in 1996, in a deal worth SKr 10.1 billion. In 1998, leadership of the company passed to Lennart Sunden. The new CEO was known for his skill in marketing. He helped focus the company's long-term strategy on non-cigarette tobacco products and smoking accessories. Key products would be smokeless tobacco, cigars, matches, and lighters. Consequently in 1999 the company made one significant divestiture and a major acquisition. In June, Swedish Match announced the sale of its entire cigarette division to Austria Tabak, for SKr 4.8 billion ($560 million). Swedish Match was Sweden's lone cigarette manufacturer at that time, where its brands made up almost half the market. It also had a large share of the Estonian cigarette market. Cigarettes were not a business the company could compete in globally. Cigars, however, were another matter. At virtually the same time it was disposing of its cigarette operations, Swedish Match spent $200 million to buy the mass-market lines of the Virginia cigar manufacturer General Cigar Holdings Inc. This purchase gave Swedish Match the well-known brands White Owl, Tiparillo, Tijuana Smalls, and GarciaVega. By that time, North America accounted for about one-fifth of Swedish Match's sales, and it hoped to use the General Cigar buy to help increase its U.S. sales, particularly in urban markets. A year later, Swedish Match made another offer to General Cigar, this time to purchase a 64 percent interest in the company. Swedish Match's leading product in the U.S. market was chewing tobacco, where it marketed the venerable Red Man brand. In 2000 the company made another major purchase in the North American market, paying $165 million for the chewing tobacco brands of National Tobacco Company. National Tobacco was a private company based in Louisville, Kentucky, that made about $50 million annually off chewing tobacco. It sold Swedish Match its Beech-Nut and Durango brands. This was expected to give the Swedish company over half the U.S. chewing tobacco market share.

Another key product in Swedish Match's stable of niche tobacco products was snuff. Snuff was a tobacco product that was used in Sweden as a passive way of absorbing nicotine. A thumbnail-sized portion of it sat in the mouth—it was not snorted or chewed. With the ascension of Lennart Sunden as CEO in 1998, the company began to change the way it presented snuff. It became not just another tobacco product but a smoking cessation aid. By 2000, Sweden had 900,000 snuff users, and according to Swedish Match, over half were former smokers. With smoking becoming less socially and medically acceptable, Swedish Match marketed its snuff as a neat, safe, effective way to enjoy tobacco while cutting down on or quitting cigarettes. The company began packaging snuff in pre-measured packets something like a teabag, so that the user did not have to contend with unattractive tobacco juice or shreds. The company saw a significant rise in its snuff sales with the new marketing campaign.

In other markets abroad, Swedish Match remained a strong seller. It dominated the cigar market in the Netherlands, where it had a host of established brands plus the new ones it bought from General Cigar. In England, the company found that, as cigarettes became more expensive, accessories for hand-rolling were a growing and profitable category. Its Swan brand had a line of papers, matches, lighters, and filters. These items had a profit margin of more than 40 percent, and the hand-rolling category was the fastest-growing segment of the entire tobacco products market in the United Kingdom. Swedish Match

re-launched its Swan brand in 1999, aiming it more at younger smokers. Overall, Swedish Match seemed to be keeping finely tuned to its stated objective of growing its niche tobacco and smoking accessories markets, particularly in Europe and North America.

Principal Subsidiaries

Swedish Match North America, Inc.; Swedish Match Philippines Inc.; General Cigar Holdings, Inc.; Wimco Ltd.

Principal Divisions

North Europe; Continental Europe; North America; Overseas; Matches.

Principal Competitors

Societe BIC S.A.; UST, Inc.; Swisher International Group, Inc.

Further Reading

Abrose, Jules, "Swedish Match Again Strikes Out in New Directions," *International Management,* October 1987, pp. 87–90.

George, Nicholas, "Swedish Group Sells Cigarette Operations," *Financial Times,* June 1, 1999, p. 24.

Hassbring, Lars, *The International Development of the Swedish Match Company, 1917–1924,* Stockholm: Swedish Match Company, 1979.

Kapstein, Jonathan, and Charles Gaffney, "Peter Wallenberg is Rebuilding a Dynasty," *Business Week,* November 2, 1987, pp. 158–59.

Loeffelhyolz, Suzanne, "Global Report: Fore Products—Outside Looking In," *Financial World,* February 20, 1990, pp. 66–67.

Moskowitz, Milton, *The Global Marketplace,* New York: Macmillan, 1987.

Ress, David, "Trying to Sell Europe on Snuff . . . and Gearing Up to Host an EC Bash," *Business Week,* April 10, 2000, p. 4.

"Richmond, Va.-Based Tobacco Business to Buy Four General Cigar Lines," *Knight-Ridder/Tribune Business News,* March 28, 1999.

"Snuff, Puff and Paper Go to Euroland," *Euromoney,* October 1999, p. 86.

"Swan's Offer is Strikes Ahead," *Grocer,* July 8, 2000, p. S10.

"Swedish Match Remains Strong," *World Tobacco,* May 2000, p. 33.

"Swedish Mismatch," *Euromoney,* July 1995, pp. 111–112.

Wikander, Ulla, *Kreuger's Match Monopolies, 1925–1930,* Stockholm: Swedish Match Company, 1980.

—Dave Mote
—update: A. Woodward

Thor Industries, Inc.

419 West Pike Street
Jackson Center, Ohio 45334-0629
U.S.A.
Telephone: (937) 596-6849
Fax: (937) 596-6092
Web site: http://www.thorindustries.com

Public Company
Incorporated: 1980
Employees: 3,520
Sales: $894 million (2000)
Stock Exchanges: New York
Ticker Symbol: THO
NAIC: 336214 Travel Trailer and Camper Manufacturing;
    336213 Motor Home Manufacturing; 336211 Motor
    Vehicle Body Manufacturing

Thor Industries, Inc., is the nation's second largest manufacturer of recreation vehicles and the largest builder of mid-size buses. The company manufacturers such popular recreation vehicles as Airstream, Land Yacht, Dutchmen, Signature, Four Winds, Tahoe and others, as well as buses under the names of El Dorado, National, and Champion. Through 13 recreational vehicle and bus manufacturing plants in the United States and two in Canada, Thor annually produces approximately 40,000 vehicles. In January 2000, Thor was named by *Forbes* magazine to its Platinum 400 list of "exceptional big corporations," based on its profitability as well as its prospects for long- and short-term growth.

Wally Byam Invents the Airstream

Thor was founded in 1980 with the purchase of Airstream, a legendary maker of aluminum trailers that had set the standard for quality in the recreational vehicle industry for half a century. These distinctive, silver, bullet-shaped trailers were immensely popular travel vehicles in the late 1940s and throughout the 1950s, becoming famous for their unique design and durability.

Airstreams would later be exhibited at both the Smithsonian Institution and the Henry Ford museum, and early models would be highly prized by collectors. More than 60 percent of all Airstreams ever built were still rolling along the nation's highways and back roads in the 21st century.

The Airstream was the creation of one man: Wally Byam. Born in Oregon on the Fourth of July in 1896, Byam was a prototypical American wanderer and inventor. As a boy, he traveled through the Northwest with his grandfather, who led a mule train in Oregon. As a teenager, he worked as a shepherd, living in a small donkey cart, outfitted with only the most basic equipment and tools. After high school, seeking adventure, Byam signed on with the merchant marine, where, in three years, he graduated from cabin boy to ship's mate. He then worked his way through Stanford University, graduating in 1923 with a law degree.

Opting not to practice law, Byam entered the booming advertising business of the late 1920s. He first worked as a copywriter for the *Los Angeles Times* and then became owner of his own ad agency. Later, he started a number of magazines, one of which published an article on how to build a travel trailer. When readers wrote to complain that their homemade trailer projects had failed, Byam tested the directions himself and found that they were, indeed, defective. So, he decided to build a trailer according to his own plans.

His first attempts were primitive. One was a plywood platform built on top of a Ford Model T chassis. Another was a cramped plywood box which was, Byam wrote in his book, *Trailer Travel Here and Abroad*, "little more than a bed you could crawl into, a shelf to hold a water bottle, a flashlight and some camping equipment." Nonetheless, the trailer attracted attention, and Byam began to receive requests to build similar models for others.

When Byam wrote an article in *Popular Mechanics* describing how to build his new, improved plywood trailer for less than $100, many readers responded with orders for the $5 plans he offered. Meanwhile, he had turned over his Los Angeles backyard to building made-to-order trailers for customers who often arrived to lend a hand in the construction process. Byam's tiny home-based business survived the stock market crash of 1929, and by 1930 he had abandoned magazine publishing to build travel trailers full time.

Continuing to modify the basic design, Byam began to introduce a more aerodynamic look to his trailers and to adopt aircraft construction methods in order to lessen wind resistance. In 1934, he christened his ovoid-shaped trailers "Airstream," because "that's the way they travel, like a stream of air." According to Bryan Burkhardt and David Hunt in *Airstream, The History of the Land Yacht,* "the single most important designer in determining the final shape of what would become the classic Airstream Clipper" was William Hawley Bowlus, whose vehicle designs and travel trailer company Byam took over in a 1935 bankruptcy auction. In 1936, the Airstream Trailer Co. introduced the famous Clipper model, named after the Pan Am Clipper, the first transatlantic plane to carry people in numbers. With the capacity to sleep four, the bullet-shaped Clipper had a shiny, riveted aluminum body, carried its own water supply, featured an enclosed galley, and was fitted with electric lights. Even with a $1,200 price tag—very expensive during the Depression—the meticulously constructed Airstream was a winner. Of more than 300 travel trailer companies in operation in 1936, Byam's company was the only one to survive.

The company closed its doors during World War II since aluminum was critical to the war, and tires and gasoline were strictly rationed. Byam spent the war working in the engineering departments of aircraft companies, and he put that experience to good use at war's end. By 1948, he had built a new manufacturing facility in Van Nuys, California, to meet the surging demand for Airstreams by returning servicemen and their young families. In 1952, the company leased a facility in Jackson Center, Ohio, to build Airstreams for the Midwest and Eastern markets, and soon thereafter, the California factory was moved to larger quarters in Santa Fe Springs.

Over the next decade, until his death in 1962, Byam continued to refine the Airstream design, and his company prospered. Putting into practice his mission "to refine and perfect our product by continuous travel-testing of the highways and byways of the world," he led a group of Airstream drivers through remote areas of Central America in 1951. This was the first of many such caravans that he and other Airstream enthusiasts made to Africa, Europe, the Soviet Union, China, Australia, New Zealand, and more. Intrepid travelers, organized as the

Wally Byam Caravan Club International, would continue to explore the world in their Airstreams through the 1990s.

Conglomerate Ownership: 1967–80

Airstream's reputation for quality solidified the company's existence, and the company continued to thrive following the death of its founder in 1962. Its design excellence placed it at the forefront anywhere trailers were required, and the vehicle proved easily adaptable to government and military needs. Specially equipped Airstream trailers, for example, were set up around the vast White Sands missile range to provide a temporary office for President John F. Kennedy when he visited the site. When astronauts Neil Armstrong, Mike Collins, and Ed Aldrin returned from the first lunar landing in 1969, they were quarantined in a specially designed Airstream Mobile Quarantine Facility aboard the *U.S.S Hornet.* An Airstream carried the crew of the space shuttle Discovery to their launch vehicle for their historic nine-day mission; in fact, every shuttle astronaut since has ridden in an Airstream.

In 1967, Airstream was acquired by Beatrice Foods, as part of that company's aggressive acquisition strategy into a bevy of non-food interests. Beatrice made Airstream a division, allowing it, however, to operate autonomously. Airstream continued to produce high quality vehicles, and in 1979, introduced its first motor home. Featuring riveted aluminum construction, like its trailer counterpart, and pioneering a new level of aerodymanic efficiency, the motor home soon became a popular addition to the Airstream line.

However, the gasoline crisis of the 1970s and the resulting economic downturn hit Airstream hard. The company reportedly lost $12 million on sales of $22 million in 1979, and similar losses continued in 1980. Moreover, parent Beatrice was struggling to manage its vast holdings and remain profitable. A new CEO in 1980, James Dutt, began selling off non-core companies, and those that could not provide Beatrice with at least a 20 percent return on net assets. Airstream was among those to go.

1980: Thor Takes Over

When Wade F.B. Thompson and Peter B. Orthwein purchased Airstream in 1980, they had been involved in the recreational vehicle business for only three years. In 1977, the two entrepreneurs had combined their marketing and financial expertise to purchase HI-LO Trailer, a small player in the industry. Under their leadership, HI-LO prospered, and the two looked around for a bigger opportunity. Airstream was an obvious target.

Combining the first two letters of their last names, Thompson and Orthwein formed Thor Industries, Inc. in order to acquire Airstream. The acquisition of the legendary recreational vehicle and motor home manufacturer and the formation of the new company occurred simultaneously on August 29, 1980. The two new owners acted immediately to reverse the downward trend of Airstream's fortunes. They moved to improve quality, reduce costs, strengthen dealer relationships, and enhance their famous product. Within a year, sales had increased to $26 million, and they had achieved net income before taxes of $1 million, a $13 million turnaround.

With Airstream again a profitable enterprise, Thompson and Orthwein searched for another likely acquisition. In 1982, they purchased the recreational vehicle operations of Commodore Corporation. Known in Canada as General Coach, this new addition to the Thor line manufactured travel trailers and motor homes in British Columbia and Ontario. Under Thor, General Coach would build Citation and Corsair travel trailers, fifth wheels, motor homes, and truck campers, and maintain one of the highest customer satisfaction indexes and lowest warranty costs of any North American recreational vehicle manufacturer.

In 1984, Thor went public, and in 1986 gained listing on the New York Stock Exchange. That year, *Forbes* magazine ranked Thor sixth out of 200 best small companies in America. In 1987, *Money* magazine named Airstream travel trailers one of 99 ''best-made products'' in America.

Growth and Expansion: 1988 and Beyond

On September 8, 1988, Thor entered the small- and mid-size bus industry with the acquisition of El Dorado, a company based in Salina, Kansas. Under Thor, El Dorado would more than quadruple its sales—all from internal growth—to become the largest manufacturer of small buses in the United States. The Thor acquisition of National Coach, a bankrupt builder of mid-size buses, followed in 1991. Under Thor, National would become its parent's most profitable bus operation. Finally, in 1998, Thor added Champion to its bus-manufacturing group.

Meanwhile, Thompson and Orthwein continued to make strategic acquisitions on the recreational vehicle side. Dutchmen, purchased in 1991, became Thor's largest towable company and a major profit center. Motor home manufacturer Four Winds International, acquired in 1992, became Thor's largest company by the turn of the century. Four Winds was a major supplier to most of the large recreational vehicle rental operations throughout the United States and Canada. CruiseAmerica, the largest of these operators, agreed to make Four Winds its primary supplier after Thor provided financing so that CruiseAmerica's former owners could repurchase their company. As a result of that transaction, Thor expected sales of some $30 million to CruiseAmerica in 2001.

In 1995, Thor introduced the lightweight Aerolite, a laminated, aerodynamic European-style travel trailer. Sold at an affordable price, the Aerolite proved ideal for towing behind smaller cars as well as mini-vans and sports-utility vehicles. Sales of this model in 2000 hit all-time records. Thor California started up in 1995 with the introduction of two new lines of travel trailers and fifth wheel vehicles, Tahoe and Wanderer. In less than five years, Tahoe or Wanderer had become the best-selling vehicle of its kind in Colorado, Arizona, Nevada, New Mexico, and Alberta, Canada.

If Thor executives had succeeded, another major addition would have taken place in 2000. That year, the company made two strong attempts to purchase Coachmen Industries Inc., a major motor home and modular home manufacturer. Had the deal gone through, it would have made Thor the second largest motor home builder in the United States. However, in April 2000, Coachmen's board rejected Thor's April 17 bid of $289.6 million in a cash and stock transaction. According to Thor's 2000 Annual Report, ''Although this offer was a substantial premium above Coachmen's price and we made it clear we wished to complete a friendly transaction, our proposal was rejected by Coachmen's board of directors and withdrawn by us.''

Acquisitions aside, Thor was also cultivating a sense of civic responsibility as part of its corporate culture. Specifically, Thor took the lead in raising the awareness level of prostate cancer and in encouraging its early detection. Its ''Drive against Prostate Cancer,'' inspired by the company's chairman, president and CEO, Wade Thompson, a cancer survivor, offered free screening to more than 8,000 men and raised significant funds for cancer research. The New York Stock Exchange recognized Thor's public service initiative by offering company executives the opportunity to ring the stock market's closing bell on June 16, 2000.

Looking Ahead

As it entered 2001, Thor believed that the $8 billion recreational vehicle industry, which included about 75 manufacturers, would continue to consolidate. Thompson and Orthwein, who retained control of the company, planned to continue to seek acquisition opportunities in recreational vehicles, buses, and related industries.

Some industry observers agreed with Thor executives that, as baby boomers move into their 50s and 60s—the target recreational vehicle demographic—sales would enjoy significant growth. They pointed out that, between 2000 and 2005, four million people, or 11,000 potential new buyers each day, would turn 50. Other analysts, however, observed an industry-wide decrease in demand for recreational vehicles in 2000, due to higher interest rates, lower consumer confidence levels, and rising gasoline prices, as a cause of concern, at least in the short run.

Meanwhile, the company's bus business was on track to continued success. In the growing $700 million mid-size bus industry, Thor had an estimated 35 percent market share and was larger than its next three competitors combined. Major bus customers included rental car companies, who used the buses to ferry customers around airports, New Jersey Transit, the Los Angeles Department of Transportation, Cal Trans, and Marriott Hotels. Believing that fuel cells were the power of the future, Thor announced in 2000 that the company would build the world's first commercially viable fuel-cell-powered, zero-emissions transit buses, in an exclusive alliance with International Fuel Cells (IFC), Inc., a United Technologies company, and ISE Research. (IFC's fuel cells had powered every NASA space shuttle mission.) The first fuel-cell-powered bus was scheduled to be built in California in 2001. Thor had exclusive rights for the use of IFC's fuel cells in the complete drive system, called ThunderPower, for all North American mid-sized buses.

Principal Divisions

Airstream; Four Winds; Dutchmen; Komfort; Thor America; Thor California; General Coach America; Aero Coach; El Dorado National; Champion; Thor Bus.

Principal Operating Units

Recreation Vehicles; Buses.

Principal Competitors

Coachmen Industries, Inc.; Fleetwood Enterprises, Inc.; Winnebago Industries Inc.

Further Reading

Burkhart, Bryan, and David Hunt, *Airstream: The History of the Land Yacht,* San Francisco: Chronicle Books, 2000.

Byam, Wally, *Trailer Travel Here and Abroad: The New Way to Adventurous Living,* New York: McKay, 1960.

Innis, Jack, ''A Legend in its Own Time,'' *Trailer Life,* February 1998, pp. 52–60.

Kachadourian, Gail, ''Coachmen Rejects Thor's Takeover Bid,'' *Automotive News,* May, 8, 2000, p. 24.

Santiago, Chiori, ''House Trailers Have Come a Long Way, Baby,'' *Smithsonian,* June 1998, pp. 76–85.

Setton, Dolly, ''Demographic Play,'' *Forbes,* August 9, 1999, p. 136.

White, Roger B., *Home on the Road: The Motor Home in America,* Washington, D.C.: Smithsonian Institution Press, 2000.

—Margery M. Heffron

THQ, Inc.

27001 Agoura Road, Suite 325
Calabasas Hills, California 91301
U.S.A.
Telephone: (818) 871-5000
Fax: (818) 871-7400
Web site: http://www.thq.com

Public Company
Incorporated: 1990
Sales: $302.36 million
Employees: 390
Stock Exchanges: NASDAQ
Ticker Symbol: THQI
NAIC: 51121 Software Publishers

THQ, Inc. is a leading developer of gaming software for use on dedicated play stations, portable game players, and computers. The company produces a combination of licensed and self-developed titles. The licensed products include games based on WWF Wrestling, Scooby-Doo, Rugrats, Power Rangers, MTV Sports, and the *Star Wars* and *Evil Dead* motion pictures. Through its recently acquired Volition, Inc., subsidiary, the company produces original games such as Summoner and Descent. THQ games are primarily sold in the United States, but the company also has distribution arms in the United Kingdom, France, Germany, and Australia. The game industry has recently been developing new products with on-line components, and THQ is following this trend, as indicated by its purchase of the online gaming firm Genetic Anomalies, Inc., in 1999, its introduction of a wrestling game in 2000 with on-line features, and its preparation of games for Microsoft's on-line-capable Xbox platform, due for release in fall 2001.

1990s Beginnings

THQ was founded by Jack Friedman, a toy industry veteran. Friedman had entered the business with LJN Toys in the mid-1960s and had risen to the position of company president 20 years later. After LJN was purchased by entertainment conglomerate MCA, Inc., Friedman grew disenchanted with work-ing for a giant corporation and left to start his own company. In April 1990 he formed THQ, Inc., investing $1 million of his own money. The name was short for "Toy Headquarters," and the company, based in Calabasas, California, planned to produce a full line of toys including dolls, board games, and electronic games.

Soon after its formation, the company purchased Broderbund Software's video games division, and the first products came to market in October. Some early offerings were Peter Pan and the Pirates board games and action figures and Videomation and Wayne Gretzky Hockey games. THQ staffers came up with ideas for the products, but contracted out the actual design and manufacturing to other firms.

Needing cash to develop new product licenses, in the summer of 1991 Friedman merged THQ with Trinity Acquisition Corporation. The publicly traded Trinity had been formed some time earlier to raise capital for as yet unrealized ventures. The new entity retained the name of THQ, Inc. and continued to trade on the NASDAQ exchange. By the end of its first full year THQ, with 16 employees, had achieved annual sales of $33 million. The company could boast of two genuine hits: a video game based on the popular movie *Home Alone* and another drawn from the successful *Where's Waldo* book series. THQ video games were licensed to run on Nintendo game stations, and the company had recently extended its contract with Nintendo to allow it to market the games beyond North America to Europe, Australia, and parts of Asia. Nintendo manufactured the games, which were designed by THQ and programmed by an outside software company. Each of these parties took a cut of the profits, as did the licensor of the game's subject matter.

In the spring of 1992, THQ began working with Nintendo rival Sega to produce games for that company's home play system. THQ was also developing games for Nintendo's portable Game Boy units. Again needing more working capital, the company issued a secondary stock offering, selling 1.5 million shares at $4 each. THQ was actively seeking more licenses from popular entertainment or sports commodities on which to base products. Although its sales were rapidly climbing, its net profits were flat, due in part to problems with the dollar in overseas markets and higher product development and promotion costs. In 1993 Jack Friedman agreed to take an 11 percent pay cut and give up his options on 2.2 million shares of stock. Nonetheless, the company's founder was still earning a handsome $850,000 per year and held options on 1 million shares. During that same year, THQ purchased a Chicago-based home and arcade software company, Black Pearl Software. Black Pearl would retain an office in Chicago but moved its headquarters to Calabasas.

A Financial Crisis in 1993

Struggling to come up with new hits in an increasingly competitive and costly marketplace, the company saw its net profits begin to shrink, then turn into losses, which mounted quickly. Sales for 1993 reached $37.5 million, but losses totaled $16.2 million. The next year was even bleaker, with revenues of only $13.3 million and losses of $17.5 million. The company attempted to stop the hemorrhaging of money by cutting costs and even selling 3.5 million shares of stock for 50 cents apiece, but this had little impact. Finally, in 1995 founder Jack Friedman departed, turning over the reins to the chief financial officer, Brian J. Farrell.

In the months preceding Friedman's departure, THQ had focused on developing games for the new Nintendo Super NES platform, but this platform wound up being less popular than Sega's Genesis system. Sitting on a huge backlog of unsold Super NES games, Farrell immediately instituted strict inventory control procedures. He also eliminated half of THQ's staff of 60.

Using a new marketing tactic, Farrell decided to focus on supplying the needs of consumers who were still using older game platforms and avoid gambling on which new system would be most popular. Meeting with creditors, many of whom also happened to be product licensors such as Walt Disney Interactive, LucasArts, MTV, and Nickelodeon, Farrell was able to convince them to cut better deals on licenses to produce software for the older 16-bit systems. THQ developed new games that would cost only $9.99 to $14.99, compared with $40 to $60 for games for the most recent platforms. The company also increased its offerings, debuting 24 new games in 1995, more than twice the number it had introduced in 1994. The results were swift and gratifying. 1995 sales rebounded to more than $33 million, with a net profit of $600,000. The company was also able to establish a distribution office in the United Kingdom during the year.

Results for 1996 were even better, with sales reaching $50.2 million and profits hitting $1.9 million. The company released more than 30 titles and also invested in a software maker, Inland

Productions, Inc., and acquired a design company, Heliotrope Studios, Inc. Deciding that the time was right to re-enter the big leagues, THQ began to design games for the newly released 64-bit systems. It struck a major new licensing agreement with World Championship Wrestling (WCW) to produce games based on its players, who included Hulk Hogan and Macho Man Randy Savage. The company was now making games for Nintendo's portable Game Boy, Sony's PlayStation, and for personal computers, in addition to Nintendo's other platforms. The Christmas shopping season of 1997 saw copies of WCW versus NWO:World Tour flying off the shelves, with nearly 40 percent of the company's $90 million in sales for the year coming from the wrestling game.

The bubble appeared to burst the following spring, however, when THQ lost the WCW license to its arch rival, Electronic Arts, in a bidding war. Within two days, THQ's stock value dropped by 40 percent. Quickly bouncing back, the ever-resilient Farrell obtained a license from Nickelodeon to make games based on the hit cartoon Rugrats and within a year had replaced the wrestling deal with a license from WCW's chief competitor, the World Wrestling Federation (WWF).

Late 1990s Acquisitions and More Sports-Based Games

During 1998 the company added two new subsidiaries. It purchased 3D graphics developer GameFX, Inc. for 246,000 shares of stock and $790,000 in cash. The Massachusetts-based firm was soon joined by German software distributor Rushware Microhandelsgesellschaft mbH, acquired for $6 million. Despite the loss of the WCW contract, THQ was allowed to produce its licensed games into 1999, and the company had successful offerings in WCW/NWO Revenge, WCW Nitro, and WCW/NWO Thunder. It conducted major advertising campaigns for the launch of these games, as well as for the company's Rugrats: Search for Reptar, targeted at children seven to 12 years old. THQ was now realizing 55 percent of its revenues from 64-bit Nintendo games, 30 percent from Sony PlayStation, and eight percent from Nintendo Game Boy. Only two percent came from sales of PC-based games. The majority of revenue, 85 percent, was earned in the United States.

THQ was also developing games that targeted fans of "real" sports, offering Brunswick Bowling, Championship Motocross, and several BASS Masters Classic fishing simulation games in 1999. That same year, THQ made another acquisition in the spring when it purchased Pacific Coast Power & Light Co., a developer of game consoles. It also signed licensing deals with motocross star Ricky Carmichael, MTV Sports, and the makers of TV's "Power Rangers" series. At the end of the year the company also acquired Genetic Anomalies, Inc., bringing THQ a developer of on-line gaming products. This area was heating up, as the possibilities of making games interactive via the Internet seemed to be the next major step for the industry. As the year ended THQ had its best Christmas sales season ever. The company had also moved to a new, larger headquarters site during the year.

The spring of 2000 saw the release of THQ's first on-line wrestling game, WWF With Authority, developed by Genetic Anomalies. The game could be played on-line in real time

<table>
<tr><td colspan="2" align="center">**Key Dates:**</td></tr>
<tr><td>**1990:**</td><td>Jack Friedman founds THQ and acquires Broderbund Software's video game division.</td></tr>
<tr><td>**1991:**</td><td>THQ becomes a public company after a merger with Trinity Acquisition Corporation.</td></tr>
<tr><td>**1993:**</td><td>The company acquires Black Pearl Software.</td></tr>
<tr><td>**1994:**</td><td>Sales stall, and losses reach $17.5 million for the year.</td></tr>
<tr><td>**1995:**</td><td>Friedman exits, and Brian Farrell is named CEO as the company's focus shifts to cheaper 16-bit games.</td></tr>
<tr><td>**1996:**</td><td>The company invests in Inland Productions, Inc. and acquires Heliotrope Studios, Inc.</td></tr>
<tr><td>**1999:**</td><td>THQ signs a deal with the World Wrestling Federation and moves to new headquarters.</td></tr>
<tr><td>**2000:**</td><td>THQ is named a key publisher of games for forthcoming Microsoft Xbox system.</td></tr>
</table>

against another player anywhere in the world. Other features included chat capabilities and a world ranking system.

The volatile nature of the gaming marketplace was affecting THQ again, however, and the company announced in May that it would lose significantly more money than it had expected during the year. A transition in game console technology was pegged as the cause. It still had new ventures in the works, including an investment in Japanese game developer Yuke's Co. Ltd., a joint venture to market games with the Communication Devices division of Siemens AG of Germany, and the opening of an Australian office. The company also completed its largest acquisition to date, purchasing Volition, Inc. of Illinois for approximately $20 million. Volition was an established designer of original game concepts such as Descent and Freespace, and THQ had earlier teamed with the company to create Summoner and Red Faction. In September, THQ announced it would begin developing games for the newly announced Microsoft Xbox game system, due out in the fall of 2001. New releases included several more WWF titles and games based on television quiz show ''Who Wants to Be a Millionaire,'' the *Star Wars* and *Evil Dead* movie series, and cartoon dog Scooby-Doo.

In only ten years, THQ had grown to become one of the top three independent video game makers in the United States. It offered what proved a winning mix of sports- and entertainment-based titles along with select original concepts. The company was now reaping the benefits of the hard lessons learned during its formative years. As the industry moved toward development of on-line gaming products, THQ appeared likely to remain a leader in its field.

Principal Subsidiaries

Black Pearl Software, Inc.; GameFx; Genetic Anomalies, Inc.; Heliotrope Studios, Inc.; Malibu Games, Inc.; Pacific Coast Power & Light Company; THQ Asia Pacific Pty. Ltd.; THQ Deutschland GmbH; THQ France; THQ International Ltd.; Volition, Inc.

Principal Competitors

The 3DO Company; Acclaim Entertainment, Inc.; Activision, Inc.; Electronic Arts, Inc.; Hasbro, Inc.; Havas SA; Infogrames Entertainment SA; Infogrames, Inc.; LucasArts Entertainment Company LLC; Microsoft Corporation; Midway Games, Inc.; Nintendo Co., Ltd.; SEGA Corporation; Take-Two Interactive Software, Inc.; The Walt Disney Company.

Further Reading

Dunphy, Laura, ''Spate of Recent Deals Boosts Video-Game Maker THQ,'' *Los Angeles Business Journal*, September 11, 2000, p. 21.
''Heavy Losses Continue for Game Maker THQ Inc.,'' *Los Angeles Times*, April 4, 1995, p. 2.
Huffstutter, P.J., ''THQ Shares Take a Hit from Video Games Console Wars,'' *Los Angeles Times*, May 26, 2000, p. C3.
''Loss of License to Wrestling Hurts THQ,'' *Consumer Multimedia Report*, March 23, 1998.
MacCallum, Martha, ''Power Lunch—THQ Chairman & CEO Interview,'' *CNBC/Dow Jones Business Video*, August 25, 1999.
O'Steen, Kathleen, ''CEO's Sense of Integrity, Ethics Cited Reputation: People Have Faith in THQ Leader Because of his Honest and Straightforward Manner, Supporters Say,'' *Los Angeles Times*, October 26, 1999, p. B6.
Peltz, James F., ''THQ Inc. to Develop Software for Sega Videos,'' *Los Angeles Times*, May 26, 1992, p. 4.
——, ''THQ's Video-Game Success Comes With Betting on Winners,'' *Los Angeles Times*, December 24, 1991, p. 9A.
''THQ Bags Developer, Inks MTV, Bodacious Rodeo and Motocross Deals,'' *mmWire*, May 18, 1999.
''THQ Chief Executive to Take 11% Pay Cut,'' *Los Angeles Times*, March 16, 1993, p. 2.
''THQ Hopes for Strike with 'Brunswick Circuit Pro Bowling','' *Multimedia Publisher*, November 1, 1998.
''THQ Shares Slide After Loss of Wrestling License to Electronic Arts,'' *Dow Jones Online News*, March 11, 1998.
Young, D.B., ''Taking Stock of the 3rd Quarter: THQ Among Valley's Top Gainers,'' *Los Angeles Times*, October 12, 1999, p. B2.

—Frank Uhle

TV AZTECA

TV Azteca, S.A. de C.V.

Periferico Sur 4121
Mexico City, D.F. 14141
Mexico
Telephone: (525) 420-1313
Fax: (525) 420-1456
Web site: http://www.tvazteca.com.mx

Public Company
Incorporated: 1993 as Contraladora Mexicana de
    Comunicaciones, S.A. de C.V.
Employees: 2,700
Sales: 4.11 billion pesos ($433.81 million) (1999)
Stock Exchanges: Mexico City; New York (for American
    Depositary Receipts)
Ticker Symbol: TV AZTCA; TZA
NAIC: 51221 Record Producers; 51312 Television
    Broadcasting; 513322 Cellular and Other Wireless
    Telecommunications; 54191 On-Line Information
    Systems; 551112 Offices of Other Holding
    Companies; 711211 Sports Teams and Clubs

TV Azteca, S.A. de C.V. is a Mexican holding company that, through its three principal subsidiaries, is engaged in the broadcasting and production of television programs and the sale of advertising time. One of these subsidiaries, Television Azteca, S.A. de C.V. (commonly called TV Azteca), operates two national networks and is the only commercial rival to Grupo Televisa, S.A. de C.V., which is the world's largest Spanish-language media company. TV Azteca also owns a soccer team, a record company, two television stations in Central America, a share in a wireless telephone company, and an Internet portal.

Televisa's First Rival: 1993–95

The story of TV Azteca may be traced to Contraladora Mexicana de Comunicaciones, S.A. de C.V., the government corporation in charge of two of Mexico City's seven over-the-air VHF television stations and their network for transmission to other Mexican stations. Founded in 1969 as a concession to Francisco Aguirre Jimenez, one of these channels, Channel 13, had been returned to public status in 1972. This station and some others, including Channel 7, were later grouped under the Instituto Mexicano de Television (Imevision). The offerings of this body were so little to the public taste that a joke ran that the best way to get away with murder was to commit it in front of Imevision's cameras, since no one would be watching. By 1988, 65 to 80 percent of Imevision's budget was going to meet its payroll, and practically no funds were available for producing programming. Much studio equipment reportedly was stolen, and what remained was largely obsolete. Some 40 percent of the regional stations that retransmitted Imevision's offerings were virtually or completely off the air.

The government put Channel 13 and Channel 7 (which was merely retransmitting 13's programming) up for auction in 1993. They were purchased by Ricardo Salinas Pliego, owner of Grupo Elektra, S.A. de C.V., a chain of stores selling electronic products, appliances, and furniture, purchased the station. Through one of his companies, Radiotelevisora del Centro, S.A., Salinas Pliego submitted the winning bid of two billion pesos ($642.7 million), which was far higher than any other offer. This money came from Salinas Pliego and the other owners of Grupo Elektra; a credit syndicate; and Alsavicion, a firm founded by the textile tycoon Alberto Saba Raffoul. It would later be alleged that conditions surrounding the sale had been unfair, with stories surfacing that the unsuccessful bidders had been told that $450 million would be the ceiling. Moreover, it would later be learned that Salinas Pliego had received about $30 million in loans during the time of the purchase from the notorious Raul Salinas, the corrupt brother of a former Mexican president who was eventually imprisoned for conspiracy to assassinate a political foe. Regardless of the conditions, the purchase was finalized and included a film studio converted to television production and a chain of unprofitable movie theaters that was later disposed of.

Named TV Azteca, the new enterprise was pitted against Grupo Televisa, which owned four of the Mexico City over-the-air VHF stations. (The seventh remained under the control of a public body.) Salinas Pliego, who assumed administrative responsibilities, set about cancelling low-rated programs, launching others that could be produced or acquired abroad cheaply, and cutting the work force from 1,500 to 750. He also offered advertisers—only 18 at the time of purchase—rates far below those of Televisa and put Channel 7 into production.

Salinas Pliego invested money in new studios and updated the transmission network. By mid-1994 Channel 13 was reaching 85 percent of Mexican homes and Channel 7 was reaching 65 percent. Moreover, the company asserted, Channel 13 had raised its market share during prime time from four to 16 percent.

While such moves clearly gave TV Azteca a strong presence in the industry, some critics found fault with the network offerings. Interviewed by the Mexican business magazine *Expansion,* Salinas Pliego defended TV Azteca's frankly commercial orientation. Declaring that "Television is the most democratic medium that there is: people decide with the channel selector what they want," he suggested that criticism of TV Azteca's programming was coming from "a small group of intellectuals who have nothing better to do."

TV Azteca first brought in such programming as soap operas from Europe, Brazil, and other Latin countries. The company also entered a partnership with NBC that gave it exclusive rights to transmit certain programs—NBC Nightly News, four television serials, and about 20-odd films—but that relationship eventually ended. To guarantee popular sports programming, the company bought professional soccer teams in Veracruz and Morelia. By the end of 1995 Channel 13 was reaching 91 percent of all Mexican households with televisions, and Channel 7 was reaching 81 percent. Revenues rose from about $60 million in 1994 to about $150 million in 1995. Also in 1995, TV Azteca hired Argos Comunicaciones to produce a popular semidocumentary police show called "Expediente 13/22:30" (File 13/22:30). This and future Argos productions were characterized by scenes filmed outside the studios, and the kind of care and technical realization more characteristic of feature films or theater than television.

TV Azteca's Golden Year: 1996–97

In 1996 TV Azteca turned to Argos for the popular *telenovelas* format pioneered by Grupo Televisa. Although of-

ten likened to U.S. soap operas, *telenovelas* had a finite life span—usually six to nine months—and appeared in prime time slots as well as during the day. TV Azteca's first *telenovela, Nada personal* (Nothing Personal), revolutionized the format by basing the show on the seamy realities of Mexican public life. In the first episode of the series a prominent politician was assassinated, reminding viewers of the recent murder of the presidential candidate for Mexico's ruling Institutional Revolutionary Party (PRI). The 150-episode prime-time show, with storylines featuring drug-dealing criminals and corrupt policemen, was largely shot in recognizable public places in and around Mexico City. TV Azteca invested $5 million in this production.

TV Azteca followed up *Nada personal* with *Mirada de mujer* (A Woman's Gaze), a popular *telenovela* about a woman who seeks to avenge her husband's philandering by taking a young lover. Another program, *Ciudad desnuda* (Naked City), a documentary, used hidden cameras to expose crimes even as they occurred, while the show *Te cache* (I Caught You) was a 1990s version of "Candid Camera." Moreover, the company introduced an Oprah-like talk show uniting guests with long-lost relatives. The company's nightly news program presented a young, irreverent anchorman to counter Televisa's establishment image—and its close ties to the ruling PRI. TV Azteca more than doubled its revenues in 1996, to about $305 million. Also in 1996, the company introduced Azteca Music, a producer of compact discs associated with Warner Music.

The founding company was reincorporated as TV Azteca in 1996 and offered shares to the public the following year, raising an impressive $604 million in Mexico City and New York for 21 percent of the shares. Shareholder Saba Raffoul then sold his stake of about 22 percent to Salinas Pliego, cashing in $400 million immediately (with $92 million more paid later in the year and still more due later) for his original investment of $180 million. Salinas Pliego ultimately increased his share of the company to 73 percent. In 1997, TV Azteca marketed $425 million in bonds abroad, most of which went to repay bank loans for the original purchase, then sold $255 million more to buy back the stock options coming due to the creditor banks.

TV Azteca reached, in this year, the zenith of its fortunes in the 1990s. Revenues climbed about 60 percent, to $511 million. Its profit margin, in terms of operating income, was a sensational 43 percent. The company's share of the prime-time weekday audience in Mexico City rose to 35 percent, compared to only 14 percent in 1994. TV Azteca also claimed to have a larger share of higher-income viewers than rival Televisa. By now it had enrolled hundreds of advertisers, including such blue-chip clients as Bayer, Burger King, DHL, Jose Cuervo, Nissan, and Volkswagen. Seeking more markets, TV Azteca purchased a 75-percent interest in an El Salvador station intended as the axis of a national network and 75 percent of a UHF station in Guatemala City.

New Shows and New Markets: 1998–2000

However, in 1998 TV Azteca surrendered some of these gains. After *Mirada de mujer* concluded in April, the company lost 15 to 20 percent of its prime-time viewers. *Tentaciones* (Temptations), a *telenovela* about a priest in love, offended some of Mexico's Catholics and failed to find sponsors. *Demasiado corazon* (Too Much Heart) was also a failure. Weekday prime-time viewership in Mexico City dropped to 25 percent for the year, resulting in disappointing advertising receipts, because such receipts were based on ratings. The company brought in a new chief financial officer during this time, 31-year-old New Yorker Adrian Steckel, who had been with the company since the beginning, serving as Salinas Pliego's assistant and then vice-president of business operations. In addition to overseeing the financial future of the company, Steckel was often tapped for public relations duties, acting as spokesperson in times of controversy. Although the company's net revenues still posted a modest gain and operating profit came to a solid 36 percent, high financing costs reduced net income to less than $7 million. Near the end of the year, TV Azteca formed a joint venture with a smaller television company to operate and provide programming for Channel 40, a Mexico City UHF station. It also negotiated an agreement with the programming division of Walt Disney Television International for rights to broadcast Disney movies, television series, and children's programming in Mexico. The company repositioned the Channel 7 network for children and young adults, retaining Channel 13 as the flagship network.

During 1999 TV Azteca retained its share of the prime-time audience, but its revenues slumped by 19 percent in real terms, to 4.11 billion pesos ($433.81 million), and it incurred a net loss of 158.96 million pesos ($16.77 million). The company blamed the revenue decline mainly on lower advertising sales in real pesos because it had not adjusted rates to compensate for double-digit inflation. A 36 percent rate increase was announced for 2000. TV Azteca also noted a lack of special events to attract viewers during the year, such as the world soccer championships in Mexico in 1998; thereafter it divested itself of its interest in the Veracruz soccer team. During 1999 Channel 13's programming was available in 97 percent of Mexican households, while Channel 7's was reaching 94 percent. All but 39 stations outside Mexico City were retransmitters; the remainder were in other metropolitan areas and were presenting some local content as well. TV Azteca was producing about half of its own programming and, during the year, sold about $20 million worth of its programming, including two *telenovelas* to Telemundo, a U.S.-based Hispanic network. Azteca Music released 32 recordings in 1999.

During the summer of 1999, popular game- and talk-show host Francisco (Paco) Stanley was brazenly gunned down in broad daylight not far from TV Azteca's studios in Mexico City. The company launched an offensive against the city's mayor, presidential candidate Cuahtemoc Cardenas, blaming him for the area's high crime rate. City prosecutors countered by arresting several of Stanley's colleagues and charging them with the murder. TV Azteca's image also suffered a blow when Stanley was linked with drug dealers, following the revelation that cocaine had been found in his pocket at the time of the murder. In 2001, however, a judge threw out the case against the defendants.

Controversy continued, as Salinas Pliego enraged minority shareholders of TV Azteca in 1999 by using company funds to buy a 50-percent stake in his low-cost fixed wireless telephone service Unefon S.A., despite repeated pledges earlier not to do

so. In 2000 TV Azteca purchased 50 percent of another Salinas company, Todito.com, S.A. de C.V., an Internet portal with the exclusive right to distribute over the Internet all TV Azteca content. Also in 2000, TV Azteca agreed to sell EchoStar Satellite Corp. exclusive rights for three years to transmit Channel 13's programming to the United States via DTH all-digital satellite technology.

TV Azteca's most popular new telenovelas in 2000 were *Todo por amor* (All for Love), *El amor no es como lo pintan* (Love Isn't How It's Painted), *La calle de las novias* (The Street of Girlfriends), and *Tio Alberto* (Uncle Albert). Continuing from 1999 was *El candidato* (The Candidate), which recalled *Nada personal* in treating formerly taboo themes such as vote buying and the links between corrupt politicians and police and drug kingpins. The last episode of that series aired three weeks before Mexico's presidential election. TV Azteca's most popular talk show during this time was *Cosas de la vida* (Real Life). Broadcast in the afternoon, it was being seen regularly in 1.5 million of Mexico's nine million households.

In 2000 Argos severed its links with TV Azteca, frustrated that Salinas Pliego would not allow it to profit from the resale of the programs it produced. TV Azteca then turned to Columbia Pictures Television Inc. and a unit of Pearson plc. The former was to co-produce films, and later, *telenovelas,* while Pearson was to continue to produce programs for TV Azteca such as the game show *La venta incredible* (Incredible Sale) and perhaps *telenovelas.* Meantime, Argos went to work for the Spanish-language U.S. network Telemundo. TV Azteca was planning to join Pappas Telecasting Cos., the largest private owner of U.S. television stations, in a new Spanish-language network, Azteca America Inc., which would debut in 2001, with TV Azteca owning 20 percent. The Salinas Pliego family controlled 62.5 percent of TV Azteca's shares in 1999, mostly through Azteca Holdings. The company's long-term liabilities came to 4.04 billion pesos ($425.9 million) at the end of 1999. As management hoped to restore the profits and reputation of TV Azteca to the heights of its 1996 season, efforts were focused primarily on new program development; game show and situation comedy formats were both being explored in the quest to captivate the Mexican audience.

Principal Subsidiaries

Azteca Digital, S.A. de C.V.; Grupo TV Azteca, S.A. de C.V.; Television Azteca, S.A. de C.V.

Principal Competitors

Grupo Televisa, S.A. de C.V.

Further Reading

Barragan, Maria Antonieta, "Asalto al cuartel azteca," *Expansion,* March 25, 1998, pp. 40–42.

"A Bunch of Angry Stockholders," *Business Week,* June 28, 1999, p. 66.

Castellanos, Camilla, "TV Titans Face Off," *Business Mexico,* July 2000, pp. 36+.

Guenete, Louise, "Sin miedo a la libertad," *Expansion,* November 22, 2000, pp. 170+.

Huerta, Jose Ramon, ''Audiencia garantizada,'' *Expansion,* January 14, 1998, pp. 24–26.

——, ''Noticias del otro imperio,'' *Expansion,* June 4, 1997, pp. 19 + .

Hope, Maria, ''Del caos, hacia donde?'' *Expansion,* May 25, 1994, pp. 142 + .

Millman, Joel, ''Mexican Billionaire Enjoys Good Timing,'' *Wall Street Journal,* August 22, 1997, p. A10.

Miro, Juan Jose, *La television y el poder politico en Mexico,* Mexico City: Editorial Diana, 1997.

Moore, Leslie, ''A Year Later, Azteca Loses Its Gold,'' *Electronic Media,* January 25, 1999, p. 100.

——, ''Youthful Spirit,'' *LatinFinance,* May 1998, pp. 49.

Paxman, Andrew, ''The New TV Azteca,'' *Business Mexico,* November 1993, pp. 39–41.

Preston, Julia, ''As Mexico Mourns TV Figure, Cocaine Clouds the Picture,'' *New York Times,* June 10, 1999, p. A3.

——, ''An Upstart Mexican Television Network Gets a Bit Personal,'' *New York Times,* July 22, 1996, pp. D1, D3.

Robertson, Anne, ''Hispanic Network Debuts,'' *Business Journal— Serving Phoenix & the Valley of the Sun,* September 15, 2000, p. 16.

Robinson, Edward A., ''Sex, Drugs, *AND* Dinero,'' *Fortune,* November 10, 1997, pp. 163 + .

Tangeman, Michael, ''TV Azteca's Global Signal,'' *Institutional Investor,* January 1998, pp. 83–84.

''TV Azteca: Mexico's Crowd-Pleaser,'' *Euromoney,* December 1998, p. 66.

Torres, Craig, ''Mexico's TV Azteca and Its Chairman Regain Their Credibility After Scandal,'' *Wall Street Journal,* February 3, 1997, p. A9.

—Robert Halasz

Ukrop's Super Market's, Inc.

600 Southlake Boulevard
Richmond, Virginia 23236
U.S.A.
Telephone: (804) 794-2401
Fax: (804) 794-7557
Web site: http://www.ukrops.com

Private Company
Incorporated: 1937
Employees: 5,600
Sales: $575 million (2000 est.)
NAIC: 44511 Supermarkets and Other Grocery (Except
    Convenience) Stores

Ukrop's Super Market's, Inc. operates a chain of 27 grocery stores in Virginia, primarily in the Richmond area, where it is the market leader. Ukrop's stores, known for their broad selection of goods, feature prepared foods made at the company's central kitchen, which produces more than 150 prepared food items, including complete prepackaged meals. Owned and managed by the Ukrop family, the chain sells no alcohol and closes on Sundays, yet it manages to dominate a market populated by large national chains. In 2000, Ukrop's controlled 38.9 percent of the market for grocery sales in the greater Richmond area.

1930s Origins

As a supermarket chain, Ukrop's began modestly, a characteristic that would describe the company's existence during its first half-century of business. The first store, started by husband and wife Joe and Jacquelin Ukrop, opened in 1937 in Richmond, Virginia. Located on Hull Street, the first store belied the grandeur of the Ukrop's that would follow in its wake, measuring 16 feet wide and 32 feet long. In their garage-sized store, the Ukrops made $23 in their first day's sales, a total that thrilled Joe Ukrop.

The store survived the last years of the century's most devastating economic crisis, eventually becoming a fixture in the Richmond area. Despite the success of the store, Joe and Jacque-

lin were in no hurry to open a second store. Instead, the Ukrops were content with running a single store and leading a simple life. Devout Baptists, the Ukrops raised their children according to their faith, closed the store on Sundays, and sold no alcohol. Jacquelin cooked lunch for the employees, and Joe frequently lent a hand to neighboring farmers, closing the store when the demands of harvest season required his help. The Ukrops demonstrated no interest in parlaying the success of one store to finance the establishment of another store. In fact, 26 years separated the opening of the first store from the debut of the second Ukrop's, time enough for the Ukrop's children to mature and take an active role in the leadership of the family business.

1960s: A Second Store and a Second Generation

James Ukrop joined the business at his father's side in 1960 and began laying the seeds for the company's first expansion. A second store opened three years later, beginning an initial expansion spree that brought the store count to five by the time James's younger brother Robert joined the family business. When Robert Ukrop joined the company in 1972—serving as manager of two Richmond stores—Ukrop's controlled seven percent of the grocery market in Richmond. By comparison, the market leader, Safeway, commanded 35 percent of the market, far outdistancing the independent and privately owned Ukrop organization. When Robert Ukrop joined the company, however, his brother, who served as chief executive officer, and his father, who served as chairman, were ready to begin another major expansion drive. In addition to new stores, the company purchased a bakery as part of its 1970s expansion program. The success of the bakery taught the Ukrops the efficiencies that they could achieve through a central production site, which served as a key lesson in later years when the company reached the defining moment in its history. By 1981, after a steady stream of new store openings, Ukrop's had closed the distance on its much larger rivals, laying claim to 26 percent of the market.

Ukrop's command of the Richmond market was impressive, especially in light of the company's insistence on remaining closed on Sundays and refusing to sell beer or wine. Observers credited the company's unwavering focus on details, which was a by-product of the Ukrop's signature trait: its attention to

Company Perspectives:

We're a chain of grocery stores. But chances are, we're unlike any other supermarket you've seen. The difference is all in our attitude. See, we all really like our jobs, and you can tell. Go ahead. Walk into one of our stores. Ask one of our associates a question about a product. You'll get a cheerful response. Make a special request. We'll do everything possible to fulfill it. Shop away. We'll take all those groceries out to the car for you, and carefully pack them in your trunk (and a small "thank you" is tip enough).

customers. Providing superior service enabled the company to differentiate itself from the deep-pocketed national chains with units in the Richmond area. "The people that know them, know them as a company that runs superb foods stores," explained Bill Bishop, a food-retailing analyst, to *Marketing News* in a June 5, 1989 interview. "I think that far and away the most important thing that Ukrop's does is to put their customer number one," Bishop continued, noting "A lot of people say that, but it's not done all that frequently, and they do that." Robert Ukrop reiterated the importance of customer service, explaining to the *Richmond Times-Dispatch* in a June 12, 1996 interview: "Our goal isn't to keep our eye on the market share, but to take care of our customers. People keep score, but that is not what is driving our business. The numbers will take care of themselves if we keep our eyes on our customers."

Perhaps as important as the company's focus on customer service was its extensive investment in employee training and its interest in developing an environment conducive to retaining its employees. As with customer service, Ukrop's success in providing an enjoyable atmosphere for its "associates" came not from articulating such a goal, but through execution—from actually achieving such a goal. The chain refused to sell wine or beer because the Ukrops were devout Baptists, but the chain remained closed on Sundays in deference to its employees. "If you want to be the best place to shop, you have to be the best place to work," Robert Ukrop remarked to *Marketing News* in a June 5, 1989 interview, referring to the long-standing policy of closing the stores on Sundays. Ukrop's ability to compete against an onslaught of national chains was attributable, so industry pundits theorized, to the chain's focus on the fundamental aspects of business. Many retailers proclaimed a commitment to customer service and employee morale, but far fewer actually succeeded in realizing their commitment. By all accounts, Ukrop's delivered on its commitment, presenting Richmond shoppers with an attractive alternative to the swarm of grocery stores in their area.

The distinction in consumers' minds was strong enough to make Ukrop's the largest grocery store operator in Richmond. By the late 1980s, the company controlled 30 percent of the metropolitan region's grocery sales, enabling it to collect nearly $275 million in annual sales. Expansion since the 1960s, pursued at a measured pace, had lifted the store count to 19 by the end of the 1980s, with two more stores in offing. Although the company was frequently presented with requests to open stores beyond the greater Richmond area, the Ukrop family resisted more far-flung

geographic expansion. "We have an advantage being local," Robert Ukrop was quoted as saying in the June 5, 1989 issue of *Marketing News,* adding "We live here, we have friends here. We're able to put our arms around our business."

Prepared Foods Debut in 1989

Despite the family's reluctance to penetrate other markets, it was preparing a bold move in another direction. Remarkably, Ukrop's had achieved its market dominance without the hallmark quality that underpinned its success at the century's end. The company's greatest contribution to grocery store innovation came from research conducted during the mid-1980s, which revealed that changing consumer demographics and lifestyles indicated a growing demand for convenient, restaurant-quality food. The Ukrops decided to tap into the demand and further differentiate themselves from competitors. The result was one of the grocery industry's most lauded success stories of the late 20th century.

Based on their experience with a central bakery, the Ukrops decided to construct a central kitchen to prepare chilled prepared food, which consumers could then re-heat. For those few grocers who offered prepared foods at the time, the common method was to prepare the food items separately at each store. Ukrop's approach ran counter to the norm and received much criticism, but a combination of past experience and financial constraints predicated the reasoning behind establishing a central kitchen. "We realized, from a kitchen point of view, that we couldn't produce out of [each store]," Robert Ukrop explained in the October 1997 issue of *Progressive Grocer.* "We needed it out of one place. Bakery gave us some experience with manufacturing and logistics. We learned that some things are better done centrally." By relying on a single, large kitchen, the chain saved money on equipment and staff, possessed greater control over food quality, and could more precisely supply each store with an accurate supply of food items.

Out of a 10,000-square-foot kitchen, Ukrop's began experimenting with proprietary recipes, concentrating on what it referred to as "homestyle" foods. On Halloween 1989, the company's prepared foods line debuted, featuring ten items that included twice-baked potatoes, lasagna, and macaroni and cheese. It took approximately three years for the kitchen operation to begin generating a profit, but the company's persistence paid off. By 1994, the roster of prepared foods had swelled to a rotating list of 125 items that included chilled soups, grilled chicken breasts, spoon bread, cobblers, meat loaf, and various potato salads. Ukrop's foray into prepared foods became the talk of the industry, accounting for nearly 15 percent of the chain's total sales and adding further incentive to shop at Ukrop's. "They are not the flashiest . . . but what they do, they do very well," a retail consultant remarked in the April 11, 1994 issue of *Supermarket News.* "It wasn't duck a l'orange," the consultant added, "It was very middle America. They obviously know who their customers are."

Expansion in the 1990s

By 1994, with the prepared foods business a confirmed success, Ukrop's began to show signs of a more aggressive approach to expanding the chain. There were 22 stores in operation, generating an estimated $420 million in sales. After doubling the size of the central kitchen, the company purchased two buildings in Richmond in 1994 with a combined 393,000 square feet of space to serve as the future site for the expanded and consolidated bakery and fresh food preparation operations that supplied the chain. Company executives also began charting the chain's expansion beyond Richmond for the first time, looking at sites to the northwest and southeast in Charlottesville and Williamsburg, Virginia. In charge of overseeing the company's expansion was 47-year-old Robert Ukrop, who was named president in August 1994, succeeding his 57-year-old brother James Ukrop, who added the title of vice-chairman and continued to serve as chief executive officer. The company also had six new sites targeted in Richmond, as it readied itself for an unprecedented pace of expansion.

Ukrop's expansion and renovation program began in earnest in 1996, financed for the first time in the company's history by taking on debt. The $125-million program, perceived as a preemptive strike against mounting competition, included relocating stores, expanding existing stores, and adding new locations. The new store openings included the August 1997 debut of a store in Fredericksburg, Virginia, a 63,000-square-foot store that represented the company's first major move beyond the Richmond area. A greater geographical leap followed a month later, when the company's 26th store opened in Charlottesville. Meanwhile, as executives focused on growth, the company's market performance continued to improve despite the distractions of expansion. In 1997, the chain's market share increased to 37.6 percent, keeping the company well in the lead amid intensively competitive conditions.

Midway through the company's expansion and renovation program, management duties among the Ukrop family evolved one more step. Family patriarch Joseph Ukrop was named chairman emeritus in 1998, making room for the appointment of James Ukrop as chairman and the promotion of Robert Ukrop to chief executive officer.

By the end of the decade, the company's expansion program was winding down. Between 1996 and 2000, four new stores were opened, three stores were relocated, and four existing stores were expanded, but the company's expansion activity was expected to diminish as it entered the 21st century. Although the company was reluctant to divulge specifics, analysts predicted three new stores would open by 2005.

One area of the company that was expected to expand in the new century was Ukrop's foray into health-oriented departments within its stores. In November 1999, the company opened its first full-blown health-focused store, which featured a store-within-a-store format. The concept integrated in-store pharmacies with wellness/patient centers that included large natural and organic foods departments staffed by a registered dietitian. The extension of the format chain-wide was expected in the decade ahead, as company executives confirmed that the ''whole-health'' approach was a major focus for the future.

Principal Competitors

Winn-Dixie Stores, Inc.; The Kroger Co.; The Great Atlantic & Pacific Tea Company, Inc.

Further Reading

Coupe, Kevin, '' 'We're Going to Fight','' *Progressive Grocer,* July 1994, p. 52.

Frederick, James, ''Ukrop's Breaking New Ground in Merging Pharmacy,'' *Drug Store News,* August 28, 2000, p. 13.

Gilligan, Gregory J., ''Ukrop's Supermarket Chain Continues Dominance of Richmond, Va., Area,'' *Knight-Ridder/Tribune Business News,* June 11, 1997.

——, ''Virginia-Based Ukrop's Super Markets Inc. Gains Market Share,'' *Knight-Ridder/Tribune Business News,* June 12, 1996.

Hammell, Frank, ''Ukrop's Journey, Outward and Inward,'' *Progressive Grocer,* October 1997, p. 108.

Harper, Roseanne, ''Ukrop's Acquires 2 Sites to Boost Bakery Output,'' *Supermarket News,* August 22, 1994, p. 19.

Kramer, Louise, ''Down-Home Pat,'' *Supermarket News,* April 11, 1994, p. 29.

''Personal Touch, Traditional Values Help Family Grocery Beat 'Giants','' *Marketing News,* June 5, 1989, p. 6.

Tanner, Ronald, ''A New Dimension in Marketing,'' *Progressive Grocer,* May 1987, p. 133.

—Jeffrey L. Covell

Universal Electronics Inc.

6101 Gateway Drive
Cypress, California 90630
U.S.A.
Telephone: (714) 820-1000
Fax: (714) 820-1135
Web site: http://www.ueic.com

Public Company
Incorporated: 1986
Employees: 232
Sales: $125 million (2000)
Stock Exchanges: NASDAQ
Ticker Symbol: UEIC
NAIC: 33431 Audio and Video Equipment
    Manufacturing

Universal Electronics Inc. develops and markets a variety preprogrammed universal control devices, including remote controls, wireless keyboards, and gaming controls. The company's devices control virtually all infrared remote controlled televisions, DVD players, VCRs, cable converters, CD players, audio components, and satellite receivers. Under the All For One brand name, Universal sells its products to retailers overseas, as well as to private label customers and original equipment manufacturers (OEMs). Domestically, the company licenses its proprietary technology and the One For All brand name to third-party companies who, in turn, market the devices to retailers. Universal sells its wireless control devices to private label customers and OEMs in the United States, having abandoned the domestic retail market in 1998. The company also markets a line of home safety and automation products under the Eversafe brand name.

1980s Origins

Incorporated in 1986, Universal began producing its signature and sole product the following year, the All For One television set remote. For founders Frank Doherty, Paul Darbee,

and Frank O'Donnell, the debut of the All For One marked the introduction of a pioneering product, one that they hoped would spark explosive growth for their entrepreneurial creation. Before Universal's remote was released, those who purchased televisions were forced to purchase remotes from the manufacturer of their television. As its name implied, the All For One operated virtually any remote-controlled television, representing a major evolutionary step beyond the capabilities of existing remotes.

The distinction proved to be a marketable one, fueling remarkable growth for the Twinsburg, Ohio-based company. Profit margins were high, enabling the company to finance further advancements in technology. After being developed at the company's research and development center in Anaheim, California, later models of the All For One allowed customers to operate their audio systems and televisions with the same remote. Under the stewardship of Thomas Tyler, Universal's first president and chief executive officer, the company grew at a dizzying pace, drawing the attention of the national business press. From $166,000 in 1988, annual revenue swelled to $50 million by 1992 and reached $89 million in 1993, the year *Business Week* listed Universal as the seventh fastest growing company in the country.

According to research sponsored by Universal, Tyler and his management team could look forward to further tantalizingly substantial growth. In 1993, the year Universal filed with the Securities and Exchange Commission for an initial public offering, the company sold 11.76 million remotes. By 1997, the retail market was expected to expand significantly, with forecasts calling for the sale of 46 million units. The projected growth, according to Universal's estimates, would lift retail sales from the $347 million generated within the market in 1993 to $751 million by 1997. Such prognostications caused a stir of excitement, both at Universal's headquarters and among investors. Company executives signed long-term production contracts, while investors flocked towards Universal's stock, lifting its per share price from $13 to a high of $30.

The enthusiasm swirling around Universal in 1993 was underpinned by the company's technology and the database of information the company had collected to utilize its technology.

Company Perspectives:

Universal Electronics Inc. (UEI) develops technology that simplifies access to entertainment and information in the home. Our company delivers this technology in a variety of ways: as licensed proprietary firmware, as custom and customizable chips, and as turnkey solutions in the form of wireless remotes, keyboards, and other devices. UEI licenses its patented technologies and sells its products to original equipment manufacturers (OEMs), private label retailers and companies involved in the cable and satellite industries worldwide.

Universal maintained a database, or "library," of infrared codes that gave the company's products their ability to communicate with a range of electronic products. The digital codes were obtained by purchasing the original remotes sold with consumer electronics manufacturers' equipment, analyzing the codes in a lab, and then storing the codes on Universal's database, which contained nearly 40,000 individual codes.

The wealth of the company's library, which was augmented on a daily basis, enabled Universal to compete on an international basis. The remotes were manufactured overseas, primarily in Korea by a company named Kimex Electronics, and distributed in 15 other countries. Universal sold its products to retailers such as Kmart, Wal-Mart, Montgomery Ward, Sears, and Circuit City, and to other manufacturers such as Bose, Goldstar, JVC, and Samsung. The company also supplied remotes to cable operators, including Comcast, TCI, Time Warner, and Continental. Although nearly all of Universal's sales were derived from the sale of remotes, the company also sold a line of home safety and automation products under the Eversafe brand name, which it had acquired in 1991 from Eversafe Battery for $1.6 million.

Profound Problems Surface in 1994

Universal's broad market reach coupled with its extensive library of digital codes pointed toward robust growth during the 1990s, particularly in light of the growth projections for the retail remote market, where the company collected more than half of its sales. The frenetic growth of the Tyler-led era screeched to halt in 1994, however, just months after the company was hailed as one of the country's fastest-growing enterprises. The high profit margins enjoyed by Universal during its first years in business were gone, stripped away by the emergence of a host of competitors who drove retail prices downward. During a six-month period ending January 1993, for instance, the retail price of remotes had plunged 40 percent. Universal was also crippled by excess inventory, a result of long-term production contracts that saddled the company with large, slow-moving supplies of merchandise. Further, Universal suffered from what it termed "production difficulties," according to a statement filed with the Securities and Exchange Commission. By December 1994, the company was hobbled by $14.7 million in backlog orders, including $2.4 million worth of orders to cable operators that it could not ship because of Universal's production difficulties.

After Universal posted a staggering loss of $12.8 million in 1994, Tyler left the company, vacating his posts as president and chief executive officer in January 1995. His replacement had joined the company one month earlier, having spent the previous five years at Mr. Coffee. At Mr. Coffee, David M. Gabrielsen had risen to the offices of executive vice-president and chief operating officer, the same posts he occupied when he was hired by Universal in December 1994. When Tyler left the company in January, Gabrielsen was promoted to president and chief executive officer, inheriting control over a company that spent the previous twelve months losing money.

Gabrielsen faced a daunting task when he took over early in 1995. The company's relationship with banks that issued lines of credit had deteriorated, as had the company's reputation among creditors, vendors, and customers. The prices of its shares had toppled from a high of $30 to $4, further eroding any confidence in the company. In an interview with the trade publication *HFN* on January 1, 1996, Gabrielsen shared his recollection of Universal's condition at the beginning of 1995: "We had issues with inventory. We had far too much. We had issues with our information systems. We had issues with turnaround time with our vendors. We had product development issues; not getting product to the marketplace. Our market share was declining."

Although Gabrielsen faced numerous problems, perhaps the most threatening challenge was presented by the complexion of the retail market. Retail sales were crucial to Universal's financial well-being, but since it had introduced the All For One, other companies had followed suit and begun producing similar products. The existence of a variety of universal remotes induced competitive pricing, making it harder to make a profit. During Gabrielsen's first three months at the helm, Universal posted another loss of $2.5 million, but he nevertheless did make progress. Gabrielsen reduced the company's direct sales force, turning instead to independent representatives, and brought in senior and middle-level executives who had worked at Mr. Coffee. Gradually, Universal's reputation among its business associates began to improve, and the company, with revamped retail lines, narrowed its losses as it slowly reduced its bloated inventories. By the end of 1995, the value of the company's stock had doubled, reinvigorated by three consecutive profitable quarters. For the year, the company posted a profit, albeit meager, of $320,000.

Although the company was far from reclaiming the vitality that described its growth during its first five years in business, Gabrielsen was convinced full recovery was near. In a January 1996 interview with *HFN,* he noted: "Phase 1 [of the restructuring in 1995] is getting the business stabilized, which I think we did a good job of. . . . 1996 should be a good year. 1997 should be a great year." In mid-1996, the company announced its decision to expand its home security electronics business, which accounted for 15 percent of sales. Management was keen to strike a more even balance between its two business segments, thereby reducing its reliance on the troublesome retail market for universal remotes. The home safety and security products, which were used to operate lighting, temperature, and thermostat control, used radio frequency and infrared technologies. "We've been perceived as a one-product company," explained Universal's senior vice-president of marketing and product

Key Dates:

1987: The All For One universal television remote debuts.
1991: The company acquires the Eversafe brand.
1995: Universal restructures after losing $12.8 million.
1997: Management decides to exit the domestic retail market.
1998: Camille Jayne assumes control over Universal.

development to *HFN* on June 10, 1996. He added: "We're looking to expand our business. Our thrust going forward is on home control. We're going to move into the wireless area." Universal planned to market its line of home security systems under the One For All and Eversafe brands, hoping to derive 35 percent of its revenues from the sale of such products by 1998.

As the company attempted to move beyond the troubles of 1994, the harsh condition of the retail market delayed its recovery. Several months after it announced the plans for a greater involvement in home control products, founders Doherty, Darbee, and O'Donnell resigned from Universal. Their departure ceded greater authority to Gabrielsen, who added the title of chairman to his posts as president and chief executive officer. Concurrent with his promotion, Gabrielsen had the unenviable task of informing analysts that Universal was failing to perform as expected. "It's going to take us a little longer to make this business profitable than we originally thought," he conceded in the September 2, 1996 issue of *Television Digest*. Net income for 1996, Gabrielsen told analysts, was expected to be half the per-share price projected by the company earlier in the year. The news delivered a crushing blow to the hope that the restructuring of 1995 had cured the company's ills. Universal continued to wade through excess inventories of outdated products and memory chips. Equally distressing, profit margins continued to shrink because of price pressures, forcing Gabrielsen to submit new, much lower, earnings projections to analysts. By the end of 1996, the news was grim. Universal lost $2.3 million during the year, reverting to the money-losing enterprise that had stumbled profoundly in 1994.

Exiting North American Retail Market in 1997

Hounded by the losses incurred from its retail operations, Universal entered its second decade of business backpedaling. In January 1997, a deal to sell the company's One For All retail remote business collapsed. In the wake of the failed divestiture, the company announced its was not actively seeking another buyer for its beleaguered retail operations. In late 1997, however, the company announced it was abandoning the North American retail business for universal remotes, which accounted for 29 percent, or $26 million, of its overall business. The company also decided to relocate its headquarters from Twinsburg to Cypress City, California, 25 miles north of Los Angeles, completing the move in 1998. Universal officially exited the North American retail market in 1998, licensing the One For All brand name and certain proprietary technology to third parties, who assumed Universal's former role of selling to domestic retailers.

Amid the drastic changes that occurred in 1998, Universal gained new leadership, marking the end of the Gabrielsen era. Camille Jayne joined Universal in February 1998 as president and chief operating officer, before being named chief executive officer in August 1998 and chairwoman four months later. Formerly the senior vice-president in charge of the digital television business unit at TCI, Jayne took control of Universal in the company's new guise. Although the company had abandoned the North American retail market, it continued to participate in retail sales in Europe, where profit margins remained sufficiently high to warrant further investment. The company was also supported by sales to OEMs, cable and satellite television operators, and by private label sales.

Analysts were encouraged by the composition of the restructured Universal, at last free of the domestic retail business that had halted the company's remarkable growth during its first five years of business. Universal's proprietary technology and its library of digital codes, which exceeded 80,000 individual codes by the late 1990s, were valuable assets in a digital age replete with consumer electronics products. No longer forced to compete as a low-cost producer of what had become a commodity product, Universal stood in a better position to reap the rewards of its technological advantages over competitors. The company's financial performance during the last two years of the 1990s demonstrated as much, ending the pattern of debilitating annual losses. After posting a $6.5 million loss in 1997, Universal recorded a $5.6 million profit in 1998, followed by a $7.7 million gain in 1999.

The difficulties of the mid-1990s appeared to have disappeared as Universal entered the 21st century. The company derived one-third of its sales from OEM customers, another third from cable and satellite operators, and the remainder from private label and international retail sales. For the future, expansion was expected on all fronts, but the company was particularly interested in increasing its cable and satellite business. Universal's new management team was exploring new distribution relationships and was intent on expanding the company's presence in Europe, Asia, South America, and Canada.

Principal Subsidiaries

Universal Electronics B.V. (Netherlands); One For All GmbH (Germany); Ultra Control Consumer Electronics GmbH (Germany); One For All Iberia S.L. (Spain); One For All Ltd. (U.K.).

Principal Competitors

Koninklijke Philips Electronics N.V.; Motorola, Inc.; Sony Corporation.

Further Reading

Adams, David, "Universal Electronics Moving Headquarters from Ohio to California," *Knight-Ridder/Tribune Business News,* December 20, 1997.

Beauprez, Jennifer, "Universal Electronics Sees Path to Underground," *Crain's Cleveland Business,* August 4, 1997, p. 9.

Bloomfield, Judy, "Universal Locks into Security," *HFN—The Weekly Newspaper for the Home Furnishing Network,* June 10, 1996, p. 63.

——, "Universal Remotes to Bow This Spring," *HFN—The Weekly Newspaper for the Home Furnishing Network,* March 10, 1997, p. 60.

"Inside Universal Electronics," *Television Digest,* March 8, 1993, p. 17.

Lieber, Ed, "Universal Packs Its Remotes; Supplier Will Pull Out of Retail in North America," *HFN—The Weekly Newspaper for the Home Furnishing Network,* December 29, 1997, p. 51.

Ryan, Ken, "Universal Electronics' Comeback," *HFN—The Weekly Newspaper for the Home Furnishing Network,* January 1, 1996, p. 66.

"Sizing Up Remote Market," *Television Digest,* June 7, 1993, p. 17.

"UE Drops One For All U.S. Retail Line," *Television Digest,* December 22, 1997, p. 19.

"Universal Electronics Cuts Losses," *Television Digest,* May 6, 1996, p. 17.

"Universal Founders Quit," *Television Digest,* September 2, 1996, p. 15.

"Universal Restructuring," *Television Digest,* May 22, 1995, p. 14.

"Universal Weighs Strategy," *Television Digest,* April 21, 1997, p. 18.

Vanac, Mary, "Ohio-Based Universal Electronics Hopes New Faces Will Restore Profitability," *Knight-Ridder/Tribune Business News,* April 30, 1995.

—Jeffrey L. Covell

Van Houtte Inc.

8300 19th Avenue
Montreal, Quebec, H1Z 4J8
Canada
Telephone: (514) 593-7711
Fax: (514) 593-8755
Web site: http://www.alvanhoutte.com

Public Company
Incorporated: 1919 as Maison A.L. Van Houtte Inc.
Employees: 1,600
Sales: C$250 million (US$161.77 million) (2000)
Stock Exchanges: Toronto
Ticker Symbol: VH
NAIC: 311920 Coffee Roasting; 417130 Manufacturing
    Industry Machinery and Equipment, Wholesale;
    533110 Franchises, Selling or Licensing; 722210
    Coffee Shops

Van Houtte Inc. is the largest gourmet coffee roasting company in Canada and one of the leading coffee service specialists in North America. The company operates in three principal areas: Coffee Services, The Coffee Group, and VKI Technologies. The Coffee Group purchases green coffee on international markets, roasts the beans, packages the product, and then markets it throughout North America under various brand names to food retailers. Van Houtte coffee is found in more than 2,000 supermarkets across Canada and in thousands of other retail outlets. VKI Technologies Inc., a wholly owned subsidiary of Van Houtte, is the largest designer, manufacturer, and distributor of single-cup coffee brewing equipment in North America. The patented VKI brewers are sold under license to manufacturers in Canada, the United States, Europe, and Japan. Coffee Services, through the operations of Red Carpet Food Systems Inc., Selena Coffee Inc., and Filterfresh Corporation, provides coffee to 63 corporate outlets and 33 franchises across Canada and in 28 U.S. states.

Early 20th Century Origins

In 1912, Albert-Louis Van Houtte emigrated from France, traveling by steamer and landing at Montreal. A short time later, he established a coffee import business in Chelsea, Quebec, near the border of Ontario. However, by 1914, with Canada involved in World War I, Van Houtte gave up his coffee activities and worked at a variety of different jobs. In 1919, after the war had ended, he purchased a store in Montreal and once again turned his attention to importing coffee. His shop specialized in the import of fine teas, coffees, and spices. The Van Houtte logo would later feature a caricature of the mustachioed founder.

At his Maison A.L. Van Houtte, Albert-Louis imported specialty coffees from Europe and roasted small batches in the back of his specialty grocery store. Eventually, he established a good reputation in Montreal, and the business prospered. After Albert-Louis' sons entered the family business, the importing and retail operations of the family business grew. In 1944, following the founder's death, the Van Houtte sons took over, and, eventually, the second son, Pierre Van Houtte, headed the enterprise. During the first 60 years of operations, Van Houtte distinguished itself for its roasting expertise and brand image in the Montreal fine coffee market. In the 1970s, the company added wholesale distribution to the food and restaurant sectors to its portfolio of activities.

Business Perks Up: 1980–92

The 1980s and early 1990s represented a time of tremendous growth and change as Van Houtte responded to the increased demand for gourmet coffee in North America. In 1980, the company strengthened itself by partnering with Paul-André Guillotte Benoît Beauregard. The new venture retained the Van Houtte name, A.L. Van Houtte Inc., as well as its original mission, according to company literature, to ''offer consumers the enjoyment of discovering fine quality coffees.''

In the 1980s, Van Houtte focused on the coffee category in the Quebec retail sector, promoting its products in grocery stores and pioneering the concept of the café-bistro. In May 1981, Van Houtte opened its first coffee bistro in Montreal.

Over the next few years, it established A.L. Van Houtte Bistros throughout Quebec. Also during this time, pursuing a goal of vertical integration, Van Houtte expanded and acquired companies involved in other areas of the coffee business.

In 1987, Van Houtte announced an initial public offering (IPO) of its stock at C$2.50 a share. With the funds raised from the IPO, Van Houtte was able to make further acquisitions, including those of the Café Orient Express and the Café Christophe Van Houtte roasters in Quebec. The IPO was regarded by the company as a major turning point in its journey toward national prominence. As the 1980s drew to a close, Van Houtte was selling coffee through supermarkets, convenience stores, and drug stores all across Canada. Annual sales of C$1 million in 1980 would increase to C$27 million by 1992.

The 1990s

One highlight of the company's early 1990s activities was its entrance into the coffee services market, in which it pioneered a new category: single-cup brewing. Single-cup brewing technology was targeted towards the office coffee market, a segment that had been largely ignored up to that point. Company CEO Paul-André Guillotte observed in an article in *Profit Magazine,* that "the industry had lost the younger generation because coffee offered in coffee shops and everywhere else was a very bland product. But companies such as Starbucks have made coffee a fun beverage again. Now people used to good coffee at home and in restaurants expect the same at work." From 1992 to 2000, pursuing its mission to provide better coffee to office dwellers, Van Houtte invested some C$175 million to acquire approximately 50 businesses (primarily coffee service operators) and expended nearly C$125 million in the purchase of single-cup coffee brewers and coffee roasting, distribution, and retailing facilities.

Perhaps the most significant acquisition during this time was that of VKI Technologies Inc, located in St-Hubert, Quebec. Van Houtte purchased 51 percent of VKI Technologies in 1994 and the remainder in 1997. VKI had developed and patented the world's first single-cup coffee machines to brew coffee the traditional way. Van Houtte made the machines available to customers on a rental basis. Also during this time, Van Houtte paid C$49 million to acquire Canada's largest coffee service company, Red Carpet Food Service, as well as a 51 percent stake in the U.S.-based coffee services company Filterfresh Corporation. The remaining interest in Filterfresh was purchased by Van Houtte in 1997, around the same time that it acquired VKI in total.

The size of Van Houtte's single-cup equipment base increased more than six-fold, as the company expanded its presence in all Canadian provinces and 28 American states. Soon Van Houtte had captured a dominant share of the Canadian market (more than 45 percent) and had established a network of 16 corporate branches in the Unites States, along with 33 franchises. One stock analyst, quoted in *Profit Magazine,* commented on the unique position of Van Houtte: "No wonder. The only thing they don't do is grow the coffee. There is no other company like it in North America."

In Canada, the Coffee Group expanded its presence and increased shipments by an average of 12 percent annually. Such growth was bolstered by its late 1990s acquisitions of Gold Cup Coffee Company Ltd., a Vancouver-based roasting outlet, and the Gerard Van Houtte roasting plant in Montreal. Meanwhile, Van Houtte's Coffee Services division realized 32 percent of its revenues from Quebec, 29 percent from Western Canada, 20 percent from the United States, 16 percent from Ontario, two percent from the Atlantic Provinces, and one percent from export.

Van Houtte's net earnings grew at an annual compound rate of 23 percent. By 1999, the company had acquired approximately 40 coffee-service companies, including Selena Coffee Inc., Red Carpet Food Systems, and Filterfresh Corp. It had a network of 61 corporate branches and 36 franchised outlets to sell, install, and service the single-cup coffee machines. Still, the company had only a three percent market share of the $3-billion U.S. coffee service market, the American market being more than ten times the size of the Canadian market. Detecting an opportunity, Van Houtte decided to focus on increasing sales to its larger neighbor to the south. Toward that end, the company launched Caffe Mondo, a workplace coffee-sampling program. The program proved an effective marketing strategy that helped increase single-cup technology sales in the United States.

2000 and Beyond

In hopes of further penetrating the U.S. market, Van Houtte developed a strategic plan that focused on repositioning itself from a Canadian company with American interests to a leader in the North American market. The plan involved four objectives: 1.) to align the Coffee Group's roasting and merchandising strengths, the Coffee Service network's expertise and VKI's product innovation capabilities to offer consumers an experience that would be unique to A.L. Van Houtte; 2.) to establish Van Houtte's brand image among North American consumers as the most accessible fine coffee roaster; 3.) to grow the number of single-cup sites through acquisitions and internal development, and increase coffee consumption per site; 4.) to complete the coverage of the retail food industry in Canada and penetrate certain target markets in the United States. To further strengthen the Van Houtte name, the company began to phase out the former names of its subsidiaries.

Van Houtte had already begun focusing on markets in the American Midwest as well as in Seattle, where it competed in the grocery stores with such big brand names as Nestlé. *Profit Magazine* reported that the first major win for Van Houtte outside these areas occurred when the company struck a deal with Florida's Publix stores, which agreed to carry Van Houtte's coffee in 300 outlets. Having identified the search for

Key Dates:

1912: Albert-Louis Van Houtte immigrates to Canada.

1919: Van Houtte opens a coffee import business and grocery.

1944: Company founder dies, and family carries on the business.

1980: Management partners with Paul-André Guillotte Benoît Beauregard and reincorporates as A.L. Van Houtte Inc.

1987: Company goes public on the Montreal Stock Exchange.

1994: Red Carpet, Canada's leading coffee service company, is acquired for C$49 million; a 51 percent stake in Filterfresh and VKI Technologies is acquired.

1995: Stock is listed on Toronto Stock Exchange.

1997: A.L. Van Houtte acquires remaining shares of Filterfresh and VKI Technologies; announces a two-for-one stock split.

2000: U.S. sales represent about 20 percent of Van Houtte's total revenues; company opts to shorten its name to Van Houtte Inc.

professional sales staff as a challenge, the company opened the Single Cup Sales Academy near Boston and prepared a manual on managing coffee services for its partners.

In its home territory, in February 2000, Van Houtte reached a commercial agreement to expand its presence in Western Canada by providing 17 additional outlets in the Calgary region, at Calgary Co-Op stores, with a selection of specialty and gourmet coffee. Later that year, Van Houtte purchased Heritage Coffee Ltd., a Vancouver-based coffee company.

Earmarking significant investment dollars for internal development and for business acquisitions that would be directed mainly towards the U.S. market, Van Houtte warned investors that net earnings might dip temporarily. Management remained confident, however, that the company would regain and then surpass its growth rates. At the annual meeting held on September 12, 2000, shareholders ratified a resolution to change the company name to Van Houtte Inc., dropping the initials of founder Albert-Louis for a corporate name that more readily reflected its brand names.

Management also introduced shareholders to a new generation of single-cup compact coffee brewers. The Caffe Mio model was targeted to groups of 20–40 users, while the Piccolina was designed for smaller groups of 20 or less. These products were regarded as superior because, in addition to the main brewing system found in all Van Houtte equipment, these products offered a packet system that allowed consumers to choose among eight different coffee blends as well as tea and hot chocolate. Company executives pointed out that in the previous five years, 90 percent of all jobs created in the United States had been in small businesses with 20 employees or less.

"This gives you an idea of the size of the potential market we are targeting," said Gerard Geoffrion, executive vice-president.

In December 2000, Van Houtte acquired the Millstone gourmet coffee roasting plant in Henderson, Kentucky. Formerly owned by Procter & Gamble, the plant was to be decommissioned to allow Millstone to centralize production facilities in New Orleans. Van Houtte acquired assets such as the roasting and packaging equipment and also hired several of the plant's key employees. The acquisition was in keeping with Van Houtte's plan to accelerate expansion in North America. "Not only will this plant yield a potential 50% increase in our fine coffee production capacity, but it is also located in the heart of Filterfresh's densest market, mid-way between Chicago and New Orleans. In fact, this location is recognized as strategic in the U.S. food distribution industry. We will therefore be able to provide our American coffee service customers with fast, efficient service, while gradually developing our presence in targeted areas of the retail food market," wrote Jean-Yves Monette, president of the Coffee Group, in the annual report.

Van Houtte set a growth objective of ten to 12 percent in net earnings for fiscal 2001, allocating $2 million to complete the implementation of the strategic plan. The money was targeted at Coffee Service development and integration, training activities, and implementation of a customer satisfaction program. Van Houtte appeared well financially stable, well managed, and working methodically towards achieving its strategic goals.

Principal Subsidiaries

Gold Cup Coffee Ltd.; Filterfresh Corporation (U.S.); Selena Coffee Inc.; Red Carpet Food Services.

Principal Divisions

Coffee Group; Coffee Services; VKI Technologies.

Principal Competitors

HDS Services; Aramark Corporation; Nestle S.A.; Starbucks Corporation.

Further Reading

"A.L. Van Houtte Buys Kentucky Coffee Roasting Plant From P&G," *MoneyGrowth News,* December 7, 2000.

"History: Because Fine Coffee is Part of Our History," Montreal: A.L. Van Houtte, 1999.

Lavay, Vic, "A.L. Van Houtte," *Vending Times,* September 25–October 24, 2000.

Pratt, Laura, "Still Feisty After All These Years," *Profit Magazine,* http://www.profitguide.com/magazine/van-houtte.html, 2000.

"Strategic Acquisition in Toronto: Van Houtte Becomes the No. 1 Coffee Service Operator in the Greater Toronto Area," *Business Wire,* July 15, 1999

"Trend-Setting Coffee-Maker A.L. Van Houtte Expands Its Presence in Western Canada," *Canada Newswire,* February 22, 2000.

"Van Houtte's Coffee Group Secures Foothold in the United States," *Canada Newswire,* December 7, 2000.

—June Campbell

VEW AG

Rheinlanddamm 24
D-44139 Dortmund
Germany
Telephone: (49) (231) 438-00
Fax: (49) (231) 438-2147
Web site: http://www.vew.de

Public Company
Incorporated: 1925 as Vereinigte Elektrizitätswerke
Westfahlen GmbH
Employees: 13,892
Sales: DM 9.42 billion ($4.80 billion) (1999)
Stock Exchanges: Frankfurt/Main
Ticker Symbol: VEWG.F
NAIC: 221112 Fossil Fuel Electric Power Generation;
221111 Hydroelectric Power Generation; 221113
Nuclear Electric Power Generation; 221121 Electric
Bulk Power Transmission and Control; 221122 Electric
Power Distribution; 22121 Natural Gas Distribution;
48621 Pipeline Transportation of Natural Gas

VEW AG is one of Germany's leading utility companies and is active throughout Europe. It consists of five independent operating companies including VEW Energie, WFG, MEAG, Edelhoff, and Harpen. VEW Energie generates and distributes electricity in the German states of Westphalia and Saxony and is involved in energy trading; WGV, a joint venture with Westfälische Ferngas AG, provides gas in Westphalia; MEAG is active in energy and gas markets through various subsidiaries in eastern Germany and Europe; Edelhoff is VEW's waste management arm; and Harpen provides heat to 65,000 German clients, runs small water-power plants and develops real estate. Following the liberalization of Germany's electricity market in 1998, VEW agreed in 2000 to merge with utility giant RWE AG based in Essen.

VEW's Founding: 1900–25

Around the turn of the century electricity generated from burning coal began to alter how things were done, in industry as well as in daily life. Electric machinery and household appliances became more and more popular and increased the demand for electricity. Power generation emerged as one of the most influential and profitable industries of the twentieth century. In the Ruhr, the heart of coal mining in Germany, the Rheinisch-Westfälische Elektrizitätswerk (RWE) had become a leader in the market for power generation and distribution by 1914. However, the idea of RWE owner Hugo Stinnes to create a company that supplied the entire Ruhr with electricity, gas, and water seemed frightening to many municipal authorities. Not only would they have to yield price control to a privately owned company, they would also give up a profitable source of income for their chronically starved public coffers. Consequently, a number of community leaders in the Eastern Ruhr decided to establish a counterweight organization to Stinnes' giant in form of power-supply companies controlled by the communities themselves.

By 1914 several large municipal power-supply companies had been established in and around the cities of Bochum and Dortmund. Bochum-based Elektrizitätswerk Westfahlen AG was founded in 1906 and served the surrounding counties. Städtisches Elektrizitätswerk Dortmund, one of Germany's biggest power stations at that time, was established in 1897 and supplied the city of Dortmund. Dortmund-based Westfälisches Verbands-Elektrizitätswerk AG, founded in 1908, served the area around the city.

World War I had major consequences for the power industry. At first, demand for electricity dropped significantly because many factories closed or reduced production. However, a shrinking supply of imported petroleum caused a rising demand for electricity in private households. Between 1914 and 1919 the number of electricity customers in Dortmund doubled from 24,000 to 50,000. In addition, the war industry increased demand. At the same time, power suppliers struggled with diminishing coal supplies, rising prices, and fewer employees. The establishment of new power supply networks in rural areas came to a halt because of high costs, giving rise to electricity-cooperatives as vehicles for interested customers to finance the hook-up.

After the war, coal production in the Ruhr was about one-third of the pre-war levels and a significant part of that was shipped to the Allied victors in reparations. Doubling electricity prices did not make up for rising costs, and lack of coal even forced power stations to close down in the winter of 1919–20. On top of that, the new German parliament, the *National-versammlung,* passed a law for the "socialization of the electricity industry" that put bigger power stations under government control and organized the country into energy districts. The law drew opposition from private and community-owned energy suppliers, which saw their influence and profits fading away. In October 1920 ten electricity providers, mostly community-owned, founded the Kommunalen Elektrizitäts-Verband Westfahlen-Rheinland (KEV), the Westphalia-Rhineland Municipal Electricity Association, based in Hagen. It intended to technically connect existing power stations and to provide means for them to assist each other, to build and run new power stations, and to lay the necessary cable. The idea was to create an organization large enough to be an independent energy district and not be dominated by RWE. The organization proved useful during the French occupation of the Ruhr and hyperinflation in the early 1920s. However, after coal supplies normalized and the "socialization" law was unable to achieve political relevance, the bonds between the different KEV members began to loosen again.

Finally, in fall 1924 Elektricitätswerk Westfahlen began negotiations with the two Dortmund-based power suppliers about a possible merger to boost its power to finance the ever growing infrastructure of cable. The three companies had a similar shareholder structure—all were owned by cities or counties. Effective the beginning of 1925, the three companies founded the Vereinigte Elektrizitätswerke Westfalen GmbH (United Electricity Works of Westphalia)—VEW for short. They leased their four power stations and all other facilities, and transferred all their other assets to the new entity. VEW was Germany's fifth-largest power supplier, supplying electricity and gas to 31 cities and counties with 2.65 million people.

Dynamic Growth and Financial Crisis: 1925–30

Although the German economy was still sluggish in 1925, VEW's top management was envisioning a bright future. The development of the energy sector in the United States showed that there was a good chance that electricity consumption would go up quickly in all areas of the economy. To be prepared for the upcoming boom, VEW had to invest in the necessary capacity and infrastructure. However, capital and long-term loans in particular, were not available on the German financial market.

In negotiations with the American banks Speyer & Co. and Harris-Forbes the issue was raised that VEW itself didn't have anything to offer in security because all the power stations it operated were only leased. In November 1925 the company's shareholders decided to increase the capital by 40 million Reichsmarks by including all production facilities in its assets. However, it took four years until the last shareholder, the city of Bochum, gave up its resistance and exchanged its shares.

VEW invested heavily in its production facilities and infrastructure between 1925 and 1929. To make production more efficient and reliable all three big power stations were connected and equipped with furnaces that were able to burn coal dust, a technology that boosted output four- to fivefold. While expanding its service territory VEW also took over some water power stations from smaller electricity providers. By the end of the 1920s VEW's 20 water power stations were contributing 7 percent of the total output. Between 1925 and 1927 the company also bought three coal mines to secure a supply of raw materials. At the same time, in mid-1926, demand for electricity started rising and in the late 1920s VEW significantly expanded its network of power lines. Within five years VEW's electricity sales went up by 150 percent and two thirds of its total sales came from industrial and commercial customers. To win less wealthy private households as customers the company introduced an installment-payment system in 1927 and between 1925 and 1929 electricity provided to private households almost doubled. A new subsidiary, the Vereinigte Gaswerke Westfahlen GmbH (VGW) was founded to promote the use of and supply gas as another field of activity.

However, financed by short- and long-term loans the expansion had its price. When short-term debt equaled four and a half times the company's annual profits in fall 1929, the still-ongoing construction work was slowed down. After negotiations with the Prussian government over the purchase of a share of VEW through its power supplier Preussenelektra fell through in spring 1930, VEW's shareholders decided to allow private capital into the business to solve its financial problems. In June 1930 the VEW Aktiengesellschaft was founded and all of VEW's assets were transferred to the new company. VEW GmbH was renamed Westfälische Elektrizitätswirtschaft GmbH (WEW) and functioned as a holding company for the community-owned shares in VEW AG. The additional share capital came from a group of German banks led by the Deutsche Bank und Diskonto-Gesellschaft (DD-Bank) and another group of American banks led by Harris, Forbes & Co. In addition to twelve representatives from the shareholding communities, VEW AG's new Board of Directors included eight members from the private banks. However, the worldwide economic crisis which began with the stock market crash in New York in October 1929 was about to reach Germany and created new challenges for VEW.

Economic Crisis and the Nazi Regime: 1930–45

Fading profits and high short-term debt caused VEW in fall 1930 to look for solutions to the company's financial dilemma. A takeover deal with RWE was almost closed, but was finally canceled out of mutual distrust and unresolved problems in connection with the possible interests of American creditor banks in VEW. Next, the company concentrated on cost cutting programs, put new construction projects on hold and reduced the number of employees by 25 percent, down from 3,341 in 1929 to 2,504 three years later. The closure of VEW's loss-making coal mines was reversed following massive protests, but workers agreed to have their wages cut by 25 percent. Despite these measures the numbers on VEW's 1931 and 1932 balance sheets remained in the red. Because of the depressed economy and the resulting mass unemployment, VEW's total electricity sales dropped by 18 percent between 1929 and 1932. However, the crisis turned out to be VEW's rescue in another way. After none of the company's two groups of creditors had taken advantage of an option allowing them to change their loans into share ownership in summer 1933, DD-Bank paid off the American partner's share of the loan in 1934 and changed VEW's short-term loan into a long-term loan. Because of the depressed dollar, the company's debt was cut by almost one third and it was able to buy back another dollar bond it had issued in 1928. By 1935 VEW was turning profits again. In late 1940 WEW GmbH was dissolved and the holding's shares in VEW were distributed directly among the 135 community shareholders, including 12 big and 102 small cities, 20 counties, and the regional community organization of the Westfalian region.

The rising mass poverty and unemployment in Germany contributed to the National Socialist Party's coming to power in 1933 which greatly influenced VEW in many ways. In mid-1933 two Nazis took the leading positions in management while about 120 people, among them members of the Social Democratic Party, were fired for political reasons. Within a short period of time the violence and repression on the part of the Nazis, coupled with compliance, adaptation and even support from the staff, made VEW a model company for the Nazis. In accordance with the Nazis' second "four Year Plan" aimed at preparing the German economy for a war, the Steinkohlen-Elektrizitäts-AG (Steag) was founded in 1937. The Essen-based company united all power-generating coal mine operators from the Rheinisch-Westfälisches Kohlensyndikat and was bound by contract to deliver all electricity to VEW which would in turn distribute and charge customers for it. VEW's own facilities and the Dortmund power station in particular, were modernized and a central control system installed in Dortmund.

The demand for electrical power as well as for gas in Germany exploded in the years before World War II and continued to rise until 1944. The industry was under strict government control. While an integrated national high-voltage cable network was strengthened, hundreds of tons of copper wire were replaced by iron wire in low-voltage networks in order to support the war economy with raw material. More and more workers from VEW's coal mines were called to the front and beginning in 1942 replaced by between 445 to 630 slave laborers and prisoners of war from Poland, Italy, Kroatia, Russia, and France. When the war came back to Germany VEW suffered significant losses such as the destruction of the Dortmund power station and of a dam in the river Ruhr for the Möhne water power station between 1943 and 1944.

Consolidation and Going Public
After the War: 1945–89

Dr. Friedrich Stiegler, one of the few company executives who were not active Nazis, became VEW's first CEO after the war and initiated the de-Nazification of the company. By

January 1946, 186 VEW employees, 12.5 percent of all white-collar workers and 3.4 percent of all blue-collar workers, were dismissed for their Nazi activities. By the time the new German currency was introduced in 1948, most of the war damage had been cleaned up. The currency exchange also freed the company from almost half of its debt. Another financial boost came from a DM 8.15 million loan with preferred conditions from the Investitionshilfegesetz, a fund that was initiated by the German government in January 1952 to accelerate reconstruction in the raw materials industries. However, VEW's growth demanded ever rising investments. The total amount invested between 1951 and 1960, DM 1.1 billion, was only sufficient to cover investments planned for five of the next decade. In addition, a law that allowed a tax exemption for municipally owned enterprises was phased out in April 1965. Consequently, VEW opened up to private capital and went public in May 1966. To ensure that the communities retained their major influence, their shares were given three votes each. In fall 1968 a group consisting of RWE, Conti-Gas, Deutsche Bank and Allianz-Lebensversicherung, the Energie-Verwaltungs-Gesellschaft mbH became a major shareholder with 25.3 percent of VEW's share capital.

In the 1950s coal was the major fuel for generating electricity. VEW's own coal mines were closed down in the 1950s and 1960s. With coal prices moving up steadily, VEW began exploring alternative options. By the mid-1960s the company was using heavy heating oil in two of its power stations as fuel supplementing coal. In October 1968 VEW's first atomic power station went into operation in Lingen. Designed as a demonstration project it was heavily subsidized by the German government. However, it ceased production in 1977 when the repair of a defect would have been too costly. A third alternative fuel competing with coal was natural gas. Based on a contract from October 1969 that guaranteed fixed prices over 20 years, VEW started buying natural gas from Dutch suppliers Amoco Netherlands Petroleum Company and Exploratie- en Produktiemaatschappij Dyas N.V., and later also from Nederlandse Aardolie Maatschappij. However, the two oil shocks of 1973 and 1978 reminded VEW that completely replacing coal as a fuel was not a good idea. The Dutch government raised prices for natural gas after the two oil crises. In April 1988 KKW Emsland, a new atomic power station with a 1,300 megawatt (MW) capacity, started operations in Lingen. However, after the catastrophic accident at the atomic power station in Chernobyl in the Ukraine on April 26, 1986, public opinion turned against the use of this risky technology. Another nuclear power generator, the THTR300 on the site of the Kraftwerk Westfahlen in Hamm-Uetrop was shut down in the late 1980s.

In addition to economic turmoil, VEW found itself under growing political pressure from the German government to buy domestic coal. As early as the mid-1960s the government issued laws that obliged German electricity suppliers to use German coal for electricity production. When coal use in the German electricity industry dropped to an all-time low of 27 percent in 1975, the government introduced the "Kohlepfennig," a de facto tax added to consumer's electricity bill to subsidize the use of German coal for energy production. In May 1977 by signing the "Jahrhundertvertrag"—"the contract of the century"—the German public electric industry agreed to buy 250 million tons of domestic coal over the next ten years, 16.5 percent of which was purchased by VEW. In September 1984

VEW took the chance to acquire over 20 percent of the shares of Ruhrkohle AG, Germany's number one coal producer. Three years later VEW's share went up to 30 percent.

By the late 1970s the higher consciousness for environmental concerns was the reason that the steady growth of electricity consumption came to a halt. Instead of building new electricity production facilities VEW invested in its power transmission infrastructure. A new power transmission line made a connection with the networks of other German power suppliers possible in 1980, and four years later a direct connection to the Netherlands was installed. New electronic remote controls and data processing equipment made the exchange of electricity with other suppliers possible. To stabilize gas supply for VEW customers a 250 mile long circle gas pipeline was built between 1974 and 1985.

Reunification, Diversification, and Market Deregulation: 1990–2000

The reunification of Germany provided VEW with an opportunity to expand its business beyond its traditional market in the Ruhr. Based on the *Stromvertrag,* an agreement between the East German government and the West German energy suppliers, VEW took over 51 percent of the share capital of the East German power supplier Mitteldeutsche Energieversorgung AG (MEAG) based in Halle, Saxony-Anhalt in 1994. Shortly after that VEW acquired shares in three East German gas suppliers in the states of Saxony, Saxony-Anhalt, and Brandenburg.

Besides expanding into new regions, VEW started pursuing a diversification strategy into utility-related service markets. In 1991 VEW Umwelt GmbH (VUG) was founded as VEW's new waste management subsidiary. In August 1992 VEW took over Dortmund-based Harpener AG, a former mining company active in the energy and transportation markets and which owned a considerable amount of real estate. In December 1992 the company acquired a 24.9 minority share in Edelhoff AG & Co., a leading German waste management company and took over the remaining shares two years later. By 1994 the percentage of sales from power generation in total sales had dropped to 85 percent, from 98 percent in the late 1980s. In mid-1995 a new company structure was introduced that enabled VEW to better manage its diverse business activities. VEW AG became a management holding for the four operating companies VEW Energie AG, MEAG AG, Edelhoff Entsorgung (waste management) and Harpen Dienstleistungen (services). In 1998 Westfälische Gasversorgung AG & Co. KG, a Westphalian gas supply company, became the fifth operating company and was transformed into Westfälische Ferngas-AG in 2000.

"European integration" and "deregulation" became buzzwords of the 1990s with significant consequences for VEW. On February 17, 1997 the new Richtlinie für den Elektrizitätsbinnenmarkt der Europäischen Union, the guidelines regulating the liberalization of the electricity markets in EU member countries, went into effect which had to become national law within two years. Germany decided to jump headfirst into the cold water and opened its entire energy market with its sudden energy reform which went into effect on April 29, 1998. At that time there were about 80 regional energy suppliers and 900 municipal power companies. The big utilities such as VEW lost traditional customers to new domestic and international players in the energy market which was allowed to trade electricity without having to generate it. VEW responded by getting involved in setting up electricity trading places like the Amsterdam Power Exchange (APX) in which the company holds a 4.9 percent share, and the Frankfurt-based European Energy Exchange (EEX) in which VEW holds two percent, and getting involved in electricity trading itself at the Leipzig Power Exchange established in 2000. To compete successfully against the tough competition, VEW Energie eliminated one level of hierarchy which resulted in the number of employees dropping from 6026 in 1996 to about 3,300 three years later. The energy division was organized in the four subdivisions generation, trade, networks, and distribution.

However, all these measures, including new marketing efforts, with the liberalization of the gas market on the horizon, did not seem to provide a basis for sustainable future growth. Within one year energy prices for businesses dropped between 25 and 50 percent and for private customers ten to 20 percent. While VEW's energy sales rose by 6.1 percent in 1999, profits dropped by 11.2 percent. After alternative plans fell through because of time constraints, VEW's top management proposed to merge with its long-time competitor RWE. On June 27, 2000 VEW's shareholders approved the decision. The name VEW was not carried over to the new entity. Effective in October 2000, the new company became Germany's number one and Europe's third-largest energy company and Europe's 12th-largest industrial enterprise.

Principal Subsidiaries

VEW Energie AG; Westfälische Gasversorgung AG & Co. KG (58.2%); Mitteldeutsche Energieversorgung AG (52.5%); RAG AG (30.2%); Harpen AG (70.6%); Edelhoff AG & Co. (75%).

Principal Competitors

E.ON AG; Bewag AG; Electricité de France SA.

Further Reading

"Das VEW-Konzernergebnis broeckelt weiter ab," *Frankfurter Allgemeine Zeitung*, November 5, 1993, p. 20.

"Die VEW-Entsorgung ist noch keine sprudelnde Gewinnquelle," *Frankfurter Allgemeine Zeitung*, November 8, 1994, p. 21.

"Edelhoff hat endlich die Gewinnschwelle ueberschritten," *Frankfurter Allgemeine Zeitung*, November 29, 1997, p. 23.

Eickeler, Rudolf, "Beim Strommonopoly stehen Sieger und Verlierer noch nicht fest," *vwd*, December 27, 1999.

"Harpener ist wieder 'blanko-kreditwuerdig'," *Süddeutsche Zeitung*, September 19, 1992.

"Klaus Knizia tritt ab," *Süddeutsche Zeitung*, December 29, 1992.

"VEW bereitet die Expansion ins Ausland vor," *Frankfurter Allgemeine Zeitung*, November 7, 1995, p. 23.

"VEW steht unter Akquisitionsdrang," *Süddeutsche Zeitung*, May 29, 1992.

"VEW strebt ins internationale Energiegeschaeft," *Süddeutsche Zeitung*, November 7, 1995.

—Evelyn Hauser

Weatherford International, Inc.

515 Post Oak Boulevard, Suite 600
Houston, Texas 77027-3415
U.S.A.
Telephone: (713) 693-4000
Fax: (713) 693-4294
Web site: http://www.weatherford.com

Public Company
Incorporated: 1998
Employees: 12,200
Sales: $1.8 billion (2000)
Stock Exchanges: New York
Ticker Symbol: WFT
NAIC: 213111 Drilling Oil and Gas Wells; 23571
    Concrete Contractors; Oil and Gas Field Machinery
    and Equipment Manufacturing

Houston-based Weatherford International, Inc. is one of the top five oilfield service companies in the world, with annual revenues exceeding $2 billion. The company was created in 1998 from the merger of EVI, Inc. and Weatherford Enterra, Inc. The emergent company now operates through three divisions—Completion Systems, Drilling & Intervention Services, and Artificial Lift Systems—offering a broad range of oil-patch services, running from well installation and completion to production enhancements. Among other things, it provides fishing services to remove debris from wells and artificial lift systems for use in oil recovery.

1940–89: Early Rise and Oil Bust Survival

Weatherford International's name can be traced back to the 1940s, when Jess Hall, Sr., formed the Weatherford Spring Company in Weatherford, Texas, a town in north central Texas, about 25 miles west of Fort Worth. The company originated as a provider of oil drilling equipment and services. Over the next couple of decades, when the Weatherford name moved into Europe, Hall's company started acquiring a global reputation as a reliable ''scratcher'' and ''centralizer,'' terms relating, re-

spectively, to its casing cleaning and directional-drilling control services. A good portion of its business came from well retrieval and fishing service contracts for removing tools and debris from wells.

Weatherford added other services as it grew. Moreover, the oil industry boom of the 1970s encouraged both expansion and diversification. In fact, by the time the petroleum bubble burst in the early 1980s, Weatherford's business had broadened considerably. It was dealing in drilling products and services, cement engineering, production equipment, and specialty items and applications. Still, despite its global range and diversified services, in 1983 the company logged the first net loss in its history.

Under Eugene L. Butler, president and CEO, the company struggled to survive the bad times that closed down a number of over-extended oil service companies. To stay in business, all of them had to compete in a market demanding up to a 70 percent discount for their services. Weatherford refused to succumb to the heaviest pressures, preferring instead to downsize and stress quality goods and services over price. As a result, its sales fell off rather sharply. It withdrew from some unprofitable markets and concentrated on the Gulf Coast, particularly offshore and abroad, where the rig count held up better than it did in the United States. It also reduced its corporate headquarters from five floors to one, cut its domestic work force by 68 percent and its international work force by 39 percent, put in effect graduated, across-the-board salary cuts, and consolidated its manufacturing operations. It was reeling badly from the economic punch, but it survived. It even added some new, specialized services tailor-made to meet some of the industry's changing needs. For example, it combined services and recent technology into a new business, that of reclaiming, stacking, and maintaining pipe taken from wells for companies contracting the service.

Primarily, the company stayed on hold throughout the 1980s. In 1987, Butler revealed that at the beginning of the recession Weatherford had actively pursued a merger with one or more other companies but, for whatever reason, never found any takers. Its only choice was to contain costs by slimming down to its core business. At the same time, Butler also indicated that the company would probably sell eventually, though, he stipulated, it was not going to be given away at ''recession prices.''

Company Perspectives:

Weatherford's mission is to be the company of choice for an extensive range of oilfield products, services and technologies that will help our customers produce oil more efficiently and profitably. By anticipating and exceeding our customers' short and long-term requirements, we expect to achieve superior profitability, growth and return to our shareholders and to expand opportunities for our employees. We will accomplish our mission through the following strategies: Growth: Weatherford's goal is market leadership in high-growth, industry segments. As a result, we constantly search for opportunities to develop, acquire and distribute, through our worldwide infrastructure, unique technologies that will give us this advantage. Performance: Weatherford is focused on delivering superior service and product quality. This commitment to performance adds the highest value to our customers' operations and our shareholders' bottom line. Innovation: Weatherford continually seeks new ways of doing business. This spirit of innovation advances the Company's capabilities and differentiates us from our competitors. An Entrepreneurial Workforce: Weatherford expects employees to play a significant role in the future of the company. To balance this responsibility and accountability, we equip employees with the tools, knowledge and training they need to excel in their jobs.

Instead, within a few years Weatherford began an aggressive growth cycle through acquisitions and mergers that transformed it into one of the world's largest oil services companies. In fact, it had already started on that path four years before its 1995 major merger with Enterra Corporation.

1990–2000: Acquisitions and Mergers

At the beginning of the 1990s, Energy Ventures, Weatherford, and Enterra—the three companies that would finally combine to emerge as the newly organized and structured Weatherford International—were all busy growing through vertical expansion and integration.

Energy Ventures (EV) was founded in 1972. It began as an offshore oil and gas explorer and producer. In 1981 it became a 50–50 partner with Northwest Energy in developing an oil field in Hockley County, Texas. By the next year, Northwest had gained about a 25 percent share of EV. Thereafter, Appalachian, EV's majority stock holder, attempted to take control of the company, but its efforts failed when the oil debacle of the mid-1980s trashed its plans. However, EV was liquidated and had to be recreated. It emerged again in 1987 and began an aggressive vertical integration. In the 12 years before its merger with Weatherford Enterra, it made over 40 acquisitions. Among these were Grant Oil Country Tubular, in 1990, and Prideco, in 1995. These two subsidiaries were combined as Grant Prideco, giving parent EV a solid position as a major producer and supplier of drill pipe and tubulars. In 1997, when the company built a manufacturing plant in Canada, it changed its name to EVI.

Enterra, the other company, was a diversified energy service and manufacturing business. It provided products and services worldwide to the petroleum exploration, production, and transmission industries. Its special service areas included the rehabilitation of older pipeline systems and the provision of services and products for drilling and serving both onshore and offshore gas and oil wells. At the time of its merger with Weatherford, Enterra was considered one of the industry's leaders in technological research and development (R&D). It had become an international business in 1988, the year in which, for $35 million, it bought out CRC Evans. In 1994, in a deal valued at over $310 million, it bought Total Energy Services Co., making it one of Weatherford's chief competitors and a logical merger target. It also had an excellent cash flow and zero debt.

Weatherford started its own shopping spree under Phillip Burguieres, who became chairman of the company in April 1991. Within two years, Weatherford bought eight small companies. Then, in the summer of 1993, it worked out a $370 million purchase agreement with Tuboscope Vetco International Inc., also a Houston-based company. The acquisition made Weatherford the sole company offering comprehensive tubular servicing to the oil industry, ranging from tubular running services to pipeline coating and inspection. Additional acquisitions followed through 1993 and into 1994, the year in which, at about the same time, Weatherford bought Odfjell Drilling and Consulting Co. A/S of Norway and Enterra purchased Total Energy Services Co.

Coverage of the two acquisitions in a single article in *The Oil Daily* seemed to hint that the two growing competitors were on a collision course.

They did not, however, collide; they simply teamed up, creating the world's sixth largest oil field services company. The deal, the first of two major events that led to the 1998 emergence of a completely restructured Weatherford International, Inc., was hammered out in 1995. Both companies had continued purchasing smaller companies through 1994 and into 1995. Then, in June 1995, they announced the proposed merger, noting that the combined company would boast over $1 billion in assets and annual revenues of more than $850 million. Although the deal was "99% to 100% sure," it required the approval of the Justice Department, with the odds on its blessing set at around 80 percent. The approval was quickly given, though, and by October the merger was a done deal, "a tax-free pooling of interests." Combined, the two companies became Weatherford Enterra Inc., if only temporarily.

Over the next two years, Weatherford Enterra continued to grow and prosper. The trend in the oil field service industry was clearly towards the consolidation of groups of companies into major conglomerates, a trend which seemed to hit one peak in 1998, when there were two important mergers. First, Halliburton Co. and Dresser Industries Inc. completed a stock-swap merger, pushing the resulting company ahead of Schlumberger Ltd. as the world's largest oil field service company. Within a week thereafter, Weatherford Enterra announced its impending merger with EVI. Weatherford's president and CEO, Thomas R. Bates, Jr., said that the joining of the two companies was "a growth story, not a consolidation story that is painful to employees." That may have been so, but the end result, EVI Weatherford, talked and

Key Dates:

1940s: Weatherford Spring Company is founded in Weatherford, Texas.

1972: Energy Ventures is founded as an offshore gas and oil exploration and production company.

1987: Energy Ventures is liquidated and re-established.

1988: Enterra acquires CRC Evans.

1990: Energy Ventures acquires Grant Oil Country Tubular.

1995: Weatherford International merges with Enterra, becoming Weatherford Enterra Inc.; Energy Ventures purchases Prideco.

1997: Energy Ventures builds a manufacturing plant in Canada and changes its name to EVI.

1998: Weatherford Enterra merges with EVI Inc. to become Weatherford EVI Inc., later renamed Weatherford International, Inc.

2000: Company spins off its Grant Prideco Drilling Products subsidiary and buys Gas Services International, Oakwell Compressor Packages, and Alpine Oil Services.

2001: Company sells Weatherford Global Compression Services to Universal Compression Holdings, Inc.

walked pretty much like a consolidated duck. The $2.6 billion stock swap had created the fourth largest oil field service company in the world, a position reflected in its November 1998 change of name to Weatherford International, Inc.

In its first whole year of operations, 1999, in addition to completing the necessary task of restructuring and reorganizing, Weatherford International arranged over a dozen acquisitions and strategic alliances. It also established a state-of-the-art, world-class R&D training and testing facility. At the site, with a derrick, two separate wells, and two additional test cells, Weatherford gained the ability to test its complete inventory of oilfield tools under fully simulated conditions.

There were growing pains, however. The petroleum industry had stagnated in the middle of the decade, and in 1998, when the rig count in North America dropped 38 percent, it went into a recession that even worsened in 1999. In 1998, even though Weatherford International's revenue was up over 1997 figures, its earnings dropped sharply, from $187.8 million to $64.8 million.

In early 1999, the decline in profits compelled Weatherford to lay off 3,300 workers, about 25 percent of its work force, and close 100 North American sales and service facilities. It also cut its capital budget to $90 million, a drop of 50 percent. Further, it shifted its focus to international markets, where the rig count drop was only 15 percent. Even with the retrenchment, 1999 proved to be a grim year. Revenues dropped from over $2 billion to $1.24 billion, producing a net loss of $20.9 million.

Made necessary by its major mergers and acquisitions, the company had known that it had to make some major consolidation and restructuring moves. The industry-wide woes simply exacerbated its reorganization problems, albeit only temporarily. As Bernard J. Duroc-Danner, Weatherford's new CEO indicated, the company's greatest challenge was to assemble all of its acquisitions into a coherent and cohesive whole. By November 1999, the number of acquisitions made since Weatherford Enterra and EVI merged in 1998 had reached 16 with an expenditure of about $500 million.

In its consolidation strategies, including its acquisitions and divestitures, Weatherford seemed to be redefining itself, particularly as it moved into the next century. Major steps included the 1999 merger of the company's gas compression services with GE Capital, a subsidiary of General Electric Co. The result was a new company, Weatherford Global Compression Services, which became the core of one of the four divisions of Weatherford International, Inc. However, two years later, for a large stake in the combined companies, Weatherford sold Weatherford Global Compression Services to Universal Compression Holdings, Inc. In the interim, Weatherford continued to acquire other companies, despite sustaining losses into 2000, when the industry finally recovered and the company returned to profitability. In 1999, it had also divested itself of its major subsidiary, Grant Prideco Drilling Products, by spinning it off to Weatherford shareholders.

Principal Divisions

Weatherford Drilling & Intervention Services; Weatherford Completion Systems; Weatherford Artificial Lift Systems.

Principal Competitors

Baker Hughes Inc.; BJ Services Company; Haliburton Company; Schlumberger Limited; Smith International, Inc.

Further Reading

Dittrick, Paula, ''The High-Tech Plumber,'' *Oil and Gas Investor*, November 1999, p. 39.

Drummond, Jim, ''Quality, Bottom Line Focus Aid Weatherford's Steady Recovery,'' *Oil Daily*, January 16, 1985, p. 8.

Fletcher, Sam, ''Weatherford International, Enterra to Merge, Creating 6th Largest Oil Field Services Firm,'' *Oil Daily*, June 27, 1995, p. 1.

——, ''Weatherford International, GE Capital to Merge Gas Compression Groups,'' *Oil Daily*, February 4, 1999.

Pybus, Kenneth R., ''Weatherford Capturing Another Market with Tuboscope Acquisition,'' *Houston Business Journal*, July 26, 1993, p. 10.

Sullivan, R. Lee, '' 'I Didn't Want to Make Another Mistake','' *Forbes*, December 20, 1993, p. 226.

Weeden, Scott L., ''Service and Supply Sector Starts Across New Frontier,'' *Oil Daily*, July 27, 1987, p. 8.

——, ''Weatherford Chief Sees Improving Outlook for Oilfield Service Industry,'' *Oil Daily*, July 12, 1987, p. 6.

—John W. Fiero

THE WINE GROUP

The Wine Group, Inc.

240 Stockton Street
San Francisco, California 94108-5325
U.S.A.
Telephone: (415) 986-8700
Fax: (415) 986-4304
Web site: http://www.winegroup.com

Private Company
Incorporated: 1981
Employees: Not Available
Sales: $300 million (1999 est.)
NAIC: 31213 Wineries

The Wine Group, Inc. (TWG), a privately owned company, is the third largest wine company in the United States in terms of sales volume. At its vineyards in California and New York, it produces a variety of wines sold under the Franzia, Corbett Canyon, Mogen David, Tribuno, and Lejon labels. Their product line is largely inexpensive, making them available to a wide audience. Franzia and Corbett Canyon, at their California vineyards, are principal producers of TWG's standard table wines. Franzia Winetaps, sold in boxes, are the best selling wines in the United States. Corbett Canyon, with wines sold in distinct, re-sealable decanters, produces very competitive, premium-grape varietals at its winery near San Luis Obispo. More specialized are the sweet concord grape and blackberry Mogen David kosher wines produced in New York, the premium vermouths sold under the Tribuno label, and the less expensive vermouths sold under the Lejon name. Most recently, TWG has begun marketing wines under the Foxhorn and Crysta labels as well as producing a line of wine coolers under the Lyrica name. The company has also purchased Turner Road Vintners, the Woodbridge production and bottling facilities of Sebastiani Vineyards Inc., which bottles medium-priced wines under a variety of brand names, including Talus, Vendange, Farallon, Nathanson Creek, Heritage, and La Terre.

The Wine Group's Origins in the 1980s

Early in the 1980s, several large conglomerates began divesting wine companies that they had acquired just a few years

earlier. Among the sellers were the Coca-Cola Company, R.J. Reynolds, Schlitz Brewing Company, and the Coca-Cola Bottling Company of New York. For whatever reason, the wineries no longer fit into the conglomerates' plans for growth and diversification. The Coca-Cola Company had in fact caused quite a stir in 1977, when it created the Wine Spectrum, a subsidiary consisting of the Monterey Vineyard and Sterling Winery in California and Taylor Wine Company and Great Western Winery in New York. Some critics questioned the advisability or propriety of the soft-drink giant's entry into the alcoholic beverage market. Whether it took such concerns seriously or not, it sold its winery holdings to the Seagram Company in 1983.

By that time, the Coca-Cola Bottling Company of New York, which had owned three wineries, had already divested itself of its holdings. These consisted of Franzia, Mogen David, and Tribuno, which were bought in 1981 by The Wine Group, a limited partnership formed for the purpose of buying the wineries. The partnership was headed by Arthur A. Ciocca, who was the president and CEO of Franzia and formerly a marketing executive with Gallo. He was joined in the venture by some other members of his team, men who had been charting Franzia's way under the ownership of the Coca-Cola Bottling Company of New York and were opposed to a buyout involving a third party.

At the time, Franzia was a well established California winery offering a range of varietal wines. It also shipped wine, grape concentrates and brandy in bulk to the Mogen David winery in Westfield, New York, to be used in such Mogen David products as MD 20–20 and Golden Chablis. Mogen David also had a long history and was noted for its regional kosher wines, notably its sweet concord grape and blackberry table wines. Tribuno vermouths, both sweet and dry, bottled in New Jersey, were also established products. The brand was the number one premium vermouth produced in the United States. It and Lejon, a leading popular-priced vermouth, were two high-volume brands of TWG. Both produced sweet (red) and dry (white) vermouth. The wines, often used in standard cocktails like martinis and Manhattans, were also used as both aperitif and dessert wines.

The Histories of the Wineries

At the time of its acquisition by The Wine Group, Franzia had been in existence for 66 years. In 1893, Giuseppe Franzia,

Company Perspectives:

The Wine Group's innovations have changed the way millions of Americans enjoy wine. Our company pioneered the wine-on-tap category with Franzia, and made this the fastest growing wine package of the 1990s. We are also a leader in developing and marketing new varietals and blends, and recently introduced freshness assurance dating to the wine industry.

its founder, immigrated to California from his native Italian city of Genoa. He worked in small truck farms around San Francisco, earning a meager salary that kept him at the poverty level for several years. He was very frugal, however, and by 1906 he had saved enough to plant and cultivate a small vineyard of his own. He founded the first Franzia family winery in 1915. It was not a particularly auspicious moment, however. The country was two years away from entering World War I and just five from passing the infamous 18th Amendment, which cleared the path for the Volstead Act, barring the manufacture, sale, or transportation of intoxicating liquors.

Franzia had no choice but to close his winery during Prohibition, which lasted from 1920 to 1933. During that period, Franzia's five sons continued cultivating the vineyard, and when the Repeal came in the form of the 21st Amendment, they reopened their father's business under the name Franzia Brothers. Initially, the sons sold their wine in bulk to eastern bottlers. Then, late in World War II, they began bottling their own branded wine, using the mass-production methods that had been introduced by their in-laws, Ernest and Julio Gallo, who had opened bottling plants in Los Angeles and New Orleans. In addition to an assembly-line method of bottling, the Gallos used screw-caps rather than corks to seal the bottles, something considered almost a criminal act by some wine connoisseurs but defended as sanitary improvement by health-conscious customers.

In 1971, a family squabble over the future of the winery resulted in its sale to a group of investors in the East who subsequently sold it to the Coca-Cola Bottling Company of New York (itself acquired by Coca-Cola Enterprises Inc. of Atlanta in 1997). However, some members of the Franzia family continued in the business, creating the JFJ Bronco Winery near Modesto, California.

The Mogen David Winery, located in Westfield, New York, also had been around a long time when TWG acquired it. Originally, the company was located in Chicago, but it relocated to upstate New York in 1967, a practical move to put it closer to its supply of grapes for its Concord wines. At the time it was purchased by TWG, it was producing about six million gallons of wine annually and was the world's largest producer of Concord wines. Not all of its wines were the kosher wines for which it was best known. Popular among a younger audience, specifically college students, was its MD 20/20 affectionately know as ''Mad Dog'' 20/20, a line marketed in several flavors that recalled non-alcoholic drinks, including pink grapefruit, wild berry, and Hawaiian blue.

1982–89: Becoming a Major Market Player

TWG faced some troubling prospects in the early going. By 1983, the California wine boom of the 1970s had ended, leaving an industry in a slump and a major marketing problem. In the decade prior to TWG's formation, California had at last won the long battle to establish itself as a world class producer of wines. State vintners, buoyed by a new optimism, added considerable acreage with new grape plantings, developed new technologies, and created new wineries, including, for example, the Lawrence Winery, the forerunner of Corbett Canyon. In 1982, after a decade of an annual average growth of ten percent, wine shipments flattened out. About half of California's leading wineries shipped fewer cases than in the previous year, and between the 1981 and 1982 harvests, wine inventories climbed by 16 percent to 685 million gallons. The 3.1 million ton grape crush of 1982 broke all previous records; it also caused wine prices to plummet, aided by a general recession that was reining in a growth in the sales of all alcoholic beverages.

The wine glut compelled wineries to use new marketing strategies, and it soon became clear that the 1980s would be ruled by the low-cost producers and marketers. TWG responded with some innovative measures for producing and marketing its array of bargain-priced wines. Notably, with Franzia, TWG pioneered the ''wine tap'' container, a box containing a pouch with a tap. It would become the fastest growing wine package of the 1990s. Because a loophole in federal wine standards allowed boxed wine producers to dilute the wine with water and still market it under classic varietal names such as Merlot and Cabernet Sauvignon, the new packaging caused some industry flack. Also with Franzia, TWG helped initiate the wine cooler craze in the 1980s.

In 1988, the company took an important expansion step, buying Corbett Canyon from Glenmore Distilleries Co. The vintner was originally established in 1979 as the Lawrence Winery but was re-established as Corbett Canyon in 1983. From grapes grown on its 350-acre Los Alamos Vineyards in the Edna Valley, outside of San Luis Obispo, California, the winery was producing a line of award-winning Coastal Classic varietals and Reserve designated wines. Its line would eventually grow to include Cabernet Sauvignon, Chardonnay, Merlot, Muscat, Muscat Canelli, Sauvignon Blanc, White Zinfandel, and Zinfandel. Growing sales would also compel it to buy some of its grapes from other producers.

1990 and Beyond: TWG Becomes the Nation's Third Largest Producer

In most ways, TWG fared very well in the 1990s. It enhanced its reputation as an innovator, introducing, for example, freshness assurance dating to the wine industry and garnering some awards for the distinct design of some of its bottles. Both its Franzia and Corbett Canyon brands were highly successful. According to A.C. Nielsen ratings, in the mid-1990s, Corbett Canyon was the fastest growing domestic wine. From 1995 to 1996, Corbett Canyon produced one million cases, a 67 percent leap in production. The wine maker—one of 19 wineries and vineyard members in the Edna Valley Arroyo Grande Valley Vintner's Association—was so successful that it had to close its doors to the public; it needed its tasting-room space for additional barrel storage to accommodate its growing product line and sales. In 1995, after cultivating additional acreage, it added Merlot and Zinfandel to its range of Californian varietals. However, the closing move made it the only winery in the Association to turn away visitors and prompted some criticism because the vintner, immensely popular, had previously drawn many visitors to the area, a benefit to all the other area wineries.

It was also in 1996 that Corbett Canyon received a *Wine Business Monthly* Clear Choice Award for package design for its 1.5 liter bottles that tapered from rounded shoulders to square bases, a distinct, innovative shape. Still, it was not just TWG's break from the traditionally shaped bottle that made Corbett Canyon a great seller. It won plenty of accolades for it caliber, and even "wine snobs" were buying some of Corbett Canyon's line, its Sauvignon Blanc, for example, that in 1997 still cost under $5 for a .75 liter bottle.

As for Franzia, in 1997 it was the top selling brand of wine in the country. In that year it recorded depletions of 18 million nine-liter cases, 6.6 million cases ahead of its closest competitor, Carlo Rossi. Even Mogen David continued to lead in its particular market sector. In 1998, 1.5 million adults were drinking Mogen David, beating out it chief competitor Canandaigua's Manischewitz wine by 100,000. Demographics indicated that the drinkers of the kosher wines produced by Mogen David and rival Manischewitz were not typically part of a kosher community or even Jewish. The non-vintage kosher wines, with their relatively high sugar content, had an appeal to a broader customer base, principally to consumers who preferred sweet dessert wines in traditional flavors like blackberry and concord. Mogen David was also tapping into a more youthful market, a mainstay of TWG.

Throughout the decade, TWG continued to develop products with a primary appeal to that market sector, one that was not hidebound by tradition and was willing to try anything at least once. In 1999, it started shipping its new, clear-bottled Lyrica brand in a variety of flavors: Raspberry Merlot, Passion Berry White Zinfandel, Peach Chardonnay. The bottles, created at the San Francisco design shop Primo Angeli, were again unique, reinforcing

the impression that TWG always did things a little differently than other wineries. However, in 2000, it appeared that TWG was also going to invest some more in standard varietals and pricier wines. Sebastiani Vineyards Inc. agreed to sell its Woodbridge production and bottling facilities, the Turner Road Vintners, the largest in the Lodi, California, area, to TWG. The facilities included a crushing and wine making complex with a 275,000 square foot bottling plant and distribution warehouse located nearby. The Turner Road Vintners produced about 7.8 million cases of wine per year (about 90 percent of Sebastiani's wine) bottled under a variety of brand names: Talus, Vendange, Farallon, Nathanson Creek, Heritage, and La Terre.

In addition to being an industry leader in the development and marketing of new varietals and blends, throughout the decade TWG played an exploratory part in the development of new markets, including Mexico. The North American Free Trade Agreement (NAFTA) that went into effect at the start of 1994 encouraged American wineries to make a serious attempt to export wines to Mexico and other south-of-the-border countries. Mexico's tariff was reduced by 20 percent and would continue to decline by two percent per year until it would finally be eliminated. Arthur Ciocca, TWG's CEO, noted that once the tariff barrier was sufficiently lowered NAFTA would give American wine makers an opening in a market with enormous potential.

The Wine Group was clearly going to remain a major industry player at the century's turn. In the first calendar quarter of 2000, The Wine Group shipped 5.47 million nine-liter cases of wine, an increase of 7.2 percent over the same period of the previous year. Its exporting volume also soared by 46 percent over the same period in the previous year. Furthermore, TWG was rapidly closing in on second-ranked Canandaigua, which shipped 5.56 million nine-liter cases. Though both trailed industry leader Gallo by a wide margin, they were way ahead of fourth ranked Robert Mondavi.

Principal Operating Units

Franzia; Corbett Canyon; Mogen David; Tribuno; Lejon.

Principal Competitors

Canandaigua Wine Company; E. & J. Gallo Winery; Sebastiani Vineyards Inc.; Sutter Home Winery, Inc.; Robert Mondavi Corporation.

Further Reading

"California Wineries Seek to Develop Mexican Consumer Market for Wines," *Knight-Ridder/Tribune Business News*, September 19, 1994.
Hardesty, Kathy Marcks, "Corbett Canyon Closes California Central Coast Tasting Room: Barrel Room Expansion Devours Public Facility," *Wine Enthusiast Online*.
Moran, Tim, "San Francisco-Based Wine Firm to Buy Vintners Division," *Knight-Ridder/Tribune Business News*, September 1, 2000.
Sewall, Gilbert T., "Trouble for California Wine Makers," *Fortune*, April 18, 1983, p. 54.

—John W. Fiero

World's Finest Chocolate Inc.

4801 South Lawndale Avenue
Chicago, Illinois 60632-3065
U.S.A.
Telephone: (773) 847-4601
Toll Free: (800) 932-3863
Fax: (773) 847-4006
Web site: http://www.wfchocolate.com

Private Company
Incorporated: 1939 as Cook Chocolate Company
Employees: 850
Sales: $170 million (1999 est.)
NAIC: 31132 Chocolate and Confectionery
 Manufacturing from Cacao Beans; Nonchocolate
 Confectionery Manufacturing; 42299 Other
 Miscellaneous Nondurable Goods Wholesalers

World's Finest Chocolate Inc. (WFC) makes candy—including chocolate bars, chocolate candies, and cocoa—that schools, churches, athletes, scout troops, and other fraternal and youth organizations use in their fundraising efforts. Although the majority of WFC's products are sold for fundraising, its products are sold for personal and corporate gift giving. By focusing on fundraising, WFC avoids the need for many traditional and expensive marketing strategies, such as in-store displays and heavy advertising. Instead, the company has concentrated its efforts on developing quality chocolate and turnkey fundraising programs for its customers. Arguably, WFC's most popular fundraising program allows fundraisers to personalize chocolate bar wrappers with information about their organizations and include coupons from local establishments as a sales incentive. The company's products are also sold via a catalog program, which includes food items other than chocolate and a gift-wrapping option. In addition to the plant located at its 11-acre Chicago headquarters, WFC owns a cocoa plant near Toronto, Canada, and another facility in Sydney, Australia. The company also operates Kinney Printing Co. and an experimental cocoa plantation called Union Vale on the island of St. Lucia in the West Indies.

Birth of a Dream

In many ways, the story of WFC is the story of its founder, Edmond Opler, Sr. As Patricia Tatro Opler wrote in her 1993 book *Something's Chocolate*, "World's Finest Chocolate is the American Dream: the story of a man's life devoted to hard work and chocolate."

Edmond Opler, Sr., was born the seventh of eight children—all of whom he outlived—to immigrant parents. Growing up in a New York City tenement, Opler experienced hardships, including the death of his father when Opler was only 12. In 1910 he sought employment to help support the family and was hired by Runkle Brothers Chocolate Company, earning $3 per week delivering cocoa to small stores by horse-drawn wagon. In addition to a stint as an office boy, Opler eventually became a salesman for the company, covering the territory of New England.

Opler enlisted in the Marines Corps and, after World War I, moved to the Chicago area at the age of 26 with his brother Arnold. (A physician had discovered a spot on Opler's lung and had encouraged him to move to an area of the country where the air was cleaner.) In 1922 Opler and his brother founded E&A Opler, a bulk cocoa-packing company that eventually evolved into WFC. He pursued night classes at Northwestern University's School of Commerce and, around this same time, was part owner of Chicago-based chocolate maker Siren Mills, a company that eventually was acquired by Nestle.

The Oplers broke into the business world when the climate was favorable, and they managed to prosper even through the difficult days of the Great Depression. In 1939, after residing in Chicago for 17 years, Edmond Opler, Sr., established the Cook Chocolate Company. Located on Ogden Avenue, the company became home to a new brand called World's Finest Chocolate. A decade later, in 1949, the brand evolved into its own company division, dedicated exclusively to fundraising efforts. As Donna Chavez explained in the *Chicago Tribune*, "Like most marriages made in heaven, the happy wedding of for-profit business fueled by not-for-profit sales zeal proved a winner from the very start."

To better serve the Canadian marketplace, Opler established World's Finest Chocolate Canada Ltd. in the 1950s, basing it in

Company Perspectives:

Making chocolate is a long and complex process that is both science and art. Just as the tropical cacao tree tolerates only a narrow range of temperature and humidity to develop its fruit, World's Finest Chocolate's standards demand perfect conditions, the most modern machinery, dedicated employees and the finest ingredients.

Campbellford, Ontario, a small town between Montreal and Toronto. According to Karl Howse, WFC's general manager and vice-president of Canadian operations, at the time several town members offered to build a plant for Opler if he agreed to locate operations there.

Focusing on Fundraising: The 1970s

The 1970s were significant for Opler. His company's fundraising division had been so successful through the 1960s that in 1972, he changed the company's name from Cook Chocolate to World's Finest Chocolate. During the early 1970s, WFC had annual sales of approximately $20 million and had become a fundraising powerhouse. According to a *Chicago Tribune* article by Leonard Wiener, in the early 1970s Opler estimated WFC had helped to raise about $180 million since the company's fundraising division was created. At that time, WFC charged $2 per pound for its chocolate, which enabled organizations to make a profit of 75 cents per item. Most of WFC's fundraising campaigns made $1,000 or less, but some made $5,000 or more. One exceptional 4-H fundraising campaign reportedly brought in $150,000.

Concerned about a shortage of cocoa beans during this time, Opler acquired Union Vale, the company's cocoa plantation. Chavez explained the move in the *Chicago Tribune:* ''Plagued by very primitive conditions exacerbated by unstable governments, the cocoa-producing regions were unable to hold their young people who, Opler said, leave to go to cities where they are untrained for jobs. In a move designed to benefit both his company and the native population, Opler bought a 238-acre failing sugar plantation on the West Indies Island of St. Lucia, south of Martinique.''

Visions, a 1992 Hinsdale Hospital newsletter, described the arrangement Opler established to obtain cocoa from the plantation: ''Opler joined a local co-op called the St. Lucia Agriculturist's Association when he purchased the plantation. World's Finest grows its own cocoa crops, sells them to the co-op, then buys back the cocoa it needs at the current price.'' Even though the plantation produced only a very small percentage of WFC's beans, Opler viewed the operation as a success because it improved living conditions for those who lived on the plantation and served as a model of what could be done in other economically troubled areas of the region.

During the 1970s Opler made it clear that his son, Edmond Opler, Jr., would eventually succeed him as company president. Years later, after nearly 20 years of marriage, Alice Opler described her husband in the *Chicago Tribune:* ''He is a totally devoted husband, father and grandfather. He's good and he's

generous and he's meticulous in every way.'' Along with Alice, Opler started the Edmond and Alice Opler foundation and provided assistance to several organizations in Chicago and abroad.

One institution that benefited from Opler's philanthropy was Illinois' Hinsdale Hospital, which in 1992 renamed its cancer center after him. At the time, the hospital issued a press release that asserted: ''Due in part to the Oplers' generosity, the Opler Cancer Center provides sophisticated technology and cancer treatments that are unsurpassed in the Chicago area, including autologous bone marrow transplants, gynecologic oncology clinic, radiation therapy, chemotherapy, hyperthermia and brachytherapy, biological response modifier therapy, therapeutic pheresis, and participation in national cancer research, experimental drugs and treatments.''

Finally, in addition to its success in the fundraising arena, WFC sold chocolates to hotels, restaurants, and private clubs during the 1970s; was involved in the personal gift market; and sold cocoa powder to cake mix and pudding manufacturers.

End of an Era: The 1980s

Edmond Opler, Jr., succeeded his father at the helm of WFC eight years before the elder Opler retired in 1988, at the age of 91. Prior to that time, Opler, Jr., had spent more than 35 years working for the company in every area, from the lab to the loading dock.

Like his father, Opler, Jr., had served in the Marine Corps. A graduate of Middlebury College in Vermont, the younger Opler had a management style that differed from his father's. ''Dad's business training came on the streets of the Lower East Side of New York, where business economics took place from a pushcart,'' he said in Chavez's *Chicago Tribune* article. ''It's a very different experience from college business management training,'' he observed.

Edmond Opler Sr. died at Hinsdale Hospital, home to the cancer center that bore his name, on August 19, 1995, at the age of 98. A long-time member of the Chocolate Manufacturers Association—and at one time its chairman—the senior Opler's influence went beyond WFC and touched an entire industry. At the time of his death, *Candy Industry*'s Susan Tiffany wrote: ''There are few individuals left in American Business who have made the kind of impact Opler did. . . . Opler attributed his success to the people in his life. He was quoted as saying on winning *Candy Industry*'s Kettle Award in 1987: 'I surround myself with the best people and hope that I'll be lucky. And, I have been lucky'.''

Sweet Horizons: 1990 and Beyond

In the 1990s, WFC remained Chicago's largest chocolate bar manufacturer and the leading national manufacturer of chocolate bars for fundraising. Toward the decade's end, 85 percent of WFC's sales came from fundraising programs. At that time, the company relied on about 200 independent distributors who sold the company's products exclusively in designated territories, handling very small individual orders as well as large standing orders for thousands of cases.

Key Dates:

1910: Edmond Opler, Sr., begins working in the chocolate industry at the age of 13, making deliveries in New York City by horse-drawn wagon.

1922: With his brother Arnold, Opler, Sr., founds E&A Opler, a bulk cocoa packing company in Chicago.

1939: Opler, Sr., founds Cook Chocolate Co., home to the brand of World's Finest Chocolate.

1949: World's Finest Chocolate becomes its own division of Cook Chocolate Co., devoted exclusively to fundraising.

1950s: World's Finest Chocolate Ltd. begins operation in Campbellford, Ontario, to better serve the Canadian marketplace.

1972: Cook Chocolate Co. changes its name to World's Finest Chocolate.

1970s: World's Finest Chocolate acquires an experimental cocoa plantation on the island of St. Lucia.

1980: Edmond Opler, Jr., succeeds his father as the company's top executive.

1988: Opler, Sr., retires at the age of 91.

2000: World's Finest Chocolate combines its sales force with QPC, a fundraising subsidiary of Reader's Digest.

In the late 1990s, WFC produced anywhere from 120,000 to 200,000 pounds of chocolate per day at its Chicago plant, where the manufacturing process involved taking cocoa beans, which arrived in 150-pound burlap bags, and turning them into chocolate bars or other candies. The process required to do this was complex and involved operations on several different floors of the plant. It included cleaning the beans, breaking off their shells (which eventually were sold as garden mulch), roasting their kernels (or nibs), and grinding the nibs into what is known as chocolate liquor. This chocolate liquor, which did not contain alcohol, was bitter and rough in texture. Some liquor was used to make more cocoa butter, and some was mixed with cocoa butter, sugar, milk powder, and granulated sugar to form a paste called crumb. This combination of ingredients was then refined and pulverized, creating a fine powder. A process called conching turned the mixture into a liquid, which was then tempered and molded into bars or other candies. After cooling for about 20 minutes, the chocolate was wrapped and packaged accordingly. Demand for WFC's products was cyclical, with manufacturing heaviest during the fall and spring, coinciding with the beginning and end of the school year.

In 2000, WFC combined its sales force with QSP, a subsidiary of Reader's Digest that focused on school and youth fundraising by selling magazine subscriptions. According to *The Wall Street Transcript*, George S. Scimone, chief financial officer of Reader's Digest Association Inc., regarded the move as an opportunity to increase productivity, emphasize complementary products, and balance the seasonal aspects of each company's business. The combination positioned WFC to be even more successful in the new millennium.

Principal Competitors

Archibald Candy Corporation; Interbake Foods, Inc.; Mars Inc.

Further Reading

"CFO of Reader's Digest Association Discusses the Integration of the Sales Force of World's Finest Chocolate," *Wall Street Transcript*, November 27, 2000.

Chavez, Donna, "World's Finest: A Lifetime Built on Chocolate." *Chicago Tribune*, November 15, 1992, p. D1.

Demetrakakes, Pan, "Sweet Charity," *Food Processing*, May 1997, p. 87.

"Edmond Opler, Sr., Candymaker," *Chicago Tribune*, August 30, 1995, Sec. 2, p. 9.

"Hinsdale Hospital Cancer Center Receives Distinguished Name," Hinsdale Hospital news release, May 7, 1992.

"Making a Difference: Edmond Opler, Sr.," *Visions* (Hinsdale Hospital newsletter), 1992, p. 2.

Opler, Patricia Tatro, *Something's Chocolate*, Chicago: World's Finest Chocolate, 1993.

Tennison, Patricia. "Talk About Fantasy! Tour World's Finest," *Chicago Tribune*, May 28, 1987, Sec. 7, p. 1.

Tiffany, Susan, "The Passing of an Era," *Candy Industry*, September 1995, p. 6.

Wiener, Leonard, "Candy Sweetens Charities." *Chicago Tribune*, January 16, 1972. Sec. 5, p. 1.

—Paul R. Greenland

The Yasuda Mutual Life Insurance Company

9-1, Nishi-shinjuku 1-chome
Shinjuku-ku, Tokyo 169-92
Japan
Telephone: 813-3342-7111
Fax: 813-3348-4495
Web site: http://www.yasuda-life.co.jp

Mutual Company
Incorporated: 1880
Employees: 20,903
Total Assets: $18.88 billion (1998)
NAIC: 524113 Direct Life Insurance Carriers

Despite severe economic conditions in Japan that have crippled the insurance industry, the Yasuda Mutual Life Insurance Company, Japan's oldest life insurer, maintains its reputation for dependability and innovation. As insurance in Japan undergoes a period of restructuring, Yasuda looks to introduce new products, expand its international presence, and perhaps restructure itself as a public company. The motivation for such moves is a matter of survival rather than a means to greater prosperity.

The Yasuda Group is Formed in 1868

Yasuda Mutual's beginnings and early history are closely tied to the founding of the Yasuda *zaibatsu,* the financial conglomerate owned and managed by the Yasuda family. The group was organized following the collapse of the Tokugawa government in 1868, which had secluded feudal Japan from the rapidly industrializing West since 1639. The victorious Meiji Restoration government reopened communications with the West. It concentrated on modernizing Japan and catching up with the technologically superior Western nations. In this context, already consolidated families, such as Mitsui, quickly took advantage of new capitalist potential and government incentives, diversifying quickly and successfully. Unlike Mitsui, Yasuda had no pre-Meiji existence as a business concern. Its founding and progress were, rather, the vision of one man, a son of a lower class samurai, Zenjiro Yasuda.

With the rise of the Meiji government, Zenjiro Yasuda became an entrepreneur with almost reckless ambition and imagination. As a member of the board of Nippon Ginko, the Bank of Japan, he was an upstart who diluted the longer established power of the Mitsui family. He quickly began to amass newly available capital, forming the Yasuda Bank, now Fuji Bank, the center of the Yasuda *zaibatsu.* Unlike the other heads of large families—Mitsui, Mitsubishi, and Sumitomo—Yasuda consolidated his empire in banking and finance, specializing in backing small- and medium-sized traders and industrialists.

In 1880, as part of his financial empire, Yasuda founded the Yasuda Mutual Life Insurance Company. Along with the rest of the *zaibatsu* concerns, the company prospered. In 1893, the Yasuda *zaibatsu* absorbed the Tokyo Fire Insurance Company (later renamed the Yasuda Fire and Marine Insurance Company), a young insurance firm unable to survive without Zenjiro Yasuda's aid.

Wartime Activities

Yasuda was also one of the largest financiers of the Russo-Japanese War from 1904 to 1905; in the aftermath of the war, the government asked Yasuda to help the troubled Hayaku Zenjiro bank survive. He proposed a government loan of ¥6 million. In 1912 the existing Yasuda Bank was incorporated with capital of ¥10 million. At the same time, the Yasuda *hozensha,* or family holding company, was formed to manage and direct all Yasuda concerns, including Yasuda Mutual. The stock for these companies was all held by family members, however, and the Yasuda group remained private.

In the 1920s, post-World War I Japan declined into severe economic depression. Nationalist radicals, many opposed to the terms of the Portsmouth Treaty that had ended the war with Russia in 1905, divided the country with rioting and political assassinations. In this tense atmosphere, Zenjiro Yasuda was not a respected man. He had been accused of profiteering after the Russo-Japanese War. In 1921, the same year Prime Minister Hara Kei was assassinated by a nationalist fanatic, Zenjiro Yasuda was killed by a disgruntled visionary incensed by the financier's refusal to fund a workers' hotel. Zenjiro's son, Zennosuke Yasuda, assumed leadership of the *zaibatsu*. Under his guidance, the conglomerate's operations were modernized; a university education, for example, became a prerequisite for many Yasuda positions.

The Yasuda *zaibatsu* survived the postwar political upheaval and economic depression to come into its own in the late 1920s. By 1928, the group was ranked behind only the Mitsui and Mitsubishi groups in total capital; in that year, the Yasuda *zaibatsu* encompassed 66 companies and reported total capital of ¥308 million. Yasuda Mutual reflected the successful trend of its parent company. By 1939 the company was reporting profit rates of 453 percent. In 1940 and 1941, those rates soared even higher, to 1,642 percent and 3,089 percent, respectively, surpassing even Mitsui Life. Although the Anti-Profiteering Law had been revised and extended in 1937, it did not apply to the insurance industry, thus allowing the kind of spectacular growth experienced by Yasuda Mutual in the 1930s and early 1940s.

World War II occasioned a change in the Yasuda *zaibatsu* structure. To fund the war effort, the Japanese government began forcing consolidation of major financial institutions. Although Yasuda avoided full consolidation, it did streamline family members' efforts. Hajime Yasuda, primary heir to the Yasuda empire and now head of the conglomerate, announced Yasuda's new structure in January 1942: all Yasuda family members would withdraw from related and subsidiary companies, assuming new leadership positions as board members over all *zaibatsu* concerns.

Postwar Rebuilding

With Japan's defeat in August 1945, the organization of Yasuda again changed, this time to check the earlier move toward amalgamation. By the end of August, occupation forces had arrived under General Douglas MacArthur, Supreme Commander for the Allied Powers (SCAP). Under the SCAP administration, economic controls reversed the consolidating trend of Japanese business and enforced democratization and deconcentration of the Japanese economy. Early directives from the Allied powers included mandates for the dissolution of the *zaibatsu*, preferably according to proposals from the *zaibatsu* themselves. Responding to what they saw as an inevitable redir-

ection of the Japanese economy, Yasuda executives assumed a leadership role in planning for the dissolution of their own group and ultimately that of other *zaibatsu* as well.

The Yasuda Plan was submitted in October 1945 and stipulated that the Yasuda *zaibatsu* would be dissolved and that Yasuda Bank would cease to control Yasuda subsidiaries. Shares held by family members in the bank, the holding company, and all other subsidiaries, including Yasuda Mutual, would be sold to a government control commission and the proceeds used to purchase ten-year government bonds. In addition, family members and executives appointed by them would resign from all Yasuda companies. The Mitsui and Sumitomo *zaibatsu* reluctantly agreed to the proposal, but Mitsubishi held out longer. The Yasuda Plan, with some revisions, was accepted by the U.S. government in November.

When the occupation ended in 1952, Japanese business reorganized itself once again along the original *zaibatsu* lines. Although the holding companies had been dissolved, the banks had remained intact; Yasuda Bank, renamed Fuji Bank, and the other *zaibatsu* banks now became the nuclei of business groups that were remarkably similar to the prewar *zaibatsu*. The families themselves never quite regained the extent of their prewar power. Mitsui was most acutely affected by the occupation; Yasuda, however, did reclaim some of its former holdings. Hajime Yasuda, the prewar *zaibatsu* chieftain who had announced the reorganization of 1942, became chairman of Yasuda Mutual after the occupation, a post he would continue to hold through the 1980s. He also promoted other businesses that had been Yasuda subsidiaries during the *zaibatsu*'s heyday.

Despite a rapidly expanding postwar economy and the reconsolidation of the *zaibatsu*, the Japanese life insurance industry was slow to recover in comparison to other industries. By 1955, life insurance in force amounted to only 40 percent of the prewar amount. In the 1960s, the rate of recovery increased, with total life insurance assets doubling in the years from 1962 to 1966. Yet by 1966, life insurance assets amounted to only five percent of total assets of all Japanese financial institutions, compared with ten percent before the war. In the tight money market then prevailing, most life insurance funds were loaned to emerging and expanding businesses rather than invested in negotiable securities, as had been the case in prewar Japan.

New Focus in the 1960s

In 1964 Japan joined the International Monetary Fund and the Organization for Economic Cooperation and Development. As a result, industry restraints were lifted and competition increased in the insurance industry. Focus over the next two decades would be on preparing to participate in an increasingly international economy.

In 1987 Yasuda purchased an 18 percent voting stake in PaineWebber for $300 million. The investment gave Yasuda two voting positions on PaineWebber's board, an advisory board position for Yasuda President Norikazu Okamoto, and up to a 25 percent share in PaineWebber's common stock. The move increased the company's exposure to international money markets.

The following year, the company established a firmer presence in the United States by forming Yasuda Life America Agency Inc., a subsidiary dedicated to strengthening and expanding insurance coverage for Japanese-affiliated companies in the United States. Internationalization through foreign investment also continued to escalate. In 1989 and early 1990, facing uncertainty in the Japanese economy, Chairman Yasuda and President Okamoto invested in foreign bonds rather than Japanese government bonds, increasing foreign bond assets to ¥821 billion, a 34 percent climb over the previous year. Such diversifying investments reflect Yasuda Life's strong commitment to becoming a truly international company in a rapidly changing global market. In the early 1990s, as Japan's fifth-largest life insurance company, Yasuda Mutual continued to search for investment opportunities.

The Mid-1990s and Beyond

Poor real estate investments and a weak Japanese economy that deflated domestic stock prices would have a crippling impact on Yasuda Mutual and the Japanese insurance industry as a whole. In April 1996 a revised Insurance Business Law went into effect in Japan to reduce government regulation, with the expectation that insurers would have more freedom to engage in global financial activities. Instead of entering a period of unprecedented prosperity, however, the industry soon witnessed the unimaginable: Nissan Mutual Life, Japan's 16th largest life insurer, went bankrupt. A year later Toho Mutual would also collapse. With no safety net provided by the government or the insurance industry, policyholders found their faith in their traditional insurers sorely tested. Deregulation also brought new players into the life insurance business, so that policyholders had more options. In effect, too many companies began to chase an ever-shrinking premium pool, as it was estimated that within two decades one-quarter of the Japanese population would be over 65. A consolidation of the insurance industry seemed inevitable.

Underlying structural flaws in the insurance industry became apparent. Mutuals in Japan were run essentially as non-profits, with most of the profits returned to policyholders. The companies also had a limited ability to increase capital. As long as the Japanese economy remained robust, insurers could count on increasing unrealized gains on domestic stocks to provide the necessary capital to offer higher dividends to policyholders. With the price of securities depressed, however, insurers were caught in a bind. Domestic interest rates were far lower than the promised benefits of policies, leaving insurers with no place to turn for an infusion of capital than commercial lenders—a stopgap measure at best. Only the strongest firms could expect to ride out the storm. The weak, as in the case of Nissan and Toho, would simply succumb.

To bolster its position, Yasuda Mutual looked to strengthen its ties to traditional members of the Yasuda Group: Fuji Bank and Yasuda Trust & Banking Co. There was even talk of combining forces under a holding company. After two straight years of a drop in the number of insurance contracts signed, Yasuda Mutual would also see its premium revenues drop by ten percent in 1998 and its credit rating downgraded, prompting the insurer to take more aggressive steps to maintain its business. It looked to the possibility of converting from a mutual form of ownership to a public company, which would allow Yasuda Mutual to raise capital through a public offering of stock. The tax laws did not provide for conversion, but the Ministry of Finance supported demutualization, and Yasuda Mutual and other insurers hired advisers to begin the process.

Yasuda Mutual also began efforts to diversify its business into the non-life area. Late in 1998 it announced that it had reached an agreement with the PaineWebber Group to form a joint venture to sell mutual funds and other asset-management products in Japan. In 1999 Yasuda Mutual, along with Yasuda Fire & Marine Insurance Co., purchased Nippon Enterprise Development Corp., a venture capital firm that specialized in high tech companies in both Japan and the United States. A few months later Yasuda Mutual announced a joint venture with Britain's Direct Line Insurance plc to sell auto insurance by telephone in Japan. Shortly thereafter, a potentially even more important alliance was established. Fukoku Mutual Life Insurance joined Yasuda Mutual in the Direct Line venture, as the two insurers began to discuss the possibility of one day merging, a move that would have a major impact on the realignment of the Japanese insurance industry.

In 2000 Yasuda Mutual turned to American International Group, Inc. to help it prepare to offer defined contribution pension plans (similar to the American 401(k)) that were scheduled to be introduced in Japan in 2001. The insurer's efforts to fortify its business were rewarded in 2000 when Standard & Poor's upgraded its rating of the company. Overall, the insurance industry began to stabilize, caused in some measure by the establishment of the Life Insurance Policyholders Protection Corporation of Japan to create a safety net for policyholders that helped to quell consumer fears. Nevertheless, Yasuda Mutual and others continued to be dependent on the volatility of the stock market, which left in doubt the future of Yasuda and the Japanese life insurance industry. If Yasuda Mutual and other insurers indeed converted to stock ownership, the results of such a change were equally uncertain.

Principal Subsidiaries

Yasuda Life International Investment S.A. (Luxembourg); Yasuda Life International Investment (Cayman) Ltd.; Yasuda Life International Investment (B.V.I.) Ltd. (British Virgin Islands); Yasuda Life Global Investment (Jersey) Ltd. (U.K.); Yasuda Life America Capital Management Ltd. (U.S.A.); Yasuda Life International (London) Ltd. (U.K.); Yasuda Life International (Hong Kong) Ltd.; Quaestor Investment Management Ltd. (U.K); Yasuda Life International (Singapore) Ltd.; Yasuda Realty America Corporation (U.S.A.); Yasuda Properties (U.K.) Ltd.; Yasuda Life America Agency Inc. (U.S.A).

Principal Competitors

Nippon Life Insurance Company; Dai-Ichi Mutual Life Insurance Company; Sumitomo Life Insurance Company; Maiji Life Insurance Company; Mitsui Mutual Life Insurance Company.

Further Reading

Completion of Safety Net Stimulates the Reorganization of Life Insurance Industry, Norinchukin Research Institute, September 2000, 12 p.

Japan Insurance Digest 2000, New York: Standard & Poors, 2000, 28 p.

Roberts, John G., *Mitsui: Three Centuries of Japanese Business,* New York: Weatherhill, 1989.

Shimbun, Asahi, ''Dismal Results for Insurance Firms,'' *Financial Times,* June 10, 1999.

''Three of Japan's Zaibatsu,'' *Oriental Economist,* December 1945.

The Yasuda Fire and Marine Insurance 1888–1988: A Century of Achievement, Tokyo: The Yasuda Fire and Marine Insurance Company, 1988.

—Lynn M. Voskuil
—update: Ed Dinger

INDEX TO COMPANIES

Index to Companies

Listings in this index are arranged in alphabetical order under the company name. Company names beginning with a letter or proper name such as Eli Lilly & Co. will be found under the first letter of the company name. Definite articles (The, Le, La) are ignored for alphabetical purposes as are forms of incorporation that precede the company name (AB, NV). Company names printed in bold type have full, historical essays on the page numbers appearing in bold. Updates to entries that appeared in earlier volumes are signified by the notation (**upd.**). Company names in light type are references within an essay to that company, not full historical essays. This index is cumulative with volume numbers printed in bold type.

Durango-Mapimi Mining Co., **22** 284
Duray, Inc., **12** 215
Durban Breweries and Distillers, **I** 287
Durham Chemicals Distributors Ltd., **III** 699
Durham Raw Materials Ltd., **III** 699
Duriron Company Inc., 17 145–47; 21 189, 191
Durkee Famous Foods, **II** 567; **7** 314; **8** 222; **17** 106; **27** 297
Durr-Fillauer Medical Inc., **13** 90; **18** 97
Dutch Boy, **II** 649; **III** 745; **10** 434–35
Dutch Crude Oil Company. *See* Nederlandse Aardolie Maatschappij.
Dutch East Indies Post, Telegraph and Telephone Service, **II** 67
Dutch Nuts Chocoladefabriek B.V., **II** 569
Dutch Pantry, **II** 497
Dutch State Mines. *See* DSM N.V.
Dutchland Farms, **25** 124
Dutton Brewery, **I** 294
Duttons Ltd., **24** 267
Duty Free International, Inc., 11 80–82. *See also* World Duty Free Americas, Inc.
Duval Corp., **IV** 489–90; **7** 280; **25** 461
DWG Corporation. *See* Triarc Companies, Inc.
Dyckerhoff AG, 35 151–54
Dyersburg Corporation, 21 192–95
Dyke and Dryden, Ltd., **31** 417
Dylex Limited, 29 162–65
Dymed Corporation. *See* Palomar Medical Technologies, Inc.
Dynaco Corporation, **III** 643; **22** 409
DynaMark, Inc., **18** 168, 170, 516, 518
Dynamatic Corp., **I** 154
Dynamem Corporation, **22** 409
Dynamic Capital Corp., **16** 80
Dynamic Controls, **11** 202
Dynamic Microprocessor Associated Inc., **10** 508
Dynamics Corporation of America, **39** 106
Dynamit Nobel AG, **III** 692–95; **16** 364; **18** 559
Dynamix, **15** 455
Dynapar, **7** 116–17
Dynascan AK, **14** 118
Dynasty Footwear, Ltd., **18** 88
Dynatech Corporation, 13 194–96
Dynatron/Bondo Corporation, **8** 456
Dynell Electronics, **I** 85
Dyno Industrier AS, **13** 555
Dyonics Inc., **I** 667
DYR, **I** 38; **16** 167

E. & B. Carpet Mills, **III** 423
E&B Company, **9** 72
E&B Marine, Inc., **17** 542–43
E & H Utility Sales Inc., **6** 487
E. & J. Gallo Winery, I 27, 242–44, 260; **7 154–56 (upd.); 15** 391; **28 109–11 (upd.),** 223
E&M Laboratories, **18** 514
E & S Retail Ltd. *See* Powerhouse.
E! Entertainment Television Inc., 17 148–50; 24 120, 123
E-Stamp Corporation, **34** 474
E-Systems, Inc., I 490; **9 182–85**
E*Trade Group, Inc., 20 206–08; 38 439
E-II Holdings Inc., **II** 468; **9** 449; **12** 87. *See also* Astrum International Corp.
E-Z Haul, **24** 409

E-Z Serve Corporation, 15 270; **17 169–71**
E.A. Miller, Inc., **II** 494
E.A. Pierce & Co., **II** 424; **13** 340
E.A. Stearns & Co., **III** 627
E.B. Badger Co., **11** 413
E.B. Eddy Forest Products, **II** 631
E.C. Snodgrass Company, **14** 112
E.C. Steed, **13** 103
E. de Trey & Sons, **10** 270–71
E.F. Hutton Group, **I** 402; **II** 399, 450–51; **8** 139; **9** 469; **10** 63
E.F. Hutton LBO, **24** 148
E. Gluck Trading Co., **III** 645
E.H. Bindley & Company, **9** 67
E.I. du Pont de Nemours & Company, I 21, 28, 305, 317–19, 323, **328–30,** 334, 337–38, 343–44, 346–48, 351–53, 365, 377, 379, 383, 402–03, 545, 548, 675; **III** 21; **IV** 69, 78, 263, 371, 399, 401–02, 409, 481, 599; **V** 360; **7** 546; **8 151–54 (upd.),** 485; **9** 154, 216, 352, 466; **10** 289; **11** 432; **12** 68, 365, 416–17; **13** 21, 124; **16** 127, 130, 201, 439, 461–62; **19** 11, 223; **21** 544; **22** 147, 260, 405; **24** 111, 388; **25** 152, 540; **26 123–27 (upd.); 34** 80, 283–84; **37** 111
E.J. Brach & Sons, **II** 521. *See also* Brach and Brock Confections, Inc.
E.J. Longyear Company. *See* Boart Longyear Company.
E. Katz Special Advertising Agency. *See* Katz Communications, Inc.
E.L. Phillips and Company, **V** 652–53
E.M. Warburg Pincus & Co., **7** 305; **13** 176; **16** 319; **25** 313; **29** 262
E. Missel GmbH, **20** 363
E.N.V. Engineering, **I** 154
E.R. Squibb, **I** 695; **21** 54–55
E. Rabinowe & Co., Inc., **13** 367
E.S. Friedman & Co., **II** 241
E.S. International Holding S.A. *See* Banco Espírito Santo e Comercial de Lisboa S.A.
E.W. Bliss, **I** 452
E.W. Oakes & Co. Ltd., **IV** 118
The E.W. Scripps Company, IV 606–09; 7 157–59 (upd.); 24 122; **25** 507; **28 122–26 (upd.)**
E.W.T. Mayer Ltd., **III** 681
EADS. *See* European Aeronautic Defence and Space Company.
Eagle Airways Ltd., **23** 161
Eagle Credit Corp., **10** 248
Eagle Distributing Co., **37** 351
Eagle Family Foods, Inc., **22** 95
Eagle Floor Care, Inc., **13** 501; **33** 392
Eagle Gaming, L.P., **16** 263
Eagle Hardware & Garden, Inc., 9 399; **16 186–89; 17** 539–40
Eagle Industries Inc., **8** 230; **22** 282; **25** 536
Eagle-Lion Films, **II** 147; **25** 328
Eagle Managed Care Corp., **19** 354, 357
Eagle Oil Transport Co. Ltd., **IV** 657
Eagle-Picher Industries, Inc., 8 155–58; 23 179–83 (upd.)
Eagle Plastics, **19** 414
Eagle Printing Co. Ltd., **IV** 295; **19** 225
Eagle Sentry Inc., **32** 373
Eagle Snacks Inc., **I** 219; **34** 36–37
Eagle Square Manufacturing Co., **III** 627

Eagle Star Insurance Co., **I** 426–27; **III** 185, 200
Eagle Supermarket, **II** 571
Eagle Thrifty Drug, **14** 397
Eagle Travel Ltd., **IV** 241
Earl Scheib, Inc., 32 158–61
Early American Insurance Co., **22** 230
Early Learning Centre, **39** 240, 242
Earth Resources Company, **IV** 459; **17** 320
Earth Wise, **16** 90
Earth's Best, Inc., **21** 56; **36** 256
The Earthgrains Company, 36 161–65
EarthLink, Inc., 33 92; **36 166–68; 38** 269
EAS. *See* Executive Aircraft Services.
Easco Hand Tools, Inc., **7** 117
Eason Oil Company, **6** 578; **11** 198
East African External Communications Limited, **25** 100
East Chicago Iron and Forge Co., **IV** 113
East Hartford Trust Co., **13** 467
East India Co., **I** 468; **III** 521, 696; **IV** 48; **20** 309
East Japan Heavy Industries, **III** 578–79; **7** 348
East Japan Railway Company, V 448–50
East Midlands Electricity, **V** 605
The East New York Savings Bank, **11** 108–09
East of Scotland, **III** 359
East Texas Pulp and Paper Co., **IV** 342, 674; **7** 528
East-West Airlines, **27** 475
East-West Federal Bank, **16** 484
East West Motor Express, Inc., **39** 377
Easter Enterprises, **8** 380; **23** 358
Easterday Supply Company, **25** 15
Eastern Air Group Co., **31** 102
Eastern Airlines, I 41, 66, 78, 90, 98–99, **101–03,** 116, 118, 123–25; **III** 102; **6** 73, 81–82, 104–05; **8** 416; **9** 17–18, 80; **11** 268, 427; **12** 191, 487; **21** 142, 143; **23** 483; **26** 339, 439; **39** 120
Eastern Associated Coal Corp., **6** 487
Eastern Australia Airlines, **24** 396
Eastern Aviation Group, **23** 408
Eastern Bank, **II** 357
Eastern Carolina Bottling Company, **10** 223
Eastern Coal Corp., **IV** 181
Eastern Coalfields Ltd., **IV** 48–49
Eastern Corp., **IV** 703
Eastern Electricity, **13** 485
Eastern Enterprises, IV 171; 6 486–88
Eastern Gas and Fuel Associates, **I** 354; **IV** 171
Eastern Indiana Gas Corporation, **6** 466
Eastern Kansas Utilities, **6** 511
Eastern Machine Screw Products Co., **13** 7
Eastern Market Beef Processing Corp., **20** 120
Eastern Operating Co., **III** 23
Eastern Pine Sales Corporation, **13** 249
Eastern Software Distributors, Inc., **16** 125
Eastern States Farmers Exchange, **7** 17
Eastern Telegraph Company, **V** 283–84; **25** 99–100
Eastern Texas Electric. *See* Gulf States Utilities Company.
Eastern Tool Co., **IV** 249
Eastern Torpedo Company, **25** 74
Eastern Wisconsin Power, **6** 604
Eastern Wisconsin Railway and Light Company, **6** 601

Nyman & Schultz Affarsresbyraer A.B., **I** 120

Nymofil, Ltd., **16** 297

NYNEX Corporation, V 311–13; 6 340; **11** 19, 87; **13** 176; **25** 61–62, 102; **26** 520

NYRG. *See* New York Restaurant Group, Inc.

Nyrop, **I** 113

Nysco Laboratories, **III** 55

NYSEG. *See* New York State Electric and Gas Corporation.

NZI Corp., **III** 257

O&K Rolltreppen, **27** 269

O&Y. *See* Olympia & York Developments Ltd.

O.B. McClintock Co., **7** 144–45

O.G. Wilson, **16** 560

O. Kraft & Sons, **12** 363

O.N.E. Color Communications L.L.C., **29** 306

O-Pee-Chee, **34** 447–48

O.S. Designs Inc., **15** 396

O.Y.L. Industries Berhad, **26** 3, 5

Oahu Railway & Land Co., **I** 565–66

Oak Farms Dairies, **II** 660

Oak Hill Investment Partners, **11** 490

Oak Hill Sportswear Corp., **17** 137–38

Oak Industries Inc., III 512; **21 396–98**

Oak Technology, Inc., 22 389–93

Oakley, Inc., 18 390–93

OakStone Financial Corporation, **11** 448

Oaktree Capital Management, **30** 185

OakTree Health Plan Inc., **16** 404

Oakville, **7** 518

Oakwood Homes Corporation, 13 155; **15 326–28**

OASIS, **IV** 454

Oasis Group P.L.C., **10** 506

OASYS, Inc., **18** 112

ÖBB. *See* Österreichische Bundesbahnen GmbH.

Obbola Linerboard, **IV** 339

Oberheim Corporation, **16** 239

Oberland, **16** 122

Oberrheinische Bank, **II** 278

Oberschlesische Stickstoff-Werge AG, **IV** 229

Oberusel AG, **III** 541

Obi, **23** 231

Object Design, Inc., **15** 372

O'Boy Inc. *See* Happy Kids Inc.

O'Brien Kreitzberg, Inc., **25** 130

Obunsha, **9** 29

Occidental Bank, **16** 497

Occidental Chemical Corp., **19** 414

Occidental Insurance Co., **III** 251

Occidental Life Insurance Company, **I** 536–37; **13** 529; **26** 486–87

Occidental Overseas Ltd., **11** 97

Occidental Petroleum Corporation, I 527; **II** 432, 516; **IV** 264, 312, 392, 410, 417, 453–54, 467, **480–82**, 486, 515–16; **7** 376; **8** 526; **12** 100; **19** 268; **25 360–63 (upd.); 29** 113; **31** 115, 456; **37** 309, 311

Occidental Petroleum Great Britain Inc., **21** 206

Océ N.V., 24 360–63

Ocean, **III** 234

Ocean Combustion Services, **9** 109

Ocean Drilling and Exploration Company. *See* ODECO.

Ocean Group plc, 6 415–17

Ocean Reef Management, **19** 242, 244

Ocean Salvage and Towage Co., **I** 592

Ocean Scientific, Inc., **15** 380

Ocean Specialty Tankers Corporation, **22** 275

Ocean Spray Cranberries, Inc., 7 403–05; 10 525; **19** 278; **25 364–67 (upd.); 38** 334

Ocean Steam Ship Company. *See* Malaysian Airlines System BHD.

Ocean Systems Inc., **I** 400

Ocean Transport & Trading Ltd., **6** 417

Oceania Football Confederation, **27** 150

Oceanic Contractors, **III** 559

Oceanic Properties, **II** 491–92

Oceanic Steam Navigation Company, **19** 197; **23** 160

Oceans of Fun, **22** 130

Ocelet Industries Ltd., **25** 232

O'Charley's Inc., 19 286–88

OCL. *See* Overseas Containers Ltd.

Ocoma Foods, **II** 584

Octek, **13** 235

Octel Communications Corp., III 143; **14** 217, **354–56; 16** 394

Octopus Publishing, **IV** 667; **17** 398

Oculinum, Inc., **10** 48

Odakyu Electric Railway Company Limited, V 487–89

Odam's and Plaistow Wharves, **II** 580–81

Odd Job Trading Corp., **29** 311–12

Odd Lot Trading Company, **V** 172–73

Odda Smelteverk A/S, **25** 82

Odeco Drilling, Inc., **7** 362–64; **11** 522; **12** 318; **32** 338, 340

Odegard Outdoor Advertising, L.L.C., **27** 280

Odeon Theatres Ltd., **II** 157–59

Odetics Inc., 14 357–59

Odhams Press Ltd., **IV** 259, 666–67; **7** 244, 342; **17** 397–98

ODM, **26** 490

ODME. *See* Toolex International N.V.

O'Donnell-Usen Fisheries, **II** 494

Odwalla, Inc., 31 349–51

Odyssey Holdings, Inc., **18** 376

Odyssey Partners Group, **II** 679; **V** 135; **12** 55; **13** 94; **17** 137; **28** 218

Odyssey Press, **13** 560

OEC Medical Systems, Inc., 27 354–56

Oelwerken Julias Schindler GmbH, **7** 141

OEN Connectors, **19** 166

Oertel Brewing Co., **I** 226; **10** 180

Oësterreichischer Phönix in Wien, **III** 376

Oetker Group, **I** 219

Off the Rax, **II** 667; **24** 461

Office Depot Incorporated, 8 404–05; 10 235, 497; **12** 335; **13** 268; **15** 331; **18** 24, 388; **22** 154, 412–13; **23 363–65 (upd.); 27** 95; **34** 198

Office Mart Holdings Corporation, **10** 498

Office National du Crédit Agricole, **II** 264

Office Systems Inc., **15** 407

The Office Works, Inc., **13** 277; **25** 500

OfficeMax Inc., 8 404; **9** 15 329–31; **18** 286, 388; **20** 103; **22** 154; **23** 364–65

Official Airline Guides, Inc., **IV** 605, 643; **7** 312, 343; **17** 399

Officine Alfieri Maserati S.p.A., 11 104; **13** 28, **376–78**

Offset Gerhard Kaiser GmbH, **IV** 325

The Offshore Company, **III** 558; **6** 577; **37** 243

Offshore Food Services Inc., **I** 514

Offshore Logistics, Inc., 37 287–89

Offshore Transportation Corporation, **11** 523

Ogden Corporation, I 512–14, 701; **6 151–53**, 600; **7** 39; **25** 16; **27** 21, 196

Ogden Food Products, **7** 430

Ogden Gas Co., **6** 568

Ogden Ground Services, **39** 240, 242

Ogilvie Flour Mills Co., **I** 268; **IV** 245; **25** 9, 281

Ogilvy & Mather, **22** 200

Ogilvy Group Inc., I 20, **25–27**, 31, 37, 244; **6** 53; **9** 180. *See also* WPP Group.

Oglebay Norton Company, 17 355–58

Oglethorpe Power Corporation, 6 537–38

O'Gorman and Cozens-Hardy, **III** 725

Ogura Oil, **IV** 479

Oh la la!, **14** 107

Ohbayashi Corporation, **I** 586–87

The Ohio Art Company, 14 360–62

Ohio Ball Bearing. *See* Bearings Inc.

Ohio Barge Lines, Inc., **11** 194

Ohio Bell Telephone Company, 14 363–65; 18 30

Ohio Boxboard Company, **12** 376

Ohio Brass Co., **II** 2

Ohio Casualty Corp., III 190; **11 369–70**

Ohio Crankshaft Co. *See* Park-Ohio Industries Inc.

Ohio Edison Company, V 676–78

Ohio Electric Railway Co., **III** 388

Ohio Mattress Co., **12** 438–39

Ohio Oil Co., **IV** 365, 400, 574; **6** 568; **7** 551

Ohio Pizza Enterprises, Inc., **7** 152

Ohio Power Shovel, **21** 502

Ohio Pure Foods Group, **II** 528

Ohio River Company, **6** 487

Ohio-Sealy Mattress Mfg. Co., **12** 438–39

Ohio Valley Electric Corporation, **6** 517

Ohio Ware Basket Company, **12** 319

Ohlmeyer Communications, **I** 275; **26** 305

Ohlsson's Cape Breweries, **I** 287–88; **24** 449

OHM Corp., **17** 553

Ohmeda. *See* BOC Group plc.

Ohmite Manufacturing Co., **13** 397

Ohrbach's Department Store, **I** 30

Ohta Keibin Railway Company, **6** 430

ÖIAG, **IV** 234

Oil Acquisition Corp., **I** 611

Oil and Natural Gas Commission, IV 440–41, **483–84**

Oil and Solvent Process Company, **9** 109

Oil City Oil and Grease Co., **IV** 489

Oil Co. of Australia, **III** 673

Oil Distribution Public Corp., **IV** 434

Oil-Dri Corporation of America, 20 396–99

Oil Drilling, Incorporated, **7** 344

Oil Equipment Manufacturing Company, **16** 8

Oil India Ltd., **IV** 440, 483–84

Oil Shale Corp., **IV** 522; **7** 537

Oilfield Industrial Lines Inc., **I** 477

Oilfield Service Corp. of America, **I** 342

Oita Co., **III** 718

Oji Paper Co., Ltd., I 506, 508; **II** 326; **IV** 268, 284–85, 292–93, 297–98, **320–22**, 326–27

OK Bazaars, **I** 289; **24** 450

OK Turbines, Inc., **22** 311

INDEX TO INDUSTRIES

Index to Industries

BEVERAGES

BIOTECHNOLOGY

CHEMICALS

CONGLOMERATES

ELECTRICAL & ELECTRONICS

ENGINEERING & MANAGEMENT SERVICES

ENTERTAINMENT & LEISURE

FINANCIAL SERVICES: BANKS

FOOD PRODUCTS

FOOD SERVICES & RETAILERS

HEALTH & PERSONAL CARE PRODUCTS

INSURANCE

MATERIALS

MINING & METALS

PUBLISHING & PRINTING

REAL ESTATE

RETAIL & WHOLESALE

RUBBER & TIRE

TELECOMMUNICATIONS

WASTE SERVICES

GEOGRAPHIC INDEX

Geographic Index

641

NOTES ON CONTRIBUTORS

Notes on Contributors

BIANCO, David. Freelance writer, editor, and publishing consultant.

BRENNAN, Gerald E. Freelance writer based in California.

CAMPBELL, June. Freelance writer and Internet marketer living in Vancouver, Canada.

COHEN, M. L. Novelist and freelance writer living in Paris.

COVELL, Jeffrey L. Seattle-based freelance writer.

DINGER, Ed. Brooklyn-based freelance writer and editor.

FIERO, John W. Freelance writer, researcher, and consultant.

GREENLAND, Paul R. Illinois-based writer and researcher; author of two books and former senior editor of a national business magazine; contributor to *The Encyclopedia of Chicago History* (University of Chicago Press) and *Company Profiles for Students*.

HALASZ, Robert. Former editor in chief of *World Progress* and *Funk & Wagnalls New Encyclopedia Yearbook*; author, *The U.S. Marines* (Millbrook Press, 1993).

HAUSER, Evelyn. Freelance writer and marketing specialist based in Northern California.

HEFFRON, Margery M. Freelance editor and writer living in Exeter, New Hampshire.

INGRAM, Frederick C. South Carolina-based business writer who has contributed to *GSA Business*, *Appalachian Trailway News*, the *Encyclopedia of Business*, the *Encyclopedia of Global Industries*, the *Encyclopedia of Consumer Brands*, and other regional and trade publications.

KARL, Lisa Musolf. Editor for LifeServ.com; freelance editor, writer, and columnist living in the Chicago area.

MEYER, Stephen. Freelance writer based in Missoula, Montana.

MILITE, George A. Philadelphia-based writer specializing in business management issues.

ROTHBURD, Carrie. Freelance technical writer and editor, specializing in corporate profiles, academic texts, and academic journal articles.

STANSELL, Christina M. Freelance writer and editor based in Farmington Hills, Michigan.

TRADII, Mary. Freelance writer based in Denver, Colorado.

UHLE, Frank. Ann Arbor-based freelance writer; movie projectionist, disc jockey, and staff member of *Psychotronic Video* magazine.

WALDEN, David M. Freelance writer and historian in Salt Lake City; adjunct history instructor at Salt Lake City Community College.

WERNICK, Ellen. Freelance writer and editor.

WOODWARD, A. Freelance writer.